D0116650

THE FACTS ON FILE
COMPANION TO

BRITISH
POETRY

17TH AND 18TH CENTURIES

VIRGINIA BRACKETT

An imprint of Infobase Publishing

The Facts On File Companion to British Poetry, 17th and 18th Centuries

Copyright © 2008 by Virginia Brackett

Facts On File, Inc.
An imprint of Infobase Publishing
132 West 31st Street
New York NY 10001

Library of Congress Cataloging-in-Publication Data

The Facts On File companion to British poetry, 17th and 18th-centuries / [edited by] Virginia Brackett.
    p. cm.
  Includes bibliographical references and index.
  ISBN-13: 978-0-8160-6328-4 (acid-free paper)
  1. English poetry—Early modern, 1500–1700. 2. English poetry—18th century. I. Brackett, Virginia. II. Facts on File, Inc. III. Title: Companion to British poetry, 17th and 18th-centuries.
  PR1209.F27 2008
  821'.409—dc22   2007026937

Facts On File books are available at special discounts when purchased in bulk quantities for businesses, associations, institutions, or sales promotions. Please call our Special Sales Department in New York at (212) 967-8800 or (800) 322-8755.

You can find Facts On File on the World Wide Web at http://www.factsonfile.com

Text design adapted by James Scotto-Lavino
Cover design by Salvatore Luongo

Printed in the United States of America

VB Hermitage 10 9 8 7 6 5 4 3 2 1

This book is printed on acid-free paper and contains 30 percent postconsumer recycled content.

CONTENTS

INTRODUCTION   v

A-TO-Z ENTRIES   1

APPENDIXES
I. GLOSSARY   468
II. SELECTED BIBLIOGRAPHY   472

INDEX   475

INTRODUCTION

HOW TO USE THIS BOOK

The Facts On File Companion to British Poetry, 17th and 18th Centuries takes its place within a four-volume set on British poetry from the beginnings to the present. As the other volumes do, this one considers British poetry to include that written by English, Irish, Scottish, and Welsh poets. Entries address a number of topics, including poets, individual poems, themes important to the period's poetry (such as *carpe diem*), genres and forms important in the period (such as the *elegy, aubade,* and *ballad*), and poetic groups and movements (including the Cavalier poets and the Tribe of Ben). The selection of poets and poems covered in the volume was based on their appearance in high school and college anthologies and textbooks. In addition, other less popular poems were chosen for their historical, cultural, or aesthetic significance. Entries avoid difficult jargon, making this work accessible to students of literature and general readers, but the aim of this book is to provide not only basic information but also appropriate critical commentary.

The 17th and 18th centuries were a particularly fruitful time for poetry, but not all of the impressive poems of the period could be included here. Readers will, however, find generous, although not comprehensive, selections by all of the better known poets of these centuries, such as Ben Jonson, John Milton, John Donne, John Dryden, George Herbert, Alexander Pope,

and Jonathan Swift. Their notable contemporaries are also included, though not quite as extensively. As for the time frame covered by this volume, the work of some poets spills from the end of the 18th century into the 19th century and the beginning of the Victorian age, reflecting the influences and conflict of their day. Arbitrarily designed periods and labels are useful in setting boundaries for reference works. However, they do little to confine poets and their thoughts; thus a smattering of poems published during that "buffer" era is included.

A few comments regarding editorial choices may prove helpful. While most entries are not demandingly long, those addressing lengthy works, such as Milton's epics, John Dryden's *The Hind and the Panther,* John Denham's *Cooper's Hill,* or James Thomson's *A Hymn on the Seasons,* must by necessity be longer. For the most part, quotations from poems retain original spellings where those spellings do not prevent understanding. This allows readers a familiarity with the dynamic nature of language that proves to be a part of the delight of a study of literature spanning multiple early-modern centuries. Line numbering references appear in discussions of longer poems; in briefer poems, every line may not be identified by number, but its position within the poem will be referenced. Quotations shorter than four lines separate those lines with the familiar slash (/); longer quotations or those requiring emphasis are set in block form. The terms *verse* and *stanza* are both used to reference the groups of lines into which some poems are divided, in order to emphasize the contemporary interchangeable use of those terms. The term *verse* for some students of poetry more correctly refers to distinct collections of lines applied to the more popular use of rhyme, such as that found in songs or greeting cards, with the term *stanza* reserved for references to what stuffy academic types label literature. These applications have gone in and out of favor in academia, where such value judgments expressed through rhetoric abound, with a basis in a long history of rhetorical hegemony. The tension on which such reference discussions thrive has strong roots in the 17th and 18th centuries in the "modern versus classics" rhetoric wars and is actually a notable aspect of some of the Companion selections.

Entries on individual works discuss the context during which the work was produced; summarize the work's salient elements, such as theme, tone, and figurative language; address the insight provided by various literary critical approaches; and outline the work's influences from previous writings and on future writings. Regarding the last, most entries reflect a work and poet's position in what we must view as a continuum of writing that swept one century's select emphases into the next, while leaving others behind to thrive more comfortably in their own age. The relationships and connections between and among poetry and its writers remain crucial to understanding them. Because literature reflects the concerns of the era in which it is produced, historical events and social and cultural movements and practices are discussed within entries and related to the poet's style, where applicable. A general glossary at the back of the book contains poetic terminology that will prove helpful to those unsure of meanings as applied within individual entries. Each individual entry contains a bibliography of works specific to its subject, and an additional bibliography containing sources of a more general nature appears as another appendix.

GENERAL SURVEY OF PERIODS, AUTHORS, AND WORKS

As in most discussions of literature, this one acknowledges the critical penchant for dividing and labeling certain periods into which literature may be loosely categorized. It is to the credit of those responsible for such matters that the divisions are not strictly applied. In this volume, entries cover and/or reference those eras labeled the Renaissance, the Restoration, the Augustan age or age of reason, the romantic period, and more. Each term *loosely* indicates what common sense tells one, that while academics and specialists find that terminology like *age* and *period* provide a handy means of discussion, literature joyfully spills from one era into another with few specific demarcations occurring in any particular year. Thus, Milton represents the Renaissance even while writing during the Restoration, and Dryden's Restoration poetry looks forward to the Augustan age. Poetry begins to slip from confining chains of logic and dictated format years before the age of reason officially concludes. Romantics, a referenced group, though they are not covered in this Companion, did not know they were such. That label only appeared years later in recognition of their pendulum swing into the glorification of imagination and the innocence of a natural state of things that rebelled against age of reason control. The pendulum would follow its natural corrective course, swinging back later when Darwin and others arrived on the scene, forcing their culture to recognize the negative aspects of nature. Once again, the British culture would long for control over a changing industrializing society that caused humans to enter an evolution of social classes, power structures, and nationalism accompanied by conflict and self-doubt.

Much poetry contains political, religious, and cultural themes, and poets of all periods surveyed in this volume provide excellent examples of this fact. For instance, the seemingly light-hearted love poetry of the Renaissance reflects the tension felt by the Cavalier poets, such as Thomas Carew, Sir John Suckling, and Robert Lovelace, who depended upon the court's pleasure for their livelihood. It also reflects in John Donne's case his struggle to overcome fleshly pleasures of his youth as he moves into a more spiritually reflective stylistic maturity. His rebellion against control appears clearly in his adoption of metaphysical references later embraced and celebrated, but viewed with great skepticism during his own time. George Herbert expressed his deep religious devotion in part through the shape poems in which form echoes sentiment, like "The Altar" and "Easter Wings," works many readers encounter during early schooldays. During the Restoration John Dryden's works, such as *Absalom and Achitophel,* reflected the political unrest and religious conflict between Protestantism and Catholicism that would continue to haunt England and its neighbors for centuries. Dryden also became a poetic chronicler in *Annus Mirabilis: The Year of Wonders, 1666,* his first major nondramatic poem. It characterized the horror of London's great fire and the glory of England's naval victories over Holland. These early works and their ideas would later be used as the basis for much poetic response, as in the early 18th-century poem "The Repulse to Alcander" by Sarah Fyge Egerton. Egerton adopts a female voice to counter the traditional seduction poem, made popular by the Renaissance Cavaliers.

In the 18th century Alexander Pope's Catholicism placed him within a group ostracized for its faith, a fact his poetry often confronts. In addition, growing contrasts between newly strengthened political parties motivated Pope and others to transfer political loyalties, their preferences made clear in their poetry. Pope's contemporary and friend Jonathan Swift, perhaps best known to readers as the essayist who produced the brilliant satiric political essay "A Modest Proposal," also produced poetry with satire's bite. That style is clearly reflected in his "Verses on the Death of Dr. Swift," in which he imagines the not-always-complimentary commentary that will follow his death. Robert Burns wrote in the vernacular of his native Scottish dialect, reflecting nationalistic pride and his belief that Scotland should remain separate from England at a time when a movement to unite the two countries proved strong. Burns also used his popularity to gain well-deserved attention for his predecessor Robert Ferguson when he discovered Ferguson was buried in an unmarked grave, thus drawing attention to another Scottish patriot poet. Songs from various musical productions often reflect political intent, as seen in John Gay's ever-popular *A Beggar's Opera.* Those songs live on as poems, some featured in this Companion.

However some of the uses of poetry change over time, this genre consistently offers a not-always-com-

fortable consideration of the human condition. Life and death, those still most mysterious states of being that continue in our advanced century to escape scientific explanation, remain enduring topics for poetry, regardless of the era. Examples in this Companion include Mary Barber's light celebration "Written For My Son, And Spoken by Him at His First Putting on Breeches"; as well as Ben Jonson's laments "On My First Son" and "On My First Daughter"; and Elizabeth Boyd's sober contemplation "On The Death of an Infant of Five Days Old, Being a Beautiful but Abortive Birth." Poetry also allows expression of the pure wonder and joy in simple pleasures that too seldom grace us, as seen in Thomas Traherne's "On Leaping over the Moon" and Katherine Philip's "Friendship's Mysteries, to My Dearest Lucasia."

Early women poets featured in this volume generally reflect a focus on either religion or love. They include the well-known Mary Sidney Herbert, countess of Pembroke, who succeeded in promoting her martyred brother's work while featuring her own, and her niece, Lady Mary Wroth, one of the first women to write popular romantic poetry. Women writing decades later are able to take up causes specific to their gender and class, such as the lack of choice suffered by females for whom nondomestic pursuits were considered improper, or scandalous working conditions endured by those women who did find employment. Aphra Behn at the end of the Restoration became a sorely needed model for women, having nerve enough to wield a pen in her position as the first woman to support herself through her writing. Still, she had to work at "marketing" a self-image that reflected the scandal about which she wrote in order to make readers feel comfortable about purchasing and reading creative work by a woman.

Those who followed Behn include courageous figures who challenged the creative status quo for women. Mary Leapor, a contemporary of Pope and Swift, produced work labeled labor-class poetry. Mary Astell used her subservient position to males to suggest in poetry such as "Ambition" that society should accept a natural equality between the sexes. Mary Robinson would take her baby with her to join her profligate husband by an arranged marriage in debtor's prison. She later became a noted actress and poet, mistress to the prince of Wales, and her family's only means of support. Additional women poets include the Renaissance "diva" poet Margaret Cavendish, duchess of Newcastle, the first female to venture into the male dominion of scientific writing, and Katherine Philips, nicknamed the Matchless Orinda, the first to write same-sex love poetry.

Over time, women received a more positive reception to their work. Upon the verge of the Restoration, the poet Anne Killigrew would be celebrated in elegy by Dryden after her tragic young death, while the age of reason's Anna Hunter Seward received the label "Swan of Lichfield" from her contemporary the poet, essayist, and critic Samuel Johnson. By the end of the 18th century, readers felt much more comfortable with writing women, some so concerned about the melancholic tone of work by Charlotte Turner Smith that they wrote to the journal in which she published, expressing concern for her evident depression. Smith's lyrical writing about the moon and madness supplied later feminist critics and teachers of literature superb examples of the imagery and symbolism important to their method of critical analysis.

The volume also points to the reincarnation of poets' works and lives in new media. One well-known example is the popular 20th-century version of Gay's 18th-century opera, Bertolt Brecht and Kurt Weill's *The Threepenny Opera*. It produced the enduring song "Mack the Knife" with which the modern singer Bobby Darin remains identified. As another example, the scandalous 18th-century poetry by John Wilmot, second earl of Rochester, gained renewed interest after a 2004 movie version of Wilmot's life, *The Libertine*, starring Johnny Depp. In addition Christopher Smart's mad poem "My Cat Jeoffrey" from his *Jubilate Agno* enjoyed rebirth when the 20th-century composer Benjamin Britten adopted a short excerpt from the poem for use in his festival cantata "Rejoice in the Lamb." Such examples make clear the enduring quality of stirring literature.

Biographical entries may vary from information related to a poet's writing to inform the reader of interesting and surprising facts. An example would be that Lady Mary Wortley Montagu introduced vaccination against smallpox to England after her travels to India, where she observed the benefits of such inoculation. In order to counter resistance of her fellow countrymen to this seemingly exotic procedure, she requested that her own children be inoculated.

Just as this discussion and this volume do not attempt to cover every poet and every work of two centuries, neither does this volume attempt to define poetry. It takes as a defense that some of humankind's most remarkable minds have grappled unsuccessfully with this conundrum. Readers may look to Samuel Johnson's discussion in his seminal *Lives of the English Poets* about Pope's consideration as an accomplished poet to gain further insight, if not complete satisfaction. Johnson urges readers who unwisely insist upon such a definition to search for it by examining those diverse individuals assigned across the ages the label *poet* by a discerning readership:

> To circumscribe poetry by a definition will only show the narrowness of the definer.... Let us look round upon the present time, and back upon the past; let us enquire to whom the voice of mankind has decreed the wreath of poetry; let their productions be examined and their claims stated.

And in considering Pope as possessing the genius necessary to a poet, Johnson describes the poet's mind as

> active, ambitious, and adventurous, always investigating, always aspiring; in its widest searches still longing to go forward, in its highest flights still wishing to be higher; always imagining something greater than it knows, always endeavouring more than it can do.

The four volumes of the Facts On File Companion to British Poetry offer the work of such minds for the reader's consideration. They invite each reader not simply to read *about* the poets and their work, but to go to the poems themselves for pleasure and enlightenment. Only then might readers develop a private and satisfactory definition of this most magical of the creative genres.

WORK CITED

Johnson, Samuel. *The Lives of the Poets.* Edited by G. B. Hill. 3 vols. Oxford: Clarendon Press, 1905.

A

ABSALOM AND ACHITOPHEL JOHN DRYDEN
(1681) JOHN DRYDEN's publication of *Absalom and Achitophel* had a specific political motivation. He wrote the poem during the threat of revolution in England, connected to the so-called Popish plot and the move to exclude the reigning King Charles II's Catholic brother, James, duke of York, from his right to follow the Protestant Charles to the throne. The protesting faction supported instead Charles's bastard son, James, duke of Monmouth, whom Charles recognized as his son but not his heir. Born in the Netherlands to Lucy Walter, James was a product of only one of many sexual liaisons of his mother's. While rumors existed that Charles had secretly married Lucy, granting legitimacy to James, others insisted that James could not even be proved Charles's son. Charles never produced an heir with his wife, the Portuguese Catherine of Brangaza. Although Lucy followed Charles to England, where James was raised a pampered member of the court and eventually made a duke, she had died before Charles married Catherine.

Dryden observed the parallel in England's situation to that of ancient Israel under the rule of King David. The story found in the biblical book of 2 Samuel contained all of the political elements in which Dryden found himself, as a citizen of England, involved. Each of the main characters corresponded to a real-life person in Dryden's time. David's bastard son, Absalom, represented Monmouth, and his evil confidant Achitophel represented Anthony Ashley Cooper, earl of Shaftesbury. Shaftesbury had introduced to Parliament the Exclusion Bill to prevent York from taking the throne. Other characters and their contemporary references included Zimri as George Villiers, the duke of Buckingham and a longtime opponent of Charles; Amiel, Edward Seymour, speaker of the House of Commons; Cora as Titus Oates, who fabricated the rumors that prompted social unease over the so-called Popish Plot; and *Shimei* as Bethel, sheriff of London. In addition the pharoah referenced in line 281, the biblical ruler of Israel's enemy Egypt, represented King Louis XIV, ruler of France, an enemy of England.

By referencing only the biblical characters to maintain his ALLEGORY, Dryden accomplished his purpose, which was to comment on the folly of the political clash between the Protestant Whigs and Catholic Tories. Reflecting his traditional middling position that tended toward compromise in the fairness with which he treated both factions, Dryden included positive passages about characters on both sides of the issue. Nevertheless he supported the Royalist cause. By 1681 the Royalists seemed to take the upper hand in the clash after Charles executed a tactical move to relocate Parliament to Oxford, where he would have more power over its members in isolation from London's rebellious forces. The people eventually lost faith in the pro-Monmouth group, and Charles remained absolute ruler, never again convening Parliament, until his sudden death from kidney infection in 1685. Ironically while on his deathbed Charles secretly called a priest to minister to him. He converted to Catholicism and received the last rites, and his Catholic brother, the duke of York, became James II of England.

While readers recognized the situation in the poem as one reflecting England's own, some were not confident about the precise present-day individuals Dryden's characters reflected. That resulted from Dryden's absolute devotion to the biblical parallel, although a close reading by those knowledgeable regarding Charles and the Jewish King David revealed some differences between the two reigns in the poem's small details. For instance, lines 438–39, "Perhaps th' old harp on which he thrums his lays, / Or some dull Hebrew ballad in your praise," distinguished Charles's love for music from David's poetic talent. However, as David had, Charles had many illegitimate offspring, as many as 14, and, as David removed himself from Jerusalem, Charles moved from his seat of power in London because of news of a possible revolt by one of his illegitimate sons. Some critics feel that Dryden may have attempted to ease public disapproval of Charles's many sexual affairs by comparing him to the highly lauded David, although the poem's speaker notes that David had his affairs "Before polygamy was made a sin" (2). In addition, according to Royalist tradition, English kings had a divine right to rule, and David likewise had been specifically chosen by God to lead his people.

Dryden's direct address "To the Reader" preceding the lengthy poem proves of interest. While he hoped to treat each political faction fairly, he acknowledged that "he who draws his pen for one party must expect to make enemies of the other. For Wit and Fool are consequents of Whig and Tory, and every man is a knave or an Ass to the contrary side." He also stated he would take comfort in the "manifest prejudice to my cause" that the opposition would surely publicize, as that prejudice would "render their judgment of less authority against me." Continuing, Dryden offers the opinion that "if a poem have a genius, it will force its own reception in the world." His supporting logic for that idea was "for there's a sweetness in good verse which tickles even while it hurts, and no man can be heartily angry with him who pleases him against his will." His tone turns sharply sober later when he informs his

readers, "I have but laugh'd at some men's follies, when I could have declaim'd against their vices, and other men's virtues I have commended as freely as I have tax'd their crimes."

Dryden's choice of the Bible as allegory proved appropriate for his era. Most educated individuals agreed that the Bible could be used as a type of gloss to reveal truths civic, as well as religious. No one else, however, had seen the artistic possibilities in the way Dryden did. The parallel story, as Earl Miner explains, granted a sense of action that the poetry itself lacked. The rhyming couplets in Dryden's 1,031 lines framed only three incidents from the story of David's retention of rule. In the first, Achitophel tempts Absalom to overthrow his father. In the second, the two together tempt the Jews to participate in a revolt. And in the third, David makes a moving speech to his reunited subjects, concluding with the lines, "For lawful pow'r is still superior found; / When long driven back, at length it stands the ground." In this couplet, Dryden expressed the belief, which a struggle with his own religious allegiance eventually confirmed, that the tradition of the Catholic Church gave it a strength his culture badly needed.

Absalom and Achitophel contains a number of strong passages in its lengthy narrative. After a history of how David came to dote on his illegitimate son, Dryden wrote, "But life can never be sincerely blest; / Heaven punishes the bad and proves the best" (43–44), preparing readers for a downward turn in the monarch's life. That turn, they soon observed, was due to the Jews,

> a headstrong, moody, murmuring race
> As ever tri'd th'extent and stretch of grace,
> God's pamper'd people whom, debauch'd with
>   ease,
> No king could govern nor no god could please
> (Gods they had tr'd of every shape and size
> That god-smiths could produce, or priests
>   devise.) (45–50)

Dryden wrote of his own readers, many of whom recognized that reference.

After the time of peace that Israel enjoyed, "David's mildness manag'd it so well / The bad found no occasion to rebel" (77–78), those "bad" factions, thanks to "the careful Devil," conjured a plot. The speaker then comments, "Plots, true or false, are necessary things / To raise up commonwealths and ruin kings" (83–84). To be fair to English subjects, Dryden added a passage intended to defend the rebellious Jews and, by extension, the supporters of anti-Catholic forces of 17th-century England:

> Submit they must to David's government;
> Impoverish'd, and depriv'd of all command,
> Their taxes doubled as they lost their land
> And, what was harder yet to flesh and blood,
> Their gods disgrac'd and burnt like common wood. (93–97)

Thus, the people stand ready to be convinced by those who plot against the king, although Dryden terms that plot a "curse" conjured up by other members of aristocracy and

> Not weigh'd or winnow'd by the multitude,
> But swallow'd in the mass, undhew'd and
>   crude.
> Some truth there was, but dash'd and brew'd
>   with lies
> To please the fools and puzzle all the wise.
> Succeeding times did equal folly call
> Believing nothing or believing all. (112–118)

Dryden emphasizes the term *lies* by giving it a line of its own, following a line that concludes with ENJAMB-MENT. That line forces the reader to run past *brew'd,* for which he or she anticipates a RHYME with *crude* in the preceding line. The fact that the anticipated rhyme is overwritten immediately awakens the sleepy reader. Dryden continues to blast the leaders of the movement as "Some by their Monarch's fatal mercy grown / From pardon'd rebels kinsmen to the throne," emphasizing that those leading the rebellion would have had no power had it not been for the actions of Charles at the RESTORATION. Of these men "the false Achitophel" (150) proves the worst, described as

> A name to all succeeding ages curst,
> For close designs and crooked counsels fit,

> Sagacious, bold, and turbulent of wit;
> Restless, unfix'd in principle and place,
> In power unpleas'd, impatient of disgrace.
>   (151–155)

Dryden will later compare Achitophel's words to snake venom, making a strong connection to the temptation by Satan in the Garden of Eden. He uses equally strong words for the son, Absalom, "that unfeather'd, two-legg'd thing, a son" (170), who "In friendship false, implacable in hate; / Resolv'd to ruin or to rule the state." Dryden also condemns Buckingham through the character of Zimri, about whom the speaker relates:

> A man so various that he seem'd to be
> Not one, but all mankind's epitome.
> Stiff in opinions, always in the wrong,
> Was everything by starts and nothing long,
> But in the course of one revolving moon,
> Was chemist, fiddler, statesman, and buffoon.
>   (545–550)

Because David had no brother to play the part in the biblical plot that York did in reality, Dryden invents one for his poem. Absalom thinks about him and the fact that he stands "secure of native right" (354) and is loyal to the king. Although Absalom understands his mind may be debased, he also feels that he deserves something for David's treatment of his mother. In attempting to rationalize his plan, he admits "Desire of greatness is a godlike sin" (372). Dryden employs PAR-ADOX in suggesting sin can be like God. Absalom con-tinues deluding himself, capturing the public's imagination and trust, as he allowed Achitophel to capture his. Dryden notes the results with beautiful control, exhibiting the art that he describes:

> Th' admiring crowd are dazzled with surprize
> And on his goodly person feed their eyes;
> His joy conceal'd, he sets himself to show,
> On each side bowing popularly low;
> His looks, his gestures, and his words he
>   frames,
> And with familiar ease repeats their names.

Thus, form'd by nature, furnish'd out with arts,
He glides unfelt into their secret hearts.
    (686–693)

Dryden's experience writing for the stage had put him into close contact with many actors. This passage reflects his familiarity with their craft. His understanding of men's natural motivation to attain power allows his characterization of Absalom some tenderness. Those loyal to David eventually must be honest regarding his beloved son's actions and the effects of bad influences upon him, as the speaker explains:

That Absalom, ambitious of the crown,
Was made the lure to draw the people down;
That false Achitophel's pernicious hate
Had turn'd the Plot to ruin church and state;
The council violent, the rabble worse,
That Shimei taught Jerusalem to curse. (927–932)

Dryden also wants his audience to understand that the monarch's pampered existence includes fearsome responsibilities, when he writes, "Kings are the public pillars of the state, / Born to sustain and prop the nation's weight" (953–954). In the biblical story Absalom strangles to death in a bizarre accident in which he becomes fatally entangled among branches. Monmouth would, after his father's death, attempt to overthrow his uncle and be executed as a result, with eight blows of the ax required to behead him. One gruesome legend has it that after his execution, someone noticed no official portrait had ever been made of Monmouth. Supposedly his head was placed back on his body and the corpse used as a model for the portrait now hanging in the National Portrait Gallery in London.

SAMUEL JOHNSON later described *Absalom and Achitophel* as a poem "in which personal satire was applied to the support of public principles." In his opinion, this caused the poem to be of interest to "every mind." He adds an interesting anecdote relating that his father, "an old bookseller," in describing the huge sales of the poem, "told me he had not known it equaled but by Sacheverell's trial." His father referenced notes on a trial sparked by arguments written by Henry Sacheverell, rector of St. Peter's, against the Whig ministry. His trial for sedition had famously been held from February 27 to March 23, 1710. The two sermons constituting his arguments were ordered burned, and Sacheverell became a martyr, advancing the cause of the Tories against the failing Whig ministry. Dryden's era and the decades beyond proved a heady time for the expression of political sentiment, when the written word bore force for change.

BIBLIOGRAPHY
Graham, W. *Absalom and Achitophel*. Oxford: B. Blackwell, 1965.
Johnson, Samuel. *Lives of the English Poets*. Vol. 1, 1777. New York: E. P. Dutton, 1958.
Miner, Earl, ed. *Selected Poetry and Prose of John Dryden*. New York: The Modern Library, 1985.
Plumsky, Roger. "Dryden's *Absalom and Achitophel*." *The Explicator* 60, no. 1 (fall, 2001): 60–63.
Selden, Raman. *John Dryden: Absalom and Achitophel*. Harmondsworth, England: Penguin, 1986.

"ADAM POSED" ANNE FINCH (1709)

ANNE FINCH, COUNTESS OF WINCHILSEA wrote at a time when poetry by women did not have a large appreciative audience; as a result she often offers an "apology" or attempts to explain her act of writing, to her readers. However, she also had strong supporters, including ALEXANDER POPE, who encouraged her efforts. She enjoyed country life and included pastoral themes in several of her poems. Even a playful attempt like "Adam Posed" reflects her affection for nature.

For Finch's usage the term *Posed* meant "Puzzled," as her speaker wonders what Adam's reaction might have been had he, after his expulsion from Eden, encountered a "nymph," a well-dressed and fashionable woman. Keeping in mind that Adam had remained naked in the Garden of Eden and had as his assignment the naming of all creatures he found there, and that he and Eve were deemed the only humans on earth, Finch's light IRONY is amusing. While in other poems she dealt self-consciously with the idea that women enslaved men for all times when Eve tempted Adam with fruit from the Tree of Knowledge, Finch's amusing fantasy in "Adam Posed" offers sheer entertainment.

Finch often incorporated rhetorical questions into her poetry, and she uses that technique in the first four lines of this poem:

Could our first father, at his toilsome plough,
Thorns in his path, and labor on his brow,
Clothed only in a rude, unpolished skin,
Could he a vain fantastic nymph have seen.

Her imagery remains strong, helping readers conjure a clear picture of a man working in the field, and the great contrast to his surroundings that a "vain fantastic nymph" would cause. The speaker continues by describing the nymph, who has "airs" and "antic graces," wearing "various fashions, and more various faces." Such an active woman would surely confuse Adam, accustomed only to Eve. The description suggests a colorful creature, such as a strutting bird or a changeable chameleon, again in contrast to the drab Adam, sweating over brown or gray dirt in a world colorless by comparison to the Garden he had left behind. The nymph would have "posed that skill, which late assigned / Just appellations to each several kind," as Finch references Adam's assigning of names, "appellations," to all living beings. The nymph would try Adam's skill in applying such labels. To enjoy the poem fully, one must keep in mind that all of the creatures Adam observed and labeled, he was seeing for the first time, with no basis for comparison. Therefore the fashionable woman would have seemed one more in a collection of mysterious creatures who moved by various means, from flying to crawling in the dirt.

Finch concludes her playful riddle with three lines:

A right idea of the sight to frame;
T'have guessed from what new element she
    came;
T'have hit the wavering form, or given this
    thing a name!

She never expresses an opinion as to whether Adam would have "hit" upon the perfect label for the nymph. Instead, she invites readers simply to enjoy his conundrum.

"AELLA" THOMAS CHATTERTON **(?date)**   Written by THOMAS CHATTERTON and published sometime after his death, "Aella" contains a popular song easily located online in electronic versions. It represents the musical,

as well as poetic, form known as a roundelay, meaning that it contains a line or phrase that is repeated as a refrain. Used as a mourning song, the poem's three-line repeated refrain is "My love is dead, / gone to his death-bed / All under the willow-tree." That refrain concludes each seven-line verse, while the first four lines of each, with a repeated rhyme scheme of *abab* and an iambic RHYTHM in four feet, falls into the BALLAD format, perfect for telling the sad tale of a maiden parted by death from her lover.

Chatterton begins by inviting readers, "O sing unto my roundelay / O drop the briny tear with me," so that the audience joins in the song as well as the grieving of its persona. Although readers are invited to sing, the voice continues, "Dance no more at holyday, / Like a running river be," indicating that the song will not be one of celebration, as no dancing accompanies it. The comparison to a river is the first of many strong images that imbue the poem with a haunting and active quality. The dead man is compared to a dark winter night, with dark a traditional symbol of death, as is winter. The winter reference is reemphasized in the next line with the phrase "summer snow," a PARADOX that represents nature's fracture of its natural order in the death of one too young to die. The lover's face is red "as the morning light," where morning should represent a new beginning, but "cold he lies in the grave below" the willow tree, itself a figure of mourning with its branches that bend to the ground.

FIGURATIVE LANGUAGE (FIGURE OF SPEECH) continues as the dead man's tongue is compared to the sweetness of "the throstle's note," or that of the thrush, while his quickness in dance reminds the speaker of a swift thought. The audience understands that the speaker is now missing her dance partner and partner in life. She continues praising him, adding, "Deft his tabor, cudgel stout; / O he lies by the willow-tree!" Regardless of his former strength, he now lies prone, felled by death. The double reference to the tree in this third verse emphasizes her grief. She calls again, beginning the first and third lines of the next verse with the exclamation "Hark!" The audience is asked to listen to a raven flapping his wings and is informed that "the death-owl loud doth sing / To the nightmares, as they go." Again with birds this time symbolizing death, the chaotic state of affairs is referenced with an allusion to nightmares, in which no natural laws apply.

The next verse emphasizes the imagery of white, with references to a white moon, traditional symbol of the female; a white morning sky; and a white evening cloud, the audience learning that the lover's shroud is whiter than any of those. The speaker identifies herself as a maid in the next stanza, comparing herself to "the barren flowers" that shall be lain on the grave, as she notes, "Not one holy saint to save / All the coldness of a maid." She may suggest that she will remain barren, her passion having become as cold as the object of her love. The following verse makes literal her reference as she notes that her own body will lie upon his grave. She calls upon a spirit and a fairy to light their fires to help her grieve. She concludes by bidding the mystical creatures,

> Come, with acorn-cup and thorn,
> Drain my heartes blood away;
> Life and all its good I scorn,
> Dance by night, or feast by day,

suggesting that her passion will drain from her body one drop at a time, a torture, while others may continue in their orderly way. She, however, rejects life and any good it might offer to others, as "My love is dead, / gone to his death-bed / All under the willow-tree."

While the speaker consistently returns to the traditional comparison of death to sleep by referring to her lover's "death-bed," she undercuts that peaceful connotation with her own unrest. Her once orderly life, directed by trustworthy icons of time, such as the moon and the morn, and the cyclical revelry sought by youth in holiday dancing and feasting, has been destroyed. No longer interested in the activities of the living, her maiden passion cold and unresponsive, she chooses to prostrate herself with grief above the corpse of her lover.

"AFFLICTION (1)" GEORGE HERBERT (1633)

GEORGE HERBERT wrote five "Affliction" poems, all contained in his collection *The Temple*. The first of the series, while not essentially autobiographical, did grow from Herbert's life and experiences. While the poem begins with positive aspects of the speaker's life, that same life quickly dissolves into the chaos caused by illness and the loss of friends. Specific to Herbert's experience is the reference to university life as well as that of the clergy. The poem consists of 11 six-line stanzas with a RHYME scheme of *ababcc*.

The persona begins by recalling "When first thou didst entice to thee my heart," referring to an initial "service brave" to God. He recalls enormous "joys," drawn from his own "stock of natural delights, / Augmented with thy gracious benefits." He continues to discuss the benefit he derived from "thy furniture so fine," meaning all the trappings of a life publicly dedicated to service. The speaker felt the "glorious household-stuff . . . entwine," with the verb *entwine* connoting, despite the upbeat tone, a trap, like that of a spider's web. Still, the speaker earned his "wages in a world of mirth." As the third stanza opens, the persona asks the rhetorical question "What pleasures could I want, whose King I served / Where joys my fellows were," meaning he lived constantly with joy and lacked nothing. Herbert makes clear that his speaker confused service to God with that to an earthly king, complete with royal trappings. However, his statements become an argument of sorts, as he claims he did not realize the responsibility that accompanied the rewards. Because all of the joy left "No place for grief or fear," when it did arrive he was caught unaware. The fourth stanza makes clear that the "milk and sweetnesses" and the satisfaction of his every "wish and way" caused him to live as if no month other than May, a time of new life and promise, existed. But as he aged, his "years sorrow did twist and grow, / And made a party unawares for woe."

When that woe arrived, it was in the form of fleshly pain, and the speaker notes that "sicknesses cleave my bones; / Consuming agues dwell in ev'ry vein," and even his breath turns to groans. Sorrow became "all my soul" to the point that he could hardly believe himself alive, "Till grief did tell me roundly, that I lived." Although his health returned, God metaphorically took his life, as his friends died. He declares, "My mirth and edge was lost; a blunted knife / Was of more use than I." Herbert's persona begins to understand that all the while he thought he had the power to choose, his actions have been undercut by a cruel deity. He accuses God directly, claiming, "Thou didst betray me to a ling'ring book, / And wrap me in a gown," where the book refers to his education and the gown to both the academic and religious communities. He also references "his birth," suggesting he was born to privilege, as was Herbert, a fact that should have afforded him some power.

In the ninth stanza Herbert employs a technique characteristic of METAPHYSICAL POETS AND POETRY, the use of contraries, as the speaker says,

Yet lest perchance I should too happy be
   In my unhappiness,
Turning my purge to food, thou throwest me
   Into more sickness.

He follows in the next stanza by wondering, "what thou wilt do with me," and finds no answers in his books. He goes so far as to wish himself a tree, which at least birds could trust, "and I should be just." While the suggestion contains some hint at humor, it also signals desperation. Herbert does not conclude on an optimistic note. His speaker can only say that he "must be meek," and in that meekness he "must be stout." He even considers seeking a new master. However, he concludes with a contradiction that nevertheless indicates he would like to remain with his present Lord: "Ah, my dear God! though I am clean forgot, / Let me not love thee, if I love thee not."

As a result of his experiences the speaker first suffers rebellion but in the end shows humility. He seems to recognize not only his personal inadequacy, but also the inadequacy of his language, particularly FIGURATIVE LANGUAGE, to express the proper relationship with God. The speaker remains frustrated, a state proper for a mere human in the presence of his Lord.

"AGAINST THEM WHO LAY UNCHASTITY TO THE SEX OF WOMEN" WILLIAM HABINGTON (1634)

WILLIAM HABINGTON first published his poem "Against Them Who Lay Unchastity to the Sex of Women" anonymously in 1634 in a collection titled *Castara*. Two further editions appeared, one in 1635, and a third, acknowledging Habington as

author, in 1640. The third edition is the one most often used for anthologized excerpts. Habington wrote to a real-life Castara, his wife, Lucy. Born into better circumstances than Habington, a fact that he makes clear in his poetry, Lucy nonetheless returned his love, and the two remained happily married. Each poem in the collection deals with one of four themes, the mistress, the wife, the friend, and the holy man. "Against Them Who Lay Unchastity to the Sex of Women" deals with attitudes against women promoted by those who judge all women unchaste, because some serve as mistresses. Habington's speaker makes the point that all women cannot be judged by the actions of a few, with Castara's virtue representing the example all should follow. While feminist critics might wish that Habington made clear male complicity in the making of a mistress, his focus is not drawn to blame and judgment. He does not judge the women who give themselves as lovers, except to describe them as slaves to male desire.

The speaker uses the FIGURATIVE LANGUAGE (FIGURE OF SPEECH) of metaphor as he references those who believe all women unchaste in the first few lines. He adopts seasons of the year usually positively associated with love to characterize the charge against all women as an unnatural one: "They meet but with unwholesome springs, / And summers which infectious are." He adds that those "Who ever dare / Affirm no woman chaste and fair" also only hear "the mermaid" sing and "only see the falling star." In other words, they must not inhabit the real world, but only one of fantasy. The second stanza bids those who remain so confused to "cure your fevers" and travel elsewhere in order to "The right ones see, / And grant all gold's not alchemy." Habington adopts the reference to alchemy, a use of magic to produce false gold, as a contrast to objects composed of the pure precious metal. He suggests that chaste women possess true value, as does gold.

In the third stanza the speaker explains that one would have to be a madman to believe that "'cause the glo-worm's flame / Is cold," "there's no warmth in fire." He extends his consideration of things false versus those true in his comparison of a worm's ability to duplicate the appearance of flame to that of fire to produce heat. The speaker next notes that just because some women choose to "forfeit . . . their name," where *name* means "reputation," "And slave themselves to man's desire," that does not mean that "the sex, free / From guilt," or women who do preserve their chastity, should be also "damn'd to the bondage." Habington asks his readers not to damn all women on the basis of the actions of a few. The fourth and final stanza addresses Castara directly, bidding her, "Nor grieve, Castara, though t'were frail; / Thy virtue then would brighter shine." The speaker reminds Castara that her commendable character shines even brighter in comparison to that of those who lack virtue. Her "example should prevail, / And every woman's faith be thine," but if women refuse to follow her example, "'Tis majesty to rule alone."

Habington's final statement represents the occasional lines of strength for which his poetry gained its reputation. His critics willingly admit that he flawlessly controlled his rhetoric. However, his format often suffers from lack of coherency, leaving parts stronger than the whole.

"AIR AND ANGELS" JOHN DONNE (1633)

JOHN DONNE admired women, as is obvious in his early poetry. Much of it focuses on monogamous love and the importance of shared dedication. It also acknowledges differences between the sexes, holding at times to the traditional beliefs of his age. Those beliefs held that women should exercise control in their lovemaking, while men could make love at will, yet proposed men's love as more pure. Much of the era's religious and civic law supported that view. While Donne's love poetry clearly differs in tone and theme from that of the religious poetry he would later write, including his *HOLY SONNETS,* he often employed biblical and religious allusions. As is obvious in the title to his poem, "Air and Angels," he believed that religion and carnal love could be considered in the same context, an unusual attitude for his day. In the poem he plays with the philosophy that described angels as able to assume human form, while constituted only of air. The airy form proved pure, but not to the degree of the angel's heavenly form. He advanced this idea in "Air and Angels," associating the different levels of purity with female and male capacities to love. As with many of the ideas Donne adapts for poetic means, he did not necessarily believe them.

The speaker begins the first of the two 14-line verses with a dreamy tone. He confesses to the object of his desire that he had previously engaged in fantasy regarding her existence: "Twice or thrice had I loved thee, / Before I knew thy face or name." He suggests the traditional Petrarchan ideal of the female, to which a real woman could never aspire. However, the next two lines suggest a tempered approach, as Donne adopts an abundance of s sounds in ALLITERATION to produce a softened effect: "So in a voice, so in a shapeless flame, / Angels affect us oft, and worshipped be." He suggests he had heard a particular timbre in a voice that attracted him, and that he visualized his love in flame, the shape of which changes too often to form a true representation. Despite man's presumed superiority to woman, her presence proves a necessity. The effect of his fantasy is that of an angel, an airy and difficult-to-recognize form that yet commands respect and reverence. The speaker continues, "Still when, to where thou wert, I came, / Some lovely glorious nothing I did see." Donne manages to use repetition of the w sound to pleasing effect, exercising an uncommon ability to make the harsh sounding term *wert* appealing. Because the reader understands the common view that angels assume forms of air, the phrase *lovely glorious nothing* makes sense, as one cannot see air. However, the speaker makes the point that just as his own soul requires a body to function, love must also assume a corporeal form, logic typical of Donne's poetic voices:

> But since my soul, whose child love is,
> Takes limbs of flesh, and else nothing do,
> More subtle than the parent is
> Love must not be, but take a body too.

By the conclusion of the first stanza the speaker has requested that love take form in a body, fixing "itself in thy lip, eye, and brow." The PETRARCHAN tradition often categorized the physical parts of the female body, an approach that Donne employs.

Donne next adopts an extended nautical metaphor, referring to his attempts to "ballast love" and steady the situation "With wares which would sink admiration, / I saw I had love's pinnace overfraught." The *wares* equate to his lover's overwhelming beauty, and *pinnace* refers to a small boat, reflecting on the previous verb *sink*. The speaker continues describing the ultimate nature of his love. If he dotes on every hair, that will be "much too much," but love cannot adhere to "nothing, nor in things / Extreme and scatt'ring bright." Donne returns to the myth regarding angels, whose earthly form might scatter diffused light, offering the only manner by which to recognize their airy presence.

The speaker concludes by commenting on the difference between the virtue of an angel while in heaven and its lesser virtue in earthly form. While he has complimented his love by comparing her to an angel, he has also suggested that she lacked purity, like an angel on Earth. Because the male was believed more constant, he suggests that her love might form a sphere around his own, based on his era's belief in the Ptolemaic theory of the universe as overlapping concentric spheres. His love, the stronger and more pure, could move within her sphere, acting as a control:

> Then as an angel, face and wings
> Of air, not pure as it, yet pure doth wear,
> So thy love may be my love's sphere;
> Just such disparity
> As 'twixt air and angels' purity,
> 'Twixt women's love and men's will ever be.

The message in this poem differed from that in much of Donne's love poetry, in which he claimed that pure love not only united two people, but made them one and the same person. His use of enchanting imagery and bewitching sounds, however, supports a thoughtful tone not typical of an insincere person. Despite the speaker's claims of male superiority, he reveals a touching vulnerability and remains susceptible to the promise of feminine attention. He also seems to fear that his love may vanish, like so much thin air.

BIBLIOGRAPHY

Grennen, Joseph, E., ed. *The Poetry of John Donne & Metaphysical Poets.* New York: Monarch Press, 1965.

Eliot, T. S. *The Varieties of Metaphysical Poetry.* Edited by Ronald Schuchard. New York: Harcourt Brace, 1994.

Wilcox, Helen, Richard Todd, and Alasdair MacDonald, eds. *Sacred and Profane: Secular and Devotional Interplay in Early Modern British Literature.* Amsterdam: VU University Press, 1996.

ALABASTER, WILLIAM (1567/8–1640)

William Alabaster was born on January 27, 1567/8, in Hadleigh, Suffolk. The eldest in a family that included six children, he matured as a Protestant in a family proud of its Norman heritage and engagement in trade. His father, Roger, was a clothier and related to the Winthrops, well-known Anglian Puritans. William's uncle, John Still, served as master of Trinity College in Cambridge and as bishop of Bath and Wells. He decided to supervise Alabaster's education, encouraging his nephew to learn classical languages. Alabaster did not disappoint his uncle, becoming a Queen's Scholar to Trinity College in 1584. While finishing his education, he wrote poetry as an active member of Cambridge literary coteries. Two poems written between 1588 and 1592 eventually attracted the attention of literary greats. Alabaster's friend Edmund Spenser alluded to his *Elisaeis,* an epic about Queen Elizabeth, in Spenser's *Colin Clouts Come Home Againe* (1595), and SAMUEL JOHNSON (1709–84) judged Alabaster's tragedy *Roxana* some of the best of English Latin verse to precede the work of JOHN MILTON. An ambitious man, Alabaster knew he was destined to join the clergy and became chaplain to Robert Devereux, earl of Essex, in 1596, accompanying Devereux on a famous voyage to Cádiz.

Upon his return to England, Alabaster experienced the first of several religious conversions when he became a Catholic. He later wrote in an autobiography that in 1596 at Michaelmas he felt more tender toward "Christes Crosse and Passion" than most Protestants, then described visions that succeeded in shaking his faith. On Easter 1597, while visiting a friend, he met Thomas Wright, an outspoken Catholic priest who had led BEN JONSON from Protestantism. Wright's arguments supported Alabaster's reading of a French publication by William Rainolds titled *A refutation of sundry reprehensions.* According to the scholars G. M. Story and Helen Gardner, he vividly described his conversion, writing, "I lept vp from the place where I satt, and saide to my self 'Now I am a Catholique,' and then fell down vpon my knees." His fascinating but damaged and often indecipherable autobiography titled "The Conversion of Alabaster" has never been printed and is at the English College in Rome.

Alabaster spent the next five months immersed in reading and study, delaying his wedding and converting family members, while writing religious poetry. His *Seven Motives,* describing how he was moved to convert, caused an order for his arrest in September 1597. He was under house arrest by the university beadle until October, when he traveled to London and suffered a light imprisonment in a private home. For six months, authorities, including his uncle John Still, in addition to a former schoolmaster urged him to recant in private conferences. He refused, and his Anglican orders were removed in February 1597/8 while further punishment was considered. Not allowed any public defense of his beliefs, Alabaster decided to escape.

Alabaster remained in hiding during summer 1597/8 and fled across the Channel in September, taking refuge in a convent in November. He planned eventually to return to London to testify in favor of Catholicism. During a visit to Spain, he was arrested and sent to England, where he was imprisoned in the Tower of London in early August 1599. He was examined for nearly a year, claiming to act as an emissary promoting peace between England and Spain, although his claims were never proved. By 1601, he had been moved from the Tower to live imprisoned in Framlingham Castle, Suffolk, until James I ascended the throne and pardoned Alabaster in 1603. He returned to prison after the Gunpowder Plot, when Catholic persecution increased. By 1606 he remained confined at the King's Bench prison, where he wrote to Robert Cecil, offering to spy on the political Catholic émigrés.

Alabaster wrote his *Apparatus in Revelationeum Iesu Christi,* essays in mystic theology, which was printed in Antwerp, in 1607. His writing and action drew the disfavor of Rome, and he was called before the Inquisition, his *Apparatus* labeled heretical in 1609/10. Ordered not to leave Rome, he denied the church and fled to Marseilles, where by July he was accusing Catholics of involvement in the Gunpowder Plot. The English authorities remained unconvinced of his denial of Rome and ordered him into confinement at the house

of the dean of St. Paul, his Cambridge fellow John Overall. By 1610/11 Alabaster regretted his separation from Rome and again declared himself a Catholic. While little detail of his life during the next few years exists, he was again a Protestant by 1613/14 and in favor with King James, who declared him a doctor of divinity at Cambridge, a benefit noted by JOHN DONNE in correspondence. John Chamberlain labeled Alabaster a "double or treble turncoat" in January 1614/15, noting that not many clergy applauded him but remarking that Alabaster was yet a "curious fantasticall piece of worke."

Alabaster at last settled into his writing over the next few decades, although in his time his fame remained that of a clergyman. He outraged many by attempting to reveal the true hidden meaning of Scripture in his interpretations, which seldom prompted positive criticism. ROBERT HERRICK offered a rare tribute to Alabaster in one of his own poems, and BEN JONSON befriended him late in life. The SONNETs in his *DIVINE MEDITATIONS* remain crucial to the new style of the METAPHYSICAL POETS AND POETRY, which first became popular in the last years of the Elizabethan age; examples include SONNET 10, SONNET 15, and SONNET 46. They also extended the devotional tradition of the 17th century that persisted, despite various religious upheavals and reformation attempts. Alabaster wrote his will in March 1640 and died on April 28.

As an English sonnet poet Alabaster did not receive much attention, perhaps because his poetry circulated mainly in manuscript form. His work was seldom referenced later, although the 1821 (Third Variorum) *Shakespeare* contained two sonnets, and John Payne Collier published an additional two in *History of English Dramatic Poetry* in 1831. In the early 20th century, 43 of his sonnets were discovered and six of those printed as the work of an "Elizabethan divine and neo-Latin Poet" along with a brief biography in a 1903 edition of the *Athenaeum.* Later an additional 164 sonnets by Alabaster were identified at St. John's College, Cambridge. A few of the sonnets were published in 1904 in *Month,* and research on his life appeared in *Recusant Poets* (1938). Two sonnets were reprinted in *Poets of the English Language* (1952) by W. H. Auden and N. H. Pearson. With the introduction of electronic postings, the University of Birmingham developed and sponsors a Web site, The Philological Museum, that carries links to a portion of Alabaster's interrogation during the Inquisition written in both Latin and an English translation, along with a hypertext Latin version of his play *Roxana*. With the revival in Donne's popularity in the 20th century, critics hoped that Alabaster's *Devine Meditations,* composed of 77 sonnets, might also be widely anthologized. That did not happen, however, and his poetry still awaits discovery by 21st-century readers.

BIBLIOGRAPHY
Story, G. M., and Helen Gardner, eds. *The Sonnets of William Alabaster.* New York: Oxford University Press, 1959.
Sutton, Dana F. "William Alabaster: Six Responses (1598)." The Philological Museum. University of Birmingham. Available online. URL: http://www.philological.bham. ac.uk/alab/. Downloaded on December 11, 2004.

ALEXANDER, SIR WILLIAM (FIRST EARL OF STIRLING) (1567–1640)

Born in Scotland, the CAVALIER POET William Alexander wrote in his youth a group of SONNETS and songs titled *AURORA, First Fancies of the Author's Youth,* but the collection was not published until 1604. He tutored King James VI's son, Henry, and after becoming a courtier in 1603, he followed King James, then the English King James I, to London. There he published The TRAGEDY OF DARIUS in about 1604. He later added *The Tragedie of Croesus* and *The Paranesis to Prince Henry* and reprinted the group. After Prince Henry's death he served Prince Charles as a courtier. The tragedies were released again in 1607 with the addition of *The Alexandrean Tragedy* and *Julius Caesar.* As part of his court duties Alexander assisted King James in his "translation" of the Psalms and received knighthood in 1621. That same year, received a charter for Nova Scotia, but his colonization attempts proved unsuccessful. In 1626 he became secretary of state for Scotland and was titled the viscount Canada in 1630, and earl of Stirling in 1633. In 1637 he published his final poem, a religious work titled *Domesday,* and issued a folio edition of his tragedies.

All of Alexander's works sold well and rated positive evaluations from contemporaries, Samuel Daniel, MICHAEL DRAYTON, and others, including his close friend WILLIAM DRUMMOND OF HAWTHORNDEN, whose work Alexander's sonnets influenced. Drummond dedicated a poem to Alexander, "Sonnet to Sir W. Alexander," in which he compared their friendship to that of "The love Alexis did to Damon bear." Despite his popularity and service to both King James I and King Charles I, Alexander died impoverished in 1640. Much detail regarding his life has been lost or was never printed; most critical sources paraphrase the information about Alexander found in Sir Humphry Ward's 19th-century volume on English poets. In his entry Ward quotes Masson, biographer of Drummond, repeating his "severe judgment" of Alexander: "There he lies, I suppose, to this day, vaguely remembered as the second-rate Scottish sycophant of an inglorious despotism, and the author of a large quantity of fluent and stately English verse which no one reads."

BIBLIOGRAPHY
Survey of British Poetry: Cavalier to Restoration. Vol. 2. Edited by the Editorial Board, Roth Publishing. Great Neck, N.Y.: Poetry Anthology Press, 1989.
Ward, Thomas Humphry. *The English Poets: Selections with Critical Introductions by Various Writers and a General Introduction by Matthew Arnold.* Vol. 2. 1880, Reprint, New York: Macmillan, 1912.

"ALEXANDER'S FEAST; OR THE POWER OF MUSIC" JOHN DRYDEN (1697)

JOHN DRYDEN wrote his second ode in celebration of St. Cecilia's Day, "Alexander's Feast; Or the Power of Music," 10 years after his first tribute, "A Song for St. Cecilia's Day." Set to music by Jeremiah Clarke, it became Dryden's most popular song.

The ode's topic was dictated by the fact that the day celebrated music, with the martyred St. Cecilia traditionally recognized as the creator of the organ. While Dryden's first effort had praised various instruments and the human passions they aroused, the second tribute focused on two classical stories. One featured Timotheus the musician and Alexander the Great, the other Alexander with his beautiful courtesan bride Thais on their wedding day. Timotheus entertains the couple and their guests and moves Alexander, the great warrior, from one passion to another. The drunken Alexander eventually dissolves into weeping, offering the audience a new view of the mighty warrior, all due to the power of music.

Critics praised the energy of the ode, which served to invigorate and renew the stories for an appreciative audience. Earl Miner sees a parallel between the manipulation of Alexander by the musician artist Timotheus and Dryden's manipulation of his audience through the art of poetry. In the narrative, St. Cecilia eventually enters toward its conclusion but plays a minor part in the presentation. Alexander remains its center and the audience favorite. The seven stanzas vary in length, with each engaging in much repetition and ALLITERATION to the pleasing effect common to musical verse. Each contains a chorus, which serves to comment on the scene, always preserving an uplifting mood despite the consideration of death and war.

The first stanza sets the scene, with Alexander described as "The godlike hero" and Thais as "like a blooming Eastern bride / In flow'r of youth and beauty's pride." The four brief lines preceding the chorus fill with a celebratory tone:

> Happy, happy, happy pair!
> None but the brave,
> None but the brave,
> None but the brave deserves the fair.

The second stanza introduces the musician Timotheus, "plac'd on high" in the middle of the choir. He plays his lyre with "flying fingers," his music ascending to the heavens, where it inspires joy. Lush imagery recreates the journey of Jove, moved by love in "A dragon's fiery form" and riding "on radiant spires" to Olympia. He then "stamp'd an image of himself, a sov'reign of the world," and the audience assumes that stamp is Alexander. Jove's act, according to the chorus, "seems to shake the spheres," a comparison of the warrior prince's birth to a portent. The third stanza praises Bacchus, god of celebration and drink. The celebration that Dryden describes had followed Alexander's attack on the Persian capital city of Persepolis. The original story stresses the greed of the looting soldiers, who lost all control in their thievery and destruction of priceless treasures. Timotheus foreshadows the increased destruction that will follow the drunken debauchery, as he sings,

> Drinking is the soldier's pleasure;
> > Rich the treasure,
> > Sweet the pleasure
> Sweet the pleasure after pain.

In stanza 4, Timotheus recalls that "the King grew vain, / Fought all his battles o'er again," and describes Alexander, as three times "he routed all his foes, and thrice he slew / the slain." He sings of the madness of battle that challenged Alexander, the passion for war eventually softened by pity for Darius, the Persian ruler. At that point, Alexander "the joyless victor sat" as he considered chance, suggesting that he might have been in Darius's place if not for fate, and he weeps. Stanza five celebrates the softening of the mighty master as "pity melts the mind to love." Timotheus sings that war "is toil and trouble, / Honour but an empty bubble," and he urges Alexander to consider that "If the world be worth thy winning, / Think, O think it worth enjoying." He reminds the ruler of his lovely bride, and then:

> The Prince, unable to conceal his pain,
> > Gaz'd on the fair
> > Who caused his care,
> > And sighed and look'd, sigh'd and look'd,
> > Sigh'd and look'd, and sigh'd again;
> At length, with love and wine at once oppress'd,
> The vanquish'd victor sunk upon her breast.

Interestingly while remaining undefeated on the field, Alexander falls under the control of a mere woman. As do many mortal women in classical stories, Thais will co-opt the power of the male, tempting men with the passions she arouses to do as she bids them.

In the sixth stanza Timotheus describes the prince awakening as he hears the lyre, amazed to "See the Furies arise! / See the snakes that they rear," with the ghastly sights explained as ghosts of those slain in battle. Traditionally women who haunted men, the Furies symbolize Thais in her control of Alexander, while the snakes suggest the temptation of Eve in the Garden of Eden that led to original sin. Dryden's audience would have been familiar with the story of Thais's tempting Alexander to burn Persepolis, after his men's drunken looting of its riches. Thais led a procession of warriors and women to the accompaniment of flutes and pipes, as if in a grand celebration, and convinced Alexander to hurl his torch into the city. Her torch followed, and then hundreds of others, and the once-glorious city was destroyed. In Dryden's ode Thais "led the way" of the revenging king "to light him to his prey / And like another Helen fir'd another Troy." The reference to Helen also reflects on the power of women to stir men's passions, even to war. That Thais used instruments during her "parade" to the city also suggests the power of music to stir passions, helping to overcome the strength of even the great Alexander.

St. Cecilia, patroness of music, does arrive in the final stanza, following all of the action, and

> Enlarg'd the former narrow bounds
> And added length to solemn sounds
> With nature's mother-wit and arts unknown
> before.
> Or both divide the crown;
> He rais'd a mortal to the skies;
> She drew an angel down.

The "narrow bounds" she enlarges with her music are those tied to the ability of mere mortals to make music. Where Timotheus praises the mortal, Alexander, raising his name to the heights reserved for celebrated individuals, St. Cecilia's music is so powerful that it tempts heavenly creatures to descend to earth.

As he did with Dryden's first effort, G. F. Handel later reset "Alexander's Feast" to new music. It made its debut in Covent Garden on February 19, 1736, proving an instant success with its audience of 1,300, and Handel's version remains a well-known song in Germany. Amadeus Mozart also set it to music in 1790. The ode has been continuously praised over the three centuries since its writing as one of the most beautiful ever written in English.

BIBLIOGRAPHY
Miner, Earl, ed. *Selected Poetry and Prose of John Dryden.* New York: The Modern Library, 1985.

ALLEGORY Allegory adopts tropes, most commonly FIGURATIVE LANGUAGE, to suggest a symbolic meaning supporting a work's literal meaning. A literal sequence in narrative allegory may correspond to psychological, spiritual, moral, or historical occurrences or ideas, usually in an attempt to clarify aspects of human nature or the material world. Although meant to simplify meaning, some poetic allegory is so dense or obscure that readers may be unable to identify its reference. Originally popular in mythology, allegory appears in all religious writings. The Middle Ages identified four aspects of meaning in biblical texts. The first was the literal, the second allegorical, the third tropological or moral, and the fourth anagogical. Edmund Spenser's *The Fairie Queene* (1590, 1596) was a popular Renaissance allegory, and JOHN MILTON would later include the allegorical figures of Sin and Death in his epic work about man's fall from grace, PARADISE LOST (1667). However, JOHN DRYDEN's use in *The HIND AND THE PANTHER* (1687) produced a rather distasteful humor, purposely contrived by the poet. Dryden felt his audience needed the occasional absurdity in order to understand references they might find obscure. In his fables of the Swallows and the Pigeons in part 3, readers had to absorb the fabulous suggestion of a Catholic Hind explaining to an Anglican Panther that Catholic Poultry, even though promiscuous, were of higher value than Anglican Pigeons. The use of serious allegory in elevated form dwindled during the 17th century, although it was put to great use in the more traditional religious sense by John Bunyan. His use of allegory in the prose *Pilgrim's Progress* (1678, 1684) was judged coarse but proved effective for the common reader.

BIBLIOGRAPHY
Bloomfield, Morton W., ed. *Allegory, Myth and Symbol.* Cambridge, Mass.: Harvard University Press, 1981.
Greenblatt, Stephen J., ed. *Allegory and Representation.* Baltimore: Johns Hopkins University Press, 1981.
Miner, Earl, ed. *Selected Poetry and Prose of John Dryden.* New York: The Modern Library, 1969.

ALLITERATION Alliteration may be defined as repetition of sound in two or more words. It may appear for effect in any type of writing and is a favorite device of poets in their concentrated medium. The repetition of initial consonants in words is the most common form of alliteration. Examples may be found in a line from WILLIAM ALEXANDER's *The TRAGEDY OF DARIUS,* "time, through Jove's judgment just," a heavy-handed use intended to call order to the sense, more than the sound, of the three *j* terms, positioned in contrived order. JOHN DONNE, on the other hand, seldom adopts alliteration except for sound's sense, as in his famous "fixt foot" reference to a compass in "A VALEDICTION FORBIDDING MOURNING," which presents an abrupt contrast to the softer sounds that surround it. ROBERT HERRICK's use with the letter *f* is more gentle in his "CANDLEMAS EVE" as he describes flowers used "To Honour Whitsuntide" as "Both of a fresh and fragrant kin." ALEXANDER POPE applied alliteration to satire for a humorous effect, as in the famous line from *The RAPE OF THE LOCK,* "But when to mischief Mortals bend their Mind." In a less common usage labeled "hidden alliteration," the sound repetition is internal and may be combined with the initial sound repetition as well. In James Shirley's "A Dirge," he makes the point, using both types of alliteration, that in battle, neither combatant may win, by labeling one such combatant a *victor-victim.* WILLIAM HABINGTON's "Nox Nocti Indicat Scientiam" contains the phrase *Almighty's mysteries,* an example of internal alliteration with the *t* sound. It also represents consonance, in which similar consonants are repeated with different vowels, the *m* and *t* in each word separated by an *i* and *y* consecutively. Another repetition, termed assonance, displays the reverse approach, with similar vowels and different consonants, as in the same poem's phrases "shoots forth" and "speaking the Creator's."

"ALTAR, THE" GEORGE HERBERT (1633)

One of GEORGE HERBERT's famous pattern or SHAPE POEMS, "The Altar" appeared as part of his collection titled *The Temple.* If one simply performs an uninformed close reading of the poem, conforming to the formalist critical school of thought, its sentiment may be seen as uncomplicated and straightforward, the speaker offering a prayer to God to sanctify his heart. Herbert uses the altar as an extended metaphor for the human heart, which, in the case of this speaker, is broken. The cement holding the stones of the altar together consists of tears, and the speaker notes that only the Lord's

power can cut the stone that is his heart. The pieces of his heart join to form the altar, meeting "in this frame" in order that he may praise the Lord's name. The penultimate line, "O, let thy blessed Sacrifice be mine," refers to the sacrifice made by God when he gave his son to save humans. The speaker desires to make such a sacrifice himself, asking that God "sanctify" his heart.

However, if one chooses instead to use the New Historical critical approach to understanding the poem, bringing to its reading knowledge of Herbert's era, its effect may differ. As Cristina Malcolmson explains, the Arminians, a group who reacted against Calvinistic aspects of the English church to assert a belief in free, not earned, grace, in 1617 removed the wooden communion table that represented Christ's last supper from its traditional east-west-facing location in the Durham Cathedral choir. They instead set it "north-south altarwise," moving it to the chapel's east end. By 1620 the wooden communion table was gone, replaced by an altar of stone. Herbert's poem suggests that the Arminians' act of moving the altar succeeded in separating the human from that altar. Their focus on ceremony and obedience differed from the traditional focus on the need for grace, a requirement for personal reform, represented by the communion table. Herbert, as one who held Calvinist beliefs, also seemed to help unite two dissenting groups by using a symbol important to Arminians but emphasizing the theme of grace, which would be appreciated by Puritans. Herbert emphasizes that "grace rather than merit breaks the resistance within and provides the willingness to obey." Only God's grace can affect the heart in this way, and Herbert again suggests a contrast between the work of man, the altar, and that of God.

The obvious skill required to form lines to shape an altar pattern remains admirable, as does the text, which supports the visual representation. The icon shape requires that the rhyming couplets vary in line length. Herbert begins with iambic pentameter for his first two lines, with the next two losing one metric foot each in order to comply with the demands of the shape. The column is constructed of eight three- or four-word lines with two beats each. The pedestal repeats the construction of the first four lines, inverting line order with the final two lines containing five feet. The suggestion of construction and stones accumulating to shape an altar is reflected in Herbert's physical construction of the image.

The Altar

A broken ALTAR, Lord thy servant rears,
Made of a heart, and cemented with teares:
Whose parts are as thy hand did frame;
No workmans tool hath touch'd the same
    A   HEART   alone
    Is   such   a   stone,
    As   nothing   but
    Thy pow'r doth cut.
    Wherefore each part
    Of my hard heart
    Meets in this frame,
    To praise thy Name:
That if I chance to hold my peace,
These stones to praise thee may not cease.
O let thy blessed SACRIFICE be mine,
And sanctifie this ALTAR to be thine

BIBLIOGRAPHY

Malcolmson, Cristina. *George Herbert: A Literary Life.* New York: Palgrave Macmillan, 2004.

"AMBITION" MARY ASTELL (1689)
MARY ASTELL proved unusual among her contemporaries in supporting personal independence for women, although within the traditional patriarchal social structure. If society accepted the natural equality of the sexes, women could benefit from expansion of economic and work opportunities. Astell defended that idea in her prose. In her poem "Ambition," written while she was a teenager on March 30, 1684, Astell proposes faith as a more traditional route to independence. In four eight-line verses composed of four couplets each, she suggests that the immortality sought by male writers and those who possess an ambition for fame pales when compared to the ideal of Christian immortality. As her biographer Ruth Perry suggests, Astell made "a virtue of necessity" as she attempted to benefit from her gender's submissive position.

"Ambition" opens with the self-questioning of the poem's persona, who asks herself, "What's this that with such vigor fills my breast?" She next compares the force she feels to that of "the first mover," alluding to the medieval astronomical plan featuring the primum mobile. It occupied the outermost sphere but affected all aspects of the universe with its movement, making, as the speaker notes, "all submit to its imperial laws!" Astell therefore equates ambition to the strongest universal force, one that did not always result in good. Her next comparison of ambition is to "what Prometheus stole," referring to the mythological story of the Titan Prometheus, assigned by Jupiter to make humans from mud and water, who gave them the forbidden gift of fire. His punishment was consignment for eternity to pushing a large stone up a steep grade only to have it roll back again, requiring continuous repetition of his movements. She thus suggests that ambition leads to futility. Astell concludes the first verse with the persona announcing she cannot control the "sophistry," or deception, of those "Who falsely say that women have no soul." Thus, she begins her argument not only in favor of religious faith, but of women's place within that faith.

In verse two, the voice strongly declares,
Vile greatness! I disdain to bow to thee,
Thou are below even lowly me,
I would no fame, no titles have,
And no more land than what will make a grave.

Astell makes clear that despite man's collection of titles and material goods, all humans must eventually bow to the universal leveler, death. She continues explaining that she has no desire to "reign" over worlds but wishes only for "empire o'er my self obtain." Self-control remained a social edict for women, who in Renaissance times were believed to have wild sexual desires that men had to control, for the good of the women themselves. One theory, inherited from the classical beliefs of the physician Galen, held that women's wombs wandered about their bodies when they lacked sexual satisfaction. Even in the Augustan age of reason, traditional views of women persisted. Astell extends the metaphor of kingship as she mentions Caesar and Alexander, the speaker declaring,

> I scorn to weep for worlds, may I but reign
> And empire o'er my self obtain,
> In Caesar's throne I'd not sit down,
> Nor would I stoop for Alexander's crown.

Astell's imagery of a person sitting and stooping suggests that rather than lowering herself by proclaiming victory over others, she would prefer to raise herself to higher moral ground by gaining self-control.

The third stanza allows the speaker to focus solely on herself, although claiming to reject public focus, asking that she may remain obscure "and never known," not "pointed at about the town," not having her name repeated by "Short-winded fame," only "that the next age may censure it." She remains demure in rejecting the attention that accompanies a false, short-lived fame, referencing the fickle nature of humankind, which may later reject what it today celebrates. Astell then references her own occupation as her speaker declares,

> If I write sense no matter what they say,
> Whether they call it dull or pay
> A reverence such as Virgil claims,
> Their breath's infectious, I have higher aims.

She implies that public opinion does not represent the true worth of one's written words. Astell, of course, does not seriously believe that her writing could be on the level of that by VIRGIL but rather refers to his status as the dominant voice of Latin literature to suggest IRONY in the fact that his value is found in the mere breath of men. She uses the word *infectious* to mean that the common man speaks of immoral, or infected, matters. When she mentions that she has "higher aims," she shocks readers by claiming her own goal to be more valuable than the reverence in which her contemporaries held Virgil.

Astell concludes her poem in her fourth verse by labeling those men who "bait at honor, praise, / A wreath of laurel or of bays" as "mean-spirited." In these lines *bait* means "stop," and the wreath extends the previous classical references, as victors of competitions in ancient Greece won crowns of laurel, of which bay is one type. Her next line echoes that imagery, "But oh a crown of glory ne'er will die!" as she skillfully moves from a classical tradition into a religious one and returns to the theme of immortality. The speaker references the title as she states, "This I'm ambitious of, no pains will spare / To have a higher mansion there," referencing the biblical statement of John 14:2, "In my Father's house are many mansions." She therefore echoes a promise, calling upon the highest of all authorities to validate her poem.

Astell concludes by emphasizing one of her favorite themes, the natural equality of the sexes, writing, "There all are kings," and makes a final request, balancing the repeated "there" with "here": "here let me be, / Great O my God, great in humility." Astell concludes with a PARADOX, informing readers that humility signals a type of greatness with which broader society is not generally impressed. She succeeds in shaming those "vile" and "mean-spirited" men who claim women cannot commune with God because of lack of a soul, as all the while those men separate themselves from God through a desire for empty earthly glory.

BIBLIOGRAPHY
Perry, Ruth. *The Celebrated Mary Astell: An Early English Feminist.* Chicago: Chicago University Press, 1986.

"ANATOMY OF THE WORLD, AN" JOHN DONNE (1611, 1633)

JOHN DONNE's "An Anatomy of the World" was one of few works published during his lifetime. Composed of two poems, "The First Anniversary" and "The Second Anniversary," they eulogize Elizabeth Drury, the 14-year-old daughter of his patron, Sir Robert Drury. Originally Donne planned to write a poem per year on the anniversary of Elizabeth's death, but he abandoned that plan when public reaction proved negative. Others agreed with BEN JONSON, who criticized "An Anatomy of the World" as profane, labeling it a blasphemy. Donne defended the poems by famously explaining that he "described the Idea of a Woman, and not as she was." Because of the work's specific purpose, it does not represent Donne's best talent. It also departs from the traditional elegy focus on praise of the dead to comment on the world's disintegration. Donne adopts imagery of decay to describe a culture no longer supported by a shared moral vision. The term *Anatomy* in the title warns readers that he will perform a rhetorical dissection of the world as he viewed it. Not original in his approach, Donne adopted various models, as did most poets. The critic Andrew Fleck has claimed that the PETRARCHAN "Sonnet 338" influenced "The First Anniversary" as both view the world empty of value as a result of a virtuous woman's death. Donne even incorporates some of Petrarch's imagery in his own work.

While seldom completely anthologized, the entire text of "An Anatomy of the World," as of Donne's other works, may be easily accessed in electronic form. The University of Oregon has included online in its *Renascence Editions* a transcribed copy by the Facsimile Text Society. It derives from the 1621 copy housed in the British Museum. Original copies exist in various rare book collections, including the Fisher Rare Book Library in Toronto.

BIBLIOGRAPHY

Donne, John. "An Anatomy of the World." Transcribed by R. S. Bear. Facsimile Text Society. 1927. *Renascence Editions.* The University of Oregon. Available online. URL: http://darkwing.uoregon.edu/~rbear/donne1.html. Downloaded on June 10, 2005.

Fleck, Andrew. "The Ring of the World: Donne's Appropriation of Petrarch's 'Sonnet 338' in 'The First Anniversary.'" *Notes and Queries* 49, no. 3 (September 2002): 327.

ANNUS MIRABILIS: THE YEAR OF WONDERS, 1666 JOHN DRYDEN (1667)

With *Annus Mirabilis* JOHN DRYDEN published his first major nondramatic poem, and his last major poem utilizing the heroic quatrain format. In addition to its subtitle, *The Year of Wonders, 1666,* the work contained an explanation beneath the title identifying those wonders: "AN HISTORICAL POEM: CONTAINING THE PROGRESS AND VARIOUS SUCCESSES OF OUR NAVAL WAR WITH HOLLAND, UNDER THE CONDUCT OF HIS HIGHNESS PRINCE RUPERT, AND HIS GRACE THE DUKE OF ALBEMARLE, AND DESCRIBING THE FIRE OF LONDON." Dryden labeled it a historical poem, explaining in his introductory material that written wit "is that which is well defin'd, the happy result of thought

or product of that imagination." He continues, "But to proceed from wit in the general notion of it to the proper wit of an heroic or historical poem, I judge it chiefly to consist in the delightful imaging of persons, actions, passions, or things."

Critics have judged Dryden's critical material almost as valuable as the verses that follow, as he continues explaining his approach by comparing it to that of the classical writers Lucan, VIRGIL, and Ovid. He notes that description must be "dress'd in such colours of speech that it sets before your eyes the absent object as perfectly and more delightfully than nature." He next describes what he calls the three elements representing the "happiness of the poet's imagination." The first happiness is "invention, or finding of the thought," while the second "is fancy, or the variation, driving or moulding of that thought, as the judgment represents it proper to the subject." In his opinion, Ovid most famously accomplishes those happinesses. Virgil best accomplishes the third happiness, which is "elocution, or the art of clothing and adorning that thought so found and varied, in apt, significant, and sounding words." All three remain crucial to proper execution, as "quickness in the imagination" remains responsible for "invention, the fertility in the fancy, and the accuracy in the expression."

Dryden well exhibits all of these ideals in his 304 four-line stanzas. He explains that he selects the quatrain "in alternate rhyme, because I have ever judg'd them more noble and of greater dignity, both for the sound and number, than any other verse." Naturally in telling of miracles, a poet would select a format that imbued a dignified sense of pride. Acknowledging the simplicity of the couplet for easy rhyme, he explains that, by contrast, in the quatrain a poet is challenged to succeed. Poets correctly using this form "must needs acknowledge that the last line of the stanza is to be consider'd in the composition of the first."

As Earl Miner discusses, Dryden's purpose was to encourage readers that the source of England's woes lay in the past, in the country's enemies, and even in human nature. This proved important when speaking to a certain faction who blamed the war and the fire on divine retribution. They conceived history as a combination of God's acts and those of nature, and many believed a natural disaster, such as the fire that devastated London, was the result of God's displeasure with the restoration of the king to the throne. Portents also proved important, and Dryden combines these ideas in Stanza 16 to suggest that God approved of the English action against the Dutch. He used the FIGURATIVE LANGUAGE of metaphor to compare two comets sighted in November and December of 1664 to candles, sent by angels to light the English way:

To see this fleet upon the oceans move
Angels drew wide the curtains of the skies,
And Heav'n, as if there wanted lights above,
For tapers made two glaring comets rise.

Dryden alludes again in stanza 22 to the fact that God took the side of the English in battle, a fact admitted by the Dutch when they lose their commander, Sir John Lawson:

Their chief blown up, in air, not waves expir'd,
To which his pride presum'd to give the law;
The Dutch confess'd Heav'n present and retir'd,
And all was Britain the wide ocean saw.

In stanza 192, however, Dryden seems to remind his readers that all sides in war may look to God as their guide, as he imagines the thoughts of the Dutch:

Their batter'd admiral too soon withdrew,
Unthank'd by ours for his unfinish'd fight,
But he the minds of his Dutch Masters knew,
Who call'd that Providence which we call'd
  flight.

As Dryden focused on four days of the second war with the Dutch, he praised Prince Rupert and James, duke of York, later to become King James II, for their part in settling it in England's favor. This aspect of the poem has caused critics also to categorize it as panegyric, a poem of praise, as Dryden writes in his introductory material of his two subjects, "it is no wonder if they inspir'd me with thoughts above my ordinary level." He devotes much praise to the duke of Albemarle as well, shaping powerful dialogue for the English:

75

Then, to the rest, "Rejoyce," said he, "today
In you the fortune of Great Britain lies;
Among so brave a people you are they
Whom Heav'n has chose to fight for such a
  prize.

76

If number English courages could quell,
We should at first have shunn'd not met our
  foes,
Whose numerous sails the fearful only tell:
Courage from hearts and not from numbers
  grows."

Dryden also examined the part of art and science in improving humans' lot in life. The poem's opening line seeks to credit art for Holland's strength: "In thriving arts long time had Holland grown, / Crouching at home, and cruel when abroad." He also inserted a section subtitled "Digression Concerning Shipping and Navigation" in which he began stanza 155, "By viewing Nature, Nature's handmaid Art, / Makes mighty things from small beginnings grow." Dryden next inserts an "Apostrophe to the Royal Society," the group formed under King Charles II, of which Dryden was a member, to investigate the many new scientific developments. He urges his audience to recognize the importance of study, writing in stanza 166,

O truly royal! Who behold the law
And rule of beings in your Maker's mind
And thence, like limbecs, rich ideas draw
To fit the levell'd use of humankind.

Just before stanza 209 Dryden inserts the subtitle "Transitum to the Fire of London." He reminds his readers of the pride the English felt after the defeat of the Dutch and the English sailors' looting of Holland's fleet, then suggests in stanza 210, "We urge an unseen fate to lay us low / And feed their envious eyes with English loss." Describing the death and devastation brought on by the fire, he focuses on the actions of King Charles and his brother, James, who received much credit for saving London. Of the king he writes in stanza 241,

> He wept the flames of what he lov'd so well
> And what so well had merited his love.
> For never prince in grace did more excel,
> Or royal city more in duty strove.

Then Dryden makes the point in line 966 that, unlike the people who could indulge in a numb terror, the king must act: "(Subjects may grieve, but monarchs must redress)." Charles ordered that several buildings be exploded with gunpowder in order to form a breech to stop the flames. Dryden describes the results, using personification in stanza 245:

> The powder blows up all before the fire;
> Th' amazed flames stand gather'd on a heap,
> And from the precipice's brink retire,
> Afraid to venture on so large a leap.

His plan worked, and some of London was saved, although the flames continued to wreak havoc, described with vivid imagery and the use of ALLITERA-TION in stanza 249: "No help avails: for, Hydra-like, the fire / Lifts up his hundred heads to aim his way." By night, when Charles is exhausted, he calls on James for help in stanza 253:

> The days were all in this lost labour spent,
> And when the weary King gave place to night,
> His beams he to his royal brother lent
> And so shone still in his reflective light.

Dryden conducts a bit of wordplay with the term *light*. Humans generally depended upon flame, in the controlled form of candles and lanterns to light their way. But in this instance, the ruler provides the metaphoric light to brighten a symbolic, as well as literal, dark hour in which London is tried by disaster. As a lesser body like the Moon reflects the Sun's light, James, a crucial person but not yet a king himself, reflects his brother's light to great advantage for them both.

As the fire at last burns out, Dryden suggests in stanza 293 that, as when fire is applied to ore to remove its impurities, London will be golden in its reincarnation:

> Methinks already, from this chemic flame,
> I see a city of more precious mold:
> Rich as the town which gives the Indies name,
> With silver pav'd and all divine with gold.

The poem concludes with an emphasis on London's future as a great trade seaport, interacting with the countries once its enemies. Mainly through Dryden's energy, the poem concludes on an optimistic note, despite the desolation it has described.

BIBLIOGRAPHY
Miner, Earl, ed. *Selected Poetry and Prose of John Dryden.*
New York: The Modern Library, 1985.

"ANSWER, THE" ANNE FINCH (1717) The friendship ANNE FINCH shared with ALEXANDER POPE was celebrated in their writing. In her poem "The Answer" it was Pope's work titled "Impromptu" to which Finch replied. Pope had at first written a poem to Finch subtitled "Occasioned by four satirical verses on women wits in *The Rape of the Lock.*" The lines in Pope's MOCK-HEROIC had suggested that certain females scribbled plays as a type of "treatment" for "hysteria," the root *hyster* derived from the Greek word meaning "womb." He humorously compared the writing by such women to the "physic" that others ingested to treat a disorder. Finch took his comments so much to heart, the two may have argued about them publicly. Pope then wrote "Impromptu," flattering Finch and implying she possessed much more talent than the female poets she often referenced in her poetry.

Finch begins "The Answer" by referencing the effect of Pope's "so genteel an air" in disarming her to the point that "The contest I give o'er." The term *contest* could refer to any conflict the two experienced, but most specifically, to that sparked by Pope's dismissive remarks about women. However, by the third line she warns, "Alexander, have a care, / And shock the sex no more," where *sex* refers to females. She warns Pope against condescension by illustrating the manner by which most men condescend to women when she writes that women well know they "rule the world" during their entire lives, while "Men but assume that right." She cleverly reverses the condescension, as women tolerate men's false assumptions. She next accuses men of immature actions in the presence of female beauty, and of inequity when their mates become annoyed by such behavior, as they establish themselves first "slaves to every tempting face, / then martyrs to our spite."

Finch also employs a classic reference to make her point, reminding Pope of "one Orpheus," referring to a mythical Greek poet. Orpheus's wife, Eurydice, was forced to remain in hell when Orpheus disobeyed instructions by the god of the underworld, Hades, not to look behind him as he departed Hades's realm. He proved too weak to resist the temptation to look, thus betraying his wife. Finch assumes a tart tone, stating that had Orpheus "been bred" in London, he would have "polished too his wit." *Wit* remained an important term in early 18th-century writing, a characteristic that distinguished excellent poets from mediocre ones; Finch uses it in IRONY. She frames a tale in which she imagines Orpheus incensing through his poetry the very "heroines," women like those who later dismembered the mythical Orpheus, whom he intends to impress. The classical heroines repaid his betrayal of Eurydice, and Finch includes gruesome imagery of the river Hebrus, which "rolled his skull / And harp besmeared with blood."

Finch's tone returns to mock-appreciative in line 25, as she makes clear Pope is nothing like Orpheus. He treats women's "follies gently." She adopts the FIGURATIVE LANGUAGE (FIGURE OF SPEECH) of metaphor to add, "And spin[s] so fine the thread, / You need not fear his awkward fate." Spinning and weaving had long been connected to storytelling and literature, especially alluding to Penelope, wife of Ulysseus, who wove her father-in-law's funeral shroud each day, then unraveled it at night in order to keep suitors at bay during her husband's years of absence. That Finch would compare Pope's work to the female art of spinning thread remains ironic. When she adds, "The lock won't cost the head," she refers to "The RAPE OF THE LOCK," in which the heroine loses a lock of her hair but retains her virginity under duress. Finch again displays wit by extending her comparison of Pope to women. She

assures Pope that all of his female readers greatly admire him, and "What next we look for at your hand / Can only raise it more." Still, she advised him to "sooth the ladies." She confesses, "We're born to wit, but to be wise / By admonitions taught." She tells Pope that wit comes naturally to women, so they will enjoy his poetry, but wisdom must be taught, through, she adds tongue in cheek, warnings by forces greater than they.

ANTITHESIS Antithesis is a rhetorical device that employs opposites for emphasis in a balanced contrast. In one example from GEORGE HERBERT's "AFFLICTION," the contrast occupies two lines: "Yet lest perchance I should too happy be / In my unhappiness," but in a chorus response in RICHARD CRASHAW's lengthy "In the Holy Nativity of Our Lord God," the contrast appears in a single line, structured as separate independent clauses: "Summer in winter. Day in night." In reference to holy forces Crashaw suggests a disturbance in the natural order. ALEXANDER POPE used antithesis to great advantage to reflect his fascination with PARADOX, a part of his neoclassicist view. In *AN ESSAY ON MAN* he follows his famous line "Hope springs eternal in the human breast;" with antithesis in "Man never Is, but always To be blest," emphasizing that human nature looks to the future for its blessings, rather than to the present. He concludes that work with several lines representing antithesis:

All Nature is but Art, unknown to thee;
All Chance, Direction, which thou canst not
  see;
All Discord, Harmony, not understood;
All partial Evil, universal Good.

He thus supports the common belief that opposites prove necessary, each supporting the understanding of the other, his overall suggestion being the importance of balance. Pope also includes in his *Imitations of Horace* antithetical phrases such as "'Tis the first Virtue, Vices to abhor / And the first Wisdom, to be Fool no more." These lines are examples of a closed couplet, which often engaged antithesis. JOHN MILTON employs antithesis in book 1 of *PARADISE LOST,* as his speaker declares that the human mind "Can make a Heav'n of Hell, a Hell of Heav'n," creating a pleasant sensation with his interchange of nouns, a prime example of sound supporting sense.

"APOLOGY, THE" ANNE FINCH (1713)
In her poem "The Apology" ANNE FINCH engages in an approach common to women writers of her era. She feels she must defend her desire to write. She does so first by questioning why she should not be allowed to write, when others take up the pen freely, and then includes other women in her verse with whom she may contrast and compare herself. Rather than a vehement declaration, the lines form a frustrated complaint, the tone never becoming petulant or accusatory, but remaining rather thoughtful, as if musing.

Finch opens with her speaker's stating that the fact that she writes is true, and asking to be told "what rule" states that "I am alone forbid to play the fool." Others can write, whether foolish or not, so why should not she? She favors the idea of following "a wandering muse" through a grove, emphasizing Finch's fondness for the country and nature. Other women, such as "Mira," paint their faces "to paint a thought; / Whilst Lamia to the manly bumper flies," where *bumper* means "a glass of wine." Those are activities deemed acceptable for women, neither requiring intellect nor imagination. Mira even attempts to pretend to think. The speaker suggests that writing surely proves more acceptable than those activities. Lamia has "borrowed spirits" of alcohol in order to make her eyes "sparkle": writing poetry does the same for the speaker, her passion needing no "borrowed spirit." Finch adopts the idea of emotion, the inspiration for art, as producing heat, when the speaker next asks, "Why should it be in me a thing so vain / To heat with poetry my colder brain?"

At line 11 her tone alters, becoming a bit more serious, as she states, "But I write ill and therefore should forbear," criticizing her own ability. However, not yet fully convinced, she adopts a name often used for a shepherdess in pastoral poetry to ask whether "Flavia" should stop letting people see her face at age 40, "Which all the town rejected at fifteen?" Perhaps Finch suggests that writing is as natural to her and as much a part of her as her appearance. If people did not like her appearance as a young woman, that would not cause her to hide herself from society years later.

Because weakness was expected in women, and they were deemed better subjects of poetry than writers of it, the speaker states in lines 15–16, "Each woman has her weakness; mine indeed / Is still to write though hopeless to succeed." Finch engages in false modesty, for her poetry was perfectly acceptable, and she did succeed in publishing it. She grows bolder in the next two lines, comparing herself for the first time to male writers: "Nor to the men is this so easy found / Even in most works with which the wits abound." Perhaps feeling she has overstepped her limits, Finch draws back in the penultimate line as her speaker acknowledges, "(So weak are all since our first breach with Heaven)." She refers to the belief that women remained responsible for the often miserable human condition because of Eve's sin, or "breach" in the garden. Feminist critics, however, would find the format as a parenthetical statement of interest, as one might theorize Finch expressed that as an afterthought, only to appease the "wits" who might feel insulted by her previous lines. She concludes that as a result of that breach, "There's less to be applauded than forgiven," where *forgiven* alludes to original sin that requires God's forgiveness.

Finch returns full circle, as she began by stating there is no reason she should not be allowed to join the ranks of other "fools" who write poetry. Men are allowed to write, even when the quality of their writing is less than admirable. If men argue that women will not write works of quality, were their statement true, it simply relegates them to the same acceptable level as those lesser male poets.

"APPARITION, THE" JOHN DONNE (1633)
JOHN DONNE's poetry includes several efforts never meant to be taken seriously, including "The Apparition." He adopts the voice of a lover scorned who imagines himself literally killed by that scorn. He then fantasizes how his spirit will revisit the woman who murdered him. The tone remains light, and because the first line turns on hyperbole, "When by thy scorn, O murderess, I am dead," the reader understands its

words are in jest. The poetic form is a single stanza of 17 lines, with the ninth and 13th lines indented and METER that varies from iambic pentameter to iambic dimeter.

In the second line the speaker lets the former lover know that just when she feels free "From all solicitation from me, / Then shall my ghost come to thy bed." He will visit her at night in the place he previously occupied. He assumes an accusatory tone, labeling her a *feigned vestal*, referencing the classical vestal virgins, sacred young women of Rome, with the adjective *feigned*, or pretended, reflecting negatively on her character and reputation for purity. He also places her in "worse arms" than his own, dooming her to find another man who does not measure up to his standard. With his visit already carefully planned, he describes how her candle, a "sick taper," will flicker in his ghostly presence, and how "he whose thou art then," her new lover, will push her away, "being tired before." The speaker suggests his replacement will be weary from earlier lovemaking, so that when the lover attempts to wake him for comfort in her fright, her partner will "think / Thou call'st for more, / And in false sleep will from thee shrink." Psychoanalytic critics would see a double meaning in the term *shrink*, which suggests a flaccid male penis, as well as the action of pulling away normally applied to a demure female. Donne often indulged in imagining role reversals, and this image falls into that tradition. Feminist critics would find interesting his gender role reversal suggestion in a woman's demanding more sex from a man who pretends sleep in order to avoid satisfying that demand. The stereotype of the reluctant female lover had long been a staple image of love poetry.

The speaker then compares his former lover to the trembling leaves on an aspen tree, so great will her fear be. Having been "neglected" by her sleeping partner, she will find herself "Bathed in a cold quicksilver sweat," frightened by the lover she killed, who has become a "verier ghost," or truer spirit, than he was a human.

By the 14th line the speaker withholds information, obviously hoping to make his "murderess" even more uncomfortable: "What I will say, I will not tell thee now." He prefers a more ready revenge: "I had rather thou shouldst painfully repent, / Than by my threatenings rest still innocent." Should he continue to badger her, she could play the innocent victim. However, his silence may drive her to regret her actions in "murdering" him and pray for forgiveness.

Readers of any era can identify with such a revenge fantasy of one human rejected by another. Donne enlivens his poetic persona's wish life with dramatic imagery and the satisfaction of having the former lover suffer rejection by his replacement.

"ASK ME NO MORE WHERE JOVE BESTOWS" THOMAS CAREW (1640)

One of the most loved songs of the dozens written by the CAVALIER POET THOMAS CAREW was "Ask Me No More Where Jove Bestows," a LYRIC poem set to music in various ways. It exists in several forms, with the five four-line verses bearing the RHYME scheme *aabbccddeeffgghhiijj*. Carew adopts nature imagery to make the point that although time passes, evidenced by changes in the natural state of earth and heaven, the beauty of a woman remains eternal. He uses repetition of the opening phrase, "Ask me no more," to emphasize the simple and effective theme of beauty as a mystery, a riddle that no one can solve.

He begins, "Ask me no more where Jove bestows, / When June is past, the fading rose," using the traditional symbol of romantic love and of woman as a sexual being, the rose. This rose fades as summer moves into fall, but the next lines make clear that they actually "as in their causes, sleep" in the beauty of the speaker's lover. The term *causes* alludes to Aristotelian philosophy that suggested objects may remain latent in whatever causes them. For example, one popular theory held that within a man's seed dwelled a tiny fully formed man, called a *homunculus*, the cause of humans. As his fellow poets did, Carew often called upon mythic and classical references to add solemnity to his subject matter.

The second verse again bids listeners not to ask the speaker "whither do stray / The golden atoms of the day," noting they become powder for his lover's hair, prepared "in pure love" by heaven. The third voice repeats the refrain "Ask me no more," this time adding, "whither doth haste / The nightingale when May is past." In this instance, although a creature seems to disappear at a certain season, in actuality it "winters" in his lover's throat. Carew softens the harsh sound and image of "throat" by including in the phrase the descriptors "sweet dividing throat," where *dividing* means "harmonious." After the repeated refrain opening the fifth verse, the speaker adds, "where those stars light, / That downwards fall in the dead of night." His readers need no longer worry about the stars' fate, as they sit in his lover's eyes, "and there / Fixèd become, as in their sphere." He not only suggests that her eyes are lit with a celestial light, but that they represent the entire universe, or sphere. The speaker concludes his rendition of answers to the question he asks others not to propose by saying, "Ask me no more if east or west / The phoenix builds her spicy nest," extending the use of birds as traditional symbols of women. The phoenix proves a crucial reference, as in mythology it builds its nest with spicy shrubbery and then immolates itself every 500 years to arise a brand new creation. Carew's last couplet reads of the phoenix, "for unto you at last she flies, / And in your fragrant bosom dies." It is a pleasing imagery if not a logical one, sustaining the suggestion of his lover as a universe unto herself, harboring in her breast a dead bird who by definition never really dies, but continually recreates itself. Whether Carew intends to suggest his lover's ability constantly to renew her attraction, or simply to suggest that her beauty does not fade, he produces a light, sonorous poem that could be easily sung by performers and audience members alike. It reflects the emotion common to Cavalier lyric poems, which sought to entertain, more than instruct.

ASTELL, MARY (1666–1731)

Mary Astell was born into a working-class family at Newcastle-on-Tyne, where her father worked as a merchant. Her early life remains a mystery, and while for a time historians believed she was educated by a clergyman uncle, that theory fell into disfavor upon the discovery that he died when Astell was quite young. She likely educated herself through reading, allowing her later to advocate the same for other women. Both of her parents died before she reached 18 years, and Astell moved to London, where she may first have occupied a small modest house and later lived with Lady Catherine Jones. Lady Catherine's activity in court circles allowed Astell's exposure to other educated females interested in changing the economic and vocational situation for women. Another close friend, Lady Elizabeth Hastings, furnished Astell a quarterly allowance, allowing her to live on Swan's Walk in Chelsea.

Astell was somewhat of an anomaly for her era, publishing tracts and literature supporting women's natural equality to men. While never a proponent of female independence from society's patriarchal structure, she believed that women should be allowed to reach their full potential within economic and legal subordination to their fathers and husbands. At age 18 she wrote the poem "AMBITION," lambasting men for their desire for earthly immortality through writing, rather than for spiritual immortality. She also commented on her disregard for those who criticized her words because they did not meet cultural expectations that women remain passive. In addition to writing two pamphlets and six books, Astell engaged in a spirited correspondence with the Reverend John Norris of Bemerton, discussing the love all Christians owe to God. In 1689 she presented a collection of her religious poetry, known to later scholars as the Rawlinson Manuscript, to the archbishop of Canterbury.

Astell's first publication, *A Serious Proposal to the Ladies* (1694), presently housed in the British Museum, suggested that women form an all-female community in which they might achieve education and share supportive friendships. In her concern for women and education, she echoed themes expressed in the previous generation by the writer and poet MARGARET CAVENDISH, duchess of Newcastle. As Ruth Perry writes, Astell's "sense of self was very much bound up in relationships with other women; she both needed and relied upon the community of friends who supported her." Her focus on female friendships carried on the tradition of the 17th-century writer KATHERINE PHILIPS, who also believed such relationships imperative to the mental and emotional health of women. One of Astell's most important relationships formed with LADY MARY WORTLEY MONTAGU, to whom she dedicated her *A Serious Proposal*. She asks her readers, "For since god has given women as well as men intelligent souls, why should they be forbidden to improve them? Since he has not denied us the faculty of thinking, why should we not (at least in gratitude to him) employ our thoughts on himself their noblest object, and not unworthily bestow them on trifles and gaieties and secular affairs?" Astell often adopted the anonymous pseudonym "a Lover of her Sex." She argued well, employing Augustan wit identifiable with her era. She adopted many of its recognizable terms and phrases, such as "an English Spirit and Genius" and "the Native Liberty, the rights and Privileges of the Subject." As her contemporaries did in the age of reason, she employed a clear logic in discussing a subject they did not often engage, the intellectual and moral lives of women.

The following year Astell published *Letters Concerning the Love of God,* dedicated to Lady Catherine Jones, and she published the second portion of her *A Serious Proposal* in 1697; in it she explained to her female audience how to pursue rational thought. Over the following decade Astell published tracts continuing to emphasize the natural equality of the sexes, managing to maintain balance between that belief and her continued support of the subjection of women to men. Her stance remained possible partly because she focused her claims on single women, remaining single herself. She lived out her life in Chelsea, supporting the founding of a charity school for girls that operated into the 19th century. A strong enough voice to be satirized by JONATHAN SWIFT in the *Tattler,* Astell was later celebrated by Richard Steele in his *The Ladies Library* (1714). She apparently died of breast cancer and was buried in the Chelsea Church cemetery.

BIBLIOGRAPHY

Perry, Ruth. *The Celebrated Mary Astell: An Early English Feminist.* Chicago: Chicago University Press, 1986.
Springborg, Patricia, ed. *Political Writings/Mary Astell.* Cambridge: Cambridge University Press, 1996.

"AT THE ROUND EARTH'S IMAGIN'D CORNERS BLOW" JOHN DONNE (1633)

"At the round earth's imagin'd corners blow" provides JOHN DONNE an opportunity in SONNET form to consider the prophecy from the Bible's book of Revelation 7:1 that angels would stand at the earth's four corners to herald the resurrection of the faithful. The term *imagined* does

not reflect on a lack of truthfulness, but rather on the apostle John's dream state as he received God's inspired vision of the future. One of the *HOLY SONNETS,* this poem has traditionally been numbered 7 and adopts its first line as its title. Its message remains simple. Donne repeats the detail from Revelation that describes angels trumpeting the beginning of eternal life for those "numberless infinities / Of souls" who will answer the call. Despite their "scattered bodies," they will arise, as did Jesus after his physical death on the cross.

Donne catalogs the many manners by which the faithful died and would continue to die:

All whom the flood did, and fire shall,
    o'erthrow,
All whom war, dearth, age, agues, tyrannies,
Despair, law, chance hath slain.

Certain translations printed the word *dearth,* appearing in the second line, as *death.* Helen Gardner discusses the dispute over that printing. As has been pointed out, because Donne enumerates several modes in which death arrives, "death" cannot be one of those modes; it would represent a circular argument. More convincingly, Gardner explains that Donne's use of the term *death* would constitute a biblical error, one he probably would not make. The Fourth Horseman of the Apocalypse as described in the biblical book of Revelation is named Death and can kill using four different plagues. Those plagues are described in Ezekiel 14:21: "The sword, and the famine, and the noisome beast, and the pestilence." While the word *death* is substituted in the Revised Standard Version of the Bible for the word *pestilence,* Gardner notes that nowhere outside that instance has she ever seen *death* without an adjective of some sort substituted for *pestilence.* In addition, because Donne has characteristically been dealing with opposites in his poem, contrasting those who die abruptly and in large numbers by war and pestilence with those who die singly and slowly, by decay, the term *dearth* acts as war's partner, a reference to something tame or unremarkable. The contrast afforded by such juxtaposition led to a pleasing balance common to Donne's poetry.

The speaker continues, noting that while the faithful have died, they "never taste death's woe," a PARADOX indicating that death remains a transient state for them. It merely prepared them for their later opportunity to join God in heaven, as Jesus' crucifixion and resurrection permit.

Donne adopts the PETRARCHAN form in this sonnet, presenting his topic in the first eight lines and then commenting on it in the remaining sixth. His comment focuses on the speaker's own status as a sinner exposed by the dead faithful, "above all these," as one whose own "sins abound." He acknowledges, "'Tis late to ask abundance of thy grace / When we are there." Donne employs ENJAMBMENT to move the reader directly from the term *grace* to the idea of an appropriate time to receive that grace, which is not "there." Rather, he asks the Lord, "Here on this lowly ground, / Teach me how to repent." Donne offers hope to those living in his own age that they may determine their own forgiveness. No matter when the speaker, or any sinner, repents, as long as it is prior to the rise of the faithful to heaven, "that's as good / As if thou hadst sealed my pardon with thy blood." The final phrase expresses IRONY, as Christ's blood flowed during his crucifixion, and the imagery of that blood washing away sin of those who lived in later ages remains common to Christian writing. In addition during Protestant communion the wine ingested symbolized Christ's blood, and its sealing of the faithful's pardon of sin.

BIBLIOGRAPHY
Gardner, Helen, ed. *John Donne: The Divine Poems.* New York: Oxford University Press, 1969.
Grierson, H. J. C., ed. *The Poems of John Donne.* 2 vols. New York: Oxford University Press, 1912.

AUBADE

The poetic form known as the aubade always adopted the morning as a setting, strongly featuring the dawn, often as an hour of parting for lovers. WILLIAM DRUMMOND OF HAWTHORNDEN's "PHOEBUS, ARISE" calls the sun to "give life to this dark world" and regrets that everything in the world seems in place, "save her." JOHN DONNE's "BREAK OF DAY" rues the presence of sunlight as a reason that he must part from his love, as he asks, "Why should we rise because 'tis light?" In "THE SUN RISING" Donne personifies the sun, famously labeling it "Busy old fool, unruly sun," as his speaker questions why it must disturb him and his

love. He suggests, instead, that it visit huntsmen, kings, and ants, but in the end he decides the sun's warmth should shine in the center of the bed. In ABRAHAM COWLEY's "HYMN TO LIGHT" the speaker welcomes the sun pulled across the sky by fiery steeds. He celebrates the dawn chasing away "Night, and her ugly subjects" and remarks of fear, "sunshine melts away his cold." ANDREW MARVELL praises the morning damp in his "A DROP OF DEW," feminizing the morning through personification, as he notes that "the orient dew" is "Shed from the bosom of the morn." As befits a CAVALIER POET, Marvell equates the morning with love quickly lost, as the "glories of the almighty sun" dissolve the dew: "How loose and easy hence to go."

AURORA WILLIAM ALEXANDER (1604)

Considered a minor poet, WILLIAM ALEXANDER produced two notable works. One of those is titled *Aurora*, a collection of 106 SONNETs written in his youth, remaining unpublished until 1604. The tradition of linking sonnets in sequences to suggest or relate a story grew from the 16th century, as did the sonnets' erotic themes. Most are written in the PETRARCHAN form and, while lacking deep emotion, exhibit a style that caused his contemporary, the poet MICHAEL DRAYTON, to label him "that most ingenious knight." In continuing conventions popular at the end of the 16th century, Alexander applied a polish to his work that tended to limit its intellectual power.

While the entire collection of sonnets is not readily available, two often published include "I Envy Not Endymion" and "Love Swore by Styx." Both draw heavily on mythology to emphasize the relationship between love and death, an association popular with early English poets. Alexander's emphasis on mythological deities insinuates that his earthly love, Aurora, is herself a goddess. His use of the Petrarchan conventions included exploration of contraries: contrary emotions felt by the lover who pursues an unattainable lady, the lady's cruelty versus her desirability, her power versus the speaker's helplessness. Other conventions adopted by Alexander were the inability of the speaker stricken by love to sleep, his lady's purity, and the pain caused by their separation.

Endymion was a youth loved by the Roman deity Diana, goddess of the moon, long a traditional symbol of women. Diana was also goddess of the hunt and a protector of women. All three aspects prove important to the poem, as Endymion slept, ostensibly beneath the moon, when Diana discovered him. Women are often characterized as hunters or predators in early modern poetry, and in much of Alexander's poetry, women prove victorious in love, as if protected and empowered by Diana's special strengths. The speaker of this sonnet declares that he no longer envies Endymion his kiss from Diana as he slept. While Diana "suck'd from his sleep-seal'd lips balm for her sore" Endymion remained a passive recipient of her grace, never experiencing real love. The poem's speaker, on the other hand, declares that he "embraced the shadow of my death" in a dream far more pleasurable than Endymion's experience. Psychoanalytic critics might suggest that the speaker's embrasure has a sexual connotation, as does the shadow of death, as the loss of control during sex and ejaculation may be viewed as a type of dying, or at least a loss of control.

In a line that would set a modern reader's teeth on edge, the speaker declares he "quaff'd with Cupid sugar'd draughts of love" that made him feel "Jove-like," like royalty. He states that Endymion did not enjoy his kiss, while by contrast, the speaker "tasted that delight / Which Venus on Adonis once bestow'd:." The speaker compares his own experience to that of Adonis, who, while loved by Venus, was later killed by a boar, after which Venus named a flower for him in remembrance. The imagery of the boar allows Alexander's emphasis on the beastly nature of human love, as well as the violence to which women may resort as they wield the only power they possess, that of romance/sex. The speaker concludes by stating his experience proved superior even to that of Adonis, as the mythological man "only got the body of a kiss, / And I the soul of it, which he did miss." Alexander adds clever wordplay in focusing on the physical and spiritual aspects of love as two separate, but equally desirable, forms of romance. The mere thought of love can be satisfying and destructive as man may sacrifice his literal and figurative life for a taste of it.

In "Love Swore by Styx" Alexander immediately associates passion with death, adopting the name *Love* for Cupid, the Roman god of romance, and imagining the winged deity swearing, a term with a possible double meaning. Cupid stands beside the river Styx, literally a river of Hate (from the Greek *stugein,* "to hate") said to circle the infernal regions nine times. Alexander's clever juxtaposition of love and hate emphasizes the similarity in two supposedly opposite emotions and suggests also that one cannot understand one concept without the other. Although Cupid was later romanticized to represent idyllic love, in his original form he was a fearsome being, a hateful child figure who shot his victims with painful arrows said to be sharpened on a stone wet with human blood.

Alexander suggests the bitter sacrifice humans make in order to experience love and all of its unpleasant accompanying emotions, especially jealousy. It steals the life blood from a man, rendering him weakened, his power drained. The vow that Cupid swears is to take revenge on the speaker's pride, "Who to his deity durst base styles impart." Alexander displays the poetic style others praised, with the use in that line of ALLITERATION in repetition of the *d* sound. He also employs three consecutive words, all beginning with hard consonants, *deity, durst, base,* in addition to the contrasting of the soft *s* sound that ends the term base with the harsher declarative *s,* paired with a hard *t* sound, which begins the next word, *styles.* He skillfully extends his use of contrast between the meanings of words to that between their sounds.

Alexander then comments on another mythological figure, Latona, mother to Apollo and Artemis by Jupiter, who had to flee the jealous wrath of Juno, queen to Jupiter. The speaker makes clear Cupid's focus when he says that Cupid "gave full leave to any for to slay me," as *slay* means to force the speaker to fall in love against his will, again linking romance with death. This eventually happens, and the speaker closes his sonnet with the couplet "Thus, thus I see that all must fall in end, / that with a greater than themselves contend." Alexander reflects on the mythological figures he employed, all of whom "fell" to stronger forces, or caused others to "fall" to their own. He simultaneously focuses on his speaker, and, by extension, his readers, suggesting humans remain victims to forces "greater than themselves." Surrender to passion is a common theme of the CAVALIER POETS.

BIBLIOGRAPHY

Survey of British Poetry: Cavalier to Restoration. Vol. 2. Edited by the Editorial Board, Roth Publishing. Great Neck, N.Y.: Poetry Anthology Press, 1989.

Ward, Thomas Humphry. *The English Poets: Selections with Critical Introductions by Various Writers and a General Introduction by Matthew Arnold.* Vol. 2. 1880. Reprint, New York: Macmillan, 1912.

B

BALLAD The first ballads grew from an oral tradition, originally to be sung as a dance accompaniment, with the term originating in the Latin and Italian *ballare,* "to dance." The ballad presented a narrative, a story eventually committed to writing, and may be placed in one of three categories, the folk ballad, the BROADSIDE BALLAD, and the literary ballad. Folk ballads generally remain anonymous, as generations of singers may have contributed to them before their production in written form. Marked by an impersonal tone, most folk ballads contain abrupt beginnings that move directly into action designed to evoke an emotional response from listeners/readers. The broadside ballad appeared in print but remained unsophisticated, used as popular, rather than formal, literature. The literary ballad proved the most sophisticated of the various versions, appeared in later centuries, was written by a recognizable poet, and generally was meant to be read, rather than sung.

The stanza in the ballad's form of four lines (a quatrain) contains alternating eight- and six-syllable lines, rhyming *abcb,* but the format may vary. An excellent form for a personal lament, some ballads were told from a first-person perspective, such as the one written by Anne Askewe while awaiting execution for heresy in 1546, under the reign of Henry VIII. Popularly called "Ballad from Newgate," Askewe's song represents a mixture of the broadside and literary ballad, its form written and author known. She wrote the words after her final examination in Newgate Prison, in which she was urged to denounce Protestantism for Catholicism in order to save herself. She declined, as she did when asked once again to recant while tied to a stake. She was martyred, burned at the stake, shortly after writing her 14 four-line stanzas of six syllables each. The fifth stanza makes clear her stance:

> Faith in the fathers old
> Obtained rightwiseness,
> Which make me very bold
> To fear no world's distress.

One early broadside ballad, "A Winter Campaign," dates to about 1600. It was written by Eochaidh Ó Heóghusa, an important Irish bardic poet who wanted to relate the hardships of war as experienced by the Irish rebel Hugh Maguire, the poet's major patron. His verse would be translated in the 19th century by the Dubliner James Clarence Mangan. While unreadable by those unfamiliar with the Gaelic tongue, it clearly represents the ballad form, as may be seen in its first of 19 verses:

> Fúar liom an adhaighsi dh'Aodh,
> cúis tuirse truime a ciothbhraon;
> mo thrúaighe sein dár seise,
> neimh fhúaire na hoidhcheise.

In a more upbeat use of the form, SIR JOHN SUCKLING wrote the literary ballad "A BALLAD, UPON A WEDDING," published in 1646, but it was based on a popular folk ballad already existent as the song "I tell thee Dick," a phrase Suckling adopted in his first line. He uses a six-line format for each stanza, with an *aabccb* rhyme scheme. The marriage celebrated was likely that of Lord Lovelace to Anne Wentworth in 1638, the "Dick" being RICHARD LOVELACE. Many of the 22 verses describe the bride, with others relating details about the food served at the celebration. The humor introduced at the bride's expense remains good humor, supporting the festive tone of the happy event, as stanza 9 demonstrates:

> He would have kissed her once or twice,
> But she would not, she was so nice,
> She should not do't in sight,
> And then she looked as who should say,
> I will do what I list today;
> And you shall do't at night.

The ballad form later helped to celebrate Lady Grisell Baillie, a Scottish poet who fled Scotland for Utrecht in the 17th century with her Jacobite father, managed all the family affairs, and later risked her life to return to Scotland for her sister. Although most of her daybooks in which she used poetry to describe the family exploits were later lost, her ballad "Were na My Heart Licht I Wad Die" is believed to have been from the lost book. A broadside ballad, published anonymously in 1726, it is spoken in heavy dialect by a young maid who loved Johnny, but Johnny's family felt her beneath his rank and interfered in their romance, as attested to by the sixth verse:

> They said I had neither cow nor calf,
> Nor dribbles o' drink rins through the draff,
> Nor pickles o' meal rins through the mill-eye;
> And were na my heart Licht, I wad die.

A prime example from the late 18th century of the literary ballad stanza may be seen in Samuel Coleridge's enduring *The Rime of the Ancient Mariner* (1798):

> Water, water, everywhere,
> And all the boards did shrink;

> Water, water, everywhere,
> Nor any drop to drink.

Ballads proved especially suitable to stories of war. While much of Robert Southey's poetry appeared in the 19th century, his literary ballad "The Battle of Blenheim" was published in 1798. He added two lines to each stanza, for a total of six lines, but adhered to the traditional ballad rhythm. Southey selected the form to demonstrate the parallel between Marlborough's 1704 victory and the British war against France in his own age, as his ninth verse demonstrates:

> They say it was a shocking sight
> After the field was won,
> For many thousand bodies here
> Lay rotting in the sun;
> But things like that, you know, must be
> After a famous victory.

Anonymous ballads including "BONNY BARBARA ALLAN" and "Sir Patrick Spens" remained popular over centuries. Oxford University's Bodleian Library makes available online to researchers a collection of more than 30,000 ballads, most of which are broadsides, dating from the 16th to the 20th century.

BIBLIOGRAPHY

"The Ballads Project." Bodleian Library. Available online. URL: http://www.bodley.ox.ac.uk/ballads/ballads.htm. Downloaded on January 6, 2005.

"BALLAD UPON A WEDDING, A" SIR JOHN SUCKLING (1640)

"A Ballad upon a Wedding" by SIR JOHN SUCKLING represents one of his best unified poems. Criticism of Suckling's poetry includes his shaping of carelessly fragmented and disjointed verses, but all 22 stanzas in this traditional BALLAD form hang together well. The speaker remains anonymous, telling his story in six-line stanzas with a RHYME scheme of *aabccb*. The persona makes clear that the Charing Cross wedding described is a special event, not one that took place in his part of town, where common laborers live. He addresses his friend Dick and begins by describing the event he witnessed as one of "the rarest things" he had ever seen. It occurred close to the place, he tells

Dick, where the two "sell our hay." The "Forty at least, in pairs" of folk he witnesses were "Such folk as are not in our town." He first describes the groom as one who, had he appeared in "Course-a-Park," would have been set upon by all the women. Then he describes the bride, noting

No grape, that's kindly ripe, could be
So round, so plump, so soft as she,
    Nor half so full of juice.

As to be expected from a court poet, Suckling spends many more lines on the subject of the bride than the groom. She had a tiny finger that the ring "Would not stay on," and her feet looked "Like little mice," while her cheeks "so rare a white was on, / No daisy makes comparison." Her red lips appeared to have been bee stung, and her eyes were so guarded, perhaps by remaining downcast, that the speaker could not catch a good view of them. Her fragile nature is clear from the description of a tiny mouth that threatens to have its teeth broken from the spoken word. Suckling's hyperbole complements the "tall tale" nature of the ballad subject matter.

The bride's appearance did not dampen the celebration when the group sat to eat, served by a number of men carrying dishes. When "all the meat was on the table," no man "was able / To stay to be intreated." Instead, they ate with relish, dispatching the food. Later, "hats fly off, and youths carouse," as everyone toasts the health of the new couple. Suckling well captures the joy of the scene, concluding,

On the sudden up they rise and dance;
Then sit again and sigh, and glance:
    Then dance again and kiss:
Thus several ways the time did pass,
Whilst ev'ry woman wished her place,
    And every man wished his.

Suckling takes the reader on LYRIC flight through his ballad, its tone never losing its airy quality.

BARBAULD, ANNA LAETITIA AIKIN
(1743–1825)   As the oldest child born to an educa-

tor named Dr. John Aikin in Kibworth, Leicestershire, Anna Laetitia Aikin matured in academic surroundings. Supposedly a prodigy who could read by age two, Anna Laetitia learned the classics, both the French and Italian languages, and English literature. Her father managed a school for boys, an environment that she later credited for teaching her how to behave in polite society. In 1758 Dr. Aikin took a position as tutor in the new Warrington Academy for Dissenters, and Anna Laetitia spent 15 years influenced by the intellectual liberal atmosphere; Aikin taught the famous economist Thomas Malthus at the academy.

Dr. Joseph Priestly, known for his learned philosophical and scientific prose, also a tutor at Warrington, encouraged Anna Laetitia to write. Her brother John matured to become a physician and well-known writer and editor who greatly influenced his sister's publishing. He requested that she contribute poetry to his *Essay on Song-Writing* (1772) and urged her to publish her own volume, *Poems,* which was well received in 1773. It contained pieces such as "The Groans of the Tankard," in which a silver water tankard sat on the sideboard in her father's school and commented on what it observed. The tankard proudly proclaimed it had served mayors and aldermen, "the furry tribe," probably alluding to the animal hair trim on many official robes, and comparing the public servants to animals who lost control when drinking too much. Written in HEROIC COUPLETS with a MOCK-HEROIC tone, it was probably modeled on ALEXANDER POPE's "The RAPE OF THE LOCK" (1712, 1714), to which it directly alludes, as well as on JOHN MILTON's poetry, as there are detailed geographical references in Milton's style. Anna Laetitia used the mock heroic to cloak serious concerns, indicting the establishment through a comic tone and adopting the domestic scene, woman's proper place, as setting. She would become an amazingly prolific writer over the next decades.

In 1774 the writer Elizabeth Montagu suggested that Aikin become a principal at an all-girl school, a position that would seem a perfect fit for a young woman with staunch opinions regarding liberal education. However, she declined, stating that she perceived no need for *femmes savantes.* In a remark supporting her lifelong attitude that women should most importantly strive to be "good wives and agreeable companions," she declared a father or brother to be the best teacher for girls, whose high passions at age 15 would prohibit learning. Later that year, Aikin married a clergyman educated at Warrington, Rochemont Barbauld, and began years of helping him serve various congregations. After moving to Palgrave in Sussex, he took on a congregation of dissenters and opened a boy's school where Barbauld taught and acted as accountant.

The couple never had children but adopted a nephew, Charles Rochemont Aikin, who later became a physician. Barbauld found time to continue her writing of letters, essays, parodies, and poetry. She published *Devotional Pieces* (1775), *Lessons for Children* (1778), and *Hymns in Prose for Children* (1781) and became part of an important London literary circle. When in the city, she visited the essayists Montagu and Hannah More and later developed supportive relationships with the playwright Joanna Baillie and the novelist Maria Edgeworth. Because of her husband's mental strain, the couple sold their school in 1785. After travel abroad, they returned to England, settling in Hampstead, where Rochemont served a small chapel and Barbauld's writing continued. She began to publish at a rapid pace as her husband's mental health deteriorated, his condition causing some friends to fear for her safety.

Over the next several years Barbauld focused on political and social matters in her writing. She published a pamphlet supporting dissenting schools over traditional universities titled *An Address to the Opposers of the Repeal of the Corporation and Test Acts* (1790), a poem attacking the slave trade for women; *Epistle to William Wilberforce* (1791); and she expressed her support of democracy and public education in *Civic Sermons to the People* (1792). Her *Sins of the Government, Sins of the Nation* (1793) took a stance against England's support of war in France. Barbauld's strongly expressed opinions prompted Horace Walpole to write a letter to Hannah More in 1791 denouncing Barbauld's efforts, a certain measure of the effect she was perceived to have on her reading public. Barbauld issued an antiwar poem, *Eighteen Hundred and Eleven* (1811), and worked on editing projects with her brother, including volumes of poetry by Mark Akenside (1794) and William Collins (1797).

The Barbaulds' 1802 move to Stoke Newington, where John Aikin lived, allowed Barbauld to be close to her brother, aiding her ability to work with him. Her husband ministered at a chapel as he grew dangerously violent. Eventually requiring physical restraint, he broke free and drowned in 1808.

Additional editing projects by Barbauld included six volumes of letters by Samuel Richardson (1804), the 50 volumes of *The British Novelists* (1810), and a collection of works for young women readers titled *The Female Speaker* (1811). A harsh 1812 review of *Eighteen Hundred and Eleven* by J. W. Croker in the *Quarterly Review* virtually ended her popular career. Barbauld remained busy writing fiction reviews for the *Monthly Review* until 1815. Her literary acquaintances by then included poets Samuel Taylor Coleridge and ROBERT SOUTHEY and the poet and novelist Sir Walter Scott.

After Barbauld's death her niece, Lucy Aikin, released a two-volume edition of her poetry, which included the popular and later well-anthologized "The RIGHTS OF WOMEN" and "WASHING-DAY." Never a feminist and one who made public through letters her lack of desire to become a "bluestocking," Barbauld yet enjoyed the company of many female intellectuals. She felt she had "stepped out of the bounds of female reserve" to write, and that act represented her only rebellion. Comprehensive collections of her poetry became available in the late 20th century with renewed interest by feminist critics in women writers. A complete collection including her prose has yet to be published.

BIBLIOGRAPHY
McCarthy, William, and Elizabeth Kraft, eds. *The Poems of Anna Laetitia Barbauld.* Athens: University of Georgia Press, 1994.

Messenger, Ann. "Heroics and Mock-Heroics: John Milton, Alexander Pope, and Anna Laetitia Barbauld." In *His and Hers: Essays in Restoration and Eighteenth-Century Literature,* 172–196. Lexington: University Press of Kentucky, 1986.

Rodgers, Betsy. *Georgian Chronicle: Mrs. Barbauld and Her Family.* London: Methuen, 1958.

Watson, Mary Sidney. "When Flattery Kills: the Silencing of Anna Laetitia Barbauld." *Women's Studies,* 28, no. 6 (December 1999): 17–43.

BARBER, MARY (1690–1757)

BARBER, MARY (1690–1757) While not a major poet, Mary Barber remains of interest because of her interaction with the far more famous poet JONATHAN SWIFT. Little is known of her life previous to marriage to Jonathan Barber, an Englishman who relocated to Dublin to begin a draper business. They had four children; their son Rupert became a miniature painter and Constantine a physician. Barber explained in a preface to her *Poems* (1734) that she only wrote poetry to aid in the education of her children, who more easily learned lessons when in verse form. She published some poetry in Dublin previous to the release of her collection and gained an important patron in the person of Lady Carteret, wife of the lord-lieutenant of Ireland. One poem she titled "A Tale Being an Addition to Mr. Gay's Fables" (1728), addressing it to the queen in support of a pension for the poet JOHN GAY.

By 1728 Barber had been introduced to Swift, who praised her in a letter to Lord Orrery printed as a preface to *Poems*. He believed her to be the most talented woman writer in their group and especially appreciated her willing acceptance of criticism. During Barber's visit to England in 1730 Swift decided to solicit subscriptions to a new edition of her poems. His letters to various English notables, including ALEXANDER POPE, referred to her as a "poeticall Genius." Despite the fact that she annoyed Pope by asking for his help in correcting her work, he subscribed to her poems, as did Gay, Sir Robert Walpole, and Swift. Barber enjoyed London so much that she hoped to settle there, and Swift tried to aid her husband in finding employment.

Barber next decided the family would move to Bath, where her husband could continue trading as a woolen draper while she rented out lodgings. In fall 1732 she returned to Ireland to organize her family to make the move but had a crippling attack of what was labeled "gout." A decreased ability to use her legs delayed her plans, and then her husband apparently died, as no further mention of him after 1733 occurs in her circle's correspondence. She returned to England in 1734, attempting to smuggle into England a forbidden manuscript written by Swift and was arrested. After her release she did settle in Bath, expanding her plans for support to include selling Irish linen. Her son Rupert had studied painting in Bath and may have lived with

or near her for a time. In 1734 Barber's *Poems on Several Occasions* was published in quarto form. Samuel Richardson, the later author of what was traditionally labeled the first epistolary novel, *Pamela,* served as her publisher. Some critics judged her work not poetic enough, a reason that the nontraditionalist Swift would have liked it.

Barber's physical condition worsened, but she stayed in England for a time, living on the subscription money. After concocting and discarding additional schemes, Barber at last returned by 1740 to Ireland, where her physician son may have cared for her. She corresponded with Richardson, thanking him for the copy of *Pamela* that he had presented her daughter, apparently expressing her opinion that the second rape attempt on Pamela was a bit strong for her taste. She wrote little later in life, publishing some comments about her illness in *Gentleman's Magazine* in 1737. Twenty-eight of her poems appeared in *Poems by Eminent Ladies* (1755), but only six were included in its 1780 revision. Not often anthologized in later centuries as a result of changing tastes, Barber's works included "WRITTEN FOR MY SON, AND SPOKEN BY HIM AT HIS FIRST PUTTING ON BREECHES," a work typical of her humorous approach.

BIBLIOGRAPHY

Canoso, Teresa, and Diana Solomon. *Teaching Comedy in Mary Barber's Poetry.* June 24, 1999. University of California, Santa Barbara. November 2000. Available online. URL: http://home.earthlink.net/~dianska/barber.htm. Downloaded on January 17, 2005.

Rowton, Frederic. *The Female Poets of Great Britain.* Detroit: Wayne State University Press, 1981.

"BATTER MY HEART" JOHN DONNE (1633)

"BATTER MY HEART" JOHN DONNE (1633) Critics feel fairly certain that one group of JOHN DONNE'S HOLY SONNETS was published in 1633, a collection that included "Batter My Heart," sometimes listed as "Batter My Heart, Three Person'd God." It gained fame as a prime example of the style of METAPHYSICAL POETS AND POETRY with markedly unusual FIGURATIVE LANGUAGE (FIGURE OF SPEECH) or comparisons. Victorian readers found Donne's comparison of God's effect on his life to the violent act of ravishment, or rape, so disturbing that the poem basically disappeared from publishing until resurrected in the 20th century through the efforts of the poet T. S. Eliot and others. The sonnet's hysterical tone grows from the tradition of meditation, which may be used as an emotional stimulus. Typical of Donne, he heavily emphasizes the first-person pronouns *I* and *me,* enabling readers to visualize the speaker's involvement and the importance of the experience to him, while the strong but simple language does not distract the reader from the poem's theme of the importance in the Christian life of total surrender to God. While critics including the Donne expert Helen Gardner insist that a true assessment of Donne's "spiritual and moral achievement" may be gained only through his sermons, the sonnets best reveal his *extreme* capacity for passion and ecstasy.

From the opening line, "Batter my heart, three-person'd God," the reader understands the speaker does not seek a Christian God who is gentle or compassionate. The three persons referenced constitute the holy trinity composed of Christ the Son, the Holy Spirit, and God the Father, and the speaker commands that all three attack his heart, the term *Batter* suggesting repeated blows. That line contains a caesura due to the semicolon that follows the apostrophe to God then continues with ENJAMBMENT into the second line: "for, you / As yet but knock, breathe, shine, and seek to mend." This series of verbs reflects on various biblical characteristics of Christ, with *knock* representing a polite request to open a door. In Revelation 3:20 Christ states, in part, "Behold, I stand at the door, and knock: if any man hear my voice, and open the door, I will come in to him." Donne will extend this CONCEIT throughout the sonnet.

The speaker does not want his deity to hesitate at the door. He explains, using PARADOX, that in order for him to "ride, and stand," God must "o'erthrow" him. As ore undergoing transformative purification into valuable metal, he needs God's "force, to break, blow, burn, and make me new." Donne moves into one of his favorite metaphors, expressing a single being as a larger geographic expanse, as the speaker continues, "I, like an usurp'd town, to another due, / Labour to admit you." He explains that another force has overtaken him, suggesting evil or the devil, and follows up on the previous reference to a knock on the door by stating he

works to "admit" the deity, but to no avail: "but O, to no end." Although logic should move him to act, "Reason your viceroy in me, me should defend," reason has been taken captive by the opposing force, "and proves weak or untrue." The speaker offers a dual explanation for his incapacity to open the door to God's gentle prod. His use of logic lacks strength or proves false, causing the speaker to be "betroth'd unto your enemy." Here Donne compares the promise through law of a woman to a man to his promise to God's "enemy," or Satan. The comparison reflects on the biblical comparison of Christ to a bridegroom, with the church his bride.

In the final four lines Donne builds to a mighty climax, avoiding the problem of a weak concluding couplet that some plagued some poets. He again turns to allusions to violence. Having introduced the idea of romantic love as a conceit, he extends that conceit, insisting that God "Divorce me, untie, or break that knot again." By Jewish law an engagement proved as strong a bond as a marriage, and the betrothal "knot" that tied two people together could only be broken through a second decree of law, a divorce. The speaker then begins the three lines that depict one of the most violent of attacks, a rape, made clear through the use of "ravish": "Take me to you, imprison me, for I / Except you'enthral me, never shall be free, / Nor ever chaste, except you ravish me." What some readers have missed is that Donne produces a double paradox, equating imprisonment with freedom and chastity with the act of sex, quite obviously not making a literal suggestion. In addition to the shocking allusion to violence, that a male would assume the role of the female as an object of attack was even more unusual, a fact of interest to later feminist and psychoanalytic critics.

Such outlandish expression proved a hallmark of metaphysical writing, and Donne would be eventually recognized as the most skillful of those who attempted it. While several centuries had to pass before society embraced his expression as art in its purest form, Donne's poetry at last received its due.

BIBLIOGRAPHY

Gardner, Helen, ed. *John Donne: The Divine Poems.* Oxford: Clarendon Press, 1969.

Johnson, Jeffrey. *The Theology of John Donne.* Cambridge, England: D. S. Brewer, 2001.

BEHN, APHRA (1640?–1689)

Although Aphra Behn's exact birth date remains unknown, it is generally recognized as between 1637 and 1643. Her baptism on December 14, 1640, makes 1640 the most likely year of birth. Further complications are caused by the number of different spellings of her name, which include *Ayfara* and *Aphara,* as well as *Aphra.* Some accounts suggest her birthplace as the small town of Weye and her parents as John Amis and Amy Amis, a barber and a wet nurse, respectively, although they may have been her foster parents. While not wealthy, the Amises had decent professions. Through various contacts Behn gained some education, picking up languages and knowledge of music. She commented in later years that the learning of classical languages was unimportant, as such learning led to a sense of superiority. In approximately 1663, Behn moved with the Amises to the West Indies, and John died en route. Amy settled there with her children, providing Behn with experiences vital to her later novel *Oroonoko, The History of the Royal Slave* (1688).

The Amis family returned to England in 1664, when Aphra married a Mr. Behn, possibly an English merchant with a Dutch background. She may have spent time at the court of King Charles II, enjoying the licentious behavior reported to have occupied certain members of the royal family, for she was known to the king's cronies who would give her employment. Behn needed that employment following her husband's death during the 1665 plague. References in her writings as well as in remarks by acquaintances appear to indicate that Behn served as a professional spy in Holland for England. In her correspondence, she refers to herself by the code name *Astrea,* which would later become a pen name. Although she acquitted herself well in a number of dangerous missions, she had to beg the English court for payment. Upon her return to England in 1668, she could not pay her debts and ended up in debtor's prison, but not for long. A man named Tom Killigrew, with whom she had corresponded from Holland, probably paid her way out of prison, as she later spoke kindly of him. Historians cite her experience with espionage as a possible explanation for her fascination with the entanglement of sex and power. This "scandalous" topic led to Behn's reputation as a writer of early 19th-century smut. ANNE FINCH, COUNTESS OF WINCHELSEA, later mentioned Behn in "The CIRCUIT OF APOLLO," and even while characterizing the god Phoebus as praising Behn, noted her improper themes: "He lamented for Behn o'er that place of her birth, / And said amongst femens was not on the earth / Her superiour in fancy, in language, or wit, / Yet own'd that a little too loosely she writ."

Later critics, such as Frederic Rowton, editor of *The Female Poets of Great Britain* (1853), referenced Behn's sometimes nickname of "a Female Wycherley." A RESTORATION playwright, William Wycherley focused on themes of debauchery, both sexual and materialistic, and Rowley pronounced the comparison to Behn sound. He described her as joining "to a fine and subtle humour . . . grossness of thought; and to a lively and laughing imagination . . . an essential coarseness of passion." Rowton found that passion a force "which disfigures and depraves" almost everything Behn wrote. He suggested she might be excused for engaging in such licentiousness because of her association with the court of Charles II, a time he describes as "a wicked era." His observations would prove true of most poets writing at the end of the 17th century, both male and female, for whom sexual love was an important topic. That male poets escaped the social censure obvious in Rowton's judgment reflected the separate spheres assigned to the genders by the 19th century with its Victorian mores. In Behn's own time, the evolution of the middle classes and Protestantism redefined male and female characters as similar, although women remained subservient to men. The fact that human nature was viewed as the same in both sexes allowed Behn to build a writing career.

Behn never remarried, though she did take lovers. Her main relationship was with a man named John Hoyle, whose attention to boys was well known. Perhaps bisexual herself, Behn was not concerned with Hoyle's affinity for the same sex but was frustrated by his reluctance to acknowledge her advances. While Behn remained obsessed, Hoyle proved cold, and the relationship eventually ended. Behn captured much of her experiences with Hoyle in her poetry. Widely anthologized selections include "The DISAPPOINTMENT," "The DREAM," "LOVE ARMED," "ON HER LOVING TWO EQUALLY," "ON THE DEATH OF WALLER," "TO THE FAIR CLARINDA," and "The WILLING MISTRESS."

Behn's first play, *The Forced Marriage* (1670), proved successful, running for six nights. She published, and saw performed, additional dramas, including *The Amourous Prince* (1671), The *Dutch Lover* (1673), and *The Town Fop, or Sir Timothy Tawdry* (1676), with varying degrees of success, over many years. Nel Gwyn, mistress to King Charles II, acted in Behn's most popular play, *The Rover* (1677), and in *Sir Patient Fancy* (1678). Although her dramas provided some social criticism of traditions such as forced marriage, overbearing parental authority, England's hypocritical moral hierarchy, and other aspects of gender inequity, many female members of the audience did not support her productions. Eventually Behn concentrated on poetry, whose impassioned themes and stark sexual imagery raised several eyebrows.

In a move important to later feminist critics Behn published the first part of *Love Letters Between a Nobleman and His Sister* (1684–87), the first major epistolary novel in English, later labeled amatory fiction. Critics used Behn's work to challenge the title of first early novel and first epistolary novel in English previously granted to Samuel Richardson's popular *Pamela* (1740). Based on a sex scandal of her day, Behn's *Love Letters* featured characters modeled after public figures, such as the duke of Monmouth, illegitimate son of Charles II. At that time prose fiction received little respect as serious literature and for that reason could be undertaken without public criticism by an uneducated woman such as Behn. Behn's amatory fiction offered more complex characters than those of her fellow writers, and her style in presenting plots heavy with sexual intrigue she distinguished with wit, irreverence, and intelligence. In her *The History of the Nun; or, The Fair Vow-breaker,* Behn emphasizes through the spouse murderer, Isabella, the dangers to beautiful women in a patriarchal society. Free from the influence of classics and traditional literature, she could produce innovative work, as seen in the realistic aspects of *Oronooko,* published successfully in 1688. Featuring a heroic African prince who engages in a slave rebellion, it became her signature work with later generations. Behn died April 16, 1689, and was buried in Westminster Abbey.

The Restoration during which Behn lived proved more accepting of sexual allusions in literature than the decades immediately following, which enjoyed an "improvement of the national delicacy and taste," according to the poet and novelist Sir Walter Scott. Scott's aunt in 1821 declared *Oroonoko* shameful reading for a lady. The marquis of Halifax actually blamed the oppression of women on Behn, remarking, "The unjustifiable freedom of some of your sex have involved the rest in the penalty of being reduced." A Victorian critic judged Behn "a mere harlot who danced through un[c]leaness." With the rise of feminism in the 1960s, Behn's poetry, drama, and fiction reemerged through feminist criticism to a more liberal generation of readers who explore them as legitimate and sensual examinations of gender, race, and class. A forward-looking Virginia Woolf commented that "all women together ought to let flowers fall upon the tomb of Aphra Behn . . . for it was she who earned them the right to speak their minds."

BIBLIOGRAPHY

Backscheider, Paula R., and John J. Richetti, eds. *Popular Fiction by Women: 1660–1730, an Anthology.* Oxford: Clarendon Press, 1996.

Bowers, Toni. "Sex, Lies, and Invisibility: Amatory Fiction from the Restoration to Mid-Century." In *The Columbia History of the British Novel,* 50–72. New York: Columbia University Press, 1994.

Day, Robert Adams. "Aphra Behn and the Works of the Intellect." In *Fetter'd or Free: British Women Novelists, 1670–1815,* edited by Mary Anne Schofield and Cecilia Macheski, 372–382. Athens: Ohio University Press, 1986.

Mendelson, Sara Heller. *The Mental World of Stuart Women: Three Studies.* Amherst: University of Massachusetts Press, 1987.

Rowton, Frederic. *The Female Poets of Great Britain.* 1853. Facsimile, Detroit: Wayne State University Press, 1981.

Todd, Janet. *The Secret Life of Aphra Behn.* New York: Pandora, 2000.

Williamson, Marilyn L. Introduction to *The Female Poets of Great Britain* by Frederic Rowton, xi–xxxii. Facsimile, Detroit: Wayne State University, 1981.

"BERMUDAS" ANDREW MARVELL (1681) ANDREW MARVELL probably wrote "Bermudas" between 1653 and 1654, although, along with his other works, it would not be published until 1681. In the early 1650s Marvell served as tutor at Eton to William Dutton, Oliver Cromwell's "ward." While doing so, he stayed with his friend, John Oxenbridge, a fellow of Eton College and vicar of New Windsor. A victim of persecution by William Laud, Oxenbridge had twice visited the Bermuda islands and was made a commissioner for the government of the Bermudas in 1653. Marvell probably wrote the poem as a tribute to the Oxenbridge family. He greatly admired Oxenbridge and his wife, Jane, and their virtuous lifestyle, and he would later compose an epitaph for Jane Oxenbridge. Marvell viewed the Bermuda islands as a refuge from religious persecution, joining other poets in characterizing them as a modern Eden.

As the critic Nigel Smith discusses, Marvell employed several sources, altering them as fit his puritanical approach to celebrating a supposed work ethic of the island inhabitants. EDMUND WALLER had written a MOCK-HEROIC poem, "The Battle of the Summer Islands" (1645), which included erotic elements in its emphasis on the great fecundity of the Bermudas. In opposition to that view, colonialist oarsmen of the boat in Marvell's version celebrate God and the paradise he has seen fit to grant to them, as "From a small boat, that rowed along, / The list'ning winds received this song." The island had long remained unsettled, not discovered until 1515 by Juan Bermudez. The next lines acknowledge God for leading religious refugees over the ocean to the islands. The refugees sing God's praises, as the poem describes elements of the islands, including whales: "Where He the huge sea-monsters wracks / That lift the deep upon their backs." Waller had described the colonists' treatment of the whales as barbaric, a detail that Marvell avoids. God has provided all the refugees need, with nothing left to chance. He sends them "fowls," "the orange bright," which Marvell compares through the FIGURATIVE LANGUAGE (FIGURE OF SPEECH) of simile to "golden lamps in a green night"; "pom'granates," "Jewels," "figs," and "melons" thrown at their feet; in addition to apples of incredible size; dispute remains regarding whether the large

apples were actually pineapples. Marvell compares the pomegranates to jewelry cases that contain seeds, natural "jewels" more beautiful than precious stones. He also references cedars "from Lebanon" and the ambergris, a sweet smelling substance secreted by sperm whales, so valued by colonists. His imagery avoids historic reports of squabbles among the settlers over the ambergris, instances of sodomy, and the natives' attempted rejection of Puritanism. He also does not make clear that some of the fruit he mentions, such as the melons, were not natural to the island, and his description belies the fact that colonists had to take with them most of the necessities of life as they knew it. Marvell's island is paradise reborn, Eden revisited.

The poem most strongly emphasizes the value of religion, as the biblical gospel is compared to a pearl, supposedly common in the Bermudas, although in reality pearls were rarely found. The line may reflect on the biblical passage Matthew 7:6, which refers to "pearls before swine," as hogs were common in the islands, having been taken there by previous colonizers. Line 32 notes that the islands possess a temple for the worship of the Lord. Voices rise from the islands in praise, and Marvell suggests that the sound arrives "at heaven's vault," from which it might rebound and "Echo beyond the Mexique Bay," referencing the Gulf of Mexico. That location would be important as a bastion of Catholicism, with the echoes of Protestant praise acting as a spiritual invasion. He concludes with the couplets

> Thus sung they, in the English boat,
> An holy and a cheerful note,
> And all the way, to guide their chime,
> With falling oars they kept the time.

Critics note that Marvell's verse imitates the METER of most entries in the biblical book of Psalms, which are also songs. While he employs the familiar meter of iambic pentameter, he occasionally varies it with insertion of spondees and trochees. The public showed little interest in "Bermudas" until the 19th century, when critics interpreted the poem as Marvell's consideration of self-exile. Later interpretations held that Marvell reflected that such a paradise was inappropriate for man in his fallen state. More modern critics believe the poem exists to celebrate nature and the harmony it encourages in human communities.

BIBLIOGRAPHY

Chambers, Alexander B. *Andrew Marvell and Edmund Waller: Seventeenth-Century Praise and Restoration Satire.* University Park: Pennsylvania State University Press, 1991.

Cummings, R. M. "The Difficulty of Marvell's 'Bermudas.'" *Modern Philology* 67 (1969–1979): 331–340.

Hardman, C. B. "Marvell's 'Bermudas' and Sandys's *Psalms.*" *Review of English Studies* 32 (1981): 64–67.

———. "Marvell's Rowers." *Essays in Criticism* 27 (1977): 93–99.

———. "Row Well, Ye Mariners." *The Review of English Studies* 51 (February 2000): 80–161.

Smith, Nigel, ed. *The Poems of Andrew Marvell.* New York: Pearson/Longman, 2003.

Yoshinaka, Takashi. "Religio-political Associations of 'The Orange' in Marvell's 'Bermuda.'" *Notes and Queries* 48, no. 4 (December 2001): 394–395.

"BETTER ANSWER, A" MATTHEW PRIOR (1718)

"A Better Answer" provides an excellent example of the simple, yet artful, LYRIC, which gained a reputation for MATTHEW PRIOR. The speaker attempts to convince his love, Cloe, identified in the subtitle, "To Cloe Jealous," that she need not suspect his dedication to her. The speaker begins by referencing his lover's distressed state, visible in her physical features: her "pretty face" is "blubbered," her "cheek all on fire," and her "hair all uncurled!" Because the tone remains humorous and light, the reader suspects that the speaker enjoys Cloe's show of passion, despite his supposed concern. He requests that Cloe "quit this caprice," offering a reference to Falstaff's comment in Shakespeare's *2 Henry IV* 5.3.101–102: "Let us e'en talk a little like folks of this world." In other words, Cloe needs to calm down so she may communicate with the speaker. Interesting to feminist critics would be the fact that Cloe is never allowed a voice; the reader hears only the speaker throughout Prior's seven stanzas of 28 lines, with every other line rhyming.

The speaker teases Cloe in the second stanza, as he tries to make her feel guilty for the destruction caused by her tears "The Beauties which Venus but lent to thy keeping." He makes clear that Cloe was "designed to inspire love and joy," whereas weeping should be confined to more "ord'nary eyes." ALEXANDER POPE would probably call this approach "damning with faint praise," as the speaker simultaneously accuses and cajoles Cloe, in essence projecting guilt onto the victim. He concedes in the third stanza that Cloe might find "a trifle or two that I writ" vexing, noting she would wrong both his judgment and passion if she did so. He again blames Cloe for taking too seriously a witty verse, asking "must one swear to the truth of a song?" What he writes, he makes clear in the next stanza, demonstrates the difference between "nature and art," as Prior alludes to a long-standing argument about whether the poet bore a duty to express truth in writing.

The speaker attempts to convince Cloe that others have his "whimsies, but thou hast my heart." The sixth stanza refers to Apollo as "The god of us verse-men," reminding her that after Apollo's journey across the sky—for he also served as the sun god—he rests at night, his head on Thetis's breast. This allusion allows the speaker to continue into the next stanza by comparing himself to Apollo. When he is "wearied with wandering all day," he tells Cloe, "To thee, my delight, in the evening I come." Regardless of the world's temptations he experiences during the day, his evenings belong to her, for such attractions "were but my visits, but thou art my home." The speaker succeeds in convincing Cloe of her place in the domestic sphere and persuades her that he will always return to share that space with her.

The speaker never specifically denies whatever caused Cloe's jealousy but rather lulls her with flattery and a seemingly rational argument. He closes his argument by referencing her anger at him as a "pastoral war," offering Prior the opportunity to introduce a classical allusion to Horace and Lydia, a story recorded in Horace's *Odes* 3:9. Prior has some fun with that reference, as Lydia castigated Horace for a dalliance with a woman named Cloe, whereas in Prior's case, Cloe is the one to be jealous. The stanza concludes with the ultimate statement of faux self-deprecation, as Prior's poet-speaker in reference to Lydia and Horace adds, "For thou are a girl as much brighter than her, / As he was a poet sublimer than me."

Prior executes his piece with what SAMUEL JOHNSON termed "sprightliness" in reference to his lighter works. He noted that Prior wrote with respect for laws of writing that aided his avoidance of "ridiculous or absurd" poetry. However, Prior paid a price for such judiciousness, as "the operations of intellect can hinder faults, but not produce excellence." In Johnson's judgment, Prior was "never low, nor very often sublime." In that, Johnson agrees with Prior's own final pronouncement in this poem.

BIBLIOGRAPHY
Johnson, Samuel. *Lives of the English Poets.* Vol. 1. New York: E. P. Dutton, 1958.

BLANK VERSE   Blank verse is poetry that lacks RHYME, although it has a set rhythm, or METER. Early poetry generally rhymed, perhaps because it grew from a spoken tradition in which rhyme could aid in memorization. Later poets retained that traditional approach in brief poems such as BALLADS as well as those of epic length, such as Edmund Spenser's *The Faerie Queene* (1590, 1596), which recalls the pastorals of VIRGIL. However, playwrights of the 1500s retained the common rhythm of iambic pentameter, but sometimes dropped rhyme. Playwrights including Christopher Marlowe, William Shakespeare, and BEN JONSON all adopted blank verse in their various dramas, retaining occasional HEROIC COUPLETS, generally spoken for emphasis. This practice was also adopted by the playwright John Webster to memorable effect as in his *The Duchess of Malfi* (1613), which concludes with the solemn warning

Nature doth nothing so great for great men
As when she's pleased to make them lords of truth:
Integrity of life is fame's best friend
Which nobly, beyond death, shall crown the end.

CAVALIER and most RESTORATION poets retained the rhyme form, but the poet JOHN MILTON, writing later in the 17th century, adopted blank verse in his spectacular epics, *PARADISE LOST* (1667) and *SAMSON AGONISTES* (1671). Rhyme remained popular in the 18th century,

as seen in multiple poems by JONATHAN SWIFT and ALEXANDER POPE, but other poets used blank verse, such as CHRISTOPHER SMART in his "MY CAT JEOFFRY" and JAMES THOMSON in "A Hymn on the Seasons." By the 19th century blank verse was commonly used, and with changing reader sensibilities in the 20th and 21st centuries, rhyme in poetry became rare.

BONNY BARBARA ALLAN ANONYMOUS **(1740)**   Published in a collection of miscellany in 1740, *Bonny Barbara Allan* had long been sung as a BALLAD. It bears many traditional ballad characteristics, falling into the narrative category. It remains anonymous, probably altered over time by various balladeers before appearing in print. It begins in the midst of action, with Sir John Graeme on his deathbed attended by Barbara Allan, a woman he had spurned in the past but still deeply loves; he even attributes his death to a broken heart. The ballad's tone remains unemotional, but the plotline and poetic elements elicit emotion from listeners/readers. It also complies with the traditional four-line verse format, and its RHYME scheme fits the usual *abcb* pattern. Composed of nine stanzas, it includes some Irish dialect, for which most anthologies in which it appears offer explanations.

The first verse sets the date of the action at about "the Martinmas time," which is November 11. The late autumn timing remains symbolic of approaching death, emphasized by the line "When the green leaves were a-fallin." Listeners learn that an aristocrat named Sir John Graeme "in the West Country" had fallen in love with Barbara Allan. Her lack of title establishes the traditional conflict between social classes that produced star-crossed lovers, couples who could not marry because of social edict against the mixing of the classes. Graeme's status is emphasized when he sends "his man down through the town." The man is his servant, and the direction indicated by *down* symbolizes that Graeme literally lives above the masses, probably on an estate, as suits his place in the social hierarchy. The servant searches for Barbara Allan, finds her, and asks that she attend "my master dear." The third verse begins, "O hooly, hooly rase she up, / To the place where he was lyin," with *hooly* meaning "gently," while *rase* means "rose." Her movement "up" represents both a literal and a metaphoric climb to a higher order. Apparently not one for subtlety, Barbara, upon seeing Sir John, tells him, "'Young man, I think you're dyin'.'" Sir John claims his illness is due to his desire for her, but she counters by asking whether he does not recall having "'slighted Barbara Allan'" while he "'the cups were fillin','" and making "'the healths gae round and round,'" meaning he bought rounds of drinks and toasted the health of his fellow drinkers. Barbara was not included in his revelry. The repentant Graeme next "turned his face unto the wall," while "death with him was dealin'," and he bids his friends, "'Adieu,'" telling them "'to be kind to Barbara Allan.'"

The seventh stanza gains emotional momentum through repetition and an ALLITERATION and rhythm especially pleasing to the ear:

And slowly, slowly, rase she up,
And slowly, slowly left him;
And sighing said she could not stay,
Since death of life had reft him,

with the term *reft,* probably a shortened form of *bereft,* meaning "deprived."

As the ballad concludes Barbara starts back toward her home, hearing "the dead-bell knellin'," with the bell personified, crying, "'Woe to Barbara Allan!'" In the final verse Barbara says,

"O mother, mother, make my bed,
O make it soft and narrow:
Since my love died for me today,
I'll die for him tomorrow."

The narrow bed evokes imagery of a grave, while calling on the allusion to death as sleep.

While *Bonny Barbara Allan* recalls a tragic scene, it is not without an edgy wit. Because Barbara is labeled *Bonny* she remains an attractive woman, probably still in her prime, an arguable truth because she refers to Graeme as "young man." As the well-resourced aristocrat, he could take her for granted, something she obviously does not. He tells her, "'O it's I'm sick, and very, very sick, / And 'tis a' for Barbara Allan,'" but she does not accept that explanation. Her sarcasm is real

when she counters, "'O the better for me ye sal [shall] never be, / Though your heart's blood were a-spillin'.'" The grief he now experiences over the loss of their relationship has no practical worth to a working girl like Barbara, a woman still living with her mother, and she basically tells him he offers too little too late. She also knows enough not to linger after Graeme's death, as a woman of her social status would not be welcome during the formal grieving rituals that would follow.

The final lines can be interpreted as expressing simply a sweet sentiment, that Barbara now has no reason to live, her love having died for her. However, they may also be seen as expressing IRONY. She did not fall down in a death swoon beside Graeme's bed but instead managed to walk home and delay her death for 24 hours. Of the duo Graeme may have possessed the material power, but Barbara's strength and will, which may be seen as positive characteristics, obviously overshadow his. Her fate remains her own choice, emphasizing the fortitude of the working class over that of the wasteful aristocracy, as well as her rebellion against his treatment of her.

BIBLIOGRAPHY
"The Ballads Project." Bodleian Library. Available online. URL: http://www.bodley.ox.ac.uk/ballads/ballads.htm. Downloaded January 6, 2005.

BOYD, ELIZABETH (ca. 1727–1745)

Not much is known of Elizabeth Boyd's life or death, although many clues have been discovered among her publications. According to a note in one publication, her father apparently served the Stuarts in some manner and enjoyed their favor. Boyd published a novel in 1732, *The Happy-Unfortunate; Or, the Female Page,* which reappeared in 1737 as *The Female Page.* She noted in its preface that she wrote and published in order to support her care for her aged mother, who had at one time taken "the Charge of many Children," indicating that Boyd matured in a large family. She mentions John, duke of Argyll, as one who encouraged her to write, and dedications included the countess of Hertford and the earl of Albemarle. The list of about 300 subscriptions sold includes a notable number of aristocrats. Those facts support the belief that her family had royal connections, and she earned enough profit from her novel to allow her to sell stationery goods from a house near Leicester Fields.

Boyd's earliest published poem appears to have been "Variety: A Poem . . . by Louisa" (1727), followed on the king's birthday by *Verses* (1730) written to celebrate that occasion. Her poem "ON THE DEATH OF AN INFANT OF FIVE DAYS OLD, BEING A BEAUTIFUL BUT ABORTIVE BIRTH" appeared in the strangely titled *The Humorous Miscellany* (1733), a collection containing many works on sobering topics. A later play titled *Don Sancho, Or The Student's Whim* (1739), while never staged, had a reading at Drury Lane Theatre.

Boyd published additional occasional poems through 1744, and in 1745 she published *The Snail: Or The Lady's Lucubrations . . . by Eloisa,* the first volume of what she had planned as a periodical. It noted that its publication had been delayed by her "unhappy State of Health." The volume focused on the scandal caused two decades earlier by the duke and duchess of Marlborough, widely believed to have manipulated Queen Anne to their personal benefit. Others had written about the unfortunate relationship, including the early novelist Mary Delarivière Manley in the popular *The Secret History of Queen Zarah and the Zarazians* (1705), the first roman à clef written in English. Boyd apparently lived near St. James's Church when she published *The Snail,* the sole volume of her intended series. She may have been unable to continue its publication as a result of poor health.

Deemed a minor poet, Boyd remains of interest because of her obvious determination to write. "On the Death of an Infant," her most easily located work, is significant for a sudden contrast in its final lines between the male and female approaches to grief over a lost baby. That thematic turn elevates the stylistically highly sentimentalized poem.

BIBLIOGRAPHY

Schofield, Mary Ann. *Masking and Unmasking the Female Mind: Disguising Romances in Feminine Fiction, 1713–1719.* Newark: University of Delaware Press, 1999.

"BREAK OF DAY" JOHN DONNE (1633)   JOHN DONNE's playful "Break of Day" reflects on the tradition of the AUBADE, a poem in praise of morning that often featured the parting of two lovers. One of the few Donne poems adopting the female point of view, it offers evidence of the use by METAPHYSICAL POETS AND POETRY of balance in terms of darkness and light. While important on their own as expressions of different times of day and the traditional activities that accompany them, the opposites also suggest as FIGURATIVE LANGUAGE (FIGURE OF SPEECH) the traditional association of two related opposites, evil (darkness) and good (light). Donne uses these metaphors to muse upon the various facets of love, its carnal facet generally believed to be evil in contrast with its spiritual. Particularly for women physical desire represented a dark spirit. Donne, however, expresses sympathy for women, who must share their men with distractions of the world. The bed represents woman's sphere, while the world of business claims men, separating the two. Donne's style includes an abundant use of ALLITERATION and repetition of words for emphasis. His simple format includes many single-syllable terms and an easy rhyme scheme of *aabbcc,* allowing an imitation of the natural speaking voice.

The female voice begins with a question put to
    her lover:
'Tis true, 'tis day; what though it be?
O wilt thou therefore rise from me?
Why should we rise because 'tis light?
Did we lie down because 'twas night?

Donne often included rhetorical questions in his poetry, the answers to which he believed would prove of universal interest. His female voice speaks for all women in questioning the need to adhere to the artificially prescribed limits of time in the exercise of passion. The fourth line in this first of three six-line stanzas makes clear that men and women do not lie down just because the darkness dictates that they do so. Donne concludes the first stanza with lines imitating a riddle, playing off the idea of opposites: "Love, which in spite of darkness brought us hither, / Should in despite of light keep us together." Clearly the persona feels that love should be dictated by neither natural nor unnatural law.

The second stanza engages in personification, as the voice characterizes light as a villain that robs her of satisfaction. The tone remains teasingly pouty, as she states,

> Light hath no tongue, but is all eye;
> If it could speak as well as spy,
> This were the worst that it could say,
> That being well, I fain would stay.

Donne incorporates the traditional view of the sun as heaven's eye, adopting an approach he also uses in his more famous "The SUN RISING." The last lines of this stanza clarify that her lover possesses both her heart and her honor. Donne's inclusion of *honor* remains crucial, as this female shows herself devoted to only one lover, an important distinction from the inconstant woman made popular in much Renaissance literature.

In the third stanza readers learn that business takes the lover away, suggesting that he also remains devoted to only one lover; this couple may be married, if the speaker intends *business* in the workday sense. The speaker terms business "the worst disease of love," explaining, "The poor, the foul, the false, love can / Admit, but not the busied man." Ironically she categorizes persons "foul" and "false" as more appropriate to love than those engaged in business. Donne may also reflect on his own method of adopting business as a topic for a love poem, rendering passion simply a part of the quotidian existence. However, the final two lines of the poem challenge the domestic bliss suggested by previous imagery. Typically of Donne, they offer a strong conclusion, leaving the reader wondering whether he/she had properly understood the poem. The previously honest voice turns coy as she states, "He which hath business, and makes love, doth do / Such wrong, as when a married man doth woo." Suddenly the man's "business" becomes questionable, as does the lovers' relationship. Again, however, the voice may simply suggest that a busy man has two lovers in the metaphoric sense, his wife and his business.

BIBLIOGRAPHY

Brown, Meg Lotta. *Donne and the Politics of Conscience.* Leiden, The Netherlands: E. J. Brill, 1995.

Mintz, Susannah B. "'Forget the Hee and Shee': Gender and Play in John Donne." *Modern Philology* 98, no. 4 (May 2001): 577.

BRETON, NICHOLAS (ca. 1555–1626)

Nicholas Breton (last name also spelled *Brittaine*) was probably born in Essex and later may have gained an education at Oxford, as indicated by diary notes of the Reverend Richard Madox. His wealthy widowed mother, Elizabeth Bacon Breton, remarried to George Gascoigne, a revered Renaissance poet, soldier, and member of Parliament, whose *Certain Notes of Instruction in English Verse* proved one of the earliest statements on English prosody and influenced Breton's writing. In 1593 he married Ann Sutton and the two raised a family. Breton moved to London and began to write labored verse, often overwrought with ALLITERATION and heavy word choice. He enjoyed the patronage of Mary, countess of Pembroke, and probably served her brother, Sir Philip Sidney, a Protestant martyr and seminal poet. Although the countess withdrew her support for unknown reasons in 1601, Breton continued to write and publish. Facts regarding his life are credited to assumed autobiographical letters signed only "N.B.," contained in *A Poste with a Packet of Mad Letters* (1603).

As Breton's poetry improved, the writer Francis Meres compared him at the close of the 16th century with the poets Edmund Spenser, William Shakespeare, and MICHAEL DRAYTON; later critics felt Breton's works did not merit membership in that group. Breton's preferred use of RIME ROYAL connects him to a past tradition including the 16th-century poets Sir Thomas Wyatt and Henry Howard, earl of Surrey, both early imitators of the PETRARCHAN SONNET. His work appeared in the important publication ENGLAND'S HELICON (1600), and his later poem "Strange News Out of Diverse Countries" (1622) is considered one of his best. His voluminous publications included religious writings, pamphlets, and satires. All of his work is supported by a moralistic tone, and, at times, an overwhelming sweetness that suited religious poetry of his age. His better known works include "Passionate Shepheard" (1604) and the lullaby "COME LITTLE BABE," the latter published in *Lyrics from Elizabethan Romance* (1890) by A. H. Bullen and a prime example of rime royal; both are easily located in electronic format. His final published work, titled *Fantastickes* (1626), helped later scholars collect information on religious festivals and customs of the day.

Occasionally a scholar will advance a new theory regarding authorship by a lesser-known writer. This happened with Breton in 1929, when a scholar named Charles Crawford proposed that a work titled *Greenes Funeralls,* a copy of which existed in the Bodleian Library, Oxford, had wrongly been credited to a writer named Richard Barnefield, to whom Crawford referred as "that much over-rated poetaster." Instead, he claimed, Breton authored the book celebrating Greene. The concealing of his name may have resulted from the animosity of his contemporaries, explained with fervent empathy by Crawford, who notes, "they condemned all he wrote, whether good, bad, or indifferent; one special point of theirs being that Breton was a rhymer, and no poet." Crawford claims Breton wrote "many anthologies," the majority "of which were assigned to others, printers and publishers being among the happy people thus honoured." Breton "loved to play practical jokes on his friends, as well as on his enemies," and he seems to have provoked William Shakespeare by "unlawfully" using his name "to gull the public" into believing he had a hand in the publication of an anthology titled *Poetical Rhapsody.* Apparently the bard did not care for Breton's habit of publishing some of his own writing under the names of others. Many of those others remained silent, however, according to Crawford, gladly accepting that credit. Crawford theorized that Breton's reticence to claim credit for his own work may be why "so little direct mention of him is made in contemporary writings."

BIBLIOGRAPHY
Crawford, Charles. "*Greenes Funeralls,* 1594, and Nicholas Breton." *Studies in Philology,* May 1929, 1–39.

BRITANNIA'S PASTORAL WILLIAM BROWNE (1613, 1616, and 1852)

WILLIAM BROWNE wrote *Britannia's Pastoral* by adopting an approach practiced since the third century B.C. when Theocritus wrote his *Idylls,* featuring the romance and laments of shepherds and shepherdesses. Their rural existence symbolized the ideal life and formed the basis for VIRGIL's later *Eclogues,* the earliest Roman example of the pastoral. The term *pastoral* became interchangeable with *idyll* and *eclogue.* Both terms derived from the Greek: *idyll* meaning "little picture," and *eclogue* meaning "selec-

tion," referring to a brief poem or a portion of a longer poem. Eventually in the 18th century the pastoral provided more of a context, while eclogue signified a specific poetic form. Although many critics feel Browne's *Pastoral* fails as a narrative, forcing the reader to move in hundreds of lines from the trials and tribulations of one fair shepherdess to those of another with little to distinguish them, it bears some fine pastoral characteristics. Browne might be excused for occasionally addressing his readers as "swaines" in an attempt to promote the pastoral pastiche because of his obvious and justified admiration of his native Devonshire, to which his references remain abundant. His love for water becomes apparent in his use of various streams for charming sensory imagery, their music imitated through metaphor. In addition, his use of models, such as Edmund Spenser and Sir Philip Sidney, proves of interest. His blend of fact and tradition creates a pleasant world appreciated by readers willing to imagine themselves a part of it. The First Book and the Second Book each contain five songs, while the Third Book is brief and fragmentary.

The plot of Book 1 derived from the playwright John Fletcher's *The Faithful Shepherdess* (1609). Its focus is a shepherdess named Marina who pines for a faithless lover named Celandine, who abandoned her. She twice attempts suicide, leaping from cliffs into water below, the natural scene an appropriately pastoral environment in which to end her life. A water god falls in love with her, rescues her during her second attempt to kill herself, and succeeds in administering a type of potion that allows her to forget Celandine. Her adventures continue as she travels with a Nymph and meets a shepherd named Doridon. Later wounded, Doridon is transported to his mother's house by the Nymph, and a Hermit heals him. Some of these details parallel those in Edmund Spenser's epic pastoral *The Fairie Queene* (1590, 1596, 1609). Doridon searches for Marina, encountering other shepherds and shepherdesses, along with pastoral dances and magical occurrences, including the appearance of the beautiful Aletheia (Truth). Aletheia springs forth from the mangled body of the shepherdess Fida's favorite hind, or deer, killed by the figure Riot, further featured in an ALLEGORY along with Truth and Time.

In the concluding Song to Book 1, popularly labeled "The poet's ambition," Browne departs from the story to reflect upon his debt to other pastoral writers. The plea to a Muse for aid may be found in much traditional poetry; Browne expands that tradition to pay homage to his models as well as to the mystical power of inspiration. Browne begins,

A truer love the Muses never sung,
Nor happier names e'er graced a golden tongue:
O! they are better fitting his sweet strip,
Who on the banks of ancor tuned his pipe.

The speaker claims his lack of worthiness to be inspired by the same Muse as his contemporary and friend MICHAEL DRAYTON, the "Who" referred to in the fourth line. He continues,

Or rather for that learned swain, whose lays
Divinest Homer crowned with deathless bays;
Or any one sent from the sacred well
Inheriting the soul of Astrophell,

where the "swain" who gained immortality through his verse represents GEORGE CHAPMAN and the one who inherited Astrophell's soul is Sir Philip Sidney. That poem concludes with the poetic appeal,

My Muse may one day make the courtly swains
Enamoured on the music of the plains,
And as upon a hill she bravely sings
Teach humble dales to weep in crystal springs.

The Muse is viewed as a teacher, and her association with Browne's models for the pastoral form proves appropriate.

In Book 2, readers again follow Marina's story as she is carried out to sea to the Isle of Auglesey by the ravisher, who leaves her sleeping under a bush. When Marina awakes and attempts to help an ugly young girl, the allegorical creature Limos (Hunger) captures Marina and carries her to his monster cave. Limos raids shepherds' flocks and will later be caught and tied to a rock, where he will perish from hunger. Browne's introduction of the ugly female character follows precedent in pastoral where a malevolent or unattractive creature or person may be introduced in order to emphasize the beauty of the main characters. Thetis, a sea goddess, appears, allowing Browne to make a moral point as the goddess ensures the welfare of the oppressed who live along the sea. Thetis meets various Nymphs and introduces the story of the nymph Walla.

In a portion of Song 3 from Book 2, aptly titled "The Description of Walla," Browne includes many lines of detail regarding the Nymph. He employs various classical allusions, including to Venus; the Zephyr, or breeze; and Cupid, and uses the popular reference to Cynthia as the sun. Most of his figurative language helps the reader picture Walla's clothing, including a "green silk frock [which] her comely shoulder clad"; a "love-knot girdle," which threatens "willing bondage"; the entire dress "lined with rich carnation silk, / And in the midst of both lawn white as milk," "a deep fringe hung of rich and twisted gold." He places her on the "green marge of a crystal brook," where "A thousand yellow flowers at fishes look," describing her "mantle, stitch'd with gold and green," adding "A silver quiver at her back she wore, / With darts and arrows for the stag and boar." The imagery of Walla as a hunter evokes the goddess of the hunt and protector of women, Diana. He concludes strongly, leaving no doubt in his readers' minds of Walla's potency, especially for one shepherd, or swain, named Tavy:

Walla, the fairest nymph that haunts the woods
Walla, beloved of shepherds, fauns, and floods,
Walla, for whom the frolic satyrs pine,
Walla, with whose fine foot the flowerets twine,
Walla, of whom sweet birds their ditties move,
Walla, the earth's delight and Tavy's love.

Tavy was in actuality the name of a river with which Browne was closely associated, with his ties to Tavistock, and Walla was a tributary. The CONCEIT of two rivers or bodies of water loving one another represented another inherited aspect of pastoral for Browne, a tradition with its roots in Ovid. Browne's makes obvious his love for the countryside where he was raised in his repeated praise of nature, while other songs emphasize his broader love for his country.

Song 3 continues with "The Song of Tavy," in which Browne departs from his dreamy presentation of Walla to adopt a new format supporting a more earthy style. While the description of Walla used 44 consecutive lines of rhyming couplets in iambic pentameter, Tavy's thoughts of her assume a less-formal format of seven iambic pentameter rhyming couplets in four-line stanzas and a concluding couplet. By dividing Tavy's fantasy into stanzas, Browne allows momentum to build, supporting the increase in Tavy's passion. Browne skillfully rendered Walla as a silent object, while Tavy's voice is strong, declaring,

> As careful merchants do expecting stand
> (After long time and merry gales of wind)
> Upon the place where their brave ship must
>   land,
> So wait I for the vessel of my mind.

Browne may have intended no double meaning in the use of the term *vessel* applied to the sensuous Walla. However, the long-popular conception of the female as a vessel shaped to accommodate the male remains one psychoanalytic critics might later note as indicative of gender stereotypes. In addition feminist and Marxist critics would immediately note the commodification of Tavy's love object as material goods, available for barter by merchants.

Browne extends the maritime metaphor, as Tavy dreams of the vessel's "great adventure" and "the East jewels of wealth she brings," followed with hyperbolic descriptions of that wealth, including "The sapphires ringed on her panting breast / Run as rich veins of ore about the mould" and

> the melting rubies on her cherry lip
> Are of such power to hold; that as one day
> Cupid flew thirsty by, he stooped to sip,
> And fastened there could never get away.

The melodrama fits the pastoral, in which all players, despite their obvious awareness of earthly delights and erotic thoughts, remain innocently caught up in passion and pining. The book continues with the exploits of Thetis and a return of the shepherd Remond, who believes his love, Fida, to be dead. In addition Walla's pursuit by a lustful Satyr results in her cries in vain to Diana for help, then to Ina. In Ovidian tradition, she pleads for transformation into a stone or tree—any metamorphosis in order to preserve her chastity. Her wish granted, Walla becomes a spring and is mourned by Tavy.

Browne repeats many of his motifs of pursuit, capture, and release throughout the pastorals. Pan enters the scene and helps introduce readers to another pair of lovers, Philocel and Caelia, in Song 5. Thetis rescues them and leaves the island but hears a lamenting voice, which belongs to Marina, still trapped by Limos in his hideous cave. She will be freed by Triton and join the lovers at "Thetis Court."

Readers quickly understand that pastoral does not emphasize character development. Reality had no relationship to the pastoral, which was created for its own sake to celebrate an idealistic manner of existence. The only realistic aspects exist in Browne's description of places, as he accurately paints his familiar countryside. In that respect he prefigured later poets such as SIR JOHN DENHAM and his *COOPER'S HILL* and ALEXANDER POPE and his *WINDSOR FOREST*.

While Tavy's song discussed here shares his hopeful expectations, in a later song from the fragmentary Book 3, Celadyne relates his grief when expectations are not fulfilled. He mourns the loss of Marina, who had, ironically, attempted suicide in Book 1 after Celadyne's abandonment of her. In one of Browne's more skillful and less precious poems, he references the pitiful figure of Philomela, who in Ovid's *Metamorphosis* is raped and mutilated, her tongue cut out. Philomela eventually regained self-expression through art, which Celadyne considers as a way to help him deal with his grief but ultimately declines. He says of his lost love,

> Marina's gone and now sit I
> As Philomela on a thorn,
> Turned out of nature's livery,
> Mirthless, alone, and all forlorn.

In two additional verses, Celadyne offers mournful comparisons of his loss to "a dying swan," the closing of marigolds, "the departure of the sun," the bee at the end of the day, and birds that suffer through winter after having enjoyed summer. The reference to art as a possible cure occurs in the fourth stanza, but Celadyne rejects its healing possibilities:

> I oft have heard men say there be
> Some, that with confidence profess
> The helpful Art of Memory.

He refers to the loss of a painful remembrance, noting that through "forgetfulness, / I'd learn, and try what further art could do / To make me love her and forget her too." Browne next employs personification of the emotion of melancholy and repetition of both sound and word to help underscore Celadyne's constant thought about his loss:

> Sad melancholy, that persuades
> Men from themselves, to think they be
> Headless, or other body's shades,
> Hath long and bootless dwelt with me.
> For could I think she some idea were
> I still might love, forget, and have her here.

Representing for modern readers one of the most thought-provoking and beautiful of Browne's verses, it leads into the song's conclusion, which advances the idea that even the way time passes has been influenced by Celadyne's relationship with Marina.

Browne's *Britannia's Pastoral* remains an excellent representative of the pastoral form. Although not as stylishly executed as those by his models, it contains all the required elements, enthusiastically and intensely executed. And when Browne focuses on the power of melancholy to alter human perceptions, he produces verse worthy of the age that fostered similar considerations by William Shakespeare and BEN JONSON.

BIBLIOGRAPHY
Moorman, Frederic William. *William Browne: His Britannia's Pastorals, and the Pastoral Poetry of the Elizabethan Age.* 1897. Reprint, New York: Burt Franklin, 1969.

BROADSIDE   Broadsides were songs sold in print for a half-penny or a penny in Britain, beginning in the 16th century. They were used in conjunction with discussions of politics or other subjects of interest at taverns and similar social gatherings. A cheap form of print readily available, existing broadsides contribute immeasurably to studies of literary, music, social, art, and printing history, although rarely dated or signed by their authors. Known for lavish woodcut illustrations, the documents can now be viewed online through projects such as that supported by the Bodleian Library of Oxford University, which has cataloged more than 30,000 ballads for research use. Broadsides celebrated legendary weddings and love affairs, as well as stirring patriotism and declaring allegiance with tales of the Jacobite rebellion and the Crimean War. They also acted as advertisements and souvenirs of events.

BROWNE, WILLIAM (1591?–1643)   Born around 1590 to Thomas Browne, William Browne matured in England and attended school at Tavistock. He attended Exeter College at Oxford and entered Clifford's Inn, the Inner Temple, in 1611 and graduated with a masters degree in 1624. A scholar, Browne admired and imitated work by Edmund Spenser, Sir Philip Sidney, and MICHAEL DRAYTON, particularly their pastoral poetry. Drayton reciprocated the admiration by prefixing some of Browne's verses in his well-known *Polyolbion*. Browne's own pastorals would later influence the poets JOHN MILTON and John Keats; twentieth-century critic W. T. Arnold compared Keats and Browne as both "being before all things an artist" with "the same intense pleasure in a fine line or a fine phrase for its own sake." Mainly known for BRITANNIA'S PASTORAL, a narrative poem published in three parts in 1613, 1616, and 1852, Browne also collaborated with other poets to produce *The Shepherd's Pipe* (1614). Drayton added commendatory verses in honor of *Britannia's Pastorals,* and Keats later included a quotation from Browne's work in the preface of his *Epistles.* Both admired Browne despite the judgment of some of his contemporaries that Browne's work lacked "invention" and the criticism of later scholars that it lacked narrative power. He also wrote an occasionally anthologized SONNET, "FAIREST, WHEN BY THE RULES."

In addition to his pastorals, Browne wrote epitaphs, his most famous celebrating the countess of Pembroke, Philip Sidney's sister, Mary Sidney:

Underneath this sable hearse
Lies the subject of all verse:
Sidney's sister, Pembroke's mother:
Death, ere thou hast slain another
Fair and learn'd and good as she,
Time shall throw a dart at thee.

That epitaph was originally credited to BEN JONSON, to whom Browne remained devoted. A member of the group popularly known as the TRIBE OF BEN, the poet received praise from Jonson in a preface to the second edition of *Pastorals*. Browne worked as a tutor and lived at various times in Oxfordshire and Dorking, although he would be buried in Tavistock. Original copies of his works exist, including a copy of *Britannia's Pastoral* at the Fisher Rare Book Library, University of Toronto. Browne's better known poems may be easily found at electronic sites.

BIBLIOGRAPHY

Arnold, W. T. "William Browne." *The English Poets,* edited by Thomas Humphry Ward. Vol. 2. New York: Macmillan, 1914.

"BUNCH OF GRAPES, THE" GEORGE HERBERT (1633)

GEORGE HERBERT included his "The Bunch of Grapes" in the posthumously published collection titled *The Temple*. He adopts a biblical metaphor, establishing grapes as the raw fruit upon which the production of wine depends. Wine occupied a central role in the life of the Hebrews, and Canaan, a location referenced by Herbert in this poem, contained vast vineyards. When the Jews departed Egypt, Canaan represented their Promised Land, the geographic location the Israelites occupied before their bondage in Egypt. When they returned to Canaan, Joshua, brother to Moses, directed that the land be divided among the 12 Jewish tribes. Herbert establishes Canaan as symbolizing God's promised life to those who will receive his grace. He uses the story of the Jews seeking God's promises to tell the story of one who at first knew "Joy," locking it safely away, but suffered when "some bad man" allowed Joy to escape.

Herbert employs the fertility of Canaan, and by extension, the Christian life, to contrast with the symbolic meaning of the Red Sea, crossed by the Israelites when they first departed their bondage in Egypt. At the place where the Israelites crossed, the land remained so flat the Egyptians could not perceive the shoreline as they chased the Israelites in the fog of night, and so they fell into the trap Moses set when he ordered that the waters part to allow the Israelites to cross the sea safely. While the Red Sea represented a new beginning for the Israelites as the first obstacle they overcame with God's help, they later rejected God to worship an idol and wandered aimlessly around the desert, doubling back to the Red Sea before God at last allowed them to complete their journey at Canaan. Herbert suggests that as the Israelites, his speaker traveled toward God's Promised Land (6), then lost his focus and was "Brought back to the Red Sea, the sea of shame" (7). While the Jews spent 40 years in their wanderings, the speaker has spent "Sev'n years" (40).

The speaker notes in the second stanza another comparison to the "Jews of old" who traveled according to God's commandment, yet along the way "saw no town." In this case he compares to the Jews "each Christian" who "hath his journeys spanned" (10), as has the speaker. The speaker suggests that Christians learn from the story penned by the Jews, that human actions remain of "small renown," while "God's works are wide" and imbued with an "ancient justice" that "overflows our crimes" (12–14). Thus although Christians embrace the promise of a new life based on God's grace, they would do well to pay attention to God's rendering of justice in another age, which was revealed through the Old Testament and its dependence on religious law.

Herbert includes several additional biblical references in his third stanza, comparing Old Testament stories to New Testament parables. Examples include sand, an allusion to the parable found in Matthew 7 of the man who built his house on sand, or worldly concerns, only to lose it when water flooded it. He stands in contrast to the man who built his house on rock, or the word of the Lord, whose house stood firm. Other biblical allusions include "serpents, tents and shrouds" (17), with the serpent primarily symbolizing evil or temptation from the story of the Garden of Eden; tents representing the nomadic life; and shrouds suggesting the linen in which Christ's body was bound, or perhaps an allusion to the fact that humans' concept of God remains clouded, as if one peered through a shroud, which rendered what he sought to see unclear. The speaker notes that such "murmurings" will not be the last ones in the name of God. Then he asks:

> But where's the cluster? Where's the taste
> Of mine inheritance? Lord, if I must borrow,
> Let me as well take up their joy, as sorrow.
>   (19–21)

Herbert appears to question why he does not enjoy the inheritance specified for the Jews as God's chosen people. That inheritance might be represented in the "cluster" of grapes, produced by Canaan.

In the final fourth stanza the voice at first answers its question with an additional question: "But can he want the grape, who hath the wine?" Herbert extends his metaphor to make the point that while the Jews who await their promised leader from God hold the grapes, or the promise, Christians, who acknowledge Christ as their savior, hold wine, the realization of the promise. He further expands on the metaphor as the speaker praises God for making Noah's vine "bring forth grapes good store." Acknowledging the grapes are worth praising, the speaker adds

> But much more him I must adore,
> Who of the law's sour juice sweet wine did
>   make,
> Ev'n God himself, being pressed for my sake.
>   (26–28)

Herbert notes that Christians no longer must abide by Old Testament law to try to earn grace, as Christ's sacrifice suffices: it is the wine pressed from God. The image proves even stronger when the reader has some knowledge of the traditional grape press found in Canaan. It consisted of two troughs cut into rock, a fact that allows Herbert to reflect on his previous allusion to the house built on rock rather than sand. The wine press itself sat on the higher level, suggesting God's position in relationship to humans. The higher level proved shallower, with the lower level that human beings would occupy much deeper, forming a reservoir to collect the abundant juice pressed from the grapes. The juice was fermented twice, once in the wine press, then in wineskins or large jars, often strained to remove impurities during the process. Thus, Herbert suggests the process of coming to God experienced by his speaker. That process may involve misdirection, disillusionment, and purification by trial before it reaches any satisfactory completion.

"BURIAL OF AN INFANT, THE" HENRY VAUGHAN (1650)

Because he believed so strongly in the possibility of human regeneration through faith, HENRY VAUGHAN did not fear death. It served as a topic for many of his poems, which often grew from his grief over his personal losses and those resulting from war. In observing part of the ritual of death in the burial of a baby, Vaughan turns to one of his occasional themes, that childhood represented a divine state. As did THOMAS TRAHERNE, he believed that all infants are born into the sinless state enjoyed by Adam, prior to his fall from grace and expulsion from the Garden of Eden. This may be seen in the opening stanza in which Vaughan adopts FIGURATIVE LANGUAGE (FIGURE OF SPEECH) to compare the "Blest infant" to a fragile blossom, its life only long enough for it to "look about, and fall / Wearied out in a harmless strife." The speaker makes clear that the world's problems may not be blamed on an innocent baby. The infant's expiration was done "Sweetly," as its "soul / Flew home unstained by his new kin," again emphasizing the baby's blameless state with the characterization "unstained." He remained untouched by sin during his brief stay with the "kin," or humans, who supplied no support for his soul. Before the child's soul "knew'st how to be foul / Death weened thee from the world and sin." Vaughan's use of the term *weened* emphasizes this person's infant state, as babies are weaned, or separated from dependence upon their mother's breast milk. In this instance the weaning was from human existence in a state of sin. The infant's remains are termed *virgin crumbs*, the adjective *virgin* again making clear the infant's innocence.

Those crumbs, all that will remain of the earthly body, anticipate arrival of "thy Savior" to "undress them, and unswaddle death." The concluding image of Christ unwrapping death, or revealing its visage and freeing the infant body, remains a strong reminder that unlike adults infants die in a state of grace and may expect salvation.

BIBLIOGRAPHY

Leishman, J. B. *The Metaphysical Poets: Donne, Herbert, Vaughan, Traherne.* Oxford: Clarendon Press, 1934.

BURNS, ROBERT (1759–1796)

Robert Burns was born in the southwestern town of Alloway, Scotland, to a poor tenant farmer. The eldest of seven children, he benefited from a spotty education in various nearby schools as well as by a tutor his father insisted on employing, regardless of the expense. Not a particularly impressive student, Burns matured quickly, assuming responsibility on Mt. Oliphant, the family's rented farm, from a young age. He also gained a reputation for drink and celebration and had a number of relationships with various women throughout his life, fathering at least three children with women other than his wife.

After his father's death in 1784, Burns joined his brother Gilbert in renting another farm, but that venture did not prove successful. He began a sexual affair with Jean Armour, who became pregnant. Although she possessed a marriage agreement signed by Burns, it did not meet the conventional requirements for marriage, prompting her father to appeal to the local Kirk session for its censure. Burns apparently then balked at the agreement with Jean, confessing to his friend Gavin Hamilton that he wanted to end the relationship, sought his freedom, and might have impregnated another woman, the Mary Campbell who inspired some later poetry. With the failure of his business and the challenges to his marriage to Jean, Burns considered moving to the West Indies and hid from a warrant issued by Jean's father. While in hiding, he learned that Mary had died in childbirth, while Jean had delivered twins, Robert and Jean. Burns had in the meantime published a collection of poetry titled *Poems, Chiefly in the Scottish Dialect* (1786), and its success spurred a move to Edinburgh. In between flings with other women, he continued to visit Jean, and a second set of twins were born, both of whom died. In a series of events that could form the plot of a melodrama, Burns at last reunited with Jean, who would eventually bear him nine children and inspire Burns to write at least 14 BALLADS.

Fascinated by Scotland's ballads and their capacity to capture both the native work ethic and the propensity to drink, Burns revised many of the traditional songs and committed them to print. Several became international favorites, including "Auld Lang Syne" and "JOHN ANDERSON MY JO." Some of the best known, such as "TO A MOUSE," may be found in his *Poems,* a publication that assured his popularity. Interested parties from Edinburgh supported repeated editions of the collection, which grew larger with each issue.

While Burns's use of dialect may challenge the untrained eye and ear, it also adds charm and authenticity to a poetry form that grew from an oral tradition. The subject matter and themes of his ballads often mirrored Burns's concerns, as is seen in "Holy Willie's Prayer." The Willie of the title accused Gavin Hamilton in 1785 of stealing from the fund for the poor that he had been appointed to manage. The poem celebrates Hamilton's acquittal, although Burns published it after his friend's death. Burns's lifestyle separated him from the Church of Scotland's Calvinistic beliefs in predestination, which promised Willie salvation. "SONG—FOR A' THAT AND A' THAT" echoes Burns's disenchantment with the events of the French Revolution, although he still believed in its causes.

Burns's writing success led him again to try to farm, this time selecting Dumfriesshire on property called Ellisland. Although his attempt again failed, he had gained the trust of Jean's family, and the couple participated in a traditional marriage. In 1791 he had to abandon Ellisland, and he supported himself as a tax inspector in Dumfries. By all reports he became bored and listless and died at the age of 38. Jean would outlive him by 38 years.

Burns's popularity remains unequaled by any other Scottish poet. His work has never been out of print, spawning a cottage industry, with many electronic Web sites, as well as printed sources, featuring his work and biography. A full Burns encyclopedia was published in 1959 and is now available online at http://www.robertburns.org/encyclopedia/index.shtml. This site, sponsored by Scotweb Marketing, Ltd., also links to 558 works by the poet. Burns tours and festivals continue to promote the poetry of this balladeer extraordinaire.

BIBLIOGRAPHY

Crawford, Thomas, ed. *Love, Labour, and Liberty: The Eighteenth-Century Scottish Lyric.* Cheadle, England: Carcanet Press, 1976.

Eyre-Todd, George. *Scottish Poetry of the Eighteenth Century.* Westport, Conn.: Greenwood Press, 1971.

Kinsley, James, ed. *Burns: Poems and Songs.* New York: Oxford University Press, 1971.

Low, Donald A. *Robert Burns.* Edinburgh: Scottish Academic Press, 1986.

Mackay, James A. *A Biography of Robert Burns.* Edinburgh: Mainstream, 1992.

BUTLER, SAMUEL (1613–1680)

Samuel Butler was born near Worcester and enhanced a spotty formal education at the King's School until age 15 with self-education through reading and study. After school he took a position as a justice's clerk at Earl's Croome in service to a Mr. Jeffries and remained in service in various clerical, secretarial, and household positions for the following three decades. He worked for the countess of Kent in Wrest, Bedfordshire, where he met John Selden, the legal scholar. He next took employment with the Presbyterian Sir Samuel Luke, a position that would become critical later in Butler's life. Luke had served Cromwell as a colonel in the Puritan revolution and was the governor of Newport Pagnell when Butler, a strong supporter of the Crown, worked for him.

Butler later expressed his Royalist sympathies through pamphlets in the 1650s and composed satiric ballads. When Charles II returned to the throne in 1660, Butler served the president of Wales as secretary and became steward of Ludlow Castle. Finally in 1662 at age 50, he published the first part of a serious work that guaranteed his fame, the mock-epic HUDIBRAS. For some time, critics knew of few additional works by Butler, but in later centuries, at least six anonymous prose pieces were attributed to him, including *The Case of King Charles I Truly Stated,* which refuted each point

in a prior pamphlet that supported regicide. However, it did not see print until 1691, when, as the publisher wrote in its preface, "A new Race of the Old Republican Stamp . . . reviv'd the Quarrel," a quarrel of Butler's era, then 40 years old. Two other of those publications were printed during Butler's lifetime. One, titled *Mola Asinaria,* bears the name *William Prynne* as its author. Prynne existed, in fact, and was used savagely by Butler as a character within the satire. Another, titled *Answer* (1659–60), supposedly John Manners' ghost-written reply to his father-in-law, Henry Pierpoint, featured a marital situation that later became a sensational scandal, commented upon by the duke of Buckingham and JOHN MILTON. None of Butler's early publications are of value, other than to prove that his writing of *Hudibras* was not an isolated act.

The lengthy poem would be completed with two more issues in 1663 and 1678. *Hudibras* proved extremely popular, as evidenced by its multiple printings within its first year of publication. It spared no one considered a pedant or a hypocritical Puritan, causing it to become favored reading by the king. Butler especially targeted his former employer, Sir Samuel Luke, believed to be the model for the character Hudibras.

By 1670 Butler had returned to service, this time in the employ of George Villiers, second duke of Buckingham and one of the five members of the king's cabinet. During the summer of 1670 Butler accompanied Villiers and other notables upon the death of Charles II's sister, wife of the French duke of Orléans, to St-Germain. Traveling with the group was Thomas Sprat, historian for the Royal Society. The one notebook that survived the trip Butler used to compile an English-French dictionary, as well as a sketch book of the people he observed along the way. He may also have traveled to the Hague on a diplomatic mission in 1672 with the duke, the earl of Arlington, and the duke of Monmouth. He remained with Buckingham while the duke served in 1673–74 as chancellor of Cambridge University. The antiquarian Anthony Wood wrote that Butler helped compose Buckingham's satire *The Rehearsal,* as early as 1663, although that cannot be proved; if he had a hand in the work, it was more probably the revision, written in 1671. Two other works written after *Hudibras* are most certainly Butler's, each bearing the phrase "Written by the author of *Hudibras*" and each executed in his style. *To the Memory of the Most Renowned Du-Vall* (1671) offered a biting ode on the famed highwayman Claude Duval, which later critics noted as a precursor to Henry Fielding's novel *Jonathan Wild* (1743). It ridiculed the English fascination with French behavior and dress, attacked certain literary styles, and savaged lawyers for their dishonesty; Du Vall allowed them to practice in "his own allow'd High-way." Butler also wrote a final satire four years after the death of William Prynne titled *Two Letters, one from John Audland a Quaker, to William Prynne. The Other, William Prynne's Answer,* another instance of his assumption of a false identity.

Various reports exist of Butler's life in his final two years. Some pronounce him impoverished, others wealthy; some report him without a means of support or a home, while others declare that he felt sufficiently stable to decline offers of aid. Surprisingly he would receive a marker in Westminster Abbey, but not until the 18th century. The fact that he received no royal pension as a reward from the king who so enjoyed his work remains puzzling. Apparently Butler did receive a one-time payment of £200, recorded on November 30, 1674, in the *Calendar of Treasury Books*. Wood and others have suggested that Butler's share of profits from the sales of *Hudibras* must have been great. A letter to his sister revealed that he did marry and spent some leisure time in writing notebooks and miscellanies, the manuscripts of which entered into the possession of one Robert Thyer.

Three volumes of Butler's writings appeared in 1715, declared mostly unimportant by later scholars, with another collection titled *Genuine Remains* published in 1759 by Thyer. SAMUEL JOHNSON included a biographical comment about Butler in *The Works of English Poets* (1779). Without doubt *Hudibras* best represents Butler, and it remains important to English poetry studies, with excerpts easily located in print and electronic form. Although challenging in its language and 17th-century references, *Hudibras* remains required reading for anyone desiring to understand the era and the development of satire, a subgenre that would become increasingly popular. Also available in anthologies is his "UPON THE WEAKNESS AND MISERY OF MAN."

BIBLIOGRAPHY

Johnson, Samuel. *The Works of English Poets, with Prefaces, Biographical and Critical.* Vol. 6. London: J. Nichols, 1779.

Penelhum, Terence. *Butler.* New York: Routledge and Kegan Paul, 1986.

Wasserman, George Russell. *Samuel "Hudibras" Butler.* Boston: Twayne, 1976.

C

"CALANTHA'S DIRGE" John Ford (ca. **1629**) John Ford included multiple songs in both his comedies and tragedies, but most critics agree his tragedies remain the superior accomplishment. One of those tragedies, titled *The Broken Heart,* features two women who both die as a result of the loss of men they loved. Calantha, daughter of a king, is courted by her cousin Nearchus, prince of Argus. Calantha later learns of her brother's murder, her father's death, and the death by self-starvation of her friend Penthea, subject of another song, titled "Penthea's Dying Song." Calantha perseveres without shedding a tear, lives long enough to crown her brother's corpse, and then falls over dead, leaving the kingdom to Nearchus. Some critics believed Ford to be reflecting on the forced passing of the Crown from a female ruler to a male, as Elizabeth I was forced to do 30 years previously for James V of Scotland. Known for his intensity of emotion, Ford produced lyrics both sad and smart, but unexpectedly quiet and calm. The characters' suffering proves intense, but their expression remains restrained. Their passionate but unyielding natures separate them from most other characters of the Caroline period (1625–49).

Ford begins his song with a series of items, including "Glories, pleasures, pomps, delights and ease," that please only the senses of an "untroubled" mind, one perhaps "by peace refined." Those descriptions in no way apply to his characters, who all become quite troubled by the drama's conclusion. Continuing in a fatalistic manner, the speaker considers life's ethereal quality:

> Crowns may flourish and decay,
> Beauties shine, but fade away.
> Youth may revel, yet it must
> Lie down in a bed of dust.

As in "Penthea's Dying Song," Ford adopts the figura-tive language of metaphor, using sleep to symbolize death, a popular dramatic trope. The theme of decay continues, as the next line notes, "Earthly honours flow and waste," as Ford seems to imply that all of life's efforts are wasted, because they disappear along with the individual who made them. Only time "doth change and last," as

> Sorrows mingled with contents prepare
>   Rest for care;
> Love only reigns in death; though art
> Can find no comfort for a Broken Heart.

Ford extends the conceit of death as the great leveler, for even royal people, alluded to in the verb *reigns,* will die. Love may rule, but only after death has had its say. While great love may be celebrated in art, such as Ford's own, after the one who loves dies, this proves little comfort to the woman who goes to death with a broken heart. Ford suggests that the death of passion leads to the death of person; fable had long implied that a broken heart, or disappointment in love, had the strength to kill the flesh.

"CANONIZATION, THE" JOHN DONNE (1633)

Critics basically agree to divide JOHN DONNE's writing into two groups related to his life stages, his romantic, or love, poetry in the stage dating prior to 1615, and the spiritual poetry emanating from the time of his ordination in 1615 to the year of his death, 1631. However, most scholars also agree that much of his romantic poetry reflects his grounding since childhood in the Catholic faith, seen often in the FIGURATIVE LANGUAGE he adopts to write of love and its erotic aspects. This combination proved unseemly to many in cultures that followed Donne's own, and for that reason his poetry did not gain popularity until the 20th century. That era proved more open to the exaggeration and surprising comparisons of METAPHYSICAL POETS AND POETRY that had so scandalized earlier readers. Donne's focus on the theme of union, both physical and spiritual, dominates his work. Supported by the logical precision in which Donne excelled, his writing emphasizes balance in relationships and between themes. In "The Canonization," he uses the relationship between the spiritual and the erotic as framework to emphasize the close ties between spiritual and physical love.

By titling his poem "The Canonization," Donne prepares his readers for a religious poem but delivers something entirely different. He often utilized that technique, as in "A VALEDICTION, FORBIDDING MOURNING," among others. Canonization in the Catholic Church occurs when individuals have proved themselves practitioners of "heroic virtue." A person labeled as heroic is believed to have acted in an exceptional manner that ranks him above the common man, while one who practices virtue possesses a soul already redeemed by Christ, enabling him to reject things material in favor of things spiritual. Canonization preceded the granting of sainthood, and those deemed saints could be called upon by humans for intervention with God in important matters. Donne's choice of *canonization* as suggesting role models and intercessors proves vital to the meaning of his poem.

The speaker begins with a dramatic address suitable to the stage, crying to an unseen provoker, "For God's sake hold your tongue, and let me love." In a few words Donne sets a scene in which his audience understands that the "hero" of his poem has been attacked through words, probably gossip, due to the hero's manner of loving. The speaker is concerned that because of the provoker's judgment, he will not be allowed to continue his love. He next offers the antagonist substitute targets for his slander, including the obviously aged speaker's physical attributes, such as his "palsy," "gout," and "five gray hairs." Donne chooses the verb *chide* to make clear that the speaker's nemesis seems a nag with so little to do, he must select an innocent person to rebuke. His next lines further allow his speaker to belittle the antagonist. Not only might the antagonist attack him simply for his age, which amounts to petty cruelty, but he might also criticize the speaker's lack of material goods and social position, saying the attacker might his "ruined fortune flout." Again Donne's word choice proves imperative for its connotation. A person who suffers "ruin" is generally reduced by an outside attack of some kind, not by profligate actions of his own. The use of ALLITERATION emphasizes that the attacker does not simply whisper about the speaker's problems but flaunts them, suggesting he shows contempt for the debt, defying laws of decency. The speaker orders his assailant, "Take you a course, get you a place," suggesting situations that at first glance seem to have high status, serving "his hounour, or his grace," or a "King." But Donne makes clear that these positions of "service" equate to simple toadyism, contemplating, for instance, the king's "real, or his stamped face," with "stamped face" probably meaning that which appeared on currency of the realm. The speaker does not care what other occupations the antagonist chooses, as long as he will "let me love." He concludes the first of his five nine-line stanzas having established himself as an innocent, set upon by undesirables who have no loves of their own.

The second stanza continues the speaker's application of logic, as he questions how his love injures or harms others. He contrasts small actions, such as a lover's sigh or tears shed, with grand events, such as the sinking of a "merchant's ships" and the floods that caused that sinking. The results escalate to the level of the absurd, with the speaker questioning,

When did my colds a forward spring remove?
When did the heats which my veins fill
Add one more to the plaguy bill?

His love has not altered the seasons or killed anyone with infection; nor has it, he adds, affected soldiers or lawyers who will continue with their normal actions even "Though she and I do love." Having reduced his attacker to the level of fool, the speaker moves into the next stanza inviting others to label him and his lover whatever they wish; labels do not alter the reality of their love:

Call us what you will, we are made such by
    love;
Call her one, me another fly,
We're tapers too, and at our own cost die.

The taper metaphor invokes thoughts of burning candles, which eventually disappear, as he and his lover might eventually die, consumed by their passion.

Donne next compares the lovers to "the eagle and the dove," alluding to the Renaissance idea of the Ptolemaic theory of the universe as concentric circles. Within those circles various creatures moved. While the eagle flew in the sublunar space, that of the sky above earth, doves ascended and descended to and from the upper heavens, according to biblical passages such as the one in which the Holy Spirit descends from heaven during the baptism of Christ by John the Baptist. Donne extends the metaphor of fire by using the phoenix, a mythological bird that recreated itself every 500 years, and suggesting its constant renewal as a riddle. The speaker proposes that the heat of passion may keep him young, despite his advancing age. The stanza concludes with an allusion to the Platonic notion that two lovers could join to form a perfect whole: "We die and rise the same, and prove / Mysterious by this love."

Donne carries the idea of love and death into the penultimate stanza, his first line reading, "We can die by it, if not live by love," suggesting that once dead, the lovers will become the subject of legend and chronicle, their story preserved as an example to others. If their story is not told in history, it will certainly be presented through art:

We'll build in sonnets pretty rooms;
As well a well wrought urn becomes
The greatest ashes, as half-acre tombs.

His suggestion of the small urn's equality to the most lavish of tombs was made famous in the title of the 20th-century formalist critic Cleanth Brooks's seminal book *The Well Wrought Urn: Studies in the Structure of Poetry.* But Donne saves his most dramatic comparison for the final two lines of this stanza, writing, "And by these hymns, all shall approve / Us Canonized for love." Here he broaches the blasphemous suggestion that his physical love bears an importance equal to that of the canonized saints. Not only do they provide an example, their names may be called upon in order to intercede with requests that their own passion be increased.

This suggestion supports the final stanza, in which the brazen speaker claims that the very antagonists attacking him, and others of his ilk, will call upon the speaker's love as a model for their own. Those for whom "love was peace that now is rage" once valued a quiet method for romance but now crave a far more passionate approach, signified by *rage.* Donne incorporates various words suggesting religion, including *invoke* and *reverend,* that would have scandalized Victorian readers. The speaker states that the *You* he addresses made the homes, or "hermitage," of others their own through their intrusion or spying. Sketching a memorable metaphysical image, Donne writes,

Who did the whole world's soul extract, and
    drove,
Into the glasses of your eyes, So made such
    mirrors, and such spies,
That they did all to you epitomize,
Countries, towns, courts; beg from above
A pattern of your love!

The speaker feels that those who spied upon others did so for vicarious needs and internalized what they observed. In the penultimate line, Donne adapts his frequent method for emphasis of an idea, expanding the individual concern or state to universal proportions.

BIBLIOGRAPHY

"Beatification and Canonization." *The Catholic Encyclopedia.* Vol. 2. Available online. URL: http://www.newadvent.org/cathen/02364b.htm. Downloaded on June 5, 2005.

Edgecombe, Rodney Stenning. "The Meaning of 'Rage' in 'The Canonization.'" *American Notes and Queries.* 14, no. 2 (April 2001): 3.

Flynn, Denis. *John Donne and the Ancient Catholic Nobility.* Bloomington: Indiana University Press, 1995.

CANTO   The canto is a group of verses that serves to subdivide lengthy poetry. In English poetry, famous examples of its use include Edmund Spenser's *The Faerie Queene,* Lord Byron's *Childe Harold's Pilgrimage* and *Don Juan,* and Ezra Pound's *The Cantos,* a group of poems published over 30 years. Lesser-known examples also appear in work by prominent poets including Sir Walter Scott, Percy Bysshe Shelley, and John Keats. The label has been used in parody and satire, such as in ALEXANDER POPE's MOCK-HEROIC "The RAPE OF THE LOCK," or in the American poet Lawrence Ferlinghetti's "Baseball Canto," in which he refers to the "Anglo-Saxon tradition" in Pound's "First Canto."

CAREW, THOMAS (?1595–?1639)   Born the son of a master in Chancery, Thomas Carew (pronounced Carey) attended Oxford, entered the Inner Temple in 1612, and studied law for one year, then began service as secretary to Sir Dudley Carleton. Carleton was ambassador to Venice, then to the Netherlands, but Carew stayed with him only three years, and reports characterized his service as "dishonourable." Carew apparently committed libel against Dudley and Lady Carleton, causing them to sever the relationship with their one-time protégé, although he may not have been aware that they had discovered the ill remarks he had written about them. That began many months of a search for employment for Carew, who had no intention of practicing law, for which he had been educated.

In 1616 Carew returned to London seeking service, on the supposed advice of Dudley, with one of his own distant cousins who was a member of the Privy Counsel, a move that annoyed Carew's father. Lord Carew refused his cousin, who then turned to the earl of Arundel, a man he had met in Florence. Rejected also by Arundel, who learned something of Carew's charac-

ter, for the next year Carew lived off the graces of his father, who revealed in letters his disgust with his "debauched" son. During this time Carew probably met the woman who inspired the figure of Celia in his later poetry, or he developed the ideal that would support an imaginary figure. After his father's death, Carew at last found service with Sir Edward Herbert, British ambassador to France. During the time Carew spent in Paris with Sir Herbert, he may have met Giambattista Marino, an Italian poet whose outrageous lyrics Carew enjoyed and modeled his own poetry upon, as had his predecessors WILLIAM DRUMMOND OF HAWTHORNDEN and Samuel Daniel. His first commendatory verses appeared in 1622 in a preface to Thomas May's "The Heir," a comedy produced for the stage in 1620.

Sir Herbert later became Lord Herbert of Cherbury, and Carew gained a reputation as a lyric poet at court, winning the attentions of King Charles and taking the title *sewer in ordinary,* meaning a waiter or usher, to Charles I. His sense of poetic style supported his popularity as a LYRIC poet along with other court writers, including SIR JOHN SUCKLING and RICHARD LOVELACE, who as a group would later be labeled CAVALIER POETS. They would also become a part of the TRIBE OF BEN, as a result their use of BEN JONSON's style.

Most critics agree only ROBERT HERRICK's more polished poetry surpassed Carew's lyricism. As are other lyricists, he is credited for preserving some of the Shakespearean tradition, when dramatists of his day had rejected the Elizabethan admiration of language for language's sake. While poets including Ben Jonson had included courtly amorous poetry in their work, Carew made an art of that approach, revealing influence, but not control, by Jonson and other predecessors. His works exude an artful and simple sensuality that the more stringent, metaphysical, remote symbolism of contemporaries such as JOHN DONNE lacks. His fellow poet CHARLES DAVENANT imagined in his poem, "To Thomas Carew," that other poets of their age despised Carew for his greater talents.

Later admirers such as CHARLES SEDLEY would attempt to imitate Carew and Herrick, but they echoed only the more mechanical aspects of those poets, such as their elegant versification. Carew completed one ambitious lengthy poem, a masque titled *Coelum Bri-*

tannicum (1634), attributing to the Caroline court (that of Charles I) an ideology that included truth, justice, and religion. However, he remains best known for his most widely anthologized short poetry, which includes "Ask Me No More Where Jove Bestows," "Celia Singing," "A Cruel Mistress," "Disdain Returned," "Epitaph on the Lady Mary Villers," "Would You Know What's Soft? I Dare," "An Elegy upon the Death of the Dean of Paul's, Dr. John Donne," "To Ben Jonson," and probably his most famous, the erotic "A Rapture." Carew gained his reputation for the organic structure afforded his lyrics by their balance and smooth flow from one movement to the next.

Carew worked at his craft, unlike some Cavaliers, who invested more energy in courtly pursuits, producing verse with little of the discords of the preceding Elizabethan school. Instead, the poems reflect a gentle muse that would influence lyrics produced mainly as an afterthought by early 18th-century poets such as Matthew Prior. Carew made a last journey in 1639 accompanying forces north in the Bishops' War and died on the return journey at an unknown location. Some accounts note his burial at St. Dunstan's church in Westminster, but no marker survives. No confirmed likenesses of Carew exist, although a 1638 portrait by Anthony Van Dyck features Thomas Killigrew and a figure identified, but not confirmed, as Thomas Carew. Carew had written a song for the 1636 wedding of Killigrew. The painting remains in the Royal Collection at Windsor.

Carew's popularity endured, evidenced by the 1640 posthumous collection published possibly by Aurelian Townshend, a poet with whom Carew had corresponded. That publication was the first public exposure many of Carew's poems received; its reprints expanded to include additional works in 1642 and 1651. The collection became the authoritative text for Carew. More than three dozen miscellanies carried his work, one with a collection of 80 Carew poems. His poetry has remained in print, despite later evaluations by critics such as Alexander Pope, who placed Carew in the "mob of gentlemen who wrote with ease." A facsimile edition of the 1640 poems appeared in 1969, and the Bodleian Library holds a manuscript. Carew's work may be easily located in both print and electronic

form, with the best-known edition published by Rhodes Dunlap in 1949.

BIBLIOGRAPHY

Dunlop, Rhodes, ed. Introduction to *The Poems of Thomas Carew with His Masque, Coelum Britannicum,* xiii–lxxvii. Oxford: Clarendon Press, 1957.

Sadler, Lynn Beach. *Thomas Carew.* Boston: Twayne, 1979.

CARPE DIEM

Carpe diem, a Latin expression meaning "seize the day," is a label applied to poetry with a certain motif. Carpe diem poetry exhorts its audience or subject to make the most of the time they have, before life passes by. Horace initiated its usage, and he was imitated by Renaissance and later poets of devotional and erotic work, including Andrew Marvell, Robert Herrick, and Edmund Waller. Marvell's "To His Coy Mistress" is a widely anthologized example of the theme, as are Herrick's "Gather Ye Rosebuds While Ye May" and Waller's "Go Lovely Rose." In those examples the speaker seeks to persuade a young woman to give up her chastity, stressing the urgency of time, as in Waller's first two lines, "Go lovely Rose, / Tell her that wastes her time and me." The use of the rosebud as a symbol of a young virgin and the rose in full bloom as a more mature and sexually aware woman was common.

CARTER, ELIZABETH (1717–1806)

Elizabeth Carter was the eldest daughter of the Reverend Nicholas Carter of Canterbury Cathedral and his wife, Margaret Swayne. She fortunately received an education equal to that of her brothers, allowing her an early grasp of classical and modern languages. She participated willingly, studying so hard that she later credited that work for headaches and her nearsighted vision, as well as a snuff addiction, as she had taken snuff to help her remain awake to read late into the night. She lost her mother when she was only 10, but her father remained attentive to her needs and talents. When his friend Edward Cave founded *Gentleman's Magazine,* her father encouraged Elizabeth's submissions, and she began to publish in that periodical in 1734. This necessitated a regular correspondence with Cave, which was later preserved in the British Library. She not only contributed the juvenilia titled *Poems upon Particular Occasions*

(1738), but also a translation of the Swiss writer Jean Pierre de Crousaz's *Examination of Mr. Pope's Essay on Man* (1738), which held that ALEXANDER POPE's fatalistic approach led to Spinozism. In addition, for *Gentleman's Magazine* she translated one of the 18th century's most famous works, Francesco Algarotti's *Sir Isaac Newton's Philosophy Explain'd, for the Use of the Ladies. In Six Dialogues on light and colours. From the Italian* (1739), which focused on the newly popular natural philosophy.

Carter met SAMUEL JOHNSON through her work for the periodical and became friendly with Thomas Birch, a critic who may have been an anonymous voice praising Carter's works; he also hoped she would marry him. She followed her father's advice to "live quietly" if she hoped to marry but had no intention of doing so, turning down one suitor because he had published poetry that exhibited "too light and licentious a turn of mind." She corresponded with the countess of Hertford and gained many admirers of her poetry. Carter arose early in the morning to study, depending upon, so the story goes, a local church sexton to pull a string hanging out her window that was attached to a bell at her bedside to awaken her. She circulated anonymously "Ode to Wisdom," and Samuel Richardson published it in his famous epistolary fiction *Clarissa* (1747) without knowing the author's identity, for which he later apologized, as he used it without her permission. In the first example of a woman's educating a man at Cambridge, she tutored her stepbrother and worked for months on the project of translating Epictetus from Greek. In addition, she contributed two essays to Samuel Johnson's periodical, *Rambler*. When Johnson printed her *All the Works of Epictetus* as a large quarto volume in 1758, it earned £1,000 from subscriptions. That was a fortune for Carter and allowed her independence from her father and the ability to live in London. Although invited to stay with friends, she preferred living alone. After her stepmother's death she rented part of her new house in Deal to her father, and he lived there until his death in 1774.

Yielding to the pressure of her circle of friends, who included LADY MARY WORTLEY MONTAGU, she published *Poems on Several Occasions* (1762), which remained in print through four editions. That would be her final publication of note. She traveled to Europe with Montagu and her friend Lord Lyttelton and later received annuities from both Montagu and another friend, William Pulteney, earl of Bath. Her literary circle expanded to include the novelists Hannah More and Joanna Baillie.

No feminist, Elizabeth Carter stated her disapproval of writing by those supporting women's rights such as Charlotte Smith and Mary Wollstonecraft. Although she enjoyed writing by women, she did not believe they should travel in the same circles as men. However, she took full advantage of the avenues open to "ladies" during her age to write. The periodical press offered new opportunity for women like Carter, a dedicated scholar who gained a positive reputation. She did not act on that reputation to serve as a role model. While her verse proved influential, it was limited to praise of its "sublime simplicity," "correctness," and "elegance," and it did not inspire other women to follow her lead. Johnson's remark that "My old friend, Mrs. Carter, could make a pudding as well as translate Epictetus" may remain the best known fact about this intelligent, but creatively inhibited, writer.

BIBLIOGRAPHY
Pennington, Montagu. *Memoirs of the Life of Mrs. Elizabeth Carter*. Boston: O. C. Greenleaf, 1809.

A series of letters between Mrs. Elizabeth Carter and Catherine Talbot, from the year 1741 to 1770. To which are added, letters from Mrs. Elizabeth Carter to Mrs. Vesey, between the years 1763 and 1787; published from the original manuscripts in the possession of the Rev. Montagu Pennington. 1809. Facsimile, New York: AMS Press, 1975.

CARTWRIGHT, WILLIAM (1611–1643)

While not the most famous of his era's writers, the Royalist poet and dramatist William Cartwright was considered a phenomenon by contemporaries. A member of the group euphemistically known as the TRIBE OF BEN, Cartwright gained public notice through his association with BEN JONSON. Although his exact birthplace remains in dispute, Cartwright lived out his adult life in Oxford, where he had been educated at the Westminster School and Oxford University. An official court chronicler, Cartwright wrote poetry that delivered blatant flattery on appropriate occasions, as well as the expected laudatory excess of elegy. Those still easily located include "On a Virtuous Young Gentle-woman That Died Suddenly" and "On His Majesty's Recovery From the Small-Pox, 1633." He dedicated verse to those returning from journeys, to wedding couples, to contemporary poets, to various court officials, and to Lucina, his favorite subject. Jonson praised Cartwright as one who wrote "like a man," reflecting admiration for Cartwright's education, which allowed him a scholarly approach and use of a great number of classical conceits. He was capable of eroticism, as in these lines:

Seal up her eyes, O Sleep, but flow
Mild as her Manners, to and fro:
Slide soft into her, yet that she
may receive due wound from thee.

He has been compared by the critic Donald Bruce to George Herbert in his talent for apothegm, as in the lines from his *Poetical Works,* "Whoever the girdle doth undoe / He quite undoes the owner too."

Cartwright also wrote several plays produced on stage. They included a comedy, *The Ordinary* (1634); two tragicomedies, *The Siege* and *The Lady-Errant,* both in 1636; and, probably his most successful, *The Royal Slave* (1636). *The Royal Slave* featured the sacrifice of kin by a powerful figure. Enacted before King Charles I and Queen Henrietta Maria at Christ Church, Oxford, the play was labeled the best ever performed. Its celebrated production included music composed by Henry Lawes, friend to John Milton, and design by the incomparable Inigo Jones.

Cartwright produced no creative work after 1638, having answered a call to the church. Gaining a reputation for his dramatic and spirited sermons, he often expressed his Royalist leanings, praising King Charles I in a Passion sermon at Oxford, where in 1642 the monarch would establish a temporary court as the Protestant revolution gathered force. Cartwright gained a reputation as a diligent scholar, spending up to 18 hours daily in study. In 1643 the plague, called camp-fever by Oxford's inhabitants, claimed Cartwright. The biographer and antiquary John Aubrey noted that "King Charles 1st dropt a tear at the newes of his death."

In 1651 an edition of Cartwright's work contained commendatory verses from 51 admirers. Although modern scholars find him of interest mainly as an extravagant writer of panegyrics, or honorary poems dedicated to particular individuals, he inspired work by the likes of John Dryden. What he lacked in imagination, Cartwright made up for with felicity and rhetorical prowess. Bruce judges him capable of occasional "intrigue or at least surprise," and at his best "capable of Donne's insolent aplomb."

BIBLIOGRAPHY
Bruce, Donald. "An Oxford Garrison of Poets in 1642." *Contemporary Review,* November 1992, 250–256.
Danton, J. Periam. *William Cartwright and His Comedies, Tragi-Comedies, and Other Poems, 1651.* Chicago: University of Chicago Press, 1942.
Evans, G. Blakemore. *The Plays and Poems of William Cartwright.* Madison: University of Wisconsin Press, 1951.

CARY, PATRICK (?1623–1657)

Patrick Cary was born into a family destined for literary and political fame. His father, Sir Henry Cary, Lord Falkland, was made first viscount by Charles I and appointed deputy minister to Ireland. Patrick, one of 11 children, was born in Dublin and raised by his mother, Elizabeth, a playwright who at 16 wrote the first closet play, one meant to be read rather than acted, published by an Englishwoman. The play was titled *Mariam, Fair Queene of Jewry* with a focus on religious freedom and freedom for women; she published it in 1613 with the encouragement of John Davies. The topic proved personal, as Lady Falkland later secretly converted to Catholicism, infuriating her husband, who convinced the king to place her under house arrest and remove her children, including Patrick, from her care. Lord Falkland was later recalled from Ireland by King Charles after attempting to banish all priests from the country. Soon after he suffered a leg injury in a horseback riding accident and died in 1633 of gangrene, his wife at his side after their reconciliation through the efforts of Queen Henrietta Maria, also a Catholic. A book titled *The History of Edward II* was discovered among Falkland's possessions at his death and credited to him, although later critics and historians gathered ample evidence to support Elizabeth Cary as its true author.

After his father's death Patrick moved in with his older brother by 13 years, Lucius, an Anglican of strict anti-Catholic views who did not speak to his mother for some time after she was cast off by his father. In 1636 Lady Falkland planned the kidnapping of Patrick and a younger brother from Lucius's estate near Great Tew, spiriting them to the Continent to St. Edmund's Priory in Paris. Patrick moved on to Rome and remained there until 1650; in Rome he met JOHN MIL-TON, the devotional poet RICHARD CRASHAW, and John Evelyn, a diarist who was one of the first elected to the Royal Academy. During his first two years in Italy Cary followed his mother's example, writing secular poetry, the *Trivial Ballads,* as well as devotional meditations.

During Patrick's absence Lucius inherited his father's title and became the second viscount, Lord Falkland. He entered Parliament in 1639 and became secretary of state in 1642. His home near Oxford entertained literati including BEN JONSON; Falkland became a SON OF BEN and would be honored in a poem by Jonson after his death at the Battle of Newbury in 1643, "TO THE IMMORTAL MEMORY AND FRIENDSHIP OF THAT NOBLE PAIR, SIR LUCIUS CARY AND SIR H. MORISON" (1629). Patrick eventually followed his brother into public service, after first entertaining the idea of priesthood. After a brief stint in a monastery, he returned to England, married, and worked in government service in Ireland, where he died of unknown causes in 1657.

Cary's poetry would not be published until 1771, when *Trivial Ballads* gained notice for its satire, lyrics, and pastoral entries, described by critics as graceful and witty. While his devotional works, never published as a collection, reflected the influence of Jonson and JOHN DONNE, they lacked the sustained quality characteristic of his models. His notable illustrations illumined his manuscripts. The poetry was published again in 1819 as *Trivial Poems and Triolets* by Sir Walter Scott, who discovered and admired Cary's work. The most recent version, published in 1978, is out of print but possible to locate.

BIBLIOGRAPHY

Chetwood, William Rufus. *Memoirs of the Life and Writings of Ben Jonson, Esq.* 1756. Facsimile, New York: Garland, 1970.

McKuen, Katharine Anderson. *Classical Influence upon the Tribe of Ben: A Study of Classical Elements in the Non-Dramatic Poetry of Ben Jonson and His Circle.* New York: Octagon, 1968.

"CASTAWAY, THE" WILLIAM COWPER (1803)

Not published until 1803, WILLIAM COWPER's "The Castaway" was written during his final year of life, 1799. It reflects his state of mind, as he had become a mental and physical invalid several years previously. With undeniable power and admirable beauty, Cowper portrays the desolation felt by a sailor eventually abandoned at sea when his crew could not reverse course in a storm to rescue him. While any death causes sadness, the thought of witnessing the slow death of a friend one is helpless to rescue is especially chilling. Although he based his poem on a true incident, Cowper adopted the drowning as a metaphor for his own debilitating condition, which became hopeless after the loss of his longtime companion, Mary Unwin. Despite the attempts of Cowper's friends, he eventually found himself isolated by a constant foreboding and sense of despair that those friends could not understand, leaving them unable to support him, a situation that mirrored that of a man lost at sea.

"The Castaway" focuses on a publication titled *Voyage* (1748) written by Lord Anson George (1697–1762), which Cowper had read decades before writing his poem. George told of the horrors of watching die a sailor who had been washed overboard during a storm. In 11 six-line verses with the RHYME scheme *ababcc, dedeff,* and so on, the reader experiences through Cowper's skill the rocking rhythm from three vantage points, that of the sailor himself, that of his mates on the ship, and that of the poet. He begins,

> Obscurest night involved the sky,
> The Atlantic billows roared,
> When such a destined wretch as I,
> Washed headlong from on board.

The speaker does not spend much energy describing how the sailor happened to fall into the sea, instead devoting all his attention to a description of death. The immediate comparison of the sailor to the "I" of the poem signals readers that the poet also felt close to death. The initial stanza concludes: "Of friends, of hope, of all bereft, / His floating home forever left," describing Cowper's own situation, as well as that of the hapless sailor.

The second verse praises Lord George as a brave chief and makes clear the boat set sail "With warmest wishes" from the sailor's home of "Albion," another name for England. Rather than proving positive, these facts only intensify the lost man's sorrow, because "He loved them both, but both in vain, / Nor him beheld, nor her again." Despite the power of the sailor's love, he would never again see his captain or his homeland. Cowper employs ALLITERATION with the *b* sound and repetition of the term *nor* for heightened effect. In the third verse the reader learns the sailor did not stay long "beneath the whelming brine," as he was an expert swimmer, filled with courage and strength, so that he "waged with death a lasting strife, / Supported by despair of life." Not willing to give in easily because he loved life, the sailor takes on death's challenge, as Cowper must have done with his mental illness. Part of the sailor's strategy is to call attention to himself, so he shouts at his "friends," a term indicating that he had more than a working relationship with others on board. Those friends had attempted "To check the vessel's course," but the elements prove too strong, exerting a "pitiless perforce," a brilliant phrase, designed so the ship "scudded still before the wind."

In the next stanza the sailor's mates try a different "succor," throwing against the wind into the water devices designed to keep their mate afloat, "The cask, the coop, the floated cord." However, not only the mates on board, but also the sailor, understand nothing will help him survive the storm. Cowper makes a statement regarding the desperation felt by humans who will continue to attempt rescue of a person or a situation, when all the while they know their efforts will prove fruitless.

In the sixth verse Cowper reflects on the abandoned man's thought process, in which he determines that his mates could do nothing else, "Aware that flight, in such a sea, / Alone could rescue them." He did not judge them cruel to save the many rather than have all perish in an attempt to save one, "Yet bitter felt it still to die /

Deserted, and his friends so nigh." ENJAMBMENT after the word *die* takes the reader immediately to *Deserted,* emphasizing the nature of the lonely death through alliteration and placement. While at first the sailor's courage and desire to survive prove admirable, they at last become pitiful. He survives an hour, a feat the speaker emphasizes as incredible, holding himself up, repelling his destiny. But as each minute "flew" by, he "Entreated help, or cried, 'Adieu!'" His sense of isolation grows, made even worse by having his friends so near.

By the eighth verse, in which the attention switches again to those on board, his voice could no longer be heard, because "For then, by toil subdued, he drank / The stifling wave, and then he sank." His disappearance is sudden even though expected, leaving the reader with a true sense of loss. Cowper notes next that "No poet wept him" but reminds readers that George's "narrative sincere" does tell the sailor's "name, his worth, his age." It is a narrative "wet with Anson's tear." Such tears, whether by "bards or heroes shed / Alike immortalize the dead."

Cowper's 10th verse comments on his act of reflecting in verse on the sailor's death so many years later. He writes,

> I therefore purpose not, or dream,
> Descanting on his fate,
> To give the melancholy theme
> A more enduring date.

Readers might wonder at those lines, as it seems the poet intends to do exactly what he denies. He explains in the final couplet of that verse, writing, "But misery still delights to trace / Its semblance in another's case." In other words, Cowper undertakes this task for himself. The sailor's condition mirrors his own, also predicting Cowper's fate. He accepts that fate, unhappily, as the sailor had to accept his. With a final verse Cowper is completely honest with his readers, as well as with himself, admitting he expects no miracle to intervene and save him. He determines that

> No voice divine the storm allayed,
> No light propitious shone,

When, snatched from all effectual aid,
We perished, each alone.

He includes all humankind in the ship of life, which will, by necessity, eventually leave them behind, struggling to survive. However, some deaths are more horrible than others, Cowper clearly concludes, as he writes his last couplet: "But I beneath a rougher sea, / And whelmed in deeper gulfs than he."

Cowper renders his story without self-pity, although he does mourn its necessity. He suggests that while all humans perish, those deaths are not necessarily equal. The loss of his mental faculties formed a terrible prelude to his physical death, clearly seen when he recovered them long enough to describe his predicament to the world.

BIBLIOGRAPHY

Greening, John. "Rescuing the Castaway: The Case of William Cowper." *Quadrant* 47, no. 12 (December 2003): 60–63.

Packer, Barbara. "Hope and Despair in the Writings of William Cowper." *Social Research* 66, no. 2 (summer 1999): 545.

Roy, James A. *Cowper and His Poetry*. Folcroft, Pa.: Folcroft Press, 1969.

CATACHRESIS

The use of a word or phrase in a manner that disrupts the norm is called *catachresis*. That use may involve a mixed metaphor, a word out of context, or a flagrant pairing of ideas that normally do not appear together, often to great effect. In ABRAHAM COWLEY's poem "The Muse," he includes catachresis when he writes, "Thy verse does solidate and crystallize," inventing the term *solidate* and comparing verse to water that may change form with changes in temperature. JOHN WILMOT, SECOND EARL OF ROCHESTER, suggests in "A SATYRE AGAINST MANKIND" that books may act as life preservers, causing men to try "To swim with bladders of philosophy," while CHRISTOPHER SMART in "MY CAT JEOFFRY" describes his feline, explaining, "he camels his back to bear the first notion of business," ironically comparing Jeoffry to a beast of burden. JOHN DONNE adopts catachresis through personification in "A NOCTURNAL UPON ST. LUCY'S DAY," as he describes the shortest day of the year: "The world's whole sap is sunk: / The general balm th' hydroptic earth hath drunk," and in "BATTER MY HEART," one individual is compared to an entire community: "I, like an usurp'd town to another due, / Labour to admit you."

CATALEXIS

Synonymous with *truncation*, catalexis describes the omission of one or more syllables from the end word in a line of poetry. It indicates the absence of an unstressed syllable at the end of a trochaic or dactylic line and the absence of a stressed syllable at the beginning of an iambic or anapestic line (see METER). An example of the latter case appears in JOHN DONNE's "A VALEDICTION FORBIDDING MOURNING" in the line "Our two souls therefore, which are one." Catalectic indicates the line lacks one syllable, while brachycatelectic indicates that two syllables are missing. Should a line contain excess syllables, it is termed hypercatalectic. Such a line appears in THOMAS CAREW's "AN ELEGY UPON THE DEATH OF THE DEAN OF PAUL'S, DR. JOHN DONNE." Carew first claims that no one can mimic Donne's style, then he does so, by inserting a line with one too many syllables in the middle of lines marked by iambic pentatmeter: "Since to the awe of thy imperious wit / Our troublesome language bends, made only fit / With her tough thick-ribb'd hoops, to gird about." Lines containing regular meter are termed *acatalectic*.

CAVALIER POETS

LYRIC poets writing during the reign of Charles I (1625–49) are sometimes classified as Cavalier poets. The label indicates their allegiance to the monarch. All were courtiers whose poetry focused on romance and Royalist sentiments, most reflecting a humorous, plaintive, or cynical tone. Many stressed the CARPE DIEM theme, providing arguments to fair maidens that love saved is love wasted. Most Cavalier poetry exhibited elegant, and often erotic, language and imagery; employed heroic couplets; and owed much by way of CONCEIT to JOHN DONNE and BEN JONSON. The group included THOMAS CAREW (?1595–?1639), SIR JOHN SUCKLING (1609–41), RICHARD LOVELACE (1618–58), and EDMUND WALLER (1606–87). Many Cavalier poets were well educated, and some performed military as well as artistic service to the king. A few died in poverty or suffered exile, due to involvement in various political schemes. All felt in friendly competition with one another, and their poetry reflects the pressure to perform well, as they often remained completely dependent on the court for their livelihoods.

CAVENDISH, MARGARET, DUCHESS OF NEWCASTLE (1623–1673) Margaret Lucas matured as a pampered young woman in a family of means, the daughter of the wealthy landowner Thomas Lucas and Elizabeth Leighton. Elizabeth, eventually a widow who learned to manage her own properties, raised her several children, educated by the help of tutors. Margaret showed creative tendencies at an early age, dressing herself in outlandish styles that would carry over into adulthood. She served Queen Henrietta Maria as a maid of honor between 1643 and 1645, a position she claimed not to enjoy. In letters Margaret begged her mother to allow her to return home, as she felt uncomfortable among members of the court, having been raised in semi-isolation. How much of her discomfort was feigned is not known, but she later claimed to have been disliked because of her attractive face and figure, which, according to her, sparked a great deal of jealousy. Despite her claim of shyness, she wore dresses revealing a generous décolletage.

Living abroad in France with the Queen, Margaret met her future husband, the exiled Royalist Marquis William Cavendish. Although he was many years older than Margaret, he persisted in courting her despite her coy response. She married Cavendish and recorded the supposed jealousy of those in the Queen's entourage who foolishly sought to prevent the union. Despite their great difference in age, the two shared many interests, and Cavendish lived to make his young wife happy, so the marriage proved blissful. Because of Cavendish's Royalist sentiments, the couple was forced to remain abroad during the Civil War, living in Paris, Rotterdam, and Antwerp, despite Margaret's repeated written appeals that they be allowed to return to England. When the couple at last could return home, they took up residence on the Cavendish family estate. Much to her sorrow, Margaret never bore children, but she seemed to have a congenial relationship with her husband's grown children. Her husband doted on her, encouraging her to write and willingly publishing her voluminous works.

Margaret Cavendish was one of the first English women who publicly sought a life of the mind. She invested her energies in intellectual pursuits, engaging in self-education in areas of science and philosophy. Her imagination, however, overshadowed her propensity for fact and logic, and she produced some outrageous fantasies, which she labeled "natural science." Along with her husband, she published nearly 12 folio volumes of essays, poetry, and drama, as well as her biography of her husband, to which she appended her own brief autobiography. She published *Poems and Fancies* (1653), which was followed by a supplementary volume in the same year titled *Philosophical Fancies*. In her first book, *The Worlds Olio* (1655), she noted that fame, a product of published writing, served as a superior substitute for children: "Fame . . . the older it groweth, the more it florishes, and is the more particularly a mans own, then the child of his loines . . . many times the child of his loines deceives the parent, and instead of keeping his father's fame, brings him infamy." The pursuit of that fame offered her a lifelong project.

Nature's Pictures (1656) was followed by many additional volumes, including *Plays* (1662); *Philosophical Letters* (1664); *Description of a New World, Called the Blazing World* (1666); *Observations upon Experimental Philosophy* (1666); *Plays* and *Grounds of Natural Philosophy* (both 1668); and *The Lotterie* (an unpublished play). In one work, titled "Melancholy and Mirth," the female character in her verse, conveniently named Margaret, claims that JOHN MILTON "was obliged for many of his thoughts in his *L'Allegro* and *Il Penseroso* to this lady's Dialogue between Melancholy and Mirth." Scholars who later studied Margaret's works, while admitting her obvious immaturity and egoism, admired her boldness in claiming herself as the inspiration for works that appeared 20 years before her own by a poet who completely overshadowed her own lively, if not overly inventive, talents. Equally clever is the rhetorical strategy of referring to her work within the work itself. William Cavendish achieved dukedom in 1665, and for the remainder of her life, Margaret enjoyed a comfortable existence.

One of the few prominent writers of her time, she protected her own interests first, as a member of her class would, but that resulted in her promoting the right of all women to become educated. She railed against the double standard that allowed men far more freedom than women. Her progressive attitude, however, did not prevent her occasional elitist attack on members of her own gender as foolish, but no one equaled her engagement with new ideas or the strong effect she had on the public. She committed the same social crime as had other women writers who supposedly assumed male traits by writing, but despite her detractors' charges of her claiming credit for works she did not author, she persevered.

In 1667 the duchess's expression of a desire to visit England's newly formed Royal Society, an all-male group dedicated to the discussion of science and philosophy, met with resistance. She did find some support in the group, but not because of her scientific writings; rather, her husband had several friends in the society who felt a political obligation to the duchess. The diarist Samuel Pepys wrote that the invitation was extended only after much debate; he noted that the event would probably become the subject of future BALLADS. Fortunately Margaret's good sense took over, and she remained silent during the meeting, simply listening and observing. However, she still expressed her individuality through her dress, as she had since a child. She often dressed in male attire, an action that modern scholars believed helped relieve her frustration over not enjoying all of the independence afforded to men. It raised eyebrows in the London social scene. Sir Charles Lytton once noted that Margaret "dressed in a vest, and instead of courtesies, made legs and bows to the ground with her hand and head." She chose her visit to England's most learned group to display again her attitude toward the double standard of her day. An attendant named John Evelyn fulfilled Pepys's prediction by writing a ballad about the occasion that included the following lines:

> Though I was half-afeard
> God bless us! when I first did see her
> She looked so like a Cavalier
> But that she had no beard.

Pepys remained fascinated by Cavendish, as evidenced by his multiple diary entries focusing on her.

He confesses in 1667 his eagerness "To see the silly play by my Lady Newcastle called *The Humorous Lovers;* the most silly thing that ever came upon the stage, I was sick to see it, but yet would not but have seen it, that I might better understand her." While the authorship of that particular play is sometimes credited to Margaret's husband, creating an especial interest in Pepys's comment, equally important is the confession by one of her severest critics to a desire to know better the estimable force that was the duchess of Newcastle. Eventually gaining the unfortunate nickname "Mad Madge" because of her well-publicized eccentricities, Cavendish often attracted curious crowds. Pepys records the anticipation of one group that gathered when they learned she was due to appear at court. Catching only a glimpse of her, he describes her arrival in a silver coach. Her footmen were all dressed in velvet, and she wore a velvet cap. For a brief moment he saw her face between her white carriage curtains, a face he describes as that "of a very comely woman." When she died, she was buried in Westminster Abbey.

Frederic Rowton pronounced her "indefatigable" in 1853, then noted of her writing, "The Duchess is not without force, and that, too, often of a picturesque and effective sort . . . but the bulk of her works are insufferably tame, common-place and prosy." By the middle of the 20th century, feminist critics would give the duchess her due as one of the first English feminists, an early dramatist who went so far as to write a play, *The Convent of Pleasure,* that focused on a lesbian relationship. Her works are widely anthologized; some of her most famous poems are "AN EXCUSE, FOR SO MUCH WRIT UPON MY VERSES," "The Poetess's Hasty Resolution," and "The HUNTING OF THE HARE."

Critics agree that the value of Margaret's books lies merely in their existence; most are available to view at the British Museum. But as scholars have looked more closely at her works, they have recognized additional values. Her *Sociable Letters* (1664) is now acknowledged as the forerunner to the epistolary novel, a credit long attributed to the English male writer Samuel Richardson and his book *Pamela* (1740). In that collection of epistles, the duchess assumed a fictional persona who wrote letters on myriad topics. One entry, Number CXXIII, anticipates JOHN DRYDEN as the first person, male or female, to write a general assessment of William Shakespeare as a dramatist. While Dryden's writings became far more famous, Cavendish's was the first and presents an interesting evaluation of Shakespeare's representation of women.

The writings of Margaret Cavendish afford a valuable record of the life of the aristocratic woman, an affirmation of the female's limited role in English life, and the ability of select individuals to overcome some of those limits. Despite Margaret's willingness to abide by the general hierarchy of male dominance, she achieved significant power within her specific domestic sphere. Granted free rein by her husband to use her time as she pleased, she suffered little under so-called social restraints. She represents one example of the inconsistencies in England's social order as she defied the social edict against writing and thinking women. Perhaps most importantly, Margaret Cavendish's prolific publishing career contributed to a significant change in the 17th century, a gradual shift from an all-male publishing world at the century's beginning to one that by the dawn of the 18th century was forced to include women.

BIBLIOGRAPHY
Bowerbank, Sylvia, and Sara Mendelson. *Paper Bodies: A Margaret Cavendish Reader.* Orchard Park, N.Y.: Broadband Press, 2000.

Ferguson, Moira. *First Feminists: British Women Writers 1578–1799.* Bloomington: Indiana University Press, 1985.

Mendelson, Sara Heller. *The Mental World of Stuart Women: Three Studies.* Amherst: University of Massachusetts Press, 1987.

Perry, Henry Ten Eyck. *The First Duchess of Newcastle and Her Husband as Figures in Literary History.* Boston: Ginn, 1918.

Reynolds, Myra. *The Learned Lady in England 1650–1760.* Boston: Houghton Mifflin, 1920.

Rowton, Frederic. *The Female Poets of Great Britain.* Detroit: Wayne State University Press, 1981.

Whitaker, Katie. *Mad Madge: The Extraordinary Life of Margaret Cavendish, Duchess of Newcastle, the First Woman to Live by Her Pen.* New York: Basic Books, 2002.

"CELIA SINGING: HARKE HOW MY CELIA" THOMAS CAREW (1640)
As did all lyricists, THOMAS CAREW wrote songs, and he wrote more

than one titled "Celia Singing." To differentiate among the songs, critics adopt the first line to follow the title. In "Celia Singing: Harke How My Celia," Carew uses his favored character of Celia. Whether Celia represented a real woman or simply an ideal remains unimportant to Carew's creative process. Greatly affected by the social scene of the court where he lived, Carew could never freely create. He had to write to meet a particular standard, and thoughts of patronage by aristocrats could never be far from his mind. Although the CAVALIER POETS as a group are deemed less important than poets like their Elizabethan predecessors Edmund Spenser and Sir Philip Sidney, or their contemporaries the METAPHYSICAL POETS such as JOHN DONNE, they produced poetry that sharply reflected the sensibility of Charles I's court, elegant, if not moving, and distinctive, if not original. Carew owed a large debt to the Italian poet Giambattista Marino, whose fantastic lyrical flights influenced English Renaissance and Carolinian poets alike. While the Elizabethan poets may have produced poetry of more substance, they lacked the light modulation in tone in which the Cavalier lyricists excelled, exemplified by Carew's songs.

The speaker of "Celia Singing" begins his 18-line rhyming couplet LYRIC tribute with a call to onlookers, "Harke," to observe how the "musique of Celia's hand and voyce" work to control natural forces, including the "loude wind" and "wilde / Incensed Bore, and Panther wilde!" Of more interest is the speaker's claim of Celia's power to animate statues and other works of art, a clear message that she acts as the poet's muse, giving life to his words. Carew expresses this in two neatly balanced couplets, admirable also for their gentle but insistent rhythm:

> Marke how those statues like men move,
> Whilest men with wonder statues prove!
> This stiffe rock bends to worship her,
> That Idoll turnes Idolater.

Through the use of opposites and verbal cues such as *This* and *That,* Carew suggests his love's power to alter both the natural and the unnatural. Thus, Celia personifies inspiration, literally the act of breathing in, and can grant life to those that are lifeless. She elevates viewers to a higher emotion, claiming a godlike power to create. That higher emotion is love, made clear by the speaker in the lyric who describes "the new inspir'd Images" as being "fir'd" with love.

Carew repeats, "Harke," adding a refrainlike quality often present in songs, which tend to repeat themes and important concepts. They also tend to present a turn of some kind, and Carew's song is no exception. As the speaker continues, he tells his audience that although the "tender marble grones" and the "late transformed stones" attempt to court Celia, "the faire Nymph," with tears, she ironically becomes "more stony then they were," her "unrelenting mind" stunning them in contrast to her "matchlesse beautie." Such "disdaine" in one so lovely causes the animated statues to be "turn'd into stones againe."

Carew suggests that beauty is worth little without a kind and supple heart, a sentiment that conflicts somewhat with the popular Cavalier CARPE DIEM theme. That theme suggests that sex remains the most important role for a beautiful female. He also demonstrates of what little use inspiration and the resultant poetry can be, if those who inspire cannot recognize and prize their effect on others.

BIBLIOGRAPHY
Dunlop, Rhodes, ed. Introduction to *The Poems of Thomas Carew with His Masque, Coelum Britannicum,* xiii–lxxvii. Oxford: Clarendon Press, 1957.

CHAMBERLAYNE, WILLIAM (1619–1689)

William Chamberlayne gained his reputation as a Caroline poet, although his vocation was the practice of medicine. His works included *Pharonnida* (1659), an epic romance in HEROIC COUPLETS at a length of 14,000 lines that occupied five books when published. Also a dramatist, he published the play *Love's Victory,* titled at one time *Wits led by the Nose,* in 1658. Because of his heavy style he is considered a minor poet, but he imbued his verse with occasional flashes of beauty, influencing the later major romantic poet John Keats. Critics note his importance lies in the fact that as a bridge between Elizabethan poetry and later styles represented by CHARLES DRYDEN, he helps promote understanding of art much greater than his own. Percy Bysshe Shelley joked that Chamberlayne never

intended anyone to reach the end of *Pharonnida,* but it represented a popular style of his era. Some excuse what may be considered incoherence with the fact that its composition was interrupted when Chamberlayne left his work to fight with the Royalists at the Second Battle of Newbury (1644).

In verse that at times seemed disorganized and unfocused, Chamberlayne remained inconsistent about the simplest of details, such as the setting for the romance featuring the damsel Pharonnida and her knights errant; one moment the characters are in Sicily, and at another in Morea. He also altered his characters' names at will. The work's excesses and lack of form disgusted Dryden, becoming one of several forces that caused him to choose a different stylistic tack; therefore, as George Saintsbury writes, *Pharonnida* must be considered influential, if ineffectual. A prose version, *Eromena, or the Noble Stranger,* was published in 1658 by an unknown author. The poem appeared in full in George Saintsbury's *Minor Poets of the Caroline Period* (1905), in which Saintsbury guardedly praises Chamberlayne as deserving of his minor, but not unimportant, status.

BIBLIOGRAPHY
Saintsbury, George, ed. *Minor Poets of the Caroline Period.* Vol. 1. Oxford: Clarendon Press, 1905–1921.

CHAPMAN, GEORGE (?1560–1634)

Little is known of George Chapman's childhood and maturation, other than that he was born near Hitchin and proved a fine classical language student. Although he did much of his writing at the close of the 16th century, he extended his work and his influence into the 17th century. As a poet he drew on his considerable education to fill his verse with allusions, making it inaccessible, because of his belief that poetry should be available only to select readers. His best known poems are two hymns that combine to serve as allegory in *The Shadow of Night* (1594), the publication that first introduced his name to the public record. Dense and complex, the poems consider philosophical, political, and poetic matters. *Ovids Banquet of Sence* (1595), a later piece, supported Platonism as superior to Ovidian eroticism. He completed and corrected Christopher Marlowe's *Hero and Leander* and in 1609 published *Euthymiae Raptus,* or *The Teares of Peace,* in which he defended the dream vision as an appropriate form for poetry written to consider often-related Platonic, Stoic, and Christian ideas. He joined his contemporaries in mourning the death of the prince of Wales in *An Epicede or Funerall Song on the Death of Henry Prince of Wales* (1612).

Probably a creative genius, he produced translations that gained him enduring fame, particularly his translations of Homer, his *Seven Books of the Iliad* (1598) and *Achilles' Shield* (1598). The romantic poet John Keats would later reference those translations, as well as Chapman's release in English of *Illiads* (1611) and *Homer's Odyssey* (1614–15), for which Chapman had been promised a reward by Prince Henry that he lost as a result of his patron's death. These last two works Chapman managed through expert translation to apply to events in his own era and culture. He also translated works of Petrarch (1612), Musaeus (1616), Hesiod (1618), and Juvenal (1629).

Chapman also wrote numerous dramas and was first mentioned in connection with the theater in records related to the performance of *Blind Beggar of Alexandria* by the Admiral's Men. The theater manager Philip Henslowe noted Chapman's efforts in that production. Francis Meres, the clergyman who helped date Shakespeare's early plays and who published a record of contemporary writers, praised Chapman's comedy and tragedy. His plays included *The Gentleman Usher* (ca. 1602), *All Fools* (1599 or 1604), *Monsieur D'Olive* (1604), *Sir Giles Goosecap, Knight* (ca. 1604), *Bussy D'Ambois* (1604), *The Widow's Tears* (ca. 1605), and *May Day* (1609). His comedies focused on the series of human errors made popular by BEN JONSON. With Jonson and John Marston, Chapman wrote *Eastward Ho* (1605) for the Children of the Queen's Revels, a child acting group. He earned Jonson's praise, placing him among a select few, but was imprisoned for a time in the tower of London by James I, who found Chapman's satire on the Scots offensive.

Chapman continued to write and focused on heroes that a later age would describe as larger than life in *The Conspiracy and Tragedy of Charles, Duke of Byron, Marshal of France* (1608); *The Revenge of Bussy D'Ambois* (ca. 1610); and *Chabot, Admiral of France* (ca. 1613). Although Chapman died in comparative poverty, the famous archi-

tect Inigo Jones designed a monument to memorialize him. Chapman wrote with an Elizabethan sensibility, fortified by his background in the classics. He often adopted historical figures for his dramas but elaborated upon history, adding ghosts and shaping more logical than true connections among events. His tragedies feature ethical discourse in the Senecan vein, but they looked forward to the metaphysical elements that became so crucial in the poetry of the next generation.

BIBLIOGRAPHY
Baskervill, Charles Read, ed. *Elizabethan and Stuart Plays.* New York: Henry Holt, 1934.
MacLure, Millar. *George Chapman: A Critical Study.* Toronto: University of Toronto Press, 1966.
Spivak, Charlotte. *George Chapman.* New York: Twayne, 1967.

CHATTERTON, THOMAS (1752–1770)

Born in Bristol, Thomas Chatterton was the posthumous son of a poor schoolmaster and at age 11 published his first poem, titled "A Hymn for Christmas Day," which later critics described as influenced by JOHN MILTON and containing some satire against the Pope. He gained his education at Colston's Hospital, a charity institution for the poor that trained pupils to serve merchants of the port town, while his mother sewed to help support her family. As popular mythology goes, he was expelled from school at age seven, not surprising his mother, who had often told him he was a fool. However, he made progress, visibly improving and surprising his mother; by age eight he had become "eager" for books, according to his biographer, John Dix. He also apparently became enthralled with the illuminated manuscripts that his mother was shredding for scrap.

By age 14 Chatterton apprenticed with an attorney named John Lambert and became interested in the historical documents of his church of St. Mary Redcliffe. He learned to recreate aristocratic pedigrees and coats of arms and transferred his interest in that hobby to his writing. He became so adept at such forgery that, according to Dix, he delighted a vain member of the community by telling him he had discovered his family pedigree traced from a remote period. When he presented a book to the man with his family's coat of arms painted on the cover, he received five times the payment he had expected, prompting the invention of a second volume, complete with a poem dated 1320.

Chatterton gained a reputation as a dabbler in the occult and became a familiar face at local taverns; some of his poems celebrate drunken carousing. Bored by his transcription duties, he found imaginative outlets by composing love poems for his inarticulate friends. Other of his poetry targeted the Bristol community, attacking what he perceived as some members' greed and hypocrisy.

Chatterton wrote a later set of poems under the pseudonym Thomas Rowley, identifying himself as "a Secular Priest of St. John's," using 15th-century Bristol as a setting. In those poems he transformed a historical figure, Bristol's merchant mayor William Canynges, into an imaginary patron for the fictional Rowley. He corresponded with the novelist Horace Walpole, who encouraged Chatterton to send more of the Rowley works. However, when Walpole showed the poems to his poet friend John Gray, Gray recognized them as forgeries and dismissed them. Walpole wrote to Chatterton, encouraging him to give up writing and focus on his apprenticeship. This enraged Chatterton, who threatened to destroy his work; instead he composed a vitriolic poem aimed at Walpole, which read, in part,

Had I the gifts of wealth and luxury shar'd,
Not poor and mean, Walpole! Thou hadst not
    dar'd
Thus to insult. But I shall live and stand
By Roywley's side, when thou art dead and
    damn'd.

In 1769 Chatterton began to publish periodicals in London and hoped to move there but was too encumbered by indentures. Lambert discovered a suicide note written by Chatterton, obviously intended to manipulate his employer, which proved effective, even though it contained such nonsense as bequeathing his humility and his modesty to various individuals. Lambert had the indentures dismissed, and in 1770 Chatterton moved to London.

At first Chatterton wrote political pieces in a progressive vein, usually in the form of letters addressed to political figures. For instance, in a letter to *Middlesex Journal* dated April 17, 1770, and signed "Decimus," he wrote to the duke G———n:

> The people are indeed to be pitied. They have a king, (the best of kings, in the language of flattery) who never hears the truth. They petition, and are not regarded; and if they assume a becoming spirit of freedom, it is licentiousness. I shall conclude with observing, that your whole administration has been derogatory to the honour and dignity of the crown; for the honour of the crown is the liberty of the subject.

However revolutionary his words proved, Chatterton remained always the pragmatist in such matters, expressing in a letter to his sister his willingness to write in support of Tory opinions.

With exuberance Chatterton wrote on May 6, 1770, to his mother, "I get four guineas a month by one magazine: shall engage to write a History of England, and other pieces, which will more than double that sum. Occasional essays for the daily papers would more than support me. What a glorious prospect!" He did pay for his rented room in Holborn until the radical presses closed and many of their editors went to prison. Sending most of the pittance he received for a few additional pieces to his sister and mother, he lived for a short time penniless and hungry. All of his poetry was rejected except a single Rowley poem, "Elinoure and Juga," which appeared in *The Town and Country Magazine* (1769). Chatterton's sensitivity led him to take arsenic. His landlady reported that he refused her offer of a meal on August 24, 1770. He then went to his locked room and committed suicide by injesting arsenic, dying days before his 18th birthday.

The circumstances of Chatterton's death, in conjunction with his poetry, caught the imagination of the later romantic poets. William Wordsworth wrote of Chatterton in "Resolution and Independence" as "the marvelous boy" who "perished in his pride," while John Keats dedicated *Endymion* to him. When Keats also met an early death, Shelley referenced Chatterton in his elegy to Keats, *Adonais*. He became the dissenting artist ideal, inspiring writing also by Samuel Taylor

Coleridge and a momentary inspiration behind a never acted upon plan by Robert Southey to found a utopia in the colonies. The artist John Flaxman composed a pen and wash drawing titled *Despair offering a bowl of poison to Chatterton,* presently hanging in the British Museum. The Victorians recharacterized Chatterton as saintly, ignoring his topics of sex and drink, and another portrait by Henry Wallis fashioned Chatterton a martyr of sorts.

The poet remained in the public eye through various biographies and a definitive two-volume edition of his works by Donald S. Hall in 1971. Peter Ackroyd's 1987 novel, titled simply *Chatterton,* aroused renewed interest, as did a collection of critical essays in 1999 edited by Nick Groom. His childhood home can be spotted on Pile Street in Bristol, across from St. Mary Redcliffe, still the largest parish church in the country. Although his works are out of print, libraries still have copies, and poems and excerpts, including a roundelay, or song, from "AELLA," are available in electronic version.

BIBLIOGRAPHY

Dix, John. *The Life of Thomas Chatterton, Including His Unpublished Poems and Correspondence.* Westmead, England: Gregg International, 1971.

Groom, Nick, ed. *Thomas Chatterton and Romantic Culture.* New York: St. Martin's Press, 1999.

Lindsay, David W., ed. *English Poetry, 1700–1780; Contemporaries of Swift and Johnson.* Totowa, N.J.: Rowman & Littlefield, 1974.

Nevill, John Cranstoun. *Thomas Chatterton.* Port Washington, N.Y.: Kennikat Press, 1970.

Taylor, Donald S. *Thomas Chatterton's Art: Experiments in Imagined History.* Princeton, N.J.: Princeton University Press, 1978.

"CHRIST'S VICTORY IN HEAVEN" GILES FLETCHER (1610)

One of the best of the 17th-century religious poets, GILES FLETCHER produced poetry mostly free of didacticism, despite his membership in the Spenserian school. With nondramatic verse modeled after that of Edmund Spenser of *The Fairie Queene* (1590, 1596) fame, the Spenserians proved serious writers intent on wise subjects, which often caused their work to dissolve into a stilted preachiness. Fletcher's approach to the topic of religion helped him avoid, for the most part, the deep moralizing that often swallowed the creative aspects of work by his fellow religious poets. His innate enthusiasm for his topic, plus his chosen themes, aided his avoidance.

Fascinated by the various stages of Christ's existence, Fletcher applied his abundant powers of imagination and intelligent grasp of language to produce elegant verse that captivated his readers. His most often anthologized (in excerpts) poem, "Christ's Victory in Heaven" presents a dispute between Justice and Mercy, as Fletcher adopts the FIGURE OF SPEECH of personification to bring those figures to life. It represents the first of four cantos, followed by "Christ's Victory on Earth," "Christ's Triumph over Death," and "Christ's Triumph after Death." Fletcher adopts a RHYME scheme of *ababbccc* with METER of iambic pentameter in 265 eight-line verses to complete his four cantos, producing a work of epic proportion.

"Christ's Victory in Heaven" resounds with the rich imagery for which Fletcher is best remembered. Although some critics note a tension between his desire to make an imaginative presentation and his compulsion to adopt some traditional rhetoric, the poem proves both LYRIC and narrative, as Mercy intercedes to prevent Justice's indictment of humankind. An excerpt well illustrates his capable talent. Mercy has convinced God to extend grace to humans, despite their state of sin, when Justice intervenes:

> But Justice had no sooner Mercy seen
> Smoothing the wrinkles of her Father's brow,
> But up she starts, and throws her self between.

The reader can clearly picture this dispute and its dramatic combatants.

Fletcher next adopts a simile to aid his reader's imagination, selecting something to which they can relate. He compares Justice's move to that of "a vapour" rising "from a moory slough." That vapor "Doth heav'n's bright face of his rays disarray, / And sads the smiling Orient of the springing day." Fletcher's use of personification in describing the sun in the sky as "heav'n's bright face" may seem cloying to some readers. However, his use of CATACHRESIS in applying the adjective *sad* in the following line as a verb proves somehow just the right grammatical form, with a stronger effect than that of the too-formal *saddens.* He employs wordplay in the phrase *rays disarray,* which makes his rhyme, but also displays Fletcher's love of language.

The admirable description continues, as the speaker notes Justice "was a Virgin of austere regard," explaining she was "Not as the world esteems her, deaf and blind; / But as the eagle" in vision. Her ears "The silence of the thought loud speaking hears," and her breast holds "No riot of affection." Fletcher again selects an image to which readers can relate, that of Lady Justice. Justice is, of course, supposed to be both blind and deaf, allowing nothing to influence her decisions. Art depicts her as a female statue holding a balanced scale and wearing a blindfold.

Fletcher employs repetition and ALLITERATION as he continues,

> But a still apathy
> Possessed all her soule, which softly slept
> Securely, without tempest; no sad cry
> Awakes her pity, but wrong'd poverty,
>> Sending her eyes to heav'n swimming in
>> tears.

He demonstrates Justice has a compassionate side, but only when an innocent is involved; she does not consider man an innocent.

So strong is the effect of Justice that when she frowns, "The flints do melt, and rocks to water roll, / And airy mountains shake, and frighted shadows howl." Justice can vanquish Ignorance, Death, and Strife, causing Shame to veil "his guilty eyes," a nice contrast to Justice's intentional blindfold. Fletcher's description of Justice's preparation to address her audience is imbued with his judgment of her strength and importance, as "she, the Living Law" proceeds to bow "herself with a majestic awe, and "All heavn' to hear her speech, did into silence draw." The description of Justice as a "Living Law" remains a powerful reminder of its presence, although that presence may often exist as only an ideal. The law, or written arbitrary creed, is not enough to produce justice, which requires moral application of that law.

Although Fletcher is noted specifically as a poet who did not write drama, he had a bent for constructing highly dramatic scenes. With well-delineated characters and a tone of respectful enthusiasm, he employs a heightened language that suits his subject.

CHUDLEIGH, LADY MARY (1656–1710)

Born the daughter of Richard Lee and Mary Sydenham in Winslade, Devon, Mary Lee married George Chudleigh in 1674 at age 17. She moved from one well-established family into another, as the Chudleighs had been members of the aristocracy since 1320. The son of Sir George Chudleigh of Ashton in Devon, a staunch Royalist, George was 13 years older than Mary. He eventually claimed his father's baronetcy and had the wealth to support his growing family.

The Chudleighs lost their first child, Mary, then had three sons, Richard, George, and Thomas; Richard died at age three. They also lost their youngest child, a daughter named Eliza Maria, an experience that provided the subject for a later poem. Church records indicated the loss of a fourth child as well. Isolated from other women, Chudleigh kept her contacts through correspondence with MARY ASTELL, whom she greatly admired; John Norris; and Elizabeth Thomas, and she also wrote verse. In 1697 JOHN DRYDEN wrote to his publisher that "I felt in my pocket, & found my Lady Chudleighs verses; which this Afternoon I gave Mr. [William] Walsh to read in the Coffee house." Referring to the commendatory verses in his own translation of VIRGIL, Dryden wrote that Mr. Walsh agreed with him regarding Lady Chudleigh's poetry, "that they are better than any which are printed before the Book." He added that the famed playwright William Wycherley agreed with his assessment.

Chudleigh responded so positively to Astell that she decided to write a poem dedicated "to Almystrea," a name that is an anagram of Mary Astell's name. The two women were part of a literary group in which they all adopted names; Chudleigh was called "Marissa" and used that name when she wrote to Thomas, who replied as "Corinna." Other women, who remain unidentified, include "Cleanthe," "Clorissa," "Lucinda," and "Eugenia." She may have followed the lead of KATHERINE PHILIPS, who enjoyed a much wider and more prominent circle of friends, most of whom also had classical nicknames.

Astell's feminist writing, especially her *Some Reflections on Marriage* (1700), inspired Chudleigh to write one of her best-known poems, a book-length work titled *The LADIES DEFENCE* (1701). She wrote in reaction to a sermon titled "The Bride-woman's Counselor" (1700) by a Nonconformist minister heard at a wedding that supported complete subordination of wives to husbands. She prefaced her poem explaining that the three male voices in the work, Sir John Brute, Sir William Loveall, and a Parson, represented males she observed rudely enjoying Sprint's debasing of the females in the gathering. The poem implies that Chudleigh's marriage proved unhappy, but her stylized approach also suggests she may have simply been following a traditional form. She wrote of *The Ladies Defence* in a preface to a collection of essays, "The whole was designed as a Satyr on Vice, and, not, as some have maliciously reported, for an Invective on Marriage." She divulged little about her own marriage and never wrote about George specifically, so readers could only infer her feelings regarding matrimony and her own situation. Later critics believed Chudleigh's exploration of life through the pen allowed her to find a harmony lacking in her own existence.

Elizabeth Thomas addressed a poem to Chudleigh, having expressed her admiration of *The Ladies Defence,* and they continued writing letters for years. Chudleigh once explained to Thomas that she "was troubl'd" when women became "the Jest of every vain Pretender to Wit" who proved "invidious Detracters" that believed women could not "be *obedient Wives,* without being *Slaves,* nor pay their *Husbands* that *Respect* they owe them, without sacrificing their *Reason* to their *Humor.*" She wrote in her preface to *Poems on Several Occasions* (1703), which included the cautionary poem "To THE LADIES," that the poetry resulted from her solitary lifestyle. "To the Ladies" proved so popular it can be found handwritten onto flyleafs of contemporary books, including the Shakespeare First Folio owned by one Elizabeth Brockett.

Chudleigh later confided in Thomas that her books and thoughts proved pleasant companions, although she added that life had little appeal, and the grave held no fear. A second edition of her poetry appeared in 1709 with *The Ladies Defence* included, although she had not granted permission for the printer to do so; that collection appeared in further editions in 1713, 1722, and 1750. She complained in *Essays upon Several Subjects in Verse and Prose* (1710), a collection of moralizations, about the affront of the printer's unauthorized action. Confined as a result of painful rheumatism, she left some unpublished writings including plays and translations upon her death in Ashton, Devon.

Thomas and Martha Sansom published some dedicatory verses to Chudleigh, and short biographies appeared in Ballard's *Memoirs* (1752), Shiells's *Lives of the Poets* (1753), and *Poems by Eminent Ladies* (1755). Renewed interest in Chudleigh arose among feminist critics in the mid-20th century, leading to the anthologizing of her poems and their abundant inclusion on electronic sites. Original manuscripts exist in Harvard University's Houghton Library and in the Huntington Library in San Marino, California.

BIBLIOGRAPHY
Ezell, Margaret J. M., ed. *The Poems and Prose of Mary, Lady Chudleigh.* New York: Oxford University Press, 1993.

Ward, Charles E., ed. *The Letters of John Dryden.* Durham, N.C.: Duke University Press, 1942.

"CHURCH MONUMENTS" GEORGE HERBERT (1633)

In "Church Monuments," GEORGE HERBERT establishes tombs as an extended metaphor to contemplate death and preparation for death. The poem appeared among the collection titled *The Temple,* and its church reference unites it in theme with others in the collection. Herbert adopts at first a somber tone that makes clear the reverential nature of his consideration. By the second stanza, however, he incorporates IRONY and suggests humor through self-deprecation as his speaker expresses a desire to acclimate his body to the impending state of death and dissolution.

The speaker begins by describing a quiet moment spent inside a tomb, where his mind and body both "practice" for the coming moment of reckoning: "While that my soul repairs to her devotion, / Here I intomb my flesh." His purpose is to allow his body to "take acquaintance of this heap of dust," as "the blast of death's incessant motion, / Fed with the exhalation of our crimes," will deliver all individuals to this state one day. He concludes the first of his four six-line stanzas with "Therefore I gladly trust," using ENJAMBMENT to carry readers into the first line of the second stanza, "my body to this school." He employs additional metaphor to compare the tomb and the various headstones to a school, a place where he will learn of his own future. His body must "learn / To spell his elements" later to "find his birth / Written in dusty heraldry and lines," a reference to perhaps a carving of his family crest, as well as engraved lines of an epitaph. He concludes that stanza noting that "dissolution" engages in "comparing dust with dust, and earth with earth," finding humor in man's erecting "Jet and Marble" as "signs" to mark their graves.

Herbert again signals readers to move into the next stanza from the concluding word, *signs,* the first line of the third stanza reading, "to sever the good fellowship of dust." As he does in several other poems, including "DEATH" and "TIME," Herbert demystifies the idea of death and subsequent decomposition by assuring that as each individual dies, he will find much company in those who have gone before. The headstones simply serve to "spoil the meeting" of dust with dust. The speaker gently derides man's tenacity in clinging to his earthly existence, adding,

> . . . What shall point out them,
> When they shall bow, and kneel, and fall down
> flat
> To kiss those heaps, which now they have in
> trust? (13–15)

He addresses his own flesh, instructing it to "learn here thy stem / And true descent," both of which are dust. Herbert repeats his previous approach of ending the final line of stanza 3 with a comma, causing the reader to continue without break into the final stanza:

> . . . that when thou shalt grow fat,
> And wanton in thy cravings, thou mayst know,
> That flesh is but the glass, which holds the dust
> That measures all our time. (18–21)

Herbert's format of continual movement through enjambment and uncompleted lines and thoughts

mimics his subject matter, that of the continual and unstoppable movement from before birth, when all are dust, to after death, when all again become dust. He concludes with a soothing thought:

> . . . Mark here below
> How tame these ashes are, how free from lust,
> That thou mayst fit thyself against thy fall.
> (22–24)

In other words, people may prepare themselves for the transformation forced by death by observing the quiet unresisting nature of what is left of those who have preceded us in death. They have been liberated from desires of the flesh and remain resigned to their destiny.

"CIRCUIT OF APOLLO, THE" ANNE FINCH, COUNTESS OF WINCHILSEA (1702)

ANNE FINCH, COUNTESS OF WINCHILSEA, cleverly asserts in her "The Circuit of Apollo" that no male would dare anger three out of four women by selecting only one to receive the traditional laurel wreath placed upon the head of the winner of a competition. When Apollo assumes the task of choosing the finest female poet in Kent, he notes not many poets exist there, and most who do are women. He establishes the competition in order to encourage their work. Finch takes the opportunity to praise two poets, APHRA BEHN and KATHERINE PHILIPS, crucial early female writers in establishing a benchmark for the women who would follow.

The poem falls into three sections, indicated by the insertion of white space at the end of the first two. The speaker explains Apollo's task in the first section. Finch also famously writes of Behn, England's first professional female poet and known for her erotic themes, that no superior to her existed "in fancy, in language, or wit," but Apollo "owned that a little too loosely she writ." Finch adds, "Since the art of the muse is to stir up soft thoughts, / Yet to make all hearts beat without blushes or faults." She uses ALLITERATION in establishing the purpose of inspiration, which is not to inflame readers or to call attention to the poet herself, but rather to delight the audience gently. With that general comment she concludes the first section.

The second section frames the comparison of the four female poets. Apollo begins his competition by asking to see their work. "Alinda" specializes in love poetry, and the speaker describes her work: "So easy the verse, yet composed with such art, / That not one expression fell short of the heart." Apollo is so struck by her "song upon love" that he decides to accompany her with his lyre, "Declaring no harmony else could be found / Fit to wait upon words of so moving a sound." Just as he moves to set the laurel upon Alinda's head, he hears "Laura" reading a paper. Finch then references "Orinda," the classical name Katherine Philips, "The Matchless Orinda," had given herself in her poetry. Another female poet who left a great legacy to those who followed in the next century, as did Finch, she specialized in same-sex love poetry, focusing without erotic suggestion on the strong friendships of women. So beautiful were Laura's words that Apollo felt Orinda might have written them. He now finds himself struggling to choose either Alinda or Laura as his winner. To complicate matters, "Valeria" then contributes her poetry, telling Apollo that only he should read her verse, and, finally, "Ardelia," the neoclassical label Finch had created for herself, enters the competition, "expecting least praise, / Who writ for her pleasure and not for the bays." Finch claims that she does not write for an audience, a common apology. In reality she remained quite concerned about her readers' reaction to her work, understanding that women were not expected to write poetry, and that such action often sparked criticism. Despite her lack of desire for attention, she

> Would sometimes endeavor to pass a dull day
> In composing a song, or a scene of a play
> Not seeking for fame, which so little does last
> That ere we can taste it the pleasure is past.
>   (46–49)

Finch self-consciously comments on her own endeavors, denying that she seeks the immortality available to writers whose works became a revered part of poetic tradition. Because she has previously referenced Behn and Philips, that tradition remains important to Finch, who, despite her protestations, probably hoped

her name might in the future be connected to theirs. Apollo agrees that Ardelia has joined the group as a likely candidate.

In the third section, Finch compares Apollo to Paris, the son of Troy's King Priam, who had to select the most beautiful woman in the world from the goddesses Hera, Aphrodite, and Athena. Obviously such a selection could only lead to grief, as the two not chosen would be angered and hurt. Apollo prevents a possible problem by choosing not to choose, a decision that shows his wisdom. He notes all are equally deserving, "And that 'twere injustice one brow to adorn / With a wreathe which so fitly by each might be worn." He judiciously decides to refer the selection to Parnassus and the female muses who lived there, as he had to depart to drive his mythical chariot across the sky, pulling the sun behind him. He leaves the choice to the female muses, as Finch explains in her final three lines,

> Since no man upon earth, nor Himself in the
>   sky
> Would be so imprudent, so dull, or so blind,
> To lose three parts in four amongst
>   womankind. (75–77)

CLEVELAND, JOHN (1613–1658) John Cleveland matured in Yorkshire, the son of a clergyman, who educated him at Christ's College, Cambridge. He took his degree in 1631, a contemporary of JOHN MILTON. By 1634 he was a fellow of St. John's College and became the University's praelector in rhetoric, following in the tradition of GEORGE HERBERT. Because of his opposition to Cromwell, he departed his position in 1643 to declare his Royalist sentiments, moving to Oxford and later joining the Royalist garrison at Newark, where his robust written defense of the Crown earned him an appointment as judge advocate to Newark. He left Oxford in 1645, prompting his decline. According to legend, he lasted through the six-month Scottish siege and then was sent home by General Leslie with the order to "go about his business and sell his ballads." Although he apparently wandered for the next nine years, his work remained extraordinarily successful, enjoying 14 editions. The next recorded

mention of Cleveland occurred in 1655, noting his imprisonment in Yarmouth by Parliamentarians. An appeal to Cromwell gained his release, after which he would survive only two additional years, dying at age 45 of "gaol fever" contracted while in prison.

Cleveland's popularity with contemporary readers as a satirist and poet grew to overshadow that of Milton, although later critics scoffed at the comparison. He wrote the type of poetry termed "masculine" and "robust," gaining the title "last of the metaphysicals" because of his employment of what JOHN DRYDEN would later term "Clevelandisms" in Dryden's *Essay of Dramatic Poesy* (1668), reducing the poet's overreaching to a syndrome. A Clevelandism was CATACHRESIS, "wrestling and torturing a word into another meaning." An additional publication, Fuller's *Worthies* (1662), adopted the poet's name as an infinitive suggesting dubious value: To *clevelandise* was to employ the "masculine" approach, using phrases "pregnant with metaphors, carrying in them a difficult plainness, difficult at the hearing, plain at the consideration thereof." Nevertheless, Cleveland's work proved popular with the public; two of his famous poems are "The Rebel Scot" and "The King's Disguise." A collection of Cleveland's poetry appeared in *The Character of a London Diurnal* (1647), and in 1651 a collection titled *The Poems* was published, to enjoy 18 editions before the poet's death. Scolar Press published a facsimile of the 11th of those editions in 1971, but the most often-used edition is that edited by Morris and Withington in 1967; selections may also be found in electronic versions. Popular anthologized selections include "UPON THE DEATH OF MR. KING," a perfect example of his clevelandizing and a painful contrast to Milton's markedly superior rendering in pastoral elegy of the same topic in LYCIDAS (1638).

Still, the critic Donald Bruce notes Cleveland's trademark wit, intelligence, "vigour, fertility of invention and imagery, and aptness of comparison." In Bruce's opinion Cleveland "trifled away transcendent gifts" in his choice of light themes. The instances in which that regrettable choice did not prove true caused Cleveland, as did other poets housed in Oxford with Charles I, to attempt to advise the king against unwise action. He expressed his dismay when Charles disguised himself as a servant to flee Oxford in 1646, running to the Scottish camp. He also believed that Charles had failed his people by not acting as an apt steward of the country's resources. Despite the attempts on his behalf by Cleveland, JOHN DENHAM, ABRAHAM COWLEY, and RICHARD CRASHAW, Charles I continued on a political path that resulted in his eventual execution.

BIBLIOGRAPHY
Bruce, Donald. "An Oxford Garrison of Poets in 1642." *Contemporary Review,* November 1992: 250–256.
Jacobus, Lee A. *John Cleveland.* Boston: Twayne, 1975.
Morris, Brian, and Eleanor Withington, ed. *The Poems of John Cleveland.* Oxford: Clarendon Press, 1967.

"COLLAR, THE" GEORGE HERBERT (1633) One of the most famous of the poems by GEORGE HERBERT, his autobiographical "The Collar" acts to protest restrictions he experienced in his life as a man of God who suffered many unwanted attentions and demands. He expressed to acquaintances his desire for an uneventful obscurity, a life in which others did not so depend upon him. His thoughts channel through his speaker, who remains burdened by expectations of others when he most desires escape. A protest poem until its conclusion, "The Collar" also serves to reassert through the obviously anguished speaker Herbert's devotion to his calling.

Herbert opens in lines depicting clear frustration as his speaker asserts, "I struck the board, and cried, No more. / I will abroad." Although the reader does not yet know what the speaker desires "no more" of, his plan to stage an escape is clear. While *abroad* literally meant to readers of Herbert's day a visit to the Continent, it could be seen in a broader sense as a term reflecting the speaker's desire to broaden his horizons. He desires a journey that will remove him from what seems to be a narrowly restrictive existence. He next questions his own statement, as the volume of his voice decreases: "What? Shall I ever sigh and pine? / My lines and life are free; free as the road." The speaker now notes that nothing physical prevents him from traveling. Herbert employs additional FIGURATIVE LANGUAGE (FIGURE OF SPEECH) with the similes "Loose as the wind, as large as store," to describe the freedom the speaker should feel. However, something restrains him. Herbert next reflects metonymy as the speaker asks another question, "Shall I still be in suit?" Here his clothing represents his lifestyle, the suit indicating his religious garb. He feels bitter that his life reaps "no harvest but a thorn / To let me blood." Rather than "cordial fruit" and "wine," he holds only a thorn from a vine. The thorn image allows Herbert to reflect on the crown of thorns worn by Christ at his crucifixion, thus associating his speaker and himself with the religious faith with which he so closely identifies.

The speaker next notes wine did exist before his "sighs did dry it," indicating sighs of mortification. He also acknowledges by line 12 that corn did exist, but that it drowned in his own tears. Extending the metaphor of crops and the round of seasons that produces them, Herbert references through the speaker the loss of a year, his speaker wondering, "Have I no bays to crown it?" Because bay was shaped into a wreath of victory for youth in the ancient Olympic Games, he suggests that as a young man, he should be scoring victories of his own in life, perhaps in romance and business. His rhetorical questions continue, as he asks about his lost year,

> Have I no bays to crown it?
> No flowers, no garlands gay? All blasted?
>   All wasted? (14–16)

By line 18 the speaker begins to recover from his mournful state, as an internal voice tells his heart, "there is fruit, / And thou hast hands." The fruit to which he refers represents the bounties of the holy life, and the speaker is urged to use his hands to pluck them. He can recover his "sigh-blown age" to enjoy "double pleasures." The voice then commands the speaker, "leave thy cold dispute / Of what is fit, and not." as he begins to focus on the rewards of a life dedicated to Christ, despite its difficulties. The voice continues with edicts, including

> . . . Forsake thy cage,
>   Thy rope of sands,
> Which petty thoughts have made, and made to thee
>   Good cable, to enforce and draw. (21–24)

Clearly the speaker has constructed his own prison, binding himself by thoughts unworthy. In a tone that has shifted from frustration to hope, the voice notes that the speaker must assume all blame for his depressed state, for it was while he "didst wink and wouldst not see." that matters seemed bleak. Herbert urges readers not to refuse to open their eyes to God's glory and the eternity promised to one to whom God extends grace.

In a last struggle of protest, the speaker repeats, "I will abroad" and adds,

> He that forbears
> To suit and serve his need,
>   Deserves his load. (30–32)

But contrition strikes the speaker as he "raved and grew more fierce and wild." That contrition is invoked by a call the speaker hears "At every word," a call of a single term, which appears italicized for effect: "*Child.*" Immediately responsive to the overwhelmingly convincing cry of a father for his son, the speaker replies without hesitation, closing the poem, "*My Lord.*" Herbert makes clear that even in one's sin and protest, an acceptance of God as Lord will open one's life to receive God's grace.

No doubt Herbert did experience just such feelings of rebellion against his lifestyle. Although he seems outwardly to have chosen his own fate, he makes repeatedly clear in his various poems that man does not have such control. Any thoughts of directing one's future prove ultimately futile. For Herbert, his future was based on a simple response to God. His poem emphasizes that God will care for all who heed his call, as a parent cares for a child.

COLLINS, WILLIAM (1721–1759)
William Collins was born on Christmas Day, the son of Chichester hat maker and twice mayor, William, and his wife, Elizabeth. The younger William Collins grew up with sisters, Elizabeth and Anne, losing his father when he was 12 years old. A few months later Collins enrolled in Winchester College, where he began to write poetry. He published the poems "To Miss Aurelia C——r" and "Sonnet" in the *Gentleman's Magazine* in

1739. Of his early educational experience, SAMUEL JOHNSON later noted, "His English exercises were better than his Latin"; Collins would become skilled in other languages, including French, Italian, and Spanish. Johnson wrote that the lack of openings in New College, Oxford, which Collins should have attended as a nominated scholar, became "the original misfortune of his life." Collins instead attended Queen's College by default. He completed his *Persian Eclogues* (1742) while still a teen. Employing the ruse that he had translated the poems from the Turkish language, Collins attempted to depart from what he termed the "strong and nervous" CONCEITS of his era, adopting a Middle Eastern approach, one enriched by more FIGURATIVE LANGUAGE (FIGURE OF SPEECH).

Collins remained determined to become a poet, and with that goal in mind, he moved while near-penniless in 1744 to London, for which Johnson labeled him "a literary adventurer." Although it did not at first gain him fame, Collins's *Odes on Several Descriptive and Allegoric Subjects* (1746) became the work for which he would be remembered. JOHN MILTON influenced his choice of the BLANK VERSE ode stanza and of some of his expressions, as the critic Arthur Johnston notes. As Milton wrote in L'ALLERGO, "Tells how the drudging Goblin sweat / To earn his cream-bowl duly set" (105–106), Collins wrote in "Ode on Popular Superstitions," "There each trim lass that skims the milky store / To the swart tribes their creamy bowl allots" (22–23).

Of a sensitive temperament, Collins lived always in fear of poverty. According to Johnson, "his great fault was irresolution," because he was "doubtful of his dinner, or trembling at a creditor." Collins decided to return to Chichester after working under contract for a brief time as a translator. A £2,000 inheritance in 1749 from his uncle allowed him the freedom to give up work on a translation of Aristotle's *Poetics,* return the advance he had received, and focus on his own writing. However, poor health prevented additional work, and Collins eventually suffered from an increase in melancholia. The heavy depression evolved into insanity, and Collins died at age 38; he was buried at St. Andrew's Church.

The few poems Collins left behind indicated the potential for a robust career, based on his success in countering convention. Johnson wrote that Collins occasionally exhibited "sublimity and splendor." The most widely anthologized of his poems include "ODE TO EVENING," "HOW SLEEP THE BRAVE," and "A SONG FROM SHAKESPEARE'S CYMBELINE." Additional popular poems are "Ode to Simplicity" and the posthumous "Ode on the Popular Superstitions of the Highlands" (1788). Much of Collins's scant work remains available in electronic format.

BIBLIOGRAPHY

Carver, P. L. *The Life of a Poet, a Biography of William Collins.* New York: Horizon Press, 1967.

Garrod, Heathcote William. *Collins.* 1928. New York: Octagon Books, 1973.

Johnson, Samuel. "The Life of William Collins." In *The Works of the English Poets from Chaucer to Cowper, including the Series edited with Prefaces, Biographical and Critical, by Dr. Samuel Johnson: and the most approved translation.* Edited by Alexander Chalmers. 21 vols. London: C. Whittington, 1810.

Johnston, Arthur. "Poetry and Criticism after 1740." *Dryden to Johnson,* edited by Roger Lonsdale, 313–349. New York: Penguin, 1993.

Sherwin, Paul S. *Precious Bane: Collins and the Miltonic Legacy.* Austin: University of Texas Press, 1977.

"COME LITTLE BABE" NICOLAS BRETON (?1593–4)

A late 16th- or early 17th century poem, NICOLAS BRETON's "Come Little Babe" offers a prime example of the extension of a popular form from one century into the next. Breton adopts his favored approach of RIME ROYAL for his lullaby, varying the common seven-line verse format to six lines. He also departs slightly from rime royal's traditional rhyme scheme of *ababbcc,* using *ababcc* instead. While best known by its first line as a title, the poem may have appeared originally as "A Cradle Song" in a work titled *The Arbor of Amorous Devices* (1593–94). Later published in *Lyrics from Elizabethan Romance* (1890) by A. H. Bullen, the poem remained anthologized into the 21st century and can be found online in electronic format.

"Come Little Babe" adopts a narrative approach, its plotline revealed in words supposedly sung to an infant, but actually written for adult readers to enjoy. Rime royal typically was meant to be read, rather than spoken. Even though this poem's lullaby form suggests that it should be sung, its subject matter counters that tradition. The speaker begins, "Come little babe, come silly soul" but immediately departs a light approach to focus in its second line on the serious adult theme of sexual indecency: "Thy father's shame, thy mother's grief." The speaker states that the infant "little think'st and less dost know / The cause of this shy mother's moan," that he "wants the wit to wail her woe." Breton's heavy use of ALLITERATION is a familiar mark of his style. While the child does cry, it "know'st not yet what thou dost ail."

By the third stanza the voice shifts from third-person point of view to first-, and the reader's suspicion that the speaker is the child's mother is confirmed. She seeks to absorb the blame for her "only joy" and declares that if God could see "O, thy sweet face!" the child could "soon purchase grace." The tone darkens in the final line of stanza 4, as with additional strong alliteration the mother remarks on her abandoned state: "For father false is fled away." She next thinks aloud of how the child's father might react should she die, and she requests her "sweet boy" to "commend" her to his father, replying to those who may "ask thy mother's name" that "by love she purchased blame." To prevent the child's assuming the worst of his father, she explains that while she may "moan," his father "is no rascal lad, / A noble youth of blood and bone," who with his smile can "beguile" even "Right honest women." Finally, she tells her child to sleep and mentions again that she will continue to weep, sitting by her child to "wail my fill." She concludes by asking that "God bless my babe, and lullaby / From this thy father's quality." Because rime royal served as a format only for loftier poems, the lullaby is likely intended as a cautionary tale for those well-born males tempted to take advantage of young women of lower social status.

COMPLAINT
The term *complaint* traditionally refers to a poetic expression popular during the Middle Ages and used often by the group labeled CAVALIER POETS who were connected to the court of Charles I. The complaint is issued by a speaker who tells of his problem, the sorrow it gives him, and its causes. The problem may be of a political, a romantic, or another personal nature, but whatever the cause, it results in a tone of general dissatisfaction with fate and fortune. For example, EDMUND WALLER in "Of English Verse" expresses concern that the words of poetry will eventually die, because of "a daily-changing tongue," and he wonders how poets can then "extend their fame." SIR JOHN SUCKLING adopts the same subject, although he adds a humorous tone of self-deprecation in his "A Sessions of the Poets," noting the debt that poets owe predecessors, but suggesting caution. He concludes a dramatic scene in which various poets and dramatists have stepped forward to testify with the lines, "Only

> The small poets clear'd up again,
> Out of hope (as 'twas thought) of borrowing;
> But sure they were out, for he forfeits his crown
> When he lends any poet about the town.

RICHARD LOVELACE's "Song: To Amarantha, That She would Dishevel Her Hair" represents the romantic complaint. The speaker complains against his love's binding her hair, a metaphor for the withholding from him her romantic attentions. On a more serious note, a BALLAD titled "Ballad: The Cavalier's Complaint" (1660), presently housed in the British Museum, expresses discontent over Charles I's seeming ingratitude toward his family's longtime supporters. WILLIAM COWPER's "The NEGRO'S COMPLAINT" offers a plea against slavery in the voice of a slave.

Application of the label *complaint* has expanded recently, applied by feminist critics to an approach to serious poetry written by females in the Renaissance, the Augustan age, and later. Reacting to both natural and civil laws that restricted their activities and expression, poets such as Mary Lee, LADY MARY CHUDLEIGH, voiced concerns in "TO THE LADIES" regarding a wife's position as little more than servant in many marriages. As another example, ANNE KILLIGREW had to join other women in defending the originality of their works, as in "UPON THE SAYING THAT MY VERSES WERE MADE BY ANOTHER."

BIBLIOGRAPHY
Mills, Rebecca M. "'That Tyrant Custom': The Politics of Custom in the Poetry and Prose of Augustan Women Writers." *Women's Writing* 7, no. 3 (2000): 391–409.

COMUS JOHN MILTON (1637) Although its subtitle (*A Masque Presented at Ludlow Castle 1634: On Michaelmas Night, Before the Right Honourable, John Earl of Bridgewater, Viscount Brackeley Lord President of Wales*) declares JOHN MILTON's pastoral drama *Comus* a masque, it was not a masque in the true sense of the word. Masques presented at court focused mainly on spectacle, with their actual message of minor importance. By contrast Milton wrote a drama with focus on good versus evil in which theme proved paramount. Good is represented in the character of the virgin Lady, while evil is presented through the erotic Comus. However, Milton believed it comparable to court entertainments and originally titled it simply *Masque*. SAMUEL JOHNSON, among others, evaluated *Comus* as lacking the dramatic unity supporting a masque. Critics believe that Dr. John Dalton first titled it *Comus* when he printed it in 1738 with the subtitle *A Masque, Now Adapted to the Stage*.

As Milton's lengthy subtitle indicates, he wrote the production for entertainment at the estate of Viscount Brackeley, designing the parts of the three travelers to be enacted by the Bridgewater children. He did so at the request of his good friend Henry Lawes, a well-known musician who wrote the accompaniment to *Comus* and who portrayed the Attendant Spirit during its enactment at Bridgewater. The production celebrated Bridgewater's appointment to Wales and would be published anonymously by Lawes in 1637 and by Milton himself in 1645. The only existing manuscript of the original presentation of *Comus* is called the *Bridgewater MS*, privately owned.

The plot offers Comus as its antagonist. An evil mythological character who through magic can assume various guises, he represents unbridled passion, while the Attendant Spirit represents rational logic. In Milton's emphasis on good versus evil, he pits reason against passion, also having the Lady support the idea of reason. However, he emphasizes more her virginity. In its Platonic sense, chastity equated to loyalty to reason, and Milton does emphasize the superiority of reason over passion. But as critics note, he presents chastity as equating to virginity, not loyalty to reason.

A female traveler and her two brothers find themselves lost in "this drear Wood, / The nodding horror of whose shady brows" threatened all travelers. The brothers leave their sister momentarily to search for a source of water, and in their absence, the Lady hears the sounds of music and celebration. Comus is celebrating with his companions, bidding them, "Come let us our rites begin, / 'Tis only daylight that makes Sin." Milton offers repeated imagery of light and dark, symbolizing good and evil.

The Lady investigates the sounds and discovers Comus, disguised as a shepherd, who invites her into his curiously quiet cottage. A son of Bacchus, Roman god of wine, and Circe, the sorceress who turned Ulysseus's crew into swine, Comus ceased his debauched revelry when he observed the Lady's approach, telling his companions that he feels "some chaste footing near about this ground." Enchanted by her great beauty, he plans to "under fair pretense of friendly ends" apply "well-pac't words of glozing courtesy, / Baited with reasons not unplausible." Milton continues to emphasize the superiority of reason above passion, as Comus will attempt to adopt reason for evil means but will ultimately fail. As the Lady approaches the cottage, now a quiet scene, she wonders whether she had simply fantasized the sounds she thought she heard. She expresses her thoughts that "may startle well, but not astound / The virtuous mind," as she calls upon "thou unblemish't form of Chastity, / I see ye visibly." Her lines support the Platonic idea that virtue is such a clear mental concept that it can be seen. Critics point out the circular logic of her argument, in which she basically claims that because she is chaste, she will remain chaste. Despite its logical flaw, its focus on chastity and purity supports the drama's theme.

The brothers return, aghast to find their sister has disappeared. The elder brother affirms the strength of her chastity to keep her safe:

> She that has that, is clad in complete steel,
> And like a quiver'd Numph with Arrows keen
> May trace huge Forests and unharbor'd Heaths,
> Infamous Hills and sandy perilous wilds,
> Where through the sacred rays of chastity,
> No savage fierce, Bandit or mountaineer
> Will dare to soil her virgin purity.

In a foreshadowing of Comus's temptation of the Lady, the older brother also notes that one with chastity is protected by "A thousand liveried Angels . . . / Driving far off each thing of sin and guilt." He adds that such a woman is able to converse with spirits whom others can neither see nor hear.

A benign Attendant Spirit informs the brothers of the Lady's fate and promises to help them. He has assumed the guise of a shepherd named Thyrsis and reveals that Comus is a malevolent sorcerer who will bewitch their sister as he does all travelers. Comus lures them into his cottage by promising hospitality, then gives them drink that converts their faces into those of beasts, when he waves his magic wand, as the speaker reveals early on in the work:

> Soon as he Potion works, their human
> count'nance,
> Th' express resemblance of the gods, is chang'd
> Into some brutish form of Wolf, or Bear,
> Or Ounce, or tiger, Hog, or bearded goat,
> All other parts remaining as they were.

Worse, those afflicted do not realize the change has taken place, not perceiving "their foul disfigurement" and still boasting "themselves more comely than before." This passage emphasizes Milton's repeated emphasis on the fact that in order for one to gain sensuality, he must sacrifice rational nature. Furnishing the brothers an antidote made from the root of the Harmony plant, the Spirit takes them to their sister.

Comus attempts to seduce the Lady with a famous speech celebrating the common CARPE DIEM theme in which he famously claims that the Lady actually blasphemes nature by preserving her virginity while Nature pours "her bounties forth, . . . covering the earth with odors, fruits, and flocks." Although she rebuffs his twisted logic, he continues, telling her, "List Lady, be not coy" in clinging to her virginity, for "Beauty is nature's coin" and "must not be hoarded." He then speaks directly to her virgin state, as Milton adopts the FIGURATIVE LANGUAGE of simile: "If you let slip time, like a neglected rose / It withers on the stalk with languish't head." She sits in an enchanted chair that will not allow her to depart, but her resolve to resist Comus remains strong, as she replies,

> I had not thought to have unlockt my lips
> In this unhallow'd air, but that this Juggler
> Would think to charm my judgment, as mine
> eyes,
> Obtruding false rules prankt in reason's garb.
> I hate when vice can bolt her arguments,
> And virtue has no tongue to check her pride.

She speaks in no uncertain terms, telling Comus of the "serious doctrine of Virginity." Comus has reinitiated the rout and passes drink that he attempts to force on the Lady. She refuses, but magic holds her to the chair and she cannot escape.

The brothers arrive at the cottage wielding swords that chase the revelers away, and Comus escapes. The Spirit scolds the brothers about letting Comus go; they "should have snatcht his wand" as only it can reverse the spell. However, the Spirit calls on Sabrina, goddess of the river Severn, for help, and she complies, telling the Spirit, "Shepherd 'tis my office best / to help ensnared chastity." Sabrina asks the Lady to look at her as she sprinkles drops from her pure fountain,

> Thrice upon thy finger's tip,
> Thrice upon thy rubied lip;
> Next this marble venom'd seat
> Smear'd with gums of glutinous heat
> I touch with chaste palms moist and cold.
> Now the spell hath lost his hold.

The travelers express their gratitude to Sabrina through song, and then follow the Spirit to arrive at their destination of Ludlow Castle.

As Stanley Fish notes, Comus represents an early example of one of many Miltonian figures involved in the act of containment. While Comus attempts to establish his own space in God's universe with his own agenda, he will be restrained. No deity or force can rival that of the Christian God or his authority to support good over evil.

BIBLIOGRAPHY

Bellamy, Elizabeth J. "Waiting for Hymen: Literary History as 'Symptom' in Spenser and Milton." *English Literary History* 64 (summer 1997): 391–414.

Fish, Stanley. *How Milton Works.* Cambridge, Mass.: Belknap Press of Harvard University Press, 2001.

Kirkconnell, Watson. *Awake the Courteous Echo: The Themes and Prosody of Comus, Lycidas, and Paradise Regained in World Literature with Translation of the Major Analogues.* Toronto: University of Toronto Press, 1973.

Lewalski, Barbara K. "Milton's *Comus* and the Politics of Masquing." In *The Politics of the Stuart Court Masque,* edited by David Bevington and Peter Holbrook, 296–320. Cambridge: Cambridge University Press, 1998.

Malpezzi, Frances. "Milton's *Comus.*" *The Explicator* 53 (summer 1995): 194–196.

Moore, Jeanie Grant. "The Two Faces of Eve: Temptation Scenes in *Comus* and *Paradise Lost.*" *Milton Quarterly* 36, no. 1 (March 2002): 1–18.

Orgel, Stephen. "The Case for Comus." *Representations* 81 (winter 2003): 31–45.

Shullenberger, William. "Into the Woods: The Lady's Soliloquy in 'Comus.'" *Milton Quarterly* 35, no. 1 (March 2001): 33–41.

Treip, Mindele Anne. "'Comus' and The Stuart Masque Connection, 1632–34." *American Notes & Queries,* July 1989, 84–90.

CONCEIT

CONCEIT   The conceit is a metaphor applied to compare two apparently unrelated concepts or objects. The term is derived from the Italian *concetto,* which means "conception," "notion," "idea," or "fancy." A conceit may extend throughout a poem, as seen in much poetry of earlier centuries, or it may be dense and focused, offering readers PARADOX as well as allusion and symbolism, a technique used in modern poetry.

Advanced by the PETRARCHAN SONNET, the conceit was adopted by English Renaissance poets. Sir Philip Sidney wrote in his seminal "Defense of Poesy" (1595) that "the poet's talents stem from the fact that he is able to create from a pre-existing idea called the fore-conceit. Poetry is the link between the real and the ideal." He continued, "the poet . . . does not learn a conceit out of a matter, but makes matter for a conceit." Many examples exist in Shakespeare's poetry, as in his Sonnet 135, in which the term *Will* is applied to desire, determination, and intellectual pursuit, concluding with a pun on the poet's name. In his famous Sonnet 130, "My mistress' eyes are nothing like the sun," he adopts beauty as a conceit to undermine traditional ideas of feminine physical attributes.

The conceit was transformed by METAPHYSICAL POETS AND POETRY, in particular by the works of JOHN DONNE, in reaction to the Petrarchan model, which they found too predictable. The metaphysical conceit was designed to undermine expectations of the reader by developing unusual analogies. Donne's well-known compass reference in "A VALEDICTION FORBIDDING MOURNING" and his comparison of the emotional effect of God to that of physical ravishment in "BATTER MY HEART" are strong examples of metaphysical conceits. GEORGE HERBERT's adoption of an altar in "The ALTAR" to represent his lonely heart as "such a stone / As nothing but / Thy power doth cut" is one of many conceits he used in his religious poetry.

RICHARD CRASHAW adopted Herbert's book on which to develop a conceit of his own in "On Mr. George Herbert's Book, *The Temple.*" He extends the temple analogy to the object of his love, comparing the "fire" in her eyes to flame that would "kindle this his sacrifice," introducing references to angels and concluding by referring to her hand as a "shrine." EDMUND WALLER, as did many CAVALIER POETS, used the conceit of a fading rose in "GO LOVELY ROSE" in an effort to convince a virgin to sacrifice her innocence to him.

BIBLIOGRAPHY

Sidney, Philip, Sir. *The Defense of Poesy: Otherwise Known as an Apology for Poetry.* Edited by Albert S. Cook. Folcroft, Pa.: Folcroft Library Editions, 1973.

COOPER'S HILL JOHN DENHAM (1642)   Most students enrolled in college English literature courses are introduced to *Cooper's Hill* by JOHN DENHAM as an important descriptive poem that influenced 18th-century poets, particularly JOHN DRYDEN, through its topographical emphasis. While Denham did focus on nature and the countryside around Windsor Castle, he used his view of geography to muse on the nature of royalty, employing his talent, as did other poets of his day, in hopes of influencing King Charles I to redeem his reign while it was still possible to prevent a Protestant revolution. Thus Denham adopts topoi, or traditional themes and literary convention, of space to reflect his Royalist leanings while remaining somewhat critical of his ruler.

Joseph Addison in his *The Annual Miscellany: For the Year 1694* (London: Jacob Tonson) praised Denham, writing, "nor Denham must we e're forget thy Strains / While Cooper's Hill commands the Neighb'ring Plains." ALEXANDER POPE, whose "WINDSOR FOREST" (1713) reflected Denham's influence, and SAMUEL JOHNSON also praised *Cooper's Hill*. They found it powerful and balanced in format, that balance resulting from Denham's rhetorical use of pairs of ideas in phrases. An example appears in lines 4 and 5, which read, "Those made not poets, but the poets those. / And as courts make not kings, but kings the court." However, later critics such as James Grantham Turner argued that such use of balance proved standard in the traditional Royalist viewpoint. He finds that rhetorical method in Royalist tracts and even in the king's writing.

Later critics also considered the poem's political content more important than had Denham's contemporaries, although the poet himself must have noticed it, because he revised much of its political content when he rereleased *Cooper's Hill* in 1655. Criticism evaluating its polemical content grew strong in the 20th century. One of the first essays to consider the lengthy poem closely was by the noted literary critic Earl Wasserman in 1959. Wasserman, executing a new criticism approach, found the poem political but also successful in balancing the tension that arose through the use of IRONY. He evaluated the work as a prime example of *concordia discors*, or balanced discourse. Other critics, including Bruce Boeckel, disagree, evaluating the poem as a failure in regard to achieving concord, seeing it instead as "highly partisan" in its successful attempt to construct a landscape in which Denham's political enemies are silenced. Boeckel achieves meaning through the application of new historicism, in which he considers the political unrest that led up to the isolation of Charles I at Oxford, where Denham lived, and eventually to his execution. That type of reading has gained strength with the popularity of a revised view of Stuart England, which began with the reign of Charles's father, James I. That view holds that the Civil War did not begin with Puritan revolution, as traditionally taught, but rather at the time that Charles took the throne. The opinion claims that a broad agreement regarding the proper manner of worship existed in England in the 1630s, but that religious leaders rejected that agreement in an attempt to impose their own more limited ideas on the populace. That meant that even though many English citizens accepted the Book of Common Prayer and the rites of the Church of England, a few power-hungry religious leaders, such as William Laud, archbishop of Canterbury, shattered that acceptance by forcing instead their own extreme Anglican view. The fact that such new views of history have spurred a reconsideration of the meaning of literature emphasizes the importance of political and social culture during the era in which poetry is written. No artist creates in a vacuum; most are strongly affected by what takes place around them. The effect of the unrest and political and religious divisions on John Denham as he wrote *Cooper Hill* should not be ignored in its reading.

The 358-line poem is composed of rhyming couplets, another factor in its format that supports the praise of its balanced presentation. It begins with a call to classical tradition as Denham mentions Parnassus and the Helicon. As are most of his additional classical allusions, this one is common. However, Denham includes PARADOX in his statements that note that poets who did not live during classical times can still produce poetry. Thus, it was not the geographical locations of Parnassus or Helicon that made the poets, but rather the poets created or made famous the geographical locations: "Those made not poets, but the poets those." As Boeckel notes, Denham's statement that the "poetic topos—a Parnassus or a Cooper's Hill—is essentially the creation of the poet, yet it functions as the poet's inspiration," remains comparable to "a serpent swallowing its tail."

The references to geography or topography prove crucial to the entire poem, which describes the English countryside but actually does something in addition. That "something" Denham suggests in his next line, which plays upon his previous comment that poets make the place. He contradicts his own remark regarding the poets' power by firmly stating the court, meaning those who serve the king, lack that power in respect to the monarch. He writes in line 5, "And as courts make not kings, but kings the court," then continues

> So where the Muses and their train resort,
> Parnassus stands; if I can be to thee
> A poet, thou Parnassus art to me.

Denham at once seems to equate the power of poetry with that of royalty but then makes clear that King Charles I acts as his inspiration. This proves a crucial political point, for if the politic body of the king inspires Denham's poetry, it must be written in order to support that inspiration. The speaker underscores the power given him by his monarch, stating that his "flight," meaning flights of fancy or imagination, takes "wing from thy auspicious height." This leads Denham into FIGURATIVE LANGUAGE (FIGURE OF SPEECH) with the use of the extended metaphor of flight, allowing the speaker to hover above the country and its people, reporting what he observes. Thus, the speaker's eye

> swift as thought contracts the space
> That lies between, and first salutes the place
> Crown'd with that sacred pile, so vast, so high,
> That whether 'tis a part of Earth, or sky,
> Uncertain seems.

This allows Denham to note that sense may be superior to intellect, a proposal that readers must accept in order to accompany him on this flight. With the term *uncertain*, Denham may offer an excuse for whatever claims he intends to make, thus allowing himself escape from censure of those he will offend.

The speaker's initial vantage point is that of London's St. Paul's Cathedral, which he praises as having survived "sword, or time, or fire," secure in the praise of many poets and "Preserv'd from ruin by the best of kings." From the top of St. Paul's the speaker sees the city as if in "a mist" where the "state and wealth the business and the crowd, / Seems at this distance but a darker cloud." He then notes that "luxury, and wealth, like war and peace, / Are each the others ruin, and increase," offering another paradox in that luxury increases wealth as it simultaneously ruins it. His view of London's populace is not flattering, as he compares

the people in his original version to "Ants" who toil to "prevent imaginarie wants." The speaker continues to praise the building itself, which invites

> A pleasure, and a reverence from the sight.
> Thy mighty master's emblem, in whose face
> Sat meekness, heighten'd with majestic grace,

suggesting the prophet Paul as the master.

Denham combines themes of politics and religion in this section, reflecting upon the state of England itself. As Boeckel discusses, a fundraising campaign to repair and preserve St. Paul's had begun in 1631, and it had not progressed well. As part of Charles I's plan to restore a decent mode of worship, he had undertaken to repair English churches, and St. Paul's should have served as a major happy symbol of that effort. However, the people soon recognized the king's plan as his demand that all accept a rigid conformity in worship, as he verbally attacked those who wished to preserve icons and the sacrament in their rituals. Most importantly, Charles eventually ordered all justices of the peace to collect pledges and donations from their counties. This resulted in not only a taxation of citizens, but also a clear message that the king intended to impose the unity the people refused to give him, quashing local powers of government. Finally, he supported the dean of St. Paul's in what became known as the St. Gregory's case. When the dean decided to relocate the communion table to the east part of the chancel and confine it behind a rail, he ordered that the same be done in St. Gregory's, a church at St. Paul's border, a move that invoked complaints from those who used the church. When the court in control of such issues stood ready to counteract the dean's command, Charles I ordered the case be heard before the Privy Council, his own court, which ruled local churches must follow the guidance of St. Paul's. In addition, as Denham wrote of St. Paul's, suggesting its spire as the highest point in London, he reflects upon another tall landmark, the Tower of London, where William Laud had been imprisoned in March 1641.

Denham's next topography of consideration is that of Windsor. He makes a smooth transition by writing of St. Paul's that the

heavenly race
Do homage to her, yet she cannot boast
Amongst that numerous, and celestial host,
More heroes than can Windsor, nor doth
  Fame's
Immortal book record more noble names.

He mentions "Caesar, Albanact, or Brute, / The British Arthur, or the Danish Knute," comparing Windsor's claim of those individuals to the famous seven cities' claims as the birthplace of Homer. He continues writing of Windsor,

But whosoere it was, Nature design'd
First a brave place, and then as brave a mind.
Not to recount those several kings, to whom
It gave a cradle, or to whom a tomb,
But thee (great Edward) and thy greater son,
The lilies which his father wore, he won.

While Denham begins with praise for Windsor, he moves into an indictment of Henry VIII, which later critics saw as a direct attack on the English Reformation. The speaker transfers his consideration specifically to Chertsey Abbey, referring to a hill

whose top of late
A chapel crown'd, till in the common fate,
The adjoining Abbey fell: (may no such storm
Fall on our times, where ruin must reform).

Denham extends the abbey's ruin into a metaphor for the impending ruin of England, which must be set right by the king. For Henry he expresses disgust, writing,

Tell me (my Muse) what monstrous dire
  offence,
What crime could any Christian king incense
To such a rage? Was't luxury, or lust?
Was he so temperate, so chast, so just?
Were these their crimes? They were his own
  much more:
But wealth is crime enough to him that's poor.

As Denham berates Henry, by extension he praises his own monarch as a different type of ruler. However, some critics view Denham's approach as warning Charles I against royal despotism. He views Henry as a monster who spent all of the funds in the treasury for his own delights, who used "devotion's name" as a way to "varnish o'er the shame / of sacrilege."

While many Protestants may have also felt that Henry's action in breaking from the Catholic Church in order to annul his marriage to Queen Catherine and marry Anne Boleyn had been wrong, they felt the break a needed one. Denham lambastes present reformist Protestants, his personal political enemies, writing of their lethargy, which causes "Religion in a lazy cell, / In empty, airy contemplations dwell." As far as the speaker is concerned, the English people have been made to "wish for ignorance" of the terrible knowledge that the Anglican Church inflicts. They would "rather in the dark . . . grope our way, / Than [be] led by a false guide to err by day." He adds that Henry's change so affected England outsiders might wonder "What barbarous Invader sack'd the land?" This section is one to which critics point who argue against the theory that Denham presents a poem of concord and unity. His argument is definitely balanced in favor of the Royalists and against Protestant reformists as well as Catholicism, in favor of the Caroline Church of England's Episcopal and sacramentalist beliefs.

Denham next moves as part of his topographical consideration to the Thames River, considered the lifeblood of London and even of England:

My eye descending from the hill, surveys
Where Thames amongst the wanton valleys
  strays.
Thames, the most lov'd of all the Ocean's sons,
By his old sire to his embraces runs.

He next compares a river to the oceans it feeds, with their foam equated to "amber, and their gravel gold." By contrast, a river is more "genuine" and offers

less guilty wealth t'explore,
Search not his bottom, but survey his shore;

O'er which he kindly spreads his spacious wing,
And hatches plenty for th'ensuing Spring.

In those and lines that follow, Denham clearly notes the importance of the river to England's international trade. What he does not make clear is the political contention that such trade had sparked, as both England's navy and its maritime trade opposed the king's policies, including the rule of "tonnage and poundage," which applied customs duties to imported goods. As Boeckel thoroughly discusses, while Charles had legitimate right to regulate commerce, many citizens viewed his customs duties as an illegal tax. They grew out of the king's inability to work with the Parliaments of 1625 and 1626 and caused uproar in the third Parliament of 1629, emphasizing Charles's inability to compromise with elected officials. He followed with an additional tax, "ship money," based on an old regulation, whereby he taxed outside Parliament all of England to support his navy and foreign policy, giving him complete control. Another example of the king's exercise of royal absolutism, the tax on shipping commerce greatly increased his unpopularity. This knowledge does not detract from the lovely sense of Denham's description in his praise of the Thames as

Though deep, yet clear, though gentle, yet not
    dull,
Strong without rage, without o'er-flowing full.
Heaven her Eridanus no more shall boast,
Whose fame in thine, like lesser currents lost,
Thy nobler streams shall visit Jove's abodes.

But even in the first two lines of this passage, the reader might see a warning to the king to express his strength without anger, not to indulge in greed. As for most of the other Carolinian poets' warnings, this one would not be heeded by Charles. When the speaker touts the wealth taken to England through its foreign trade, however, Denham's contemporaries would be quick to note and counter that claim.

Denham's description continues, as he focuses on nature, first noting a paradox: "Wisely she knew, the harmony of things, / As well as that of sounds, from discords springs." He includes lines supporting an argument of balance for the poem, such as

While the steep horrid roughness of the wood
Strives with the gentle calmness of the flood.
Such huge extremes when nature doth unite,
Wonder from thence results, from thence
    delight.

Those wonders include a stream "transparent, pure, and clear." The speaker then turns to focus on a variety of mystical beings that arise from, and celebrate, the water, including "fairies, satyrs, and the nymphs their dames, / Their feasts, their revels, and their amorous flames."

Denham then transitions into a consideration of the realistic creatures that dwell in the nearby woods and fields and describes a famous hunt scene, also considered strongly polemic:

The stag now conscious of his fatal growth,
At once indulgent to his fear and sloth,
To some dark covert his retreat had made,
Where no man's eye, nor heaven's should
    invade
His soft repose.

However, the stag will be aroused by the sounds of dogs and hunters and employ "his strength, and then his speed, / His winged heels, and then his armed head" to escape, only to be traced through the scent of his hooves. When he seeks shelter in a herd, it "chases him from thence, or from him flies," so that

Like a declining statesman, left forlorn
To his friends' pity, and pursuers' scorn,
With shame remembers, while himself was one
Of the same herd, himself the same had done.

In a metaphoric hunt for liberty, Denham seems to reverse the land's guarantee of protection for all, based on the Magna Carta, creating an England where no mutual security exists and one portion of the population is desperate for protection. The shooting begins, and none of the stag's past triumphs can save the "Prince of the soil." As he turns to the water for solace, "fearless they pursue, nor can the flood / Quench their dire thirst; alas, they thirst for blood." The stag at least has the honor of dying by the king's "mortal shaft," and remaining "Proud of the wound," he resigns his blood. Denham then uses color imagery to suggest a curious reversal of victims when the speaker notes that the stag "stains the crystal with a purple flood." Because purple long symbolized royalty, he equates the king with the stag, again perhaps as a signal to Charles. The political rhetoric strengthens as the speaker notes that

the happier style of king and subject bear;
Happy, when both to the same center move,
When kings give liberty, and subjects love,

as he continues to reflect on the importance of the Magna Carta, writing, "Therefore not long in force this charter stood; / Wanting that seal, it must be seal'd in blood." He emphasizes through italicized print, "Who gives constrain'd, but his own fear reviles / Not thank'd, but scorn'd; nor are they gifts, but spoils." After that balanced thought, Denham offers advice: "Thus kings, by grasping more than they could hold, / First made their subjects by oppression bold." Again, he cautions against royal tyranny, but he insists that subjects share the blame, continuing,

And popular sway, by forcing kings to give
More than was fit for subjects to receive,
Ran to the same extremes; and one excess
Made both, by striving to be greater less.

He concludes by comparing political forces to the natural forces that cause a river to overrun its banks, noting that if "husbandmen" have wisely "with high-rais'd banks" secured "Their greedy hopes," the king can endure the rising. However, if "bays" and "dams" are employed in an attempt "to force

His channel to a new, or narrow course;
No longer then within his banks he dwells,
First to a torrent, then a deluge swells:
Stronger, and fiercer by restraint he roars,
And knows no bound, but makes his power his
    shores.

Denham cautions power-hungry individuals not to force the king, as the monarch will react by extending his powers until boundaries remain unrecognizable.

As Boeckel notes, *Cooper's Hill* remains applicable to any era that experiences a culture war. He characterizes Denham and the Royalists as "belligerents" who exclusively claim ideals and symbols that others may also value. Their opponents are not allowed also to lay claim, as the belligerents monopolize ideology to make themselves appear legitimate, the only group allowed to represent "national authority and identity." Readers may recognize belligerents in their own cultures.

Whichever one of the multiple readings of *Cooper's Hill* one may accept, it remains important for its effect on 18th-century writers. Had it not been for this poem, Denham's loss of popularity might have been complete.

BIBLIOGRAPHY
Boeckel, Bruce. "Landscaping the Field of Discourse: Political Slant and Poetic Slope in Sir John Denham's 'Cooper's Hill.'" *Papers on Language & Literature* 34, no. 1 (winter 1998): 57–93.
O'Hehir, Brendan. *Expans'd Heiroglyphicks: A Critical Edition of Sir John Denham's Cooper's Hill.* Berkeley: University of California Press, 1969.
Scanlon, Thomas. "Overcoming History: Topicality in Denham's 'Cooper's Hill.'" *Renaissance Papers,* 1991, 43–52.
Turner, James Grantham. *The Politics of Landscape: Rural Scenery and Society in English Poetry, 1630–1660,* 49–61. Oxford: B. Blackwell, 1979.
Wallace, John L. "Cooper's Hill: The Manifesto of Parliamentary Royalism, 1641." *English Literary History* 41, no. 4 (1974): 494–540.
Wasserman, Earl. "Denham: Cooper's Hill." In *The Subtler Language: Critical Readings of Neoclassical and Romantic Poems,* 45–88. Baltimore: Johns Hopkins University Press, 1959.

"CORINNA'S GOING A MAYING" ROBERT HERRICK (1648) ROBERT HERRICK wrote "Corinna's Going a Maying" as a contribution to the popular CARPE DIEM poems of his day. Those verses urged readers or listeners to make the most of the present, as time would produce a sure decline followed by death. They urged their audiences to accept today as the best day during which to act, because one could never positively count on another day to follow. Such poetry often incorporated imagery of growing things already threatened in their prime by death. The traditional idea had been present in ancient poetry, including that of the Hebrews, as well as in Roman and Greek poetry. However, the latter groups stressed the positive aspect of accepting death as inevitable and then enjoying all that life had to offer. Horace, Tibullus, Propertius, Ovid, Publius Syrus, and Seneca all celebrated the pleasure of the moment, according to the Herrick biographer George Walton Scott. Horace provided a direct descent for carpe diem, derived from the Latin infinitive *carpere,* in many instances representing the action of gathering fruits or flowers, just as one would gather, or pluck, a "ripe" day. In "Corinna," Herrick does conclude on a serious note, alluding to death after a celebration of the promise of May. In the end, time will cheat even the most abundant of lives; thus, one must extend time by thoroughly enjoying each available moment.

The poem's structure includes 70 lines of rhyming couplets with varying METER. Five stanzas of 14 lines each contain two lines of iambic pentameter, followed by three lines of tetrameter, with that pattern repeated in a second set of five lines. The season is spring, specifically at the beginning of the month of May, and the speaker urges his audience, every "budding Boy, or Girlie," to "bring in May," an admonition to harvest time.

The opening line labels the morn as "Blooming," as the speaker calls all sleepers to arise and celebrate day. Herrick references "Aurora," the goddess of the dawn, and calls on imagery of the dawn's "fresh-quilted colors" and "The Dew-bespangling Herbe and Tree," as well as "Each Flower" and birds, including the traditional singer of the day, the Lark, "to fetch in May." While the tone remains light and teasing, it also betrays a sense of urgency. If the audience remains in bed an hour after the dawn, precious time will be wasted. Herrick also references Virgins in line 13, a traditional reference, used seductively by CAVALIER POETS, but simply indicating an untried and as yet immature being in this poem. Herrick extends his use of FIGURATIVE LANGUAGE with plant and growth metaphors. The second stanza suggests those the speaker calls "put on your Foliage" and "come forth, like the Spring-time, fresh and greene." Participants in the celebration may eschew

"Jewels for your Gowne, or Haire," as "leaves will strew / Gems in abundance upon you." In addition, the young day retains "some Orient Pearls unwept," an allusion to dew, whose sparkling diamondlike appearance in the bright sun was often compared to jewels. Herrick does not insist that the maidens to whom he speaks ignore their faith. His speaker merely bids them to "be brief in praying: / Few Beads are best," with the beads referencing prayer beads. In the third stanza the speaker addresses Corinna, a representative of all young virgins, bidding her to notice "How each field turns a street; each street a Parke / Made green, and trimm'd with trees," while each house is decorated with boughs or branches. Herrick references biblical verses that describe the use of parts of trees and bushes in celebrations and mentions the "white-thorn," a traditional symbol of both joy and pain. The stanza concludes with the command to "sin no more," as spring represents a new beginning, or a life without sin.

By the fourth stanza, all boys and girls are intent on bringing in May, having gone into the fields and returned with the white-thorn after eating "Cakes and Cream." They may later dream or weep or plight their troth, choosing their priest, exchanging kisses and glances, and telling jokes. In short, a celebration of coupling and, by extension, propagation of the human race is under way. Herrick strongly emphasizes the carpe diem philosophy in his fifth stanza, which reads:

> Come, let us go, while we are in our prime;
> And take the harmless follie of the time.
>> We shall grow old apace, and die
>> Before we know our liberty.
>> Our life is short; and our dayes run
>> As fast away as do's the Sunne:
> And as a vapour, or a drop of raine
> Once lost, can ne'r be found againe: (57–64)

Herrick uses stock references to the popular theme of fleeting time, including the sun running across the sky as the mythical Apollo, driving his fiery horse-pulled chariot that hauls the sun from east to west. He next references art as the only way to beat time at his own game, writing, "So when or you or I are made / A fable, song, or fleeting shade." However, little satisfaction exists today in the knowledge that one may remain alive as a literary reference or a recognized spirit. Rather, humans favor "All love, all liking, all delight," but that joy "Lies drown'd with us in endlesse night," the night symbolizing the dark of the unknown represented by death. The penultimate line loses some of the upbeat tone in a solemn reference, "Then while time serves, and we are but decaying," which alludes to the theory that organisms begin to die as soon as they are born. It also allows further extension of the comparison of humans to plant life, each having its specific life cycle. Herrick does conclude with a repeat call to enjoy the day as his speaker bids, "Come, my Corinna, come, let's go a Maying."

A priest as well as a poet, Herrick called upon Hebrew tradition in addition to classical tradition in which to ground his theme. As noted by G. W. Scott, the second book of *The Wisdom of Solomon,* a poetic discourse in Greek, probably written by a Hellenistic Jew assuming the identity of the biblical Solomon, may have provided a model. It carries the admonition that "in the death of man there is no remedy," and the spark that represents his life will be extinguished. Therefore, man should "enjoy the good things that are present; and let us speedily use the creatures like as in youth . . . and let no flower of the spring pass by us."

BIBLIOGRAPHY
Scott, George Walton. *Robert Herrick.* New York: St. Martin's Press, 1974.

"CORRUPTION" HENRY VAUGHAN (1650)

In his poem "Corruption," HENRY VAUGHAN offers comfort to Christians living in a corrupt era filled with the woes predicted by the biblical book of Revelation to precede the return of Christ and his earthly reign. The poem opens with a sad but accepting tone, as the speaker states of man's early days on Earth, immediately following his eviction from the Garden of Eden,

> Sure it was so. Man in those early days
>   Was not all stone and earth;
> He shined a little, and by those weak rays
>   Had some glimpse of his birth.

In other words, despite his sinful state, man could recall something of his once-sinless nature, prior to his fall from God's grace through sin. The allusion to light with "weak rays" contrasts to the strong light often referenced in the Bible as a product of knowledge or epiphany. Light also symbolized Christ, particularly as it is used in the opening to the Gospel of John. While man's knowledge at that early point remained "weak," it was at least present.

The poem's imagery emphasizes man's transient state, as when Vaughan compares him to plants, which die at the end of each growing season. He avoids references to nature's abundance of fruits and flowers present in the garden, instead suggesting everything after the fall proved worthless and even harmful, as "a thorn or a weed," adding "Nor did those last, but (like himself) died still / As soon as they did seed." Adopting PARADOX, Vaughan emphasizes IRONY in the fact that as soon as a birth occurs, whether human or vegetation, death immediately takes hold and disintegration begins. This long and sure death results from man's sinful nature, which separates him from God. Rather than providing man easy nourishment, as the plants did in Eden, these plants that man must toil and suffer to cultivate "seemed to quarrel with him" because of "that act / That felled him" and "foiled them all." Man's actions in disobeying God drew a curse on every aspect of the world. In Vaughan's imagination, man longed for the time of his creation, believing that "still Paradise lay / In some green shade or fountain" where angels existed.

Eden remains a dim memory, and man's actions have all but destroyed the once beautiful and supportive earth, as well as man's originally divine nature. Vaughan suggests that, as a result of man's sinful acts, the time of troubles predicted by Revelation has arrived. He saw it in the raging of the Civil War that took the life of his brother and disillusioned many. The biblical Gospel of Mark noted that brother would betray brother, as in the domestic conflict that pitted family against family. The speaker describes a scene of insanity representing a loss of control causing man to engage in self-destructive and illogical acts. He begins by questioning where God has hidden his love for man, as he writes in lines 29–32,

> Almighty Love! Where art thou now? Mad man
>   Sits down and freezeth on;

He raves, and swears to stir nor fire, nor fan,
>   But bids the thread be spun.

In this passage, the final line may be interpreted to mean that man takes no action to change his fate, simply accepting it, as one allowing a thread to be spun on a wheel. Vaughan illustrates this idea by describing man as choosing to freeze when he might instead build a fire to prevent his own destruction. The fire also represents purification of man's sinful soul, something God cannot accomplish unless man repents and turns from his corrupt ways.

The poem emphasizes one of several paradoxes that inform Christianity, in this case, that the worse circumstances become, the greater hope Christians may have of improvement, as those circumstances will preface the end of time as man knows it. That ending would be followed by the new beginning that supported the most important of the Christian paradoxes; one must die in order to live. The poem's conclusion alludes to chapter 13 in Revelation with the lines describing the triumph of sin and the sinking of man below "The center," with the world described as being in "deep sleep and night;" in which "thick darkness lies / And hatcheth o'er thy people." This description of the present time marked by a lack of light, or knowledge and redemption, is tempered by the final two lines. Although couched in question form, they allude to Revelation 14:15, where an angel commands one "that sat on the cloud, 'Thrust in thy sickle, and reap.'" The reaping results in a time of harvest, and Vaughan suggests that the time of God's harvest of human souls is near, as he questions, "But hark! What trumpet's that? What angel cries, / 'Arise! Thrust in thy sickle'?" Vaughan's readers would have been well informed about the book of Revelation and would know the words that follow his quotation.

BIBLIOGRAPHY

Rudrum, Alan. *Henry Vaughan*. Cardiff: University of Wales Press, 1981.

"COTSWOLD ECLOGUE" Thomas Randolph (?)

The "Cotswold Eclogue" by Thomas Randolph appears in excerpts in many anthologies as a beautiful example of the pastoral. Randolph's early death prevented his having much of an impact on British poetry, but many critics believe that had he lived, his influence would have been great. Contrary to his odes, such as "Ode to Master Anthony Stafford," which seemed more exercises in the classical approach, his eclogue is deemed creative and written with seeming ease.

The eclogue format is traditional, with Colin, a common name for a shepherd, in dialogue with others, including Thenot. In one section, the two discuss the high price to pay should the typical celebratory atmosphere of the shepherds' domain shift to that of melancholy. Colin describes the May celebration of times past as "the jolly rout," with young men literally jumping through the air. As one was "coursing" from a beech to a mulberry tree, "A second leap'd his supple nerves to try; / A third was practicing his melody," the latter a reference to the pipe playing often celebrated in the pastoral. Young women crown the winners of the celebration that culminates in a winning of a bell to honor "the nut-brown lady of the May." The crowns consist of flower garlands "With daisies, pinks and many a violet, / Cowslip, and gillyflower."

The joyful ceremony to welcome spring is in no manner a debauched celebration. Colin makes this clear when he notes the rewards of the sporting games are small, but they "Encourage virtue." Then he cautions lest virtue "languisheth and die" if continued support for sport is withdrawn. The "dull and general lethargy" practiced by those of more melancholy nature endangers the virtue for which the country folk remain well known. Thenot's reply is to the point: "I'll thrive the lout that did their mirth gainsay! / Wolves haunt his flocks that took those sports away!" The threat against the flock remains important in the context of the pastoral.

Colin continues his support of the celebration, characterizing the "phlegm and sanguine" of those discouraging celebration as personality aspects that should "no religions be." The naysayers equate dancing to the work of "Jezebel," a reference to the biblical woman of the world who was fated to be torn apart in the streets by dogs, while the songs and dances are "profane relics." This misplaced "zeal" that the shepherds intend to counter Colin blames on the influence of the city, where "sport" is considered "a dish proper to th' Court." Randolph employs a favored description of city and court life as "foppery," closing that section by noting that courtiers should avoid mirth, while the swains, or shepherds, were born to the life of sport:

Mirth not becomes 'em; let the saucy swain
Eat beef and bacon, and go sweat again.
Besides, what sport can in the pastimes be,
When all is but ridiculous foppery?

COWLEY, ABRAHAM (1618–1667)

Abraham Cowley was born in London after the death of his father, who had been a successful stationer. At 10 years of age he published the romantic epic *Pyramus and Thisbe* and before age 15 published a collection of poems titled *Poetical Blossoms,* which gained considerable notice. By age 20 Cowley had also written a Latin comedy titled *Love's Riddle* (1638). He attended Westminster School and Trinity College in Cambridge, his precocious reputation having preceded him; completed his bachelor's degree in 1639; became a fellow in 1640; and completed his master's degree in 1643, the same year he published his satire *The Puritan and the Papist.* He joined other writers, including the devotional poets RICHARD CRASHAW and JOHN CLEVELAND, in the loss of his status as a fellow when anti-Royalist forces took over Parliament. By the time of the Civil War, Cowley had left Cambridge of his own volition, supported the king at Oxford, and eventually joined Queen Henrietta Maria in exile in 1644 in France, where he served as her secretary. According to Thomas Humphry Ward, he became "so famous at thirty that pirates and forgers made free with his name on their title-pages." While living in France with the court, he may have met Margaret Lucas, later MARGARET CAVENDISH, DUCHESS OF NEWCASTLE, who served as the queen's lady in waiting in 1643–45. Upon her return to England she would gain fame as one of the first women poets to publish voluminously.

Cowley published a collection of approximately 100 lyrics in 1647 titled *The Mistress: or Several copies of Love Verses.* It would be included in a larger 1656 collection, containing additional poetry titled *Miscellanies, Pindaric Odes,* as well as four books based on Old Testament writings about King David titled *Davideis.* That first folio of his *Works* would go through eight editions, indicating his popularity.

When Cowley returned to England in 1654, he was imprisoned for a time until he apparently agreed to comply with the Cromwellians, although historians believe he may have served as a Royalist spy. He used the opportunity to earn an additional degree in medicine, graduating from Oxford in 1657. After the Restoration, the queen made a land grant to Cowley and he regained his Cambridge fellowship. In 1660 he published "Ode upon the Blessed Restoration" and a year later, *A Discourse By Way of Vision Concerning the Government of Oliver Cromwell.* Later in 1661, he published *Proposition for the Advancement of Experimental Philosophy,* having moved to Chertsey to study botany and write essays. One year after his death a folio edition of his works appeared, *Several Discourses by way of Essays, in Verse and Prose,* on which his reputation was later based.

Although the popularity evidenced by Cowley's grand burial in Westminster Abbey near Chaucer and Edmund Spenser did not last, he greatly influenced later writers, including ALEXANDER POPE. CHARLES DRYDEN noted about Cowley in 1700, "Though he must always be thought a great poet, he is no longer esteemed a good writer." Ironically some critics feel it was Dryden's adaptation and advancement of Cowley's methods that reduced the highly intellectual poet's popularity; as Humphry notes, "Dryden absorbed all that was best in Cowley, and superseded him for the readers of the 18th century, and the nineteenth century, which reads Dryden little, naturally reads Cowley less." Nevertheless, Cowley became the first entry in SAMUEL JOHNSON's *The Lives of the Poets* (1779).

Modern sentiment would concur with Dryden's opinion. Today's readers, for example, would not find much to admire in Cowley's love lyric "Written in Juice of Lemon." The title in itself introduces unintentional humor through the jarring juxtaposition of a sour liquid with the emotion of love. Cowley's CONCEIT of written poetry that will be made visible only through contact with his love's body heat proves clumsy at best. His awkward vision of a paper on which,

. . . when a genial heat warms thee within,
A new-born wood of various lines there grows;
Here buds an A, and there a B,
Here sprouts a V, and there a T,
And all the flourishing letters stand in rows,

offers little for an ear tuned to graceful expression. Rather than softened and sweet, the poet's love appears angular and rough, his tone not at all sensitive or receptive. A more widely anthologized example of a tepid lyric is "The SPRING," discussed in this volume for the sake of illustration.

However, Cowley did produce poetry that pleases the more sophisticated reader of later ages. He proved at his best in the verses that conclude his essay on solitude, titled simply "ON SOLITUDE"; in his odes, such as "ODE TO THE ROYAL SOCIETY"; and in "HYMN TO LIGHT." All in all, the 21st century finds Cowley of interest mainly as a historic figure, and his art of note for its wide variety and strong voice. But as a poet prefiguring a century that would, for a time, embrace rationality to a fault, Cowley in his habit of calm, unemotional reflection and sound judgment proved empowering to his own new scientific era, that of the Restoration.

BIBLIOGRAPHY

Ward, Thomas Humphry, ed. "Thomas Cowley." In *The English Poets: Selections with Critical Introductions by Various Writers*. Vol. 2, 234–243. New York: Macmillan, 1914.

COWLEY, HANNAH PARKHOUSE (1743– 1809)

Hannah Parkhouse Cowley was born in Tiverton, Devon. Her father, Philip, sold books, and her mother may have been related to the poet JOHN GAY. She married Thomas Cowley, a Stamp Office clerk, at age 25 and soon after began writing plays. Living in London, she went often to the theater and decided to try her hand at drama. According to some accounts, she declared that she could easily match the quality of the plays she and her husband watched. The famous actor David Garrick read and revised her first effort, *The Runaway*, and recommended it to Richard Cumberland, and it enjoyed a successful run at Drury Lane in 1776. The 800 guineas Cowley received encouraged her to produce additional plays, as her family needed the income. Twelve additional comedies, tragedies,

and farces were produced by 1795, including a favorite of the court, *The Belle's Strategem* (1780), which Cowley dedicated to the Queen; she reportedly received 1,200 guineas for that drama. Although not a popular figure and often described as vulgar and ill behaved, Cowley became the most successful female playwright at the end of the 18th century. She earned her negative reputation in part as a result of her sensitivity, at one point making a public complaint to Garrick regarding his servant's actions toward her and her husband. She also accused the popular writer Hannah More of plagiarizing from her drama *Albina*. She did not take part in "literary society" and apparently enjoyed reading travel books far more than reading poetry.

For unexplained reasons, Cowley's husband signed on to serve with the East India Company and departed England in 1783. The marriage seems to have been a contented one, as Cowley dedicated a comedy, *More Vows Than One* (1784), to her husband, and *The Fate of Sparta* (1788) to a brother-in-law. The Cowleys had two daughters, who studied in France, where their mother visited them in 1788; one daughter died in 1790, still a teenager. Cowley dedicated her final play, *The Town Before You* (1795), to a woman in Calcutta, leading historians to surmise that she may have visited the country.

Cowley's poetry did not enjoy the level of fame her drama achieved. She first published *The Maid of Aragon: A Tale* in 1780, followed by *The Scottish Village, or Pitcairne Green* (1786); then wrote for *The World* under the name Anna Matilda, leading some critics to ridicule her work. Florid and characterized by high sentiment, works such as *The Poetry of Anna Matilda* (1788), *The Poetry of the World* (1788), and *The British Album* (1790) earned derision by other poets, most especially William Gifford in *The Baviad*. Her husband died in India in 1797, after an attempted visit to his daughter, who was in Calcutta at the time. A short time later, Cowley moved back to Tiverton. While she did not participate in others' societal gatherings, she invited "ladies only" to gather at her house weekly. After her death, her *Works* (1813) were published in three volumes and included a brief memoir written by Cowley, as well as the later anthologized poem "Departed

Youth," written in 1797 and possibly inspired by the loss of her husband.

BIBLIOGRAPHY

Lonsdale, Roger. *Eighteenth-Century Women Poets.* New York: Oxford University Press, 1990.

COWPER, WILLIAM (1731–1800)

William Cowper (pronounced Cooper) was born in Herfordshire, where his father was a rector. He attended private school as a child, his sensitive nature suffering from bullying, and later continued his education at Westminster School and the Middle Temple in London. Although called to the bar in 1754, he chose not to practice, because of the onset of depression, which eventually led him into periods of madness. He would have married his cousin, Theodora Cowper, except for his father's interference. His father feared the results of a union of two so closely related people.

By age 32, Cowper suffered from grave mental illness, apparently arising from his belief that he was eternally damned. An uncle hoped to help him by nominating him as clerk of the Journals of the House of Lords, but he so feared the process that he attempted suicide. The depression seemed relieved by writing poetry, which never hinted at Cowper's madness. After Cowper's first bout of depression, his doctor managed to convince him that his preoccupation with sin was a product of delusion. Cured temporarily of his dementia, he settled at Huntingdon, enjoying a small income and the constant support of friends.

Cowper turned to religion for comfort and lived for a time with an Evangelical clergyman, Morley Unwin, and his family. Mrs. Unwin allowed Cowper to remain after her husband's death, and he stayed with her until 1796. In 1765, the two relocated from Huntington to Olney and became followers of John Newton, another Evangelical preacher. Under Newton's influence, Cowper contributed entries, such as "God Moves in a Mysterious Way," to Newton's *Olney Hymns,* which would still be sung by Methodist congregations centuries later. Cowper planned to marry Mary Unwin but suffered another attack of delusions, in part due to the intellectual challenge he felt from Newton. He again believed himself a sinner, forever condemned by God.

With Mary Unwin's care Cowper recovered enough by 1776 to interact with friends. He responded to a book written by a cousin, Martin Madan, supporting polygamy with *Anti-Thelypthora: a Tale in Verse* (1781) and began a series of satires titled *Poems* (1782) at Mary's urging. Cowper wrote in a fury, attempting to counteract his despair, producing six books of BLANK VERSE titled *The Task* (1785), which would make him famous. As the story goes, he had complained over the lack of a subject for his poetry. Supposedly one Lady Austen challenged him to write about his own sofa. He began that task and gained a title for his book, constructing a humorous MOCK-HEROIC about the sofa's early life as a stool. The verse metamorphosed into more than 5,000 lines of meditative verse, filled with details about his surroundings and his political era. Although in a delicate and modulated tone, Cowper indicted so-called civilized man for his involvement in slavery and war, and for the corruption that grew from a desire for every luxury. For distraction he also tended a garden, enjoyed animals, and carried on a voluminous correspondence, his letters later admired for their clear, straightforward style. Not artful as the mode of the day required, the correspondence reflected Cowper's life in the country, captured in vivid detail.

Cowper wrote the comic *The Diverting History of John Gilpin* (1782) and individual poems including "The Poplar Field," "On the Loss of the Royal George," and a well-received sonnet, "To Mrs. Unwin." Additional work included "LIGHT SHINING OUT OF DARKNESS" and "The NEGRO'S COMPLAINT," the latter expressing his conviction regarding the evils of slavery. It had a first printing as a BROADSIDE and was set to music as a BALLAD. He began a translation of Homer and gained solid subscriptions to the project, which would be published in 1791. Additional translations would include works from Latin, Italian, and French. After Mary's death in 1794 he sank into complete dejection and became an invalid, although he managed to write the powerful but depressing "The CASTAWAY," published posthumously. He lived on a pension after 1794, dying six years later at East Dereham, Norfolk.

Anthologized selections from *The Task* include "A LANDSCAPE DESCRIBED. RURAL SOUNDS," "CRAZY KATE," "The STRICKEN DEER," and "The WINTER EVENING, A

BROWN STUDY." Some early critics judged Cowper's works lacking in intellect, but later critics and readers found much to appreciate in his quiet verse, which never claimed to do more than examine and expose the quotidian. His work proved important in the evolution of poetic style and theme from the 18th century's focus on neoclassicism to the new concerns of the next century.

BIBLIOGRAPHY

Baird, John D., and Charles Ryskamp, ed. *The Poems of William Cowper.* New York: Oxford University Press, 1996.

Brunstrom, Conrad. *William Cowper.* Lewisburg, Pa.: Bucknell University Press, 2004.

Heller, Deborah. "Cowper's 'Task' and the Writing of a Poet's Salvation." *Studies in English Literature, 1500–1900* 35 (summer 1995): 575–598.

Huntley, Dana. "Newton and Cowper: The Olney Hymns." *British Heritage* 26, no. 1 (March 2005): 28–33.

King, James, ed. *The Letters and Prose Writing of William Cowper.* 5 vols. Oxford: Clarendon Press, 1979–1986.

Packer, Barbara. "Hope and Despair in the Writings of William Cowper." *Social Research* 66, no. 2 (summer 1999): 545.

CRABBE, GEORGE (1754–1832)

Born in the Suffolk seaport of Aldeburgh, George Crabbe knew poverty much of his life. His father worked collecting salt duties and could not send his son to private school, but George was educated in Bungay and Stowmarket. He learned the surgeon's craft but began to publish verse in 1772, placing a poem in *Wheble's Magazine* and publishing anonymously a more important piece, *Inebriety,* in 1775. In the latter he imitated ALEXANDER POPE's satiric approach, focusing on the perils of alcohol. He tried to earn a living in Aldeburgh after his surgical internship but continued to read and write, with one of his favorite topics being botany. He finally decided he could never support himself in the small village and moved to London in 1780. Crabbe hoped to earn a decent wage and marry his longtime love, Sarah Elmy, to whom he had been engaged since 1772. Unable to find employment and reaching desperation, Crabbe maintained faith in his writing abilities. He decided to ask the famous philosopher and politician Edmund Burke for help. Crabbe clearly impressed Burke, appealing to him as a stranger on the verge of entering debtors' prison. Burke, who first became a member of Parliament (M.P.) in 1774, was able to use his influence to promote Crabbe.

Thanks to Burke's efforts, Crabbe published *The Library* (1781) and then stayed with Burke at Beaconsfield. There he continued writing while Burke introduced him to important individuals, including Sir Joshua Reynolds, who convinced Crabbe to consider serving the church. He agreed and took holy orders, becoming an Anglican minister. His service to the duke of Rutland as chaplain from 1782 to 1785 allowed him at last to marry Sarah Elmy in 1783. His *The* VILLAGE (1783) confirmed his reputation as a poet, after revision by none other than SAMUEL JOHNSON who praised the lengthy collection of heroic couplets. His next effort was a 1784 memoir of Lord Robert Manners, brother to the duke of Rutland, killed at sea. He followed that effort with a 1785 satire, *The Newspaper.* Crabbe wrote nothing of note for more than two decades, destroying some of his work during that time. In 1789 he moved to Muston, Leicestershire, and worked there until 1814 but took up a living at Suffolk from 1792 to 1805. At some point his wife began to suffer from mental illness.

Crabbe began a second productive writing phase, publishing *The Parish Register* (1807), judged a fine example of verse narrative. It included the critically praised "Sir Eustace Grey" in eight-line stanzas, a poem focusing on the hallucinations of an insane asylum inhabitant, suggesting that Crabbe may have been under the influence of opium as he wrote. He published *The Borough* in 1810, a poem composed of 24 "letters" featuring small town life, and *Tales* two years later. Sarah died in 1813 after a long period of manic depression, and Crabbe fell ill for some time. He took up the vicarage of Trowbridge, Wiltshire, in 1814 and was engaged to Charlotte Ridout, but that relationship quickly ended.

Frequent visits to London acquainted him with notables including Thomas Moore and the poets Robert Southey and William Wordsworth, who, along with George Gordon, Lord Byron, admired his work. They found particularly admirable Crabbe's realistic approach, narrative, and characterization. His son would later publish a story of his father's life that included Crabbe's *London Journal* (1817); Crabbe also published in 1817 *The World of Dreams* followed by *Tales of the Hall* (1819). He later became friends with the novelist and poet Sir Walter Scott, and the novelist Jane Austen publicly admired Crabbe's work. He continued to publish, releasing *In a Neat Cottage* (1822) and a collected edition of his *Works* (1823) in several volumes. At his death he left several unpublished pieces, which would later be published as part of the eight-volume *The Poetical Works* (1834).

Although much of Crabbe's publishing occurred in the 19th century, his *The Village,* excerpts of which are widely anthologized, is a product of 18th-century sensibilities. He exhibited Augustan characteristics in his value of the heroic couplet and in his sustained focus on judgment, rationality, and moderation. While 21st-century readers may find some of his language stilted and outmoded, it remains notable for its negative tone, as well as its skill in form. Crabbe's realistic pessimism contrasted with the traditional idyllic approach to rural description, such as that found in work by his predecessor WILLIAM COWPER. He introduced originality in his unrelenting investigation of the tension between the suffering of poverty, which he knew all too well, and the supposed ideal of country living. In 1945 an opera titled *Peter Grimes* was produced with a prologue based on Crabbe's *The Borough.*

BIBLIOGRAPHY

Crabbe, George. *The Life of George Crabbe, by His Son.* London: Cresset Press, 1947.

Faulkner, Thomas C., ed. *Selected Journals and Letters of George Crabbe.* New York: Oxford Press, 1985.

Nelson, Beth. *George Crabbe and the Progress of Eighteenth-Century Narrative Verse.* Lewisburg, Pa.: Bucknell University Press, 1976.

CRASHAW, RICHARD (1613–1649)

RICHARD CRASHAW was born the only child of William Crashaw, a Puritan preacher and rabid anti-Catholic. His father's vocation probably helped determine the tumultuous nature of his later spiritual life, although both of his parents died while he was still a teenager. Educated at Pembroke College, Cambridge, a High Church college, Crashaw graduated in 1634. That same year he published Latin epigrams on scriptural matters titled *Epigrammatum sacrorum liber,* which helped him win a fellowship in 1635. When the Royalists were defeated in the Civil War, Crashaw lost his fellowship in 1644, but he had already left Cambridge. He had long preferred ritual and ceremony to the barrenness of his father's religion; that preference contributed to his conversion to Roman Catholicism after two years in exile from England, along with fellow exiles WILLIAM COWLEY, the countess of Denbigh, and Queen Henrietta Maria. He lived as a Catholic for his last five years, taking up residence on the Continent and ultimately in Rome. He held a minor position at the Loreto cathedral at the time of his death.

An admirer of GEORGE HERBERT, Crashaw wrote religious poetry, although he did not emulate Herbert. Herbert's influence as a fellow Cambridge graduate who achieved an academic reputation with his spiritual poetry proved obvious in the title of Crashaw's *Steps to the Temple* (1646). However, where Herbert's verse exhibits grace and intimacy, Crashaw's verse is a study in hyperbole that often results in grotesque imagery. His passionate nature and expressive faith affected his diction and resulted in what the critic George Simcox refers to as an "epidemic of conceits," often with a ludicrous result. For example, in his brief poem "To the Infant Martyrs," he focuses on infants who have been murdered for a cause, a group who should elicit pity and admiration. Instead, Crashaw offers them a bad pun on mother's milk in his final line: "Go, smiling souls, your new-built cages break / In heaven you'll learn to sing, ere here to speak / Nor let the milky fonts that bathe your thirst / Be your delay / the place that calls you hence is, at the worst, / Milk all the way." One almost wishes not to recognize in the final line a play on the celestial Milky Way. On the other hand, Crashaw also produced poems admirable for their simple rhythm and sound, such as "DESCRIPTION OF A RELIGIOUS HOUSE," and has been described as having a style smoother and more fluent than those of the tame Herbert, with whom his ferocious energy contrasted.

Crashaw published *Sacred Epigrams* in Latin (1634), a posthumous version of which contained some epigrams in Greek translations as well. With the help of a person identified only as "an English friend," he combined *Steps to the Temple* and a collection of secular poems, *The Delights of the Muses,* for publication in 1646; his last work would be a collection titled *Carme Deo Nostro,* published in Paris in 1652. Additional individual works were later discovered. Anthologized selections include "I AM THE DOOR," and "ON THE WOUNDS OF OUR CRUCIFIED LORD," both excellent examples containing grotesque metaphors, and "IN THE HOLY NATIVITY OF OUR LORD GOD: A HYMN SUNG AS BY THE SHEPHERDS," "The FLAMING HEART UPON THE BOOK AND PICTURE OF THE SERAPHICAL SAINT TERESA," and "To the Noblest & Best of Ladies, the Countess of Denbigh."

Other influences included Jesuits specializing in Latin epigrams and the Italian writer Giambattista Marino, another poet who embraced the grotesque. Among Crashaw's several translations was a portion of Marino's *The Massacre of the Innocents,* a poem whose violent topic would have attracted him. His blatant focus on torture and death at times verged on the sadistic, with no redemption to be found in any well-turned phrase. However, his zeal cannot be denied, nor his energy; he was known to engage in constant revision. He produced among his scant work only one secular lyric, "Wishes: To His (Supposed) Mistress."

Much of Crashaw's work elicited scorn from readers in later centuries. However, his excesses remained so consistent that they admitted the skill he exhibited in following a format similar to the baroque. All of his works boast elaborately drawn titles containing varied lettering and stacks of lines that have been compared to baroque architecture. Twenty-first-century readers may be ready to embrace Crashaw as an accomplished artist with sensibilities found more acceptable in a post-postmodern culture. He produces a disturbing collage of topics at once spiritual and erotic, innocent and cynical, his tone verging on exhibitionism. Although his works were once received with derision, Crashaw's poetry gained favor from a more widespread understanding of the manner by which one art affects another, offering insight into Crashaw's greatly embellished style. He intended that his form reflect that of the baroque, and he achieved his goal.

BIBLIOGRAPHY

Bennett, Joan. *Five Metaphysical Poets: Donne, Herbert, Vaughan, Crashaw, Marvell.* Cambridge: Cambridge University Press, 1964.

Bertanasco, Marc F. *Crashaw and the Baroque.* Tuscaloosa: University of Alabama Press, 1971.

Di Cesare, Ed. *George Herbert and the Seventeenth-Century Religious Poets: Authoritative Texts Criticism.* New York: W. W. Norton, 1978.

Roberts, John R. *New Perspectives on the Life and Art of Richard Crashaw.* Columbia: University of Missouri Press, 1990.

Simcox, G. A. "Sandys, Herbert, Crashaw, Vaughan." In *The English Poets: Selections with Critical Introductions,* edited by Thomas Humphry Ward, 192–198. New York: Macmillan, 1914.

Williams, George Walton. *Image and Symbol in the Sacred Poetry of Richard Crashaw.* Columbia: University of South Carolina Press, 1967.

"CRAZY KATE" WILLIAM COWPER (1785)

WILLIAM COWPER included the poem "Crazy Kate" in book 1 of his six-volume BLANK VERSE collection *The Task.* As did the other poems, "Crazy Kate" provided readers with a glimpse of Cowper's village environment, populated with figures such as Kate. Her story is a traditional tale of a woman driven insane by the loss of love; in this case, Kate's sailor lover dies at sea. She spends the remainder of her days in tattered formal clothing, living in the fantasy world of madness, as she awaits his return. Cowper begins in the midst of action, writing in the style of the folktale,

> There often wanders one, whom better days
> Saw better clad, in cloak of satin trimmed
> With lace, and hat with splendid ribband
>   bound.

Repetition of the term *better* emphasizes a change in fortune for the "one" he describes, with the term *wander* connoting an aimless movement. Cowper employs repetition in sound as well, making abundant use of the letter *s* and practicing ALLITERATION with the consonant *c.*

This poor soul had been a "servingmaid" who loved "one who left her, went to sea, and died." The speaker supplies no details regarding the sailor but offers instead a fatalistic series of actions: the sailor left, he went, he died. Such brevity allows focus to remain on the woman left behind. She immediately dissolves into "fancy," imagining her lover sailing "foaming waves / To distant shores," weeping at the idea that he might suffer at sea. As the speaker points out, imagination most deludes "where warmest wishes are," and she often anticipated "his glad return." Kate becomes a sympathetic figure, lacking the strength that one might believe a servant to possess, dreaming "of transports she was not to know." She never smiled after hearing "the doleful tidings of his death," her blank mind leading her to roam

> The dreary waste; there spends the livelong day,
> And there, unless when charity forbids,
> The livelong night.

Kate is trapped in an endless longing, emphasized by Cowper's repetition of the term *livelong* in describing the endless cycles of day and night. A pitiful figure, her

> . . . tattered apron hides
> Worn as a cloak, and hardly hides, a gown
> More tattered still; and both but ill conceal
> A bosom heaved with never-ceasing sighs.

In these four lines Cowper demonstrates his rhetorical skill, repeating the words *hides* and *tattered* for emphasis and including internal rhyme with the words *still* and *ill,* both of which resound in close proximity to the off rhyme in *conceal*. The speaker next relates that while Kate will ask fellow travelers for an "idle pin," which she "hoards," by sticking them in her sleeve, she will not request what she really needs, food and clothing, "Though pinched with cold." This fact alone causes the speaker to exclaim after a pause, or caesura, forced midline by a dash, "—Kate is crazed!"

Such madwomen were common topics for BALLADS and stories, relayed as cautionary tales for young women or just as entertainment in a gathering. Ironically Cowper often sank into depression, eventually becoming completely disabled through insanity. His madness, however, was not sparked by love lost, but rather by delusions that led him to believe he was eternally damned for his sinful nature.

BIBLIOGRAPHY
Heller, Deborah. "Cowper's 'Task' and the Writing of a Poet's Salvation." *Studies in English Literature, 1500–1900* 35 (summer 1995): 575–598.

"CRUEL MISTRESS, A" THOMAS CAREW (1640) THOMAS CAREW wrote "A Cruel Mistress" firmly within the CAVALIER tradition. At a time when the CARPE DIEM theme remained popular, lyricists like Carew wrote lively light fare that mostly focused on women, particularly their coy and fickle natures. Despite their drawbacks, women held supreme attraction for Cavaliers, who echoed concern of the court of King Charles II with romantic relationships, whether consummated or star-crossed. In "A Cruel Mistress" Carew focuses on love scorned as his male persona bemoans his mistreatment by his love. He adopts an 18-line format with rhyming couplets.

The speaker begins by emphasizing the importance of his topic, accomplished by the comparison of his love's behavior to that of royalty and deities:

> We read of Kings and Gods that kindly took
> A pitcher fill'd with water from the brook
> But I have daily tendered without thanks
> Rivers of tears that overflow their banks.

The persona makes clear that his copious tears have met with no gratitude or pity from his love, although they would have well satisfied even a god. He continues by remarking on various sacrifices acceptable to mythological deities, such as a bull for the "angry Jove"; a horse for the god of the sun, Phoebus; and a lamb for the god of love, Cupid. But when he offered his "pure heart" at "her altar," she "disdains the spotless sacrifice." Thus the speaker notes that while lesser sacrifices of dumb beasts could satisfy gods, his own proffered heart is found unworthy, not only rejected, but rejected with *disdain,* a favorite term of Carew and his contemporaries to express pure and cruel disregard.

As the speaker continues the LYRIC in this vein, he notes that "Vesta is not displeas'd if her chaste urn / Do with repaired fuel ever burn," but his love, "my Saint," will frown should he light an eternal flame in her honor. He next notes with a tone of wonder, "Th'

Assyrian King did none i' th' furnace throw, / But those that to his Image did not bow," a reference to the mighty King Nebuchadnezzar and his treatment in the biblical book of Daniel of the Old Testament prophets Meshack, Shadrach, and Abednego. Because they refused to worship a statue, he placed them in fire to destroy them. Carew's point is that the king only punished in that way those who would not participate in the worship. The speaker of his poem, however, "With bended knees" worships his love every day, a willing participant in that ritual, "Yet she consumes her owne Idolater." The reference to consumption reflects back on Nebuchadnezzar's furnace, where those who failed to obey him were consumed by fire. The poem's speaker remarks on the IRONY of the fact that his love is so disdainful and cruel as to destroy the very person who worships her.

After having called forth a veritable catalog of mythical figures, Carew can conclude his poem by writing, "Of such a Goddess no times leave record, / That burnt the temple where she was ador'd." Carew succeeds in incorporating numerous references to religious traditions, including the term *temple*. In the Old Testament tradition, the temple referred not only to a place of worship but also to one's literal body. Had Carew intended that double meaning for *temple,* he would have suggested that his love's rejection resulted in a type of self-consumption for her. Her haughtiness literally would have destroyed her along with her worshipper.

D

"DAFT DAYS, THE" ROBERT FERGUSSON (1771)

ROBERT FERGUSSON is credited as one of the most important Scottish poets for his revival of the traditional Scots language in late 18th-century poetry. Before writing "The Daft Days," he had attempted to adopt the English approach to verse, producing some unexceptional poetry. However, in "The Daft Days," published in Ruddiman's *Weekly,* Fergusson returned to his true talent. He writes of the power of holiday celebrations to lift human spirits depressed by life's hardships, expressing his great affection for "Auld Reikie," or Edinburgh, as the scene of celebration. He adopted the "standart Habbie" tail RHYME stanza. The term *Habbie* derived from Robert Sempill's poem "Life and Death of Habbie Simson" (ca. 1640), in which the poet both praises and pokes fun at his subject. Tail rhyme, or, as coined by the French, *rime couée,* indicates a stanza concluded by three lines. The first and third of the three concluding lines rhyme and are short lines, separated by the longer second line.

"The Daft Days" is the first in modern Scottish poetry to use a six-line stanza in a poem that is neither comic elegy nor epistle in verse form. Fergusson's contribution to the "Habbie" or "Habby" form remained important, extending its use into the next century. ROBERT BURNS, who openly expressed his debt to Fergusson, would pick up the form soon after Fergusson's early death. "The Daft Days" contains the quickly executed transitions and lively description that would mark Fergusson's best work. Although he frames specific description within abstract ideas, he does not sacrifice unity to his method. Later critics would comment on the poem's skillful form and Fergusson's ability to echo the harmony inherent to the poem's theme in its overall construction, mainly through the use of sharp imagery.

Falling naturally into three sections, the poem opens with description of the gloomy winter day, establishing a tone of drear, as the speaker asks his listeners to "mirk," or mark, December's "dowie," or gloomy face:

> Now mirk December's dowie face
> Glours our the rigs wi' sour grimace,
> While thro' his minimum of space,
>   The bleer-ey'd sun,
> Wi' blinkin light and stealing pace,
>   His race doth run.

Even the sun cannot enliven the darkened day. Fergusson adopts the FIGURATIVE LANGUAGE (FIGURE OF SPEECH) of personification for both the sun and the month. December has a face that "glours" or glowers, "our the rigs," over the ridges, managing to prevent the sun from reaching into many of the dark wintry spaces. The second stanza extends the dark imagery, in which "nae birdie sings," and no "shepherd's pipe" sounds. The breeze supplies "nae od'rous flavour," or scent

>   Frae Borean cave;
> And dwynin' Nature droops her wings,
>   Wi' visage grave.

95

The third stanza offers more of the same negative tone, emphasizing the fact that "Mankind but scanty pleasure glean" from the barren landscape. Concluding the first section of the poem, which sets the scene, Fergusson takes his reader in the fourth stanza into Edinburgh in a delightful contrast to the hostile external environment. The speaker salutes "Auld Reikie!" as "the canty hole," which offers a snug and warm escape in its pubs to humans weary of winter.

As the fifth stanza moves into the poem's second section, the tone appears considerably lightened. Holiday has arrived, and all enjoy it:

When merry Yule-day comes I trow,
You'll scantlins find a hungry mou;
Sma' are our cares, our stamacks fou
    O' gusty gear,
And kickshaws, strangers to our view.
    Sin' fairn-year.

No one hungers during Yule-day, as cares grow small when one enjoys a full stomach, and "kickshaws," or worries, are things of the "fairn," or past, year. The sixth stanza calls upon "Ye browster," or brewer, "wives!" to "fling your sorrows far away,'" while the seventh stanza explains "we'll never quarrel," and "Discord" cannot "spoil our glee." The eighth stanza builds on this joy as fiddlers play, banishing "vile Italian tricks." Those fiddles in the ninth stanza beckon revelers to respond to Scottish music:

For nought can cheer the heart sae weel
As a canty Highland reel;
It vivifies the heel
    To skip and dance:
Lifeless is he wha canna feel
    Its influence.

One would have to be dead not be affected by the uplifting music; nothing else can "sae weel," or so well, cheer a sad heart. Fergusson adds balance to his stanza by contrasting a heel that music "vivifies," or brings to life, with the "lifeless" person who cannot feel the music's inspiration.

In those five middle verses, the reader enjoys vignettes of feasters, musicians, and dancers, with the mention of specific instruments. Fergusson increases the poem's momentum as the movement that he describes picks up speed, partially by his choice of consonants. Hard sounds such as *b* and *k*, achieved in part through the hard *c* usage, result in sharp verbal explosions within frequent ALLITERATION that increases the pace.

The last two stanzas form the poem's third section and conclusion. The activity tapers off in stanza 10, emphasized by Fergusson's switch to Standard English:

Let mirth abound; let social cheer
Invest the dawning of the year;
Let blithesome innocence appear
    To crown our joy;
Nor envy, wi' sarcastic sneer,
    Our bliss destroy.

The speaker returns to his opening strategy, speaking in generalizations, all of the distinctive specific detail that so enlivened the middle section of the poem replaced by an empty philosophy. The vacuous words reflect the disappointment the New Year is destined to cause. Critics find this stanza the weakest, particularly the tail rhyme lines, which remain lackluster. They also comment on the half-hearted approach to incorporate the neoclassical abstractions that so contrast with the previous sharply defined imagery.

However, the final stanza recovers strength in its biting indictment of Edinburgh's so-called law enforcers, the City Guard. Ironically, Fergusson refers to them as "that black banditti" and calls on the "great god of aqua vitae" for protection of the poor against those who should support the common man's best interests but who do not. The Guard remained an ever-present military force that had degenerated into a group with little regard for justice. Thus, Fergusson characterizes them in his stanza as a force that abused the very people they should have protected.

Fergusson would follow "The Daft Days" in Ruddiman's periodical with "Elegy on the Death of Scots Music," another example of traditional language and form. While his output remained small because he died at age 24, it proved vital to development of the poetry that Robert Burns would make famous. It also provided the humanist historical, political, and literary continuity promoting Scottish traditions, important to poets such as Fergusson for the stability and self-knowledge those traditions provided. Emphasis of tradition reminded readers of their past, as well as the future to which they should aspire. The Whig philosophy promoted materialism as the path to happiness and contentment, contrasting greatly with the Scots humanist traditional philosophy. It encouraged man to look within, assess his limitations, then develop a new sense of self-awareness, rejecting the idea of defining one's self on the basis of one's possessions.

BIBLIOGRAPHY
Freeman, F. W. *Robert Fergusson and the Scots Humanist Compromise.* Edinburgh: Edinburgh University Press, 1984.
Maclaine, Allan H. *Robert Fergusson.* New York: Twayne, 1965.

"DANCE, THE" SIR JOHN SUCKLING (1648)

In "The Dance," SIR JOHN SUCKLING adopts the FIGURATIVE LANGUAGE of personification to transform the emotions love, hate, and pride, and the mental configurations reason, fancy, and folly, into characters. The dance to which the title refers describes their interactions, as each changes partners several times, except the couple Love and Folly, who remain together throughout the three six-line stanzas. The RHYME pattern is *aabbcc,* with the final line of each stanza concluding with the word *hell.* Suckling emphasizes that people experience all of these emotions and states, simply forming varying combinations depending upon circumstances. However, while other permutations occur, love and folly always remain together. The poem's message that love is always doomed by foolish acts remains bleak, although its sprightly form moves with a jolly momentum that promotes reader pleasure.

The first stanza opens with imagery of "Love, Reason, Hate" speaking as "Three mates to play at barleybreak." They form couples: "Love Folly took; and Reason, Fancy; / And Hate consorts with Pride." "Love coupled last," and its choice will prove disastrous, as it can never separate itself from Folly. In the second stanza, as readers continue to visualize partners dancing, "Love would Reason meet, / But Hate was nimbler on her feet," and "Fancy looks for Pride." Although Love hoped to couple with Reason, Hate, Fancy, here meaning desire untempered by intelligence, and Pride all interfered, leaving Love again with Folly as a result of the other couplings. By the third stanza, all partners rest briefly. When they execute another change, "Pride / Hath now got Reason on her side" and "Hate and Fancy meet," all remaining "Untouched by Love." Love only touches Folly again, despite Folly's "dull" nature, "So Love and Folly were in hell."

Suckling is considered by modern critics at times an adept poet, at other times one who presents disjointed and unreadable lines. In "The Dance," he establishes a strong metaphor for human interactions that become ritual, with scripted steps. That allows him to offer his philosophy regarding love and the likelihood that engagement in that most common of human emotions will lead to success for any random couple. A person who loved games, Suckling probably would not bet on the chance that love can ever win out, because of the folly of human nature, a fact made clear in his sentiments expressed in this seemingly light-hearted poem. The repeated word *hell* rings loudly as literally the last word about love, for it closes each stanza and the entire poem. The connotation of hell as a place not only of punishment but of no escape throughout eternity, an endless dance in Suckling's construction, remains inescapable.

DAVENANT, SIR WILLIAM (1606–1668)

The critic Edmund Gosse wrote, "There is not a more hopelessly faded laurel on the slopes of the English Parnassus than that which once flourished so bravely around the grotesque head of Davenant." Despite the later unkind treatment by his critics, Sir William Davenant, also spelled *D'Avenant,* remained enormously popular during his era, a theater manager, playwright, and poet. Apparently William Shakespeare's godson, he was rumored also to have been the bard's illegitimate offspring, born to Jane Shepherd Davenant, wife of an innkeeper at Oxford's Crown Tavern, frequented by Shakespeare. The rumor may have arisen from a remark made by SAMUEL BUTLER that Davenant strove to imitate Shakespeare and would have been pleased to be called the poet's son; the rumor was later discredited. Davenant's father became mayor of Oxford in 1621, later sending his son to Lincoln College, which he left before taking a degree in order to begin service at court. He first served the duchess of Richmond, and later Fulke Greville, Lord Brooke, who encouraged Davenant's interest in the stage.

After Greville's murder Davenant left service and in 1629 wrote and staged his first play, *The Tragedy of Albovine.* He was asked to write a royal masque, and Queen Henrietta Maria and her ladies performed his *The Temple of Love* at Whitehall on Strove Tuesday 1634. Davenant then took charge of all such court entertainments. His playwright career was launched, and his best known romances included *The Wits, The Platonic Lovers,* and *Love and Honour,* all appearing between 1634 and 1639. In 1638 he published *Madagascar, with Other Poems* and he became, after BEN JONSON's death, poet laureate.

As a Royalist Davenant was accused in 1642 before the Puritan Parliament of activity in a scheme to overthrow the Commonwealth, leading to a two-month internment in the Tower of London. His successive acts in support of the Royalist cause led to a knighthood after the 1643 siege of Gloucester. He lived in France with the queen and other political exiles from 1646 until 1649, when he received an appointment as governor of Maryland. Not far off England's coast, his ship was captured by Cromwell's forces. He used the time of his imprisonment (some reports say in Cowes Castle on the Isle of Wight and others in the Tower) from 1650 to 1652 to write a romantic epic poem titled *GONDIBERT.* Davenant's 1654 pardon was probably due in part to the interference on his behalf by the poet and statesman JOHN MILTON.

When Charles II was restored to the throne, he granted Davenant one of the few patents available to form an acting company. Davenant is generally considered the first composer of the English opera, his most famous titled *The Siege of Rhodes,* the first part of which appeared in 1656, and the second part produced in 1659. Its performance marked the return of theater to England after 14 years of suppression under Cromwell. Davenant and JOHN DRYDEN adapted Shakespeare's *The Tempest* to the opera for its first production in 1667 and followed its performance with several additional adapted Shakespeare plays. Their productions angered many because of their variance from the originals, but historians credit Davenant for the return of Shakespeare to the stage. Despite such reaction to his work by his contemporaries, Davenant was later included among those important playwrights aiding the transition from Elizabethan to Restoration drama.

Davenant continued to produce poetry along with his plays. He would be remembered partly for *Madagascar,* which focused on the plan of the prince of the Rhenish Palatinate, Charles I's nephew, to colonize the island of Madagascar. His poetry appeared in a large folio edition of works published posthumously in 1673. Critics later held that application of the grand term *works* in the fashion of Jonson to Davenant's poetry proved the only parallel that could be drawn between the two poets; everything positive the reader has been led to expect from poetry by Jonson is absent in Davenant's extraordinarily derivative verse. He imitated widely, including Jonson and Shakespeare as models, and he best enjoyed writing in the classical mode. By the 19th century he became important for his historical significance, rather than for his art.

While many of his works proved ponderous and pedantic, Davenant's unfinished *Gondibert* is generally thought of more positively. Its narrative of chivalry in Lombardy contains individual strong lines, with some inspired imagery, although its plot is at times difficult to follow because of its narrative incoherence. The 70-page preface to *Gondibert* is an address to Thomas Hobbes, to whom the poem was dedicated. It focused on the art and nature of poetry and was followed by 19-page reply from Hobbes. *Gondibert* also contained prefatory poems by EDMUND WALLER and ABRAHAM COWLEY and later inspired an 18-line satirical poem by JOHN DENHAM that makes reference to Hobbes, Cowley, and Waller, and to the destructive effect of syphilis on Davenant's nose.

Selected quotations from Davenant, including, from *Gondibert,* "The assembled souls of all that men held wise," appeared in John Bartlett's *Familiar Quotations,* 10th edition (1919). Seldom anthologized in depth, Davenant's poetry remains available in printed and electronic excerpts, mainly because of *Gondibert*'s influence on Dryden, seen most notably in the form of his *Annus Mirabilis*. Also occasionally anthologized is a song from *Gondibert*, "The Lark Now Leaves His Watery Nest," classified as an AUBADE.

BIBLIOGRAPHY

Gosse, Edmund W. "Sir William Davenant." In *The English Poets*, edited by T. H. Ward. Vol. 2, 289. New York: Macmillan, 1914.

Herbage, Alfred. *Sir William Davenant, Poet Venturer*. New York: Octagon Books, 1971.

Schiffer, Edward. "Sir William Davenant: The Loyal Scout Lost at Sea." *English Literary History* 59, no. 3 (fall 1992): 553–576.

"DEATH" GEORGE HERBERT (1633)

Along with the poems "Dooms-day," "Judgement," "Heaven," and "LOVE (3)," "Death" closes the sequence titled "The Church" within the collection *The Temple* by GEORGE HERBERT. Taken together, the poems feature the Christian individual's movement from earthly existence into heaven. "Death" resembles JOHN DONNE's "DEATH BE NOT PROUD" in its rendering of death as something to be welcomed, rather than feared. Donne probably influenced Herbert directly, not only because both served as religious leaders and shared spiritual beliefs made clear in poetry, but also because Donne had been a family friend. Both sought to explain death from a nontraditional perspective in order to promote a more positive earthly experience for those who awaited that final stage of life.

Herbert's speaker directly addresses Death through the FIGURATIVE LANGUAGE of personification, as had Donne. Not only in his opening comment, "Death, thou wast once an uncouth hideous thing / Nothing but bones," does he devalue Death, his direct address serves to demystify the act of dying. He builds to completion of Death's transformation when he notes that for ages people suffered from thoughts of the effects of death on those who had passed on, "Flesh being turned to dust, and bones to sticks," as well as those left behind, who turn to "dry dust" that sheds no tears. This same dust will later reappear in the poem transformed into a reference to bodies preparing for reassembly and resurrection.

The speaker now begins his transformation of Death in earnest, noting that "since our Saviour's death" Death had become more human, with "blood" put in his face. He has even "grown fair and full of grace, / Much in request, much sought for, as a good." Herbert uses hyperbole but makes his point. Christ's death yielded redemption, allowing humans to hope for a better existence after death than their earthly one. Only by dying can they attain this "good" state. By the fifth and penultimate stanza, Death is beheld as "gay and glad," just as souls will be "at doomsday," wearing "their new array, / And all thy bones with beauty shall be clad." The dead bodies at doomsday will reassemble, bones and all, to become more complete and beautiful than at any time during their earthly existence.

Death's transformation and rebirth parallel those of the humans he had so terrified. Even this most feared state has been redeemed and resurrected by Christ's sacrifice. The result of this new manner of thinking is, the speaker concludes, that "we can go die as sleep," with people trusting "Unto an honest faithful grave; / Making our pillows either down or dust." Dust, which began the poem with a negative connotation, closes it as part of a desirable state of pleasant suspension akin to sleep, a state in which humans may await their day of resurrection.

"DEATH BE NOT PROUD" JOHN DONNE (1633)

While discussion continues over the order in which JOHN DONNE wrote the individual poems that compose his HOLY SONNETS, the critic Helen Gardner has argued convincingly that "Death Be Not Proud" was published in 1633. Structured as a variant of the Italian, or PETRARCHAN, SONNET, the poem's RHYME scheme is *abbaabbacddcee*. Donne became popular while serving as the dean of St. Paul's, writing and preaching sermons that also occupy an important position in his works. As one who tended to the spiritual life of others, he dealt regularly with death, and the sonnet probably reflects the theme of hope he attempted to pass to the grieved. He had two strict views about the soul. He believed it immortal by the will of God and believed that a virtuous soul is taken to heaven at the moment of death; it does not linger to arise with the body on the last day, described by the Bible as the day of reckoning.

Donne could turn to the Bible for a model in his opening apostrophe to death, which he personifies through FIGURATIVE LANGUAGE: "Death be not proud, though some have called thee / Mighty and dreadful, for, thou art not so." Christian tenets held that a person need fear death only when burdened by sin. Because Christ had assumed that burden during his own death by crucifixion then arose from that death state, humans who accepted him as their savior stood redeemed from sin. The King James Bible (1611) translation of 1 Corinthians 15:55–57 reads, "O death, where is thy sting? O grave, where is thy victory? The sting of death is sin; and the strength of sin is the law. But thanks be to God, which giveth us the victory through our Lord Jesus Christ." Donne could call on verses such as these to support his claim against the power of death. The sonnet's third line continues the speaker's direct address of Death, stating, "For, those, whom thou think'st, thou dost overthrow, / Die not, poor death, nor yet canst thou kill me." By adopting a pitying attitude toward "poor death," which cannot hurt true believers, the speaker co-opts the power that even the term *death* possesses to frighten humans.

Donne next adopts a familiar trope for death, that of sleep, one that Shakespeare used in Hamlet's famous soliloquy that begins, "To be or not to be." In his thoughts, Hamlet noted that death must offer an opportunity to men "perchance to dream." However, because no communication from beyond the grave has ever occurred, he cannot be confident that his hope for a peaceful sleep will be fulfilled. Donne, however, has no doubts, as his speaker tells death, "From rest and sleep, which but thy pictures be, / Much pleasure, then from thee, much more must flow." The poem's persona remains completely and calmly convinced that death merely imitates a pleasurable sleep, and because it is long-lasting, humans will derive even more pleasure from death. The speaker even repeats the term *much* to convince his audience. When he acknowledges in the next lines that "soonest our best men with thee do go," he describes that journey as rest for "their bones," or flesh, but "delivery" for the soul, their spirit that will be released from its confines. This line concludes the first grouping of eight, which in the Italian sonnet propose

a problem or issue. The secondary grouping of six lines will act as response.

Momentum in the final six lines gathers initially not only through Donne's driving use of two series, but through the rising realization by the audience that death, indeed, is to be pitied. The speaker presses the idea of the reversal of power, with those in a position of strength, the humans, indulging in pity of death, which is weak. Death serves as merely one small part of a general plan of transitory earthly existence and attends humans only when circumstances determine. He acts as a slave, and as such, lacks any control over humans: "Thou art slave to fate, chance, kings, and desperate men, / And dost with poison, war, and sickness dwell." Death keeps desperate company and draws no joy from his companions. The speaker makes clear that death's power to promote sleep is nothing remarkable. It is shared by drugs concocted from nature by humans, as opium is derived from the poppy flower: "And poppy, or charms can make us sleep as well, / And better than thy stroke; why swell'st thou then?" Not only can such drugs and "charms" help people sleep, they prove superior to death. Donne chides death as if he were a child, asking why he would swell with pride over power not exclusively his own. The final couplet brilliantly declares victory over death as a transitory state, as the speaker claims the promise of eternal life made by God to all Christians: "One short sleep past, we wake eternally, / And death shall be no more, Death thou shalt die." Donne concludes with a stunning PARADOX, declaring that death shall suffer the only permanent destruction.

In the 1940s the American journalist John Gunther adopted Donne's opening line, "Death be not proud," as the title of what critics term an "illness narrative." He wrote in memoir form about the 15-month fight with cancer and subsequent death of his teenage son. As Donne, he chose to believe that death proved only a beginning of life beyond that experienced by mortal humans. Donne's sonnet remains popular into the 21st century, read often at funeral services and readily available in electronic and print form.

BIBLIOGRAPHY
Gardner, Helen, ed. *John Donne: The Divine Poems*. Oxford: Clarendon Press, 1969.

Lancashire, Ian. "John Donne." *Representative Poetry on Line.* The Department of English, University of Toronto. Available online. URL: http://eir.library.utoronto.ca/rpo/display/poem658.html. Downloaded on June 2, 2005.

"DEFINITION OF LOVE, THE" ANDREW MARVELL (1681)

Judged the best example of the works of METAPHYSICAL POETS AND POETRY, ANDREW MARVELL's work "The Definition of Love" remains a source of discussion for literary critics. As does most of Marvell's LYRIC poetry, it lacks a specific date of composition and appeared first in his posthumous 1681 collection, *Miscellaneous Poems.* Contextually similar to Marvell's "TO HIS COY MISTRESS" and containing echoes of poetry from the late 16th century and the early decades of the 17th century, "The Definition of Love" probably can be dated between 1649 and 1651; most critics feel confident it is one of the poet's early works. While many identify it with metaphysical poetry by JOHN DONNE, in particular his "A VALEDICTION: FORBIDDING MOURNING" and "A VALEDICTION: OF WEEPING," others see resemblance to works by GEORGE HERBERT, ABRAHAM COWLEY, and RICHARD LOVELACE. Some judge Marvell's geometric imagery superior to that of Donne, while others feel his presentation lacks the personal passion of Donne and other predecessors. He may have produced the poem as an exercise in imitation, a common practice in his day, emphasizing the FIGURATIVE LANGUAGE (FIGURE OF SPEECH) of hyperbole and including ANTITHESIS, the latter approach resulting in a poor attempt to reproduce Donne's notable use of PARADOX. Geometry provides its framework, on which he builds his argument through logic and the inversion of logic through the use of oxymoron and paradox, resulting in the type of IRONY that distinguished Socratic dialectic. Its structure rests on the METER and feet of iambic tetrameter arranged in nine quatrains with the rhyme scheme of *abab.*

The first stanza presents the idea of logic, or illogic, as the speaker compares his love to a rare birth and to an "object strange and high." Oxymoronically, it is "begotten by Despair" and based "Upon Impossibility." An oxymoron opens the second stanza, as Marvell begins, "Magnanimous Despair alone / Could show me so divine a thing" and defines Hope as "feeble," like an inept angel that "vainly flapped its tinsel wing." Where Donne designs his love as not only possible, but realistic, Marvell notes the presence, yet vain nature, of his passion. The third stanza notes the speaker's inability to "arrive / Where my extended soul is fixed," echoing the compass imagery from Donne's verse but inverting it by rendering the speaker incapable of challenging that fixed position. He cannot act on his love, because of the obstruction caused "iron wedges," which "Fate" drives between him and his goal, only one approach apparently used by Fate as it "crowds itself betwixt." The fourth stanza explains that Fate's "jealous eye" moves it to separate the lovers, and the imagery of "perfect loves" reflects the Platonic ideal of love. Should the lovers unite, Fate's "tyrannic power" would be deposed. Stanza 5 follows stanza 4's explanation with the logic of a reaction to every action:

> And therefore her decrees of steel
> Us as the distinct poles have placed,
> (Though Love's whole world on us doth wheel)
> Not by themselves to be embraced:

This view of Fate originates in Horace's *Carmina,* a view that Marvell intensifies through Fate's power to place the speaker and his love at opposite magnetic poles. The speaker parenthetically suggests the world's dependence on such perfect spiritual love, as its rotation depends upon the magnetic poles. He broadens his explanation in stanzas 6 and 7 through use of the geometric figures compared to those from Donne:

> Unless the giddy heaven fall,
> And earth some new convulsion tear;
> And, us to join, the world should all
> Be cramped into a planisphere
>
> As lines so loves oblique may well
> Themselves in every angle greet:
> Bout ours so truly parallel,
> Though infinite, can never meet.

In Marvell's vision, in order for these lovers to unite, heaven must experience a mighty upheaval that would result in the squashing flat of earth. That remains an impossibility, echoing that term in the opening stanza.

Until such an upheaval occurs, the lovers remained star-crossed, destined like parallel lines never to meet; although such lines may extend forever, they will never cross. The speaker suggests the imperfection of oblique lines that do intersect, suggesting lovers that "in every angle greet" lack the perfect spiritual love that he shares with his lover. This creates the paradoxical conditions that first, while they share, they never meet, and second, perfection, a desired state, equates to eternal separation, an undesirable state. The final stanza concludes that these lovers enjoy only a mental intercourse, a perfect way to unite. Their relationship is compared to that of the "opposition of the stars," the final phrase of the poem. While his reference to astronomy remains unclear, he may suggest that the two share a position within the same astrological plane, like two planets within the same zodiac sign, although positioned at opposite ends.

Most modern criticism focuses on the poem's curiously impersonal tone when dealing with such a personal subject.

BIBLIOGRAPHY

Ray, H. Robert. *An Andrew Marvell Companion.* New York: Garland, 1998.

Rees, Christine. *The Judgement of Marvell.* New York: Pinter, 1989.

Smith, Nigel, ed. *The Poems of Andrew Marvell.* New York: Pearson/Longman, 2003.

Sokol, B. J. "The Symposium, Two Kinds of 'Definition,' and Marvell's 'The Definition of Love.'" *Notes and Queries* 35 (1988): 169–170.

Toliver, Harold E. "Marvell's 'Definition of Love' and Poetry of Self-Exploration." *Bucknell Review* 10 (1961–1962): 263–274.

"DELIGHT IN DISORDER" ROBERT HERRICK (1648)

When ROBERT HERRICK wrote "Delight in Disorder," he followed the tradition that celebrated nature's "orderly disorder" and suggested that one might take pleasure from a disruption resulting in aesthetic chaos. His mentor, BEN JONSON, utilized that belief in the song "Still to be neat" from his drama *Epicoene*, I.i. The song praises "Robes loosely flowing, hair as free," noting that "Such sweet neglect more taketh me, / Than all the adulteries of art." Herrick's speaker shares that sentiment, as he begins, "A Sweet disorder in the dress / Kindles in clothes a wantoness," then supports his opening statement by describing common articles of clothing in disarray. They include "A Lawne about the shoulders thrown / Into a fine distraction," as well as errant lace and "A cuff neglectfull, and thereby / Ribbands flowing confusedly." The subject matter supports a playful tone and the use of abundant alliteration to lend a songlike quality to the verse, as in 9–10, "A winning wave (deserving Note) / In the tempestuous petticote," lines also sexually suggestive, yet innocently expressed. Herrick includes an OXYMORON in the phrase "wilde civility," in describing "A careless shoestring." His use of contradictory terms echoes that of the "orderly disorder" tenet he follows. He concludes his simple 14-line collection of rhyming couplets clarifying that such wild civility does "more bewitch me, then when Art / Is too precise in every part." The speaker seems to find most becoming that woman whose appearance predicts a loss of control. However, his final line notes that even such loss remains an art, suggesting that a woman may design such an appearance after all. It also suggests an additional oxymoron, "disartful art."

DENHAM, SIR JOHN (1615–1669)

John Denham was born in Dublin and attended Trinity College at Oxford, where he studied law at Lincoln's Inn. Called to the bar in 1639, he inherited his father's Surrey estate that same year. In 1641 he published two works, a tragedy in BLANK VERSE titled *The Sophy* and the poem that gave him enduring fame, COOPER'S HILL, supposedly written on brown wrapping paper. The lengthy poem's description of the countryside surrounding Denham's home at Egham and nearby Windsor Castle greatly influenced verse of the next century describing topography. In recent decades, its political tone and content have been reevaluated as equally important as the topographical approach.

In November 1642, Denham became part of a temporary court that included other Royalist poets, such as ABRAHAM COWLEY, RICHARD CRASHAW, and JOHN CLEVELAND, when King Charles I moved with many of his followers to Oxford. He withdrew from a contentious Parliament and growing Protestant forces. Queen Henrietta Maria and her ladies eventually joined Charles, and with them entertainment and frivolity; the queen would become pregnant with her ninth child while at Oxford. A temporary Parliament was established in Oxford's Divinity Schools and Shakespeare's plays were enacted, while in London drama had been curtailed. Although many found the King's stay in Oxford exhilarating, his poets, including Denham, tried to transmit their advice and disapproval of certain of his causes through their poetry. According to the critic Donald Bruce, Denham had focused in *Cooper's Hill* on royal despotism, an aspect of the poem not commented upon until centuries after its publication. Although Denham was not totally skeptical, he did attempt, as did his fellow poets, to dissuade Charles from the path of certain disaster. Their attempts failed, and Charles would be executed as his queen and followers fled to France.

Devoted to the Royalist cause, Denham moved to the Continent when the Civil War broke out, living in exile 1648–53. He later received a knighthood when King Charles II was restored to the throne. Additional rewards for his loyalty included his office as surveyor of the Royal Works and his seat in Parliament representing Sarum. He republished *Cooper's Hill* in 1655, with the later version muting some of the former polemical content. In 1665 Denham married a much younger woman named Margaret Brooke, who became mistress to James II, possibly contributing to the poet's famous emotional breakdown episode in which, believing he was the Holy Ghost, he proclaimed as much to the king. In addition to writing poetry and drama, Denham translated some classical works and wrote essays expressing theories regarding translation, including "To Sir Richard Fanshaw Upon his Translation of Pastor Fido" (probably 1643–44) and a preface to "The Destruction of Troy" (1656). He also completed the translation of the French dramatist Corneille's *Horace,* left incomplete by the poet and playwright KATHERINE PHILIPS at her untimely death. JOHN DRYDEN would later reference Denham's attitude toward translation as one in which poets from all eras prove contemporaries as they attempt to transmit the same message to their own ages.

Denham's views strongly influenced Dryden's approach to translation and his views on 17th-century literature. Twentieth-century critics suggest that Denham also influenced Dryden's grounding in Royalist poetics. Although Dryden did not often specifically reference Denham, according to the critic Tanya Caldwell, "key tenets of Dryden's critical and political stances have their roots in Denham's poetry and critical proclamations." Denham's writing during a time of political unrest when one's political and personal aesthetics often proved indistinguishable allowed Dryden, in similar conditions, to recognize a commonality with his predecessor. As had Horatio, Denham cautioned against word-for-word translation, and Dryden referenced the earlier poet in the preface to Ovid's *Epistles* (1680), writing, "Too faithfully is indeed pedantically: 'tis a faith like that which proceeds from Superstition, blind and zealous: Take it in the Expression of Sir John Denham, to Sir Rich. Fanshaw, on his Version of Pastor Fido." Denham's words quoted by Dryden read,

> That servile path, thou nobly do'st decline,
> Of tracing word by word and Line by Line;
> A new and nobler way thou do'st pursue,
> To make Translations and Translators too:
> They but preserve the Ashes, thou the Flame,
> True to his Sense, but truer to his Fame.
>   (1:115)

Dryden also quotes a later statement by Denham in his preface before the translation of the *Aeneid:* "Poetry is of so subtil a Spirit, that in pouring out of one Language into another, it will all Evaporate; and if a new Spirit be not added in the transfusion, there will remain nothing but a Caput Mortum."

Despite multiple viewpoints claiming *Cooper's Hill* was not the mild descriptive piece praised by notables including ALEXANDER POPE and SAMUEL JOHNSON, most anthologies continue to emphasize Denham's contribution to the poetry of place. Additional attention is given to his adoption of the couplet for its versatility in establishing rhythm and his use of rhetorical balance as his greatest legacy. However, 20th-century critics have also disputed that the idea of balance was peculiar to Denham, claiming instead that rhetorical balance appeared commonly in Royalist writings, even those by Charles I himself. In addition, they have challenged

18th-century praise of Denham's tone of peaceful concord, claiming that the poem actually projects acrimony and discord. The fact that *Cooper's Hill* continues to promote such animated discussion remains proof of its importance, not only to literature, but also to a revisionist historical view of the era of Charles I.

BIBLIOGRAPHY

Boeckel, Bruce. "Landscaping the Field of Discourse: Political Slant and Poetic Slope in Sir John Denham's 'Cooper's Hill.'" *Papers on Language & Literature* 34, no. 1 (winter 1998): 57–93.

Bruce, Donald. "An Oxford Garrison of Poets in 1642." *Contemporary Review,* November 1992, 250–256.

Caldwell, Tanya. "John Dryden and John Denham." *Texas Studies in Literature and Language* 46, no. 1 (spring 2004): 49–72.

O'Hehir, Brendan. *Harmony from Discords: A Life of Sir John Denham.* Berkeley: University of California Press, 1968.

"DEPARTED YOUTH" HANNAH COWLEY

(1813) Published as part of HANNAH COWLEY's posthumous *Works,* "Departed Youth" had been written years before. Cowley composed the 34 lines of rhyming couplets in 1797, the year her husband died while serving in India. The poem's theme of youth's fleeting existence, expressed through a description of physical change, is written with a contemplative tone, edged by regret and sadness. That tone, however, will be overridden by appreciation for spirit, the true measure of a person's condition.

The poem begins with the speaker's insisting that although "the rosebuds from my cheek / Have faded," they are the same cheeks that once "Spoke youth, and joy, and careless thought." Whether because of "guilt, or fear, or shame uncaught," her soul "uninjured, still hath youth, / Its lively sense attests the truth!" The idea that one's physical demeanor does not necessarily mirror one's spiritual or emotional makeup becomes the focus of the poem. The voice declares, "Oh!" with the exclamation point as evidence of passion and energy, "I can wander yet, and taste / The beauties of the flowery waste," with the term *waste* adding a realistic balance to the imagery of flowers, which, as the speaker, lose their beauty with time's passage. Her passion can still be aroused by "The nightingale's deep swell," its

song bringing tears to her eyes. Cowley suggests bittersweet emotion with the imagery of tears that "steal" to the speaker's eyes, unbidden. Another exclamation begins the fifth line, balancing the previous one, as the speaker declares,

> Rapt! Gaze upon the gem-decked night,
> Or mark the clear moon's gradual flight,
> Whilst the bright river's rippled wave
> Repeats the quivering beams she gave.

Taken for its surface meaning, the imagery is simply that noticed most often by young lovers. The allusion to the moon, a traditional symbol for woman, supports the speaker's identity as a female. The fact that the moon shines on a river, rather than a lake, suggests the deeper meaning of time's movement, rapid and constant like that of a river. The reflection of the moon, or woman, quivers, uncertain in the moving water.

Next Cowley selects "Painting" and her passionate reaction to it to prove that she may still enjoy "the lofty passions of the mind." It does not "strive in vain" to "hint the sentiment refined," for the speaker declares she continues to "bow" to art's "sweet magic," just "As when youth decked my polished brow." One's physical appearance remains secondary to the ability to appreciate art. The speaker next alludes to the power of sculpture, "The chisel's lightest touch," to move her. Using repetition to advantage, Cowley adds, "Through the pure form, or softened grace, / Is lent me still; I still admire." Art offers her greater pleasure, through its "pure" nature, than ever did her physical beauty. Cowley includes a self-reference in the imagery of a poet, as the speaker testifies to the power of literature, which causes her yet to "kindle at the Poet's fire—." The fact that she continues to react to art remains her salvation, as she convinces herself that, regardless of what happens to her physical state, she can yet enjoy life.

The speaker at last directly addresses Time, as Cowley adopts the FIGURATIVE LANGUAGE of personification. The speaker notes that since time has not destroyed art, she does not mind the physical changes. That change includes a loss of "luster from my eye," and graying hair, her "tresses sprinkle o'er with snow," although her hair once "boasted" its "auburn glow."

Finally, she advises Time, "Break the slim form that was adored," the slim form being her, "By him so loved, my wedded lord," but concludes, "leave me, whilst all these you steal, / The mind to taste, the nerve to feel."

Cowley may have feared that she might become numb to all the joys of the world in her grief over the loss of her husband. She requests control of her thoughts, so that she might indulge in mental delights, as well as retention of her natural emotions, so that she can still experience passion over natural delights. Her own art, that of writing poetry, will help her in that experience.

"DESCRIPTION OF A CITY SHOWER, A" JONATHAN SWIFT (1710)

In his mock tribute to the aggravation that a heavy rain inflicted upon London, JONATHAN SWIFT used some elevated language in "A Description of a City Shower," casting it in the satirical light shared by most of his poetry. Examples may be found in its opening lines:

Careful observers may foretell the hour
(By sure prognostics) when to dread a shower;
While rain depends, the pensive cat gives o'er
Her frolics and pursues her tail no more.

His use of the terms *foretell, prognostics,* and *depends,* meaning in this instance "impends," contrast with the image of a thoughtful cat that has stopped chasing her tail. Swift intends to promote humor with his description of the revolting contents of the sewers, which washed onto the city streets during this common occurrence.

Definitely not considered traditional subject matter for the typically high language of poetry, the shower allowed Swift to make fun of those poets who took themselves and their art too seriously. He writes of physical signals of the approach of rain, such as "shooting corns," or foot pain caused by the horny growths that should not be a topic of civil conversation, as well as of a raging "hollow tooth" and "Old aches" that throb in signal of rising humidity and barometric change. He continues this approach in lines 14–16, which contain heightened terminology including "A sable cloud" and "the welkin" then compare the swollen rain cloud to a drunk, as it "swilled more liquor than it could contain." The lovely shepherdess of traditional pastoral poetry, which often celebrated nature, is replaced by "some careless quean," defined in Swift's day as a slut, flinging mop water that might splatter on the passer-by. Even that water would be cleaner than the drops that dampen the city dweller during this sprinkle. The speaker remarks, "Ah! Where must needy poet seek for aid, / When dust and rain at once his coat invade?" While those dwelling in the city may tout its advantages over country living, Swift's imagery makes clear that dust and rain mix to form mud, whatever the location.

Additional verses build the few drops into a flood, "Threatening with deluge this devoted town." Women walking on the streets take refuge in shops, where they pretend to bargain for goods but actually have little interest in purchases. As "every spout's abroach," or streaming water, students and seamstresses alike must seek cover and become unwilling acquaintances as they share shelter. Even "Triumphant Tories and desponding Whigs / forget their feuds, and join to save their wigs." Swift cannot resist a reference to the political unrest that cheated him after the death of Queen Anne of the government appointment that he so richly deserved.

Finally "from all parts the swelling kennels," meaning open gutters, "flow, / And bear their trophies with them as they go." The speaker includes little of a subtle nature as he observes of the mock "trophies," that "Filth of all hues and odors seem to tell / What street they sailed from, by their sight and smell." He then makes specific for the perhaps unwilling reader what floats from the sewers and into the streets, including "sprats," or small herring fish:

Sweepings from butchers' stalls, dung, guts, and
blood,
Drowned puppies, stinking sprats, all drenched
in mud,
Dead cats, and turnip tops, come tumbling
down the flood.

According to critics, Swift designed his concluding triplet with its final alexandrine as a burlesque on poetry by JOHN DRYDEN, as well as formal poetry by other Restoration writers. The editor of a 1735 edition of Swift's writings claimed that by using the triplet and alexandrine in such low manner, Swift ended its use permanently. "A Description of a City Shower" perfectly fits the 18th-century approach in which poets sought to subvert the reader's traditional expectations of poetry.

"DESCRIPTION OF A RELIGIOUS HOUSE" RICHARD CRASHAW (1646)

Known for his abundant descriptive excess, RICHARD CRASHAW occasionally produced work not overburdened by hyperbole, as in "Description of a Religious House." His use of what was later labeled the baroque style for its ornate diction fit well his religious energy. It is that passion for spirituality that inhabits this poem, which lacks the abundant and often bizarre FIGURATIVE LANGUAGE for which Crashaw gained a reputation. The idea of a house as an eternal reward he draws from the King James version of the Bible in John 14:2–3, which reads, "In my Father's house, are many rooms; if it were not so, would I have told you that I go to prepare a place for you? And when I go and prepare a place for you, I will come again and will take you to myself, that where I am you may be also."

The tone is one of praise and deep devotion as Crashaw begins by describing what is missing from a house in which religion is practiced:

No roofs of gold o'er riotous tables shining
Whole days and suns, devour'd with endless
   dining;
No sails of Tyrian silk, proud pavements
   sweeping,
Nor ivory couches costlier slumber keeping.

He creates vivid imagery of overindulgence, his rich diction making clear his broad training in languages. Words such as *riotous* and *devour'd* and *proud* suggest not simple luxury but decadence in the use of the material. The table is a traditional symbol for the center of a house, its spirit and life force, as used in the Bible. Crashaw also uses from these beginning lines the ALLITERATION that continues throughout his 39

lines. He continues in this vein, noting "flaring gems" that produce "False lights," offering near-PARADOX in coupling terms such as *tumultuous joys* and introducing what some critics identify as homoeroticism in the line "Halls full of flattering men and frisking boys." This house, which could be a metaphor for the human body as used commonly in the Bible, is home to corrupting influences. It offers "false shows of short and slippery good" that "Mix the mad sons of men in mutual blood," the eye rhyme of *good* and *blood* calling attention to their strong contrast in effect on the reader.

The ninth line begins with the transition "But," signaling a long rendition of descriptors applied to a more desirable lifestyle. They tumble one over the other, the continuing alliteration promoting a momentum in form that imitates the personal drive the speaker feels. Souls are "unforc'd and genuine," lodgings are "hard and homely" as fare that is "chaste and cheap," just like the clothes those who live in a religious house wear. He adds,

Obedient slumbers, that can wake and weep,
And sing, and sigh, and work, and sleep again;
Still rolling a round sphere of still-returning
   pain.

G. A. Simcox judges the skill in construction of the line "Obedient slumbers that can wake and weep" worthy of ALEXANDER POPE. Crashaw's inclusion of eight sibilants or *s* sounds in all three of those lines suggests a whisper as well as a smooth and sliding movement supporting the imagery of the pain that acts as an ever-turning sphere. A sphere is a slippery shape, lacking corners and angles, an image Crashaw skillfully contrasts with the idea of unrelenting pain and its often stabbing effect on the human body. The reader encounters pain again in the next line, one of several words that begin with the letter *p*, reinforcing the idea of its constant repetition, or return, to intrude into the human condition: "Hands full of hasty labours; pains that pay / And prize themselves." Crashaw pulls readers up short with the insertion of a semicolon after the word *themselves*, forcing a caesura. He continues with much additional repetition of sounds and imagery, again reinforcing the idea of a turning sphere, which alludes to the earth and its natural forces that man cannot control: "do much, that more they may, / And work for work, not wages." Regardless of the harsh scene he constructs, Crashaw makes clear that work for the sake of work yields a more desirable reward than that of things material. He invokes thoughts of baptism with the line "New drops wash off the sweat of this day's sorrows" and continues emphasizing the fact that we are basically born to die with the next two lines, "A long and daily dying life, which breathes / A respiration of reviving deaths."

With the use of another transition, *But,* to begin his next line, Crashaw moves into the unrhyming line, number 27, inserted to shatter the effect of the accompanying 19 sets of couplets. He writes, "But neither are there those ignoble stings / That nip the blossom of the word's best things, / And lash Earth-labouring souls." At this point, the reader is asked to focus on the fact that alternatives exist, that humankind may make important choices regarding lifestyle that might ennoble the constant movement toward death. In the religious house, "reverent discipline, and religious fear, / And soft obedience, find sweet biding." In addition, "Silence, and sacred rest; peace, and pure joys; / Kind loves keep house, lie close, and make no noise." Again using sibilants, Crashaw allows readers to glide through this house, to contrast the rest it promotes to the jangling, jarring life one finds surrounding those "riotous tables" mentioned in the first line. The center of the religious house proves magnetic, drawing all of those who need not only the physical nurture suggested by tables bearing food, but also nurture for the spirit, too often distracted by the "long and daily dying" of life alluded to earlier.

Crashaw continues his use of biblical allusions, calling to mind Christ's promise of his father's mansion, which has many rooms to house the faithful after death: "And room enough for monarchs, while none swells / Beyond the kingdoms of contentful cells." The imagery of a heavenly house remains strong in the two concluding couplets, which offer readers hope for life that is bound not by the physical constraints of geography, the cultural constraints of lifestyle, or the arbitrary constraints of time. Rather, its metaphysical existence expands the manner by which humans may define themselves:

The self-remembring soul sweetly recovers
her kindred with the stars; not basely hovers
Below: but meditates her immortal way
Home to the original source of Light and
    intellectual day.

At last, the house has become a home, with all of its connotations of life. Where a house is simply a structure that could stand vacant, a home is a happily inhabited place. This Home is further distinguished by note as the "original source of Light," where the uppercase *L* indicates this Light as distinctive and distinguished, the term often applied to Christ in the Bible. A notable reference appears in the King James Bible (1611) translation of John 1:4–5, as the writer describes God's creation of the Earth and his introduction of Christ, present as both "the Word" and "the light." The verses read, "In him was life; and the life was the light of men. And the light shineth in darkness; and the darkness comprehended it not." In John 8, Christ himself declares, "I am the light of the world."

BIBLIOGRAPHY
Simcox, G. A. "Sandys, Herbert, Crashaw, Vaughan." In *The English Poets: Selections with Critical Introductions,* edited by Thomas Humphry Ward, 192–198. New York: Macmillan, 1914.

"DESCRIPTION OF COOKE-HAM, THE"
AMEILIA LANYER (1611) This poem predates "TO PENSHURST" (1616) by BEN JONSON, long credited as the first country house poem. Drawing on classical generic features, Lanyer expresses the virtue of Margaret, countess of Cumberland, by creating imagery that includes her honoring by the plants and animals of the estate. Feminist critics find the poem of great interest in its focus on the custom that did not allow women to inherit property. Rather than featuring the countess and her daughter, Anne Clifford, enjoying the estate, Lanyer describes their taking leave of their home. Its ownership remained in doubt after the death of the earl, George Clifford, as Anne and her mother entered a lengthy legal battle with Clifford's brother and nephew, who sought to deny Anne Clifford's claim to her own father's estates. The preferred manner for existence of women of Lanyer's day depended on the largesse of

male heirs. As with other of Lanyer's works, "The Description of Cooke-ham" offers a vision of an all-female community with little need for traditional male authority. Her challenge of the gender hierarchy fore-shadowed her own later legal battles with her dead husband's brothers as she fought for an income from his former business promised to her by her in-laws.

While Lanyer's country poem is often compared to that of Jonson, they did not work with the same assumptions regarding inheritance of property. The critic Marshall Grossman suggests that Jonson may have been credited improperly for the first country house poem because males received preference in matters of ownership. He theorizes that the country-house genre itself "was gendered at its inception," and he sees Jonson as suggesting a relationship between the order of nature and man, rather than between nature and all of humankind. Lanyer's 210 lines of rhyming couplets paint an elegant picture of a female paradise that grays and withers upon the forced removal of its inhabitants. The poem also informs readers that Lanyer may have begun her career as a poet through the influence of the Countess of Cumberland.

The speaker opens with praise, bidding farewell to "sweet Cooke-ham" and acknowledging she "first obtained / Grace from the grace where perfect grace remained," suggesting that she gained favor from the perfectly virtuous Margaret, countess of Cumberland, who inhabited Cooke-ham. The voice makes clear that the grounds of Cooke-ham shone in response to the countess's presence, "From whose desires did spring this work of grace." Grace, or conferred merit, becomes a theme of the poem, as that term is repeated multiple times.

Lanyer employs the FIGURATIVE LANGUAGE (FIGURE OF SPEECH) of personification in line after line to make her point that Cooke-ham is nothing without the presence of the countess. For instance, she writes in lines 35–45,

> The very hills right humbly did descend,
> When you to tread upon them did intend.
> And as you set your feet, they still did rise,
> Glad that they could receive so rich a prize.
> The gentle winds did take delight to be

> Among those woods that were so graced by thee.
> And in sad murmur uttered pleasing sound,
> That pleasure in that place might more abound:
> The swelling banks delivered all their pride,
> When such a Phoenix once they had espied.

Lanyer also adds imagery of the countess's studying her Bible among the friendly elements, further emphasizing her pious purity:

> In these sweet woods how often did you walk,
> With Christ and his Apostles there to talk;
> Placing his holy writ in some fair tree,
> To meditate what you therein did see. (82–85)

The countess converses with Moses, David, and Joseph, seeking heavenly counsel. Lanyer next references the countess's daughter, Anne Clifford, whose account of her legal wranglings with her family proved invaluable to later feminist critics. She refers to Clifford as a "sweet lady," "noble," "honorable," with a "fair breast" that housed "true virtue."

After establishing the natural elements as reacting to the countess, Lanyer can express their reaction upon learning she would have to leave. The trees, previously "so glorious," "Forsook both flowers and fruit, when once they knew / Of your depart, their very leaves did wither." (134–135). All vegetation pleads that the countess and her daughter remain, but finding their pleas in vain, "they cast their leaves away" (141). The nightingale, "Fair Philomela," which previously sang joyfully, "leaves her mournful ditty, / Drowned in dead sleep, yet can procure no pity" (189–190), while trees turn "bare and desolate" and even "The sun grew weak, his beams no comfort gave." (195).

As Lanyer closes, she hopes, "When I am dead thy name in this may live" (206), expressing the traditional desire for immortality for her subject that literature could afford. While the influence of the countess on her estate proved great, that on the poet proved even greater, as Lanyer concludes about her subject, "Whose virtues lodge in my unworthy breast, / And ever shall, so long as life remains, / Tying my heart to her by those rich chains" (208–210).

BIBLIOGRAPHY

Grossman, Marshall. *Aemilia Lanyer: Gender, Genre, and the Canon.* Lexington: University Press of Kentucky, 1998.

DESERTED VILLAGE, THE OLIVER GOLD-SMITH (1770)

When OLIVER GOLDSMITH wrote his 431-line poem in rhyming couplets *The Deserted Village,* he exhibited the talent for shrewd observation and scene for which he had gained a reputation. He also imbued this idealization of English rural life with the simplicity and unforced grace critics later found his most appealing attributes. He mingles his idealized scenes with memories of his own careless youth in Ireland. While the tone remained light, Goldsmith had a serious concern, that of the effects of the agricultural revolution, which resulted in the enclosure of arable land, often to form private parks or gardens. The Enclosure Acts caused small farmers whose families had earned their living from the land for generations to lose everything. Goldsmith's sad vision of that displacement incorporates hyperbole, as he exaggerates the resultant migration of yeoman farmers to British cities and to America, as well as the heartless characters of the wealthy. However, his opposition to "luxury" and support of "rural virtue" remained sincere, and his nostalgic tone results in a strong sense of longing for a lifestyle already doomed.

Goldsmith begins in a voice of praise, writing, "Sweet Auburn! Loveliest village of the plain," then praises in his second and third lines the abundance of village life, not only because it produces material results, but because it is a place "Where health and plenty cheered the laboring swain, / Where smiling spring its earliest visit paid." He adopts the FIGURATIVE LANGUAGE of personification to demonstrate that nature proved kind to Auburn, heavily suggesting that kindness as a result of right living. The speaker notes that summer, slow to part, leaves behind many flowers that offer "lovely bowers of innocence and ease" and informs readers this was where he spent his youth. That adds an authority to the description of a place "Where humble happiness endeared each scene," Goldsmith's use of ALLITERATION calling attention to the fact that the inhabitants were marked by humility. His selection of adjectives, as in "sheltered cot," "never-failing brook,"

and "decent church," all suggest the sterling character of those who reside at Auburn, as well as of nature, which supports it. Readers will later notice a marked contrast between the "laboring swain" and the aggressive, greedy individuals whom, despite laws permitting their actions, Goldsmith envisions as no better than poachers raping the land and destroying its abundance. Many of the early details support this method, suggesting contrast with the descriptions that will occur later in the poem. He concludes the first part of his poem with "These were thy charms—But all these charms are fled" in order to signal transition.

In line 36, Goldsmith adds details, which abruptly convert the positive tone to negative, balancing the opening portion. Readers learn that "sports are fled, and all thy charms withdrawn," that "the tyrant's hand" has invaded the bower and "desolation saddens" the green of the village. A new "master grasps the whole domain" (39), while a half-tilled field "stints" the plain. The adjectives turn dark, that rhetorical change echoing the change to Auburn. The brook is "choked"; the bittern, a local bird, is "hollow-sounding"; and even the ruin done to the land is "shapeless." Conditions become so bad that "trembling, shrinking from the spoiler's hand, / Far, far away thy children leave the land." The personal possessive pronoun, *thy,* connotes days past and represents a reverent attitude toward that past. The accumulating wealth of the present leads to human decay. The speaker's attitude toward the encroachers is one of disdain, then warning, as he notes:

> Princes and lords may flourish, or may fade;
> A breath can make them, as a breath has made;
> But a bold peasantry, their country's pride,
> When once destroyed, can never be supplied.
>   (53–56)

The speaker then calls on history to remember a time when "every rood of ground" could support a worker, requiring only "light labor" to spread the earth's bounty. Goldsmith uses repetition to good effect when he writes of the losses resulting from the arrival of "Unwieldy wealth, and cumbrous pomp":

These gentle hours that plenty bade to bloom,
Those calm desires that asked but little room,
Those healthful sports that graced the peaceful
   scene. (69–71)

They have all disappeared along with "rural mirth and manners."

The speaker next mourns the loss of a peaceful retirement, as his late life stage fills him with concerns. He cannot celebrate the wonderful sounds he used to love, as he recalls at evening's close,

The swain responsive as the milkmaid sung,
The sober herd that lowed to meet their young,
The noisy geese that gabbled o'er the pool,
The playful children just let loose from school.
   (117–120)

Now "No cheerful murmurs fluctuate in the gale" and the earth yields a fraction of the bounty it once did. The speaker feels an especial loss when he remembers the village preacher who never sought power, but rather spent his time with vagrants and beggars, considering it an honor as he "relieved their pain." He extols the virtue of this forgotten individual, remembering the great service he supplied, filling almost an additional 50 lines. This allows Goldsmith not merely to praise the preacher with gushing hyperbole, but to make his case that no such individual exists among the grasping group that displaced the preacher and those to whom he ministered. He does the same for the "village master," who "taught his little school," praising the teacher's good humor and love of learning. A strong example of Goldsmith's exaggeration may be found in lines 213–216:

While words of learned length, and thundering
   sound,
Amazed the gazing rustics ranged around;
And still they gazed, and still the wonder grew,
That one small head could carry all he knew.

The speaker next recalls "transitory splendors," including physical details about not only the village's inhabitants but also their homes, with "whitewashed wall" and "nicely sanded floor," as well as furnishings and a hearth decorated with "aspen boughs, and flowers, and fennel gay" when not being used to protect against the chill. The nostalgic tone proves touching as well as moving, causing the reader to remember his own home. Goldsmith again attacks the intruders, then calls on "Ye friends to truth, ye statesmen," who witness the change to judge which is superior, the "splendid" and "happy land" or an area to which "rich men flock from all the world around," purporting to have a wealth that

Takes up a space that many poor supplied;
Space for his lake, his park's extended bounds,
Space for his horses, equipage, and hounds;
The robe that wraps his limbs in silken sloth
Has robbed the neighboring fields of half their
   growth. (276–280)

Not only have the intruders ruined the property, they have driven the rightful inhabitants away, moving the speaker to ask, "Where then, ah where, shall Poverty reside, / To 'scape the pressure of contiguous Pride?" He answers his own grim question with an equally grim reply. Some move to the city, where they find only work at a trade that cannot support them, and they suffer mightily. Others leave the country, traveling to a place inhabited only by terrors, including "blazing suns that dart a downward ray," "Matted woods where birds forget to sing / But silent bats in drowsy clusters cling;" and "the dark scorpion gathers death around." He notes the destruction to local lands but does not ask readers to interfere. Rather, he bids the scene farewell, asking that it continue to remind humans of its existence:

Still let thy voice, prevailing over time,
Redress the rigors of the inclement clime;
And slighted truth, with thy persuasive strain
Teach erring man to spurn the rage of gain.
   (421–424)

Goldsmith's hope made clear in his last few lines is that nature itself can teach man the folly of his ways. His speaker hopes man will eventually learn that "states of native strength," although "very poor, may still be very blest" and remain far preferable to the devastation caused by the base desires of an arrogant few. Goldsmith's close friend and confidant SAMUEL JOHNSON composed the final four lines:

That Trade's proud empire hastes to swift
   decay,
As ocean sweeps the labored mole away;
While self-dependent power can time defy
As rocks resist the billows and the sky.

While Goldsmith's "Auburn" was based on his childhood home of Athlone, Ireland, Auburn was another name for Lissoy Parsonage, where he lived. *The Deserted Village* inspired the name *Auburn* for towns the world over. As are others of Goldsmith's works, the poem is available in both print and electronic form.

"DIALOGUE BETWEEN THE SOUL AND BODY, A" ANDREW MARVELL (1681)

While ANDREW MARVELL's "A Dialogue Between the Soul and the Body" contains a traditional medieval COMPLAINT of the soul against the tyranny of the body, critics do not consider it a marked example of the soul-body dialogue genre. It lacks several traditional elements, including reference to sin and differentiation between will and action. Marvell establishes a philosophical debate, rather than a religious debate, and he makes no attempt to resolve the debate. Rather, he focuses on the dependence of the soul on the body, and vice versa. Marvell echoes sources as disparate as WILLIAM COWLEY's "The Despair" and scientific writings like those focusing on anatomy by William Harvey. He adopts the FIGURATIVE LANGUAGE of personification to allow the soul and body to address one another, devoting two 10-line stanzas to the Soul and one 10-line and a final 14-line stanza to the Body. All stanzas incorporate IRONY, hyperbole, and PARADOX, along with additional figures of speech to elicit amusement in the reader.

The first stanza, spoken by the Soul, notes its imprisonment in "this dungeon," a reference to the body, its binding achieved "with bolts of bones, that fettered stands / In feet; and manacled in hands." Marvell adopts paradox in the phrases "blinded with an eye"

and "Deaf with the drumming of an ear," noting the soul is "hung up . . . in chains / Of nerves, and arteries and veins." He uses a pun on *vein* in the stanza's final line, writing the soul is tortured most of all "In a vain head, and double heart." The soul's accusatory tone and the use of ALLITERATION and exaggeration amuse readers.

The body replies, asking who will deliver it "From bonds of this tyrannic soul?" Although it "warms and moves this needless frame; / (a fever could but do the same)." Marvell includes ANTITHESIS and paradox, noting on the body's part, that the soul "Has made me live to let me die." The body lacks rest, as a result of possession by the soul, the term *possession* generally applied to a satanic effect upon bodies. Not to be outdone, the Soul returns, asking, "What magic" could have confined it "Within another's grief to pine?" The body's constant complaints are felt by the soul, which, by definition, should not feel fleshly reactions. Continuing his use of paradox, Marvell notes that the soul must work "to preserve" that "which me destroys." Not only must the soul endure physical disease, but it must also take the cure along with the body.

In the final stanza, the body takes up the idea of disease by noting that "physic yet could never reach / The maladies thou me dost teach." Marvell characterizes a feeling of hope of the body as a "cramp," fear as "palsy shakes," love as a "pestilence," hatred as a "hidden ulcer," joy as "cheerful madness," and sorrow as an additional madness. The final four lines characterize the body as blaming the soul for original sin, which affects the body in a negative manner, and compares that situation to architects who "square and hew / Green trees that in the forest grew." These "architects" cut down trees and destroy them in order to produce lumber. The reference to "square" echoes one of Marvell's common complaints against garden designs that employ the unnatural angles preferred by some in the Renaissance, a COMPLAINT echoed in his "The Mower against Gardens." Most critics feel that Marvell also alludes to the Garden of Eden, where sin first inhabited the body, destroying its perfect state.

BIBLIOGRAPHY
Bossy, Michel-Andé. "Medieval Debates of Body and Soul." *Comparative Literature* 28 (1976): 144–163.

Osmond, Rosalie. "Body and Soul Dialogues in the Seventeenth Century." *English Literary Renaissance* 4 (1974): 364–403.

Smith, Nigel, ed. *The Poems of Andrew Marvell.* New York: Pearson/Longman, 2003.

Toliver, Harold. "The Strategy of Marvell's Resolve against Created Pleasure." *Studies in English Literature, 1500–1900* 4 (1964): 57–69.

"DISAPPOINTMENT, THE" APHRA BEHN (1680)

APHRA BEHN's lengthy poem "The Disappointment" features the well-known tale of the shepherd Lysander and his unsuccessful attempt to rape the not unwilling nymph Cloris. Its source was likely the French poem *Su rune impuissance* by Jean Benech de Cantenac, published in 1661 in Amsterdam in the collection *Recueil de diverses poésies choisies.* While that work presented the problem from the male viewpoint, Behn relates the incident from the female point of view. Highly erotic, the poem supports Behn's reputation as a female poet bold enough to use topics considered by her contemporaries only appropriate to male writers. In a preface to one of her several RESTORATION plays, she defended her use of sexual themes in all of her writing, noting that society unfairly labeled her talents "my masculine part, the poet in me." Ignoring such criticism, Behn became the first English woman to support herself with writing, gaining popularity, but later dying in poverty. She remained an obscure writer until later 19th-century critics renewed interest in her, and Virginia Woolf declared all women writers to be in Behn's debt. By the mid-20th century, feminist critics revived her works, and her poetry became widely anthologized.

In "The Dream" Behn sketches in detail in 14 10-line stanzas "the amorous" Lysander's surprising of Cloris as he was "By an impatient passion swayed." What happens next represents at first a sexually charged rape scene, but by the poem's conclusion, Behn has subverted with IRONY the tale's traditional theme to suggest it tells of an attempted seduction by Cloris of Lysander. Behn complements the verse format with dramatic dialogue that clearly reflects her dramatist background as she replaces the original urban French setting with a pastoral English one.

When Cloris realizes that she cannot escape from "a lone thicket made for love," she

. . . permits his force, yet gently strove;
Her hands his bosom softly meet,
But not to put him back designed,
Rather to draw 'em on inclined.

Cloris reacts in a manner traditionally credited to the female, long seen as a temptress, whose charms in the Garden of Eden doomed men to a life of misery. The narrator tells readers, "She wants the power to say—*Ah! What d'ye do?*," italicizing her silent plea for emphasis and using the term *wants* to mean "lacks." Cloris immediately regains her voice, first "breathing faintly in [Lysander's] ear," then crying to him,

Cease, cease—your vain desire.
Or I'll call out—what would you do?
My dearer honor even to you
I cannot, must not give—Retire.
Or take this life, whose chiefest part
I gave you with the conquest of my heart.

Although Cloris makes the traditional plea to one for whom she willingly has pledged her metaphoric body and soul not to steal by force her physical virginity, that plea characterizing her as a victim allows her to exercise a peculiar power over Lysander. Readers not knowing the story of the famous duo at first might fear that Lysander will follow Cloris's command to kill her, especially in view of the fact that he is a shepherd, for whom the sacrificial lamb was a fact of life. He presses a "burning, trembling hand . . . Upon her swelling snowy breast," as Behn uses ALLITERATION for momentum to support the action and employs the traditional image of snow to suggest purity. Later feminist critics question whether Behn intended such imagery as ironic, as Cloris may be seen to take charge of the situation, her very surrender promoting Lysander's defeat. Cloris is completely exposed,

. . . her rising bosom bare;
Her loose thin robes, through which appear
A shape designed for love and play;

The speaker adds that "her pride and shame" seem to have abandoned her, as Lysander cannot complete the act. Playing upon the sacrifice theme, Behn adds that Cloris offers "her virgin innocence / A victim to love's sacred flame." That fact makes clear that Cloris is the active party, while Lysander remains a pawn to passion's whim, passively following his physical instincts without any thought to match Cloris's cunning. In the end, it is Lysander who is "o'er-ravished," "Ready to taste a thousand joys," but, "too transported," he loses his erection. Behn does not mince words as Cloris reaches for "that fabulous Priapus. That potent god," but instead encounters "a snake," supporting the familiar use of the serpent as a phallic symbol and again calling to mind the Garden of Eden scene of the temptation of Eve. Interestingly, this temptation originates with the man, not Satan.

In a clever switch of the center of desire from the male to the female, Behn describes Cloris as withdrawing her hand, "Finding that god of her desires / Disarmed of all his awful fires." Cloris becomes the figure filled with potency, while Lysander's potency has abandoned him. Cloris runs away, and the speaker inserts herself into the poem, commenting, "The nymph's resentments, none but I / Can well imagine or condole," as Behn calls attention to herself, a typical act on her part. Lysander curses every god he can think of, although as the speaker makes clear in the final lines, "the shepherdess's charms" became a "bewitching influence" that "damned him to the hell of impotence."

The poem remains of interest on several levels. First Behn updates a classic tale, enhancing its inherent erotic power with blatant sexual references. Second, she recasts the tale as a tension-filled drama, including a dramatic climax, reflecting her experience as a playwright. Third, in a feminist critical approach, the title "The Disappointment" could become a subtext, referring not to Lysander's feelings of impotence in an attempted rape, but rather to Cloris's disillusionment as Lysander cannot fulfill her sexual expectations; he is a disappointing combatant, leaving her with too easy a victory. Finally, another way of viewing Cloris is as one who uses her sexual allure, which ostensibly leaves her open to victimization, instead as a trap for the unsuspecting male. Of importance is the phrase "bewitching influence," in which the male's disappointing performance can only be caused by a monstrous female, a witch. Behn slyly reflects this traditional belief only in a final line, after having convinced readers that Lysander was, no pun intended, simply not up to the task.

BIBLIOGRAPHY
Duffy, Maureen. *The Passionate Shepherdess: Aphra Behn 1640–89*. London: Methuen, 1989.
Survey of British Poetry: Cavalier to Restoration. Vol. 2. Edited by the Editorial Board, Roth Publishing. Great Neck, N.Y.: Poetry Anthology Press, 1989.
Ward, Thomas Humphry. *The English Poets: Selections with Critical Introductions by Various Writers and a General Introduction by Matthew Arnold*. Vol. 2. New York: Macmillan, 1912.

"DISCIPLINE" George Herbert (1633) In "Discipline," George Herbert pleas with God gently to correct man's errant acts, rather than use violence. He appeals to God's mercy, utilizing a New Testament vision of God, rather than the Old Testament image of a punisher filled with wrath. As in many of Herbert's poems form becomes important in shaping the eight four-line stanzas. Lines 1, 2, and 4 depend on iambic trimeter for rhythm, while line 3 contains only two feet with a trochaic rhythm. Herbert employs repetition of words and phrases for emphasis and effect. The first stanza makes a direct request:

> Throw away thy rod,
> Throw away thy wrath:
>   O my God,
> Take the gentle path. (1–4)

In making the request, the speaker could be seen as impudently attempting to instruct God. However, the acknowledgment "O my God" acts at once as recognition of God's power and as praise of that power. Herbert suggests that he well understands God's enormous capacity for punishment, indicated by the strongly descriptive term *wrath*. He also understands that God's power to control his wrath remains admirable. Unlike man, he can exert self-control when needed. The second stanza supports the request by making clear the person does not speak from a sense of entitlement, but rather from humility:

> For my heart's desire
> Unto thine is bent:
>   I aspire
> To a full consent. (5–8)

The speaker possesses a heart willing to comply with God's demands, although his flesh may not have that strength. The third stanza declares that the speaker has learned all he knows through "thy book alone," meaning the Bible; the speaker "affect[s] to own" (11–12) nothing of his own. The fourth stanza offers imagery of a man on his knees, constantly trying to gain God's grace:

> Though I fail, I weep:
> Though I halt in pace,
>   Yet I creep
> To the throne of grace. (9–12)

The speaker then returns to his original request, suggesting that rather than wrath, "Love will do the deed," causing "Stony hearts" to bleed. He praises Love as "swift of foot" and contradicts traditional visions of Love, describing it with FIGURATIVE LANGUAGE (FIGURE OF SPEECH) as "a man of war" that "can shoot, / And can hit from afar." Herbert emphasizes the terrible and awesome strength of love as an emotion. The speaker then notes that love's "bow . . . brought thee low," meaning because God loved man, his son died on the cross. As love has worked miracles previously, it can surely work to discipline the speaker.

The poem concludes with an echo of its opening lines, with alterations:

> Throw away thy rod;
> Though man frailties hath,
>   Thou art God:
> Throw away thy wrath. (29–32)

By requesting that God "throw away" wrath, Herbert notes God's role as an active deity and one fully capable of making choices of sacrifice. His previous reference to the sacrifice made by Christ on the cross confirms this tremendous power.

"DISDAINE RETURNED" THOMAS CAREW (1640)

THOMAS CAREW's "Disdaine Returned" falls firmly into the CAVALIER poet tradition. Its light, lyrical feel is intended, as Carew and his contemporaries at the court of Charles II focused mainly on themes of love: love thwarted, love accepted, love disdained, love engendered, love proposed, love rejected. Heightened emotion became their goal, and they achieved it through a musical cadence that allowed many of their poems to be set to music, as was true of much LYRIC verse. The poetry often featured romantic games played by an idealized female and the male voice that explained the give and take between a couple. Carew formats his three stanzas with varying length, the first two composed of six lines and the third of eight. The RHYME scheme also varies, with the first two stanzas adhering to an *ababcc* format and the third formatted *ababccdd*. The rhyme variance allows sound to support sense, as Carew's poem features a shift in feeling from admiration to disdain.

The speaker of "Disdaine Returned" begins with the familiar conceit of a catalog of female body parts, the beauty of each revealed through FIGURATIVE LANGUAGE (FIGURE OF SPEECH), or comparison. The cheek is compared to a rose, the lip to coral, and the eyes to stars. The speaker cautions that "He" who seeks such attractions as "Fuel to maintain his fires" must remain aware that "As old Time makes these decay, / So his flames must waste away." In the second stanza, Carew departs from the traditional CARPE DIEM theme for which Cavalier poets gained fame, preaching the preference of a "smooth, and stedfast mind, / Gentle thoughts, and calme desires" over that of changeable beauty. While the coral may fade from lips and the rosy glow from cheeks, "Hearts, with equall love combind / Kindle never dying fires." The speaker urges equality between lovers, favoring its longevity. Where these elements prove absent, the speaker declares, "I despise / Lovely cheeks, or lips, or eyes." In the final stanza the speaker boldly addresses Celia, Carew's favorite female persona, making clear that her tears will prove useless in convincing his "resolv'd heart to returne." Celia has apparently rejected the speaker as a lover. He has "searcht" her soul and found "nought, but pride, and scorne," in addition having learned her "arts." Those discoveries afford him strength to "disdaine" Celia in the same way she has disdained him. He concludes by admitting that having conveyed as part of his revenge his love to her, he does lose a bit of his power. However, the poem claims victory for the speaker. His lack of regret over the loss of Celia proves his resolve to find a greater worth in constancy than beauty.

DIVINE MEDITATIONS, THE WILLIAM ALABASTER (1597–1598?)

Some question remains regarding the period in which WILLIAM ALABASTER composed the 77 SONNETs included in his *The Divine Meditations*. Critics believe they were written during Alabaster's imprisonment between 1597 and 1598 after his first conversion to Catholicism. They appear in two manuscripts, and the manuscripts have some sonnets in common. While many are titled and numbered, others are only numbered. Alabaster's work represents a look forward to the 17th century, in which the sonnet form would remain a popular vehicle for occasional poems, including devotionals. They are collected into sequences later titled by critics *The Portrait of Christ's Death, Penitential Sonnets, Resurrection, Upon the Ensigns of Christ's Crucifying, Miscellaneous Sonnets, New Jerusalem,* and *Personal Sonnets*. A final grouping of two poems, *Questionable Sonnets,* for a total of 79 sonnets, cannot be attributed to Alabaster with complete confidence. They were found, according to Helen Gardner, in the only known copy of "the 1613 edition of *Boys, An Exposition of the Festivall Epistles and Gospels,* preserved in the Library of Lambeth Palace."

Written in both the PETRARCHAN and the Elizabethan form, with the Petrarchan Alabaster's favored approach, the sonnets' first purpose appears to be that of meditation, as the group title given the collection indicates. Alabaster's purpose causes the sonnets to lack the universality that promoted the sonnet form's appeal (although JOHN DONNE would later successfully adopt the same form for his meditations), and it may in part be responsible for the categorization of Alabaster as a minor poet. As noted by the critics Story and Gardner,

if not always "good," Alabaster's poetry "is usually interesting." The sonnets' most commonly shared weakness is reflected in their concluding lines, as if Alabaster did not quite understand how to complete his thought, such as in Sonnet 10. Number 9 also bears a weak conclusion, possibly due to its emotionally charged topic of Protestantism and Alabaster's vituperative attack against Luther. After lambasting "damned Luther, swollen with hellish pride" for his presumption, offering a contrast with St. Peter's devotion evidenced through his shunning of "world and goods and wife," Alabaster concludes,

> And who might less than Luther, that did dwell
> In such acquaintance with the fiends of hell,
> And married (incest!) with a sacred nun?

Even if such an attack suited the sonnet—and it does not—Alabaster's emotionally wrought hyperbole destroys the grace inherent to the form. While in praise of God in number 61, "Incarnatio Divini Amoris Argumentum," Alabaster stumbles over a final line, burdened by the need to provide an awkward rhyme. After utilizing the metaphor of romantic love to describe God's love for man, a CONCEIT later also adopted by Donne, Alabaster adds a fairly successful five lines:

> But man did love the gift, and not the giver,
> Yet see how God did in his love persever:
> He gave himself, that as a gift he might
> Be loved by taking, putting on our feature
> So to be seen in more familiar sight,

but concludes with a decidedly awkward thud: "How must we love him that so loves his creature!" In some cases, Alabaster's choice of metaphor dooms his effort, as in SONNET 64, which begins, "Jesu, the handle of the world's great ball." The jarring contrast between the imagery evoked by the formal address, *Jesu,* with that of a common tool, not to mention the ball, a sporting object, renders the line a failure. He echoes the conceit in line 5, "Jesu, the handle consubstantial," which also contains an eye rhyme that results in unintentional humor.

All of the sonnets do not share such problems, as demonstrated in Sonnet 43, considered one of the more superior. Alabaster uses as an extended metaphor the concept of the "threes," based on the traditional Christian understanding of God, Christ, and the Holy Spirit as the triumvirate. He begins,

> Thrice happy souls and spirits unbodied,
> Who in the school of heaven do always see
> The three-leaved bible of one Trinity,
> In whose unfolded page are to be read
> The incomprehended secrets of the Godhead.

The next lines explain that love remains necessary to the act of reading and learning God's life lessons, with the final couplet admonishing, "From word to word: for all is but one letter, / Which still is learnt, but never learnt the better." The conclusion benefits from repetition of the term *learnt,* as well as the placement of a preponderance of syllables in the second phrase, emphasizing its heady message.

Many of the sonnets incorporate the expected PARADOX notable in the approach of METAPHYSICAL POETS AND POETRY, including SONNET 15. Much of that paradox reflects the mystery implicit in Alabaster's subject of Christianity, described by Story and Gardner as an infinite God's assuming of man's finite form. An example appears in Sonnet 54, titled "Incarnationem Ratione Probare Impossibile": "Two, yet but one, which either other is, / One, yet in two, which neither other be / God and man in one personality." Alabaster's obvious delight in the mystery that is the deity is evident in his production of a word riddle emphasizing the act of riddle solving often depicted in mythology as a test of courage and mettle. He also suggests the inadequacy of the human mind, easily deceived by what appear to be simple concepts, which upon consideration challenge comprehension. He employs paradoxes familiar to Christians, such as water that burns, "The smouldering brimstone and the burning lake" (Sonnet 46, "Of His Conversion") and maternal imagery to evoke God's nurture, "O holy mother, New Jerusalem" (Sonnet 42).

As might be expected the poems adopt abundant Christian symbolism, some of which remains accessible by the common Christian reader because of its physical presence in church iconography. For example, Alabaster uses the grape cluster as symbolic of Christ; the grapes often appear in stained-glass windows, easily observable by worshipers. He also enjoys enticing readers to admire his wordplay, manipulating sound and meaning to high effect, as in his final lines of Sonnet 48, "That fire may draw forth blood, blood extend fire, / Desire possession, possession desire."

BIBLIOGRAPHY
Story, G. M., and Helen Gardner, ed. *The Sonnets of William Alabaster.* New York: Oxford University Press, 1959.

DONNE, JOHN (1572–1631)

John Donne was born on Bread Street into a devoutly Catholic family, his father a wealthy ironmonger, his mother the daughter of the dramatist John Heywood. Educated at Hart Hall, Oxford, he did not complete his studies there because he refused to take the Oath of Supremacy, a declaration of "allegiance, fidelity and obedience to His Majesty the King alone . . . and not to any foreign power." It disallowed loyalty to the pope, required of all affirmed Catholics.

Traveling abroad for a time, Donne would forever remain conscious of his Catholic background. By all accounts he proved a womanizer and became a poet after entering Lincoln's Inn in 1592. While exact dating of his early poetry is not assured, he produced in this period his famous romantic poetry as well as his *Satires,* using formal verse in five poems to produce some of the first verse satires in English. Critics like Helen Gardner feel he began a serious consideration of faith at that time, evident particularly in the third satire, when he recognized only the authority of conscience, rather than that of any specific religious faith. However, he demonstrated a continued belief in the importance of religion, for "true Religion" he saw as the responsibility of any individual who considered himself a moral being. He did not criticize various approaches to Christianity, but rather the reasons that men choose to practice those approaches. Donne acknowledged that "the intellect, which is made for truth, can attain truth and, having attained it, can keep it, can recognize it, and preserve the recognition." He offered a famous allegory in which he places Truth on a hill, reminding men who may have lost their way that they still have knowledge of the general direction toward faith; Truth acts as a beacon to remind them.

Donne's Catholic family heritage included an uncle who led a Jesuit mission in England and a brother who died in a prison in 1593, having been accused of and convicted for harboring a priest. As for Donne, he fought with Robert Devereux, earl of Essex, at Cadíz in 1596 and accompanied Sir Walter Raleigh in the Azores on a treasure hunting expedition in 1597; both events become subjects for his poetry. Upon return to England, he enjoyed the patronage of Sir Thomas Egerton, lord keeper of the seal, serving him as chief secretary until Donne's secret marriage to Ann More, the 17-year-old niece of Lady Egerton, whom he had known for three years. The family severed ties with Donne after they discovered the marriage, and Egerton ordered him imprisoned for a short time. Because Donne's dismissal by Egerton cut him off from "polite society," he lived with the fear of poverty for years. He learned that he enjoyed city life more than that of the country after traveling again to the Continent with Sir Walter Chute. Upon his return to England, he made unsuccessful bids for patronage to both the countess of Bedford and the countess of Huntingdon.

Donne's struggle with faith continued, evident in his prose *Biathanatos,* written in 1607. It focused on Christianity and suicide, revealing his deep consideration of faith and his gradual separation from the beliefs of Catholicism. Probably in 1608 he wrote "A Litanie," a poem brimming with the physical imagery that so offended later generations. Examples of lines exhibiting Donne's developing recognizable style include "O be thou nail'd unto my heart, / And crucified againe" and

Double in my heart thy flame,
Which let devout sad teares intend; and let
(Though this glasse lanthorne, flesh, do suffer
   maime)
Fire, Sacrifice, Priest, Altar be the same. (24–27)

Notably, in verse number 10 he wrote, "Oh, to some / Not to be Martyrs, is a martyrdome," reflecting his awareness of the sacrifices of his family for their faith and his perceived lack of that faith.

Donne declined a friend's proposal that he become ordained and published in 1610 his noted prose *Pseudo-Martyr,* in which he discussed the strong allegiance he held toward Catholicism. Much of his feeling emanated from his respect for his early teachers, who, Donne wrote, "seem'd to me justly to claime an interest for the guiding, and rectifying of mine understanding" in religious matters. He argued that English Roman Catholics take the Oath of Supremacy, a direct turn from his early thought. His next work, a satire on the Jesuits titled *Ignatius His Conclave* (1611), caught the attention and approval of King James I. Soon after, Donne suffered a depression during which he wrote the HOLY SONNETS, later to become a celebrated collection. One of his Divine Poems is "La Corona," composed of seven linked SONNETS, each celebrating one of the Joyful Mysteries of Faith. As described by Gardner, the final line of each was repeated as the first line of the next and followed the form of Sir Philip Sydney, containing only two rhymes in each octave, the rhymes contained in two closed quatrains. Donne then alternated between two different rhyme formats in the remaining *sestet* of each sonnet. His choice of a more difficult approach than that of most Elizabethan sonneteers, such as Shakespeare, indicates his view of his work as an intellectual challenge. Each of his poems represents a thorough self-examination and a wish to be open to accepting whatever faith might give him. Helping combat his mental state, he developed a circle of friends including MICHAEL DRAYTON, BEN JONSON, and the architect Inigo Jones, who all met regularly at the Mitre Tavern. Donne traveled again to Europe, this time with Sir Robert Drury, and returned to England a year later in 1612, settling in Drury Lane.

Donne's feelings of guilt over subjecting his family to poverty after further unsuccessful attempts to attract patronage for his writing prompted him in 1615 to pursue a career in the Anglican Church, taking holy orders. His continuing devotion to his wife and family testifies to his seriousness of purpose and the lifelong effect of his early grounding in religion. Shortly thereafter James I appointed him royal chaplain, and he became reader in divinity at Lincoln's Inn in 1616. While his income at last offered respite from the family's poverty, Ann would enjoy it only for a year, dying in the delivery of their 12th child, stillborn, in 1617. He had married her at a terrific sacrifice, and her loss plunged him into grief. He seemed never to recover but her death did cause his focus on spiritual matters to deepen. Of their 12 children, seven survived.

Donne turned again to traveling for a few months, this time with Viscount Doncaster on a mission to find consensus between Germany's Catholic leader and some of his Protestant followers. He proved unsuccessful. He wrote at one point to his friend Sir Tobie Mathew, who had converted from Anglicanism to Catholicism, that lack of faith had become so rampant that he was relieved to be united with men of any faith "in a serious meditation of God, and to make any Religion the rule of our actions." He returned to England somewhat revived, his depression having abated. When he was later made dean of St. Paul's, Donne's spirits elevated, and he became a favorite figure in the church. He experienced no sudden inspiration, but rather a slow evolution into spiritual maturity. His daughter Constance made a good marriage to the well-known actor Ned Alleyn, and the family seemed secure until 1623, when Donne fell ill along with many others during an epidemic. He used the time to work on a collection of various mediations and prayers, which became *Devotions Upon Emergent Occasions* (1624). He enjoyed appointment as vicar of St. Dunstan's-in-the-West in 1624. On the day of James I's death, March 27, 1625, Donne preached before King Charles I. In retirement at Chelsea, he continued delivering notable sermons but fell ill again in 1630. Despite his deteriorating and painful condition, he preached at Whitehall before the king one last time on the first Friday in Lent, 1631. He died soon after, on March 31. When St. Paul's burned, Donne's self-designed monument, erected above his grave, survived the Great Fire. His marble effigy was one of the few relics to survive; it resides in the South Quire Aisle of St. Paul's Cathedral, scorch marks still visible on the statue's base.

Forty years of writing produced a remarkable outpouring, in not only poetry and sermons, but also songs, including "GO AND CATCH A FALLING STAR"; hymns, including "HYMN TO CHRIST," "HYMN TO GOD MY GOD," and "A HYMN TO GOD THE FATHER"; and elegies, including "ON HIS MISTRESS" and "TO HIS MISTRESS GOING TO BED," the elegies offering a new approach to English literature. In addition, he wrote the satires; occasional poems, including "GOOD FRIDAY, 1613. RIDING WESTWARD"; verse letters; divine meditations, and devotions. Often anthologized poems include "The FLEA," "The GOOD-MORROW," "The UNDERTAKING," "The SUN RISING," "The INDIFFERENT," "The CANONIZATION," "AIR AND ANGELS," "BREAK OF DAY," "A VALEDICTION: OF WEEPING," "The APPARITION," "A VALEDICTION FORBIDDING MOURNING," "DEATH BE NOT PROUD," "BATTER MY HEART," and "An ANATOMY OF THE WORLD." A large number of readers' favorites appeared in *Songs and Sonnets,* including, "I AM A LITTLE WORLD MADE CUNNINGLY," and hail from Donne's wild days prior to marriage.

Many of Donne's phrases became part of the vernacular, including "Death Be not Proud," "For Whom the Bell Tolls," and "No Man Is an Island." His poetry, never published during his lifetime, first appeared in published version in 1633. Twenty-first-century readers may find hard to believe the fact that Donne suffered a decline in popularity in the centuries after his own, due to beliefs that ran counter to his metaphysical approach. The aspects of Donne appreciated by a modern audience, including his passion and intellect, uneven rhythms, PARADOX, and riddle, annoyed 18th and 19th-century readers. They also found little to admire in his arrogant and irreverent nature, or his lack of focus on the natural world, or the lack of tenderness in his love poetry. Interest in him revived, in large part, as a result of efforts in the early 20th century of the poets William Butler Yeats and T. S. Eliot.

BIBLIOGRAPHY

Carey, John. *John Donne: Life, Mind, and Art.* Boston: Faber & Faber, 1990.

Clements, Arthur L. *Poetry of Contemplation: John Donne, George Herbert, Henry Vaughan and the Modern Period.* Albany: State University of New York Press, 1990.

Edwards, David L. *John Donne: Man of Flesh and Spirit.* Grand Rapids, Mich.: William B. Eerdmans, 2002.

Gardner, Helen, ed. *John Donne: The Divine Poems.* Oxford: Clarendon Press, 1969.

Johnson, Jeffrey. *The Theology of John Donne.* Cambridge: D. S. Brewer, 2001.

Marotti, Arthur F. "John Donne's Conflicted Anti-Catholicism." *The Journal of English and Germanic Philology* 101, no. 3 (July 2002): 358–378.

Mintz, Susannah B. "'Forget the Hee and Shee': Gender and Play in John Donne." *Modern Philology* 98, no. 4 (May 2001): 577.

Parfitt, George A. E. *John Donne: A Literary Life.* Basingstoke, England: Macmillan, 1989.

DRAMA AND POETRY   Poetry was abundant in 16th- and 17th-century English drama, such as that written by William Shakespeare, Christopher Marlowe, BEN JONSON, and others. Most playwrights were also poets, so the incorporation of one genre into another came naturally. Renaissance writers shared concerns for art's form with those of their era. The improvement of nature, an idea that would become foreign to literature of later centuries, extended to all aspects of life in Elizabethan England. Just as the culture appreciated a formally designed garden in which humans executed control over plants by forcing them into various elaborate and intricate shapes and designs, they appreciated the form that poetry represented.

While later realistic writers shaped dialogue to reproduce the spoken word perfectly, early dramatists used the poetic METER of iambic pentameter to format dialogue, adopting the every-other-syllable stress that most closely matched the rhythm of speech. Poetry also allowed control over logistical concerns, such as an actor's delivery, as well as concerns of a more artistic nature, such as his portrayal of emotions. At a time when the English language continued to develop and exhibited various spellings of the same words (Shakespeare spelled his name at least three different ways), dramatists experimented in poetry with new words, contriving pleasing phonetic effects at times.

The concern with models also affected the adaptation of poetry into drama. Elizabethan aesthetics dictated that dramatists look to the classics, adopting Plautus and Terence for comedy, and Seneca for tragedy. Sir Philip Sidney would draw from Aristotle's opinion when he wrote in his *The Defence of Poesy* (1595) that the poet does not faithfully imitate true "fallen nature," but rather an ideal, a "golden" nature. Sidney wrote his defense in reaction to Puritan attacks against poetry as having low social and moral values. Using classical conventions as springboards, dramatists expressed their originality with a combining of forms,

as noted in the comic lines from Shakespeare's *Hamlet* (1600–1601) when Polonius describes the visiting actors as "either for tragedy, comedy, history, pastoral, pastoral-comical, historical-pastoral, tragical-historical, tragical-historical-comical-pastoral" (2.2.392–97).

Literary decorum demanded that drama adapt the ideal genre of poetry for communication with its audience. Not all verses rhymed; those that did generally indicated a shift to a serious and formal subject by the dramatist. Because the early plays were staged outside, often victim to changing weather conditions, they moved rapidly, lacking the breaks at scene and act changes to which modern audiences are accustomed. The use of poetry in dialogue aided in audience understanding of rapidly spoken speeches. Many plays also incorporated songs, naturally structured as poetry. In the Elizabethan court, as well as that of the two Stuarts to follow, James I and Charles I, the contents of drama were dictated by courtly concerns, which also affected their form. Aristocrats patronized dramatic presentations and helped support the poets who wrote them. Courtly romances generally proved long-winded affairs, elegant but artificial, with a high-toned poetry supporting formal conventions. In part, the poetry met political demands, imitating the order and hierarchy that the court represented. Because honor proved the most desirable courtly human attribute, and because of its connotation of a highly developed sensibility, poetry proved the best manner for its use as a theme. Discipline was highly valued and the universal truth that the higher power ruled the lower could be easily adapted to poetry. Because most tragedies at the end of the 16th century and many in the early 17th century focused on noble characters, dialogue in verse proved appropriate to their high stations. Comedies were considered a lower art form and produced a mix of prose and verse, with middle- and lower-class characters speaking in prose.

Tragedy, such as John Webster's *The Duchess of Malfi* (1614), incorporated the rhyming couplet throughout to conclude serious speeches, as in the two lines that conclude the third scene of the second act: "'though lust do mask in nev'r so strange disguise, / She's oft found witty but is never wise.'" Jonson employed poetry to open his dark comedy *Volpone; or, The Fox*

(1616), creating wordplay by using the letters of the character name *Volpone* to begin each of the first seven lines:

> V olpone, childless, rich, feigns sick, despairs,
> O ffers his state to hopes of several heirs,
> L ies languishing; his Parasite receives
> P resents of all, assures, deludes, then weaves
> O ther cross plots, which ope' themselves, are
>   told.
> N ew tricks for safety are sought; they thrive,
>   when, bold,
> E ach tempts th'other again, and all are sold.

Thomas Middleton's satirical dramas used the rhyming couplet to create epigrams, or wise sayings that concluded mock-moralistic dialogue. Examples from *A Chaste Maid in Cheapside* (1630), which focused on the seven deadly sins, include "He has both the cost and torment; when the strings / Of his heart frets, I feed, laugh, or sing" (1.2.52–53) and "so say I; Though they strive more, / There comes as proud behind as goes before" (2.4.15–16). JOHN FORD commonly incorporated songs into his tragedies, his wonderfully cynical *The Broken Heart* (ca. 1629) a good example, containing "PENTHEA'S DYING SONG" and "CALANTHA'S DIRGE."

However, as the century progressed, and civil wars and revolt proved that no universal truth existed, those individuals with social and political power promoted the idea that a universal truth proved unnecessary. Differing views could easily exist within the same culture, so drama began to focus more on questions than answers. Society showed an appreciation for difference, eschewing the old foundation of hierarchy and uniformity. But during the Interregnum, the years between the execution of Charles I in 1649 and 1660, the Commonwealth became England's government. Within the Commonwealth Oliver Cromwell served as lord protector from 1653 to 1659, and during those years the government was properly referred to as the Protectorate. His self-assigned mission to protect the masses included shielding them from the decadence of art. For 11 years, most drama and art was censored, mirroring the lack of free expression supported by Cromwell and his Protestant faction. While writers

such as JOHN MILTON continued to produce polemical prose and some poetry, drama basically disappeared.

During the Restoration, the period 1660–1700, drama reappeared under the patronage of Charles II. An affable monarch who encouraged art, Charles chartered two acting companies in 1660, the King's Players and the Duke's Players. In 1662 he showed his intellectual bent by chartering the Royal Society of London for the Improving of Natural Knowledge, a display of the monarch's approval of the emerging scientific age. When Charles died in 1685 his brother, James II, succeeded to the throne, only to be chased from the country in 1688 during the Jacobite rebellion. James's daughter, Mary, and her husband, William, took the throne, demanding an oath of allegiance that many artists who supported James found impossible to sign as long as their monarch lived, even in exile.

While Milton wrote as the last Renaissance poet, with great state and formality, JOHN DRYDEN ushered in a new era of elegance. All art reflected the conflict of values that characterized the latter half of the 17th century but most often represented the interests of the wealthy, who could afford to patronize it. The long revered religious orthodoxy was challenged by philosophic skepticism, which had its roots in ancient Greece, reflected in contemporary work by the French writer Michele Montaigne. He and others argued that because humans gain knowledge through their senses, that knowledge will always remain incomplete. That is because senses do not exactly duplicate through human experience what actually occurs in nature. Man should declare nothing as absolute truth and should rely on custom in politics and in ethical and intellectual matters. All of these ideas influenced themes of drama and its incorporation of poetry, but probably none more than science. It seemed to promise that one day all mystery would disappear, and everything about nature and God would stand revealed.

Dryden, a man who wrote in literally every important form, can be used as representative of literary thought from 1660 to 1700. His preference for a simple natural wit guided his choice of format in drama. He turned from the elaborate styles of Milton and JOHN DONNE's metaphysical CONCEITS to embrace a BLANK VERSE that imitated urbane conversation. While FIGURA-

TIVE LANGUAGE remained acceptable for poetry when emotions should be engaged, it was intolerable in the rational exchanges then imitated on the stage. Some exceptions existed in works by minor dramatists. They included Nathaniel Lee (ca. 1649–92), whose wildly violent plots featured characters enduring great emotional swings and using extravagant rhetoric, and the poet and playwright THOMAS OTWAY (1652–85), who specialized in pathos.

In his *An Essay of Dramatic Poesy* (1668) Dryden explained ideas summarized in the 20th century by the critic Earl Miner. According to Miner, Dryden's essay noted that

> the first danger is represented by modern innovations, by English and especially Spanish variety or violence, and by heightening through rhyme. The second danger is exemplified by the example and "rules" of the ancients, by the "correct" practice of the French, and by a narrow idea of verisimilitude that will exclude rhymed verse from the stage.

Dryden's drama masterpiece in blank verse was his tragedy *All for Love* (1677). He also wrote masques, dramatic performances based on mythological tradition, incorporating poetry, music, and dance. In his *The Secular Masque* (1700), written for public performance, the character Momus provides light-hearted rhyming commentary in lines 13–20:

> Ha! ha! ha! ha! ha! Well hast thou done
>   To lay down thy pack,
>   And lighten thy back;
> The world was a fool, e'er since it begun,
> And neither Janus, nor Chronos, nor I
>   Can hinder the crimes,
>   Or mend the bad times,
> 'Tis better to laugh than to cry.

Critics agree that the 18th century produced no high-quality tragedy. The best drama of the Restoration and the 18th century was comedy. With witty plots presenting a cynical view of human nature, characterized by sexual intrigue, most dramas of the period fall into the category "the comedy of manners." Such drama featured morality and social commentary, with the intent of making its audience laugh. William Congreve's *The Way of the World* (1700), a prose drama with some inset lyrics, is still performed in the 21st century. It contains a traditional verse prologue, spoken by the character Mr. Betterton, to introduce the drama. The prologue reflects comically on those who write poetry, particularly the author of the drama itself, reading, in part

> Of those few fools, who with ill stars are curst,
> Sure scribbling fools, called poets, fare the
>   worst:
> For they're a sort of fools which fortune makes,
> And, after she has made 'em fools, forsakes.
> With Nature's oafs 'tis quite a diff'rent case,
> For Fortune favours all her idiot race.
> In her own nest the cuckoo eggs we find,
> O'er which she broods to hatch the changeling
>   kind:
> No portion for her own she has to spare,
> So much she dotes on her adopted care.

The same approach may be found in William Wycherley's *The Country Wife* (1672–74), whose rhyming prologue spoken by the character Mr. Hart reads in part

> Poets, like cudgelled bullies, never do
> At first or second blow submit to you;
> But will provoke you still, and ne'er have done,
> Till you are weary first with laying on.
> The late so baffled scribbler of this day,
> Though he stands trembling, bids me boldly
>   say,
> What we before most plays are used to do,
> For poets out of fear first draw on you;
> In a fierce prologue the still pit defy,
> And, ere you speak, like Castril give the lie.

In the 1690s certain members of society, including Anglicans and Noncomformists, demanded reforms in literature, particularly in the bawdy nature of the Restoration comedy. Dryden and Congreve both came under attack by an Anglican clergyman named Jeremy

Collier, who expressed his outrage over the "subversive" wits writing for the stage.

By the 17th century's end, society as a whole demanded more respectable dramatic presentations. Satire seeking social reform emerged as the most common poetry. The old comedies were replaced by highly sentimental presentations, which moved their audience to tears, rather than laughter at the characters' expense. This would change later in the 18th century, although sentiment remained popular, with enormous successes such as the poet JOHN GAY's *The Beggar's Opera* (1728) and comedies by the novelist, poet, and playwright OLIVER GOLDSMITH and by Richard Sheridan.

The Beggar's Opera introduced the BALLAD opera, which would give birth to Sheridan's style and proved important in the much later development of the musicals of Gilbert and Sullivan. Because of its songs, the ballad opera contained much rhyming verse. A comic farce, it promoted a serious theme. It sent a message to the authorities who encouraged some crime in order to collect a percentage of the receipts. The message was that that tenuous control could be lost at any moment, victim to the greed of those who believed themselves in charge. Gay's opera also satirized Italian opera through its parody of grand musical presentations to highlight London's low life. He featured characters representing the real-life criminals Jonathan Wild and Jack Sheppard and also caricatured the prime minister, Sir Robert Walpole. During the prosperous era of the Hanoverian rule (1714–60), in which the Kings George spent as much time outside England in Hanover as possible, Walpole assumed extreme power. Although Walpole conducted a competent and peaceful government, he increased corruption in Parliament through the use of flagrant bribes. He remained indifferent to art, offering little in the way of patronage, thus becoming a prime target for artists.

Gay presented three acts, rather than the traditional five, in 45 rapid scenes. Poetry helped strengthen the drama's momentum. As an example, the rascal Peacham early in the presentation ponders the inner workings of society:

Through all the Employments of Life
Each Neighbour abuses his Brother;

Whore and Rogue they call Husband and Wife:
All Professions be-rogue one another:
The Priest calls the Lawyer a Cheat,
The Lawyer be-knaves the Divine:
And the Statesman, because he's so great,
Thinks his Trade as honest as mine.

Richard Sheridan in his *A School for Scandal* (1777) uses a mixture of prose and poetry to introduce his drama and to ridicule his characters, as seen in an excerpt from his second act. The character Sir Ben attempts to impress his simple audience with his supposed artistic prowess:

Sir Ben. But, ladies, you should be acquainted with the circumstance. You must know, that one day last week, as Lady Betty Curricle was taking the dust in Hyde Park, in a sort of duodecimo phaeton, she desired me to write some verses on her ponies; upon which, I took out my pocket-book, and in one moment produced the following:—

Sure never were seen two such beautiful ponies;
Other horses are clowns, but these macaronies;
To give them this title, I'm sure can't be wrong,
Their legs are so slim, and their tails are so long.

Crab. There, ladies, done in the smack of a whip, and on horseback too.

Jos. Surf. A very Phœbus, mounted—indeed, Sir Benjamin!

Sir Ben. Oh dear, sir!—trifles—trifles.

Oliver Goldsmith's plays, including *She Stoops to Conquer* (1773), were later characterized by critics as a refreshing contrast to the dull sentimental dramas of the period. *She Stoops to Conquer* worked against stereotypes of the day, such as that of country dwellers as dull bumpkins, not on intellectual par with city dwellers. The character Mr. Woodward introduces the drama with a rhyming prologue, a few lines from which are the following:

Pray, would you know the reason why I'm
   crying?

The Comic Muse, long sick, is now a-dying!
And if she goes, my tears will never stop;
For as a player, I can't squeeze out one drop:
I am undone, that's all—shall lose my bread—
I'd rather, but that's nothing—lose my head.

The play also contains verse songs, such as "The Three Pigeons," in addition to lines excerpted from other tunes, and rhymes are used to conclude dramatic asides delivered to the audience. While the use of poetry in 18th-century drama remained common, it had immensely changed from the formal application of the Renaissance to use in promoting farce almost two centuries later.

As the 18th century progressed into the 19th, public tastes shifted. Poetry began to disappear altogether from drama, influenced by one of the greatest threats to poetry: the development of the novel, a genre that quickly became a favorite form of entertainment for all classes.

BIBLIOGRAPHY

Clare, Janet. *Drama of the English Republic, 1649–1660.* New York: Manchester University Press, 2002.

Cordner, Michael, ed. *Court Masques: Jacobean and Caroline Entertainments, 1605–1640.* New York: Oxford University Press, 1999.

McMillan, Ian. *Perfect Catch: Poems, Collaborations, and Scripts.* Manchester, England: Carcanet, 2000.

Miner, Earl. Introduction to *Selected Poetry and Prose of John Dryden,* ix–xxxiv. New York: The Modern Library, 1969.

Rose, Mary Beth. *Perspectives on Renaissance Drama.* Evanston, Ill.: Northwestern University Press and the Newberry Library Center for Renaissance Studies, 1995.

DRAYTON, MICHAEL (1563–1631) Michael

Drayton was born at Hartshill near Atherstone in Warwickshire. Not much is known of his early years, but he may have served Sir Walter Aston as his esquire and temporarily attended Oxford University. Records do show that as a young man he entered service with Sir Henry Goodeere of Powlesworth, who in turn provided Drayton's education. Goodeere also introduced Drayton to the great arts patron Lucy Russell, the countess of Bedford, in an attempt to help support his writing. During this time, Drayton apparently fell in love with Anne Goodeere, Sir Henry's daughter, who influenced the poet's later work by serving as inspiration for the figure "Idea" that appeared on more than one occasion in his poetry. She eventually married and became Anne Rainsford, offering hospitality to Drayton later in his life. Drayton may have served in the army and by 1590 had settled in London. He seemed to prefer the country to the city, often visiting with various members of the landed gentry for pleasure as well as for patronage. He probably tutored Elizabeth Tanfield, the future Viscountess Falkland, the first English woman to produce a closet drama (one meant only to be read aloud, rather than acted on the stage), *Mariam, Fair Queene of Jewry* (1595), and mother to the poet PATRICK CARY.

Drayton first published in 1591, launching a career that would not end for 40 years. He sampled all poetry forms, including pastoral, eclogue, SONNET, and epyllion, a poem with a mythological and/or romantic theme, as well as historical poetry. He adopted both RIME ROYAL and OTTAVA RIMA, according to the seriousness of his subject. Drayton proved adept at serving society's poetic tastes, drawing on a variety of sources and models. He gained a reputation for his meticulous attention to detail, constantly revising and reissuing poems, at times changing their titles, with some of his work existing in five versions. He published two collections of his own poetry, one in 1605 and another in 1619.

Drayton's first publication, *The Harmony of the Church* (1591), was a collection of spiritual verse, which later critics described as overburdened with ornate language. Dedicated to the wealthy Lady Devereaux, the poems probably provided a vehicle for Drayton to seek patronage. The book's version of Song of Solomon offended some, and the archbishop of Canterbury ordered it destroyed. Drayton's first critically worthy work was *Idea, The Shepherds' Garland* (1593), a secular pastoral containing nine separate eclogues and obviously influenced by Edmund Spenser's well-known *The Shepheardes Calender* (1579). Drayton dedicated his poem to Robert Dudley, son of one of Spenser's patrons, the older Robert Dudley, duke of Leicester. It would be revised and reissued in 1606, but the second version did little to correct its trite approach, which was probably the result of Drayton's attempt to adhere to convention. While he took inspiration from fellow poets, Drayton would in turn inspire those who followed him as the courtier tradition continued into the 17th century.

Mindful of the court's interest in the sonnet form, Drayton published his 64-sonnet sequence *Idea's Mirror* (1594), later reissued as *Idea*. His 1595 erotic mythological poem, ENDIMION AND PHOEBE, resembled works by Christopher Marlowe (*Hero and Leander*), William Shakespeare (*Venus and Adonis*), and George Chapman. Drayton acknowledged influence also by Thomas Lodge, who would later reciprocate in his *Fig for Momus*. Although highly romantic by nature, as evidenced by his poetry, Drayton never married. Capturing the wistful tone of one who desires love but has been disappointed, his SONNET "SINCE THERE'S NO HELP, COME LET US KISS AND PART" remains his most accomplished and famous poem in that form. It avoids the cloying heavy language and CONCEITS of much of his other poetry.

In the 1590s Drayton first attempted what would become a favorite form, historical poetry. He based *Piers Gaveston* (1594) on legends regarding the homosexual relationship between the historical royal sycophant Gaveston and King Edward II. According to the scholar Richard Hardin, Drayton followed convention in introducing Gaveston to his readers "From gloomy shadow of eternal night," as many writers had introduced the main characters of their verse tragedies. However, a few verses later, Gaveston appears to be a figure of light, signaling the fact that Drayton seemed unable to decide which of the two Gavestons belonged in his poem. The revised version in 1596 had a stronger moral tone, emphasized with the addition of 26 stanzas. Also in 1594, Drayton published *Matilda,* an epic poem in rime royal. Additional work during the 1590s included *Robert Duke of Normandy* (1596, revised 1605 and 1619), which was one of the final English dream visions, according to Hardin. In this medieval drama, the protagonist is visited by his own ghost as well as the spirit of Fame and Fortune.

Always a careful researcher Drayton often consulted accounts written by the chronicler Ralph Holinshed. His *Mortimeriados* (1596) focused on the Wars of the Roses and would reappear in a much altered version as the well-known *The Barons' Wars* (1603), again considering the subject of Edward II and probably heavily influenced by Marlowe's drama *Edward the Second* (1594). It is likely that Drayton was influenced by a writer he greatly respected, the historian Samuel Daniel, who had written *Civil Wars* (1595), focusing on the fall of Richard II through the fall of Edward IV. Unlike Daniel, however, Drayton limited his topic to one event to add dramatic unity, an element Daniel's prose vision lacked. Hardin explains that *Mortimeriados* allowed Drayton to focus on a topic that he would study for the next decade, "the relation between national destiny and the personal human spirit." As did other writers of English history, Drayton believed that men act, whether for good or evil, as part of a pattern established by a divine power. Important changes made to the second version included the addition of hundreds of lines and a move from rime royal to ottava rima. His interest shifted from individual relationships to the civil war as a topic, and the leader of the revolt against the king, Mortimer, along with Queen Isabel, became major figures. The history contained a gruesome scene of regicide, meant, some later critics believed, as a caution for King James I. Critics disagree over the quality of *The Barons' Wars* as compared to *Mortimeriados*. Some feel the revision proved superior, mainly because of its strengthening in narrative structure. Hardin disagrees, arguing that Drayton mishandled the ottava rima and diminished his presentation in an obvious attempt to impress readers with his scholarship. A further revised text appeared in 1619.

A playwright as well as a poet, Drayton may have written several dramas, but only one survived, *The First Part of Sir John Oldcastle* (1600). Drayton probably collaborated with others on its writing and followed the success of Shakespeare's *Henry IV* plays, in which the Falstaff figure was based on the real Sir John Oldcastle. He earned the nickname "Our English Ovid" after publishing *England's Heroical Epistles* in 1597. Based on Ovid's *Heroides,* which focused on mythological characters, it was composed of a series of 24 love letters in heroic couplets written by actual historical figures. Later critics praised Drayton's skillful use of conceits and his rhetorical balance, aspects that made it the most palatable of his voluminous works to later generations of readers. His next publication, *The Legend of Great Cromwell* (1607), based on the radical Protestant John Foxe's *Acts and Monuments,* focused on Thomas Cromwell, earl of Essex, and his service to Henry VIII. Despite his source, Drayton did not exhibit any bias toward Protestantism. It would be included in the 1610 edition of the important *The Mirror for Magistrates.* Drayton's pastoral poetry also joined that of Sidney, Spenser, Lodge, Nicholas Breton, Christopher Marlowe, and many others, in 1600 and 1614 editions of the prestigious ENGLAND'S HELICON, later considered the finest of the Elizabethan poetic miscellanies.

Drayton had long enjoyed the patronage of Queen Elizabeth and became a familiar figure at her court, known to have shared a friendship with BEN JONSON. However, after her death, when he dedicated a poem to her successor, James I, the King rejected it. Drayton responded in the form of a beast fable, *The Owl* (1604, 1619). He lacked the biting wit for satire, though, and turned more successfully to the ode, becoming the first English poet to produce a collection of work inspired by Horace's *Odes.* That collection, titled *Poems Lyric and Pastoral* (1606), also contained eclogues. In 1612 and 1622, Drayton published the two parts of his major work, *Poly-Olbion,* the first part dedicated to Henry, prince of Wales, who had granted the poet a small bequest. That work had occupied him for some years, as he remained determined to produce a complete history of England; the first part contained 18 volumes, and the second part contained 12 volumes. Probably his most important project, it remains his least readable. He structured it in the French style with alexandrines, lines with METER of iambic hexameter. To English readers accustomed to five feet per line, the additional sixth foot causes reading difficulty. By the time the second part was published, Drayton seemed to have lost his enthusiasm. The poetry appeared more topographical with historical passages that contained little more than description. However, that description would later act as a source for the poet JOHN DYER in his attempt to construct a "Commercial Map" of England.

Drayton issued next a 1627 collection of new poems titled *The Battle of Agincourt,* an epic. His sources for Agincourt again included Holinshed as well as Shakespeare. This volume also contained his most popular piece, *Nimphidia,* a MOCK-HEROIC series of fairy poems, also called "Nimphalls," obviously influenced by Shakespeare's *A Mid-summer Night's Dream* (1596). Also in 1627, he published *The Moon-Calf,* a lengthy satire that focuses on the vices of London, including, according to Hardin, "whoring, gambling, homosexuality, [and] buying Flemish shirts," as well as a "confusion of masculine and feminine dress." In Drayton's final work, *The Muses' Elizium* (1630), he returned to the pastoral.

A popular and revered poet, Drayton was buried in Westminster Abbey. Lady Anne Clifford Herbert, the countess of Dorset, Pembroke, and Montgomery, supplied a monument, and its lines have been attributed to Jonson. His life and works filled an entire chapter in an early edition of *The Cambridge History of English Language,* but he was soon displaced by the METAPHYSICAL POETS AND POETRY, such as that of JOHN DONNE. As Hardin explains, Donne's personal, ahistorical poetry replaced for a modern readership the historical poetry for which Drayton gained fame in his own age. Where Drayton desired to raise English verse and the country of England itself to greater fame than any other country's, his belief in England's destiny making him an "Elizabethan poet," Donne sought simply to surprise his reader with his control over language. Despite later judgments of Drayton's work as overwritten and ponderous, critics praise his pastorals as excellent representatives of that genre. Little read in later years, his works remain available in electronic and print form.

BIBLIOGRAPHY

Brackett, Virginia. "Elizabeth Cary, Drayton and Edward II." *Notes and Queries* 21, no. 4 (December 1994): 517–519.

Davie, Donald. "From Drayton to Dryden: Shifting Tales in Seventeenth-Century Verse." *Times Literary Supplement,* December 27, 1991, 6–7.

Elton, Oliver. *Michael Drayton: A Critical Study.* New York: Russell & Russell, 1966.

Hadfield, Andrew. "Spenser, Drayton, and the Question of Britain." *The Review of English Studies* 51, no. 204 (November 2000): 582–599.

Hardin, Richard F. *Michael Drayton and the Passing of Elizabethan England.* Lawrence: University of Kansas Press, 1973.

Rollins, Hyder Edward, ed. *England's Helicon: 1600, 1614.*
Vol. 1. Cambridge, Mass.: Harvard University Press, 1935.

"DREAM, THE" Aphra Behn (1640?–1689) In

Aphra Behn's "The Dream," a four-beat line alternates
with a three-beat line and projects a rhyming pattern
of *ababcdcdefef*, continuing the every-other-line RHYME
for a total of 36 lines. Behn adopts traditional mythological references to write of thwarted love and incorporates the erotic suggestions for which she became
infamous in her era. As the 19th-century critic Edmund
Gosse wrote of her dramas, "Living among men, struggling by the side of Settle and of Shadwell for the dingy
honours of the stage, she forgot the dignity of her sex,
and wrote like a man." Her dramatic bent surfaces in
the dialogue and wide, sweeping gestures of the characters featured in her poetry. Later critics, most
famously Virginia Woolf, would praise the eroticism
that Behn's contemporaries publicly censored.

Dreams and visions remained an important device
of classical literature, seen as early as Homer's *Odyssey*
and widely present in religious writings as well. Behn
adopts the dream as a trope for free, unfettered thought,
a manner by which restrained desire could be released.
Cupid, the god of love, is the main figure in her dream
sequence, and Behn employs ALLITERATION and imagery
to set a negative tone in her opening line, "The grove
was gloomy all around," supported in the second line
by a stream that does not bubble or flow, but murmurs
instead, as if scolding. The speaker follows in the steps
of Astraea, a nickname applied to Behn herself, who
had occupied a "bed of grass" previous to the speaker's
arrival. After falling asleep, as befits the dream theme,
the speaker sees a

    . . . piteous sight,
    Cupid a-weeping lay,
    Till both his little stars of light
    Had wept themselves away.

The dreamer mentions pity again, deciding to ask
Cupid why he cries, to which

    . . . the sad boy replied,
    "Alas! I am undone!

    As I beneath yon myrtles lay,
    Down by Diana's springs,
    Amyntas stole my bow away,
    And pinioned both my wings."

Cupid refers to the bow he uses to inflict a deadly
wound through the human heart, causing his victims
to fall in love with the next person they see, while
Amyntas is the speaker's lover. Diana, goddess of the
hunt, was also goddess of the moon, a traditional symbol for women, as well as protector of women. That
she had taken Cupid's bow should have been a warning to the female speaker, but she does not heed the
warning. Instead, she focuses on the fact that Amyntas
apparently had control of Cupid's darts, which he in
turn used to wound her. The imagery of penetration
by the arrows or darts may be perceived as a sexual
reference.

Angered that Amyntas had used Cupid's power
against her, the speaker labels him an "amorous swain"
and tells Cupid,

    I'll set thy wings at liberty,
    And thou shalt fly again;
    And, for this service on my part,
    All I demand of thee,
    Is, wound Amyntas's cruel heart,
    And make him die for me.

Behn enjoys wordplay with the use of the word *die*,
suggesting love or passion as the cause of death, a common trope of her time in reference to male ejaculation,
as well as the vulgarized connotation of desire as a type
of death. The speaker acts on her promise, although
Cupid never confirms that he will do his part, saying,
"His silken fetters I untied." Behn's adaptation of silk
as the material that binds Cupid suggests erotica, as
does her act of untying the love god, the act underly-
ing the freedom from normal physical forces one may
experience in a dream. Psychoanalytic critics would
interpret the next lines as highly sexually suggestive,
as Cupid's "gay wings" are "displayed," then "gently
fanned," with Cupid "mounting" as he cries out. True
to his male character, he betrays the speaker, crying,
"'Farewell, fond easy maid!'" She blushes "and angry

grew / I should a god believe." The speaker acknowledges her own foolishness, as Cupid labels her "easy," another term with a pointed sexual connotation. Upon awakening, the speaker discovers her "dream too true," noting that she remained "a slave," ostensibly to love, or more concretely, to Amyntas.

Behn's vocation as a playwright is obvious in her dramatic scene setting and her use of dialogue. One interesting factor is her subdued use of fantasy elements. Although the poem represents a dream, its details remain realistic. The fantasy characters, Cupid and Diana, would not be of great interest, as they were common characters in 17th-century love poetry.

BIBLIOGRAPHY

Gosse, Edmund. "Mrs. Behn." In *The English Poets: Selections with Critical Introductions by Various Writers and a General Introduction by Matthew Arnold,* edited by Thomas Humphry Ward. Vol. 2, 419–421. New York: Macmillan, 1912.

Rowton, Frederic. *The Female Poets of Great Britain.* 1853. Fascimile, Detroit: Wayne State University Press, 1981.

DRUMMOND OF HAWTHORNDEN, WILLIAM (1585–1649)

Considered the last worthy Scottish poet of the 17th century, William Drummond was born to John Drummond, a gentleman usher to King James V, and to Susannah Fowler, whose father was a burgess in Edinburgh. Drummond was educated at the University of Edinburgh, where he graduated with a master's degree in 1605. He then traveled to Paris and to London, assuming the family title of laird of Hawthornden upon his father's death in 1610. Drummond remained for the rest of his life at the family's estate near Edinburgh, focusing upon writing. Once a great center of culture, the Scottish court suffered from the loss of James when he ascended to Great Britain's throne as James I in 1603. James had served as a great patron of poets, his support legitimizing the Scottish language in poetry. Much of Drummond's poetry focused on death and retreat, reflecting the wound left by the absence of Scotland's monarch, as HENRY VAUGHN's poetry would do for England during the later Interregnum. He joined the British world in mourning the death of Prince Henry with his 1613 poem "Teares on the Death of Moliades." In 1614 he

published *Poems,* which he revised two years later. That collection included "Teares on the Death of Moliades," as well as love poetry to a woman identified as Auristella, epigrams, madrigals, and sonnets in the vein of Sir Philip Sidney's *Astrophil to Stella,* and his senior contemporary and fellow Scot WILLIAM ALEXANDER'S SONNET sequence "AURORA." Auristella represented the real-life Euphemia (Mary) Cunningham, a beautiful neighbor who died just before her planned marriage to Drummond. His prose tract *The Cypresse Grove* focuses on death and is considered some of his finest writing. One influence on Drummond's baroque approach was that of the Italian poet Giambattista Marino, who also influenced Samuel Daniel and THOMAS CAREW, a later Caroline poet; Drummond translated more than 20 of the Italian's poems.

Through his contacts in 1614 with Alexander, to whom he would later dedicate a sonnet, Drummond began a correspondence with MICHAEL DRAYTON and made the acquaintance of BEN JONSON when Jonson hiked to his estate from London in 1618. Soon afterward, Drummond published his notes on their meeting as the well-known and praised *Conversations with Ben Jonson,* reprinted in 1832. In 1623 Drummond extracted the religious poems from his earlier collection to publish as *Flowres of Sion.* In addition to engaging in his pastime of writing, he fancied himself an inventor of machines, applying for one patent in 1626. Continuing to mourn Euphemia Cunningham, he fathered three children by a mistress before marrying Elizabeth Logan in 1632, 50 years after his first love's death; together they produced nine offspring. He continued to publish, releasing *The Entertainment of the high and mighty monarch Charles* (1633) and *The Exequies of the Honourable Sir Anthony Alexander, Knight* (1638). Later in life, Drummond began work on a Scottish history from the Royalist view and wrote political tracts against the Covenanters, a reaction to the Bishops' Wars between Charles I and the Scottish Presbyterians. He died a debtor in 1649, emotionally crushed by the execution of Charles. A posthumous edition of most of his works appeared in 1711.

The critic Thomas Humphry Ward noted in his 1880 edition of *The English Poets* that Drummond held interest for readers as a rare breed, "one of the earliest instances in our literature of the man of letters" who wrote not to support himself or simply to pass his leisure time, but rather "for the sake of writing." He was so closely associated with his beloved estate that he was for ages referred to as Drummond of Hawthornden. While not celebrated for more than 100 years after his death, he remains of interest as one of the first Scottish poets, like Alexander, who chose to write in English instead of his native tongue. He presented many valuable books to the University of Edinburgh, and Ward notes that he once wrote to a Dr. Arthur Johnston of "poesy," that her "beauty" appealed to any era, and that "in vain have some men of late, transformers of everything, consulted upon her reformation, and endeavoured to abstract her to metaphysical ideas and scholastical quiddities, denuding her of her own habits, and those ornaments with which she hath amused the world some thousand years." Drummond did not count himself among that group.

BIBLIOGRAPHY

Dunlop, Rhodes, ed. Introduction to *The Poems of Thomas Carew with his Masque, Coelum Britannicum.* xiii–lxxvii. Oxford: Clarendon Press, 1957.

Ward, Thomas Humphry. *The English Poets: Selections with Critical Introductions by Various Writers and a General Introduction by Matthew Arnold.* Vol. 2. New York: Macmillan, 1912.

DRYDEN, JOHN (1631–1700)

John Dryden was born in the Aldwinckle, Northamptonshire, vicarage to parents who could be labeled country gentry. Although they offered some support to the Royalist cause, they also favored Puritan practices, refusing at one point to pay taxes demanded by Charles I. With a huge appetite for reading and study, Dryden attended the best school available, Westminster, benefiting from the talents of its headmaster, Richard Busby. Critics later described Busby as "redoubtable," so strict a taskmaster that the lord protector, Oliver Cromwell, never even challenged him. Under Busby, Dryden learned Latin and fell in love with languages; he would later learn French well and could read Italian and possibly Spanish and Dutch, also translating passably in Greek.

Dryden published an ELEGY titled "Upon the Death of Lord Hastings" in 1649 at the age of 18 years. However, he was not yet ready to begin his prolific publishing career. He earned a B.A. at Trinity College, Cambridge, in 1654, the same year his father, Erasmus, died. While he received an annual income of about £70, adequate for one person, it proved a small sum with which to support his mother and siblings. Not much is known of his activities over the next several years; however, it is likely worked for the Interregnum government.

In 1659 Dryden wrote *Heroic Stanzas,* a poem that took as its subject Cromwell's death. Critics later found the stanzas so superior to Dryden's scant earlier work that they believed other writing, serving as transition, must have been lost. Despite the stanzas' topic, Dryden found much to appreciate about the Restoration and the return of the monarchy. As a result, he published *Astraea Redux* (1660), like, as SAMUEL JOHNSON later wrote, "the other panegyrists of usurpation," probably more for the income patronage promised than as an expression of any ideology. Such practicality, earning Dryden what Johnson labeled "the reproach of inconstancy" from others, would mark the poet's future, as he favored compromise in all of his interests, which were many. He also preferred to investigate human nature in terms of art, religious beliefs, and history, rather than by analysis of the private being. A man of extreme talent, Dryden would later represent more than any other single writer England's literary scene from the Restoration until the 17th century's end. Yet for such a prolific and publicly visible figure, Dryden did not leave behind much evidence regarding his private life.

Dryden continued to produce occasional poetry, written to celebrate or mourn a specific event, throughout the Restoration, at last beginning a serious writing career at age 32. His penchant for tailoring his work to the moment would lead him later to become poet laureate. For the crowning of Charles II, he wrote "To His Sacred Majesty, A Panegyric" (1661) and the tactful "To My Lord Chancellor" (1662). He became a playwright at a fortuitous time, as many London theaters closed under Cromwell reopened and flourished with the renewed interest in drama by the king and the public. An astute observer of fashion, Dryden adopted the French tastes of the new court to write the unremarkable prose *The Wild Gallant* in 1661. That same year he fell in love with his business partner's sister, Lady Elizabeth Howard, and married her. They would have three sons. Charles became an usher of the palace for Pope Clement XI and drowned in 1704 as he swam across the Thames. John also became a dramatist, and Erasmus-Henry entered a religious order.

For Dryden's 1664 production *The Rival Ladies*, he altered his style to adopt the rhyming couplet and garnered minor success. When the plague forced theater closing and the temporary relocation of the court to Oxford, Dryden wrote the extremely successful *The Indian Emperor*. That play made his reputation and established a signature style for Dryden.

Popular and modest, Dryden had many friends, but SAMUEL JOHNSON, among others, believed that he never made a friend whom he did not want to use. Whether an opportunist or simply a shrewd man, Dryden quickly ascended socially. After accepting an invitation to join the new Royal Society, he published one of his best-known works to later generations, ANNUS MIRABILIS: THE YEAR OF WONDERS, 1666 (1667). The wonders referred to in the title included the Second Dutch War and the Great Fire of London, with its tone one of optimism for the future, after those two events. His first really ambitious attempt, *Annus Mirabilis* anticipated as a narrative poem by a few months JOHN MILTON's PARADISE LOST. Dryden's accompanying material proved almost as valuable as the poem itself. In it he provides a definition of historical poetry and discusses his heroic quatrain format as well as various poetic tropes and methods, with classical references. In the year following its publication, England's first poet laureate, SIR WILLIAM DAVENANT, died, and Dryden advanced to that appointment. Johnson later wrote, "The salary of the laureate had been raised in favour of [Ben] Jonson, by Charles the First, from a hundred marks to one hundred pounds a year and a tierce of wine; a revenue in those days not inadequate to the conveniences of life." Dryden's fortunes continued to rise as in 1668 he accepted appointment to the post of Historiographer Royal. Over the next few years, Dryden continued to publish critical as well as creative writing.

Dryden wrote many plays that went to the stage, his best including *Secret Love* (1667), *The Conquest of Granada* (1668), *Tyrannic Love* (1669), and his most enduring comedy, *Marriage à la Mode* (1672). One of his most valuable and famous works of critical prose, *Essay of Dramatic Poesy,* appeared in 1668, later to be followed by the also excellent *Essay of Heroic Plays* (1672). Some other efforts proved of dubious value, including *The State of Innocence,* the never performed curious musical adaptation of *Paradise Lost.* Of much higher quality were the dramas *Aureng-Zebe* (1676) and the BLANK VERSE *All for Love* (1678). Despite some successes on the stage, Dryden suffered strong critical attacks that he found discouraging. Written to blast the heroic style, a satiric play titled *The Rehearsal* (1671) by George Villiers, second duke of Buckingham, first parodied Davenant but was revised to focus on Dryden. A serious physical attack on December 1679, its perpetrator never identified, badly injured Dryden; he never fully recovered. The poet and wit JOHN WILMOT, SECOND EARL OF ROCHESTER, was rumored to have been involved, along with other members of his "Merry Gang," which included Villiers. Later that year Dryden produced a final low-quality drama in an attempt to adapt Shakespeare's *Troilus and Cressida,* prompting deserved public ridicule.

In an attempt to redeem his reputation and in his own personal interest, Dryden turned to the form that would grow immensely popular into the 18th century, the political poem. Despite the fact that he was not Catholic, Dryden wrote an admirable defense of James, duke of York, as the rightful successor to the king. Titled *ABSALOM AND ACHITOPHEL* (1681), the poem used biblical characters to represent current political figures. A masterful work, it took to task the moral rationalist and philosopher Anthony Ashley Cooper, earl of Shaftesbury, and the supporters of James Scott, duke of Monmouth, Charles II's illegitimate son. Monmouth would later be executed for his part in an unsuccessful rebellion against James II. The poem concluded with a passage based on a speech by Charles given at Oxford, where he had temporarily relocated Parliament. The critic Earl Miner later characterized the work as the only exemplary English poem to be written in the midst of revolution, as a response to that revolution. Dryden's anti-Whig stance pleased King Charles II, who also appreciated the poet's next pro-Royalist political work, *The Medal* (1682).

Although such highly politicized writing earned Dryden new detractors and counterattacks, such as *The Medal of John Bayes* by Thomas Shadwell, Dryden met the challenge. He responded to Shadwell with MAC FLECKNOE, another enduring work still widely anthologized. Written in 1678, it went through pirated printings and appeared in an approved version in 1684. Johnson would later write that the attacks on Dryden by both critics and rivals did little to damage his reputation but did succeed in vexing him into a famous temper at times. Johnson characterized Dryden as always "angry at some past or afraid of some future censure"; however, his ever-present "shield of adamantine confidence" protected him.

Dryden's focus on political matters caused him to question his spiritual practices. His religious allegiance had begun to change during the previous decade when, as many of his contemporaries had, he wondered how to choose between the established Church of England and the Roman Catholic Church, the latter the more likely to satisfy a need for central authority. Dryden expressed his questions in his Anglican confession, the enduring RELIGIO LAICI; OR A LAYMAN'S FAITH (1682), although his wife and perhaps his children were all Catholic. But his uncertainty led him to convert to Catholicism in 1686. When Charles II died in 1685 and his brother took the throne as James II, Dryden wrote the ode *Threnodia Augustalis,* in celebration of the two brother monarchs. Unlike Dryden, many feared James's Catholic zeal, and his attackers accused the poet of hypocrisy, labeling his conversion to Catholicism simply an opportunistic move. Whatever the naysayers' opinions regarding his motivations, Dryden's poetry appealed to the public. Undoubtedly influenced by his writing for the stage, he attempted to align his language more closely with natural speech, so that it became colloquial at times, proving accessible to his readers. During the years of his religious questioning, he wrote additional poems with less social impact, such as "TO THE MEMORY OF MR. OLDHAM" (1684), celebrating a poet whom Dryden followed in using satire.

In 1686, Dryden again employed the ode to write the moving *"TO THE PIOUS MEMORY OF . . . MRS. ANNE KILLIGREW,"* referring to ANNE KILLIGREW, a painter and poet who died tragically young. He not only celebrates

her life cut short by drowning, but also asserts his faith in art and the artist. That poem would be adopted by feminist critics in the distant 20th century as a defense of Killigrew, whose talents those critics believed were unfairly ignored by later generations. Dryden used *A SONG FOR ST. CECILIA'S DAY* (1687), ostensibly an occasional poem celebrating a historic event, to express his faith in humans, rather than in the predictive power of history. Also written in 1687, one of Dryden's readily available, but not easily understood, works, titled THE HIND AND THE PANTHER, offered an allegory in fable form. It focused on the conflict between Protestant and Catholic beliefs, criticizing the Anglican Church. Dryden's open criticism of Protestantism caused the revocation of his laureate title when James II's Protestant daughter, Mary, and her husband, William, gained control of the throne in the Revolution of 1688. The removal of the laureateship proved all the more insulting when Shadwell assumed it. Because profession of the Catholic faith was legally treasonous, Dryden could have been executed for his religious practice. But as John Milton's political connections had spared his persecution under Catholic rule, Dryden's friendships protected him under the Protestant rule. He continued work, contributing anonymously in 1688 an "EPIGRAM ON MILTON" to the first illustrated edition of *Paradise Lost.*

Never long without a voice, Dryden returned to his roots in drama, rapidly producing new work for the stage. Two of his plays were staged in 1690, a religious-themed tragicomedy titled *Don Sebastian,* along with a comedy titled *Amphitryon.* The next year, Henry Purcell's celebration of the English monarchy, *King Arthur,* contained a Dryden libretto. However, the social satires of prolific playwrights including William Congreve, whose first play, *The Old Bachelor* (1693), Dryden ironically helped to shape, began to compete with Dryden's own work. Despite their competition with Dryden, the younger playwrights became devotees, and Congreve would produce an edition titled *The Dramatic Works of John Dryden* in 1717 as tribute to his mentor. Dryden enjoyed one additional moderate success, *Cleomenes: The Spartan Hero* (1692), before staging a final unsuccessful work, *Love Triumphant* (1694). His dramatic output included about 30 pieces, a mix of tragedies, comedies, tragicomedies, heroic plays, a masque, operas, and oratorios.

Although he had ended his career as a playwright, Dryden never considered ending his writing career. He began translating his beloved classics, issuing editions of translations from Persius and Juvenal (1693), as well as from Virgil (1697), the *Georgics* later proclaimed a marvel. Centuries after Dryden's death, Miner pronounced his translations as the finest in English. Dryden eventually translated more than 38,000 lines of verse and 2,000 prose pages. The critical commentary included with the Persius and Juvenal satires, titled *Discourse Concerning the Original and Progress of Satire,* became a hallmark of such criticism. Dryden published a second ode for St. Cecilia's Day in 1693, titled "ALEXANDER'S FEAST; OR, THE POWER OF MUSIC," followed seven years later by his acclaimed rendering of tales from Ovid, Boccacio, and Chaucer, *Fables, Ancient and Modern* (1700), a work twice the length of *Paradise Lost.*

As the new century began, Dryden was buried in Westminster Abbey, having exercised tremendous influence through his poetry, prose, drama, and critical writings. He perfected the use of the heroic couplet for his era, and although it would fall into disfavor, the change in public taste did not diminish his accomplishment. The only genre to develop post-Dryden would be the novel, a form he, no doubt, would have attempted, had it been in existence in his lifetime. For a single writer, he had an outstanding output, and he wrote in every 17th-century literary form except the prose romance; even that he produced in a translation of Boccaccio. Yet Dryden rarely repeated his own approach or that of others. While many of his century's poets, including Milton, produced versions of Horace's first satire, in which the classic poet encounters a boar, Dryden resisted. His capacity to focus on craft and format remained unrivaled, and his persistence and resilience in the face of public challenge of his political and religious views was impressive.

ALEXANDER POPE, among many others, paid homage to Dryden; Pope imitated his predecessor's format using a triplet and alexandrine, saluting his variety and energy. Pope wrote in his 1733 *Epistle i of Satires, Epistles, and Odes of Horace,*

Dryden taught to join
The varying verse, the full resounding line,
The long majestic march, and energy divine.
     (2.267)

Pope would extend Dryden's work with the couplet, adding balance and ANTITHESIS and perfecting it in a way Dryden chose not to in his own particular control of "energy divine." Johnson would label Dryden the father of English criticism and Congreve would write of his love for the man who helped introduce him to the world of drama. Perhaps the best measure of a poet's influence is the longevity of his works. The fact that John Dryden's works are studied and read for pleasure more than three centuries after their creation speaks to their excellence.

BIBLIOGRAPHY

Brady, Jennifer, and Earl Miner, ed. *Literary Transmission and Authority: Dryden and Other Writers.* New York: Cambridge University Press, 1993.

Caldwell, Tanya. "John Dryden and John Denham." *Texas Studies in Literature and Language* 46, no. 1 (spring 2004): 49–72.

Gelber, Michael Werth. "John Dryden and the Battle of the Books." *The Huntington Library Quarterly* 63, no. 1–2 (winter 2000): 139–156.

Hall, James M. *John Dryden: A Reference Guide.* Boston: G. K. Hall, 1984.

Johnson, Samuel. *Lives of the English Poets.* Vol. 1. New York: E. P. Dutton, 1958.

Kinsley, James, and James T. Boulton. *English Satiric Poetry, Dryden to Byron.* Columbia: University of South Carolina Press, 1970.

Miner, Earl, ed. *Selected Poetry and Prose of John Dryden.* New York: The Modern Library, 1985.

Pechter, Edward. *Dryden's Classical Theory of Literature.* New York: Cambridge University Press, 1975.

Walker, Keith, ed. *John Dryden: The Major Works.* New York: Oxford University Press, 2003.

Zwicker, Steven. *Dryden's Political Poetry: The Typology of King and Nation.* Providence, R.I.: Brown University Press, 1972.

DUNCIAD, THE ALEXANDER POPE (1723) ALEXANDER POPE has long been acknowledged as one of the leading satirists of his age. Adopting the 18th-century

belief that the "lash" of satire could lead to change, he applied that lash liberally in various works targeting those who established themselves as leaders, politically, artistically, and socially, but whose wrong-headed approach simply misled the public. This method proves especially strong in his celebrated *The Dunciad*, a poem in four books.

The Dunciad was born from discussions among Pope and other members of the informal literary society called the Scriblerus Club. Various voices of the Tory Party, including Pope, JONATHAN SWIFT, and John Arbuthnot, enjoyed concocting satires called the "Memoirs of Martinus Scriblerus" that cleverly ridiculed certain individuals. Arbuthnot contributed the most to the "memoirs," although they would be published under Pope's name in the 1741 edition of his works. Pope and Swift worked together in 1727–28 to publish three volumes titled *Miscellanies,* also satire containing Pope's "Treatise on the Bathos, or the Art of Sinking in Poetry." All of the writings took sharp aim at inferior poets and critics who had gained the eye and ear of the public, establishing themselves as of much greater importance than their work merited. Those individuals reacted as expected, releasing vitriolic responses to Pope's satire. They would all see themselves in unfortunate characterizations in Pope's rebuttal, *The Dunciad*. Based in form on a Latin treatise, it labels the poetasters "dunces" and contains much detail regarding their individual exploits. Pope demonstrates through his own admirable execution everything wrong with the writing of poets like Colley Cibber, John Dennis, the Reverend Laurence Eusden, Lord Hervey, and others. No poet better represented the conservation of words and clean expression admired by the 18th century nor worked better in heroic couplets, preserving the fixed form, yet adding variations in rhythm.

The Dunciad continues to earn much literary critical attention. The critic Brean S. Hammond sees Pope and other Scriblerians, including Swift, JOHN GAY, Henry Fielding, and SAMUEL JOHNSON in his early writing days, as wishing to provide a countercultural force. They opposed the Whig forces, often represented in what they perceived as a low-brow popular culture, overburdened by artifice, while bereft of art. *The Dunciad* dramatizes the struggle between the Scriblerian values and those of the duncres. As Hammond points out, the characters in the poem struggle over actual physical territory, making Pope's presentation concrete, rather than simply abstract. The "Smithfield muses," a derogatory reference to the dunces, gather around St. James's Palace and Westminster, an area hosting Bartholomew Fair and public amusement considered of a low nature.

Pope's friend William Cleland supposedly wrote "A Letter to the Publisher," which precedes the poem, although many believe Pope himself wrote it. In part, he discusses the fact that some have questioned why Pope spends so much energy writing about such weak subjects, persons "too obscure for satyr." He responds that their obscurity "renders them more dangerous, as less thought of: Law can pronounce judgment only on open facts; Morality alone can pass censure on intentions of mischief." He agrees with Pope that "no public punishment" remained, other than "what a good Writer inflicts." Alluding to attacks on Pope's physical condition, he notes, "Deformity becomes an object of Ridicule when a man sets up for being handsome; and so must Dulness when he sets up for a Wit." Pope felt that such "vain pretenders" had to receive their due from a pen far sharper than their own.

The fictional character Martinus Scriblerus writes an introduction to the poem, advising readers that *The Dunciad* is fashioned after a poem by Homer featuring Margites, recorded "to have been Dunce the first." He describes the desperate times in which the author existed, when paper proved so cheap that anyone could write and publish, and the public remained at the mercy of the dullards. He does the only thing he can, which is to write a satire in the heroic fashion, selecting a main hero; Pope will establish Colley Cibber as that hero. Cibber helped operate a drama house and eventually became poet laureate, although his works proved offensive, unimaginative, and miserably executed in the opinion of many. The support he gained by garnering wealthy and powerful patrons allowed his continued public exposure to ridicule.

Each of the four books begins with an Argument that describes its action. In the first, the Goddess in the City of the great Empire of Dulness must find a successor to the present Poet Laureate. "Bays," an allusion to

Cibber, sits among his books, contemplating whether to go to church, gaming, or a party, finally settling on raising an altar of "proper books." Pope places Cibber first close to the walls of Bedlam, linking the dunces with madness to emphasize their irrational behavior. As the critic David Morris notes, satire consists of a moral, a psychological, and a literal study of the irrational. Pope suggests that people could choose madness or rationality. Madness can prove entertaining, a fact suggested in the characterization, from the "Cave of Poverty and Poetry," that bards "Escape in Monsters, and amaze the town."

Pope establishes Fortitude, Temperance, Prudence, and Poetic Justice as allegorical figures who behold the development of a "nameless something," more precisely masses of unidentifiable material called poems or plays. The product of the new poet monsters, they represent "new-born nonsense," mere "Maggots half-form'd in rhyme" that "learn to crawl on poetic feet." Cibber, or "Bays," sinks "from thought to thought" into "a vast profound," plunging as if to the bottom of an abyss or pool to locate his sense. Pope suggests that Cibber will go to any lengths, or depths, to become famous. Unable to locate the bottom limit of his despair or to work out any plan of his own, he steals from the writings of others, as the great heroes of literature observe him from a heavenly vantage point.

Pope returns repeatedly in many of his works to reflect upon the concept of "wit." A popular term in his era, it suggests a talent all writers hoped to be described critically as possessing and exhibiting. However, Pope cautions that simply because one person deems another witty, that does not make him so. Wit remains a difficult commodity to gain, and Bays [Cibber] becomes fearful he will not produce any. One character in the poem urges Bays to seek a place in the dark of dullness, so as not to be judged by the measure of true wit:

> And lest we err by Wit's wild dancing light,
> Secure us kindly in our native night.
> Or, if to Wit a coxcomb make pretence,
> Guard the sure barrier between that and Sense.

"Cibberian forehead, and Cibberian brain" will reduce the art of writing to a shameful shambles. The narrator then turns to Thomas Shadwell, the unfortunate subject of JOHN DRYDEN'S "MAC FLECKNOE: A SATIRE UPON THE TRUE-BLUE PROTESTANT POET T.S.," a satirical poem similar in approach to *The Dunciad*. Dryden had taken Shadwell to task for his *The Medal of John Bayes,* as Pope now singled out Cibber, the "Bays" of his poem. The Mother goddess crowns Cibber "king colley" in the closing lines of the first book, as he measures down to her lowly qualifications.

"Book the Second" focuses on the games played in celebration of Cibber's "coronation," a parody of the Olympic Games. Pope models his mockery after Virgil, who used the games as a serious subject to represent a peaceful enactment of war. As Morris explains, Pope does this precisely to debase the meaning of ceremony. Poets and critics attend the competition in honor of the new poet king, trailed by their patrons and booksellers, representatives of the latter group also receiving a lambasting by Pope in *The Dunciad* for scurrilous business practices. Various accidents occur during the gaming, all designed to make the participants look as foolish as possible. The "Exercises for the Poets" consist of "tickling, vociferating, diving." The lines describing the poet Arnall's dive well represent the tone of the second book, clarifying even further Pope's assessment of the writing efforts of the dunces:

> Furious he dives, precipitately dull.
> Whirlpools and storms his circling arm invest,
> With all the might of gravitation blest.
> No crab more active in the dirty dance,
> Downward to climb, and backward to advance.
> He brings up half the bottom on his head,
> And loudly claims the Journals and the Lead.

Pope based that character on William Arnall, "bred an Attorney, [and] a perfect Genius in this sort of work," according to Pope's footnote. Because Arnall had misused Pope's friends, he landed in the satire. The imagery in this passage clearly suggests that Arnall creates metaphoric "waves" to distract from the fact that he remains unrepentantly dull. As a crab does, he retreats rather than advances, and moves downward, suggesting participation in low culture, rather than to the higher ground that would symbolize value.

At the second book's conclusion, critics read aloud, causing everyone to fall asleep and concluding the games. Pope implies that critical activity results in simple regurgitation, requiring absolutely no creativity. The result proves so dull that even the dunces cannot appreciate it.

In the third Book, *The Dunciad*'s hero naps. Pope again draws on classical sources, as sleep proved crucial to Homer's hero, Odysseus, who enjoyed visits from his guide, Athena, while asleep. The nap echoes the classical pattern of the sleep journey, when the hero descended into Hades to consult dead warriors regarding how he might proceed. However, in Cibber's case, he forgets the past, rather than awakening with a renewed understanding that might guide his future actions. The act clarifies nothing for him; rather, he will awaken believing himself the most fit to rule over the dull kingdom he sees in his vision. Pope emphasizes Cibber's lack of metaphoric vision, as well as a material vision that might awaken in him any semblance of intellectual curiosity.

As summarized, in this book the ghost of Settle visits in Cibber's sleep to show him the wonders of his kingdom. From the Mount of Vision, Settle displays the "past triumphs of the empire of Dulness." They next view the present and then the future, discussing the failures of science. Cibber receives a miraculous vision and learns that the throne of Dulness "shall be advanced over the Theateres, and set up even at Court; then how her Sons shall preside in the seats of Arts and Science." Pope makes the point that a lack of imagination in one area of culture may promote that same lack in another. While Arts differs greatly from Science, both may be equally destroyed by men of Cibber's ilk.

Pope achieves his purpose to demonstrate through satire the quite serious effects of shallow thinking on all aspects of culture. Again Cibber makes an apt representative, as he was a comanager of Drury Lane Theatre and partially responsible for its popular farces. An example of Pope's use of imagery in this section is his insertion of multiple images of owls. While viewed as representing wisdom in classical times, owls were thought stupid creatures in the age of reason. He thus employs the great birds, which have a magnificent appearance but no intellectual

capacity, to emphasize the dark nature of the dunces' power, as in this passage:

> There, dim in the clouds, the poring Scholiasts
>   mark,
> Wits, who like owls, see only in the dark,
> A Lumberhouse of books in ev'ry head,
> For ever reading, never to be read!

No matter how much reading the "Scholiasts," a term that suggests perverted scholars, undertake, they will never be able to write like the masters.

As all heroes do, Cibber must encounter monsters during his sleep vision. Most monsters are fantastical miscreants, the product of a fearsome creativity. However, the monsters Cibber encounters during his dream are the same as those of his day-to-day life, indicating he lacks imagination, and fantasy and reality are the same in his world. This is illustrated in the line spoken to Cibber, "Each Monster meets his likeness in thy mind." Pope references himself, Swift, and Gay in this section, as losers in this "Revolution of Learning" led by Cibber. He also references the great architect Inigo Jones, whose marvels stood under great disrepair, neglected by London's leaders during Pope's time. The book concludes with Cibber's celebrating a vision in which education has all but disappeared:

> "Proceed, great days! 'till Learning fly the shore,
> 'Till Birch shall blush with noble blood no
>   more,
> 'Till Thames see Eaton's sons for eve play,
> 'Till Westminster's whole year be holiday,
> 'Till Isis' Elders reel, their pupils' sport,
> And Alma mater lie dissolv'd in Port!"

The fourth book of *The Dunciad* is most often seen anthologized in excerpts. The Goddess makes her ascent in great majesty to oversee the destruction of Order and Science, replacing them with the Kingdom of the Dull. She silences the Muses, while her children, various "Half-wits, tasteless Admirers, vain Pretenders, the Flatterers of Dunces, or the Patrons of them," gather about, discouraging all progressive thought and activity. The instructors under her sway promise to bombard their charges with words in order to discourage thought: "Since Man from beast by Words is known, / Words are Man's province, Words we teach alone."

Pope especially slams the meaningless ritual demanded by those who seek an Oxford education. Those in charge "vest dull Flatt'ry in the sacred Gown; / Or give from fool to fool the Laurel crown." As the parade of miscreants continues, "There march'd the bard and blockhead, side by side, / Who rhym'd for hire, and patroniz'd for pride." Pope again satirizes those who attempt to balance their lack of talent with paid tributes to pompous patrons. He again blasts critics, echoing lines from his AN ESSAY ON CRITICISM suggesting that they attempt to see the whole work when reviewing it, not simply small parts:

The critic Eye, tht mircroscope of Wit
See hairs and pores, examines bit by bit:
How parts relate to parts, or they to whole,
The body's harmony, the beaminig soul,
Are things which Kuster, Burman, Wasse shall
  see,
When Man's whole frame is obvious to a *Flea*.

With reason lost, the next step is to "doubt of god / Make Nature still incroach upon his plan," substituting a "Mechanic Cause" in the creator's place, to "Make God Man's Image, Man the final Cause," and "See all in *Self*, and but for self be born." In AN ESSAY ON MAN Pope cautioned man not to fixate on himself at the expense of God and Science.

While passing judgment on various disputes, the Goddess suggests those involved "find proper employment . . . in the study of Butterflies, Shells, Birds-nests, Moss, etc., with particular caution, not to proceed beyond Trifles, to any useful or extensive views of Nature, or of the author of Nature." Now the dunces may truly enjoy their position, having been actually ordered not to engage in creative or intellectual activity of note. The poem closes as the group answers the Goddess's call to make "One Mighty Dunciad of the Land!" Night and Chaos reign, evoking thoughts of Milton's PARADISE LOST, in a once creative and intelligent world:

Lo! Thy dread Empire, Chaos! Is restor'd;
Light dies before thy uncreating word;
Thy hand, great Anarch! Lets the curtain fall;
And Universal Darkness buries All.

As Aubrey Williams writes, "Pope's poetry can move us deeply because it so often stirs a sense of the innate precariousness of all things." While his satire contains much humor, it also succeeds in projecting Pope's belief that all "delights" remain transitory. He consistently stresses the relationship of art to everyday life and emphasizes that man's unrelenting moral failure will lead to great losses, of both a material and a spiritual nature. *The Dunciad* stands as an inversion of the Christian vision, rule converted to misrule. Pope understands the occasional necessity for a shake-up in order; however, he strongly cautions against crowd mentality and radical change simply for the sake of change. He understands the courage required for those in the minority, as he and his fellow Scriblerians were, to refuse to accept mediocrity, although the loudest and best-placed voices in society demand it in the name of the people.

BIBLIOGRAPHY

Broich, Ulrich. *Mock-Heroic Poetry, 1680–1750.* Tübingen: M. Niemeyer, 1971.

Brower, Reuben A. *Alexander Pope: The Poetry of Allusion.* Oxford: Oxford University Press, 1986.

Guilhamet, Leon. *Satire and the Transformation of Genre.* Philadelphia: University of Pennsylvania Press, 1987.

Hammond, Brean S. "*The Dunciad* and the City: Pope and Heterotopia." *Studies in the Literary Imagination* 38, no. 1 (spring 2005): 219–232.

Heaney, Peter, ed. *Selected Writings of the Laureate Dunces, Nahum Tate (Laureate 1692–1715), Laurence Eusden (1718–1730), and Colley Cibber (1730–1757).* Lewiston: E. Mellen Press, 1999.

Milton, John. *Paradise Lost.* Edited by Roy Flannagan. New York: Macmillan, 1993.

Morris, David P. *Alexander Pope, the Genius of Sense.* Cambridge, Mass.: Harvard University Press, 1984.

Odell, W. "Pope's *The Dunciad.*" *The Explicator* 64, no. 2 (winter 2006): 71–73.

Sutherland, James, ed. *The Dunciad.* 3d ed. New York: Yale University Press, 1963.

Vermeule, Blakey. "Abstraction, Reference, and the Dualism of Pope's *Dunciad.*" *Modern Philology* 96, no. 1 (August 1998): 16–51.

Weinbrot, Howard D. *Alexander Pope and the Traditions of Formal Verse Satire.* Princeton, N.J.: Princeton University Press, 1982.

Williams, Aubrey. *Pope's Dunciad: A Study of Its Meaning.* Hamden, Conn.: Archon, 1968.

DYER, JOHN (ca. 1700–1758)

John Dyer was born in Dyfed, Wales. His ancestor Hugh Dyer was named by James I in the Charter of 1618 as an alderman of Kidwelly. The daughter of the first vicar of Kidwelly, Elinor, married Hugh Dyer's son, Robert. Robert eventually became the 21st mayor of Kidwelly and John Dyer's great-grandfather. Dyer did not complete his education at Westminster School and, unlike his older and younger brothers, did not go on to Oxford. He returned to Aberglasney and studied law. After his father's death, he moved to London and studied painting as an apprentice to the landscape artist Jonathan Richardson. The talent he lacked on the traditional canvas emerged in his poetic landscapes. Dyer made several close friends who later became noted artists, as he continued to work at painting. One popular artist, Arthur Pond, was later referenced by Dyer in his poem "The Fleece" (1757), a work characterized by his biographer Belinda Humphrey as Dyer's "most eighteenth century poem."

Dyer traveled to Italy soon after April 1724, ostensibly to improve his painting; he copied Correggio's famous *Madonna Adoring the Christ Child.* More importantly, he continued to write, producing several poems including the personal "Written at Ocriculum, in Italy" (1725) in the style of JOHN MILTON's *LYCIDAS.* Dyer's religious considerations in that contemplative poem probably anticipated his later commitment to a religious life. He also continued work in Italy on a poem he had begun in Dyfed, "GRONGAR HILL" (1726). The first of his landscape poetry, it became his most anthologized work in the 21st century. The poem features the valley of the river Towy in Dyfed and the house of Aberglasney, which Dyer praised for their power to inspire.

After a year in Italy, Dyer appeared ready to return home. According to a letter he wrote to his mother, he had discovered "the follies of many distinctions and the greatest heights of people," his understanding of those follies allowing him to "sit me down with much ease in a very firm opinion that you are happier at Grey House than if you practiced all the formalities of greatness in courts and palaces."

Dyer split his time between Wales and London, where one of his most important city friendships was with the older poet JAMES THOMSON. As did Dyer, Thomson showed interest in local landscape poetry, evidenced in his "A HYMN ON THE SEASONS," the first portion on winter published in 1725. While SAMUEL JOHNSON later labeled SIR JOHN DENHAM's "COOPER'S HILL" (1642) the first English local poetry, critics, including Humphrey, dispute that credit. They argue that Denham's description is masked by his political and moral reflections, and that even ALEXANDER POPE's "WINDSOR FOREST" (1713), another touted local poem, cannot compete with the geographic detail for detail's sake found in the poetry of Thomson and Dyer. The relationship of the two poets is evidenced by the only copy of a poem that Dyer wrote in Thomson's honor, probably in 1727, found in the commonplace book of their mutual patroness, the countess of Hertford. The friendship with Thomson seems to have ended a few years later when Dyer returned to the country, although he maintained contact with the countess into the next decade.

Dyer returned briefly to Aberglasney in 1727 and soon afterward apparently became estranged from his brother, Robert. He spent the next several years in London, where accounts indicate he had become wealthy, perhaps through an inheritance after his mother's death in 1735. In that year he began a poem titled "The Cambro-Briton," which would remain unfinished, and began a new project in 1737, the construction of "The Commercial Map of England." He explained his project in a letter to a friend, noting, "I am at present very unfit for Poetical subjects."

In 1738 Dyer purchased two farms at Higham on the Hill in Leicestershire, later moved two miles away to Nuneaton, and married. His 26-year-old wife, Sarah Ensor, was a widow and apparently descended from Shakespeare. Dyer would at last in 1740 publish the mainly descriptive "The Ruins of Rome," begun during his stay in Italy. It is considered less successful than his other efforts because of its generality and lack of emotion, although he wrote enthusiastically while in Italy of the art and architecture that inspired him. In 1741 he sent Pope some special stone for his Twickenham grotto, a hideaway made famous in Pope's writing.

Dyer traveled to Worcester between 1740 and 1741 to paint the portrait of Bishop Hough, a move that would change his life. There he began a serious consideration of his religious beliefs. The meditations contained in his notebook suggest he focused on the nature of morality, recording some pessimistic ideas regarding human behavior. In September 1741, he became ordained as an Anglican deacon and in October as a priest. Dyer served at Coningsby and Kirby in Lincolnshire and gave up his farms to his tenants but began learning about sheep farming at his parish. He used his experience to write four books that composed "The Fleece," all published in 1757, leaving his mapping project unfinished although it had influenced his writing of "The Fleece." In this, his final major work, Dyer again proved himself a landscape painter's poet, writing of British landscape and farming activities with great emotion and imagination. Humphrey describes that work as "a tapestry or living landscape of his own life." By all accounts he proved a conscientious and respected parson, remaining at the parish until his death from consumption in 1757.

William Wordsworth praised Dyer's imagination and "purity of style," comparing him quite favorably with Milton, but later generations found less to appreciate. Little critical work on his poetry exists; edited versions were published in 1770 and in 1903, and select poems are available in electronic and print form.

BIBLIOGRAPHY
Humphrey, Belinda. *John Dyer*. Cardiff: University of Wales Press, 1980.
Lindsay, David W., ed. *English Poetry, 1700–1780: Contemporaries of Swift and Johnson*. Totowa, N.J.: Rowman & Littlefield, 1974.

E

"EASTER" GEORGE HERBERT (1633) In his poem "Easter" GEORGE HERBERT celebrates a Christian tradition of redemption through the use of familiar references. His purpose is not to surprise, but to engage in pleasant instruction, as he constructs a song of praise and celebration of Christ's resurrection. Herbert often employed music as a theme in his poetry, and it perfectly suits the occasion of this LYRIC.

"Easter" contains 30 lines divided into two sections by format. Lines 1–18 are arranged in three groups of six lines. Each group contains a first and third line with the rhythm of iambic pentameter, and a second and fourth two-beat line; the RHYME scheme is *aabb*. That four-line grouping is followed by an additional rhyming iambic pentameter couplet. Thus, the first verse, in which Herbert emphasizes Christ's act of rising from the grave by bidding the Christian heart to "rise" with emotion, reads:

> Rise heart; thy Lord is risen. Sing his praise
> Without delays,
> Who takes thee by the hand, that thou likewise
>   With him mayst rise;
> That, as his death calcined thee to dust,
> His life may make thee gold, and much more
>   just.

His focus in the third stanza shifts to that of song, as he writes, "Consort both heart and lute, and twist a song / Pleasant and long," noting that "all music is but three parts vied / And multiplied," that description suggesting the three members of the Godhead, the Father, the Son, and the Holy Ghost. The sentiment of each verse remains equally clear and simple, calling for recognition of Christ's sacrifice of his life for that of the eternal life of all those who receive his grace.

Herbert divides lines 19–30 into three four-line verses with a METER of four beats per line and a rhyme scheme of *abab*. The presentation slips into narrative, as the speaker tells the Easter story. He begins by describing the triumphant Palm Sunday entrance into Jerusalem of Christ, when crowds lined his path with flowers and palm boughs: "I got me flowers to straw thy way; / I got me boughs off many a tree." Herbert employs CATACHRESIS in his use of the term *straw* as a verb, calling attention to the poor material.

On Good Friday Christ suffered crucifixion, but, as the narrator relates, he rose on Easter Sunday. In the fifth stanza, Christ is compared to "The Sun arising in the East," but its light, along with the perfume from the East, should not presume "to contest / With thy arising." He closes by asking joyfully, "Can there be any day but this," then extends the sun reference, adding, "Though many suns to shine endeavour?" Herbert concludes by suggesting the homonym *son*, for the Son of God, in his allusion: "We count three hundred, but we miss: / There is but one, and that one ever." While men may note hundreds of suns rise, only one Son exists, he who arose to resume an eternal existence, purchasing eternity also for those humans who enjoy God's grace.

"EASTER WINGS" George Herbert (1633)

George Herbert included the well-known shape poems, "The Altar" and "Easter Wings," in his collection *The Temple*. The unity and harmony suggested by the wing shape support Herbert's message about the importance of man's acceptance of grace. As in "The Holdfast" and other such poems, he emphasizes that man can do nothing to earn grace; it must be granted by God. The wings create a sense of freedom, suggested by the act of flying, and Herbert emphasizes that act in references to birds and flight. The poem consists of two 10-line stanzas, with each line varying in length to fit the wing shape. As the lines diminish in length, their content suggests that act, revealing Herbert's skill in using form to reflect sentiment.

The first line is a direct address to God, although the speaker refers to humankind in third-person point of view: "Lord, who createdst man in wealth and store." The speaker notes that man "foolishly lost the same," the line length shrinking with the statement of loss. By the still shorter third line, the speaker suggests man's "Decaying," and in the next lines he adds, "Till he became / Most poor." The fifth line, with only two

words, represents the smallest, poorest point for man. The sixth line, "With thee," balances the fifth line but begins expansion into lines that now increase in length, balancing the first five lines in appearance. Only with God's help can the speaker "rise / As larks, harmoniously," and sing of God's "victories." The final line of the first stanza balances the first in length. Herbert uses a metaphysical approach to express his thought through contradiction, as his speaker notes that "the fall," referring to man's fall from grace in the Garden of Eden, is what will ultimately allow him to fly. This "fortunate fall" sentiment held that had man not engaged in original sin, he would never have had the chance to recover through Christ's sacrifice and experience the glory of redemption.

Repeating the same shape as the first stanza, the second stanza emphasizes that man's age, or history, began in sorrow, another reference to the fall, which brought on "sicknesses and shame" as God's punishment of sin. In the middle of the verse, in its two-word line, the speaker notes he became "Most thin," the thought expressing the thin shape of the wing image. Balancing the sixth line in the first stanza, Herbert

Easter wings.

Lord, who createdst man in wealth and store,
Though foolishly he lost the same,
Decaying more and more,
Till he became
Most poore:
With thee
Oh let me rise
As larks, harmoniously,
And sing this day thy victories:
Then shall the fall further the flight in me.

My tender age in sorrow did beginne:
And still with sicknesses and shame
Thou didst so punish sinne,
That I became
Most thinne.
With thee
Let me combine
And feel this day thy victorie:
For, if I imp my wing on thine
Affliction shall advance the flight in me.

The shape poem "Easter Wings" by George Herbert, as it was originally published in 1633.

again begins the recovery stage with the sixth-line phrase "With thee," followed by a plea, "Let me combine, / And feel this day thy victory." The speaker asks to become a part of Christ, to meld into him, concluding, "For if I imp my wing on thine, / Affliction shall advance the flight in me." The man's affliction, or weakness, will actually strengthen him, as it causes him to seek God's support.

Herbert's concluding line reflects on the wing and flight image of the poem, as well as on its theme, that man must remain completely dependent on God, paradoxically a prisoner of God's strength, in order to enjoy freedom. This conclusion can be reached only after the in-depth self-examination the speaker undergoes, with his confession of lack proving crucial to his gain of power through faith. As the critic Cristina Malcolmson suggests, Herbert's poem achieves the great harmony suggested by its shape. She considers this shape poem more successful than "The Altar," which "never quite escapes the problems associated with hardness of the heart."

BIBLIOGRAPHY

Malcolmson, Cristina. *George Herbert: A Literary Life.* New York: Palgrave Macmillan, 2004.

EGERTON, SARAH FYGE (LATER FIELD) (1670–1723)

Born into a family of six daughters, Sarah Fyge showed feminist sympathies at an early age. Her father, Thomas, practiced as a physician at Winslow, Buckinghamshire. He descended from well-to-do landowners and married Mary Beacham, who died in 1704. Not much is known of Fyge's childhood; more is known of her teen years. By age 14 she had begun to write, and at 16 she saw her first work published. She titled the poem *The Female Advocate* (1686), writing in reply to Robert Gould's *Love Given O're: Or, A Satyr Against the Pride, Lust and Inconstancy, etc., of Woman* (1682). In the reply that may have been published without her consent, Fyge vented her disgust over Gould's, and society's, marginalization of women and the gender-based double standard, offering a new interpretation of the Garden of Eden story. She reimagined the beginning of humankind in an attempt to convince men to look upon women as sources of pleasure, not sin and treachery. She cleverly argued that man was

created of dull inert matter, while woman originated in the far more noble source of man himself. Her act infuriated her father, who exiled her to country living with relatives, an action Fyge found unfair.

Fyge's first marriage, to the attorney Edward Field, may have been arranged. It ended with his death before 1700, but she seemed happy with Field, as indicated in her later poetry. Left a well-off widow, in 1700 she published an ode to JOHN DRYDEN, which appeared in *Luctus Britannici.* Whether she personally knew Dryden remains unclear. A second piece in his honor was among those dedicated to him in Delariviére Manley's *The Nine Muses,* which Fyge, then Fielding, signed "Mrs. S.F." In 1703, she wrote a dedication to the earl of Halifax indicating her remarriage through its signature of "S.F.E."; it appeared in her *Poems on Several Occasions, Together with a Pastoral.*

Fyge married her second cousin, a minister much older than she, the Reverend Thomas Egerton. He had children by a first marriage and could offer Fyge wealth and stability in his long-term position as rector of Adstock, Buckinghamshire. However, continuing to exhibit the early independence that had landed her in trouble with her father, she continued during her marriage a sexual affair with Henry Pierce. A friend of Edward Field, Pierce remained dedicated to the new Mrs. Egerton, who had immortalized him in previous verse as "Alexis." Their relationship caused conflict in Egerton's marriage, and divorce proceedings began as early as 1703. Although accusations flew on both sides, including claims by Field's children of her attempt to take their rightful inheritance, the legal suit was never resolved and no divorce occurred. Her tempestuousness led her into a later falling out with Manley, a writer of popular scandalous fiction, and Manley immediately created an unflattering rendition of Egerton from the point of view of her tormented husband in her *Secret Memoirs . . . from the New Atalantis* (1709–10). Manley titled that section "A Fury of a Wife," constructing a farcical battle of the sexes. In it, the male narrator declares of his wife, "She looks as if she had been buried a twelve-month," and "Deliver me from a poetical wife." He complains of her genius as Manley alludes to some of Egerton's works, including "To One Who Said I Must Not Love," as mere "rumbles

... foreign to all fashionable understanding." The Egertons' unfortunate marital battles were apparently common knowledge, satirized again in a 1711 BROADSHEET titled *The Butter'd Apple-Pye*. Thomas Egerton died in 1720, and she followed in 1723, never having achieved the poetic fame for which she longed.

While a minor female poet, Egerton remains important for her support of women's right to artistic expression. Her support of the intellectual equality of women to men and of education for both sexes earned her the enmity of many readers, particularly those insulted by Egerton's attack on the idea that women remained morally inferior to men. Her *The Female Advocate* may be found in complete version on microfilm in many university library collections.

BIBLIOGRAPHY
Clark, Constance. Introduction to *Poems on Several Occasions* by Sarah Fyge Egerton. 1703. Facsimile, Delmar, N.Y.: Scholars' Facsimiles & Reprints, 1987.
Egerton, Sarah Fyge. *The Female advocate, or, An ansvver to a late satyr against the pride, lust and inconstancy, &c. of woman / written by a lady in vindication of her sex.* London: Printed by H. C. for John Taylor . . . , 1686.
Manley, Delariviére. *Secret Memoirs and Manners of Several Persons of Quality, of Both Sexes, from the New Atalantis, an Island in the Mediterranean.* Edited by Rosalind Ballaster. New York: New York University Press, 1992.

ELEGY An elegy is a poem written specifically in remembrance of the dead. In the 17th and 18th centuries, families of the bereaved might hire poets to compose elegies. In many instances the poets did not personally know the individual who had died, and they used traditional formats and phrases, as seen in WILLIAM CARTWRIGHT's "ON A VIRTUOUS YOUNG WOMAN THAT DIED SUDDENLY." Poets also composed elegies either in admiration of a model or in praise of their own family member or friend. They could be brief with no hidden agenda, such as JOHN DRYDEN's "TO THE PIOUS MEMORY OF THE ACCOMPLISH'D YOUNG LADY MRS. ANNE KILLIGREW" and THOMAS CAREW's "ELEGY UPON THE DEATH OF THE DEAN OF PAUL'S, DR. JOHN DONNE." They might also be lengthy and formal, such as JOHN MILTON's *LYCIDAS*, in which Milton adopts the pastoral ALLEGORY to mourn the drowning of his friend and crit-

icizes the clergy. Touchingly personal elegies include BEN JONSON's "ON MY FIRST SON" and "ON MY FIRST DAUGHTER," and KATHERINE PHILIPS's "ON THE DEATH OF MY FIRST AND DEAREST CHILD, HECTOR PHILIPS." THOMAS GRAY adopted a mournful tone in his "ELEGY WRITTEN IN A COUNTRY CHURCHYARD," in which he considers human potential, the duties of the state, and mortality in general. Poets may also adopt the form for satiric reasons, as does JONATHAN SWIFT, who imagines his own death in "VERSES ON THE DEATH OF DR. SWIFT."

"ELEGY OVER A TOMB" EDWARD HERBERT **(1665)** EDWARD HERBERT, Lord Herbert of Cherbury, adopts a thoughtful, contemplative tone to begin his "Elegy over a Tomb." Readers can easily envision the speaker, who loved the figure in the tomb, asking gently probing questions that rise in strength to demand a reason for his loss. He becomes an everyman, a universal figure, in his attempt to understand death. His six six-line stanzas adopt a RHYME scheme of *abbacc* with varied METER that promotes a driving momentum. In all except the final stanza, the six lines equate to one lengthy question.

With his grief clearly reflected in his words, the speaker wonders why he must "see, alas! Eternal night / Sitting upon those fairest eyes." Herbert offers a nice contrast between the speaker, who can see all, and the possessor of the "fairest eyes," who can only view death, referred to through traditional FIGURATIVE LANGUAGE as "Eternal night." The beams from the beloved's eyes "once did rise / So radiant and bright" their "light and heat" converted into "Knowledge and love." Again, Herbert contrasts the deceased's previous condition, in which beams of light and life shot from her eyes, to her present condition, in which she sees only the darkness of death. The speaker then questions the deceased herself, asking whether she "did delight no more to stay / Upon this low and earthly stage," selecting instead "an endless heritage," where she has stored "all the beauty that those ashes ow'd." Herbert makes the point that beauty is ethereal and all things human will one day be reduced to elements, such as those represented by ashes.

The third stanza suggests that the sun might now enjoy her light, extending the earlier CONCEIT. Herbert adds additional nature references as the speaker surmises that ocean waves have claimed the curls from her hair, and that she has restored "unto the sky and air, / The red, and white, and blue." She may also have passed her "sweetest breath" along to the flowers. Continuing to seek the cause of what appears to have been an early death, the speaker wonders whether heaven demanded her light, or the "sky and air have else conspired" along with the flowers to steal her gifts. He continues to surmise that she may have so "enriched" the natural elements that she "changed the course they held before, / And broke their proper laws." He seems to want to draw some comfort from the obvious answer to whether her beauty gave "this second birth to Heaven and Earth?" Herbert bases his ideas on the natural philosophy presented in his philosophical treatise in Latin *De Veritate* (1625). In that work he theorized on the necessity of harmony between man's thoughts and his environment. He also believed in pantheism, the idea that multiple deities existed in nature, a belief projected through his poem.

The speaker concludes by begging for some word from the dead, with the first, third, and fifth lines of the final stanza all beginning with the phrase "Tell us." He wants her to explain "where are those beauties now become, / And what they now intend." Herbert ends his poem with two lines that make clear the occasional brilliance in his work remarked upon by critics: "Tell us, alas, that cannot tell our grief, / Or hope relief." Herbert's sincere emotion unifies the poem, as does his extended use of nature imagery.

"ELEGY TO THE MEMORY OF AN UNFORTUNATE LADY" ALEXANDER POPE (1717)

"Elegy to the Memory of an Unfortunate Lady" is considered, along with *ELOISA TO ABELARD,* one of the two greatest LYRIC poems written by ALEXANDER POPE. He deals ostensibly with the subject of a young woman, dead possibly by her own hand, whom no one mourns. However, the ghost he supposedly sees acts only as the triggering topic, while the ELEGY's true topic is the mortality that remains the heritage of all humans, even, or perhaps more especially, poets who celebrate the death of others. Historians do not know whether the woman who inspired Pope's musing actually existed. His speaker identifies her in the opening line only as a "Beck'ning ghost, along the moonlight shade."

She invites the speaker to move close and points to a nearby glade. Then the speaker notices her "bleeding bosom," in which "the visionary sword" gleams. He stops to wonder whether heaven considers loving too well a crime, particularly if it results in one's acting "a Lover's or a Roman's part." He references a Roman to suggest suicide. The Catholic Church, of which Pope remained a devout member, considered suicide a mortal sin, but Pope reveals his compassion in questioning that edict for the sake of the homeless spirit.

If heaven does not approve of one human's loving another beyond bearing, and the death by one's own hand that might result, why then, the speaker wonders, would heavenly "Pow'rs!" allow, or even cause "Her soul aspire / Above the vulgar flight of low desire?" Pope searches for someone or something to blame for the folly of love that ends in death. He accuses heavenly forces of first producing the "Ambition" for love. It "first sprung" as the "glorious fault of Angels and Gods," their images flowing down to earth to inhabit the breasts of humans. In adopting the term *image,* Pope recalls the biblical description of the creation of man, a creature made in his creator's image. He considers the fact that as a result of human frailty, most souls only "peep out once an age," the rest of the time remaining "sullen pris'ners in the body's cage." He adopts FIGURATIVE LANGUAGE by using the traditional image of a heart either imprisoned or set free by passion.

The speaker imagines the young woman's soul snatched by fate into "the pitying sky. / As into air the purer spirits flow." That would allow her soul to fly "to its congenial place," leaving no virtue behind to "redeem her Race." However, instead, a force took her life, because he can "See on these ruby lips the trembling breath," her "cheeks, now fading at the blast of death." All positive imagery disappears as the speaker contrasts his previous flight of fancy with what he now envisions, a once-warm breast turned cold, and love deserting her once-passionate eyes. The speaker places a curse on whatever being caused the apparition's death, declaring that "frequent herses" should "besiege your gates" while his children and other family members die. So many should die that neighbors behold a veritable parade of hearses, in order to compensate for the death of the innocent maiden who could not be buried in hallowed ground because of her manner of death.

Because the young woman will not be allowed a traditional funeral, no one will cry for her. Instead, the speaker tells her, in order to show that he understands:

> By foreign hands thy dying eyes were clos'd,
> By foreign hands thy decent limbs compos'd,
> By foreign hands thy humble grave adorn'd,
> By strangers honour'd, and by strangers
>   mourn'd! (51–54)

Pope captures a dirgelike RHYTHM through the use of repetition, also imitating the delivery of a sermon in which a speaker would repeat points for emphasis. The speaker tries to comfort the spirit, basically asking what it matters that the rituals of burial are not observed. Rather than humans' furnishing the flowers to mark her solitary grave, nature, a far purer force, will care for her, preserving her memory. While flowers dress her grave, "the green turf" will "lie lightly on thy breast," and the morning dew will act as tears, promoting the growth of the season's first roses. True angels will hover over her grave, a superior substitute for the statuary marker that no one furnished.

The speaker at last notes the peace of the spirit's unmarked resting place, as Pope moves into the poem's closing lines. All humans will one day be "A heap of dust," and as with this young woman, that will be the only "art" each person leaves behind. He comments on the value of art to outlive its creator, here disagreeing with that idea. "Poets themselves must fall, like those they sung," meaning that the poets who write of the great achievements of those who have died must also die. While the poet now weeps for those about whom he writes, soon he will have need for someone to weep for him. His death will then cause the previously dead to be forgotten for good, as with "The Muse forgot," they shall be "belov'd no more!"

While Pope likely did not actually believe that one day no poet would exist to celebrate those who went before, he may have been commenting on the very personal nature of poetry and art. No one poet may substitute for another, as their approach varies. While

great art may bear resemblance to other great art, each exertion results in a unique creation. The death of an artist puts an end to his art. Pope may have meant the spirit to represent his poetry, with his lyric representing his premonition regarding the future of his work.

"ELEGY UPON THE DEATH OF THE DEAN OF PAUL'S, DR. JOHN DONNE, AN" THOMAS CAREW (1640)   THOMAS CAREW was obviously influenced by the poet JOHN DONNE, but he remained incapable of achieving Donne's metaphysical resonance and elegance. Most critics agree his lighter LYRIC touch and gentler tone did not permit the serious approach of Donne. However, in Carew's "An Elegy upon the Death of the Dean of Paul's, Dr. John Donne," he demonstrates the benefit he reaped from familiarity with Donne's work. Rhodes Dunlap includes in his discussion of Carew's achievements a comparison and contrast between poems by both poets that adopt the same conceit. Donne wrote in his poem "The Dampe,"

> When I am dead, and Doctors know not why,
> And my friends curiositie
> Will have me cut up to survey each part,
> When they shall finde your Picture in my
>   heart."

The speaker of the Donne poem seriously challenges his mistress with a cynical tone that adds strength supporting his accusation against her as the cause of his death. In Carew's later "Secresie Protested," he imitates Donne's theme but adopts a contrasting stylistic approach, more in keeping with the frivolity often present in CAVALIER poetry:

> If when I dye, Physicians doubt
> What caus'd my death, and there to view
> Of all their judgements which was true,
> Rip up my heart, Oh then I feare
> The world will see thy picture there.

The stirring emotion that informs each line for Donne makes a quick appearance only in Carew's final couplet. He avoids the stronger metaphysical approach that caused many to label Donne eccentric but then can never achieve the older poet's strength of purpose. As a member of the Caroline school, Carew depended more on light wit than innovation, gaining him the ire of later critics, who deemed his type of ingenious FIGURATIVE LANGUAGE the result of a corrupt and immoral society. Nevertheless, in Carew's tribute to Donne, he turns his inability to equal the master to his advantage.

Carew begins his elegy with a CONCEIT, "widowed poetry," recognizing poetry as Donne's spouse. He also addresses the dead poet, asking four questions in his first 10 lines that create a tone of wonder and subservience, as a servant might question a dead master. The speaker wonders whether the living have "nor tune, nor voice" left to speak in honor of Donne, who may have used "all our language" to "dispense . . . both words and sense." He then skillfully slides into the tribute, for which he has just questioned whether he had the skill, adopting Donne's approach to do so, mimicking the student imitating the master. He uses the metaphysical approach to contraries, writing, "Of thy brave soul, that shot such heat and light / As burnt our earth and made our darkness bright." Carew continues by adopting Donne's famous, and to many distasteful, conceit of ravishment from his "BATTER MY HEART," adding that Donne "Committed holy rapes upon our will," and

> Did through the eye the melting heart distil,
> And the deep knowledge of dark truths so teach
> As sense might judge what fancy could not
>   reach.

He informs readers that without Donne, a man of God whose sermons reached many, but whose poems may have reached more, they will all be left with a desire that can never be satisfied.

Carew includes various classical references, such as to Prometheus, suggesting that Donne's verse proved as vital to human life as the fire Prometheus presented to man. He references the Muses' garden, from which Donne removed all weeds, representing the more traditional approach to poetry. Because of Donne, "the lazy seeds / Of servile imitation [were] thrown away, / And fresh invention planted," as Donne paid "The

debts of our penurious bankrupt age," more than meeting the cost of classical poetic devices incurred by present poets. Carew spends many lines criticizing those writers who do little more than imitate others, suggesting that some prefer Pindar's passion to their own. He makes clear the disagreeable approach of

> The subtle cheat
> Of sly exchanges, and the juggling feat
> Of two-edg'd words, or whatsoever wrong,
> By ours was done the Greek or Latin tongue.

Donne redeemed all of those wrongs by drawing "a line / Of masculine expression." Carew also proves adept at the rules by breaking them when he purposely disrupts rhythm to prove a point. After writing of Donne that to "thy imperious wit / Our troublesome language bends, made only fit," he demonstrates by disrupting the smooth iambic pentameter of previous lines: "With her tough thick-ribb'd hoops, to gird about." The thing the language had to gird was "Thy giant fancy, which had prov'd too stout / For their soft melting phrases." Carew thus reflects on the contrast between his own approach, that of the "soft melting phrases," and Donne's far more fantastical. He concludes his 96-line poem by offering a four-line elegy, calling on others to express in a more complete way their grief for Donne, while he "on thy grave this epitaph incise":

> Here lies a king, that rul'd as he thought fit,
> The universal monarchy of wit;
> Here lie two flamens, and both those the best,
> Apollo's first, at last the true God's priest.

Carew's epitaph does not skirt the issue that later fascinated literary critics, the curious mix in Donne's poetry of the religious and the profane.

BIBLIOGRAPHY
Dunlop, Rhodes, ed. Introduction to *The Poems of Thomas Carew with His Masque, Coelum Britannicum*, xiii–lxxvii. Oxford: Clarendon Press, 1957.

"ELEGY WRITTEN IN A COUNTRY CHURCHYARD" THOMAS GRAY (1751) THOMAS GRAY may have begun writing "Elegy Written in a

Country Churchyard" as early as 1746. He discarded four stanzas of an early version, which were probably read by his friend Horace Walpole, and planned to title the work simply "Stanzas" until his friend William Mason suggested "Elegy" instead. A meditation in a burial ground proved a popular theme of that era, and Gray may have first thought of recording his thoughts about a graveyard while living next door to a cemetery in Peterhouse. However, the description of the grounds matches those of the churchyard at Stoke Poges, where his mother and aunt lived and he often visited. He mentions "unhonoured dead," which suggests members of a rural community, rather than the distinguished occupants of graves in Cambridge; in addition, the scenery as described by Gray matches the Stoke Poges cemetery, particularly that of two yew trees. Although Gray did not at first intend the poem for publication, it so impressed Walpole that he immediately began to circulate it in manuscript form.

While the sharing of his poem dismayed Gray, he became even more dismayed when contacted by an editor of a disreputable periodical titled the *Magazine of Magazines* who planned to publish the work. He appealed to Walpole to help prevent an initial publication in that source, at which point Walpole immediately published the elegy in a quarto-sized pamphlet, which sold for the cost of sixpence, the day before the magazine published a copy filled with spelling errors. The quarto sold out, to be reprinted multiple times over the following years. In the opinion of the critic A. L. Lytton Sells, no such brief poem has ever received the attention garnered by Gray's work; for decades English schoolchildren had to commit it to memory. The language, more than theme, captured the imagination of not only the ordinary reader, but also poets including George Gordon, Lord Byron, and Alfred Lord Tennyson. Gray borrowed liberally for his creation, the most often quoted line, "The paths of glory lead but to the grave," from his good friend Richard West, to whom the poem proved a tribute.

With a total of 32 four-line stanzas in iambic pentameter, the ELEGY contains three voices, with the first 23 stanzas spoken by the dead youth, a voice many imagine to be fashioned on that of West. The following five lines Gray speaks, while lines 98–116 are spoken

by a "hoary-headed swain," or country man, and Gray supplies the concluding 12-line epitaph. Some critics have ventured that Gray imagined his own final days and writing his own epitaph. Most of the lines represent a mixture of Gray's and West's expressions, but they also borrow heavily from Latin, Italian, and English poets who wrote during the 1740s. Although some feel the length to be excessive, Gray desired to include multiple variations on his main idea, which suggested that although the dead in the graveyard are uncelebrated, they also lie peacefully, having enjoyed uneventful lives filled with no crime, guilt, or anguish. The poem may be envisioned in four balanced sections following the first three stanzas that so wonderfully describe the churchyard setting. The first of the four deal with the humble nature of the lives of the dead, the second four contrast their lives with the lives of the celebrated, the third four focus on fate's depriving any of the dead villagers of greatness, while the final four celebrate the fact that the villagers did not have to suffer the effects of crime or negative emotions.

The poem opens with the melancholic tone most readers immediately notice, as words and phrases such as "curfew" and "tolls the knell of parting day," "The plowman homeward plods his weary way, / And leaves the world to darkness and to me" prepare for the topic of death. In the second stanza, "the glimmering landscape" fades, while the air holds "a solemn stillness," again emphasizing endings. Even the sound imagery creates a sense of life winding down, as the beetle drones and "drowsy tinklings lull" the herds of sheep, the tinklings referring to bells tied around some of the sheep's necks and inspired by the Italian poet Dante. The pastoral scene soon is bathed in moonlight, its stillness broken only by a "moping owl" complaining to the moon. By the third stanza the reader understands that a graveyard is the subject. The speaker describes an area "Beneath those rugged elms, that yew tree's shade, / Where heaves the turf in man a moldering heap," the heaps being graves. Each body lies in its own "narrow cell" and the group are identified as "forefathers of the hamlet," with Gray adopting the traditional FIGURATIVE LANGUAGE of metaphor to compare death to sleep.

The next stanzas describe all that the forefathers no longer experience, including sounds of the "swallow twittering" from a shed, a cock's call, and an "echoing horn," that of a hunter. They will no longer experience a "blazing hearth" at home or observe a "busy house-wife" plying "her evening care," nor hear children or enjoy those children climbing into their laps. Gray describes various activities in which the dead partici-pated, including harvesting and chopping down woods with "their sturdy stroke." After noting these unsingu-lar images and duties, the voice cautions against "Ambi-tion" mocking "their useful toil" or "Grandeur" listening "with a disdainful smile / The short and simple annals of the poor." Gray begins to emphasize his theme, praising the simple life of those now at rest in the churchyard. They may never have experienced "The boasts of heraldry, the pomp of power" or immense wealth, but those who did trace "paths of glory" will find those paths also lead "to the grave."

The 10th stanza offers a strong example of Gray's moving language and his skill in establishing a solemn pace fitting the occasion described:

Not you, ye proud, impute to these the fault,
If memory o'er their tomb no trophies raise,
Where through the long-drawn aisle and fretted
    vault
The pealing anthem swells the note of praise.
    (37–40)

The speaker continues to stress that those who achieved more than the men at his feet have no effect on Death. Even if the dead at some time dreamed of greatness or knew a "celestial fire," they were not allowed to act on that passion. Comparisons to gems lost in the "unfath-omed caves of ocean" and flowers "born to blush unseen" note the unfulfilled promise to be merely one more trick of nature. However, as expressed in the 17th stanza, that may not be a bad thing:

Their lot forbade: nor circumscribed alone
Their growing virtues, but their crimes confined;
Forbade to wade through slaughter to a throne,
And shut the gates of mercy on mankind. (65–69)

They avoided a guilty conscience, shame, and pride, that thought leading to a line with a phrase later made

famous when Thomas Hardy selected it as a title for a novel, "Far from the madding crowd's ignoble strife, / Their sober wishes never learned to stray." He urges listeners not to have concern for these uncelebrated lives, as

Their name, their years, spelt by the unlettered
    Muse,
The place of fame and elegy supply:
And many a holy text around she strews,
That teach the rustic moralist to die. (81–84)

The swain begins by relating facts he knows regard-ing one of the dead, and Gray adds quotation marks to signal dialogue. The swain notes that he often saw the individual going about his daily activities until

"One morn I missed him on the customed hill,
Along the heath and near his fav'rite tree:
Another came; nor yet beside the rill,
Nor up the lawn, nor at the wood was he."
    (109–112)

Following the swain's dialogue, Gray inserts white space, then the title "The Epitaph," inserting three itali-cized verses that conclude his consideration of death in a quiet churchyard. They represent some of the most famous of 18th-century verse:

Here rests his head upon the lap of Earth
A youth to Fortune and to Fame unknown.
Fair Science frowned not on his humble birth,
And Melancholy marked him for her own.
    (117–120)

The imagery remains peaceful, as Gray extends the sleep metaphor representing death. The speaker explains the dead youth will never be wealthy or famous, he was not blessed with any particular knowl-edge, and he was possessed by melancholy since birth. The second stanza adds:

Large was his bounty, and his soul sincere,
Heaven did a recompense as largely send:
He gave to Misery all he had, a tear,

He gained from Heaven ('twas all he wished) a
   friend. (121–124)

Contradicting what readers might think, the dead youth did enjoy the bounty of friendship and a sincere soul, riches equal to material goods. The speaker concludes that no further knowledge of the dead man is necessary, as he now rests with God:

No farther seek his merits to disclose,
Or draw his frailties from their dread abode
(There they alike in trembling hope repose),
The bosom of his Father and his God. (125–128)

Gray's "Elegy" provided tremendously successful. *The Monthly Review* noted, "This excellent little piece is so much read, and so much admired by every body, that to say more of it would be superfluous." It enjoyed multiple reprinting and wide imitations in English as well as other languages. In addition to the familiar version, an earlier shorter version later labeled the Eton manuscript exists, containing four stanzas eventually removed by Gray. It is one of three surviving original manuscripts. A second rendition appears in Gray's commonplace book, while the third exists in the British Museum as Egerton MS 2400.

BIBLIOGRAPHY
Lonsdale, Roger, ed. *The Poems of Thomas Gray, William Collins, Oliver Goldsmith.* New York: Longman, 1969.
Sells, A. L. Lytton. *Thomas Gray: His Life and Works.* London: George Allen & Unwin, 1980.

ELISION In poetry, elision occurs when the poet omits parts of words, usually for the sake of rhythm/METER, allowing the altered word to slide into the word that follows. Elision allows for ease of pronunciation as well as for emphasis. A common elision is the dropping of end vowels, such as the *e* from the word *the,* as in MARY WORTLEY MONTAGU's "EPISTLE FROM MRS. YONGE TO HER HUSBAND" in the line: "Th' oppressed and injured always may complain." Elision also occurs within a word, as seen in this line from JOHN DENHAM's "COOPER'S HILL": "Crown'd with that sacred pile, so vast, so high / That whether 'tis a part of Earth, or sky, / Uncertain seems." For simpler pronunciation, the *e* is omitted

from the traditional past tense *ed* ending in *Crown'd,* while *i* is omitted from the two-word phrase, *it is* to form *'tis,* retaining the rhythm of iambic pentameter.

"ELOISA TO ABELARD" ALEXANDER POPE (1717)
ALEXANDER POPE prefaces his "Eloisa to Abelard" with an "Argument" that begins with this statement about the French couple: "Abelard and Eloisa flourish'd in the twelfth Century; they were two of the most distinguish'd persons of their age in learning and beauty, but for nothing more famous than for their unfortunate passion." Their story was well known. The 38-year-old Peter Abelard (1079–1142) served as tutor to Héloïse, with whom he fell in love when she was 17. A philosopher and theologian, Abelard nevertheless followed his passion and the couple had a son, after which they married. However, the canon Fulbert, uncle to Héloïse, hired ruffians to punish Abelard through a physical beating and castration. The act drove Héloïse into an Argenteuil convent, while Abelard lived in a hermitage. It later became a school for monks called the Paraclete, which in biblical terms meant "Comforter." Abelard later presented Paraclete to Héloïse in order for her to house a sisterhood there. The two former lovers began corresponding, their letters later collected and published in 1616 in their original Latin version. They appeared in French in 1607, and in 1713 John Hughes translated that version to English, which Pope read. His poetic version appeared in his *Works* (1717).

Pope presents a sympathetic casting of Eloisa, although many believed she did not rate that characterization, because of her sin. Later critics have proposed that Pope may have done so with a feeling of identification with a fellow marginalized individual; Pope's physical condition caused his exclusion from normal romantic activities and his enemies to create jokes at his expense. In addition, both he and Eloisa were writers, and she remained cloistered, as he often did in his garden. Others suggest he could not engage in sex or marry, because of his twisted body, which effectively castrated him, helping him to identify with Abelard as well.

As for format Pope uses imperfect RHYME, a style contrary to his traditional presentation, perhaps to balance the soft effect of the rhyming couplets, which also drew criticism. Some felt the couplets an improper format, much too tame to express Eloisa's magnificent passion. Pope's speaking for Eloisa also prompted commentary by later feminist critics, who viewed it as another co-opting of the female voice by a male for political and artistic purpose. Critics identify inspiration by Shakespeare and the Petrarchan tradition, which generally objectified women as heavenly objects, as Pope does with Eloisa.

When in the poem's opening lines Eloisa considers a letter received from Abelard, she demonstrates her passion remains very much alive, even after the many years that have passed since they were together. She kisses the name on the letter, after wondering, "Why rove my thoughts beyond this last retreat? / Why feels my heart its long-forgotten heat?" Some found her comparison of her love for God to her love for Abelard repulsive, but she clearly bids, "Hide it, my heart, within that close disguise, / Where, mix'd with God's, his lov'd Idea lies." Pope's choice of the term *idea* results from his use of classical models, particular Ovid's heroic epistles. The term will reappear multiple times, establishing a pattern that also suggests Eloisa's strong use of the imagination.

Eloisa admits her struggle, wailing at "Relentless walls! Whose darksome round contains / Repentant sighs, and voluntary pains." The knees of penitents have scraped against the stones, and Eloisa feels as enshrined as if she were already buried, her grave decorated with "pitying saints, whose statues learn to weep!" Pope will return to this image in the poem's conclusion, adding a satisfying balance.

No matter how devoted Eloisa remains to God, she has not yet turned to stone, and "All is not Heav'n's while Abelard has part, / Still rebel nature holds out half my heart." That nature made her an attractive and even admirable figure to readers, despite her past sin. Pope makes clear her conflict, as the letters do not evoke happiness along with the passion. Instead, they awaken something hidden that she believed her solitary lifestyle had destroyed: "There stern religion quench'd th' unwilling flame, / There dy'd the best of passions, Love and Fame." Eloisa reviews their past and reminds herself through a direct address of Abe-

lard, "how guiltless first I met thy flame, / When Love approach'd me under Friendship's name." She admits to not loving the saint, "nor wish'd an Angel whom I lov'd a Man." She questions the civic rule of marriage, declaring her reaction: "Curse on all laws but those which love has made?" She prefers nature's law, that of love, to man's arbitrary codes. She bemoans the fact that when her lover "bound and bleeding" lay, she could not help him. Adopting for a moment what critics identify as a male voice, she declares, "The crime was common, common be the pain."

Although Eloisa realizes a reunion is impossible, she still fantasizes that Abelard might relieve her woe simply with "thy looks, thy words," so that "Still on that breast enamour'd" she might lie, and "Still drink that delicious poison from thy eye." As critics have noted, Eloisa moves in confusion from God to Abelard, and from referring to herself in the third person to adopting first person. Thus, Pope emphasizes her internal conflict and sense of self-division. Pope's vivid imagery makes clear the effect of the structures in which Eloisa remains imprisoned:

> In these lone walls (their day's eternal bound)
> These moss-grown domes with spiry turrets
>   crown'd,
> Where awful arches make a noon-day night,
> And the dim windows shed a solemn light;
> Thy eyes diffus'd a reconciling ray,
> And gleams of glory brighten'd all the day.
>   (140–145)

The shadowy walls allow strong contrast to the light represented by Abelard's imagined presence. Pope also offers a metaphor for Eloisa's heart, into which the light of passion has found entrance after decades of absence. She at last acknowledges that death will be her only escape from "the lasting chain," her pledge of her life in service to God, after which her dust will remain in her cell. Still her being will "wait, till 'tis no sin to mix with thine." Pope suggests a CONCEIT OF METAPHYSICAL POETS AND POETRY in the vision of two souls mingling as one.

Eloisa then admits her wretched feelings, as she has mistakenly believed she was Christ's bride, the traditional title adopted by nuns. Pope uses a familiar trope of fire and ice as representative of passion, for although Eloisa thought she was safe from sin and passion in the nunnery, she muses, "Ev'n here, where frozen chastity retires, / Love finds an altar for forbidden fires." She deals with PARADOX as she wonders, "How shall I lose the sin, yet keep the sense / And love th' offender, yet detest th' offence?" She notes the fortune of the truly chaste nun who can focus on prayer and God. Instead, for her, "Fancy restores what vengeance snatch'd away."

As a poet, Pope naturally admired the power of imagination that restores Eloisa's passion. Her imagination, her sense of place, and her memory all make her heroic in 18th-century terms. She struggles to forget but cannot and muses how nice it might be if "The world forgetting, by the world forgot," as this would equate to "Eternal sun-shine of the spotless mind!" The 21st-century scriptwriters Charlie Kaufman and Michel Gondry would adopt that line as the title for a movie about a process through which individuals could choose to erase bitter memories.

Pope returns to previous imagery when Eloisa says, "What scenes appear where-e'er I turn my view! / The dear Ideas, where I fly, pursue." She cannot escape the Ideas, which cause the imagined to seem real, another reference to classical philosophy.

Eloisa's final fantasy begins with Abelard's presence at her funeral, "The hallow'd taper trembling in thy hand." Then he dies, and the two at last reunite, sharing a single grave. She looks into the future, musing that ages later, "When this rebellious heart shall beat no more," wandering lovers will read their story on "the pale marble" that marks their grave. She imagines heavenly redemption, reward for the lovers' sacrifice, as from a heavenly choir "loud *Hosanna's* rise, / And swell the pomp of dreadful sacrifice." More importantly, a sympathetic "future Bard" who shares her grief will "our sad, our tender story tell." Pope concludes with a comment on his own action, "He best can paint'em, who shall feel 'em most." He makes an interesting admission of sharing the lovers' passion, painting for readers a portrait of a woman who transcends, rather than resolves, her conflict.

BIBLIOGRAPHY

Atkins, G. Douglas. *Quests of Difference: Reading Pope's Poems.* Lexington: University of Kentucky Press, 1986.

Cooksey, Thomas L. "Pope, Eloisa, Milton: A Possible Source." *Notes and Queries* 51, no. 1 (March 2004): 40–41.

Damrosch, Leopold, Jr. *The Imaginative World of Alexander Pope.* Berkeley: University of California Press, 1987.

Fabricant, Carole. "Defining Self and Others: Pope and Eighteenth-Century Gender Ideology." *Criticism* 39, no. 4 (fall 1997): 503–526.

Ferguson, Rebecca. *The Unbalanced Mind: Pope and the Rule of Passion.* Philadelphia: University of Pennsylvania Press, 1986.

Francus, Marilyn. "An Augustan's Metaphysical Poem: Pope's 'Eloisa to Abelard.'" *Studies in Philology* 87, no. 4 (fall 1990): 476–491.

Hagstrum, Jean H. *Sex and Sensibility: Ideal and Erotic Love from Milton to Mozart.* Chicago: University of Chicago Press, 1980.

Leissner, Debra. "Pope, Petrarch, and Shakespeare: Renaissance Influences in 'Eloisa to Abelard.'" *Philological Quarterly* 74, no. 2 (spring 1995): 173–187.

Mews, Constant J. *The Lost Love Letters of Heloisa and Abelard: Perceptions of Dialogue in Twelfth-Century France.* New York: St. Martin's Press, 1999.

Morris, David P. *Alexander Pope, the Genius of Sense.* Cambridge, Mass.: Harvard University Press, 1984.

Winn, James. "Pope Plays the Rake: His Letters to Ladies and the Making of the 'Eloisa.'" In *The Art of Alexander Pope.* 106–107. New York: Harper & Row, 1979.

"EMULATION, THE" SARAH EGERTON (1703)

In SARAH FYGE EGERTON's "The Emulation," the poet addresses the common topic of custom, coupling with it the traditional adjective *tyrant* in her first line. The characterization of societal customs as tyrannical, exerting an iron-fisted control over society stronger than any formal civic law, was a frequent CONCEIT used since the Restoration. Poets such as JOHN MILTON had confronted the topic in a far more sophisticated manner than did Egerton, in the formal context of addresses to Parliament. However, Egerton's poetic use of the topic to advance her profemale sensibility remains of great interest to feminist and new historicist critics. She argues that only custom, an arbitrary construct, supports the gender inequity that women suffer. Customs are easily altered; therefore, society should reconsider a tradition so odious that it binds women in slavery to culture. The term *emulation* used in her title means an attempt to equal or surpass another, generally through imitation. Egerton intends IRONY in her use of that term. In testimony to her dogged attempts to change the view of women, and of women poets in particular, often at her own expense, an anonymous poet wrote in Egerton's defense in 1706, "No more let haughty man with fierce disdain / Despise the product of a female brain."

Egerton begins by adopting the FIGURATIVE LANGUAGE of personification as her speaker addresses Custom, asking, "Say, tyrant Custom, why must we obey / The impositions of thy haughty sway?" The speaker notes, "From the first dawn of life unto the grave, / Poor womankind's in every state a slave." Those states include that of "nurse, the mistress, parent and the swain," with the speaker noting that love accompanies a slave state, and "there's none escape that pain." Egerton immediately makes clear her agenda of support for advancing equity for women. Most stupefying her speaker notes that the point is that "the fatal slavery" is support by "The husband with insulting tyranny," he "justified" in enslaving his wife "by law." As she arrives at her 10th line of rhymed couplets, Egerton adds that men "join" in conspiracy to "keep the wife in awe." She next turns to a discussion of biblical history because the attitude toward woman as the source of sin and pain derives from the biblical story of Adam and Eve in the Garden of Eden. She had made the same point in her *The Female Advocate* (1686), writing at age 16 in reply to Robert Gould's *Love Given O're: Or, A Satyr Against the Pride, Lust and Inconstancy, etc., of Woman* (1682). In her poem, she accuses Moses, the first to "rebuke" women's "freedom," as a married man "when he writ the Pentateuch," suggesting that he so constructed his writings as to retain control in his marriage, thereby extending it to all males.

The speaker next notes, still speaking to Custom, "They're wise to keep us slaves, for well they know, / If we were loose, we soon should make them so." While those lines appear humorous on the surface, the suggestion that women might divorce their husbands, loosing them, represented a transgression against society in her era. She next compares women to "vanquished kings whom fetters bind" who yield to their captives when war is threatened. While the women

agree to "Submit in form," the speaker expresses outrage over the fact that men want also "our thoughts to control, / And lay restraints on the impassive soul." Egerton presents a serious and borderline blasphemous charge. She claims that men not only desire legal controls over women, but also spiritual, suggesting that males pretend to have the power of God. The speaker believes men do so in order not to be bested by women, who might "excel their sluggish parts, / Should we attempt the sciences and arts." She notes that men believe such studies an exclusively male privilege, invoking another of Egerton's common themes, that education should be available to both sexes.

The comparisons grow stronger and more threatening as the speaker next notes that men are no better than medieval priests who taught in the Latin tongue for centuries in order to mystify their congregations. The men shared priestly concerns that "vulgar eyes would sacred laws profane," where *vulgar* refers to the common (wo)man and the common language. "Mysteries" were screened from the sight of the ordinary populace in order to promote the power of the church. However, the speaker notes,

> In this blessed age such freedom's given,
> That every man explains the will of heaven;
> And shall we women now sit tamely by,
> Make no excursions in philosophy,
> Or grace our thoughts in tuneful poetry?
>   (27–31)

Egerton references her own activity of writing, demonstrating that she is not willing simply to "sit tamely by," despite her era's attacks on women in the arts.

In her final lines, Egerton calls to all women, so that "Wit's empire now shall know a female reign," urging that her audience "Divinely imitate the realms above." She reflects on her previous reference to the attempt of men to control even women's spiritual lives. However, in the midst of her call to action, she remains cynical. She concludes that "finite males" will never "reverse their rules," because of their fear of the results: "we'll be wits, and then men must be fools." She demonstrates ANTITHESIS, or the use of opposites, to add balance to her line and to make her point.

Sarah Egerton remained a product of her era, caught between the emotional presentation of the Restoration and the incorporation of traditional Augustan appeal to logic. Her intent, though, remained anything but traditional, as she made an argument that would continue to fall on deaf ears for more than two centuries.

ENDIMION AND PHOEBE Michael Drayton
(1595)   As with many of his poems, Michael Drayton fashioned the theme of his erotic pastoral, *Endimion and Phoebe,* on others' work, including the decade's most famous poets and playwrights, Christopher Marlowe (*Hero and Leander*) and William Shakespeare (*Venus and Adonis*). In form, however, it reflected influence by the playwright George Chapman. Drayton's version more closely resembled those of Marlowe and Chapman in the use of heroic couplets. According to the Drayton scholar Richard Hardin, he also manipulated their styles so they would allow his emphasis on his Platonic theme, "that the way to spiritual perfection begins in the study of the created universe." It reflects Marlowe's approach as it opens with a focus on the beauty of the pastoral setting, shaping an Arcadian paradise. Later, it reflects Chapman's philosophical style by focus on celestial matters. Hardin suggests that Drayton's poem offered something new to the world of poetry: "A philosophical epyllion: sexual love, the principal concern of earlier epyllions, is here a means to the end of communion with the beauty and truth of all nature."

Drayton's lengthy poem remains of interest in its sharp reflection of the traditions of the pastoral genre, which will be noted in description of a brief excerpt. The poem features as its pastoral hero Endimion, a young shepherd who lives an idyllic life, as tradition demanded. In the first few lines of the poem's iambic pentameter format, Drayton includes multiple mythological references, mixing the Greek with the Roman. Examples include the ubiquitous nymphs, lesser nature divinities; Pan, the Greek nature god; and Pan's Roman counterpart, Silvanus. Silvanus inspired the often-employed poetic descriptor *sylvan,* meaning of nature, and the corresponding name *Sylvia.* Drayton's poem is heavy with adjectives that appear pretentious to the 21st-century reader but in his era were necessary to the genre.

The poem opens with the introduction of the shepherd Endimion, who dwells on Latmus, also spelled in other references *Latmos*. Latmos was a mythological mountain where Diana, Roman goddess of the moon, protector of women, and the great mother goddess of nature, fell in love with Endimion.

The excerpt will preserve for the sake of reader experience the original italics and spelling, in which a symbol, called a *glyph,* which looks like the letter *v,* appears for the letter *u,* and vice versa, and in doubled uppercase form, *VV* substitutes for the modern English alphabet letter *W.* In addition, the vowel *e* appends to words that later dropped it, and words that would later include vowels, such as *e,* appear phonetically spelled. The lowercase letter *y* often substitutes for the more familiar letter *i.* Drayton also invented some terms, such as *imparadize* as a verb indicating conditions had been shaped as they were in Paradise, the perfect world. Lines 11–22 of Drayton's poem read:

> *Latmus,* where young *Endimion* vsd to keepe
> His fairest flock of siluer-fleeced sheepe.
> To whom *Siluanus* often would resort,
> At barly-breake to see the Satyres sport;
> And when rude *Pan* his Tabret list to sound,
> To see the faire Nymphes foote it in a round,
> Vnder the trees which on this Mountaine grew,
> As yet the like *Arabia* neuer knew:
> For all the pleasures Nature could deuise,
> Within this plot she did imparadize;
> And great *Diana* of her speciall grace,
> With *Vestall* rytes had hallowed all the place:

In the next excerpt Drayton describes a grove of trees, including cedars and pines, whose branches met to form a bower, hidden from the sun's heat. In that bower Phoebus, an epithet for the Greek sun god, Apollo, visited the paradise, as did Venus, Roman goddess of beauty and love. Also present in this retreat at one time or another were Mars, Roman god of war; Minerva, Roman goddess of wisdom and patroness of arts and trades; and Alcides, another name for Hercules, the Greek hero and son of Jupiter and Alcmena. Drayton references additional trees, such as the Olive, the weeping Myrtle, the Palm, and the Poplar. All of those trees represented ancient times, as well as temperate climates, suitable to a paradise. Drayton includes such details to emphasize the importance of setting in the pastoral in lines 23–36:

> Vpon this Mount there stood a stately Groue,
> Whose reaching armes, to clip the Welkin
>   stroue,
> Of tufted Cedars, and the branching Pine,
> VVhose bushy tops themselues doe so intwine,
> As seem'd when Nature first this work begun,
> Shee then conspir'd against the piercing Sun;
> Vnder whose couert (thus diuinely made)
> *Phœbus* greene Laurell florisht in the shade:
> Faire *Venus* Mirtile, *Mars* his warlike Fyrre,
> *Mineruas* Oliue, and the weeping Myrhe,
> The patient Palme, which thriues in spite of
>   hate,
> The Popler, to *Alcides* consecrate;
> VVhich Nature in such order had disposed,
> And there withall those goodly walkes inclosed,

As is appropriate to pastoral, Drayton spends many lines preparing the reader for the romantic tale that will follow. He introduces Phoebe, who in Greek mythology was one of the original Titans, the enormous offspring of Uranus and Gaia. Apollo's grandmother, Phoebe was traditionally associated with the moon. She represents Drayton's second moon reference, emphasizing the celestial body that eventually became a symbol for woman. Phoebe wants to romance Endimion, as had her grandson, Apollo, who believed that because of Endimion's beauty, he must have been a nymph in shepherd disguise. Drayton's contemporary readers, all educated members of the aristocracy, would have recognized the many references and understood how focused on the sexual aspects of humans the deities remained. This prepared them for the erotic themes of Drayton's work.

Because Phoebe does not want to frighten Endimion with her Titan attributes, she assumes a disguise in order to pursue their romance. The next excerpt begins with line 81, which references Phoebe's plan to visit Endimion and concludes with line 92. New mythological references include dancing fairies, naked as befitting the innocent tone of the pastoral. Also included are satyrs, hairy, hooved goatmen, lesser deities of the woods and fields, whose heads sprouted short horns. Because they, like Apollo, were male, their enthrallment with the beautiful youth introduces an element of homosexuality as well as bestiality. But because shepherd boys featured in pastorals were innocents, such references did not carry a negative moral connotation. This passage also provides examples of the cloying sensory imagery abundant to pastoral in its comparison of Endimion's breath to nectar so sweet that those who kissed him might fall into a death swoon:

> Endimion, the louely Shepheards boy,
> *Endimion,* great *Phœbes* onely ioy,
> *Endimion,* in whose pure-shining eyes,
> The naked Faries daunst the heydegies.
> The shag-haird Satyrs Mountain-climing race,
> Haue been made tame by gazing in his face.
> For this boyes loue, the water Nymphs haue
>   wept
> Stealing oft times to kisse him whilst he slept:
> And tasting once the Nectar of his breath,
> Surfet with sweet, and languish vnto death;

By line 100 the reader observes Pheobe's transformation from a figure so bright that no mortal eye could bear to look on her to a nymphlike being. Drayton includes the abundant overwrought detail appropriate to his tale, including focus on Phoebe's azure mantle, or garment, using the FIGURATIVE LANGUAGE of simile to compare it to a boat's sail. Composed of silk, the garment bears embossed rainbows as well as streamers as white as milk. The garments are lifted by gentle breezes to produce a romantic effect, and to set off Phoebe's necklace, composed of 20 gold chain loops with rubies around her neck. Finally, garment is pleated to emphasize her breasts, the image that closes line 119:

> But like a Nymph, crown'd with a flowrie
>   twine,
> And not like Phœbe, as herself diuine.
> An Azur'd Mantle purfled with a vaile,
> Which in the Ayre puft like a swelling saile,

Embosted Rayne-bowes did appear in silk,
With wauie streames as white as mornings
  Milk:
Which euer as the gentle Ayre did blow,
Still with the motion seem'd to ebb and flow:
About her neck a chayne twise twenty fold,
Of Rubyes, set in lozenges of gold;
  Trust vp in trammels, and in curious pleats,
With spheary circles falling on her teats.

Drayton extends Phoebe's description through line 131 and at 132 describes Endimion. As a shepherd should, he plays the popular pipe music of the roundelay, a song with a regularly recurring refrain, later called simply a *round:*

Thus came shee where her loue *Endimion* lay,
VVho with sweet Carrols sang the night away;
And as it is the Shepheards vsuall trade,
Oft on his pype a Roundelay he playd.

Next is more description of Endimion, appropriately compared to a lamb with dainty snow-white hands ironically untouched by the challenges of physical work. A fortunate swain indeed, he has a sheep hook that is not the normal wooden affair, but instead is silver gilded, studded with exotic coral, bearing a black ebony tip:

As meeke he was as any Lambe might be,
Nor neuer lyu'd a fayrer youth then he:
His dainty hand, the snow it selfe dyd stayne,
Or her to whom *Ioue* showr'd in golden rayne:
From whose sweet palme the liquid Pearle dyd
  swell,
Pure as the drops of *Aganippas* Well:
Cleere as the liquor which fayre *Hebe* spylt;
Hys sheephooke siluer, damask'd all with gilt.
The staffe it selfe, of snowie Iuory,
Studded with Currall, tipt with Ebony

Lines 146 through 151 include further physical description of the shepherd boy whose "tresses" shine black like those of ravens in curls that straggle "along his manly back." His eyes are "balls" that "nature . . .

had set / Lyke Diamonds inclosing Globes of Jet." They "sparkled" beneath "milky lids out-right," fit to be compared to the constellation of "Orions heaven-adorning light."

This excerpt barely introduces readers to Drayton's subject, but curious readers may learn of the lovers' adventures online. Long in the public domain, *Endimion and Phoebe* may be found in its entirety at the Renascence Editions Web site, sponsored by the University of Oregon. As the notice at the Web site states, it bases its version on the 1595 edition, transcribed as closely as possible to the original.

BIBLIOGRAPHY
Drayton, Michael. *Endimion and Phoebe.* Renascence Editions. Available online. URL: http://darkwing.uoregon.edu/~rbear/drayton1.html. Downloaded on July 20, 2005.
Hardin, Richard F. *Michael Drayton and the Passing of Elizabethan England.* Lawrence: University of Kansas Press, 1973.

END-STOPPED LINE   An end-stopped poetry line concludes with a natural pause, due to the insertion of punctuation. The pause caused by a comma, semicolon, exclamation point, question mark, or period represents the most common conclusion to a poetic line. A pause may also be signaled by the inclusion of a parenthetical statement. A verse in which all lines are end-stopped may be seen in ANNE KILLIGREW's "UPON THE SAYING THAT MY VERSES WERE MADE BY ANOTHER," where she writes:

Orinda (Albion's and her sex's grace)
Owed not her glory to a beauteous face;
It was her radiant soul that shone within,
Which struck a luster through her outward
  skin;
That did her lips and cheeks with roses dye,
Advanced her height, and sparkled in her eye.
Nor did her sex at all obstruct her fame,
But higher 'mong the stars it fixed her name;
What she did write, not only all allowed,
But every laurel to her laurel bowed!

An opposite treatment of a line's end in which no signal for a natural pause occurs is known as ENJAMBMENT.

ENGLAND'S HELICON

The collection, possibly assembled by John Bodenham, of mostly pastoral poems printed in 1600 titled *England's Helicon* contained work by England's best known poets of the day. They included George Peele and Robert Greene, dramatists whose lyrics were also printed as verse; Sir Philip Sidney; MICHAEL DRAYTON; Christopher Marlowe; Thomas Lodge; NICOLAS BRETON; Henry Howard, earl of Surrey; Shepherd Tony; perhaps William Shakespeare; Sir Edward Dyer, Sir Walter Raleigh; Fulke Greville; and Edmund Spenser, author of *The Fairie Queene*. Only entries by Bartholomew Young, also spelled *Yong,* were later judged too weak to merit inclusion. Several questions still exist regarding the authorship of some entries, labeled simply *Ignoto.* Poems by Sidney include excerpts from *Astrophel and Stella* and *Arcadia;* Spenser's contributions draw from his *Shepheardes Calendar* and *Astrophel,* Drayton's from *Eclogues* and *Idea.* Its collection made it the finest of the English miscellanies, containing abundant imagery of love, music, and dance. Some individual poems were later set to music, their titles indicating the type of composition, such as the roundelay, jig, and madrigal. It proved popular enough to warrant a second printing with nine additional entries in 1614.

BIBLIOGRAPHY

England's Helicon. 1600. Facsimile, Menston, England: Scolar Press, 1978

ENJAMBMENT

The term *enjambment* applies to a line of poetry that signals at its end no natural pause. Unlike the END-STOPPED LINE, the enjambed line lacks punctuation, prompting the reader to move directly into the next line. In the following lines from JOHN DONNE's "AIR AND ANGELS" lines 1, 2, and 4 illustrate end-stopped lines, and line 3 illustrates enjambment:

> But since my soul, whose child love is,
> Takes limbs of flesh, and else nothing do,
> More subtle than the parent is
> Love must not be, but take a body too.

In an additional example excerpted from "The Introduction" by ANNE FINCH, COUNTESS OF WINCHILSEA, the first line represents enjambment, while the additional three lines are end-stopped:

> Alas! A woman that attempts the pen
> Such an intruder on the rights of men,
> Such a presumptuous creature is esteemed,
> The fault can by no virtue be redeemed.

"EPIGRAM ON MILTON" JOHN DRYDEN (1688)

That JOHN DRYDEN would contribute to the first illustrated version of JOHN MILTON's *PARADISE LOST* surprised no one. He had long admired his older contemporary and that particular epic poem, which his own *ANNUS MIRABILIS* (1667), had anticipated as a narrative poem by only a few months. Dryden wrote a simple six-line epigram, which proved elegant and meaningful, its brevity supporting its strong effect. He published it anonymously, writing,

> Three poets in three distant ages born
> Greece, Italy, and England did adorn,
> The first in loftiness of thought surpass'd;
> The next in majesty; in both the last.
> The force of nature cou'd no farther go:
> To make a third she join'd the former two.

One of the best ways to honor a poet was in comparison to classical writers. As Milton did, Dryden favored the classics as models, learning Latin and Greek and in the 1690s engaging in accomplished translation of Persius, Juvenal, and Virgil. In his epigram, Milton is the third poet, while the first is Homer and the second Virgil. Dryden's use of repetition of the term *three* allows emphasis on the number of poets as well as calling attention to the fact that they spanned different eras, thus suggesting a continuum in which Milton occupied the most recent position. He elevates Milton by placing him in such lofty company and does the same for his own country by placing it in a series with Greece, home to the golden age of poetry, and Italy, home to the Continental Renaissance.

The two characteristics used as major criteria by which to measure the excellence of a poet are "loftiness of thought" and "majesty." The effect of Dryden's final three lines actually is to boost Milton above the revered classical poets. The phrase "in both the last" indicates that the better of "the first," Homer, and "The next," Virgil, existed in Milton. The final two lines make clear that at first, all of nature's forces could not find a way to exceed their own previous creations of Homer and Virgil. However, they eventually found a way to do so by simply combining those two estimable forces; the result was Milton. Dryden may have known of a previous suggestion of this sentiment by the Italian poet Selvaggi, written when Selvaggi met Milton in Rome. WILLIAM CONGREVE would later translate Dryden's epigram into Latin.

"EPISTLE FROM MRS. YONGE TO HER HUSBAND" LADY MARY WORTLEY MONTAGU (1724)

Although LADY MARY WORTLEY MONTAGU wrote "Epistle from Mrs. Yonge to Her Husband" in the 18th century, its subject matter prevented publication until almost 200 years after its writing. Montagu adopted the voice of one Mary Yonge, whose husband, William, quite publicly sued her for divorce on the grounds of adultery. The well-publicized relationship of Mrs. Yonge with a Colonel Norton followed William Yonge's own affair. A noted womanizer, Yonge separated from Mary in 1724 and revealed in great detail her adulterous relationship, including having her love letters read aloud during legal proceedings. While he paid no penalty for his betrayal, the court found Mary Yonge guilty and ordered that her dowry and an additional large financial sum be paid to her husband. She was also held guilty in the eyes of a judgmental public who practiced a double standard where adultery was concerned.

Ever reactive to unfair situations, Montagu made the scandal the basis of her poem, although not every fact she includes is true. She attacked the double standard her culture held dear and its tendency to punish women for acts men were not only allowed, but, in some situations, encouraged to do. Her characterization of a hypocritical society desiring the very behavior it censures would not have been well received in her time. The poem would only be published as a result the interest of feminist critics many years later. Montagu writes 80 lines in iambic pentameter with rhyming couplets, shaping an appealing persona.

The poem opens as if Mary Yonge writes a letter to her husband, a form known well to Montagu, judged one of the superior letter writers of her era. The speaker makes clear she writes not to move her husband to pity or ask for excuse for her "offense," with Montagu adopting a sarcastic tone to add, "Nor can a woman's arguments prevail, / When ever your patron's wise example fails." She referred with the term *patron* to Sir Robert Walpole, a friend to Yonge and rumored to accept his wife's penchant for affairs.

Montagu arrives quickly at her point in lines 9–10, writing, "Too, too severely laws of honor bind / The weak submissive sex of womankind," then notes that, regardless of the circumstance of a marriage, society expected a wife to devote herself entirely to her husband. She makes the point that civil law will not execute justice. Instead, one must turn to heaven: "Just heaven! (for sure in heaven does justice reign, / though tricks below that sacred name profane)." Not only do men behave in an unjust way, the speaker claims that they do so in heaven's name, perhaps referencing the use of the Bible in court. Montagu next lists examples of lawbreakers who do gain justice, such as "Defrauded servants" who are freed and the "wounded slave" who "regains his liberty." By contrast, "For wives ill used no remedy remains, / To daily racks condemned, and to eternal chains," the *racks* and *chains* referring to the tortures of having to face a condemning public as well as to suffer under the prejudiced legal system.

Montagu then compares the passion of women to that of men, finding them alike. Their minds are just "as haughty, and as warm our blood," but while men take joy in a wide range of activities, women must remain silent. The speaker acknowledges women are not strong, for which men accuse them of weakness, and then blame them when they lose control or commit a weak act, an unacceptable contradiction. She has been ruined, losing her "small fortune," which causes her to have to "quit the woman's joy to be admired," suffering instead a "low inglorious state," although her conscience remains clear. However, she cannot hide from her vengeful husband, who desires not only her wealth, but also her pride, making her a public spectacle: "Dragged into light, my tender crime is shown / And every circumstance of fondness known." Montagu pointedly accuses Mr. Yonge of seeking shelter from the law and of urging all politically connected men to move against his wife, a force she has no chance of withstanding.

The speaker finally describes herself as "wretched" and "abandoned" but able to take some comfort in the "mean conduct" of her "infamously loose" husband, feeling secure that those with "just and reasonable" minds have mentally acquitted her, even though their "lips condemn" her. She takes solace in the "brittle friendships" her husband cultivates with "the great" but predicts his new-found freedom will be tainted by yet another disloyal bride. In actuality, William Yonge would marry well, his new-found wealth allowing him to wed the daughter of a baron. Mary Yonge also remarried, but little else is known of her.

"EPISTLE TO DR. ARBUTHNOT" ALEXANDER POPE (1735, 1751)   ALEXANDER POPE spent some time considering the choice of form for his late-career rebuttal of those who had most demeaned him in print. He selected a poetic letter, "Epistle to Dr. Arbuthnot," which later critics would deem a rhetorical masterpiece. Because Arbuthnot held the public's esteem, his choice as the ostensible recipient of Pope's remarks proved brilliant strategy, as it lent instant credibility to Pope's words. In its originally published form, the poem did not contain dialogue by Arbuthnot, once a royal physician, a spirited member of the Martinus Scriblerus Club, and one of Pope's best friends. When the poem was published in Warburton's 1751 edition, the form most familiar to readers, Arbuthnot's direct remarks had been introduced, changing the form from epistle to dramatic dialogue.

Arbuthnot apparently had urged Pope to take aim at his detractors, applying the "lash" represented by satire. In 1733 when his friend lay close to death, Pope decided to act on his urging. The 18th century considered satire a desirable form of social punishment, believing it might actually lead the subject to change his ways. However, as Pope began to understand late in his career, such change rarely occurred. He writes in this poem of some of his own satire, particularly that found in The DUNCIAD (1728), "You think this cruel? Take it for a rule, / No creature smarts so little as a Fool," to which he adds,

Who shames a Scribler? Break one cobweb thro',
He spins the slight, self-pleasing thread anew;
Destroy his Fib, or Sophistry; in vain,
The Creature's at his dirty work again;
Thron'd in the Centre of his thin designs;
Proud of a vast Extent of flimsy lines. (89–94)

While Pope suffered various criticisms over his lifetime to which he skillfully reacted, the year 1733 yielded some of the more vicious attacks. Once Pope's friend, MARY WORTLEY MONTAGUE took offense at Pope's unfounded comment about her in his The First Satire of the Second Book of Horace (ll. 83–84), joining Lord John Hervey to publish the vitriolic Verses Addressed to the Imitator of Horace (1733). Montague had in truth been provoked to take action. However, Hervey, an effeminate unpopular courtier and adviser to Queen Caroline, made assumptions regarding some of Pope's allusions with no true evidence they pertained to him. He published on his own a second attack on Pope during 1733 titled Epistle to a Doctor of Divinity from a Nobleman at Hampton Court. Pope would characterize Hervey in subsequent work as Lord Fanny, while Montague appeared under her own name, as well as the name Sappho. Pope included Lord Fanny among the dunce poetasters in his satires, most specifically in the The Dunciad.

"Epistle to Dr. Arbuthnot" opens in an even tone with a small vignette with which most readers could identify. The speaker urges his friend to sit quietly and talk with him, as they hide from public concerns: "Shut, shut the door, good John! fatigu'd I said, / Tye up the knocker, say I'm sick, I'm dead." The speaker engages "John" with a rendition of his troubles, as his attackers seem to be able to find him no matter where he goes, even in his beloved grotto: "They pierce my Thickets, thro' my Grot they glide." The vague they later becomes quite specific, as Pope takes on many individuals who had caused him conflict, both by name and allusion. They include the Reverend Laurence Eusden, poet and clergyman, whose drunkenness while serving as poet laureate became legendary; James Moore Smythe, who adopted some of Pope's work into poorly written drama and joined the dunces in their attacks; Edmund Curll, who published unauthorized work by others as well as notorious literature; and Bernard Lintot, a publisher of most of Pope's early writing. However, Pope reserves his most skillfully expressed and contained fury for those weak opportunistic individuals who claimed most publicly to be poets:

And has not *Colly* still his Lord, and Whore:
His Butchers *Henley,* his Free-masons *Moor?*
Does not one Table *Bavius* still admit?
Still to one Bishop *Philips* seem a Wit?
Still *Sapho*—"Hold! For God-sake—you'll offend;
"No Names—be calm—learn Prudence of a Friend." (97–102)

In this passage, the voice of Arbuthnot interrupts Pope as he names Sapho, whom all readers would recognize as Montague. However, his satire emphasizes the fact that the other names he has used would be just as well recognized. His subjects include "Colly," or Colley Cibber, long Pope's deserved target and an actor, playwright, and eventual poet laureate, the hero of *The Dunciad;* John Henley, an orator who publicly held forth on unsuitable topics; "Moor," James Moore Smythe, known for his practice of freemasonry; "Bavius," a catch-all label, actually a poet who attacked VIRGIL and Homer, an act ridiculous in the extreme; and Ambrose Philips, minor poet and dramatist who served the archbishop of Armagh, Dr. Hugh Boulter, as secretary. The incorporation of Bavius proves an exceptional rhetorical strategy, as Pope places himself in the company of Virgil and Homer by extension.

Pope next discusses why he became a poet, inserting the now-famous line "I lisp'd in Numbers, for the Numbers came" (128), where the term *numbers* refers to METER in poetry. His description makes clear that poetry came naturally to him, by instinct, something he argued as far more important than training in his *ESSAY ON CRITICISM.* He balances his attacks on the dullards with praise for those he considers exemplary poets, such as Virgil; George Granville, Lord Lansdowne, who served Queen Anne as secretary of war, and to whom Pope dedicated *WINDSOR FOREST;* William

Walsh, a poet and critic who encouraged Pope in his youth; Sir Samuel Garth, author of "The Dispensary" (1699), a satiric poem on apothecaries that Pope enjoyed; the playwright William Congreve; his friends the poets JONATHAN SWIFT and JOHN GAY; and the celebrated JOHN DRYDEN, among others. He next engages in self-censure when he writes that he at first wrote purely descriptive poetry, lacking "Sense," or meaning, comparing himself to Lord Hervey. He notes that the critics, whose advice he meekly attempted to follow, had never written a word of poetry themselves. How then could they claim to evaluate JOHN MILTON and Shakespeare, much less the work of Pope and his contemporaries? His narrative notes that he learned from others, particularly Joseph Addison, esteemed poet and essayist with whom Pope had a brief falling out, but would later write of in a more positive manner. Here Pope inserts a description of Addison that became one of the most famous lines of poetry written in the English language, when he describes him as one who tends to "Damn with faint praise" (201), wounding, rather than striking. Addison had publicly criticized Pope for his satiric "strokes" against John Dennis, whose bad-natured criticism Pope had attacked. Pope also takes on those poets who write only to praise certain patrons, labeling such a patron *Bufo,* the Latin word for "toad."

Most important to Pope is to make clear that he would not use poetry simply to attack a worthy individual who had wounded his vanity, as his enemies had him: "Curst be the Verse, how well soe'er it flow, / That tends to make one worthy Man my foe" (183–184). A dunce is one "Who reads but with a Lust to mis-apply, / Make Satire a Lampoon, and Fiction, Lye." However, "A Lash like mine no honest man shall dred, / But all such babbling blockheads in his stead" (303–304). Then he includes the lines later attributed to Arbuthnot that caused some critics to believe Pope took advantage of his friend by placing in his mouth words he probably would not utter. The poem's speaker mentions Sporus, or Lord Hervey, as one who should tremble in fear that Pope might satirize him. Arbuthnot replies,

". . . What? That Thing of silk,
Sporus, that mere white Curd of Ass's milk?

> Satire or Sense alas! Can Sporus feel?
> Who breaks a Butterfly upon a Wheel?"
>   (305–309)

Pope provides a spirited answer to Arbuthnot's protest, explaining just why such poetasters do deserve his lash. The low quality of their work remains obvious to the trained eye, but they take advantage of the public by establishing themselves as experts. He concludes that group of lines with a description of Sporus, whose "virtues" even prove repulsive: "Beauty that shocks you, Parts that none will trust, / Wit that can creep, and Pride that licks the dust" (332–33). He continues to blast Hervey as a libeler and a Plagiarist. Worse yet, Hervey had viciously attacked Pope's family and his heritage, characterizing his parents as having weak characters when the opposite proved true. Pope's mother lived to read their vindication in her son's poem; she died at age 93, shortly after its publication. The final lines close the poem with a reverent tone in acknowledging Pope's dear friend's illness and wishing him the best, a method modeled after that of Horace.

Of this much published and repeated poem, SAMUEL JOHNSON would write:

> The *Epistle to Arbuthnot,* . . . is a performance consisting, as it seems, of many fragments wrought into one design, which by this union of scattered beauties contains more striking paragraphs than could probably have been brought together into an occasional work. As there is no stronger motive to exertion than self-defence, no part has more elegance, spirit, or dignity than the poet's vindication of his own character.

While one requires references to understand fully the identities of Pope's targets and the context in which they wrote, the beauty and skill of his expression remain obvious.

Alexander Pope believed in the power of poetry, supported by a man's character, to reveal the truth. He took great offense at those who used it for dastardly purposes. Unfortunately for them, he expressed that offense in a manner guaranteeing their deeds would live in infamy, long after their words had been forgotten.

BIBLIOGRAPHY

Clark, John. "Pope's Epistle to Arbuthnot, 189–90." *The Explicator* 46, no. 2 (winter 1988): 11–13.

Grundy, Isobel. "A Skirmish between Pope and Some Persons of Rank and Fortune: *Verses to the Imitator of Horace.*" *Studies in Bibliography* 30 (1977): 96–119.

The Lives of the Poets. Edited by G. B. Hill. 3 Vols. Oxford: Clarendon Press, 1905.

Mengel, Elias F. "Pope's Imitation of Boileau in Arbuthnot." *Essays in Criticism* 38. no. 4 (October 1988): 295–307.

Radner, Sanford. "Pope's Epistle to Dr. Arbuthnot." *The Explicator* 46, no. 1 (fall 1987): 11–14.

"EPISTLE TO MISS BLOUNT" ALEXANDER POPE (1712, 1735)

ALEXANDER POPE originally published "Epistle to a Young Lady" in 1712. His subject may have been imaginary or real, but in 1735 he changed the poem's title to reference his dear friend, Martha Blount: "Epistle to Miss Blount." They had been close since 1711, when Pope left London at age 23 after a vicious attack on his character and physical features by the critic John Dennis. He settled for a time in a rural community around Binfield and met the Blount sisters, described as possessing two of the finest faces in the universe. Whether Martha Blount became Pope's lover is unknown, but they enjoyed a lifelong relationship.

Pope subtitled the poem "With the Works of Voiture," a reference to Vincent de Voiture, a French poet whose gallantry in letter writing proved legend. Much of Pope's own "epistle" focuses on the act of writing, and he opens,

> In these gay thoughts the Loves and Graces
>   shine,
> And all the Writer lives in ev'ry Line;
> His easie Art may happy Nature seem,
> Trifles themselves are Elegant in him.

While he writes ostensibly of Voiture, Pope references himself by extension. He expresses the opinion that excellent writers make their efforts appear slight, as if natural. However, the smallest matters, "trifles," they may transform into the elegant simply through the power of the word. Pope continues through line 20 bemoaning the loss of Voiture, describing how his absence will affect his admirers. Their hearts will heave with sighs to have lost "The Smiles and Loves" that "dy'd in Voiture's death, / But that for ever in his Lines they breath." Pope emphasizes a familiar theme, that art grants immortality to its creator, as it lives on after the creator's death.

In the next section, Pope adopts a voice of morality, noting that mere mortals deserve the strict life of "A long, exact, and serious Comedy," in which each scene will teach a lesson. This sentiment remains fitting to the 18th century, which believed in female propriety and in woman's position as a moral authority. The speaker does allow that each scene might "both Please and Preach," following Sir Phillip Sidney's edict, and that of the classics, that poetry should both teach and delight. The speaker declares his desire that his own life might be "an innocent gay Farce" with more diversion than found on regular days, containing "Humour, Wit, a native Ease and Grace." After the verbal beating Pope took at the hands of lesser writers, he expresses his honest judgment of his work as worthy. The notion of "wit" proved crucial to readers and critics in Pope's time. It sometimes meant an edgy humor, but it had additional meanings, one of which was an intellectual nature. Pope wished to remind his detractors that possession of wit alone was insufficient; one must also have an ease and grace of expression, as he demonstrates. He makes clear that wit is not bound "to Time and Place," meaning he can write as easily in a rural setting as a city setting, adding, "Criticks in Wit, or Life, are hard to please, / Few write to those, and none can live to these," a direct slam against Dennis and others like him.

Beginning with line 31, he speaks directly to his female audience, as he cautions Miss Blount that women allow critics too much effect on their choices. While critics prove rough on him as a writer, women remain the most vulnerable to their effects. Women must abide by custom, which no longer knows why it laid down the edicts that it holds, again alluding to his era's belief in the necessity of virtuousness in women. Custom forbids many pleasures in the misplaced desire for virtue. Women are "Made Slaves by Honour, and made Fools by Shame." While marriage chases away some "petty Tyrant," that of gossips who would accuse the unmarried woman of impropriety, it proves an even greater tyrant. It leaves women still in "Constraint / . . . Or bound in formal, or

in real Chains." Once "caught" by marriage, women have few social choices open to them. A double standard applies where men are concerned; they neglect their wives to fawn on their servants. Critics believe that Pope may have been defending his relationship with Martha Blount, explaining that he will not marry her in order that she may keep her independence.

Pope includes much detail to describe the material benefits a woman gains through a good marriage, such as a "gilt Coach and dappled *Flanders* Mares, / The shining Robes, rich Jewels, Beds of States," and the activities she might enjoy, such as balls, opera boxes, and a good seat at the boxing ring. However, these reach only her outward appearance and leave her "wretched"; she remains "no Dutchess at her Heart" (56).

However, should Miss Blount decide to marry, the speaker advises her not to trust to her beauty and physical charms to make the union, as they will not last. What may provide "A Morning's Pleasure" is "at Evening torn." In the speaker's opinion, "Good Humour only teaches Charms to last," and allows women to continue making conquests, even as they age. Again, Pope touches on the idea of wit, implying that of Miss Blount to be superior to that of certain critics. He emphasizes that Good Humour "binds in Ties more easie, yet more strong, / The willing Heart, and only holds it long." His critics had certainly exhibited bad humor in their tasteless criticism of Pope's physical malformation. He clearly intimates that his application of charming rhetoric and easy wit proves superior as a romantic, as well as rhetorical, approach.

The lasting relationship Voiture made through his words caused his "early Care" to "still shone the same," drawing and holding true lovers together through his language. In death he abides "on th' Elysian Coast, / Amid those Lovers, joys his gentle Ghost." Pope employs CATACHRESIS to shorten the verb *enjoys* to the noun *joys,* utilizing it as a verb. He concludes by comparing Miss Blount's British eyes to the French eyes that caused Voiture to love and concludes with another comment on the power of the well-written word: "And dead as living, 'tis our Author's Pride, / Still to charm those who charm the World beside." While the author has died, his work, his "Pride," abides, continuing to charm young women, who then charm the world.

BIBLIOGRAPHY

Combe, Kirk. "A Contradiction Still: Representations of Women in the Poetry of Alexander Pope." *Notes and Queries* 47, no. 2 (June 2000): 254–256.

Nakanishi, Wendy Jones. "Classical and 'Augustan' Notions of the Literary Letter." *English Studies* 71, no. 4 (August 1990): 341–352.

"EPITAPH, AN" MATTHEW PRIOR (1718)

When MATTHEW PRIOR wrote his satire "An Epitaph," he had in mind a chorus from Seneca's *Thyestes*, "All I seek is to lie still," and its theme of the danger of living a life unfulfilled. In the 62 lines of rhyming couplets, Prior's speaker examines a "marble stone" that marks the grave of "sauntering Jack and idle Joan." He notes that whether "human things went ill or well," or "changing empires rose or fell," Jack and Joan remained exactly the same. They "walked and ate," did it again, then "soundly slept the night away," and after burying four children did not try for more. They lived with both economic and ethical boundaries, which served to separate them from one another, so neither "trespassed on the other's ground." They did not punish or reward their footmen or maids, allowing each servant to "take his course," causing all to become undesirables. Eventually, "slothful disorder filled his stable, / And sluttish plenty decked her table," as they enjoyed beer and wine with meals prefaced by a "short" grace. The speaker does not admire the pair's treatment of the poor, for they gave away the remnants of their "meat / Just when it grew not fit to eat." Prior employs many single-syllable terms, emphasizing the elementary aspects of a life devoid of challenge and change. Because Jack and Joan never grew to know anyone well, they "never made themselves a foe." They also never commended a "man's good deeds," so they had no friends; avoided knowing their relations, as those relations might require aid; and did not keep their house or barn in good repair, as it might "oblige their future heir." The litany of all the pair did not do continues:

> They neither added, nor confounded;
> They neither wanted, nor abounded.
> Each Christmas they accompts did clear;
> And wound their bottom round the year.

Here Prior refers to the personal accounts the couple took care of on an annual basis, using the holiday for practical, rather than spiritual reasons. The term *bottom* refers to a skein of thread, as Prior adopts the FIGURATIVE LANGUAGE of metaphor to describe the way the couple put things right.

The couple were "Nor good, nor bad, nor fools, not wise; / They would not learn, nor could advise." Prior finishes the tale of vacant lives with the final four lines:

> Without love, hatred, joy, or fear,
> They led—a kind of—as it were;
> Nor wished, nor cared, nor laughed, nor cried;
> And so they lived and so they died.

Prior warns against the balanced, seemingly perfect life, in which risk plays no part. It results in boredom and vacuity, a deadly-dull procedure that kills one's spirit.

SAMUEL JOHNSON wrote in his *Lives of the English Poets* that Prior's "epigrams and lighter pieces are, like those of others sometimes elegant, sometimes trifling, and sometimes dull; among the best are the *Camelion* and the epitaph on *John and Joan*." According to Johnson, Prior made little effort at originality, having borrowed most of his ideas. However, his execution remains often admirable, because of his diligence and measured judgment on what he chose to imitate.

BIBLIOGRAPHY

Johnson, Samuel. *Lives of the English Poets.* Vol. 1. New York: E. P. Dutton, 1958.

"EPITAPH ON S.P., A CHILD OF QUEEN ELIZABETH'S CHAPEL" BEN JONSON (1616)

Unlike many professionals who wrote epitaphs for a fee, BEN JONSON undertook to write "Epitaph on S.P., a Child of Queen Elizabeth's Chapel" for personal reasons. He had known the "S.P." of the title as Salomon Pavy, one of the child actors in a troupe called the Children of Queen Elizabeth's Chapel. A playwright as well as a poet, Jonson had observed Salomon on the stage for three years, and the boy had performed in some of Jonson's plays. Unlike the professionally written epitaphs that distanced themselves from their subjects because of unfamiliarity, this poem reflects Jonson's affection for the boy. While understandably not as poignant as epitaphs he composed for his own children, "ON MY FIRST DAUGHTER" and "ON MY FIRST SON," "Epitaph on S.P." reflects a genuine sadness at the loss of such a young life. Written in 24 lines with the RHYME scheme *ababcdcdefef*, and a METER alternating between iambs of four feet and two feet, the poem matches the rhythm of everyday speech. Although dealing with an elevated subject, Jonson opted to adopt direct simple language, resulting in a clean, elegant style.

Aspects of the poem reflect an address to the audience from a stage, thus suggesting the child's brief acting career. As a Greek chorus to its audience, the speaker begins with a call to readers:

> Weep with me, all you that read
>> This little story:
> And know for whom a tear you shed,
>> Death's self is sorry.

Salomon's remembrance is couched as a narrative designed to elicit a single tear from those who hear it and even to make death, personified here through the use of FIGURATIVE LANGUAGE (FIGURE OF SPEECH), feel regret. The reference to the tear, rather than to uncontrolled weeping, suggests the story is so common that its very familiarity provokes a sentimental reaction, even from those who do not know its subject; such is the power of excellent storytelling.

The next four lines describe S.P. as a child who so thrived "In grace and feature" heaven stood in competition with nature as to which of their influences he reflected. Although "When Fates turned cruel," he was "scarce thirteen" the speaker emphasizes his few years were well spent, for "three filled zodiacs had he been / The stage's jewel." He acted so well, the speaker surmises, that "Parcae," or the Fates, likely perceived him as a veteran, thus mistaking him as an old man whose time had come. When they discovered their error, nothing could be done; thus, as the fourth line had stated, Death was sorry. They might have attempted a rebirth for the boy, or tried "In baths to steep him," a reference critics believe may have been to mystical

baths, such as that of Medea, which restored youth to Jason's father. However, his "being so much too good for earth, / Heaven vows to keep him," indicates nothing could restore the child to life.

Jonson concludes on a positive note, adopting the traditional view that some souls prove too highly valued by heaven to be left on earth for a full lifetime. Resigned to that simple fact, much easier to accept than the reality of a cruel loss, the speaker gives hope to listeners that S.P. resides in a better place than he had among men.

"EPITAPH ON THE LADY MARY VILLERS" THOMAS CAREW (1640)

A strong representative of a common type of verse during the Carolinian period, THOMAS CAREW's "Epitaph on the Lady Mary Villers" was probably written in part to cultivate patronage from the deceased's family. Poets had to earn a living, and epitaphs supplied an income. Neither original nor particularly moving, the epitaph does exactly what it should in commiserating with the family of its subject and in reminding readers that such losses remain ubiquitous and may visit their own families. Epitaph writers did not even need to know the deceased, as the approach often proved so general it could apply to anyone.

Carew begins by noting that the Lady Mary Villers lies "under this stone," as the epitaph literally appeared on a grave marker. He adds that "with weeping eyes" her parents and friends placed her "in earth." He next speaks directly to those who will in the future view the stone, writing, "If any of them (Reader) were / Known unto thee, shed a tear," inviting those who may have known Mary Villers or any in the funeral party to feel sympathy. He extends his invitation to readers to identify with the bereaved, whether they had personal knowledge or not, continuing,

> Or if thyself possess a gem,
> As dear to thee, as this to them,
> Though a stranger to this place,
> Bewail in theirs, thine own hard case.

In other words, while passers-by may not be familiar with that particular grave or graveyard, they may know of one that cradles their own beloved. With terms such as *bewail*, Carew invites readers to share the heightened emotion of grief that remains a universal human experience because of death. He concludes with a couplet that modern readers may find imbued with unintentional humor, due to a forced RHYME: "For thou perhaps at thy return / Mayest find thy Darling in an Urne."

ESSAY ON CRITICISM, AN ALEXANDER POPE (1711)

ALEXANDER POPE wrote *An Essay on Criticism* at an early age yet created a work worthy of a far more experienced hand. He involves himself in the ongoing dispute between the values of the traditional as compared to the contemporary, the ancient to the modern. A didactic piece, *An Essay on Criticism* offers much opinion and judgment regarding the occupation of publicly expressing one's opinion regarding art. While the poem exudes a negative tone, it resulted more from Pope's attempts to shape a witty piece than from his true dislike of those upon whom he depended for exposure to the public. The public listened to those critics; otherwise, Pope would not have spent the energy in advising them how to go about their criticism.

SAMUEL JOHNSON wrote that although Pope often "professes contempt of the world" and "pretend[s] indifference," such "dispositions" were merely "counterfeited" for effect. He asks, "How could he despise those whom he lived by pleasing, and on whose approbation his esteem of himself was superstructed? Why should he hate those to whose favour he owed his honour and his ease?" Johnson pronounced Pope "sufficiently 'a fool to Fame'" that he would not really place himself at risk with critics. If accurate, Johnson's summation of Pope's satiric approach counters much of modern criticism, which assumes Pope's honesty in his evaluation of others: "His scorn of the Great is repeated too often to be real: no man thinks much of that which he despises; and as falsehood is always in danger of inconsistency he makes it his boast at another time that he lives among them."

An Essay on Criticism was the first comprehensive statement in English regarding literary criticism and was celebrated by Pope's fellow writers. He discusses terms seen repeated constantly in criticism, such as *wit,*

Nature, and *genius,* as he imitates Horace's approach in his *Art of Poetry.* In so doing, he answers his own query as to the importance of the classics to contemporary writing. Should they act as models, or should writers take inspiration only from natural knowledge, that gained through intuition? If one continued to utilize the masters, should it be only as a suggested pattern, or as prescriptive instruction? He divides his poem into three sections, each with a different purpose. The first portion suggests a compromise between warring opinions, the second provides analysis of weak criticism, and the third offers praise for the classics. Pope's purpose is not to find a solution, but rather to offer his opinion. He creates some of the great maxims of the English language, including "A little Learning is a dang'rous Thing" (215), "To Err is *Humane;* to Forgive, *Divine*" (525), and "*Fools* rush in where *Angels* fear to tread" (625).

Pope opens with a statement that pits the effect of weak writing against that of faulty criticism:

'Tis hard to say, if greater Want of Skill
Appear in *Writing* or in *Judging* ill;
But, of the two, less dan'rous is th' Offence,
To tire our *Patience,* than mis-lead our *Sense.*
(1–4)

The speaker notes the importance of standards to act for comparison purposes, using watches, and our ability to compare the time of our own watch to that of another, as an analogy. This requires little judgment of us. However, judgment, such as that applied by critics, may be arbitrary, consisting in the definition of fixed and theoretical standards. Thus, "by *false Learning* is *good Sense* defac'd" for "In search of *Wit*" some "lose their common *Sense*" Pope suggests varied definitions for the term *wit,* from a cleverly framed expression to an intelligent suggestion. The speaker next notes that those who fail as wits try poetry, and failing poetry, they become "*Cricks* next," proving "plain *Fools* at last." He turns to Nature to consider the concept of "wit," an important one in the 18th century. Men should conform to nature's limits, but their pride often causes them to feel they may move beyond nature, attempting to become accomplished in areas for which they are not fit: "One *Science* only will one *Genius* fit; /

so vast is Art, so narrow Human Wit" (60–61). While "Wit and Judgment often are at strife," they are "meant each other's Aid, like Man and Wife." Pope notes the conflict has not always been present, as in ancient times, "Criticism the Muse's Handmaid prov'd" (102). However, in later times, critics focused on trying to display their own learning, with the result that they "explain[ed] the Meaning quite away." He makes clear that in order to retain coherency in critical method, one needs a standard by which to judge excellent poetry, suggesting that poetry by classical writers well qualifies. Their natural beauty remains admirable, as one may develop fine guidelines from their execution, although such guidelines should not be converted into enforceable rules. Otherwise, critics will force all poets to write according to the laws of criticism. The section concludes with the maxim that society has a duty "To teach vain Wits a Science little known, / T' admire Superior Sense, and doubt their own!" (200).

The second, much lengthier section focuses on the multiple errors in human judgment exhibited by faulty criticism. Generally the pride of the critic interferes with true judgment, and all sense is abandoned, along with truth. Pope stresses his belief that limited human understanding will never grasp the vast amount of knowledge that waits to be claimed. Crucial to valuable criticism is the critic's reading "each Work of Wit / With the same Spirit that its Author writ," and digesting the entire piece and measuring its effect on the reader, rather than counting its small errors. The speaker also notes that critics often reflect the political attitudes of their day. As a Catholic, Pope had suffered negative criticism that had little to do with his talent at a time when anti-Catholic sentiment ran high. He includes a famous statement regarding wit:

> True Wit is Nature to Advantage drest,
> What oft was Thought, but ne'er so well Exprest,
> Something, whose Truth convinc'd at Sight we find,
> That gives us back the Image of our Mind."
>   (303–306)

In other words, the fewer tricks and trappings used in self-expression, the better for the poet. According to Pope, "True Expression, like th' unchanging Sun, / Clears, and improves whate'er it shines upon." Faulty criticism focuses on one aspect only of a poem, such as its rhythm or one imperfect line. Pope includes some of the most famous lines written in poetry about criticism, in which he formats the lines to match their topics. For instance, in order to demonstrate a slow-moving line, he writes, "that like a wounded Snake, drags its slow length along," inserting syllables difficult to pronounce or rush. In an attempt to explain why some find weak poetry acceptable, he describes the approaches used by poetasters. They insert a line here and there that catches the reader's interest, while supplying little of true value. He cautions critics against allowing this approach to fool them:

> Yet let not each gay Turn thy Rapture move,
> For fools Admire, but Men of Sense Approve,
> As things seem large which w thro' Mists descry,
> Dulness is ever apt to Magnify. (390–393)

Pope takes up many additional pitfalls he warns critics to avoid. They include allowing the passage of time to tarnish fine poetry, criticizing it only because it no longer satisfies contemporary taste; he uses Chaucer and Dryden as examples. The passing of time may actually cause "ripe Colours [to] soften and unite" (490), improving the poem in the eyes of the astute reader. His caution extends to poets who sacrifice the quality of their work to a feeling of competition with one another for critical praise: "And while Self-Love each jealous Writer rules, / Contending Wits become the Sport of Fools" (516–517). Petty competition shatters friendship, and critics attack humanity, rather than poor art. Thus, the speaker cautions, never "in the Critick let the Man be lost!" He points to the reigns of Charles II and William III as examples of "the fat Age of Pleasure, Wealth, and Ease," in which "Sprung the rank Weed, and thriv'd with large Increase," that weed being dullness evidenced in obscene verse. Critics should take aim at such blasphemy: "Here point your Thunder, and exhaust your Rage!" (555).

Pope opens his final section in which he will discuss the personal and ethical aspects of the practice of criticism by writing, "LEARN then what MORALS Criticks ought to show, / For 'tis but *half a Judge's Task, to Know*" (560–561). Critics must most of all "let Truth and Candor shine," as evidence of their own good characters. He stresses the ability of critics to be generous in their praise and to admit they may not possess all knowledge. The single idea that borders on original arises when Pope insists that each artistic work exists as an entity separate from all others, and the critic should know the creator's intent before judging. Thus,

'Tis best sometimes your Censure to restrain
And *charitably* let the Dull be vain;
Your Silence there is better than your *Spite,*
For who can *rail* so long as they can *write*?
  (596–599)

Pope supplies a history lesson, noting specific poets of the past as models of judgments. He concludes his essay with a final caution to critics to be

Careless of *Censure,* nor too fond of *Fame,*
Still pleas'd to *praise,* yet not afraid to *blame,*
Averse alike to *flatter,* or *Offend,*
Not *free* from Faults, nor yet too vain to *mend.*

BIBLIOGRAPHY

Johnson, Samuel. *The Lives of the Poets.* Edited by G. B. Hill. 3 Vols. Oxford: Clarendon Press, 1905.
Morris, David P. *Alexander Pope, the Genius of Sense.* Cambridge, Mass.: Harvard University Press, 1984.

ESSAY ON MAN, AN ALEXANDER POPE (1733)

By the time ALEXANDER POPE chose to publish his *An Essay on Man,* he had received thorough and undeserved criticism from the poetasters, or "dunces," whose activities he so often correctly lambasted, most notably in *The* DUNCIAD (1723). Still smarting from Pope's satire, his enemies turned the public against his *Epistle to Burlington* (1731), misrepresenting it as a personal attack on Burlington, one of Pope's close friends. A biased public did not take the poem as Pope intended, as a satire on the vanity of nobility as a whole. In reaction to that misunderstanding, Pope devised a clever and, as it proved, wildly successful plan to publish *An Essay on Man* anonymously, allowing the public and

the dunces themselves to render an honest evaluation. Pope published through his known bookseller two poems in 1733 clearly under his own name, "Epistle to Bathurst" and the *First Satire of the Second Book of Horace.* He then chose a different bookseller for *An Essay on Man,* and because his precise RHYMES were so well known, even inserted one weak rhyming couplet to mislead his readers. Pope hoped for a fair reception of a poem that he knew would draw charges of religious unorthodoxy if printed under his name. His plan worked beautifully, and his usual critics raved about the genius evident in this work by a new poet.

Later critics did not evaluate the poem as one of Pope's stronger pieces, claiming that Bolingbroke influenced Pope to adopt some of his own metaphysical views and an ideology of natural theology. The fatalistic and naturalistic themes were the result, as they saw Pope reducing man to little more than a puppet with no free will. He attempted to consider man and his experience apart from Christian revelation, the more familiar and acceptable approach used by poets including JOHN MILTON. Thus, he ignores those events of history considered crucial by many, such as the creation, man's fall from grace in the Garden of Eden, the birth of Christ, Christ's death and resurrection, and the final days as predicted by the biblical book of Revelation. He also excluded references to myths and their explanations for man's condition. Pope instead perceived of man as making discoveries through his experience based on reason. He also hoped to demystify some language with which the church had embedded specific symbolic meaning. As Locke did, Pope believed that words simply referred to our ideas, not to any hidden essence. Pope would add in 1738 the "Universal Prayer" to the end of further editions of *Essay on Man,* but he never escaped that early judgment of religious unorthodoxy in his lifetime.

Later evaluations found the poem nothing short of brilliant, with Pope's desire to challenge the value of what passed for 18th-century "wit" even beyond what he had in his *An* ESSAY ON CRITICISM and to reconcile philosophy with man's perception of "sense." Pope wrote in "The Design" that precedes the poem:

The science of Human Nature is, like all other sciences, reduced to a *few clear points:* there are not *many certain truths* in this world. It is therefore in the Anatomy of the Mind as in that of the Body; more good will accrue to mankind by attending to the large, open and perceptible parts, than by studying too much such finer nerves and vessels, the conformations and uses of which will for ever escape our observation.

Structured in four epistles, the poem stretches to slightly more than 1,300 lines. Pope originally conceived it as an introduction to an extended work that would include the MORAL ESSAYS. According to Pope's notes, the additional sections would cover themes including "Knowledge and its limits," "Government, both ecclesiastical and civil," and "Morality, in eight or nine of the most concerning branches of it; four of which would have been the two extremes to each of the Cardinal Virtues." He eventually gave up the plan, for unknown reasons. Pope provides an "Argument" that precedes each epistle, making clear the various points each will attempt to make.

The First Epistle clarifies, according to its argument, "the Nature and State of Man, with respect to the Universe." Major points include the fact that man can only judge other systems, of which he remains ignorant, in relation to his own system. In addition, he should not be considered imperfect, but suitable to his rank within the general order of things. All present happiness depends upon ignorance of the future. Aiming to know more than is possible causes "Man's error and misery." Man is part of an order and suborder that extend above and below him, and if any part is destroyed, the entire order disintegrates. If any individual wished that to take place, it would be the result of pride and madness. Man must assume his proper place in Providence.

Pope opens the First Epistle by addressing Henry St. John, Viscount Bolingbroke, telling him, "leave all meaner things / to low ambition, and the pride of Kings." The speaker invites Bolingbroke to join in study instead of "all this scene of Man / A mighty maze! but not without a plan." He makes clear his belief that we can only reason from what we know; only God can know all the secrets of the universe. He then references "the great chain" (33), imagery he will return to later. This traditional concept would be familiar to his read-

ers, who shared the vision of man in the most crucial central position on a ladder of creation. At the top is God, followed by other superior ethereal creatures, then humans, then angels, then "Beast, bird, fish, insect!" and finally, "what no eye can see" (239). Man represents a combination of beastly sensual instinct and spiritual intelligence. He needs to resist the temptation of pride to rise above his natural place, and he must resist surrender to animal instinct. Man reflects all parts of his world, resulting in a condition labeled by the ancients *concordia discors,* or the harmonization of opposites: "But All subsists by elemental strife; / And Passions are the elements of Life." This First Epistle yields one of Pope's most quoted lines as he writes of hope, encouraging man to nurture that emotion as he awaits death and future blessings:

Hope humbly then; with trembling pinions
    soar;
Wait the great teacher Death, and God adore!
What future bliss, he gives not thee to know,
But gives that Hope to be thy blessing now.
Hope springs eternal in the human breast:
Man near Is, but always To, be blest;
The soul, uneasy and confin'd from home,
Rests and expatiates in a life to come. (90–98)

Man's bliss "Is not to act or think beyond mankind." He lacks "a microscopic eye . . . / For this plain reason, Man is not a Fly." Pope closes the First Epistle by inserting a basic axiom of philosophy, "All *x* is *y*." He includes PARADOX as he writes:

All Nature is but Art, unknown to thee;
All Chance, Direction, which thou canst not
    see;
All Discord, Harmony, not understood;
All partial Evil, universal Good:
And, spite of Pride, in erring Reason's spite,
One truth is clear, "Whatever IS, IS RIGHT.
    (289–294)

The Second Epistle notes as its argument "Of the Nature and State of Man, with respect to Himself, as an Individual." Points include that man should study himself, rather than prying into God's business; that his capacity remains limited; and that Two Principles remain necessary to man: Self-love and Reason; Self-love is stronger. He examines the passions and how reason should override them and concludes by noting "the ends of Providence and general Good are answered in our Passions and Imperfections," and they are well distributed and useful.

The epistle opens with another famous line, as its second, "The proper study of Mankind is Man." The speaker urges man to try to do things he supposes he cannot, such as instructing "the planets in what orbs to run" and teaching "Eternal Wisdom how to rule," after which he will "drop into thyself, and be a fool!" (30). He urges man, "Trace Science then, with Modesty thy guide; / First strip off all her equipage of Pride" (44–45). All man needs to heed are two principles: "Two Principles in human nature reign; / Self-love, to urge and a Reason, to restrain." Neither is good or bad on its own, and both are required in the government of man. Expressing a typical 18th-century thought, Pope writes that habit and experience strengthen Reason and help restrain Self-love. All passion results from Self-love:

Love, Hope, and Joy, fair pleasure's smiling
   train,
Hate, Fear, and Grief, the family of pain;
These mix'd with art, and to due bounds
  confin'd
Make and maintain the balance of the mind.
  (117–120)

Concordia discors appears again as "lights and shades," which may cause strife, but that strife "Gives all the strength and colour of our life" (121–122). Reason may even help in overcoming madness. He suggests that each individual nurtures his or her own virtue, which is closest to his or her vice, for "Extremes in Nature equal ends produce, / In Man they join to some mysterious use" (205–206). Pope closes by noting the stages of life and including another well-known phrase as a metaphor for death, "Life's poor play is o'er!" (282), drawing on the familiar allusion since the Renaissance to life as a performance, men the players. The final line offers the comfort "tho' Man's a fool, yet God is Wise."

The Third Epistle argues "Of the Nature and State of Man, with respect to Society." Pope discusses the Universe as a single social system, "Nothing made wholly for itself, nor yet wholly for another" and asserts that animals know happiness and that Reason and Instinct operate for the good of each individual and for Society. While Instinct proves good for Society, Reason proves better, the origins of Monarchy, Religion, and Government, all from the Principle of Love, and Superstition and Tyrany from Fear. Finally, he discusses the various forms of government and their true ends.

Pope offers a theory in his first few lines based on a "chain of Love" that all men can observe. They can see "The single atoms each to other tend" and can see that "All forms that perish other forms supply." In other words, he concludes, "Parts relate to whole" (21), a line critics suggest relates to the various parts of the poem relating to its whole. As he describes monarchs, wits, and tyrants, he describes two types of discord. One is warlike and violent, the other benevolent and creating peace; neither is good on its own. Instinct causes men to feel compassion for others and results in service, an aspect that Reason, "cool at best" (85), ignores. God sets the proper bounds of each and "On mutual Wants built mutual Happiness" (112), linking all creatures and all men. The speaker notes that left to his instincts, man might allow his greed to lead to destruction and savagery, and that he can learn control by observing nature. The bees can teach arts of building, "the mole to plow, the worm to weave" (176). Such statements draw from classical sources, in which efficient creatures were posed as examples for human society to imitate.

The speaker states that men never possessed any divine right (236) and supplies various examples of the effect of fear on others. Pope returns to what at first seems to be a PARADOX, writing,

So drives Self-love, thro' just and thro'unjust
To one Man's pow'r, ambition, lucre, lust:
The same Self-love, in all, becomes the cause
Of what restrains him, Government and Laws.
  (269–272)

However, as Pope critics later explained, what he writes contains no true contradiction. The sharing of self-interest makes for proper government. In the end, "Self-love forsook the path it first pursu'd, / And found the private in the public good" (281–282). The final couplet reads, "Thus God and Nature link'd the gen'ral frame, / And bade Self-love and Social be the same."

In the Fourth and final Epistle Pope's focus is happiness, including false notions of happiness; that happiness is the end of and attainable by all men; that God intends happiness to be available to all; thus, it must be social, governed by general laws. Happiness does not consist in external goods; is kept even by providence, through Hope and Fear; and the good man will have an advantage. We should not judge who is good, and external goods are often inconsistent with or destructive of virtue. He also deals with the nobility, with superior talents, with fame, and concludes that "the perfection of Virtue and Happiness consists in a conformity to the ORDER OF PROVIDENCE here, and a Resignation to it here and hereafter."

The reader has no doubt regarding Pope's major topic after reading the first line, which declares, "Oh Happiness! Our being's end and aim!" Line 3 describes that state of being as "That something still which prompts th'eternal sigh, / For which we bear to live, or dare to die" (4–5). Discussion with others regarding the location of bliss will evoke varied responses. Some believe it exists "in action, some in ease, / Those call it Pleasure, and Contentment these" (22–23), as Pope makes the point that we cannot learn of bliss; we must experience it for ourselves in order to recognize it. Most importantly, happiness must "Subsist not in the good of one, but all" (38). Because of order, some will enjoy more happiness, or bliss, than others; however, "Condition, circumstance is not the thing; / Bliss is the same in subject or in king" (57–58). The speaker notes unequivocally that "all the good that individuals find" (77) "Lie in three words, Health, Peace, and Competence" (80). These elements are composed of, and supported by, further elements and the consideration of all results in the truth that he "Who sees and follows that great scheme the best, / Best knows the blessing, and will most be blest" (95–97). He then makes clear that those who are virtuous and just may die too soon, but their deaths are not caused by their virtue.

In order to enjoy a true kingdom on earth, everyone must cooperate, even though "What shocks one part will edify the rest, / Nor with one system can they all be blest" (147–148). Again, discord may evoke harmony, as evidenced by the fact that "sometimes virtue starves, while Vice is fed" (149). Humility, Justice, Truth, and Public Spirit deserve to wear a Crown, and they will, but one must wait to receive the rewards of possessing such traits. In the meantime, "Honour and shame from no Condition rise; / Act well your part, there all the honour lies" (193–194). Pope assembles an honor code for all to follow, as he attempts to convince individuals not to feel jealousy toward others who seem to have more possessions, as these do not lead to bliss. One should also avoid a desire for fame, which Pope defines as "a fancy'd life in others breath" (237). Rather, "An honest Man's the noblest work of God" (248), and "'Virtue alone is Happiness below'" (310). Pope has managed, through various examples, to lead from his opening request for a definition of happiness to the conclusion that virtue equates to that state, and, because virtue is available to all, everyone can enjoy happiness. He echoes his previous sentiments, including that self-love must be pushed from the private to the public, or social level, and that "God loves from Whole to Parts; but human soul / Must rise from Individual to the Whole" (361–362). As any worthy lesson does, this one bears repeating, and Pope closes with that emphasis:

That REASON, PASSION, answer one great aim;
That true SELF-LOVE and Social are the same;
That VIRTUE only makes our BLISS below;
And all our Knowledge is, OURSELVES TO KNOW.
    (395–398)

BIBLIOGRAPHY
Hammond, Brean S. Pope and Bolingbroke: A Study of Friendship and Influence. Columbia: University of Missouri Press, 1984.
Morris, David P. Alexander Pope, the Genius of Sense. Cambridge, Mass.: Harvard University Press, 1984.

"EVE'S APOLOGY IN DEFENSE OF WOMEN" AEMILIA LANYER (1611) As part of AEMILIA LANYER's larger work, Salve Deus Rex Judaeorum, "Eve's Apology in Defense of Women" sets for

itself a remarkable agenda. Lanyer reenvisioned the traditional view of woman as the cause of all mankind's misery as a result of Eve's sin in the Garden of Eden. She adopts two approaches in attempting to redeem Eve and, by extension, all women. First Lanyer contrasts Eve's innocent betrayal of Adam to man's active betrayal of Christ in his crucifixion to argue the far greater degree of man's betrayal. Second she argues that man's self-proclaimed position of lord of the earth, a being stronger than woman, made Adam far more culpable than Eve in eating of the forbidden fruit, which she offered in innocent love. While unremarked upon in any public venue by Lanyer's contemporaries, her revised myth of the Garden of Eden proved an extraordinary feminist work. In 12 eight-line stanzas, with RHYME scheme of *abababcc*, Lanyer makes a thorough case in defense of Eve.

The speaker begins by describing the part of Pontius Pilate as judge of Christ. She inserts the plea of Pilate's wife for her husband to spare Christ, it is based on her dream, a telling consistent with the biblical version of the story. Pilate's wife pleads,

> "O noble governor, make thou yet a pause,
> Do not in innocent blood imbrue thy hands;
> > But hear the words of thy most worthy wife,
> > Who sends to thee, to beg her Savior's
> > life." (5–8)

Lanyer reverses the tone of the request made by Eve of Adam to partake of the fruit, when Pilate's wife begs him not to act. She can later make the point that men gathered to kill Christ, while a woman attempted to halt his murder. Pilate's wife continues at the conclusion of the second stanza emphasizing that women should not celebrate man's fall, referring either to the fall of Adam, Christ's death, or Pontius's part in his death: "Let not us women glory in men's fall. / Who had power given to overrule us all." Lanyer makes clear that men have always had power, by their own claim, over women, thus suggesting Adam neglected his duty in allowing Eve's innocent gift to corrupt all of mankind. The third stanza states,

> Our mother Eve, who tasted of the tree
> Giving to Adam what she held most dear,

> Was simply good, and had no power to see;
> The after-coming harm did not appear. (20–23)

In contrast Pilate had been warned by his wife, as a result of her power to see the terrible consequences of Christ's persecution.

The speaker notes that Eve employed neither "guile nor craft" in offering the forbidden fruit to Adam; rather her ignorance had allowed Satan to confuse her. Although Eve's blame was great, Adam's proved greater, for "What weakness offered, strength might have refused; / Being lord of all, the greater was his shame." Lanyer's tone remains respectful but firm, as she relates that Adam had been created perfect by God and "received that straight command" not to eat from the forbidden tree directly from God's mouth. Furthermore, Adam understood, as Eve did not, that betrayal of that order would result in death. Adam begins to appear more and more the dupe, as Lanyer reminds readers that Eve silently offered Adam the fruit without any attempt to persuade him, and the fruit's "fair" appearance acted as the persuasion: "No subtle serpent's falsehood did betray him; / If he would eat it, who had power to stay him?" Lanyer proposes that Eve's only fault was loving Adam too much; love prompted her to give him what she believed to be a wonderful gift.

Having constructed her comparison of Eve's act to the potential sin of Pilate, Lanyer states bluntly in lines 72–73; "Her weakness did the serpent's words obey, / But you in malice god's dear son betray." Clearly, man's sin far overshadows Eve's. Lanyer further presses her point, asking, "Your fault being greater, why should you disdain / Our being your equals, free from tyranny?" She follows that question with a stinging indictment: "If one weak woman simply did offend, / This sin of yours hath no excuse nor end." Lanyer closes in her final stanza by restating the fact that women were in no way complicit with man's murder of Christ. The warning by Pilate's wife proves the opposite.

As noted by Barbara K. Lewalski, Lanyer "challenges patriarchal ideology" as well as "the discourses supporting it." She succeeds in "displacing the hierarchical authority of fathers and husbands," quite a feat for a 17th-century female poet. Her combination of narration and religious meditation results in an informed challenge to traditional views of women and their place in society. Aemilia Lanyer became an important force in women's literature in the 20th century, and her small body of writing continues to attract more attention in the 21st century. It remains easily obtainable, in both electronic and print versions.

BIBLIOGRAPHY

Beilin, Elaine V. *Redeeming Eve: Women Writers of the English Renaissance.* Princeton, N.J.: Princeton University Press, 1987.

Lewalski, Barbara K. "Seizing Discourses and Reinventing Genres." In *Aemilia Lanyer: Gender, Genre, and the Canon,* edited by Marshall Grossman, 49–59. Lexington: University Press of Kentucky, 1998.

"EXCUSE FOR SO MUCH WRIT UPON MY VERSES, AN" MARGARET CAVENDISH, DUCHESS OF NEWCASTLE (1653)

When MARGARET CAVENDISH, DUCHESS OF NEWCASTLE, wrote "An Excuse for So Much Writ upon My Verses," she joined her contemporary, the American poet Anne Bradstreet, in referring to her poetry as her offspring. Unlike Bradstreet, Cavendish had no children of her own and expressed the seeming tension between that absence and her mainly healthy self-image by noting that the fame one attained through writing proved more satisfying than children, who could become treacherous to their parents. While Cavendish may have suppressed her anxiety about publishing with a brash approach contrasting greatly with Bradstreet's humility, they shared concern over how the public might receive writing by a woman. Unlike Bradstreet, who wrote mainly of her domestic sphere, Cavendish's topics often proved more ambitious, as she focused on her own brand of science. She then suffered attack by those who accused her of placing her name on writings by her husband and brother-in-law. She adamantly denied the claim, although she had somewhat invited it by carefully excusing her female "ignorance," then presuming to write about scientific and philosophical topics whose familiarity was generally gained only by upper-class males through formal education. She had enjoyed a tutored education as a child in a wealthy family, but not over an extended time, as she and her rowdy siblings succeeded in driving away several tutors. Thus, some readers did not understand how she might have acquired certain knowledge expressed in her poetry.

In this brief 10-line poem of rhyming couplets, Cavendish adopts a light tone. The apology would become a common convention for women, who spent 200 writing years making excuses for their activity. Thus, she calls to readers, "Condemn me not for making such a coil," where *coil* meant "trouble" or "turmoil," "About my book, alas it is my child." By adopting FIGURATIVE LANGUAGE comparing her words to offspring, she plays upon public sympathy; anyone could understand the motherly impulse to protect her children. She also manages to identify herself with women who enjoyed motherhood, something she did not. The fact that she remained childless while married to a once-widowed duke who had already fathered multiple children no doubt raised public suspicion about her femininity.

Cavendish then extends her metaphor of her writing as offspring by using imagery of a mother bird who must eventually urge her fledglings to fly from the nest, offering the woman-as-bird symbol that would become important to later feminist critics in their study of early women writers. As she identifies herself with a mother bird that pursues unceasing honest labor on behalf of her babies, she asks the public to approve of her own activity nurturing her creation. She also suggests that she achieves a personal freedom as her words, so intimately identified with her, achieve independence:

> Just like a bird, when her young are in nest,
> Goes in, and out, and hops, and takes no rest;
> But when their young are fledged, their heads
>   out peep,
> Lord what a chirping does the old one keep.

She humorously implies that just as baby birds create a disturbance that forces the mother to push them out and onto their own, her writing clamored for public reception, to be allowed a chance for exposure to readers. Because that exposure carried the threat of destruction while exposed to, in her case, critical elements, she must cry out a warning to her own words. She explains her position, writing,

So I, for fear, my strengthless child should fall
Against a door, or stool, aloud I call,
Bid have a care of such a dangerous place:
Thus write I much, to hinder all disgrace.

Although Cavendish remains unassuming with a teasing tone, her noting the reading world is a "dangerous place" reveals her real concern over public reaction to her words. The public had already made clear their attitude toward her as an eccentric in both dress and preoccupation with the intellectual life, which had remained theretofore a male arena. The danger for women who overstepped socially established boundaries separating females from males proved quite real. However, with her husband's devoted protection and support, Cavendish flourished as a writer, becoming astoundingly productive and outspoken on behalf of freedom for her sex, or at least those in her own social class.

"EYAM" ANNA HUNTER SEWARD (1788) ANNA HUNTER SEWARD wrote "Eyam" as she visited her birthplace, Eyam in Derbyshire, where her father had served as pastor. The poem sadly recalls the happier days of her childhood. At the time Seward visited Eyam, she had lost two siblings as infants, her younger sister and best friend as an adult, her adult foster sister, and her mother. Most important to the poem, her father had fought a long battle with mental illness, during which Seward acted as full-time caregiver; he would die two years after she wrote "Eyam." The form of the poem is seven eight-line stanzas, each with the RHYME pattern *ababccdd*.

After noting that she is allowed "one short week" for her visit, the poem's speaker remarks in the second line on the responsibility she bears for her father, writing that she leaves the "Source of my filial cares, the Full of Days." Although Seward probably intended the brief escape from nursing duties as a respite, it seems to have had more of a melancholy than an uplifting effect. Her strong use of descriptive detail may be seen as she describes the nearby Derwent River: "I trace the Derwent's amber wave, / Foaming through umbrag'd banks." Even the river suggests sad memories, as an

acquaintance distraught over financial difficulties had committed suicide by jumping into the river. She continues by describing the countryside as "The soft, romantic valleys, high o'er-peered, / By hills and rocks, in savage grandeur reared." Seward's use of past tense may indicate that she remains lost in memories, rather than immersed in the present. She mentions "Thy haunts, my native Eyam, long unseen" and remarks on the "lov'd inhabitants" that she imagines she sees "again." She notes their gaze is from "the eyes of Friendship," but that they inspire in her "pain'd sighs" and a "spontaneous flow" of tears. She recalls that she had viewed everything while "by a Father's side," now "pastor, to this human-flock no more," while "Distant he droops, and that once gladdening eye / Now languid gleams." The melancholy tone heightens as the speaker remarks on the change in the walk from one "once smooth, and vivid green" to one of "weedy gravel . . . / Rough, and unsightly," as she makes her way to the now "deserted rectory."

Knowing that she may never return, the speaker walks through the church and her "vital spirits freeze, / Passing the vacant pulpit" where the ashes of her infant sister "sleep." She describes the church beams "with paper garlands hung / In memory of some village youth, or maid," adding that the sight draws from her "the soft tear" as she recalls how often her "childhood mark'd that tribute paid." Here Seward reflects on the many deaths that were a part of the life of her youth. She adds a touching description of a pair of "gloves, suspended by the garland's side, / White as its snowy flowers." She concludes the penultimate verse by addressing her onetime home: "Dear village, long these wreaths funereal spread, / Simple memorials of thy early dead!" in which her own siblings would have been included.

Seward concludes her poem by returning to the "blank, and silent pulpit!" a metaphor for her own father, whose "precepts, just, and bland, / Didst win my ear, as reason's strength'ning glow." She describes his "eloquence" as "paternal, nervous, clear," and imagines him before her "sad, suffs'd, and trembling gaze" as a "Dim Apparition" that draws from her a "bitter" tear. The contrast of the dim apparition to her father's once-sharp expression is achieved with lucid imagery, and Seward emphasizes her deepening gloom with the adjective *bitter* to describe tears she earlier described as "soft."

Seward's autobiographical poem remains the one that critics most favor. It well illustrates her sentimen-tality, yet also exhibits a modicum of restraint, as if Seward sought to pay tribute to her father's "just, and bland" pronouncements through her own words. The speaker's voice remains abject, calm, and completely despondent.

F

"FAIREST, WHEN BY THE RULES" WIL-
LIAM BROWNE (n.d.) WILLIAM BROWNE gained his
reputation as a writer of pastoral poetry; *BRITANNIA'S PAS-
TORAL* is his best known work. As most 17th-century
poets did, he also wrote SONNETs, and "Fairest, When by
the Rules" is one that is occasionally published in modern poetry collections. He adopts the traditional RHYME
scheme for the Shakespearean, or English, sonnet,
ababcdcdefefgg, with the three quatrains establishing and
extending a theme through metaphor and the final couplet commenting upon it. The theme is that of prediction, as Browne adopts a metaphor of palmistry, one
means of fortune telling. The object of the prediction is
the speaker's happiness and how he might achieve it.

The speaker proposes the question as he addresses
his love in the first quatrain:

> Fairest, when by the rules of palmistry
> You took my hand to try if you could guess,
> By lines therein, if any wight there be
> Ordained to make me know some happiness.

Because his love reads his palm and he uses the term
ordained, the speaker seeks to connect the cause for
his contentment with fate or a religious decision made
for him by an unseen source. By doing so, the speaker
suggests that neither he nor the object of his affection
has the power to change that which has been ordained.
He continues, "I wished that those characters could
explain, / Whom I will never wrong with hope to win,"
making clear that he feels unworthy to reveal the name
of the person he desires, the *characters* referring to the
lines in his palm. He especially does not want "Fairest"
to know, as he coyly says, "Or that by them," meaning
the "characters," "a copy might be seen, / By you, O
love, what thoughts I had within." The speaker moves
from the examination of his hand to that of his mind.

Browne executes a clever double meaning concerning his hand and fortune in the next line, "But since the
hand of Nature did not set," and then again refers to
fate or providence, suggesting that nature did not want
his need clearly revealed, although he tries to minimize
the remark by making it a parenthetical one: "(As prov-
idently loth to have it known)." The next two lines
pursue the idea of future occurrences as a type of riddle, its solution hidden at first glance, as Browne writes,
"The means to find that hidden alphabet, / Mine eyes
shall be th' interpreters alone." Now the speaker has
told the "Fairest" that she looks to the wrong part of his
body to reveal his needs. She should look into his eyes,
which will interpret for her his emotions and communicate what will make him happy. He makes this quite
clear in the concluding couplet: "By them conceive my
thoughts, and tell me, fair, / If now you see her that
doth love me there?" He playfully suggests that she will
see her own physical reflection in his eye, while searching for his mental reflection, or thought.

Browne appropriately adopts a light approach in
developing this flirtatious scene as he makes use of the
sonnet in the manner in which it was intended.

FERGUSSON, ROBERT (1750–1774) Born in Cap-and-Feather Close, Edinburgh, Robert Fergusson was the second son of a clerk named William and his wife, Elizabeth. Respectable members of the lower middle class, Fergusson's parents could not have afforded to educate him. After he attended a private school in Edinburgh, he was able to enroll in the Grammar School of Dundee through a bursary, or scholarship, which also allowed him to attend four years at St. Andrews, 1764–68. Before leaving for school in 1764, Fergusson traveled with his mother to Roundlichnot, near Aberdeenshire, to visit his wealthy uncle, John Forbes, who would later prove a disappointment to his future. While at St. Andrews Fergusson studied with the brilliant poet and professor William Wilkie and proved a promising student, reading voraciously Latin, English, and Scots poetry. Despite undesirable accommodations and not much in the way of food, Fergusson thrived in the environment. He wrote two high-quality poems in the Scots language, including the satire "Elegy on the Death of Mr. David Gregory," but before he could develop a writing career, his father died in 1767. While Fergusson stayed on at school for a short time, he had to interrupt his education in 1768 in order to care for his family.

Fergusson's uncle, Forbes, invited the young man to live with him for a time, promising to find him work, but did little on his nephew's behalf. After six months passed with no prospects, Fergusson returned to Edinburgh, feeling desperate in regard to his future. He found a position copying legal documents for Charles Abercrombie, deputy clerk of the Comissary Office, Edinburgh. In the only position he would ever hold, Fergusson performed the most dull and tedious work imaginable. Probably in hopes of increasing his income, he returned to writing. When he attempted to write in the popular English mode in order to sell, he produced several poems unworthy of his talent. As did others tempted away from their native tradition, Fergusson failed in his efforts. Only when he returned to the Scots language did his talent become clear.

As Allan H. MacLaine, writer of the first book-length study on Fergusson, explained, Scotland's native poetic tradition was in peril in the mid-18th century. While the 15th and early 16th centuries had produced a

"golden age" of Scots poetry, three particular changes caused its near-demise. First, the Calvinist beliefs of John Knox became popular in Scotland, convincing its populace that poetry should be categorized, along with other entertainments, as a "lewd" pursuit. Second, the Scottish court, long a center of traditional arts, moved in 1603 from Edinburgh to London, removing its strong support. Third, the influence of English poetry caused native poets, such as WILLIAM DRUMMOND of Hawthornden, to adopt not only the English style, but the language. A renewed interest in the Scottish poetic heritage did not occur until an upsurge of nationalism early in the 18th century. That upsurge was ironically propelled by the insult of the parliamentary Union of 1707, which citizens viewed as a reduction of Scotland to little more than a British province. Led by their queen, Mary Scott, Scottish citizens resisted assimilation, resulting in an astounding resurgence of all cultural aspects, including writing; the Scottish Enlightenment was born. While various outstanding poets, including James Watson and Allan Ramsay, published in the century's first decades, no excellent poet worked during the four decades between 1730 and 1770. When Fergusson returned to his native style, the prospect of a new Scots writer appeared strong.

With publication of a few of his poems, Fergusson gained reputation. He contributed regularly by 1771 to *The Weekly Magazine, or Edinburgh Amusement.* While his first work was in the hackneyed English vein, probably influenced by the undeservedly praised William Shenstone, in 1772 Fergusson returned to the native language to produce the traditional and much lauded "The DAFT DAYS." That began a brilliant series of 31 Scots language poems. He became famous but received no offers of support and continued work at his copying job. In fall 1772 he was proclaimed in letters from delighted readers successor to Allan Ramsay. This led to election to the prestigious Cape Club of Edinburgh and the publication of *Poems,* a volume of his few works, in 1773.

A celebrity, Fergusson did not long enjoy his position. Overworked and strained by a tedious occupation and heavy social commitments, he became ill, collapsing in January 1774; the doctors diagnosed a nervous disorder. As he seemed in recovery, a fall down stone steps caused irreversible damage from a concussion that permanently injured his brain. Fergusson became violently insane, requiring institutionalization by his frantic mother. He moved into Edinburgh's house for the insane, nicknamed "the Schelles," or "Cells." Shortly after his 24th birthday, Fergusson died.

According to the scholar F. W. Freeman, by the early 19th century, the critic James Sibbald agreed with others in dismissing the Scots Vernacular Revival as provincial, the poetry too debased and common. But an understanding of Fergusson as a highly educated and traditional man, a practicing Tory, debunks the idea that colloquial writers were uneducated dolts. The debate over the value of a national language art had existed for some time, hearkening back to the ancient versus modern controversy of the 16th century. One group supported the idea that one's national language provides a unique way to express the "natural genius" of a nation and that poetry's language is that of the common man. Fergusson well exemplified that belief.

Robert Fergusson's memory and work were unnoticed for the next two centuries, except by the poet who would eclipse his importance, ROBERT BURNS. Burns greatly appreciated Fergusson's talent and sent a respectful letter to the Honorable Bailies of the Canongate, Edinburgh, in 1787. He wrote, in part, of his sorrow upon learning that "the remains of Robert Fergusson, the so justly celebrated Poet, a man whose talents, for ages to come, will do honor to our Caledonian name," lay unrecognized in their churchyard. Burns asked, and was granted, permission to mark Fergusson's grave with a stone. Burns recognized what it would take scholars decades to acknowledge, that Fergusson was an artist deserving of the dignity and respect of the poetry world.

BIBLIOGRAPHY

Freeman, F. W. *Robert Fergusson and the Scots Humanist Compromise.* Edinburgh: Edinburgh University Press, 1984.

Maclaine, Allan H. *Robert Fergusson.* New York: Twayne, 1965.

FIGURATIVE LANGUAGE (FIGURE OF SPEECH)

Figurative language, also called figure of speech, involves a nonliteral reference to both animate and inanimate objects. The purpose of such a figure is to suggest an imaginative relationship between things that are in reality different. Figurative language proves essential to the dense form of poetry, and its abundant usage helps distinguish poetry from prose. Figurative language always involves comparisons.

Many figures of speech exist, including the common *metaphor,* or direct comparison. An example is seen in JOHN CLEVELAND's "UPON THE DEATH OF MR. KING," when the speaker states that his eyes "weep down pious beads: but why should I / confine them to the Muses' rosary?" He adopts the term *beads* instead of *tears* in order to suggest a religious ritual, made clear in the next line, as he compares his weeping to the Catholic rite of praying the rosary. A second common figure of speech is the *simile,* or indirect comparison, in which the word *like* or *as* is used. An example appears in ANDREW MARVELL's "UPON APPLETON HOUSE," when Marvell writes, "But all things are composed here / Like Nature, orderly and near." In *irony,* the figure of speech means the opposite of what the poet intends. CHRISTOPHER SMART demonstrates IRONY in his "MY CAT JEOFFRY." In that poem he seems seriously to characterize his cat as a devotee of God, supplying many examples as to why he feels that characterization to be accurate:

> For I will consider my cat Jeoffry.
> For he is the servant of the Living God duly and
>   daily serving him
> For at the first glance of the glory of god in the
> East he worships in his way.
> For is this done by wreathing his body seven
>   times round with elegant quickness.

In the figurative language of *personification,* human characteristics are projected onto nonhuman things. A common approach in early poetry, its use diminished later. JOHN DONNE often employed personification, as in his poem, "THE SUN RISING," in which he begins with an *apostrophe,* yet another figure of speech, in an address to the sun:

> Busy old fool, unruly sun,
> Why dost thou thus
> Through windows, and through curtains call on
>   us?

Another example appears in ROBERT FERGUSSON's "THE DAFT DAYS," as he opens with the lines "Now mirk December's dowie face / Glowrs owr the rigs wi' sour grimace." *Hyperbole* represents exaggeration for effect, as in KATHERINE PHILIPS's poem "TO MY EXCELLENT LUCASIA, ON OUR FRIENDSHIP." In order to stress the unusually important nature of the relationship she shares with Lucasia, the speaker states, "for thou art all that I can prize, / My joy, my life, my rest." In the figure of speech known as *metonymy*, the name of that being described is substituted for a term closely related. An example may be found in the title of GEORGE HERBERT's "THE COLLAR," as well as in a line from that poem, "Shall I be still in suit?" Herbert uses parts of his official dress as a priest to represent the duties that religious station demands from him. RICHARD LOVELACE writes in "To Lucasta, going to the Wars,"

> True; a new mistress now I chase,
> The first foe in the field;
> And with a stronger faith embrace
> A sword, a horse, a shield.

All three items referenced in the fourth line of this stanza, "a sword, a horse, a shield," represent war, which in its turn represents allegiance to a certain country or political power fighting in the war. Finally, *synechdoche* is a type of metonymy, in which a part stands for a whole, a whole stands for a part, and a species may represent an entire genus. Synecdoche proved common in Renaissance SONNETS and in the work of the CAVALIER POETS, when parts of women's bodies, such as their hands, or part of their clothing, represented them. An example appears in EDMUND WALLER's "On a Girdle," where the girdle represents a woman the speaker has loved. Donne used his heart to represent his physical and spiritual life in "BATTER MY HEART." He employed synecdoche in the opposite way, allowing a large object, the earth, to represent a small object, him, in his "I AM A LITTLE WORLD MADE CUNNINGLY." He writes that "black sin hath betrayed to endless night / My worlds' both parts, and, O, both parts must die." Another example of using a part to represent a whole appears in "TO THE MEMORY OF MY BELOVED, THE AUTHOR, MR. WILLIAM SHAKESPEARE," by BEN JONSON. The speaker states in the first line, "To draw no envy, Shakespeare, on thy name," where *name* represents Shakespeare's poetry and dramas, above which appear his name as author. These are examples of the more common types of figurative language.

FINCH, ANNE, COUNTESS OF WINCHILSEA (1661–1720)

Anne Finch was born at Sydmonton near Newbury. Her father, Sir William Kingsmill, hailed from an established Hampshire family whose fortunes suffered a downturn during the Civil War. He showed great interest in educating not only his son, William, but also his daughters, Bridget and Anne. He instructed in his will that rent from his property be set aside to do so, leaving each daughter more than £1,000 in inheritance. After his death when Anne was five months old, her mother, Anne Haslewood, remarried, providing a stepfather, Sir Thomas Ogle, and new stepsister, Dorothy, to her three children. At age three Anne lost her mother, and when she was 10 years old, Sir Thomas died. An uncle named Sir William Haslewood raised William, while Anne and Bridget lived with their grandmother, Lady Kingsmill. When she died in 1672, the girls moved in with their uncle, who died 10 years later. Their extended family continued the siblings' education, and Anne matured versed in Greek and Roman mythology, history, poetry, and drama and acquainted with French and Italian.

As Anglicans, the Kingsmills supported the Stuarts. In 1682 Anne moved to London and served Mary of Modena, married to the duke of York, later King James II, as a maid of honour. She may have known the poet ANNE KILLIGREW, who also served Mary. While at court Anne began writing poetry in secret and later reflected fondly in writing on her mistress. She met her future husband, Captain Heneage Finch, at court, where he served the duke as gentleman of the bedchamber. They married in 1684 and lived happily pampered lives, Anne writing of their playfulness and intimacy. Almost 40 years later, her husband wrote in his journal of their marriage day as a blessed one. Both staunch Royalists, they lost that fine lifestyle when James fled the country. Captain Finch tried to follow his monarch and was arrested, but later released. He became a colonel, and the Finches left London in the late 1680s or early

1690s to settle at Eastwell Park, Kent. It was the seat for Heneage Finch's nephew, Charles, earl of Winchilsea. The earl served as a patron of the arts and encouraged Anne in her writing. Hineage also supported her, transcribing some of her poetry.

While Anne's marriage produced no children, the couple remained active, wintering in London and enjoying visits to the Continent. Her husband became an antiquarian of sorts, while Anne began to write seriously, extending an activity she had enjoyed for more than a decade. Feminist critics would later find of interest Finch's complaints in "The Introduction" of the male-dominated world of writing and the chauvinistic view of women writers as frivolous, presumptuous females who did not know how to keep their place in the domestic sphere. Her gloomy outlook on a future of writing prevented her publishing more than one collection, although she found her country surroundings inspiring, as reflected in her "A Nocturnal Reverie," published in her 1713 collection.

After her poetry had been read in circulation, Finch published 30 pages of four poems, including her famous "The SPLEEN," in *New Collection of Poems on Several Occasions* (1701). Identified in 18th-century tradition with the neoclassic name *Ardelia,* Finch received high praise from the actor Nicholas Rowe, who wrote that she would "redeem poetry" and save the empire. She became part of a wide literary circle that included her fellow female poets Elizabeth Rowe and Frances Seymour, countess of Herford and later duchess of Somerset; JONATHAN SWIFT, who addressed his 1709 "Apollo Outwitted" to Finch; and ALEXANDER POPE, who corresponded with her regarding his RAPE OF THE LOCK. She eventually returned to court to serve Queen Anne as lady of the bedchamber, and her husband in 1712 assumed his nephew's title as earl of Winchilsea but did not sit in Parliament.

Finch continued writing, adopting the mode of JOHN MILTON in "Fanscomb Barn" (1713), a satire that alludes to PARADISE LOST. Her work appeared within that of others, including Delarivière Manley's "Secret Memoirs . . . from the New Atalantis," a roman à clef and a predecessor to the newly developing novel genre. She published anonymously her own 1713 collection titled *Miscellany Poems on Several Occasions,* which included an original drama. Its reissue later in the year identified her by name. A protracted illness two years later may have prompted her to turn to religious verse. In 1717 her poetry was among that introducing Pope's *Works,* and he also included her verse in his *Poems on Several Occasions.* Although Pope obviously felt positively toward Finch, her caricature as a mad writer in his 1717 *Three Hours after Marriage,* a farce cowritten with JOHN GAY and John Arbuthnot, confirmed some of her fears regarding the acceptance of her poetry. Finch refused, however, to be silenced. She declared on more than one occasion that those occupations her society approved for women remained on the whole foolish and highly dissatisfying to any intelligent woman. This theme may be found in her poem about depression and melancholy "The Spleen." She left many poems to be published posthumously in various collections, including *Poems by Eminent Ladies* (1755); however, her style lost favor in later generations. Still, William Wordsworth greatly admired her work, including 17 of her poems in an 1819 collection of 50 that he presented to Lady Mary Lowther.

The noted feminist critic Myra Reynolds reintroduced Finch to academe in an edition of her works titled *Poems* (1903). A manuscript by Finch stored at Wellesley College, Massachusetts, was edited in the 1980s and again a decade later, and several valuable additions to work on Finch were added in the late 20th century. While a comprehensive scholarly collection of, and commentary on, her works has not yet been undertaken, her poetry remains available in both print and electronic form. In the University of Pennsylvania's online digital library, *A Celebration of Women Writers,* edited by Mary Mark Ockerbloom, readers may find a complete transcription of Finch's poetry that appeared in the 1713 *Miscellany Poems on Several Occasions.* Favorites often made available by various sources, in addition to excerpts from "The Spleen," include "ADAM POSED," "The ANSWER," "The APOLOGY," "CIRCUIT OF APOLLO," "FRIENDSHIP BETWEEN EPHELIA AND ARDELIA," and "TO THE NIGHTINGALE."

BIBLIOGRAPHY

Hinnant, Charles. H. "Feminism and Femininity: A Reconsideration of Anne Finch's 'Ardelia's Answer to Ephelia.'" *The Eighteenth Century* 33 (1992): 119–132.

———. *The Poetry of Anne Finch: An Essay in Interpretation.* Newark: University of Delaware Press, 1994.

———. "Song and Speech in Anne Finch's 'To the Nightingale.'" *Studies in English Literature, 1500–1900* 31 (1991): 499–513.

Mallinson, Jean. "Anne Finch: A Woman Poet and the Tradition." In *Gender at Work: Four Women Writers of the Eighteenth Century,* edited by Ann Messenger. Detroit: Wayne State University Press, 1990.

McGovern, Barbara. *Anne Finch and Her Poetry: A Critical Biography.* Athens: University of Georgia Press, 1992.

———, and Charles Hinnant, eds. *The Anne Finch Wellesley Manuscript Poems.* Athens: University of Georgia Press, 1998.

Mermin, Dorothy. "Women Becoming Poets: Katherine Philips, Aphra Behn, Anne Finch." *English Literary History* 57, no. 2 (summer 1990): 335.

Messenger, Ann. "Heroics and Mock Heroics: John Milton, Alexander Pope, and Anna Laetitia Barbauld." In *His and Hers: Essays in Restoration and Eighteenth-Century Literature,* 172–196. Lexington: University Press of Kentucky, 1986.

Ockerbloom, Mary Mark, ed. "Anne Finch." *A Celebration of Women Writers.* The University of Pennsylvania. Available online. URL: http://www.digital.library.upenn.edu/women/finch/finch-anne.html#. Downloaded on June 25, 2005.

Reynolds, Myra, ed. *The Poems of Anne, Countess of Winchilsea.* Chicago: University of Chicago Press, 1903.

Rogers, Katharine M. "Anne Finch, Countess of Winchilsea: An Augustan Woman Poet." In *Shakespeare's Sisters,* edited by Sandra M. Gilbert and Susan Gubar, 32–46. Bloomington: Indiana University Press, 1979.

———. *Before Their Time: Six Women Writers of the Eighteenth Century.* New York: Frederick Ungar, 1979.

———. "Finch's 'Candid Account' vs. Eighteenth-Century Theories of the Spleen." *Mosaic* 22 (winter 1989): 17–27.

———. *Selected Poems of Anne Finch.* New York: Frederick Ungar, 1979.

"FLAMING HEART UPON THE BOOK AND PICTURE OF THE SERAPHICAL SAINT TERESA, THE" RICHARD CRASHAW (1652)

RICHARD CRASHAW became enthralled as many High Church enthusiasts did with the mythology surrounding Teresa of Avila. A 16th-century Spanish Catholic convert of Jewish heritage, she founded the ascetic order of Carmelite nuns and became a focus for members of the Inquisition, in part because of her Jewish blood and in part her mystic experiences. One of those experiences included a vision in which she was stabbed in the heart by an angel as she related in her popular autobiography. A famous statue sculpted by the Italian sculptor and architect Gian Lorenzo Bernini became one of the most famous of the baroque, or ornate, school. Although not unveiled until after Crashaw's death, the statue existed while he lived in Rome, and it may have inspired his poem.

Crashaw imagines a painting featuring the details Teresa supplied, repeated in his title. A parenthetical subtitle adds, "As she is Usually Expressed with a Seraphim biside [sic] her." Famous for his gauche metaphor-burdened and often hyperbolic poems, Crashaw could not have found any better material to shape into his own poetic vision of passionate faith. The eroticism suggested in Teresa's description of her experience appealed to Crashaw, a proponent of passionate spirituality. As did many of those faithful to the church, he hoped one day to experience the rapturous union with the divine that Teresa had. Although raised by a Puritan minister who would have found the fleshly representation repugnant, Crashaw found the description of Teresa's wounding intriguing.

Crashaw begins his poem by playfully suggesting that the artist responsible for a picture of Teresa reversed the situation, inserting the dart in the angel's hand. He proposes that Teresa had complete control and plunged the dart deep into her own heart. He never makes clear the purpose of the reversal, other than in the statement the speaker makes directly to the young angel in lines 47–48: "Give her the dart, for it is she / (Fair youth) shoots both thy shaft and thee." In order to construct RHYME, Crashaw refers to the single angel as a Seraphim, ignoring the fact that *Seraphim* is a plural reference.

The speaker begins with ALLITERATION as he bids readers to "catch the precious name this piece pretends." He cautions against those who gaze on the picture admiring the young angel, "That fair-cheeked fallacy of fire." He calls upon his audience to look instead at Teresa and then confronts the artist, explaining that his characterization is incorrect: "Painter, what didst thou understand, / To put her dart into his hand!"

Instead, he says of Teresa, "This is the mistress-flame; and duteous he, / her happy fire-works here comes down to see." He continues a few lines later chiding the artist,

> One would suspect thou meant'st to paint
> Some weak, inferior, woman saint.
> But had thy pal-faced purple took
> Fire from the burning cheeks of that bright book,
> Thou wouldst on her have heaped up all
> That could be found seraphical.

He continues in this vein for many lines, ordering the painter:

> Do then as equal right requires,
> Since his the blushes be, and hers the fires,
> Resume and rectify thy rude design
> Undress they seraphim into mine.
> Redeem this injury of thy art,
> Give him the veil, giver her the dart.

Crashaw does not leave this game until line 58, when the speaker states, "For all the gallantry of him, / Give me the suffering Seraphim," making clear he prefers to view Teresa as an angel. The seraphim may keep his "glowing cheeks, the glistering wings, / The rosy hand, the radiant dart," but "Leave her alone the Flaming Heart." Crashaw begins an ecstatic declaration:

> Leave her that, and thou shalt leave her
> Not one loose shaft, but love's whole quiver.
> For in love's field was never found
> A nobler weapon than a wound.

His words seem to allude to the Roman God of love, Cupid, famous for wounding lovers by shooting an arrow through their hearts.

The speaker crescendos into his own rapture as he proposes a dual PARADOX, "Love's passives are his activ'st part, / The wounded is the wounding heart," then declares,

> O heart! The equal poise of love's both parts,
> Big alike with wounds and darts,

> Live in these conquering leaves, live all the
> same;
> And walk through all tongues one triumphant
> flame.

Crashaw's mention of the leaves of Teresa's book emphasizes the importance of written celebration, a reference to his own occupation.

The momentum of Crashaw's praise grows as lines 79–80 read, "Live here, great heart; and love and die and kill, / And bleed and wound; and yield and conquer still." Although Teresa's heart has been pierced, an injury that should lead to death, instead it leads to the ultimate victory of eternal life through her union with the divine. The speaker next claims Teresa's heart as his own and asks that she

> . . . at once break in
> And take away from me myself and sin!
> This gracious robbery shall thy bounty be,
> And my best fortunes such fair spoils of me.

He continues suggesting that only through death in the name of a deity will he truly live. He uses repetition in lines 94–97 to advance toward his conclusion:

> By all thy dower of lights and fires;
> By all the eagle in thee, all the dove;
> By all thy lives and deaths of love;
> By thy large draughts of intellectual day,
> And by thy thirsts of love more large than
> they . . .

He returns to the "By all" and "By thy" usage in lines 99–101. The eagle and dove were traditional symbols, the eagle representing wisdom and the dove mercy.

Crashaw introduces references to God for the first time in his final seven lines, noting that Teresa seals God's soul, adding, "By all the heavens though hast in Him, / Fair sister of the seraphim, / By all of Him we have in thee," at last stating that she and the Lord have joined as one. He concludes by pleading that he be allowed such a divine rapture, writing, "Leave nothing of myself in me! / Let me so read they life that I / Unto all life of mine may die!" Crashaw incorporates the hyperbole characteristic of the works of METAPHYSICAL POETS AND POETRY.

Richard Crashaw never hesitated to express his spirituality in as rich a manner as possible, with descriptors tumbling over descriptors and metaphors tripping over metaphors. The result is too much of all facets for some readers, who prefer subtlety and grace to Crashaw's enthusiasm. However, even those critical of Crashaw's bombast acknowledge his dedication to both sense and sensibility.

"FLEA, THE" JOHN DONNE (1630)   Most critics agree that JOHN DONNE wrote "The Flea" during his youth, before becoming an ordained minister. It was first published as part of "Songs and Sonnets" in a posthumous collection that appeared in 1630, 1635, 1650, and 1669. As does his other romantic poetry, it contains a tone marked with IRONY and playfulness. He adopts the popular convention of using the flea as an object of humor, due to the fact that such a tiny creature could inflict such misery on a human being. The flea became a subject not only of literature, but also of art, as seen in the 1630 painting *Woman Catching Fleas* by Georges de la Tour. In "The Flea" the speaker notes the insect's activity of blood sucking as symbolic of sex between romantic partners. He creates a parody of the approach used by CAVALIER POETS, who through flawed logic attempted to convince virgins to engage in sex. Donne presents a circular argument that focuses on the flea's activity as an excuse for conjugal relations. He uses a closed form in three stanzas, each with a RHYME pattern of *aabbccddd*.

The poem begins with a plea for attention to the speaker's love, assumed to be a male voice speaking to a female: "Mark but this flea, and mark in this, / how little that which thou deny'st me is." Donne uses repetition of *mark* for emphasis, insisting that his audience note his main point. When he uses the term *little* in describing the act of sex that his love denies him, he does not intend to diminish the importance of that act. Rather, he attempts to convince her that engaging in sex would not be the enormous sin that she perceives it to be. He uses the flea's diminutive size to help make his point.

Donne supports his argument by noting that the flea has sucked blood from both of their bodies, allowing it to commingle with his own, inside his body. Because the lovers' juices have already mixed, the speaker suggests, they have theoretically already engaged in sexual union: "Me it suck'd first, and now sucks thee, / And in this flea our two bloods mingled be." That act caused no shame he argues, saying, "Confess it, this cannot be said / A sin, or shame, or loss of maidenhead." Donne purposely indents the final three rhyming lines, or triplet, of each of his three stanzas, making clear the importance of his summary of the points made in each. His stance is that of a barrister arguing a case, each stanza concluding with summation. In the first stanza, the speaker points out in the conclusion that the flea has already enjoyed the lovers' fluids, "And pamper'd swells with one blood made of two," adding that it is a shame that the lovers will not do the same: "And this, alas, is more than wee would doe."

The second stanza begins with a second plea, this to save the life of the flea. The speaker projects concern that the woman has moved to kill the pest, which she sees as no more than vermin. As some critics note, the three stanzas offer readers a miniature drama, as between each stanza, the speaker engages the silent partner. Feminist critics mark with interest the silence of the female, who nevertheless assumes power over the speaker through her ability to act.

The speaker beseeches, "Oh, stay, three lives in one flea spare, / When we almost, nay more than married are." When he bids her "stay," or stop, he tries to convince her that the flea must be spared because it represents their union or marriage. Donne adopts marriage as a CONCEIT, represented in an unusual manner through the actions of a mere flea. Because marriage was a holy sacrament, Donne flouts the need for religious approval before sex between willing partners may occur. He adopts elevated terminology, such as the biblical reference to the human body as a temple, to advance his ironic and playful tone, equating the "marriage bed" with a "marriage temple." The man tells the woman that, while she and her parents may "grudge" the fact, the young lovers have become a married pair, via the flea.

In the concluding three lines of stanza 2, the speaker equates killing the flea to a double murder and suicide, with suicide a mortal sin. He suggests that act would then constitute a greater sacrilege than their having sex:

> Though use make thee apt to kill me,
> Let not to this, self murder added be,
> And sacrilege, three sins in killing three.

The first couplet in stanza 3 makes clear the speaker's argument has failed, as the murder he had feared has occurred. Donne includes imagery of the flea's blood, enriched to a purple color by the human blood his body contains: "Cruell and sodaine, has though since / Purpled thy naile, in blood of innocence?" The speaker melodramatically labels his lover's act both cruel and violent, the meaning of the word *sodaine*. The speaker continues to maintain the flea's innocence, again suggesting that the mingling of the lovers' fluids should not be censured. The fact that the offender could be dispatched by a mere fingernail maintains the emphasis on the tiny, but complete, world that Donne has attempted to create in his representation of the flea. He wrote in the tradition of "man as microcosm," extending that idea to the tiny flea. The speaker must admit that his love has won, "thou triumph'st," in making clear that neither she nor the speaker remains weakened by the blood loss, symbolic for his own loss of the argument. However, in a final desperate attempt to convince his love, the speaker cleverly turns even the flea's death to his favor, suddenly acknowledging that the loss has minimal results, as would his love's loss of her virginity:

> 'Tis true, then learne how false, feares bee;
> Just so much honor, when thou yeeld'st to me,
> Will wast, as this flea's death tooke life from
>   thee.

What she will lose in honor equates to what the world has lost in the death of one flea. This popular poem may be found in both print and electronic forms.

BIBLIOGRAPHY

Baumlin, James S. *John Donne and the Rhetorics of Renaissance Discourse.* Columbia: University of Missouri Press, 1991.

Chambers, E. K., ed. *Poems of John Donne.* Vol. 1. London: Lawrence & Bullen, 1896.

FLETCHER, GILES (?1585–1623)

Giles Fletcher was born to the diplomat and poet Giles Fletcher, Sr., and educated at Westminster School. Cousin to the well-known dramatist John Fletcher, Fletcher went on to Trinity College, Cambridge, and became a formal reader of Greek grammar (1615) and Greek language (1618). A highly religious individual, he later received appointment as rector of Alderton in Suffolk and wrote religious poetry. Fletcher's most famous and widely anthologized poem is "CHRIST'S VICTORY IN HEAVEN," published in 1610 as the first canto of four. Some historians of his era suggested his death was in part due to depression over a lack of appreciation of his efforts in work with his parishioners. His final work was "The Reward of the Faithful" (1623). His brother Phineas also wrote poetry in the Spenserian vein, and the work of both was admired by JOHN MILTON. Giles Fletcher's influence on Milton may be seen in a comparison of Fletcher's lines describing Satan, "To be in heaven, the second he disdains / So now the first in hell and flames he reigns," with Milton's line from PARADISE LOST spoken by Satan, "Better to reign in hell, than serve in heaven."

In Fletcher's day the best known nondramatic poets previous to Milton were Chaucer and Edmund Spenser, the latter the author of the allegorical *The Fairie Queene* (1590, 1596). Fletcher became a member of the Spenserian school, which focused on serious poetry that had a didactic purpose. This focus often resulted in stilted moralizing and a lack of art. However, Fletcher did not produce such dull and predictable poetry, because of his authentic enthusiasm for verse and his genuine religious ardor. Fletcher selected religious themes that complemented his natural eloquence, enjoying most a vivid contemplation of Christ's career. The cantos following "Christ's Victory in Heaven," in which mercy and justice argue in heaven, include "Christ's Victory on Earth," an allegory depicting Christ's temptation by Satan; "Christ's Triumph over Death," which follows the Passion; and "Christ's Triumph after Death," focusing on Christ's resurrection and eventual ascent to heaven.

As many critics suggest, poets who engage in religious writing assume a difficult burden. They do not enjoy the liberty in relation to their topic that nonreligious poets do. The profound mysteries religious poets attempt to define often lead to more questions than answers, and their tone must remain one of reverence in deference to the strong regard in which they hold their subject. In addition, they may become overly emotional, using overblown language and hyperbole in an attempt to write in the high style demanded by their topic. The language can escape control as they fail to resist the tone of adoration demanded by their faith. Religious poets must translate their passion into one that readers can understand, even if they do not share that devotion. Fletcher died at age 38, having in his short life contributed superior verse to the religious writing tradition.

BIBLIOGRAPHY

Survey of British Poetry: Cavalier to Restoration. Vol. 2. Edited by Editorial Board, Roth Publishing. Great Neck, N.Y.: Poetry Anthology Press, 1989.

Ward, Thomas Humphry. *The English Poets: Selections with Critical Introductions by Various Writers and a General Introduction by Matthew Arnold.* Vol. 2. New York: Macmillan, 1912.

"FLOWER, THE" GEORGE HERBERT (1633)

GEORGE HERBERT used the FIGURATIVE LANGUAGE of extended metaphor when he wrote "The Flower," in which a flower represents the spiritual effect of God's grace. Herbert declared early on that he intended to use approaches traditional to writing about erotic love in his writing of religious love. The flower had long symbolized women in sexual terms and appeared often in work by the CAVALIER POETS, as well as other LYRIC poetry. Herbert used that same symbol throughout his collection, *The Temple,* to represent instead spiritual or, occasionally, professional growth and development.

A member of a literary coterie that included his extended family, Herbert wrote at times in reaction to the poetry of others in his group, one example of which is "JORDAN" written as an "answer poem" to Sir Philip Sidney. Sidney's sister, MARY SIDNEY HERBERT (COUNTESS OF PEMBROKE), served as a patron to poets, as did her son, William. Critics feel that LADY MARY WROTH,

niece to the countess, may have influenced "The Flower" with her poems "Forbear Dark Night" and "The Spring Now Come at Last." Still, the work most reflects Herbert's oft-expressed belief that man cannot earn God's grace.

Herbert structures his poem in seven seven-line stanzas with a RHYME scheme of *ababccb* with varied METER and line length. His opening stanza compares the effect of the Lord's "sweet and clean" return to that of the annual return of the flower, which upon its arrival in spring causes grief to melt "Like snow in May, / As if there were no such cold thing." With *return,* Herbert references the act of God's reentering a human life after an absence of spirituality. The speaker reveals in the second stanza that his "shriveled heart" had for a time suffered separation from God, comparing his heart to the flowers that go "Quite underground" for a time,

> To see their mother-root, when they have blown;
> Where they together
> All the hard weather,
> Dead to the world, keep house unknown.

But with the return of God, his shriveled heart, as the flower in spring, recovers its "greenness."

The third stanza notes example of the Lord's "wonders," including "Killing and quik'ning, bringing down to hell / And up to heaven in an hour," where *quik'ning* refers to giving life. Herbert perhaps references the belief by some groups that Christ descended into hell after his crucifixion before ascending to heaven. His point is that God remains changeable and powerful enough to reverse the course of natural processes, such as death. In the fifth stanza Herbert uses a theme he had employed many times, that of man's foolishness in believing he can make himself worthy of God. The speaker says,

> But while I grow in a straight line,
> Still upwards bent, as if heavn'n were mine own,
> Thy anger comes, and I decline . . .

God's force is such that a killing frost cannot compare; even a "pole," meaning a location frozen by ice, becomes a place "Where all things burn . . ." if God wills it so.

However, in the sixth stanza, the speaker adds that "in age I bud again, / After so many deaths I live and write," once more enjoying the scents of "dew and rain." Herbert's reference to writing emphasizes a rebirth of creativity and acts as an autobiographical reference. The speaker can hardly believe he is the same individual "On whom thy tempests fell all night."

The final stanza expresses Herbert's awe over God's wonders, one of which is "To make us see we are but flowers that glide," and to understand that God "hast a garden for us." However, that garden exists only for those "Who would be more." Individuals who felt the false self-confidence that the speaker had previously known "Forfeit their Paradise by their pride."

While Herbert seemed to share beliefs from both Arminianism and Calvinism, he leaned more heavily toward the idea of Calvinistic predestination. That man could earn grace, through good works, for instance, he adamantly denied.

BIBLIOGRAPHY
Pritchard, R. E. "George Herbert and Lady Mary Wroth: A Root for 'The Flower'"? *Review of English Studies*. n.s. 47, no. 187 (1996): 386–389.

FORD, JOHN (ca. 1586–ca. 1640)

While not much is known about the childhood and youth of John Ford, he was born in Devon and probably attended Oxford's Middle Temple. Best known as a playwright, he had first published prose and poetry, but little of note. His first play, *The Witch of Edmonton* (1621), was probably a joint effort with Thomas Dekker and Samuel Rowley. He collaborated again with Dekker on *The Welsh Ambassador* (1623) and *The Sun's Darling* (1624), the latter a masque. He favored extreme cynicism, and his characters were notable for their suffering.

Ford's first independent attempt, *The Lover's Melancholy,* appeared in print in 1628. Its subject matter revealed his fascination with the human propensity for sorrow. He famously stated that he wrote for private satisfaction and felt no need to satisfy audiences or focus on the ordinary virtues and idealistic themes of his fellow poets and playwrights. His two comedies, *The Fancies, Chaste and Noble* (ca. 1636) and *The Lady's*

Trial (1638), were unremarkable, having little effect on audiences. However, his tragedies proved more successful, especially *The Broken Heart* (ca. 1629) and *'Tis Pity She's a Whore* (ca. 1631). His chronicle play *Perkin Warbeck* (1634) also had more lasting value, and all three of those works continue to be read into the 21st century.

The Broken Heart contains the song, "CALANTHA'S DIRGE" and "PENTHEA'S DYING SONG," revealing Ford's background in poetry. Both reflect his trademark morbid attitude toward life and love, projecting the idea that love only adds to life's suffering and often leads to both a metaphorical and a literal death, because it so often produces only disappointment. His character's suffering was not due to fate, but rather to a flaw in their basic natures. Heroism for Ford was resistance, and his characters' refusal to comply with society's demands proved both their folly and their heroism.

BIBLIOGRAPHY
Anderson, Donald K., Jr. *John Ford.* New York: Twayne, 1972.
Huebert, Ronald. *John Ford: Baroque English Dramatist.* Montreal: McGill-Queen's University Press, 1977.

"FOR THE BAPTIST" WILLIAM DRUMMOND (1616)

WILLIAM DRUMMOND gained a reputation for poetry that focused on death and surrender, often associated with love or religion. He adopts the biblical tale of John the Baptist as his subject in "For the Baptist." A spiritual radical who lived in the wilds of the desert, John achieved fame for recognizing and baptizing Christ as the Son of God, thus earning his title of Baptist. His story later turned gruesome when the dancer Salome requested his head on a platter as reward for dancing at Herod's palace.

Drummond employs the PETRARCHAN SONNET form to sketch John's early life, labeling him "The last and greatest herald of heaven's King" in the opening line. He describes John as "Girt with rough skins," living apart from civilization as he "hies to the deserts wild." There he will live "Among that savage brood" that the woods breed, a brood John finds "more harmless . . . and mild" than mankind. Drummond suggests that previous to the existence of the grace Christ gives to humans, they proved more base than forest creatures.

John's life, supported by "honey that from virgin hives distill'd," leaves him with "Parch'd body, hollow eyes," as "some uncouth thing." Thus, he is perceived as alien, "long since from earth exil'd." Drummond's skillful retelling of the biblical story prepares readers for John's harsh end, lessening its terror by suggesting the prophet had never belonged on earth anyway.

When John at last speaks, he bursts forth, "All ye, whose hopes rely / On God, with me amidst these deserts mourn," allowing Drummond to suggest that man has suffered a loss through his separation from God after the temptation in the Garden of Eden. He uses repetition for emphasis as he builds momentum through John's persistent cry, "Repent, repent, and from old errors turn," then also emphasizes man's lack of response as the next line rhetorically asks, "Who listen'd to his voice, obey'd his cry?" The answer, of course, is no one, calling to mind the biblical allusion to a voice crying in the wilderness. The closing couplet puts that reply into words: "Only the echoes, which he made relent, / rung from their marble caves, 'Repent, repent!'" Drummond employs IRONY, as John's command is not received by man and repeated only by nature, emphasizing again John's isolation and distance from humankind.

FORM AND FORMAT

Form refers to the physical aspects of a poem, its shape and pattern. In *stanzaic form,* a poem may be divided into repeated units called *stanzas,* or *verses.* Generally, stanzas share the same METER and RHYME scheme and may contain the same number of *lines.* Lines may appear in various groupings and are labeled for those groups. For example, a *couplet* indicates two lines that rhyme with one another, while a *tercet* is a three-line grouping, and the common *quatrain* contains four lines. *Continuous form* indicates that all lines follow one another without any formal grouping. *Fixed form* refers to a poem with a pattern prescribed by tradition that never varies. Examples include the SONNET, with a constant 14-line format, adopted by JOHN DONNE and many other Renaissance poets, and the far more complicated *villanelle.* The villanelle's form contains 19 lines, consisting of five tercets rhymed *aba* and a concluding quatrain rhymed *abaa.* Its first and third lines of the first tercet serve as refrains, alternating through line 15 and then repeated as lines 18 and 19. A famous example is Dylan Thomas's "Do Not Go Gentle." In *free verse,* a poem remains nonmetrical, its basic rhythm unit is simply the line, and any formal pattern develops as a result of the demands of the individual work, not tradition or prescription.

Fixed forms are more closely associated with centuries prior to the 20th century. The 20th and 21st centuries produced more free verse than previous eras. Some forms proved more suitable to certain subject matter, such as the sonnet, which was used often in the Renaissance, generally to suggest erotic themes. Donne adopted it to religious themes, as did JOHN MILTON, but it would fade from the scene until 19th-century romantic poets revived it. The METAPHYSICAL POETS AND POETRY of the Renaissance favored intricate stanzaic form, but the style lost favor as the couplet gained it through use by poets including BEN JONSON and EDMUND WALLER. Because the couplet proved an excellent METER to combine the stinging effect of the simple epigram with strong momentum, it was ideal for discursive argument in poetry, causing during the RESTORATION period the decline of the more elegant LYRIC approach. Couplets continued in favor throughout the 18th century, proving particularly useful to satirists including ALEXANDER POPE and JONATHAN SWIFT.

"FRIENDSHIP BETWEEN EPHELIA AND ARDELIA" ANNE FINCH, COUNTESS OF WINCHILSEA (1713)

Feminist and queer theory critics find ANNE FINCH of interest not only for her consideration of the limitations placed on women who wanted to publish their writing, but also for her vision of female community. According to the critic Carol Barash, representative of new historical critics, Finch was marginalized as a result of her perceived ideal relationship, that between women, which the Augustan canon did not accept. Even later so-called admirers, including the poet William Wordsworth, did not consider the political and religious themes that support Finch's poetry because of the authoritative voice in which she wrote. While she echoed ideas made common in the poetry of the esteemed KATHERINE PHILIPS, her more forceful attitude toward same-sex love and friendship some readers found troubling. Her poem "Friendship between Ephelia and Ardelia" appeared in her 1713 collection titled *Miscellany Poems on Several Occasions*. Barash believes that collection represents Finch's attempt to create a feminine heroic. Written as dramatic dialogue between two women's voices, the 20-line poem contains rhyming couplets with a METER of iambic tetrameter.

Ephelia challenges, "What friendship is, Ardelia, show." Finch seems to ask for not only a new definition of the term, but also a demonstration, indicating the relationship she refers to is an active one. Ardelia decides to define friendship in personal terms, replying, "'Tis to love, as I love you." Friendship advances to love, a term emphasized by its repetition. However appreciative Ephelia may be, referring to Ardelia's response as "kind," she notes, "This account . . . Suits not my inquiring mind." She instructs Ardelia to go "farther," asking her to "now repeat: / What is friendship when complete?" Finch uses the term *complete* in the sense of "perfect."

Ardelia finds herself up to Ephelia's challenge. She does not hesitate, but instead elaborates on her earlier version, again emphasizing the active aspects of their relationship. Not only does friendship mean "to share all joy and grief," it is also "to lend all due relief / From the tongue, the heart, the hand." Finch adopts the FIGURATIVE LANGUAGE known as synecdoche in her series of three body parts to reference whole bodies, or individuals. By *tongue* Finch may refer to women or men who gossip, slander, or use verbal abuse, where the *heart* refers to subjects of romance. However, when she refers to the *hand* she suggests something more serious. If one requires relief from a hand, she may have been struck, ostensibly by a husband or other male. Ardelia believes a community of women can provide relief for one another, the basis of the temperance movement in its beginnings a century later. Women joined to demand laws to banish alcohol, as it led to so many instances of abuse by men of wives and children.

Ardelia then becomes more emphatic, noting that sacrifice is immediate and complete between true friends. One should "mortgage house and land; / For a friend to be sold a slave." Finch adopts a metaphor of commodity in referencing the barter of humans, one

feminists would note as an allusion to the objectification of women, many of whom became slaves to their husbands. Men on occasion literally purchased wives through the promise of property to their families. Finally, even the ultimate sacrifice is not too much, as Ardelia declares, "'Tis to die upon a grave, / If a friend therein do lie."

While Ephelia obviously appreciates her friend's gesture, she notes that Ardelia's "high" words have all been spoken before, even if they describe ideals seldom acted upon, as "more than e'er was done / Underneath the rolling sun." She asks Ardelia one more time whether she can "say no more." Ardelia takes the poem back to the point where it began, by gently repeating herself to Ephelia. She concludes the stanza, "Words indeed no more can show: / But 'tis to love, as I love you." Finch brings balance to the poem, not only by returning full circle to her original idea, but through repetition of her second line in her final line.

Finch's focus on friendship makes the point that at times we attempt to complicate simple straightforward matters. The strength of feminine friendship should not be underestimated; its passion equals that of love. That simple yet poignant reply should satisfy even an "inquiring mind" like that of Ephelia. She had asked Ardelia to "show" her the meaning of friendship, not realizing that through their existing relationship, her friend had already done just that.

BIBLIOGRAPHY
Barash, Carol. "The Political Origins of Anne Finch's Poetry." *The Huntington Library Quarterly* 54, no. 4 (autumn 1991): 327–351.

"FRIENDSHIP'S MYSTERIES, TO MY DEAREST LUCASIA" KATHERINE PHILIPS (1655)

The first English woman to write same-sex love poetry, KATHERINE PHILIPS employed this approach to celebrate her closest friendships, particularly with Anne Owen, the Lucasia of many of her poems. "Friendship's Mysteries, to My Dearest Lucasia" would be set to music by the esteemed musician Henry Lawes, who also worked with the verse of JOHN MILTON. Philips took friendship so seriously that she explored the topic with the noted religious leader Jeremy Taylor, and her poetry reflects the attitude that true friendship remains a spiritual matter. Philips's liberal use of metaphysical CONCEITS aligns her with JOHN DONNE and others who incorporated hyperbole to express their romantic passion, shaping it to support her declaration of the passion of friendship. This poem takes the form of six five-line stanzas, each with a RHYME scheme of *ababb*.

The first stanza classifies the speaker's love shared with Lucasia as a practice of faith, as the speaker tells Lucasia that, since the faith of men is moved by miracles, they should prove "To the dull, angry world" that "There's a religion in our love." Having established their spiritual relationship, the speaker asks Lucasia to agree in the second stanza "That fate no liberty destroys," so their "election is as free / As Angels" who may determine their own joys. Philips makes clear that this relationship is not forced, but the product of free choice. She introduces the first of several metaphysical conceits in stanza 3, writing in the first line, "Our hearts are doubled by their loss" to continue emphasis on the benefits of their relationship. They do not each lose a heart; rather, they each gain one in addition to their own. The mix causes growth even as the hearts appear to be spread thin, as "We both diffuse, and both engross." Philips also emphasizes the intellectual aspect of their relationship and extends the metaphysical nature of her poem as her speaker adds, "And we,

whose minds are so much one, / Never, yet ever, are alone." Stanza four turns on the idea of the captive heart as a positive:

> We court our own captivity,
> Then thrones more great and innocent:
> 'Twere banishment to be set free,
> Since we wear fetters whose intent
> Not bondage is, but ornament.

Philips adds PARADOX by stating that banishment is equivalent to freedom and release, not a disgraceful dismissal.

The fifth stanza continues praising the strength gained through shared love, as "griefs united easier grow." The two friends are "Both princes, and both subjects too," as Philips again offers a paradox. The friends enjoy the wealth of royal people yet remain subject to one another. It is in their subjection that they gain a privileged life. The final stanza emphasizes in a parenthetical remark that through the power of friendship, the two hearts become "altars, priests, and offerings." This means that "each heart which thus kindly dies, / Grows deathless by the sacrifice." The act of friendship becomes akin to a religious act, conquering death as does submission to God.

G

"GARDEN, THE" ANDREW MARVELL (1681)
"The Garden" remains a favorite among critics of poetry
by ANDREW MARVELL. Although he most probably wrote
it during retirement between 1650 and 1652, some
critics have argued convincingly it may have been produced earlier in his career. Because of Marvell's lack of
comment regarding his work, questions linger as to the
dates of origin of his various poems. Most appeared in
print for the first time in the posthumous 1681 collection titled *Miscellaneous Poems.*

Marvell drew on a rich tradition of garden writing
for this work, including that by classical poets. One of
the poets most imitated by Marvell was Horace, who
associated gardens with epicurean delights and the
contemplative life. In addition, VIRGIL's ideas of the
garden as a source of themes of wisdom and philosophy in poetry, rather than of public virtue, surface in
"The Garden." The reader may also recognize echoes of
BEN JONSON's amplified description used to persuade
readers to his point of view in the country house poem
"TO PENSHURST"; of ABRAHAM COWLEY's early LYRIC
poetry; and of the biblical Song of Solomon in which
the bridegroom (an allegory for Christ) compares his
bride (the church) to a garden. He employs the familiar
octosyllabic METER of iambic tetrameter seen also in his
"The DEFINITION OF LOVE" in nine eight-line stanzas
with rhyming couplets.

Marvell's speaker begins by indicting "vainly men"
who seek recognition from "uncessant labours," which
earn them a crown "from single herb or tree, / Whose

short and narrow vergèd shade" produces an insult to
their efforts. He suggests the paucity of their reward
when compared to the lush "garlands of repose" woven
by "all flow'rs and trees." This fixes attention firmly on
the garden to begin the second stanza, in which Marvell uses the FIGURATIVE LANGUAGE of personification,
writing "Fair Quiet, have I found thee here, / And
Innocence thy sister dear!" By converting the advantages of the garden setting into female figures, he suggests a greater reward for the men described in the first
stanza, in whose company the speaker had mistakenly
sought the garden figures. He also suggests that the
company of plants are preferable to the company of
women, a suggestion he extends throughout the poem.
The garden holds "sacred plants," while human "Society is all but rude, / To this delicious solitude." *Rude*
meant not only injurious or insulting actions or language, but was also defined as "uncultivated," suggesting potential lack of attention and sophistication.
Marvell's critical attitude toward the meaningless activity rewarded by society remains clear.

The third stanza describes the "white" and "red,"
meaning the lily and rose, of the "green" garden as
"am'rous." These are positive images of love, whereas
the names cut into the bark of the trees by lovers "cruel
as their flame" is by comparison a waste of time as an
attempt to cultivate love. The passion's flame is destructive, rather than constructive. The speaker issues an
indictment of such thoughtless lovers through a self-
comparison, concluding that stanza with "Fair trees!

Wheres'e'er your barks I wound, / No name shall but your own be found." Marvell continues his comparison of man's errant expression of passion to the preferable quiet contemplative life offered by the garden. He extends his metaphor of passionate love by noting that when Apollo loved Daphne, he hunted her purposely to cause her transformation into a laurel, and Pan did the same with Syrinx, whose nymph form would become a reed. The plant forms are obviously superior to the female beings' original forms in Marvell's new version of the mythological stories. The speaker is so caught up in the garden that its various fruits force their pleasures upon him, the "ripe apples" dropping around his head, grape clusters crushing wine "Upon my mouth," and "The nectarine, and curious peach, / Into my hands themselves do reach." The body reaps great bounty from the garden scene.

After noting the physical benefits of the garden, the speaker notes benefits to the mind as well, including withdrawal "into happiness" as Marvell shows the value of the contemplative life. He also projects onto the mind creative powers, like those God exercised in the Garden of Eden. The mind may transcend earthly bounds, as Marvell adopts an extended metaphor of the ocean to demonstrate the mind's far-reaching powers:

> The mind, that ocean where each kind
> Does straight its own resemblance find;
> Yet it creates, transcending these,
> Far other worlds, and other seas.

The mind's creative activity engages in "Annihilating all that's made / To a green thought in a green shade." Marvell's age sometimes employed the term *annihilation* in a religious sense, to indicate obliteration of self in order to unite with God. His speaker notes the mind annihilates in order later to resurrect everything not connected with a garden into "green" entities or thoughts, to unite with the garden's life.

Stanza 7 considers the soul's benefit from the garden, where "like a bird it sits, and sings, / Then whets, and combs its silver wings." The soul draws sustenance from the garden, which prepares it for "longer flight," and "Waves in its plumes the various light."

The imagery suggests the flight the soul will take to heaven when it later joins the deity, often compared to light in biblical imagery. Marvell extends the biblical imagery into stanza 8 with a consideration of the original "happy garden state" of man. Feminist critics find of interest that Marvell characterizes man's state as happy when he "walked without a mate," suggesting that he might have been better off without the help-meet, or female partner, promised to him in the biblical rendition found in Genesis. However, the speaker notes that man could not bear "To wander solitary there" and enjoy the double paradise of the garden and solitude. As Marvell previously suggests, the plants prove superior to women, their company more comforting than that of the female. His tone remains humorous, and he does not expect readers to take that suggestion seriously.

The final stanza references the passing of time by noting that the "skillful gard'ner" fashioned "Of flow'rs and herbs the dial new," suggesting God as the ultimate gardener and timekeeper and the world the ultimate clock. The sun's movement causes "the milder sun / . . . through a fragrant zodiac [to] run," where flowers represent the belt in the celestial sphere around which the planets organize. The speaker concludes with a classical reference to the presence of bees and a recommendation that man reckon "sweet and whole-some hours" not with a time piece of metal and springs, but with "herbs and flow'rs!"

Critical consideration of the poem has varied, including that of psychoanalytical theories that see the ocean in a Freudian sense, suggesting a return to the womb. Many consider it humorous and reject theories that it reflects serious philosophical or religious thought.

BIBLIOGRAPHY

Kermode, Frank, ed. *English Pastoral Poetry: From the Beginnings to Marvell.* New York: Barnes & Noble, 1952.

Ray, H. Robert. *An Andrew Marvell Companion.* New York: Garland, 1998.

Smith, Nigel, ed. *The Poems of Andrew Marvell.* New York: Pearson/Longman, 2003.

Whitaker, Curtis. "Andrew Marvell's Garden—Variety Debates." *The Huntington Library Quarterly* 62, nos. 3–4 (summer–fall 2000): 297–311.

GAY, JOHN (1685–1732) John Gay was born in the port town of Barnstaple, Devon, on Joy Street, into a family with three siblings, Joanna, Jonathan, and Katherine. His father, William, was probably a member of the newly distinguished merchant middle class, as the location of the house in the middle of town indicated Mr. Gay worked with goods unloaded at the port. Gay's first few years proved happy ones in an agreeable climate with a contented family. Far from scenes of dissent, the Gays remained little touched by political upheaval. The children probably knew little about the conflict between Protestants and Catholics and the challenge of King James II by William, prince of Orange, in the Glorious Revolution of 1688. At age six Gay attended Barnstaple Grammar School. At age nine, he lost his mother to a mysterious illness, and barely a year later his father died. All four children moved in with an uncle, Thomas Gay, who had a large family of his own. John Gay's experience as part of a cohesive affectionate family had effectively ended.

Tradition in the 18th century led families with more than one son to direct the eldest into the military and the younger into apprenticeship; thus, a teenaged John Gay became a silk-merchant apprentice in London. Gay embraced the city, especially enjoying the lively social scene. The temptations of the city resulted in Gay's applying minimal energy to learning the silk trade, leading to the loss of his position at age 16. He requested his uncle to allow him to stay in London but was refused. Uncle Thomas instead moved Gay into the household of a maternal uncle, the Reverend Jonathan Hanmer. No record exists of Gay's activities over the next six years, and when he became of age in 1706, he immediately returned to London. Once again in his element, Gay through his gentle nature and sharp sense of humor became friendly with other young men with excellent imaginations known as "wits." Gay worked for a time as a secretary to an old school friend as he turned his attention to writing.

In 1708 Gay published his first poem in BLANK VERSE. titled "Wine," a forgettable celebration of Scotland's union with England, an act that made Queen Anne during her fifth year as monarch the first ruler over Great Britain and an emerging two-party system of Tories and Whigs. While "Wine" lacked all of the lightness that would later mark Gay's work, its obvious influence by JOHN MILTON resulting in a style inappropriate for Gay's era, it did secure him the title of poet-author, a title he took seriously. Gay's place in the writing continuum would interest later critics, as he produced work with romantic tendencies, while attempting to adopt an Augustan sensibility.

Soon Gay's social circle expanded to include ALEXANDER POPE, and he became a common sight on the coffeehouse scene. That scene changed the face of English writing, as the coffeehouse supplied under a single roof a place of refreshment, a public library, and a debating culture. The artistic company in which Gay circulated inspired his continued writing efforts. Again without success, he wrote a drama, *The Mohocks* (1712), which never saw the stage. Its focus on aristocratic thugs, however, foreshadowed his later extraordinarily popular stage production *The Beggar's Opera* (1728). In addition to the coffeehouse, another new development affected Gay, that of serious journalism. The journalism scene supplied a lucrative outlet for Gay, as he continued to develop his more creative material. While working toward successful poetry and drama, he wrote essays for Lintot's *Miscellany* and *The Examiner,* creating a minor stir with one essay titled "The Present State of Wit" (1711).

By the second decade of the new century, Gay moved into service with the duchess of Monmouth as secretary, thereby supporting his burgeoning career. He published an imitation of Pope's MOCK-HEROIC, "The RAPE OF THE LOCK" (1712), titled "The Fan" (1713). Pope cautioned Gay against publishing too hastily, writing, according to Gay's biographer David Nokes, "I would have you varnish and glaze it at your leisure, and polish . . . as much as you can." Gay took Pope's advice to heart and proved more successful with a tribute to Pope titled "Rural Sports." According to his biographer Phoebe Fenwick Gaye, Pope wrote to JONATHAN SWIFT that Gay, whom Pope labeled affectionately "an unhappy Youth," wrote pastorals "in Divine Service," a reference to the duchess, while lavishing away "all that silver he should have reserved for his soul's health, on buttons and loops for his coat."

While Pope and other members of his circle adopted an indulgent stance toward Gay, SAMUEL JOHNSON had little tolerance for Gay's sometimes outlandish behavior. Johnson wrote in his *The Lives of the Poets* that although Gay proved a favorite of the wits, "they regarded him as a playfellow rather than a partner, and treated him with more fondness than respect." Gay achieved measured success with an additional essay published in the *Guardian*, "Art of Dress." However, as Nokes points out, it suffered the fate of many of Gay's early writings, as "the wit of this piece is spoilt by a kind of literary showing-off." Gay's obvious desire to let readers know he had read Aristotle, Ovid, Horace, Milton, and Boileau resulted in a simple "parade" of "knowing references."

In 1713 Gay also wrote the first English "town eclogue," "Araminata." The eclogue represented a mix of pastoral and burlesque with a bit of classicism added. Not a particularly memorable work on its own, "Araminta" gained the later attention of feminist critics, because of its suggestions of connection to work by Gay's contemporary LADY MARY WORTLEY MONTAGU. He published five eclogues, one of which bore a great resemblance to an eclogue by Montagu. Best known for her letters from Constantinople, Montagu spent about 18 months in London before accompanying her husband abroad. Both eclogues bore the title "The Toilette" and shared other characteristics, suggesting the two poets not only knew one another's work, but might also have collaborated.

Not until Gay published "The Shepherd's Week," which contained his series of eclogues, did he garner the attention he had craved. Then a part of the elite Scriblerus Club, Gay joined a "pastoral war" begun by Pope against Ambrose Philips, a lesser poet demolished by Pope in print. After that well-discussed event, Gay produced "The Shepherd's Week" in support of his friend and mentor, Pope. The public enjoyed Gay's witty parody of Philips, presented as a pastoral cycle. He hoped to ride the public attention to even greater success, ending his service to the duchess in 1714 to become secretary to Lord Clarendon during a mission to Hanover. However, with the death of Queen Anne later that year, any political aspirations held by Gay were quashed, as the Tory Party, also Pope's political party, fell.

With Queen Anne's death, and the political stability brought on by the new Hanoverian King George I, as well as by the controlling Whig influence, the era of the politically inspired wit had ended. Gay turned again to drama and soon scored a hit with a play he described as a tragic-comic-pastoral farce. When his aptly named "The What d'ye Call It" was staged at Drury Lane in 1715, his satire proved so strong that his audience at first wept. Many members of the audience had recently been ousted from Tory privilege and took to heart the play's tender melancholy, which Gay meant as satire. When they at last recognized the play as a mixture of genres that resembled nothing else they had ever seen, the audience was delighted by its foolishness. The ever-critical Johnson wrote of that play, "Of this performance the value certainly is but little; but it was one of the lucky trifles that give pleasure by novelty." Nokes writes that both "The Shepherd's Week" and "The What D'Ye Call It" "possess an anarchic spontaneity" that some of Gay's work lacked. Gay's excellent ear for detail, tuned during his jaunts through London streets, gave realism to his next work, the poem "Trivia, or, The Art of Walking the Streets of London" (1716). In the following year, he collaborated with fellow Scriblerians Pope and John Arbuthnot to produce a flop play, "Three Hours after Marriage." When the curtain went down, Gay actually scuffled with its main actor, the infamous Colley Cibber, often insulted by Pope for his dullness, who had not realized Gay's lampoon focused on him until the play had concluded.

The year 1720 gave Gay success with the publication of his collection *Poems on Several Occasions*. Most of those poems, including "To a Young Lady, with Some Lampreys," remained popular centuries later. Hoping to turn his profits into even greater income, Gay decided to invest them in the doomed South Sea Company. When it famously failed, he lost everything along with many other famous investors, and he also began to lose his good health. Continuing a voluminous and energetic correspondence with Swift, he lived for a time with Pope and other friends, took the cure at Bath, and again attempted to gain a court position by addressing to Prince William in 1726 his *Fables*, the first volume appearing in 1729. It proved popular and convinced him to finish the second volume, which would not be published until after his death.

It was Gay's longtime friend Swift who suggested the idea that developed into *The Beggar's Opera*.

According to Johnson, "Dr. Swift had been observing once to Mr. Gay what an odd pretty sort of a thing a Newgate Pastoral might make. Gay was inclined to try at such a thing for some time; but afterwards thought it would be better to write a comedy on the same plan." Johnson referred to the infamous Newgate Prison, an unlikely topic for a serious pastoral, but one that might be used satirically. Gay asked Swift, Johnson, and the playwright William Congreve to read the resulting play, and none believed it would succeed.

Despite Gay's having written 13 different dramas, *The Beggar's Opera* would be the work for which he would be always remembered, and it would inspire in the 20th century the equally successful musical satire *The Threepenny Opera* (1928) by Bertolt Brecht. Written in BALLAD form to make fun of the pretension of "real" opera, *The Beggar's Opera* celebrated London's underworld and suggested the hypocrisy of high-placed politicians and social figures who used criminal activity to their own benefit. Ironically, its original performance could not have taken place without support from the very class that Gay lampooned, the funds from the duchess of Queensbury. She fronted the needed cash and John Rich agreed to stage *The Beggar's Opera*. A phrase developed to describe the play's stunning effect: it made "Gay rich, and Rich gay." First performed at Lincoln's Inn Fields in January 1728 and running for 62 consecutive nights, it proved an unprecedented success. Johnson wrote that it succeeded in driving all traditional Italian opera out of England. The songs from *The BEGGARS'S OPERA* remain the poetry by which most readers best know Gay.

Although Gay wrote a sequel titled *Polly* (1729), Robert Walpole, Britain's first prime minister and a figure roundly satirized in *The Beggar's Opera,* suppressed it. Gay's biographer David Nokes states, however, that "*Polly* is a relatively innocuous work presenting a sentimental contrast between Old World corruption and New World innocence." One passage in the opening scene to which Walpole took exception, spoken by the character Ducat, who might have acted as Walpole's representative, read, "I have a fine library of books that I never read; I have a fine stable of horses that I never ride; I build, I buy plate, jewels, pictures, or anything that is valuable and curious, as your great men do, merely out of ostentation." Walpole's action in preventing the staging of *Polly* only succeeded in calling attention to Gay's newest play, which finally saw production in 1777. Gay's resultant frivolous lifestyle, marked by indulgences such as gambling and drinking, probably advanced his death in 1732. He was buried in Westminster Abbey, his marker bearing the epitaph that he wrote: "Life is a jest, and all things show it; / I thought so once—and now I know it."

Critics continue to argue Gay's value to the advancement of literature, perhaps because of his flippant attitude and needy character. However, his poetry is considered accomplished, with his mastery of the heroic couplet and his natural ear for lyrics resulting in sophisticated and stylistic productions. As his biographer David Nokes writes Gay has too often been "the victim of his own ambivalence," suffering from a "fatal lack of self-belief." Johnson agreed, noting that Gay was a man "easily incited to hope and deeply depressed when his hopes were disappointed." He allowed, however, that while Gay did not deserve a place among the great Augustan geniuses, including Swift and Pope, he should not be forgotten. As Johnson explained,

> Much, however, must be allowed to the author of a new species of composition, though it be not of the highest kind. We owe to Gay the ballad opera, a mode of comedy which at first was supposed to delight only by its novelty, but has now, by the experience of half a century, been found so well accommodated to the disposition of a popular audience that it is likely to keep long possession of the stage. Whether this new drama was the product of judgment or of luck, the praise of it must be given to the inventor; and there are many writers read with more reverence to whom such merit or originality cannot be attributed.

John Gay's work remains easily accessible through print anthologies as well as online collections.

BIBLIOGRAPHY

Gaye, Phoebe Fenwick. *John Gay: His Place in the Eighteenth Century.* Freeport, N.Y.: Books for Libraries Press, 1972.
Johnson, Samuel. *Lives of the English Poets.* Vol. 2. New York: E. P. Dutton, 1958.

Lindsay, David W., ed. *English Poetry, 1700–1780: Contemporaries of Swift and Johnson.* Totowa, N.J.: Rowman & Littlefield, 1974.

Nokes, David. *John Gay: A Profession of Friendship.* New York: Oxford University Press, 1995.

"GO, LOVELY ROSE!" EDMUND WALLER (1645)

EDMUND WALLER proved an immensely popular poet in his day, although his precise and unoriginal style could not sustain that popularity in later centuries. Still, 18th-century poets appreciated his insistence on correct diction and balance, seen in his song "Go, Lovely Rose!" He adopts the common theme of CARPE DIEM in the best tradition of CAVALIER POETRY, utilizing the easily recognizable symbol of the rose for a woman ripe for romance. In this version Waller establishes the rose as a go-between for the poet to his love, adopting the FIGURATIVE LANGUAGE of personification. The speaker bids the rose in the first line, also the title line, "Go, lovely rose!" The next lines make clear the rose's destination and its charge:

> Tell her that wastes her time and me
> > That now she knows
> When I resemble her to thee,
> How sweet and fair she seems to be.

In this instance, the word *resemble* means "compare," as the speaker wants his lover to understand he thinks her as beautiful as the rose. Waller inserts that word as the only term that contains more than a single syllable, calling the reader's attention to it. Although the speaker is generous in his praise of the woman's beauty, he makes clear his impatience by accusing her of wasting her time and by resisting his efforts at romance. The second stanza emphasizes traditional Cavalier logic, or lack thereof. The speaker bids the rose to tell the young woman who "shuns to have her graces spied" that had the rose grown "In deserts, where no men abide," it would "have uncommended died." The message remains obvious: if the young woman hides her beauty, or graces, they might as well not exist. The false logic insists that unless praised by a lover, her physical attributes prove worthless.

The speaker presses this point in the third stanza, where Waller writes

> Small is the worth
> Of beauty from the light retired;
> > Bid her come forth,
> Suffer herself to be desired,
> And not blush so to be admired.

The speaker urges the young woman not to be shy. Not only will it not harm her to be admired, it will prove to her benefit. She should "come forth" as the rose does, when the bud matures and opens for the world to enjoy. That pleasure, however, remains fleeting, as the speaker next commands the rose, "Then die!" This startling command has its basis in the speaker's desire to teach the young woman that even the greatest beauty remains limited by time. Her own beauty will also fade with age, "The common fate of all things rare." Waller concludes the fourth stanza with the admonition "How small a part of time they share / That are so wondrous sweet and fair!"

"Go, Lovely Rose!" remains one of the most widely anthologized carpe diem poems.

"GO AND CATCH A FALLING STAR" JOHN DONNE (1630)

JOHN DONNE enforced a tight structure on his song "Go and Catch a Falling Star," with three stanzas each containing sestets with a RHYME scheme of *ababcc* and concluding with a rhyming triplet. That controlled format contrasts with the light tone used throughout, appropriate to a song about romance. However, as might be expected from Donne, the lyrical approach is undercut by a cynicism regarding the constancy of women. The speaker suggests that women who can be trusted are rare in lines Donne uses ironically to mimic the serious romance poetry of his age.

The first stanza begins with an order, the imperative, "Go and catch a falling star," an obviously impossible task but presented as if it could be accomplished. The second line, "Get with child a mandrake root," appears nonsensical, but Donne is probably referring to the mandrake root because of the mythology that surrounded it. In fables the mandrake took on human characteristics. Its three-to four-foot brown root mimicked the shape of a human, was said to scream when jerked from the ground, and in medieval times was said to be used in witchcraft. Old drawings often depicted the root as male or female, depending on the number of branches it bore. The mandrake produced flowers that developed into fruit, nicknamed "Satan's apples."

The allusion to Satan connects the plant imagery with the next two lines: "Tell me where all past years are, / Or who cleft the devil's foot." The gently taunting voice continues with mythological references, "Teach me to hear mermaids singing, / Or to keep off envy's stinging." Because mermaids were believed to be half-woman and half-beast and to lure sailors to their death, the theme of temptation, supported by the devil imagery, extends through those lines. Feminist critics would later find interesting the presumably male speaker's requesting that a female teach him to hear the mermaid's deadly song, "Or," conversely, teach him not to be jealous in resisting the sting of envy. That male attitude contradicts the attitude of distrust found in the remainder of the stanza. However, if the reader accepts that Donne's topic was the inconstancy of women, the idea of a dishonest female's tempting man may also be suggested through IRONY in the final rhyming triplet, "And find / What wind / Serves to advance an honest mind." Things carried on the wind proved insubstantial, suffering a fleeting existence, conditions the speaker bestows on honesty in a female.

In the second stanza, Donne continues his suggestion of the mystical as the speaker declares,

> If thou be'st born to strange sights,
> Things invisible to see,
> Ride ten thousand days and nights,
> Till age snow white hairs on thee.

He parodies the theme of eternal love found in traditional romance poetry with the use of an enormous number to illustrate the lengths to which a true lover's dedication extends. Appropriate to the work of the METAPHYSICAL POETS AND POETRY, Donne inserts a surprising use of words, converting the adjective and noun phrase *snow white hairs* to a verbal, with "*hairs*" becoming a verb suggesting aging over time. The line might be paraphrased, "Until age, which is snow white, places

hairs on thee." The speaker mocks his listener through repetition of the term *thou* in the next line, noting that when she returns, she must tell him her tale: "Thou, when thou return'st, wilt tell me, / All strange wonders that befell thee." He may ironically suggest that, because of her inconstancy, she is not likely to return, and if she does, she will lie about the "strange wonders" that drew her away. Donne then makes another skillful turn as the speaker concludes, "And swear / No where / Lives a woman true and fair." He suggests that out of all the wonders his listener observed over the thousand days, one of those was not a constant woman; she does not exist, even as a curiosity.

At the beginning of the final verse, Donne keeps alive hope for the discovery of a faithful woman, which would be a highly valued goal for any long journey: "If thou find'st one, let me know, / Such a pilgrimage were sweet." By using the term *pilgrimage,* he evokes thoughts of religion or a spiritual creed requiring a quest. However, the speaker declares that while his listener might travel far for such a prize, he would not even step next door to meet such a woman should the traveler write to him of her existence, as she would probably have changed by the time he arrived. Thus, no news of that discovery need be sent to the speaker:

> Yet do not, I would not go,
> Though at next door we might meet,
> Though she were true, when you met her,
> And last, till you write your letter.

The stanza ends with another simple, but this time more forceful, triplet that leaves no doubt regarding woman's inherent temperament: "Yet she / Will be / False, ere I come, to two, or three." Because the last stanza deals with a search for a woman, a traditional prize of classic and medieval quests, Donne may suggest the speaker addresses a man in the final stanza, rather than the woman he has addressed in the first two stanzas. However, his sense of irony could be strengthened were a woman sent on the "pilgrimage," as the woman embarking on the search would not be a "true" one.

In his song, Donne comes full circle. He began urging his listener to attempt an impossible feat, that of catching a star in the process of falling. He concludes by warning that same listener that as soon as one believes a true woman has been located, she will also fall, quicker than "one, two, three," disproving his theory that an honest woman exists.

BIBLIOGRAPHY

Chambers, E. K., ed. *Poems of John Donne.* Vol. 1. London: Lawrence & Bullen, 1896.

GOLDSMITH, OLIVER (1728–1774) Oliver Goldsmith was born in 1728 in West Meath, Ireland. His father, a man of English ancestry, served as Anglican clergyman in the Church of Ireland. Goldsmith was later said to have inherited both his father's geniality and his improvident nature. He spent his early childhood near a village called Lissoy but later left the village to take an education at several grammar schools. Because his face was disfigured by smallpox and his stature was small, he suffered much bullying as a child. When he entered Trinity College in Dublin, Goldsmith had little enthusiasm for education but graduated, barely obtaining a bachelor of arts degree; his tutors viewed him as dull and unintelligent. After failing at several professions, he engaged in a half-hearted attempt to pass medical school at Edinburgh and then in Holland but failed in both places. He wandered about Flanders, France, Switzerland, and into Italy, earning a living by playing his flute. When he arrived in London in 1756 and applied for medically related jobs, he lacked the competence to pursue any of them. After miserable service assisting a schoolmaster, he lived in poverty resulting from his poor attempt to make a living as a freelance journalist.

Goldsmith at last in 1759 published his first important work, *An Enquiry into the Present State of Polite Learning in Europe,* while also writing for various publications, including the novelist Tobias Smollett's *Critical Review,* as well as *The Busy Body, The Weekly Magazine, The Royal Magazine,* and *The Lady's Magazine.* He found some success when he copied an approach made popular by Voltaire and assumed the persona of a Chinese mandarin visiting England, sending reports regarding his experiences home to Peking. Published in 1762, Goldsmith's work was titled *The Citizens of the World,* after appearing first as "Chinese Letters" in John Newbery's *The Public Ledger.* Goldsmith's astute description of London's local color gained a readership, and the public warmed to the adventures, some of which he set in Persia and Russia.

Goldsmith's works prior to the 1760s appeared anonymously and included essays, histories, anthologies of poems, and biographies. His rise in success gained him entry into the select coterie dominated by Dr. Samuel Johnson called "The Club." Although always in need of money, Goldsmith favored expensive attire and enjoyed gambling. He also enjoyed giving his money away to those he felt less fortunate than he, attributes that annoyed friends who knew of his constant indebtedness. In order to support his activities, he sold a manuscript in 1764 at a pittance to pay his rent, and the bookseller who purchased it ignored it for a time. As the story goes, Goldsmith was in danger of going to debtor's prison and called his friend Johnson to peruse his manuscripts, and Johnson selected a novel-length work, which he deemed high enough quality to sell. The novel did not particularly impress its purchaser because it was short and devoid of the currently popular melodrama, lacking characters who suffered endless agony. In addition, it offered a much gentler humor than the satire and obscene burlesque that seemed to hold public attention. However, after Goldsmith's successful publication of "The Traveller" (1764), a lengthy poem and the first work published under his own name, the seller decided to market the manuscript. Thus, one of the most enduring 18th-century novels, *The Vicar of Wakefield* (1766), which contained the poem "When Lovely Woman Stoops to Folly," found an enthusiastic audience. Its tale of a simple good man forced to bear up under worldly challenges struck a chord with the reading public, despite its variance from the normal reading fare. It would be Goldsmith's only novel but would gain the reputation of one of his century's most important works.

The novel's great success inspired Goldsmith in 1770 to publish his best and most lengthy poem, *The Deserted Village,* which gave him an income. His monetary success proved brief, as his gambling habits depleted his support, but allowed him to live well for a time and travel to France. He was joined by family friends, the Horneck sisters and their mother. He was later rumored to have fallen in love with 17-year-old Mary Horneck. Understanding the impropriety of such a romantic relationship, Goldsmith remained determined to keep their friendship platonic.

When he returned to England, Goldsmith needed to generate more cash. He began to research a new project and published *History of England* in 1772; it was not well received. However two years later he again enjoyed great success through the performance of his wildly popular play *She Stoops to Conquer*. While he never again published a successful piece, his drama and select poems remained popular. His poetry achieved its popularity through his departure from the stiff rule of the heroic couplet and his presentation of the seemingly simple and pleasurable themes of childhood, based on memories of his travels and his childhood home.

As a result of a kidney infection rumored to have been badly self-treated, Goldsmith died in London in 1774 and was buried in the Temple churchyard. His cohorts in "The Club" felt moved to recognize Goldsmith's genius properly by erecting a monument in Westminster Abbey bearing an epitaph composed in Latin by the great Johnson. All of his works remain popular centuries later, and many are available in both hardcopy and electronic format.

BIBLIOGRAPHY

Lucy, Sean. *Goldsmith: The Gentle Master.* Cork: Cork University Press, 1984.

Wibberley, Leonard. *The Good-Natured Man: A Portrait of Oliver Goldsmith.* New York: William Morrow, 1979.

GONDIBERT (EXCERPT) William Davenant

(1651) WILLIAM DAVENANT remains most important for his involvement in restoring drama to the stage after the long Cromwellian moratorium on public performance. However, he was also a poet, who wrote the incomplete romantic epic poem *Gondibert* while imprisoned as a Royalist by Cromwell's forces. Set in Lombardy, *Gondibert* followed the adventures of feudal knights. Davenant based the poem's quatrain form on Sir John Davies's *Nosce Teipsum,* or, *Know Thyself* (1599), a poem of natural philosophy that considered the relationship of the soul to the human body and senses, as well as the soul's immortality. In turn, *Gondib-ert* later served as a model for JOHN DRYDEN's ANNUS MIRABILIS: THE YEAR OF WONDERS, 1666. While Davenant's poetic capabilities were limited, he exhibited occasional flashes that were, if not brilliant, commendable.

In the sixth canto of Book 1, Davenant uses the quatrain form for multiple verses, of which 12 will be considered here. He applies an *abab, cdcd, efef*, and so on, RHYME scheme and adopts iambic pentameter as rhythm. The action frames a chivalric journey through a beautiful land. Davenant includes certain classical approaches, such as adopting the FIGURATIVE LANGUAGE (FIGURE OF SPEECH) of personification for nature and including references to ancient figures. His heroes, who include a duke, reach the palace of Astragon,

> Which had its beauty hid by envious night,
> Whose cypress curtain, drawn before the sun,
> Seemed to perform the obsequies of light.

The use of repetition, as with the *s* sound, and emphasis on light and dark imagery result in a dreamy effect. In addition, Davenant employs the term *obsequies,* a word derived from Middle English meaning "funeral rites." It might seem clumsy on its own and suggest a negative connotation, but in this stanza it fits smoothly into the rhythm, supports the sound repetition, and reflects the medieval setting. The next stanza also employs repetition to its benefit, as the speaker describes "a passage through a gate" that the travelers spot, "Whose height and space showed ancient ornament, / And ancients there in careful office sate." The idea of age and wisdom is strongly suggested, although the final word, chosen to rhyme with *gate,* does not prove graceful. It does lead directly into the next stanza, which describes exactly what those offices were. The learneds used "weights and measures" to record "Such numerous burdens as were thither brought / From distant regions, to their learned lord, / On which his chymics and distillers wrought." That description allows contrast in the next stanza, which begins by informing readers that the travelers "refrain" from the "common business" just described, having observed "bloody marks" showing the distress of the house within.

A character named Ulfin arrives, familiar to the travelers, and he provides torches to light the travelers' way to Astragon. Ulfin greets them cheerfully, then discovers several wounded among their group. He leads the duke to his own apartment and sees that the wounded are settled in. One stanza features the hospitality medieval castles were expected to provide to travelers, but because of the physical ailments of the guests, it is subdued:

> Then thin digestive food he did provide,
> More to enable fleeting strength to stay,
> To wounds well-searched he cleansing wines
>   applied,
> And so prepared his ripening balsam's way.

The next stanza represents Davenant's tendencies to become pedantic as he praises the

> Balm of the warrior! Herb Hypernicon!
> To warriors, as in use, in form decreed,
> For, through the leaves, transparent wounds are
>   shown,
> And rudely touched, the golden flower doth
>   bleed.

The hyperbole causes a semihysterical tone that does not benefit his description. He extends his discussion of the effective application of the yellow flower into his next verse but fortunately mutes the rhetoric.

In the penultimate stanza to be considered here, Davenant provides a glimpse of the redeeming qualities noted by later critics. He returns to his former dreamy tone and in describing sleep achieves the effect through elevated and skillful word choice that he previously sought to force on readers by rhetorically yelling at them. He begins, "And now the weary world's great medicine, Sleep, / This learned host dispensed to every guest," perpetuating the wistful tone through the phrase *weary world,* employing ALLITERATION to advantage. The next two lines extend the effect as Davenant adds, "Which shuts those wounds where injured lovers weep, / And flies oppressors to relieve the opprest." As critics point out, Shakespeare's influence is strong throughout the stanza, but especially in these two lines with the use of alliteration and emphasis on mostly single-syllable simple words until the final phrase,

which resembles an epigram. A familiar example may be drawn from Shakespeare's "Sonnet 116," "Let me not to the marriage of true minds," in which the third and fourth lines read, "Which alters when it alteration finds, / Or bends with the remover to remove."

As quickly as Davenant achieves poetic grace, he loses it in the final stanza, incorporating in the first two lines a heavy use of alliteration that calls attention to sense, rather than sensibility: "It loves the cottage and from court abstains, / It stills the seaman though the storm be high." He continues plodding forward through a group of *c* and *s* sounds that bog down the reader, "Frees the grieved captive in his closest chains," finally increasing the oppression of the *s* sound and forcing a three-syllable word in a line ruled by single-syllable terms: "Stops Want's loud mouth, and blinds the treacherous spy." The concluding metaphor of the mouth remains as unpleasant in its suggestion as in its sound and precedes a clumsy phrase forcing readers to stagger to the stanza's end.

"GOOD FRIDAY, 1613. RIDING WEST-WARD" JOHN DONNE (1633)   One of JOHN DONNE's most often anthologized pieces, "Good Friday, 1613. Riding Westward" represents occasional verse. In this case that occasion was the Friday before Easter Sunday, the day traditionally honored by Christians as the time of Christ's crucifixion; it fell on April 2 in 1613. Donne captures his thoughts regarding Christ's death and his own sinful nature from which Christ's sacrifice rescued him.

Donne opens his 42-line poem with a METER of mostly iambic pentameter, by adopting the FIGURATIVE LANGUAGE of extended metaphor. This comparison may be classified as characteristic of the style of METAPHYSICAL POETS AND POETRY in that Donne wants to examine man's soul by comparing it to the cosmos:

> Let man's soul be a sphere, and then, in this,
> The intelligence that moves, devotion is.
> And as the other spheres, by being grown
> Subject to foreign motions, lose their own,
> And being by others hurried every day,
> Scarce in a year their natural form obey;

While the poem for the most part adheres to iambic pentameter, its first five words all receive the same emphasis. The format of words in single syllables for effect proved a common approach for Donne. His punctuation also serves a specific purpose; for example, the period that concludes the second line with a pronounced end-stopped effect. Donne signals readers that they should pause for a moment to consider those first two lines carefully as a complete thought. However, he begins the third line with the conjunction *And,* which allows readers to connect the following thought with the first.

Helen Gardner relates "Let man's soul be a sphere" to the Ptolemaic theory of the universe, one referenced often by Donne. In his poem, the soul is the moving force or principle, the *form,* in Platonic terms. The Angel who causes a sphere to move is its "natural form," while devotion serves as the soul's intelligence or "form."

As he continues, Donne completes the thought regarding men's not obeying their "natural form" to explain that their souls instead adopt "Pleasure or business," which they substitute "For their first mover, and are whirled by it." The image of planets whirling outside their orbits proves a strong comparison for man's misguided actions. The speaker next notes that while his "soul's form bends toward the East," he is "carried towards the West." As Gardner explains, while the natural motion of spheres was west to east, the force of the primum mobile could move them instead from east to west. The spheres also suffered other forces that served to deflect them from their proper motions. Donne had used this CONCEIT, as Gardner notes, in a letter to a friend in which he contrasted true friendship with false, writing, "which is not moved primarily by the proper intelligence, discretion, and about the naturall center, virtue . . . returns to the true first station and place of friendship planetarily, which is uncertainly and seldome." The letters were collected into *Letters to Severall Persons of Honour,* published in 1651.

The speaker admits, "I should see a Sun by rising, set, / And by that setting endless day beget." Donne engages dual wordplay, using the traditional reference to "Sun" as a pun on the "Son" of God, who is Christ, and invoking PARADOX in his description of an "endless day." As the speaker considers "But that Christ on this cross did rise and fall, / Sin had eternally benighted all," additional wordplay occurs. First, in the allusion to the natural course of the sun in the phrase "rise and fall," Donne describes Christ's life, as God's son, and death. In addition, his emphasis on night in "eternally benighted" strengthens the former reference to an "endless day." In other words, without Christ's sacrifice, humans would have remained eternally in the night of sin. He notes he would "almost be glad I do not see / That spectacle, of too much weight for me." He calls on the biblical references to death for one "Who sees God's face," a fact emphasized in the biblical book of Exodus, chapter 3, when Moses went to the mountain top to receive the command to lead the Hebrews from Egypt and had to speak with a burning bush, rather than be face to face with the Lord. However, the speaker adds, if seeing God is such a terror, "What a death were it then to see God die?"

The next lines continue to focus on Christ's crucifixion, during which supposedly an earthquake and an eclipse simultaneously occurred. The speaker alludes to those events that happened while God's "own lieutenant, Nature" shrunk: "It made his footstool crack, and the sun wink." Donne returns to his sphere metaphor as the speaker wonders, "Could I behold those hands which span the poles / And tune all spheres at once, pierced with those holes?" The holes refer to those made by the spikes hammered through Christ's hands to hold him on the cross. Some discussion exists regarding the term *tune,* which appears in line 22; some versions read instead *turn,* a product of the ongoing problems that occur in Donne scholarship. H. J. C. Grierson adopted the word *turn* in his edition of Donne's poetry, explaining that Donne described Christ as "first mover," adding that *tune* could also refer to *turn,* as the rate of turning produces music. In line 26, Donne refers to "The Seat of all our Souls," echoing, according to Gardner, a reference in *LXXX Sermons* (1640) to blood as "the seat and residence of the soule," and to Christ's blood as "the seat of his [Donne's] soule." He wonders whether he could look on the height that Christ represents "Or that blood which is / The seat of all our souls, if not of his."

Donne continues for several lines questioning how he could in his sin face his God. Although the speaker cannot literally see the events of Christ's death, he forms a mental image that causes his memory to look "towards them; and thou look'st towards me." The speaker explains that he must "turn my back to thee but to receive / Corrections, till thy mercies bid thee leave." In an approach Donne also famously employed in "BATTER MY HEART," he asks his Lord to punish him physically: "O think me worth thine anger, punish me: / Burn off my rusts and my deformity." Only such treatment will "Restore thine image so much, by thy grace, / that thou may'st know me, and I'll turn my face." The poem concludes with the speaker's acknowledging he may turn his face toward God only when God's image is clearly restored in him, alluding to the biblical explanation found in the creation story in the book of Genesis that man was made in God's image.

BIBLIOGRAPHY
Chaney, C. R., ed. *Handbook of Dates for Students of English History.* London: Royal Historical Society, 1970.
Gardner, Helen, ed. *John Donne: The Divine Poems.* New York: Oxford University Press, 1969.
Grierson, H. J. C., ed. *The Poems of John Donne.* 2 vols. New York: Oxford University Press, 1912.

"GOOD-MORROW, THE" JOHN DONNE (1630)

"The Good Morrow" was first published in JOHN DONNE's posthumous collection *Songs and Sonnets* and ranks among his best known love poems. Critics have developed various theories regarding the poem's symbolism, many relating to the Platonic theory of love. Donne's metaphoric vision of two lovers who join as one to reach completion supports their theories. Christopher S. Nassaar believes Plato's cave allegory also influenced Donne's construction. He uses as evidence Donne's reference to a cave in the first stanza, the speaker's reference to his lady as the Idea of Beauty, and the lovers' later emergence from the cave into awareness of their love as perfection, as if emerging into light. As suits the approach of the METAPHYSICAL POETS AND POETRY, Donne includes unusual FIGURATIVE LANGUAGE in describing the lovers' relationship. His format includes three stanzas, each composed of two couplets followed by a triplet.

The first stanza opens with the speaker's musing to his partner about existence prior to their relationship:

I wonder by my troth, what thou, and I
Did, till we loved? Were we not wean'd till then,
But suck'd on country pleasures, childishly?

Donne naturalizes the dialogue by using ENJAMBMENT at the end of his first line and inserting a caesura caused by a question mark in the middle of the second line. The speaker suggests that previous to romance, the two lovers were as babies, still dependent upon their mothers' breasts for nourishment. Donne creates an unusual phrase in "suck'd on country pleasures," perhaps indicating that the country, where the lovers matured, provided an unsophisticated environment. His next line employs the disrespectful verb *snorted* in conjunction with reference to a Christian miracle, when he writes, "Or snorted we in the seven sleepers' den?" The "seven sleepers' den" refers to Christian mythology, in which seven Christian youths from Ephesus hid in a cave during the persecution of Diocletian in A.D. 250. While they slept, the opening to the cavern was blocked, leaving them entombed. Supposedly they were discovered, still living, in A.D. 479. Donne's lack of respect in use of this reference suggests he did not want the love shared by the subjects of his poem compared to a miracle of faith, but simply to be perceived as a miracle of life. The speaker continues,

'Twas so; but this, all pleasures fancies be.
If ever any beauty I did see,
Which I desired, and got, 'twas but a dream of thee.

The lover acts as a fantasy, fulfilling all of the speaker's desires for pleasure. In cliché form, one could paraphrase the end of the stanza as "My love, you're a dream come true."

In the second stanza, the speaker remains fixed on the movement of time, which is so important to their realization, and to their emotional awakening. He bids their souls good morning, stating,

And now good morrow to our waking souls,
Which watch not one another out of fear;

For love, all love of other sights controls,
And makes one little room, an everywhere.

Donne employs one of his favored approaches, envisioning small areas as equivalent to enormous landscapes, as in his "The FLEA," where a tiny creature momentarily represents a universe, and in one of his sonnets, "I AM A LITTLE WORLD, MADE CUNNINGLY." His use of ALLITERATION and word repetition adds auditory pleasure to these lines, as the reader watches the lovers discover one another completely unabashed, as a result of the purity of their emotion. The concluding triplet expands the room as "an everywhere" into the sea and entire worlds, then multiple worlds, meant to be explored as the lovers explore their feelings: "Let sea-discoverers to new worlds have gone, / Let maps to others, worlds on worlds have shown." However, the lovers desire only the single world they form when they unite, as Donne develops a delightful PARADOX in his final line of stanza two, "Let us possess one world, each hath one, and is one."

The third stanza indisputably acknowledges that each lover requires the other in order to be whole, as they literally reflect one another: "My face in thine eye, thine in mine appears, / And true plain hearts do in the faces rest." Not only does Donne establish a metaphysical CONCEIT with the melding of the two represented in physical dimensions, but his internal RHYME, with the repetition of *thine* and the inclusion of *mine,* creates an echo effect that underscores the idea of two separates that are in reality identical. Extending the geography conceit, the speaker adds, "Where can we find two better hemispheres / Without sharp north, without declining west?" Their world remains superior to the geographical world, as their orientation toward one another is defined by neither dimension nor direction.

The final triplet references a theory of the physician Galen, who held that physical death was caused by an imbalance—"Whatever dies, was not mixed equally"—then continues with the concluding epigrammatic statement, "If our two loves be one, or, thou and I / Love so alike, that none do slacken, none can die." Donne again uses enjambment to suggest the continuity that he describes. Because the two lovers are so alike, all aspects, emotional and physical, will remain perfectly combined, leading to eternal life.

BIBLIOGRAPHY
Nassaar, Christopher S. "Plato in John Donne's 'The Good Morrow.'" *American Notes and Queries* 16, no. 1 (winter 2003): 20–21.

GRAY, THOMAS (1716–1771)

Although his parents had 12 children, Thomas Gray was the only to survive. His father, Philip, worked as a scrivener in Cornhill, while his mother, Dorothy, and his aunt, Mary Antrobus, operated a milliner's shop. Gray enjoyed an education at Eton, where two of his uncles, Robert and William Antrobus, served as assistants. There he became one member of the so-called Quadruple Alliance, which included Horace Walpole, later fourth earl of Oxford and the author of the novel *The Castle of Otranto,* credited as the first of the gothic genre. The group of four also included Richard West and Thomas Ashton. While at Eton Gray produced a few verses, the product of Latin exercises.

Gray moved on to Peterhouse, Cambridge, where he considered a legal career and in 1734 sent his first existing English verse to Walpole, who was at King's College. Gray was admitted at the Inner Temple a year later. In 1736 he received a small inheritance from an aunt and later that year published his "Hymeneal," celebrating the wedding of the prince of Wales, in the Cambridge publication *Gratulatio.* He continued writing and toured France and Italy between 1739 and 1741 with Walpole, visiting Paris, Rheims, Lyon, Florence, and Rome. The two eventually quarreled, apparently over Gray's resentment of Walpole's assuming Gray depended on his largesse.

Gray returned to England, where he continued work on Latin verses and intended to study law, all the while corresponding with West. When Gray's father died in 1741, his inheritance left him free to focus on writing, and he began work in 1742 on a drama titled *Agrippina.* Shortly after mailing a poem, "Ode on the Spring," to West, he learned that his friend had died. At the time Gray was at work on *De Principiis Cogitandi,* a translation of Locke's "Essay Concerning Human Understanding." He included with his translation *Liber Quartus,* a lament on the loss of West. Returning to Peterhouse in fall 1742, Gray divided his time between London and Stoke Poges, where his mother and aunt had retired. While visiting his mother he wrote "Sonnet on the Death of Richard West," additional odes titled "On Adversity" and "Ode on a Distant Prospect of Eton College," and an uncompleted work titled "Hymn to Ignorance."

By the close of 1743, Gray had his bachelor of law degree in hand and two years later reconciled with Walpole; the two would remain lifelong friends. When Walpole's cat died in 1747, the poet sent his friend a poem titled "Ode on the Death of a Favourite Cat, Drowned in a Tub of Gold Fishes." However, it was not until 1750 that Gray completed the poem that would secure his reputation, "ELEGY WRITTEN IN A COUNTRY CHURCHYARD." He probably began the poem prior to his aunt's death in 1749, after which he visited the church celebrated in his verse. He sent a copy to Walpole, who circulated it in manuscript form; it would be published in 1751.

Correspondence between Walpole and a friend indicated that Gray seemed to remain on the defensive when in the company of aristocrats, evincing a melancholy and "a little too much dignity" that Walpole later noted he found oppressive. However, although Walpole found Gray disagreeable, he found his friend's writing admirable. Whatever Walpole's personal feelings toward Gray, he would remain a major force encouraging Gray to write. Friends observed Walpole remained more interested in publishing Gray's work than his own.

By 1752 Walpole had collected five of Gray's poems and set the excellent illustrator, Richard Bentley, to work designing art to accompany the verses in publication. Although Gray at first resisted the idea, he eventually responded positively, writing to Walpole regarding one illustration, "I am surpriz'd at the Print, which far surpasses my Idea of London Graving." He commented on a copy of Bentley's rendering of the funeral made famous in the "Elegy." In 1753 Gray's mother died on March 11, causing him to draw small joy from the appearance of *Designs by Mr. R. Bentley for Six Poems by Mr. T. Gray* on March 29. He wrote the words on his mother's tombstone, a portion of which described her as "the careful tender mother of many children, one of whom alone had the misfortune to survive her." Gray would publish no additional major works. Although he had remained in good health through his 37 years, he suffered a slow decline beginning in 1754, and friends noticed an increase in his eccentric behavior.

Invited to serve as secretary to the earl of Bristol in 1755, Gray declined. In 1757 Walpole published through his own Strawberry Press Gray's two Pindaric odes, "Progress of Poesy" and "The Bard," and in December of that year, Gray declined the offer of the poet laureate title. Over the next few years he wrote several epitaphs; his connection to Stoke Poges ended in 1758 with the death of his last friend who resided there.

Gray relocated to London in 1759 to focus on research at the British Museum in order to write a history of English poetry. He toured England and Scotland, continuing his letter writing, adding to a collection of correspondence that would be of extreme value after his death. He wrote imitations of Celtic and Norse verse, which became part of his collection titled *Poems* (1768). While he failed to obtain the post of Regius Professor of Modern History at Cambridge in 1763, he gained that sinecure in 1768. The next year he wrote *Ode,* honoring the duke of Grafton as the new chancellor of the university. Continuing research, Gray made another trip to the Lake District that year, all the while writing in his *Journal,* which would be published posthumously in 1774. After he died at Cambridge in 1771, he was buried in the churchyard that made him so famous at Stoke Poges.

Despite his small output, Gray remained known for his distinctive voice and polished verse. Although he never published his history of verse, his study of the work of many others supported the development of his own introspective style. "Elegy Written in a Country Churchyard" continues to be frequently published and remains readily available in both electronic and print form.

BIBLIOGRAPHY
Lonsdale, Roger, ed. *The Poems of Thomas Gray, William Collins, Oliver Goldsmith.* New York: Longman, 1969.
Sells, A. L. Lytton. *Thomas Gray: His Life and Works.* London: George Allen & Unwin, 1980.

"GRONGAR HILL" JOHN DYER (1726) JOHN DYER made his reputation as a landscape painter poet

with "Grongar Hill," a richly descriptive poem that praised his home in his native Wales. He published three versions, the first in Richard Savage's *Miscellaneous Poems* (1726), which contained five additional Dyer poems. The second revised version appeared in the first volume of *A New Miscellany, Written Chiefly by Persons of Quality. To Which is added Grongar Hill, a Poem,* dated 1725, although it appeared later. Dyer's patroness, the countess of Hertford, may have supported its publication. The final revision was published in the first volume of *Miscellany* (1726), compiled by a friend from Westminster, David Lewis. The poem later influenced the Romantics in their view of nature, and William Wordsworth would express his admiration of Dyer's technique.

Dyer did not use the traditional HEROIC COUPLET of JOHN DRYDEN and ALEXANDER POPE for "Grongar Hill." He chose instead to imitate the Welsh *cywdd* couplet, closer to seven syllables per line, although it is commonly described as an "octosyllabic couplet." When he began the poem as a teen, he had used the heroic couplet but later became enthralled with JOHN MILTON's poems "L'ALLEGRO" and "IL PENSEROSO," adopting a similar METER. The poem's theme is best expressed in the line "quiet in the soul," a quiet that poetry allowed Dyer to feel as he valued personal harmony with the world at large. His abundant use of *I* centers his modern thought, couched in a neoclassical approach, in the typical 18th-century format of including personal detail within more general observation, suggesting that the poet's experience parallels that of his readers.

Dyer begins his 158-line poem in the classical vein, his speaker calling on a Nymph to "aid thy sister Muse" as Phoebus, or the sun, rises and "Grongar Hill invites my song." The intimacy with which the speaker embraces his surroundings is reflected in a reverent tone. It remains a special place, as he explains:

> Grongar, in whose mossy cells,
> Sweetly musing, Quiet dwells;
> Grongar, in whose silent shade,
> For the modest Muses made. (15–18)

The speaker then describes himself at times, "With my hand beneath my head," observing his surroundings "'Till Contemplation had her fill." Dyer employs ALLITERATION as the speaker references "groves, and grottos where I lay" (29) and notes that "Wide and wider spreads the vale," soon skillfully repeating his allusion to circular movement. Dyer adopts the FIGURATIVE LANGUAGE of simile, comparing the spreading vale in the next line to "circles on a smooth canal." As the reader learns of the round tops of mountains disappearing against the sky, Dyer further extends his CONCEIT, writing

> Still the prospect wider spreads,
> Adds a thousand woods and meads,
> Still it widens, widens still,
> And sinks the newly-risen hill. (37–40)

He employs chiasmus (inversion) in the line "Still it widens, widens still," the second phrase reversing the second, and uses ANTITHESIS by implying opposite ideas in describing a "newly-risen" hill, which simultaneously is sinking.

Once the speaker climbs "the mountain's brow," a phrase in which Dyer employs personification, he describes the scene before him. After again noting in wonder nature in terms of its hues and light, he becomes more specific, his voice rising to a note of reverential praise. In lines 49–56 Dyer employs alliteration, consonance, assonance, and participle verb forms (*towering* and *rushing*), all of which build momentum, imitating in form the building emotion obvious in multiple exclamations:

> Old castles on the cliffs arise,
> Proudly towering in the skies!
> Rushing from the woods, the spires
> Seem from hence ascending fires!
> Half his beams Apollo sheds
> On the yellow mountain-heads!
> Gilds the fleeces of the flocks,
> And glitters on the broken rocks!

When Dyer reaches line 77, he begins a contemplative stage, his speaker observing the decay of a once-fine tower with protective walls, built into the mountain side. He celebrates all manner of creatures, again employing repetition to strong effect. He uses alliteration in line 83 to repeat the *h* sound, choosing the adjective *hoary* to imbue a sense of age to the scene:

'Tis now the raven's bleak abode;
'Tis now the apartment of the toad;
And there the fox securely feeds;
And there the pois'nous adder breeds,
Conceal'd in ruins, moss, and weeds;
While, ever and anon, there falls
Huge heap of hoary moulder'd walls. (77–83)

Such contemplation allows his focus on fate, the ultimate power over men's best plans. Lines 84–85 are especially heavy with alliteration of the letter *l,* causing a lumbering effect that suggests the ever-steady passage of time: "Yet time has seen, that lifts the low, And level lays the lofty brow." The speaker reminds readers that "A little rule, a little sway, /A sunbeam in a winters day," may be fate's only gift to "the proud and mighty" as they move from cradle to grave.

In lines 121–122 Dyer cautions through his speaker, "So we mistake the Future's face, / Ey'd thro' Hope's deluding glass." However, he does not intend his message to be negative. Rather he urges his audience to do what he tries to do:

O may I with myself agree,
And never covet what I see:
Content me with an humble shade,
My passions tam'd, my wishes laid;
    (129–132)

The speaker cautions those who search for peace behind "the lofty door" or "on the marble floor" that they will be disappointed. He points them, instead, toward nature, and more specifically toward Grongar Hill, where "Quiet" and "Pleasure" abide. It serves as his touchstone, a place of quiet in which he has learned to observe as much about himself as he does in the scenes of nature that surround him:

Grass and flowers Quiet treads,
On the meads, and mountain-heads,
Along with Pleasure, close ally'd,
Ever by each other's side
And often, by the murm'ring rill,
Hears the thrush, while all is still,
Within the groves of Grongar Hill. (152–158)

BIBLIOGRAPHY

Humphrey, Belinda. *John Dyer.* Cardiff: University of Wales Press, 1980.

H

HABINGTON, WILLIAM (1605–1654) William Habington was born in Worcester. His father, Thomas, was a Roman Catholic gentleman imprisoned for a time for his involvement in the Gunpowder Plot. Not much detail of Habington's youth is known; nor has it greatly interested later critics. A second-tier poet known for incongruity in form, he nevertheless could produce the occasional remarkable line. He used the HEROIC COUPLET with flawless execution, inserting CONCEITs sparingly as he focused mainly on one subject, that of his love "Castara." The real Castara, Lucy Herbert, daughter of William, Lord Powis, while occupying a social level above that of Habington, reciprocated his affection. The two enjoyed what appeared to be a loving marriage.

In addition to his collection *Castara* (1634), published anonymously, Habington collaborated with his father to write and publish three works, *The History of Edward the Fourth* (1640), *Observations Upon History* (1641), and a drama, *The Queen of Aragon* (1640). He also published a second edition of *Castara* in 1635, which contained elegies, and in a third (1640), he at last acknowledged himself as author. *Castara* became the work upon which Habington made his reputation. Divided usually into three or four sections by modern editors, it remains easy to locate in anthologies, which often print excerpts. Selections might include "To Roses in the Bosom of Castara," "To Cupid, upon a Dimple in Castara's Cheek," and "To Castara, upon the Death of a Lady." One of the better known of the group is "AGAINST THEM WHO LAY UNCHASTITY TO THE SEX OF WOMEN." *Castara* focuses on four themes, the mistress, the wife, the friend, and the holy man. Some critics find Habington's lack of sensuality annoying, but they agree his love verses remain powerful, even though imbued with a Platonic sensibility. For instance, in "To Castara, in a Trance," he writes,

> Forsake me not so soon; Castara, stay,
> And as I break the prison of my clay
> I'll fill the canvas with my expiring breath,
> And sail with thee o'er the vast main of Death.
>   (1–4)

BIBLIOGRAPHY
Allot, Kenneth, ed. *The Poems of William Habington*. Liverpool: University Press of Liverpool, 1948.

HALL, JOHN (1575–1635) John Hall was probably born in 1575 in Bedfordshire, England, his father, William, a property owner. He presumably spent his childhood at Carlton, a small and pleasant village, leaving at age 14 along with his brother, Dive, to attend Queen's College at Cambridge. He received a bachelor of arts in 1593 and continued study for a master's degree, awarded in 1597. Records containing his name dated 1600 indicate his presence in Stratford, then a busy market town of about 2,000 people. At age 32, he became William Shakespeare's son-in-law, marrying Susanna Shakespeare, the eldest Shakespeare child, on June 6, 1607; they had a daughter, Elizabeth. Susanna's epitaph hints at her character: "Witty beyond her sex, but that's not all / wise to salvation was good Mistress Hall," where *witty* refers not to humor, but wisdom. That they shared an agreeable marriage is indicated by lines added to his tombstone, after her death:

Lest anything be wanting to his tomb,
His most faithful wife is with him,
And the companion of his life he has also in
    death.

Records indicate Hall spent time with Shakespeare, although details remain scant. Scholars have wondered whether Hall might have influenced his famous playwright father-in-law's medical knowledge, as revealed in Shakespeare's plays.

While practicing medicine, Hall also worked as an essayist, poet, pamphleteer, and translator. Although his creative works were later little read, contemporaries including ROBERT HERRICK, Henry More, and Thomas Hobbes praised his poetry. Best known for his prose, he published a collection of essays titled *Horae Vacivae* (1646) and the first English translation of Longinus, in addition to his *Poems* (1647). In 1648 he was hired to write the *Mercurius Brittanicus* and *Mercurius Censorius,* works defending Parliament against attack by other writers. Such an attack was represented in one work titled *Mercurius Elencticus.* A collection of rebel biographies, its authorship was claimed by Samuel Sheppard, but Sir George Wharton, imprisoned at the time, probably wrote it.

Hall practiced medicine for 35 years both in and around Stratford with a legendary dedication to his patients. In 1626 when King Charles I offered Hall a knighthood, he declined, worried that his duties might interfere with his practice, causing him to be fined £10. He did serve one of three times he was elected burgess to the City Council at Stratford. A dedicated Puritan, he spent much time in service to his church. Hall's death at age 60 was due to his contracting plague as he treated victims.

Hall left behind manuscripts, one a notebook containing 178 medical case descriptions in Latin, which was eventually published as "Select Observations on English Bodies of eminent Persons in desperate Diseases" (1657). Second and third editions followed in 1679 and 1683, and it may be found in facsimile in Harriet Joseph's biography of Hall. One entry mentions "Mr. Drayton, an excellent poet," referring to MICHAEL DRAYTON, celebrated poet and friend to Shakespeare.

BIBLIOGRAPHY
Joseph, Harriet. *Shakespeare's Son-in-Law: John Hall, Man and Physician.* Hamden, Conn.: Archon Books, 1964.

HERBERT, EDWARD, LORD HERBERT OF CHERBURY (1583–1648)

Born in Eyton, Shropshire, Edward Herbert was older brother to the much better known poet GEORGE HERBERT. Educated at University College, Oxford, he married in 1599 and settled in London after 1600. Made Knight of the Bath by James I, he enjoyed the company of others of his aristocratic rank. He served as ambassador to France from 1619 to 1624, traveled widely, and became a philosopher and diplomat. His philosophical treatise written in Latin *De Veritate* (1625) gained him fame because of his views on the principles of natural religion; he was later dubbed the "father of deism." Herbert believed that virtue should combine with piety as the chief part of worship. He also proposed four degrees of truth, based on his theory of the necessity for harmony between the human mind and its surrounding world.

Herbert first became part of the Irish peerage, then received a baronetcy from King Charles I, after which he joined the Council of War. After completing military service, he welcomed retirement to Montgomery Castle in 1644, receiving a pension from Parliament the following year. He published the respectably written *The Life and Reign of Henry VIII* (1644) from a Royalist point of view. In addition, he supplied some interesting detail about his era when he wrote his life's story through the year 1624. Titled *Autobiography,* it was published by Horace Walpole, famous for his gothic fiction.

Herbert's poetry was not published until a slim posthumous volume was issued in 1665. The SONNETS, epitaphs, satires, madrigals, and odes would never have been revealed to the world if not for the efforts of his uncle, Henry Herbert (some sources claim his son published his poetry). He shared his brother's bent for metaphysical poetry, but not for religious topics. An example of his use of metaphysical references employing PARADOX may be found in his "An ODE UPON A QUESTION." Judged by various critics intelligent, graceful, musical, vigorous, and fresh, Edward Herbert's verse did not reach the excellence of his brother's work; some critics feel he never reached his potential. However, critics note that with superior versification and strong topical themes, Herbert's poetry easily finds a place among that of the better known poets of his age. An additional example of his skill and talent for the musical line may be found in "ELEGY OVER A TOMB."

BIBLIOGRAPHY

Bedford, R. D. *The Defence of Truth: Herbert of Cherbury and the Seventeenth Century.* Manchester: Manchester University Press, 1979.

HERBERT, GEORGE (1593–1633) George Herbert was born in Wales, the seventh child of 10 to Richard and Magdalene Herbert. His father died when Herbert was about three, and the family moved to live with George's maternal grandmother in Eyton, Shropshire. Two years later, they again relocated, this time to Oxford, only to move yet again in 1601 to Charing Cross, London. Having reached the proper age, Herbert began his education at Westminster School, where he enjoyed the honor of being elected scholar. The poet JOHN DONNE knew Herbert's brother, the poet EDWARD HERBERT, and wrote to Herbert's mother in 1607, and the following year may have sent her the poems that later formed his collection, *La Corona;* he dedicated to her his ELEGY "Autumnal Beauty."

Magdalene remarried at age 40 in February 1609 to the 20-year-old John Danvers, who a month later was knighted. George Herbert entered Cambridge as king's scholar that same year and in December matriculated to Trinity. He presented his first sonnets to his mother on New Year's Day 1610. Of interest is his relation to Sir Philip Sidney, a fourth cousin, who originated the form of the SONNET sequence. Some critics argue the hints at misogyny in two of Herbert's sonnets may have been induced by jealousy of his mother's young husband. He countered the PETRARCHAN standard that praised fair women with golden hair. However, he

announced in 1610 his intention to write religious verse reflective of the Sidney-Herbert group.

In 1612 Herbert published Latin poetry in a Cambridge volume on the death of Prince Henry of typhoid fever. Those first printed poems reflected his talent for writing with a nationalistic tone. The fact that at only age 19 he was asked to contribute to such an important collection indicates his serious consideration as a Latin scholar. In addition to Latin, he learned Greek and became fluent in Italian, Spanish, and French. No doubt Herbert participated in literary coteries, gatherings during which poets shared their work. Those coteries were supervised by MARY SIDNEY HERBERT, countess of Pembroke, sister to Philip and a poet in her own right. Because publication by members of the upper class was considered vulgar, the coterie provided a manner by which wealthy poets could recite or sing their poetry with musical accompaniment; Herbert also proved an accomplished musician. An auspicious writing career thus began, as Herbert supported the use of religious love as a topic for the sonnet.

Herbert earned his bachelor of arts in 1613 and looked forward to a privileged life, suitable to his high social rank. He cultivated the patronage of the duke of Richmond and the marquis of Hamilton in hopes of political advancement. He contributed occasional poems to help celebrate a visit to Cambridge by Frederick, elector Palatine, husband to Princess Elizabeth, and Prince Charles. Herbert clearly demonstrated a commitment to Protestantism in his two contributions. He does advise Elizabeth against war, suggesting instead that she remain patient until God restores her to the throne; Herbert's antiwar stance would be a lifelong trait. By 1614 he was a minor fellow at Trinity. The following year Donne was ordained and probably wrote a Latin poem to Herbert at that time. Herbert became a major fellow at Trinity one year later and took his master of arts in 1616. By 1617 Herbert was a lecturer at Trinity but suffered a loss with the death of two of his brothers. He wrote a congratulatory letter in 1618 to the duke of Buckingham on his becoming a marquis and apparently requested by letter funds from Sir John Danvers for books and the expenses of settling in Cambridge. In 1619 a poem on the death of Queen Anne was published, and Herbert asked Danvers to assist him in gaining a public oratorship, later assuring his stepfather that appointment would not interfere with his ordination. Herbert had become a celebrant of sacred love in his poetry amd eventually became the best known religious poet in the English language.

In October Herbert enjoyed an appointment as deputy orator at Cambridge, undergoing official election to public orator in May 1620. He sent a letter of gratitude to King James for the monarch's gift of 13th-century philosopher and theologian Ramon Lull's *Opera Latina*. Other letters reflecting his distinguished position went to Robert Naunton, secretary of state; Francis Bacon, lord chancellor; and Fulke Greville, expressing his gratitude for their support in a local dispute over whether the Bedford fens should be drained. After Bacon delivered the *Instauratio Magna,* his plan to restore man to mastery over nature (Great Instauration), at Cambridge, Herbert sent another letter of thanks. Herbert's brother Edward dedicated a 1622 manuscript titled *De Veritate* to him and also to his secretary, William Boswell, requesting their help in editing any reference that seemed inappropriate to their faith and morals. Herbert's brother Henry became a servant to King James in 1622, while another brother, Richard, died at the siege of Bergen-op-Zoom. Throughout that year Herbert made clear his devotion to Protestantism, and most of his works were later characterized by critics as written with a purpose to flatter those in high places who could promote his ambitions.

The year 1623 marked a busy time for Herbert, who delivered an oration to the Spanish and Austrian ambassadors and received an honorary master of arts. An epigram written to King James in farewell as he departed Cambridge was later published by command, presumably of a member of court. He lost a sister, Margaret, to death and in October delivered an antiwar speech to Prince Charles and the duke of Buckingham, an oration later published. He continued writing poetry and performing some translation and became a member of Parliament in 1624. By November 3, Herbert received a dispensation for immediate ordination as a deacon and was granted a sinecure in Montgomeryshire. Presumably, he saw his opportunity for preferments dwindle as his two patrons died. Much scholarly writing about Herbert traditionally held that

when King James died in 1625, all hopes of an appointment for Herbert died with him, characterizing him as a man without a focus. However, newer scholarship, including that by Cristina Malcolmson, suggests that Herbert remained quite active as part of a literary coterie, not engaging in the isolationism of private contemplation long believed to occupy his last years.

Ineligible for Parliament in 1625, Herbert visited Donne, who stayed in Chelsea with Danvers to escape the plague. Bacon dedicated his *Translation of Certaine Psalmes into English Verse* to Herbert. Bacon died the following year, and Herbert probably helped collect contributors to a volume in his memory, in addition to publishing his own Latin poem. He became canon of Lincoln Cathedral and lived for a time with his brother Henry in Essex as he recovered from an illness. When Magdalene Herbert Danvers died in 1627, Donne delivered the funeral sermon. The next year Herbert lived for a time with Danvers's brother, the earl of Danby, near Chippenham, Wiltshire.

Herbert at last married in 1629, wedding Jane Danvers, the earl's cousin, and the two resided in Wiltshire with her family according to some critics; others claim they lived with the earl. The following year he was ordained as a priest in Salisbury Cathedral, and he lived the next two years peacefully. He fell ill and, confident of impending death, sent a copy of his collection of poetry, later titled *The Temple,* to his lifelong friend Nicholas Ferrar. He famously requested that Ferrar pass judgment on the work, burning or publishing it, whichever he felt the manuscript deserved. Ferrar published two editions after Herbert's death of consumption in 1633. The volume contains all of the poems still read centuries later. The collection appeared in 13 editions between 1633 and 1679, followed by a loss of scholarly and reader interest in Herbert. A 1799 edition rekindled public interest, and the poems have never been out of print.

The Temple is divided into three sections. The first section, titled "The Church-porch," is composed of a number of precepts that help in directing typical behavior, such as transactions requiring the exchange of money, drinking, and quarreling. The subtitle, "Perirrhaneterium," refers to the sprinkling of holy water by a specific implement, which suggests the

"Church-porch" aphorisms are designed to prepare Christians for a spiritual state. For example, the first line of "2" reads, "Beware of lust: it doth pollute and foul," while that of "5" cautions, "Drink not the third glass, which thou canst not tame." The second portion of the collection titled "The Church" contains all those popular lyrics most often associated with Herbert. Select widely anthologized selections include "The ALTAR," "REDEMPTION," "EASTER," "EASTER WINGS," "AFFLICTION," "PRAYER," "JORDAN," "CHURCH MONUMENTS," "The WINDOWS," "VIRTUE," "MAN," "TIME," "The BUNCH OF GRAPES," "The PILGRIMAGE," "The HOLDFAST," "The COLLAR," "The PULLEY," "The FLOWER," "DISCIPLINE," "DEATH," and "LOVE." The third and final portion, titled "The Church-militant," refers to a community of believers who must constantly battle evil. Apocalyptic in nature, it little resembles Herbert's other works. Some critics argue it represents the poet's immature attempts, written at an early stage of his life. Others feel it represents his disappointment with the Church of England and with the Stuart court; it acts as a type of protest.

Critics continue to debate details of Herbert's biography and authorship; aspects of *The Temple* particularly generated debate. Because no evidence exists that Herbert titled his collection, arbitrary choices, such as its title, were made by someone, probably Ferrar. This suggests other important details may have been altered. Even Herbert's appearance remains in question. The most famous reproduction of Herbert's likeness was cast years after his death; many believe it was based on a lost portrait. The biography held as seminal for years, written by Izaak Walton in 1670, was subsequently found to contain various errors, later corrected by Amy Charles's *A Life of George Herbert* (1977). As with any life and work that existed centuries ago, complete details remain missing, and some questions may never find satisfactory answers. Herbert's importance to the genre of religious poetry, however, has never been in doubt. His works remain readily available in print and electronic form, and a *George Herbert Journal* also exists.

BIBLIOGRAPHY

Charles, Amy. *A Life of George Herbert*. Ithaca, N.Y.: Cornell University Press, 1977.

Clements, Arthur L. *Poetry of Contemplation: John Donne, George Herbert, Henry Vaughan and the Modern Period*. Albany: State University of New York Press, 1990.

Endicott, Annable M. "The Structure of George Herbert's Temple: A Reconsideration." *University of Toronto Quarterly* 34 (1965): 226–237.

Gottlieb, Sidney. "The Social and Political Backgrounds of George Herbert's Poetry." In *The Muses Commonweale*, edited by Claude Summers and Ted-Larry Pebworth. Columbia: University of Missouri Press, 1978.

Malcolmson, Cristina. *George Herbert: A Literary Life*. New York: Palgrave Macmillan, 2004.

Summers, Joseph. *George Herbert*. Cambridge, Mass.: Harvard University Press, 1968.

Tobin, John, ed. *George Herbert: The Complete English Poems*. New York: Penguin Books, 1991.

HERBERT, MARY SIDNEY, COUNTESS OF PEMBROKE (1562–1621)

Mary Sidney was born the third of seven children to a privileged family of aristocrats at Tickenhill Palace in Worcestershire. Her parents both had strong court connections, her father the godson to Henry VIII and friend to Edward VI and serving three times as lord deputy of Ireland, while her mother served Queen Elizabeth as a lady in waiting. Mary served Elizabeth in the same capacity between 1575 and 1577 after an excellent education that included instruction in Latin, French, and Italian. She shared her love for learning and poetry with both of her brothers, Sir Philip Sidney and Sir Robert Sidney. Both brothers wrote poetry, and Robert and his wife, the Welsh heiress Barbara Gamage, had a daughter named Mary, later LADY MARY WROTH, who also became a poet. Robert would be celebrated in BEN JONSON's famous poem "TO PENSHURST."

Married in 1580 at age 15 to Henry Herbert, earl of Pembroke, Mary began many years of what appeared to be a happy union, despite an apparent love affair with the younger Matthew Lister. Their four children matured also to appreciate and provide patronage to writers; in 1623 Shakespeare's first folio was dedicated to the earls of Pembroke and Montgomery, her two sons. The countess opened their estate, Wilton House near Salisbury, to host many meetings of her literary coterie. The magnificent house gained a reputation for its learned gatherings, and Philip Sidney probably worked on his *Arcadia* and *Apology for Poetry* while visiting. The poet SAMUEL DANIEL served as a tutor for the Herbert children, and the countess influenced many poets through her patronage and support, including her cousin, GEORGE HERBERT; JOHN DONNE; and Jonson. The aristocratic members of the circle were able to share their work through manuscripts, as publication was considered too vulgar for those of their social status. Her support of artistic endeavors gained dedications of works from Edmund Spenser, MICHAEL DRAYTON, John Davies, and Daniel.

Devastated by Philip's 1585 death fighting in the Netherlands, the countess edited and published his poetry. By the 1590s she produced her own work, beginning with translations including Philippe de Mornay's *A Discourse of Life and Death* (1592) and a version of Seneca's *Antonie* based on Robert Garnier's *Marc Antonie* (1592). Her continuation of Philip's English version of the Psalms beyond the 43rd became her greatest contribution to literature, and the 150-psalm sequence circulated privately. It received praise from Donne, among others, and would be first published as a complete collection in 1823. Scholars found it invaluable for its inclusion of many verse strategies used by Elizabethan poets. Its dedication, "TO THE THRICE-SACRED QUEEN ELIZABETH," and Psalm 58, "Si Vere Utique," offer excellent examples of her range in style. She also honored her brother's memory with her poem "The Most Angel Spirit of the Most Excellent Sir Philip Sidney," a work that reflects a love expressed in such intimate terms, some imagined their relationship might have been sexual. While most scholars dismiss that idea, they agree on the poem's extreme emotion, which supports Herbert's revision of the Christian myth regarding the union and resultant offspring of a human and a spiritual being.

While Mary Sidney Herbert may have written other poetry, it has never been found and may have been lost in a fire. Admired by all who knew her and praised in print by poets such as AMEILIA LANYER, Mary Sidney Herbert played a pivotal role in 17th-century poetry production. Her contributions became better known as feminist critics in the mid-20th century insisted on her inclusion in anthologies and texts, which had long contained information regarding her brother Philip.

Recent scholars have even added Herbert's name to those proposed as the true author of works credited to William Shakespeare. That theory would explain the dedication to her sons of his first folio, Shakespeare's sonnets written to a younger man, and Jonson's eulogy in his first folio of 1623 praising the "sweet swan of Avon," as the Herbert estate sat on the river Avon, and Herbert adopted the swan as her personal emblem.

BIBLIOGRAPHY
Bennett, Lyn. *Women Writing of Divinest Things: Rhetoric and the Poetry of Pembroke, Wroth, and Lanyer.* Pittsburgh: Duquesne University Press, 2004.
Clarke, Danielle. "'Lover's Songs Shall Turne to Holy Psalmes': Mary Sidney and the Transformation of Petrarch." *The Modern Language Review* 92 (April 1997): 282–294.
Hannay, Margaret. *Philip's Phoenix: Mary Sidney, Countess of Pembroke.* New York: Oxford University Press, 1990.
Pritchard, R. E. "Sidney's Dedicatory Poem: 'To the Angel Spirit of the Most Excellent Sir Philip Sidney.'" *The Explicator* 54 (fall 1995): 2–4.
Underwood, Anne. "Was the Bard a Woman? A New Contender for Authorship of Shakespeare's Works." *Newsweek International,* 28 June 2004, 58.

HEROIC COUPLET The heroic couplet consists of two rhyming lines with a METER of iambic pentameter. Although the heroic couplet appeared as early as in Chaucer's verse, it gained its name through its frequent use in 17th-century heroic, also labeled epic, drama. It proved a favorite of JOHN DRYDEN, who used it in his 1697 translation of VIRGIL. Its use continued into the 18th century, when master poets including ALEXANDER POPE applied it to works including his translation of the *Iliad,* as well as popular works such as *An ESSAY ON MAN* (1711). An example from that work demonstrating Pope's magnificent use of the heroic couplet is "A little learning is a dang'rous Thing / Drink deep, or taste not, the Pierian spring." In the hands of lesser poets the form proves disastrous, promoting tedium and unintentional humor.

HERRICK, ROBERT (1591–1674) Robert Herrick's father died one year after his son's birth in Cheapside, London. Raised by an uncle who shared his father's goldsmith and banker trade, Robert was destined to follow in the family tradition. However, after a brief apprenticeship to his uncle in 1607, he elected instead to continue his education at Cambridge. There he first attended St. John's College and later matriculated to Trinity Hall, moving at a leisurely, good-natured pace that biographers note reflected his disposition. After ordination in 1623, he served as chaplain to the duke of Buckingham during his 1627 expedition to Isle de Rhé. He moved to a parish at Dean Prior in Devonshire, reluctantly accepting a living that forced him away from his beloved London into a country life he did not enjoy. However, true to his happy nature, he eventually accepted his position, enjoying the bachelor life.

Herrick had begun to write and publish and received an extraordinary tribute in 1625 from the writer Richard James. James wondered in print why no remarkable writer had ever paid tribute to King James during his lifetime, famously noting in "The Muse's Dirge" that "Some Jonson, Drayton or some Herrick" should "Before this time have charactered the mould" of the monarch. As critics remark, for Herrick to be named as equal to BEN JONSON and MICHAEL DRAYTON was high praise, indeed; he would later express his feelings about Jonson in "An ODE FOR HIM" and "HIS PRAYER TO BEN JONSON." Approximately 10 poems had been published before 1648, although others circulated in manuscript, "The Curse" and "Welcome to Sack" proving favorites, the latter balancing his later "HIS FAREWELL TO SACK." Herrick began to produce poetry at an extraordinary rate, although he had little interest in publishing it.

With Civil War, the Puritans came to power and removed Herrick's appointment. He moved to London, where in 1648 he published a volume with dual titles, *Hesperides,* which included secular verse, and *Noble Numbers,* containing sacred. Dedicated to the future monarch, Charles II, it contained an astonishing number of poems on various subjects, many of which are no more than epigrams. They included the later widely anthologized "CORINNA'S GONE A MAYING," considered a major contribution to LYRIC poetry. Many other of his poems proved reader favorites, including "A THANKS-GIVING TO GOD," "DELIGHT IN DISORDER" "TO THE VIRGINS, TO MAKE MUCH OF TIME," "THE MAD MAID'S SONG," "UPON JULIA'S CLOTHES," "UPON THE LOSSE OF HIS MIS-TRESSES" (the mistresses all being imaginary), "THE VINE," "UPON THE NIPPLES OF JULIA'S BREAST," "UPON JACK AND JILL," "THE NIGHT-PIECE, TO JULIA," and "UPON HIS VERSES." Additional selections included epigrammatic poems, such as "Dreams," complete in two lines: "Here we are all, by day; by night, we're hurled / By dreams, each one into a several world," where the term *several* means "separate," and "To His Conscience," in which he wrote, "Can I not sin, but thou wilt be / My private protonotary," *protonotary* referencing the chief recording clerk of a court. Herrick celebrated nature, both environmental and human.

Although he was a practicing cleric, much of Herrick's attitude resembled that of a pagan. The opening to his collection, titled "The Argument of His Book," presented a catalog of songs, as he wrote in part, "I sing of brooks, of blossoms, birds, and bowers, / Of April, May, of June, and July flowers." Some entries in this catalog did not please his Puritan peers, including "I write of youth, of love, and have access / By these to sing of cleanly wantonness," as they believed wantonness nothing to joke about, even in PARADOX form. His volume contained more than 1,400 separate poems, none of which proved well received by a public not inclined to enjoy his playful approach. Herrick's good humor informed all of his work, about 60 selections of which appeared in *Wit's Recreations* (1650), although the remainder of his works sat unpublished for some time. Despite the fact that his poetry was ignored, Herrick survived the period until King Charles took the throne, regaining his former employment and dying at age 83.

Only in the 19th century did critics embrace Herrick in an era ready to celebrate his self-effacing work. Despite characterizations of Herrick's work as "light" by well-respected critics such as Louis Untermeyer, they remain widely read and cited, readily available in both print and electronic form.

BIBLIOGRAPHY

Guffey, George Robert. *Elizabethan Bibliographies Supplements: Robert Herrick, Ben Jonson, Thomas Randolph.* London: Nether Press, 1968.
Patrick, J. Max. *The Complete Poetry of Robert Herrick.* New York: New York University Press, 1963.
Scott, George Walton. *Robert Herrick.* New York: St. Martin's Press, 1974.

Untermeyer, Louis. *The Love Poems of Robert Herrick and John Donne.* New Brunswick, N.J.: Rutgers University Press, 1948.

HIND AND THE PANTHER, THE JOHN DRYDEN (1687)

JOHN DRYDEN wrote *The Hind and the Panther* in order to contribute to an ongoing dispute between Protestant and Catholic factions. While his exact date of conversion from devotion to the Church of England to Catholicism remains uncertain, it happened sometime during 1686, as in July of that year he was known to have attended mass. Many doubted his motivations, most believing he was moved by the practicality that had ruled his life, rather than by a passion for the Catholic faith.

When Charles II died in 1685, he was succeeded by his Catholic brother, James, duke of York, a figure celebrated by Dryden in his poetry. Detractors accused Dryden of converting in order to gain religious favor. SAMUEL JOHNSON would write later in *Lives of the English Poets* (1779) while considering Dryden's conversion, "He that never finds his error till it hinders his progress towards wealth or honour, will not be thought to love Truth only for herself." However, Dryden had questioned publicly in his *RELIGIO LAICI; OR A LAYMAN'S FAITH* (1682) the proper authority for faith and salvation. As the scholar Earl Miner notes, "Like many before him, he could say 'my doubts are done' only when he had trusted the guidance of his faith to a Church whose claim to authority was complete and whose government (like monarchy?) was continuous in legitimate succession." Johnson was willing to believe Dryden an honest convert of conscience, as he continued, "Yet it may easily happen that information may come at a commodious time; and as truth and interest are not by any fatal necessity at variance, that one may by accident introduce the other."

In the third portion of *The Hind and the Panther* Dryden supplies history for beast fables, in which animals assume characteristics of humans, noting examples from real life in which humans behaved like animals and concluding, "If men transact like brutes, 'tis equal then / For brutes to claim the privilege of men." The pure white hind, or deer, represented Catholicism while the equally beautiful, but impurely spotted and black,

panther represented the Church of England. Dryden's employment of an animal tale to express the sober truths of faith provoked ridicule from the reading public. Yet in his traditional approach, Dryden fashioned his poem on various models that dealt with sacred zoography, a religious study of animals. He may also have been influenced by Wolfgang Franzius's *Historia Animalium Sacra* (1612), a discussion of, according to Miner, "the moral, ecclesiastical, and typological significances of quadrupeds and birds." The Renaissance and Middle Ages had both utilized animals for religious allegory. While all of Dryden's scenes of interaction between the animals are not absurd, those that are generally feature the panther. Readers had to suspend the normal rules governing existence to adopt the anthropomorphological approach. Indulging the poet by accepting that animals can engage in serious discussion, readers might still smile in the poem's third part when the Catholic Hind informs the Anglican Panther that Catholic Poultry, even though involved in unapproved sexual behavior, still prove superior to Anglican Pigeons.

The lengthy poem is divided into three parts. "The First Part" runs to 572 lines, "The Second Part" to 722 lines, and "The Third Part" to 1,298 lines, with a format of rhyming couplets. The beginning lines introduce various animals and make clear their allegorical significance. That the poem focuses on religion and faith is made clear by 27 references to *grace* or variant terms, such as *mercy, kindness,* and *forgiveness,* where grace is superior to nature. Dryden describes "A milk white Hind, immortal and unchang'd," adding she is "unspotted, innocent within" as contrast to the spotted panther. Because she knows "no sin," she does not fear danger. He describes a history of her being hunted by "horns and hound" but offers a PARADOX in line 8, "And doom'd to death through fated not to die," at which point the reader understands she is not a typical deer. Dryden will focus on other animals as well, supplying information that alerts readers to their allegorical significance, with several representing different religious organizations or affiliations:

> The bloody *Bear,* and *Independent* beast,
> Unlick'd to form, in groans her hate express'd.
> Among the timorous kind the *Quaking Hare*

Profess'd neutrality but would not swear.
Next her the *Buffoon Ape,* as atheists use,
Mimic'd all sects and had his own to choose;
Still when the Lion look'd, his knees he bent
And pay'd at church a courtier's compliment.
    (1.35–42)

Additional references include the "Baptist Bore" (43), on which Dryden spends much description. He later includes a wolf and a fox, each representing heresy present in the Anglican Church. The wolf believes God's essence is man's will, not his wisdom, and the fox denies supernaturalism, a central premise to true faith. These heresies corrupt what Dryden views as an otherwise true church. Lines 62–149, which center on the fox's Socinianism, or denial of Christ's supernatural divine state, are the best known of the poem. The "wolfish race" (160) refers to Presbyterians, such as Shaftsbury, described as "Never was so deform'd a beast of Grace. / His ragged tail betwixt his legs he wears" (162–163) and he also "pricks up his predestinating ears" (166), referring to predestination, a major tenet of Presbyterianism. Dryden makes the point that when men turn from the Catholic faith, they deny God's greatest gifts, which served to distinguish man from animals as each was created:

And mercy mix'd with reason did impart,
One to his head, the other to his heart;
Reason to rule, but mercy to forgive;
The first is law, the last prerogative. (1.259–262)

While the lion, or the crown, holds the other animals at bay, the Panther, described from line 327, is something different. After the hind, she is "the noblest," the "fairest creature of the spotted kind." Dryden wants to differentiate clearly the unspotted, and therefore pure, Hind and the Panther, or Church of England. By the end of part 1 the Hind and the Panther begin a discussion.

In part 2 the two animals discuss Church authority and religious controversy. Of the three parts, the second contains the most theology. The controversy it examines includes the Anglicans' reluctance to relate to the new king and to his Catholic subjects; church tradition and especially the Rule of Faith, the Catholic Church as the only true church, and the Catholic tradition of embracing all who desire to enter. Dryden pauses along the way to praise James's tolerance, again comparing the monarch to a lion, who, "when his foe lies prostrate on the plain, / He sheaths his paws, uncurls his angry mane," and remains "pleas'd" with "bloodless honours" (2.269–271). He continues,

So JAMES, if great with less we may compare,
Arrests hs rolling thunderbolts in air,
And grants ungrareful friends a lenghten'd
    space
T'implore the remnants of long suff'ring grace.
    (2.273–276)

Dryden alludes to James again toward the section's conclusion, ending with the Hind and Panther still in conversation. For that reason, modern readers may find it uninteresting, but it contains excellent examples of Dryden's artistic passion.

The poem's third portion begins with the allusion to animal tales noted earlier and continues to focus on social and political influences on the religious climate during the second half of England's 17th century. It includes some skillful logic of Dryden's that through the Hind traps the Panther into admitting that the Catholic faith is the only true faith. The allegory continues through the use of birds, including martins, crows, and ravens, but most especially swallows. Dryden's source is John Ogilby's Aesop-style fable "The Parliament of the Birds," in which the swallow is the true, or Catholic, Church. As Miner notes, Dryden's argument proves complicated, as he counsels care of James, as the king has been advised rashly in the opinion of many Catholics. They hoped that James could deal fairly with the Anglicans. Dryden then caricatures the Anglicans, through the Panther character, as cruel, wishing death to the Catholics. However, the fact that the swallow survives a bitter winter in the Panther's tale is an admission by him that the Catholic Church will survive. Still the Hind reacts vigorously to the Panther's cruel suggestion of death to Catholics:

The patience of the Hind did almost fail,
For well she mark'd the malice of the tale,

Which ribald art their Church to Luther owes;
In malice it began, by malice grows;
He sow'd the Serpent's teeth, an iron-harvest
   rose.

Dryden's use of ALLITERATION and repetition supports momentum, while his brilliant imagery of the serpent's teeth as seeds birthing an iron-hard rose proves he deserves his reputation as his era's finest poet.

The Hind and the Panther proves crucial to reader understanding of Dryden's religious stance. Never a revolutionary, he always preached a middling philosophy in political dealings. While his dedication to the Catholic Church remains clear, so does his humanism in his desire that Anglicans should receive the respect English subjects deserve. The reign of the Catholic James II lasted a brief three years, after which Protestant rule returned to the throne through James's daughter, Mary, and her husband, William. James was forced into Continental exile, and Dryden remained true to the Catholic faith, even though he risked persecution for so doing. Perhaps his dedication put to rest rumors that his conversion to Catholicism had been merely a move of expedience.

BIBLIOGRAPHY

Johnson, Samuel. *Lives of the English Poets.* Vol. 1. New York: E. P. Dutton, 1958.
Miner, Earl, ed. *Selected Poetry and Prose of John Dryden.* New York: The Modern Library, 1985.

"HIS FAREWELL TO SACK" ROBERT HERRICK (1648)

"His Farewell to Sack" proved one of ROBERT HERRICK's most popular poems. Herrick's devotion to alcohol, particularly to "Sack," or wine, was legendary; he most often enjoyed the drink with his mentor, BEN JONSON. Jonson's literary circle enjoyed drink, discussion, and literature in various London taverns. That Herrick would give up an important part of that relationship, the alcohol that flowed so freely at such events, seemed tragic to his audience. He imbues his 54 lines of rhyming couplets in iambic pentatmeter with IRONY, as he addresses Sack in the manner of a best friend from whom he regretfully separates.

The speaker begins by making clear how strongly he feels regarding the impending end of his relationship with Sack: "Farewell thou Thing, time-past so known, so dear / To me, as blood to life and spirit:" Herrick stresses the urgency in this parting by using ENJAMBMENT, forcing the first line to flow rapidly into the second. As the Herrick biographer and scholar J. Max Patrick explains, the comparison of the relationship with Sack to that of blood to life and spirit carried a specific meaning. In the 17th century, blood, phlegm, black bile, and choler represented primary humors. Together they determined the human temperament. The heart contained pure blood, known as the *vital spirit,* which conducted heat, essential to life, to all body parts. When it reached the brain, the blood became the even more refined *animal spirit,* which, "like a messenger," flowed to the nerves, carrying important signals that linked mind and body. Use of these concepts in metaphor allowed Herrick to demonstrate his strong feelings regarding his drink. He adds more FIGURATIVE LANGUAGE (FIGURE OF SPEECH) in comparing his relationship to Sack with that of "friend, man, wife, / Male to the female, soul to body" as well as "The kisse of Virgins; First-fruits of the bed: / Soft speech, smooth touch, the lips, the Maiden-head," the sexual references helping the lines qualify as excellent recitation for a rowdy group enjoying a round at Herrick's expense.

The speaker declares Sack "the drink of Gods, and Angels! Wine / That scatter'st Spirit and Lust," noting it outshines summer. As do comets and other portents,

'Tis thou, above Nectar, O Divinest soule!
(Eternal in thyself) that canst control
That, which subverts whole nature, grief and
   care;
Vexation of the mind, and damn'd Despair.

Sack proves more magical and powerful than "Wisdome, Art, or Nature," in its mysticism rousing "sacred madness" and awakening "The frost-bound blood, and spirits." Even those frosty spirits could be made frantic by Sack as it flashed "through / The soule, like lightning." The hyperbole builds until the speaker references classical deities, including Apollo, and the three muses, as well as Horace and Anacreon, all relating to art and literature. The speaker gives credit for such creative forces to the influence of Sack, soaring into praise by labeling it "thou Thespian spring!" After additional lines of glorification, the speaker wonders why he continues to address the subject of his adoration when he knows he must leave it. He accuses its bewitching nature for his lingering and explains that

> Nature bids thee go, not I
> 'Tis her erroneous self has made a brain
> Uncapable of such a Soverainge,
> As is thy powerful self. (42–45)

The speaker eventually resigns himself to the fact that others will continue to indulge, drinking freely, while he must admire from afar. In the future his Muse must do without Sack's support, and he concludes, "what's done by me / Hereafter, shall smell of the Lamp, not thee."

Herrick's critics note that he wrote to be enjoyed, his whimsy intentional and his earthiness a crucial aspect of his style. When he balanced this poem with his later "The Welcome to Sack," his readers enjoyed it almost as much as his farewell. Although later generations lost patience with what some considered Herrick's insipid tendencies, the 20th and 21st centuries, with a penchant to embrace multiple approaches to art, have rediscovered much to appreciate in a poet who could wax rhapsodic about being in his cups.

BIBLIOGRAPHY

Patrick, J. Max. The Complete Poetry of Robert Herrick. New York: New York University Press, 1963.

"HIS PRAYER TO BEN JONSON" ROBERT HERRICK (1648)

ROBERT HERRICK's affection for the poet and playwright BEN JONSON is well known. He celebrated his mentor in a number of poems, including "An ODE FOR HIM," all meant to praise Jonson's talent and his willingness to associate with and cultivate younger poets. Herrick's debt to Jonson proved great, as the older man introduced Herrick to his TRIBE OF BEN, allowing Herrick to join their gatherings. In "His Prayer to Ben Jonson" Herrick establishes Jonson as a saint figure. Because individuals were encouraged to pray to saints for protection and intercession, that metaphor allowed Herrick to depict Jonson as not only a mentor, but also a type of divine inspiration. In three simple four-line stanzas composed of rhyming couplets, Herrick extends his use of FIGURATIVE LANGUAGE (FIGURE OF SPEECH) to great effect. The first stanza reads:

> When I a Verse shall make,
> Know I have prayed thee,
> For old Religions sake,
> Saint Ben to aid me.

The speaker emphasizes that poetry is not created in a vacuum, as poets require inspiration for their spiritual endeavor. Some critics propose that Religion, as Herrick uses it here, may equate to the sacred nature of an oath, which would allow the poet to repledge his loyalty to his departed mentor. The second stanza acts as a request as Herrick adopts the tone of a supplicant as he asks for Jonson's guidance in his writing:

> Make the way smooth for me,
> When I, thy Herrick,
> Honouring thee, on my knee
> Offer my Lyrick.

The speaker kneels, as befits one requesting a favor from a near-deity. The phrase thy Herrick allows the poet to remind readers and himself of his close relationship with Jonson. In the third and final stanza, Herrick references the lighting of candles, an important part of religious ritual designed to honor a departed soul, as well as an altar, an icon representing sacrifice by humans to God:

> Candles Ile give to thee,
> And a new Altar;
> And thou Saint Ben, shalt be
> Writ in my Psalter.

A psalter is a book containing the Psalms, or lyrics, from the Bible, used in worship. That Herrick's Psalter will include Ben Jonson extends the metaphor of worship and praise connected with religious ritual. Herrick sought to exalt Jonson through his personal art, the highest honor a poet could offer.

"HOLDFAST, THE" GEORGE HERBERT (1633)

In his SONNET "The Holdfast," GEORGE HERBERT summarizes the ideas regarding grace presented in poems that appear earlier in his collection, *The Temple,* including "The ALTAR." He also employs the methods of METAPHYSICAL POETS AND POETRY, suggesting contradiction reveals the truth. In addition, Herbert departs from the traditional Elizabethan sonnet technique of employing the final couplet as summation. In "The Holdfast," the concluding couplet represents an outside voice, convincing the poem's persona of his error.

The speaker begins, "I threatened to observe the strict decree / of my dear god with all my power & might." It is the first of several declarations of intent by the speaker. This one reflects on the Arminian belief, which countered Herbert's own Calvinistic leanings, that civil authority should be respected and served. Such declarations will be undercut by responses from an outside "one," as evidenced in the third line, "But I was told by one, it could not be." The speaker will be told repeatedly that none of his actions will result in his salvation. Specifically the counter to his first idea is "Yet I might trust God to be my light." The speaker accepts this idea, that trust will prove superior to observation of decree, responding, "Then I will trust, said I, in him alone." However, no sooner does he agree to what he sees as a countermand than he learns that also will not do, because trust "was also his: / We must confess that nothing is our own," where the possessive pronoun *his* refers to God. Predictably, when the speaker agrees to make that confession, "that he my succour is:" the rejoinder is "But to have nought is ours, not to confess / That we have nought." Herbert's use of caesura occurs in the middle of line 10, effectively stopping the reader with the thought that man has nothing and can claim or confess nothing. That line continues, "I stood amaz'd at this," with the forced pause emphasizing the phrase that precedes the comma. The speaker remains "Much troubled," but a friend explains the contradiction by stating another seeming contradiction:

That all things were more ours by being his.
What Adam had, and forfeited for all,
Christ keepeth now, who cannot fail or fall.

Herbert challenges the idea that one can earn grace through merit; the speaker cannot contribute to his own salvation, but instead must hold fast to Christ. Although the speaker makes a valiant attempt in his declarations of action at morality, he learns that his personal goodness does not matter. Even confession does not reflect obedience but rather acknowledges a lack of power and control. A force from outside the speaker, in this case a "friend," represents grace, which the speaker can neither generate nor earn.

BIBLIOGRAPHY

Malcolmson, Cristina. *George Herbert: A Literary Life.* New York: Palgrave Macmillan, 2004.

HOLY SONNETS JOHN DONNE (1617)

Although the precise year when JOHN DONNE wrote his *Holy Sonnets* remains unknown, historians make a "best guess" at the year 1617, feeling confident that they were composed after the death of Donne's wife, as some are written about that sad occasion. They help compose a group of verse known as Donne's "Divine Poems," the term *Divine* referencing a deity. One problem critics point out with any attempt to date the SONNETS is the assumption that Donne composed all 19 during one condensed period, as if he envisioned a sequence. Some support of that theory exists, as thoroughly discussed by Helen Gardner in her book on the topic. While some of the sonnets will be considered individually within this Companion, they merit discussion as a group.

Various manuscripts of Donne's poems exist, most copied from originals. All have specific names, generally based on their owners or the institution in which they reside. They are commonly placed in groups, with Group I containing five manuscripts and Group II containing four manuscripts. Another group of five manuscripts exists, but the individual poems do not appear to descend originally from the same collection, as do the other two. What unites them into a group is that the text in certain poems differs from that found in Group I. While certain differences also occur between Groups I and II, they are of an occasional nature; in the third group, the differences remain constant from poem to poem. In addition, Group III contains several poems not written by John Donne. Experts also note various types of "contamination" in the Group III entries, where changes were made to the text. The Divine Poems, including some Holy Sonnets, which appear in the third group, cannot safely be labeled part of the Donne tradition. Various "interpretations" by an unknown person of Donne's phrases have been inserted, several of which reflect a lack of understanding of what later critics believed to be Donne's meaning. Those changes may represent preparation for publication. One critical theory holds that the works in Group III represent early versions of poems that exist in a revised form in Groups I and II.

The sonnets were first published along with most of Donne's additional poetry in 1633. That edition was enlarged in 1635, and other editions appeared in 1639, 1649, 1650, 1654, and 1669. Of the 19 sonnets, 16 share easily recognized thematic elements, all proper for use in meditation. Meditation existed as a long tradition in religious exercise, separate from spoken prayer, which also offered a common approach for religious poetry. The sonnets' tendency toward hyperbole, or exaggeration, correctly reflects the highly emotional quality of meditation. Unlike the earlier poet WILLIAM ALABASTER, Donne avoids overdramatizing his topic, the spiritual life, by a focus on the difficulty natural man has in obtaining that life. He expresses feelings of incompetence to embrace his own desire for spirituality, establishing some emotional distance from the theme. His sonnets manage simultaneously to project a great anguish and a great desire, based on Donne's feeling of personal inadequacy. His voice is that of a real, live person with whom readers may identify.

Donne's tone of despair proves appealing, simply for its pure nature. He often asks questions, chooses simple words, many of single syllables but heavy with meaning, and often followed by terms with secondary stresses. An example may be found in the first lines of Divine Meditation 8 (1633):

Why are we by all creatures waited on?
Why do the prodigal elements supply
Life and food to me, being more pure than I,
Simple, and further from corruption?

He also proclaims, using *Ah* or *Oh,* sounds as in the second line of Divine Meditation 9 (1633), "Mark in my heart, O Soul, where thou dost dwell," and exclaims, as in the first line of Divine Meditation 11 (1633): "Wilt thou love God, as he thee!" The simplicity remains disarming and effective; any art within the sonnets lies in their fixed form. That dictated form forces both Donne and the reader to remain focused and contains his momentum, acting as a strict taskmaster, which echoes Donne's desire for just such a master in his spiritual life.

The final couplet, required by the form, could seem an afterthought, weakening the sonnet in the hands of a less skillful writer, such as Alabaster. That does not happen to Donne, who offers in all of the couplets ringing climactic statements, such as in Divine Meditation 2 (1633), which opens with the lines "Oh my black Soule! now thou art summoned / By sickness, deaths herald, and champion," and concludes with the four lines:

Oh make thy self with holy mourning black,
And red with bushing, as thou art with sin;
Or wash thee in Christs blood, which hath this
   might
That being red, it dyes red souls to white.

Most critics agree that Donne takes full advantage of the sonnet's 14 lines. He so thoroughly draws in the reader that he or she may not even notice the form familiar through Renaissance love poetry. Donne requires for his meditative purposes a form that allows tension to build, accommodates both intellect and emotion, one in which no one line ever appears more important than another.

As Gardner notes, Donne's religious poetry grew from "conflict between his will and temperament" in which he drew language from the Bible, hymns, and prayers. While the truths of his "love poetry are truths of the imagination, which freely transmutes personal experience," the religious poetry contains "truths of revelation," in which Donne's imagination is curtailed. Its intensity, contrasting with the passion of the love poetry, "is a moral intensity." The critic Paul Cefalu has argued that Donne, as did Calvin, stressed a cause/ effect link "between godly fears, as reverence for God, and sanctification." He believes that Donne's focus on deathbed repentance and terror in the face of eternal damnation may metaphorically represent the sonnets' speakers;' and, by extension, Donne's own, experience of conversion. However, other critics, including Gardner, argue that Donne had no one specific emotional moment of conversion. Rather, he developed his beliefs in a slow, steady manner over his lifetime.

BIBLIOGRAPHY

Cefalu, Paul. "Godly Fear, Sanctification, and Calvinist Theology in the Sermons and 'Holy Sonnets' of John Donne." *Studies in Philology* 100, no. 1 (winter 2003): 71–156.

Gardner, Helen, ed. *John Donne: The Divine Poems.* Oxford: Clarendon Press, 1969.

Smith, A. J., ed. *John Donne: Essays in Celebration.* London: Methuen, 1972.

Wilcox, Helen, Richard Todd, and Alasdair MacDonald, eds. *Sacred and Profane: Secular and Devotional Interplay in Early Modern British Literature.* Amsterdam: VU University Press, 1996.

HORATIAN ODE UPON CROMWELL'S RETURN FROM IRELAND, AN ANDREW MARVELL (1681)

ANDREW MARVELL wrote *An Horatian Ode upon Cromwell's Return from Ireland* between June and July 1650. He celebrates in rhyming couplets the fact that Oliver Cromwell had distinguished himself in military expeditions to both Ireland and Scotland, becoming commander in chief of parliamentary forces. Marvell begins by establishing a comparison of Cromwell to a scholarly youth who had to "forsake his Muses Dear" and "leave the books in dust," instead oiling "th'unused armour's rust." This proved Cromwell's fate, as described in the third verse when Cromwell uses war to help succeed in peace, as Marvell suggests a PARADOX:

> So restless Cromwell could not cease
> In the inglorious arts of peace,
>   But through adven'trous war
>   Urgèd his active star.

Cromwell, "like the three forked-lightning" that broke through the clouds, "Did through his own side / His fiery way divide." Cromwell echoes a tradition of comparison of great warriors to Jove, the god king who threw thunderbolts at the earth.

The poem circulated first in manuscript form, probably supporting Marvell's hopes for patronage from Cromwell. Marvell's political reversals of loyalty from Royalist to republican cause, a stand he reversed again during the later Restoration, caused some critics to term him an opportunist, others to see him merely as an individual sensitive to political climate. Marvell's conflict may have surfaced as the ode presents the history of the ensuing execution of Charles I, famously described with compassion and admiration:

> He nothing common did, or mean,
> Upon that memorable scene;
>   But with his keener eye
>   The axe's edge did try.
>
> Nor called the Gods with vulgar spite
> To vindicate his helpless right;
>   But bowed his comely head
>   Down, as upon a bed. (57–64)

Marvell continues describing the creation of the new republic under Cromwell and the Irish campaign. In addition lines 109–112 anticipated the invasion of Scotland, with *Caldonia,* the Roman name for northern Britain, commonly used in Marvell's time to refer to Scotland. He characterizes Cromwell as a hunter pursuing elusive game:

> Happy if in the tufted brake,
> The English hunter him mistake,
>   Nor lay his hounds in near
>   The Caledonian deer.

A "tufted brake" could indicate several bushes in a group, but a brake was also a barred cage and a trap or a snare, according to the *Oxford English Dictionary.* Either usage, or perhaps both, fit Marvell's lines.

Marvell's adoption of Horace's approach proved logical, as Horace, who at first defended his era's republicans, later had to accept Augustus Caesar as his ruler, celebrating in verse the peace that Caesar gained for Rome and its territories. Marvell employs the comparison to Caesar, noting of Cromwell, "And Caesar's head at last / Did through his laurels blast"

(23–24). He extends that metaphor when he adds about Cromwell in line 101, "A Caesar he ere long to Gaul."

Marvell also used as models additional Horatian odes that celebrated heroic feats. In one such ode Nero defeats Hannibal, who must eventually accept that defeat. Similarly Marvell's lines 77–80 read about the Irish, who "are ashamed / To see themselves in one year tamed,"

> They can affirm his praises best,
> And have, though overcome, confessed
>> How good he is, how just,
>> And fit for highest trust.

Later he extends that comparison, as he had the one to Caesar, when he writes that Cromwell was "To Italy an Hannibal" (102). Marvell probably also used the work of Lucan, considered a poet whose depiction of war was superior, as a model. According to the scholar Nigel Smith, Marvell's "recollection of Horace and Lucan serve to evoke Roman responses to the ambiguities of power and right."

Greatly admired for its style, Marvell's ode was regarded differently through the following centuries. The 19th century viewed Marvell as a patriot and omitted the ode's sympathetic characterization of Charles I, as the French Revolution spurred admiration for Cromwell's seeming support of the overthrow of the Crown. Lines 81–88 provide evidence supporting the view of Marvell as a man of republican, sympathies, as he employs the FIGURATIVE LANGUAGE (FIGURE OF SPEECH) of synecdoche to characterize Cromwell's sacrifice of personal glory to the good of the common man:

> Nor yet grown stiffer with command,
> But still in the Republic's hand:
>> How fit he is to sway
>> That can so well obey.

> He to the Common's feet presents
> A kingdom, for his first year's rents.
>> And, what he may, forbears
>> His fame to make it theirs.

The ode appeared in Marvell's posthumous *Miscellaneous Poems* (1681) but would be omitted from later editions in which the political nature of the work was considered inappropriate. Marvell's lyrics grew in popularity, and for a time his ode was characterized also as especially lyrical, although critics puzzled over its contradictory political messages. Later in the 20th century, readers and students focused on the lyrics to the exclusion of Marvell's other works, including this ode.

BIBLIOGRAPHY

Greene, Thomas M. "The Balance of Power in Marvell's 'Horatian Ode.'" *English Literary History* 60 (1993): 379–396.

Harkins, Matthew. "'Forward Youth'" and Marvell's 'An Horatian Ode.'" *Criticism* 45, no. 3 (summer 2003): 343–359.

Hayes, Thomas H. "The Dialectic of History in Marvell's *Horatian Ode.*" *Clio* 1 (October 1971): 26–36.

Moore, Peter R. "The Irony of Marvell's 'Horatian Ode.'" *English Studies* 84, no. 1 (February 2003): 33–56.

Norbrook, David. "Marvell's 'Horatian Ode' and the Politics of Genre." In *Literature and the English Civil War,* edited by Thomas Healy and Jonathan Sawday, 147–169. Cambridge: Cambridge University Press, 1990.

Richards, Judith. "Literary Criticism and the Historian: Towards Reconstructing Marvell's Meaning in 'An Horatian Ode.'" *Literature and History* 7 (1981): 25–47.

Smith, Nigel, ed. *The Poems of Andrew Marvell.* New York: Pearson/Longman, 2003.

Syfret, R. H. "Marvell's 'Horatian Ode.'" *Review of English Studies* 12 (1961): 160–172.

Wortham, Christopher. "Marvell's Cromwell Poems: An Accidental Triptych." In *The Political Identity of Andrew Marvell,* edited by Conal Condren and A. D. Cousins, 16–52. Aldershot, England: Scolar Press, Gower, 1990.

"HOW SLEEP THE BRAVE" WILLIAM COLLINS (1746)

WILLIAM COLLINS selects British soldiers killed in battle as a subject for his "How Sleep the Brave." He honors them in two simple verses composed of six lines of rhyming couplets, employing no surprises in either form or fashion. The speaker begins, "How sleep the brave who sink to rest / By all their country's wishes blest!" reminding his audience that everyone owes a great debt to the dead soldiers' courage. Collins employs sleep as the traditional symbolic reference to death, suggesting a peaceful afterlife for the soldiers. However, the verb *sink* guarantees the tone will not be altogether positive, as the sleep is not the choice of the dead. He employs FIGURATIVE LANGUAGE personifying spring as having "dewy fingers cold," rather than suggesting the traditionally sunny season imbuing warmth. However, the positive imagery of dew connotes the morning, a time of rebirth, cleansing, and new beginnings and offering hope that the dead will find a new life elsewhere. He also notes that when Spring returns

> . . . to deck their hallowed mold,
> She there shall dress a sweeter sod
> Than Fancy's feet have ever trod.

The speaker references spring's covering the mold, or grave, with its usual blessing of flowers, which will mature in earth made sweeter than any other through the great sacrifice of the dead beneath the ground. He also seems to reflect on his own occupation as a writer dependent upon imagination, or "Fancy." In this case, even the finest imagination could not conjure a greater gift to its audience than these men have made to their fellow humans.

In the second and final verse the nature references continue, as "fairy hands" ring the death knell and "By forms unseen their dirge is sung"; one of those forms is Honor, which "comes, a pilgrim gray / To bless the turf that wraps their clay." Thus these graves will be covered by more than spring flowers; they will be attended by the Honor that the soldiers earned through their sacrifice. Honor's characterization as a pilgrim suggests that a special journey has been undertaken with a specific goal in mind. Its dress in "gray" becomes a more hopeful image than had it worn traditional black mourning garb. Finally "Freedom shall awhile repair, / To dwell a weeping hermit there!" Collins makes clear that before the living may enjoy the liberty purchased by these soldiers' deaths, they must reflect upon those bodies that proved the currency for the purchase of that liberty, offering tears for their loss.

"HOW SOON HATH TIME" (SONNET VII) JOHN MILTON (1632) JOHN MILTON suppos-

edly wrote his Sonnet VII, "How Soon Hath Time," after receiving a letter from a friend who took him to task for continuing his education instead of becoming a productive member of society. Milton was not the first poet to be accused of excessive affection for learning. As scholars note, Edmund Spenser served as a model, as did Sir Philip Sidney, both of whom had to defend themselves, as Milton did, against the charge. His SONNET reflects the Elizabethan form.

Milton opens using FIGURATIVE LANGUAGE (FIGURE OF SPEECH) to refer to Time as "the subtle thief of my youth." The second line notes Milton's age, as he continues his accusation, writing of Time, "Stol'n on his wing my three and twentieth year!" It extends the metaphor of time as a thief, with the reference to the wing suggesting Time's rapid flight. He continues his allusion into the third line, writing, "My hasting days fly on with full career," a sly nod to the fact that he has no career, other than watching his days pass. Suggesting his "spring" is simply a late one, he admits that it shows "no bud or blossom." After introducing the situation of his dwindling youth, the speaker ponders on his "semblance," which "might deceive the truth," which is that he nears maturity and "manhood." He also wonders whether he might possess an "inward ripeness" less visible to the exterior gaze, resembling that of "some more timely-happy spirits," the spirit allusion one that critics believe to be to Edmund Spenser. However, whether "less or more, or soon or slow," his future must be measured against his fate, "toward which Time leads me." He closes with the serious hope that that fate be "the will of Heav'n," and that he will possess the "grace to use it" as it should be, "As ever in my great task-Master's eye." A highly religious man, Milton uses a light tone that does not diminish his serious musing about his purpose on earth and his desire to serve God.

HUDIBRAS SAMUEL BUTLER (1662, 1663, 1678) Indisputably the most important work by SAMUEL BUTLER, the mock-epic satire *Hudibras* appeared in three parts. An attack against Puritans, especially Butler's former employer and a colonel in the Puritan War, Sir Samuel Luke, it nevertheless focused on the masses as rabble, and any leader as vain and equally ignorant to the common man. He did, however, charge

the dissent movement on six counts according to the scholar Edward Ames Richards: "hypocrisy, greed, lust, intellectual narrowness, low social status, and foolish mysticism." Richards is quick to explain that Butler did not write as "a bigoted Anglican or a blind royalist," as his "intellectual designs" proved much broader than those of the mere pamphleteer. "Isolated in his own cold and scornful mind," Butler lacked the capacity for identity with "current concerns," a fact Richards associates with his "remote tempers." Believing in neither spirituality nor science/logic as a source of truth, Butler did believe that truth existed and that it could be discovered through an application of human intelligence and a close observation of nature. The work proved so successful that the first part merited nine editions in the year it appeared, at least two of those pirated.

Later scholars described the poem as too lengthy, discursive to an extreme, and challenging to readers of later generations. While 21st-century aficionados and students generally experience *Hudibras* in excerpts, some critics adamantly declare it can be understood only when read in its entirety. Butler probably gathered much material during his employment with Sir Luke, who became the model for the character Hudibras. Influences may have included the *Satire Ménippée,* an anonymous French pamphlet that first circulated in Paris in the 1590s. A cunning political satire, it attacked leaders of the Catholic League at the 1593 States General and supposedly helped gain public support for Henry IV. Butler also looked to works featuring companions such as Don Quixote and Sancho Panza in Miguel Cervantes's 1605 satire *Don Quixote* in fashioning his Hudibras and Ralpho. Capturing perfectly the tone of malice suitable to such a satire, Butler spent little effort in developing any high drama in the dialogue/diatribes of his subjects. He understood the importance of avoiding humanization of his characters, who remained monstrous in their perfidy and arrogance, never achieving any three-dimensional development, both man and master too vile to imagine within a real world. Its wit has supported its continued reading in a century that rates much of Butler's style tedious and even trivial. Its vocabulary and self-aware use of rhythm continue to recommend the poem, as do

Butler's skillful incorporation of colloquialisms, philosophies, and detailed sense of place.

Butler alerts readers from part I, Canto I that his targets include easily swayed public opinion, as he suggests people will take up a cause without realizing its import or even its origin. The speaker hearkens back to the time when civil arguments began, emphasizing that men often "fell out they knew not why; / When hard words, jealousies and fears / Set folks together by the ears," explaining they fought as if "mad or drunk, / For dame religion, as for punk." Into the middle of such chaos, based on religious disagreement sounded from the pulpit and by "drum ecclesiastic," a leader appeared: "Then did Sir Knight abandon dwelling, / And out he rode a-colonelling," with Butler creating a verb from the noun *colonel* to indicate how seriously Sir Knight took his rank. The ensuing description does not prove complimentary, as readers learn that authors remain divided over "Whether he were more wise or stout," making clear that "The diff'rence was so small, his brain / Outweigh'd his rage but half a grain." This unfortunate circumstance "made some take him for a tool / That knaves do work with, call'd a fool." The Knight's attempts to speak Greek resembled "pigs squeak," his Latin the noise made by blackbirds. He was so skilled in analysis that "He could distinguish, and divide / A hair 'twixt south and south-west side," emphasizing the trivialities some confuse for wisdom. In hundreds of lines, Butler adds descriptions of the Knight's talents including that

> For he a rope of sand could twist
> As tough as learned Sorbonist;
> And weave fine cobwebs, fit for skull
> That's empty when the moon is full.

He operates in the group that

> Call fire and sword and desolation
> A godly, thorough Reformation,
> Which always must be going on,
> And still be doing, never done.

The IRONY in that last line consists partly in its implication that the church never achieves reform, because of the pleasure men take in dramatic gestures that result in little change. The members of this group

> Compound for sins they are inclined to,
> By damning those they have no mind to. . .
> All piety consists therein
> In them, in other men all sin.

Butler concocts skillful RHYME to label the pro-Cromwell force hypocritical.

In part II Butler demonstrates admirable style by adopting a lively PARADOX in his description titled "Night," when he first compares the sun's setting to the lowering of a lady's eyes, then references the moon, a traditional symbol of woman, writing,

> The moon pulled off her veil of light
> That hides her face by day from sight
> (Mysterious veil, of brightness made
> That's both her luster and her shade!).

By referencing the duplicity of woman in proposing the veil as something that both reveals and hides, Butler emphasizes dishonesty as a theme. He continues to prove his satiric prowess with topics other than the Knight and his ilk in a parody of the classics. As many ancient writers had, the speaker greets the dawn, saying, "The sun had long since in the lap / Of Thetis taken out his nap," alluding to the goddess who gave birth, with a human, to the great Greek warrior Achilles. However, Butler immediately undercuts any signs of serious design when he uses FIGURATIVE LANGUAGE in a decidedly undesirable metaphor, writing, "And, like a lobster boiled, the morn / From black to red began to turn." He inverts the normal symbolism of morning as new life by alluding to death, both in the boiling alive of the lobster and the use of red, a traditional symbol for blood. In addition, the night is described as black, a traditional symbol of death. In part III Butler reveals an unflattering view of wedlock in "Marriage," describing the "matrimonial tie"

> That binds the female and the male,
> Where the one is but the other's bail.
> Like Roman jailers, when they slept
> Chained to the prisoners they kept.

BIBLIOGRAPHY

Jack, Ian. "Low Satire: *Hudibras.*" In *Augustan Satire: Intention and Idiom in English Poetry: 1600–1750.* Oxford: Clarendon Press, 1952.

Parker, Blanford. *The Triumph of Augustan Poetics: English Literary Culture from Butler to Johnson.* New York: Cambridge University Press, 1998.

Richards, Edward Ames. *Hudibras in the Burlesque Tradition.* New York: Octagon Books, 1972.

"HUNTING OF THE HARE, THE" MARGARET CAVENDISH, DUCHESS OF NEWCASTLE (1653)

MARGARET CAVENDISH, duchess of Newcastle, gained a reputation based on the writing of often fantastic poetry filled with unpleasant metaphors, including the comparison of body parts to sewers and pipes in a city. However, she varies from her more common presentation of pseudoscientific and philosophical musing in her "The Hunting of the Hare" to consider the sad plight of a rabbit named Wat. She presents a narrative poem that describes Wat hiding by day "Betwixt two ridges of ploughed land." She describes his nose resting on his forefeet, as he glares "obliquely" with "great grey eyes," working to keep warm by turning himself into the wind to prevent the ruffling of his fur. Although described as "wise" in the ways of nature, Wat cannot compete with man and by the 14th line has been discovered "By huntsmen with their dogs who came that way." Fate brought death to Wat in the form of sport of which Cavendish apparently does not approve. She includes no excitement in her tone, rather renders a somewhat objective view of Wat's eventual destruction. The fact that it is eventual, following a lengthy terrifying pursuit, becomes a pivotal part of the story. Instinct spurs Wat to use his natural talents and run, but the dogs also exercise their instincts and talents to give chase, following his scent.

By the second stanza, Cavendish introduces a little more emotion, using FIGURATIVE LANGUAGE to personify Wat, who hides "underneath a broken bough," where "every leaf what with the wind did shake / Did bring such terror, made his heart to ache." He eventually runs again, unable to remain in hiding, and traces a wandering path in hopes of slowing the hounds that must search for his scent. Wat grows weary, and the "snuffling" hounds find his track. Cavendish includes an interesting catalog of the various types of dogs who hunt in the pack. They include "the great slow hounds," whose voices are in the bass range; "the swift fleet hounds, as tenors next in place;" and "the little beagles," who add their treble voices to the mix. She thus compares the pack to a type of choir, although this group is bent on death and destruction. Finally Cavendish inserts what appears to be a note of judgment against the hunters, writing, "The horns kept time, the hunters shout for joy / and valiant seem, poor Wat for to destroy." That the hunters should spur their horses through water and over obstacles, unafraid, "to endanger life and limbs, so fast will ride, / Only to see how patiently Wat died" devalues their efforts. As the dogs mercilessly set "their sharp teeth" into Wat's body, he tumbles and with "weeping eyes, / Gives up his ghost, and thus poor Wat dies."

As a member of aristocracy and as wife to a master horseman, Cavendish would probably have witnessed such hunting scenes firsthand. Her sympathy unmistakably lies with the hare, while she expresses disdain for the hunters. She even seems to admire the dogs, who are merely instruments put to use for human entertainment. Her poem departs from a simple country tableau to become instead a proanimal statement. Never one to be without an opinion, Cavendish makes clear her attitude toward such activity and its misnomer as sport.

HYMN ON THE SEASONS, A James Thomson (1726–1730)

JAMES THOMSON produced an extremely popular work in his lengthy poem "The Seasons," sometimes referred to as "A Hymn on the Seasons." He included several themes, all of which excited the imagination of his readers. As the Thomson biographer and critic Mary Jane W. Scott writes, *The Seasons* has many dimensions, "religious, philosophical, sociopolitical, neoclassical," all of which represent Thomson's "Scottishness." He considers man's place in nature, nature as a conduit for knowledge of God, country life as superior to city life, the idea of harmony between recent scientific claims by Newton and religious ideas, and the poet's duty to transmit God's word to readers, among other themes. However, support of religion remains Thomson's primary motivation in writing this poem. Critics claim that "The Seasons" served as a challenge to the artifice found in poetry by ALEXANDER POPE, among others of the Augustan age; it would influence THOMAS GRAY and WILLIAM COWPER, both forerunners of 19th-century romanticism. Thomson first published the poem over four years, "Winter" in 1726, "Summer" and "Spring" in each of the following two years, and "Autumn" in a collected edition published in 1730. However, the poem remained a living, breathing creation for Thomson, who would spend 16 years in continuous revision.

Known for his descriptive talent, Thomson incorporates detail about nature to support his claims that religion should prove a significant focus for man, and that man's place in nature is extremely important. He supports his claims with personal observation, as well as with biblical allusion and reference. The Psalms especially influence his praise style, while the Latin writer VIRGIL, the official poet of ancient Rome, informed his focus on geography, or place. In an example of that praise early in "Summer," Thomson writes,

> Welcome, ye shades! Ye bowery thickets, hail!
> Ye lofty pines! ye venerable oaks!
> Ye ashes wild, resounding o'er the steep!
> Delicious in your shelter to the soul.

Thomson presents the time spent by Adam and Eve in the Garden of Eden as a golden age, incorporating the classicism that informed his admiration of ancient Rome as one of man's greatest achievements. While doing so, he emphasizes nature's place as a backdrop for all of man's best efforts. His esteem for Rome and its leaders' abilities to unify many separate cultures into an empire inspired Thomson to imagine a united Britain, in real life as well as in references to unity included in "The Seasons." He calls to mind classical times in "Spring" when he writes that even those who "live / In luxury and ease, in pomp and pride" should keep in mind the importance to civilization of toil on the land. The speaker reminds readers, "Such themes as these the rural Maro sung / To wide-imperial Rome," whose "elegance and taste" had been "by Greece refined." Thomson recalls ancient verse in his format as he invites his audience to compare themselves to such civilizations which found greatness in their turning of the earth:

In ancient times the sacred plough employ'd
The Kings, and awful fathers of mankind:
And some, with whom compared your
    Insect-tribes
Are but the beings of a summer day.
Have held the scale of empire, ruled the Storm
Of mighty war; then, with victorious hand,
Disdaining little delicacies, seized
The Plough, and, greatly independent lived,
Scorned all the vile stores corruption can
    bestow. (58–66)

Later in "Summer" Thomson emphasizes the connection of his own culture to the land in a strong statement of nationalism. Although the farms yield "A simple scene," because of them Britannia observes a rise of "solid grandeur," allowing her to command "The exalted stores of every brighter clime," all due to her reaping of the sun's treasures. Because of that sacred land the country has become a leader in the world, building a mighty navy that already has allowed control of France and has affected the entire world:

Hence, fervent all with culture, toil, and arts,
Wide glows her land: her dreadful thunder
    hence
Rides o'er the waves sublime, and now, even
    now,
Impending hangs o'er Gallia's humbled coast;
Hence rules the circling deep, and awes the
    world. (427–431)

Continuing with his theme of the importance of nature and an understanding of its seasons to the development of a superior culture and philosophy, Thomson uses the "Winter" section to reflect on classic thought. He references Socrates, Solon, Lycurgus, Aristides, Cimon, leading up to a consideration of the "heroes," who include "Numa," "the Light of Rome." He expands consideration of those who contributed to the greatness of Rome, naming Servius, Camillus, Fabricius, Scipio, Tully, and others. Thomson con-

cludes with a reference to Brutus, noting that history and literature must give such heroes their due, "but who can count the stars of heaven / Who sing their influence on this lower world?" (528–529). The poet requests that such stars continue to visit his dreams, so he may pay tribute to their accomplishments. Winter, or death, may remove them from the earth, but others may study their lives in hopes of improving their own.

As Thomson writes of nature, he constantly makes the point that it yields both blessings and curses. He believed that while Eden represented man in perfect harmony with nature, man's fall from grace through sin represented a disturbance of nature, leading to his expulsion from the garden. Among the images of death and destruction in "Winter" he includes lines that offer hope to man. While winter challenges man, it also

Refines our spirits through the new-strung
    nerves
In swifter sallies darting to the brain
Where sits the soul, intense, collected, cool,
Bright as the skies, and as the season keen.
    (700–703)

As always Thomson sought to praise God, but also to seek God's truth through nature and his own art. He viewed his work as crucial to promoting man's understanding of God, holding that the poet served as an arbitrator, translating nature, much as one would a book's message, for his readers. Scott points to lines 192–196 in "Summer" as an example:

To me be Nature's Volume broad-display'd;
And to peruse its all-instructing Page,
Or, haply catching Inspiration thence,
Some easy Passage, raptur'd, to translate,
My sole Delight.

Also in "Summer" Thomson focuses on the sun as a life-giving force, but in addition as a threat to man through its powerful heat. He divides "Summer" into groupings of lines centered on the sun's description: "Sun-rising," "Hymn to the Sun," "Noonday," and "Sunset." The first portion focuses strongly on the order the sun's rising gives to the earth, as the speaker celebrates its arrival:

"But yonder comes the powerful king of day / rejoicing in the East" (81–82). He establishes the sun as a ruler, a metaphor he will use to reflect nature's majesty and connection to God throughout this season's section. However, in "Hymn to the Sun" he seems to focus on scientific, rather than religious, theory regarding the Sun's force and effect on Earth, drawing from Newton's *Principia* and his *Optics*. In reality Thomson's lines suggest that the cyclical order imposed by the sun results in a spiritual harmony, thus offering a balance of scientific theory and religious thought. In "Noonday" one most clearly sees the possible threat of the sun to earth, suggesting that God's creation may prove a blessing or a scourge to man, depending upon man's reception of it:

> 'Tis raging noon; and vertical the sun
> Darts on the head direct his forceful rays.
> O'er heaven and earth, far as the ranging eye
> Can sweep, a dazzling deluge reigns; and all
> From pole to pole is undistiguish'd blaze.
>   (432–436)

The personification of the sun suggests a mythical connection, supporting the claim of some critics that Thomson incorporates the topic of deism. In "Sunset" the imagery again seems to support that claim, when Thomson ignores science to praise the sun in the colorful sky, as the clouds "in all their pomp attend his setting throne" (1622). Critics counter the claim of deism, by pointing out the fact that Thomson honors only one God during most of the poem. God's existence and interaction with man remain one aspect of Thomson's poem that does not change through its many stanzas, although Thomson's view of God's basic nature undergoes some transition. Because the poem took several years to complete, the reader can observe that transition. For instance in "Spring" beginning at line 1727, Thomson depicts God in the Old Testament manner, fully capable of showing his wrath and inflicting violent judgment on man. However, in later lines, he invokes a happier vision of a smiling God, one more benevolent, as in the New Testament characterization.

Thomson regarded God as active in man's world, rather than as a deity who merely observed man's fate,

remaining removed from human activity, the classic watchmaker who winds the mechanism and then lets it run. He continuously emphasizes the revelation of God through nature, a theme common to most of his poetry. In "Winter" he writes:

> Then is the Time,
> For those, whom Wisdom, and whom Nature charm,
> To steal themselves from the degenerate Croud,
> And soar above this little Scene of Things:
> To tread low-thoughted Vice beneath their Feet:
> To lay their Passions in a gentle Calm,
> And woo lone Quiet, in her silent Walks.
>   (33–39)

Clearly an escape into nature allows humans to escape sin, evident in the phrases *degenerate Croud* and *low-thoughted Vice*. Traditionally a physical move to a higher position, as indicated in the phrase *And soar above*, symbolizes a moral or spiritual ascent to a higher plane of recognition. However, nature's face changes, and man must learn to survive. Nature's place is to teach man, as seen when the wayfarer fights his way through a storm seeking shelter, crying out,

> Father of Light, and Life! Thou Good Supreme!
> O! teach me what is Good! teach me thy self!
> Save me from Folly, Vanity and Vice,
> From every low Pursuit! and feed my Soul,
> With Knowledge, conscious Peace, and Vertue pure,
> Sacred, substantial, never-fading Bliss!
>   (217–222)

An additional crucial theme throughout "The Seasons" is whether the primitive, or rural, life is superior to that of the more cultured, or city, life. Because many British readers viewed the Scottish life, Thomson's background, as primitive, he took a self-conscious aspect to his approach. He remains ambivalent as to superiority, not adopting a black or white, bad or good, approach to either lifestyle. However, he does imply that country living proves more moral, or perhaps innocent, than city life. Thomson remains honest about the challenges of primitivism, including examples of the ways in which living things suffer from extreme weather. One example drawn from his own experience often referred to by critics is the description of the shepherd found dead in the snow in "Winter." Another is the evil that results in "Summer" from man's passion, which leads to violence. Cities also contained violence and vices not found in the wilds. Close living presented an opportunity for humans to hurt one another, the result of human nature's tendency toward greed and selfishness.

Virgil's influence caused Thomson to see both types of living as having advantages and disadvantages. Thomson himself had moved from small town life, to Edinburgh, then to London, a series of moves that he believed represented progress. His practice of Calvinism held that man should progress throughout his lifetime, mainly through God's influence. While a man could not earn a place in heaven, he could live a good and productive life while on earth. Such a progressive view he tempered in "The Seasons" with his attitude toward Scotland, an attitude at times conflicted. While he viewed Scotland's union with England as progress, he also remained concerned that his native country retain its uniqueness. With a strong nationalistic approach he praises the Scots' varying contributions to Europe, including their efforts at making war and peace and in forming a cultured society. In "Autumn" he issues a call for stronger leadership in Scotland, beginning with line 910:

> Oh is there not some Patriot, in whose Power
> That best, that godlike Luxury is plac'd,
> Of blessing Thousands, Thousands yet unborn,
> Thro' later Posterity?

As noted by Scott, "Thomson's sociopolitical vision in *The Seasons* embraced human rights, individual and national liberty, nostalgic progressivism, involvement in Scottish affairs, and positive patriotism for both Scotland and Great Britain." A lengthy and carefully planned epic poem that thoughtfully considers a multitude of topics, only a few of which have been touched on in this entry, *The Seasons* remains a popular work for critical consideration.

BIBLIOGRAPHY

Chalker, John. "Thomson's *Seasons* and Virgil's Georgics: The Problem of Primitivism and Progress." *Studia Neophilologica* 35 (1963): 41–56.

Corder, Jim W. "A New Nature in Revisions of *The Seasons*." *Notes and Queries,* December 1966, 461–464.

Grant, Douglas. *James Thomson: Poet of the Seasons.* London: Cresset Press, 1951.

Hayes, Lindsay. "James Thomson's *The Seasons*: Summer." *Studies in Poetry* (October 2004). Available online. URL: http://ocw.mit.edu/NR/rdonlyres/Literature/21L-704Fall-2004/A56F7BAC-4767–41A 7–99C5–86EADC6FFD0C/0/thomson_summer.pdf. Downloaded on August 8, 2006.

Kinsley, Zoe. "Landscapes 'Dynamically in Motion': Revisiting Issues of Structure and Agency in Thomson's *The Seasons*." *Papers on Language & Literature* 41, no. 1 (winter 2005): 3.

Lancashire, Ian. "The Seasons: Winter, Excerpts." University of Toronto Web Development Group. Available online. URL: http://rpo.library.utoronto.ca/poem/2211.html. Downloaded on August 8, 2006.

Scott, Mary Jane W. *James Thomson, Anglo-Scot.* Athens: University of Georgia Press, 1988.

Stormer, Phillip Ronald. "Holding 'High Converse with the Mighty Dead': Morality and Politics in James Thomson's 'Winter.'" *English Language Notes* 29, no. 3 (March 1992): 27–40.

Tomlinson, Janis A. "Landscape into Allegory: J. M. W. Turner's 'Frosty Morning' and James Thomson's 'The Seasons.'" *Studies in Romanticism* 29, no. 2 (summer 1990): 181–196.

"HYMN TO GOD MY GOD, IN MY SICKNESS" John Donne (1635) While its year of publication may be correctly dated to 1635, the year in which John Donne wrote the hymn titled "Hymn to God My God, in My Sickness" remains under question. This is true of many of his poems, as most were published posthumously, but this work more than others seems to have sparked the imagination of critics. One may consult the Donne scholar Helen Gardner's seminal discussion for a fascinating account of the dispute. While some critics believe that Donne wrote the poem while dying, others look to a note from a well-known witness, Sir Julius Caesar, for a definite dating to 1623. Caesar wrote on the back of a copy of the poem, "D. Dun Dene of Pauls / his verses in his greate / siknes. / in Decemb. 1623."

Donne's six-stanza poem, each stanza composed of five iambic pentameter lines, proves quite traditional in its references. Replete with the FIGURATIVE LANGUAGE (FIGURE OF SPEECH) of metaphor, the verses project the humility and acceptance of one on the verge of death. The first metaphor extends from line 1 through line 5, as the speaker notes,

> Since I am coming to that holy room
> Where, with thy choir of saints for evermore,
> I shall be made thy music; as I come
> I tune the instrument here at the door,
> And what I must do then, think now before.

To represent heaven with musical allusions suggests the music enjoyed in church services, as well as that written of in the Bible, both from instruments and voices. The speaker will join a "choir" of "saints," with *saints* meaning true believers. The transformation the spirit shall undergo is here depicted as a conversion into song. That conversion connotes a transition into joy and reverence, each often serving as the inspiration for songs, particularly those of praise. When the speaker refers to tuning "the instrument," he means he should try to prepare himself before entering the "door," or entrance to heaven. The final line of the first stanza contains language of balance, with the verb *do* balancing *think,* and the adverb *then* balancing *before.*

The speaker next compares his doctors to "cosmographers" and himself to their "map" on which will be distinguished a "southwest discovery," a metaphor for the Strait of Magellan, according to most critics. They support their theory with Donne's later references to various nautical locations and straits. Others feel the reference is not to a known geographical point, but rather to some spiritual point in the body. The fourth line concludes with ENJAMBMENT, or lack of punctuation. It moves the reader directly into that stanza's final statement, *"Per fretum febris"* (literally through the strait of fever) "by these straits to die." In adopting nautical references, Donne suggests that death represents a journey into a place of mystery, but for which Christians need no physical map, as they will not chart the journey; Christ has done that for them through his self-sacrifice.

The third stanza begins with Donne's converting the noun *joy* to a verb as his speaker states, "I joy, that in these straits, I see my West." The sun sets in the west, and the sun setting served as a traditional symbol for the end of life. Donne continues his use of metaphysical CONCEIT in the conception of his body as a map. His speaker proclaims that on "flat maps (and I am one)" the opposite directions of east and west become one, a physical impossibility in man's universe. He concludes, "So death doth touch the resurrection," suggesting that while humans view death and life as opposites, to the Christian, death and the rising from the dead to embrace everlasting spiritual life become one concept.

The speaker next questions his reader as to which location, "the Pacific Sea," "The Eastern riches," "Jerusalem," "Anyan" (the Bering Strait), "Magellan," or "Gibraltar," represents his "home." The reference to existing geographical points allows Donne to express the anxiety felt by those who seek to know heaven's exact location. He concludes his fourth stanza comforting readers that "All straits, and none but straits, are ways to them / Whether where Japhet dwelt, or Cham, or Shem." He refers to the sons of the biblical Noah, who all settled different parts of the world after the great flood. This informs his audience that heaven's exact location is unimportant. More important is the "way" into heaven, the strait allowing passage, which is man's faith.

The sixth verse references additional locations, "Paradise" and "Calvary," where Paradise represents the first man, Adam, and Calvary represents Christ. This allows Donne to continue his expression of the idea of unity, as the speaker describes "both Adams met in me." As the first Adam's "sweat" covered the speaker's face, the "last Adam's blood," the blood of Christ, "my soul embrace." He clearly differentiates between man and God, even though Christ inhabited a human body to dwell on the earth for 33 years. God punished Adam and Eve for the original sin of eating from the forbidden Tree of Knowledge by evicting them from the garden to support themselves through their own sweat. Christ's blood, however, will cleanse that sin.

Donne concludes with the first line of the final stanza again referencing Christ's blood, this time through the use of the color purple as a metaphor.

Purple as the royal color of kings and rulers had long been associated with Christ. When Donne writes, "So, in his purple wrapped, receive me, Lord," he takes the reader back to the blood referenced in the former verse, creating a unity of purpose for the two stanzas. The line "By these his thorns give me his other crown" recalls the description of Christ's crucifixion, during which he wore a piercing circle of thorns on his head, having been labeled "The King of the Jews" by his persecutors. The title proved an epithet at the time but was later converted by the faithful into a positive image, allowing Donne to extend the conceit of a royal authority who wears the "other crown." Donne concludes with a personal reference to his position as dean of St. Paul's, adopting the traditional sermon administered by a preacher to a congregation as another extended metaphor:

And, as to others' souls I preached thy word,
Be this my text, my sermon to mine own;
Therefore that he may raise the Lord throws
    down.

Donne notes that where he has been the preacher delivering the text in the past, he must adopt as his own "text" or personal "sermon" to his soul the ideas contained in his poem. His final line depends on its format for strong effect. He omits the expected punctuation of a comma after the word *raise*. This allows emphasis on the idea that in order to raise (a human being), the Lord first "throws down" that human. In other words, humans must first be tried and ultimately humbled through death in order to arise to the glory God promises them. Donne again adds balance to a line by dealing in opposites.

BIBLIOGRAPHY

Gardner, Helen, ed. *John Donne: The Divine Poems.* New York: Oxford University Press, 1969.

"HYMN TO GOD THE FATHER, A" JOHN DONNE (1633)

Scholars of the works of JOHN DONNE continue the search for various elements in his poetry to aid in the dating of their creation and even in the ways to refer to the poems. As Donne did not title his own poems, most titles derive from their first lines.

However, "A Hymn to God the Father" gained its title from its subject matter. Its similarity to other hymns, such as "Hymn to Christ," seems to challenge the affording of a title, with its opening stanza asking forgiveness making it appropriate as a hymn to God or Christ. A close reading of the poem's three six-line stanzas, with a traditional METER of iambic pentameter, reveals why critics have concluded that the hymn is appropriately a prayer to God the Father.

As the speaker asks forgiveness, he refers to the theory of original sin, committed first by Adam in the Garden of Eden, dooming all men to repeat that commission: "Wilt thou forgive that sin where I begun, / Which is my sin, though it were done before." In these lines, Donne makes clear that although worshippers may wish to blame Adam and Eve for the sin, they must take credit for their own sinful acts. The speaker continues, "Wilt thou forgive those sins through which I run, /And do them still: though still I do deplore?" Donne repeats the verb *do* to emphasize again the active nature of sin. He also requires those who sing the hymn to admit their own hypocrisy, as they "do" their sins "still," even thought they hate the fact that they continue. In the final line of the first stanza he inserts a play through PARADOX on the word *done,* extending his use of the verb "do": "When thou hast done, thou hast not done, / For, I have more." The speaker admits to the deity to whom he prays that when the deity is "done" forgiving him, he is not truly "done," as the sinner will continue to commit his sins. Typically of Donne, most words consist of a single sentence, simplicity in format producing a carefully planned effect.

In the second stanza the speaker pursues the same topic, as Donne employs repetition often seen in hymns. He asks again:

Wilt thou forgive that sin by which I have won
Others to sin? And made my sin their door?
Wilt thou forgive that sin which I did shun
A year or two, but wallowed in a score?

This stanza emphasizes the extent of the speaker's sin more strongly than the first. Not only has the speaker sinned, he has led others to sin as well. Donne employs the FIGURATIVE LANGUAGE (FIGURE OF SPEECH) of meta-phor, using a door to represent the entrance he offers others into a sinful life. The speaker also apparently repeats a previous sin, probably forgiven in the past but returned to haunt him. Donne's choice of the verb *wallowed* proves effective, making clear the abandon with which the sinner embraces his sin. The term *wallow* is often attached to animals such as pigs, which enjoy rolling in mud and slime, sometimes composed of their own waste. Donne clearly connects men's baser instincts to those of animals, suggesting that without God's grace, men would be no better than such irrational beasts. The speaker repeats the final two lines of the first stanza, which act as a refrain for those singing; "When thou hast done, thou hast not done, / For I have more."

The third stanza departs from the previous pattern of questioning, beginning with a statement, "I have a sin of fear." As the speaker describes his sin, Donne's use of metaphor proves particularly effective: "that when I have spun / My last thread, I shall perish on the shore." He adopts imagery of spinning that could add meaning to the poem on several levels. First, Donne comments on his own activity of writing literature, as spinning was traditionally associated with storytelling, that is, "spinning a yarn." Second, and of interest to feminist critics, the act of spinning calls to mind the mythological figure of Penelope. As Odysseus's wife, she had to weave a funeral shroud each day, and then pulled it apart at night to keep her suitors at bay as her wayward husband made his way homeward. She constantly destroyed her daily work, in the end creating nothing, as a sinner might daily commit destructive acts. Finally, Donne also suggests a spider weaving a web, a structure that never lasts long but must be constantly reconstructed. If the speaker spins webs, he daily repeats the same actions in a futile pursuit of happiness.

Donne's reference to the shore also suggests multiple meanings. The first is that of a journey by sea like that mythological heroes such as Odysseus embarked upon with unknown destinations. Thus, the journey could be simply that represented by life, with the act of reaching the shore suggesting a conclusion to life, or death. A second allusion through the shore imagery could be to the river Styx, literally "river of hate," one of five mythological rivers surrounding Hades. Travelers had to traverse those rivers after death.

At this point, the speaker asks the one to whom he prays, "Swear by thy self, that at my death thy Son / Shall shine as he shines now and heretofore." This vow would cancel the fear felt by the speaker, were he a believer. The reference to Abraham's promise in this final stanza also allows scholars to characterize the hymn as addressed to God the Father. In addition the speaker references "thy Son," meaning Christ, a reference that proves appropriate only if the speaker addresses God. In some older versions, the word *Sunne* is employed, allowing a double meaning in the suggestion of the sun shining; without the warmth of the sun, man would perish. However, Christ as God's Son was also referenced many times in the New Testament as a light revealing truth to man, allowing Donne to suggest the shining caused by wisdom, realization, or knowledge. The speaker concludes, "And, having done that, thou hast done, / I fear no more." Here Donne reflects on the previous lines, declaring that when God forgives a sinner, he is not "done," as the sinner will continue to sin. However, the promise of Christ as savior removes the speaker's fear. Without fear, he will sin no more, and God is truly "done."

BIBLIOGRAPHY

Gardner, Helen, ed. *John Donne: The Divine Poems*. New York: Oxford University Press, 1969.
Grierson, H. J. C., ed. *The Poems of John Donne*. 2 vols. New York: Oxford University Press, 1912.

I

"I AM A LITTLE WORLD MADE CUNNINGLY" JOHN DONNE (1635)

For one of his HOLY SONNETS, "I Am a Little World Made Cunningly," JOHN DONNE adopted the familiar CONCEIT of man as a microcosm. He extended that allusion through the FIGURATIVE LANGUAGE (FIGURE OF SPEECH) of metaphor, contrasting the human body with the entire cosmos. As he had in other poems, he focused on the Ptolemaic theory of the universe to produce imagery of spheres that he could apply to his own physical and spiritual microcosm. However, some of the precise meanings of Donne's allusions remain under discussion.

Donne begins simply enough on a positive note, writing in his first two lines, "I am a little world made cunningly / Of elements, and an angelic sprite." He employs ENJAMBMENT to run the first line into the second, intimately connecting the idea of his private, cleverly made world with that of both the body, or physical "elements," and the soul, "angelic sprite," where *sprite* means "spirit." Then Donne executes a neat reversal in tone, which becomes suddenly negative in the third line. The speaker reveals "but black sin hath betrayed to endless night / My world's both parts, and o, both parts must die." Terms such as *black, sin, night,* and *die* reflect on the previous term *cunningly* to suggest an evil, rather than a wise, force that exposes man to harm in its construction of an interactive body and soul. Because of original sin, inherited by all humans, the speaker knows not only his material body, but his spiritual soul, will suffer death. In addition, the speaker's announcement that both his body and soul must die prepares readers for Donne's conclusion.

In the next lines, the speaker appeals to those without sin to help him:

> You which beyond that heaven which was most high
> Have found new spheres, and of new lands can write,
> Pour new seas in mine eyes, that so I might
> Drown my world with my weeping earnestly.

Donne uses a CONCEIT characteristic of METAPHYSICAL POETS AND POETRY with his request that the powers pour "seas" in his eyes. Although outrageous, the image works well, in its juxtaposition with imagery of exploration, as in seeking new spheres and new lands. Lesser poets attempting this type of metaphor succeeded only in developing revolting references that repelled, rather than fascinated, the reader.

The reference to "new lands" is one of those that critics continue to discuss. According to the Donne expert Helen Gardner, C. M Coffin noted the phrase *new lands* referred to Galileo's description of the Moon's landscape, helping date the sonnet after 1610, when the astronomer's work *Sidreus Nuncius* was published. Donne refers to it in *Ignatius His Conclave,* noting that Galileo "instructed himselfe of all the hills, woods, and Cities in the new world, the *Moone*." If true, that would indicate Donne's support of the Copernican hypothesis of the universe. However, Gardner believes Donne refers, as he does in many poems, to the Ptolemaic system, with the outermost heaven the eighth sphere, that of the "fixed stars." She explains that Donne used this as a metaphor suggesting any new discoveries and the explorers who make them.

Donne extends his conceit, the speaker declaring, "Drown my world with my weeping earnestly, / Or wash it if it must be drowned no more." Donne alludes to God's promise to Noah after the flood that destroyed all living things on earth that he would never flood the world again. Donne next turns from the idea of water to fire as a cleansing element, offering a balance through those opposing elements. But he does more He distinguishes three types of fires. First, he alludes to the fires of human passion that lead to sin and destruction and ultimately to the fires of the Last Judgment. Next, he refers to those of the soul, which result in redemption through the destruction of sin. Finally, he calls on the Lord to burn him with the fire of zeal, its fuel faith, as referenced in the biblical Psalm 69:9:

> But O, it must be burnt! Alas, the fire
> Of lust and envy have burnt it heretofore,
> And made it fouler; let their flames retire
> And burn me, O Lord, with a fiery zeal
> Of thee and thy house, which doth in eating
>   heal.

The psalm also uses the imagery of eating, as the Psalmist notes that the zeal in "thine house," meaning the Lord's house, has "eaten me up." Here the reference serves as another metaphysical conceit for Donne. As flames consume his body, so will zeal consume his flesh and spirit, in a transformative effort. The robust physicality of such conceits appealed to Donne's passionate and dramatic nature.

BIBLIOGRAPHY

Gardner, Helen, ed. John Donne: *The Divine Poems*. New York: Oxford University Press, 1969.

IAMB/IAMBIC   See METER.

"I AM THE DOOR" RICHARD CRASHAW (1646)

"I Am the Door" represents well the type of poetry produced by RICHARD CRASHAW that engendered hostility toward his work for centuries after his death, not for its topic, but for its style. It focuses on Christ's symbolism as the entrance by which believers may reach heaven, a traditional CONCEIT, its source found in the King James Bible (1611) translation of John 10:9, "I am the door; by Me if any man enter in, he shall be saved." Challenged then by how to incorporate elegantly the term *open* as verb or adjective in describing Christ's act of invitation to grace, Crashaw exhibits creativity in form but disregards sound and its effect, as he twice employs the shortened and awkward form *ope*. That term alone undermines any hope for poetic unity, as it shatters both sound and sense in the brief poem, printed here in its entirety:

> And no wh' art set wide ope, the spear's sad art,
> Lo! Hath unlocked thee at the very heart;
>   He to himself (I fear the worst)
>   And his own hope
>   Hath shut these doors of heaven, that durst
>   Thus set them ope.

Crashaw begins in the middle of the act of Christ's crucifixion in a line that recalls the spear plunged into Christ's side to promote his death. It gathers momentum through the use of single-syllable words that pull the reader along. However, the line's flow stumbles over the abbreviated form for *open,* distracting the reader: "And now th' art set wide ope, the spear's sad art, / Lo! Hath unlocked thee at the very heart." The title has introduced the extended metaphor of the door, which Crashaw supports admirably with reference to a door standing unlocked and wide open. It offers sustenance to the faithful dismayed by the stab into Christ's body as they realize his death leads directly to their own redemption. Only through his sacrifice can they enter heaven. While the thought proves strong, Crashaw destroys the sensibility he works to establish by allowing an unidentified voice to step into his work with a parenthetical remark, which could be attributed to either the poet himself or a poetic persona, in the third line: "He to himself (I fear the worst)," then continues in a reversal of his optimistic tone. In a four-word indented line, he writes, "And his own hope," adding no punctuation at the line's end to create ENJAMBMENT. Crashaw then moves back to the left margin for the fifth line, once again indenting the final, sixth line: "Hath shut these doors of heaven, that durst / Thus set them ope." His ending with the shortened *open* prevents an effective conclusion. Crashaw does remain true to the Bible verse that clearly notes that a man must by his own volition enter. Thus, Christ's death will not profit the man who continues to doubt, choosing to close the door to an afterlife.

While none doubted Crashaw's fervent faith, and it remains in evidence in "I Am the Door," the verse supports his categorization as a second-tier poet. However, Crashaw could produce much more harmonious and less self-conscious poetry, as in his celebrated, DESCRIPTION OF A RELIGIOUS HOUSE.

BIBLIOGRAPHY
Williams, George Walton. *Image and Symbol in the Sacred Poetry of Richard Crashaw.* Columbia: University of South Carolina Press, 1967.

"IL PENSEROSO" JOHN MILTON (1632)

JOHN MILTON's solemn, yet comforting, "Il Penseroso," meaning "the contemplative man," was written to balance "L'ALLEGRO," a title translating to "the cheerful man." He likely wrote the two poems early in his career, perhaps while still at Cambridge, a natural outgrowth of student rhetorical practice with traditional themes of opposites, such as day and night. William Blake would add stunning illustrations to later editions of the two poems.

After the introductory nine lines of "Il Penseroso," Milton employs with some variance a familiar octosyllabic format and uses rhyming couplets. The introduction suggests a dark tone, supported, for example, by "vain deluding joys" and "The brood of folly." The speaker makes clear that melancholy is a product of the mind, a theory supported by Robert Burton's *The Anatomy of Melancholy* (1621). He tells his audience that one's "fancies" may possess "gaudy shapes . . . / As thick and numberless / As the gay motes that people the Sunbeams." The speaker clarifies that such fancies remain difficult to restrain, because of their infinite property. While the opening references suggest threat, Milton will show that melancholy, when defined as a thoughtful state, proves desirable.

Milton conjures a goddess of Melancholy so bright that human sense can only perceive her as dark, suggesting PARADOX. He uses the descriptor *black* twice in two lines, labeling it "Wisdom's hue." He intends to contrast the simplicity of darkness to the often hectic state revealed by light, playing on the "thick" and "numberless" "gay motes," or dust particles, previously referenced as found in sunbeams. He also references Saturn, and readers would understand that those with Saturn present in their horoscope were said to be austere, sullen, and black.

As the critic Merritt Y. Hughes explains, in classical writing the mythological figure of Vesta was the virgin daughter of Saturn, but Milton chooses to make her the mother of Melancholy in this poem. Because melancholia was connected to contemplation, he may have made that choice because of another myth that placed Vesta in the heavens, suggesting her to be part of the Orphic, or wisdom, tradition. The speaker describes her as a "pensive Nun, devout and pure, / Sober steadfast, and demure," wearing a dark robe and a "sable stole." She lives in the skies, her "rapt soul sitting" in her eyes. She casts a glance that is "sad Leaden," as she considers the earth. Her companions are the figures of Leisure, "the Cherub contemplation / And the mute Silence." Philomel, or the nightingale, greets the dark with song, as Cynthia, goddess of the moon, "checks her Dragon yoke." Milton offers appealing imagery to describe nightfall.

The description of the night world continues with pleasant details including singing enchantresses of the wood, "the wand'ring Moon," "a fleecy cloud," and the "far-off Curfew sound" moving across a body of water. One finds no source of "mirth" in this still world, other than the cricket's chirp. The Bellman, or night watchman, has a "drowsy charm" as he blesses "the doors from nightly harm." While Milton's world is dark, it offers no threat. Rather, the imagery shapes a welcome retreat from the day's business. In this retreat, absent are the "Daiemons that are found / In fire, air, flood, or underground," probably a direct reference to Burton's "Digression of Spirits" within *Melancholy*.

The speaker remains fascinated with the "sage and solemn tunes" sung by Bards who tell "Of Tourneys and of Trophies hung, / Of Forests, and enchantments drear." He prefers night to day, contrasting the sun's appearance with that of the moon. Where the moon imbues her arrival with mystery and sophistication, the sun bursts out flinging "His flaring beams" and casting "Day's garish eye." He requests a haven from such an attack, preferring "the dewy-feather'd Sleep" and the "strange mysterious dream" that will "Wave at his Wings in Airy stream / Of lively portraiture display'd." Apparently the speaker prefers fancy to reality, made all the more harsh by the sun's unforgiving glare.

If the speaker must awake from his night fancies, he requests that "sweet music breathe / Above, about, or underneath," a gift from a sweet spirit. He remains fixed on the spiritual, imagining a church with "antic Pillars" and "storied Windows," those with representations of biblical stories cut into stained glass. The windows will cast "a dim religious light" as a "full voic'd Choir" responds to a "pealing Organ" producing "Anthems" designed to "dissolve me into ecstasies, / and bring all Heav'n before mine eyes." He dreams of a time when he may join the stars in heaven, drawing on the traditional belief that, as Sir Walter Raleigh wrote in part 1 of his *The History of the World* (1614), God had granted "every star, a peculiar virtue and operation, as every herb, plant, fruit, and flower adorning the face of the earth hath the like."

Milton's melancholy represents a desirable state, clear in his conclusion. After having expounded upon the many delights of that condition, he closes with the couplet "These pleasures Melancholy give, / And I with thee will choose to live."

BIBLIOGRAPHY

Hughes, Merritt Y., ed. *John Milton: Complete Poems and Major Prose*. New York: Macmillan, 1957.

"IMPERFECT ENJOYMENT, THE" JOHN WILMOT, SECOND EARL OF ROCHESTER (1680)

Known for his pornographic poetry, JOHN WILMOT, second earl of ROCHESTER, couched his bawdy presentations in humor. Although he was often drunk and intolerably rude, court regulars appreciated his great wit, which often involved taking others to task for their hypocrisy. His poems included graphic descriptions of the sex act and often demeaned those involved. While in "The Imperfect Enjoyment" the speaker at one point compares the whores to pigs, he also elevates his present partner to a position of power.

The couple described by the speaker begins on even terms, both naked, he "filled with love, and she all over charms; / Both equally inspired with eager fire." As their love-making progresses, the narrator proves at first an equal partner. His mind sends a message to "The all-dissolving thunderbolt below," and his "fluttering soul . . . / Hangs hovering o'er her balmy brinks of bliss" as they rapidly complete the sex act, Wilmot imitating the momentum through his use of quick-moving ALLITERATION. However, when the woman responds with "a thousand kisses," she also asks, "'Is there then no more?'" His initial ejaculation has been "'to love and rapture's due,'" but she wonders, "'Must we not pay a debt to pleasure too?'" The narrator then describes his inability to comply:

Eager desires confound my first intent,
Succeeding shame does more success prevent,
And rage at last confirms me impotent.

He does not blame his partner but rather rages against his "dead cinder," a "dart of love, whose piercing point, oft tried," at that moment proves unresponsive. Rochester adds interest with much FIGURATIVE LANGUAGE (FIGURE OF SPEECH), although he also uses specific vulgar terms for various body parts.

As the poem continues, the reader understands that the speaker accounts for his failure as the expression of a desire for pleasure from his partner. He rants:

Thou treacherous, base deserter of my flame,
False to my passion, fatal to my fame,
Through what mistaken magic dost thou prove
So true to lewdness, so untrue to love?

He proceeds to explain the lewd manners for which he has become so famous, comparing the female reaction to his invitation to have sex to "hogs," which "do rub themselves on gates and grunt." The speaker confesses to having enjoyed sex with "ten thousand" virgins. His organ "Stiffly resolved, 'twould carelessly invade /

Woman or man, nor aught its fury stayed." Yet in this instance when true love, rather than mere desire, is involved, it betrays him: "But when great Love the onset does command, / Base recreant to thy prince, thou dar'st not stand." In a send-up of the serious pastoral love poetry of the previous era, Rochester concludes by including a classical name familiar to those who read such poetry, as his speaker curses his traitorous sex organ, calling on "ten thousand," which are more able, "To do the wronged Corinna right for thee."

Not appearing in print until long after his death, most of Rochester's poetry is now available and has promoted a respectable amount of critical inquiry.

"INDIFFERENT, THE" JOHN DONNE (1633)

JOHN DONNE's love poetry has been categorized by some critics, including Theodore Redpath, according to its positive or negative tone. "The Indifferent" falls into the latter grouping. Donne adopts the prevalent attitude that women almost always proved inconstant. Men did as well, but they did not suffer the same social stigma as did women who engaged in multiple sexual relationships. Religious dogma blamed women's treacherous nature for the ills of the human race, based on Eve's sacrificing the future happiness of man by indulging her appetites in the Garden of Eden. In addition, civil laws of inheritance made clear the importance of monogamy of women, who produced sons who would inherent family property.

As might be expected of Donne, his "attack" against women proved ironic. After supporting the idea of women's inconstancy, he praises that trait, rather than condemning it. Much of his writing was a reaction against social and poetic traditions, including the PETRARCHAN tradition that praised the perfect woman, an ideal, rather than viewing women in a realistic manner. Shakespeare countered that tradition in his famous Sonnet 130, which begins, "My mistress' eyes are nothing like the sun," and Donne does the same in "The Indifferent." He does not use the sonnet form, instead writing three nine-line stanzas with a RHYME scheme of *abbacccdd*, his METER varying.

The speaker begins expressing his open-minded approach, telling his female audience,

I can love both fair and brown,
Her whom abundance melts, and her whom
  want betrays,
Her who loves loneness best, and her who
  masks and plays.

He first describes opposites in terms of physical appearance, with "fair and brown" meaning both blonde and brunette, and continues describing opposites in desires and appetites. Some of his phrases incorporate exaggerated and unpleasant comparisons to help make his point, such as "And her who is dry cork, and never cries." He concludes his first stanza, again making clear he is an equal-opportunity lover by stating, "I can love her, and her, and you, and you, / I can love any, so she be not true." The final line is contrary to traditional ideas, in that this man specifically desires a false woman.

The playfully taunting tone continues into the second stanza as the speaker asks a representative woman why "no other vice" contents the female. He wonders, "Doth a fear that men are true torment you?" Donne's use of ALLITERATION and hidden rhyme in the insertion midline of the word *true* prove enjoyable and call attention to his method, emphasizing the importance of wordplay. The speaker immediately makes clear his jest in telling the woman that men are not true, adding, "be not you so." He invites her, "Rob me, but bind me not, and let me go." His next lines emphasize the importance of his personal freedom. He does not want expectations of true devotion to burden his relationship.

In his final stanza, Donne allows his speaker an allusion to Venus, goddess of love, who becomes complicit in his quest to free all women from the burden of constancy. Upon first hearing the speaker's "song" Venus "swore, / She heard not this till now; and that it should be so no more." Convinced that women should not hold men captive by remaining true to them,

She went, examined, and returned ere long,
And said, Alas, some two or three
Poor heretics in love there be,
Which think to 'stablish dangerous constancy.

Donne extends his reversal of societal expectations through the end of his poem, with a parody of the method of romantic poets who called on classical tradition to support their idealization of women. His Venus remains as practical as Donne's speaker, concluding, "But I have told them, Since you will be true, / You shall be true to them who are false to you." She tells women they are foolish to be constant with inconstant men. Repeating the word *true,* Donne offers a double meaning of the term, considered in terms of constancy, as well as in the speaking of truth. He obviously believes that society does not speak the truth regarding men and constancy.

Thus, Donne concludes his tongue-in-cheek presentation by indicting members of his own sex for the sin that they had traditionally employed to condemn women. Most of his romantic poetry presented women in a positive light, or at least not a negative one. As a young man, Donne seemed to enjoy women almost as much as he enjoyed writing witty poetry.

BIBLIOGRAPHY
Gardner, Helen, ed. John Donne: *A Collection of Critical Essays.* New York: Prentice-Hall, 1962.

Grennen, Joseph, E. ed. *The Poetry of John Donne & Metaphysical Poets.* New York: Monarch Press, 1965.

Redpath, Theodore, ed. *The Songs and Sonnets of John Donne.* Cambridge: University Printing House, 1976.

"IN THE HOLY NATIVITY OF OUR LORD GOD: A HYMN SUNG AS BY THE SHEPHERDS" RICHARD CRASHAW (1646, 1652)

RICHARD CRASHAW first published "In the Holy Nativity of our Lord God: A Hymn Sung as by the Shepherds" in 1646. When it was published again in 1652 several changes had been made to the poem, and it is that version most often anthologized. Crashaw shares his theme with notables including JOHN MILTON, as Christmas celebratory religious poems proved popular among poets. He formats his poem with speaking parts by two shepherds, borrowing from a classical tradition to name the shepherds Tityrus and Thyrsis. In his enthusiasm for his topic, Crashaw apparently saw no IRONY in adopting shepherds' names from a pagan era for his characters present at the birth of the Christ child. He includes all of the traditional aspects of Christ's birth, such as the baby's being born in a manger and the presence of angels announcing and attending his birth.

Crashaw's background in the Italian language and literature led him to use the format recognized during the Restoration as an oratorio. He presents three stanzas to be sung as a chorus by a group of shepherds and then breaks into individual parts extending over nine stanzas for two specific shepherds, whose statements are answered by the chorus. The final five stanzas are presented by full chorus. The format resembles that of JOHN DRYDEN's later "ALEXANDER'S FEAST: OR, THE POWER OF MUSIC." Always passionate in his presentation, Crashaw charges this piece with the joyful energy fitting its subject.

The chorus begins in an opening four-line stanza with a call to one another to gather together to celebrate their "blest sight," which encountered "Love's noon in Nature's night," planning to lift their voices in order to "wake the sun that lies too long." This begins the notion that the order of existence has been permanently altered by Christ's arrival. Night was converted to day through the "Heaven's fairer Eye," an allusion to the star that tradition stated shone above Christ's birthplace. They continue alluding to the lack of the presence of nature's sun, now replaced by a spiritual light, jovially making light of the sun's absence through Crashaw's use of the FIGURATIVE LANGUAGE of personification. They repeat references to the sun as "him," singing, "Tell him he rises now too late / To show us aught worth looking at," continued into the third verse: "Tell him we no can show him more / Than he e'er showed to mortal sight." Finally, the chorus bids, "Tell him, Tityrus, where th' hast been; / Tell him, Thyrsis, what th' hast seen." The two shepherds then take charge of relating the story. Tityrus begins by recalling the "Gloomy night" that, when

> . . . the babe looked up and showed his face:
> In spite of darkness, it was day.
> It was thy day, Sweet! And did rise,
> Not from the East, but from thine eyes.

Then the chorus repeats the final lines of that stanza, as it will certain others that follow. The child's power is proved by the fact that winter sent "the angry North to wage his wars," but the North forgot his duty upon seeing the child, leaving "perfumes instead of scars."

The shepherds tell of seeing the child and feeling inadequate to do anything for him, ashamed that only a lowly manger had been furnished.

While Crashaw continues to impress upon listeners the fact that the natural order of the universe shifted with Christ's appearance, he also remains true to doctrine by emphasizing Christ has always been present. He calls on the image of the phoenix, a mythological bird that destroyed itself by fire every five hundred years in order to be reborn. The phoenix remained a traditional symbol of Christ, who not only reportedly arose from the dead but also promised new life to all men through redemption of their sins. The child "made his own bed ere he was born." Crashaw likely had in mind the powerful opening of the Gospel according to John in the King James (1611) translation of the Bible. It celebrates the beginning of the world, using "the Word" as a metaphor for Christ, the first line reading, "In the beginning was the Word, and Word was with God, and the Word was God." The passage continues three lines later, "In him was life: and the life was the light of men. And the light shineth in darkness; and the darkness comprehended it not."

> Crashaw continues with nature imagery, as in
>   the ninth verse Tityrus says,
> I saw the curl'd drops, soft and slow,
> Come hovering o'er the place's head,
> Offering their whitest sheets of snow
> To furnish the fair Infant's bed;
> Forbear (said I), be not too bold;
> Your fleece is white, but 'tis too cold.

The term *fleece* used to describe snow links the imagery with that of sheep and, by extension, the shepherds themselves. Christ was often referred to as a shepherd in the Bible's New Testament, and his followers to sheep. He was also represented symbolically as a lamb, destined to be sacrificed for man's sin.

In the next stanza Seraphim, angels known for their fiery composition, appear, but the shepherd questions whether their warmth is needed. Crashaw executes a skillful riddle as in the following verse Tityrus notes that the child's "new-bloomed cheek"

> Twixt mother's breasts is gone to bed.
> Sweet choice (said we), no way but so
> Not to lie cold, yet sleep in snow,

referring to the virgin's snow white skin. Both shepherds repeat their observation of the light Christ gave to the world, and then the full chorus sings together:

> Welcome, all wonders in one sight!
> Eternity shut in a span.
> Summer in winter. Day in night,
> Heaven in earth, and God in man."

Crashaw has anticipated the most powerful evidence of a new order in the world by noting nature's inversions through PARADOX finally to declare the greatest wonder, which is that God has appeared on earth in a human form.

In verse 14 the chorus makes clear the welcome is in earnest; although the scene lacks "gold" and "silk," the child is deserving to "more than Caesar's birthright," the reference to the Roman ruler emphasizing the divine right of kings theory introduced by King Henry VIII. Rather than earthly riches and courtly beings, the child is welcomed by "poor shepherds, homespun things, / Whose wealth's their flock, whose wit to be / Well read in their simplicity." Here Crashaw suggests the pastoral tradition, which emphasizes the simplicity and purity of rural life that resulted in a type of wisdom that city dwellers should admire. They promise in the penultimate verse to crown the child with May's "first-born" flowers, expressing their gratitude "To thee, dread Lamb! Whose love must keep / The shepherds more than they the sheep." The hymn concludes with a final blissful welcome, tempered by the realization that humans must choose to give themselves over to Christ in order to attain the purity gained through the fire of personal sacrifice:

> Each of us his lamb will bring,
> Each his pair of silver doves,
> Till burnt at last in fire of Thy fair eyes,
> Ourselves become our own best sacrifice.

Crashaw includes an additional important biblical symbol in his reference to the dove. Doves symbolized peace and were used as sacrificial birds. Most important, however, according to biblical accounts, the Holy Spirit had descended from heaven in the form of a dove on the occasion of Christ's adult baptism by John the Baptist.

As a poet, Crashaw achieves his goal of a retelling of one of Christianity's most celebrated stories in song form, incorporating abundant applicable imagery and symbolism familiar to those who would be singing as well as their audience. His imagery emphasizes the importance of the moment, and his use of ALLITERATION and repetition calls attention to crucial narrative elements. As a man devoted to God, he achieves the separate but related goal of worship, guiding a choir of individuals gathered for the specific purpose of praise through an exercise of ritual crucial to the practice of Christianity.

BIBLIOGRAPHY

Williams, George Walton. *Image and Symbol in the Sacred Poetry of Richard Crashaw.* Columbia: University of South Carolina Press, 1967.

"IN THIS STRANGE LABYRINTH HOW SHALL I TURN?" LADY MARY WROTH (1621)

LADY MARY WROTH included in her prose romance *The Countess of Montgomery's Urania* a SONNET sequence "PAMPHILIA TO AMPHILANTHUS." Within that sequence, she embedded a "corona," the Italian word for "crown," of sonnets titled "A Crown of Sonnets Dedicated to Love." The crown form demanded that the last line of each poem serve as the first line of the next. By the end of the grouping of poems, the last line of the final poem will be the same as the first line of the first poem, thus forming a crown of sorts. Wroth's corona contained 14 separate sonnets. The use of the labyrinth as the opening imagery compliments this fixed form, which, while set and predictable, proved difficult to execute.

The numbering of the first sonnet in this sequence is 77, the first and title line reading, "In this strange labyrinth how shall I turn?" The labyrinth represents life and passion, the topic that occupies Wroth throughout her romance and sonnet sequence. Pamphilia, a virtuous young woman who grapples with the double standard of proper decorum established in Wroth's era, insists that her lover, Amphilanthus, abandon the common practice of male infidelity. The labyrinth imagery allows Wroth to comment on the perils present for women in romance. As her speaker enters the labyrinth, she notices that "Ways are on all sides," meaning she has many paths as options, but no guarantee that the option she selects will benefit her. Pamphilia notes that if she selects the path on the right, "there in love I burn: / Let me go forward, therein danger is," and if she turns to the left, "suspicion hinders bliss." None of these possibilities promises a positive result. In addition, shame bids her to turn back and not lose heart when facing adversity. She could also choose not to move at all, but she remarks that "is harder" and will also leave her with regrets.

Pamphilia decides in the final six lines that she must simply choose a way and move on, enduring her doubts, the "travail" or suffering the only reward on which she can depend. Critics point out that in Wroth's original printing, she substituted the word *travel* for *travail* and probably had in mind a pun when she later made the change. The sonnet closes with Pamphilia's statement "Yet that which most my troubled sense doth move / Is to leave all, and take the thread of love." As Wroth scholars explain, she is probably alluding to Ariadne's gift of thread to Theseus, which she bid him to unwind as he searched for a way through the labyrinth at Crete. His assignment was to slaughter the minotaur that lived in the labyrinth's center; he could retrace his steps to freedom by following the thread that marked the escape route. Such mythological references in Wroth's work were abundant, helping well-informed readers of her day to understand her meanings through the allusions.

"INVITING A FRIEND TO SUPPER" BEN JONSON (1616)

In "Inviting a Friend to Supper," BEN JONSON imitates Horace but writes with an English sensibility. He had famously discussed speech as primarily an instrument for social interaction, noting, "Pure and neat language I love, yet plaine and customary." While Jonson ostensibly communicates only with one close acquaintance in this poem, he retained not only a sense of his broader audience but also a responsibility toward communicating with them. He leaves little room for ambiguity, applying his traditional approach to the construction of strong surface imagery that lodges with the observant reader and helps that reader distinguish the poem's theme. This method ran contrary to that of writers who dealt with deep subconscious suggestion. Jonson also commented, "Words are the Peoples; yet there is a choise of them to be made," making clear his belief in the writer's responsibility to choose wisely.

When he invites his friend, a "grave sir," into his "poor house," desiring company, the reader is not prepared for the sumptuousness of the feast the speaker then describes. He notes that the guest's presence "will dignify our feast / With those that come," a display of ritual modesty. The speaker notes that "the fair acceptance, Sir, creates / The entertainment perfect: not the cates," where *cates* means food. Thus, company makes the meal. Jonson's open acceptance of his guest has caused some critics to identify that guest as Jonson's former teacher, the historian William Camden.

The speaker next begins to provide for his would-be guest a litany of delights designed to tempt him through the door. They will eat olives, capers, salad, mutton, "a short-legged hen, / If we can get her, full of eggs," as well as "Lemons and wine for sauce" and a rabbit. He notes that "though fowl now be scarce, yet there are clerks," adding humor with his reference to scholars, and then continuing, "The sky not falling, think we have larks." He tells of "partridge, pheasant, woodcock" and "Knot, rail, and ruff, too," all various game birds. Not only will they sup handsomely, the speaker's manservant will read VIRGIL, Tacitus, and Livy, "or of some better book to us, / Of which we'll speak our minds amidst our meat." He promises not to repeat aloud any verses, with a droll urbanity, and notes that if any paper is seen, it will be lining a pie pan. In other words, they will turn full attention to the food, leaving work aside for a time. While they will enjoy cheese and fruit, the speaker most anticipates "a pure cup of rich Canary wine," which best stirs his muse but presently sits at an inn. Jonson identifies the inn as the Mermaid, a popular drinking stop for London poets where Canary wine, a favorite of Jonson and of ROBERT HERRICK, was served.

Jonson next references two famous figures, the Latin Horace and the Greek Anacreon, and declares the lines they wrote had lasted a long time, a second example in this poem of his frequent use of the classics. His hospitality is neither formal nor stuffy, but rather framed by a good-natured tone, that of one accustomed to sharing with others in intimate circumstances. Jonson had much practice on the social scene, as he and his TRIBE OF BEN were staples of the London tavern scene. While drink remained important, so did bright verbal exchange regarding the aesthetics of poetry and drama and an interest in events of the day.

The speaker remains confident that other intoxicants cannot prove as enjoyable as the wine, and they need not worry about "Pooly or Parrot," probably a reference to state spies, as Jonson had to be careful regarding public display of his Catholic faith. He concludes, noting that their "cups" will not make them feel guilty,

> But at our parting we will be as when
> We innocently met. No simple word
>   That shall be uttered at our mirthful board
> Shall make us sad next morning, or affright
>   The liberty that we'll enjoy tonight.

By the poem's conclusion, one remains confident that the speaker did not use the term *friend* lightly. His companion was a close acquaintance who could be taken into confidence, who could share a jest without insult, and who proved perfect company for a liberating evening of pleasure.

BIBLIOGRAPHY
Herford, C. H., Percy Simpson, and Evelyn Simpson, eds. *Ben Jonson.* 11 vols. Oxford: Clarendon, 1954–1970.

"I PRITHEE SEND ME BACK MY HEART" SIR JOHN SUCKLING (1648)

"I Prithee Send Me Back My Heart" was published after the suicide of SIR JOHN SUCKLING in the posthumous collection *Fragmenta Aurea.* In a fashion POETS typical of the CAVALIER the five four-line stanzas incorporate hyperbole in an attempt by the speaker to convince a young woman to yield her heart. His tactic is to bid her farewell, in hopes that she will change her mind after having rejected him.

The speaker begins with a bid that his love return to him his heart, "Since I cannot have thine:" adding a faux attempt at logic by noting that if she will not part from her heart, "Why then shouldst thou have mine?" With a moment's thought, however, he changes his mind, bidding her simply to "let it lie." Were he to find his heart, her "thief in either eye" would "steal it back again." Suckling incorporates a metaphysical CONCEIT in the third stanza in imitation of the style of JOHN DONNE. The speaker continues his questions, asking:

> Why should two hearts in one breast lie
>   And yet not lodge together?
> O love, where is thy sympathy,
>   If thus our breasts thou sever?

Suckling does not assume a serious attitude toward his metaphysical proposition, as did Donne. The double entendre remains as much a physical as a spiritual sentiment. He next incorporates PARADOX, as the speaker confesses that love remains such a mystery to him he cannot figure it out, "For when I think I'm best resolv'd, / I then am in most doubt." His confusion actually benefits him, as illustrated in the final stanza, where he notes,

> Then farewell care, and farewell woe,
>   I will no longer pine:
> For I'll believe I have her heart,
>   As much as she hath mine.

Suckling incorporates into his poem the devil-may-care-attitude that distinguished him from other Cavalier poets, who spent multiple lines regretting an impossible romantic situation. At once impudent and sympathetic, the persona of this poem appeals to those who envision love as a state to be enjoyed, not suffered.

IRONY Irony indicates a discrepancy or incongruity, suggesting simply that matters are not as they appear. It may be in the form of *verbal irony,* in which FIGURATIVE LANGUAGE/a figure of speech indicates an opposite meaning of what is said. An example of verbal irony may be seen in BEN JONSON's touching tribute to his firstborn son, who died at age seven, "ON MY FIRST SON." After expressing his grief at his loss, the speaker notes that in the future, "what he loves may never like too much." Obviously one cannot dislike what one loves; Jonson actually suggests that too great a love may have been fatal to the loved one, whereas love generally is believed to be a nurturing emotion. A second type of irony is *situational irony,* in which the incongruity exists between actual circumstance and what might seem appropriate, or in the case of the following lines from JOHN DONNE's "Good Friday, 1613. Riding Westward," between what is anticipated and what actually occurs: "And as the other spheres, by being grown / Subject to foreign motions, lose their own." Finally, in *dramatic irony* a discrepancy exists between what the speaker tells us and what the poem actually means, as in JOHN DRYDEN's masterful "MAC FLECKNOE," a satire meant to belittle the playwright Thomas Shadwell. The speaker supposedly relates an event of great importance, that of the selection by Mac-Flecknoe, a character based on the real-life poet Richard Flecknoe, of his successor to write doggerel. Mac Flecknoe selects Shadwell to inherit the throne of dullness, suggested by Dryden's insertion in his poem of "Sh—" in place of the honored successor's name. Adopting mock-epic approach with a ridiculous comparison of a second-rate poet to one of the greatest kings who ever lived, Dryden's speaker states with ironic grandeur:

> All human things are subject to decay,
> And when fate summons, monarchs must obey.
> This Flecknoe found, who, like Augustus, young
> Was called to empire, and had governed long.
>   (1–4)

J

"JANUARY, 1795" MARY ROBINSON (1806)
When MARY ROBINSON wrote "January, 1795," she was within five years of death after ill health and a life that included imprisonment for her husband's debts; a year-long love affair with the prince of Wales, who then rejected her with no compensation; and a miscarriage followed by paralysis. Those circumstances combined with the gloomy winter atmosphere to support the disillusioned tone of the poem. It takes the form of 11 four-line stanzas composed of rhyming couplets.

While January may have represented a new beginning to many as it opened a new year, Robinson notes instead the season's challenges as worse for some than others, beginning, "Pavement slippery, people sneezing, / Lord in ermine, beggars freezing." Sentiment for the poor, marginalized, and downtrodden parallels the speaker's disgust for the wealthy, arrogant, and undeservedly powerful throughout the poem. Robinson compares glutinous "titled" individuals with starving geniuses, left to perish in untended garrets, and contrasts in the second stanza "Lofty mansions, warm and spacious"; "voracious," meaning greedy, courtiers; and misers with "the wretched" whom they ignore. She also notes that soldiers fight gallantly, dying unappreciated, in order that the privileged may enjoy what they believe to be their due.

By the third stanza, Robinson becomes more specific, viewing London society through an unforgiving microscope. She writes in the same stanza of spoiled wives, theaters, meeting houses and balls, contrasting them with hospitals, filled with "groans of anguish." The fourth stanza notes harsh economic factors, such as failing credit and appointed government representatives who ignore those who depend on their services for support. The fifth stanza expresses indignation for "Authors who can't earn a dinner," while rogues are rewarded, and for "fugitives" who lack shelter while misers hoard their wealth and tradesmen do not pay what they owe. The speaker expresses the opinion in the sixth stanza that "Taste and talents" have been "quite deserted; / All the laws of truth perverted," while arrogance soars and merit proves lacking. The seventh stanza takes on gambling and the culture's tendency to scorn "works of genius" while lauding foolish ones. When the speaker notes that older women are "for girls mistaken, / and Youthful damsels quite forsaken," Robinson may allude to the use of cosmetics by wealthy older women to fool young men desirous of patronage. Those in the ninth stanza delight in luxury, would rather talk than take action to support their ideals, and are equivalent to "Lovers old, and beaux decrepit; / Lordlings empty and insipid." The term *Lordling* proves especially negative, a reductive term with the suffix *-ing* indicating something small and insignificant that considers itself of higher worth than it is.

Robinson continues expressing displeasure over her society's artists, as well as its "Lawyers, doctors, politicians," all of whom seek renown not through merit, but rather through false publicity. Those true "Gallant souls" have "empty purses," and all the real "Generals" have grown old and are "only fit for nurses." In the opinion of the speaker, "School-boys" with no experience, but only a false sense of "martial spirit," have made false claim to the "veteran merit" that should go only to those who have earned it. The final stanza sums up with

> Honest men who can't get places,
> Knaves who show unblushing faces;
> Ruin hastened, peace retarded;
> Candor spurned, and art rewarded.

Robinson obviously felt strongly that in 1795, just before the new century, artifice had replaced art, complacency had replaced the inquisitive spirit, and the false sense of entitlement of a few caused many to suffer.

"JOHN ANDERSON, MY JO" ROBERT BURNS (1789)

"John Anderson, My Jo" has been called one of the most moving of all love poems recorded by the Scottish poet ROBERT BURNS. The song had existed in the oral tradition for some time before Burns committed it to writing. Its appealing voice is that of an elderly woman expressing her love for her equally aged "jo," or sweetheart. Its appeal in two brief eight-line stanzas lies in its simplicity.

Transparent in its heartfelt expression, nothing in the poem confuses the reader except perhaps for the native dialect, always present in Burns's poetry. The first line replicates the title as the speaker addresses her love, "John Anderson, my jo, John." She reminds him that a great deal of time has passed since their first acquaintance by describing his appearance as a youth:

> When we were first acquent,
> Your locks were like the raven,
> Your bonnie brow was brent,

meaning his forehead lacked wrinkles. The lines include ALLITERATION, common to songs, which lends a pleasant effect and enhances rhythm. The next two lines describe John's present appearance, offering a striking contrast to the previous description: "But now your brow is beld, John /," or bald, "Your locks are like

the snow." Then the speaker concludes the first eight-line stanza by declaring, "but blessings on your frosty pow, / John Anderson, my jo," with *pow* corresponding to the English term *pate*. In a graceful moment, the speaker counteracts time's ravages by declaring John's bald head blessed, a simple gesture brimming with grace and an easy redemption.

In the second stanza, the speaker repeats the affectionate opening line, then reminds her love, "We clamb the hill thegither; / And mony a cantie day, John," where *cantie* means "cheerful," and the climbing of the hill represents the exertions that their lives together comprised. Despite having to surmount many problems, they remained cheerful and positive, mainly because they shared life's demands by meeting them head on as a team. She looks toward their imminent and predictable physical demise and eventual death, easing the moment's solemnity by reminding him they will face the end together, just as they have the rest of their existence:

> We've had wi'ane anither:
> Now we maun totter down, John,
> And hand in hand we'll go,
> And sleep thegither at the foot,
> John Anderson, my jo.

Terms such as *totter* and *sleep* counter the harsh realities all humans must eventually face by setting a light and positive tone, leaving both the characters within the BALLAD and its listeners/readers feeling hopeful. The poem clearly makes the point that both the pains of life and the fear of death can be eased through companionship and love. Human interaction remains a saving grace.

BIBLIOGRAPHY
Kinsley, James, ed. *Burns: Poems and Songs.* New York: Oxford University Press, 1971.

JOHNSON, SAMUEL (1709–1784)

Samuel Johnson, a sickly child whose father was a bookseller, was born in Lichfield. In 1728 he entered Pembroke College, Oxford, and began his literary life with a translation of a collection of religious writings by ALEXANDER POPE (1731). He could not afford to complete his education and would later be awarded an honorary "Dr." title. After his father's death in 1731, Johnson taught grammar school to ease his family's debt during 1732 and then spent three years in Birmingham, where he published his first essays in the *Birmingham Journal*. His first book, a translation from a French account of a Portuguese missionary, appeared in 1735 under the title *A Voyage to Abyssinia*. He also married Mrs. Elizabeth "Tetty" Porter, a wealthy widow 20 years his elder, beginning a lifelong romance. The couple's efforts at starting a school failed, so they moved to London in 1737. One of their students, David Garrick, accompanied the Johnsons. He would later become one of England's most celebrated actors.

Johnson at last earned a stable living, making numerous contributions to Edward Cave's journal *The Gentleman's Magazine*. His famous poem "London," an imitation of Juvenal's Third Satire, appeared in 1738, offering commentary on Johnson's favorite themes: social degeneracy, the self-importance of the wealthy, and economic abuses against the poor. It was one of a very few superb poems Johnson would publish. He then published biographical commentary on Richard Savage, a friend, who died in 1744, the first of many biographical writings, which would become as famous as his creative work. A series of such biographies later were published in a volume titled *The Lives of the Poets*, material that would be studied centuries later for its insights not only into human nature, but also into the England of his day. Urged by a publisher named Robert Dodsley to help codify the ever-shifting English language by writing a dictionary, Johnson published his *Plan* for the dictionary in 1747 and applied for financial support to Lord Chesterfield but received none. He decided to undertake the project anyway and worked on it for eight years, using varied sources for terms. He quoted from religious works, offering advice for a moral life, using, for example, more than 100 quotations from the religious poetry of GEORGE HERBERT.

In 1749 Johnson published his most accomplished poem, "The VANITY OF HUMAN WISHES," an imitation of Juvenal's Tenth Satire. It emphasized the folly of allowing hopes to distort reality, crippling man's ability to cope with everyday life. He would consider the same theme again a decade later in his only novel, *The History of Rasselas, Prince of Abissinia* (1759). Also in 1749 Garrick staged Johnson's forgettable play *Irene*. While not his most accomplished work, *Irene* earned £300 for Johnson, who always needed funds.

In 1750 Johnson began publication of *The Rambler*, a twice-weekly periodical that he almost single-handedly wrote. The essays contained in *The Rambler* established Johnson's distinctive style as he considered moral issues echoed in his later novel. James Boswell later wrote in the most famous biography in English, *Life of Samuel Johnson L.L.D.* (1791), about the essays, which "in no writings whatever can be found more bark and steel for the mind."

Johnson's *A Dictionary of the English Language*, a momentous and vitally important work, at last was published in 1765. When Chesterfield stepped forward to "support" the project, Johnson blasted him by including in the work the definition of *patron* as "Commonly a wretch who supports with insolence, and is paid with flattery." Despite the work's popularity, Johnson could hardly stay ahead of his debts. Finally after 1762, Johnson received a state pension and some measure of financial security. He became known famously as an arbiter of taste, labeled "The Great Cham" by Tobias Smollett, and led an artistic group called simply "The Club." Its membership included the painter Sir Joshua Reynolds, the politician and writer Edmund Burke, the novelist Oliver Goldsmith, and David Garrick, as well as Boswell. Johnson continued his voluminous writing, which included an eight-volume edition of *The Plays of William Shakespeare* (1765). A deservedly famous figure, he toured Scotland with Boswell and published his observations in 1775 as *A Journey to the Western Islands of Scotland* (1775). *The Lives of the Poets* appeared in 1782, offering 52 studies that featured his acute literary criticism and showcased his totally absorbing understanding of the human condition.

Suffering ill health, Johnson fought bouts of depression in his later years. He died in 1784 and was buried as a celebrated hero of letters in Westminster Abbey. For the most part as a result of Boswell's detailed and eminently readable biography, Johnson enjoyed more fame after his death than he had during his life. The rational practicality he gave to his critiques of literature and philosophy guaranteed Johnson a reputation as one who applied an insightful knowledge of his own human weakness and strength to his assessment of others. In his creative work he fulfilled his stated requirements of a true poet, to observe and reflect upon the quotidian with fresh understanding.

BIBLIOGRAPHY

Boswell, James. *Life of Johnson.* Edited by R. W. Chapman. New York: Oxford University Press, 1998.

Hardy, John. "Samuel Johnson." In *Dryden to Johnson,* edited by Roger Lonsdale, 279–312. New York: Penguin, 1993.

Lindsay, David W., ed. *English Poetry, 1700–1780; Contemporaries of Swift and Johnson.* Totowa, N.J.: Rowman & Littlefield, 1974.

Redford, Bruce. *Designing the Life of Johnson.* New York: Oxford University Press, 2002.

JONSON, BEN (1572–1637) Most probably born in Westminster, Ben Jonson would become one of the best-known poets and playwrights of his day. Educated at Westminster School, he may have spent some time learning bricklaying, his stepfather's craft. He wrote little of his childhood, so few facts are known. He may have wanted to distract attention from a family that held little status during his own day, but one that he believed had at one time enjoyed the favor of Henry VIII. As a Protestant Jonson's father had suffered under the rule of Mary Tudor, losing the family's fortune and dying before Jonson's birth, leaving his mother, a courageous and resourceful woman by Jonson's accounts, to care for her family. Her remarriage saved the family, but her choice of husband mortified her son. His stepfather's common labor would later embarrass Jonson as he attempted to lead the life of a member of the lettered social class.

Westminster proved the major force in developing Jonson's attitudes toward education and art, as well as in cementing his lifelong friendship with his teacher and mentor William Camden. Jonson would praise Camden in "To WILLIAM CAMDEN" and the teacher was most likely the subject for his poem "INVITING A FRIEND TO SUPPER." Lacking a sponsor, Jonson would not follow the traditional path after Westminster to Oxford, or other advanced schooling, a fact that added to his bitterness. Much of what is known regarding Jonson's

attitudes is drawn from his correspondence with his lifelong friend the poet WILLIAM DRUMMOND OF HAWTHORNDEN. Jonson's poem "MY PICTURE LEFT IN SCOTLAND" probably followed a visit to Drummond during which the poet apparently became attracted to an unidentified woman. The 1632 published notes of Drummond contain conversations with Jonson and reflect Jonson's prose style.

While details of Jonson's early life prove sketchy, he seems to have served in the military in Flanders and upon his return to England probably supported himself through the hated craft of brickwork. However, he continued his studies on his own and in 1594 married and later fathered children he adored. Not much is known of his wife, Anne Lewis, other than that Jonson once referred to her as a "shrew, yet honest." The couple would lose both their beloved daughter Mary and their son Benjamin, immortalized in Jonson's poignant epitaphs "ON MY FIRST DAUGHTER" and "ON MY FIRST SON." His poetry was deeply affected by the publication of Sir Philip Sidney's *Apology for Poetry* (1595), a work that put into words many of Jonson's attitudes regarding art. He would later salute the Sidney family through the poem long considered the first of the estate poems, "TO PENSHURST."

Jonson attempted acting but was apparently unsuccessful and began to mingle his poetry writing with that of drama. In 1597 the theater manager Philip Henslowe mentions Jonson in his papers. Jonson would gain a reputation for a fiery temperament that may have landed him in prison along with other actors after a 1597 performance of *The Isle of Dogs.* That temper led him to kill a fellow actor, Gabriel Spencer, in a 1598 duel, although reports indicate it was in self-defense. He avoided execution by claiming benefit of clergy, a claim of clerical standing used to the advantage of many criminals.

With the staging in 1598 of his second play, a comedy named *Everyman in His Humor,* Jonson's reputation grew. A not so successful sequel, *Every man out of His Humour,* followed in 1599, along with *Cynthia's Revels* (1600), both satires that displayed the knowledge of classical language and literature of which Jonson remained so proud. His elitist attitude caused him to become entangled in the popularly known "war of theaters," in which his poorly written *The Poetaster* (1601) was meant to answer playwrights who he felt had misused his reputation, most notably John Marston and Thomas Dekker. He characterized himself as Horace, making clear his great admiration for the classical writers whose work he would translate; his Horace's *Art of Poetry* appeared posthumously in 1640. Clashing with his reputation for a detached sense of privilege was a tenderness that emerged in elegies, not only in those for his own children but in works such as "EPITAPH ON S.P., A CHILD OF QUEEN ELIZABETH'S CHAPEL," celebrating the brief life of a child actor. "Giles and Joan" well represented Jonson's not-so-celebrated ability to capture playful humor.

Jonson continued writing for the stage with *Sejanus, His Fall* (1603), which again drew him to the attention of the authorities. Although Jonson's political plays, such as *Sejanus* and the later *Caitiline His Conspiracy* (1611), lacked the grace of Shakespeare's political works, they still stood as political statements. Jonson had to reply to accusations of "popery and treason" before the Privy Council. Jonson had converted in 1598 to Catholicism, a practice not popular in the days of James I. Many critics have commented on the unwise choice of conspiracy and assassination as topics for Jonson's play during the same year that James I had agreed to sponsor a group of players, the King's Men. Jonson landed in trouble yet again through his part in the collaborative drama *Eastward Ho* (1604). That could have proved disastrous to the patronage he sought at James's court.

Jonson's bid to become a court writer improved with *The Masque of Blackness* (1605), which advanced his eventual reputation as the best of the masque writers. However, his combative nature again gained him an enemy, this time in the powerful Inigo Jones. His attitude toward the life of the courtier was sharply expressed in "ON SOMETHING, THAT WALKS SOMEWHERE" (1616), reflecting his ambivalence over the fawning necessary to the courtly life. As many writers did, he felt pressured to seek patronage, and his poem "Lucy, Countess of Bedford," along with "A SONNET TO THE NOBLE LADY, THE LADY MARY WROTH" he wrote in hopes of gaining support. He continued to move in court circles until he felt drawn again to focus most of his energies on the stage in 1609.

In the world of drama Jonson's comedies did more to distinguish him than his tragedies. His best included *Volpone* (1605), *Epicoene, or The Silent Woman* (1609), *The Alchemist* (1610), and *Bartholomew Fair* (1614). They offered audiences sharp criticism of human nature, with greater emphasis placed on deception than honor and ethics. Even the minor devil Pug, title character for Jonson's *The Devil is an Ass* (1616), learns that humans can inflict more serious harm on one another than Satan.

Jonson had often employed his marked poetic talents in his masques and in songs for the stage, such as his "SONG: TO CELIA," "SLOW, SLOW, FRESH FOUNT," "QUEEN AND HUNTRESS," and "STILL TO BE NEAT." He was rewarded in a singular manner for his long service to the Crown in 1616 when James presented him not only a lifetime pension but the title of England's first poet laureate. That year Jonson published his collected verse in his famous *Works,* which included the collections *Epigrams* and *The Forest,* in which the majority of his best known poetry appears. More serious in tone than the poems included in *Epigrams,* the 15 works in *The Forest* included "TO PENSHURST" and the less successful "TO HEAVEN." The year 1616 held an added significance with the death of Jonson's peer, William Shakespeare. Jonson contributed to a later first folio printing of Shakespeare's works "TO THE MEMORY OF MY BELOVED, THE AUTHOR, MR. WILLIAM SHAKESPEARE, AND WHAT HE HATH LEFT US" (1623). In a later final return to the stage, Jonson did not repeat his earlier success. His rocky relationship with his audience is made apparent in "ODE TO HIMSELF," in which he castigates the public for its rejection of his comedy *The New Inn* (1629). Additional drama included *The Staple of News* (1625) and *A Tale of a Tub* (1633). Jonson's 1628 appointment as city chronologer would have allowed optimal use of his in-depth knowledge of London. Unfortunately that year he suffered a stroke that weakened his ability to work. He maintained a devoted following until his death in 1637. Jonson was buried in honor in Westminster Abbey, and a collection of memorial elegies, *Jonsonnus Virbius,* was published in 1638. Jonson's posthumous *Timber, or Discoveries made upon Men and Matter* appeared in 1640, offering the public a valuable collection of Jonson's notes, observations, and short essays, as well as adaptation of Latin works into English, further evidence of Jonson' place in history as England's first great critic. In 1641 an additional collection of poetry titled *The Underwood* appeared.

Although he made several enemies with his superior attitude, Jonson also attracted a strong following of young writers with whom he met regularly in pubs. The group included the poets WILLIAM BROWNE, WILLIAM CARTWRIGHT, Sir Lucius Cary, and Cary's best friend, Henry Morison. Jonson celebrated the latter pair in his "TO THE IMMORTAL MEMORY AND FRIENDSHIP OF THAT NOBLE PAIR, SIR LUCIUS CARY AND SIR H. MORISON" (1629). The phrase TRIBE OF BEN is often applied to that group erroneously. They should be properly labeled the SONS OF BEN, as should the poets who succeeded him, such as THOMAS CAREW, ROBERT HERRICK, RICHARD LOVELACE, and SIR JOHN SUCKLING. Later playwrights specifically influenced by Jonson's writing, including Francis Beaumont and John Fletcher, Richard Brome, Nathan Field, Philip Massinger, and James Shirley, are more correctly labeled Tribe of Ben. As those writers felt a debt to Jonson, he also realized his debts to predecessors, obvious in poems such as "TO JOHN DONNE."

Surely one of the greatest forces in British literature, Jonson remains widely read and anthologized, supporting ongoing criticism. However, many critics believe he has yet to receive the attention due such a prolific genius.

BIBLIOGRAPHY

Brock, D. Heyward. *A Ben Jonson Companion.* Bloomington: Indiana University Press, 1983.

Craig, D. H. *Ben Jonson, The Critical Heritage: 1599–1798.* New York: Routledge, 1995.

Enck, John J. *Jonson and the Comic Truth.* Madison: University of Wisconsin Press, 1957.

Greene, Thomas M. *The Light in Troy: Imitation and Discovery in Renaissance Poetry.* New Haven, Conn.: Yale University Press, 1982.

Guffey, George Robert. *Elizabethan Bibliographies Supplements: Robert Herrick, Ben Jonson, Thomas Randolph.* London: Nether Press, 1968.

Miles, Rosalind. *Ben Jonson: His Life and Work.* New York: Routledge & Kegan Paul, 1986.

Parfitt, George. *Ben Jonson: Public Poet and Private Man.* New York: Harper & Row, 1977.

Peterson, Richard S. *Imitation and Praise in the Poems of Ben Jonson.* New Haven, Conn.: Yale University Press, 1981.

Riggs, David. *Ben Jonson: A Life.* Cambridge, Mass.: Harvard University Press, 1989.

"JORDAN" (1) GEORGE HERBERT (1633)

GEORGE HERBERT's two "Jordan" poems, published posthumously in the collection *The Temple,* differ from some of his other work in that they represent responses to members of his literary coterie. His extended family included Sir Philip Sidney and his sister, MARY SIDNEY HERBERT (COUNTESS OF PEMBROKE). The countess was a poet herself and also patronized the arts, passing her appreciation of poetry to her son, the third earl, William Herbert. He would also serve as literary patron to Shakespeare, BEN JONSON, Samuel Daniel, and WILLIAM BROWNE, among others. Her son took over her position as head at Wilton House when George Herbert was 10 years old, and their Protestant coteries would greatly influence Herbert. The coteries offered a manner by which the upper class could make public their creative work, as publication was considered too vulgar an act in which to engage.

Within the coterie, members exchanged verses and honored one another's works through replies, or *Repartee,* commonly known as "answer poems." The reply answered the first poem through imitating it but also often by challenging its ideas or attempting to best its wit. Herbert's "Jordan" poems offered a reply to Sidney's *Astrophil and Stella,* as well as to his *Apology for Poetry.* Sidney designed *Astrophil and Stella* as a sequence of 108 SONNETS with the addition of 11 songs. As the sonnets relate the unsuccessful romance of Astrophil and Stella, they also comment on poetic conventions. For instance, in the 15th sonnet, Astrophil declares himself independent of PETRARCHAN conventions. It offers an account of 16th-century attitudes toward love poetry and the topic of love. Without some knowledge of Sidney's works and "answer poems," a reader might find Herbert's "Jordan" poems inaccessible. Herbert early declared he would use the sonnet form to celebrate sacred love, rather than erotic love, the traditional topic of most lyric poetry. Sidney had written in his *Apology* that in addition to romantic love poetry, another type existed, but that of it "almost have we none." It should be employed, according to him, "in singing the praises of the immortal beauty: the immortal goodness of that God who giveth us hands to write and wits to conceive." Herbert agreed.

As Cristina Malcomson explains, Herbert selected the title *Jordan* for the biblical river important to Christian imagery. He found it a logical substitute for the Greek Helicon, fountains of sacred water that provided inspiration to classical poets. Herbert included no references to erotic love in his work, and, because he wished to compliment Sidney's work, which he greatly admired, incorporated wit, rather than argument, into "Jordan." Herbert imitates Sidney's sparse style but incorporates allusions that are anything but simple.

The poem opens with four rhetorical questions, including "Who says that fictions only and false hair / Become a verse? Is there in truth no beauty?" Herbert questions the idea that only things untrue and fake ("false hair") make strong topics for poetry. He urges his readers to admit that "truth," or what is real, also has beauty. He includes phrases that allow him to parody the excess of FIGURATIVE LANGUAGE favored by the courtiers, including a "painted chair," a special lash against the PETRARCHAN aesthetic. He also executes a neat pun, employing the phrase *a winding stair,* to refer to the structure of the sonnet, writing, "Is all good structure a winding stair?" In the second stanza, Her-

bert also questions the value of "enchanted groves / And sudden arbours," as well as "purling streams," playing on conventions of pastoral verse. While Sidney also celebrated true emotion over complex verbosity, Herbert departs from his model by noting that pastoral love, a specialty of Sidney's verse, represents the fiction he proposes as undesirable.

Herbert's third stanza drives relentlessly toward his point, noting that the shepherds of pastoral convention "are honest people," who should be allowed to sing. However, he shall "envie no mans nightingale or spring," a direct reference to conventions pastoral and the works of the CAVALIER POETS; nor will he allow men to "punish me with losse of rime, / Who plainly say, *My God, My King.*" When he concludes with praise of his God, he makes clear the sentiment is poetic enough; it requires no RHYME. Even the final phrase may be interpreted in different ways, as Malcomson points out. Herbert might mean "my God is my King," but he also could suggest, "My God and King," meaning that he recognizes both his heavenly and his earthly ruler. If the latter interpretation proved the true one, Herbert could diplomatically pay homage to both the Cavalier poet tradition and his own religious belief.

BIBLIOGRAPHY
Malcolmson, Cristina. *George Herbert: A Literary Life.* New York: Palgrave Macmillan, 2004.

K

KILLIGREW, ANNE (1660–1685) Born the daughter of Dr. Henry Killigrew, Master of the Savoy and a prebendary of Westminster, Anne Killegrew would mature during the restoration of Charles II. Her father, an accomplished dramatist, served as chaplain for the duke of York, his position allowing Killigrew to mature in an atmosphere where her art was encouraged. Killigrew served as maid of honor to Mary Modena, the duchess of York, and enjoyed a broad education, although not at the level of her male counterparts. That education remained responsible for what some critics judged the masculine tone of her poetry. However, for a person of status, Killigrew did not leave behind much information on her early years. Letters written from her father to her uncle William were later used to glean some information by the antiquarian Anthony Wood for his monumental work, *Athenae Oxoniensis*. The letters are still with Wood's manuscripts in the Bodleian Library. Dr. Killigrew's letters reveal an obvious love for Anne, and a strong feeling she remained worthy of the biography that Wood wanted to write. He began a letter dated November 4, 1691, "You have pitched upon a subject in my daughter far worthier to be registered to posterity than to me her father."

According to the scholar Marilyn L. Williamson, Killigrew enjoyed the same publishing privileges as males of her era, as a result of her social status. She chose to model her approach after that of KATHERINE PHILIPS, nicknamed "The Matchless Orinda," a cele-

brated woman poet and playwright who met an early death of smallpox, as would Killigrew. More comfortable than Philips with her role as a poet, Killigrew stated her hope that art would give her immortality when she wrote in *Poems by Mrs. Anne Killigrew* (1686), "When I am Dead, few Friends attend my Hearse, / And for a Monument, I leave my verse." She still had concerns about public reaction to her work, as expressed in "UPON THE SAYING THAT MY VERSES WERE MADE BY ANOTHER." In that poem she acknowledged her debt to Philips, writing that she "Owed not her glory to a beauteous face; / It was her radiant soul that shone within." Adopting the rhetorical stance of the late 17th century, she engaged in extreme modesty in writing "TO MY LORD COLRANE, IN ANSWER TO HIS COMPLEMENTAL VERSES SENT TO ME UNDER THE NAME OF CLEANOR," probably anticipating criticism from those who still did not feel women should be writing poetry. Her modest demeanor protected her from those who would accuse her of engaging in masculine pursuits.

Killigrew's work achieved high praise when published after her death at age 25, including that contained in the famous ode "TO THE PIOUS MEMORY OF [. . .] MRS. ANNE KILLIGREW" (1686), appended to the collection by JOHN DRYDEN. She is probably best remembered because of Dryden's ode. His praise would provoke as much later critical comment as did Killegrew's slight collection of works, which her father published in a slim 100-page posthumous volume. Critics question Dryden's lavish words, in part because, despite his praise, he also characterized Killigrew's poetry as neither artful nor skillful. However, he quickly softened that characterization by adding that she did not need art, as nature supplied her treasures:

Art she had none, yet wanted none;
For nature did that want supply,
So rich in treasures of her own,
She might our boasted stores defy:
Such noble vigour did her verse adorn,
That it seem'd borrow'd where 'twas only born.

Some characterize Dryden's excessive approach as traditional for his era, which engaged in, according to David Vieth, as quoted by the Restoration literature expert Ann Messenger, "extremes-without-a-mean." Interestingly, Dryden connected Killigrew to Philips in that ode, as Killigrew herself had in her own verse.

Feminist critics reclaimed Killigrew's small body of works in the 1970s as part of their emphasis on the importance of subtext in writing by early women writers. However, Killigrew seems to have worried little about burying her true meaning beneath the literal and immediately evident meaning of her words. While she engaged in the common apology expected of women who wrote and published in her age and assumed a humble stance, real or feigned, regarding her work's quality, she dealt with strongly autobiographical concerns in an honest manner. But as Messenger explains, one must adopt caution when attempting to identify autobiographical concerns in Augustan poetry. Allusions may simply fulfill the demands of the era's shared rhetorical stance by poets, "the power of genre to control meaning," and most especially, "that a poet is a teacher, a legislator, a public rather than a private voice." The two poems discussed in this *Companion* remain widely anthologized; Killigrew's complete works are available through the University of Pennsylvania–sponsored Web site *A Celebration of Women Writers*.

BIBLIOGRAPHY
"Anne Killigrew." *A Celebration of Women Writers*. University of Pennsylvania Digital Library. Available online. URL: http://digital.library.upenn.edu/women/killigrew/biography.html. Downloaded August 20, 2005.
Messenger, Ann. "A Problem of Praise: John Dryden and Anne Killigrew." In *His and Hers: Essays in Restoration and Eighteenth-Century Literature,* 14–40. Lexington: The University Press of Kentucky, 1986.
Rowton, Frederic. *The Female Poets of Great Britain.* Detroit: Wayne State University Press, 1981.
Williamson, Marilyn L. Introduction to *The Female Poets of Great Britain* by Frederic Rowton, xi–xxxii. Detroit: Wayne State University Press, 1981.
———. *Raising Their Voices: British Women Writers, 1650–1750.* Detroit: Wayne State University Press, 1990.

L

LADIES DEFENCE, THE LADY MARY CHUD-LEIGH (1701)

LADY MARY CHUDLEIGH wrote *The Ladies Defence* in response to a wedding sermon titled "The Bride-Woman's Counselor" delivered by John Sprint in 1700. The sermon so incensed Chudleigh that she wrote her lengthy poem with a strong feminist bent, indignant over Sprint's popular suggestion that women should focus on little else other than obedience to their husbands. She wrote to a friend that she could hardly bear the snickering reception of the sermon by the males in the congregation. Before launching into the poem, Chudleigh wrote an address to her female readers explaining she wrote the *Defence* because of her "Love of Truth" and the high regard in which she held her readers' honor. She also expressed her indignation, directly addressing her readers, at seeing "you so unworthily us'd," which prompted her to apply her pen in her readers' service. She feared her defense might be too weak, exposing readers to further attacks from the type of person "who has not yet learnt to distinguish between Railing and Instruction, and who is so vain as to fancy, that the Dignity of his Function will render everything he thinks fit to say becoming." However, after hearing certain men actually defend the offensive sermon, expressing "an ill-natur'd sort of Joy to see you ridicul'd, and that those few among 'em who were Pretenders to more Generosity and good Humour, were yet too proud, too much devoted to their Interest, and too indulgent to their Pleasures, to give themselves the Trouble of saying any thing in your Vindication, I had not the Patience to be Silent any longer."

Chudleigh voiced several complaints regarding the negative attitude of males and their demanding natures, which they defended with points of religion. She also made clear the church's shameful role in propagating such behavior, couching ills against women in the language of morality, encouraging the silencing of women in the face of abuse. She most strongly voiced her dissatisfaction with the lack of education for women, who were then punished for that very lack.

In order to emphasize her point of view, Chudleigh invents three male voices, Sir John Brute, Sir William Loveall, and a Parson, fashioned to represent real men whom she had observed during that gathering. Of Sir John Brute, she explains, in part, in her preface to the reader, "those Expressions which I thought would be indecent in the Mouth of a Reverend Divine, are spoken by Sir John Brute, who has all the extraordinary Qualifications of an accomplished Husband; and to render his Character compleat, I have given him the Religion of a Wit, and the good Humour of a Critick." She adds that she fears "the Clergy will accuse me of Atheism" because Sir John makes various irreverent remarks about the church and clergy. However, she asks those who would condemn her "to consider, that I do not speak my own thoughts, but what one might rationally suppose a man of his Character will say on such Occasions." Sir William, still single and desiring a wife, defends women but employs an undercutting manner, as ALEXANDER POPE would later write, "damning with faint praise." The Parson most certainly represents Sprint himself. Excerpts serve to demonstrate Chudleigh's outrage and act as examples of traditional poetic format, written with rhyming couplets in iambic pentameter.

In an excerpt of lines 512–564 titled "A Dialogue between Sir John Brute, Sir William Loveall, Melissa, and a Parson: Melissa's Answer," Chudleigh's approach becomes clear. The voice of Melissa, the representative female who finds herself under attack by the three males in the poem, begins,

'Tis hard we should be by the men despised,
Yet kept from knowing what would make us
   prized:
Debarred from knowledge, banished from the
   schools,
And with the utmost industry bred fools.

Melissa claims that men create the very female traits they seem so to hate. The fact that the large majority of women could not obtain any formal schooling by law ensured that most would little grasp what proved the most common knowledge to their male counterparts. She notes the IRONY of the fact that ignorance is actually "bred" into women, the result of a very specific program that withheld the solution to the famous "woman problem." She continues by stressing that men make women the objects of derision, laughing at their "native innocence" and taunting them for being "incapable of wit," when that condition is the only possible result of men's specific actions to oppress women. She compares women to "slaves" whom men keep in ignorance in order that their own "luxury and pride" be served. Melissa remains brutally honest in remarking that the only release women have from male-inflicted pain is death. She fashions death as heaven's reaction to women's complaints because "Th'ill-natured world will no compassion show." That same world "gratifies its envy and its spite; / The most in others' miseries take delight," with *others* indicating the women who request that some pity be spared for them. The reaction from men to their pleas is a patronizing audience during which the men may "look grave

and sigh" and even show signs of friendship. However, when away from their wives, males demonstrate their hypocritical characters as they

fan the flame, and our oppressors aid;
Join with the stronger, the victorious side,
And all our sufferings, all our griefs deride.

She sketches a completely undesirable picture of marital relationships.

Melissa continues by referencing a minority of males who desire the happiness of all, but even those few

think if we our thoughts can but express,
And know but how to work, to dance and
   dress,
It is enough, as much as we should mind,
As if we were for nothing else designed.

She then uses the FIGURATIVE LANGUAGE (FIGURE OF SPEECH) of simile to compare women to puppets, mere toys designed "to divert mankind."

At line 548, Melissa executes a turn, diverging to consider what women might do to lessen their own burden. She wishes that

my sex would all such toys despise;
And only study to be good, and wise:
Inspect themselves, and every blemish find,
Search all the close recesses of the mind,
And leave no vice, no ruling passion there,
Nothing to raise a blush, or cause a fear.

Only then "they will respect procure, / Silence the men, and lasting fame secure" and prove the best possible companions to one another. Feminist critics would note that the solution proves an unrealistic one, as Melissa suggests that only through perfection will women satisfy men and end male taunts. Because no woman could, or, more importantly, should have to strive to be perfect, little hope seems to exist for any type of a tolerable life.

Naturally Chudleigh adopted a strident tone to express her complaint, knowing full well that not every woman suffered the indignities Melissa describes.

However, enough of her words ring true that many readers of her day recognized themselves among that hapless group to whom Melissa refers.

BIBLIOGRAPHY
Ezell, Margaret J. M., ed. *The Poems and Prose of Mary, Lady Chudleigh.* New York: Oxford University Press, 1993.
Ferguson, Moira. "Mary Lee, Lady Chudleigh." In *First Feminists: British Women Writers 1578–1799,* 212–213. Bloomington: University of Indiana Press, 1985.

"L'ALLEGRO" JOHN MILTON (1632)   JOHN MILTON adopted a joyful tone to write "L'Allegro" as a celebration of mirth, its title translating to "the cheerful man." It balances a second piece, "IL PENSEROSO," which focused on the solemn contemplative man and employed a melancholy tone. Milton may have drawn as a creative source on verse written by Robert Burton as a prefix to his *The Anatomy of Melancholy* (1621). That happy poem supported Burton's theory that mirth could combat the type of prolonged melancholy that might lead to madness. Milton's playful approach supports a simple familiar format of octosyllabic rhyming couplets. He begins by describing the dwelling place of "loathed Melancholy," born at "blackest midnight" as a cave with "horrid shapes, and shrieks, and sights unholy" for company. Although the imagery is dark, Milton's employment of ALLITERATION with repetition of the s sounds suggests a sense of the lighthearted, as if one were telling a ghost tale for fun.

The speaker calls upon the "Goddess fair and free" named Euphrosyne, or Mirth, to combat the effect of Melancholy. He notes she is daughter to Venus and Bacchus and sister to two Graces. Milton supports the classical allusion by simply making up his own story, uniting Zephyr (the wind) with Aurora (the dawn) to produce a "blithe" and "debonair" Nymph daughter. This offspring is accompanied by "Jest and youthful Jollity," contagious to others and causing the speaker to sing aloud:

> Come, and trip it as ye go
> On the light fantastic toe,
> And in thy right hand lead with thee,
> The Mountain Nymph, sweet Liberty.

Milton continues his joyous salute to carefree abandon for a total of 152 lines. Their effect has managed to elude the critical approach, and experts who attempt to analyze Milton's work have a problem reducing its happy effect to a matter of METER, RHYME, or form. Its language and arrangement prove too simple, and one must simply enjoy its sounds and imagery.

Milton's speaker celebrates the quotidian in order to include audience members from lower social groups. He describes as delights flowers such as the Sweet-Briar and the Eglantine, the morning cacophony created by the Cock and "his Dames," and "the Hounds and horn." With the rise of the "great Sun," described as robed "in flames, and Amber light," come the shepherds, milkmaids, and mowers, not only to work, but to tell stories and enjoy one another's company. The speaker notes his eye catches "new pleasures /

> Whilst the Landscape round in measures
> Russet Lawns and Fallows Gray,
> Where the nibbling flocks do stray;
> Mountains on whose barren breast
> The laboring clouds do often rest.

The speaker celebrates the pastoral scene through the day and into the evening, when all the country folk and creatures "creep" to bed, "By whispering Winds soon lull'd asleep."

Not to end his celebration so early, the speaker then makes his way to the city "And the busy hum of men." There he may observe knights, barons, and ladies, all entertained by "Wit, or Arms, while both contend" to win a Lady's favor, offering "Such sights as youthful Poets dream." He then joins the audiences of dramas by Shakespeare and BEN JONSON. Milton also celebrates music, but not the traditional Dorian chaste notes. Instead, he praises Lydian music, although some believe it to be immoral. He salutes the Lydian ability in "Untwisting all the chains that tie / The hidden soul of harmony," continuing to emphasize the theme of liberty available through mirth.

In the closing lines Milton again includes classical references, as he continues to describe the effect of the glorious music. The final couplet allows the speaker to sum his thoughts: "These delights if thou canst give, / Mirth, with thee I mean to live."

BIBLIOGRAPHY

Hughes, Merritt Y., ed. *John Milton: Compete Poems and Major Prose.* New York: Macmillan, 1957.

"LANDSCAPE DESCRIBED. RURAL SOUNDS, A" WILLIAM COWPER (1785)

As he did in other poems contained in his six-volume collection *The Task,* WILLIAM COWPER expressed his appreciation of the quotidian, or the everyday aspects of our lives, in "A Landscape. Rural Sound." It appeared in Book 1, offering readers a glimpse into not only Cowper's geographical environment, but also his personal environment. He begins his 60 unrhymed lines by addressing his lifelong companion, Mary Unwin, and, by extension, his audience, when he begins,

Thou knowest my praise of nature most sincere,
And that my raptures are not conjured up
To serve occasions of poetic pomp,
but genuine, and art partner of them all.

This seemingly simple statement reveals much of Cowper the poet. Readers understand that he is a nature poet but has no grandiose design to achieve his goal of praise of his physical surroundings. He prefers simple language, not that suitable for grand occasions, such as for the praise of monarchy or celebration of a holiday. However, because he labels his poems his *raptures,* they are brimming with emotion, emotion that is real. He next allows readers to continue eavesdropping on him as he chats with Mary by noting that they have often "slackened to a pause" in their stroll in order best to observe a favorite "eminence." At such times, they

. . . have borne. The ruffling wind, scarce con-
scious that it blew,
While admiration, feeding at the eye,
And still unsated, dwelt upon the scene.

Cowper adopts FIGURATIVE LANGUAGE (FIGURE OF SPEECH), using a technique known as *synesthesia,* in which one sense perception is used to describe another, in "feeding at the eye / And still unsated." Here he suggests taste in the act of feeding, yet the eye is "fed" through vision. Cowper and Mary gorge on the scenery, unable to be satisfied, such is its visual attraction. However, when he informs readers what they observed with such pleasure, it is nothing more than

The distant plow slow moving, and beside
His laboring team, that swerved not from the
track,
The sturdy swain diminished to a boy!

Poetic skill guides Cowper's juxtaposition of the terms *plow* and *slow,* creating an eye RHYME, in which two words look as if they would rhyme but do not. In addition, Cowper inserts ALLITERATION, as he often does, in the pairing "sturdy swain," scattering additional *s* sounds throughout those lines. Finally, he alludes to the most delightful aspect of the view based upon perspective, a term important to painting, allowing him to reflect on nature as natural art.

The next lines note the presence of the river Ouse, on which his village is located, noting that it "Conducts the eye along its sinuous course / Delighted." His use of ENJAMBMENT, followed by the caesura invoked by his insertion of punctuation after the term *Delighted* that brings the reader to a full stop, emphasizes pointedly human response to natural phenomena. Further description praises the "sloping land," the "hedgerow beauties," "groves," and "heaths," interspersed among which one may note a "Tall spire, from which the sound of cheerful bells / Just undulates upon the listening ear" and "smoking villages." He praises such sights daily over the years, as their "novelty survives" even a poet's "scrutiny."

Cowper then begins praise not of "rural sights alone, but rural sounds," as they also "Exhilarate the spirit, and restore / The tone of languid Nature." Winds carry music to a "far-spreading wood / Of ancient growth," which the poet compares to music made by "The dash of ocean on his winding shore." As he does in "THE WINTER EVENING: A BROWN STUDY," he then observes that they act to "lull the spirit while they fill the mind," nature serving a dual purpose. He also enjoys "leaves fast fluttering," although his alliteration prevents the line's rapid reading, and "the roar / Of distant floods," as well as "the softer voice / Of neighboring fountain, or of rills that slip / Through the cleft rock, and, chiming as they fall / Upon loose pebbles, lose themselves at length / in matted grass." Cowper references rural sounds then recreates them with the use of sound imagery as well as through his word choice, for example, in the close proximity of the terms *loose* and *lose*.

Cowper goes on to consider the creatures in nature, introducing them with another nicely turned phrase that uses repetition of sound and words, while inverting the word *order*: "nature inanimate employs sweet sounds, / But animated nature sweeter still." That sweetness includes "The thousand warblers," which "Nice-fingered art must emulate in vain," as well as "cawing rooks, and kites that swim sublime," "The jay, the pie, and even the boding owl / That hails the rising moon." All charm the poet, despite the seeming contradiction on which he concludes his poem:

> Sounds inharmonious in themselves and harsh,
> Yet heard in scenes where peace forever reigns,
> And only there, please highly for their sake.

One might say the same of Cowper's efforts, which "please highly for their" own poetic "sake."

BIBLIOGRAPHY
Peake, Charles. *Poetry of the Landscape and the Night: Two Eighteenth-Century Traditions.* Columbia: University of South Carolina Press, 1970.

LANYER, AEMILIA (1569–1645) Records indicate that Aemilia (also spelled *Amelia* and *Emilia*) Lanyer was christened at St. Botolph, Bishopsgate, on January 27, 1569. While her father was the well-known English court musician Baptista Bassano, little is known regarding her mother, Margaret Johnson. The Bassanos became court musicians after emigrating from Venice as Henry VIII's reign came to a close. None of Aemilia's three siblings, Angela, Lewes, and Phillip, survived to adulthood, and Bassano died when she was only seven. She became an orphan with her mother's death in 1587 and, according to evidence from Lanyer's later poetry, was probably taken in as a foster child by Susan Bertie Wingfield, countess dowager of Kent. She later became close with the family of Margaret, countess of Cumberland, and knew her daughter, Anne Clifford, whose writings regarding her family's legal dealings

later became an important part of the early women writers' canon. Lanyer would pay tribute to the countess and Clifford by writing one of the first poems of place about the family estate of Cookham Dean in "The DESCRIPTION OF COOKE-HAM." This poem predates "TO PENSHURST" (1616) by BEN JONSON, long credited as the first country house poem. Her writing indicates some education, probably gained through time spent at the court of Elizabeth I.

As a young woman, Lanyer became mistress to Henry Carey, Lord Hunsdon, 45 years her senior. Hunsdon apparently provided well for Lanyer, who may also have been, according to A. J. Rowse and other historians, mistress to William Shakespeare. Little evidence exists to support that theory, or another, which claimed Lanyer was the "dark-eyed lady" of Milton's sonnets. At age 23, Lanyer conceived a child with Hunsdon, who apparently paid her a large sum for her silence. She then married her cousin, Alphonso Lanyer, a musician for Queen Elizabeth. Alphonso had been one of five members of a recorder consort founded by Lanyer's father and his family and enjoyed a royal stipend originally paid to Lanyer's father. He volunteered in the Essex Islands Voyage (1597) and served in Ireland. A favorite of Queen Elizabeth's adviser William Cecil, Lord Burghley, Alphonso played at the queen's funeral and received a position as the sole weigher of hay and straw, for which he received a commission per pound. The couple probably enjoyed a comfortable income, enough to own a house. Lanyer again was left without immediate family when Alphonso died in 1613. She signed over the weighing monopoly to Innocent Lanyer, Alphonso's brother, and was supposed to receive a commission. However, the financial agreement would later be disputed, and she received little income from what had been her husband's business.

Lanyer may have had several miscarriages, and she claimed to have borne at least two children. Her first, the son of Lord Hunsdon, she named Henry; her daughter, Odillya, born in December 1598, died when 10 months old. Henry became a court flautist, married Joyce Mansfield in 1623, and then died 10 years later. Lanyer later wrote that she had to provide for two grandchildren, suggesting that her daughter-in-law had also died.

Lanyer began consulting an astrologer named Simon Forman in 1597, and much of the information known about her is from him. Because he was a man who had a tendency to jealousy and possessiveness, that information cannot be completely trusted. He apparently hoped that he might become romantically involved with Lanyer, but no evidence exists that such a relationship developed. She apparently rejected his advances, leading Forman to wonder whether she was sexually competent and to label her a "whore." Lanyer lived at that point in a fashionable area of Westminster.

Lanyer first published at age 42, issuing a volume of poetry in iambic pentameter titled *Salve Deus Rex Judaeorum (Hail, God, King of the Jews)* (1611). She added two prefatory pieces and an afterword in prose. Her later famous description of Cookham was probably written between February 25, 1609, when, according to several sources including Barbara Kiefer Lewalski, Anne Clifford took her married name, *Dorset,* by which Lanyer refers to her friend in the poem, and October 2, 1610, the date of recording of the poem in the Stationers' Register. The book went through a second issue, but confusion remains regarding its exact publication history. One version, which may be formed of parts of both issues, contains 11 addresses to figures of note in its preface. Some critics find the addresses curious and even overreaching, as Lanyer enjoyed neither their position nor wealth. They include Queen Anne; Princess Elizabeth; "all vertuous Ladies in generall"; Arabella Stuart; Susan, countess of Kent; MARY SIDNEY HERBERT (COUNTESS OF PEMBROKE); Lucy, countess of Bedford; Margaret, countess of Cumberland; Katherine, countess of Suffolk; Anne, countess of Dorset; and "the vertuous reader."

Salve Deus Rex Judaeorum became important to feminist criticism during a later revival of early writing by women by virtue of its radical theological and political stance arguing for religious and social equality for women. It also contains an attack on class privilege in the poem to Anne Clifford. Of great interest to feminist critics is Lanyer's "EVE'S APOLOGY IN DEFENSE OF WOMEN," in the book, which offers a revisionist view of the Eden mythology, which had for centuries proclaimed women guilty for the suffering of all mankind. Lanyer argues that Eve acted in innocence, while men

later proved far more culpable in their crucifixion of Christ. She makes a remarkable statement in the entry "To the Virtuous Reader," warning women not to support male misogyny by speaking against their own gender. In this small excerpt, she explains why she decided to write her "small volume, or little book, for the general use of all virtuous ladies and gentlewomen":

> And this have I done, to make known to the world, that all women deserve not to be blamed though some forgetting they are women themselves, and in danger to be condemned by the words of their own mouths, fall into so great an error, as to speak unadvisedly against the rest of their sex; which if it be true, I am persuaded they can show their own imperfection in nothing more: and therefore could wish (for their own case, modesties, and credit) they would refer such points of folly, to be practiced by evil disposed men, who forgetting they were born of women, nourished of women, and that if it were not by the means of women, they would be quite extinguished out of the world, and a final end of them all, do like vipers deface the wombs wherein they were bred, only to give way and utterance to their want of discretion and goodness.

Lanyer supported herself by operating a children's school in a leased house owned by Edward Smith, an attorney, in summer 1617. Records show the two became involved in a lawsuit over repairs for which Lanyer had herself paid and sought recompense. Smith reacted by having Lanyer arrested, probably causing the immediate withdrawal from school by most of her pupils. She remained in the house for two years and was arrested again when she departed in 1619 without paying rent. Those legal records, along with ones that recorded her attempts to sue her brother-in-law for income owed her, add to Lanyer's scant official history. Apparently Innocent had passed the income from the weighing business along to another brother, named Clement, who was ordered by King Charles I to pay Lanyer her due; however, she had to sue again, and it is not known whether Lanyer ever received her rightful income. She did enjoy a regular pension, information recorded at the time of her death in 1645.

Whatever the true facts about Lanyer's personal life, her publication proved critical to the history of early writing women. For a woman whose works were never mentioned by a contemporary, she has assumed a markedly important place in the consideration of writing by women of her era. Her revision of the common myth regarding man's fall from God's grace remains remarkable for its period, as does her bidding to women to support and protect one another. An obviously intelligent and spirited woman whose works for too long did not receive their due, Ameilia Lanyer made a contribution to writing about women that cannot be overestimated in importance.

BIBLIOGRAPHY

Barroll, Leeds. "Looking for Patrons." In *Aemilia Lanyer: Gender, Genre, and the Canon,* edited by Marshall Grossman, 29–48. Lexington: University Press of Kentucky, 1998.

Beilin, Elaine V. *Redeeming Eve: Women Writers of the English Renaissance.* Princeton, N.J.: Princeton University Press, 1987.

Bennett, Lyn. *Women Writing of Divinest Things: Rhetoric and the Poetry of Pembroke, Wroth, and Lanyer.* Pittsburgh: Duquesne University Press, 2004.

Bevington, David. "A. L. Rowse's Dark Lady." In *Aemilia Lanyer: Gender, Genre, and the Canon,* edited by Marshall Grossman, 10–28. Lexington: University Press of Kentucky, 1998.

Goldberg, Jonathan. "Canonizing Aemilia Lanyer." In *Desiring Women Writing: English Renaissance Examples,* 16–41. Stanford, Calif.: Stanford University Press, 1997.

Grossman, Marshall, ed. *Aemilia Lanyer: Gender, Genre, and the Canon.* Lexington: University Press of Kentucky, 1998.

Lasocki, David, and Roger Prior. *The Bassanos: Venetian Musicians and Instrument Makers in England, 1531–1665.* Aldershot, England: Scolar Press; Brookfield, Vt.: Ashgate, 1995.

Lewalski, Barbara Kiefer. "Of God and Good Women: The Poems of Aemilia Lanyer." In *Silent but for the Word: Tudor Women as Patrons, Translators, and Writers of Religious Works,* eduted by Margaret Patterson Hannay, 203–224. Kent, Ohio: Kent State University Press, 1985.

Prior, Roger. "Was Emilia Lanier the Dark Lady?" *Shakespeare Newsletter* 25 (1975): 26.

Rowse, A. L., ed. *Shakespeare's Sonnets: The Problems Solved.* 2nd ed. New York: Harper & Row, 1973.

———. *Simon Forman: Sex and Society in Shakespeare's Age.* London: Weidenfeld and Nicolson, 1974.

Seelig, Sharon Cadman. "'To All Vertuous Ladies in Generall': Aemilia Lanyer's Community of Strong Women." In *Literary Circles and Cultural Communities in Renaissance England,* edited by Claude J. Summers and Ted-Larry Pebworth, 44–58. Columbia: University of Missouri Press, 2000.

Woods, Susanne. "Aemilia Lanyer and Ben Jonson: Patronage, Authority, and Gender." *Ben Jonson Journal* 1 (1994): 15–30.

LEAPOR, MARY (1722–1746)

Born in Marston St. Lawrence in Northamptonshire, Mary Leapor would become one of the first English working women to produce poetry. Although none of her verse was published in her lifetime, it would later give critics and historians an astounding view of the working woman's world, in which a life lived as an outsider to privilege remains a dominant theme. Nothing is known of Leapor's mother, but her father, Philip, served prominent families as a gardener, including the family of John Blencowe, a member of Parliament. Philip Leapor's name appears in various business notations and especially in *The Purefoy Letters 1735–1753,* edited by George Eland. Henry Purefoy was another of Philip Leapor's employers, and his accounts reflect Leapor's income as comfortable.

Most facts about Leapor's life are from a letter written by Bridget Freemantle, Leapor's mentor as well as friend, to a London gentleman, believed to be either John Duncombe or John Blencowe, which served as a preface to the second volume of Leapor's verse (1751). Freemantle's letter describes Mary Leapor as a voracious reader and writer, so much so that her preoccupation troubled her parents. She probably attended Free School in the town of Brackley. The school was operated by Magdalen College School and resided in that school's chapel. As the biographer Richard Greene explains, the note about Leapor that prefaced the first version of her poems minimized her reading experience, probably to support the idea of Leapor's being a natural genius, in order to promote book sales. While Leapor owned works by both ALEXANDER POPE and JOHN DRYDEN, along with volumes of drama, she likely read many more than the fewer than 20 books that belonged to her. She became a servant employed by a woman named Susanna Jennens, probably related to John Blencowe. The library of Weston Hall at Northamptonshire contains three original volumes of Leapor's works, and the first volume bears the line "One Kitchen maid at Weston." Jennens and her family apparently engaged in informal writing, allowing Leapor to work in an atmosphere that appreciated language.

Leapor left Jennens to take a job described in a letter published in the *Gentleman's Magazine,* 1784. The note in the periodical answered a previous query as to the location of Mary Leapor, describing her as a "some time cook-maid in a gentleman's family." It also describes her "fondness for writing." The identification of her place of service may be revealed from one of her poems, "Crumble Hall," as Edgcote House, an estate containing carved heads described in Leapor's verse. In addition, the poem describes Sopronia, who appeared in other of Leapor's poems as well, as making cheese cakes. The number of domestic positions occupied by Leapor remains unknown, but, according to evidence in her "Epistle to Artemisia. On Fame," Leapor describes her dismissal from what must have been her final work position at Edgcote House.

Leapor returned home to Brackley to care for her father and lived there the remainder of her brief life. Her move to Brackley proved crucial, as she met Freemantle, who encouraged her poetry. Leapor named herself *Mira* and Freemantle *Artemisia* in her poetry, the use of classical names a common 18th-century poetry trope. Freemantle's first reading of Leapor's work was a play, which so impressed her that she asked to see additional work. She urged Leapor to consider printing some of her works through subscriptions that Freemantle felt confident she could help sell. Greene assumes Freemantle to have been well read, the daughter of an Oxford don and a woman who would know how to pursue publication. While a play by Leapor submitted first to the poet laureate Colley Cibber was never performed, subscriptions for a publication of Leapor's poetry were mounting shortly before her death. She had a lingering illness about which she wrote, but a swift infection of measles killed her. One of her final requests of Freemantle was to use subscriptions to her work to support her aging father, who she

feared to be in poor physical condition. Ironically her father would outlive Leapor by many years.

Two months after Leapor died, The *London Magazine* printed her poem "To Lucinda." In January 1746–47 the proposal for a printing by subscription of her works was issued and attracted more than 600 subscribers. Leapor's work was praised by the novelist Samuel Richardson, who wrote of one poem that it "exceeds every Thing of that kind, which has yet been exhibited by the Male Authors, and I think does a supreme Honour to our Sex." Richardson's friend the poet Thomas Edwards decided to issue a second volume, delivered in March 1751. Less than half the number of subscribers to the first volume could be interested, probably because the appeal of poetry by a kitchen maid had run its course. Although no longer a novelty, Leapor's poetry did appear in a second volume, which some critics agree confirmed her reputation. Leapor eschewed popular forms, such as the ode, and included few abstractions in her poetry. Instead she focused on a life of exclusion from polite society, one that resulted in an even stronger gender discrimination than that experienced by even the wealthiest female in 18th-century society. She stresses poverty and injustice suffered by the poor. Her position as an outsider to the culture that would read her poetry resulted in a compelling poetic voice.

That her work appeared in *Poems by Eminent Ladies* (1755), edited by George Colman and Bonnell Thornton, proved its worth, particularly as Leapor's verse occupied more pages than any other poet's; the same was true of the 1775 edition. She was praised by Robert Southey and WILLIAM COWPER, and her poems remained available through the 20th century in various forms. By the 1980, she began to receive the attention she deserved, particularly in research by Betty Rizzo. Feminist critics consider her a true discovery, as she demonstrated that poets of the laboring class could tackle formal verse with the same accomplishment as the best-known Augustan poets. An example of Augustan graveyard poetry is her "MIRA'S WILL," which critics have compared to Swift's "VERSES ON THE DEATH OF DR. SWIFT." A shift in 18th-century studies to admit lesser known poets, particularly those whose works represent women and the poor, has worked to Leapor's benefit. Because so few women poets published in 18th-century

England as a result of gender discrimination, Leapor's works remain particularly important. While a modern critical edition of Leapor's poetry has yet to be written, Greene's biography proves highly informative.

BIBLIOGRAPHY
Dalporto, Jeanne. "Landscape, Labor, and the Ideology of Improvement in Mary Leapor's 'Crumble-Hall.'" *Eighteenth Century: Theory and Interpretation* 42, no. 3 (fall 2001): 228–244.
Greene, Richard. *Mary Leapor: A Study in Eighteenth-Century Women's Poetry.* Oxford: Clarendon Press, 1993.
Mandell, Laura. "Demystifying (with) the Repugnant Female Body: Mary Leapor and Feminist History." *Criticism* 38, no. 4 (fall 1996): 551–582.
Powell, David. "Five Best Poets of Northamptonshire." *Northamptonshire and Bedfordshire Life* 2 (April–May 1972): 22–24.
Rizzo, Betty. "Molly Leapor: An Anxiety for Influence." *The Age of Johnson* 4 (1991): 313–343.

"LIGHT SHINING OUT OF DARKNESS"

WILLIAM COWPER (1773) WILLIAM COWPER's "Light Shining out of Darkness" testifies to his evangelical faith, a faith that convinced him he was evil and condemned by God as he sank into a depression that eventually resulted in insanity. It adopts the traditional Christian metaphor of light as knowledge, grace, and Christ and includes familiar lines from the Bible, such as its opening, "God moves in a mysterious way."

The poem's format is six stanzas of four verses each, with a RHYME scheme of *ababcdcdefef*, and so on, and alternate line rhythms of iambic tetrameter and iambic trimeter. In each stanza Cowper offers assurance. He follows his description of God's mysteries, adding,

> His wonders to perform;
> He plants his footsteps in the sea,
> And rides upon the storm.

While he includes nothing surprising in this poem, Cowper paraphrases the familiar to pleasing effect, creating an imagery of a grand deity.

The second stanza reads,

> Deep in unfathomable mines
> Of never-failing skill

> He treasures up his bright designs
> And works his sovereign will.

The speaker assures readers with the term *unfathomable* that the human mind can never understand God's efforts, thereby relieving them of any burden to try to do so. They understand a mine as a place deep in the earth, beyond the normal reach, where "treasures" might be discovered. The fact that God's will is "sovereign" makes him something more than an earthly king, who reigns but remains limited.

The speaker addresses the faithful in the third stanza, stating,

> Ye fearful saints fresh courage take,
> The clouds ye so much dread
> Are big with mercy, and shall break
> In blessings on your head.

He comforts the audience by explaining that while clouds often signal a storm, a metaphor for the problems that plague man, these clouds will rain with blessings. In the fourth stanza the speaker commands readers,

> Judge not the Lord by feeble sense,
> But trust him for his grace;
> Behind a frowning providence,
> He hides a smiling face.

Cowper continues his assurance by clarifying that our human natures cannot comprehend the Lord, because of his spiritual existence. The fearful God of Old Testament teachings, often seen as a vengeful parent, is actually prepared to offer man a gentle grace, rather than punishment. As the next stanza attests, that is part of an overriding plan, which man may at first not understand:

> His purposes will ripen fast,
> Unfolding ev'ry hour;
> The bud may have a bitter taste,
> But sweet will be the flow'r.

Cowper offers the flower as metaphor, reminding readers that an immature bud remains bitter, but if one remains patient and waits until it matures and flowers, he will be rewarded by a sweet scent, or taste. Cowper concludes with a final statement urging blind faith, not "Blind unbelief," which

> . . . is sure to err,
> And scan his work in vain;
> God is his own interpreter,
> And he will make it plain.

While Cowper's surface message, that one must remain attentive to signs from the Lord, is clear, he suggests an additional idea. He speaks to others like him, poets, preachers, and all diviners of the spirit, warning them that God can best represent himself to those who will only listen. Therefore, Cowper exhibits an understanding of the limitations of language and art. While they may move men's emotions, only the Lord can move a soul.

"LOVE (3)" GEORGE HERBERT (1633)

"Love (3)" joins the poems "Dooms-day," "Judgement," "Heaven," and "DEATH" as the closing sequence to the grouping titled "The Church" within the collection *The Temple* by GEORGE HERBERT. These final poems serve to complement some of the first poems, such as "The ALTAR." Herbert opens using the altar, an icon that traditionally represented sacrifice and later the communion service. In "Love (3)," he closes reflecting on that same communion, a sacramental service that celebrates Christ's sacrifice for the sake of man. The poem is structured in 18 lines divided into three six-line stanzas. Lines 1, 3, and 5 in each stanza have a METER scheme of iambic pentameter, while lines 2, 4, and 6 are much shorter and reflect iambic trimeter. Herbert often used such a format, emphasizing contrast, perhaps between God's greatness and man's lack of such.

As Christina Malcolmson explains, the Church of England had since the Reformation used the communion table to represent the last supper, where worshippers kneeled to accept the sacrament. Puritans preferred a seated posture, and Arminians, post-1617, used altars. In the absence of an altar, they moved a communion table to the east end of the church, placed it in the direction of the altar, and enclosed it with rails

as a sign of respect for the clergy. Herbert agreed that participants in the holy ceremony should kneel, representing man's confession of unworthiness. However, he envisions the supplicant in this poem as seated at the table, emphasizing Christ's humility in his invitation for mere mortals to join him in a celebration of souls. Herbert establishes Love as a figure of ALLEGORY, hearkening back to the cautionary drama of medieval times. Yet he simultaneously undermines those stories of doom and gloom by revealing that Love aids Christ in the salvation of man.

The first line states, "Love bade me welcome: yet my soul drew back," indicating that the speaker feels unworthy, his emotion described in the second line as "Guilty of dust and sin." However, "quick-eyed Love" observes the sinner's hesitation and "Drew nearer to me, sweetly questioning, / If I lacked anything." Love plays a gracious and (for)giving host to his guest. In the second stanza the speaker makes clear to Love that he feels unworthy to be in Love's presence. Although Love assures the guest "you shall be he" who will join Love at the table, the speaker continues to resist, unable even to look upon Love. Love takes the speaker's hand "and smiling did reply, / Who made the eyes but I?" Love assumes the speaker's burden by claiming responsibility for the gaze the speaker wishes to withhold. The sincerely humble speaker continues in the third stanza by countering that while he understands he is God's creation, he has "marred" his eyes. He tells Love, "Let my shame / Go where it doth deserve." At that point Love makes clear that such shame and blame have been borne by Christ. He concludes by gently insisting that the sinner "sit down" and "taste my meat." The sinner acquiesces, completing the poem by stating, "So I did sit and eat." Herbert stresses that all sinners are welcome at the communion table, providing they have a contrite heart and approach with proper humility.

BIBLIOGRAPHY
Malcolmson, Cristina. *George Herbert: A Literary Life.* New York: Palgrave Macmillan, 2004.

"LOVE A CHILD IS EVER CRYING" LADY MARY WROTH (1621)

Among the SONNET sequence titled "PAMPHILIA TO AMPHILANTHUS" in LADY MARY

WROTH'S prose romance *The Countess of Montgomery's Urania* are songs, including 74, "Love a child is ever crying." Wroth wrote of the perils to virtuous women in dealing with unscrupulous men in matters of romance. One topic she emphasized was the lack of control one may experience over one's passions. Her narrator, Pamphilia, sought to convince her love, Amphilanthus, that he could control his passions but only with the maturity and judgment women were required to exercise. In this song she compares love to a child who, lacking of maturity, makes unreasonable and illogical demands. The title line opens the song, and Pamphilia's first ideas about love follow:

> Love, a child is ever crying;
> Please him, and he straight is flying;
> Give him, he the more is craving,
> Never satisfied with having

Her characterization of love as a child also brings to mind the Roman god of love, Cupid, depicted as a winged child. She includes additional allusions to mythology throughout the sonnet sequence.

After making the point that the child's appetite remains endless, and he can never be satisfied, Pamphilia reemphasizes this idea in the next several stanzas, stressing that "His desires have no measure, / Endless folly is his treasure," noting that he breaks all of his promises and one should "Trust not one word that he speaketh." When applying these characteristics to human passion, Wroth has used the term *folly,* a word often linked with love in Renaissance poetry. In the third stanza, Pamphilia continues criticizing the untrustworthy love: "He vows nothing but false matter, / And to cozen you he'll flatter." Critics note that Wroth may have intended a pun on the word *cozen.* While its common meaning is "cheat," she may have also wanted to bring to mind the word *cousin.* She was involved for many years in an affair with her married cousin, William Herbert, the earl of Pembroke, after a period of financial difficulty that followed the death of her young husband. In this depiction Wroth makes clear that if love gains the upper hand, he will leave, having satisfied his desire. Not only will he desert the sufferer, he will "glory to deceive" her. Her comments were probably autobiographical.

Wroth continues to extend love's comparison to a spoiled child by noting he will enjoy the wailing of others, causing them to fail. She summarizes in the fourth stanza, "These his virtues are, and slighter / Are his gifts, his favors lighter." Love proves worse than worthless, without virtue, gift, or favor. She paints a bleak picture of the state of romance, emphasizing, "Feathers are as firm in staying, / Wolves no fiercer in their preying" than love will be in its destruction. The image of a wolf represents the first truly frightening image of the sonnet, as wolves are hunters that track and surprise their victims. She concludes with approbation, "Nor seek him, so given to flying." Pamphilia's point is clear. When one seeks love, it will surely depart and do so only after wreaking havoc on its victims.

"LOVE ARMED" APHRA BEHN (1676) APHRA BEHN included several songs in her various dramas, with "Love Armed" first heard in a performance of her *Abdelazer; or, The Moor's Revenge,* one of about 14 plays written and produced in the 1670s and early 1680s. While Behn had to cease writing plays when the London theaters that produced them suffered a series of financial challenges, she continued publishing her poetry and began a new career writing prose fictions. Among them was *Oroonoko, The History of the Royal Slave* (1688), a tale, like *Abdelazer,* with a black character at its center. Seemingly fearless in the face of criticism by her contemporaries for writing openly about sex and marginalized individuals, Behn constantly fought against her era's refusal to view all humans as worthy of dignity and personal freedom.

The song is a simple tale in which the god of love, Cupid, is given the traditional name *Love;* he is the individual referred to as being "armed" in the song's title. The song will explain just how the deity manages to gather his weapons, freely admitting that he succeeds only because humans allow it. The speaker depicts Cupid in a procession, a "triumph," surrounded by all of those he had wounded with his arrows or darts: "Whilst bleeding hearts around him flowed." He inflicts "fresh pains" and has a "strange tyrannic power," a reference to the power of romantic sex, often associated in song since the Middle Ages, and in later literature, with pain and death.

In the second stanza the speaker clearly connects the idea of tyranny to her passion for her lover and his lack of feelings for her; in other words, she feels betrayed, not by Cupid, but by her lover. The speaker accuses her lover in two lines: "From thy bright eyes he took the fires / Which round about in sport he hurled." In a neat turn Behn depicts Cupid as drawing his power from humans, rather than vice versa. The speaker goes on to admit her complicity in arming Cupid with her own passion: "But 'twas from mine he took desires / Enough t'undo the amorous world." The female equals the male in her capacity for sexual passion, an admission that demure women of Behn's era were socially forbidden to verbalize.

The third stanza offers rhetorical balance, as Cupid takes from the speaker and her lover additional emotions contributing to the speaker's feeling of rejection. While she contributes grief, as well as her passion, her lover's contributions continue to be ones with a negative, even sinful, connotation. Behn shapes him as near-inhuman in his disregard for the speaker, a skillful intersection with Cupid's lack of humanity in lines balanced by pleasing repetition: "From me he took his sighs and tears, / From thee his pride and cruelty." Behn then pursues the perceived inequity of the speaker in two lines that finally equate her lover's cruelty to the physical wounds inflicted by Cupid, as her speaker states of the sources of Cupid's weapons, "From me his languishments and fears. / And every killing dart from thee." While in the final stanza of the song the speaker clarifies that she and her lover have armed their own enemy, and worse, "set him up a deity," she alone is victimized: "But my poor heart alone is harmed, / Whilst thine the victor is, and free." The male character is perceived as victorious, while the female speaker remains a victim, albeit partially as a result of her own efforts.

BIBLIOGRAPHY
Duffy, Maureen. *The Passionate Shepherdess: Aphra Behn 1640–89.* London: Methuen, 1989.
Gosse, Edmund. "Mrs. Behn." In *The English Poets: Selections with Critical Introductions by Various Writers and a General Introduction by Matthew Arnold.* Vol. 2, Edited by Thomas Humphry Ward, 419–421. New York: Macmillan, 1912.

LOVELACE, RICHARD (1618–1658)

Richard Lovelace was born in either Kent or Holland, the privileged son of a Kentish knight blessed with the advantages of wealth. A handsome young man, he attracted attention through his charm and intelligence. After graduating from Oxford with an M.A. at 18 years of age, he moved in court circles and enjoyed London's artistic offerings. He probably first served King Charles I on Sutton's foundation at Charterhouse upon petition of his mother, Anne Barne Lovelace, and in 1631 became "gentleman wayter extraordinary" in service to the king. His first creative work was a comedy titled *The Scholars,* written in 1635. He entered Cambridge in 1637 and was back at court by 1638. That year his first poems appeared in print, including "An Elegy on Princess Katherine."

Lovelace fought for the Crown in the Bishops' Wars during 1639 and 1640 under General George, Lord Goring, prompting his later poem, "SONG: TO LUCASTA, GOING TO WARS." By 1640 Lovelace enjoyed a commission as captain in the second Scottish expedition, writing a tragedy during that year titled *The Soldier.* His drama detailed the decidedly unromantic realism of war, as Charles's forces had faced 20,000 well-organized Scottish troops, forcing the king to compromise. Lovelace returned home to claim what was left of his family's estate, which allowed him to live comfortably, if not lavishly. He retained his Royalist loyalty, along with his three brothers, William, Francis, and Dudley, despite the Covenanters' victory.

With political debate remaining heated a year later, Lovelace during a public meeting destroyed a pro-Parliament petition that also reflected anti-Episcopalian sentiment and in 1642 sponsored a petition to retain the bishops. That act resulted in several weeks of imprisonment in Gatehouse Prison at Westminster, during which he wrote the endearing "TO ALTHEA, FROM PRISON," considered one of the finest LYRICS in the English language, and probably also "To Lucasta, from Prison." During the height of his career he sat for a portrait, which later hung in the Dulwich Collection.

Lovelace used his inheritance to support the interests of King Charles I upon his release and followed the life of an artist. He also continued to serve, probably in Holland and France. Those events likely inspired his

"To Lucasta, going beyond the Seas," and "The Rose." Wounded at Dunkirk in 1646, he continued service and was honored with admission to the Freedom of the Painter's Company in 1647. After traveling the Continent in 1648 he was imprisoned upon his return for 10 months because of his family's Royalist loyalties but gained liberty after the execution of Charles. A CAVALIER POET, he joined THOMAS CAREW, ROBERT HERRICK, and SIR JOHN SUCKLING as a member of the TRIBE OF BEN.

Lovelace published a collection of verses, *Lucasta: Epodes, Odes, Sonnets, Songs, etc.* after his release from prison in 1649. The title may have referred to his one-time fiancée Lucasta Sacheverell, although Lucasta's identity remains debatable. Little is known about the final years of his life, during which he continued to write poetry, other than that he continued to support his brothers and sisters as needed. A second posthumous volume of his work, published by his brother, was titled *Posthume Poems.*

Although Lovelace published few poems, his reputation extends into the 21st century with often anthologized works. According to his biographer Manfred Weidhorn, he remains the best known Cavalier poet, although his work was never as accomplished as that by poets such as ANDREW MARVELL. His LYRICS best express the tragedy of his era and a dying ideal, that of the nobleman dedicated to family and king.

BIBLIOGRAPHY

Anselment, Raymond A. "'Clouded Majesty'": Richard Lovelace, Sir Peter Lely, and the Royalist Spirit." *Studies in Philology* 86, no. 3 (summer 1989): 367–380.

Weidhorn, Manfred. *Richard Lovelace*. New York: Twayne, 1970.

"LOVING AND BELOVED" SIR JOHN SUCKLING (1646)

"Loving and Beloved" represents one of the weaker LYRICS by SIR JOHN SUCKLING. Critics often write of the uneven quality of his work, despite its attractive tone and distinct moments of brilliance. While some reflect unity and coherence, others, such as this poem, strain toward completion. Two of its four six-line stanzas reflect clumsy concluding rhythms, one the result of forced RHYME. Its subject matter of the difficulty of love was a traditional one, particularly for the CAVALIER POETS. Suckling makes the point that in order both to give and receive love, one must be completely honest, a condition he believes impossible in romance. Therefore love is doomed. As he sums up in his final line, "Love's triumph must be Honor's funeral."

The speaker opens with the two-line declaration "There never yet was honest man / That ever drove the trade of love." The stanzas reflect a rhyme scheme of *ababcc*, with the first four lines each having four feet. Preservation of that METER in the final rhyming couplet places demands on Suckling, and he moves to five beats instead. To conclude the first stanza he writes, "For kings and lovers are alike in this, / That their chief art in reign dissembling is." The transition from four feet to five causes an unpleasant sound and challenges the reader. In addition, placement of the verb *is* as the final word of the stanza in order to rhyme with the word *this* proves clumsy at best and results in a disappointing rhyme. Stanza 2 concludes more smoothly with "So we false fire with art sometimes discover, / And the true fire with the same art do cover." This stanza proves the most successful, as the closing lines, through repetition of the terms *fire* and *art,* provide balance. In addition, the ALLITERATION afforded by repetition of the *f* sounds is pleasant. Finally, the rhyme is an identity rhyme, as the same words are used at the lines' ends, generally an unchallenging approach. However, because *cover* in the first usage appears as part of the longer term *discover,* the rhyme satisfies more than had each line concluded with *cover.* The third stanza is not difficult to read once the reader accomplishes the rhythm shift, as the final line contains only single-syllable words: "And which the harder is I cannot tell, / To hide true love, or make false love look well." While the sense of the final line in the fourth stanza remains strong, its rhythm forces the reader to pronounce all three syllables of the term *funeral* separately. Suckling may have designed this intentionally to call attention to the negative connotation of death.

LYCIDAS JOHN MILTON (1638)

JOHN MILTON had known Edward King at Cambridge and wrote *Lycidas* as an ELEGY for his friend's death. When word arrived that King had drowned in the Irish Sea returning to

Dublin in 1637, his many friends were strongly moved. They combined their poems to honor their fallen friend, Milton terming his piece a *Monody* in which he "bewails" the loss of his friend. He also puts his elegy to political use, employing it to foretell "the ruine of our corrupted Clergy then in their height." The collection adds little personal information regarding King, other than that he had proved a decent scholar who had chosen to serve the church. That choice allowed Milton to characterize King in his pastoral as a good shepherd caring for his sheep, the familiar biblical analogy that applied to Christ.

Milton begins the elegy in the traditional praise mode, calling on Myrtles and Laurels, traditional plants used to crown heroes. However, these plants will never fulfill their destiny, as they have grown brown and will "Shatter" their leaves before they mature. The speaker explains, "Bitter constraint, and sad occasion dear, / Compels me to disturb your season due," emphasizing that King, as the plants, died far too young, "dead ere his prime."

Critical reaction to *Lycidas* has long been mixed. Milton's highly stylized approach incorporates frequent syncope, or the omission of letters from the middle of words, for the sake of rhythm, a technique that seems unnecessary and distracting. Some find unintentional humor in the heavy pastoral tradition that incorporates hyperbole, as the speaker continues speaking of King,

He must not float upon his wat'ry bier
Unwept, and welter to the parching wind,
Without the meed of some melodious tear.

He calls on the Muse for guidance, including what some find an annoying self-portrait as shepherd, joining King in guarding his flock:

Together both, ere the high Lawns appear'd
Under the opening eyelids of the morn,
We drove afield, and both together heard
What time the Gray-fly winds her sultry hour,
Batt'ning our flocks with the fresh dews of
     night.

Milton continues by including the *pathetic fallacy,* so labeled later by John Ruskin, personifying nature to mourn the passing of Lycidas. He uses FIGURATIVE LANGUAGE to compare the hero's obliteration by death to nature's cruel method, sending canker to kill the rose, "Or Taint-worm to the weanling Herds that graze, / Or Frost to Flowers." SAMUEL JOHNSON added his voice to those critical of Milton's style for the overwrought lines.

Others criticized the piece for lack of unity. Milton constructs the poems in three distinct sections, the first with a theme of loss of poetic fame, the second focusing on the corrupt clergy, and the third the deification of Lycidas, with the result that the sections do not hang well together. The voice that expresses concern over the survival of Lycidas's poetic words contains a supplicant, almost groveling tone, speaking of the poets' hope to burst into a "sudden blaze" of inspiration, only to be dashed when "Comes the blind Fury with th'abhorred shears, / And slits the thin spun life." Jove's voice enters to assure the speaker that the only true judgment of a man's earthly deeds will take place in heaven. The speaker then summarizes Lycidas's life, recalling his matriculation through Cambridge and describing the shipwreck.

The speaker then moves into a rant regarding the "foul contagion" of the clergy. In contrast to the good shepherd Lycidas, these clergy "shove away the worthy bidden guest;" have "Blind mouths!" a skillful use by Milton of *synesthesia;* and "scarce themselves know how to hold / A Sheep-hook." Lines 128–129 adopt the metaphor of a wolf to expand criticism of the Catholic Church: "Besides what the grim Wolf with privy paw / Daily devours apace, and nothing said." As the critic Eric C. Brown explains, etymology informs us that the name *Lycidas* is derived from the Greek *lukos,* or "wolf," with the ending *idas* meaning "son of." That knowledge suggests that Milton inexplicably deconstructs his own positive construction of Lycidas. However, critics have also suggested that Milton intends for a connection to be made, not to the church and the twin wolves appearing on the Jesuit coat of arms, but rather to the formal appellation *Lycus* or *Lucos,* names appearing in Ovid's *Metamorphoses.* Another view suggests simply that Lycidas may be a son of the church, his roots in ancient teachings, but one who has broken away from that heritage.

Critical evaluation deems the passage more interesting in a historical context than a poetic one. Much effort has been spent on study of the lines concluding that section, "'But that two-handed engine at the door / Stands ready to smite once, and smite no more.'" The image of the two-handed engine is taken from the biblical St. Peter, who notes the engines will smite evil within the church. At least 40 different explanations of the engines have been critically summarized, including the suggestion that the two handles represent the judgment of death and damnation. That symbolism echoes Milton's earlier use of the image of St. Peter's gold and iron keys as fitting the locks on heaven and hell.

Milton next includes a list of flowers that critics continue to discuss, as their meaning is not clear in the context of his poem. Some believe the poem represents a simple exercise in the use of as many poetic techniques as possible. In this section Milton adopts the approach of *anthimeria*, converting the adjective *purple* to a verb, describing rain showers that "purple all the ground with vernal flowers." That conversion to an unexpected form also constitutes CATACHRESIS. He next begins the catalog of flowers, as seen in lines 143–147:

> . . . the rathe Primrose that forsaken dies,
> The tufted Crow-toe, and pale Jessamine,
> The white Pink, and the Pansy freakt with jet,
> The glowing Violet,
> The Musk-rose, and the well-attir'd Woodbine,
> With Cowslips wan that hang the pensive head.

Milton concludes with praise for Lycidas, including the well-known phrase "Look homeward Angel." The speaker bids "woeful Shepherds weep no more," one of many phrases loaded with ALLITERATION, assonance, and consonance. Adopting ANTITHESIS the speaker notes, "So, Lycidas, sunk low, but mounted high," describing heaven's celebration of the shepherd's arrival and his conversion into "the Genius of the shore" to protect others from his fate. Milton draws on the tradition of VIRGIL, who imagines in his *Eclogues* Julius Caesar in the guise of Daphnis to be "good" to men below.

Critical reception of *Lycidas* remains mixed. Observant scholars have found multiple weaknesses in the poem. Added to those already noted is Russell Fraser's observation that Milton has not written the "monody," or poem in a single voice, that he claims because a second distinctive voice enters at the poem's conclusion. A seemingly disapproving voice tells us, "Thus sang the uncouth swain," suggesting Milton's dismissive evaluation of his own voice. Fraser's suggestion that Milton remains a poet "still at odds" with his own material may account for the uneven presentation others have observed.

BIBLIOGRAPHY

Brown, Eric C. "Ovid's Rivers and the Naming of Milton's *Lycidas*." *Early Modern Literary Studies* 7, no. 2 (September 2001): 51–53.

Fraser, Russell. "Milton's Two Poets: Voices in John Milton's *Lycidas*." *Studies in English Literature, 1500–1900* 34, no. 1 (winter 1994): 109–118.

Horton, Alison. "An Exploration into the Etymology of *Lycidas*." *Milton Quarterly* 32, no. 3 (1998): 106–107.

Kaminski, Thomas. "Striving with Vergil: The Genesis of Milton's 'Blind Mouths.'" *Modern Philology* 92, no. 4 (May 1995): 482–485.

Kirkconnell, Watson. *Awake the Courteous Echo: The Themes and Prosody of Comus, Lycidas, and Paradise Regained in World Literature with Translation of the Major Analogues.* Toronto: University of Toronto Press, 1973.

Womack, Mark. "On the Value of *Lycidas*." *Studies in English Literature 1500–1900* 37, no. 1 (winter 1997): 119–136.

LYRIC   Poetry may be divided for convenience into two broad categories. One category is the narrative poem, which tells a story, complete with plot and characters. Examples include the BALLAD and the epic. The second category, representing the majority of poetry, is the LYRIC, generally a brief poem that focuses on expression of emotion or thought. The term *lyric* derives from the fact that in classical Greece, lyrics usually took the form of songs accompanied by a musical instrument, the lyre. Formal examples of lyric include the ode and the ELEGY, in which thought and feeling are expressed in a complex way. A more simple and popular fixed form of the lyric is the 14-line SONNET, in both the PETRARCHAN and the Shakespearean or Elizabethan constructions.

M

"MACFLECKNOE: A SATIRE UPON THE TRUE-BLUE PROTESTANT POET T.S." JOHN DRYDEN (1684)

Although a first authorized published edition of "MacFlecknoe" by JOHN DRYDEN appeared in *Miscellaney Poems* in 1684, it had been circulated in unapproved versions since 1682. Critics cannot pinpoint the year that Dryden wrote it, but he may have done so as early as 1678. Written in 218 lines of rhyming couplets, it represents satire in which Dryden takes to task the poet and dramatist Thomas Shadwell, the *T.S.* indicated in its subtitle. Dryden critics still puzzle over the poet's motivation in writing the poem. Although he had quarreled publicly with Shadwell over political matters, the two appeared still to hold one another in regard, and Shadwell proved a talented writer, undeserving of Dryden's judgment that his work was dull and unworthy of commendation. Equally puzzling is the poem's tone, which, for all of the work's clever references, remains, as Earl Miner notes, not biting but rather "curiously affectionate." Dryden intimates that Shadwell is part of an inner circle of writers struggling under specific political and religious upheaval in the London environment. Unable to stand the pressures, he bows to outside forces and sacrifices his art. Exposure to the upheaval and its resultant pressures led to obvious tension among factions, and jealousy or suspicion may have prompted a quarrel that led Dryden to expose Shadwell to ridicule.

The two poets had their political differences. The Protestant Shadwell supported Anthony Ashley Cooper, earl of Shaftesbury, in the dispute over who should succeed King Charles II to the English throne. Shaftesbury championed Charles's illegitimate son, the Protestant James Scott, duke of Monmouth, while Dryden supported the Catholic brother of Charles, James, duke of York. Dryden had caricatured Shaftesbury in his ABSALOM AND ACHITOPHEL (1681). Dryden also attacked Shaftesbury in his satire *The Medall* (1682), which parodied the Whigs who celebrated Shaftesbury's verdict of innocence when he was tried for his part in an attempt to overthrow Charles. Dryden characterized the jurors who freed Shaftesbury as ignoramuses, and his followers, who cast a medal celebrating his "innocence," as ignorant revelers. The poem caused immediate response from poets supporting Protestant interests, Shadwell included. He attacked Dryden in his *The Medal of John Bayes* (1682). "MacFlecknoe" appeared for the first time about six months later. The tensions present in London over not only religion, but also trade, created a paranoia supporting rumors such as the so-called Popish Plot. Dryden refers to London as Augusta in the poem, alluding to its nervous environment when he inserts a quiet parenthetical statement as line 65, "(The fair Augusta much to fears inclin'd)."

The name given to the poet in Dryden's verse was from an Irish Catholic priest and minor poet, Richard Flecknoe, who had died in 1678. Dryden sets the scene as if Flecknoe appointed Shadwell to succeed him as the ultimate poet. Dryden employs "Sh——" to represent Shadwell throughout the poem, selected as Flecknoe's successor to "realms of Nonsense" just prior to his death; the *Mac* prefix means "son of." Why Dryden selected Flecknoe as the vehicle for his attack remains unclear. As the country worried about a successor to their monarch, the poem satirized succession issues and exposed various London figures to ridicule.

"MacFlecknoe" opens in Augusta with its ruler, Flecknoe, forced to determine who will assume his place as leader of the empire. The reference to Augustus recalls Julius Caesar's choice of Octavius, later called Augustus, as his successor. Dryden thus shapes his poem as a MOCK-HEROIC, while parodying groups dedicating themselves to various poets and adopting the celebrated's name, such as the TRIBE OF BEN [Jonson]. Flecknoe concludes that he must select the one who most resembles him, noting

> Sh——alone my perfect image bears
> Mature in dullness from his tender years.
> Sh——alone of all my sons is he
> Who stands confirm'd in full stupidity. (15–18)

Dryden compares Sh——to the contemporary dramatists Thomas Heywood and James Shirley, again puzzling critics, as neither proved deserving of so derogatory a characterization.

Flecknoe continues considering the fact that he has prepared the way for his "son," alluding to John the Baptist, who prepared the way for the arrival of Christ. Dryden employs *sententia* as blown-out terminology, intended for use in high praise, but here applied to a low subject:

> When thou on silver Thames did'st cut thy way
> With well tim'd oars before the royal barge,
> And big with hymn, commander of an host,
> The like was ne'er in Epsom blankets toss'd.
>   (38–42)

In the next few lines Dryden extends his CONCEIT by comparing MacFlecknoe to the fabled Arion, a Greek musician rescued while at sea by dolphins, and then employs the term *Sh*—— as a scatological reference, made clear from the term *toast,* an allusion to sewage floating on the top of the water. Critics sometimes argue Dryden did not intend such a reference, as he maintains the demand for a two-syllable term, *Shadwell,* in his rhythm. However, others disagree:

> Methinks I see the new Arion sail,
> The lute still trembling underneath thy nail.
> At thy well sharpen'd thumb, from shore to
>   shore
> The treble squeaks for fear, the basses roar;
> Echoes from Pissing Alley, "Sh——" call,
> And "Sh——" they resound from Aston Hall.
> About thy boat the little fishes throng,
> As at the morning toast that floats along.
>   (43–50)

Preparations are made for the coronation, and the speaker describes in lines 67–75 a brothel district in Augusta where a watchtower, an allusion to the grandeur of Rome, once stood, and "now, so Fate ordains, / Of all the pile an empty name remains." Nearby "a Nursery erects its head / Where queens are formed and future heroes bred." This nursery produces actors, and Dryden employs the contemporary association of acting with prostitution, as the nursery is near the brothel. Scholars explain that such imagery allows continuous contrast between the glorified past and a debased present. Dryden invents the term *Maximins* in line 78 to describe the inhabitants of Augusta who challenge the gods. He engages in wordplay on a classical term: Where *Maximus* means "greatest," his term represents the opposite. The coronation celebration, involving a parade through the streets of Augustus, connotes the type of empty drama, all artistry and no art, of which Dryden accuses Shadwell and his ilk.

Dryden repeatedly uses the term *dull* in various forms, as Sh—— must take a vow to defend his father's realm of "dullness." As he continues, he adds to his multiple references or allusions ones to contemporary dramas, their characters and lines; to playwrights, including BEN JONSON, George Etherege, and Sir Charles Sedley; to the minor poet John Ogilby; to JOHN MILTON and *PARADISE LOST*; to Romulus, one of Rome's founders; to VIRGIL's *Aeneid*; to Hannibal Barca, enemy of Rome; to the duke of Newcastle and his duchess, the poet MARGARET CAVENDISH; to shape poems, such as those written by GEORGE HERBERT; as well as to biblical stories and images. Many of his references serve to juxtapose the tawdry existence of the individuals who serve as targets of his poem against that of the high values held by classic and 17th-century laudatory writers. He signals readers that a heroic past has dissolved into a debased present, when artists are wasting a once noble heritage.

Both print and electronic versions of the poem supply exhaustive keys to Dryden's multiple references. As with all satires, a thorough understanding of Dryden's era is required in order to appreciate "MacFlecknoe." Shadwell represented political values that Dryden found anathema, but, possibly more importantly, he represented the sacrifice of art to social pressures, an act of which Dryden himself had stood accused.

BIBLIOGRAPHY

Broich, Ulrich. *Mock-Heroic Poetry, 1680–1750*. Tübingen: M. Niemeyer, 1971.

Donnelly, Jerome. "MacFlecknoe." *The Literary Encyclopedia.* Available online. URL: http://www.litencyc.com/. Downloaded August 1, 2005.

Miner, Earl, ed. *Selected Poetry and Prose of John Dryden.* New York: The Modern Library, 1985.

"MAD MAID'S SONG, THE" ROBERT HERRICK (1648)

During the time that ROBERT HERRICK spent serving Dean Prior in Devon he grew to know country folk well. Not enamored of the rough ways of those he encountered in rural life, he nevertheless succeeded in reproducing their dialect in some of his verse while showing sympathy for their concerns. In "The Mad Maid's Song" Herrick chooses as his topic the universal concern over the loss of a loved one. The speaker of his poem, the maid referenced in its title, sings her bitter song with remorse over the death of her beloved. She is termed mad, or insane, because she continues to look for her love, although she seems to understand he has been buried. She fixates on exhuming his body but in her longing remains without joy or hope.

Herrick captures his subject's madness by showing her engaged in everyday rituals, such as greeting all those she meets with a "Good morrow to the Day so fair; / Good morning Sir to you" while demonstrating her imbalance when she adds, "Good morrow to mine own torn hair / Bedabled with the dew." The image of her damp hair suggests that she has been out all night and into the early morning, perhaps lying on her lover's grave and caught by the morning dew. Normally a sign of cleansing and new life, the dew creates IRONY in its symbolizing death in this instance.

In the second stanza the mad maid bids good morning to a primrose and then to several other maids, noting those maids "will with flowers the Tomb bestrew, / Wherein my Love is laid." Confused, she repeats, "woe is me" and begs a man to take pity, asking that he "find out that Bee, / Which bore my Love away." At first the reader might think she does not refer to the flying insect, as that makes little sense, but in the fourth of the four-line stanzas, she continues, "I'le seek him in your Bonnet brave," confirming that she must have been referring to the common bee. Her madness becomes all the more clear as she determines to seek her love in the eyes of others, then declares, "th' ave made his grave / I' th' bed of strawburies." Her love has died in the warm comfort of summer, indicated by the presence of the berries, rather than during winter, a traditional season of death, making her loss even harder to accept.

In the fifth stanza the maid declares that she will seek out her love, as "The cold, cold Earth doth shake him." Talking more nonsense, she says she might simply send a kiss, rather than go see her love, sending "By you, Sir, to awake him." Because she feels sure he understands "who do love him," even though he is dead, she asks that he be moved gently, remaining intent on physical contact with the body. She closes the song with a request that "bands of Cow-slips" bind him, as "He's soft and tender." However, she concludes by noting that even should he be transported home, "'tis decreed, / That I shall never find him."

Herrick's poem captures the sense that most country villagers remained acquainted with one another. Even so, one feels isolated in grief, no matter how sympathetic friends may be. Herrick also understood isolation during his early months in Devon, where his disappointment over separation from city life must have proved bitter.

"MAN" GEORGE HERBERT (1633)

In his LYRIC poem "Man" GEORGE HERBERT adopts the popular characterization of man as a microcosm, representative of an entire world, an idea that is common in the work of METAPHYSICAL POETS AND POETRY such as that of JOHN DONNE. He does so to make a point regarding man's position in the universe. While man may claim such a close relationship with all aspects of the material world that he is simultaneously in it and of it, he still owes service to his God. Herbert counters the human self concept as a self-contained universe, fully functional on its own. He opens with a call to the Lord and based on something the speaker heard, shares the thoughts that will follow:

> My God, I heard this day,
> That none doth build a stately habitation,
> But he that means to dwell therein.
> What house more stately hath there been,
> Or can be, than is Man? To whose creation
> All things are in decay.

Herbert uses FIGURATIVE LANGUAGE (FIGURE OF SPEECH) to compare man to a stately habitat, suggesting that God, as man's builder and creator, intended to dwell within man, that is, to become an integral part of his being. To the speaker man is not only everything, he is more, a PARADOX stated in the second stanza. That "more" includes a tree, but one that does not produce fruit, and a "beast," but man should outshine the beast. "Reason and speech" should set humans apart from beasts, but the speaker makes the point that even the simple parrot can mimic the sound of speech, with no involvement of intellect. Therefore, speech and reason alone do not support man's self-realization.

The third stanza continues the description of man, a symmetric being with limbs in proportion to one another, "And all to all the world besides." Herbert's use of repetition and imitation of his own description in the format of his poem, featuring in his line structure the symmetry he praises in regard to man, proves skillful. Not only do the limbs relate to one another as do family members, they also "hath private amity . . . with moons and tides," making clear man's close connection to the universe and to the heavenly movements. The fourth stanza stresses the fact that man has "caught and kept" everything, including "the highest star," because "He is in little all the sphere,"

meaning that he represents a microcosm, a small world of his own. The sixth stanza notes that all forces, including wind, earth, heaven, and fountains, act only for man's benefit; everything man sees proves for his own good. In a playful and indulgent tone, Herbert adds

> As our *delight,* or as our *treasure*:
> The whole is, either our cupboard of *food,*
> Or cabinet of *pleasure.*
> The stars, sun, music and light stir "our head,"
> while
> All things unto our *flesh* are kind
> In their *descent* and *being*; to our *mind*
> In their *ascent* and *cause.*

The eighth and ninth stanzas continue in this vein, offering a catalog of services the universe provides to man and for man, as all aspects of life are servants in the human cause. But Herbert returns attention to God and to his house metaphor in the final stanza as he writes:

> Since then, my God, thou hast
> So brave a Palace built; O dwell in it,
> That it may dwell with thee at last!

The speaker invites the Lord to live within each man, the verb *dwell* emphasizing a long-term and intimate relationship. If the Lord dwells within the "Palace" that is man, then man will dwell with the Lord. Until that time, the speaker adds, "afford us so much wit," meaning an awareness of the situation. He concludes by reversing the imagery of man as master, making him instead a servant, stressing until the Lord dwells in man, "That, as the world serves us, we may serve thee, / And both thy servants be."

Herbert does not want to detract from the grand position on earth afforded to man by God. He readily admits the wonder of the human as a creation. However, that wonder will become all the more glorious through service to God.

"MARRIED STATE, A" KATHERINE PHILIPS (1667) Although dated 1667, "A Married State" was

a part of the juvenilia, or youthful writings, of KATHER-
INE PHILIPS. While Philips remained self-deprecating to
the extreme in her later public life, always bowing to
masculine needs, this poem may reflect her private
thoughts regarding the effect of marriage upon a
woman. The 16 lines in rhyming couplets exhibit
IRONY, adopting a warning tone.

The speaker notes that "A married state" offers "little
ease," as even "The best of husbands are hard to please."
She observes the challenge of caring for those hard-to-
please men in the faces of wives, although they carefully arrange their expressions in order not to reveal
their displeasure, as "they dissemble their misfortunes
well." Virgins are content, their state "always happy as
it's innocent." Philips emphasizes that the opposite is
true of wives by beginning three successive lines with
the usually negative term *No* to note what virgins lack.
However, in this case, lack is a positive:

No blustering husbands to create your fears,
No pangs of childbirth to extort your tears,
No children's cries for to offend your ears.

As long as one retains the virginal state, she has few
"worldly crosses to distract" her prayers. The poem
concludes with three lines of advice, incorporating
ALLITERATION as well as metaphor and a Shakespearean
reference:

Turn, turn apostate to love's levity.
Suppress wild nature if she dare rebel,
There's no such thing as leading apes in hell.

The speaker urges virgins to abandon, or run away,
from love, and Philips personifies wildness as female,
warning virgins to suppress any rebellion by passion,
which might demand love. Her final allusion is from
Shakespeare's play *The Taming of the Shrew*, about a
recalcitrant and spirited woman who refuses marriage
until her father marries her off to Petruchio in what
amounts to a commercial trade. In the second scene
the courtier Baptista rejects Katherine, the shrew of
the play's title, for her younger sister, Bianca, to which
Katherine with great vitriol responds,

She is your treasure, she must have a husband;
I must dance barefoot on her wedding-day,
And for your love to her lead apes in hell.
  (2.1 33–35)

Philips uses Shakespeare's comedy, the reference to
which readers of her day would identify, to represent
a woman opposed to marriage who was eventually
overcome by a man's attentions, reducing her to little
more than servitude.

MARVELL, ANDREW (1621–1678)
Andrew
Marvell was born at Winestead, Holderness, Yorkshire.
His father, also Andrew, served as the vicar of Winestead, and young Andrew matured under the close
care of his parents. The Reverend Andrew Marvell took
an appointment as master of the Grammar School and
Charterhouse at Hull and served Holy Trinity Church
as lecturer. Young Andrew probably attended Hull
Grammar School from 1629 to 1633 and received an
allowance from the Trinity College, Cambridge, foundation beginning in 1633. In 1637 he published his
first verse, an occasional poem in a congratulatory volume celebrating the birth of a child to Charles I and
Queen Henrietta Maria. He was elected to a scholarship at Trinity College in 1638, the same year that his
mother, Anne, died. The vicar remarried, and Marvell
earned his BA. Debate exists over whether he may have
been influenced by "kidnappers" to convert for a brief
time to Catholicism, much to his father's dismay. The
Reverend Andrew Marvell drowned in 1641 in the
Humber, possibly accompanying the daughter of a
member of his congregation, who also drowned.

Marvell decided to leave Cambridge, relocating to
London, where he lived in Cowcross. During the years
1642 to 1647 he traveled to the Continent, visiting Holland, France, Italy, and Spain, and became acquainted
with Richard Flecknoe in 1646 in Rome. A minor poet,
Flecknoe would later become the object of ridicule in
JOHN DRYDEN'S satire "MACFLECKNOE: A SATIRE UPON THE
TRUE-BLUE PROTESTANT POET T.S.," and Marvell would
write of him in "Flecknoe, an English Priest at Rome"
(1681). The poem reflects Marvell's anti-Catholic views
as he mocks Flecknoe's poverty, in which he has only
"consecrated Wafers" for food.

Marvell published *An Elegy Upon the Death of My Lord Francis Villiers* in 1648 and in 1649 published "To his Noble Friend Mr. Richard Lovelace, upon his Poem's published." He seems to have returned to London by that time and published also in 1649 "Upon the Death of Lord Hastings." In the years 1650–55 he wrote and circulated several poems, including *An HORATIAN ODE UPON CROMWELL'S RETURN FROM IRELAND* and "UPON APPLETON HOUSE, TO MY LORD FAIRFAX." Reflecting what would be a lifetime spent in apparent political conflict, Marvell's ode for Cromwell also expressed compassion toward the executed monarch, King Charles I.

JOHN MILTON recommended Marvell for a Latin secretaryship in 1653, the same year in which Marvell published *The Character of Holland.* He worked as a tutor at Eton for Oliver Cromwell's ward, William Dutton, at the house of John Oxenbridge. Marvell continued to write and publish prose prolifically and in 1656 accompanied Dutton to visit France. The following year he published "On the Victory Obtained by Blake over the Spaniards" and enjoyed an appointment as Latin secretary to John Thurloe. He also became an assistant to Milton in 1657, as the older poet was losing his sight. He wrote "A Poem upon the Death of his Late Highness the Lord Protector" in 1658 and joined Cromwell's funeral procession, where he, according to legend, led the blind Milton. But within a year he would join the RESTORATION and write pamphlets in support of King Charles II. Such changes in allegiance caused later critics to question whether or not Marvell was simply an opportunist. However, most agree that his LYRICS do reflect the political fractures and confusion of the era.

In 1659 Marvell began his political career in earnest with election as joint member of Parliament (M.P.) for Hull. He lost his seat at the restoration of the Rump Parliament but remained Latin secretary, taking residence at Whitehall. After his reelection in 1660 he gained a reputation for his spirited representation of his political views. His passion led to blows with the rabidly Catholic and aggressive Sir Thomas Clifford in the House in 1662. That physical fight revealed that, despite his normally quiet demeanor, Marvell had a temper. Such altercations were rare; in 19 years of parliamentary service only on six occasions did the record reflect a verbal quarrel between Marvell and another politician. Later that year Marvell traveled to Holland, representing the earl of Carlisle. He served the earl as secretary during travels to Russia, Sweden, and Denmark, 1663–65, contributing to his reputation as one "acquainted with Intrigues of State at Home," as noted by a detractor named Samuel Parker. Russian accounts of English insolence disturbed Charles II, who requested a full report by the earl; Marvell would never write about the trip.

In 1666 Marvell contributed to *The Second Advice to a Painter* (1667) as well as *The Third Advice to a Painter.* This genre of instruction had begun in 1656 when in Venice elation over a naval victory prompted the selection of Pietro Liberi to record the scene in the Doges' Palace. The Italian poet Giovanni Francesco Busnello addressed an instructive poem to the artist. After the poem's translation in 1658, the English poet EDMUND WALLER decided to imitate Busnello's approach in his "Instructions to a Painter" (1666), and the genre began to flourish in English. Several poets contributed to succeeding poems, including Marvell. Because the contributions were in some cases anonymous, and later incorrectly attributed by critics and editors, later antiquarians, including the incomparable Anthony Wood, reattributed certain poems. In 1667 Marvell wrote "Clarendon's Housewarming," at first incorrectly attributed to SIR JOHN DENHAM. The only entry in the Instructions series verified as absolutely Marvell's was "The Last Instructions to a Painter"; four editions of "The Advice to a Painter" poems and associated poems were printed. Also in 1667 Marvell became embroiled in another political debate. Parliament sought to punish those felt responsible for various unethical acts during war, and because Lord Clarendon held most power, he became a target for impeachment. At first Marvell supported the impeachment, but he later spoke against it, reflecting the turns in sentiment that had become characteristic. Increasingly active politically, Marvell took up various causes over the next several years and in 1669 was included on a list of names of supporters of the duke of York.

Work written between 1670 and 1674 included "The Loyal Scot" and Latin and English versions of

"Epigram: Upon Blood's attempt to steal the Crown." While living at Highgate, he published translations from Seneca and entered into a controversy with Samuel Parker, his old nemesis, in 1672. In 1674, he produced the popular "ON MR. MILTON's PARADISE LOST" and continued writing politically charged materials. In 1677 Marvell spoke against a bill to secure the Protestant succession in the House of Commons and moved to Great Russell Street in order to sequester bankrupt relatives. He published *An Account of the Growth of Popery and Arbitrary Government* anonymously in 1677 and in 1678 traveled to Hull. During his return to London he became ill and died of "ague" at home. He was buried in St. Giles-in-the-Fields.

A 1681 publication of *Miscellaneous Poems,* with a notice "To the Reader" written by his wife, Mary, contained most of the lyrics for which Marvell is best known, including "The BERMUDAS," "The DEFINITION OF LOVE," The GARDEN," "A DIALOGUE BETWEEN THE SOUL AND BODY," "The NYMPH COMPLAINING FOR THE DEATH OF HER FAWN," "TO HIS COY MISTRESS," and the four poems often considered together as *The MOWER POEMS,* "The Mower against Gardens," "Damon the Mower," "The Mower to the Glowworms," and "The Mower's Song." This publication exists in several different states, causing problems for critics who seek to authenticate its contents. Some editors have excluded some poems on the basis of internal inconsistencies that suggest they do not belong to Marvell. The 1681 collection first appeared as part of a Whig propaganda campaign, according to Nigel Smith. Editions printed soon after lacked the Cromwell poems and indicate interference, possibly by printers or other editors, probably for political reasons. He remains a secretive person, never referencing literature or poetry in correspondence. Unlike Milton, he did not intend to become a major poet who would change forever English verse; nor did he, as JOHN DRYDEN did, seek a set of new principles to guide English letters. His poetry, however, did reflect philosophical thought regarding the nature of poetry and of those who wrote it, as well as the differences between the public and the private person. He enjoyed exploring the relationship of various forms of art to one another, as well as the meaning of authority, of both a civil and a religious nature.

Most critics agree that Marvell's best poetry did not appear until after his death, and he did not became famous for his lyrics until the 20th century. The 18th century regarded him as a satirist and pamphleteer, a patriot who encouraged religious tolerance, while two centuries later his prose would hardly be read. Augustan sensibilities could not stomach his poetry, much of which reflected characteristics of METAPHYSICAL POETS AND POETRY T. S. Eliot's seminal essay on Marvell in 1921 compared the poet's ability to speak of his age to that of Milton, praising his metaphysical wit. An outpouring of critical study of Marvell's works followed and continues, his poetry easy to find.

BIBLIOGRAPHY

Berthoff, Anne. *The Resolved Soul: A Study of Marvell's Major Poems.* Princeton, N.J.: Princeton University Press, 1970.

Condren, Conal, and A. D. Cousins, eds. *The Political Identity of Andrew Marvell.* Aldershot, England: Scolar Press, Gower, 1990.

Kermode, Frank, and Keith Walker, eds. *Andrew Marvell.* New York: Oxford University Press, 1994.

Murray, Nicholas. *World Enough and Time: The Life of Andrew Marvell.* New York: St. Martin's Press, 1999.

Patrides, C. A., ed. *Approaches to Marvell: The York Tercentenary Lectures.* London: Henley, and Boston: Routledge & Kegan Paul, 1978.

Ray, H. Robert. *An Andrew Marvell Companion.* New York: Garland, 1998.

Rees, Christine. *The Judgment of Marvell.* New York: Pinter, 1989.

Roberts, John R., ed. *New Perspectives on the Seventeenth-Century English Religious Lyric.* Columbia: University of Missouri Press, 1994.

Smith, Nigel. "Introduction." In *The Poems of Andrew Marvell,* edited by Nigel Smith, xii–xvii. New York: Pearson/Longman, 2003.

METAPHYSICAL POETS AND POETRY

Metaphysical poetry rose to prominence in the 17th century, primarily through the work of JOHN DONNE. However, other poets also proved important to the metaphysical approach. Most critics include as crucial to the method ANDREW MARVELL, THOMAS TRAHERNE, HENRY VAUGHAN, and GEORGE HERBERT, with ABRAHAM COWLEY occasionally mentioned. The phrase *metaphysical poetry* did not appear until the 18th century and may have been coined by SAMUEL JOHNSON, applied as a pejorative term. Metaphysical poetry developed, in part, as an artistic reaction against traditional Elizabethan poetry's mild and predictable sentiments. It also represented a political reaction to the intellectual and spiritual challenges poets experienced during the transition from the Renaissance to the modern period. Highly philosophical, metaphysical poetry seldom focused on nature or the concrete and adopted different verse forms, none of which became a convention. Herbert produced some of the most famous SHAPE POEMS, using format as a metaphor to suggest his topic; a prime example is his "The ALTAR," in which the lines are formatted in the shape of an altar. The metaphysicals appreciated the precise phrase, making select lines worthy of the dramatic epigram; as critics have noted, many individual poems resemble dramatic monologues. Their poetry dealt with simple but common emotions, such as love, anger, jealousy, and sorrow, but used uncommon FIGURATIVE LANGUAGE to construct surprising metaphors that compared two things not usually thought of as comparable. It also adopted rationality to discuss phenomena, rather than the intuition or mysticism common to Elizabethan poetry. Donne, as a metaphysical, may have been rejected in the centuries that followed him for his lack of tenderness in his romantic poetry or for a perceived lack of solemnity and respect in his religious poems. The metaphysicals' use of comparisons, rather than straightforward statements about their topics, caused the 18th century, which valued clarity, to scorn their approach. The 20th-century poet T. S. Eliot revived interest in the metaphysicals, appreciating their intellect and their revolutionary natures, with which he could identify.

Donne's poem "The CANONIZATION" represents the metaphysical metaphor. While it suggests a focus on religion, the poem instead focuses on romantic love, with the speaker desiring that others accept his attitude about romance, which contrasts with their own. He includes lines scolding those who would judge him, who had turned love from peace into rage, "Who did the whole world's soul extract, and drove, / Into the glasses of your eyes, / So made such mirrors, and such spies." The odd imagery constitutes use of CATACHRESIS by Donne. He includes a violent image of an object boring into human eyes and then compares the eyes to mirrors that reflected the deeds of others, as a spy might do. Such wit was expected of poets, and the metaphysicals often applied a clever approach to discussion of religious matters, astrology, and early science, such as theories of alchemy. They employed PARADOX in a similar way, framing seemingly contradictory statements that contained a startling truth. Vaughan's poem "THEY ARE ALL GONE INTO THE WORLD OF LIGHT" couples the term *beauteous* with the term *death,* an unusual pairing supporting his metaphor of death as "the jewel of the Just." Readers accustomed to death's characterization as something to be feared and avoided would find this more positive characterization puzzling. However, it helped transmit Vaughan's message that only through death does one achieve true liberty and need no religion or philosophy to understand the ultimate truth.

METER   The term *meter* refers to rhythm in poetry created by syllabic stresses or the lack of stresses. Groups of syllables may be organized into various patterns, which are labeled feet. Generally one foot consists of one stressed syllable plus one to two unstressed syllables. In order to determine which syllable is stressed, its sound is compared to other syllables within the same foot. Many feet forms exist; the most popular are the iambic, trochaic, anapestic, dactylic, spondee, and pyrrhic, the terms originating in the Greek language. When feet appear in multiples, the rhythm is labeled according to the number of feet per line, as in dimeter (two feet), trimeter (three feet), tetrameter (four feet), pentameter (five feet), and so forth. While most lines of poetry consist of one type of foot, that may vary.

In the iambic foot the first syllable is unstressed and the second stressed. While the term *iamb* derives from Greek, its meaning has been lost. The most common type of foot, it often appears in a series of five, labeled *iambic pentameter,* and is familiar to many readers through Shakespeare's SONNETS. By far the most popular meter, iambic pentameter closely resembles natural speech patterns and was used almost to exclusion of all other meter by 17th- and 18th-century poets. An example may be seen in the first line from "ON MY FIRST

SON" by BEN JONSON. Inserting a vertical line between feet, and a *breve* (˘) for the unstressed syllable and an *ictus* (´) for the stressed syllable, the line appears as: "Fare well| thŏu child| ŏf mý | right hand| and joy," with a stress falling on the second syllable of each foot. *Troche* means "running" or "belonging to the dance" in Greek and is often used in classical comedy. The trochaic is the opposite of the iambic, with a stressed syllable followed by an unstressed syllable. It often appears in groups of four as seen in the first two lines of "The LADIES DEFENSE" by LADY MARY CHUDLEIGH, which also include an example of a variance: "Wife and | ser vant| are the | same, / But on | ly dif | fer in |the name." The anapestic foot contains two unstressed syllables with one stressed syllable. Clement Moore's familiar "'Twas the Night Before Christmas" represents an example of anapestic tetrameter: "Twas the night| be fore Christ | mas and all | through the house." *Anapest* means "beat back" in Greek, referencing the fact that it is the reverse of the dactylic. Dactylic, meaning "finger" in Greek, indeed reverses the stress in anapestic, containing one stressed syllable followed by two unstressed syllables, as in the words múl tĭ plĕ and ín tĕr vĕne. Homer often employed dactylic hexameter. The *spondee*, meaning "used in libation" in Greek, offers equal stress on two or more syllables and was often used in religious rituals. In "BATTER MY HEART" by JOHN DONNE the fourth line contains a spondee in the series "break, blow, burn," each single-syllable word receiving identical stress. The pyrrhic foot, used in war dances, which reverses that pattern, most commonly contains two unstressed syllables. Neither the spondee nor the pyrrhic is employed repeatedly.

BIBLIOGRAPHY
Preminger, Alex, ed. *Encyclopedia of Poetry and Poetics.* Princeton, N.J.: Princeton University Press, 1965.

"METHOUGHT I SAW MY LATE ESPOUSÈD SAINT" (SONNET XXII) JOHN MILTON (1658)

Critics continue to debate the subject of the SONNET by JOHN MILTON "Methought I Saw My Late Espousèd Saint." While probably one of Milton's first two wives, who both died of complications of childbirth, on the basis of lines 4–5, "Mine as whom washt from spot of child-bed taint," even that theory

remains under question. Those who accept the theory then argue whether the subject is Mary Powell Milton, who died three days after giving birth, or Katherine Woodcock Milton, who died three months afterward. An additional theory holds that because the term *Saint* indicates simply a "soul in heaven," any interpretation is further complicated.

Critics note Milton's reference to the classical character of Alcestis, Admetus's wife and the title character in Euripides' play, "Methought I saw my late espoused Saint / Brought to me like Alcestis from the grave," to suggest Milton's general, rather than personal, interest in the topic. Admetus does not recognize his wife, who had a veil over her face, which Milton notes in line 10, writing, "Her face was veil'd." The second part of that line, "yet to my fancied sight," has been interpreted by some to indicate Milton's blindness. Others believe the entire poem references the *donna angelicata* of Dante and Petrarch, which was the feminine poetic ideal, a heavenly vision in concrete form, explaining the reference to Milton's fancy, or imagination.

The sonnet remains appealing for its simple descriptive elements of a dream. The final four lines read:

Love, sweetness, goodness, in her person shin'd
So clear, as in no face with more delight.
But O, as to embrace me she inclin'd,
I wak'd, she fled, and day brought back my
     night.

In these lines Milton expresses the plight of the blind through use of PARADOX, as the light of day gives way to the dark of night. The speaker's suggestion that his vision returns only in the dream state makes his a sympathetic voice, one filled with longing for the touch, or embrace, of a person present only during repose.

BIBLIOGRAPHY
Hughes, Merritt Y., ed. *John Milton: Complete Poems and Major Prose.* New York: Macmillan, 1957.

METONYMY   See FIGURE OF SPEECH.

MILTON, JOHN (1608–1674)

Born on Bread Street in Cheapside, London, John Milton matured in a family of practicing Puritans. His father, a scrivener and composer of music, had converted from Catholicism and moved to London from Oxfordshire. Milton benefited from his father's substantial income in gaining an excellent early education at St. Paul's School. He entered Christ's College at Cambridge in 1625; there he earned a reputation as a malcontent and was dubbed by the other students "the Lady of Christ's." Although he did not find college challenging, he continued study for his M.A., graduating in 1632 having written a fair number of poems. They included one of his best-executed poems, an ode titled "ON THE MORNING OF CHRIST'S NATIVITY."

At one point Milton had planned to enter the church but elected instead to enjoy a life of leisure, much to his father's annoyance. He relocated with his family to Horton and then to Buckingham, continuing to write verse and to follow a private plan of study. In 1632 he published "ON SHAKESPEARE" in the Second Folio of Shakespeare's plays and collaborated with the musician Henry Lawes on two masques. The first was "Arcades" (1633), written for the dowager countess of Derby. The second and more familiar to later audiences was later titled COMUS (1634), written to honor the newly appointed lord lieutenant of Wales, the earl of Bridgewater, who had married the countess's daughter. In 1638 Milton wrote one of the best known of the tribute poems in English from the Renaissance era, LYCIDAS. He composed the verse to contribute to a poetry collection written in memory of his fellow student and friend Edward King, who drowned at sea. Milton next traveled to Italy, where he met Galileo and enjoyed a more receptive audience for his work than he had in England. He toured the Continent but returned home upon the death of another good friend, Charles Diodati. In 1639 he honored Diodati in a lengthy Latin poem titled *Epitaphium Damonis.*

Milton began in 1641 what would become a long-time career as a pamphleteer, joining the fray in the second Bishop's War to publish against the Episcopalians. Pamphlets included *Of Reformation, Of Prelatical Episcopany,* and *Animadversions.* The first pamphlet that bore his name, *The Reason of Church Government,* became one of his most famous. He followed it with *An Apology for Smectymnuus,* published in 1642, as England grappled with the threat of civil war.

When not embroiled in the public turmoil over religion, Milton tutored his nephews, Edward and John Phillips, and finally married in 1642. His wife, a Royalist sympathizer named Mary Powell and younger than Milton by 16 years, left him as a result of unexplained circumstances after six weeks. Milton next published four pamphlets supporting divorce, arguing that when two people do not agree on spiritual matters, separation proves the only remedy; he ranked spiritual conflict between members of a couple above adultery and sexual incompatibility in severity. The public did not receive the divorce pamphlets well, but Milton remained undaunted. In his traditional manner, once he fixed on a cause, his enthusiasm proved unshakable.

Milton's next project, a treatise titled *Of Education* (1644), described what he believed to be a superior curriculum for a young man's training. That same year he published his strongest argument in support of civic rights in *Areopagitica,* which defended freedom of the press. A 1645 collection of poetry, *Poems of Mr. John Milton,* which included the famous paired poems "L'ALLEGRO" and "IL PENSEROSO," was basically ignored by the public. However the cool reception affected Milton, he continued to publish, his works including politically themed poetry such as the SONNET "ON THE NEW FORCERS OF CONSCIENCE UNDER THE LONG PARLIAMENT" (1646?).

Milton's personal life at last improved. Mary returned to Milton in 1645 after an apparent resolution of their conflict, and the Milton family grew with the births of their four children, Anne in 1646, Mary in 1648, John in 1651, and Deborah in 1652. The family was not to remain happy for long, as tragedy struck in 1652. Milton lost both his wife and his only son, and the family relocated to Petty France, Westminster.

Milton continued to champion civil liberties and attacked King Charles I, supporting the monarch's execution, in *The Tenure of Kings and Magistrates* and *Eikonaklastes.* The latter he wrote as a reply to the king's purported publication *Eikon Bastilke.* His political connections allowed him to begin a career translating foreign documents in 1649 when he accepted the appointed post secretary of foreign tongues to the Council of State. The poet ANDREW MARVELL became his assistant when Milton began losing his sight in 1651. He continued answering Royalist propaganda with a steady stream of prose, later blaming those writing efforts for his blindness. Critics learned much of a personal nature about Milton in one of those pamphlets, titled *Defense of Himself* (1651). He also wrote several politically themed sonnets during the interregnum, including "To the Lord General Cromwell, May 1652." In another Milton expressed his anger over the killing of Protestants. He composed "On the Late Massacre in Piedmont" as he also wrote correspondence on Cromwell's behalf expressing outrage over the event. He remarried in 1656 to Katherine Woodcock and they had a daughter, but Milton again suffered an enormous loss when both child and wife died in 1658. He wrote of his sorrow over the loss of one of his first two wives (critics disagree over which wife acts as subject) in "Methought I Saw My Late Espousèd Saint," and over the loss of his sight in the later widely anthologized "When I Consider How My Light Is Spent."

After the dissolution of the Protectorate Milton protested the looming Restoration in his pamphlet *The Ready and Easy Way to Establish a Free Commonwealth.* Never one to temper his enthusiasm, he risked severe punishment, and copies were destroyed after Charles II's return to the throne. Although imprisoned and threatened with death, Milton managed to pay a hefty fine and gain his release, in part through support from his friends Marvell and Sir William D'Avenant.

Milton married for a third time in 1663 to Elizabeth Minshull and resided with her in London for the remainder of his life, except for a brief interruption. In 1665 they had to live for a time in Chalfont St. Giles because of the threat of plague. Milton began an extraordinarily productive late period, especially in consideration of his loss of sight. He published *Paradise Lost* in 1667 and *Paradise Regained* and *Samson Agonistes* in 1671; most scholars believe he had begun these major works decades earlier. Although he continued to write, most critics consider *Samson Agonistes* his final great poem. In 1673 he published a new edition of his early poems, at last gaining the fame that had eluded him, and continued writing pamphlets, dying of gout in 1674; he was buried in St. Giles, Cripplegate. Posthumous works included *The History of Moscovia* and the second edition of *Paradise Lost*

with a preface poem, "On Mr. Milton's Paradise Lost," by Marvell.

Milton's output proved enormous, encompassing in addition to his published works detailed plans for projects never completed. The 18th century looked to his work as a model of divine poetry, but later critics attacked his challenging language as too inaccessible for general enjoyment. The 19th-century romantics favorably viewed him as a revolutionary, and the 20th century again embraced Milton's work for its artistic and aesthetic sense. *Paradise Lost* became his signature work, reprinted multiple times and written in drama form, much to Marvell's distress, by John Dryden. Milton had himself originally planned it to be a drama, rather than an epic poem. Additional popular poems include "On His Blindness," "The Psalm Poems," and "How Soon Hath Time."

BIBLIOGRAPHY

Fallon, Robert T. *Divided Empire: Milton's Political Imagery.* University Park: Pennsylvania State University Press, 1995.

Fallon, Stephen. *Milton in Government.* University Park: Pennsylvania State University Press, 1993.

Fish, Stanley. *How Milton Works.* Cambridge, Mass.: Belknap Press of Harvard University Press, 2001.

———. *Surprised by Sin: The Reader in Paradise Lost.* New York: St. Martin's Press, 1969.

Hale, John K. "Milton's Self-Representation in Poems . . . 1645." *Milton Quarterly* 25 (1991): 1–48.

Hanford, James Holly. *John Milton Poet and Humanist.* Cleveland, Ohio: Press of Western Reserve University, 1966.

Hill, John Spencer. *John Milton: Poet, Priest and Prophet: A Study of Divine Vocation in Milton's Poetry and Prose.* London: Macmillan, 1979.

Hughes, Merritt Y., ed. *John Milton: Complete Poems and Major Prose.* New York: Macmillan, 1957.

Hunter, William B., C. A. Patrides, and J. H. Adamson. *Bright Essence: Studies in Milton's Theology.* Salt Lake City: University of Utah Press, 1971.

Lewalski, Barbara K. *The Life of Milton: A Critical Biography.* Oxford: Blackwell, 2000.

Loewenstein, David. *Milton and the Drama of History: Historical Vision, Iconoclasm, and the Literary Imagination.* Cambridge: Cambridge University Press, 1990.

Moseley, C. W. R. D. *The Poetic Birth: Milton's Poems of 1645.* Aldershot, England: Scolar Press, 1991.

Norrington, Charles. *Shakespeare, the Bible, Milton and Others.* Edinburgh: Pentland, 1994.

Parker, William Riley. *Milton: A Biographical Commentary.* Oxford: Clarendon, 1996.

Patrides, C. A. *Milton and the Christian Tradition.* Hamden, Conn.: Archon Books, 1979.

Potter, Lois. *A Preface to Milton.* New York: Longman, 1986.

Revard, Stella P. *Milton and the Tangles of Neaera's Hair: The Making of the 1645 Poems.* Columbia: University of Missouri Press, 1997.

Samuel, Irene. *Plato and Milton.* Ithaca, N.Y.: Cornell University Press, 1947.

Schiffhorst, Gerald R. *John Milton.* New York: Continuum, 1990.

Shawcross, John T. *Rethinking Milton Studies: Time Present and Time Past.* Newark: University of Delaware Press, 2005.

Thorpe, James Ernest. *John Milton: the Inner Life.* San Marino, Calif.: Huntington Library, 1983.

Walker, Julia M., ed. *Milton and the Idea of Woman.* Urbana: University of Illinois Press, 1981.

Wilson, A. N. *The Life of John Milton.* New York: Oxford University Press, 1983.

Wolfe, Don Marion. *Milton and His England.* Princeton, N.J.: Princeton University Press, 1971.

"MIRA'S WILL" MARY LEAPOR (1748) A writer whose work has been termed labor-class poetry, the house maid MARY LEAPOR may have written "Mira's Will" based on the model of JONATHON SWIFT's well-known satire "VERSES ON THE DEATH OF DR. SWIFT." As noted by Leapor's biographer Richard Greene, Leapor's lines express the same "black humor" as do Swift's. In fine Augustan tradition Leapor writes of her own death, adopting the idea of balance and order in distributing her possessions at her death, then satirizing those ideas through emphasis of the fact that she has no material possessions. Instead she catalogs in 18th-century tradition aspects of her personality, which she bequeaths to those who remain behind. The poem reflects Leapor's knowledge of civil law, an important aspect of Augustan order, in her opening term, *IMPRIMIS,* (in the first place) as well as in a later direction to her executors. The poem also reflects a strong sense of self in the poet's ability to turn her own impending death into humor. Long in poor health, Leapor correctly predicted her early death at age 24.

Leapor's 16 sets of HEROIC COUPLETS are as elegant as any constructed by Swift or ALEXANDER POPE. Lacking material goods to leave behind, she instructs the distribution of other elements without a hint of sentimentality:

My name to public censure I submit,
To be disposed of as the world thinks fit;
My vice and folly let oblivion close,
The world already is o'erstocked with those;

Her gifts turn more positive in later lines, as she gives her "truth" to "modish lovers," her "cool reflection to unthinking youth," and "some good-nature" to "surly husbands, as their needs require." She concludes the first section of gifting with her own pursuits in mind, as "To the small poets" she leaves her pen.

Beginning at line 17 she instructs the design of her funeral and procession, as was common for wills of her era. Although it is meant to be a mock-description, she includes many traditional aspects, such as the carrying of evergreens, believed to represent the soul's immortality: "Let a small Sprig (true Emblem of my Rhyme) / Of blasted Laurel on my Hearse recline." Additional details include the employ of a "grave wight" who desires fame by "chanting dirges through a market-town," carrying a "broken flute." She also includes "six comic poets" as well as a "virtuoso, rich in sun-dried weeds" and "The politician, whom no mortal heeds." Other individuals are noted, as Leapor constructs a crowd scene, quiet and orderly. As Greene writes, one could describe the scene as formal, except that Leapor undercuts that idea by offering "figures of folly or contradiction." She even includes directions for the paid mourners that eyes may be wiped and "widowed husbands o'er their garlic cry," making light of the false nature of such mourning. She concludes with the typical statement that declares herself "In body healthy, and composed in mind" at the time she recorded her will.

BIBLIOGRAPHY
Greene, Richard. *Mary Leapor: A Study in Eighteenth-Century Women's Poetry.* Oxford: Clarendon Press, 1993.

MOCK-HEROIC The mock-heroic poem, most popular in the post-RESTORATION and Augustan eras, satirizes stereotypes of heroes popular in modern and romantic mythology. Classical writers including Homer used the form to comic effect. The 17th-century poet

JOHN DRYDEN employed mock-heoric in his "MACFLEC-KNOE: A SATIRE UPON THE TRUE-BLUE PROTESTANT POET T.S." but the most famous poet to employ mock-heroic was ALEXANDER POPE. His parodies took aim at traditional ideas of courage and acts of greatness. Probably the most familiar mock-heroic is Pope's "The RAPE OF THE LOCK," in which the speaker tells with elevated language and in epic form the tale of Belinda, a decidedly nonsympathetic heroine, who defends her honor against an admirer who clips a lock of her hair.

BIBLIOGRAPHY
Broich, Ulrich. *Mock-Heroic Poetry, 1680–1750.* Tübingen: M. Niemeyer, 1971.

MONTAGU, LADY MARY WORTLEY
(1689–1762) Lady Mary Wortley Montagu was the daughter of the first duke of Kingston, born in London as Lady Mary Pierrepoint. Her father, although a youngest son, would inherit his grandfather's fortune and the Evelyn estates. He obeyed his parents, taking part in an arranged marriage to Lady Mary Fielding; the couple had three daughters, Mary the eldest. She enjoyed an excellent education, although she had to seek it for herself, as her father took an active part in the court of King George I. As a young woman Lady Mary wrote essays and poetry, which she boldly passed about to members of her circle as a lark; she had no desire to become a professional writer. She also showed her independent spirit early in rejecting her father's selection of a husband. Instead she eloped with Edward Wortley Montagu in 1712, infuriating her father, but she enjoyed life as the wife of a member of parliament (M.P.). While untitled, Montagu would become one of the wealthiest men in England.

The couple became friends with various writers, their literary circle including MARY ASTELL, ALEXANDER POPE, and Joseph Addison, although Montagu would become Pope's enemy years later. When Lord Montagu became an ambassador to Constantinople in 1716, Lady Mary willingly joined him to live abroad for two years, her letters about their experiences gaining her fame when they were published in 1724. She became the first English woman to write of experiences in a non-Christian, nonwhite country. Her biographer Isobel Grundy notes Montagu's interest in the "melting pot" surroundings, writing of her family, "They had Arab grooms, Russian housemaids, French, English, and German footmen, miscellaneous Greek servants, and an Italian steward." More adventurous than many of her female friends, she visited Constantinople, delighting in its landscape.

One letter reveals Montagu's logical approach to life as she advises her friend Phillipa, who wonders whether to marry an unattractive man for wealth or a handsome man for love. She writes, "Believe from my experience there is no state so happy as with a man you like," encouraging Phillipa that she could learn to love a man, regardless of his physical form, if he could make her secure. Should Phillipa sacrifice security for love, Montagu asks, "The cares, the self denial, and the novelty that you will find in that manner of living, will it never be uneasy to you?" She continues, asking, "When time and cares have changed you to a downright housekeeper, will you not try," a question she completes with a stanza of poetry that asks whether Philippa will not return to her "father's hospitable gate." Montagu concludes by sensibly telling her friend to use her best judgment: "If you would avoid Mr. C. only because he is not well made, don't avoid him; if you would marry another only because you like him, don't marry him."

While in Turkey Lady Montagu learned of the scratch method designed to inoculate humans against smallpox. Having suffered deep scars from her own encounter with that disease, she had her children inoculated against it and publicized the method upon her return to England, although English physicians did not support it. In 1723 whatever disagreement she had with Pope caused him to include an unflattering representation of Montagu in print, a technique in which she also indulged. Facts have never revealed the source of their problems, although modern critics believe they were based on gender expectations. Pope's letters objectify Montagu as mere flesh, in the 18th-century way, while Montagu constructs herself as a reader and a writer. Despite their falling out, Pope was said to have had her portrait in his room at his death.

Lady Mary's interaction with other contemporary writers also proved interesting. While best known as a playwright, JOHN GAY wrote the first English "town eclogue," "Araminata" (1713). The eclogue represented a mix of pastoral and burlesque with a bit of classicism. He published five eclogues, one of which bore a great resemblance to an eclogue by Montagu, published in her *Town Eclogues* (1716). Both eclogues were titled "The Toilette" and shared other characteristics, suggesting the two poets not only knew one another's work but might also have collaborated. Montagu's six eclogues appeared first as a group in 1747, but she had composed them between 1715 and 1716. Her "The Toilette" she calls her "Friday poem," as her group is arranged like the days of the week and includes her often anthologized "SATURDAY: THE SMALL POX." Gay's *Shepherd's Week* with a similar arrangement had appeared in 1714. Critics continue to wonder over the exact relationship between the two poems and their writers. The two works differ in length, Gay's poem 106 lines and Montagu's 78. Both provide the lament of a 35-year-old woman named Lydia, rejected by her lover, Damon, for his younger wife, Cloe. Some critics have judged Montagu's poem wittier, providing clever PARADOX in her vigorous approach. Gay's version has been described as too gentle. Both attempt to provide a satiric picture of marriage, juxtaposing country virtue with urban vice.

Additional familiar poems by Montagu include "EPISTLE FROM MRS. YONGE TO HER HUSBAND" and "Epitaph," contained in her *Court Poems by a Lady of Quality* (1716). In 1737 she launched a periodical in favor of Sir Robert Walpole titled *The Nonsense of Common Sense,* which included a feminist essay that critics believed was inspired by her friend Mary Astell. Her relationship with Lord Montagu turned sour, and she fell in love with a bisexual Italian count named Francesco Algarotti. Montagu had always believed that Italians respected women, while the English held them in contempt. Although she had never believed that women should usurp the power of men, she did believe they should receive an education and not be penalized for their intelligence. As Grundy notes, she had written of women in a letter, "We are educated in the grossest ignorance, and no art omitted to stiffle [sic] our natural reason; if some few get above their Nurses' instructions, our knowledge must rest conceal'd and be as useless to the World as Gold in the Mine." Her work became exposed through publication in *Dodsley's Collection* and the *London Magazine,* although Montagu claimed little interest in publication. She also claimed pieces she had not written had appeared under her name, while some of those she had written appeared under the names of others.

Montagu's husband agreed to divorce her if she would leave England. She complied, although she found painful the separation from her daughter, Lady Bute, and the grandchildren she would not meet for years. Novels such as one by John Cleland, author of *Memoirs of a Woman of Pleasure,* better known as *Fanny Hill,* featured a false portrayal of Montagu. Titling his novel *Memoirs of a Coxcomb,* Cleland featured as hero Lady Bell Tavers, a corrupt woman of fashion clearly modeled on Montagu.

Despite the separation from her family and public vilification, Montagu made a successful independent life for herself for more than 20 years, a unique situation for a woman of her era. Letters written in order to preserve her relationship with Lady Bute and her family during her long absence prove an important part of Montagu's literary legacy. In 1741 the scholar Joseph Spence interviewed her in Rome with interest in her relationship with Pope. She described Pope's style, which at one time she had greatly admired, as only "a knack," just "all tune and no meaning," an approach that he himself had criticized in others. Spence claimed to have seen more than 50 letters written from Pope to Montagu, all of which were later lost. She lived in France and Italy after 1738, not returning home until 1762, the year after her husband's death. Montagu died shortly after returning to England while living with her daughter.

While Montagu seemed to live a charmed life in many ways, she expressed displeasure over feeling trapped in a man's world. As Grundy writes, "Most of the potential benefits of her rank came with a 'Men Only' label." That included the wealth with which she was always surrounded but that she never controlled. She lived as an intellectual woman in an era when rationality proved the rage, yet was anathema to the female blessed with it. The emotional sensitivity thought proper for a young woman that Montagu also possessed was used against her, an ironic punishment for compliance with her era's demands. She succeeded, however, in her struggle against the male dominance that threatened to suppress her intellectual expression. Her publications in the 20th century fill multiple volumes, including *Complete Letters, 1965–7; Essays and Poems, 1977, 1993;* and *Romance Writings, 1996.* Montagu interested later critics both as a writer and as a personality. They continue to search for unpublished pieces, which she mentioned and to produce scholarship based on Montagu's fascinating life and works.

BIBLIOGRAPHY

Campbell, Jill. "Lady Mary Wortley Montagu and the Historical Machinery of Female Identity." In *History, Gender, and Eighteenth-Century Literature,* edited by Beth Fowkes Tobin. Athens: University of Georgia Press, 1994.

Carrell, Jennifer Lee. *The Speckled Monster: A Historical Tale of Battling Smallpox.* New York: Dutton, 2003.

Crawford, Patricia. "The Construction and Experience of Maternity." In *Women as Mothers in Pre-Industrial England: Essays in Memory of Dorothy McLaren,* edited by Valerie Fildes. New York: Routledge, 1990.

DelPlato, Joan. "An English 'Feminist' in the Turkish Harem: A Portrait of Lady Mary Wortley Montagu." In *Eighteenth-Century Women and the Arts,* edited by Frederick M. Keener and Susan E. Lorsch. New York: Greenwood Press, 1988.

Fernea, Elizabeth Warnock. "An Early Ethnographer of Middle Eastern Women: Lady Mary Wortley Montagu." *Journal of Near Eastern Studies* 40 (1981): 329–338.

Grundy, Isobel. *Lady Mary Wortley Montagu.* New York: Oxford University Press, 1999.

———. "The Politics of Female Authorship: Lady Mary Wortley Montagu's Reaction to the Printing of Her Poems." *Bodleian Library Record* 10 (1988): 237–249.

———. "A Skirmish between Pope and Some Persons of Rank and Fortune: *Verses to the Imitator of Horace.*" *Studies in Bibliography* 30 (1977): 96–119.

Nokes, David. *John Gay: A Profession of Friendship.* New York: Oxford University Press, 1995.

Pick, Christopher, ed. *Embassy to Constantinople: The Travels of Lady Mary Wortley Montagu.* New York: New Amsterdam, 1998.

Rogers, Katherine M. *Before Their Time: Six Women Writers of the Eighteenth Century.* New York: Frederick Ungar, 1979.

MOWER POEMS, THE Andrew Marvell (1681)   Andrew Marvell may have written the four poems constituting the collection most editors refer to as *The Mower Poems* during his stay at Nun Appleton, an experience that would also inspire his "Upon Appleton House, to My Lord Fairfax." The poems, generally printed in the sequence in which they appeared in the posthumous *Miscellaneous Poems* (1681), are "The Mower against Gardens," "Damon the Mower," "The Mower to the Glow-worms," and "The Mower's Song." As the critic Nigel Smith explains, sources for all of the poems have connections not discernible until one closely studies the four pieces. As he often did, Marvell drew on the classics. In "The Mower against the Garden," the speaker remarks about tree grafting, a procedure that Pliny noted should take place before the intense summer heat, when the dog star is most prominent in the night sky. Both that heat and the star are referenced by the speaker in "Damon the Mower."

The settings of the poems reflect the seasons in which one would see mowers in the fields, beginning in late spring, to early summer, to later summer, with the grass mowing preceding harvest. With each poem the tone darkens until finally facing autumn the mower finds himself unable to work, the result of an unrequited love, which he feels will lead to his death. Other critics analyze the voice as the poet's own. In their view Marvell begins celebrating the pastoral tradition but turns against it by the fourth poem, when the theme remains death and his mower no longer finds sustenance in his pastoral surroundings. Marvell knew from his study of the classics that mowers were traditional figures in pastoral form, as were shepherds. In some translations *reaper* is substituted for *mower.* Mowers, as well as reapers, represented death in some pastorals, as they were associated with the passage of time and seasonal activities. Many critics see the poems as a contrast of innocence with experience, a common theme for poetry.

In "The Mower against the Garden" the mower represents wisdom and experience pitted against learning and experiment, as he chastises those who would not allow a garden to retain its natural state but rather insisted on unnatural ornamentation and changes, which are the product of horticultural experiments. The speaker describes "Luxurious man" as using his "vice" to "the world seduce," enclosing naturally beautiful spaces into gardens shaped into squares, producing "A dead and standing pool of air." Marvell extends his metaphor of man as seductive oppressor through the entire poem. The speaker argues for the higher value of natural, versus "luscious earth," fortified with unnatural nutrients that "stupefied" the plants while feeding them. With their nutrients altered, the roses take on "strange perfumes" and even the "flowers themselves were taught to paint," while "The tulip, white did for complexion seek," indicating that a tulip lacking color, or "complexion," is unnatural.

The gardener then declares man might have been excused such trespass had he left alone the trees, but instead man places "between the bark and tree" an unknown domestic plant. "He grafts upon the wild the tame," producing adulterated fruit. He also persuades the cherry "To procreate without a sex," such enforcements removing the natural beauty from plants and trees. The gardener prefers nature and its innocence, where "The gods themselves with us do dwell."

"Damon the Mower" was probably written during the unusually hot summer of 1652. In addition to that natural inspiration, Marvell turns to Theocritus as a source, his mower's humiliating lack of erection mimicking that of the cyclops Polythemus in wooing Galatea, a story also retold by other poets. VIRGIL's shepherd Corydon, as does Damon, offers gifts that are ignored by the object of his love, who happens to be a boy. Although Damon imagines death as the proper reaction for his rejection, Corydon simply returns to his pastoral life for sustenance. A more modern source may have been Thomas Randolph's "An Eclogue to Master Jonson," in which heat plays a crucial part in his depiction of mowers. Marvell's poem assumes a formal format, divided into 11 eight-line stanzas of rhyming couplets. The speaker is not Damon, but a storyteller who begins, "Hark how the mower Damon sung, / With love of Juliana stung!" The heat first plays a part as symbolic of Damon's passion:

Like her fair eyes the day was fair;
But scorching like his am'rous care.
Sharp like his scythe his sorrow was,
And withered like his hopes the grass.

Marvell establishes imagery of death, including the scythe, emblematic of the grim reaper. Sexual references, including one to "the snake, that kept within, / Now glitters in its second skin," suggest Damon's erection as he fantasizes about the shepherdess Juliana. However, when he approaches her with gifts rejected, the snake is "harmless" and "Disarmèd of its teeth and sting"; he has apparently become self-conscious and flaccid in her presence. Damon can find no relief for "the fires / Of the hot day, or hot desires." He can find no moisture other than that of his own tears, "Nor cold but in her icy breast," a reference to Juliana's rejection of him. Damon notes that he might have continued to be content as a mower, except for the "thistles" sown by Love:

"But now I all the day complain,
Joining my labour to my pain;
And with my scythe cut down the grass,
Yet still my grief is where it was:
But, when the iron blunter grows,
Sighing I whet my scythe and woes."

Distracted by love, he accidentally slices his own ankle, "By his scythe, the mower mown," as Marvell makes a pun, suggesting the term *moan*, representing Damon's agony. He knows the natural plant antidotes for his problem, which include "shepherd's-purse and clown's-all-heal," but even though he can halt the bleeding, he will not heal. Marvell closes as Damon explains:

"Only for him no cure is found,
Whom Juliana's eyes do wound.
'Tis Death alone that this must do:
For Death thou art a mower too."

The final line supplies an explicit aligning of the mower with death and with time, which traditionally carried a scythe when represented in iconic form.

The third poem in the series, "The Mower to the Glow-worms," is the most brief with only four four-line stanzas and a RHYME scheme of *abab*. The speaker expresses his grief over the fact that Juliana has so confused him that he will never find his way home. None of the natural guides, which include the glow-worms, beautifully referred to in FIGURATIVE LANGUAGE as "Ye living lamps," can assist him. He describes the meditative nightingale and "country comets." The comets "portend / No war, nor prince's funeral" but instead light the grass that has been cut by the mower, another death reference. While the glow-worms' "officious flame" often showed wandering mowers the way, they will no longer act as this mower's salvation. Critics note the escalation of the sorrowful tone, as the speaker no longer finds solace in his pastoral surroundings. They also find suggestive the fact that the speaker never refers to himself as a mower; no self-reference at all appears until the conclusion of the poem, when alienation from his world is complete.

The group of four poems concludes with "The Mower's Song," labeled by some a dirge, or song to accompany a funeral procession. The refrain "When Juliana came, and she / What I do to the grass, does to my thoughts and me" repeats as the final two lines of each of the five six-line stanzas, holding the focus firmly on death. This format remains unique among Marvell's work, with the first through fifth lines of each stanza reflecting the METER of tetrameter, while the final line is an alexandrine containing 12 regular monosyllable terms. Juliana represents life's experience, where his former pastoral existence prior to his passion for her represents his innocent age. Before Juliana, the speaker recalls,

My mind was once the true survey
Of all these meadows fresh and gay
And in the greenness of the grass
Did see its hopes as in a glass.

Marvell adopts a common approach, seen in work by Edmund Spenser, among many others, in featuring nature as a reflection of human thought. The speaker describes his surroundings as growing ever lusher and more luxurious, filled with flowers, while he pines away, filled with sorrow. He queries the "Unthankful meadows" as to how they could "A fellowship so true forgo," holding "gaudy May-games" while he "lay trodden under feet?" The speaker ruefully declares that he will have his revenge on nature for ignoring him. All that is green, along with him, "Will in one common ruin fall." As do classical heroes, he hauls his world, or parts of it, into Hades along with him. The mower now merges into his surroundings, not only identifying with the pastoral scene, but becoming that scene. In that manner Juliana may do to his thoughts and body what he has done to the grass, striking it down with his scythe. The green will become mere "heraldry" to "adorn his tomb," the color an emblem like that appearing on a coat of arms.

BIBLIOGRAPHY

Anderson, Linda. "The Nature of Marvell's Mower." *Studies in English Literature, 1500–1900* 31, no. 1 (winter 1991): 131–146.

Edgecome, Rodney. "*Pastorale à clef*: A Tentative New View of Marvell's 'Mower Poems.'" *Durham University Journal* 55 (1994): 209–217.

Kegl, Rosemary. "'Joyning My Labour to My Pain': The Politics of Labor in Marvell's Mower Poems." In *Soliciting Interpretation: Literary Theory and Seventeenth-Century English Poetry,* edited by Elizabeth D. Harvey and Katharine Eisaman Maus, 89–118. Chicago: University of Chicago Press, 1990.

Sessions, W. A. "Marvell's Mower: The Wit of Survival." In *The Wit of Seventeenth-Century Poetry,* edited by Claude J. Summers and Ted-Larry Pebworth, 183–198. Columbia: University of Missouri Press, 1995.

Smith, Nigel. "Introduction." In *The Poems of Andrew Marvell,* edited by Nigel Smith, xii–xvii. New York: Pearson/Longman, 2003.

Wortham, Christopher. "Marvell's 'The Mower to the Glowworms.'" *The Explicator,* spring 1991, 142–144.

"MY CAT JEOFFRY" CHRISTOPHER SMART (1763)

The brilliant but mentally disturbed CHRISTOPHER SMART wrote his famous passage from his *Jubilate Agno*, "My Cat Jeoffry," while confined in a mental hospital between 1759 and 1763. As Smart's only companion, Jeoffry provided a focus for his religious energy. The poem presents Jeoffry as a feline, but also as an emblem of God's divine greatness. Smart incorporates the complicated numerology and abrupt declarations for which he became famous in later centuries; he received little critical acknowledgment in his own lifetime. At 75 lines in length the poem adopts the form of the Psalms, antiphonal in its cryptic statements designed to answer one another. Each line begins with the word *For,* establishing a cause/effect relationship between God and the beasts of his creation, which include man.

The speaker begins, "For I will consider my Cat Jeoffry. / For he is the servant of the Living God duly and daily serving him." Smart's work viewed the human world as a reflection of the Supreme Being, and he filled his verse with praise for that power. The speaker describes the cat as one who "worships in his way," allowing Smart to launch a brilliant description of typical cat activity that he relates to the ritual of worship. The cat "performs in ten degrees" after having received God's blessing, and he begins to "consider himself." Smart suggests that the cat possesses a power of introspection that humans lack. He establishes Jeoffry as one from which humans might learn positive behavior, an idea that extends throughout the poem.

In the next 10 lines Smart follows the word *For* with a number in adverb form: *first, secondly, thirdly,* and so on. Each action Jeoffry takes remains familiar to the reader, so Smart proceeds to teach with simple illustration. For example, he writes of his cat, "Thirdly he works it upon stretch with the fore-paws extended," "For fifthly he washes himself," and "For Eighthly he rubs himself against a post." After Jeoffry's 10 actions "he will consider his neighbor," as in kissing "in kindness" another cat that he meets. He also takes time to enjoy his world, "dallying" frequently enough that "one mouse in seven escapes."

At the conclusion of Jeoffry's day "his business more properly begins. / For he keeps the Lord's watch in the night against the adversary." In Smart's view the cat "counteracts the powers of darkness by his electrical skin & glaring eyes. / For he counteracts the Devil, who is death, by brisking about the life." Smart contradicts the common view of cats as creatures linked with the devil and Satanic ritual. Not only is Jeoffry not a creature of Satan, he actually helps protect his cell mate against evil forces. Smart introduces the idea of electricity in this imagery, an allusion to natural power to which he will return later in the poem. Jeoffry's use of his natural powers supports his life spirit. Smart's transformation of the adjective *brisk* to the verb form *brisking* demonstrates an adept use of wordplay and proves delightful to the ear. The term will later reappear.

Although Jeoffry helps fight the devil, "the Cherub Cat is a term of the Angel Tiger. / For he has the subtlety and hissing of a serpent, which in goodness he suppresses." The phrase *Angel Tiger* acts as ANTITHESIS to demonstrate the contradiction between the state of grace and the natural state. In other words the cat has learned to suppress any natural evil instincts, but only through God's help and in desire for the peace God's presence allows. As the speaker explains:

> For he will not do destruction if he is well-fed, neither will he spit without provocation.
> For he purrs in thankfulness, when God tells him he's a good Cat.
> For he is an instrument for the children to learn benevolence upon.

Smart next skillfully inserts cats into biblical history, although the Bible never mentions a cat, claiming that "the Lord commanded Moses concerning the cats at the departure of the / Children of Israel from Egypt" that every household must have one. He then moves abruptly to the present scene, writing of the Hebrews, then the English: "For every family had one cat at least in the bag. / For the English Cats are the best in Europe." He again adopts wordplay in his wry use of the common phrase *in the bag,* with its connotation of something assured. Smart follows with a delightful catalog of reasons why Jeoffry as an English cat deserves the title *best in Europe:*

> For he is the quickest to his mark of any creature.
> For he is tenacious of his point.
> For he is a mixture of gravity and waggery.
> For he knows that God is his Saviour.
> For there is nothing sweeter than his peace when at rest.
> For there is nothing brisker than his life when in motion.

Smart creates another ingenuous term with *waggery,* as Jeoffry's natural force of motion is compared to that of gravity. As surely as Jeoffry coexists with gravity's constraints, he also exists and gains power from the knowledge of his state of grace. Smart continues to contrast the natural with the divine, simultaneously establishing the two states of being as closely related.

In addition, Smart continues to loop back on previous imagery, as in the use again of the root *brisk,* a technique that helps provide unity for his poem. The cat is also "of the Lord's poor," and "the divine spirit comes about his body to sustain it in compleat cat." Readers find the use of ALLITERATION pleasing and can enjoy the celebration of Jeoffry for being a cat's cat.

The cataloguing of Jeoffry's positive aspects continues, as the speaker cites the purity of the cat's tongue by noting, "so that it has in purity what it wants in music." Sharp suggests a whimsical thought that leads the reader to associate Jeoffry's cleaning of his fur to music. Jeoffry also is praised for his docility, which allows him to "learn certain things." Smart may be contrasting the cat to humans, who, despite their superior mental capacity, allow their emotions to interfere with intellectual development. The speaker notes that the cat "can catch the cork and toss it again. / For he is hated by the hypocrite and miser." The hypocrite "is afraid of detection," while the miser "refuses the charge." Smart engages in more wordplay as he again adopts a noun, *camel,* as a verb in a description of Jeoffry: "For he camels his back to bear the first notion of business." The poet accentuates the image of Jeoffry's arched back not only through FIGURATIVE LANGUAGE in comparing the arch to a camel's hump, but also through alliteration in the repeated use of the hard sound *b.* He suggests that Jeoffry has developed a technique by which to bear life's burdens.

In the final lines of the poem Smart again turns the reader's attention to the divine, noting that when he strokes his cat, he learns about electricity: "For I perceived God's light about him both wax and firs. / For the Electrical fire is the spiritual substance, which god sends from heaven." The reader can mentally visualize sparks flying from Jeoffry's fur as the speaker runs his hand along the cat's back. The "spiritual substance" God designs "to sustain the bodies both of man and beast." Clearly the cat provides support through his substance to the poet who strokes and admires him.

Jeoffry's body is perfect for his needs, as "God has blessed him in the variety of his movements." Although "he cannot fly, he is an excellent clamberer," so excellent that "his motions upon the face of the earth are more than any other quadrupede." In those lines Smart suggests that Jeoffry has learned a secret of life, to utilize perfectly his natural abilities, rather than wasting energy pursuing goals he can never fulfill, a lesson that humans have yet to learn. He also makes clear that God provides the source of Jeoffry's physical superiority to man.

The final three lines provide a magnificent conclusion, in both sense and form. Smart ends with quiet thunder, pouring into those lines all of the lessons he has learned from his cat. While Jeoffry can leap through the air and wreak havoc upon smaller creatures according to his natural instincts, he has also learned to tread, swim, and creep when needed, life skills gained only through restraint. Smart considers his cat a life artist, as he recalls the former imagery of music. Because music remains an art closely associated with the science of mathematics, the poet's obsession with numbers may again be seen in his use of the term *measures.* The term works on multiple levels, as it also relates in poetry to divisions into distinct rhythmic units and may be applied to any equivalents that can be meted out, including time and energy:

> For he can tread to all the measures upon the
>   music.
> For he can swim for life.
> For he can creep.

The 20th-century composer Benjamin Britten adopted a short excerpt from the poem for use in his festival cantata "Rejoice in the Lamb."

BIBLIOGRAPHY

Curry, Neil. *Christopher Smart.* Horndon, England: Northcote House, 2005.

Guest, Harriet. *A Form of Sound Words: The Religious Poetry of Christopher Smart.* New York: Oxford University Press, 1989.

"MY MUSE, NOW HAPPY, LAY THYSELF TO REST" LADY MARY WROTH (1621)

LADY MARY WROTH added to her prose romance *The Countess of Montgomery's Urania* a SONNET sequence, "PAMPHILIA TO AMPHILANTHUS." The concluding sonnet signaled the end of the reader's process, but also of the writer's process. Wroth's speaker addresses her muse, a common trope to place at the beginning of Renaissance poetry, as poets call for the muse's guidance in their writing. In this stanza Wroth instead dismisses her muse, bidding her "lay thy self to rest," after a job well accomplished that left her muse happy. She tells her, "Sleep in the quiet of a faithful love," a reference to the topic, in part, of Wroth's romance and sonnets. They do not focus on love alone, but on the crucial aspect of fidelity in love.

As a poet the speaker understands that her words no longer belong to her once on the page and digested by readers. Instead "these fantasies" should now "move / Some other hearts." The speaker emphasizes that her muse has faithfully presented the truth to her readers and now must focus on that topic herself. She should address truth, and its "eternal goodness" will lead the muse, and the poet by extension, to the "Enjoying of true joy the most and best, / The endless gain which never will remove." Love alone does not lead to joy; it must be bolstered by truth and fidelity to prove beneficial. Wroth emphasizes joy as the result of practicing truth through its repetition as an internal RHYME. Her muse cannot be responsible for teaching young lovers about passion; they must turn to "the discourse of Venus and her sun," where the term *sun* acts as a pun for *son*, referencing Venus's son, Cupid, the Roman god of love. Those figures sought only to cause humans to fall in love. They had no interest in making the lovers remain faithful to one another, as the poet does.

Wroth notes that Venus's "stories of great love" must ignite the fire that will cause young lovers to "Get heat to write the fortunes they have won." She emphasizes the power of literature, "the story," in inspiring passion in others. The speaker concludes by telling her muse, by extension Lady Wroth herself, "And thus leave off; what's past shows you can love; / Now let your constancy your honor prove." It was not enough to tell of love or to fall in love. Only protracted fidelity to the loved one over time could prove one's honor and allow the one who loved the pure joy a faithful love could yield.

"MY PAIN, STILL SMOTHERED IN MY GRIEVÈD BREAST" LADY MARY WROTH (1621) LADY MARY WROTH included in her prose

romance *The Countess of Montgomery's Urania* a SONNET sequence titled "PAMPHILIA TO AMPHILANTHUS." Scholars refer to her sonnets by their first lines, with Sonnet 68 opening, "My pain, still smothered in my grievèd breast." The topic of this sonnet is clear: The speaker has suffered a loss that she tries to conceal from others. Wroth uses frequent ALLITERATION in this poem with frequent repetition of the s sound for emphasis. In her opening she emphasizes the degree of her speaker's suffering with the phrase *still smothered,* where *smothered* indicates an act involving great effort by the speaker. While her breast "Seeks for some ease," it finds no "passage" to be able to discharge "this unwelcome guest." Here Wroth adopts the FIGURATIVE LANGUAGE of personification to increase the immediacy of her statement. All readers would understand the idea of a guest who, although not welcome to his host, expects hospitality.

The greater the effort the speaker expends to rid herself of grief, the "most fast his burdens bind, / Like to a ship on Goodwin's cast by wind," where she refers to Goodwin Sands, a group of shoals that marked the entrance to the Strait of Dover. She extends the metaphor of the ship, describing herself as struggling as a stuck ship might, only to be "more deep in sand" as a result of striving for release. Finally "she be lost" and "so am I, in this kind, / Sunk, and devoured, and swallowed by unrest." The grounded ship, assaulted by the oceans and eaten by some enormous beast, works well as a metaphor to aid the reader's understanding of the full measure of the speaker's suffering. She has no hope, enjoys "Nothing of pleasure," and has thoughts that wander helplessly. She decides to send those thoughts away, telling them, "cry / Hope's perished, Love tempest-beaten, Joy lost." In a thoroughly convincing statement, the speaker notes, "Killing Despair hath all these blessings crossed." Here the term *Killing* acts as an adjective, again emphasizing the devastation Despair can cause.

The speaker concludes by emphasizing that one may secretly hope for relief from any pain, whether the hope is logical or not: "Yet Faith still cries, Love will not falsify." The faith to which she refers is a foolish trust, proved so by the preceding lines. Foolish or no, it remains as stubbornly as does the grief, trying to convince the speaker that love cannot be false. Despite evidence to the contrary, the speaker may at first glance seem to believe her own propaganda, that any such pure passion can not be sullied by distrust or betrayal. It is, however, upon closer consideration an ironic statement.

"MY PICTURE LEFT IN SCOTLAND"

BEN JONSON (1619, 1640–1641)   Although historians do not know the identity of the woman depicted by BEN JONSON in his poem "My Picture Left in Scotland," they feel confident he wrote it after having visited his friend and fellow poet WILLIAM DRUMMOND. It holds the ninth position in the group of 18 poems constituting *The Underwood*. Jonson does more than rue his age and soft physique as impediments to a relationship with the apparently desirable female. He also demonstrates in some instances through rhythm and format his topic as he writes about it.

The poem opens with a speaker speculating that "I now think Love is rather deaf than blind." He will spend 16 lines supporting his theory, finally returning to it in the poem's last line. He bases this theory on the fact that a mysterious "she" slighted him and cast away his love. Jonson varies the poem's METER, imitating the speaker's feeling off balance, or out of order:

> For else it could not be
> That she
> Whom I adore so much should so slight me
> And cast my love behind.

Jonson skillfully challenges the reader as he moves from the iambic pentameter of the first line, into iambic trimeter in line 2, dimeter in line 3, and back to iambic pentameter in line 4. Despite the fluctuating rhythm, ALLITERATION incorporated through the repeated *s* sound advances the reader swiftly through the lines. The speaker then expresses confidence in his sweet language and continues:

> And every close did meet
> In sentence of as subtle feet,
> As hath the youngest he
> That sits in shadow of Apollo's tree.

In these lines Jonson most clearly reflects the topic of poetry writing. He uses the term *close* to mean "cadence," or *meter,* "feet," to reflect the line unit containing one stressed syllable accompanied by one to two unstressed syllables, and the reference to a young man sitting under Apollo's tree to indicate a young poet. The fact that the younger poet sits in shadow reflects the speaker's attitude that his art not only equals, but overshadows that of the immature and unaccomplished youth.

Jonson inserts white space after his 10th line, after which he includes an additional eight lines. He reflects upon his "conscious fears / That fly my thoughts between," stating that although his thoughts remain rational, they are interrupted by irrational emotion, his fears. Those fears inform him that she has observed "My hundreds of gray hairs, / Told seven and forty years," and suddenly maturity becomes a liability. Jonson makes a pun on the word *waste,* writing, "Read so much waste as she cannot embrace / My mountain belly and my rocky face" as he emphasizes through imagery what she sees when she looks at the speaker. Unfortunately his appearance proves of greater effect than his well-wrought words, and he concludes in the final line, "And all these through her eyes have stopped her ears." Jonson has moved full circle, reflecting on his opening line, "I now think love is rather deaf, than blind."

N

"NEGRO'S COMPLAINT, THE" WILLIAM COWPER (1788)

WILLIAM COWPER was known for his vigorous support of various moral causes, one of which was the abolition of slavery. "The Negro's Complaint" was popular in its first printing as a BROADSIDE. Its four-beat lines allowed easy later conversion to a BALLAD, set to music.

Adopting the voice of an individual "Forc'd from home, and all its pleasures," Cowper imagines what a slave might yearn for in his foreign captivity. The speaker continues, "Afric's coast I left forlorn," making clear his origins. The next line speaks to man's inhumanity, as the speaker notes his misery is "To increase a stranger's treasures, / O'er the raging billows borne." The term *raging* in reference to the sea suggests that even the natural elements find the white man's enslavement of the black man intolerable. Cowper points a finger at the guilty as he continues, "Men from England bought and sold me, / Paid my price in paltry gold," offering the PARADOX "paltry gold" to remind readers that the value of a human life exceeds that of even the most precious metal. He calls attention to this important point using ALLITERATION in the repetition of the consonant *p*.

At this point the speaker reveals his superiority to his captors by concluding the opening stanza, "But, though theirs they have enroll'd me, / Minds are never to be sold." A common misperception, or simply an excuse used by slavers, was that slaves lacked the ability to reason, equating them with animals. The ability to think and reason equates to the slave's independence, as stated in the second stanza,

> Still in thought as free as ever,
> What are England's rights, I ask,
> Me from my delights to sever,
> Me to torture, me to task?

Cowper uses the slave's voice to ask some hard questions of his contemporaries, repeating the word *me* as the object of the slavers' heinous action. The voice next notes that although his physical appearance differs from that of his captors, he remains their equal in the ability to feel emotion:

> Fleecy locks, and black complexion
> Cannot forfeit nature's claim;
> Skins may differ, but affection
> Dwells in white and black the same.

Cowper continues to pound home his message that blacks and whites have much more in common than not. All the passions that the slaver feels, he should recognize in his captive. In addition he should understand that "Nature" did not intend plants to be nurtured through "sighs," "tears," and "sweat," although perhaps the landowner's "iron-hearted" nature enjoys the fact that "backs have smarted / For the sweets your cane affords." By suggesting that for mere plants slaves have suffered beating or caning, Cowper again makes clear the poor judgment of those who favor slavery.

In the fourth stanza the speaker appeals to his captor's religious faith, questioning, "Is there, as ye sometimes tell us, / Is there one who reigns on high?" Cowper's repetition proves effective, strengthening the condemnation in the gentle interrogative approach. He obviously hopes to shame his audience with relentless questions:

> Has he bid you buy and sell us,
> Speaking from his throne the sky?
> Ask him, if your knotted scourges,
> Matches, blood-extorting screws,
> Are the means which duty urges
> Agents of his will to use?

The speaker clearly suggests slavers are hypocrites. Then he adopts the voice of a prophet, predicting death and destruction for the culture that desecrates God's children through such vile practice:

> Hark! He answers—Wild tornadoes,
> Strewing yonder sea with wrecks;
> Wasting towns, plantations, meadows,
> Are the voice with which he speaks.

If any justice exists, man's deity will extract a heavy payment for the insolence that leads him to harm any of that deity's creations:

> He foreseeing what vexations
> Afric's sons should undergo,
> Fix'd their tyrants' habitations
> Where his whirlwinds answer—No.

Cowper concludes with two verses that suggest the greatest crime committed against those enslaved was the breaking of their hearts. Their blood wasted in Africa before their "necks receiv'd the chain," they then experienced the horrors of a ship's hold, prior to the "man-degrading mart" where they would be sold like dumb beasts. Cowper returns to the idea of marketing human flesh as unthinkable. The speaker notes that those who survived those terrors had to learn patience.

Finally, the voice retains its pride as it beseeches its audience, "Deem our nation brutes no longer," having proved that the slavers are the real brutes. The slavers must prove they "have human feelings, / Ere you proudly question ours!" The poet's own passion emerges through that of his speaker. He likely adopts the familiar CONCEIT of a COMPLAINT in an ironic manner, as traditional complaints often focused on frivolous, barely troublesome matters, such as a courtier's frustration in romance.

BIBLIOGRAPHY

Baird, John D., and Charles Ryskamp, eds. *The Poems of William Cowper.* New York: Oxford University Press, 1996.

"NIGHT, THE" HENRY VAUGHAN (1650) First printed in the collection *Silex Scintillans,* "The Night" by HENRY VAUGHAN uses a common 17th-century trope by imagining man as a microcosm, or tiny representative of the larger world, as he meditates on Christ's life. However, rather than employ the approach of contrasting the unchanging universe with human instability, Vaughan employs the vitality of the world to emphasize man's lack of spirituality. Many critics consider "The Night," which appeared in the second portion of the collection, as Vaughan's masterpiece. J. B. Leishman describes it as "one the most exquisitely tender and sensitive of all religious poems." The poem emphasizes contradictions inherent to Christianity. These contradictions include the ideas that one must lose one's self in order to be found, one must die in order to live, and one can achieve victory only through defeat. Such PARADOX allows Vaughan to incorporate the sort of CONCEIT characteristic of METAPHYSICAL POETS AND POETRY in dealing with the seeming contradiction he proposes, that darkness may reveal more than light.

A challenging piece, "The Night" is based on the biblical Gospel of John 3:2. In that verse John describes interaction between a Pharisee, a devout adherent to Torah law, and Jesus. The Pharisee, Nicodemus, tells Jesus during a nighttime visit, "Rabbi, we know that thou art a teacher come from God." He was one of only a few members of his group who recognized Jesus as God's son. Vaughan establishes the night setting as crucial to the dawning of true light, or knowledge, for Nicodemus and, by extension, for all of mankind.

The poem opens by setting a vivid scene:

> Through that pure virgin-shrine,
> That sacred veil drawn o'er thy glorious noon,
> That men might look and live as glowworms shine
>   And face the moon,
> Wise Nicodemus saw such light
> As made him know his God by night.

The line "Through that pure virgin-shrine" has provoked various critical explanations. Alan Rudrum explains the phrase *Virgin-shrine* as referencing God's son in his human existence as Christ. His body, or "that sacred veil," may be seen as a PARADOX as both revealing God to man and shielding God from man, as the night may hide the brilliance of the sun, a pun on the term *Son,* seen at "thy glorious noon" by man. The later allusion to glow worms may suggest that while man cannot directly view God's full light, he can view a diminished version through Christ. The worms cannot glow in sunlight; they need the night to do so. Thus paradoxically the dark produces light. The term *live* suggests physical life, but also spiritual life.

The second stanza praises Nicodemus for believing while others of his group remained blind to Jesus' identity. Although the savior had been "long-expected," most could not recognize his "healing wings" as he rose, as if he were a midnight sun.

Stanza 3 contains two questions, the first "O who will tell me where / He found thee at that dead and silent hour?" Some interpret the "dead and silent hour" as an allusion to the era of civil unrest in England experienced by Vaughan and made the subject of much of his poetry. However, the reader should note that Vaughan's attention remains on Christ, not as an aspect of man's history, but rather as a vital presence in nature. The ability of nature to reflect God for man's benefit remained another of Vaughan's traditional themes. Vaughan next references the Ark of the Covenant, so important to the Jewish people, writing that "No mercy seat of gold, / No dead and dusty cherub nor carved stone" greeted Nicodemus. Rather, Christ represents God's "living works," revealed to his believers while the Jews, Christ's own people, "did sleep" in ignorance,

represented in the poem by night. Vaughan's skillful use of imagery remains strong in his contrast of light and dark. The speaker broods while viewing the night landscape, its darkness allowing a contrast to the light provided by the heavenly stars, symbolic of God's saving grace. The fourth stanza builds on the story of Solomon's temple, with its architectural references. The speaker suggests more meaning is to be found in the natural world, "Where trees and herbs did watch and peep," than in human achievement.

The fifth stanza seems to some critics out of character with the others, but, as did GEORGE HERBERT, on whose poem "Prayer" Vaughan's fifth and sixth stanzas may be based, Vaughan worked with a variety of formats and approaches. His address to the night—"Dear night! This world's defeat"—acts as transition into the next stanzas, in which interpreters, including Rudrum, see night as a geographic location, rather than a specific time of day. However, one could disagree with the geographic theory based on repetition in the sixth stanza of the term *When,* which specifically suggests time:

> When my Lord's head is filled with dew, and all
> His locks are wet with the clear drops of night;
>   His still, soft call;
> His knocking time; the soul's dumb watch,
> When spirits their fair kindred catch.

That stanza alludes to the biblical passage in which Christ knocks on the door that has no lever or pull on the outside, awaiting its opening from the inside, which will signal human acceptance of his grace. Stanzas 7 and 8 make clear that the speaker's ecstatic experience remains transitory, that he will soon wake from night to enter day, "where all mix and tire / Themselves and others," and he runs "To every mire" as a result of "this world's ill-guiding light."

Vaughan concludes with a prayer as he focuses firmly on the contrast and interaction of dark and light that have provided a framework for the poem. He begins with the use of ALLITERATION in repetition of the *d* sound for emphasis on the ability of night to reveal truth/God, where the false light of the world may hide it, writing, "There is in God (some say) / A deep but dazzling darkness." Paradox exists in the suggestion that darkness can dazzle, an attribute generally limited to light. He returns to his emphasis on the fact that the sun lends physical, not spiritual, light, writing that men on earth "Say it is late and dusky, because they / See not all clear." While they believe they require the daylight to see clearly, they are mistaken. As for the speaker, he waits "Oh for that night, where I in him / Might live invisible and dim!"

BIBLIOGRAPHY

Leishman, J. B. *The Metaphysical Poets: Donne, Herbert, Vaughan, Traherne.* Oxford: Clarendon Press, 1934.

Matar, Nabil I. "George Herbert, Henry Vaughan, and the Conversion of the Jews." *Studies in English Literature, 1500–1900* 30, no. 1 (winter 1990): 79–92.

Peake, Charles. *Poetry of the Landscape and the Night: Two Eighteenth-Century Traditions.* Columbia: University of South Carolina Press, 1970.

Post, Jonathan F. S. "Vaughan's 'The Night' and His 'Late and Dusky' Age." *Studies in English Literature* 19 (1979): 127–141.

Rudrum, Alan. *Henry Vaughan.* Cardiff: University of Wales Press, 1981.

"NIGHT-PIECE, TO JULIA, THE" GEORGE HERRICK (1648)

When GEORGE HERRICK wrote "The Night-piece, to Julia," he used as the object of his poem the ideal female figure of Julia, who appeared repeatedly in his writing. Critics have noted that this poem in particular owes much to Herrick's mentor, BEN JONSON, in its use of subtle rhythm. Herrick manages to imitate the action and subject matter of his poem in his varied METER, which moves from four feet to three feet to two feet, then returns to four feet in its four five-line stanzas. His speaker woos Julia at night, as indicated by the poem's title. Thus the first line incorporates imagery of the "Glow-worme," "Shooting Starres," and "Elves also, / Whose little eyes glow," their glowing compared to "the sparks of fire." While the glow worm lends Julia her eyes, indicating that her eyes appear to shine in the dark, the stars and elves "attend" her, suggesting Julia remains a child of nature. However, the reference to "sparks of fire" suggests the passion that love promotes, contradicting the theme of apparent innocence.

The second stanza well illustrates the superior use of rhythm, reading:

No Will-o'th'-Wispe mis-light thee;
Nor Snake, or Slow-worme bite thee:
　　But on, on thy way
　　Not making a stay,
Since Ghost ther's none to affright thee. (6–10)

In these lines Herrick employs repetition and beat to imitate the movement of the long skirts that Julia wears in his longer lines, while the shorter lines reproduce the quicker movement of creatures of the night. His reference to the "Slow-worme," probably meaning an adder, offers contrasts in imagery to the fireflies and other night life. The speaker does his best to convince Julia she will suffer no harm in the dark, most probably because of his presence as well as the supposed absence of threat from beasts and ghosts. Psychoanalytic critics, however, might view the worm imagery as a phallic reference, supporting the claim that the speaker attempts to seduce Julia by assuring her of her safety at night. The darkness offers assurance that certain actions may proceed unobserved; thus the speaker may reference a different type of security, that of a discrete cover for any socially censored actions.

In the third stanza the speaker urges Julia not to feel burdened by the night's darkness. The hidden moon in its "slumber" may not be available to cast light before her, but "The Starres of the night / Will lend thee their light," a light compared through the FIGURATIVE LANGUAGE of simile to "Tapers cleare without number" (11–15). While the moon proved a romantic figure and symbolic of woman, the stars also proved romantic. The speaker notes that the moon is hidden, as Julia might also be hidden from inquisitive eyes. In addition the speaker suggests that the moon's natural light might be replaced by man's invention, the candle, whose flame represents the heat of passion.

The need for the romantic setting becomes clear by the final stanza, in which the speaker requests, "Then Julia let me wooe thee." Verse 17 contains another repetition, producing a sound that mimics the rustle of silk skirts, the entire line producing a beat near that of the waltz: "Thus, thus to come unto me." A dance step provides a metaphor for the courting ritual, its idea again suggested as the speaker notes,

And when I shall meet
Thy silv'ry feet,
My soule Ile poure into thee. (18–20)

Upholding a rich tradition, the poet has already offered his soul through his verse in this lightly seductive poem.

"The Night-piece, to Julia" represents what critics have recognized as Herrick's fascination with the fairy world, a realm found between human and divine existence. While this poem is not strictly of the "faerie lore," incorporating objects that included dew on toadstools and gossamer webs, its close view of creatures that lived low to the ground qualifies it as related to that genre. In addition its dreamy other-world quality, accomplished through imagery and references to Elves, a Ghost, and Julia's "silv'ry feet," suggests the world of fairies with which Herrick proved so enthralled.

BIBLIOGRAPHY

Scott, George Walton. *Robert Herrick*. New York: St. Martin's Press, 1974.

"NYMPH COMPLAINING FOR THE DEATH OF HER FAWN, THE" ANDREW MARVELL (1681)

The date when ANDREW MARVELL wrote "The Nymph Complaining for the Death of Her Fawn" remains unknown. Some of its vocabulary may be traced to the 1640s and some possible associations can be made, especially with a poem published in 1642 by Rowland Watkins. However, its only secure date is that of 1681, the date of publication along with most of Marvell's lyrics in the posthumous *Miscellaneous Poems*. It represents the traditional format known as the lover's complaint, as Marvell frequently echoes Ovid's *Metamorphoses*. Mythology on which Ovid drew included Agamemnon's killing of Diana's hind, or deer. It also featured Cyparissus, who loves, then kills, her own deer. Sylvanus is Cyparissus's lover, and Marvell's inconstant lover named *Sylvio*. Edmund Spenser in *The Faerie Queene,* Book I, also follows the tradition, describing the murder of a deer by a character named Sylvanus. In addition Marvell echoes Renaissance Continental drama and pastoral poetry. He adopted a format of 11 verse paragraphs, indicated by line indention; those paragraphs vary from four to 20 lines in length.

Some critics view the poem as divided into four sections corresponding to speech modes; ANTITHESIS, repetition, ALLEGORY, and epigraph. Critics have judged the poem an aesthetic failure, because of its mixing of genres and voices. They have also viewed it as questioning not only the pastoral form, but also the value of the contemplative life. The latter is a contradiction for Marvell who seems to value highly contemplation in other poems, such as "The GARDEN."

Psychoanalytic critics view "The Nymph Complaining for the Death of Her Fawn" as a lover-scorned tale, and they find interesting the nymph's apparent substitution of the fawn as a lover after Sylvio's betrayal. After expressing 24 lines of regret over the loss of the fawn, killed by "wanton troopers," the nymph explains that "Unconstant Sylvio" had given her the fawn prior to her discovery of his "counterfeit" nature. The fawn wore a "silver chain and bell," the silver symbolizing the supposed value of Sylvio's feelings for the nymph. Marvell uses a pun on the term *deer* as the nymph recalls that Sylvio said, "'Look how your huntsman here / Hath taught a fawn to hunt his dear.'" The hunt becomes an important thematic. Sylvio's later betrayal invokes the image of an opportunist hunting a naive female; it also echoes the earlier description of the fawn's shooting death by "wanton troopers riding by."

Recalling the pleasant gift giving, the nymph notes that Sylvio "Quite regardless of my smart, / Left me his fawn, but took his heart," with Marvell again including wordplay on the term *hart*. Because the nymph's nature prevents her treating others unkindly, she cannot recognize cruelty in Sylvio. Later Marvell references "swans and turtles," meaning turtledoves, "milk-white lambs" and "alabaster," the compounding white imagery symbolizing the nymph's innocence.

The nymph concludes by noting that she will soon die, ostensibly of a broken heart. She requests that an engraver create her image in marble, but not engrave tears, for she "shall weep though I be stone," supplying the tears, which will drop on her breast and engrave themselves there. She then requests that Sylvio be laid at her feet, carved from alabaster. Marvell concludes with PARADOX, writing in the nymph's voice, "for I would have thine image be / White as I can, though not as thee." The nymph fantasizes that Sylvio remains as pure and innocent as her fawn, creating a false image in order to satisfy her desire.

Some critics view the nymph and fawn as one and the same, the nymph's sacrifice and eventual death in the name of love similar to those of the fawn. Feminist critics note the violence inflicted on the nymph and the fawn by men. They both represent innocence, as the nymph notes the fawn is whiter than she, and the male world of experience kills them. Imagery of the fawn in a garden calls to mind the original Garden of Eden, and Marvell may suggest that as every individual gains knowledge or wisdom, he or she moves closer to death.

Additional interpretations include political and religious meaning in the poem. "Wanton troopers" reflects a new term, *trooper,* which appeared first in the English language in 1640 in reference to soldiers of the Scottish Covenanting Army that invaded England to support Presbyterianism. The fawn could be seen as the English church doomed to death by civil war, or as England itself when life under a monarchy is destroyed by Cromwell's new order. Charles I himself may be the fawn, its death mirroring Charles's execution. His death was treated delicately by Marvell even in a poem written as a salute to the new leader of England, his "A HORATIAN ODE UPON CROMWELL'S RETURN FROM IRELAND." The fawn's dying "calmly as a saint" brings to mind lines from the ode about Charles: "He nothing common did, or mean, / . . . But bowed his comely head / Down, as upon a bed," submitting to the executioner's axe. Others view the fawn as Christ, the line in which it feeds "Among the beds of lilies" echoing such imagery from The Song of Solomon.

BIBLIOGRAPHY

Berek, Peter. "The Voices of Marvell's Lyrics." *Modern Language Quarterly* 32 (1971): 143–157.

Empson, William. *Seven Types of Ambiguity.* 2nd ed. London: Chatto & Windus, 1947.

Hartwig, Joan. "Tears as a Way of Seeing." In *On the Celebrated and Neglected Poems of Andrew Marvell,* edited by Claude J. Summers and Ted-Larry Pebworth, 70–85. Columbia: University of Missouri Press, 1992.

Ray, H. Robert. *An Andrew Marvell Companion.* New York: Garland, 1998.

O

OBSERVATIONS IN THE ART OF ENGLISH POESIE THOMAS CAMPION (1602)

In his *Observations in the Art of English Poesie* Thomas Campion sought to do something unique, as expressed in the subtitle to his work: "Wherein it is demonstratiuely prooued, and by example confirmed, that the English toong will receiue eight seuerall kinds of numbers, proper to it selfe, which are all in this booke set forth, and were neuer before this time by any man attempted." By *numbers,* Campion means he will focus on substituting certain classic rhythms or METER, mainly combinations of iambs and trochees, for rhyme.

Campion introduces his discussion by writing, "But when we speake of a Poeme written in number, we consider not only the distinct number of the sillables, but also their value, which is contained in the length or shortnes of their sound." Until Campion's observations poets had not much concerned themselves with defining or discussing RHYME. They understand some traditional conventions, which they followed. Campion's serious attack proves humorous to later readers, as when he states that he understands he may be challenged by those with the worst of weapons, poets themselves, who might rhyme him to death. He also understands that a broad use of rhyme in various cultures means custom stands against him. However, he writes, "All this and more can not yet deterre me from a lawful defence of perfection, or make me any whit the sooner adheare to that which is lame and vnbeseeming. For custome I alleage, that ill vses are to be abolisht, and that things naturally imperfect can not be perfected by vse." He later continues, "The eare is a rational sence, and a chiefe iudge of proportion, but in our kind of riming what proportion is there kept, where there remaines such a confused inequalitie of sillables? *Iambick* and *Trochaick* feete which are opposed by nature, are by all Rimers confounded, nay oftentimes they place in stead of an *Iambick* the foote *Pyrrychius,* consisting of two short sillables, curtalling their verse, which they supply in reading with a ridiculous, and vnapt drawing of their speech. As for example: *Was it my desteny, or dismall chaunce?*"

Campion follows this procedure throughout his document, discussing various stresses and supplying examples. Samuel Daniel replied to Campion's proposal in his 1603 *A Defence of Rhyme,* in which he argued that its use and practice justified its existence. Campion's entire work may be found online in the University of Oregon's *Renascence Editions* at http://darkwinguoregon.edu/~rbear/ren.htm.

BIBLIOGRAPHY

Harrison, G. B., ed. *Samuel Daniel / Defence of Rhyme / 1603 / Thomas Campion / Observations in the Art of English Poesie / 1602.* New York: Dutton, 1925.

"ODE FOR HIM, AN" ROBERT HERRICK (1648)

The "Him" alluded to in ROBERT HERRICK's poem "An Ode for Him" was indubitably BEN JONSON, poet and playwright extraordinaire, who served as mentor for Herrick. Although never a "sealed member" of the celebrated TRIBE OF BEN, Herrick enjoyed a close friendship with Jonson. He often joined the older poet's group in city taverns, as Jonson greatly enjoyed mixing drink and food with talk. While the favorite haunt was the first floor of the Devil and St. Dunstan at Temple Bar, in the Apollo Chamber, the group of poets also frequented other haunts, some of which Herrick mentions in the first of his two-stanza poem. Using the ode, or praise, form, to join others in celebrating Jonson after his death in 1637, Herrick begins with an appeal:

Ah, Ben!
Say how, or when
Shall we thy Guests
Meet at those Lyrick Feasts. (1–4)

With the frequent meetings for food and drink that included both serious and light discussions of intellectual and artistic matters on his mind, Herrick wonders "how, or when" the group can ever again meet. The suggestion remains that they can never duplicate that experience. He next alludes to various meeting places in lines 5 and 6, "Made at the Sun, / The Dog, the triple Tunne?" As George Walton Scott explains, *Sun* was a common name for taverns and makes the exact location to which Herrick refers difficult to know, while *Dog* likely referred to a tavern on Talbot Street, later known as the Sun. For some reason, Herrick omits reference to the clubroom in the Apollo Chamber, where Jonson famously sat near a bust of Apollo. He also neglects the best-known of the literary taverns, the Mermaid in Bread Street, which had an entrance facing Cheapside, an area with which Herrick was quite familiar. Founded by Sir Walter Raleigh, it remained a favorite haunt, although its canary wine so loved by Jonson and Herrick cost twopence more than at other taverns. The triple Tunne, also known as Three Tuns, represented the Vintner's Company coat of arms, appearing on a popular establishment standing near the Gate in Guildhall Yard.

Herrick completes that 10-line stanza by comparing the effect of Jonson's contribution to that of the friends consuming drink. He notes that the groups held "clusters" at the various drinking venues, which made the poets "nobly wild, not mad," as "each Verse

of thine / Out-did the meat, out-did the frolic wine." As the old saying goes, man's spirit needs sustenance, as does his body. Jonson tended to the needs of the soul, while the taverns cared for the needs of the flesh. Obviously Jonson's contribution proved the more important. Any drinking establishment could serve the material need, but only Jonson could satisfy the more crucial requirement.

In the second stanza Herrick repeats his apostrophe, "My Ben," making clear the affectionate quality of their relationship, adding a request that Ben "come agen," or instead "send to us, / Thy wits great over-plus" (13–14). He may mimic the classical request for inspiration, seeking motivation from Jonson, now a spiritual muse. The speaker adds, however, a request that Ben's spirit "teach us yet / Wisely to husband it" (15–16), meaning they must learn to distribute carefully in increments whatever they receive from Jonson. Otherwise they will too quickly "that Tallent spend" (17). Once that happens, they will bring "to an end / That precious stock" (18–19), and "Of such a wit the world sho'd have no more" (20).

While Herrick's ode is not unusual, he successfully frames it in a tone of unmistakable longing that gives believability to his sentiment. Not only did Herrick legitimately admire Jonson's work, he owed to that poet his acceptance into the tavern life, an important step up in artistic status. Therefore he expresses not only longing, but gratitude.

BIBLIOGRAPHY
Scott, George Walton. *Robert Herrick.* New York: St. Martin's Press, 1974.

"ODE TO EVENING" WILLIAM COLLINS (1746)

WILLIAM COLLINS published a collection titled *Odes on Several Descriptive and Allegoric Subjects* (1746), of which "Ode to Evening" was one. His LYRIC poem demonstrates the characteristic traits of an ode, including its focus on a particular occasion or event and its formal tone and form. Collins selects a traditional topic, as salutes to both the evening and the morning, the latter termed an AUBADE, were plentiful. At the same time he takes a unique approach by writing 52 lines with no RHYME. That may have been a characteristic that caused SAMUEL JOHNSON to write of Collins's poetry that it often received commendation, gathering "praise when it gives little pleasure." Collins uses FIGURATIVE LANGUAGE to personify the evening as a female named Eve. The association of that name with the first woman, according to biblical tradition, and her garden serves Collins well in his many references to nature. He opens with the hope that "chaste Eve" will welcome his "pastoral song," that his words might "soothe thy modest ear, / Like thy own solemn springs, / Thy springs and dying gales." Reference to the gales and the solemnity of the spring represents the poet's recognition of the power of natural forces, and of man's arbitrary limits of time. He also personifies "the bright-haired sun," which "sits in yon western tent," beneath "cloudy skirts" in deference to evening's arrival.

The speaker's reference to a creature, a bat, and his use of ALLITERATION exemplifies Johnson's criticism that the poet's "cluster of consonants" often "impeded" the movement of his verse: "Now air is hushed, save where the weak-ey'd bat / With short shrill shriek flits by on leathern wing." While Johnson may have reacted negatively in an Augustan age accustomed to the application of reason over fancy, later readers would appreciate Collins's more original approach. The poem's persona compares his own song to that of the bat, or of a beetle that "winds / His small but sullen horn," often ignored by a wandering "pilgrim" as a "heedless hum." The speaker wants "To breathe some softened strain," as Collins perhaps suggests the topic of inspiration, which means literally "to breathe into." Many poets were inspired by nature, and so the speaker hopes to offer music "Whose numbers," or rhythm,

> stealing through thy darkening vale
> May not unseemly with its stillness suit;
> As musing slow, I hail
> Thy genial loved return!

Collins lives up to his reputation, as assessed by Johnson, using both consonance and assonance in his lines. Although Johnson found Collins's slow-moving lines annoying, the poet admits that he purposely engages in "musing slow," finding it appropriate to his topic.

The speaker next references the evening star, whose "warning lamp" arouses elves and nymphs, bearing

"The Pensive Pleasures sweet" to "Prepare thy shadowy car." Again Collins references slow thought by adopting the term *pensive.* His imagery supports the quiet tone as he describes "some sheety lake" that "Cheers the lone heath, or some time-hallowed pile, / Or upland fallows grey." However, he makes clear that Eve may also bear "chill blustering winds or driving rain" that confines the speaker to a hut where "from the mountain's side" he "Views wilds and swelling floods." He also notes how evening differs according to the season: Spring "pour[s] his showers" and "bathe[s] thy breathing tresses," while Summer "loves to sport / Beneath thy lingering light," and "sallow Autumn fills thy lap with leaves," but winter yells "through the troublous air, / Affrights thy shrinking train," and "rudely rends thy robes." His personification of the seasons equates each one's effect on evening with its effect on man, with preference given to the three seasons that are not winter, as they all entail longer, more enjoyable evenings. This establishes sympathy between man and evening. He concludes by assuring evening that "Fancy, Friendship, Science, rose-lipped Health" own her "gentlest influence" and sing hymns to her name.

This ode shows why some critics feel that, had he lived a sane life and reached creative maturity, Collins might have joined the top tier of poets, Johnson's criticism notwithstanding.

BIBLIOGRAPHY
Johnson, Samuel. "The Life of William Collins." In *The Works of the English Poets from Chaucer to Cowper, including the Series Edited with Prefaces, Biographical and Critical, by Dr. Samuel Johnson: And the Most Approved Translation.* Edited by Alexander Chalmers. 21 vols. London: C. Whittington, 1810.
Lonsdale, Robert, ed. *The Poems of Thomas Gray, William Collins, Oliver Goldsmith.* New York: Norton, 1972.

"ODE TO HIMSELF" BEN JONSON (1631, 1640–1641)   In "Ode to Himself" BEN JONSON castigates the public for its rejection of his comedy *The New Inn* (1629). He expresses himself in a manner that supports some critical estimates of him as, in the words of George Parfitt, "truculent, arrogant, uncertain of temper, narrow-minded, dogmatic, ungenerous." Had this been the only Jonson poem in existence, that description would seem accurate. Fortunately, the body of Jonson's poetry mitigates against such a negative vision of the poet. The so-called ode appeared as an epilogue to the 1632 printed version. Many reacted to the epilogue, some urging him not to act upon his impulse to end his playwright career, others confirming the low popular opinion of the play. Jonson probably felt sensitive about this work as it was his first to be staged after he suffered a stroke in 1628, and he was anxious that it not be seen as inferior to his previous works.

"Ode to Himself" wastes no time in advancing the poet's opinion of his audience and his plan of action, as he tells himself,

> Come, leave the loathèd stage,
> And the more loathsome age,
> Where pride and impudence, in faction knit,
> Usurp the chair of wit,
> Indicting and arraigning every day
> Something they call a play.

Jonson's bitter tone well supports his self-righteous point of view. After chastising further, he concludes his 10-line verse with ANTITHESIS, writing, "They were not made for thee, less thou for them." Jonson repeatedly evaluates his subject, interjecting limiting terms, such as *more, less, large,* and criteria points, including *simple, common, best,* and his traditional ethical measure, *good.* No question exists as to whether his drama was worthy; the audience simply does not deserve his efforts.

The second stanza proves at once skillful and vituperative as Jonson adopts the FIGURATIVE LANGUAGE of extended metaphor to compare his audience to pigs. The creatures prefer base foods, or art, to the processed product Jonson would offer:

> Say that thou pour'st them wheat,
> And they will acorns eat;
> 'Twere simple fury still thyself to waste
> On such as have no taste!

Jonson's aggressive use of language includes the first of two puns on the term *taste.* The second use is discussed later.

The speaker notes that were he to offer the swines bread, they would reject it as they possess no appetite for refinement. Instead, they prefer "grains," "husks," and "swill" and "love lees," the dregs, rather than the "lusty wine" that represents Jonson's refined art. The metaphor extends into the third stanza, where readers learn that for the ingrate audience, "There, sweepings do as well / As the best-ordered meal." In the 1640 quarto version of the poem Jonson proved so out of humor that he even insulted Richard Brome, described by Parfitt as Jonson's "most faithful and successful disciple in stage comedy." The lines read, "Brome's sweeping do as well / There, as his master's meal. . . ." The pun on Brome's name is the second and more cruel within that stanza. The suggestion that Brome's efforts prove mere crumbs compared to those of Jonson proved that anyone might fall unfortunate victim of the senior poet's ire.

Throughout the remaining three stanzas, Jonson repeatedly notes his superiority to those in his audience, claiming he will depart and does not need them, the voice attempting indifference. However, certain lines counteract that attempt, including

> Ere years have made thee old,
> Strike that disdainful heat
> Throughout, to their defeat,
> As curioius fools, and envious of thy strain,
> May, blushing, swear no palsy's in thy brain.

They emit such forceful passion that they negate Jonson's claim to remain unruffled by audience attitude toward his drama.

Jonson concludes by noting that when he writes about King Charles I, "His zeal to God and his just awe o'er men," that same audience will be "blood-shaken" and experience "a flesh-quake" that will lead them to proclaim Jonson a wonder. They would have to do so, as Jonson's words will serve to elevate the king's chariot, emblematic of his power, above his "Wain," the seven stars of the constellation Ursa Major.

Jonson had claimed that only a limited circle could fully appreciate his work, while even fewer could judge it, and "Ode to Himself" seems to support that claim. He did have a temper and suffered several failed attempts at friendship; he had also killed a man in his youth, so his reputation was somewhat deserved. On the other hand, most of his plays proved popular and he surrounded himself with devoted friends much of the time. As did any writer dependent on the public for his livelihood, he experienced the constant tension between the desire to write to his own convictions and the desire for a positive critical reception. His high standards caused a reaction against Jonson in the 18th century when a mythology arose that included his supposed hatred of Shakespeare, which a reading of his "TO THE MEMORY OF MY BELOVED, THE AUTHOR, MR. WILLIAM SHAKESPEARE, AND WHAT HE HATH LEFT US" should dispel, as well as charges of plagiarism and a lack of decency. His reputation recovered with the effort of critics such as J. A. Barish.

BIBLIOGRAPHY

Barish, J. A. *Jonson and the Language of Prose Comedy.* Cambridge, Mass.: Harvard University Press, 1960.

Barish, J. A., ed. *Ben Jonson: A Collection of Critical Essays.* Englewood Cliffs, N.J.: Prentice-Hall, 1963.

Harp, Richard. "Jonson's Late Plays." In *The Cambridge Companion to Ben Jonson,* edited by Richard Harp and Stanley Stewart. New York: Cambridge University Press, 2000.

Parfitt, George. *Ben Jonson: Public Poet and Private Man.* New York: Harper & Row, 1977.

"ODE TO MASTER ANTHONY STAFFORD" THOMAS RANDOLPH (n.d.)

THOMAS RANDOLPH wrote "Ode to Master Anthony Stafford," considered one of the most beautiful odes in the English language. Critics characterize it as a strong example of Randolph's use of Latinisms, demonstrating his study of Roman classics such as those by Ovid and Martial. In typical ode form the poem is constructed in rhymed stanzas. The speaker directly addresses his subject, Master Stafford, in a plea to go to the country from the town, beginning:

> Come, spur away,
> I have no patience for a longer stay,
>   But must go down,
> And leave the chargeable noise of this great
>   town.

He follows with four three-feet lines with a RHYME scheme of *aabb*, writing,

> I will the country see,
> Where old simplicity,
> Though hid in grey,
> Doth look more gay.

The speaker's contrast is to aspects of the city, "foppery in plush and scarlet clad." He casts the city in a negative light, describing its "wits" as "Almost at civil war." That allows the speaker to offer as more beneficial the seductive advantages of the country. The fifth stanza notes some of those attractions specifically, including the cool shade and music famously made by the many birds of the field. Randolph mentions "Philomel," the classic reference to a nightingale and the tales she tells, as well as the thrush and blackbird. His beautiful phrasing may be seen in the description of the birds who "lend their throats / Warbling melodious notes" with the open vowels adding assonance pleasing to the ear.

Randolph reflects the traditional high emotion and expression expected of an ode, including more classical references in his final stanza. The speaker promises Stafford that they will "taste of Bacchus' blessings now and then," referring to the drinking of wine. He also says he will "take my pipe and try / The Phrygian melody," where Phrygian refers to music of praise. That formula, commonly used in the 16th and 17th centuries, involved a move downward of a minor second from the main virtual pitch. The music he promises will be "Doric," referencing the Dorian mode in music, named for the Dorian Greeks. Doric Greek music is based on the Dorian tetrachord, a series of rising intervals of semitones followed by whole tones.

"ODE UPON A QUESTION MOVED WHETHER LOVE SHOULD CONTINUE FOREVER, AN" EDWARD HERBERT (1665)

"An Ode Upon a Question Moved Whether Love Should Continue Forever" by EDWARD HERBERT, Lord Herbert of Cherbury, reflects the style of METAPHYSICAL POETS AND POETRY. In ode form its 15 four-line stanzas are divided into two sections, with the METER of iambic tetrameter and the RHYME scheme *abba*. The first section proposes a question with both a philosophical and religious basis: What happens to an enduring love when the people who share it die?

Herbert begins with an account of a couple, Melander and Celinda, after setting the scene with abundant imagery of spring. It is a time of "Infant-birth" for the ground that "late did mourn," as "well-accorded birds" sing "hymns" to the time. Evidence of Herbert's strong belief in deism may be observed in his use of the religious reference to songs of praise, "hymns," and his emphasis on the springing to life of all the parts of nature. The wind emits "soft whistles," while "warbling murmurs" may be heard from a brook, and leaves shake in the breeze. Herbert concludes his third stanza with the line "An harmony of parts did bind." That sentiment echoes his strong belief that in order for man to live correctly, the human mind must experience harmony with nature. He made famous his theories in his philosophical treatise *De Veritate* (1625).

The reader next meets "That mutually happy pair, / Melander and Celinda fair," who enjoy "a love none can express." Their love remained so great and pure that "No glass but it could represent"; even a mirror could not properly reflect it. The first section of six stanzas concludes with Celinda's musing,

> "Dear friend,
> O that our love might take no end,
> Of never had beginning took."

She expresses the thought that if their love had to end, perhaps it would have been better for them never to have shared it.

The poem's second portion reflects Melander's reply, and it is lengthy and thorough. He notes his belief that their "virtuous habits" are "with the soul entire" and, therefore, "Must with it evermore endure." If it were not so, he continues, that would make vain "Heaven's laws," which would "to an everlasting cause / . . . give a perishing effect." God will not exclude Love, and, he adds, "These eyes again thine eyes shall see, / These hands again thine hand enfold." Melander's argument depends upon one's faith in God, as he explains,

> For if no use of sense remain
> When bodies once this life forsake,
> Or they could no delight partake,
> Why should they ever rise again?

Herbert imbues Meander's voice with such a sincere tone that the reader must admire his beliefs, even if that reader does not share them. He then reflects his later categorization as a metaphysical poet when Meander states confidently,

> And if every imperfect mind
> Make love the end of knowledge here,
> How perfect will our love be where
> All imperfection is refin'd.

The argument reads like a riddle, where the answer might be that heaven will preserve the superior emotions.

Meander adopts a tender approach in the penultimate stanza, assuring Celinda that no doubt should "touch, / Much less your fairest mind invade," because "Were not our souls immortal made, / Our equal loves can make them such." The religious purist might raise an objection to Meander's last statement, as Herbert suggests that man can make his own soul immortal through sharing an equal and pure love. However, the sharing of the idealistic love that Herbert celebrates would represent a state of grace on earth, causing those sharing it to feel they had already achieved a heavenly state. He concludes with a roundly metaphysical sentiment, as Meander declares,

> "So when from hence we shall be gone,
> And be no more, nor you, not I:
> As one another's mystery
> Each shall be both, yet both but one."

His final line contains as skillfully developed a PARADOX as any from the metaphysical master who slightly predated Herbert, JOHN DONNE.

OLDHAM, JOHN (1653–1683)

John Oldham was born in Gloucestershire, the son of a Nonconformist minister. After graduating from Oxford, he began his career as a teacher, an Usher at Archbishop Whitgift's Free School, and a satirist. His few works, received well, included *A Satire upon a Woman, Who by Her Falsehood and Scorn Was the Death of My Friend* (1678), *A Satire against Virtue* (1679), plus *Satires upon the Jesuits* (1681). The latter composed of four poems, was inspired by Titus Oates's "Popish Plot," a concoction of a Catholic plot to murder the king. He later also wrote an ode, "Upon the Works of Ben Jonson"; Horatian satires; and translations from Juvenal. Although today's critics do not particularly value Oldham's work, his early death of smallpox caused his contemporaries, including JOHN DRYDEN, to mourn the abrupt end to what seemed a career of great promise. Dryden expressed his thoughts in "TO THE MEMORY OF MR. OLDHAM," perhaps empathizing with Oldham as a fellow satirist and adopter of political and religious themes. Oldham's poems remained popular through the 18th century.

BIBLIOGRAPHY

Hammond, Paul. *John Oldham and the Renewal of Classical Culture.* New York: Cambridge University Press, 1983.
Zigerell, James. *John Oldham.* Boston: Twayne, 1983.

"ON A DROP OF DEW" ANDREW MARVELL (1681)

As did most poetry by ANDREW MARVELL, "On a Drop of Dew" first appeared in published form in his *Miscellaneous Poems* (1681) after his death. Various critics argue that it was written between 1650 and 1652 or in 1640, but no one can be sure of the year in which Marvell created it. He drew on a tradition of writing about dewdrops, descendants from heaven that were regarded as microcosms of the entire world, a technique popular in religious writing. Written as a companion piece to a Latin version titled "Ros," "On a Drop of Dew" has complicated syntax, perhaps as a result of the dual-language presentation. Influences on Marvell may have included JOHN DONNE's reference to the dew while reflecting upon the immortality allowed through faith in Christ, and Marvell uses it to represent the human soul. Dewdrops also had represented drops of blood from martyrs, and 16th-century poets used dew in erotic imagery. For example the dew is described as "penetrating" a rose, a traditional symbol for woman, in this case Mary, with that action in turn compared to God's slipping into the womb in Ippolito Capilupi's *Carmina* (1574).

Marvell presents his poem in two parts, the first describing the dewdrop's relationship to man and earth and the second its emblematic representation of the human soul. The rhythm shifts frequently as the number of syllables often varies in the 20 lines of the first section. He begins,

> See how the orient dew,
> Shed from the bosom of the morn
> Into the blowing roses,

then notes that the drops eschew their heavenly mansions. Each drop is a world unto itself: "round in itself incloses: / And in its little globe's extent, / Frames as it can its native element." Lines 14–18 describe the dew's feeling of alienation as it is "so long divided from the sphere," and that division causes its "Trembling lest it grow impure." This allows a transition into his comparison of the soul to the drop of dew. Each section concludes with two rhyming couplets, their formality signaling a conclusion and unity of thought. The first pair leads into the second section, with the sun acting on its sympathy to evaporate the drop of dew, so that it may again enter Heaven, allowing the comparison offered in the poem's second portion:

> Till the warm sun pity its pain
> And to the skies exhale it back again.
> So the soul, that drop, that ray
> Of the clear fountain of eternal day.

The soul recalls "its former height" and "Shuns the swart leaves and blossoms green," remembering "its own light." Marvell inserts a skillful ANTITHESIS to describe the soul's activities while on earth separated from God and heaven, as in its "pure and circling thoughts" it expresses "The greater Heaven in an heaven less" (26). He includes imagery of dark and light, further contrast of the earth, not naturally graced with God's light, to heaven. The soul's location affects its attitude, as on earth it remains "disdaining," but in heaven it loves. The soul is "girt and ready to ascend," with the term *girt* implying enclosed within, just as the dewdrop was self-enclosed.

Marvell references in line 37 the biblical story of the miracle of manna, or bread, which appeared with the morning dew to sustain the Israelites as they wandered in the desert on the way to the Promised Land. In emphasizing the dew's sacred properties, Marvell more closely ties it to the redeemed soul. As the manna was congealed in the dew, the soul remains congealed while earth-bound but will melt and return to heaven when exposed to Christ's redemption. The poem ends with a pair of couplets:

Such did the manna's sacred dew distil;
White and entire, though congealed and chill.
Congealed on earth; but does, dissolving, run
Into the glories of the'Almighty Sun.

Marvell uses wordplay with his pun on the word sun, as in God's son, Christ, as he extends the FIGURATIVE LANGUAGE (FIGURE OF SPEECH) of the sun metaphor. God is also referred to as "a sun and shield" in Psalm 84:11. Other critical approaches compare the dew to sin, which must be burned out of the soul.

BIBLIOGRAPHY

Jaeckle, Daniel. "Bilingual Dialogues: Marvell's Paired Latin and English Poems." *Studies in Philology* 98, no. 3 (summer 2001): 378.

Looney, Barbara A. "Marvell's Dewdrop: Two Possibilities for the Soul." *John Donne Journal* 8 (1989): 191–193.

Rosa, Alfred F. "Andrew Marvell's 'On a Drop of Dew': A Reading and Possible Source." *Concerning Poetry* 5 (spring 1972): 57–59.

Smith, Nigel, ed. *The Poems of Andrew Marvell.* New York: Pearson/Longman, 2003.

"ON A VIRTUOUS YOUNG GENTLE-WOMAN THAT DIED SUDDENLY" WILLIAM CARTWRIGHT (1651)

WILLIAM CARTWRIGHT gained fame for his panegyrics and elegies, although critics and readers in later centuries found them florid and overblown. Judged of poor quality mainly as a result of changing tastes, the poems still represent excellent examples of the type. "On a Virtuous Young Gentlewoman That Died Suddenly" contains many traditional elements of the ELEGY, a prescriptive form that allowed poets who did not even know the deceased to praise that person.

Cartwright begins with a classical comparison of the dead woman to the sun, "the old flaming Prophet," crossing the sky, and then seemingly vanishing. While the sun would return, "He made more preface to a death than this; / So far from sick, she did not breathe amiss." In other words the sun's exit from the sky calls much attention to itself with the sunset. The young woman apparently gave no sign of her impending death, suffering from no illness. Cartwright next praises her virtue with a skillful double use of the idea of Heaven, writing, "She, who to Heaven more heaven doth annex," stating that she will actually make heaven a better place for her presence, bearing her own heaven with her. He continues noting that her "lowest thought" was higher than that of any man and again mentions that she "died as free from sickness as she liv'd."

In an attempt to make her death seem better by comparison to others, he reminds readers that "Others are dragg'd away, or must be driven," while "she only saw her time and stepp'd to heaven." He comforts the family with thoughts of how easy her passing had been, with no suffering by her or her loved ones for her sake. He assures that angels, the "Seraphims," will view her glories as if she had returned to heaven, having left it only for a brief time, a Platonic idea. As he begins to close his 18 lines of rhyming couplets, he notes

Her body seem'd rather assum'd than born:
So rarefied, advanc'd, so pure and whole,
That body might have been another's soul.

This great praise of her earthly form also comforts her family, suggesting that she had always seemed but a spirit, a being of greater purity than other mere humans. He concludes by declaring her life an equal miracle to her sudden passing, writing, "And equally a miracle it were, / That she could die, or that she could live here."

"ON GILES AND JOAN" BEN JONSON (1616)

BEN JONSON has fun with his ditty "On Giles and Joan," offering a study in contrasts. Although the married Giles and Joan agree on everything, suggesting they live in harmony, nothing could be further from the truth. Jonson demonstrates the power of rhetoric as he describes two people who eschew one another's company yet remain perfectly matched.

The 18-line poem of rhyming couplets opens with a question, "Who says that Giles and Joan at discord be?"

The speaker then gives examples that prove the couple in complete accord, although simultaneously at odds:

> Indeed, poor Giles repents he married ever,
> But that his Joan doth too. And Giles
> would never
> By his free will be in Joan's company;
> No more would Joan he should.

Next the reader learns that Giles proves an early riser, and that pleases Joan, who wants him out of the house as soon as possible. Giles feels sad to have to return home at day's end, and Joan is sad to have him return. In addition,

> . . . Ofttimes, when Giles doth find
> Harsh sights at home, Giles wisheth he were
> blind;
> All this doth Joan.

Jonson sets a pattern, first stating a truism regarding Giles, then demonstrating Joan's agreement with that truism. However, the ultimate truth is that both could easily do without the another. He employs a metaphor in describing Giles's wish that his "long-yearned life / Were quite outspun," with the yearned referring as a pun to long skeins of yarn, generally both wound up and unwound again by housewives, such as Joan. The term *outspun* serves as FIGURATIVE LANGUAGE for death, suggesting that Joan has control over his life. Naturally Joan shares his wish that Giles's life be outspun sooner, rather than later. In addition as Giles swears the children whom he must support do not belong to him, "so swears his Joan." And, finally,

> In all affections she concurreth still.
> If now, with man and wife, to will and nill
> The self-same things a note of concord be,
> I know no couple better can agree.

Jonson concludes with a tongue-in-cheek pronouncement. Both witty and satirical, "Giles and Joan" allows readers to enjoy Jonson's skill as well as his sometimes unnoted marginalized sense of humor.

"ON HER LOVING TWO EQUALLY"
APHRA BEHN (1684) Feminist critics believe that APHRA BEHN wrote "On Her Loving Two Equally" as a parody of the men of her era who were not socially censured for having both a wife and a mistress. Most of the humor of her three six-line stanzas is based on the fact that women ould not escape such censure if they publicly kept both a spouse and a lover, or if a single woman openly adopted multiple lovers. Wives were supposed to excuse or, even better for their husbands, disregard sexual arrangements outside marriage. Thus Behn highlights the gender inequality of her time, adopting a fickle voice that fits this light verse. While somewhat ironic, the poem is not meant to be taken seriously and thus lacks the edginess IRONY often gives to poetry.

The poem's persona begins with a rhetorical question, asking, "How strong does my passion flow, / Divided equally twixt two?" She responds that without one, the other would not appear so attractive:

> Damon had ne'er subdued my heart
> Had not Alexis took his part;
> Nor could Alexis powerful prove,
> Without my Damon's aid, to gain my love.

The uneven rhythm caused by awkward wording draws attention to the awkward nature of the situation. Behn suggests by the need for opposite lovers the theory that one cannot experience love without experiencing hate or the more concrete rule that heat cannot be understood without cold. She thus implies that a woman's taking multiple lovers is a natural impulse, governed by natural causes. The argument that man's natural character created a greater need for sexual satisfaction than that of woman provides the basis for her parody.

In the second stanza the fickle tone grows more prominent, the persona openly declaring,

> When my Alexis present is,
> Then I for Damon sigh and mourn;
> But when Alexis I do miss,
> Damon gains nothing but my scorn.

These lines support a claim that without Damon, Alexis could not successfully romance the speaker, a false logic that cleverly supports Behn's humorous tone. The ridiculous quality of the claim peaks in the final couplet as the speaker mourns, "But if it chance they both are by, / For both alike I languish, sigh, and die," as Behn uses the traditional comparison of love and sex to death to support her point.

The poem's third stanza opens with a plea to Cupid, "thou winged god," to solve the speaker's conundrum, as she will never be able to choose between her lovers. Behn extends her comparison of love to disease, leading to death, as her speaker begs for Cupid to cure "This restless fever in my blood." According to legend Cupid possessed both lead and gold darts; the lead darts he shot at false hearts, the gold at true hearts. The lover bases the next part of her plea on this tradition, requesting, "One golden-pointed dart take back:" then wonders, "But which, O Cupid, wilt thou take?" She concludes with a statement in which the reader can almost hear her pout: "If Damon's, all my hopes are crossed," meaning her desire for future love will be ruined, "Or that of my Alexis, I am lost." The never-spoken solution to her problem remains a suggested PARADOX, a common poetic CONCEIT.

This slight poem aids reader understanding of RES-TORATION period social mores, as well as of the poet's struggle for equality in her patriarchal world.

"ON HIS MAJESTY'S RECOVERY FROM THE SMALL-POX, 1633" WILLIAM CART-WRIGHT (1651)   WILLIAM CARTWRIGHT's "On His Majesty's Recovery from the Small-Pox, 1633" represents a strong example of the panegyric, a poem designed to praise an individual, combined with occasional verse, poetry designed to celebrate a particular occasion, the identity of both person and occasion made clear in the title. Most critics judge this celebratory approach to be Cartwright's strongest, with his lyrics and elegies superior to his drama. His staunch Royalist position and his favor at court made his choice of topic predictable, and he proved a favorite of King Charles I.

The poem begins with a beguiling confession by a speaker who wonders how later ages will receive his era's focus on the disease of its ruler. The group of 22 rhyming couplets opens with "I do confess, the over-forward tongue / Of public duty turns into a wrong" but makes clear the term *wrong* is used ironically, for that tongue is recording not only the king's disease, never specifically identified, but his recovery. Incorporating a muted RHYME in the middle of his fifth line, Cartwright continues,

> And after-ages could ne'er conceive
> Our happy Charles so frail as to receive
> Such a disease.

Here he makes clear that future generations will recall only Charles's strength, meaning his physical constitution, but also alluding to strength of character. Later critics, however, would view Cartwright's poetry, along with that of other poets of the time, as ironic, critical of the king's choices and behavior, but little affecting Charles.

Having effectively ended focus on the illness with the pause forced by the comma that follows the word *disease,* he completes the fifth line and then focuses again on the burden of those whose duty it is to report, writing,

> . . . will know it by the noise
> Which we have made in shouting forth our
>   joys;
> And our informing duty only be
> A well-meant spite, or loyal injury.

Obviously Cartwright does not see the focus on the monarch's well-being as spiteful but includes such a description in order to correct it, accomplished in the phrase *loyal injury.* In other words no injury to Charles's reputation was intended by the concern expressed in verse for his physical well-being.

Having completed his apology, Cartwright shifts to more of a panegyric tone. While he continues to retain the topic of the comments made about the king's illness, he uses the CONCEIT of classical references to the heavens to balance any negative connotation. He also demonstrates that Charles's royal personage far outshines those of his reporters, comparing the king to the "Milky-way," while those who reported were only "small stars fix'd" within that broad celestial sweep. In a second use of FIGURATIVE LANGUAGE he compares the reporters to

faithful turquoises, which Heaven sent
For a discovery, not a punishment;
To show the ill, not make it; and to tell
By their pale looks the bearer was not well.

Again Cartwright employs a midline pause by inserting a semicolon after the term *punishment,* forcing attention on the phrases that follow.

Cartwright again shifts focus toward the future, suggesting that the king's recovery be the source of an annual celebration and that further "computes," or the calculations of time, be based on "His recovery." In this manner the poet compares his ruler to Christ himself, whose birth established a new method of date calculations. He pursues his suggestion, noting, "Let not the Kingdom's Acts hereafter run / From His (though happy) Coronation, / but from His Heath, as in a better strain. / That plac'd Him on His throne; This makes Him reign."

Cartwright displays the intelligent craftsmanship that made him a favorite of his day. He offers an excuse not only for himself, as court chronicler, but for others who may have written of the king's ailment. He also uses punctuation for emphasis in a manner that asks the reader of his poem to focus attention on the king's strengths, not his illness, intimating what he predicts will happen in the future. Also of note is Cartwright's acceptance of his own immortality through writing and, equally important, through his relationship to the king and the court. His conscious consideration of future generations betrays his hope that his poetry's existence will extend far beyond his own, a desire that was fulfilled.

BIBLIOGRAPHY
Bruce, Donald. "An Oxford Garrison of Poets in 1642." *Contemporary Review,* November 1992, 250–256.

"ON LEAPING OVER THE MOON"
THOMAS TRAHERNE (ca. 1660) Although THOMAS TRAHERNE wrote in the 17th century, much of his work was not recovered and published until the 20th cen-

tury. In 1910 a group of poems labeled "The Burney sequence" was published as *Poems of Felicity,* and it included the often-anthologized "On Leaping over the Moon." That poem conveys Traherne's traditional sense of wonder in celebration of God's creation.

Two childhood anecdotes inform the poem, as Traherne describes his brother leaping over a stream in which the moon's reflection appeared and incorporates his brother's remark that the moon once followed him as he walked to town. From the poem's title a reader may anticipate Traherne's contrast of earth and sky. Traherne also employs imagery of space and location to unify his praise of, and gratitude toward, God for erasing the necessity to distinguish between high and low, up and down, as his brother enjoys transcendence of earthly bondage. In addition critics note Traherne used as a source a quotation from the work *Christian Ethics,* 445, quoting *Hermetica,* 11 (2): "A Discourse of Mind," also a source for other of his work. In that discourse the speaker tells his audience that all they need do is bid their soul to travel about the universe, and it will comply. The emphasis on faith as superior to human imagination remains strong, as the speaker begins by noting that

I saw new worlds beneath the water lie,
    New people; yea, another sky,
        And sun, which seen by day
        Might things more clear display. (1–4)

The poem's honest and solemn tone reflects the naiveté of a child who considers such trivial occurrences as jumping a stream and noting what he sees there of utmost importance. Some critics mention the poem's lack of IRONY as a defect, noting that lack causes it to hold little reader interest. Others disagree, arguing that the speaker's literal attitude allows Traherne to touch the sublime through acceptance of God's power. Those who praise the poem note its balance and unity, as in lines 7–10, which balance lines 1–4. They follow the two transition lines, "Just such another / Of late my brother":

Did in his travel see, and saw by night,
A much more strange and wondrous sight:

Nor could the world exhibit such another,
So great a sight, but in a brother.

Traherne establishes an idea of an alternate universe and then supports that idea with the example of his brother's experience. This pattern of a four-line introduction, a two-line transition, and a four-line conclusion, or comment on the first four lines, appears in each of the seven 10-line stanzas.

The speaker next stresses the fact that one can find in simple observation of God's creation greater wonders than in any stories fabricated by man. His brother seemed still on earth yet ascended to heaven, as "Up in the skies / His body flies," by means of an "open, visible, yet magic, sort." Once in heaven the young boy goes "tripping o'er the King's highway," soaring without wing over a "pearly river," which he crossed without an oar. He does not trust "Icarian wing," a reference to Icarus of mythology, who wore wings fashioned of wax by his father. The wings melted when Icarus flew too close to the sun, and he plunged to the earth and his death. By contrast the speaker's brother does not drop "through that thin element / Into a fathomless descent" but instead overcomes the danger, and "as he leapt, with joy related soon / How happy he o'erleapt the moon."

Traherne expresses his vision of God and man, the creator and the created, as one being, reflecting his belief that God is manifested everywhere in the world. Nature gives to the observant man an illumination available also through study of the cosmos. Such natural creations offer a pathway to knowledge. The poet does warn that

. . . whoever falls,
Through a long dismal precipice,
Sinks to the deep abyss where Satan crawls
Where horrid death and Despair lies.

Those who open their minds to their surroundings, like the speaker's brother, will avoid this fate. Those who remain in the fallen state caused by sin will spend eternity after death in hell. Sharing in his brother's experience helps open Traherne's own consciousness, as made clear in his final four lines:

Thus did he yield me in the shady night
A wonderous and instructive light,
Which taught me that under our feet there is,
As o'er our heads, a place of bliss.

In using the adjective *shady,* Traherne not only emphasizes a lack of light or illumination but may reference the mythological term *shade,* a label for the state of those who descended into Hades after death. Traherne closes with emphasis on the fact that God has informed nature, which informs those humans who choose to observe and learn.

BIBLIOGRAPHY
King, Francis. "Thomas Traherne: Intellect and Felicity." *Restoration Literature: Critical Approaches,* edited by Harold Love, 121–143. London: Methuen, 1972.

"ON LUCY, COUNTESS OF BEDFORD"
BEN JONSON (1616) BEN JONSON wrote "On Lucy, Countess of Bedford" in honor of one of the great patronesses of her era. Jonson probably fashioned the part of a lady in waiting to Queen Elizabeth I in his *Cynthia's Revels, or the Fountain of Self Love,* performed in 1600, on the countess who had been a lady in waiting. He also probably owed his commission in 1604 as masque writer for Queen Anne to the patronage of the countess. The poem is included in the *Epigrammes* division of Jonson's works, with the number title LXXVI. He also wrote "To Lucy, Countess of Bedford, with Mr. Donne's Satires," celebrating her within a manuscript collection of JOHN DONNE's poetry that he asked Jonson to present to the countess. Manuscripts often circulated among reading groups, as aristocrats considered publication vulgar. John Donne had also praised the countess and profited from her generosity.

Jonson's 18-line poem adopts traditional iambic pentameter, with every other line rhyming. Its formal format fits the subject, as the poet praises the countess as a muse. He opens by adopting FIGURATIVE LANGUAGE (FIGURE OF SPEECH) to describe the morning's dawn as "holy fire," noting that in the early hours,

I thought to form unto my zealous muse,
What kind of creature I could most desire,
To honour, serve, and love;

Jonson forces hesitation by inserting a semicolon mid-line, forcing the reader, for a brief moment, to wonder about the nature of the speaker's desire. However, as he continues, he makes clear he seeks an inspiration for the art he demonstrates as he muses "as poets use. / I meant to make her fair, and free, and wise, / of greatest blood, and yet more good than great." As scholars point out, Jonson often employed the terms *good* and *great* as part of his moral vocabulary. Here he emphasizes through all of his descriptors the high state of the countess's ethical nature and causes the reader to recognize *great* as simply a higher state of goodness. One of his consistently stressed beliefs held that moral goodness proved far more important than great birth. Fortunately the countess enjoyed both. He continues that emphasis when he writes,

> I meant the day-star should not brighter rise,
> Nor lend like influence from his lucent seat
> I meant she should be courteous, facile, sweet,
> Hating that solemn vice of greatness, pride.

The 10th line, borrowed from a Latin source, Claudian, expresses a favorite belief for Jonson, that empty pride proves worthless. The speaker continues to wish various virtues on his muse, including "a manly soul," indicating she must possess strong convictions. So talented is this muse

> that should, with even powers,
> The rock, the spindle, and the shears control
> Of destiny, and spin her own free hours.

Jonson praises the countess's strength and power over varied situations, using an image that calls to mind the child's game of "rock, paper, scissors." The spindle most probably refers to a part of a loom, an image carried into the next line's reference to spinning, a traditional artistic activity for women and a metaphor for telling a story. The countess is no ordinary woman, as her power allows her "free hours" in which she may do as she pleases. While she did not write, she remained free to support those who did, controlling the destiny of others. The poet concludes by noting that just as he desired to see this perfect creature, "My muse bad,

Bedford write, and that was she." In this final line, the poet's muse bade, or commanded, him to write the word *Bedford,* and he suddenly realized that the countess embodied his dream.

A conventional praise poem, "On Lucy, Countess of Bedford" allows Jonson to display his skill in applying the ethical thought of classicism, in which he adopts commonplace ideas of many predecessors. He does not merely express a moment of individual experience but rather universalizes his thought by adopting a classical foundation. He borrows freely, unafraid that he might be accused of a lack of originality. Rather he adopts a public truth and applies it to considerations of his own culture. He complied with the aesthetic principle of 17th-century England that honored the value of models and conventions but did not encourage a slavish imitation.

BIBLIOGRAPHY
Harp, Richard, and Stanley Stewart, eds. *The Cambridge Companion to Ben Jonson.* New York: Cambridge University Press, 2000.

"ON MR. MILTON'S *PARADISE LOST*" ANDREW MARVELL (1681)
ANDREW MARVELL wrote "On Mr. Milton's *Paradise Lost*" for inclusion in the second edition of PARADISE LOST (1674) by JOHN MILTON. It would be published for a second time in the posthumous collection of Marvell's work, *Miscellaneous Poems* (1681). Marvell's voice is his own in this verse, which considers Milton's ability to encompass vast topics and themes in a single work, eventually concluding the superior poet is well equipped to do so. Eighteenth-century readers knew the poem as the one that assured Marvell's reputation. Later critics found it a remarkable use by Marvell of Milton's various forms in order to distinguish those forms, thus reflecting Marvell's imitative talent. The poem also allowed Marvell to voice many of the beliefs he most cherished. One of those beliefs was the power of reading to create unique experiences through the application of the reader's imagination. He adopts the METER scheme of iambic pentameter with rhyming couplets, cleverly employing the very RHYME that Milton had rejected in his BLANK VERSE format. Simultaneously he criticizes rhyme as an approach adopted by only lesser poets.

Marvell begins, "When I behold the poet blind," echoing the sense of Milton's own words in his famous Sonnet XIX: "WHEN I CONSIDER HOW MY LIGHT IS SPENT." He immediately adds to the descriptive term *blind* the phrase *yet bold.* Milton remains bold for his attempt to a "vast design unfold" in a "slender book." He lists some of the many topics that Milton will try to cover, including "Messiah crowned, God's reconciled decree, / Rebelling angels, the forbidden tree, / Heaven, hell, earth, chaos, all." Marvell follows with a statement of doubt, explaining that before reading the work he had feared Milton would ruin "The sacred truths to fable and old song." He then references another of Milton's works, SAMSON AGONISTES, with a satiric comparison of Milton's strength, drawn from a desire to revenge his loss of sight, to that of Sampson. However, he changes his mind and likes the "project," although he remains fearful it will not succeed. He wonders about Milton, "Through that wide field how he his way should find / O'er which lame Faith leads Understanding blind." Milton might misunderstand and render "perplexed" his explanation.

In line 18 Marvell as the speaker admits to jealousy that "some less skillful hand" might, through "ill imitating," think to excel the original story by changing "in scenes" the act of creation "and show it in a play." Here Marvell criticizes JOHN DRYDEN, who had adopted Milton's poem to opera, thus "a play," and used rhyme rather than Milton's blank verse. Again Marvell casts a pointed glance at his own activity in using rhyme, as he, as Dryden, lacks Milton's skills. He then confesses that his concern over Milton's attempts lacked basis, and he knows that "none will dare / Within thy labours to pretend a share." Milton's book does what sacred writings do; it "Draws the devout, deterring the profane." Marvell's use of ALLITERATION further emphasizes the power of Milton's text.

Marvell employs the phrase *delight and horror* to describe the reaction of readers to *Paradise Lost.* In so doing, he draws on the classic tradition of Lucretius, who, according to Nigel Smith's commentary, had written "from all these things a sort of divine delight gets hold upon me and a shuddering, because nature thus by thy power has been so manifestly laid open and uncovered in every part" (*De Rerum Natura* 3, ll. 28–30).

Next Marvell notes, "Thou sing'st with so much gravity and ease," then refers to "The bird named from that Paradise you sing." The former line reflects on Milton's narrator in the first book of *Paradise Lost,* "Thou singst . . . aloft," while the second suggests the Bird of Paradise. That bird did not appear in Milton's book but remained an emblem of perfection in poetry. Marvell eventually compares Milton to the blind Tiresias, writing "just heaven . . . to requite / Rewards with prophecy thy loss of sight." In mythology Tiresias received the power of prophecy from Jupiter, after his blinding by Juno. The final lines employ IRONY to make Marvell's point regarding rhyme:

I too transported by the mode offend,
And while I meant to praise thee must
    commend,
Thy verse created like thy theme sublime,
In number, weight, and measure, needs not
    rhyme.

Critics agree that Marvell notes that his attempt to be fashionable by employing rhyme renders him unable to use the term *praise* at the end of line 52. He is forced to insert the weaker term *commend,* as it must rhyme with the previous line. In eschewing rhyme, Milton's format matches the sublime nature of his topic.

BIBLIOGRAPHY
Gross, Kenneth. "'Pardon Me, Mighty Poet': Versions of the Bard in Marvell's 'On Mr. Milton's *Paradise Lost.*'" *Milton Studies* 16 (1982): 77–96.
Parker, G. F. "Marvell on Milton: Why the Poem Rhymes Not." *The Cambridge Quarterly* 20, no. 3 (1991): 183–209.
Ray, H. Robert. *An Andrew Marvell Companion.* New York: Garland, 1998.
Smith, Nigel, ed. *The Poems of Andrew Marvell.* New York: Pearson/Longman, 2003.
Weller, Barry. "The Epic as Pastoral: Milton, Marvell, and the Plurality of Genre." *New Literary History* 30, no. 1 (winter 1999): 143–157.

"ON MY FIRST DAUGHTER" BEN JONSON (1616)

As would any bereaved father, BEN JONSON adopts a solemn, touching tone for this tribute to his dead child. While the poem was included in his *Works* published in 1616, the date of its writing remains unknown. A religious man, and a Catholic at the time of this poem's creation, Jonson adopts the attitude that all humans remain on loan from God, to whom they must return at his pleasure. As George Parfitt notes, Jonson held a specific moral vision constantly revealed in his poetry. He supported that vision through use of a recurrent "ethical vocabulary," including terms such as *virtue*. In this poem he celebrates the preservation of his daughter's innocence, and, by implication, her virtue. The 12-line poem composed of rhyming couplets remains simple in sentiment, yet imbued with all of the complicated emotions a grieving parent would feel.

Jonson opens as if standing over a new grave, stating, "Here, lies, to each her parents' ruth /," where *ruth* means grief, "Mary, the daughter of their youth." The second line signals the loss as especially hurtful, as the parents are young and inexperienced, probably doting on their first girl child. The third line reflects the father's faith as the transitional term *Yet* allows the statement of faith to balance the grief, "Yet all heaven's gifts being heaven's due," with the repetition of *heaven* emphasizing the speaker's belief that his daughter has returned to the place she left. Because all human life as God's gift will eventually depart earth, this "makes the father less to rue." He also takes solace in the fact that "At six months' end she parted hence / With safety of her innocence," suggesting that as an infant, she had not yet exhibited any sinful behavior, a point of comfort for her parents. His next lines engage in delicate imagery, as he and her mother take comfort also in the fact that his daughter's soul is now a part of those serving the baby's namesake, the Virgin Mary, mother of Jesus and queen of heaven:

> Whose soul heaven's queen, whose name she
> bears,
> In comfort of her mother's tears,
> Hath placed amongst her virgin-train:

Jonson concludes by shifting his attention back to the material reality of the grave that cradles the child:

> Where, while that severed doth remain,
> This grave partakes the fleshly birth;
> Which cover lightly, gentle earth!

He employs the harsh verb *severed* to describe a forced separation of such pain that he feels he has lost a part of himself, contrasting with the previous imagery of comfort provided by visions of his daughter in heaven. The *Where* refers to heaven, where the child's soul remains, while her earthly body lies under ground. However, Jonson concludes on a positive note, employing the terms *lightly* and *gentle* to personify the earth as a place that will respect her tiny form. That concept proved, according to Parfitt, "commonplace, both in classical and Elizabethan contexts," the classical context here that of the Latin poet Martial, although Jonson manipulates Martial's paganism to give his adaptation "a distinctively Christian connotation."

BIBLIOGRAPHY
Parfitt, George. *Ben Jonson: Public Poet and Private Man.* New York: Harper & Row, 1977.

"ON MY FIRST SON" BEN JONSON (1616) As does another of BEN JONSON's elegies, "ON MY FIRST DAUGHTER," "On My First Son" draws its power from the stark purity of Jonson's emotions expressed with a simple clarity found in much of his work. The child died in 1604 of the plague, and Jonson noted he had a vision of the boy while in Paris with his mentor and friend William Camden at the time of young Benjamin's death. In his vision the boy had a mark on his forehead resembling a bloody cross.

The poet wears his heart on his poet's sleeve, hiding nothing from the reader as he addresses "thou child of my right hand, and joy," where "child of my right hand" represents the Hebrew meaning for the name *Benjamin*. He projects the raw guilt of a parent who wonders how he might have contributed to his child's death, as he writes, "My sin was too much hope of thee, loved boy." The speaker expresses contrition over his sin of pride in his son. "Seven years thou wert lent to me," the voice continues, adopting the formality of the pronoun *thou* to extend the religious sensitivity of the address. The speaker then declares that he wishes to shed himself of parental feelings: "O could I lose all father now!" Jonson employs the exclamation point to stop the reader before the end of his fifth line, so that he may lead through ENJAMBMENT directly into the next thought, couched as a question. He asks why he should feel sad for death, a state that his Christian faith bids him anticipate as an escape from life's burdens, or perhaps, simply from the misery of growing old:

> . . . For why
> Will man lament the state he should envy,
> To have so soon 'scaped world's and flesh's
>   rage,
> And, if no other misery, yet age?

One who excelled in effective use of punctuation, Jonson inserts two nouns with possessive apostrophes after an apostrophe representing a dropped letter, all calling attention to a masterful use of repetition of the persistent and seething s sound. As George Parfitt explains, Jonson often anchored abstract ideas, in this case, lamentation, envy, rage, and misery, through the presence of concrete imagery, here that of an impossible bid for escape from both microcosm, the corporeal prison of the flesh, and macrocosm, the world at large.

The speaker's voice lowers to say, "Rest in soft peace," and then he explains to his son that if asked, he should tell others, "'Here doth lie / Ben Jonson his best piece of poetry.'" Jonson's use of poetry as a metaphor for his child proves especially poignant, if not original. However, his final two lines ring more strongly to echo the regret found in the first lines: "for whose sake henceforth all his vows be such / As what he loves may never like too much." He concludes with a PARADOX in declaring he should not in the future like that which he loves, ostensibly because its loss remains crushing. The sentiment is based on the thought expressed in his second line, that too much hope resulted in a sin, and perhaps the loss of his son represents God's punishment.

Jonson shared with others the thought that one should never consider life as anything other than something "lent," advice directly from Seneca. He was said to have marked such passages in his copy of Seneca's work. However, he did not restrict his own inquiry into the effects of death.

BIBLIOGRAPHY
Parfitt, George. *Ben Jonson: Public Poet and Private Man.* New York: Harper & Row, 1977.

"ON SHAKESPEARE, 1630" JOHN MILTON (1632)

Despite the date included in its title, "On Shakespeare, 1630" by JOHN MILTON did not appear in print until 1632. A SONNET, it was printed beneath the title *An Epitaph on the Admirable Dramatic Poet W. Shakespear* in the Second Folio of William Shakespeare's plays. As do other tribute poems, it declares its subject unmatched by mortal efforts and eternal in nature. Milton focuses on the image of stone monuments, probably with the Stratford Monument to Shakespeare in mind.

The sonnet's first two lines question the need of Shakespeare's "honor'd bones" to be represented in "piled Stones," while lines 3 and 4 continue the inquiry, wondering that "his hallow'd relics" would "be hid / Under a Star-ypointing Pyramid." The speaker makes clear that for poetry's "great heir of Fame" no "such weak witness" as a stone monument is needed. Milton adopts a traditional sentiment in line 8 to note the poet had built himself "a livelong Monument" in his poetry, or "thy easy numbers." The lines have made "deep impressions" in the hearts of their readers, suggesting that Shakespeare is the engraver. The allusion becomes fact in lines 11 through 12, when Milton writes, "Then thou our fancy of itself bereaving, / Dost make us Marble with too much conceiving," perhaps suggesting that with Shakespeare went man's ability to imagine, leaving him no more creative than cold hard stone. However, the clearer suggestion is that Shakespeare's readers will become his last resting place, as the sonnet closes, "And so Sepulcher'd in such pomp dost lie, / That Kings for such a Tomb would wish to die." Even the most powerful ruler would be jealous of one laid to rest in the hearts of his admirers.

"ON SOMETHING, THAT WALKS SOMEWHERE" BEN JONSON (1616)

Known for his biting wit, BEN JONSON showcases his talent for sarcasm in his poem "On Something, That Walks Somewhere." The fact that the speaker will not deign to identify the "Something" of which he writes indicates from the title that he holds his subject in great disdain. As did most poets, Jonson depended upon the aristocracy for patronage and yet did not hold many noblemen in high esteem. Thus he had to negotiate the tension between the need for court approval and his low opinion of many of the privileged who supported his work. The brief poem at only eight lines of rhyming couplets qualifies as an epigram, one of several easily distinguished groups into which Jonson's poetry fell. Traditionally the epigram provided a vehicle for personal attack, which is the manner in which Jonson uses it here, although he also included in his collected *Works* of 1616 epigrams of a positive tone.

Jonson immediately diminishes his subject's importance by labeling the courtier an *it* and using a tone of derision in describing its clothing as *brave,* or fine enough to pass: "At court I met it, in clothes brave enough / to be a courtier." However, he finishes his second line and uses ENJAMBMENT to move into the third, by describing the courtier's looks as "grave enough / To seem a statesman," after which he inserts a colon, causing the reader to pause as the speaker seems to pause to consider his subject. He continues the third line and moves into the fourth, only to stop again midline, then add a brief sentence describing the speaker's reaction: "as I near it came, / It made me a great face. I asked the name." Here the speaker gives the *it* under consideration the chance to distinguish itself by assuming a specific identity. In what follows, Jonson constructs a brief scene, calling on his experience as a playwright to use rhythm as timing for the interchange. The fifth line through the first half of the final eighth line includes dramatic dialogue, as the courtier replies:

> "A lord," it cried, "buried in flesh and blood,
> And such from whom let no man hope least
>   good,
> For I will do none; and as little ill,
> For I will dare none."

Jonson depicts the courtier as afraid to praise or attack, his spirit "buried" within his body. The repetition of the term *none* emphasizes the lack of identity of the courtier, who seems to represent a type for the poet. The eighth line concludes with the simple statement "Good lord, walk dead still." Not couched as dialogue, that line indicates the speaker's thought in a PARADOX, as he silently bids the lord to continue his walk, or life, lacking his own self-identity, an existence that compares to death. Jonson suggests, perhaps, that any group such as courtiers owe their existence to others, as they depended entirely upon the favor of the monarch for their daily livelihoods. His harsh judgment of such men exhibits IRONY in light of the fact that poets remained almost as dependent as courtiers on the favor of others. Of course artists live through their work, while courtiers had little to show for their time spent on earth.

"ON THE DEATH OF AN INFANT OF FIVE DAYS OLD, BEING A BEAUTIFUL BUT ABORTIVE BIRTH" ELIZABETH BOYD (1733)

The high sentiment reflected by ELIZABETH BOYD's "On the Death of an Infant of Five Days Old, Being a Beautiful but Abortive Birth," was entirely appropriate to its era and form. By the third decade of the 18th century traditional religion began to lose its hold on the English imagination, prompting development of a cult of sentimentality that believed in human benevolence. Such sentimentality would give impetus a few years after publication of Boyd's poem to a seminal event in the development of the novel, Samuel Richardson's highly moralized and melodramatic bestseller *Pamela* (1740). John Locke had proposed that all knowledge derived from sensual experience, helping women in later decades to feel free to describe in writing personal experiences that molded their emotional and intellectual development. Both male and female characters on the stage indulged in emotional portrayals as society began to accept a kind of pluralism associated with the rise of scientific knowledge. Boyd's choice of terminology, such as *symptoms, convulsions, embryo,* and *abortive,* reflects an acute awareness of scientific ideas regarding physical phenomena. She also includes an idea prevalent since publication of Thomas Hobbes's *Leviathan* (1651) and its focus on matriarchy, that men did not have natural ownership of a child. The development of a middle-class readership helped boost the popularity of literature that reflected their own experiences.

Boyd's poem appeared in a collection titled *The Humorous Miscellany,* its hopeful title not reflective of some of its subject matter, including Boyd's poem. She adopts a plaintive and sympathetic voice, that of a mother deep in mourning over the death of her baby boy. The speaker begins by declaring, "How frail is human life! How fleet our breath, / Born with the symptoms of approaching death!" intriguing in its consideration of the tremulous nature of life as merely a prelude to death. The tone is one of inconsolable grief, its word choice both sharp and disturbing:

What dire convulsions rend a mother's breast,
When by a first-born son's decease distressed,
Although an embryo, an abortive boy,
Thy wond'rous beauties give a wond'rous joy.

The tone softens by the sixth of 22 lines, as the persona considers the beauty and joy observed, even in a life cut short. After an emotional protestation the voice lapses into longing, further considering how human hope pits itself uselessly against the sure science of death: "Still flattering Hope a glittering idea gives / And, whilst the birth can breathe, we say it lives." The sound repetitions include ALLITERATION, assonance, and consonance, which support the voice's softer, wistful tone. The tone extends several more lines as the speaker muses about the "warmth" with which "the dear-loved babe was pressed," referring to the child as "darling man" and "the fond embrace" he received as "dear" and "innocent."

The speaker then mentions the infant's father for the first time as the tone turns more upbeat while considering that the baby possessed "The father's form all o'er, the father's face," which may account for the power of "the sparkling eye, gay with a cherub smile" to "mother-pangs beguile." If the next two lines seem cloying, one must consider the physical pain alluded to: "The pretty mouth a Cupid's tale expressed, / In amorous murmurs, to the full-swoll'n breast." The mother's breast would quite literally be swollen with fluid for which it could gain no release after the infant's death, other than through manual manipulation. Because milk does not immediately cease flowing when the sucking stimulation ends, the mother would suffer the discomfort of the insistent pressure in her breasts for some time. An almost magical sympathy exists between a suckling mother and her infant; his cry, or, in this case, *murmurs,* cause milk to flow spontaneously in a pure cause/effect phenomenon. Such physical empathy remains impossible between a man and a baby, preparing readers for future references to the contrast of the male attitude toward personal loss.

After two lines containing the requisite angel references, the tone again gains strength in its statement regarding striking gender differences: "Oh! Could the stern-souled sex," meaning men, "but know the pain," obviously referring to both physical and emotional discomfort, "Or the soft mother's agonies sustain, / With tenderest love the obdurate heart would burn, / And the shocked father tear for tear return." Boyd obviously believed that males had no inkling as to the suffering of women who carried a child to near term, endured labor and birth agonies, often damage to torn flesh, and additional complications, only to be left without a child and with breasts tender from milk that would not be used. The fact that fathers would be "shocked" out of their stern demeanor supports the theory that Boyd and other women of her age felt trivialized by male ignorance regarding their situations, which led to marginalization of their needs.

BIBLIOGRAPHY

Schofield, Mary Ann. *Masking and Unmasking the Female Mind: Disguising Romances in Feminine Fiction, 1713–1719.* Newark: University of Delaware Press, 1999.

"ON THE DEATH OF MY FIRST AND DEAREST CHILD, HECTOR PHILIPS, BORNE THE 23D OF APRIL, AND DIED THE 2D OF MAY 1665" KATHERINE PHILIPS (1667)

KATHERINE PHILIPS expresses the grief expected by any mother upon the loss of a child in her "On the Death of My First and Dearest Child, Hector Philips." In this ELEGY readers may conflate the speaker with the poet. Her five four-line verses were set to music by the great Henry Lawes, the musician who convinced JOHN MILTON to write the celebratory masque COMUS, which he set to music for performance for an aristocratic family.

In the first stanza Philips measures her time spent as a wife and as a mother in months and days. Previous to her son's birth, she had been married for "Twice forty months," after which her marriage vows were "crowned with a lovely boy." She often uses the metaphor of a crown in her poems to indicate her blessings of friendship, family, and love, equating the change to the maximal elevation in social status one could achieve. The speaker next notes of the infant that after "forty days he dropped away; / O! swift vicissitude of human joy!" Philips was a religious woman and may have adopted the number 40 from biblical references. For example the Hebrews, God's chosen people, wandered for forty years in the desert before arriving at the Promised Land. In addition Christ endured 40 days of fasting during one of his three temptations by Satan, a scene Milton recreated in PARADISE REGAINED. The final line of the first stanza refers to the fleeting nature of human joy, dashed, in this case, by the unanticipated death of the child.

The second stanza emphasizes the speed with which the speaker's joy died, as she states, "I did but see him, and he disappeared, / I did but touch the rosebud, and it fell. . . ." Philips uses the FIGURATIVE LANGUAGE of metaphor through reference to a rosebud, further stressing the infant's perfection and his youth, as well as the fragile nature of life. While a mature flower might be expected to fall from a bush when touched, the stem having naturally prepared for its release, a bud should remain tightly attached. That stanza concludes as the speaker notes that humans cannot understand "A sorrow unforeseen," something that had been "scarcely feared." Again Philips makes clear how unprepared she was for her loss, indicating the child had been healthy until shortly before his death.

In the third stanza the speaker questions how she can "right" her own fate or that of her child. Because the answer must be that she cannot, she can find no inspiration for action other than to write the ELEGY. As she explains, "Tears are my muse, and sorrow all my art," thus commenting on her vocation as a poet and concluding, "So piercing groans must be thy elegy." Philips metaphorically depicts her expression of grief in terms that reflect her efforts as a poet. Because the act of motherhood remains just as creative as the act of creating a poem, Philips is able to balance both as legitimate creative pursuits.

The fourth stanza notes the isolation Philips feels, suffering "whilst no eye is witness of my moan" and noting that the "unconcerned world . . . / neither will, nor can refreshment give." Life outside her private chamber offers no support. She ends the poem by offering for "thy sad tomb" the "tribute" of "gasping numbers," the numbers referencing the lines of her poem. The elegy represents her gift to her dead child, "The last of thy unhappy mother's verse."

Feminist critics have noted the absence of reference to the father in the poem as representing the private deprivation Philips endured.

"ON THE DEATH OF WALLER" APHRA BEHN (1687)

APHRA BEHN suitably honored the poet EDMUND WALLER by imitating his style in a panegyric she wrote to commemorate his death. The label for the type of poem written to praise an individual publicly derived in part from the Greek term *panēgurikos*, meaning a "speech for a public festival." One of the most popular and influential poets of his day, Waller had himself written panegyrics for both Oliver Cromwell and King Charles II, symbolizing the reversals of his political loyalties that resulted in his temporary exile from England. Upon his return he staunchly supported the Stuart reign, joining the ranks of RESTORATION Royalists to which Behn also belonged. His smooth and effective use of the HEROIC COUPLET was proclaimed a superior legacy to later poets; JOHN DRYDEN declared that he and his contemporary poets owed their very existence to Waller, echoing Behn's sentiment. She readily agrees with Dryden's estimation of Waller, as she characterizes him as the force reviving her "languished muse."

The poem contains nothing remarkable, serving as an excellent example of the traditional panegyric form. The first line calls upon the departed, while the second suggests through a question to the deceased that the writer of the poem is unworthy by comparison, a trope often used in praise poetry: "How to thy sacred memory shall I bring, / Worthy thy fame, a grateful offering?" Behn then compares her "toils of sickness" to the illness that overcame Waller, declaring "every soft and every tender strain / Is ruffled and ill-natured grown with pain." As her muse revives at the mention of

Waller's name, "a new spark in the dull ashes strives," and the poet hears Waller's "tuneful verse" and his "song divine," inspiring her. In a two-word line formatted for effect, she cries, "But oh!" following her exclamation with a rhetorical question, with the answer again calling attention to the deceased's importance: "What inspiration, at the second hand, / Can an immortal elegy command? / Unless, like pious offerings, mine should be / made sacred, being consecrate to thee." Behn follows the traditional approach of deeming her own work acceptable only through its association with that of Waller.

Behn continues with the classical allusion to immortality gained by writers through their words, Waller's expressions described as "wit sublime" with "judgment fine and strong." The name *Sacharissa* in line 20, "Soft as thy notes to Sacharissa sung," refers to Lady Dorothy Sidney, Waller's love in the 1630s and the subject of many of his lyrics. Behn then compares her own writing to decaying flowers, contrasting it with Waller's immortal words. She claims that the world did long "in ignorance stray," its writers producing nothing of worth until Waller arrived to show "the true poetic way," endowing a world that suffered only "dull and obscure" poetry, lacking the power to move readers to passion. She adopts a religious comparison of Waller saving the world of literature to Moses rescuing the Jews from Egyptian oppression and leading them to the Promised Land: "Darkness was o'er the Muses' land, displayed, / And even the chosen tribe unguided strayed, / Till, by thee rescued from the Egyptian night, / They now look up and view the god of light, / That taught them how to love, and how to write." In Behn's opinion Waller remains a deity, without whom poets would never have found a voice. She reemphasizes his immortality by labeling him a *god* and his importance by again suggesting that he led the world of poetry, and the poets who would inhabit it, from the dark into the light.

Writing in the heroic couplets that Waller so favored, Behn executes a fitting final tribute to a celebrated poet.

"ON THE LATE MASSACRE IN PIEDMONT" JOHN MILTON (1655) JOHN MILTON wrote the SONNET "On the Late Massacre in Piedmont" in order to protest the brutal treatment of the Waldensian sect on Easter 1655 in the Piedmont. A group founded in the 12th century that practiced poverty and austerity, the Waldensians had been persecuted for centuries all over the Continent, with the Italian Peninsula no exception. Anti-Catholic in belief, a group in the Piedmont had been ordered not to practice their faith and were subsequently brutalized, the survivors left to freeze and starve in the mountains. Milton wrote letters protesting their treatment on behalf of Cromwell and in his sonnet declared the Waldensians the true followers of Christ, making clear his own well-known anti-Catholic sentiment.

The sonnet's opening line calls for revenge by the Lord for "thy slaughter'd Saints," whose bones had been scattered in the cold Alps. The speaker aligns the faithful dead with Christ by labeling the Waldensians in line 3, "them who kept thy truth so pure of old / When all our Fathers worship't Stocks and Stones," making clear the superiority of the ancient group. Adopting what some label an Old Testament voice, Milton continues requesting the Lord not only to remember the martyrs, but to "record their groans." He makes his request on behalf of those "Who were thy Sheep and in their ancient Fold / Slain by the bloody Piemontese." Although Milton includes vivid imagery of death, describing "Mother with Infant" rolled down the mountain, his poem remains spiritual, rather than political. He makes clear that the martyrs' spirits remain in the form of "blood and ashes" sown "O'er all th'Italian fields where still doth sway / The triple Tyrant." The speaker hopes that from that sowing a crop "may grow," resulting in "A hundredfold" of the faithful. Critics compare Milton's allusion to the legend of Cadmus, a warrior who sowed teeth from a killed dragon in the earth, from which sprouted a crop of warriors. Milton's fantasizing that the crop of Waldensians in the final line will make "fly the Babylonian woe" echoes Petrarch's labeling of the papal court a Babylon and "fountain of woe." Thus Milton hopes Catholics may be chased from the peninsula, replaced by the group he depicts as the Lord's true followers.

BIBLIOGRAPHY

Hughes, Merritt Y., ed. *John Milton: Complete Poems and Major Prose.* New York: Macmillan, 1957.

"ON THE NEW FORCERS OF CONSCIENCE UNDER THE LONG PARLIAMENT" JOHN MILTON (ca. 1646)

As is evident by the phrase *New Forcers of Conscience* in "On the New Forcers of Conscience under the Long Parliament" by JOHN MILTON, the poem was written as a protest. Milton wrote against the Parliament that opened on July 1, 1643, and its domination by Presbyterians, or the "great rebukers of non-residence," who made up the Westminster Assembly of Divines. That group convened after the abolition of episcopacy and dictated religious matters in the name of reform, charged by Parliament to do so. The assembly then pressured Parliament to form a national Presbyterian Church, according to Barbara K. Lewalski, which would help the government "suppress heresy, sects, and schisms." The assembly undertook revision of the Thirty-nine Articles in addition to abolishing the Book of Common Prayer, among other actions that infuriated many. Milton's *Areopagitica* (1644) took on the topic of censorship and contributed to the debate over religious toleration by insisting on a free press and free discussion. However, by February 1645 the assembly recommended that Parliament institute a National Presbyterian Church Government, "with synods, classes and provincial and national assemblies." Parliament passed the recommendations with some amendments to satisfy Independent churches.

During the early years of dictates by the assembly, Milton remained focused on his private study and tutoring, publishing tracts about marriage and divorce. But his growing disillusionment with the Long Parliament and the course that religious and civic reform took moved him to action. He then became publicly involved with the toleration controversy and religious tensions created by the assembly. Parliament at last ordered the assembly's dissolution on February 22, 1649.

Milton describes the assembly's actions in the first two lines as throwing "off your Prelate Lord, / And with stiff Vows renounc'[ing] his Liturgy," his tone becoming virulent in the next two lines when he adds, "To seize the widow'd whore Plurality / From them whose sin ye envied, not abhorr'd." He turns to the true topic of the piece in the next lines, noting the group used the

"Civil Sword / To force our consciences that Christ set free." Milton vilifies the assembly by characterizing it as a group acting contrary to Christ. He later uses a comparison to the Council of Trent, famous for its tendency to compromise, to insult the group further, writing, "Your plots and packing worse than those of Trent."

Milton adopts FIGURATIVE LANGUAGE in describing members of the assembly as wearing "Phylacteries," a reference to small boxes worn by Jews on their foreheads, an outward sign of their piety; Milton uses the reference to reflect the hypocrisy of the assembly. He writes with hope that Parliament will "clip" the phylacteries, stopping short of clipping the ears of those who wear them. Mosaic law ordered that punishment for priests who broke faith, after which they could no longer serve. Milton concludes his 20-line poem by charging that the "*New Presbyter* is but *Old Priest* writ Large." As Merritt Y. Hughes explains, the terms *Presbyter* and *Priest* derive from the identical Greek word, although *Priest* entered the language prior to *Presbyter*. Milton accuses the Presbyterian leaders of being no better than Catholic priests inflicting Rome upon the English Protestants.

BIBLIOGRAPHY

Corns, Thomas. "Milton and the Characteristics of a Free Commonwealth." *Milton and Republicanism*, edited by David Armitage, Armand Himy, and Quentin Skinner, 25–42. Cambridge: Cambridge University Press, 1995.

Dobranski, Stephen B., and John P. Rumrich, eds. *Milton and Heresy*. Cambridge: Cambridge University Press, 1999.

Hughes, Merritt Y., ed. *John Milton: Complete Poems and Major Prose*. New York: Macmillan, 1957.

Lewalski, Barbara K. *The Life of Milton: A Critical Biography*. Oxford: Blackwell, 2000.

"ON THE WOUNDS OF OUR CRUCIFIED LORD" RICHARD CRASHAW (1646)

RICHARD CRASHAW commonly employed what would later be described as baroque style in much of his poetry. The label described stylistic hyperbole and employment of outrageous FIGURATIVE LANGUAGE, his extended metaphors often alienating readers, who might find them inappropriate to his religious subject matter. "On the Wounds of Our Crucified Lord" well represents his approach, and full verses are included here in order to clarify the style that resulted in Crashaw's elimination from the group of poets considered the most accomplished in the 17th century. Crashaw's has been classified with that of METAPHYSICAL POETS AND POETRY, but the label does not relieve the harshness in contrast that results from his often shocking metaphors.

The wounds referred to are traditionally those inflicted during Christ's crucifixion from a crown of thorns that pierced his scalp, from nails hammered into his hands and feet to hold him on the cross, and from a final stab in his side to hasten his death. "On the Wounds of Our Crucified Lord" contains five four-line verses of rhyming couplets, with form presenting no challenge to the reader. However, the second line introduces the jarring extended metaphor that employs imagery of human eyes and mouths to refer to the wounds sustained by Christ on the cross:

> O these wakeful wounds of thine!
>   Are they mouths? Or are they eyes?
> Be they mouths, or be they eyne,
>   Each bleeding part some one supplies.

Crashaw often employs ALLITERATION in his poetry, as observed in the first line with the *w* sounds. By using the traditional biblical personal reference *thine,* he establishes the solemn formality of the occasion. Once he establishes his subject as Christ's wounds, he moves directly into the mouth and eye comparison, questioning Christ as to which each of his wounds represents, using in the third line an older plural form for eyes, *eyne.* The final line basically states that each wound is either an eye or a mouth.

The second verse introduces images generally reserved as references to romance, such as "full-bloomed lips" and "roses." The description of the lips as "full-bloomed" connotes maturity, traditionally seen in references to women mature enough to engage in sex. In Crashaw's use he refers to Christ's maturing into his role as a sacrifice for man's sin. The mixture of what might be termed the erotic with the sacred proved a specialty of JOHN DONNE, but Crashaw lacks Donne's art as he writes:

> Lo! A mouth, whose full-bloomed lips
>   At too dear a rate are roses.
> Lo! A bloodshot eye! That weeps
>   And many a cruel tear discloses.

Crashaw's imagery remains true to the King James Bible (1611) translation of John 19:34, which reads about Christ on the cross, "But one of the soldiers with a spear pierced his side, and forthwith came there out blood and water." Although later scholars felt the *water* referred to plasma, the yellowish product of blood that has separated into its physical elements, Crashaw's comparison to tears is understandable. However, readers attempting to picture a wound as a pair of full lips or a bloodshot eye, a condition common to those who overindulge in alcohol, might encounter some dissonance.

As Crashaw moves into the third verse, he refers to wounds caused by what was traditionally believed to be either a metal or wooden stake driven through Christ's feet to hold him onto the cross. While none of the four gospels in the New Testament of the Bible makes clear that detail, simply stating that Christ was crucified, the methods used during crucifixion were well known. Crashaw notes that Christ's foot has received "Many a kiss and many a tear," and that those who honored him in such a way will have all their sins forgiven, "have all repaid, / Whatsoe'er thy charges were."

After this encouraging thought Crashaw further extends his metaphor in the fifth verse:

> This foot hath got a mouth and lips
> To pay the sweet sum of thy kisses;
> To pay thy tears, an eye that weeps
> Instead of tears such gems as this is.

Crashaw establishes an additional metaphor to that of the mouth and eyes with the reference to *gems,* connoting something of great value, which he will extend into his final verse. He in effect stacks one metaphor on top of another, as, having referred to the liquid flowing from Christ's wounds as tears wept by eyes, he will now convert those tears into jewels. That final verse concludes the poem with

The difference only this appears
(Nor can the change offend),
The debt is paid in ruby-tears
Which thou in pearls didst lend.

Crashaw achieves with his metaphors the unity he desires. His final reference to debt reflects on the third verse reference to Christ's death's constituting payment of all debts for the faithful. The use of the term *ruby* also serves double duty, acting to support the gem metaphor, reflecting on the inestimable value of Christ's gift to mankind through his death. In addition it reemphasizes the color red, which readers have attached to Christ's blood, the "full-bloomed" lips of the mouths that represent his wounds, and the roses previously mentioned. The concluding reference to *pearls* supports the idea of the value to man of Christ's death.

Crashaw remained a passionate writer, as evidenced by "On the Wounds of Our Crucified Lord." His emotions are made clear in his poetry, leaving readers to admire his determined enthusiasm and devotion to his faith, if not always his manner of expressing that passion.

BIBLIOGRAPHY

Williams, George Walton. *Image and Symbol in the Sacred Poetry of Richard Crashaw.* Columbia: University of South Carolina Press, 1967.

OTTAVA RIMA A verse form used to some extent during the Renaissance, ottava rima became popular in the 19th century when adopted by the romantics, particularly George Gordon, Lord Byron. An Italian creation employed by Tasso, Ariosto, and others, it consists of eight-line stanzas, each line containing 11 syllables, with a RHYME scheme of *ababbcc*.

OTWAY, THOMAS (1651–1685) Thomas Otway was born in Trottin, Sussex, and raised at nearby Woolbeding, where his father, Humphrey, served as rector. Educated in Winchester and Oxford, Otway failed at acting, trying his luck in the drama *Forc'd Marriage, or the Jealous Bridegroom* by APHRA BEHN. Supposedly gripped by paralyzing stage fright, he later became a decent writer of tragic drama, his first two plays titled *Alcibiades* (1675) and *Don Carlos* (1676). While he adopted for his early work the popular Restoration period format of rhymed couplets with elevated rhetoric, his later dramas, especially *The Orphan* (1680) and *Venice Preserved, or a Plot Discovered* (1682), reflect nontraditional elements. These include BLANK VERSE format supported by an honest emotional character portrayal and stylistically reflecting Otway's cynical view of life in satire. Critics feel Otway's exposure to works by the French writers Racine and Moilère supported his tone of resignation toward life's trials. JOHN DRYDEN later commented on *Venice Preserved,* a widely translated piece with an antipapal theme. Later dramas proved less successful because of weak plotting that did not complement his heavy style. In his 1692 play *The History and Fall of Caius Marius* he adopted the main plot of Shakespeare's *Romeo and Juliet* into a retelling of the story of Marius found in *Plutarch's Lives.*

Although a popular writer, Otway lacked success in both romantic and financial matters. His devotion to the actress Elizabeth Barry, supposedly mistress to the JOHN WILMOT, 2nd earl of Rochester, was not reciprocated, and Otway died alone and in poverty. According to some sources, he choked while eating ravenously, the result of starvation. Described as a tragic genius and a splendid writer, Otway remains important as a poet for his imitation of JOHN DENHAM's COOPER'S HILL in a 1685 poem titled "Windsor Castle." However, his best remembered verse appears in excerpts from his Pindaric poem "The POET'S COMPLAINT OF HIS MUSE." It presents a satirical self-portrait, lacking charm or sophistication, but admirable for its strength of purpose. Its force and vivid description compensate for its lack of art. Letters from Otway appeared in the two-volume *Familiar Letters* (1697) by Tom Brown and Charles Gilden. The letters reveal not only Otway's unrequited love, but also his firm anti-Whig political views. Critics continue to show interest in Otway; David Bergman, for example, suggests possible influence by Otway's drama *The Soldier's Fortune* (1680) on T. S. Eliot's *The Wasteland.*

BIBLIOGRAPHY

Bergman, David. "Otway in the Wasteland: A Dog Story." *American Notes & Queries* 4, no. 4 (1991): 184.

Ham, Roswell Gray. *Otway and Lee: Biography from a Baroque Age.* New Haven, Conn.: Yale University Press, 1931.

Schumacher, Edgar. *Thomas Otway.* New York: B. Franklin, 1970.

Summers, Montague, ed. *The Works of Thomas Otway: Plays, Poems, and Love Letters.* Oxford: Clarendon Press, 1932.

"OUT UPON IT!" SIR JOHN SUCKLING (1648)

SIR JOHN SUCKLING'S LYRIC poem "Constancy" is more commonly known by the title that also is the poem's first line, "Out upon It!" Probably the most widely anthologized of his verse, this poem well represents the work of the CAVALIER POETS. It establishes a complaint about love and incorporates hyperbole and IRONY in the speaker's address to his lover. The speaker's character becomes clear from the first of the four four-line stanzas:

> Out upon it, I have loved
>> Three whole days together;
> And am like to love three more,
>> If it prove fair weather.

The reader quickly discovers that the speaker's idea of remaining constant is to attach his attention for an entire three days, the extension of his favor dependent upon the weather. Suckling thus makes immediately obvious he does not expect his reader to take him seriously. The popular CARPE DIEM theme continues into the second verse, in which Suckling adopts FIGURATIVE LANGUAGE to refer to Time, using a traditional image of a winged being whose wings shall "moult" before he ever discovers "In the whole wide world again / Such a constant lover." Suckling incorporates ALLITERATION with repeated use of the letter *w* to add pleasure for readers who enjoy the IRONY of the suggestion that the speaker represents a "constant lover." The statements are so saucy that readers may easily visualize the speaker as an energetic dandy, charming and devilish. He continues in the third stanza by declaring that he deserves no "praise" for his ability to stay with one lover. Instead the credit goes to her, for "Love with me had made no stays, / Had it any been but she." Suckling skillfully evokes admiration from his audience for this speaker cad by impressing readers with the fact that three days actually is a long period in his world. The fact that this dandy could stop his gallivanting for three whole days on end he gallantly attributes to the virtue of his affection's object.

The final stanza further reveals the speaker's honesty as he explains that had his lover been any other woman, with anything other than "that very face," he would already have had a "dozen dozen" additional women "in her place." Because of the speaker's exaggeration and obvious braggadocio, the audience begins to wonder whether or not he might just be serious about his lover. Had he noted he would have replaced her with one other lover, rather than many, the effect for readers would have been never to take him seriously at all. For audiences conditioned to expect Cavalier poetry to focus on women as objects to be conquered, the poem's subject matter would have proved quite familiar.

OXYMORON

The oxymoron is a figure of speech combining contradictory terms not usually placed together. ROBERT HERRICK included the oxymorons *wilde civility* and *disartful art* in his poem "DELIGHT IN DISORDER" to achieve an incongruous effect. In ANDREW MARVELL's "The DEFINITION OF LOVE," he employs the oxymoron *Magnanimous Despair*. The effect of the oxymoron resembles that of PARADOX.

P

"PAMPHILIA TO AMPHILANTHUS" LADY
MARY WROTH (1621)   LADY MARY WROTH produced
the extraordinary prose romance titled *The Countess of
Montgomery's Urania* while in great need of income.
"Pamphilia to Amphilanthus" was a SONNET sequence
within the work. Her husband, Robert Wroth, had
died, and she inherited many debts but little of his
estate, leaving her to wonder how she might meet her
creditors' demands. While enjoying time at court
through her family connections, she had begun to
write and to record details about various individuals
there. Some of those details she thinly disguised in
The Countess of Montgomery's Urania and "Pamphilia to
Amphilanthus," much to the chagrin of many readers,
especially certain courtiers who recognized themselves in the unflattering depictions. They and their
supporters criticized Wroth for the improper sexual
bent of her work, which included content of a lascivious nature.

Ironically Wroth's romance focused on the lack of
fidelity in men, as contrasted with women, and her
heroine and narrator proved the height of virtue.
Although her name means a lover of all, Pamphilia represented constancy and chastity, virtues that she
insisted her male lover, Amphilanthus, also practice
before she would agree to a long-term commitment to
him. Despite her casting women in such a pure role, or
perhaps because of it, the London community insisted
Wroth recall the romance. Although she fought against
the charges in print, through the publication of "Rail-

ing Rimes," Wroth finally submitted to the pressure
and withdrew her publication; little is known of her
life after that act.

In addition to the prose, Wroth's remarkable sonnet
sequence represented an accomplishment unequaled in
her age by any other woman. The well-known "IN THIS
STRANGE LABYRINTH HOW SHALL I TURN?" well represents
Pamphilia's confusion and the conflict shared by many
women as they had to determine whether to fall victim
to male demands or heed the demands of their culture
to remain pure. Additional commonly published sonnets from "Pamphilia to Amphilanthus" include "MY
MUSE, NOW HAPPY, LAY THYSELF TO REST," "WHEN NIGHT'S
BLACK MANTLE," "MY PAIN, STILL SMOTHERED IN MY GRIEVÈD
BREAST," and the songs "LOVE A CHILD IS EVER CRYING" and
"SWEETEST LOVE, RETURN AGAIN."

BIBLIOGRAPHY

Dove, Linda L. "Mary Wroth and the Politics of the House-
    hold in *Pamphilia to Amphilanthus*." In *Women, Writing
    and the Reproduction of Culture in Tudor and Stuart Britain,*
    edited by Mary E. Burke et al., 141–156. Syracuse, N.Y.:
    Syracuse University Press, 2000.
Laroche, Rebecca. "Pamphilia across a Crowded Room:
    Mary Wroth's Entry into Literary History." *Genre* 30, no.
    4 (1997): 267–288.
Moore, Mary. "The Labyrinth as Style in *Pamphilia to
    Amphilanthus*." *Studies in English Literature 1500–1900* 38,
    no. 1 (1998): 109–125.
Roberts, Josephine A. "The Biographical Problem of *Pam-
    philia to Amphilanthus*." *Tulsa Studies in Women's Literature*
    1 (1982): 43–53.

Swift, Carolyn Ruth. "Feminine Identity in Lady Mary Wroth's Romance *Urania*." *English Literary Renaissance* 14 (1984): 328–346.

Warner, J. Christopher. "Talking Back to Catullus: Lady Mary Wroth's *Pamphilia to Amphilanthus* 13." *Explorations in Renaissance Culture* 23 (1997): 95–110.

PARADISE LOST JOHN MILTON (1667, 1674)

When JOHN MILTON first published his epic poem *Paradise Lost,* it appeared in 10 books. After revision he reissued the work in 1674, reorganized into 12 books. It proved a massive undertaking, and as Milton's nephew Edward Phillips later explained, Milton composed the whole in "parcels" of 20 to 30 lines at a time. While Milton began his epic in 1658, his work was twice interrupted, first by the Great Plague, when he had to relocate with his wife to Chalfont St. Giles in 1665, and again by the Great Fire of London in 1666. He had a lofty goal, explained in the opening lines of Book 1, where he references his own blindness as well as his objective in his appeal for help to the "Heav'nly Muse" (6):

> . . . What in me is dark
> Illumine, what is low raise and support;
> That to the highth of this great Argument
> I may assert Eternal Providence,
> And justify the ways of God to men. (22–26)

Milton's work strikes most readers as a drama, but one too massive for a stage to hold. Its artistic expanse equals its physical vision and has served as the basis of some critics' entire careers. The epic has produced an industry of criticism focusing on aspects including the architecture of Milton's cosmos; his debt to VIRGIL, Plato, and other classicists; his focus on the heroics of Christianity and Christian doctrine; his application of the tradition of nature and the garden; the heroic nature of Satan; his view of things angelic; his belief in "theistic materialism"; his relation to Catholic Neo-Platonism; and the baroque aspects of his style, to mention only a few. Through the ages critics tended to see Milton in two different ways. One group viewed him as sympathetic to Satan, in the tradition of 19th-century romantic poets, while others viewed him firmly in God's camp, as had writers such as C. S. Lewis. In

1967 the Milton scholar Stanley Fish in *Surprised by Sin* forever changed the view of Milton by approaching *Paradise Lost* from the view of reader response criticism. He declared the poem is simply about readers and their fallen natures, confirmed each time they felt sympathy with Satan or bristled at something that God said. Fish is said to have ushered Milton criticism into the modern age, proving that a Renaissance work can continue to challenge its readers. In his later study of Milton, *How Milton Works,* Fish makes clear that Milton does not insist that humans "shun" material mortal existence, but rather "appreciate it for the right . . . reason . . . as testimony to the goodness of its creator."

Milton organizes his book according to the Bible's story of the world's creation, the creation of the Garden of Eden, Satan's eviction from heaven, the creation of Adam and Eve, their temptation and eventual eviction from the garden. He adds much detail on his own, particularly with the subject of Satan, a so clearly and dramatically drawn figure that many postromanticism readers viewed him as a heroic figure, a Byronic hero of sorts. This view remains easily understood, particularly as Satan proudly declares his preference for the position of ruler of hell to servant in heaven. Graced with slick wit, he, however, lacks the imagination to see any possibilities outside himself, perhaps the ultimate sin in a poet's view.

Book 1 opens with an argument focusing on man's fall, particularly the reason why he disobeyed God, with Milton's laying the blame at Satan's feet. Platonic argument and reason play a large role in this book and others, but particularly as Satan argues against his fallen position and in favor of reigning in hell and on earth, should heaven remain irredeemable. It sets the scene, describing Satan and his angel minions "lying on the burning Lake, thunder-struck and astonish't." They will later hold counsel, in which various devils are identified by name. They gather in the tradition of a procession of heroes, entering "like a Deluge" (353), their leaders appearing as

> . . . Godlike shapes and forms
> Excelling human, Princely Dignities,
> And Powers that erst in Heaven sat on Thrones.
> (357–359)

The long list of supernatural beings will include Moloch, who best conveyed power and lust in his Old Testament characterization; Chemos, described as "th' obscene dread of Moab's Sons" (406); Astoreth, called by the Phoenicians "Queen of Heav'n, with crescent Horns" (439); the fish deity Dagon, whose image supposedly fell before the Ark of the Covenant, losing its head and palms; and Belial marching in the rear position, "than whom a Spirit more lewd / Fell not from Heaven" (490–491). They lead their troops across scalding terrain that burns their feet, lacking "anguish and doubt and fear and sorrow and pain" (558) that haunt humans, freeing them to breathe as one force with a single thought. Milton redefines traditional heroism and offers a chilling description of Satan, their "dread commander" (589), who stood "In shape and gesture proudly eminent," a tower, having not yet lost its "Original brightness, nor appear'd / Less than Arch-Angel" (592–593). The next lines play on the notion of immortal monarchy, the illusion that rulers achieve an "earthly permanence" according to Richard Hardin. However, his face bore "Deep scars of Thunder" (601) and his eyes projected cruelty and a desire for revenge, but he still is moved by the appearance of his fellow fallen angels. He rallies his troops, explaining he had heard of a new kingdom called Earth, and declared they would all return to Heaven or investigate the new kingdom. The book concludes with a call to council and the building of Satan's palace, Pandemonium.

Book 2 begins with Satan's debate over the wisdom of launching another attack against Heaven, as he describes its wealth and beauty. Moloch, characterized by Milton as "the fiercest Spirit . . . now fiercer by despair" (44–45), stands and urges "open War" (51). Milton uses the tradition of the Homeric counsel in this scene, as Belial next stands to add his opinion. He disagrees with Moloch, because of God's obvious power and omnipotence, and applies a sophist argument, as Milton clarifies that Moloch was "false and hollow" (112), although "his tongue / Dropt Manna, and could make the worse appear / The better reason," through his low thoughts expressed in a manner that yet "please'd the ear" (115–117). He urges the company to look to the future and learn to accept Hell, as "This horror will grow mild, this darkness light" (220),

as Milton employs PARADOX to make clear the futility of the argument. Mammon adds his idea that the group can be sufficient unto itself, not requiring God for existence, proposing they will eventually be able to imitate God's Light, as their "torments" will "Become our Elements" (274–275). After great applause for Mammon, Beelzebub, second only to Satan, speaks, countering the previous arguments with the opinion that their ejection into Hell was their doom, not their rescue; that God will rule Hell as well as Heaven. He proposes a third suggestion, following up on the hint in the previous book regarding a new kingdom:

> . . . There is a place
> (If ancient and prophetic fame in Heav'n
> Err not) another World, the happy seat
> Of some new Race call'd Man, about this time
> To be created like to us. (349)

The group will accept his plan as a way to "surpass / Common revenge" (370–71). Satan agrees to make the journey to the "unknown Region" (443) alone, after which the group praises Satan for volunteering and disregarding his own safety. As the speaker notes, "neither do the Spirits damn'd / Lose all their virtue" (482–483). They worship Satan, allowing Milton to emphasize his belief that monarchy was by nature a form of idolatry.

Satan makes his journey through a brilliantly described landscape "of fierce extremes, extremes by change more fierce" echoing Dante's description of Hell's circles, "From Beds of raging Fire to starve in Ice" (599–600). This book contains the well-known scene of Satan's meeting his own daughter, Sin, whose description interests feminist critics. A fair woman from the waist up, her shape "ended foul in many a scaly fold / Voluminous and vast, a Serpent arm'd / With moral sting" (650–652). Her connection with serpents foreshadows Satan's later conversion to serpent form after his temptation of Eve. Sin is famously surrounded by hell hounds that bark continuously. However, Milton's description of Death far outdoes that of Sin:

> . . . The other shape,
> If shape it might be call'd that shape had none

Distinguishable in member, joint, or limb,
Or substance might be call'd tht shadow seem'd,
For each seem'd either; black it stood as Night,
Fierce as ten Furies, terrible as Hell." (666–671)

Milton follows Renaissance tradition, as seen in the writings of Sir Francis Bacon and Edmund Spenser, of characterizing death as fearsome and negative. It is further described as an execrable, a miscreant, a Goblin, and a "grisly terror" (704) intent on chasing Satan back into the depths of Hell. As Death confronts Satan it grows "tenfold" (705) and Satan intends to slay Death. Sin thrusts herself between the two, informing Satan that Death is their son, a product of Satan's act of incest with Sin. Readers learn of their history, and then Satan again reveals his talent in reasoning, convincing Death that he will liberate them all if allowed to pass. Sin explains she holds the key to the gates, given to her by God, who hates her but who has commanded her not to unlock the gate. She pulls out the key, "Sad instrument of all our woe" (872), and releases Satan, who flies over a seemingly limitless ocean into night and chaos to cross an abyss. Critics have written much about the layers of Milton's cosmos, as Heaven's angels pursue Satan, who eludes them and sees earth. It hangs from Heaven, "fast by hanging in a golden Chain," a "pendant world compared to a star in size" (1052–1053). Hardin writes of Books 1 and 2 that they contain "Fear [as] the dominant chord," with imagery of "fire and darkness, hugeness, heights and depths, wandering, dislocation, dissonance—all the terrors of the night." The result is an emphasis on dread, terror, all that is terrible and "horrid," the last term with its roots in the Latin *horridus,* meaning "bristling," first used by Shakespeare in this sense.

This account of the first two books offers a sampling of Milton's style and format. His tale continues in Book 3 with God's observation of Satan and his prediction of man's fall, along with a description of how he plans to punish the betrayal, but also of his accepting of man's need for grace, which he will offer in the future. Satan flies by the Limbo of Vanity and transforms at the Gate of Heaven to fool Uriel, Guardian of the Sun. After gaining admission in Book 4, Satan discovers the Garden of Eden and observes the humans, eavesdropping on their discussion of the Tree of Knowledge. He selects Eve to receive his attention. Uriel hears that a devil has escaped Hell and warns the archangel Gabriel, who finds Satan tempting Eve in a dream. Although she rejects that first temptation, Satan will not give up. In Book 5, Eve shares her troubled dream with Adam, who then is counseled by the archangel Raphael about Satan's evil nature and the necessity of man's obedience to God. Adam hears of Satan's revolt and in Book 6, Raphael describes in detail the war in Heaven. God's Son attacks and triumphs over Satan and his devils at the exact midpoint of the poem. Book 7 contains Raphael's explanation to Adam about God's creation of earth and humans, who may aspire to join him in Heaven. In Book 8, Adam requests more knowledge, particularly of the universe, but Raphael explains he should only desire knowledge of his own world. Adam shares with Raphael the passion he feels for Eve, causing Raphael before he departs to warn Adam to tend to higher instincts, as well as the base ones. This section contains a passage in which Milton imagines how angels experience emotion and passion. As Adam and Raphael talk, Satan has returned in the form of a mist that slips under a barrier to tempt Eve again in Book 9. He enters the form of a sleeping serpent, arousing Eve's curiosity that a creature can speak when he later praises her beauty. Applying his logic, he convinces Eve to eat from the Tree of Knowledge, which she carries to Adam after Satan slips from the Garden. Adam discerns that Eve is already lost, and he eats in order to share her sin, so they will fall together. No longer innocent, they become concerned with their nakedness. The angels who had guarded the humans return to Heaven in Book 10, as the Son of God enters the Garden to tell the humans of their fate. He takes pity on them and gives them clothing. The narrator tells of Satan's triumphant return to Hell and the opening of a direct path for Sin and Death to travel into the human world. Doom will be the future of Adam and Eve's children, and they beg God's Son for mercy. This causes the Son to agree in Book 11 to serve as an intercessor with God. However, the couple must still leave the Garden, and the archangel Michael returns to evict them. As Eve sleeps, the angel tells Adam of man's future on earth, describing the later great Flood that will rid Earth temporarily of sinful humans. Book 12 extends Michael's description, encompassing the arrival of God's Son to sacrifice himself for man's redemption. The book concludes with Adam somewhat comforted by knowing of his progeny's redemption. He awakens Eve, and they leave the Garden.

The fact that Milton scholars have continued to study *Paradise Lost* for centuries proves it has lost none of its allure. Fish holds in *How Milton Works* that the poet believed a poem's value was grounded in the poet himself, not in any external evaluation of his writing. Milton never prioritized narrative or style or plot above what he considered divine inspiration. According to Fish Milton's tenacious belief energized his writing; by placing his faith first, he resisted the temptation to experiment with the aesthetics that other poets highly valued.

BIBLIOGRAPHY

Bennett, Joan S. *Reviving Liberty: Radical Christian Humanism in Milton's Great Poems.* Cambridge, Mass.: Harvard University Press, 1989.

Blessington, Francis C. *Paradise Lost and the Classical Epic.* Boston: Routledge & Kegan Paul, 1979.

Bowra, C. M. *From Virgil to Milton.* New York: St. Martin's Press, 1967.

Curry, Walter Clyde. *Milton's Ontology, Cosmogony and Physics.* Lexington: University of Kentucky Press, 1957.

Daiches, David. *Milton.* London: Hutchinson University Library, 1966.

Fish, Stanley. *How Milton Works.* Cambridge, Mass.: Belknap Press of Harvard University Press, 2001.

———. *Surprised by Sin: The Reader in Paradise Lost.* New York: St. Martin's Press, 1969.

Frye, Roland Mushat. *God, Man, and Satan: Patterns of Christian Thought and Life in Paradise Lost, Pilgrim's Progress, and the Great Theologians.* Princeton, N.J.: Princeton University Press, 1960.

———. *Milton's Imagery and the Visual Arts: Iconographic Tradition in the Epic Poems.* Princeton, N.J.: Princeton University Press, 1978.

Hardin, Richard. *Civil Idolatry.* Newark: University of Delaware Press, 1992.

Lewalski, Barbara K. *Paradise Lost and the Rhetoric of Literary Forms.* Princeton, N.J.: Princeton University Press, 1985.

Steadman, John M. *Milton and the Renaissance Hero.* Oxford: Clarendon Press, 1967.

PARADISE REGAINED John Milton (1671)

Written in four books, John Milton's *Paradise Regained* tells the story of Christ's temptation by Satan and ultimate victory, using as a historical basis the version of the tale found in the Gospel of Luke. Milton preferred Luke's version to that found in Matthew for the order of the three temptations, placing the temptation of the tower last and allowing for a dramatic conclusion. In the first book Satan asks Christ to transform a stone into bread after fasting for 40 days, and in the second Satan extends the invitation to Christ to receive "all the kingdoms of the world" as a gift. Milton intended the climax and the denouement, when the two characters of Christ and Satan realize the truth about one another, to conform to the recognition by hero and adversary that Aristotle considered essential to well-written tragedy. As Satan tells Christ in *The Fourth Book,*

> Good reason then, if I beforehand seek
> To understand my Adversary, who
> And what he is; his wisdom, power, intent,
> By parle, or composition, truce, or league
> To win him, or win from him what I can.
> (526–530)

By the conclusion of the heroic epic the speaker informs the audience, "The Son of God, with Godlike force endu'd" (602) and "regain'd lost Paradise" (608). Milton reflects on Adam's expulsion from the Garden of Eden by making clear, "for though that seat of earthly bliss be fail'd, / A fairer Paradise is founded now" (612–613). Although Satan may control man from hell for a time, he remains defeated and tormented by Christ's victory and will ". . . hereafter learn with awe / To dread the Son of God" (625–626).

While not as well known as Milton's *PARADISE LOST* (1667), to which it acts as sequel, this briefer epic has sparked much critical consideration. In *The First Book* readers learn that the speaker intends "to tell of deeds / Above Heroic" (14–15) that have remained untold too long. Discussion focuses on not only Christ as a heroic figure, but also the romantic view of Satan as a type of hero, as well as antihero. Most critics agree this Satan does not mimic the far more confident, blunt, and ill-informed Satan of *Paradise Lost.* He refers to himself as "th' Arch Fiend . . . / . . . that Spirit unfortunate" (356–357) who through "rash revolt" sacrificed his "happy Station" in heaven to be driven "from bliss to the bottomless deep" (359–361). Seemingly not as intelligent as his former incarnation, this Satan needs to mumble Christ's words to himself in a type of translation and at times engages in what some critics characterize as double talk, as in his explanation of his relationship to man:

> . . . by them
> I lost not what I lost, rather by them
> I gain'd what I have gain'd, and with them dwell
> Copartner in these Regions of the World,
> If not disposer. (389–393)

Some see Satan as a parody of Christ, but others argue against that view, characterizing Satan as too diminished a figure to qualify. Most critics and readers find the final temptation, which concludes with Satan's falling from the spire from which he tempts Christ to attempt flight, as the most interesting plot aspect. However, they also view the middle section and its argument over the value of human learning as crucial. Milton devoted most effort to this section. Some critics believe Milton reduces Christ to more of a human figure, something less than divine; some see nothing that might counter the idea of God's dual nature, at once human and divine; others admit that Milton preserves Christ's divinity but depicts Christ as dull and egotistical, an unattractive demigod.

Milton believed as other Protestant reformers of his age in Christ as an example for humans to imitate in order to regenerate their fallen nature. The very act of reading the holy word would stimulate better instincts and lead to obedience of God. The didactic nature of the poem is expected in light of Christ's position as a teacher, or enlightener, of humans. Whether this Christ held any expectation that Satan would consider his teachings remains doubtful as he in *The First Book* "sternly" (406) replies to Satan's logic. Christ calls up Job, the long-suffering biblical figure, as an example of a heroic figure that he will imitate. When he reveals Satan as a liar, the fiend counters, "Hard are the ways of truth, and rough to walk, / Smooth on the tongue discourst, pleasing to th' ear" (478–479) as he admits,

"Most men admire / Virtue, who follow not her lore" (482–483), arguing that admiration of the truth does not necessarily result in its pursuit.

Feminist critics find of interest that when Satan returns to hell to hold counsel with his demons prior to the second temptation, Belial suggests using women to tempt Christ. Milton adds humor to the scene when Satan rebuffs him by noting that he "weigh'st / All others by thyself" (173–174). When he returns to tempt Christ a second time, he leads with a description of food delights, in order to establish man's hunger for not only material sustenance, but power over others. He reminds Christ of the wonders of wealth, to which Christ replies, with a foreshadowing of his future crucifixion, "Riches and Realms" are like a crown "Golden in show," but in reality "a wreathe of thorns" (458–459). *The Third Book* involves Satan's attempt to seduce Christ with flattery and the offer of all knowledge, but not before he returns again to the subject of fame and the praise of the masses as a reason to reject God's plan. Christ's reply reflects Milton's own leanings, for he blamed the people for the collapse of the republic and the Restoration of the monarchy. That belief rings clearly in Christ's statement,

> And what the people but a herd confus'd
> A miscellaneous rabble, who extol
> Things vulgar, and well weigh'd scarce worth
>   the praise?
> They praise and they admire they know not
>   what. (49–52)

Christ then notes all of the virtues valued by Milton, wisdom, patience, and temperance, as preferable to "ambition, war, or violence" (90). Christ later tells Satan that suffering is requisite before any action may be taken: "who best / Can suffer, best can do" (194–195). Satan will be completely defeated in *The Fourth Book*, left "perplex'd and troubl'd at his bad success" (1). The speaker explains his failure, telling the audience that the "persuasive Rhetoric" had "sleek't his tongue, and won so much on Eve." However,

> . . . Eve was Eve,
> This far his over-match, who self-deceiv'd

And rash, beforehand had no better weigh'd
The strength he was to cope with, or his own.
    (6–9)

Stanley Fish explains Milton's approach, clear in *Paradise Regained,* as not establishing a tension between a choice of God and a choice of the material. In Milton's belief system these are not independent alternatives. Rather Milton theorizes that "the persons, things, and values that form one pole of this opposition are without coherence and shape if severed from that to which they are supposed alternatives." To attempt to enjoy the world God created without belief in God offers a bitter result.

BIBLIOGRAPHY

Fish, Stanley. *How Milton Works.* Cambridge, Mass.: Belknap Press of Harvard University Press, 2001.
———. *Surprised by Sin: The Reader in Paradise Lost.* New York: St. Martin's Press, 1969.
Hughes, Merritt Y., ed. *John Milton: Complete Poems and Major Prose.* New York: Macmillan, 1957.
Lewalski, Barbara K. *The Life of Milton: A Critical Biography.* Oxford: Blackwell, 2000.
———. *Milton's Brief Epic: The Genre, Meaning, and Art of Paradise Regained.* London: Methuen, 1966.
———. "Time and History in *Paradise Regained.*" In *The Prison and the Pinnacle,* edited by Galachandra Rajan, 49–81. Toronto: Toronto University Press, 1972.
Steadman, John. *Milton and the Renaissance Hero.* Oxford: Clarendon Press, 1967.
Webber, Joan. *Milton and His Epic Tradition.* Seattle: University of Washington Press, 1979.
Wittreich, Joseph A., ed. *Calm of Mind: Tercentenary Essays on Paradise Regained and Samson Agonistes.* Cleveland, Ohio.: Case Western University Press, 1971.

PARADOX   In literature a statement classified as paradox appears to be true but simultaneously contains a contradiction that defies reader intuition. Upon examination the statement, or group of statements, or lines in poetry, may not be true or may not all be true within the same proposition. In another situation a group of lines upon closer study do not actually contradict each other. Paradox is common in FIGURATIVE LANGUAGE (FIGURE OF SPEECH) and proved especially popular with Renaissance and 18th-century poets.

METAPHYSICAL POETS AND POETRY excelled in the use of paradox, as in this example from JOHN DONNE's "A HYMN TO GOD THE FATHER": "When thou hast done, thou hast not done." In this example the seeming contradiction disappears when the various usages of the term *done* are considered. The first use indicates action, while the second use indicates completion of an action. In *ABSALOM AND ACHITOPHEL* JOHN DRYDEN uses paradox to counteract reader expectation when he writes, "Desire of greatness is a godlike sin," as God remains incapable of sin. He offers another marked paradox in a line from *ANNUS MIRABILIS: THE YEAR OF WONDERS, 1666,* "And doom'd to death though fated not to die." BEN JONSON's touching ELEGY for his dead son, "ON MY FIRST SON," notes that the bereaved must learn to think less of the departed, because doing so will prove emotionally crushing, writing, "As what he loves may never like too much." WILLIAM ALABASTER included a paradox in multiple lines when he wrote in his Sonnet 54, titled "Incarnationem Ratione Probare Impossibile," "Two, yet but one, which either other is, / One, yet in two, which neither other be / God and man in one personality." He reflects the Christian belief that man and God became one in God's son, Christ.

PEMBROKE, COUNTESS OF   See HERBERT, MARY SIDNEY, COUNTESS OF PEMBROKE.

"PENTHEA'S DYING SONG" JOHN FORD (ca. 1629)   The Renaissance dramatist JOHN FORD included "Penthea's Dying Song" in his tragedy *The Broken Heart.* As befits the death the song heralds, the poem remains sad, but it does not specifically mourn the loss of Penthea. Rather it is used to focus on death in a more general way. Ford employs repetition in phrases intended as song lyrics, beginning,

Oh no more, no more, too late
    Sighs are spent: the burning tapers
Of a life as chaste as fate,
    Pure as are unwritten papers.

Ford advances the imagery of life ended, not employing the term *death* or *dead* until his seventh line. Instead he adopts the FIGURATIVE LANGUAGE (FIGURE OF

SPEECH) of metaphor in traditional references to death, seen in the phrases "too late / sighs are spent" and the image of the taper burning, its wax melting into a pile like pale flesh. Life is compared to fate, both deemed chaste, suggesting that one's fate remains unsullied by human desire; it is what it is. Ford's use of the END-STOPPED LINE forces his singer(s) to move directly into the next, which is interrupted by a caesura, the colon causing a near full stop, emphasizing the alliteration in the *s* sounds of *sighs* and *spent*. After the pause performers move into another end-stopped line, and Ford uses consonance and assonance to achieve the necessary musical tone. The fourth line emphasizes the pure nature of death as well as life, as Ford compares the lost life to papers never written, noting they also remain pure in their lack of creation. He may reflect on his own artistic bent by referencing writing. Ford extends his CONCEIT of flame as life when in the fifth line he notes that all is "burnt out" in death, "no heat, no light / Now remains," and "'tis ever night." One also associates sleep, another metaphor for death, with the night.

As Ford begins the final six lines of his brief song, he mourns the death of love, with no human directly referenced. Instead he repeats the term *love* in various forms five times, building momentum:

> Love is dead; let lovers' eyes,
> Locked in endless dreams,
> Th' extremes of all extremes,
> Ope no more, for now Love dies.
> Now Love dies—implying
> Love's martyrs must be ever, ever dying.

Ford subverts the tender image of lovers' eyes locked in passion to note they lock in the endless dream that is death, and he skillfully extends his use of sleep further as a metaphor for death. He closes with additional repetition of terms for emphasis.

Sweet and poignant, "Penthea's Dying Song" expresses no fear of death of the one dying. Rather it stresses the double loss in death when a great love is involved. Passion dies along with the flesh, regardless of its intensity. The play reveals multiple broken hearts. One belongs to Penthea, who is forced into marriage with a man she does not love and driven to distraction by her husband's jealousy, which leads him to accuse her of incest with her brother. She stoically rejects her original lover's attentions and then starves herself. As other of Ford's characters do, she controls a passion through her uncompromising focus on her own destruction. For Ford that refusal to yield to fate, even at the risk of death, defined heroism. Penthea visits her brother's love, Calantha, the subject of another song, "CALANTHA'S DIRGE," and urges Calantha to love her brother, then dies, the martyr to love referenced in the final line of "Penthea's Dying Song."

PETRARCHAN   See SONNET.

PHILIPS, KATHERINE FOWLER (1632–1664)
Katherine Fowler was born in London, daughter of a merchant. A precocious child, she had read the Bible by age four, according to family mythology. She attended school in Hackney, where she probably studied French, as she would later translate from that language. She began writing as a teenager and made important friendships at school, including that of Mary Harvey, niece of William Harvey, credited with describing the circulatory system.

After her father's death Katherine's mother married Sir Richard Philips of Wales, the country with which Katherine would later be associated. A widower, Philips had first married Elizabeth Dryden, aunt of JOHN DRYDEN, and Katherine became acquainted with the poet. As would Dryden, she would change religion several times. Raised a Presbyterian, she later become an Anglican. Those Anglican sympathies caused her to identify with the monarchy, rather than Oliver Cromwell's Puritans, who took power after the 1649 execution of King Charles I. She remained a staunch lifelong Royalist and later converted to Catholicism, although her stepfather supported Parliament over the king. He would lose his Wales estate for a time during the RESTORATION, but later regained it.

Through Sir Richard Katherine met Colonel James Philips, the 54-year-old widower who had been married to Sir Richard's deceased daughter. The 16-year-old Katherine found Philips, a prominent Puritan Parliament member, attractive. The two married in

1647, despite the tremendous difference in their ages and religious leanings, not to mention Katherine's earlier declaration regarding the desire to marry a learned Royalist. Philips did meet Katherine's desire for a husband "not too well read," and yet not illiterate either. She had described such a man as the perfect husband in a childhood poem titled "No blooming youth shall ever make me erre." He allowed her to avoid a "blooming youth," offering instead the maturity to perform those "Moderate, grave & wise acts" that she valued. An affectionate husband, Philips later allowed Sir Charles Cotterell, who served Charles II as master of ceremonies, to become his wife's intellectual patron with no apparent resulting friction. Philips remained dedicated to his young wife, and from indications in her later poetry and her correspondence theirs appears to have been enough of a love match to satisfy the practical Katherine. She staunchly supported her husband during the Restoration, probably saving his life through her Royalist sympathies.

Katherine Philips proved an unusual figure for the 17th century, in that she earned public approval as a writer, despite being a woman. While MARGARET CAVENDISH, DUCHESS OF NEWCASTLE, suffered criticism for her writing, Katherine enjoyed great acclaim. Her dignity and regal bearing, noteworthy attributes in a commoner, had much to do with her public acceptance. She represented the ideal of woman: meek, chaste, and quietly intelligent. If she knew how to avoid the ire of men, she also knew how to gain the love of women. Katherine celebrated women in same-sex love poetry, praising particular women with whom she shared apparently platonic relationships. A question she posed regarding the topic of friendship inspired the Anglican spiritual writer of the day, Jeremy Taylor, to produce a tract on that topic in which he mentions Katherine as his motivation for writing. Her society of friendship embraced men as well as women, and many members received romantic classical names used in Katherine's poetry and correspondence. Calling herself Orinda, she would later receive public acclamation as the "Matchless Orinda," a phrase that endured beyond her early and tragic death of smallpox.

A translator as well as a poet, Philips translated the French tragedy *Morte de Pompeii* (*The Death of Pompey*) by Pierre Corneille into HEROIC COUPLETs. In 1662–63 it became the first drama translated by an Englishwoman to appear on stage, produced in Dublin and securing Katherine's fame. However, her reputation grew from the circulation of her unpublished poems in manuscript, few of them published during her life time.

Reserved and humble by nature, Philips expressed embarrassment over the popular reception of her works and only published with reluctance. Apparently hoping to reap benefits from her soaring popularity, a printer released a pirated version of her poetry in November 1663. As expected of a woman in the Renaissance, she reacted violently to what she felt was a great injustice. Not only had her modesty been insulted, some of the poems contained errors, and the printer attributed work to Katherine that she had not written. Even ABRAHAM COWLEY's ode attached to the collection that praised Katherine in elegiac terms did not ease her discomfort. Cowley wrote, in part,

> For, as in angels, we
> Do in thy verses see
> Both improved sexes eminently meet,—
> They are than Man more strong, and more than
>   Woman sweet.

Katherine Philips never openly competed with men, denying any wish for public approval, causing men to support her efforts and allowing her to claim that she published at their urging. She skillfully manipulated them into urging her to do what she considered improper to do on her own. Men liked her for her deferential nature. In addition to Cowley, supporters included Roger Boyle; Lord Orrery, chief justice of Ireland; and the earl of Roscommon. The public welcomed her humility, as it perpetuated the traditional ideal of womanhood to which 17th-century English culture clung. The public preferred the more feminine Philips to the brash Cavendish, as well as to the new wave of women writers that would follow, including the outspoken and bawdy APHRA BEHN. Early women writers reflecting her influence included ANNE KILLIGREW; LADY MARY CHUDLEIGH; ANNE FINCH, COUNTESS OF WINCHILSEA; MARY BARBER; MARY ASTELL; and SARAH FYGE EGERTON.

By the 18th century Philips's work would pass from favor, although the 19th-century romantic poet John Keats would ask a friend whether he had seen "a book of poetry written by one beautiful Mrs. Philips, a friend of Jeremy Taylor's and called The Matchless Orinda." The work of Katherine Philips received renewed and deserved attention in the 20th century, as feminist studies rejuvenated interest in women writers of the early modern period. Widely anthologized works include "A MARRIED STATE"; "FRIENDSHIP'S MYSTERIES, TO MY DEAREST LUCASIA"; "ON THE DEATH OF MY FIRST AND DEAREST CHILD, HECTOR PHILIPS"; "TO MY EXCELLENT LUCASIA, ON OUR FRIENDSHIP"; and "Upon the Double Murder of King Charles."

BIBLIOGRAPHY

Gosse, Edmund. "The Matchless Orinda." In *Seventeenth-Century Studies,* 205–229. London: Kegan Paul, Trench & Co., 1883.
Hageman, Elizabeth. *Katherine Philips: "The Matchless Orinda."* Saskatoon: Peregrina, 1986.
Limbert, Claudia. "Two Poems and a Prose Receipt: The Unpublished Juvenilia of Katherine Philips." *English Literary Renaissance* 16 (1986): 383–390.
Llewellyn, Mark. "Katherine Philips: Friendship, Poetry and Neo-Platonic Thought in Seventeenth-Century England." *Philological Quarterly* 81, no. 4 (fall 2002): 441–468.
Reynolds, Myra. *The Learned Lady in England 1650–1760.* Boston: Houghton Mifflin, 1920.
Souers, Philip Webster. *The Matchless Orinda.* Cambridge, Mass.: Harvard University Press, 1931.
Taylor, Jeremy. *The Measures and Offices of Friendship.* 1662. Reprint, New York: Scholars' Facsimiles and Reprints, 1984.
Thomas, Patrick. *Katherine Philips.* Cardiff: University of Wales Press, 1988.
Thomas, Patrick, ed. *The Collected Works of Katherine Philips: The Matchless Orinda.* Vol. 2. Cambridge: Stump Cross Books, 1990.
Williamson, Marilyn. *Raising Their Voices: British Women Writers 1650–1750.* Detroit: Wayne State University Press, 1990.

"PHILLIS IS MY ONLY JOY" SIR CHARLES SEDLEY (1719)

SIR CHARLES SEDLEY gained a reputation for his bohemian lifestyle. Independently wealthy and a political figure, he found support from King Charles II, who enjoyed his frequent public antics. A

dramatist, Sedley included many songs in his performances, several of which remain interesting as lyrics included in modern anthologies. One of those is "Phillis Is My Only Joy," a playful poem with a light tone fitting its subject. The speaker follows the first line, which repeats the title, with the seemingly disapproving description, "Faithless as the winds or seas," but he obviously enjoys her being, as the third line notes, "Sometimes cunning, sometimes coy." The use of repetition and ALLITERATION, as well as the stanza form, indicates the poem was originally a song. The fourth line, "Yet she never fails to please," precedes a refrain of sorts in two sets of rhyming couplets, followed by the first stanza summary line:

> If with a frown
> I am cast down,
> Philis smiling
> And beguiling
> Makes me happier than before.

The second stanza notes the speaker's dismay at discovering "too late I find / Nothing can her fancy fix," where *fancy* means her wandering eye. However, he adds that as soon as she does him one kind turn, he "forgives her with her tricks." A second refrain follows, along with a concluding summary line:

> Which though I see,
> I can't get free,—
> She deceiving,
> I believing,—
> What need lovers wish for more.

Sedley stresses that an important part of love for his characters is game playing, in which deceit had a great part. His writing career focused on human foibles, something of which he knew a great deal through his own infamous lifestyle.

"PHOEBUS ARISE" WILLIAM DRUMMOND OF HAWTHORNDEN (ca. 1616)

WILLIAM DRUMMOND OF HAWTHORNDEN wrote "Phoebus Arise" in the tradition of the AUBADE, a poem that features morning. The aubade also often focused on lovers who had to part as the sun rose. Drummond varies his theme from that of parting lovers to that of unrequited love, featuring a male whose female lover is expected with the dawn but fails to appear. The poem's voice may imply that she has died, as Drummond often featured death and defeat in his works.

In the classical tradition Drummond's speaker calls in the first line, "Phoebus arise," to the sun god Apollo, sometimes called Phoebus. According to mythology Apollo rode a golden chariot across the sky, which pulled the sun into place. The poem's speaker bids Phoebus "paint the sable skies / With azure, white, and red," then asks him to "Rouse Memnon's mother from her Tithon's bed," referring to Aurora, the goddess of the dawn. Aurora is to spread roses about the earth as the nightingales sing their greetings to Phoebus in a setting with "an eternal spring," alluding to the life in springtime that becomes abundant beneath the sun. The positive tone turns brooding in the eighth line, as the speaker, still addressing Phoebus, requests, "Give life to this dark world which lieth dead," hinting that death closely accompanies life and is symbolized by the night, or lack of natural light. Drummond personifies the deity, writing

Spread forth thy golden hair
In larger locks than thou wast wont before,
And, emperor like, decore
With diadem of pearl thy temple fair.

Drummond adopts a formal approach and uses hyperbole in describing the world's beauty by comparing it to human beauty and the value of gems. He then again suggests the manner by which humans understand opposites when he writes, "Chase hence the ugly night, / Which serves both to make dear thy glorious light, / This is that happy morn." As the speaker mentions that the day is a "long-wished one" in his own dark life, he makes clear man's position as fortune's pawn, writing that the day will reward his patience "(If cruel stars have not my ruin sworn, / And fates not hope betray)," then compares that hope to diamonds, extending the gem metaphor. The morning's true value is its ability to "bring unto this grove" his lover, "to hear and recompense my love." He does not merely want the gods to hear of his love for another, he wants them to reward him by forcing her to feel the same for him.

In the remaining 24 lines the speaker reminds Phoebus of a time when he also may have waited for a lover, but makes clear that "two sweeter eyes / Shalt see, than those which by Peneus' streams / Did once thy heart surprise." Therefore the speaker's mortal lover surpasses in beauty even Apollo's idealized lover. Drummond continues a classical tradition, as his speaker bids "zephyrs," or breezes, to play in the hair of his lover, then praises Phoebus again for banishing stars, offering a simile: "Night like a drunkard reels / Beyond the hills to shun his flaming wheels." The poem concludes on a wistful note, as all is prepared for the absent lover:

The fields with flow'rs are deck'd in every hue,
The clouds bespangle with bright gold their blue
Here is the pleasant place,
And every thing, save her, who all should grace.

Drummond's speaker appears destined not to see his lover, playing on the popular poetic CONCEIT of unrequited love. He suggests that all the forces in the universe cannot control human emotion, although the speaker hopes that, by calling upon mythological deities who often altered man's fate, his wish for his lover's presence will be granted. Regardless of how well the speaker sets the scene, even calling upon the gods for aid, his lover cannot be forced to reciprocate his feelings.

"PILGRIMAGE, THE" GEORGE HERBERT (1633)

GEORGE HERBERT wrote "The Pilgrimage" as part of his collection *The Temple*. His six six-line stanzas depict a weary traveler who experiences an allegorical journey, never reaching his goal. Throughout his poetry Herbert stressed the futility of man's efforts to achieve grace, emphasizing the Calvinistic belief that only God may grant grace through predestination. "The Pilgrimage" serves to support this theme, with a hill, the traveler's illusive destination, symbolizing that grace.

The speaker begins in the middle of action, giving readers the impression that he has already long been at this journey: "I traveled on, seeing the hill, where lay / My expectation." Herbert makes clear that the expectation is solely that of the traveler; it is his own invention. This becomes important in making the point that man's attempts to order his own life only serve to separate him from God. Herbert then employs a conundrum popular since classical times when the speaker must pass between two dangerous geographic points. On his left lies "The gloomy cave of Desperation," and "on the other side / The rock of Pride." As Odysseus had to steer his ship between Scylla, a man-eating sea monster, and Charybdis, a deadly whirlpool, the speaker has to navigate with special agility. The cave reference calls to mind Plato's analogy in which inhabitants of a cave find their knowledge of the world limited, as their perceptions are based on illusion. Herbert suggests the same idea and implies that pride aids in man's confusion, not allowing him to choose a path separate from his ego. The uppercase *P* in *Pride* personifies that emotion, and Herbert will use the FIGURA-TIVE LANGUAGE of personification throughout the first verses of his poem, as in allegory.

In the second stanza, the traveler encounters "Fancy's meadow," where he is tempted to stop for a time but decides to move on in order to remain on schedule. He next reaches "Care's copse," a restful stand of trees that he passes "through / With much ado." Herbert incorporates IRONY in the suggestion of pride in the traveler's accomplishments, although he supposedly conquered pride early in the poem. The third stanza tells of "the wild of Passion, which / Some call the wold," where a *wold* means an "upland," an area generally devoid of trees. The traveler describes it as "A wasted place, but sometimes rich," then tells of being robbed of his gold. However, remaining is "one good Angel, which a friend had tied / Close to my side." As with all heroes on odysseys, this traveler requires a guide, a service the Angel may provide.

The traveler at last reaches his "gladsome hill," a place "Where lay my hope, / Where lay my heart." Herbert inserts a semicolon after the word *heart,* forcing a caesura for effect. The traveler continues his climb but suffers disappointment when he finds only "a lake of brackish waters." Apparently even his Angel has not been of aid. Herbert makes the point that man's expectations will always fail him. He must depend instead on God. The traveler falls, "abashed and struck with many a sting / Of swarming fears," recalling the biblical 1 Corinthians 15:55, in which the apostle Paul questions Death regarding the strength of its "sting." This sting is nothing to be ignored; it drives the traveler to tears. He cries out to his lord, wondering whether tears remain his destiny. When he arises, he suddenly "perceived I was deceived." He has not reached his goal after all; his "hill was further," so he "flung away." He does not get far and tells the audience that he

> Yet heard a cry
> Just as I went, *None goes that way*
> *And lives.*

The poem concludes with the traveler's deciding, "After so foul a journey death is fair, / And but a chair." While the reference to the chair may seem odd to modern readers, Herbert had used it elsewhere. In his poem "Mortification" Herbert employs an allusion to a chair as a conveyance to death, writing, "A chair or litter shows the biere, / Which shall convey him to the house of death."

"The Pilgrimage" retains its bleak tone throughout, as man persists in self-delusion, receiving no reward of eternal life. Herbert's message remains clear. Man cannot find eternal life on his own, regardless of the well-meaning effort he exerts. God must grant that grace.

"POET'S COMPLAINT OF HIS MUSE, THE" THOMAS OTWAY (ca. 1685)

"The Poet's Complaint of His Muse" by THOMAS OTWAY cannot be specifically dated, but it was written sometime during the 1680s. Best known for his dramatic tragedies, Otway produced some verse, including this Pindaric ode. A challenging model, the Pindaric ode contains three parts. The first, a strophe, consists of two or more lines arranged as a unit that might shift from one metrical foot to another, its name derived from the Greek for "to turn." The second portion, called an antistrophe, was constructed in the same way as the strophe, often "answering" it. In a classical chorus the strophe might be sung as the chorus moved left to right, while the antistrophe might be sung as the chorus turned to move right to left. The third and final portion, called an epode, contrasted in form with the strophe and antistrophe. In Greek tragedy it would be sung as the chorus stood still. Otway also reflects his knowledge of Pindar's focus on the hero and verbal mythology.

In an occasionally anthologized excerpt Otway demonstrates the varying format of the Pindaric approach as his speaker tells of a poet driven mad for lack of inspiration. He seeks the traditional pastoral scene that acted as the focus of much traditional poetry. Instead he encounters a bleak landscape, barren of life and unable to inspire a bard. He climbs up a "high hill where never yet stood tree" and "Where only heath, coarse fern, and furzes grow." The elements prove dismal as the sheep are "nipped by piercing air" and bear "tattered fleeces" with no grass on which to graze. The negative effect on the bard, already mad, is made clear:

> Led by uncouth thoughts and care,
> Which did too much his pensive mind amaze,
> A wandering bard, whose Muse was crazy grown,
> Cloyed with the nauseous follies of the buzzing town,
> Came, looked about him, sighed, and laid him down.

The lines demonstrate ALLITERATION and vivid imagery and establish a cynical tone toward the bard, or poet, and toward the writing occupation.

Otway counters the traditional pastoral presentation of the poet wandering among serene herds of sheep, taking inspiration from the shepherd's simple way of life. This pastoral employs IRONY and lacks the traditional lush greenery that promotes the health and happiness of the stock, which in turn supports not only the shepherd, but also the poet who wants to write of their existence. Otway presents a bleak physical landscape that supports the desperate mental landscape of his poet subject. His bard suffers from his contact with his subjects, rather than benefiting from that interaction. As a result madness is his only inspiration and nausea the effect of those with whom he interacts. Otway's stage experience surfaces in the final line of this section, which amounts to stage directions for his poet.

In the poem's antistrophe Otway uses FIGURATIVE LANGUAGE (FIGURE OF SPEECH) to personify the earth. His speaker notes that the poet was "far from any path," instead lying

> where the earth
> Was bare, and naked all as at her birth
> When by the Word it first was made,
> Ere God had said:—

At this point the tone shifts from a negative view to a positive one, as the poet recalls God's command that "grass and herbs and every green thing grow, / With fruitful herbs after their kinds, and it was so."

However, the positive imagery exists only in the speaker's imagination, fueled by madness. The reader is quickly called back to reality through the startling contrast of "whistling winds," which blow "fiercely" around the wandering poet's head, and the speaker notes that "Cold was his lodging, hard his bed." The poet looks to "the wide heavens" as the only source of peace and will find that peace only after death. The final two lines from this excerpt reflect Otway's cynicism, as the speaker notes of the poet, "And as he did its hopeless distance see, / Sighed deep, and cried 'How far is peace from me!'"

In this landscape of hopelessness Otway prefigures later works, such as T. S. Eliot's *The Wasteland*. Had Otway lived in better circumstances and beyond his 33 years, he might have produced more poetry with the dramatic flare evident in "The Poet's Complaint of His Muse."

BIBLIOGRAPHY
Grant, Mary Amelia. *Folktale and Hero-Tale Motifs in the Odes of Pindar*. Lawrence: University of Kansas Press, 1967.

POPE, ALEXANDER (1688–1744) Alexander Pope was born in London to a Roman Catholic father who worked as a linen draper. After a sketchy early education Pope could not attend university because of his religious faith. He compensated with an extraordinary self-education, augmented by studies of classical languages with a local priest begun while he was still a child. He later learned French and Italian, expanding his knowledge of languages beyond Greek and Latin. He began early paraphrasing and imitating of classical poets, biblical writers, and English language models, including ABRAHAM COWLEY and Chaucer. He may have written *The Pastorals,* a significant work, as early as age 16; it would be published in 1709. Technically astute, *The Pastorals* reflect his ability to draw upon the tradition of VIRGIL and Edmund Spenser. In 1700 Pope contracted tuberculosis, a disease that would leave him permanently weakened with a bent spine. His condition, exacerbated by asthma, shortened his stature. At less than five feet tall Pope required aid in dressing and had to wear a supporting brace. Also in 1700 his family relocated to Binfield in Windsor Forest.

After moving to London as an adult, Pope joined various literary circles and began the career that would make him the most acclaimed man of letters of his day. He published *An ESSAY ON CRITICISM* in 1711 and gained the support of the politically powerful English essayist Joseph Addison, a member of the Whig Party and member of Parliament for whom Pope would later write "TO MR. ADDISON." Pope was drawn into Addison's group for a time and with the members' support published in 1712 the religious eclogue "Messiah" in Addison's publication with Richard Steele *The Spectator.* That same year he also published the original version of his later famous "The RAPE OF THE LOCK," a mock-epic, MOCK-HEROIC poem that would interest feminist critics in centuries to follow. This witty work established his reputation in London, where he began to feel more secure in his art. Continuing to move in high literary company, he became friendly with the playwrights William Wycherley and William Congreve. He began to drift from his Whig friends, who held anti-Catholic views, drawn toward the Tory point of view. By 1713 he had met JONATHAN SWIFT, the leader of the Tory conclave, with whom he would remain a lifelong friend. That year he joined the Scriblerus Club, a group born form discussions of literature headed by Swift.

Pope's next major publication, *WINDSOR FOREST* (1713), reflected his Royalist sentiments through pastoral. The poem celebrates Queen Anne and her peaceful tenure. As that publication attracted Pope additional notice, he worked to complete his ambitious translation of Homer's *Iliad,* its first volume published in 1715. Complete in 1720, it contained extraordinary

descriptive elements, although the narrative did not remain completely true to the original. Extremely well received, it, along with the less successful *The Odyssey* (1725–26), allowed Pope a financial freedom never before enjoyed by a poet.

By 1717 Pope's collected works made him a celebrated man. The works included several important pieces, such as Chaucer's *The House of Fame,* "Ode for Music on St. Cecilia's Day," and "ELOISA TO ABELARD," one of his later most-studied works. Its melancholy tone extended also to "ELEGY TO THE MEMORY OF AN UNFORTUNATE LADY." Some scholars think the poems' haunting tone reflected Pope's conflict in his relationship with LADY MARY WORTLEY MONTAGU, once a friend, but with whom Pope interacted with little after 1723, after a quarrel. SAMUEL JOHNSON wrote of Pope:

> He was fretful and easily displeased, and allowed himself to be capriciously resentful. He would sometimes leave Lord Oxford silently, no one could tell why, and was to be courted back by more letters and messages than the footmen were willing to carry. The table was indeed infested by Lady Mary Wortley, who was the friend of Lady Oxford, and who, knowing his peevishness, could by no intreaties be restrained from contradicting him, till their disputes were sharpened to such asperity that one or the other quitted the house.

He did find a happy relationship with Martha Blount, inspiring his "EPISTLE TO MISS BLOUNT." Pope experimented in drama, collaborating with fellow members of the Scriblerus Club, John Arbuthnot, to whom he would write "EPISTLE TO DR. ARBUTHNOT," and JOHN GAY. Their play *Three Hours* enjoyed a modicum of success.

Anti-Catholic sentiment that buoyed the Jacobite rebellion of 1715 resulted in legal measures that prompted Pope to leave London. During a period of self-doubt and rejection of literature, he moved in 1719 to Twickenham, an estate that would remain his lifelong home, inspiring later verse. His relations with Lady Mary were still positive at that time, and Pope embraced horticulture and landscaping, designing his famous grotto. During the next happy years he enjoyed his surroundings and often entertained friends, particularly Swift, whom he advised on *Gulliver's Travels.*

Resuming literary activity, Pope published *Shakespeare's Works,* criticized especially by Lewis Theobald in a counterwork titled *Shakespeare Restored* (1726). However, Pope also completed *Odyssey* in 1726 to strong acclaim. He continued publishing by contributing to volumes by the Scriblerians, with two titled *Miscellany* in 1727 and another the following year. The volumes contained an early edition of the "Epistle to Dr. Arbuthnot," as well as an attack on William Broome, Pope's collaborator on the Shakespeare piece, with whom he had a falling-out, and others titled *Martinus Scriblerus peri Bathous, or the Art of Sinking in Poetry.* As other 18th-century satirists did, Pope used his genre to lay a metaphoric whip on the back of those who insulted him or whom he viewed as lesser literary lights. He continued by illustrating what he considered the low elements in contemporary verse in a comic send-up of Longinus's treatise on the sublime *Peri Hupsous.* Simultaneously he worked on another criticism of popular writing and writers titled *The Dunciad,* originally featuring Theobald in its first three books published in 1728. Pope enlarged it a year later and added a fourth book in 1743 by which time its antihero had become Colley Cibber, poet laureate.

Constantly imagining new work, Pope planned an "Opus Magnum" to include four books. He would never complete it, but his timeless *An Essay on Man,* written in four epistles, was published 1733–34. The second book was to be yet another version of *The Dunciad,* and the third he never wrote. However, the fourth, *Moral Essays* or *Ethics,* was published between 1731 and 1735. In 1733 Pope produced miscellaneous *Imitations of Horace,* which consisted of translations and adaptations of Horace's *Odes, Satires,* and *Epistles.* He was yet to produce the poem considered his masterpiece.

An Epistle from Mr. Pope to Dr. Arbuthnot reflected all the important elements of 18th-century poetry and served as a prologue to Pope's Horatian satires. Written as a celebration of Pope's personal physician and best friend, who lay on his deathbed at the time, it beautifully reflects the theme of perfect friendship, while countering that image of his relationship with Arbuth-

not with several attacks on onetime friends who had betrayed him, including Addison and Montagu. In 1735 an edition of Pope's correspondence appeared that he claimed to be pirated, although he had arranged for its publication himself.

A man of vast interests and talents that extended beyond literature to landscaping, architecture, and painting, Alexander Pope proved the consummate Augustan poet. Johnson wrote that JOHN DRYDEN had to be judged Pope's superior, were the two compared, but he qualified that statement, writing of Dryden, "What his mind could supply at call, or gather in one excursion, was all that he sought, and all that he gave." He then illustrated how difficult the choice of the better poet had been for him when he added:

The dilatory caution of Pope enabled him to condense his sentiments, to multiply his images, and to accumulate all that study might produce, or chance might supply. If the flights of Dryden therefore are higher, Pope continues longer on the wing. If of Dryden's fire the blaze is brighter, of Pope's the heat is more regular and constant. Dryden often surpasses expectation, and Pope never falls below it. Dryden is read with frequent astonishment, and Pope with perpetual delight.

Johnson clearly could not declare Dryden superior in all areas.

While subsequent generations found little to admire in Pope's sharp, driven delivery, the 20th century embraced his work with great appreciation. A major topic of academic study, Pope's work also remains available to the general public, who often quote him unawares. Lines such as "A little learning is a dangerous thing" and "Hope springs eternal in the human breast" are among many of Pope's often repeated lines.

BIBLIOGRAPHY
Erskine-Hill, Howard, ed. *Alexander Pope: World and Word.* New York: Oxford University Press, 1998.
———. *The Social Milieu of Alexander Pope: Lives, Example, and the Poetic Response.* New Haven, Conn.: Yale University Press, 1975.
Fairer, David. *Pope: New Contexts.* New York: Harvester Wheatsheaf, 1990.

Foster, Gretchen M. *Pope versus Dryden: A Controversy in Letters to the Gentleman's Magazine.* Victoria, Canada: University of Victoria, 1989.

Goldsmith, Netta Murray. *Alexander Pope: The Evolution of a Poet.* Hants, England: Ashgate, 2002.

Griffin, Dustin H. *Alexander Pope, the Poet in the Poems.* Princeton, N.J.: Princeton University Press, 1978.

Hammond, Brean. *Pope amongst the Satirists, 1660–1750.* Tavistock, England: Northcote House, 2005.

Johnson, Samuel. *The Lives of the Poets.* Edited by G. B. Hill. 3 vols. Oxford: Clarendon Press, 1905.

Kinsley, James, and James T. Boulton. *English Satiric Poetry, Dryden to Byron.* Columbia: University of South Carolina Press, 1970.

Lonsdale, Roger. "Alexander Pope." In *Dryden to Johnson,* edited by Roger Lonsdale, 77–116. New York: Penguin, 1993.

Mack, Maynard. *The Garden and the City: Retirement and Politics in the Later Poetry of Pope, 1731–1743.* Toronto: University of Toronto Press, 1969.

Noggle, James. *The Skeptical Sublime: Aesthetic Ideology in Pope and the Tory Satirists.* New York: Oxford University Press, 2001.

Williams, Aubrey. Introduction to *Poetry and Prose of Alexander Pope,* ix–xxiv. Boston: Houghton Mifflin, 1969.

"PRAYER (1)" GEORGE HERBERT (1633) The first of two poems that focus on the same topic, "Prayer (1)" by GEORGE HERBERT is a SONNET, which preserves the traditional buoyant tone of the form but focuses on religious passion rather than erotic passion. Herbert uses FIGURATIVE LANGUAGE in the first 12 lines to compare the act and nature of prayer to many other aspects of religion. He labels it, for example, "the Church's banquet, Angels' age," in the first line, with the food reference reminding readers of the vital nature of prayer to promote a healthy soul, and the angel imagery connecting prayer with service to God. It is "The soul in paraphrase, heart in pilgrimage," in line 3, a skillful pairing of two important human "organs," the soul and heart, in reference to faith. While the soul can speak, the heart journeys away from flesh, seeking God. Prayer acts in line 6 as "Reversed thunder," an intriguing suggestion, in that thunder generally issues from the heavens, whereas in this case, it issues from earth and is aimed at the heavens. In that same line prayer is also "Christ-side-piercing spear," referencing

the spear with which a soldier stabbed the crucified Christ to speed his death. Because Christ's death meant life for humans, a prayer may do the same. It is likewise "A kind of tune, which all things hear and fear," a bit of a contradiction. The word *tune* invokes a familiar feeling, an association with an informal and common song, not likely to promote "fear." Here Herbert may intend the meaning to be "awe," a component of which may be fear. The ninth line offers a series for comparison: "Softness, and peace, and joy, and love, and bliss," all products of prayer. Herbert's insertion of the conjunction *and* between the items in his series, instead of a mere comma, emphasizes the large number of pleasures to which prayer compares. It is also "Heaven in ordinary, man well dressed," meaning the common language for Heaven, which opens its lofty ears to hear man's "well dressed" supplication and praise. The speaker also compares prayer to another unexplained wonder, "The milky way," which has been identified but remains unexplained by man, who lacks the necessary language and tools to do so.

Herbert includes further reference to the stars in the concluding couplet, traditionally a summation of a proposal presented in the sonnet's first 12 lines: "Church-bells beyond the stars heard, the soul's blood, / The land of spices; something understood." The final phrase acts as unification for the concept of prayer that precedes it. Herbert suggests that in whatever form it is delivered, a prayer will be heard and understood. Its delivery remains important, not its form.

"PRESSED BY THE MOON" CHARLOTTE SMITH (1789) As a result of trying circumstances CHARLOTTE SMITH often imbued her poems with a melancholy tone, as in "Pressed by the Moon," written in the SONNET form on which Smith built her reputation. She focuses on one of her favorite subjects, nature, as metaphor for her turbulent feelings.

The somber tone begins with the sonnet's first word, *Pressed,* a verb that indicates the power of one entity over another. In this case Smith expresses the moon's power over the ocean's tide. Because the moon has long served as a symbol of the female, one might guess it is referred to in this poem as something that empowers the poet. However, the speaker remains frightened by the effect of the "mute arbitress of tides," as she refers to the moon, because under its influence, "The sea not more its swelling surge confines, / But o'er the shrinking land sublimely rides." In this instance the sea gains its power because the moon no longer controls it, having, when full, released that power. Smith's use of ALLITERATION with the s sound at the beginning of words is echoed as well at the end of the verbs *confines* and *rides*. The sound supports the visual image of water sliding forward and back again over vulnerable land. The water's power is clear as well in the fact that the land shrinks, as the water "sublimely" covers it. Psychoanalytic critics might view this imagery as sexual, particularly in light of the water's energetic power over the unmoving and silent landscape.

Smith's evocative description continues as she notes a "wild blast" that rises "from the western cave, / Drives the huge billows from their heaving bed." Her continual use of strong verbs, such as *rises* and *drives,* adds to the power of the scene. A destructive bent continues, as the speaker notes that the "village dead" are actually torn "from their grassy tombs" as the sea "breaks the silent sabbath of the grave!" In this usage, *sabbath* means "rest." The ocean commits a true atrocity by disturbing the sacred sleep of the dead.

The remaining narrative presents in vivid horror the scene, beginning with the declarative "Lo! Their bones whiten in the frequent wave; / But vain to them the winds and waters rave." Smith uses IRONY in her description of the washing clean of the bones by water, often seen as a symbol of cleansing or rebirth. However, in this case those to whom the bones originally belonged do not benefit from the cleansing. They remain deaf to the raving of wind or water. As Smith notes with italics for emphasis, "*They* hear the warring elements no more." The emphasis shifts the attention back to the speaker, for while the dead cannot observe the frightening scene, which Smith emphasizes by using FIGURATIVE LANGUAGE (FIGURE OF SPEECH) to compare it to the destruction of war, the observer can.

In the Shakespearean or Elizabethan form the final rhyming couplet of the sonnet comments on the 12-line topic that precedes it. Smith closes her sonnet with a personal comment by the speaker that reads, "I am doomed—by life's long storm oppressed, / To gaze

with envy on their gloomy rest." The melancholy tone turns completely cynical, as the speaker conceives of her situation as worse than death. Smith deftly adopts the extended metaphor of the storm to aid readers in understanding the conflicted nature of her own existence. She feels doomed and oppressed, so much so that she envies those who are dead. However, she never romanticizes death. She remains completely realistic in calling the rest of the dead *gloomy*.

Critics in Smith's day were said to have found her work so disturbingly melancholy that they feared for her mental and emotional health. Trapped in a bad marriage with many children to support, Smith did at times share the feelings of her speaker.

PRIOR, MATTHEW (1664–1721)

Matthew Prior was born into a poor family in Stephen's Alley, Westminster. While he began school, his father's death left him in the care of an uncle, probably named Arthur, who determined Prior should not complete his education because of a lack of funds. He began writing poetry early, dedicating a poem at age 12 to Arthur Prior. While at his uncle's Rhennish Wine House in Channel (later Cannon) Row, Prior met many patrons from the court of King Charles II. Supposedly Charles Sackville, earl of Dorset, a well-known patron of the arts, "discovered" Prior and sponsored his education and future career. Through the earl's generosity Prior matriculated through St. John's College, Cambridge, completing studies at age 18 and becoming a lifelong fellow in 1688. His publishing career began a year earlier when he attacked JOHN DRYDEN's *The HIND AND THE PANTHER* through satire. His parody coauthored by Charles Montague titled *The Hind and the Panther Tranvers'd to the Story of The Country Mouse and the City Mouse* was extremely popular. According to SAMUEL JOHNSON Dryden stated his distress over the fact that "an old man should be so treated by those to whom he had always been civil." The reference is probably an allusion to the fact that Dryden had included several of Prior's poems in his *Miscellanies*; Prior became well known, writing simply as "Matt."

In 1690 Prior began service as secretary to the British ambassador at The Hague. His diplomatic career flourished through the reign of William III, who made

Prior a gentleman of his bedchamber and supported the poet's study. Prior enjoyed the life of the courtier and assumed the title *commissioner of trade.* At the king's death Prior wrote the eulogy, *Carmen Secolare* (1700). Johnson wrote in his *Lives of the English Poets* that Prior made public the fact he had "praised others in compliance with the fashion, but . . . in celebrating King William he followed his inclination."

Prior lost his post when Queen Anne ascended the throne, but his career revived through the efforts of Robert Harley, earl of Oxford, a Tory. He contributed to *The Examiner,* a publication developed for the purpose of revealing government abuses in the hopes of driving the Whigs from power. The Tories proved successful and desired to end the war with France; Prior was dispatched in secret to develop a treaty. His failure in acting as a peace emissary would receive a public accounting by JONATHAN SWIFT, Prior's friend, in his *A Journey to Paris* (1711).

However, Prior later became an important connection between Britain and France and was named minister plenipotentiary in 1712. When negotiations appeared to be souring, Bolingbroke wrote to Prior, "Dear Mat, hide the nakedness of thy country, and give the best turn thy fertile brain will furnish thee with to the blunders of thy countrymen, who are not much better politicians than the French are poets." The signing of the Treaty of Utrecht gave Prior fame, and he enjoyed the company of luminaries and members of the royal family, including Louis XIV. Not all of his business and political ventures succeeded, and his friend ALEXANDER POPE judged Prior best fit "to make verses." He was known for cohabitating with various women of questionable character. According to Johnson one "despicable drab of the lowest species" stole from Prior, the consequence of his fascination with people of lower social status.

Prior again lost favor when Queen Anne died and she was replaced by the Hanoverian prince George Louis as King George I; he led a Whig administration. After returning to England, Prior was imprisoned for more than a year, mainly as a result of the efforts of Sir Robert Walpole. While in prison Prior wrote *Alma, or, the Progress of the Mind* (1718), judged "imperfect" by Johnson. After his release at age 53, he retired to private study and writing, working to improve his country house, Down Hall. The efforts of his old supporter Harley prevented his suffering poverty and allowed the purchase of the hall.

A relatively young man, Prior felt his life had all but ended with the loss of his political appointments, evidenced by some remarks in his correspondence. Through the efforts of his friends a plan was created to sell a collection of Prior's works. According to his biographer Francis Bickley, Erasmus Lewis wrote to Swift that he feared "Our friend Prior" would "end his days in as forlorn a state as any other poet has done before him, if his friends do not take more care of him than he has done of himself." Those friends included Pope, Pope's friend John Arbuthnot, JOHN GAY, and Mr. Lewis, all of whom would procure subscriptions to print Prior's work.

Prior's collection included epistles, LYRICS, odes, BALLADS, and various imitations of the classics, all of which appeared in the planned 1718 collection, supported by subscriptions and Harley's continued patronage. His *Solomon on the Vanity of the World* (1718) employed HEROIC COUPLETS and appeared in three volumes that Prior believed would assure continuing fame after his death but readers found tedious. His lyrics would stand as his best works, judged graceful in their simplicity. He left incomplete imagined dialogues between Montaigne and Locke in *Dialogues of the Dead,* considered brilliant by later critics. Prior suffered from deafness and poor health in his last years and died of cholera. He was buried as he had famously requested at the feet of Edmund Spenser, many times his poetic model, in Westminster Abbey. Popular anthologized works include "An EPITAPH," "A TRUE MAID," and "A BETTER ANSWER."

BIBLIOGRAPHY

Bickley, Francis Lawrence. *The Life of Matthew Prior.* London: Sir Isaac Pitman & Sons, 1977.

Eves, Charles Kenneth. *Matthew Prior, Poet and Diplomatist.* New York: Columbia Press, 1939.

Johnson, Samuel. *Lives of the English Poets.* Vol. 1. New York: E. P. Dutton, 1958.

Legg, L. G. Wickham. *Matthew Prior: A Study of his Public Career and Correspondence.* New York: Octagon Books, 1972.

Lindsay, David W., ed. *English Poetry, 1700–1780: Contemporaries of Swift and Johnson.* Totowa, N.J.: Rowman & Littlefield, 1974.

Nelson, Nicolas H. "From 'Reason's Dazzled Eye' to Diving Love and Omnipotence: Matthew Prior's Poetry of Faith." *Christianity and Literature* 48, no. 1 (autumn 1998): 5–27.

"PSALM 58 *SE VERE UTIQUE*" MARY SIDNEY HERBERT, COUNTESS OF PEMBROKE (1599)

"Psalm 58 *Se Vere Utique*" by MARY SIDNEY HERBERT, COUNTESS OF PEMBROKE, translates as "Psalm 58 If Indeed Holy." It is one of more than 100 psalm translations included in the collection started by Herbert's poet brother, Sir Philip Sidney, who was killed in battle before he could complete his task of translating all the Psalms. Herbert took up her brother's work where he had stopped at Psalm 43 and continued through number 150. While the manuscript was completed in 1599 and presented to Queen Elizabeth I, to whom it was dedicated, it would not be published through traditional means until 1820. Members of the 16th-century aristocracy rarely made public their work, an act believed to be vulgar. "Psalm 58" well illustrates Herbert's wide stylistic range and her confidence in attempting difficult rhythm and expression. The poem consists of four eight-line stanzas, each with a METER of iambic pentameter and RHYME scheme of *ababcdcd*.

The first stanza opens with a consideration of the Psalm's theme of justice, as the speaker questions, "And call ye this to utter what is just / You that of justice hold the sovereign throne?" The speaker assumes an accusatory tone, demanding of a group termed in the third line "O sons of dust" how exactly they define justice. Their definition, based on a "long malicious will," obviously does not please the speaker, who accuses that group of oppressing others, while serving justice only to themselves. The second stanza continues utilization of the rhetorical question, opening with "But what could they, who even in birth declined / From truth and right to lies and injuries?" The speaker suggests that those who demonstrate injustice have never known "truth and right" but were born to lie and injure others. The Psalmist adopts the traditional biblical honoring of one's birthright, adding an ironic twist to that concept. The FIGURATIVE LANGUAGE of metaphor

is used in an extended comparison of such individuals to serpents, who "show the venom of their cankered mind," where *cankered* means "infected with evil." Even an "aspic," or poisonous asp, could not "contend" with this perfectly abhorrent group. The snake charmer "all in vain applies / His skilfull'st spells," to no avail, "While she," a personification of justice, "self-deaf and unaffected, lies." Herbert uses the term *lies* in wordplay, as it reflects on the previous accusation of prevarification and injury against the group the Psalmist castigates.

In the third stanza the speaker calls upon the Lord to exact vengeance, to "crack their teeth!" and "crush these lions' jaws!" A simile requests that the evil ones "sink as water in the sand," suggesting they will be absorbed in a way that leaves no trace they had ever existed. Herbert incorporates extraordinary imagery as she imitates a fearful voice:

> When the deadly bow their aiming fury draws,
> Shiver the shaft ere past the shooter's hand.
> So make them melt as the dishousid snail,
> Or as the embryo whose vital band
> Breaks ere it holds, and formless eyes do fail
> To see the sun, though brought to lightful land.

The Psalmist's violent tendencies are revealed in the allusion to a deadly bow, which he hopes will kill the one who draws it. Herbert adopts ALLITERATION with the repetition of the *sh* sound three times, the "shooshing" effect imitating the swish of the arrow in a skillful use of *onomatopoeia*. The speaker does not wish mere destruction, but rather hopes for revenge, made plain by the wish for a death comparable to a snail allowed to bake and melt in the heat without protection of its shell. Readers might react with revulsion at the image of a fetus whose umbilical cord breaks to cut off life-giving support, its eyes never formed and never exposed to the sun as intended. However, reflecting on the previous description of these wicked souls as born to evil, the image proves effective in supporting the speaker's purpose of calling for total destruction of such miscreants.

The final stanza inflicts the speaker's desire for death also on the offspring of the evil, "a brood of springing thorns," whom he wishes to "Be by untimely rooting overthrown." Finally,

> The good with gladness this revenge shall see
> And bathe his feet in blood of wicked one
> While all shall say, "The just rewarded be;
> There is a God that carves to each his own."

The Psalmist exhibits the traditional Old Testament attitude to justice, fantasizing that God will turn the evil men's ways back upon themselves. That such death and destruction could fill the "good with gladness" marks the stanza as pre-Christian; no thoughts of mercy or redemption haunt the Psalmist's dreams.

"PSALM POEMS, THE" JOHN MILTON (1648 and 1653)

JOHN MILTON transformed a total of 17 psalms into poetry, meant to be set to music and used as praise in worship. He translated Psalms 80–88 in April 1648, noting, "Nine of the Psalms done into Meter, wherein all but what is in a different Character, are the very words of the Text, translated from the Original." Psalms 1–8 followed five years later in April 1653. Critics disagree about the importance of the Psalms, some claiming them valuable evidence that Milton could read and translate Hebrew, and others disputing that claim.

Barbara K. Lewalski explains that Milton may have used the Psalms in 1653 to express his anxieties and hopes, both personal and political. In politics he observed a chasm that developed between those virtuous few who craved liberty and proved capable of heading the government and the ignorant masses. In his personal life he found his work *Eikonoklastes* under attack by forces whose beliefs he did not understand and could not tolerate. The translations of Psalms 1–8 thus prove more meditative than the earlier Psalms, written during the second Civil War. Psalms 80–88 bid God to exact revenge from those who threatened his "dear Saints" who fought the evil Royalists and Catholics. They focus on God's displeasure with the chosen ones who occupied a country filled with conflict between friends and threatened by enemies from beyond its borders, a state Milton felt paralleled that of England.

Milton adopted the form of the psalter, alternating octosyllabic lines with lines containing six syllables. He may have written with a view that they be included in a revised psalter. In any event he selected the form that would most closely match that of "Hebraic psalmic parallelism," according to Lewalski.

One may compare a few lines from the familiar Psalm 8 in the King James Version to Milton's translation and take away a sense of his approach. In the King James Version, the first two lines read: "O Lord, our Lord, how excellent is thy name in all the earth! Who hast set thy glory above the heavens. Out of the mouth of babes and sucklings hast thou ordained strength because of thine enemies, that thou mightest still the enemy and the avenger." Milton devotes the first two four-line stanzas of his translation to those lines:

> O Jehovah, our Lord, how wondrous great
>   And glorious is thy name through all the
>   earth!
> So as above the Heavens thy praise to set
>   Out of the tender mouths of latest birth,
>
> Out of the mouths of babes and sucklings thou
>   Hast founded strength because of all thy
>   foes,
> To stint th'enemy, and slack th' avenger's brow
>   That bends his rage thy providence to
>   oppose.

BIBLIOGRAPHY

Hale, John K. "Why Did Milton Translate Psalms 80–88 in April 1648?" *Literature and History* 3 (1994): 55–62.

Hughes, Merritt Y., ed. *John Milton: Complete Poems and Major Prose.* New York: Macmillan, 1957.

Hunter, William B. "Milton Translates the Psalms." *The Philological Quarterly* 40 (1961): 458–494.

Lewalski, Barbara K. *The Life of John Milton: A Critical Biography.* Oxford: Blackwell, 2000.

"PULLEY, THE" GEORGE HERBERT (1633)

In "The Pulley" GEORGE HERBERT explains why God could not make life on earth a perfect existence for man. He presents a minidrama, allowing readers to picture the man's beginnings, with God described as "Having a glass of blessings standing by." Herbert will extend the FIGURATIVE LANGUAGE (FIGURE OF SPEECH) of metaphor in comparing the anointing of man with fortune by God to the pouring of liquid from a container. God declares that he will "pour on him all we can," gathering all of the world's riches, which he will "Contract into a span." Herbert concludes the first of his four five-line stanzas with God depicted as a generous benefactor. In the second stanza he catalogues the blessings that God poured onto man. They include strength, beauty, "wisdom, honour, pleasure." Then God hesitates, saving a bit, as he perceives that "alone of all his treasure / Rest in the bottom lay." Herbert reflects on God's edict in Genesis that man shall not enjoy rest but instead must work for his sustenance, as a result of original sin committed in the Garden of Eden. The speaker explains God's logic at holding back rest, supposedly in God's own words:

> For if I should (said he)
> Bestow this jewel also on my creature,
> He would adore my gifts instead of me,
> And rest in Nature, not the God of Nature:
> So both should losers be.

Herbert executes a play on words with the concept of rest, noting that man would take his rest and relaxation in the material natural world, were rest given to him. God's edict is that man seek spiritual relief in him, "the God of Nature." Herbert emphasizes the value of rest by first terming it a *treasure* and then reemphasizing the fact that it is a jewel.

The final verse begins extending play on the word *rest*. Herbert employs it in the opening line 16 to mean "Yet let him keep the rest," then incorporates it into the term *restlessness* in line 17: "But keep them with repining restlessness." Herbert manages to depict the lack of rest as good, as God notes that man may "be rich and weary," so that "If goodness lead him not, yet weariness / May toss him to my breast." Herbert skillfully makes his point that man need not—actually cannot—be good enough to deserve God's grace. Rather the recognition of his weakness and the lack of satisfaction offered by an earthly existence shall successfully bind him to his Lord. Thus God's withholding of rest from man acts as a natural "pulley," an irresistible force in moving him closer to his creator.

PYRRHIC See METER.

Q

"QUEEN AND HUNTRESS" BEN JONSON
(1601) "Queen and Huntress" is a song included by
BEN JONSON in his satiric stage comedy *Cynthia's Revels*.
The play focused on the sin of self-love, incorporating
as its major vehicle the myth of Narcissus, who fell in
love with his own reflection. Jonson based the character of Criticus on himself, while Cynthia represented
Queen Elizabeth I, who received Criticus after his valiant struggle to escape knaves and courtly scoundrels
to reach her. Elizabeth often appeared in literature as
Cynthia, also known as Diana, the virgin goddess of
the moon. The god of the evening star, Hesperus, ser-
enades Cynthia with the lyrics. With a RHYME scheme
of *ababcc* the poem is structured as tetrameter; it serves
as a modified heroic sestet.

Jonson addresses Cynthia / Queen Elizabeth as "Queen
and huntress, chaste and fair," placing those words in the
mouth of Hesperus. The second line incorporates traditional imagery for males in the reference to the sun, which
"is laid to sleep," while Cynthia is "seated in thy silver
chair." The inference is that the queen holds power even
over males. The god of the evening star references himself, singing, "Hesperus entreats thy light, / Goddess
excellently bright." In a role reversal the male voice
requests help from the female. The second stanza demands
that Earth not allow its "envious shade" to "interpose," as
"Cynthia's shining orb was made / Heaven to clear, when
day did close." In other words the moon should clear, or
pass across, heaven, without the Earth blocking its path.
"Goddess excellently bright" concludes all three stanzas.
The third stanza contains imagery of the huntress with
details fitting a queen, "Lay thy bow of pearl apart, / And
thy crystal-shining quiver," requesting that the queen
"Give unto the flying hart / Space to breathe, how short
soever." The hart, or deer, requires a respite, which the
gracious queen will probably grant by turning day into
night. Jonson employs ANTITHESIS as Hesperus says, "Thou
that mak'st a day of night, / Goddess excellently bright."

R

RANDOLPH, THOMAS (1605–1635) Born in Northamptonshire, Thomas Randolph gained an education at Westminster and moved to Trinity College, Cambridge, taking his degree in 1628. He was awarded a master's degree in 1632 and became a fellow before publishing well-received comedy and becoming one of the TRIBE OF BEN. While living at home with his father, Randolph completed a brief and promising career writing drama and poetry; he dedicated three poems to BEN JONSON, including "To Ben Jonson." His earliest work, *Aristippus, Or, the Joviall Philosopher. Presented in a Private Shew, To which is Added, The Conceited Pedlar* (1626), was a burlesque debating the merit of sack, or wine, over small beer. Students at Trinity College, Cambridge, staged his *The Jealous Lovers* (1632) for the king and queen; additional stage plays included *The Muses Looking-Glass* (1630), which reflects influence by Jonson, and *Amyntas, or The Impossible Dowry* (1630). The latter included several poems, some in Latin, and while beautifully conceived, has been judged incapable of staging.

Debate continues over whether Randolph might have written *Hey for Honest, Down with Knavery.* His early death has also left critics to debate what might have been his eventual influence on British literature had he lived out a normal span. Considered brilliant and highly intelligent by many, he has been characterized as one who might have threatened the popularity of JOHN DRYDEN had he enjoyed a longer career. Several of his lovely LYRICS and occasional poems have been regularly anthologized, including excerpts from the pastoral "COTSWOLD ECLOGUE," labeled one of the best eclogues in the English language, and his. "ODE TO MASTER ANTHONY STAFFORD." Randolph died before age 30 and was buried in Blatherwick Church on the property of his friend William Stafford of Blatherwick.

BIBLIOGRAPHY
Forster, Leonard. "An Unnoticed Latin Poem by Thomas Randolph, 1633." *English Studies* 41 (1960): 258.
Tannenbaum, Samuel A., and Dorothy R. Tannenbaum. *Thomas Randolph: A Concise Bibliography.* New York, 1947.

"RAPE OF THE LOCK, THE" ALEXANDER POPE (1712, 1714, 1717) As have other of works by ALEXANDER POPE, "The Rape of the Lock" has inspired many full-length books of critical consideration, so important was its effect upon Pope, his readership, the genre of poetry, and Pope's legacy. The new historicist critical approach demands that works be placed within their author's political, social, and biographical contexts in order not only to offer readers a better understanding of their words and allusions, but also to suggest what might have motivated a writer to produce a specific work. With Pope's "The Rape of the Lock" the motivation remains clear, explained by Pope himself.

The mock-epic developed in reaction to a real social event that estranged two previously cordial families and a friend's request that Pope take a part in defusing the anger that led to that estrangement. While attending a party, a certain young Lord Petre had as a joke clipped a ringlet from the head of Arabella Fermor. Miss Fermor saw no humor in the act, and her negative reaction caused a break in relations between the Petres and the Fermors. As prominent families in a small Catholic community, of which Pope himself was a part, they threatened to disrupt relationships beyond their own through their quarrel. Lord Petre's teacher contacted Pope and asked that he write a poem in jest about the event. As Pope wrote to a friend, the tutor John Caryll hoped Pope's work might for the two families "laugh them together again."

Fortunately, "The Rape of the Lock" had the desired effect upon its publication in original version as part of *Miscellanies* in 1712. Feeling his work was incomplete, Pope continued revision and published a version expanded to five cantos in 1714 to which he added the sylphs and gnomes that exaggerated the classical effect, as well as engravings. A further 1717 revision included a "moral" spoken by the character Clarissa, and it became one of the most popular published in England's history.

As for its form Pope specifically selected the mock-epic and HEROIC COUPLETS in order, as Wall explains, to "emphasize PARADOX, inversion, and ironic slippage between appearance and reality, and a tension between containment and escape." Pope incorporates absurdity through the FIGURATIVE LANGUAGE (FIGURE OF SPEECH) of comparison and contrast specifically to emphasize the "friction" between his humorous version and the true heroic epic. His not-so-subtle message to readers, especially those involved in the incident that inspired the poem, is to take themselves less seriously. Pope successfully transmitted this message because his readers were familiar with the patterns and conventions of heroic epic through their knowledge of Homer's *Iliad* and *Odyssey,* the *Aeneid* by VIRGIL, and *PARADISE LOST* by JOHN MILTON. Appearing in a mock version, such patterns and conventions highlight the poem's thematic absurdity.

In summary "The Rape of the Lock" opens as its heroine, Belinda, awakens from a most pleasantly sensuous dream. In the late morning she is attended at her boudoir by her pet dog and the sylphs who arm her against temptation, bolstering her mental and physical chastity. They recall the magical attendants of classical

figures as they prepared to enter the battlefield. Belinda's battle will be fought on the social scene, as she attends a party at a royal palace where she will be called upon to defend her honor carefully. Belinda wins a game of cards and brags a bit too much, and the baron she has beaten decides to take revenge. Another member of the party, Clarissa, "arms" him with a pair of scissors as his "weapon," and he engages in symbolic "rape" by snipping off Belinda's curl as she leans down to drink her coffee. Her lead sylph, Ariel, deserts her in impotency, having discovered she may be falling in love. Belinda's reaction is swift disgust and outrage, and she descends into a psychological Hades, mirroring the descent to gain wisdom prevalent in the classical heroic quest. She inhabits for a time the Cave of Spleen, while other young people "fight" over the event. The lock of hair rises as a star visible only to "quick, poetic eyes."

A rich and rewarding presentation, "the form and imagery" of the poem act, as scholar Cynthia Wall writes, as to "reveal and re-enact the sexual, social, political, and poetic energies, and the efforts to control and contain them, in early-eighteenth-century England." Pope successfully manages to reflect in his mock epic a miniature of his own world in which war threatened trade, making conquest all-important; authority remained in question, as royal power fell to the Hanoverians; two political parties sought to define themselves further in relation to the throne and one another; Catholicism remained at odds with Anglicanism; and a feeling of separation and displacement haunted England.

Identified on the title page as "An Heroic-Comical Poem" in the 1714 five-canto edition, "The Rape of the Lock" opened with a letter from Pope to Arabella Fermor, to whom he dedicated the poem. His motivation for writing the poem becomes immediately evident, as he writes that "it was intended only to divert a few young Ladies, who have good Sense and Good Humour enough, to laugh not only at their Sex's little unguarded Follies, but at their own." Although meant to be a private venture, as Pope notes the poem had "been offer'd to a Bookseller." The reader gains some insight into Fermor's character as Pope adds, "You had the good Nature for my Sake to consent to the Publication of one more correct." He then discusses the introduction in this latest version of the "machinery" that includes the mythological characters of the sylphs and demons. Pope concludes with conventional flattery, writing that if his poem "has as many Graces as there are in Your Person, or in Your Mind," he still could not have hoped "it should pass thro' the World half so Uncensured as You have done."

Pope opens in mock-heroic tone, his speaker calling upon the Muses to guide his pen. In this case rather than mentioning one of the nine traditional muses, he notes "Caryll," meaning John Caryll, as his inspiration. He sets the scene as "a tim'rous Ray" of sun "op'd those Eyes that must eclipse the Day," beginning his characterization of Belinda. She is still in her bed, her "Guardian Sylph" lingering over her head, as is the memory of a dream that features "A Youth . . . / (That ev'n in Slumber caus'd her Cheek to glow)." In the first canto Pope must make clear that Belinda remains a sexually mature, yet virginal young woman, who dreams of love and sex but knows those subjects need to remain in the realm of fantasy for now. As part of the classical tradition Pope had to make clear the purpose of the sylphs, writing,

> Know farther yet; Whoever fair and chaste
> Rejects Mankind, is by some Sylph embrac'd:
> For Spirits, freed from mortal Laws, with ease
> Assume what Sexes and what Shapes they
>   please. (67–70)

Only with assistance can Belinda be heroic, retaining her purity "In Courtly Balls, and Midnight Masquerades" (72).

Discussion follows of different types of Nymphs, some possessed of a "vacant Brain" who give in to the spectacle of "Peers and Dukes, and all their sweeping Train" (83–84). Clearly Belinda will not be one of those. The sylphs, who include one specifically identified as Betty, attend Belinda at her toilette, which Pope imbues with mock importance. Taking gentle advantage of the acknowledged vanity of young women, he creates a catalog of everything involved in the preparation, from "Files of Pins" to "Puffs, Powders, Patches, bibles, Billet-doux" (138–39). An increase in Belinda's

charm and a calling forth of "all the Wonders of her Face are the results."

Canto 2 opens with a description of Belinda's effect on others, making clear that behind her beauty, charm, and inoffensive manner is a quick mind. The description of her hair foreshadows impending disaster, as one sylph has dutifully tended "two Locks" (20) so that "With shining Ringlets" that "smooth" Belinda's "Ivry Neck," love "in these Labyrinths his Slaves detains, / And mighty Hearts are held in slender Chains" (22–24). Pope continues using hyperbole to capture the heroic tone designed to convince readers of the humor in such social situations. Exaggeration abounds in blown-out description and a skillful address by Ariel to "Sylphs and Sylphids . . . / Fays, Fairies, Genii, Elves, and Daemons" regarding their duties on the battlefield that the social gathering represents (73–74). The call to arms results in a swarming of mystical beings, all intent on preserving Belinda's honor:

> Some, Orb in Orb, around the Nymph extend,
> Some thrid the mazy ringlets of her Hair,
> Some hang upon the Pendants of her Ear;
> With beating Hearts the dire Event they wait,
> Anxious, and trembling for the Birth of Fate.
>   (138–143).

Pope sets the scene for the third canto, in which Belinda will enter the battle that determines her fate. He describes the playing cards as if they are powerful figures gathered for her support, including "four Kings in Majesty rever'd," four fair queens whose hands sustain a Flow'r," "four Knaves in Garbs succinct," and "Paricolour'd Troops, a shining Train," all of which "Draw forth to Combat on the Velvet Plain" (37–44). The next lines establish Belinda's foe in the ensuing battle as a Baron, to whom "Fate inclines the Field," following two triumphs by Belinda. The cards become soldiers who struggle for victory: "Th' Imperial consort of the Crown of Spades. / The Club's black Tyrant first her Victim dy'd" (68–69), while later "The Baron now his Diamonds pours apace" (75). When Belinda wins the hand, the speaker cries:

> Oh thoughtless Mortals! ever blind to Fate,
> Too soon dejected, and too soon elate!

Sudden these Honours shall be snatch'd away,
And curs'd for ever this Victorious Day.
   (101–104)

Clarissa aids the Baron in wreaking vengeance by supplying him with scissors. Pope describes them and Clarissa's act: "A two-eg'd Weapon from her shining Case; / So Ladies in Romance assist their Knight" (129–130). The Sprights gather by the thousands in a vain attempt to protect Belinda's curl, managing to twitch her diamond earrings and cause her to turn her head three times. However, Ariel suddenly "watch'd th' Ideas rising in her Mind" and saw, "in spite of all her Art, / An Earthly Lover lurking at her Heart." Defeated, he and the other magical elements abandon the field as "The meeting Points the sacred Hair dissever / From the fair head, for ever and for ever" (154–155). Belinda screams as the Baron exults over his prize, having executed "The conqu'ring force of unresisted Steel" (177–178).

In the fourth canto Belinda dissolves into depression and ends up in the Cave of Spleen. Pope has more fun in describing a Region that knows "No cheerful Breeze," where Belinda "sighs for ever on her pensive Bed, / Pain at her side, and Megrim at her Head" (23–24), where the term *Megrim* indicates a migraine headache, believed to be a product of the spleen. One fantastical being, a gnome called Umbriel, approaches a goddess, petitioning her for a solution to Belinda's problem. He notes that she can "rule the Sex to Fifty from Fifteen" and "give th' Hysteric or Poetic Fit," inspiring some to become doctors and others playwrights (59–62). Pope turns to satiric regarding the muses, who inspire mortals to various achievements.

This goddess will furnish the gnome with "Sighs, Sobs, and Passions, and the War of Tongues" (83), which he pours over Belinda's head, as if anointing her. Pope introduces the fop character of Sir Plume, based on the real-life Sir George Brown, whom Belinda bids wage war on her part. His attempts fail, and she suffers the hysterical effects of Umbriel's vial from which sorrows flow. She curses her day of infamy and wonders aloud why she ever attended the party. Instead she should have "kept my Charms conceal'd from mortal Eye, / Like Roses that in Desarts bloom and die" (157–158). Pope adopts the common CARPE DIEM imagery of CAVALIER POETS, who argued with virgins they should not hide their roselike beauty, as it would simply die unappreciated. She wails in comic form over the loss of one of her two sable "Beauties," its "Sister-Lock" left to sit alone on her neck, perhaps to tempt another rape. The canto concludes with her cry to the perpetrator of the crime, "Oh hadst thou, Cruel! Been content to seize / Hairs less in sight, or any Hairs but these!" Pope makes clear the dubious nature of the slight in revealing Belinda's concern as sheer vanity in the loss of her prominent and well-groomed curls, rather than a lock of less visible hair.

Canto 5 consists of a 150-line statement by Clarissa, partner to the crime, in which she acts as a chorus to summarize the action and expound on the cruel fate that resulted from human passion. Discussion ensues over the fate of the lock itself, and she reveals that some believe it took its place in heaven, where "Partridge soon shall view" it as a portent of "the fall of Rome" when he "looks thro' Galileo's eyes." Pope references a known prognosticator named John Partridge. Partridge annually predicted the pope's downfall, as well as the fall of the king of France, by reading the heavens through his telescope; he was a publicly acknowledged foolish figure. The poet himself steps into the poem at its conclusion, bidding Belinda no longer to mourn her "ravish'd Hair / Which adds new Glory to the shining Sphere!" (141–142).

By selecting such a low subject as the clipping of a curl to elevate through epic poetry, Pope makes the point that humans often take themselves too seriously. He also made clear the power of poetry to teach, as well as delight. His work translating Homer's *Iliad,* a six-year project begun in 1713, would inform the mock version of the heroic story that would eventually gain him financial independence. "The Rape of the Lock" remains a crucial part of Pope's early career, its perfectly controlled execution and jubilant tone reflecting the cautiously happy security he would not long enjoy. It continues to inspire much critical examination. When feminist criticism gained importance in the 20th century, this new critical approach considered the poem's misogyny in its depiction of women.

BIBLIOGRAPHY
Broich, Ulrich. *Mock-Heroic Poetry, 1680–1750.* Tübingen: M. Niemeyer, 1971.

Creehan, Stanley. "'The Rape of the Lock' and the Economy of 'Trivial Things.'" *Eighteenth-Century Studies* 31, no. 1 (fall 1997): 45–68.

Crider, Richard. "Pope's 'The Rape of the Lock.'" *The Explicator* 49, no. 2 (winter 1991): 80–82.

Edgecombe, Rodney Stenning. "Belinda's Coiffure in *The Rape of the Lock*." *English Language Notes* 42, no. 1 (September 2004): 40–42.

Jones, John A. *Pope's Couplet Art*. Athens: Ohio University Press, 1969.

Kroll, Richard. "Pope and Drugs: The Pharmacology of 'The Rape of the Lock.'" *English Literary History* 67, no. 1 (spring 2000): 99–141.

Rumbold, Valerie. *Women's Place in Pope's World*. Cambridge: Cambridge University Press, 1989.

Singh, Brijrah. "Pope's Belinda: A Feminist Rereading." *College Language Association Journal* 34, no. 4 (June 1991): 467–485.

Spacks, Patricia Ann Meyer. *An Argument of Images: The Poetry of Alexander Pope*. Cambridge, Mass.: Harvard University Press, 1971.

Varney, Andrew. "Clarissa's Moral in 'The Rape of the Lock.'" *Essays in Criticism* 43, no. 1 (January 1993): 17–32.

Wall, Cynthia. *Alexander Pope: The Rape of the Lock*. Boston: Bedford Books, 1998.

Weinbrot, Howard. "Fine Ladies, Saints in Heaven, and Pope's *Rape of the Lock*: Genealogy, Catholicism, and the Irenic Muse." In *Augustan Subjects: Essays in Honor of Martin C. Battestin,* edited by Albert J. Rivero. Newark: University of Delaware Press, 1997.

"RAPTURE, A" Thomas Carew (1640)

"A Rapture" by THOMAS CAREW is perhaps his best-known poem, because of its erotic nature. Carew attacks man's arbitrary ideal of honor as it pertains to the preservation of female virginity. The poem circulated before its printing and was referred to in Parliament in discussion of shocking and licentious works. Modern critics find it fascinating, Earl Miner pronouncing it "the most genuinely poetic of all the erotic poems of the century." Ada Long and Hugh Maclean comment on the poem's obvious CARPE DIEM theme, labeling it "a witty discourse . . . directed to a society that has lost its sense of moral equilibrium." Renée Hannaford analyzes the poem as a reaction against the social controls that court poets and courtiers suffered. Through their position as inferiors, they complied with the expectations of court aristocrats and even found themselves in competition with one another for attention that translated into patronage and financial support. Most Carolinian poetry reflects the effects of other poetry, rather than that of social and political forces, as poets remained so acutely aware of contemporary rivals. Hannaford suggests that Carew's characteristic exploration of opposing forces, his use of hyperbole and diminution, even distortion, reveals his specific view of the social order in which he operated. He envisioned himself in relationship to more powerful forces and social institutions.

The poem's speaker fantasizes about a love utopia where no one suffers restraint by the "giant, Honor," a "Collosus" whose legs lovers valiantly sail through daily. While Honor appears horrifying, the speaker makes clear that "He is but form and only frights in show," thus commenting on the arbitrary nature of the ideal, as well as the hypocrisy of those who claim, but do not actually possess, honor. The speaker voices the disillusionment felt by his fellow men, who discover that Honor is not

> The seed of Gods, but a weak model wrought
> By greedy men, that seek to enclose the common,
> And within private arms empale free woman.

The speaker shapes himself as a champion of the marginalized and restrained, employing the term *empale* as a specifically sexual allusion. He invites his Celia to mount with him

> on the wings of love, We'll cut the flitting air
>   and soar above
> The monster's head

landing where "the Queen of Love, and Innocence, / Beauty, and Nature" will "banish all offense." Then Carew catalogs his lover's parts through erotica, writing lines such as "There my enfranchis'd hand on every side / Shall o'er thy naked polished ivory slide." As the lovers lie in the "shade of cypress groves" on a bed of roses and myrtle, Carew evokes a connection to a pastoral poetic tradition through setting, but his scene does not echo the innocence normally a hallmark of that tradition. He probably models his approach on that of Christopher Marlowe's erotic "Hero and Leander," also a pastoral. The speaker and Celia have "panting limbs" as they lie beside the "bubbling stream" and the "chirping wood-choir," which sings tunes to "the Deity of Love," meaning Cupid.

After a reference to the bee, an insect popular especially in writings by VIRGIL, which deflowers "the fresh virgins of the spring," the speaker notes he will use his own "bag of honey" to

seize the rose-buds in their perfum'd bed,
The violet knots, like curious mazes spread
O'er all the garden, taste the ripen'd cherry,
The warm, firm apple, tipped with coral berry.
Then will I visit with a wandering kiss
The vale of lilies and the bower of bliss.

Carew converts Celia's body to a garden in a metamorphosis consistent with themes of change and conversion found in Renaissance poetry. By line 69 the speaker leaves the allusions and becomes more graphically specific about the female anatomy. A few lines later he again adopts symbolic language, but it remains strongly suggestive. Lines 85–90 describe how his

tall pine shall in the Cyprian strait
ride safe at anchor and unlade her freight;
My rudder, with thy bold hand, like a tried
and skillful pilot thou shalt steer, and guide
My bark into love's channel.

The speaker then declares

No wedlock bonds unwreathe our twisted loves;
We seek no midnight arbor, no dark groves
To hide our kisses; there, the hated name
Of husband, wife, lust, modest, chaste, or shame
Are vain and empty words.

Carew clearly indicts his guilt-ridden society for its attempts to control physical bliss through arbitrary laws and social edict.

By the conclusion of his 166 lines of rhyming couplets the speaker has noted that false Honor, the tyrant, should be deposed, allowing lovers to walk free

With necks unyok'd; nor is it just that he
Should fetter your soft sex with chastity
Which nature made unapt for abstinence.

Thus Carew promotes the carpe diem message prevalent in the works of the CAVALIER POETS and goes on to point out the lack of logic that causes men to fight one another over a woman's honor. While Honor demands that the speaker shed blood, religion forbids it and even damns the speaker for it. The poem concludes, "Then tell me why / This goblin Honor which the world adores / Should make men atheists, and not women whores." Carew has prepared readers for the injection of logical argument at the poem's conclusion through his use of classical allusions, myth, and historical facts to legitimize statements that follow a fantasy sequence.

BIBLIOGRAPHY

Hannaford, Renée. "'My Unwashed Muse': Sexual Play and Sociability in Carew's 'A Rapture.'" *English Language Notes* 27, no. 1 (September 1989): 32–39.

Long, Ada, and Hugh Maclean. "'Deare Ben,' 'Great Donne' and 'My Celia': The Wit of Carew's Poetry." *Studies in English Literature 1500–1800* 18 (1978): 89.

Miner, Earl. *The Cavalier Mode from Jonson to Cotton.* New York: Princeton, 1970.

"REASON WHY THE THOUGHTS ARE ONLY IN THE HEAD, THE" MARGARET CAVENDISH, DUCHESS OF NEWCASTLE (1653)

MARGARET CAVENDISH, DUCHESS OF NEWCASTLE, had good reason to write specifically of the thought process. In her age scientific theory had begun to exert an influence, and as an independent woman filled with curiosity, Cavendish was under that influence. The Royal Academy of Science, to which Cavendish was the first female allowed a visit, was newly founded for learned men to gather and discuss theories such as those put forth by Robert Burton in *The Anatomy of Melancholy* (1621). As a precursor to the study of psychology Burton's work engaged in some fanciful explanation of the source of thoughts and the purpose and function of the brain, a lead that Cavendish followed. She included "The Reason Why the Thoughts Are Only in the Head" in her *Poems,* reflecting a favorite approach, the use of

FIGURATIVE LANGUAGE (FIGURE OF SPEECH). In this instance she begins by comparing what we know today as the thought process to a system of sinews resembling pipes in a building. She then muses on the possibilities of thoughts' being located in the extremities, rather than the head.

Burton had written "Nerves or sinews, are membranes without, and full of marrow within; they proceed from the brain, and carry the animal spirits for sense and motion." Cavendish could relate to such a definition and a source, as Burton's work would not be classified as hard science. She contrasted with JOHN DONNE, who wrote in "The Funeral" that "the sinewy thread" from his brain tied all his parts together, uniting them in response. Cavendish rejected the idea of any sympathy among human parts, viewing each as separate and complete entities. Her beliefs in fairies as muses, expressed in "The Fairies in the Brain May Be the Causes of Many Thoughts" (1664), would dismay another scientist, Thomas Hobbes. A famous essayist of Cavendish's era with connections to her husband's family, Hobbes had met Galileo in 1636. He then developed a social philosophy based on principles of geometry and natural science that viewed the world as in constant motion. He wrote in his most famous work, *Leviathan* (1651), of detesting "the demonology of the heathen poets, that is to say, their fabulous doctrine concerning demons, which are but idols, or phantasms of the brain . . . such as are dead men's ghosts, and fairies, and other matter of old wives' tales."

Cavendish's 22-line poem of rhyming couplets begins with a comparison of "Each sinew" to "a small and slender string," then explains the sinew use, "Which to the body all the senses bring." She then compares the sinews to hollow "pipes or gutters" ushering through "animal spirits continually." Despite their small size, "they such matter do contain, / As in the skull doth lie, which we call brain." Cavendish displays her knowledge of anatomy, which was accomplished for its time. She continues, explaining that if "one doth strike the heel, / the thought of that sense in the brain doth feel." However, she states emphatically, "It is not sympathy, but all one thing, / Which causes us to think, and pain doth bring." The action of the nervous system becomes an adequate topic for rhyming verse in her plain-spoken manner.

Cavendish continues her consideration by projecting the brain's duties onto other parts of the body, including the heel, which if it contained "such quantity of brain" as the head and skull, then thoughts that presently "in the brain dwell high" would "Descend into our heels, and there would lie." She muses that brain actually lies "scattered" about in the small sinews, meaning nerves, wanting "both room and quantity no doubt." Her final conclusion is that if the sinews proved large enough with "a skin" that could "enfold" as much as the skull does,

> then might the toe or knee,
> had they an optic nerve, both hear and see;
> Had sinews room, fancy therein to breed,
> Copies of verses might from the heel proceed.

While Cavendish chooses a rather indelicate topic, her rhythm and RHYME support smooth movement, literally transforming science to art. Although she at times sacrificed sound for sense in her verse, in this instance she succeeds in finding the proper balance between the two.

BIBLIOGRAPHY
Breitenberg, Mark. *Anxious Masculinity in Early Modern England.* New York: Cambridge University Press, 1996.
Skinner, Quentin. *Reason and Rhetoric in the Philosophy of Hobbes.* New York: Cambridge University Press, 1996.

"REDEMPTION, THE" GEORGE HERBERT **(1633)** GEORGE HERBERT proved that the SONNET form could be used to accommodate religious poetry, an example his "The Redemption." He manages to retain the light tone generally used in the love sentiments the sonnet generally served, although that tone proves marked by IRONY in the poem's conclusion. In an exploration of Calvinist theology Herbert creates a speaker who suffers shock at what he discovers to be the truth reflected by Christ's crucifixion, an effect similar to that in his "The HOLDFAST" and "Dialogue." Some critics believe that the speaker represents human movement from the Old Testament to the promise of the New Testament, which is salvation through the sacrifice of Christ.

Herbert adopts the persona of a man who was "tenant long to a rich Lord" but who had not made much of his landlord's investment in him. Still he "resolved to be bold" and try to convince the Lord through "a suit" to offer him "A new small-rented lease, and cancel th' old." Herbert adopts the FIGURATIVE LANGUAGE (FIGURE OF SPEECH) of extended metaphor to compare God's redemption of a man's soul to the redemption of land where a renter had been "not thriving." Foolishly the tenant throws the responsibility for his failure on the landlord and, instead of working harder to become successful, decides to abandon his first project to take on a second one, which is less demanding. His arrogance leads him to believe that the "rich Lord" should simply forgive one debt and immediately pick up another. In this manner Herbert explains what he believes is Christ's interaction with man, the repeated forgiving of sins, with an ultimate relief of all human death through sacrificing his life after taking the form of man on earth.

By the fifth line the speaker has traveled "In heaven at his manor" but is told the Lord "was lately gone / About some land, which he had dearly bought." That land, of course, belongs to the speaker, who conveniently ignores that possibility. More importantly the meaning of *dearly bought* makes no impression, so the tenant, representing man in his ignorance, cannot conceive of the price Christ has paid in order to redeem man. The tenant returns to earth where the Lord has gone "to take possession." He searches for the Lord in great resorts; "In cities, theaters, gardens, parks, and courts," assuming that the Lord's great stature would require such environments. However, the tenant then hears "a ragged noise and mirth" as "thieves and murderers" make up the company of the great Lord. The Lord tells the tenant /speaker, "Your suit is granted" then dies. The speaker has caused the Lord's death through his suit; he will not survive without the grace that humans receive through that death.

Herbert employs an analogy common to the Bible, in which various characters use material goods unwisely, approach God or Christ for additional benefits, then again fail to be good stewards. But he alludes

to a far more valuable treasure than material goods, that of the human soul. Through Christ's ultimate sacrifice man receives the ultimate redemption, eternal life. Above all Herbert seeks to undercut the doctrine of grace through merit, held by Arminians, by characterizing it as a product of man's ignorant self-involvement.

BIBLIOGRAPHY
Malcolmson, Cristina. *George Herbert: A Literary Life.* New York: Palgrave Macmillan, 2004.

"REGENERATION" HENRY VAUGHAN (1650)

As did most of HENRY VAUGHAN's religious poetry, "Regeneration" first appeared in his collection titled *Silex Scintillans.* Although the poems in the collection were written several years before its publication, *Silex Scintillans* was probably held back from publication by a publisher wary of its political allusions. At a time of civil unrest when emotions ran high, Vaughan supported the king. Deeply affected by the war and its devastation, Vaughan underwent a change in religious consciousness due to what the biographer and critic Alan Rudrum terms his "pain . . . of public and private grief, intermingled and running together." The collection has as its title page emblem a heart-shaped flint, which an arm strikes with a thunderbolt, suggesting the hardened heart awakened through a spiritually inflicted trial by fire. Vaughan's forceful resistance of God's call is met by God's own force, as a spiritual power overcomes that resistance. Vaughan's penitence as he bends to God's demands represents the theme of "Regeneration." This posture may be seen from the first line, "A ward, and still in bonds," as the speaker fashions himself a shackled prisoner stealing abroad on a spring day. The imagery of rebirth seen in primroses and details such as *infant buds* are tempered by the speaker's internal frost, in which "sin / Like clouds eclipsed my mind."

Greatly influenced by GEORGE HERBERT's "The PILGRIMAGE," "Regeneration" is constructed of 10 eight-line stanzas with a RHYME scheme of *ababcdcd* and a concluding couplet that serves as an epigram of sorts. The poem focuses on Vaughan's conversion and remains autobiographical, its experience personal and specific to the poet himself. Critics have characterized it as Vaughan's move of attention from the church to nature with an emphasis on the relationship of nature to God. It contains narrative as the speaker moves through and describes a symbolic landscape, although Rudrum cautions against interpreting natural references as allegory only, because of Vaughan's well-recorded interest in mysticism, and its a sharpened awareness of the natural world. It may be seen immediately in the second stanza as Vaughan adopts the verb *Stormed* to describe his being. In that stage he perceives his "spring / Mere stage and show," while his walk was "a monstrous, mountained thing, / Roughcast with rocks and snow." Terrain holds the reader's focus.

Vaughan's keen awareness of nature informs many of his poems, including "The WATERFALL," where the water remains important for the imagery it provides, but also as a traditional biblical symbol of rebirth. As nature regenerates annually, so has the speaker of "Regeneration," his being a spiritual rebirth. As do others of Vaughan's poems, "Regeneration" contains the CONCEITs and hyperbole characteristic of the works of METAPHYSICAL POETS AND POETRY as it alludes to the intersection between natural and spiritual activities. For example the second stanza concludes with a "pilgrim's eye" described as one that "drops and rains for grief."

The scales in the third stanza recall the heart emblem of *Silex Scintillans* as they remain emblematic as well:

> I found a pair of scales;
> I took them up and laid
>   In th' one, late pains;
> The other smoke and pleasures weighted,
> But proved the heavier grains.

In this passage the speaker has not yet achieved grace, as the pleasures of the worldly life outweigh those of the redeemed life. In the next stanza he will receive some guidance, obeying commands of an unseen voice as he begins to walk a path generally used only by "Prophets and friends of God." After a brief rest he enters a grove "Of stately height" and finds himself suddenly caught up in "a new spring," which "Did all my senses greet." The speaker's rebirth is gradual, as he requires assistance before he can recognize God. This situation characterizes God as one who desires to give an opportunity to man to realize the truth with the help of nature.

In the grove in stanza 6, Vaughan incorporates the imagery of precious metal, that of gold, and colors of ultimate strength, such as the *azure,* rather than mere blue, of the sky to emphasize the contrast between the spiritual life and that of a sinner. The righteous life offers a vivid existence, not one lacking passion, as those who resist redemption might believe. In the seventh stanza the speaker hears only the flow of water, an additional symbol of rebirth and new life, as it moves over "divers stones, some bright and round, / Others ill-shaped and dull." Critics disagree on the significance of the stones, some proposing they represent human souls in myriad forms, others that they are important simply for their own contrasting imagery.

In a lovely concluding two stanzas the speaker searches for the source of a new sound. Because nature has caused his renaissance, he looks at flowers and notices a curious fact. Some are open to the sun, while others remain closed. He finally recognizes the source of the sound to be the wind, but he wonders about the source of the wind. His mind then asks about the origin of the wind, in order to gain ease "By knowing where 'twas, or where not." But it offers a surprising answer: "It whispered, 'Where I please.'" The wind, symbolizing God's power, may travel anywhere at any time, uncontrolled by any other force. That response clarifies that while nature reflects God's presence, it has no strength without him. In some of Vaughan's poetry he makes clear that the creator and created are one. However, in this poem he distinguishes between the two.

Departing from its established form, the poem adds a concluding couplet separate from any stanza that reads, "'Lord,' then said I, 'on me one breath, / And let me die before my death!'" Vaughan offers PARADOX suitable to the contradictions inherent to Christianity, one such contradiction that man must die in order to live. In this case the death is that of man's sinful nature. Thus the speaker asks that his sin die before he physically dies, so that he may die in a state of redemptive grace and achieve spiritual life.

BIBLIOGRAPHY
Rudrum, Alan. *Henry Vaughan.* Cardiff: University of Wales Press, 1981.

RELIGIO LAICI; OR A LAYMAN'S FAITH

JOHN DRYDEN (1682)   JOHN DRYDEN spent years in self-debate regarding his religious beliefs. His conversion from Anglicanism to Catholicism at the time James II, a Catholic, rose to the throne in 1686 provoked much criticism from those who believed it simply an expedient move. Dryden remained a Catholic, however, after the exile of James II and his replacement by his Protestant daughter, Mary, and her husband, William, although to do so could have meant imprisonment. But in 1682 Dryden was still Protestant, and *Religio Laici; Or a Layman's Faith,* acted as his Anglican confession. In its 457 lines he examines the conflict many felt regarding religious divisions within England, leading him to write in lines 10–11, "so pale grows reason at religion's sight, / So dies, and so dissolves in supernatural light," with that light referring to faith. He expressed the opinion that reason could never replace faith and saw as man's error the use of logic in the choosing a suitable religion to follow.

The search for a religious authority troubled many as they groped to understand and distinguish between various religious beliefs. Dryden examined three approaches in his poem, that of deists, Catholics, and those who exercised private judgment, apart from any creed. He finally deems the Anglican Church to be superior to all three.

Many believed the deists to be excessive in their rationalization, a thought Dryden expresses as his speaker muses, "But what, or who, that UNIVERSAL HE" (15) who created earth might be. He proposes two possibilities. First he writes of what later would be called the "clockmaker theory," in which God was characterized as a power that created earth, set it in motion, then abandoned it, surveying its development but not interfering to right wrongs. Dryden writes, "Whether some soul encompassing this ball, / Unmade, unmov'd, yet making, moving all:" (16–17), then adds the deist approach as a second possibility: "Or various atoms' interfering dance / Leap'd into form (the noble work of chance)" (18–19). Dryden personally found repugnant the belief that no ultimate power controlled the combining of atoms into the matter of earth and man, and he adopts an incredulous tone as he expresses that possibility. As always Dryden dresses his thoughts in admirable expression, using ALLITERATION and repetition, as well as ANTITHESIS, to engage readers.

The traditional choice for worship was Catholicism, but the scandal and corruption within that church bothered many. Dryden points out that the tradition offered by the Catholic Church should be desirable, providing stability in its recorded historical precedent, when he writes in lines 350–353,

> Tradition written therefore more commends
> Authority than what from voice descends;
> And this, as perfect as its kind can be,
> Rolls down to us the sacred history.

However, the Church did not revere its own tradition. Newer splinter divisions, to whom Dryden refers as "partial Papists," wandered from the church's original values. In so doing, they convinced themselves they were the "whole" church, rather than just one faction:

> The partial Papists wou'd infer from hence
> Their church, in last resort, shou'd judge the
>   Sense.
> But first they wou'd assume, with wondrous art,
> Themselves to be the whole who are but part.
>   (355–359)

Dryden also has harsh words for those who claimed to be traditionalists within the church. He took to task Catholic leaders for abusing their sacred duties. Because certain individuals imagined themselves the only worthy communicators with God, the "Mother Church did mightily prevail: / She parcel'd out the bible by retail" (377–378), and, far worse, kept "it in her power to damn and save" (379) so that "Poor laymen took salvation on content, / As needy men take money, good or bad" (381–382). The judgmental nature of the church obviously bothered Dryden, while the commercialism introduced through purchased penance he found disgusting. Although he would later decide the Catholic Church represented the least of the evils, offering traditional ideals promoting stability needed in unstable political times, he had not yet arrived at that belief when he wrote those lines.

As for those who would decide themselves capable of making their own judgments about religion instead of remaining within the fold of a church, Dryden had great concerns. He presented that approach as one of a mob that has broken away from civil law. Without formal guidance, chaos would prevail:

> The Book thus put in every vulgar hand,
> Which presum'd he best cou'd understand,
> The common rule was made the common prey
> And at the mercy of the rabble lay. (400–403)

Although he may have admired their "great zeal," the "little thought" (416) supporting it he found anathema. His revulsion produced one of his century's great extended CONCEITS. Dryden characterized the independent approach as a decay of decency, comparing its results to that of rotting meat in lines 417–420:

> While crowds unlearn'd, with rude devotion warm,
> About the sacred viands buzz and swarm,
> The fly-blown text creates a crawling brood
> And turns to maggots what was meant for food.

Dryden's summary makes clear his belief that every individual man's developing his own creed was far more dangerous than organized religion. He continued in his personal search for an answer, as evidenced in the question he poses in lines 276–277, "'Oh,' but says one, 'tradition set aside, / Where can we hope for an unerring guide?'" Dryden did not yet feel certain that "truth in church tradition must be found" (281); however, he would within a few years reach that certainty.

BIBLIOGRAPHY

Durant, Jack D. "*Religio Laici*: The Poem as Product." *College Language Association Journal* 35, no. 4 (June 1992): 448–466.
Kenshur, Oscar. "Scriptural Deism and the Politics of Dryden's *Religio Laici*." *English Literary History* 54, no. 4 (winter, 1987): 869–892.
Miner, Earl, ed. *Selected Poetry and Prose of John Dryden.* New York: The Modern Library, 1985.

"REPULSE TO ALCANDER, THE" SARAH FYGE EGERTON (1703)

"The Repulse to Alcander" by SARAH FYGE EGERTON adopts a female voice to counter the traditional seduction poem, made popular by Renaissance CAVALIER POETS. Egerton adopts the values that would become important in the Augustan age, as the new 18th century introduced a focus on proper behavior and logic. Rather than embracing the weepy sentimentality that gripped 17th-century literature, the new century would produce satire aimed at women's vice and, at times, a celebration of their virtue. But Egerton wrote in the century's first decade, when attacks on women writers and female artists in general remained frequent. The confusion between the bawdy adventures of the characters populating writing by women during the Restoration and their authors, often encouraged by the authors themselves in order to promote sales, no longer remained the rule. In "The Repulse to Alcander" Egerton's persona rebukes a man for his attempts at seduction, producing a strong, sure female voice that no reader could mistake as foolish or naive. In 56 lines of rhyming couplets with a METER of iambic pentameter, a woman castigates her would-be seducer without mercy.

Egerton begins with a direct question couched in a tone of disgust, demanding, "What is't you mean, that I am thus approached? / Dare you to hope that I may be debauched?" The voice makes clear that she recognizes duplicity of the man she rebukes as plying "seducing words," then attempting to beg for "pity, with a soft surprise." Egerton applies to her male subject the same indictment that had been applied to women for ages, expanding it by describing him as "one who loves, and sighs, and almost dies." Her persona reveals him as a hypocrite, at first holding seeming "vast respect" for her, yet then with an "excess of manners" growing "too bold." In no uncertain terms she tells him, "I hate and blush to see or hear" everything he does and says. She then gives as an example of the mannerly excess of her subject, playing, kissing, and pressing her hand, to the point of alarm. In a damning indictment she adds that "sacred laws and vows confine / Me to another," noting that he then framed his "lewd abuse" in "a thousand" excuses, including that of "Bacchus," indicating that he blamed his indiscretion on drunkenness.

Egerton makes several references to figures of mythology in addition to Bacchus, including to "amorous Phylaster," "Hymen," and "Cupid," to make the point that claims of instant attraction are based on fantasy. The object of her ire cannot claim to have been placed under a magical spell, such as that inflicted by Cupid, intended to "force a fondness which was ne'er designed"; nor can he blame his actions on a "foreign mode of complaisance." Even though she may have at first been tricked into believing such reasons supported his acts, his repetition of "amorous crimes" convinced her that he did not have her best interest in mind. She notes, "That to permit you would make mine [her own crimes] as great." For those who might be looking on, she makes clear that she did nothing to encourage his actions. Reflecting on her own personality, she explains,

I must confess I am not quite so nice
To damn all little gallantries for vice
(But I see now my charity's misplaced,
If none but sullen saints can be thought chaste):
Yet know, base man, I scorn your lewd amours,
Hate them from all, not only 'cause they're
    yours. (35–40)

She appeals to "sacred Love!" not to allow the world to "profane / Thy transports, thus to sport and entertain; / The beau."

Finally, the speaker regrets her former false feelings of security, having experienced the invasion of privacy her attempted seducer represents. When the speaker notes that he "Affronts my virtue, hazards my just fame," Egerton speaks to a serious problem for women. Because female virtue remained so highly prized, slander could cause women to be excluded from polite society. Whether gossip proved true or not, the fact that a woman's virtue raised any question could literally ruin her future. Her poem asks of men a question that had plagued women for centuries, "Why should I suffer for your lawless flame?" where *flame* represents the heat of passion. Egerton's use of the adjective *law-*

less allows it to carry a double meaning. Not only did the male subject of her poem prove out of control by society's measures, but because the speaker was a married woman, he also transgressed civic law in approaching her. Because of her culture's double standard, however, Egerton knew that in such a situation the woman was far more likely to be held to those laws than men. Her speaker confirms the seriousness of the matter by adding,

For oft' tis known, through vanity and pride,
Men boast those favours which they are denied;
Or others' malice, which can soon discern,
Perhaps may see in you some kind concern,
So scatter false suggestions of their own. (49–53)

The vicious attacks against women often lacked basis in truth, undertaken by men whose romantic approaches the women had denied. Their lies regarding sexual conquest quickly permeated the woman's social circle. The speaker concludes by noting that her choice of action is simply inaction: "No, I'll be wise, avoid your sight in time, / And shun at once the censure and the crime." Egerton's final couplet serves as advice to her female readers. The unfortunate truth, however, was that most women proved unable, through financial dependency on a husband, brother, or father, to "shun" "censure," regardless of whether a crime had been committed.

Poems such as Egerton's "The Repulse to Alcander" had a specific purpose. They promoted caution by women, forced to live in a society supported by a double standard. Women engaging in actions approved, or at least tolerated, when taken by men, would undergo immediate censure. Egerton often spoke out in her writing against such inequality, provoking the ire of some readers.

RESTORATION, THE   The term *Restoration* refers to the restoration of royal rule to England and the period that followed, roughly 1660 through 1700. After tremendous political and religious upheaval with a focus on the supposed divine right of kings to rule, Charles I was executed in 1649. His beheading drove his son and successor, along with loyal Royalists, to live in exile. The Protectorate headed by the Puritan Oliver Cromwell assumed power, and the Commonwealth was born. When Cromwell's son, Richard, assumed control of Parliament and the country at his father's death, the Commonwealth suffered an upheaval, civil war broke out, and the period labeled the Interregnum ended in 1660. Political forces removed the Cromwell faction, and Charles II returned to England from France to assume power. The cheerful king's return proved crucial to both drama and poetry, as the sober and repressive Cromwell group had outlawed and restricted into nonexistence most creative expression. While occasional and religious poetry supportive of Cromwellian control was encouraged, any anti-Cromwellian expression could result in punishment including imprisonment and death. For the most part an amiable monarch, Charles II enjoyed entertainment and supported it not only with his presence, but also with funds. A fan of bawdy drama, often enhanced with sexually explicit poetry, the king championed the return of all levels of creative expression.

Theaters reopened and dramatic portrayals encouraged sexual and social freedom. Imbued with a new energy, poetry flourished, first in the extremes seen in libertine poetry, such as that by JOHN WILMOT, second EARL OF ROCHESTER. Disasters within a decade of Charles II's taking power, the plague of 1665 and the Great Fire of 1666, also affected artistic expression, which often reflected the social and political atmosphere of its day. London enjoyed a rebirth after the destruction of disease and flame, resulting in increased financial prosperity for those involved in trade and colonialism. However, it also produced an increasing separation of the wealthy from the poor, firmly supporting class division in England and subsequent government corruption. England's tumultuous relationship with Ireland and Scotland also affected poets, both Royalist sympathizers and nonsympathizers, of all three countries. British poets reflecting Restoration events and social and religious mores included ANDREW MARVELL; ABRAHAM COWLEY; RICHARD CRASHAW; JOHN CLEVELAND; JOHN MILTON; KATHERINE PHILIPS; MARGARET CAVENDISH, DUCHESS OF NEWCASTLE; JOHN DRYDEN; THOMAS OTWAY; APHRA BEHN; ANNE KILLIGREW; SARAH EGERTON; SIR CHARLES SEDLEY; ALEXANDER POPE, and JONATHAN SWIFT.

BIBLIOGRAPHY

Messenger, Ann. *His and Hers: Essays in Restoration and Eighteenth-Century Literature.* Lexington: University Press of Kentucky, 1986.

Pinto, V. De Sola. *Sir Charles Sedley, 1639–1701: A Study in the Life and Literature of the Restoration.* Folcroft, Pa.: Folcroft Library Editions, 1973.

Sedenberg, H. T., Jr. *English Poetry of the Restoration and Early Eighteenth Century.* New York: Knopf, 1968.

Survey of British Poetry: Cavalier to Restoration. Vol. 2, edited by the Editorial Board, Roth Publishing. Great Neck, N.Y.: Poetry Anthology Press, 1989.

Wu, Duncan. *Poetry from 1660 to 1780: Civil War, Restoration, Revolution.* Oxford: Blackwell, 2002.

"RETREAT, THE" HENRY VAUGHAN (1650)

Found in HENRY VAUGHAN's religious poetry collection *Silex Scintillans,* "The Retreat" employs one of his favorite themes of the uncorrupted days of childhood, a theme shared noticeably by only one other poet of his era, THOMAS TRAHERNE. Vaughan believed that during innocent youth the world could be seen as an extension of God, beautiful and wholly glorious and in no way corrupt. "The Retreat" stresses that belief from its opening lines, "Happy those early days! When I / Shin'd in my Angell-infancy." As a believer in hermetic Christianity, which held that matter is constantly rejuvenated, Vaughan repeatedly used the theme of rebirth and innocence in the newly born. A child represented the results of that creative process of rejuvenation, filled with all of the potential of a future not yet needing God's grace for redemption.

The speaker's "infancy" represents a time "Before I understood this place / Appointed for my second race," as the second line indicates that the speaker believes he may have existed in another state prior to human birth. In his original state his fancy turned to "white, celestial thought," where white acts as the traditional symbol of purity and *celestial* may be equated with the adjective *heavenly.* At that time he had moved both spiritually and physically only a short distance from his origin, or "my first love." "And looking back, at that short space," the speaker glimpses "His bright face." The upper case *H* in the possessive pronoun *His* indicates reference to a deity. As a child the speaker could gaze on "weaker glories," such as clouds and flowers, and see "Some shadows of eternity." Vaughan begins to add detail regarding his developing earthly existence in which he indulges in a human "black art" and learns every sin possible. But previous to that time he could feel through his human flesh "Bright shoots of everlastingness."

The poem offers a natural division after the 20th line, as the remaining 12 lines declare the speaker's desire to "travel back, / And tread again that ancient track!" He cannot do so, of course, and Vaughan develops a strong analogy of a person drunk with whisky, the alcohol blunting his senses, as he writes, "But, ah! My soul with too much stay / Is drunk, and staggers in the way." His unusual use of the term *stay* as a noun draws reader attention to the expression. Although most men desire to move forward, meaning toward success and maturity, the speaker admits that if offered the choice, "I by backward steps would move." Vaughan shapes a PARADOX in that movement backward in this case represents a gain, rather than the traditional sense of loss. While most humans think of burial as the end of their life, the speaker will regard the interment of his body as the manner by which he may return home, as Vaughan concludes, "And when this dust falls to the urn, / In that state I came, return." He alludes to the biblical verse about death that characterizes the human body as moving from "dust to dust" and "ashes to ashes" in the birth and death cycle.

BIBLIOGRAPHY

Leishman, J. B. *The Metaphysical Poets: Donne, Herbert, Vaughan, Traherne.* Oxford: Clarendon Press, 1934.

RHYME *Rhyme* refers to two or more words in poetry containing identical or similar sounds in their final syllable. The Greek term *rhythmos*, from which the word *rhyme* derived, was refined by old French to *rime*, also an acceptable modern spelling. Several types of rhymes exist, the more common of which will be explained here.

In *perfect rhyme* the words sound identical with the same vowel sounds preceded by different consonants, an example seen in the terms *pine* and *fine*, employed by ROBERT HERRICK in his "The Mower's Song" from *The MOWER POEMS*: "But these, while I with sorrow pine, / Grew more luxuriant still and fine." These lines also represent *masculine rhyme* in which the final syllables

are stressed, as well as *tail rhyme*, the most common form of rhyme, occurring at the lines' ends. In *feminine rhyme* the penultimate syllable rhymes, as at the end of these lines from ALEXANDER POPE's *An ESSAY ON MAN*: "To sigh for ribbands if thou art so silly, / Mark how they grace Lord Umbra, of Sir Billy." *Eye rhyme* indicates two words that look as if they should be *perfect rhymes* but are pronounced differently. In some cases pronunciation changes over time, causing a once-perfect rhyme to become eye rhyme. In *oblique* or *slant rhyme* the words sound similar but are not identical. In these four additional lines from Herrick's "The Mower's Song" the first two end in eye rhyme, while the second two end in oblique or slant rhyme:

> And thus, ye meadows, which have been
> Companions of my thoughts more green,
> Shall now the heraldry become
> With which I shall adorn my tomb.

In *internal rhyme* words within the line rhyme, or a word within the line rhymes with the line's final term. An example may be seen in the words *to* and *due* in a line from Pope's *An ESSAY ON CRITICISM*: "That not alone what to your Sense is due." *Identity rhyme* means the use of identical words, as in a line from Herrick's "The NYMPH COMPLAINING FOR THE DEATH OF HER FAWN," also an example of internal rhyme: "Twould stay, and run again, and stay." *Imperfect rhyme* is seen in words in which an unstressed syllable rhymes with a stressed one, as in another line from that same poem, "The brotherless Heliades / Melt in such amber tears as these." In *dactylic rhyme* stress occurs on the third from the last syllable, seen in these lines from Pope's *An Essay on Man,* "In Faith and Hope the world will disagree, / But all Mankind's concern is Charity."

Rhyme has been used to help dictate fixed form poetry, as in RIME ROYAL, a format in which each seven-line stanza adopts the METER of iambic pentameter with the set rhyme scheme *ababbcc*. The lines may be set either in tercet and two couplets, *ababbcc*, or a tercset with one quatrain, *ababbcc*.

"RIGHTS OF WOMEN, THE" ANNA LAETITIA BARBAULD (1795) ANNA LAETITIA BARBAULD wrote "The

Rights of Women" as a formal declaration regarding the lack of women's civil rights in early 19th-century England. She addresses her audience as "injured Woman!" urging that woman to "rise, assert thy right!" To emphasize the fact that only females will profit from the advice that follows, she repeats the personal exclamation "Woman!" at the beginning of her second line, followed by a discouraging description of that woman as "too long degraded, scorned, oppressed." Her railing focuses on legal restrictions as instruments of degradation and oppression. Because such legalities are controlled by the patriarchal culture, she suggests the only way a woman may rise above civil control is through responsibility for herself; a female can only experience liberty within her private sphere. The poem's speaker concludes the first four-line verse with a lament, followed by a call to action: "O born to rule in partial Law's despite, / Resume thy native empire o'er the breast!" Again with the phrase in partial Law's despite she urges her audience to defy an unjust law using whatever manner is available.

The poem's persona next instructs women in how to claim their personal independence. Adopting FIGURATIVE LANGUAGE (FIGURE OF SPEECH) in the extended metaphors of religion, royalty, and the military, Barbauld suggests that women march together, that they "Go forth arrayed in panoply divine" to project an "angel pureness which admits no stain." Readers will recognize the allusion to biblical angels, often known for their combative natures, as well as their purity. Of course angels lack humanity, a concept that promotes IRONY in the suggestion that women would have to be inhuman in order to assume an angelic mantle. The next order focuses on male pride, as Barbauld uses ALLITERATION for effect: "Go, bid proud Man his boasted rule resign / And kiss the golden scepter of thy reign." While men suffer pride, women must resist a temptation to do the same, retaining a pure stance in their personal kingdom. The third stanza continues, "Go, gird thyself with grace, collect thy store / Of bright artillery glancing from afar," making clear that women will face resistance and must arm themselves for battle. However, theirs will be a nontraditional method, stressed by Barbauld through the use of PARADOX in "Soft melting tones thy thundering cannon's roar." She then adopts the Victorian consid-

eration of women as overly emotional, describing what will provide their ammunition: "Blushes and tears thy magazine of war."

The fifth stanza suggests that women also employ "wit and art" to try to bring men, "thy imperial foe," to their knees, the third line offering the wisdom, "Make treacherous Man thy subject, not thy friend." Barbauld makes clear that woman must employ her wiles to conquer man, that he cannot be trusted as a friend. Even such a victory gives little comfort as women "mayest command, but never canst be free." Barbauld again offers a paradox, declaring that women may bid men to do their will, but that does not constitute to freedom outside the domestic sphere. In the next stanza the voice continues suggesting ways to gain freedom, bidding the audience,

Awe the licentious and restrain the rude;
Soften the sullen, clear the cloudy brow:
Be, more than princes' gifts, thy favors sued;—
She hazards all, who will the least allow.

Barbauld creates a skillful riddle, playing off the idea of risk. That sixth stanza's final line basically tells readers that those women who do not accept men as they are, working to curb undesirable behavior by giving of themselves, risk losing personal contentment.

In a surprising turn the poem's tone softens in its final two stanzas, where the speaker admonishes that pride will not remain where a true sympathy exists between two people. Through her action, the woman controls not only the man, but herself, and "subduing and subdued, thou shalt find / Thy coldness soften, and thy pride give way." Barbauld suggests that while the pride she mentioned earlier comes naturally to man, women's warmer natures will not sustain it. Her final stanza focuses even more closely on the natural differences between women and men, noting that women will "abandon each ambitious thought," that they are not moved by "Conquest of rule." Women learn not from mankind's arbitrary rules, but rather from "Nature's school" through "soft maxims. . . . That separate rights are lost in mutual love."

Barbauld's poem supports the idea held by many historians that women were allowed power within the home, if not in public. In most instances women controlled domestic issues, even though they could not, by law, have any ownership rights in the household they managed. Important to note in her final line is that she does not suggest that in the end woman must surrender to man. She emphasizes in closing not winning and losing, but rather the mutual respect that renders individual, civically determined privilege moot. Although she wrote into the 19th century, Barbauld remained grounded in 18th-century thought, and that century's emphasis on moderation and toleration as paths to prosperity framed her writing. While women of her youth had lost economic independence as a rural existence transformed into an urban one, they gained the privilege of education and expansion of middle-class opportunity that allowed the emergence of thoughtful writing women like Barbauld. Not yet ready to march for women's rights, nor even considering doing so a necessity, Barbauld focused on themes in her writing that emphasized the strength women could draw from their relationships with men as a manner by which to counter public forces that sought to control them.

RIME ROYAL

Rime royal, a format probably created by Chaucer, remained a favorite with Renaissance writers, including MICHAEL DRAYTON. Usually in seven-line verses its rhyme scheme was ababbcc. Verse length could vary, however, as in NICHOLAS BRETON's "COME LITTLE BABE," a late 16th- or early 17th-century lullaby containing six-line verses that omitted one of the middle b rhymes. Rime royal did not insist on distinct verses, often appearing in lengthy poems with no verse organization. Not appropriate to common verse, rime royal appeared in more elevated, courtly poetry. William Shakespeare employed it in his "Rape of Lucrece." Its use declined after the 17th century, as a result of changes in reader tastes and an increase in the production of poetry that focused on more common subjects for the more common reader.

ROBINSON, MARY (1758–1800)

Mary Darby was born in Bristol and raised in London. A younger sister died of smallpox before Mary's birth. One younger brother, William, died at age six years, and a brother, George, matured along with Mary. She writes of herself in her memoir that upon learning to read she delighted in epitaphs and "monumental inscriptions." She adds, "A story of melancholy import never failed to excite my attention," a trait that may later have affected her decision to become an actress.

Robinson memorized poetry by ALEXANDER POPE and enjoyed BALLADS by JOHN GAY. Her younger years proved happy ones in elegant surroundings supported by her American-born father. However, she would later move to London with her brother and mother when her parents separated. There she attended school taught by Meribah Lorrington, an "extraordinary woman," with whom Robinson credited "All that I ever learned." The family began to experience financial difficulties as her father did not supply the support he had promised. Her mother began a small school, but her father demanded that she end that occupation. He had taken a mistress, about whom Robinson writes in her memoir. At age 15, she began to take acting lessons from David Garrick and described that pursuit: "the drama, the delightful drama, seemed the very criterion of all human happiness."

Mary's mother decided she should "relinquish [her] theatrical prospects" and marry while still in her teens. In 1774 she wed Thomas Robinson, a man who during his courting had proven "indefatiguable in his attentions." The couple had a daughter named Maria Elizabeth before he went to debtors' prison. Mary and the baby lived with him for 10 months, and other family members were free to come and go from the prison. She wrote in her memoir, "During nine months and three weeks, never once did I pass the threshold of our dreary habitation." She includes a description of her initial reaction to incarceration, writing that she cared little for herself but remained anxious for the baby's health. While "Mr. Robinson was expert in all exercises of strength or activity" and could use the exercise area, she occupied herself with her "beloved and still helpless daughter." Tom Robinson received some financial support from his father, who helped to pay for the two rooms required by the family in jail. Because of her beauty Mary began receiving offers of money from men in exchange for "favors," a situation that would only increase in her future. She remained loyal to her husband in spite of overwhelming evidence of his infidelity, but that devotion would ebb over the next five years.

Robinson began her writing career in prison, later publishing a collection of poems that earned her the support of the duchess of Devonshire. When the family left prison, she began a stage career with the help of Garrick and encouragement including from playwright Richard Brinsley Sheridan. In an early performance the audience hissed at the actors, causing her to freeze on stage. The other actor fled, leaving her "to encounter the critic tempest." As she reported, the duke of Cumberland (fifth son of George III) called to her to "take courage: 'It is not you, but the play, they hiss.'" His assessment proved correct, and she became incredibly successful. Graceful as well as beautiful, she was a natural on stage and earned the pseudonym *Perdita* with her famed portrayal of that character in Shakespeare's *The Winter's Tale.* Her memoir includes mention of 22 parts that she played during her first year. By 1779 her marriage proved a sham, but she continued to be seen with her husband off and on over many years. As she drily described her feelings in her memoir, "His indifference naturally produced an alienation of esteem on my side."

The prince of Wales, later to become King George IV, fell in love with Robinson and kept the celebrated actress as his mistress for one year; she was the first of many for the then 17-year-old prince. Her memoir concludes at the point when their relationship turned stormy, and it would later be continued by her daughter. Robinson had kept what she described as "almost daily letters" of the prince's confession of love, which afforded her some leverage in bargaining for an income. While he attempted to leave her with no support and a sullied reputation, she managed to procure a bond that acted as a promise of £20,000 when the prince became of age. While she never received the full amount, she would eventually receive sporadic annual support, and Maria Elizabeth would receive a pledge of £200 per year upon Robinson's death.

Robinson returned to her writing career and continued in various relationships with men, including the politician Charles James Fox and the soldier famous for his actions in the American Revolution Colonel Banastre Tarleton. She had become fully involved in what she described in her memoir as "the perils attendant on a dramatic life." Her pursuit of Tarleton as he fled to the Continent to escape his debts became legendary, inspiring later fiction. However, none of her romantic ventures proved lasting or satisfying. Her great beauty made her a favorite subject of the four most famous portrait artists of her era, Sir Joshua Reynolds, Thomas Gainsborough, John Hoppner, and George Romney, and her portraits remain on display into the 21st century. Her name appeared constantly in print, her every move made public. Her wearing of breeches on the stage confirmed for many Robinson's fallen nature, and the public followed her various relationships with great interest.

Robinson suffered partial paralysis at age 25, probably from acute rheumatic fever. Shortly after she had a miscarriage, losing Tarleton's baby as Maria Elizabeth cared for her. In 1792 Tom Robinson reappeared after a long absence with the news that his brother, William, had agreed to support Maria Elizabeth. The news cheered Robinson, who could not hope to give her daughter many advantages. However, William Robinson demanded that Maria Elizabeth renounce legal ties to both parents. She refused, remaining to care for her ailing mother until Robinson's death.

Even while ill, Robinson continued to write, as she was always in debt. Her poetry enjoyed multiple publications, including an erotic sequence of SONNETS, "Sappho and Phaon" (1796); a verse comedy, "Nobody" (1794); and a tragedy, "The Sicilian Lover" (1796); as well as eight novels. She adopted a number of voices, adopting pseudonyms such as *Horace Juvenal, Tabitha Bramble, Laura Maria, Sappho,* and *Anne Frances Randall.* Despite her continued poor health, she managed a social literary life, with her friends including the romantic poets William Wordsworth and Samuel Taylor Coleridge and the feminist Mary Wollstonecraft and her husband, William Godwin, parents to Mary Shelley. Robinson would carry on a spirited correspondence with Godwin, with whom she quarreled at one point. Despite their disagreements, Godwin would be one of only two people, in addition to Maria Elizabeth, who attended Robinson's funeral. She died at age 42 on December 26, 1800, of "dropsy in the chest," meaning fluid on the lungs, with her work surviving her.

Although her exact age remained in question for a time, Robinson's correspondence helped later critics determine facts about her life, as did her unfinished *Memoir*. Popularly anthologized poems include "London's Summer Morning," "JANUARY, 1795," which expresses her disillusion with her culture and its seeming lack of values, and "TO THE POET COLERIDGE." Robinson remained known into the 19th century for her relationship with King George IV during his youth, as the couple were the subject of various novels. In 1826 Robinson's publisher, Sir Richard Phillips, attempted to sell back to the royal family a lock of the king's hair that Robinson had retained as a keepsake.

Robinson received little scholarly attention until the 1990s, when feminist critics rediscovered her work. However, she still has not received the serious notice of other women writers of her era. Although Coleridge labeled her a genius, Mary Robinson is still not known in the way she had hoped, as a woman of letters, a wish she had expressed in her memoir. Paula Byrne produced the first recent biography, containing a bibliography of early references to Robinson.

BIBLIOGRAPHY

Bolton, Betsy. "Romancing the Stone: 'Perdita' Robinson in Wordsworth's London." *English Literary History* 64 (1997): 727–759.

Byrne, Paula. *Perdita: The Literary, Theatrical, Scandalous Life of Mary Robinson.* New York: Random House, 2004.

Cracian, Adrianna. "Violence against Difference: Mary Wollstonecraft and Mary Robinson." *Bucknell Review* 42 (1998): 111–141.

Labbe, Jacqueline M. "Selling One's Sorrows: Charlotte Smith, Mary Robinson and the Marketing of Poetry." *Wordsworth Circle* 25 (1994): 68–71.

Lee, Debbie. *The Wild Wreath*: Cultivating a Poetic Circle for Mary Robinson." *Studies in the Literary Imagination* 30 (1997): 23–34.

Mollow, J. Fitzgerald, ed. *Beaux & Belles of England: Mrs. Mary Robinson Written by Herself with the Lives of the Duchesses of Gordon and Devonshire by Grace and Philip Wharton.* London: The Grollier Society, n.d.

Robinson, Daniel. "From 'Mingled Measure' to 'Ecstatic Measures'": Mary Robinson's Poetic Reading of 'Kubla Khan.'" *Wordsworth Circle* 26 (1993): 4–7.

Setzer, Sharon. "Mary Robinson's Sylphid Self: The End of Feminine Self-Fashioning." *Philological Quarterly* 75 (1996): 501–520.

ROCHESTER, JOHN WILMOT, SECOND EARL OF (1648–1680)

John Wilmot was born near Woodstock, the son of a loyal Royalist father and a mother who was a Puritan sympathizer. The first earl of Rochester, reputedly a hard drinker, had remained devoted to Charles II in exile. He earned his title in 1652 for meritorious service to Charles II. The younger Wilmot lost his father in 1658 as the first earl died abroad, never to enjoy the Restoration. Wilmot spent a short time at Oxford in Wadham College, beginning at age 12, where he reportedly first displayed his penchant for all manner of debauchery. He matriculated by age 14, earning his M.A. degree granted by the University's chancellor, the earl of Clarendon, who happened also to be Wilmot's uncle.

After completion of the fashionable Continental tour Wilmot joined the Royalist forces, distinguishing himself in battle against the Dutch. His military skill and Royalist sympathies made him a favorite of Charles II. After returning to England, Wilmot earned a reputation as the most famous womanizer and master of public perversion of his era, and his constant intoxication was legend. His kidnapping of his future bride, the wealthy Elizabeth Malet, in 1665, became a part of the local mythology. The famed diarist Samuel Pepys wrote details of the kidnapping to his wife. He described Wilmot's hiring horsemen to pull the young heiress from her carriage into his own, where two female escorts waited. Although Wilmot was captured, Elizabeth's whereabouts remained unknown for some time, causing an angry King Charles to order Wilmot to imprisonment in the Tower. Once Elizabeth returned safely to her father, Wilmot was released; he married Elizabeth two years later. The two remained oddly devoted to one another, despite her fury and disgust over his long absences and well-publicized affairs, many with the most tawdry of partners.

Wilmot became a popular poet and wit, specializing in pornographic poetry in the libertine tradition, that is, a tradition reflecting the values of the intelligent skeptic who constantly questioned traditional ideas regarding morality. Libertine poetry and drama drew from the political ideas of Hobbes and Machiavelli, applying those ideas to sexual encounters. It also took inspiration from the writings of Epicurus, popular during the

Restoration, in their consideration of hedonism. Their lyrics also were based in the courtly tradition of poetry by JOHN SUCKLING, RICHARD LOVELACE, and THOMAS CAREW. Wilmot and others used undisguised sexual references, in some critics' opinions, in order to express disgust. In 20th-century criticism such blatant terms were viewed as part of the language or terminology of eroticism.

The libertines took an extreme interest in women, preferring their company in most cases to that of men. Wilmot's involvement in the theater led to promotion of the stage career of one of his many mistresses, Elizabeth Barry; she became the most famous female actor of the Restoration. Wilmot set upon a self-destructive course of sex and drink, once claiming to have been drunk for five uninterrupted years. He frequently read his poetry at court, where its content, overly bawdy even for Restoration tastes, proved at once scandalous and attractive to the court circle. He at last overstepped civil boundaries in a poetic lampoon of the king and was banished from court for several years. Eventually Charles relented and requested that Wilmot, who by that time was in poor health, return to court.

Wilmot patronized various poets, including George Villiers, earl of Buckingham, who engaged in a public dispute with the poet laureate JOHN DRYDEN. Villiers was a member of Wilmot's "Merry Gang," so dubbed by the poet ANDREW MARVELL. That group was believed to have executed the savage physical attack against Dryden that almost killed him. Despite such suspicions, the group held the public's fascination from about 1666 to 1680, the year of Wilmot's death, a result of advanced syphilis and the effects of alcohol. Returning home to die in Elizabeth's care, he apparently underwent a religious conversion, something long desired by his mother. This supposed act of piety became a useful weapon for the church, which publicized it widely.

Little of Wilmot's poetry was published in his lifetime, deemed too sexually explicit, and instead circulated in manuscript form. Despite his choice of unbridled sexual pleasure as a subject, Wilmot's skilled use of satire became a model for later far more conservative poets, including ALEXANDER POPE. His best known and most published poem is his "A SATYRE AGAINST MANKIND."

While Wilmot's poetry most certainly objectified women and clearly identified their sexual organs by profane name, feminist critics find interesting the power he assigns women. They not only control weaker men who engage in sex indiscriminately, in most poems they also prove the better lovers and have much stronger physical constitutions and capacity for sexual enjoyment than do their male lovers, for example in "The IMPERFECT ENJOYMENT." Wilmot made clear his great contempt for cultural mores, taking delight in insulting the ideals others professed to value. He did not hesitate to take aim in his poetry at the hypocrisy that produced the double standard in regard to sex from which women's reputations might suffer, while men's reputations benefited. His poetry remained on a list of works too scandalous for public consumption; in the early 20th century his writings were burned by New York Customs. Graham Greene wrote a biography suppressed for more than 40 years prior to publication because of Wilmot's reputation. Wilmot's work attracted interest in the later 20th century as sexual mores relaxed and remains readily available in both print and electronic form. His life was the subject of a 2004 film, *The Libertine,* with Johnny Depp in the leading role.

BIBLIOGRAPHY

Adlard, John, ed. *The Debt to Pleasure: John Wilmot, Earl of Rochester, in the Eyes of His Contemporaries and in His Own Poetry and Prose.* New York: Routledge, 2002.

Campion, Peter. "Rochester's Honesty." *New Criterion* 23, no. 8 (April 2005): 17–20.

Caterson, Simon. "The Devil Is an Englishman." *Quadrant* 50, nos. 7–8 (July–August 2006): 91–92.

Combe, Kirk. "'But loads of sh– almost choked the way': Shadwell, Dryden, Rochester, and the Summer of 1676." *Texas Studies in Literature and Language* 37, no. 2 (summer 1995): 127–164.

Farley-Hills, David, ed. *Rochester: The Critical Heritage.* New York: Barnes & Noble, 1972.

Goldsworthy, Cephus. *The Satyr: An Account of the Life and Work, Death and Salvation, of John Wilmot, Second Earl of Rochester.* London: Weidenfeld & Nicolson, 2001.

Greene, Graham. *Lord Rochester's Monkey: Being the Life of John Wilmot, Second Earl of Rochester.* New York: Penguin Books, 1988.

Holton, Robert. "Sexuality and Social Hierarchy in Sidney and Rochester." *Mosaic* 24, no. 1 (winter 1991): 47–65.

Johnson, James William. *A Profane Wit: The Life of John Wilmot, Earl of Rochester.* Rochester, N.Y.: University of Rochester Press, 2004.

Lamb, Jeremy. *So Idle a Rogue: The Life and Death of Lord Rochester.* London: Allison & Busby, 1993.

Narain, Mona. "Libertine Spaces and the Female Body in the Poetry of Rochester and Ned Ward." *English Literary History* 72, no. 3 (fall 2005): 553–576.

Sisk, John P. "The Letters of John Wilmot, Earl of Rochester." *American Scholar* 51 (winter 1982): 116–118.

"RULE BRITANNIA" James Thomson (1740)

"Rule Britannia," the popular British song and ode, originated in *Alfred, A Masque,* a collaborative work by James Thomson and David Mallet. First performed to celebrate the birthday of August, Prince Frederick's daughter, the masque proved political in its failure to include a reference to the current king of England, George II. It was the final work in which Thomson expressed overt Whig sentiment, projecting the patriotic themes that "Rule Britannia" so well captured. Stanza 4 declares,

> Thee haughty tyrants ne'er shall tame;
> All their attempts to bend thee down
> Will but arouse thy generous flame;
> But work their woe, and thy renown.

Viewed by most as an attack on the Stuart monarchy, the masque received little later attention, other than in 1745, when its producers may have hoped it would provoke anti-Jacobite feelings. However, "Rule Britannia" would become a public institution of sorts. While Thomson wrote the lyrics, Thomas Arne's music gave the song its true appeal. Each of its six six-line stanzas concludes with the two-line refrain "Rule, Britannia, rule the waves; / Britons never will be slaves." Mallet would revise *Alfred* after Thomson's death and claim full credit for the altered "Rule Britannia."

BIBLIOGRAPHY
Scott, Mary Jane W. *James Thomson, Anglo-Scot.* Athens: University of Georgia Press, 1988.

S

"SATTURDAY: THE SMALL POX" LADY MARY WORTLEY MONTAGU (1747)

Written during LADY MARY WORTLEY MONTAGU's 1716–17 stay in London prior to traveling to Constantinople with her husband, her "Satturday: The Small Pox" is one of a collection of six eclogues. Intended as satiric, the eclogue remained a mixture of multiple conventions, including those of the pastoral, classic, and burlesque. Others of her era, such as the poet and dramatist JOHN GAY, attempted eclogue, but Montagu has been credited with some of the best examples. Her forceful, autobiographical style marked her eclogues with spirit and the sharp biting tone appropriate to satire.

The eclogue features Flavia, who takes her position as the Saturday entry among five others also marked as days in the week to organize the group as a series. Flavia's complaint focuses on her loss of beauty, her lamentation echoing Montagu's own. As her heroine, had, Montagu had experienced the ravages of smallpox, suffering from a disfigured face. The value of beauty remains Montagu's target, as fashionable society believed that a lovely physical appearance made a woman a valued commodity. While money could purchase a husband, beauty allowed a woman greater choice and might ensure a greater degree of dedication of her mate. Montagu reinforces the idea that despite the ephemeral nature of beauty, as the critic Ann Messenger explains, it translates into power and perhaps wealth, and that fact remains evidence of a corrupt world. While it may prove aesthetically valuable, in a moral sense beauty lacks worth.

Montagu's genuine belief in that fact remains a crucial aspect of her poem.

"Satturday" consists almost completely of Flavia's dialogue lament. As ALEXANDER POPE, another of Montagu's contemporaries, did in his "The RAPE OF THE LOCK," Montague adopts a MOCK-HEROIC tone to tell her tale. Flavia remains distressed, noting in line 5 her great change since the beauty of her youth. With the loss of her fine appearance, she has also lost "The promis'd Happyness for Years to come." She had spent much time in front of the mirror, as had Pope's heroine Belinda, and had reaped various treasures from her period of social success, including opera tickets and china. The most difficult loss was that of the attention of men, who were known to leave activities such as debates just to catch a glimpse of the beautiful Flavia. She reminisces,

> For me, the Soldier has soft verses writ,
> For me, the Beau has aim'd to be a Wit,
> For me, the Wit to Nonsense was betraid,
> The Gamester has for me his Dun delaid. (28–33)

Flavia obviously took pride in her ability to provide a distraction and control the actions of others, particularly males. As Flavia assesses the possessions in her room, she notes with longing the presence of her portrait at her prime, as well as her now-little-used toilette. The main reason "Meaner beauties," as she labels other women in line 55, attract attention is lack of competition from Flavia. Her condition will force her to retire to hide her face "in shades," as Montagu establishes the pastoral, or innocent rural life, as mere escape from the more attractive city life. Flavia dreams of hiding where "Gentle streams will weep" over her sadness.

While Montagu emphasizes the vacuity of Flavia's former life, suggesting that beauty occupies her society to the extreme, her obvious longing for what she feels to be a real loss remains poignant. Perhaps most sad, as Messenger notes, is the fact that while Flavia may hide in nature, the pastoral remains merely a poetic concept. Montagu could find no such refuge in her real world.

BIBLIOGRAPHY

Messenger, Ann. "Town Eclogues." In *His and Hers: Essays in Restoration and Eighteenth-Century Literature*, 84–107. Lexington: University Press of Kentucky, 1986.

"SATYRE AGAINST MANKIND, A" John Wilmot, second earl of Rochester (1680)

Known for his focus on sexual matters in his poetry, John Wilmot, 2nd earl of Rochester, also wrote the libertine-style satire "A Satyre against Mankind," considered among his highest achievements. Probably written around 1675, the poem has among its sources works on rationality by Hobbes and Montaigne. The copy later published and now best known appeared in its basic version in the 1680 *Poems on Several Occasions*, presently housed in the Huntington Library. A portion of the modern version also appeared in a 1679 broadside and another in *Miscellaneous Works of Rochester and Roscommon* (1707). The poem's format varies, with its 225 lines appearing in stanzas composed of two to 26 lines, occasionally departing from rhyming couplets. Rochester considers the folly that he sees as inherent in man's attempts to lead rational lives.

The opening seven lines make clear the speaker's opinion, that animals live superior lives to those of men:

> Were I—who to my cost already am
> One of those strange, prodigious creatures,
>   man—
> A spirit free to choose for my own share
> What sort of flesh and blood I pleased to wear,

> I'd be a dog, a monkey, or a bear,
> Or anything but that vain animal,
> Who is so proud of being rational.

The speaker notes that man ignores his five senses to adopt a sixth, that of reasoning. Believing his power to reason superior to that of instinct in guiding his actions, he leaves "light of nature, sense, behind" and instead "Pathless and dangerous wand'ring ways" takes. He stumbles from one thought to the next and finally falls "Into Doubt's boundless sea where, like to drown, / Books bear him up awhile," keeping man afloat through "bladders of Philosophy." Rochester makes a major point early on, noting that most of man's attempts at rational thought are made to delay having to face his own mortality, that is, "In hopes still to o'ertake the escaping light." Expert at the use of figurative language (figure of speech), Rochester enhances reader interest with abundant use of metaphors and similes. He finally uses the term *death* when closing the second stanza, writing,

> Then old age and experience, hand in hand,
> Lead him to death, make him to understand,
> After a search so painful, and so long,
> That all his life he has been in the wrong.

That said, the speaker continues to expound on man's error, supplying examples and trying to explain human behavior.

The third stanza proposes that pride acted upon man, "drew him in, as cheats their bubbles catch," causing him to seek a wisdom that destroyed his happiness. Wit supplies a "frivolous pretence / Of pleasing others, at his own expense," he claims, as wits are regarded as no better than whores. Rochester probably reflects on his own position in society, as he was considered one of his era's greatest wits. His bitter statements reveal that when "fops," the wits like himself "escape," "'Tis not that they're beloved, but fortunate, / And therefore what they fear, at heart they hate." Rochester introduces the idea of fear, a term that will reappear multiple times in his poem for emphasis. Popular thinking held that rationality helped overcome fear of the unknown; according to Rochester's speaker, instead it actually promotes fear. His cynical attitude proved typical of the libertine approach to poetry.

The next section introduces a second voice, which wonders of the speaker, "'What rage torments in your degenerate mind, / To make you rail at reason, and mankind.'" This outside voice concludes by repeating the prevalent attitude toward reason, that it helps dignify man, distinguishing him from beast. It allows him to "take a flight beyond material sense" and "Dive into mysteries, then soaring pierce / The flaming limits of the universe." The speaker takes issue with this comment, but, as God spoke to the prophet in the Bible regarding his plans to destroy Sodom and Gomorrah, tells the adviser that if he can find one man fitting the description of "reasonable," he may relent.

Rochester includes references to several figures known to his readers, which he believes represents the false reason against which he argues. They include the Reverend Nathaniel Ingelo, author of a popular religious allegory in the romance tradition titled *Bentivolio and Urania* (1660); Simon Patrick, bishop of Ely, whose work resembling Bunyan's *Pilgrim's Progress, The Parable of the Pilgrim,* was published in 1664; and the Puritan Richard Sibbes, who published various inspirational pieces labeled *Soliloquies* by Rochester. The references are not flattering, as the speaker describes Ingelo's "pathetic pen" and notes that because of the types of writing produced by these three individuals, he despises "This supernatural gift that makes a mite / Think he's an image of the infinite." The speaker continues in this stanza to reflect on what he sees as a ridiculous and arrogant claim by man to resemble God. In his opinion such belief offers a false promise that makes "a whimsical philosopher / Before the spacious world his tub prefer," a reference to Diogenes' belief that one practices virtue by resisting all pleasure. The speaker uses this example to note that many retire from life simply to think, but that thought should be "given for action's government," and to cease action results in impertinence. Thus "Our sphere of action is life's happiness, / And he that thinks beyond thinks like an ass."

In the next stanza the speaker labels his own reason *right* and claims to obey it, as it is distinguished from false reasoning by sense, giving "us rules of good and ill" and boundaries for "desires, with a reforming will /

To keep 'em more in vigour, not to kill." Further stanzas hold that the wisest creatures attain reason "By surest means." He refers to Sir Thomas Meres, a political figure and prominent Whig Party member, whom he compares to a hound to indicate that the dog is more reasonable. The speaker argues through many lines the superiority of beasts, who kill only for practical reasons, to man, who lacks reason for various atrocities he commits. Man betrays his fellow man through fear:

Not through necessity, but wantonness.
For hunger or for love they [beasts] bite, or tear,
Whilest wretched man is still in arms for fear.
For fear he arms, and is of arms afraid:
From fear, to fear, successively betrayed.
Base fear, the source whence his best passions came.
His boasted honour, and his dear-bought fame.

The speaker notes that if a reasonable man may be discovered, he will recant. Among places where he believes no "just man" exists are the court, a place for bribes and avarice, and the church, where pastors commit adultery with drunken women, gossip, "rail at men of sense," and view their bastard progeny from the pulpit. He defines a good man, a godlike man, as

. . . a meek, humble man, of honest sense,
Who preaching peace does practice continence;
Whose pious life's a proof he does believe
Mysterious truths which no man can conceive.

Rochester concludes with a couplet that adds a caveat, should such a godlike man exist. He writes, "If such there are, yet grant me this at least, / Man differs more from man than man from beast." Critics note Rochester's influence on writers who may have disagreed with his sentiment but drew from his style, most notably ALEXANDER POPE. Such influence may be seen in a comparison and contrast of Rochester's "A Satyre against Man" with Pope's *An Essay on Man.*

BIBLIOGRAPHY

Fisher, Nicholas. "The Contemporary Reception of Rochester's 'A Satyr against Mankind.'" *Review of English Studies* 57 (2006): 185–200.

Sanchez, Melissa E. "Libertine and Romance in Rochester's
Poetry." *Eighteenth-Century Studies* 38, no. 3 (spring
2005): 441–459.

SCANSION
Scansion is the act of analyzing a
poem for its METER and stresses, or rhythm. When
"scanning," one marks syllables as stressed and
unstressed; then divides the lines into feet, units containing one stressed syllable and one or more unstressed
syllables; and counts the number of resultant units.

SEDLEY, SIR CHARLES (1639–1701)
Charles Sedley was born at Aylesford in Kent, matricu-
lating through Wadham College, Oxford, in 1656
without a degree. He succeeded to his title as baron
upon the death of his elder brother that same year and
became member of Parliament for New Romney, serving terms through 1701. Characterized by critics as
one of a "mob" of aristocrats who dabbled in writing,
Sedley produced some popular songs in his RESTORA-
TION drama. During his near-40-year public career, he
gained a reputation as a poetry patron as well as a dramatist. His best work included *The Mulberry Garden*
(1668), and he staged two additional comedies and
two tragedies. His works were bawdy and indelicate,
causing those at the Duke's Theater to refuse to stage
his comedy *Bellamira, or, The Mistress* (1687), which
he based on the *Eunachus* of Terence.

The dashing and scandalous JOHN WILMOT, second
EARL OF ROCHESTER, proved one of Sedley's favorite companions. The editor Charles Wells Moulton includes
many comments about Sedley in his second volume of
*The Library of Literary Criticism of English and American
Authors* (1959). The famous diarist Samuel Pepys wrote
of "the late frolick and debauchery" of Sedley and others who ran "up and down all the night, almost naked
through the streets; and at last fighting and being beat
by the watch and clapped up all night," adding that
King Charles II always defended him. Sir George Etheredge praised Sedley, writing "Few of our plays can
boast of more wit than I have heard him speak at a
supper. Some barren sparks have found fault with
what he has formerly done, only because the fairness
of the soil has produced so big a crop." While ALEXAN-
DER POPE noted, "Sedley is a very insipid writer," he

added, "except in some few of his little love-verses."
Edwin Whipple wrote that Sedley distinguished himself by "writing poems of considerable impurity of idea
and considerable purity of language." Songs that
received critical acclaim and continue to appear in
anthologies include "PHILLIS IS MY ONLY JOY" and "Love
Still Has Something of the Sea."

BIBLIOGRAPHY
Pinto, V. De Sola. *Sir Charles Sedley, 1639–1701: A Study in
the Life and Literature of the Restoration.* Folcroft, Pa.: Folcroft Library Editions, 1973.

SEWARD, ANNA HUNTER (1742–1809)
Anna Seward's father was the Reverend Thomas
Seward, rector of Eyam, Derbyshire. Her father,
described as witty and agreeable, matriculated through
Westminster and Cambridge and served as private
chaplain to the duke of Grafton, whose son he tutored.
Anna's mother, described as a handsome woman, was
Elizabeth Hunter, daughter of a rector who taught
SAMUEL JOHNSON in school, who would later become an
important person in Anna Seward's career.

After the late marriage for both the Sewards settled
at Eyam near the peak featured in the novel *Peveril of
the Peak* by Sir Walter Scott. Seward later began corresponding with Scott, who would also play a crucial
role in her later life. Anna, also listed as *Anne* and
Nancy in various accounts, was the first of four children, one of whom died as an infant; her mother also
experienced two stillborn births. At age seven Seward
moved with her family to Lichfield, Staffordshire,
where her father became prebendary of Salisbury
and canon residentiary of Lichfield, allowing him to
become a permanent part of the local clergy. He
entertained many important people, exposing his
daughter to social graces and expected behavior. A
writer, Mr. Seward contributed to Dodsley's *Collection* (1748), one piece titled "The Female right to Literature." He also served as editor for *Works*, a
10-volume collection of writings by Beaumont and
Fletcher.

Seward's desire to read and write alarmed her parents, who knew a "scribbling woman" often acquired a
dubious reputation. They also felt concern over what
would be a lifelong weight problem for Seward,

although, according to her biographer Margaret Ash-mun, Sir Walter Scott would chivalrously describe her as "a majestic presence." When the Sewards offered to provide foster care for a friend's five-year-old daughter, Honora Sneyd, they hoped the child's presence would occupy Anna's energies and shape her into a young woman desirable as a wife. The scientist Dr. Erasmus Darwin, a friend and neighbor, advised Mr. Seward that "no more verses were to be allowed," advice that Seward followed. However, when Darwin read verses by Anna so well done that he at first believed them written by her father, he changed his mind and encouraged her writing. Darwin and Anna Seward remained lifelong friends; in 1804 she published *Life of Dr. Darwin,* which would be roundly criticized as a poor presentation, a charge that she would counter. Seward's father, in some accounts jealous of her talent, upheld his edict against her writing, insisting that she spend her time in more suitable pursuits, such as needlework. Just before the age of 20 Seward lost her closest companion and older sister, Sarah, who died just prior to her wedding. Supposedly Seward had been involved at one point with Sarah's fiancé, setting a pattern for future complicated relationships. While she would enjoy several romances, about which she wrote in correspondence, she would never marry.

Seward visited London and began her writing career in earnest, encouraged by Darwin and other fellow writers in the neoclassicist school. As was her foster sister Honora, Seward was judged by many to have "more intellect than was deemed actually necessary for feminine perfection." By 1770 she enjoyed interacting with a broad intellectual circle who became familiar with her poetry, although she had not yet published. Samuel Johnson dubbed her "the Swan of Lichfield," as her career later flourished. She published "A Rural Coronation" in F. N. C. Mundy's *Needwood Forest* in 1776 and began to attend poetry sessions led by Anna Miller at Bath-Easton. Encouraged by Miller, in 1778 Seward entered a poetry competition with "Invocation of the Comic Muse," a poem influenced by JOHN MILTON's "L'ALLEGRO." Her "Elegy on Captain Cook" followed the death of the adventurer in 1779 and sold for one shilling and sixpence, although a theory that Dr. Darwin had written the poem later emerged. However,

the rumor began in writings by the novelist Maria Edgeworth, whose relative Richard Lovell Edgeworth had married Honora after having been rejected by Seward. This fact leads some critics to believe that the hard feelings in the Edgeworth family may have contributed to the claim.

By the mid-1770s Seward's father suffered poor mental health, and his care contributed to the 1780 death of her mother. Honora also died that fall, leaving Seward again to grieve what she felt to be a great loss; she later wrote several odes to honor her foster sister. She continued to produce poetry including elegies, and the *Gentleman's Magazine* described Seward as "a poetess of the age, in whom almost every poetical excellence seems to be united." In 1781 she published a poem mourning the loss in the American Revolution of Major Andre, a soldier and purported spy who had a relationship with Honora. She attacked George Washington in her *Monody on the Unfortunate Major Andre,* who had been executed as a spy. Washington would years later through an emissary defend himself to her for his part in the major's death.

Seward's reputation grew, and her name appeared in multiple references in the 1780s into the 1790s, particularly as she often commented critically on work by her fellow poets. Her popular verse novel in four epistles titled *Louisa* (1784) enjoyed five editions. The year of its publication she became close friends with the poet William Hayley, and the two were popularly conceived for a short time as the best poets of the day. However, readers quickly tired of their letters written in support of one another.

In 1785 Johnson's famous companion and biographer James Boswell contacted Seward for quotations to include in his *Life of Samuel Johnson* (1791). Although he rejected what she wrote, Boswell interviewed Seward in order to collect additional facts about Johnson. Seward continued to care for her father, whose health declined until his death in 1790. She had lived in the family home supported by the bishop in Lichfield in a type of servitude attending to his needs, only briefly escaping in 1788 to visit her birthplace. There she wrote her most often-anthologized poem "EYAM," a somber remembrance of her father in better days. After her father's death she stayed on at Lichfield, well supported on an annuity of £200 that allowed her comfortably to continue her highly visible existence.

In one of her many public literary criticisms, Seward responded to what she viewed as a hagiographic presentation of Johnson in Boswell's biography in letters printed in the *Gentleman's Magazine* in 1793 and 1794. Later critics termed her efforts foolish, the product of an irritable and bored woman, who published her criticism far too long after the biography's publication for it to be meaningful. Boswell's response was swift, described as "malicious and insulting," and Seward backed out of the public debate after a few exchanges with the formidable biographer. She followed a visit to Lady Eleanor Butler and Sarah Ponsonby with a collection containing an entry about her visit, *Llangollen Vale, With Other Poems* (1796).

Seward printed some SONNETs in 1799, which she hoped would secure her lasting fame. Increasingly melancholy, she continued her year's-long correspondence with Sir Walter Scott. While he described her letters as too sentimental for his tastes, he wrote, "When I did see her, however, she interested me very much." Confident that subsequent generations of readers would remain interested in her work, in 1784 Seward wrote to Scott's publisher, Mr. A. Constable. She informed him that he would receive after her death "exclusive copyright of Twelve Volumes, quarto, half-bound" of her correspondence. She followed with a proposal for a posthumous collection of her poems, which would result in the two-volume *Poetical Works*, its introduction written by Scott. Scott would refuse to contribute to the collection of her correspondence, as he, as did others, believed that she had considerably altered the letters through careful editing. Despite failing health, Seward continued to read avidly. She wrote public commentary and private correspondence about poetry by Samuel Taylor Coleridge and Robert Southey, to whom she referred as "Our rising stars."

Contrary to her expectations, Seward remained mostly forgotten after her death until she caught the interest of 20th-century feminist critics. While she was not considered a major poet, her participation in criticism and publication during an era when such activities remained the prerogative of men gained Seward well-deserved attention.

BIBLIOGRAPHY

Ashmun, Margaret. *The Singing Swan: An Account of Anna Seward and Her Acquaintance with Dr. Johnson, Boswell, and Others of Their Time.* New York: Greenwood Press, 1931.

Eger, Elizabeth et al., eds. *Bluestocking Feminism: Writings of the Bluestocking Circle, 1738–1785.* London: Pickering & Chatto, 1999.

Heiland, Donna. "Swan Songs: The Correspondence of Anna Seward and James Boswell." *Modern Philology* 90, no. 3 (February 1993): 381–391.

Jung, Sandro. "Two New Poems by Anna Seward." *American Notes & Queries* 16, no. 3 (summer 2003): 19–21.

Lucas, E. V. *A Swan and Her Friends.* London: Methuen, 1907.

SHAPE POEM

A shape poem is so named because its typographical shape represents its subject. The form existed since Hellenistic times and continues to be occasionally used. Typically critics consider such presentations weak poetry, as the shape, or physical form, supersedes skill of expression. Famous exceptions may be found in work by GEORGE HERBERT, a religious poet whose widely anthologized shape poems define that approach for most readers. Examples include "The ALTAR," and "EASTER WINGS," neither of which falls into the category of "false wit" assigned to more feeble approaches. A 20th-century example of the shape poem is Dylan Thomas's "Vision and Prayer."

"SILENCE, AND STEALTH OF DAYS!"

HENRY VAUGHAN (1650) Included in HENRY VAUGHAN's religious poetry collection *Silex Scintillans*, "Silence, and Stealth of Days!" expresses the poet's grief after the death of his brother, William, in the civil wars. Critics note it is one of the few poems by Vaughan that contain its own internal dating, as he writes, "'tis now / Since thou art gone, / Twelve hundred hours." This means 50 days had passed since William Vaughan's death, dating the poem during the first week of September 1648. After the time reference Vaughan incorporates light and dark imagery, as the speaker notes that "clouds hang on," but like one in a cave "Locked from the light" who "Fixeth a solitary lamp, / To brave the night," he retreats back into time, "Unto that hour / Which showed thee last." This second reference to time involves a flashback, as "that hour" has defeated his brother's "light, and power."

Vaughan attempts to recall his brother's existence by having his speaker imagine him still alive. The speaker eventually understands the futility of such an approach and instead turns for comfort to a new spiritual awareness. Vaughan extends the light metaphor, referring to the deceased as composed of "Those beams" that have been snuffed. He who dies may suffer "That dark," and death "sleeps in its known, / And common urn," where the term *urn* refers to a coffin or burial container. However, he introduces a note of hope for believers in God through redemption, writing, "But those fled to their Maker's throne / There shine, and burn." The image of humans' burning remains positive, playing on the previous metaphor of light and fire as equal. His own soul "tracks" that of his brother, allowing the two to remain united for all time. While the allusion to souls' tracking one another was not original to Vaughan, his application proved stronger than that of other poets who employed it:

> O could I track them! But souls must
> Track one the other.
> And now the spirit, not the dust
> Must be thy brother.

Vaughan concludes with positive imagery, writing,

> Yet I have one pearl by whose light
> All things I see,
> And in the heart of earth, and night
> Find Heaven, and thee.

Critics disagree over the meaning of, "one pearl by whose light / All things I see." The pearl may refer to Vaughan's first wife, or it may refer to the Bible, in which "light" commonly suggested knowledge through spiritual awakening and symbolized Christ.

BIBLIOGRAPHY
Rudrum, Alan. *Henry Vaughan*. Cardiff: University of Wales Press, 1981.

"SINCE SHE WHOME I LOVED, HATH PAID HER LAST DEBT" JOHN DONNE (1633)

Probably JOHN DONNE's most tender SONNET, "Since she whome I loved, hath paid her last debt" marks his loss of his wife. Ann Donne died on August 16, 1617, at age 33 one week after the stillbirth of their 12th child. As do all of his HOLY SONNETS, this SONNET focuses on Donne's relationship with God. He often used death as a vehicle for investigation.

In this poem he considers whether God might have used his wife to test him. Donne marks his tone with resignation rather than anger or great grief, a sign, according to the scholar Helen Gardner, that he probably had not written it immediately after his wife's death. His attempt to see his life's burdens as God's love in action by characterizing them as a lover's strategy resembles the approach he took in "A Hymn to Christ." Gardner sees the sonnet to Donne's wife as an initial attempt at the method that appears more sophisticated in the later hymn; therefore, she feels the sonnet should be dated prior to Donne's journey to the Continent in 1619. He had expressed the sentiment in a letter three years earlier to his mother after "the death of her Daughter," writing that God seemed to "repent" of having afforded her joy on earth, "that he might keep your Soul in continuall exercise, and longing, and assurance, of coming immediately to him." The purpose, according to Donne, of God's strategy was to remove from the hearts of the faithful affection for the world, better allowing them to depart their material life.

The speaker begins,
> Since she whom I loved hath paid her last debt
> To Nature, and to hers, and my good is dead
> And her soul early into heaven ravished,
> Wholly on heavenly things my mind is set.

Gardner notes a traditional format for Donne exhibited in the opening lines "Since she whom I loved, hath paid her last debt / To Nature, and to hers, and my good is dead," allowing "speech stress and metrical stress [to] pull against each other." In the second line his reference to "my good" as "dead" either provokes the thought that death precludes the possibility of acting "good" any longer or may suggest that her death has yielded "good" to both her and Donne, through her entrance into heaven and the happiness God's presence will afford. While he misses her, his understanding that she has been received blameless by God comforts him. She died young, "early," but that allows the speaker to focus now only on his religious life. However, he has not had much success in that focus. He adopts the metaphysical CONCEIT of thirst to explain his longing for his wife, a thirst that study of his faith does not relieve:

Here the admiring her my mind did whet
To seek thee, God; so streams do show the head;
But though I have found thee, and thou my
    thirst hast fed,
A holy thirsty dropsy melts me yet.

Because the speaker at first believed his love for "she" would have moved him even closer to God, the fact that he remains thirsty causes him to wonder whether she did not prove a hindrance.

As the speaker continues, he asks, "But why should I beg more love, whenas thou / Dost woo my soul, for hers offering all thine." The simple lines express a simple sentiment, that because God has claimed, first "wooing" his soul, the speaker need not ask for another love. The spiritual love proves superior to physical love. Typically of Donne, he uses mostly single-syllable words to great effect. Donne uses the PETRARCHAN style in his sonnet, with the first eight lines outlining the subject or question and the final six lines responding. By beginning the ninth line with the word *But,* both a conjunction that joins the preceding ideas to the following and a signal that a contradiction will follow, Donne helps readers make the turn into the second part of the sonnet.

The final four lines provide a gentle picture of the speaker's fear, that God may be jealous of his lingering love for his wife. He suggests that he perhaps gave in to temptation by enjoying a worldly relationship of the flesh, one that would preempt God's position in his life:

And dost not only fear lest I allow
My love to saints and angels, things divine,
But in thy tender jealousy dost doubt
Lest the world, flesh, yea, devil put thee out.

BIBLIOGRAPHY
Gardner, Helen, ed. *John Donne: The Divine Poems.* New York: Oxford University Press, 1969.

"SINCE THERE'S NO HELP, COME LET US KISS AND PART" MICHAEL DRAYTON

(1594) The SONNET titled "Since there's no help, come let us kiss and part" remains the best known poem by MICHAEL DRAYTON. In the Elizabethan sonnet form it first appeared as number 61 in Drayton's 64-sonnet sequence titled *Ideas Mirror.* As did his contemporaries, Drayton differentiated between his sonnets only by number; their first lines were later adopted as titles. Widely anthologized, this sonnet proves far more readable than many of Drayton's poems, which tended to be burdened with elevated terminology and heavy with FIGURATIVE LANGUAGE (FIGURE OF SPEECH) that obscured, rather than clarified, their themes.

The first line of the sonnet serves as its title, presenting also its topic. The speaker finds himself in a relationship that no longer proves satisfying, and he wishes that both lovers might separate with a minimum of pain. As is common to the Elizabethan format, the sonnet's first 12 lines, in iambic pentameter, present and elaborate upon the problem or topic, while the final couplet acts as a summary or final epigram. The *help* referred to in the first line is used as if the speaker says, "We cannot solve our problem or mend what has become a permanent rift." His tone remains bitter in the second line, as he adds, "Nay, I have done, you get no more of me."

Drayton fashions a seemingly angry lover who declares in lines 3 and 4, "And I am glad, yea glad with all my heart / That thus so cleanly I myself can free." He wants to make what later would be termed a "clean break," in the sense that nothing will remain to burden him emotionally in the future; thus he can be free of all attachments to his love. As if confirming a business deal, he commands his onetime love, "Shake hands forever, cancel all our vows." She remains silent, not allowed a response, so the reader is unsure of her reaction. However, the speaker's intent cannot be mistaken, as he suggests, his tone softening a bit,

And when we meet at any time again,
Be it not seen in either of our brows
That we one jot of former love retain.

He wants to guard against any public display of regretted affection, instructing his lover not so much as to wrinkle her brow should they pass one another as they move about their business in town or attend social events.

Drayton then uses personification to transform love into a dying figure, complete with a death scene also attended by the personified figures of Passion and Faith:

> Now at the last gasp of Love's latest breath,
> When, his pulse failing, Passion speechless lies,
> When Faith is kneeling by his bed of death,
> And Innocence is closing up his eyes—

The lover has completely lost his tough demeanor, as he grieves in advance the loss of innocence represented by their love, perhaps a first for both. The dash at line 12's conclusion suspends the reader momentarily. It is neither an END-STOPPED LINE that ends with a period, nor an ENJAMBMENT, as the reader is to hesitate before continuing. As the reader moves ahead to read the concluding couplet, Drayton's IRONY remains clear. The final lines contradict the sentiment the speaker had so carefully constructed in the preceding 12 lines, as he admits that hope might linger, after all. It is the guest present, but not mentioned, at Love's deathbed:

> Now, if thou wouldst, when all have given him
>   over,
> From death to life thou mightst him yet recover.

After all of his stern resignation, the speaker reveals that his lover might yet resuscitate their passion. Only she has the power over life and death, and he hopes that she will exercise it.

"SLOW, SLOW, FRESH FOUNT" BEN JONSON (1600)

BEN JONSON included "Slow, Slow, Fresh Fount" as a LYRIC in the first act of his satiric comedy *Cynthia's Revels.* The play was one used by Jonson in a heated rivalry to lampoon Thomas Dekker and John Marston, who had done the same to Jonson. It focused on the theme of self-love, and Jonson created a character named Criticus based on himself. Criticus must navigate through the company of arrogant men to the virtuous Cynthia, a representation of Queen Elizabeth I, upon whom Jonson focuses an additional song in the comedy, "QUEEN AND HUNTRESS." The poet incorporates aspects of myth with recognizable details of court intrigue and speculates upon the life of a virtuous man amid scoundrels and profligates. These fops and court toadies have extraordinary egos, inflated through proximity to the Fountain of Narcissus; Narcissus was a mythological character charmed by his own reflection and eventually transformed into a flower. Before his transformation Echo had loved him, and she sings, mourning his absence.

"Slow, Slow, Fresh Fount" remains a strong example of the use of form to reflect a poem's meaning. The lines are worded so as to make them move as slowly as the fount of Jonson's title. The first line opens with four equally stressed syllables, or double spondees, in pairs marked by ALLITERATION, a difficult series to pronounce rapidly, which is followed by three iambs: "Slow, slow, fresh fount, keep time with my salt tears." The second line provides an even greater challenge to a quick tongue Jonson's word choice and arrangement. It suits the grieving manner of Echo: "Yet slower, yet, O faintly, gentle springs!" These heavy lines are followed by two lines of iambic pentameter that describe music as a "heavy part," employing marked alliteration. Jonson uses the *w* sound, an unusual choice for repetition, again because of its forced lengthy pronunciation when coupled with the required vowel: "Woe weeps out her division, when she sings." As Echo mourns the effects of her shower of grief upon the plants on which her tears fall, Jonson uses rhythm to emphasize her sentiment. Two short lines of iambic dimeter are followed by a single line of iambic trimeter, then a line that opens with a spondee in trimeter:

> Droop herbs and flowers;
> Fall grief in showers;
> Our beauties are not ours.
>   O, I could still.

The song concludes with three lines of varied length, the 10th line echoing the sound of melting snow, and the final line noting the withering of beauty. Recalling the myth of Narcissus, Jonson compares deflated pride to a flower trapped in freezing water from melting snow:

Like melting snow upon some craggy hill,
Drop, drop, drop, drop,
Since nature's pride is now a withered daffodil.

Jonson retains focus on water imagery as a symbol of grief and death, rather than as the traditional symbol of new life or rebirth. He later incorporates into *Cynthia's Revels* aspects of the medieval masque in order to focus on the price of sin, reflected by Narcissus's punishment for his pride.

SMART, CHRISTOPHER (1722–1771) Christopher Smart was born at Shipborne in Kent. He moved to Durham at the age of 11 years when his father died. In 1742 he graduated with a B.A. from Pembroke Hall, Cambridge, as a classics scholar and won a Craven Scholarship. In addition to classical languages Smart could read and write Hebrew and gained a reputation as brilliant and insightful. His later work carried marked influences by Horace's *Ars Poetica,* an extremely challenging Latin work Smart translated in 1756. He was elected a Cambridge Fellow in 1745. Two years later he wrote, produced, and acted in *The Grateful Fair, or, A Trip to Cambridge.* However, in November that year, he appeared to be gripped by religious obsession, which expressed itself in public prayer. Falling to his knees to pray loudly in parks and on the streets, Smart was judged a nuisance and imprisoned for debt. His obsessive behavior increased, but he was released from prison and returned to Cambridge in 1748 with the support of dedicated friends.

Smart moved in 1749 to London, where he worked as an editor for the printer John Newbery and later married Newbery's stepdaughter, Anna Maria Carnan. From 1750 to 1753 Smart worked as editor of, and contributed to, *The Student, or the Oxford and Cambridge Miscellany,* as well as *The Midwife, or, the Old Woman's Magazine.* His behavior suggested an alcohol problem during 1751–52 when he wrote a revue, *The Old Woman's Oratory,* and performed in it during its staging at the Haymarket Theater. He won five consecutive Seatonian Prizes for poetry between 1750 and 1755, his subject matter always the Supreme Being. His *Poems on Several Occasions* (1752) was well received, but his satiric epic poem on Dr. John Hill

titled *The Hilliad* published one year later proved unsuccessful. In 1753 he celebrated the birth of his first daughter, Marianne, or Polly, and a year later, that of his younger daughter, Elizabeth, or Bess. Information on Smart's activities between 1753 and 1755 remains scant. Although some writings still surface, critics believe they may have been written earlier and printed as needed. Although as his publisher Newbury should have been sending him funds, any income was probably intercepted by Smart's creditors. He did not enter the Seatonian competition in 1753 and may have been ill or traveling, fearing reprisal for his debts.

Although Smart published "Hymn to the Supreme Being" (1756), in which he praised God for healing him, his mental condition continued to deteriorate. The following year he was removed from his wife and children and intermittently confined to various institutions for the insane for several years, most often St. Luke's Hospital. He first left the hospital in 1758, although pronounced "uncured," but returned in 1759 to Mr. Potter's Private Madhouse in Bethnal Green. Anna Smart moved to Dublin and then on to Reading, where she managed the *Reading Mercury.*

Even while incarcerated, Smart continued to write. The mythology associated with the poet held that he sometimes composed on the walls of his rooms, scratching lines with a key. His mania revealed itself in his writing in cryptic and bold convolutions of form, pattern, pun, and use of numbers, and he continued to pray aloud and shout out at times. The creativity in his poetry proved undeniable, and SAMUEL JOHNSON, among others, became his friend and defender. His most exceptional poems included *A Song to David* (1763), still the most often discussed and anthologized of his works, and *Jubilate Agno,* translated *Rejoice in the Lamb,* reflecting the antiphonal style of the biblical Psalms and not published until 1939. The latter became an original among 18th-century poetry, an invocation on the divine patterns revealed in nature. Critics cite its sophisticated linguistics, unusual vocabulary, and prophetic nature. One of its more popular excerpts is the poem "MY CAT JEOFFRY," in which Smart describes his cat as an advocate and watchman for the Lord. He wrote the *Jubilate Agno* a few lines at a time in what critics describe as a scholarly notebook. In addition to describing similarities between

England and the biblical world, the piece acted as Smart's own testament to his faith.

When released from the hospital in 1762, Smart returned to a profligate lifestyle and was threatened with debtors' prison one year later. Additional writings included *Translation of the Psalms of David* (1765), *The Works of Horace. Translated into Verse* (1767), and *The Parables of our Lord and Savior Jesus Christ, done into Familiar Verse,* and *Abimelech, an Oratorio,* both published in 1768. Again incarcerated in 1770, this time in King's Bench Prison, he wrote *Hymns for the Amusement of Children* shortly before his 1771 death of "liver disorder." Although he knew he had not much longer to live, Smart invested his final poems with the same sense of joy and celebration afforded to all of his poems of praise. He dedicated it to the king's second son, Prince Frederick Augustus, but gained no royal support by doing so. The biographer Neil Curry notes that Smart's nephew wrote to a friend after his troubled uncle's death, "I trust he is now at peace; it was not his portion here."

Interest in Smart was renewed at the end of the 19th century through the efforts of Robert Browning, and by the 20th century Smart received deserved attention. For example, using psychoanalytic criticism, Clement Hawes writes of *Jubilate Agno* that the horn, a central image in this "jubilee" poem, reveals Smart's "preoccupation with and revision of the concept of cuckoldry," as the poet believed his wife had been unfaithful to him. Hawes uses this idea to support Smart's inclusion of "wordplay" that he describes as "bawdy" in order "to reiterate his [Smart's] reconstructed masculinity." The brief but excellent biography by Neil Curry supplies solid critical consideration of the *Jubilate Agno, The Psalms of David, A Song of David, Hymns and Spiritual Songs,* and *Hymns for the Amusement of Children.* The 20th-century composer Benjamin Britten adopted the *Jubilate* for use in his festival cantata, "Rejoice in the Lamb."

BIBLIOGRAPHY

Anderson, Frances E. *Christopher Smart.* New York: Twayne, 1974.

Blaydes, Sophia B. *Christopher Smart as a Poet of His Time: A Reappraisal.* The Hague: Mouton, 1966.

Costa, Dennis. "Language in Smart's *Jubilate Agno.*" *Essays in Criticism* 52, no. 4 (October 2002): 295–313.

Curry, Neil. *Christopher Smart.* Horndon, England: Northcote House, 2005.

Dearnley, Moira. *The Poetry of Christopher Smart.* London: Routledge & Kegan Paul, 1968.

Devlin, Christopher. *Poor Kit Smart.* London: R. Hart-Davis, 1961.

Greene, D. J. "Smart, Berkeley, the Scientists and the Poets." *Journal of the History of Ideas* 14 (1953): 327–352.

Guest, Harriet. *A Form of Sound Words: The Religious Poetry of Christopher Smart.* New York: Oxford University Press, 1989.

Hawes, Clement. *Mania and Literary Style: The Rhetoric of Enthusiasm from the Ranters to Christopher Smart.* New York: Cambridge University Press, 1996.

———. "Smart's Bawdy Politic: Masculinity and the Second Age of Horn in *Jubilate Agno.*" *Criticism* 37, no. 3 (summer 1995): 413–442.

Hawes, Clement, ed. *Christopher Smart and the Enlightenment.* New York: St. Martin's Press, 1999.

Keymer, Thomas. "William Toldervy and the Origins of Smart's *A Translation of the Psalms of David.*" *Review of English Studies* 54, no. 213 (February 2003): 52–66.

Lindsay, David W., ed. *English Poetry, 1700–1780: Contemporaries of Swift and Johnson.* Totowa, N.J.: Rowman & Littlefield, 1974.

Mounsey, Chris. *Christopher Smart: Clown of God.* Lewisburg, Pa.: Bucknell University Press, 2001.

Rizzo, Betty, and Robert Mahony, eds. *The Annotated Letters of Christopher Smart.* Carbondale: Southern Illinois University Press, 1991.

Spacks, Patricia Meyer. *The Poetry of Vision: Five Eighteenth-Century Poets.* Cambridge: Cambridge University Press, 1967.

SMITH, CHARLOTTE TURNER (1749–1806)

Charlotte Turner was born in London, where she matured as the elder daughter of a father, Nicholas Turner, and mother, Anna Towers, who encouraged her creativity. She gained a sister, Catherine, and then her mother died giving birth to a brother, Nicholas, when Charlotte was three years old. Her father went abroad for several years in order to deal with his grief, and the children were raised by an aunt named Lucy Towers. Charlotte's early surroundings of Bignor Park in Sussex appeared as a setting for some of her later novels and poems. Her aunt allowed the children to attend school, although she held the popular view that excessive education, as well as the reading of novels, was inappropriate for young women. A precocious child, Charlotte showed a talent for art, but vision problems curtailed her painting efforts. A voracious reader, she began to write poetry at age seven. She returned to London with her aunt under her father's support to attend a fashionable school in Kensington. The family reunited with her father by 1751. While the family was happy together, Nicholas Turner's debts threatened their security. He sold property in order to continue to support the comfortable lifestyle to which his children became accustomed.

Encouraged by her family, Charlotte submitted her early attempts at poetry to the *Lady's Magazine,* but none were published. She entered an arranged marriage at age 15 to Benjamin Smith, son of Richard Smith, a wealthy West Indian merchant and director of the East India Company. At age 23 Benjamin appeared to have great potential for accomplishment and financial security. Although she seemed later to adjust to her situation, Charlotte was not happy about the marriage, writing in a letter that she was "sold, a legal prostitute" to her husband. After a few years spent with their in-laws, the couple at last enjoyed privacy when Benjamin's mother died, Richard Smith remarried, and the newlyweds relocated to a farm in Hampshire. Richard Smith wanted his son to take part in the farm operations and those of his private firm, but while Benjamin showed a strong inclination toward spending the profits, he had little desire to work. When Richard Smith died in 1776, Charlotte and Benjamin hoped to benefit from an inheritance, but complications in settlement of the estate continued for some years.

As for their personal endeavors Charlotte became quite interested in the American Revolution, the quest for national independence developing into a topic that would continue to intrigue her. Benjamin was appointed high sheriff for Hampshire in 1781, but such appointments incurred expenses. When her profligate husband landed in debtors' prison, Charlotte Smith decided to accompany him. In a letter she describes their experience, writing in part that "for more than a month I had shared the restraint of my husband, in a prison, amidst scenes of misery, of vice and even of terror." She describes the prisoners' attempts to escape on two occasions, which greatly frightened her. She calmed herself by sitting at the barred windows, writing of the effect, "how deliciously soothing to my wearied spirits was the soft, pure air of the summer's morning, breathing over the dewy grass." The passage predicted her focus on nature in her future writing career, a career she had to consider seriously. Her biographer Loraine Fletcher notes that Smith had always envisioned the world as divided into masters and servants and included herself in the former group. The shock of having to consider working in order to support her family proved profound. The family was able to leave prison through the efforts of Benjamin's brother. However, Benjamin soon resumed to a lifestyle that doomed the family to poverty, and he moved to Normandy in hopes of escaping his creditors. Charlotte joined him with the children, believing life in France would be less expensive.

Smith's sense of melancholy imbued her early SONNETS printed in the *European Magazine.* Her collection, *Elegiac Sonnets, and Other Essays* (1784), appeared shortly before her husband's release from prison and proved an immediate success. It caused reviewers and readers concern over its desperate tone, a concern expressed in printed comments and letters. While some reviewers considered her sonnets equal to the best by Shakespeare, others, including the poet and critic ANNA SEWARD, judged them weak and ineffectual.

In 1785 Smith published some ill-received translations, their criticism probably deserved, because she had not studied the original languages. The criticism did not diminish her popularity, and she continued to publish in order to support her nine (some reports note 10) children. At age 38 she left Benjamin, who later demanded her financial assistance, and became the most popular novelist of her day. By 1793 she had also achieved high rank as a poet, but day-to-day living proved a struggle.

Smith's work influenced both minor poets, such as W. L. Bowles, and major poets, such as ROBERT BURNS and William Wordsworth, both of whom wrote tributes to her. In addition Samuel Taylor Coleridge praised her crucial role in reestablishing the sonnet as an important form. Smith even hinted that she believed the poet Robert Southey had plagiarized her words. Later critics considered her an important precursor to romantic poetry, and she also influenced Elizabeth Barrett Browning. As Seward did, Smith became a great friend of the poet William Hayley, visiting him along with other artists including the poet WILLIAM COWPER and the painter George Romney. An idealist, she supported the French Revolution for a time, eventually suffering the disillusionment of many in the English artistic community. She expressed that disappointment in her lengthy BLANK VERSE poem *The Emigrants* (1793). She would become known as a "Jacobin," one who supported change through revolution, placing her in the company of such notables as the feminist Mary Wollstonecraft; her husband, William Godwin; Helen Maria Williams; Thomas Holcroft; and Elizabeth Inchbald.

Necessity made Smith a prolific writer. Between 1788 and 1802 she published 10 popular sentimental and gothic novels and novellas, including *Emmeline, the Orphan of the Castle* (1788), *Ethelinde* (1789), *Celestina* (1791), *Desmond* (1792), *The Old Manor House* (1793), and *The Young Philosopher* (1798). Her contributions to the gothic genre included the adoption of a castle to represent England itself. As some of her novels questioned who should manage the castle, or great house, Smith asked metaphorically who should be managing her country. Her *Elegiac Sonnets, and Other Essays* was published in 11 editions by 1851, and she also published children's books. Suffering from poor health and the grief caused by the deaths of a daughter and a son, Smith died in Surrey in 1806. The last of her writings, titled *Beachy Head; With Other Poems,* she delivered to a publisher five months before her death; the collection was published posthumously in 1807. In that work Smith described herself in the subtitle to one section as "an early worshipper at nature's shrine," and critics noted that she sought to honor nature, rather than transcend it, as the romantics upon whom she had such great influence would do.

Letters not discovered until 1952 revealed that Smith had at one point suffered eviction from her home, her goods seized by the landlord. She had appealed publicly to those working on Richard Smith's estate to settle it, so that his grandchildren might receive the support they deserved. The settlement would at last be finalized in April 1813, when the court of Chancery distributed £4,000, all that was left after 35 years of legal fees, to an obscure relative. However, Smith was able to leave to her children a £7,000 fortune of her own, gained from her publications.

Twentieth-century critics including her biographer Fletcher characterized Smith's work as witty and vigorous, as she focused on satire and political analysis. With a lack of factual information about Smith, her biographers freely admit to drawing from her fictionalizations of herself as a young woman. An excerpt from a letter Smith wrote regarding her travel in 1784 to Normandy with all of her children to meet her husband does read as if part of one of her novels:

> My children, fatigued almost to death, harassed by seasickness, and astonished at the strange noises of the French postillions, whose language they did not understand, crept close to me, while I carefully suppressed the doubts I entertained whether it were possible for us to reach, without some fatal accident, the place of our destination.

In addition Fletcher found helpful an anonymous entry in the series *British Public Characters* and an obituary appearing in *The Monthly Magazine,* April 1807. Anthologized poems include "PRESSED BY THE MOON," and "THIRTY-EIGHT." Smith's work is readily available in both electronic and print forms.

BIBLIOGRAPHY

Fletcher, Loraine. *Charlotte Smith: A Critical Biography.* Houndmills, England: Palgrave Macmillan, 2001.

Hilbish, Florence May Anna. *Charlotte Smith, Poet and Novelist.* Philadelphia: University of Pennsylvania Press, 1941.

Hunt, Bishop C., Jr. "Wordsworth and Charlotte Smith: 1970." *Wordsworth Circle* 35, no. 2 (spring 2004): 80–91.

Kelley, Theresa M. "Romantic Histories: Charlotte Smith and 'Beachy Head.'" *Nineteenth-Century Literature* 59, no. 3 (December 2004): 281–314.

Labbe, Jacqueline M. *Charlotte Smith: Romanticism, Poetry, and the Culture of Gender.* New York: Palgrave, 2003.

Stanton, Judith Phillips. *The Collected Letters of Charlotte Smith.* Bloomington: Indiana University Press, 2003.

Thierfelder, Bill. "Smith's Elegiac Sonnets." *The Explicator* 64, no. 1 (fall 2005): 28–30.

"SONG—FOR A' THAT AND A' THAT"

ROBERT BURNS (1794)   Arguably the greatest balladeer who ever lived, ROBERT BURNS not only committed to paper longtime oral favorites, but also wrote many original BALLADS. He used the form as it was intended to express his opinion on various topics, adopting an unemotional presentation designed to elicit emotion from his readers. In his "Song—For A' That and A' That" he writes about the marginalized and the powerless whose suffering had prompted the French Revolution. In a more general sense he contrasts the man of character who may suffer poverty with the man who arbitrarily controls him through class divisions. While Burns had much sympathy with the cause of those who revolted against the control of arrogant aristocrats, he ultimately expressed disillusionment with fighting that killed so many and did not seem to accomplish the sweeping changes for which he and others had hoped. His repeated use of the phrase *a' that* (all that) emphasizes the frustration the powerless feel when encountering forces they can never defeat. He also uses the phrase to express disdain, dismissing certain aspects of existence not worth considering. Finally, it is used with a sense of weariness produced by the seemingly endless abuse of some humans by others.

Burns opens with the FIGURATIVE LANGUAGE known as personification, as he addresses Poverty as if a human:

Is there, for honest Poverty
That hings his head, and a' that'
The coward-slave, we pass him by,
We dare be poor for a 'that!

The tone remains sarcastic, as the speaker suggests that those trapped in poverty could not be anything other than poor. By a mere accident of birth, they find themselves with little means of support. By those for whom they are forced to work, they are conceived of as a commodity, a means to an end. The working man's worth is equated only to the gold earned through his "toils obscure." The next stanza declares that regardless of the food the poor eat, "What though on hamely fare we dine," or the sad clothing they don, "Wear hoddin grey, and a' that," that neither equate to a man's character. "Fools" have their silks and "knaves" their wine and

"A Man's a Man for a' that. / For a' that, and a' that." Those with money may dress themselves up in "Their tinsel show," the term *tinsel* indicating that such a show is without substance, but "The honest man, though e'er sae poor, / Is king o' men for a' that—." Honesty distinguishes a man far beyond fancy clothing.

The next verse parodies the lord of the manor, "What struts, and stares, and a' that," making clear that even though "hundreds worship at his word," a man with a title can still be a "coof." He may wear a "ribband, star and a' that," suggesting battle decorations, but "The man of independent mind," one who enjoys free thought, "looks and laughs at a' that.—" Through repeated references to false symbols of value Burns makes clear that possessions and awards are not equal to true power, whose source is human spirit and character.

Stanza 4 hammers home Burns's message regarding the arbitrary nature of titles as he writes,

A prince can mak a belted knight,
A marquis, duke, and a' that'
But an honest man's aboon his might,
Gude faith he mauna fa' that,

the fourth line meaning that the bearing of an aristocratic title does not allow a man to claim honesty or good faith. The final four lines support that statement, as the poet makes clear that "dignities" based on "Sense" and "pride o' Worth," characteristics that grow from a pure nature, convey a rank far higher than that of man-made titles. That men fight and kill one another in a struggle for power that affords them such titles and control over other men who are in many ways their betters indicates IRONY.

Burns concludes with a call to readers to pray that "That Sense and Worth, o'er a' the earth / Shall bear the gree [degree], and a' that," adding a note of optimism that

For a' that, and a' that,
Its comin yet for a' that,
That Man to Man the warld o'er,
Shall brothers be for a' that.

In the final line Burns uses the phrase *for a' that* to mean in spite of class divisions that falsely empower some and marginalize others, men may one day recognize their shared humanity.

BIBLIOGRAPHY
Kinsley, James, ed. *Burns: Poems and Songs*. New York: Oxford University Press, 1971.

"SONG FOR ST. CECILIA'S DAY, A" JOHN DRYDEN (1687)

JOHN DRYDEN wrote "A Song for St. Cecilia's Day" at the request of the stewards of a musical society in charge of annual November 22 festivities celebrating the patroness of music. The custom of requesting LYRICS from poets had begun in England in 1683 in imitation of the Continental ritual. Drayton's ode was set to music by Giovanni Baptista Draghi, designed for a five-part chorus with orchestra. It would later be reset by G. F. Handel.

Dryden opened the song with the traditional creation scene and closed with the world's end. His theme focused on the power of music to uplift as well as to settle the passions, described traditionally as to "raise and quell." His stanzas represent a progress piece of instruments in a survey of the history of the human race, beginning with Jubal. According to the biblical book of Genesis 4:21 Jubal was the father of all harpists and organists. Dryden concluded with homage to the martyred St. Cecilia, who supposedly invented the organ. He drew on multiple sources for this most traditional of songs, arousing varying emotions with each stanza, as befitted the "raise and quell" theme. The poem's gathering momentum is skillfully supported by Dryden's beginning with a long stanza, shortening succeeding stanzas, and then lengthening them again.

The opening 15-line stanza employs ALLITERATION and word repetition, common to songs, in its first line as it focuses on the beginning of time: "From harmony, from heav'nly harmony / This universal frame began." God is equated with music, his "tuneful voice" from the heavens organizing what was at first simply "a heap / Of jarring atoms." Dryden adds God's dialogue, understanding its stunning effect when delivered by a full choir: "Arise, ye more than dead." The four basic elements respond to God's cry, and the earlier line regarding harmony, symbolic of the creation of the world, is again repeated. Dryden's use of ENJAMB-MENT propels the reader/singer forward, supporting the mounting excitement:

> Then cold, and hot, and moist, and dry
> In order to their stations leap
> And Music's pow'r obey.
> From harmony, from heav'nly harmony
> This universal frame began;
> From harmony to harmony
> Through all the compass of the notes it ran.

Stanza 2 asks in nine lines, "What passion cannot Music raise and quell!" with a reference to Jubal's striking "the corded shell" suggesting to readers another beginning, that of the playing of instruments. So stunned are Jubal's listeners by the "celestial sound" that they fall "on their faces." Dryden again associates music with divinity, as his speaker notes Jubal's audience believed no "Less than a god" dwells "Within the hollow of that shell." That stanza ends with a declaration of the theme, "What passion cannot music raise and quell!"

The third stanza introduces the trumpet, which "Excites us to arms / With shrill notes of anger," emphasizing anger as a passion. Dryden imitates sound with words when he next describes "The double double double beat / Of the thund'ring drum." Eight lines complete that stanza, with only four lines completing stanza 4, which focuses on the flute. It discovers the passion of "woe" of "hopeless lovers" through its soft complaint. Dryden offers a contrast in stanza 5 by introducing violins, their passion jealousy. They express

> Fury, frantic indignation,
> Depth of pains and height of passion
> For the fair, disdainful dame.

Dryden continues to move the song forward with alliteration and the use of enjambment, in which the fourth of the five lines carries the reader into the next.

As the stanzas begin again to expand in length, the sixth praises in six lines the human voice, its "Notes inspiring holy love," finding their way up to heaven "To mend the choirs above." In the last seven-line stanza before the chorus Dryden alludes to Orpheus, a mythological musician whose music charmed not only animals, but also inanimate objects in nature, as "trees unrooted left their place" in response to the music of his lyre. However, Cecilia occupies the highest place of praise, her organ moving humans to contemplate the divine:

When to her organ vocal breath was giv'n,
An angel heard and straight appear'd,
　　Mistaking earth for Heaven.

The chorus in nine lines concludes the song, reminding their listeners that the world will end with the blast of a trumpet, as predicted in the Bible. Dryden uses the FIGURATIVE LANGUAGE (FIGURE OF SPEECH) of metaphor to refer to life on earth as "This crumbling pageant." The song concludes with the triumphant declaration "The dead shall live, the living die, / And music shall untune the sky."

A decade later Dryden would write a second song in celebration of St. Cecilia's Day, "ALEXANDER'S FEAST; OR, THE POWER OF MUSIC." Handel would also set this second song to music.

BIBLIOGRAPHY
Miner, Earl, ed. *Selected Poetry and Prose of John Dryden.* New York: The Modern Library, 1985.

"SONG FROM SHAKESPEARE'S CYMBELINE, A" WILLIAM COLLINS (1746) WILLIAM COLLINS used a Shakespeare play known for its beautiful songs as source material for his "A Song from Shakespeare's *Cymbeline*." First published in the Folio of 1623, *Cymbeline* was mislabeled a tragedy as that publication had no romance classification, which is the correct one for *Cymbeline*. Shakespeare based the play on several sources familiar to his audience, which told stories of mistaken identity, disguise, and misrepresentation, all in the name of love. In the play set in the pre-Christian period of English history, its deities are the Roman gods, and Jupiter even makes an appearance. It contained the song considered the most beautiful AUBADE of its time, "Hark, hark, the lark," as well as the dirge "Fear no more the heat o' th' sun," the latter found in act 4, scene 2, of *Cymbeline*, verses 258–281.

The mourning song is delivered by two characters over the supposedly dead body of Fidele, in actuality Princess Imogen, very much alive and disguised as a page. Collins incorporates some imagery from the dirge, including that of storms, along with the declaration by the devoted men that Fidele shall never be forgotten. However, he also includes imagery from a recitation by Arviragus that occurs previous to the dirge in lines 218–29 of the same scene. In those lines Arviragus tells Fidele's body that "fairest flowers / Whilest summer lasts" will "sweeten" her "sad grave." He promises the grave will be decorated with "pale primrose," which resembles her complexion; "azur'd harebell," which is blue like her veins; and "The leaf of eglantine," sweet as her breath. He explains, "The raddock would, / With charitable bill" deliver the flowers, along with moss, where a *raddock* refers to a robin. He is interrupted by Guiderus, who accuses him of being "wench-like" in expressing beautiful thoughts, when the thoughts should be more serious.

Collins combined elements from Arviragus's too-feminine verses with the dirge imagery and references. The result is "A Song from Shakespeare's *Cymbeline*," with the explanatory subtitle "Sung by Guiderus and Arviragus over Fidele, Suppos'd to be Dead." He constructed six verses of four lines each with a RHYME scheme of *abab, cdcd, efef, ghgh, ijij, klkl.* Its iambic quatrameter rhythm makes it easy to set to music, along the lines of a BALLAD.

The first line promises,
To fair Fidele's grassy tomb
Soft maids and village hinds shall bring
Each op'ning sweet, of earliest bloom,
And rifle all the breathing spring.

This echoes the dirge promise by the two men "All lovers young, all lovers must / Consign to thee and come to dust" (4.2. 274–275). Collins paraphrases Arviragus's promise that the grave shall be graced with flowers, although delivered by humans; the robin will be mentioned later in the poem.

The second verse promises that "no wailing ghost" will "vex with shrieks this quiet grove." Instead shepherds will assemble along with "melting virgins," meaning emotional young women, to declare their love. At the same time the grave will not be disturbed by a "wither'd witch" or "goblin" but rather shall be haunted by "female fays," who will decorate it "with pearly dew." The dirge from *Cymbeline* had likewise stated, in the words of both men,

> No exorciser harm thee.
> Nor no witchcraft charm thee.
> Ghost unlaid forbear thee.
> Nothing ill come near thee (4.2. 276–280)

The robin appears in Collins's fifth stanza, which promises,

> The redbreast oft at ev'ning hours
> Shall kindly lend his little aid,
> With hoary moss, and gather'd flow'rs,
> To deck the ground where thou art laid,

These lines directly imitate those of Arviragus.

The fifth stanza adopts Shakespeare's storm imagery. The men had told Fidele, "Fear no more the lightning-flash, / Nor th' all-dreaded thunder-stone / Fear not slander, censure rash" in lines 270–272; Collins writes in his fifth verse,

> When howling winds, and beating rain,
> In tempests shake the sylvan cell,
> Or midst the chace on ev'ry plain,
> The tender thought on thee shall dwell.

Collins concludes by writing that tears will be constantly shed and thoughts will focus on Fidele, who will be "Belov'd, till life could charm no more; / And mourn'd, till Pity's self be dead." Fidele will enjoy immortality through thoughts and words. Collins does his part, although Shakespeare's verse achieved an easy immortality on its own, to guarantee that the two characters' devotion to Fidele, and Fidele himself, shall never be forgotten.

SONGS FROM *THE BEGGAR'S OPERA*

JOHN GAY (1728) JOHN GAY found phenomenal success with the production of his BALLAD opera *The Beg-*

gar's Opera. The idea for the play, written partially to lampoon serious-minded Italian opera, was apparently suggested to Gay by his friend the Irish poet JONATHAN SWIFT. SAMUEL JOHNSON later described the interchange as follows: "Dr. Swift had been observing once to Mr. Gay what an odd pretty sort of a thing a Newgate Pastoral might make. Gay was inclined to try at such a thing for some time; but afterwards thought it would be better to write a comedy on the same plan." Newgate was an infamous London prison, well known to the public. Because Gay reveled in parody, the idea of applying the gentle pastoral form to a story about common thieves and murderers stimulated his imagination.

Part of the mythology that arose around the play's development and presentation included the "fact" that Gay's financial supporter, the duchess of Queensbury, at the last moment suggested the addition of music to Gay's satire, although no evidence supports that idea. Gay wrote lyrics, while music was arranged by John Christopher Pepusch, also the composer of the opera's overture. Staged at Lincoln's Inn Fields by its manager, John Rich, *The Beggar's Opera* proved an immediate success, with an unprecedented run of 62 performances.

To summarize the play's action: Peachum, father to Polly, receives stolen goods. Supposedly based on the real thief Jonathan Wild, made popular through fiction as well, Peachum proves a disreputable scoundrel. However, even his sense of justice is insulted by the marriage of Polly to the highwayman Macheath, with whom Peachum has conducted nefarious dealings. Peachum turns informer against Macheath, who ends up in Newgate sentenced to death. Macheath remains irresistible to women, as illustrated when the warden's attractive daughter, Lucy Lockit, becomes Polly's rival for Macheath's affection. Her feelings for the scoundrel cause her to secure his freedom. When Macheath is recaptured at a brothel, an actor, supposedly representing the audience, demands his release. Much of the action reflected the corruption of leading figures in government and society, including Britain's first prime minister, Sir Robert Walpole, although the references were not stressed. However, in one reference by Peachum to members of his gang, he recites of one member that his name is "Robin of Bagshot, alias Gorgon, alias Bluff Bob, alias Carbuncle, alias Bob Booty." Walpole had gained a reputation for gaining personal wealth at the country's expense, and the nickname "Bob Booty" stuck with him for the remainder of his career.

Because Gay wrote a ballad opera, most of its songs were set to popular tunes. The audience's recognition of the tunes made it a simple matter for them later to sing the songs as well. In addition the simplicity of the sentiments allowed further audience recognition and identification with the themes. For instance in the first act Macheath accompanies Polly in singing a song, "Were I Laid on Greenland's Coast" to the familiar tune "Over the Hills and Far Away." All the characters imagine themselves in different circumstances as they wait, newly married, in a tavern for whores to arrive. While Macheath imagines himself on the coast of Greenland, "Warm amidst eternal frost" in the arms of his "lass," Polly imagines herself "sold on Indian soil," where as soon "as the burning day was closed," she would plan to "mock the sultry toil, / When on my charmer's breast reposed." Their light repartee continues as each speaks every other one of the final four lines:

Macheath. And I would love you all the day,
Polly.   Every night would kiss and play,
Macheath. If with me you'd fondly stray
Polly.   Over the hills and far away.

Gay's biographer David Nokes notes the IRONY in Gay's choice of the tune for "Over the Hills and Far Away" as the one in which Macheath pledges his loyalty to Polly, an empty pledge indeed. Titled "Jockey's Lamentation," the original version protested female infidelity.

Additional song titles included "If the Heart of a Man Is Depressed with Cares," set to the air "Would you Have a Young Virgin," and "Since Laws Were Made for Every Degree," set to the extremely popular tune "Green Sleeves." In the latter Macheath wonders why, with "laws made for every degree," meaning every social rank, "to curb vice in others, as well as me," he and his fellow criminals lack "better company / Upon Tyburn tree!" Tyburn tree references the gibbet on which executions took place. He continues by noting,

But gold from law can take out the sting
. And if rich men like us were to swing,

'Twould thin the land, such numbers to sting
Upon Tyburn tree!

He clearly insinuates that criminals of means can bribe crooked wardens, barristers, and judges to pardon them. If the number of the well-to-do suffered their proper sentences, England's population would drop precipitously.

In addition to popular ballads Gay included a serious anthem written by Handel and clearly recognizable by his audience. As explained by Nokes, the juxtaposition of music from low culture with that of high culture, of street music with that of music from religious worship, was to reveal the sharing of "vanities, affectations, and vulnerabilities" by individuals of every social strataum. Gay's aim was not to elevate ballads or invalidate Handel, but rather to emphasize the irony of the presence of "parallel and symbiotic motifs" at all levels of human life.

Gay's opera would influence others, including Bertold Brecht, who wrote *The Threepenny Opera* in 1928 with music composed by Kurt Weill. The song named for his main character, "Mack the Knife," was recorded by notable singers such as Bobby Darin and remains popular into the 21st century.

BIBLIOGRAPHY
Johnson, Samuel. *Lives of the English Poets.* Vol. 2. New York: E. P. Dutton, 1958.
Nokes, David. *John Gay: A Profession of Friendship.* New York: Oxford University Press, 1995.

"SONG: TO CELIA" BEN JONSON (1616) BEN JONSON drew on classical tradition to write "Song: To Celia," which first appeared in one of his dramas. It would become a famous drinking song when set to new music in the 18th century. He based his lines on five different passages written by the third-century Greek philosopher Philostratus. Philostratus practiced sophistry, which did not have in his day the negative connotation that it does today. *Sophistry* meant literally "knowledge from wisdom," and its practice conflicted with the traditional use of logic and reason in order to arrive at a truth that would convince an audience. The sophists instead held that the audience alone could determine truth, and that audience could be manipulated through an appeal to emotion.

The song is divided into two thematic sections of eight lines, opening with the famous sentiment

> Drink to me only with thine eyes,
>   And I will pledge with mine;
> Or leave a kiss but in the cup,
>   And I'll not look for wine.

Celia exchanges gazes with the speaker, leaving him uninterested in wine. His thirst is an emotional one that can be quenched only by her love. The speaker notes, "Thirst that from the soul doth rise / Doth ask a drink divine," as Jonson employs ALLITERATION to emphasize Celia's divine nature, which makes the nature of the speaker's affection also divine, by extension. However, even should "Jove's nectar," drink fit for a deity, be offered to the speaker, he gallantly declares he would not exchange that drink for Celia's cup.

The second eight lines offer a new vignette in which the speaker sends "a rosy wreath" to Celia. He does so with the "hope that there / It could not withered be." So great is Celia's effect that the wreath flowers will never die, because roses had long been a symbol for romance involving a mature woman. However, Celia merely breathed on the wreath and returned it to the speaker. He describes a miracle in that "Since when it grows and smells, I swear, / Not of itself, but thee." Celia did breathe life into the wreath, whose flowers continue to grow, emanating not the scent of a rose, but that of Celia, suggested to be even sweeter.

SONG TO DAVID, A CHRISTOPHER SMART (1763)

Although CHRISTOPHER SMART's poem *A Song to David* contains 86 six-line stanzas, it appears in its entirety in many anthologies. At the time Smart published the poem, it received negative to tepid reviews, which Smart exacerbated with cryptic responses. It was first released in quarto form to 736 subscribers. Unfortunately prospective readers heard the story that Smart had scratched his verses into the wainscoting of his insane asylum cell with a key. The hint at mental illness turned readers away, particularly in light of Smart's highly emotional response to its less-than-

stellar reception. That reception had nothing to do with the poem's focus, as 18th-century readers remained quite interested in the biblical figure of King David; Smart had checked out books from the library on the topic. But the mean-spirited attacks on Smart as an individual by the *Monthly Review* and the *Critical Review* in response to his own bitter invectives against their initial evaluations caused the work to be ignored for centuries. As Smart's biographer Neil Curry notes in a chapter devoted to *A Song to David,* the *Critical Review* quoted from "Mr. Churchill's Epistle to Hogarth" to give readers a sense not of the value of the work, but of its writer. It implied that Smart was "deep sunk, in second childhood's night!" meaning insanity, or "this evil," left "To drivel out whole years of idiot breath, / And sit the monuments of living death." Robert Browning's attention in 1887 turned the public tide of thought, and *A Song to David* gained deserved critical esteem.

One characteristic of the poem emphasized by most scholars is Smart's tendency to focus only on David's positive aspects. His traditional joyous tone celebrates much about the ruler, as evidenced by its fourth stanza description of David using the same 12 adjectives he had employed in his *Jubilate Agno* to describe the 12 Jewish tribes. Here David individually reflects all that was good about the tribes:

> Great, valiant, pious, good, and clean,
> Sublime, contemplative, serene,
>   Strong, constant, pleasant, wise!
> Bright effluence of exceeding grace;
> Best man!—the swiftness and the race,
>   The peril, and the prize!

The poet glosses over David's well-known adultery, which led to what amounted to murder of Bathsheba's husband; he never even mentions Bathsheba's name. Instead his next 12 stanzas elaborate on each of David's 12 virtues.

Because of what has been described as Smart's manic interest in numbers, as well as his membership in the Freemasons, many architectural references exist, including one to Solomon's Temple, which had been planned by King David. Smart also elaborates on

David's talent as a poet, establishing a connection between his own work and that of the Hebrew king. He especially emphasizes that both use man's language to praise God's creation, a technique closely related to Smart's traditional praise of nature as a result of divine action. Smart thus also includes a catalog of flora and fauna in stanzas 22 through 25. The "Trees, plants, and flowers" are "of virtuous root," yielding both "blossom" and "fruit," while the "fowl" are of "every beak and wing," some making music, others mocking. "Every size and shape" of fishes exist, and "the beaver plods his task; / While the sleek tigers roll and bask." He will later describe the seasons as a form of praise, sharply separating his method, as Curry points out, from that of other Anglican poets, who looked not to the world for evidence of God but only to a life after death.

One section of the poem that has long puzzled critics is the group of seven stanzas that begin with the Greek letters *alpha, gamma, eta, theta, iota, sigma,* and *omega.* Curry's discussion points out that the letters form no word and do not represent an anagram. Some scholars have looked to numerology for an explanation, while others believe the letters may correspond to various psalms, and others that the answer lies in Masonic imagery or architectural symbolism. As Curry writes, "The only thing clear is that in choosing them Smart overturned a cornucopia of both orthodox and esoteric religious thought and that there seems no end to the possibilities." The stanzas each reflect Smart's often expressed belief that man must articulate his gratitude to God, as the poet does constantly through his praise works. He continues through the poem emphasizing the positive aspects of the New Testament God as compared to the Old Testament God of vengeance, where the objective commandments that constituted Mosaic law are superseded by the moral law of the Sermon on the Mount.

The momentum of the poem increases through use of sound and form as Smart approaches its conclusion. ENJAMBMENT and the rhythm inherent to repetition draw the reader forward as letter sounds begin to explode, rather than smoothly glide, when the words are read aloud. Stanza 76, in which most words contain only one or two syllables, provides a strong example:

Strong is the lion—like a coal
His eyeball—like a bastion's mole
    His chest against the foes:
Strong the gier-eagle on his sail,
Strong against tide, the enormous whale
    Emerges, as he goes.

Smart drives his poem to a frenzy of praise with eight repetitions of the term *beauteous,* seven repetitions of *precious,* and, in stanzas 84 through 86, 13 repetitions of *Glorious* placed at the beginning of every line. He leaves the earth to describe the heavens, God's domain. Stanza 84 reads:

Glorious the sun in mid career;
Glorious the assembled fires appear;
    Glorious the comet's train;
Glorious the trumpet and alarm;
Glorious the almighty stretched-out arm;
    Glorious the enraptured main;

At the last David's purpose becomes clear; he is a progenitor of Christ. Curry compares the final stanzas of *A Song to David* to a Handel chorus, which the audience does not want to end, but simultaneously cannot endure any longer. When Smart concludes, he does so with three simple terms meant to echo and resound through the church of the reader's mind: "DETERMINED, DARED, and DONE."

BIBLIOGRAPHY
Curry, Neil. *Christopher Smart.* Horndon, England: North-cote House, 2005.
Guest, Harriet. *A Form of Sound Words: The Religious Poetry of Christopher Smart.* New York: Oxford University Press, 1989.

"SONG: TO LUCASTA, GOING TO WARS" RICHARD LOVELACE (1649) RICHARD LOVELACE participated in a common 16th-century amatory poetry tradition by celebrating a woman, her identity veiled by a pseudonym, in many of his poems, 27 to be exact. By the 17th century many poets, including ROBERT HERRICK, referenced more than one woman, but others, including EDMUND WALLER and THOMAS CAREW, adhered to the tradition as Lovelace did.

Lucasta's true identity remains under discussion and may never be settled. At one time Lucasta was believed to be Lucy Sacheverel, referred to by Lovelace as *Lux Casta* (chaste light), who married another man, as she supposedly believed Lovelace had died of war wounds. The scholar C. H. Hartmann believed her to be a real person because Lovelace referred to Lucasta in the ode "You Are Deceived" along with WILLIAM HABINGTON's Castara and Waller's Sacharissa, both confirmed to be actual women. Whether Lucasta was a real person or an ideal, she inspired Lovelace to adopt the courtly PETRARCHAN format for his SONNETs, with one exception, thus avoiding erotic themes that appear in his other poems.

Lovelace's participation in the Bishops' Wars during 1639 and 1640 inspired his 12-line three-stanza farewell poem. The speaker addresses his love in the first stanza with a plea that she not believe him cruel for leaving her behind. He begins to unfold one of the most logical, beautiful arguments in the English language, setting a dramatic scene:

> Tell me not (Sweet) I am unkind,
> That from the Nunnery
> Of thy chaste breast, and quiet mind,
> To War and Arms I fly.

The reader may easily imagine a man quietly speaking to his love, a woman who had, previous to the poem, possibly expressed dismay upon learning that her lover would be leaving. Lovelace employs the term *Nunnery* as FIGURATIVE LANGUAGE (FIGURE OF SPEECH), establishing a metaphor for a woman's world untouched by the violence that his speaker will experience. The related terms *chaste* and *quiet* emphasize how foreign the idea of combat would be to her. His simple language works to soothe his love as he remains in control of his emotions. The male voice moves away from the female presence, emphasizing his independence, to enter a man's world. While the woman's role in Lovelace's time is passively to preserve her virtue, the male lover must fulfill his courtly role as an active defender of the faith. Lovelace establishes a pun with the term *Arms,* which he will extend later in the poem.

The second stanza plays on the pun of *Arms* to advance war as a mistress, shattering the speaker's loyalty to his love:

> True, a new Mistress now I chase,
> The First Foe in the Field;
> And with a stronger Faith embrace
> A Sword, a Horse, a Shield.

Lovelace employs ALLITERATION to emphasize the connections among the words that begin with the letter *F,* the word *Faith* acting as a pun on a woman's name. He also executes wordplay with the term *embrace,* not using it to mean romantic physical contact, but rather acceptance of the tools of battle. The fact that this faith is "stronger" than the one he has for his love indicates it does not reflect an erotic emotion.

The third stanza adopts IRONY in the speaker's tone as he suggests that his ladylove will also embrace his new endeavor, and why she will:

> Yet this inconstancy is such,
> As you, too, shall adore;
> I could not love thee (Dear) so much,
> Lov'd I not Honor more.

Lovelace balances his LYRIC with the parenthetic insertion of a fond address "(Dear)," echoing the first line address "(Sweet)," and he skillfully unifies his poem by relating romantic love to honor and country. His silent partner remains unable to protest his "unfaithfulness," as it is inspired by a cause equally sacred to their love. He does not leave her; he moves toward his duty as a man of honor, to defend his country and, by extension, to defend her. His exquisite logic leaves her not only unable to protest, but actually grateful to play a part in his endeavor.

SONNET In the 17th and 18th centuries the traditional fixed sonnet form always included 14 lines with a rhythm of iambic pentatmeter, although in the hands of 20th-century poets the form became less strict. Its subject matter often was light romance but it could also reflect a serious tone. The first popular sonnet form was called PETRARCHAN because of its use by the Latin poet Petrarch; it often focused on the female form and romance. The Petrarchan sonnet consists of a grouping of eight lines, an octave, which may outline a situation upon which the final six lines, a sestet, comments. Occasionally a white space appears between the two sets of lines. The octave's rhyming pattern is usually *abbaabba*, although that may be altered, while that of the sestet might contain two to three RHYME patterns, such as *cdcdcd* or *cdecde*. The octave might also offer the reader an idea, while the sestet follows with an example, or vice versa. LADY MARY WROTH's extraordinary sonnet sequence "PAMPHILIA TO AMPHILANTHUS" illustrates the Petrarchan technique. Sonnet 43 in this grouping offers an octave describing night as "welcome" to the speaker's "mind distressed," because of its nature as "Dark, heavy" and "sad." In the final sestet the speaker requests night's friendship, as she remains "as sad and dark as though canst be, / Hating all pleasure or delight of life." Thus the two can "live, companions without strife."

A second popular sonnet form is the Elizabethan or Shakespearean. While Henry Howard, earl of Surrey, is credited for inventing this alteration, Shakespeare popularized it. As does the Petrarchan, the Shakespearean sonnet contains 14 lines, usually in iambic pentatmeter, but with the form of three quatrains and a concluding couplet. The rhyme pattern is *abab*, *cdcd*, *efef*, and *gg*. It might offer three examples, followed by a summary statement, or three ideas, followed by an application of that idea. ROBERT HERRICK commonly used the Shakespearean form, as seen in his "DELIGHT IN DISORDER." Herrick offers several examples of disorder in dress in the first 12 lines, including "An erring lace," "A cuff neglectful," ribbons that "flow confusedly," a "tempestuous petticoat," and "A careless shoestring." His concluding couplet notes that these articles of disarray "do more bewitch me than when art / Is too precise in every part." Often employed to urge young women to romance, this form was also used for serious purpose, as in JOHN MILTON's somber Sonnets VII ("HOW SOON HATH TIME") and XIX ("WHEN I CONSIDER HOW MY LIGHT IS SPENT").

SONNET 10 ("THOUGH ALL FORSAKE THEE, LORD, YET I WILL DIE") WILLIAM ALABASTER (1597–1598?)

Those who study META-PHYSICAL POETS AND POETRY cannot help but enjoy WILLIAM ALABASTER's Sonnet 10 from his group of the first 23 SONNETs in *The DIVINE MEDITATIONS*, numbers 1–11 of which focus on Christ's death. Alabaster's use of PARADOX and ANTITHESIS is skillful, if his summary statement in his final two lines is not. He writes in clear metaphysical style:

> Though all forsake thee, lord, yet I will die,
> For I have chained so my will to thine
> That I have no will left my will to untwine,
> But will abide with thee most willingly.

The wordplay reflecting the multiple meanings of the term *will* remains reminiscent of a riddle, and Alabaster's subtle insertion of RHYME in the terms *thee* and *willingly* within the same line entices readers to say the words aloud. Alabaster extends the Renaissance devotional tradition to consider the great paradox of Christianity: that God became man in order for man to find God. Whatever one may think of Alabaster's multiple conversions between Protestantism and Catholicism, the poet's faith cannot be questioned.

The imagery of chains suggests slavery and imprisonment, but not in the sense of one will forced into service by another. Instead the speaker has voluntarily assumed the chains and has no will, or intent, to extricate himself. His abiding with his "lord" is done not in spite of his will, but actually, "willingly." The release of the will supports Alabaster's exercise in meditation, an activity undertaken to promote the realization of Divine Truth. In an allusion to St. Peter's denial of Christ at his Passion, Alabaster writes, "Though all forsake thee, lord, yet cannot I," again making clear that because of his collapse of will, he has not the power; he "cannot" forsake his lord. The speaker explains why, extending the metaphor of imprisonment and loss of essential identity:

> For love hath wrought in me thy form divine
> That thou art more my heart than heart is mine:
> How can I then from myself, thyself, fly?

Alabaster not only plays with sense, he also indulges in sound manipulation through repetition of *my, thy,* and *fly* and an echo effect with *heart* and *self.* He extends the CONCEIT of God as man, man as God. He does warn readers, however, "Thus thought St. Peter and thus thinking fell, / And by his fall did warn us not to swell," and with the term *swell* begins the reduction in graceful execution that marks many of his sonnets. Although *swell* accomplishes its sense purpose by suggesting the sin of pride, its sound proves offensive, dismaying the sensitive reader.

The final quartet does not redeem Alabaster, as his speaker declares, "Yet still in love I say I would not fall / And say in hope I trust I never shall," the eye rhyme of *fall* with *shall* serving its purpose to communicate the importance of trust, but not quite successfully convincing the reader. His penultimate line, "But cannot say in faith, what might I do," attempts to resume the wordplay that first draws the reader into the sonnet with the multiple interpretations possible for *faith*. However, they turn away again on the weak note of the concluding line, "To learn to say it, by hearing Christ say so!"

Alabaster might better have concluded with some term allowing stress to remain on the verb *say*. He might then have extended his emphasis on repetition of terms and remained fixed on his vision of man and God as one, with Christ's voice also that of man. Without the final forced *so,* needed for the eye rhyme with *to* in Alabaster's couplet, and without the exclamatory voice a reader can envision Christ quietly speaking from within man's body, mind, and soul.

BIBLIOGRAPHY
Story, G. M., and Helen Gardner, eds. *The Sonnets of William Alabaster.* New York: Oxford University Press, 1959.

SONNET 15 ("MY SOUL A WORLD IS BY CONTRACTION") WILLIAM ALABASTER (1597–1598?)

Despite critics' negative assessment of some of WILLIAM ALABASTER's work, his Sonnet 15 appeals to aficionados of METAPHYSICAL POETS AND POETRY as a prime example of its early form. The SONNET, like the rest of Alabaster's works unpublished in his lifetime, has been placed by scholars among numbers 12–19, labeled the *Penitential Sonnets,* within his *DIVINE MEDITATIONS* for their marked tone of regret. In 15 the CONCEIT of tears is used to represent the cleansing Christians receive through the sacrament of baptism, with water long a traditional symbol of new life or rebirth. The penitent's tears are compared to "april showers" converted by natural forces to "vapours," suggesting Christ's transformative power in the imagery of water becoming gas. Alabaster cleverly contrasts faith with logic, anticipating the polarization by poets of a later age of religion and science, demonstrating faith's power literally to vaporize rationality.

He opens with a strong metaphysical conceit that establishes his metaphor of physical transformation by writing, "My soul a world is by contraction," suggesting not a miniaturization of the physical world, but rather an expansion of the spiritual soul. His speaker continues, "The heavens therein is my internal sense / Moved by my will as an intelligence," introducing intuition and desire as ways of knowing the world. This contracted world operates in a cosmic manner revolving around God, represented here by the sun and ever-expanding through faith and love:

> My heart the element, my love the sun,
> And as the sun about the earth doth run,
> And with his beams doth draw thin vapours thence,
> Which after in the air do condense
> And pour down rain upon the earth anon,
> So moves my love about the heavenly sphere.

Alabaster skillfully portrays a religious conversion as the extraction of love from man's heart by God's power, which then literally vaporizes that love.

The following line demonstrates what happens to those "thin vapours" as the speaker moves into the sonnet's final six-line response. The sun's heat becomes "an attractive fire" that draws from human love "The purest argument wit can desire." Such suggestion presents another paradox, the derivation of wit, or intelligence, from love, an emotion believed to have no basis in thought or wit. Only then, according to the speaker, can a human develop devotion to God, "Whereby devotion after may arise," with the verb *arise* recalling the previous imagery of a "vapour." These lines adequately sustain the contraction conceit that began the sonnet.

The concluding couplet offers the sonnet's weakest lines, a common problem with Alabaster's poetry. The penultimate line self-consciously comments on the poet's work when it refers to the metaphorical figure called a conceit, "And these conceits, digest by thoughts' retire," appearing a clever attempt to compare the artist's creativity to the sacred creative act. However, the interest that line arouses is drowned, both literally and figuratively, in the concluding comparison of the conceits to the natural phenomenon of rain: "Are turned into april showers of tears." Alabaster seems to have chosen an easy escape by aligning the nurture of the soul by thought, devotion, and even regret, with that of spring flowers sustained by rain. Perhaps wishing to suggest the simplification often inherent to the process of contraction, he instead offers a summation of heady thoughts in lines reminiscent of a child's verse.

SONNET 46 ("OF HIS CONVERSION")
WILLIAM ALABASTER (1597–1598?)   Within WILLIAM ALABASTER's SONNET sequences that compose his The DIVINE MEDITATIONS, Sonnet 46 falls into the category critics later labeled "Personal Sonnets." All of the poems are categorized as devotional poetry, a subgenre abundant since the Middle Ages, producing a tradition of allegory that carried into the beginning of the 17th century as poets such as JOHN DONNE used it liberally. The sonnet form proved especially conducive to religious consideration, particularly in the PETRARCHAN version, Alabaster's favored type. Highly dramatic, the Petrarchan sonnet introduces a problem or question in its first eight lines to which the final six lines respond. A poet could introduce a soul-searching plea in the first part of the poem, to which his own, or another voice, might reply in the closing lines.

Alabaster employed symbolism, repetition, rhetorical questions, ANTITHESIS, strong verbs, and vivid imagery drawn from traditional Christianity in an attempt to stir his readers. The 14-line fixed sonnet format encouraged concentration of emotion and thought, proving an excellent vehicle for Alabaster's high passion. Despite their often weak conclusions, the poems work beautifully as a sequence to characterize the poet's approach to meditation. The "Personal Sonnets" unite many of the themes represented by the six sonnet sequences that precede this grouping.

Titled "Of His Conversion," Sonnet 46 is a ringing testimony to the power of Alabaster's faith. Although he moved from Protestantism to Catholicism more than once, the changes seemed more in reaction to fear for personal safety caused by the politics of the day than testimony to any weakness of conviction. His first lines ward fear away, declaring "no false fire / Which thou dost make can ought my courage quail," a valid declaration from a man once threatened by the Inquisition. He establishes the traditional imagery of fire as symbolic of damnation, a CONCEIT he will extend throughout the sonnet. He adds that he will not "run or strike my sail" and declares he will not be moved by public sentiment when he writes, "What if the world do frown at my retire," employing the term world to distinguish man's domain from that of God. In a skillful use of repetition and ALLITERATION to establish a pulsating rhythm, the next lines declare "What if denial dash my wished desire, / And purblind pity do my state bewail," building dramatic tension through repetition of the conjunction And until he challenges death: "And wonder cross itself and free speech rail, /And greatness take it not and death show nigher!"

In the six-line rejoinder Alabaster bids his soul reply to explain "the fears that make me quake," those fears firmly rooted in traditional imagery of hell. In a cascade of multiple rapid syllables he notes that he fears "The smouldering brimstone and the burning lake, / Life feeding death, death ever life devouring," adopting the participle verb form to suggest ongoing processes and employing strong ANTITHESIS as he illustrates how life and death literally feed on one another. He offers a PARADOX and adopts the FIGURATIVE LANGUAGE (FIGURE OF SPEECH) of personification in the 12th line, "Torments not moved, unheard, yet still roaring," challenging readers who might deny the existence of hell, whether it be in this life or the next. The final couplet sustains tension better than many of Alabaster's conclusions, as his persona seems not only to accept, but actually to invite, a chance for martyrdom, suggesting that conversion from one faith to another does not promise peace: "God lost, hell found,—ever, never begun: / Now bid me into flame from smoke to run!"

BIBLIOGRAPHY

Story, G. M., and Helen Gardner, eds. *The Sonnets of William Alabaster.* New York: Oxford University Press, 1959.

"SONNET TO THE NOBLE LADY, THE LADY MARY WROTH, A" BEN JONSON (1640–1641)

BEN JONSON's Elizabethan SONNET "A Sonnet to the Noble Lady, the Lady Mary Wroth" appeared in his group of poems known as *The Underwood,* published after his death. LADY MARY WROTH was a member of the distinguished family that included the poets Philip Sidney and his sister, MARY SIDNEY HERBERT (COUNTESS OF PEMBROKE). As did others including GEORGE CHAPMAN and Jonson's friend WILLIAM DRUMMOND OF HAWTHORNDEN, Jonson sought Wroth's patronage and praised it publicly. Jonson also publicly declared Wroth's mother a generous woman and praised her hospitality; he had experienced much kindness in patronage by the extended family. In addition to this sonnet he appended to his popular play *The Alchemist* a Dedicatory Epistle to Wroth. He extended to her a high compliment by writing of her judgment, "(which is a Sidney's)." He later expressed his opinion of Wroth's husband, Sir Robert Wroth, labeling him "jealous" and implying what later came to be known as accurate, that the forced marriage was not a happy one. He would, however, also dedicate a poem to Sir Robert, "To Sir Robert Wroth," later labeled by critics Jonson's countryside poem. Some scholars have suggested that Jonson had Lady Mary Wroth in mind when writing about a secret romance in his drama *To the World;* Wroth probably had an affair with her cousin, William, earl of Pembroke. Wroth had a crucial connection to the sonnet format as the first English woman to compose a sonnet sequence, appended to a prose romance.

Jonson begins by praising that sequence. His speaker opens the poem by noting that while he has been a lover, he became both a better lover and a poet by copying Wroth's sonnets: "Since I exscribe your sonnets, [I] am become / A better lover, and much better poet." He adds that neither he nor his muse is

. . . asham'd to owe it
To those true numerous graces, whereof some

But charm the senses, others overcome
Both brains and hearts.

Jonson praises Wroth's verses not only for engaging the reader's imagination, but also for engaging their intellect. The speaker describes Wroth's verse as encompassing "all Cupid's armory," referencing the god of love. He explains that Cupid's "flames, his shafts, his quiver, and his bow, / His very eyes are yours to overthrow." In other words Wroth trumps Cupid at his own game.

To prevent readers from imagining Wroth as a masculine warrior type, the speaker adds a reference to Cupid's mother, Venus, whose beauty was well known, comparing Wroth to the mother, as well as the son: "But then his mother's sweets you so apply." This leads Jonson into the traditional closing sonnet couplet, designed to summarize the 12 lines preceding it:

Her joys, her smiles, her loves, as readers take
For Venus' ceston every line you make.

The ceston was Venus's girdle, which supposedly gave the one who wore it power to inspire love in another.

BIBLIOGRAPHY

Brennan, Michael G., "'A SYDNEY, though un-named': Ben Jonson's Influence in the Manuscript and Print Circulation of Lady Mary Wroth's Writings." *Sidney Journal,* 17, no. 1 (1999): 31–52.

SONS OF BEN

The label *Sons of Ben* referring to students of the work of BEN JONSON is often applied incorrectly. Those poets who worked at the beginning of the 17th century, including THOMAS CAREW, ROBERT HERRICK, RICHARD LOVELACE, SIR JOHN SUCKLING, and some minor writers, are more properly labeled the TRIBE OF BEN. Playwrights specifically affected by Jonson's writing, including Francis Beaumont and John Fletcher, Richard Brome, Nathan Field, Philip Massinger, and James Shirley, are more correctly considered members of the Sons of Ben.

SOUND

When most people consider sound in relation to poetry, they think of RHYME. Although an important aspect of 17th- and 18th-century poetry, rhyme is not the only important sound effect available to the poet. In cohort with rhythm sounds may appear in multiples to a pleasing effect. Several examples of the use of repeated sound may be seen in the opening four lines of "To the Nightingale" by Anne Finch, countess of Winchilsea:

Exert thy voice, sweet harbinger of spring!
This moment is thy time to sing,
This moment I attend to praise
And set my numbers to thy lays.

Finch uses alliteration, identical consonant sounds appearing at the beginning of words in a series, as in *sweet, spring, sing,* and *set.* The excerpt also includes an illustration of *consonance,* close repetition of consonants as the final sound of important terms. Again the *s* sound acts as example, as it concludes the repeated term *This* and the terms *praise* and *numbers* and *lays,* with *praise* and *lays* also acting as rhyme. Although it is not obvious to the eye, the ear also hears the *s* sound in the opening term *Exert,* because of pronunciation of the *x* as an *s,* and in the term *voice,* because of pronunciation of the *ce* ending as an *s* sound. In addition the four lines contain abundant assonance, or the close repetition of vowel sounds within words. The short *e* sound is repeated several times in *Exert, harbinger, moment,* and *set.* The long *a* sound in *praise* and *lays* produces rhyme. Additional repetition includes that of the long *i* sound in *thy* and *I.* Exact repetition of words also occurs, in this case in the repeated phrase *This moment.* Finally, the eye detects repetition of the group of letters *ing* in not only *spring* and *sing,* but also *harbinger.* However, *harbinger* carries a different pronunciation, här-bən-jar, with the first syllable stressed.

Finch also captures the essence of poetry in structuring sound to support the sense, or meaning, of her poem. While no true *onomatopoeia,* the use of words that sound like what they mean such as *buzz* and *hiss,* appears, *phonetic intensives* do. Phonetic intensives are words whose sound in some degree connects with their meaning, simply because of the way the human brain interprets sound. Examples in these lines include *Exert, sweet, spring, praise,* and *set.* In addition, the repeated *o* sound forces the reader's mouth open,

emphasizing the idea of singing or praise. The mouth's shaping itself as an *o* is a phenomenon easily observed in a religious choir, where one often hears the words *Lo, Holy, O, So,* and *soul.* Those open-mouth words appear repeatedly in the Psalms, a biblical book composed of 150 songs written in order to praise God. Psalm 150 is subtitled "A Psalm of Praise," with the term *Praise* beginning 12 of its 13 lines. Finally, Finch comments on her the process of writing poetry as she identifies the Nightingale as inspiration for her own *numbers,* or poetic rhythms.

"SPLEEN, THE" Anne Finch, countess of Winchilsea (1713)

When Anne Finch, countess of Winchilsea, chose the title "The Spleen," she referred to the medical classification of the four "humors" thought to compose the body. The humors equated to those passions controlling human behavior, the term *humor* derived from Latin and meaning "liquid." The four humors, as defined in the 16th century, were blood, phlegm, choler (yellow bile), and melancholy (black bile). When all four liquids were in balance, an individual enjoyed splendid health. However, should any exist in greater volume than another, chaos could ensue.

Spleen was another name given to black bile, and it was believed to accompany melancholia, or depression. Shakespeare had referenced humors in application to human temperament in his tragedy *Julius Caesar,* and Finch alludes to the dramatic and real-life character of Brutus, associated with Caesar's murder. Because solid evidence exists that Finch suffered from depression, the topic proved an appropriate choice. Critics suggest her seeming obsession with woman's supposed part in committing original sin in the Garden of Eden and the subsequent "fall" of the human race, may have added to her sense of melancholy.

Brimming with clear allusions and evocative detail, "The Spleen" is fashioned as a Pindaric ode. The formality of the ode serves to elevate Finch's topic, perhaps necessary in order for Finch to prevent claims of "hysteria" against her. A catch-all medical term, *hysteria* was applied to a variety of illnesses of women. More importantly it was also used to trump up charges of mental illness against women, leading to many documented cases of inappropriate female interment in insane asylums. Derived from the Greek word *hyster,* meaning "womb," hysteria became strongly associated with women in "out of control" states of being, whether mental, emotional, or physical. In lines of uneven METER but regular RHYME Finch questions the nature of this beast, melancholy, that haunted her and a host of others. Her interwoven references and images provide an admirable unity, while her tone reflects the melancholy about which she writes.

Finch begins as her speaker's asks the question that seemed to have no answer, "What art thou, Spleen, which ev'ry thing dost ape," where *ape* means "imitate." She describes the spleen as "Proteus," referencing a mythological lesser god of the sea who could change shape and form, and notes that because of its changeable nature, the cause of spleen remains undetermined. Melancholy may be found everywhere, in all places at any time of the day. Finch adopts the FIGURATIVE LANGUAGE (FIGURE OF SPEECH) of metaphor, writing,

Now a Dead Sea thou'lt represent,
A calm of stupid discontent,
Then, dashing on the rocks, wilt rage into a
   storm. (6–8)

By comparing spleen to the sea, she reflects on the reference to Proteus, while offering imagery of complete calm with a sea dead to life versus one of nature's rage to help readers comprehend spleen's terrible and awesome range. Readers understand this poet has experienced the ravages of spleen, as she describes its effects in various ways, including "Panic fear" and "gloomy terrors round the silent bed," which yield it the power to prevent sleep, when sleep is most desired. Instead of slumber its victim experiences hallucinations, including "antic specters" (17), "Unusual fires" (18), "airy phantoms" (19), all generating a "monstrous vision" (20). That vision Brutus saw when visited by the ghost of Julius Caesar in Shakespeare's play about the Roman emperor. Although Brutus should have become Rome's ruler, he was instead "vanquished by the spleen," as Finch evidences its power over even a warrior. She makes clear that spleen does not prefer women; nor should men feel shame when they suffer its torment.

In the second stanza Finch makes a point stressed centuries later by physicians, that humans tend to blame physical problems for emotional distress: "Falsely the mortal part we blame / Of our depressed and pond'rous frame." She then returns to a theme common to her poetry, that of original sin, a concept that seemed to haunt her. She notes that until "the first degrading sin" spleen existed in balance with the other humors. It did not clog "the active soul, disposed to fly" while "man his Paradise possessed / His fertile garden in the fragrant east." In Eden man never appeared "flushed" or "unhandsome," and it was only after the fall that a scent such as that of the jonquil could overcome "the feeble brain." Now man requires a more "offensive scent," possibly referring to smelling salts, in order to gain even a "nauseous ease."

The second stanza clarifies that each person may react differently to spleen's possession. Its "motions," or effects, change, as do its symptoms. It may distract a friend in a calm grove, attempting to listen to another speak. Instead, he "must attend" spleen's "false suggestions," including "Thy whispered griefs, thy fancied sorrows," until imagined problems cause the victim to weep. In contrast it may appear in a "light and vulgar crowd" causing people to laugh at inappropriate moments. She continues describing other victims, including an "imperious wife" and her soft-hearted husband who attempts to accommodate her condition, offering peace, rather than argument.

Stanza 3 reveals the speaker's lack of patience with "fools" who would pretend to suffer from melancholia, blaming it for their inherent "dullness." The fool can only do so because spleen is known to enter "the ablest heads," who are then forced to leave their friends and retire from discourse. The speaker explains their momentary loss of verbal dexterity as "Such slow returns, where they so much dispense," again making the point that spleen attacks everyone, regardless of mental acuity. Finch describes the effects on her art of that unwelcome guest:

O'er me alas! Thou dost too much prevail:
   I feel thy force, whilst I against thee rail;
I feel my verse decay, and my cramped
   numbers fail.

Through thy black jaundice, I all objects see,
  As dark, and terrible as thee,
My lines decried, and my employment thought
An useless folly, or presumptuous fault. (74–80)

Finch had previously termed herself "presumptuous" for attempting to write, probably to preempt men from leveling that claim against a writing woman. Women were intended subjects for poetry, not meant to be poets. She concludes the stanza by referencing the idle and useless pseudoartistic pursuits women were urged to undertake, producing "an ill-drawn Bird, or paint on glass." In Finch's opinion such vacuous attempts could lead to depression as well as act as symptoms.

The fourth lengthy stanza continues providing abundant detail regarding the powers of spleen. It acts as "patron" to "ev'ry gross abuse," examples including verbal abuse; heavy drinking, alluded to with a reference to Bacchus, the Roman god of wine; and changeability in personality, as in a coquette, whose personality changes from "light, impertinent, vain" to "withdrawn." She describes symptoms, including "The thoughtful, and composed face / proclaiming the absent mind," as evidence of spleen's "fantastic harms, / The tricks of thy pernicious stage," in which "the weaker sort" engage. Most serious is the charge against spleen relating to religion. Whereas religious faith should provide freedom and joy, translated through melancholic minds it instead generates guilt, "anxious doubts," which cause biblical verses to be incorrectly read as restraints:

Whilst touch not, taste not, what is
    freely giv'n
Is but thy niggard voice, disgracing bounteous
    heav'n.
        From speech restrained, by thy deceits
            abused,
        To deserts banished, or in cells reclused.
        (121–125)

Those affected worship at the "shrine" of spleen, rather than at the true spiritual shrine humans were intended to benefit from.

Finally, Finch focuses on the practice of medicine and its feeble and useless attempts to explain and treat the condition. She notes with IRONY that "skilful Lower" (142), referencing the famous British physician Richard Lower (1631–91), not only failed at finding a cause of spleen, but then suffered himself from spleen, became its prisoner and slave, and was driven to his death by depression.

In her well-crafted presentation Finch imitates in tone the melancholia, or spleen, she seeks to describe. While not evident in all of her poetry, Finch's bitterness and negativity about what she perceived, realistically or not, as the public's negative attitude toward her remains persistent in every line of "The Spleen."

BIBLIOGRAPHY
Rogers, Katharine M., ed. *Selected Poems of Anne Finch.* New York: Frederick Ungar, 1979.

"SPRING, THE" ABRAHAM COWLEY (1647)

ABRAHAM COWLEY published a collection of about 100 love poems in 1647 titled *The Mistress.* "The Spring" exemplifies the negative assessment the collection received in later generations. SAMUEL JOHNSON, who admired Cowley, remarked of his unromantic love lyrics, "The compositions are such as might have been written for penance by a hermit, or for hire by a philosophical rhymer who had only heard of another sex." Most critics of centuries after Cowley's would agree that he attempts to intellectualize emotion and so dooms himself to fail. He adopts traditional comparisons, particularly those from nature, but then uses them in a cold fashion, his style lacking the appropriate tone for expression of passion.

As the speaker addresses his love in the first of six eight-line stanzas with rhyming couplets, he notes that even though she is absent, the trees and flowers remain as "beautous" as always, and the bird's "rural music" remains as "melodious and free" as if she were present. He concludes with a statement regarding the rosebud, traditional symbol of a young virginal woman, made unpleasant by clumsy repetition of terms referencing the morning: "I saw a rose-bud ope this morn; I'll swear / The blushing morning open'd not more fair." When the speaker seeks to compare her to a beautiful dawn he fails, because his comparison moves from that of a rose, or his love, to a sunrise, to that of a morn to a morning, rendering the FIGURATIVE LANGUAGE moot.

The second verse asks the question hinted at in the first, "How could it be so fair, and you away?" rather than allowing the subtle suggestion to stand on its own. Such blatant statement remains more appropriate to essay than poetry. The speaker wonders whether the trees and flowers remember the previous year, when "How you did them, they you delight," which becomes a pleasant inversion. However, it is followed with harsh sounds, including that of "sprouting leaves," personified to have seen her there during a previous season. When they are not rewarded with her sight, they simply withdraw, suggesting a lack of motivation for spring. Again Cowley mitigates against a pleasing image through diction, as the leaves "Creep back into their silent barks again," suggesting a lowly insect, hiding within tree bark, that sometimes speaks. Cowley's error is in focusing on trees and leaves, rather than on flowers.

The CONCEIT continues in the third verse, which begins, "Were'er you walk'd trees were as reverend made," suggesting that her presence deified the vegetation. Without that deification they should not "smile and flourish now, / And still their former pride retain." He then references mythology: "she, / Who fled the god of wit, [and] was made a tree." That reference clashes with the previous imagery of trees who admire women, as he suggests trees are themselves of female sensibility. As Cowley extends the tree imagery, he continually fails to introduce any graceful diction or imagery into his lyric. The trees should be "wiser" and more "learned," actually following the poem's subject: "You would have drawn them, and their poet too." However, the trees are not to be blamed, for "since you're gone," they must "shine alone. / You did their natural rights invade." At this point his love is vilified as one who works against nature, rather than inspiring it. Even "fairest flowers could please no more, near you, / Than painted flowers, set next to them, could do." As Cowley concludes, "'Tis you the best of seasons with you bring; / This is for beasts, and that for men the spring," he sparks confusion with his nonspecific pronoun *This*. It seems to refer to the season that his love brings, saying it serves beasts well. In actuality he is probably referring to the present condition of spring in her absence as good only for animals, while "that," the "best of seasons with you bring," would benefit "men." The conclusion not only remains confusing, it also lacks personalization.

Cowley's lyric seems to pit sense against sensibility throughout, therefore never achieving a lyric tone. The lyric dwindles to a laborious exercise, perhaps not surprising when one considers Cowley's pronounced scientific intellect.

BIBLIOGRAPHY

Ward, Thomas Humphry, ed. "Thomas Cowley." In *The English Poets: Selections with Critical Introductions by Various Writers.* Vol. 2, 234–243. New York: Macmillan, 1914.

"STELLA'S BIRTHDAY, 1721" JONATHAN SWIFT (1727)

Literary historians remain unsure of the nature of the relationship between JONATHAN SWIFT and Esther Johnson, the "Stella" of his poetry and the famous letters published in 1766 as *The Journal to Stella.* He became acquainted with Johnson when he served as secretary to his kinsman, Sir William Temple, living in his household from 1689 to 1699. Swift tutored Johnson, daughter of Temple's steward, and the two became lifelong friends. Some believed they secretly married, while others continue to debate their relationship. Whatever its form, they both found it crucial and satisfying.

Swift wrote "Stella's Birthday, 1721" to celebrate what she claimed as her 36th birthday, although Swift avowed it to be her 40th. He gently chides her in the poem, which openly and honestly celebrates her charms and intelligence as far more important than the mere physical beauty that accompanies youth. Swift works to undermine the idea that a woman's worth is based on youth and physical attributes. He develops as a younger character for contrast to the mature Stella the dull young "Cloe," a name popular in poetry that incorporated the romantic and pastoral traditions. He also references two new friends, Thomas Sheridan and his wife, Elizabeth; the latter Swift identifies in his poem as "a new Angel." The couple had proved kind to Swift, impressing him with their gracious hospitality. Sheridan's grandson, Richard Brinsley Sheridan, distinguished himself as one of the Restoration's best playwrights.

Swift begins by adopting the FIGURATIVE LANGUAGE of extended metaphor, representing Stella's house as a welcome escape from daily cares, the type of place all weary travelers and those seeking satisfying interaction would value. Such travelers will return often to a place where "they find the chambers neat, /And like the liquor and the meat." Not only will they return, they will recommend these accommodations, which Swift dubs "The Angel Inn," to others. He makes a subtle humorous reference to Stella's age when he adds of the inn, "And though the painting grows decayed / The house will never lose its trade." The next lines refer to the Sheridans, whose home with "a new Angel" proves a possible distraction from the travelers' original focus. However, even "the treacherous rascal Thomas" and his wife "think it both a shame and sin / To quit the true old Angel Inn."

At line 16 Swift begins a new section, describing Stella physically. With obvious fondness he notes that her "angel's face" remains "a little cracked," adding slyly, "(Could poets or could painters fix / How angels look at thirty-six)." Stella's "angel's mind" filled with every virtue stands as her most important feature. She entertains "With breeding, humor, wit, and sense," putting at ease her guests and costing them "so small expense." Retaining the metaphor of Stella's home as an inn designed to afford comfort to others, the speaker adds that she "So little gets for what she gives, / We really wonder how she lives."

Swift inserts a four-line transition, proclaiming, "Then, who can think we'll quit the place / When Doll hangs out a newer face," or when Cloe opens an inn "With scraps and leavings to be fed." Line 37 begins the final section, in which Swift contrasts Stella with the younger Cloe, who engages in the "trade of scandal picking," through "innuendoes" suggesting that "Stella loves to talk with fellows." The speaker suggests Cloe's desperation in turning to lies to undercut her competitor. He firmly warns Cloe "to believe / A truth for which thy soul should grieve." That truth is that even when Stella's hair turns gray and "age must print a furrowed trace / On every feature of her face," she will prove superior to Cloe, though the younger woman might pretend through artifice to remain forever age 15. The speaker tells the would-be usurper with relish, "No bloom of youth can ever blind / The cracks and wrinkles of your mind." Men will still walk past Cloe's

establishment to attend Stella even when Stella reaches the age of "fourscore."

This 1721 birthday poem was the second of seven written for Stella and is the most anthologized. Its affectionate tone and soft, but sure, execution counter the common perception of Swift as a bitter misanthrope who had little use for women other than as objects of derision.

"STILL TO BE NEAT" BEN JONSON (1609)

The song "Still to Be Neat" was heard in BEN JONSON's play *Epicoene*. When the play's character Clerimont requests the song, which he supposedly wrote, it is in order to stress the theme of feminine artifice. Clerimont makes the request because of his impatience with another character, Lady Haughty, a woman known for heavy makeup. The speaker begins by addressing the lady, "Still to be neat, still to be dressed / As you were going to a feast," implying that she need not always appear to be on her way to a celebration. He would obviously prefer her in less formal attire, without her makeup. The repetition that recurs in line 3, "Still to be powdered, still perfumed," is typical of lyrics and reinforces the continuing state of adornment of the lady's person. The message to her at the conclusion of the first of two stanzas is that while what is beneath the art has yet to be discovered, those gazing at the lady presume "All is not sweet, all is not sound." The fact that she requires so much makeup signals she hides something unpleasant. The lyrics imply that such subterfuge suggests a flawed character beneath a possibly flawed face.

In the second stanza the speaker expresses his desire that the lady "Give me a look, give me a face / That makes simplicity a grace." In other words he would like to peek behind her mask to observe her in her simple natural state. In addition he wants her dress also to be marked by "sweet neglect," with her hair hanging free and her robes flowing, rather than caught up, as by belts and ties for false support. His final pronouncement is that such lack of artifice

> . . . more taketh me
> Than all the adulteries of art.
> They strike mine eyes, but not my heart.

By using the term *adultery* to mean an act of falsehood or a ruination of a state of innocence, Jonson connects the artifice involved with cosmetics to sexual infidelity. If one is not true to one's self, expressing a true identity, she cannot be true to others. Finally, while makeup and fancy hairstyles may initially attract the male gaze, ultimately they will not win his affection.

"STRICKEN DEER, THE" WILLIAM COWPER (1785)

"The Stricken Deer" is among the poems included by WILLIAM COWPER in his six-volume collection *The Task,* where it appears in book 3. Self-reflexive and thoughtful, the poem allows Cowper to compare himself to a deer, struck from his herd after wandering away. As a result of recurrent mental illness the poet also felt separated from his friends and cheated by his deteriorating mental acuity of achieving all he desired before dying. The FIGURATIVE LANGUAGE (FIGURE OF SPEECH) of the extended metaphor works well, reflecting through the suffering animal the agony Cowper experienced. As he shows, the alienation from one's familiar mental and physical surroundings can prove terrifying. The only time he knows hope is when he turns to spiritual faith.

Cowper begins by stating

I was a stricken deer, that left the herd
Long since; with many an arrow deep infixed
My panting side was charged, when I withdrew
To seek a tranquil death in distant shades.

Abundant use of caesura and ENJAMBMENT establishes a rhythm that pulls the reader forward through Cowper's 26 lines of BLANK VERSE. Where the deer has been "deep infixed" by multiple arrows, Cowper felt stricken, or attacked without provocation, by deep delusions that rendered him unable to function. He would eventually be cheated of the tranquil death that he imagines as a possibility for the deer. In this poem Cowper actually becomes the animal, and his speaker relates,

There was I found by one who had himself
Been hurt by the archers. In his side he bore,
And in his hands and feet, the cruel scars.

The description of the wounds makes clear that the speaker references Christ, whose side was pierced by a spear and hands and feet by nails as he hung on the cross. This poetic Christ figure uses "gentle force," as Cowper applies PARADOX to describe how "the darts" were withdrawn from his metaphorical body. The figure then "healed, and bade me live." The experience drives the speaker away from his former companions and concerns, wandering into a "remote / And silent woods." He has few "associates" and states, "Here much I ruminate, as much I may," with Cowper's use of repetition and ALLITERATION again adding a pleasing effect.

With his healing the speaker can "see that all are wanderers, gone astray / Each in his own delusions," a line quite personal to Cowper. The speaker notes that these wanderers are lost, chasing

. . . fancied happiness, still wooed
And never won. Dream after dream ensues;
And still they dream that they shall still succeed,
And still are disappointed.

Cowper's continuing interruption of the line's flow with insertion of punctuation prevents the reader becoming comfortable. The series of the word *And* connotes an endless progression, as does repetition of *still,* meaning a "continued state." The soft sounds allow Cowper to retain an appropriately gentle and melancholy tone. The adjective *disappointed* is especially poignant in its understatement. He ends with an observation, made more powerful by the continuing negative emphasis of the term *dream*:

I sum up half mankind
And add two-thirds of the remaining half,
And find the total of their hopes and fears
Dreams, empty dreams.

While Cowper may have found peace in his faith, it proved only a temporary relief from his tortured delusions of damnation. However, because in his final lines the speaker suggests that at least a fraction of mankind does not suffer empty dreams, Cowper seems to imagine the possibility that some men's hopes and fears will not amount to the empty dreams he holds.

STRUCTURE See FORM AND FORMAT.

SUCKLING, SIR JOHN (1609–1641) John

Suckling was born in Norfolk. His father had served as comptroller of James I's household and was knighted on 1616; thus the family was wealthy and well connected. After education at Trinity College, Cambridge, and Gray's Inn, Suckling joined military campaigns at the age of 19. He traveled the Low Countries, where he studied astrology at Leyden University and may have served Lord Wimbledon. Suckling acted as an emissary in Europe, wandering for several years through France, Italy, Germany, and Spain, receiving knighthood in 1630. Through 1632 he served Sir Henry Vane, the king's ambassador to Germany. By 1634 he had experienced failure in romance with Anne Willoughby, with whom he quarreled.

Suckling proceeded to practice a profligate lifestyle, becoming well known for his penchant for games; the biographer and antiquarian John Aubrey claimed that Suckling invented the card game cribbage. He gained equal notoriety for his ability to exhaust his fabulously large inheritance. The large sum of money allowed him to dress extravagantly and indulge his many aesthetic tastes. He lived such a public existence that his life can hardly be separated from his art. A member of the TRIBE OF BEN, he spent time with fellow poets and wits in the company of BEN JONSON. The group earned the title as a way to distinguish their poetry from the concentrated style of METAPHYSICAL POETS AND POETRY, as exemplified by JOHN DONNE.

Suckling became famous as both a poet and a playwright; his first satire, The Wits (or Sessions of the Poets) (1637) gained him early attention when it was sung to the king. Audiences appreciated his good sense of humor in including himself as a character who chooses not to compete in a poetry contest for a laurel, preferring a game of bowls. He made the perfect courtier, small in stature but large in spirit. His tragedy Aglaura, An Account of Religion by Reason received two separate elaborate stagings in 1638; audiences appreciated his revision of its conclusion to a more positive outcome. However, the only one of his four plays later critics judged of any merit was Brennoralt.

More than any other of the CAVALIER POETS he gained a reputation for his stubborn support of the monarch and became a leader of the Royalists. In 1639 a "troope of 100 very handsome proper men" joined the first bishops' war. He entered Parliament for a few months until it was dissolved on May 5, 1640. Suckling returned to military service to participate in the second bishops' war and the Scots' 1641 defeat of Charles I. He continued his writing, turning out the plays The Goblins and Brennoral along with a political tract, To Mr. Henry German, in the Beginning of Parliament, 1640. As a result of his part in the discovered "Army Plot" to liberate the earl of Strafford from imprisonment, Suckling had to flee England. In some accounts he underwent torture in Madrid during the Inquisition before moving to Paris. There, according to Aubrey, he committed suicide by poison at age 34.

In 1642 additional stage works were acted by the King's Men and later printed in 1646 in Fragmenta Aurea. That work included the popular poems later widely anthologized, such as "A BALLAD UPON A WEDDING," "THE DANCE," "I PRITHEE SEND ME BACK MY HEART," the song "WHY SO PALE AND WAN, FOND LOVER?" "LOVING AND BELOVED," and "OUT UPON IT!" It also contained poems critics judged of near-worthless quality, marred by incoherent passages and stylistic lapses that Suckling's contemporaries appreciated but modern audiences find impossible. One final publication appeared in 1659, The Last Remains of Sir John Suckling. Being a Full Collection of All His Poems and Letters Which Have Been So Long Expected, and Never Till Now Published.

Suckling remained a popular persona; a dramatic character shaped by William Congreve in his The Way of the World (1700) praised the poet for his "easy" approach to life. The term proved an apt descriptor of Suckling's attitude toward art as something natural and easy. Edward Phillips in Theatrum Poetarum (1675) described Suckling as "a witty and elegant Courtier. . . . His poems . . . have a pretty touch of a gentile Spirit, and still keep their reputation." The biographer Charles Squier writes of Suckling that "he is the embodiment of the Cavalier spirit of unstrained, negligent wit, charm and grace." Surprisingly a smattering of lyrics and four plays that he apparently produced with little effort outlived the labored work of many others. His gallantry and comparatively masculine approach to verse contrasted with the obsequious pliancy of his fellow Cavaliers.

BIBLIOGRAPHY

Scodel, Joshua. "The Pleasures of Restraint: The Mean of Coyness in Cavalier Poetry." *Criticism* 38, no. 2 (spring 1996): 239–279.
Squier, Charles L. *Sir John Suckling.* Boston: Twayne, 1978.
Swann, Marjorie. "Cavalier Love: Fetishism and Its Discontents." *Literature and Psychology* 42, no. 3 (summer 1996): 15–35.
Van Strien, Kees. "Sir John Suckling in Holland." *English Studies* 76, no. 5 (September 1995): 443–454.
Wilcher, Robert. "John Suckling in the Summer of 1628." *Notes and Queries* 51, no. 1 (March 2004): 21–23.

"SUN RISING, THE" JOHN DONNE (1630)

JOHN DONNE's "The Sun Rising" serves as a perfect example of the style of the METAPHYSICAL POETS AND POETRY, written early in Donne's career as part of his romance oeuvre. In three 10-line verses with the RHYME scheme *abbacdcdee,* the poet uses FIGURATIVE LANGUAGE (FIGURE OF SPEECH) to personify the sun. In addition he incorporates one of his most often used themes, that an entire world may exist within a single organism, as in "The FLEA," or that the union two lovers experience constitutes an entire universe. Because of the sun's omnipresence, Donne may utilize it to comment on the state of the entire world in discussing the relationship shared by the male speaker and his lover. Also typically of Donne's love poetry, the female love interest does not speak, yet remains quite obviously present during what could constitute a dramatic monologue on stage.

The speaker begins by scolding the morning sun for intruding into a happy bedroom after a night of lovemaking in the famous opening apostrophe,

> Busy old fool, unruly sun,
> Why dost thou thus
> Through windows, and through curtains call on
>   us?

The fact that the sun must enter the bedroom by intruding through barriers that human sight cannot, the curtained windows, establishes it as the only force brazen enough to invade. Donne uses IRONY to make fun of lovers who believe that the sun sets and rises on their emotions; time should literally stand still in honor of their emotion, leaving them to determine their own heavenly motions and seasons. The speaker makes this plain in the next line, "Must to thy motions lovers' seasons run?" Lovers should not have to cease their lovemaking in the light. In lines delightfully laced with humorous reproach, the speaker suggests other tasks for the sun as he continues,

> Saucy pedantic wretch, go chide
> Late schoolboys, and sour prentices,
> Go tell court-huntsmen, that the King will ride,
> Call country ants to harvest offices.

The sun may pursue traditional duties of moving others, but not the speaker and his love. As the speaker explains, "Love, all alike, no season knows, nor clime, / Nor hours, days, months, which are the rags of time." Donne's use of a serious tone emphasizes the boundless nature of love, which cannot be measured in the units the sun is used to measure. The speaker's awareness of his own folly contributes to the reader's pleasure in knowing the address is for the benefit of the lover only. Donne establishes a natural rhythm for a voice that rises and falls with emotion by varying the METER stresses in the lines. While in each stanza lines 1, 5, and 6 are iambic tetrameter, line 2 is reduced to dimeter, and all other lines are in pentameter.

The second stanza turns on the boast by the speaker that through his emotion he can outshine the sun's beams. He brags:

> Thy beams, so reverend, and strong
> Why shouldst thou think?
> I could eclipse and cloud them with a wink,
> But that I would not lose her sight so long.

As with most braggarts, he must offer an excuse not to complete the impossible deed he has promised; he will not eclipse the sun with his wink, because he does not want to close even one eye and miss an opportunity to gaze at the beauty of his love. He further declares that the brightness in his lover's eyes might blind the sun, source of all light. If the sun has not yet experienced that blindness, the speaker bids him to

> Look, and tomorrow late, tell me,
> Whether both th'Indias of spice and mine
> Be where thou left'st them, or lie here with me.

He equates his lover's value with that of all the spices that England had to import from India. The speaker increases his claim by noting that "those kings whom thou saw'st yesterday, / And thou shalt hear, all here in one bed lay." Donne insists that love creates its own universe and yields more than all of the material wealth and royal power of the world to those who experience it. The wordplay with exact rhyme in the homonyms *hear* and *here* again emphasizes that the lover possesses an entire universe, equivalent to all the sun hears in his omniscient position, literally in the bed.

The braggadocio reaches crescendo in the third stanza, as he claims that his love "is all states, and all princes I, / Nothing else is." Not only do the two lovers represent all that is worthy, nothing else even exists outside their own universe. "Princes" simply masquerade as the lovers, and compared to them "All honour's mimic; all wealth alchemy." Finally, the speaker continues his apostrophe, "Thou sun art half as happy as we." Donne uses ALLITERATION to his advantage, emphasizing *half* and *happy*. He could have dismissed the sun as enjoying no happiness; instead he suggests that even the sun's happiness, in his position as supreme ruler of all hemispheres, is only half that of the lovers. Donne's next line emphasizes the ability of two people to represent their own world:

> in that the world's contracted thus,
> Thine age asks ease, and since thy duties be
> To warm the world, that's done in warming us.

The ultimate claim that the lovers not only are as important as the rest of the world, but *are* that world, allows the speaker to ease into an acceptance of the sun's presence. Thus he gracefully avoids failure in his order to the sun to depart by graciously accepting its warmth. Donne's concluding couplet acts as a blessing, not only to the poem's lovers, but to all those who enjoy such a pure emotion: "Shine here to us, and thou art everywhere; / This bed thy center is, these walls, they sphere." By retaining attention to the bed throughout the poem, Donne makes clear that sex remains an integral part of love.

BIBLIOGRAPHY
Zunder, William. *The Poetry of John Donne: Literature and Culture in the Elizabethan and Jacobean Period.* Brighton, England: Harvester, 1982.

"SWEETEST LOVE, RETURN AGAIN"
LADY MARY WROTH (1621) LADY MARY WROTH included in her SONNET sequence "PAMPHILIA TO AMPHILANTHUS" part of her prose romance *The Countess of Montgomery's Urania,* a song as stanza 28 generally titled by its first line. The speaker asks her lover to return as soon as possible, comforting him by assuring him that her heart will remain true. He may even take her heart with him, a use of FIGURATIVE LANGUAGE (FIGURE OF SPEECH) that begins the inclusion of the hyperbole and allusion that characterized the works of METAPHYSICAL POETS AND POETRY. Scholars mention JOHN DONNE as one of the few poets whose work Wroth may have used as a model, and the metaphysical allusions she includes echo his. In the third stanza as an example of metaphysical PARADOX the speaker tells her lover that if he takes her heart on his journey, "in part we shall not part, / Though we absent be." She includes additional paradox by noting that while she may be bound and tied, her lack of freedom actually constitutes a benefit:

> Time, nor place, nor greatest smart
> Shall my bands make free.
> Tied I am, yet think it gain:
> In such knots I feel no pain.

She concludes by adopting the common trope of fire as symbolizing passion, writing, "Yet dear heart go, soon return: / As good there as here to burn."

SWIFT, JONATHAN (1667–1745) Born in Dublin into a poor Irish family headed by a widowed mother, Jonathan Swift gained an education through

the assistance of an uncle who cared for him from the age of three. He attended Kilkenny School and entered Trinity College, Dublin, in 1682. His academic career remained undistinguished according to Swift's own comments, but he graduated at age 14 with a bachelor's degree. He remained at Trinity until 1689, when the Revolution of 1688 caused political turmoil that interrupted his studies.

Swift then decided to visit his mother in England, where he spent a good deal of time at the home of the Whig statesman and diplomat Sir William Temple, whom he served as secretary. He nourished political ambitions, which he hoped his connections with Temple would serve, and he soon relocated to Moor Park, Surrey. Although he did enjoy an audience with William III and represented Temple in Ireland, no prospects developed. Swift spent his time in the pleasant pursuit of reading, consuming everything in Temple's large library, and enjoyed a cultured atmosphere, making connections with individuals who would later prove of importance to his career and personal life. One of those individuals was Esther Johnson, daughter to Temple's steward, whom Swift tutored. He would later characterize her as Stella in his poetry, including "STELLA'S BIRTHDAY 1721," and in his *Journal,* eventually developing what may have been a romantic relationship with her. During his years of service to Temple he also began writing two important works, *A Tale of a Tub* and *The Battle of the Books.* In 1692 he achieved his first publication in *The Athenian Mercury* with a Pindaric ode.

Also in 1692 Swift decided to complete his M.A. degree at Hart Hall, Oxford, and in 1694, he chose to enter the church. Doing so would allow him the practical means for support and was a common strategy for young scholarly men lacking financial means and future political prospects. He looked forward to a promised desirable appointment but instead was sent to serve on the northeastern coast of Ireland as vicar of three poor parishes. His main occupation was with the parish of Kilroot, near Belfast, where the bleak landscape and lack of career promise proved depressing. Kilroot had recently suffered a scandal leading to the excommunication or suspension of several clergymen for charges ranging from adultery to public drunkenness. These

facts complicated Swift's acceptance into the community, as did the growing popularity of the rival Presbyterian sect. However, Swift's service to the Anglican Church would last more than a half-century, a testimony to the unshakable loyalty that would become an important aspect of his reputation. Subsisting on a modest prebend, or church allowance, he continued work on *A Tale of a Tub,* which would reflect through satire the religious hypocrisy Swift so despised.

Remaining still hopeful of a political appointment, Swift departed Ireland to return to Sir Temple's employ in 1696; there he edited his employer's correspondence. Hopes faded for any political progress with Temple's death in 1699. Once again disappointed, Swift returned to Ireland, cynical and unhappy, smarting from the injustice of his fate. Having resigned his previous prebend, he served the lord justice, Lord Berkeley, as chaplain and obtained the living of Laracor. Granted another prebend in St. Patrick's Cathedral, Dublin, he looked forward to a promised reunion with Stella Johnson and her companion Rebecca Dingley, his youth allowing him to shrug off bitter feelings over his poor appointments. Stella would remain an important part of his life until her death, although exact details of the nature of their relationship remain sketchy.

Swift worked to become well known at St. Patrick's and was viewed as a clergyman with excellent prospects. Still in touch with his English connections, Swift in 1701 published a political pamphlet, *A Discourse of the Contests and Dissensions between the Nobles and the Commons in Athens and Rome*; it would be the first of several such pamphlets that made clear his political leanings. It gained him a positive reputation with some Whig statesmen, including Lord Somers, to whom Swift would dedicate *A Tale of a Tub.* Over the next few years as he visited London, Swift became acquainted with important writers, including Joseph Addison and Richard Steele, both highly political essayists, contributors to *The Tatler* and cofounders of *The Spectator.*

When *A Tale of a Tub* was published in 1704, Swift gained the attention of Whig literary circles. After the Whig rise to power in 1707, Swift became a representative of the bishops of Ireland to present a plea to Queen Anne to discontinue clerical taxes paid to the English

Crown. While he did well with his suit in Parliament and was encouraged by several powerful politicians, the one he most needed to win over, the earl of Godolphin, the lord treasurer, he could not. The earl requested that in return for the remission of the taxes, Swift act in a way that would endanger the future of the Anglican Church in Ireland. His loyalty to the church would not permit him to negotiate, and he sacrificed great personal gain when he rejected the earl's demands.

Although terribly disappointed by his inability to negotiate his goal, Swift continued to write, hoping to press his case later. In 1711 he published *Argument against Abolishing Christianity,* a work that reflected the tone of IRONY for which he would gain fame. In 1710 he published unflattering pieces featuring a character based on the astrologer John Partridge named Isaac Bickerstaff and published short poems in *The Tatler.*

Despite his early Whig connections, Swift began to associate with Tory wits after 1710, becoming editor of the Tory journal *The Examiner.* That post sealed his connection with the Tories, as he supported in print the Tory minister, Robert Harley, earl of Oxford. His new political alliance helped soothe his disappointment at not rising to a desirable position while associating with the Whigs. Tory ideology more easily supported Swift's convictions than had that of the Whigs, and to his great delight, he made quick progress in appealing the Irish clergy's case with Harley. Only two weeks after a meeting with Harley, Swift learned that Queen Anne was acting on his mission. He wrote to Stella with an ecstatic account of the victory, savoring the moment when he would at last receive his due credit for the withdrawal of the clergy tax. However, his hope would again be dashed. Ironically the Irish bishops decided that Swift was not, after all, the appropriate emissary on their behalf, and they removed him just before receiving the positive news from the queen. Worse, once they had learned of his success in pleading their case, they expressed public gratitude to the queen, to Lord Harley, and even to the lord lieutenant of Ireland, although he had not been involved in negotiations, but said no word about Swift. This pointed lack of recognition left Swift again discouraged and bitter.

Swift left his post of editor after a year to concentrate on writing a political pamphlet supporting proposals for peace on the Continent titled *The Conduct of Allies,* a work considered superb by later critics. As his literary reputation grew, his circle of friends expanded to include ALEXANDER POPE; Pope's best friend, the brilliant physician-to the queen John Arbuthnot; JOHN GAY; and the playwright William Congreve. A series of upbeat letters filled with information about the next heady years written to Stella would later be published as *Journal to Stella.*

Swift then began a second mysterious relationship with a woman, this one named Esther Vanhomrigh. Soon Vanessa, as Swift nicknamed Esther, fell in love with him, and he at first encouraged, but later rejected, her. He wrote of their affair in *Cadenus and Vanessa,* a work that added fuel to speculation regarding Swift and his relationships with various women, including Stella. One theory claimed he and Stella married in 1716, but another claimed they were blood relations as a result of ancestral incest and could not conduct a romance. While his various entanglements with women supported the characterization of Swift as a misogynist, some of his more charming writings disprove that characterization. Whatever his romantic entanglements, his popularity grew with his appointment as dean of St. Patrick's, and his political connections remained strong. However, power Swift drew from those connections ended with the queen's 1714 death and the Whig return to power, prompting Swift to retreat to Ireland for a long period. Although no doubt disappointed over yet another denial of a preferment, Swift took up the cause of Irish rights, producing several well-known writings, including *Proposal for the Universal Use of Irish Manufacture* (1720) and probably the most famous of his political efforts, *A Modest Proposal* (1729). His leadership in resisting the 1724 effort by England to force upon Ireland £100,000 in new copper coins minted by the corrupt William Wood made him a legendary figure. Fearful that the coin would debase the value of Irish coinage, leading the country even deeper into poverty, Swift published a series of letters encouraging readers to refuse to accept the coins. He wrote under the name *M. B. Drapier,* and the government offered a reward of £300 for information regarding the true identity of the letter writer. While all of Dublin knew his identity, and many of its poverty-stricken inhabitants could have greatly bene-fited from such a reward, no one identified Swift as the leader of the successful resistance.

Although some biographers have depicted Swift as unhappy in his self-exile in Ireland, he remained pro-ductive and conducted a spirited correspondence with his London friends. Around 1720 he began work on the book that would gain him long-lasting fame, *Gulliv-er's Travels,* published in 1726; it was the sole work for which Swift received any payment. He eventually returned to London and saw his friends again but upon learning of Stella's illness traveled quickly to Ireland. When she died in 1728 Swift lived a lonely, but con-tinuously productive life. *A Modest Proposal* was pub-lished in 1729, along with various poems and *Verses on His Own Death* (1739). Popular anthologized poems include "A DESCRIPTION OF A CITY SHOWER" and "VERSES ON THE DEATH OF DR. SWIFT."

While Swift's works continue to be studied and rep-resent some of the most important English language writings of the 18th century, a general misperception regarding him continues to exist. The characterization of Swift as a cynical misanthropic, even perverted, misogynist proves unfortunate. The Victorian age had much to do with that viewpoint, as notables including William Makepeace Thackeray encouraged readers to avoid certain parts of Swift's writing, because of its uncouth crudity. But Swift's certain pessimism cannot be considered separately from what Louis Landa terms "the intellectual currents of his time, certain philo-sophical and theological influences, which may have shaped his conception of man and the world." Writers of his age commonly focused on man's evil nature and tendencies toward corruption. Not many church divines proved optimists; their fellow church leaders would have been skeptical of such an outlook. While critics have attempted to make many things of *Gulliv-er's Travels,* from a children's story, minus the "unfor-tunate" scatological references, to a religious tract, most now agree it is a secular examination of man's moral and social tendencies. Swift was hardly alone in his observation of cultural imperfection and loss of val-ues that he felt marked his age. Regardless of his per-sonal ideology and publicly aired views, Swift produced a body of work that forever secures his reputation as a literary force.

BIBLIOGRAPHY

Fauske, Christopher. *Jonathan Swift and the Church of Ireland, 1710–1724.* Dublin: Irish Academic Press, 2002.

Glendinning, Victoria. *Jonathan Swift: A Portrait.* New York: Henry Holt, 1999.

Kelly, Ann Cline. *Jonathan Swift and Popular Culture: Myth, Media, and the Man.* New York: Palgrave, 2002.

Kinsley, James, and James T. Boulton. *English Satiric Poetry, Dryden to Byron.* Columbia: University of South Carolina Press, 1970.

Landa, Louis A. Introduction to *Jonathan Swift: Gulliver's Travels and Other Writings,* vii–xxvi. Boston: Houghton Mifflin, 1960.

Lindsay, David W., ed. *English Poetry, 1700–1780; Contem-poraries of Swift and Johnson.* Totowa, N.J.: Rowman & Littlefield, 1974.

McMinn, Joseph. *Jonathan Swift: A Literary Life.* New York: St. Martin's Press, 1991.

Nokes, David. *Jonathan Swift: A Hypocrite Reversed.* New York: Oxford University Press, 1985.

Williams, Kathleen. "Jonathan Swift." In *Dryden to Johnson,* edited by Roger Lonsdale, 41–76. New York: Penguin, 1993.

T

"THANKSGIVING TO GOD, FOR HIS HOUSE, A" ROBERT HERRICK (1648) The speaker of "A Thanksgiving to God, for his House" by ROBERT HERRICK acknowledges the many blessings represented by his house and its contents in order to praise God for those blessings. Herrick's inclusion in the title of the possessive pronoun *his* makes clear his view that anything the speaker, and by extension he, owns belongs properly to God, its source. The house imagery provides a metaphor for God's protection of the speaker. The poem's format proves appropriate to the apostrophe, an address to an unseen entity. Herrick constructs 29 sets of two lines each, in which the first line contains a primary comment with a METER of four beats, while the indented second line adds detail to the description of the first in only two beats. Thus, the first six lines read

> Lord, Thou hast given me a cell
> > Wherein to dwell;
> And little house, whose humble Roof
> > Is weather-proof
> Under the spares of which I lie
> > Both soft, and drie;

The speaker continues in this vein, describing God, or "Thou," as "my chamber" guarded by "harmlesse thoughts, to watch and keep / Me, while I sleep." The reader understands the speaker's humility is real, as he notes that both his porch and his fate are "void of state," with their measure of worth being their attendance by the poor, whom he freely supplies with "Good words, or meat." Other rooms in the house hold similar stores of food, all representing gifts from God. The speaker notes that his realization of God's kindness in supplying his needs makes everything, even "my beloved Beet, / To be more sweet." The speaker also moves outside the house proper, noting he takes in ample crops and enjoys a hen that lays each day as well as sheep that bear twin lambs each year.

Herrick concludes the poem with the speaker's understanding that God sends him blessings for a purpose; so that he may develop "A thankfull heart" and note openly that its full state is "wholly Thine," that is, that the emotions that overflow his heart originate in God. However, as the final two lines emphasize, Christ must also accept the thanksgiving in order for it to prove valid.

Such thanksgiving and praise verse contrast with Herrick's more worldly works, such as "The VINE" and several of his poems about Julia, his ideal woman. This variety of themes and approaches marks the large collection of Herrick's poetry titled *Hesperides* (1648). It contained in excess of 1,000 works, both sacred and secular, demonstrating the poet's versatility of expression.

"THEN IS SHE GONE?" WILLIAM DRUMMOND OF HAWTHORNDEN (1616) WILLIAM DRUMMOND OF HAWTHORNDEN adopts the PETRARCHAN SONNET form for the poem that begins, "Then is she gone? O fool and coward I!" published among his sonnet collection in his *Poems* (1616). The male speaker expresses regret over having been foolish and too timid to take advantage of an opportunity for love. Drummond presents an interesting twist on the CARPE DIEM, or seize the day, theme that would, a short time later, become a favorite of CAVALIER POETS. Rather than bidding a virgin to enjoy love and sex while at her physical peak as the carpe diem pleas would, Drummond's speaker chides himself for not having engaged in that bidding. This complaint will engage the first eight lines of the sonnet, while the concluding six will analyze why the speaker behaved as he did, and how he might alter his future behavior.

The speaker laments the loss of opportunity when he says in the second line, "O good occasion lost, ne'er to be found!" then continues his self-reproach, asking, "What fatal chains have my dull senses bound, / When best they may that they not fortune try?" The speaker recognizes that he has killed his own chance, or fortune, by not having been observant enough to know that he needed to act, but he is not sure exactly what "chained" him. He sketches the scene, reciting,

> Here is the flow'ry bed where she did lie,
> With roses here, she stellified the ground,
> She fix'd her eyes on this yet smiling pond,
> Nor time, nor courteous place, seem'd ought
>   deny.

In other words the young lady led the speaker to a perfect setting, the roses acting as a traditional symbol for a sexually active woman, or one prepared to be.

Then readers learn what held the speaker back: "Too long, too long, Respect, I do embrace / Your counsel, full of threats and sharp disdain." The speaker understands that the respect he felt for the would-be lover's virginity has cost him an opportunity. Drummond personifies the abstract idea of respect, using an uppercase first letter, as with a proper name. The speaker listened to the common wisdom that he should not try a young woman, because the consequences were too great to bear. He now knows that his lover did not share his reticence. Drummond skillfully builds momentum

with repetition of the word *disdain* that concludes the 10th line, placing it also at the beginning of the 11th line: "Disdain in her sweet heart can have no place, / And though come there, must straight retire again." He feels that while she may have brief doubts, momentarily sharing his disdain, they depart, because of her naturally sweet heart. The speaker concludes in the final couplet with a vow: "Henceforth, Respect, farewell, I oft hear told / Who lives in love can never be too bold." He will listen to a new common wisdom, trading the respect that made him hesitate and miss an opportunity for love for a new boldness, overcoming his former cowardice. Thus the male ironically overcomes an innocence or naivete that would traditionally be that of a female.

Drummond's sonnet proves highly dramatic, with an intensity that would support the speaking of his lines on stage. The reader can easily imagine an actor playing the distressed young man and, like one of Shakespeare's characters, striding back and forth as he expresses his regret.

"THEY ARE ALL GONE INTO THE WORLD OF LIGHT!" HENRY VAUGHAN (1655)

In the collection by HENRY VAUGHAN titled *Silex Scintillans* Vaughan includes a number of poems that focus on death. Among these is "They Are All Gone into the World of Light!" which provides a strong example of Vaughan's positive attitudes toward death. He has no fear of dying, as he inevitably expresses death as resulting in an opportunity for humans to experience rebirth through Christ's regenerative sacrifice. Critics note that this poem focuses on the death of Vaughan's brother, William, as had "Silence, and stealth of days!" However, Vaughan wrote it later and universalized the death theme to apply to the many others he knew who had also died. This speaker does not so much grieve for those lost as wish he could join them, opening with the title line, the next three lines noting, "And I alone sit lingering here." The participle *lingering* is a passively active verb, indicating a result of indecision.

The traditional use of light to symbolize Christ and man's redemption is from the New Testament of the Bible, particularly from the first lines of the opening chapter of the Gospel according to John. In the second of Vaughan's 10 four-line stanzas he extends the light metaphor with terms such as *glows* and *glitters* and FIGURATIVE LANGUAGE (FIGURE OF SPEECH) such as the similes

> Like stars upon some gloomy grove,
> Or those faint beams in which this hill is dressed,
> After the sun's remove.

His use of ALLITERATION and personification enhances the nature imagery, as does the contrast between *glows* and *glitters* and *gloomy* and *faint*. He continues this technique as the speaker describes his vision of the dead in the third stanza, contrasting their "air of glory" walking in "light" with his own "days, which are at best but dull and hoary, / Mere glimmering and decays." Alliteration appears again in the fourth stanza, when the speaker praises "O holy Hope! And high Humility, / High as the heavens above" for allowing him to see a future that he may possibly claim. The fifth stanza equates "beauteous Death" with "the jewel of the just," which requires darkness in order to shine. The speaker makes clear in the sixth stanza that men's faculties remain diminished as he is figuratively left in the dark on so many matters. He illustrates by noting that a man may see a bird's nest and know the fledgling has flown, but where the bird sings now, "That is to him unknown." Man's thoughts, however, may be penetrated, as angels appear in "brighter dreams," calling man's soul during sleep, allowing "strange thoughts to transcend our wonted themes," allowing him to "peep" at "glory."

Vaughan incorporates further effective imagery in the eighth stanza, asking readers to imagine a star "confined to a tomb" where "her captive flames" would "burn." When the same "hand that locked her up" opens the door, her light will "shine throughout the sphere." This serves as a reference to God's grace, which releases man's soul after death if he has accepted that grace, which leads to redemption. The penultimate stanza serves to praise God as "Father of eternal life," the giver of "true liberty," while in the final stanza the speaker requests that the mists through which he envisions life after death be dispersed. As an alternative, and obviously the desired act, God may "remove me hence unto that hill, / Where I shall need no glass." The last line reflects on Corinthians 13:12, commonly known as the Love Chapter, in which the disciple Paul writes, "For now we see through a glass, darkly; but then face to face."

BIBLIOGRAPHY

Rudrum, Alan. *Henry Vaughan.* Cardiff: University of Wales Press, 1981.

"THIRTY-EIGHT" CHARLOTTE SMITH (1787)

CHARLOTTE SMITH addressed her poem "Thirty-Eight. To Mrs. H—y" to Eliza Hayley, a friend one year younger than she. Separated from her husband and attempting to raise her nine children alone, Smith counters the convention that a mature woman of 38 years might have nothing to which to look forward in her life. As young women the two friends had made fun of older ladies, and Smith revises their view in her poem.

The speaker addresses her friend, reminding her that in "early youth's unclouded scene" on the "brilliant morning of eighteen," with both "health and sprightly joy elate / We gazed on youth's enchanting spring." At that time the friends did not understand "how quickly time would bring / The mournful period—*thirty-eight*!" She will conclude nine of the 10 six-line stanzas with the number that had proved anathema to the young women.

The second stanza gives the reader insight into how the two friends thought of maturity at the age of 18. They pictured those of 38 as "the starch maid, or matron sage," viewing them with "mingled scorn and hate." She adds that the two "loved to trace" the "sad effects" of aging, which would include "sharp words, or sharper face." The strength of Smith's terms could at first glance indicate regret that she now fulfills the prophecy. However, the reader quickly sees that the poem is actually designed to show just how incorrect the girls' conception proved.

The third stanza begins in the negative vein but will turn positive, probably to emphasize the contrast between the speaker's present-day reality and the silly fancies of children. She incorporates the terms *saddening, sickening,* and *dread,* writing that the friends might have preferred death to the "neglect" that they anticipated would be the lot of any as old as 38. However, in stanza 4, the speaker introduces a note of reality, as she writes, "Time, in spite of wishes, flies" and "Fate our simple prayer denies," with death forced to wait the correct hour for its visit. Their auburn hair becomes marked by gray, and the fading roses usher in a time of "Reason" "at—thirty-eight!" Smith employs the FIGURATIVE LANGUAGE (FIGURE OF SPEECH) of personification to make Reason female, a figure that instructs the mature women's hands in "new pleasures," opening a view to "Prospect less bright—but far more true." That prospect includes the capacity to enjoy a man's friendship without scandal, as well as the capacity to see youth's follies for what they were, a scorning "of sober sense the plan / Which gives content—at *thirty-eight*." Further stanzas note that in addition to content, maturity confers joy in friendship and science, "the luxuries of mind," as well as the calm in which to enjoy their accomplishments.

The biographer Loraine Fletcher points out that the term *we* used in the stanzas to refer to the young women's youth remains general, as Smith, already married for more than two years at 18, had not been carefree. Nor was she able at age 38 to enjoy much contentment or any luxuries of note. Fletcher believes that Smith may have been trying to convince Eliza to reevaluate her present situation as an unhappy wife, a young woman viewed by many of their acquaintances as extravagant. Eliza enjoyed extended visits to Bath, which took her from her home for extended periods. Smith may allude to her friend's irresponsibility, suggesting that her habits, rather than a true dislike of her husband, are to blame for marital difficulties. However Eliza viewed the poem, she and her husband would separate permanently in 1789.

In the final stanza Smith moves forward. Having considered the past and the present, the speaker looks to a future when

> With firmer souls and stronger powers,
> With reason, faith, and friendship ours,
> We'll not regret the stealing hours
> That led from *thirty-e'en* to *forty-eight*!

Fletcher describes the poem as "amusing," but "conventional." In her view Smith's shift to a different form in her concluding stanza did provide an "effective ending."

BIBLIOGRAPHY
Fletcher, Loraine. *Charlotte Smith: A Critical Biography.* Houndmills, England: Palgrave Macmillan, 2001.

THOMSON, JAMES (1700–1748)

Born in Scotland, James Thomson was raised a Scottish Calvinist. He was exposed early to a range of literature, influenced by the social and political atmosphere that followed the Union of Scotland with England. He matured in a family of gardeners and appreciated that occupation as an art. Thomson's keen observation of nature would be reflected in his poetry, especially his detailed observation of landscapes. Most critics viewed him as an English poet for some time, but later criticism regarded Thomson's Scottish background as crucial to his art. While some argued his style was too intellectual for the common man, others noted that only a Scottish peasant could relate to his description, as they had a shared experience with Thomson. His poetry continued to provoke such varying consideration into the 21st century. Later criticism holds that his natural descriptions reflect Scottish enlightenment aesthetic philosophy, which held that specific geography proved crucial to a sense of nationalism. He drew on his own experience, such as writing about a shepherd found frozen in the snow, to reveal how the elements challenged a productive life in Scotland. Thomson celebrated that challenge in his poetry, revealing how humans, the crops, and animals suffered from seasonal changes. The isolated nature of Southdean, where Thomson spent his childhood and youth, complemented his shy nature.

He attended local school and at age 12 entered the prestigious and challenging Jedburgh Grammar School, a 15th-century Latin school. Students also studied Greek, history, and math with the natural philosophy that passed for science in that era. Thomas began to write poetry as he studied, although none of his early work survived. He was probably inspired by the school stage plays, although his shy nature gained him a reputation as a dull and noncreative student. Sir William Bennett of Grubbet, a member of Parliament, adopted Thomson as his protégé. Thomson eventually adopted political views of the Whig Party, which was allied with the Presbyterian Church. It developed to represent support for Great Britain and Anglicization, rather than the militant Scottish nationalism practiced by some of his fellow poets. Bennet would encourage him to write poetry in English. Other supporters included the Elliots of Minto, Sir Gilbert and the younger Gilbert Elliot. Robert Riccaltoun also influenced Thomson through his philosophical "Essays on Human Nature." These many influences may be seen in Thomson's most enduring work, "A HYMN ON THE SEASONS" (1726–30), a copy of which was said to be found in every cottage in Scotland, despite Thomson's writing in English, rather than his native Scots tongue. He continuously revised the poem over the next 16 years.

Thomson matriculated to Edinburgh University in 1715 and became a passable student in theology, philosophy, and science, writing "A Poem Sacred to the Memory of Sir Isaac Newton" (1727) just after graduation. It reflected the influence of Newton's *Principia* as well as his *Optics*. Thomson completed the four-year M.A. program in 1719, delaying taking his degree until 1720. He continued divinity studies and after 10 years left the university in 1725, having become a member of the literary and political group the Grotesque Club. He soon began to publish in The *Edinburgh Miscellany.*

Thomson's father, Thomas, was minister and lived in the parish of Southdean and remained there all his life. While Thomson later openly displayed his love for his mother in his writings, he never mentioned his father, suggesting a difference in approach to faith and politics between the two men. Supposedly while performing an exorcism, Thomas Thompson was hit by a ball of fire that robbed him of the power of speech; shortly thereafter he died. According to records he probably died of apoplexy or a heart attack, although his death was blamed on Satan. In part because of his father's death, Thomson later adopted superstition as a theme for his writings. He continued his close relationship with his mother until her death two weeks after his move to London in 1725.

In London Thomson joined a heady literary circle, as his patrons, Lord Minto and Duncan Forbes, introduced him to ALEXANDER POPE; Pope's best friend, Dr. Arbuthnot; and JOHN GAY. As he wrote, he also tutored

Thomas Hamilton, son to Charles, Lord Binning. In 1726 "Winter," the first part of *The Seasons,* was published, followed by "Summer" (1727), "Spring" (1728), and "Autumn," the latter appearing in a collected edition published in 1730. Many of the best writers subscribed, and Thomson's reputation was assured. He continued to revise the work, perhaps with help from Pope and George Lyttleton, and a corrected, enlarged edition was published in 1744. Thomson's poetry, such as "The Castle," reflect his belief as a member of the first generation of moderates of the Scottish church that the work ethic was part of Christian social concerns, and that good works positively affected society as a whole. As a Scottish Calvinist he believed it his religious duty to work hard. While such work could not earn salvation, material rewards resulting from it were a sign that one belonged to those predestined, or elected, to merit salvation.

Thomson produced a tragedy in 1730 titled *Sophonisba,* then escorted as tutor Charles Talbot abroad. Talbot died unexpectedly, and his father expressed his fondness and gratitude to Thomson by giving him the secretaryship of briefs as a sinecure. This allowed Thomson to retire to Richmond, where he enjoyed his gardens and published a lengthy patriotic poem titled *Liberty* from 1734 to 1736. Marked by exaggeration and verbal extravagance, it was unsuccessful. After the death of his patron, Lord Talbot, Thomson focused again on the stage, producing a series of tragedies. None did particularly well. They included *Agamemnon* (1738), *Edward and Eleanora,* and *Tancred and Sigismunda* (1745). *Coriolanus* (1749) received a posthumous staging.

Through the efforts of George Lyttleton, Thomson was granted an annual pension of £100 from the prince of Wales. He contributed the famous lyrics to "RULE BRITANNIA" as part of *The Masque of Alfred* (1740). In 1748 Thomson published a poem 15 years in the writing, *The Castle of Indolence.* A clever imitation of work by Edmund Spenser and admired by many, it reflected Thomson's belief that wasted time was near-sinful and incorporated more of the natural description valued in *"The Seasons."* Labeled by the biographer Scott "a religious and sociopolitical allegory," as well as Thomson's "most compact and formally controlled poem," it represented a return to the Scottish themes crucial to

Thomson's work. He died after a brief illness that followed a boat outing, said to have caused him to "chill." Thomson was buried in the Richmond parish church and later celebrated by WILLIAM COLLINS in the ode "In Yonder Grave a Druid Lies."

BIBLIOGRAPHY

Campbell, Hilbert H. *James Thomson*. Boston: Twayne, 1979.

Griffin, Dustin. *Regaining Paradise: Milton and the Eighteenth Century*. Cambridge: Cambridge University Press, 1986.

Scott, Mary Jane W. *James Thomson, Anglo-Scot*. Athens: University of Georgia Press, 1988.

"TIME" GEORGE HERBERT (1633) As he does in "DEATH," GEORGE HERBERT demystifies man's mortality by converting death's threat into a promise. In this case he shows that man's loss of time as he ages will actually work to his benefit, as his heavenly reward will become available only after his time on earth. Therefore man need not fear his mortality but should instead embrace aging as not only a necessary, but a welcome, transformation.

Herbert begins with an apostrophe, using the FIGURATIVE LANGUAGE of personification to convert Time into a being, whom his speaker addresses. The speaker labels Time a "slack thing," telling Time, "Thy scythe is dull; whet it for shame." Herbert adopts the image of death as the grim reaper bearing a scythe, helping readers make the connection between death and time. He also sets up an extended metaphor of man as a cultivated crop, which Time will gather as lives end. Time explains to the speaker that he is not ashamed of his dull scythe, because "where one man would have me grind it, / Twenty for one too sharp do find it." In other words rarely do men want to speed time's movement toward their death; they prefer the scythe remain dull and unable to reap human lives. The speaker in the second stanza explains that perhaps that used to be man's view of time when he loved life more than anything else. Then the scythe seemed "a hatchet," but now it has become a mere "pruning-knife," made to disconnect man from his earthly life in order to speed him toward his meeting with Christ. He explains, "Christ's coming hath made man thy debtor, / Since by thy cutting he grows better." Herbert emphasizes that

Christ's death on the cross redeemed man, who can look forward to eternal life. Once time cuts him free of earthly existence, he can at last enjoy his reward.

In line 13, which begins the third stanza, the speaker adds that now Time is also blessed, benefiting from Christ's blessing of men. Before Christ Time served as "An executioner at best," but now he is "a gard'ner" as well as "An usher to convey our souls / Beyond the utmost stars and poles." Christ's death and subsequent redemption of man have also transformed Time, affording him new roles. Herbert reflects on the idea of time in line 19 writing, "And this is that makes life so long, / While it detains us from our God." He offers readers a new perspective on time, something they used to fear as leading to the terrifying prospect of death and loss of life. In his view it is life itself that is the problem, delaying the reunion with God. Waiting for that reunion can make man feel "already half of hell." The final stanza begins, "Of what strange length must that needs be, / Which ev'n eternity excludes!" He again suggests that readers adjust their concept of time. Herbert cleverly concludes his drama with the character of Time "chafing" as he waits for a man who obviously "deludes." His delusion is summarized in PARADOX, as Death questions, "What do I here before his door? / He doth not crave less time, but more." The speaker does not chase Time away in order to see less of him; rather he wants to enjoy more of Time, but as a reaper of souls, not as an extension of his earthly existence.

"TO ALTHEA, FROM PRISON" RICHARD LOVELACE (1649) "To Althea, from Prison" by the CAVALIER POET RICHARD LOVELACE is considered one of the most beautiful and balanced lyric poems in English. The famous line from its final stanza "Stone Walls do not a Prison make" supports a theme not original to Lovelace, that physical confinement may be transcended by imagination. Lovelace experienced imprisonment for his Royalist sympathies on more than one occasion, so he knew of what he wrote. In this carefully constructed poem he celebrates the fact that the human will has the capacity to triumph over adversity. Considered the finest of the "prison poems," it is valuable for its simple expression of a complex truth.

Each of Lovelace's four stanzas contains two quatrains and a rhyme scheme of *ababcdcd*, with repetition of *Liberty* as the concluding word. The first three stanzas open with the word *When,* and in each seventh line, the speaker compares himself to another being, over whom he triumphs in his feelings of liberation. Only in the concluding stanza does he note the being who shares his feelings of victory, an angel. He uses imagery that supports his theme of spiritual freedom.

In the first stanza he describes "Love with unconfined wings," which "hovers within my Gates," or his metaphorical prison. He fantasizes that Althea arrives at the prison grates to "whisper" her love, and he notes his only "fettered," or chained, state is when he lies "tangled in her hair." Even "Gods that wanton in the Aire / Know no such Liberty." The second stanza employs imagery of flowing wine, by reference to *Cups* that flow so freely they may be compared to the Thames itself. He describes a time of celebration when are "Our careless heads with Roses bound, / Our hearts with Loyal Flames." Again the prisoner imagines drowning his "thirsty grief" in wine during a time when all celebrants toast one another's health. He concludes that stanza by reflecting on the notion of the flowing river and the drunkenness that accompanies times of joy. Even "Fishes that tipple in the Deep, / Know no such Liberty."

The third stanza features a singing bird, the "linnet," to which the speaker compares himself as he sings "The sweetness, Mercy, Majesty, / And glories of my King." ALLITERATION helps emphasize the positive aspects of his ruler, making clear the speaker feels his incarceration is a worthy sacrifice. Not only will he sing, he "shall voice aloud" the king's goodness and his potential for greatness with the effect of "Enlarged Winds that curl the Flood," which "Know no such Liberty." The emotions of loyalty and devotion to his cause grant the speaker more freedom than the strongest winds, which obviously roam at will.

The imprisoned speaker makes his summary pronouncement in the final stanza, "Stone Walls do not a Prison make, / Nor Iron bars a cage," stressing that it is not physical confinement that defeats a man, but rather a lack of mental freedom. Instead of suffering in prison, "Minds innocent and quiet take / That for an Hermitage," meaning his prison becomes a refuge, allowing

him to expand his thoughts. Lovelace concludes his poem with four lines of shining simplicity that summarize his truth:

If I have freedom in my Love,
And in my soul am free;
Angels alone that sore above,
Enjoy such Liberty.

By referencing angels and heaven, Lovelace elevates human love and imagination to a divine level, reminding readers that God created men superior to the angels and in his image. Rarely has a poet so concisely and skillfully undercut the power of his oppressors. Lovelace demonstrates through his art his topic, that of the power of the imaginative word.

BIBLIOGRAPHY
Weidhorn, Manfred. *Richard Lovelace.* New York: Twayne, 1970.

"TO A MOUSE" ROBERT BURNS (1785) ROBERT BURNS included one of the most famous lines of poetry in his "To a Mouse: On Turning Her Nest, With the Plough, November, 1785." His well-known sentiment regarding mice and men would later be adopted by the American author John Steinbeck for his novel *Of Mice and Men* (1937). The title evoked the theme of the poem regarding a search for home and the propensity of fate to render the most carefully exacted plans chaotic. He employs tail RHYME in his six-line stanzas, in which the fourth and sixth lines are much shorter than the others. This format reflects the traditional Scottish technique of "standart Habbie," the term derived from Robert Sempill's poem "Life and Death of Habbie Simson" (ca. 1640), in which the poet both praises and makes fun of his subject. Another Scottish poet, ROBERT FERGUSSON, had earlier done the same in his "The DAFT DAYS," and Burns acknowledged his debt to Fergusson.

Burns set the scene with his title, and readers understand that the speaker has destroyed the home of a mouse while plowing his field. He begins with a sympathetic, yet humorous tone, as he assures the mouse, a "Wee, sleeket, cowran, tim'rous beastie," that she need not scream in fear "Wi' bickering brattle," as he will not chase her down "Wi' murd'ring pattle!" The speaker apologizes for the fact that "man's dominion / Has broken Nature's social union," then fashions himself as "thy poor, earth-born companion, / An' fellow-mortal." His address turns more serious as he considers the mortality of all living creatures, and his own problems that grow from his poverty. The speaker shows his empathy by telling her he understands that she "may thieve," as that is the only way she can live. The morsel she would require remains "a sma' request," one the farmer will grant. Then he bemoans "Thy wee-bit housie, too, in ruin! / It's silly wa's the winds are strewin!" as he watches the remnants of her nest scattered by "bleak December's winds." Assuming the mouse's perspective, he notes that she must have observed "the fields laid bare an' wast" and acknowledged "winter comin fast" by preparing a cozy home and thinking herself safe from the "blast," "Till crash! The cruel coulter past / Out thro' thy cell." He laments the fact that she is now exposed to "sleety dribble" then begins the seventh stanza by informing her she is not alone

> In proving foresight may be vain:
> The best laid schemes o' mice and men,
>   Gang aft agley,
> An' lea'e us nought but grief an' pain,
>   For promis'd joy!

As the poem concludes, the speaker muses that he may be even worse off than a field mouse, which only suffers in the present. He, on the other hand, has to suffer from his past, as well as fear his future:

> But och! I backward cast my e'e,
>   On prospects drear!
> An' forward, tho' I canna see,
>   I guess an' fear!

"To a Mouse" showcases Burns's talent for depicting the demanding life of the Scottish peasant class. In many of his poems he succeeded in convincing the reader that problems could be overcome through the efforts of the human spirit. That his speaker embraces the mouse as a fellow creature worthy of concern when Burns freely and often rejected those who believed themselves his social superiors says much about his attitude toward life.

BIBLIOGRAPHY
Kinsley, James, ed. *Burns: Poems and Songs.* New York: Oxford University Press, 1971.

"TO HEAVEN" BEN JONSON (1616) In his 1616 poetry collection *Works* BEN JONSON included a grouping of 15 poems, known as *The Forest*. More serious-minded than his collection of *Epigrams,* they reflect a stiffness that critics agree prevents most from reaching excellence, with the exception of "TO PENSHURST." Still some contain a fine individual line or two, and all exhibit skill, if not brilliance. In "To Heaven" Jonson displays his ability to imitate other writers in a manner that reflects intimacy with their works, rather than a desire to appropriate ideas improperly. As the Jonson biographer Rosalind Miles notes, he includes flashes of the metaphysical inspired by JOHN DONNE, as his speaker addresses God.

Jonson opens adopting the moral abstract terms he often used, the words *good* and *great:*

> Good and great God, can I not think of thee
> But it must straight my melancholy be?
> Is it interpreted in me disease
> That, laden with my sins, I seek for ease?

The speaker wonders whether his "disease," a tendency toward depression, might simply represent avoidance of taking responsibility for his transgression. In the next lines he acknowledges that God will know the truth and will understand whether he remains simply self-indulgent, putting on a show, and that God will later judge him. He actually invites the judgment, suggesting that if he "pretend / to aught but grace" God will know his true inclination. Beginning in line 9 he develops a CONCEIT that clearly echoes Donne:

> As thou art all, so be thou all to me,
> First, midst, and last, converted one and three,
> My faith, my hope, my love; and in this state,
> My judge, my witness, and my advocate.

While other poems in *The Forest* deal with concerns of friendship and community, as the final poem in the sequence, "To Heaven," focuses squarely on the poet's relationship with God.

Lines 13–16 contain the stilted style noted by critics. It lacks the tone of unmitigated awe that frames the preceding lines, and the terminology labors to make its point:

> Where have I been this while exiled from thee,
> And whither rapt, now thou but stoop'st to me?
> Dwell, dwell here still: Oh, being everywhere,
> How can I doubt to find thee ever here?

The internal RHYME, as seen in the terms *while* and *exiled* and *now* and *thou,* is so contrived it almost introduces unintended humor, and the eye rhyme of *here* and *everywhere,* followed by a second *here,* proves distracting.

Despite these challenges, Jonson later regains his rhetorical poise in three smooth lines, graced with skillful alliteration. They reflect a tone as melodic as that of the previous lines was harsh:

> I know my state, both full of shame and scorn,
> Conceived in sin and unto labor born,
> Standing with fear, and must with horror fall,
> And destined unto judgment after all.

The first 21 lines lack for the most part the melancholy edge that should support the speaker's claim to that emotion in the opening lines. However, Jonson achieves a respectful wistfulness in the four closing lines that evokes reader sympathy and respect:

> Yet dare I not complain or wish for death
> With holy Paul, lest if be thought the breath
> Of discontent; or that these prayers be
> For weariness of life, not love of thee.

The ENJAMBMENT that drives one line into the next only to be interrupted by a caesura imitates the speaker's hesitancy to proclaim his emotions. Rather he concludes with the very weariness he denies, in a whimper of restrained discontent.

BIBLIOGRAPHY

Miles, Rosalind. *Ben Jonson: His Life and Work.* New York: Routledge & Kegan Paul, 1986.

"TO HIS COY MISTRESS" ANDREW MARVELL **(1681)** One of his best poems, "To His Coy Mistress" is the most read of all work by ANDREW MARVELL, characterized by some critics as the best metaphysical poem in English. Widely anthologized, this poem appears often in undergraduate poetry survey courses. Its CARPE DIEM, or "seize the day," theme, was a popular one in English Renaissance poetry, drawing on a classical tradition exemplified by Catullus in his "Vivamus, mea Lesbia, atque amemus," or "Let us live, my Lesbia, and love." Adopted widely, it appeared in poetry including that by BEN JONSON, ROBERT HERRICK, and JOHN DONNE. Some critics label the poem a near-parody on the theme, as Marvell incorporates so liberally the FIGURATIVE LANGUAGE (FIGURE OF SPEECH) of hyperbole. He probably wrote this courtly LYRIC between 1640 and 1650; it first appeared in published form in his 1681 posthumous collection, *Miscellaneous Poems.* It shares the classic octosyllabic line format with others in the carpe diem group, as well as some attributes employed by METAPHYSICAL POETS AND POETRY; both of those techniques were common in Marvell's work. Its form is that of the logical argument, divided into three sections: the first premise, the second premise, and the conclusion. Because in Marvell's era *coy* could mean modest or shy, the subject of his poem requires convincing in order to overcome her shy nature and her modesty.

Marvell's argument begins with a supposition and its effect, that if he and the "lady" he addresses had "but world enough, and time," they would surely love at some point. The fallacy in his statement, of course, is that space and time are both always finite. However, he continues to imagine, playing with this fantasy to place both him and his love at specific points of geography during specific eras. Marvell's precision adds to the absurdity of his notion. He creates imagery in which "We would sit down, and think which way / To walk, and pass our long love's day." Marvell's use of the letter *w* to begin multiple terms in those two lines, as well as the assonance in *long love's,* physically slows the reader, imitating the leisurely action the speaker describes.

The speaker imagines his love in India beside the Ganges River, where she might discover rubies, while he would pass his time by the Humber River in England complaining of their separation. Marvell inserts self-reflection in the reference to the Humber, as he was born close by and enjoyed his education in Hull, on the north bank. As for time the speaker muses that he might have loved her "ten years before the flood," or the world's beginning, and she could love him after "the conversion of the Jews," an action predicted to occur at the end of the world. His "vegetable love," an allusion to an erect penis, could continue to outgrow empires and move with slow luxury; Marvell's wit remains prominent in the adoption of the vegetable metaphor. He could take "An hundred years" to praise her eyes and look upon her forehead and "Two hundred to adore each breast: / But thirty thousand to the rest." He adopts the approach of the PETRARCHAN tradition in praising the woman's body parts, reducing her to an object of admiration. Not only would he like to take this time, he tells her, "Lady you deserve this state."

The fantasy dissolves with Marvell's insertion of the transition term *But* in line 21, when the second part of his argument begins. He follows his warm fantasy with cold reality, declaring he always hears "Time's wingèd chariot hurrying near," a reference to Apollo's crossing the heavens each day pulling the sun behind him and symbolizing the unstoppable passage of time. He attempts to manipulate his love's determination not to give in to him by referencing what he believes that she most values: her beauty. In reality he reveals its value to him, noting that once she dies and is "in thy marble vault" her beauty will disappear, and she will no longer hear his "echoing song." He follows this realistic thought with a harsh accompanying note, that at that point "worms shall try / That long preserved virginity." The astute reader notes that he is setting her up to make a choice—give her virginity to him or allow it to become worm fodder—drawing on a classic logical fallacy for support, that only two choices exist. His lust will also become "ashes" at that point, a reference phrase in the 16th-century Book of Common Prayer (1559), "ashes to ashes, dust to dust." Marvell injects IRONY into the speaker's tone as the second section concludes, "The grave's a fine and private place, / But none I think do there embrace."

The final section adopts logical terminology, beginning, "Now, therefore," as if the speaker has made a perfectly rational point on which he will base a final conclusion. The seductive language is well designed to beautiful effect. The speaker makes note of his would-be lover's "youthful glow," comparing its effect on her skin to that of "morning dew." He supposes she possesses a "willing soul," one that "transpires / At every pore with instant fires." Because they both feel such passion, symbolized by fire, they should act on it, lacking the infinite time and space he earlier mentioned and facing sure death in the future. They should "like am'rous birds of prey" their own "Time devour," a reference to the consuming nature of passion. Marvell ends with another reference to Apollo, concluding, "Thus, though we cannot make our sun / Stand still, yet we will make him run." They cannot stop time, but they use it in a way that will leave them victorious.

BIBLIOGRAPHY
Belsey, Catherine. "Love and Death in 'To His Coy Mistress.'" In *Post-Structuralist Readings of English Poetry*, edited by Richard Machin and Christopher Norris, 105–121. Cambridge: Cambridge University Press, 1987.
Halli, Robert W., Jr. "The Persuasion of the Coy Mistress." *Philological Quarterly* 80, no. 1 (winter 2001): 57–70.
Karon, Jeffrey W. "Cohesion as Logic: The Possible Worlds of Marvell's 'To His Coy Mistress.'" *Style* 27, no. 1 (1993): 91–105.
Ray, H. Robert. *An Andrew Marvell Companion*. New York: Garland, 1998.
Reiff, Raychel Hangrud. "Marvell's 'To His Coy Mistress.'" *The Explicator* 60, no. 4 (summer 2002): 196–198.
Sokol, B. J. "Logic and Illogic in Marvell's 'To His Coy Mistress.'" *English Studies* 71 (1990): 244–252.

"TO HIS MISTRESS GOING TO BED" JOHN DONNE (1669)

By far JOHN DONNE's most erotic poem, "To His Mistress Going to Bed," also known as "Elegy 19," is composed of 48 lines of rhyming couplets with a METER of iambic pentameter. Not an ELEGY at all in the traditional sense of a poem written to commemorate a death, it instead celebrates the end of a woman's resistance to the speaker's sexual advances. Most critics believe Donne composed it before marriage, during a rather energetic youth. The poem in part parodies the 14th-century PETRARCHAN emotional romance tradition that objectified women, cataloging their body parts, advancing that tradition by adding explicit references. He follows the lead of popular Continental writers who improved the Petrarchan technique by imbuing it with an intellectual aspect. The tone remains that of a male wooing a female in order to seduce her. The poem involves little romanticism, other than in its FIGURATIVE LANGUAGE (FIGURE OF SPEECH). Donne offers an admirable balance in the poem, evidenced by individually balanced terminology and phrasing, as well as by the fact that the speaker does not request that his lover do anything that he is not also willing to do. By the final couplet the reader learns the speaker has already disrobed in anticipation of his lover's doing the same, after his very convincing argument.

The speaker begins, "Come, Madam, come, all rest my powers defy, / Until I labor, I in labor lie." The second line offers an example of balance in language, as well as a clever play on words. The first use of the term *labor* indicates man's physical work, while the second connotes the type of labor women undergo during birth, connoting both physical and emotional work or anguish. The term of address Donne adopts, *Madam,* indicates the speaker does not deal with an inexperienced maiden, countering the traditional seduction poem, which generally focused on a virgin. He continues with balance in mind, writing in the third line, "The foe oft-times, having the foe in sight, / Is tired with standing though he never fight." The fourth line appears to offer a PARADOX, as when one encounters a "foe," it is generally in anticipation of a battle. However, the "fight" the speaker faces is one of logic. He must convince his lover to ignore conventional social rules regarding gender behavior, as those rules represent the true "foe."

The speaker then begins ordering the removal of clothing, beginning with "that girdle, like heaven's zone glistering," where the *zone* referenced is the zodiac, or all the stars in heaven. However, his lover's girdle is "a far fairer world encompassing." Donne engages in the hyperbole, or exaggeration, characteristic of METAPHYSICAL POETS AND POETRY. The speaker also requests she remove her "spangle breastplate," which he understands she wears in order to stop "th' eyes of busy fools," suggesting that she "unlace herself" as the clock's "harmonious chime" alerts him to "bed-time." Next she may remove her "happy busk," or bodice,

which he envies "That still can be and still can stand so nigh." He compares what he views when she removes her gown to the "flowery meads" revealed when the shadow moves from a hill. Next she must remove "that wiry coronet and show/ The hairy diadem which on you doth grow." Next he requests removal of her shoes so that she may "safely tread / In this love's hallowed temple, this soft bed." He compares her white robe to that of the angels, then notes that she bears with her "A heaven like Mahomet's paradise," referring to the reward of beautiful maidens promised to attend dedicated Muslims after death. Donne becomes playful and constructs a passage assuring the lover that their white robes differ from those worn by ghosts, as the nearness of an "evil sprite" sets their hairs "uprite," but those by worn by angels do the same to their flesh. He refers to the effect of fear in hair-raising moments, and to the effect of an event of awe in causing the reaction commonly referred to as "goose bumps" on one's flesh. However, psychoanalytic critics might view the reference to rising flesh as a blatant sexual suggestion.

By line 25 the speaker asks his lover, "License my roving hands, and let them go / Before, behind, between, above, below," then incorporates an allusion to land waiting to be conquered by exclaiming, "O my America!, my new-found-land." He extends this CONCEIT, referring to himself as an emperor, where she remains his kingdom and a "mine of precious stones," all of which are "safeliest when with one man manned." Donne inserts another bit of wordplay but also suggests monogamy. He suggests another paradox by noting, "To enter in these bonds is to be free; / There where my hand is set, my seal shall be." With strongly erotic suggestion Donne also reflects on the idea of civic law, often made official by a seal.

Donne rarely wrote without reflecting on the human soul. His speaker next exclaims as if singing a hymn, "Full nakedness! All joys are due to thee. / As souls unbodied, bodies unclothed must be, / To taste whole joys." He profanely compares the release at death of the soul to sexual freedom allowed by the release of clothing. Donne includes a reference to the mythological figure of Atalanta, a woman racer who remained undefeated until challenged to a race by Hippomenes, who was in love with her. During the race he threw down some golden balls to distract her, causing her to lose the race. However, Donne reverses the story, declaring that women distract men by their arraignment, "Like pictures, or like books' gay coverings." He extends the book metaphor when his speaker compares women to "mystic books" that must be revealed. The speaker concludes his seduction by stating that he would like to know his lover just as a "midwife" might, requiring her to "cast all, yea, this white linen hence, / There is no penance due to innocence." He assures her she need make no penance, or atonement, due to innocence; in other words she is not an innocent maid. His final statement shows his sense of equality as he explains, "To teach thee, I am naked first; why then / What need'st thou have more covering than a man?"

As the Donne expert Helen Gardner has thoroughly discussed, Donne's love poetry greatly exceeds his religious poetry in style and presentation. While the religious poetry grew from self-conflict, the love poetry does not focus on whether the speaker is right to feel what he does; it focuses on the process of feeling. He seeks to explore a full range of emotions free of the judgment of Christianity or any religious creed. Gardner writes, "As a love poet he seems to owe nothing to what any other man in love had ever felt or said before him; his language is all his own." Unlike religious truths, the truths Donne uncovers in his love poetry belong to him alone.

BIBLIOGRAPHY

Edwards, David L. *John Donne: Man of Flesh and Spirit.* Grand Rapids, Mich.: William B. Eerdmans, 2002.
Gardner, Helen, ed. *John Donne: The Divine Poems.* Oxford: Clarendon Press, 1969.

"TO JOHN DONNE" Ben Jonson (1616)   BEN JONSON proved one of the most accomplished writers of his age, producing work in several genres. His poetry fell into recognizable categories, one of which is the ELEGY. While his writing could prove bawdy, for elegies he took care to preserve the appropriately respectful tone, producing clean, clear language simply of celebration. Jonson especially aspired to clarity, adopting deceptively simple language to express complex sentiments. In writing of JOHN DONNE, he adopted a humility unusual in Jonson the man, but

completely applicable to the situation, as Donne represented the epitome of the poet for most writers who followed.

The speaker opens the 10-line single stanza in rhyming couplets by labeling Donne "the delight of Phoebus and each Muse, / Who, to thy one, all other brains refuse," meaning that the muses, or inspiration, preferred Donne to all other poets. In the next two lines Jonson notes that each of Donne's works, thanks to his "most early wit, / Came forth example and remains so yet." In other words Donne remains a model for all poets and has since his first word graced a page. He possessed a self-knowledge that outreached most wits, "And which no affection praise enough can give." Jonson notes he cannot do justice to an artist of Donne's stature, even as he attempts to do so. If one then adds "thy language, letters, arts, best life, / Which might with half mankind maintain a strife," Donne represents an overwhelming subject, with a body of work to rival that of many other men. After all of this fashioning of acute praise, the poet concludes by saying he cannot do well enough to honor Donne: "All which I meant to praise, and yet I would, / But leave because I cannot as I should." The speaker notes it is one thing to praise a man as a poet, but when the praise also must include the other aspects of a career identified by Jonson, language does not have the necessary power to laud such a life accurately. Ironically Jonson could be writing of himself in the way critics would see him centuries later. Also a man of wide accomplishments that had an enormous part in the development of drama and poetry, Jonson would challenge others later as Donne had challenged him. In addition he remained persistent in employing speech as what he termed "the Instrument of Society," concerning himself with decorum in speech. Thus he may suggest that verbal praise of a man who was expert at his own expression would simply prove in poor taste.

BIBLIOGRAPHY

Herford, C. H., Percy Simpson, and Evelyn Simpson, eds. *Ben Jonson.* 11 vols. Oxford: Clarendon Press, 1954–1970.
Parfitt, George. *Ben Jonson: Public Poet and Private Man.* New York: Harper & Row, 1977.
Peterson, Richard S. *Imitation and Praise in the Poems of Ben Jonson.* New Haven, Conn.: Yale University Press, 1981.

"TO MY EXCELLENT LUCASIA, ON OUR FRIENDSHIP" KATHERINE PHILIPS (1667)

KATHERINE PHILIPS gained a reputation for her same-sex love poetry, which circulated in manuscript form for the most part. Her open admiration of her women friends found approval among her own circle of acquaintances, both male and female, the members of whom she assigned classical names. Anne Owen, viscountess of Dungannon, was the Lucasia of "TO MY EXCELLENT LUCASIA, ON OUR FRIENDSHIP," one of many poems dedicated to her. Philips incorporated metaphysical aspects in much of her work, including this piece. Four lines constitute each of six stanzas, arranged in an alternating RHYME pattern of *abab*, *cdcd*, and so on.

In the first stanza the speaker claims not to have lived until "this time / Crowned my felicity." Philips establishes a metaphor using the term *crown* to suggest royalty, FIGURATIVE LANGUAGE (FIGURE OF SPEECH) that will recur later in the poem. The speaker notes that she can claim without falsehood, "I am not thine, but thee." In suggesting that she has no existence of her own but exists only in her friend, Philips injects a metaphysical essence into the poem. The second stanza refers to the speaker's body as a "carcass," suggesting death, "a soul the motions kept," meaning the soul controlled bodily movements, thereby deceiving those who observed. Philips next adopts the figurative language of simile in the third stanza, as she compares her mechanical movements prior to meeting Lucasia to the works of a watch, powered by artificial means. The speaker lacked a true soul until she found that of Lucasia to make her own. In the fourth stanza the speaker describes the soul as something that "inspires, cures and supplies, / And guides my darkened breast," with the friendship her dearest "prize," her "joy . . . life . . . rest." The speaker notes in the penultimate stanza that neither "bridegroom nor crown-conqueror"—the second reference meaning a warlike king and echoing her initial mention of a crown—can compare his *mirth*, or satisfaction, to her own. They own "pieces of the earth," but the speaker has "all the world" in Lucasia. Philips concludes with a reference to "flames" as the passion shared by the two women. The flames remain uncontrolled by any "false fear" but are "As innocent as our design," or intention, and "Immortal as our soul."

Although some queer theorists have analyzed Philips as writing with sexual intent, other critics deny her tone suggests an erotic relationship between the speaker and Lucasia. Rather her passion resembles a religious attachment, revealed by the multiple references to the soul by a highly religious poet.

BIBLIOGRAPHY
Faderman, Lillian. *Surpassing the Love of Men: Romantic Friendship and Love between Women from the Renaissance to the Present.* New York: William Morrow, 1981.

"TO MY LORD COLRANE, IN ANSWER TO HIS COMPLEMENTAL VERSES SENT ME UNDER THE NAME OF CLEANOR" ANNE KILLIGREW (1686)

ANNE KILLIGREW takes special care in her "To My Lord Colrane" to appear grateful for a poem written to her by Henry Hare, second baron Colrane. While the occasion for the poem remains unclear, Killigrew obviously felt a burden to respond. Her effuse praise in comparing the baron to the greatest poets, including VIRGIL, cannot be taken seriously. She engaged in the over-writing that would become popular with males as well as females in the 18th century; her contemporary JOHN DRYDEN used in lavish overstatement in his odes written to various persons, including to Killigrew after her untimely death. What appears obsequious to modern sensibilities was simply a convention, especially crucial for women in Killigrew's era. By adopting a tone of utter humility, Killigrew might prevent the criticism commonly voiced against women writers.

Killigrew describes in the first line her own muse as "dull . . . in heavy slumbers" and "Indulging sloth . . . fancying little worthy her employ" (1–2). Nothing could be further from the truth for Killigrew herself, but her self-deprecating stance proved necessary to the occasion. "Cleanor's obliging strains," where *Cleanor* is the neoclassical name assigned to Hare, supposedly shake the poet from her stupor as she reads his lines "with fancy richly fraught, / Re-read, and then revolved them in her thought" (29–30). Her second stanza remains almost laughable in its fawning attempts to elevate the baron's verse. The speaker's muse asks rhetorically, "And can it be? She said, and can it be? / That 'mong the Great Ones I a poet see?" (11–12). Killigrew next praises the baron for not allowing politics, "formal pride" (14), or "Destructive vice, expensive vanity" (15) to distract him from his art, as they do other poets. She concludes that stanza,

> But here with wonder and with joy I find,
> I'th' noble born, a no less noble mind;
> One, who on ancestors, does not rely
> For fame, in merit, as in title, high!

Killigrew continues in this complimentary manner through her third stanza, in which she notes that Virgil wrote *A Smothered Gnat,* referencing a MOCK-HEROIC thought to be written by Virgil that Edmund Spenser had reproduced. She makes the point that verse is sometimes meant for instruction, to show by its perfection the weakness in others.

A genuine Augustan poet, Anne Killigrew could adapt herself to her situation. A great part of the Augustan tradition was the relation of the poet's personal experience to universal moral principles. Women supposedly lacked the capacity to do so, but Killigrew proved she possessed more than enough capacity, both intellectual and artistic, to join the chorus of male voices of her age. Projecting an image of vulnerable modesty in her salute to the baron Colrane helped protect her against attack by those voices.

"TO PENSHURST" BEN JONSON (1616)

Critics agree that BEN JONSON sought to fashion the Sidney family estate of Penshurst into an emblem representing his own ideals. He writes one of the first poems of place in "To Penshurst" and attempts to show how an aristocratic property may manifest grace without pretension when managed by a family noble in habits, as well as bloodlines. He had long admired the Sidneys, especially Robert Sidney, who eventually inherited the family title, earl of Leicester, after the death of his older brother, the famous poet Philip. Although Robert had financial problems, he never failed to welcome the poet to the family home of Penshurst in Kent. Jonson also became friends with Sir Robert's children, particularly Mary, named for her poet aunt, MARY SIDNEY HERBERT, COUNTESS OF PEMBROKE. As LADY MARY WROTH Mary Sidney would later take up the family pen and become

a prose and poetry writer. Jonson would dedicate poems to Mary and her sister, Philip (named for her uncle, whom the family adored), and brother, William, as well as to Wroth's husband, the earl of Pembroke.

Jonson believed that greatness was revealed through graceful and proper living, rather than inheritance, and he stresses that theme in this, one of his most famous poems. He writes in 102 lines of rhyming couplets in what critics term his finest effort to express his personal belief in social justice and individual responsibility. His tone is one of reverence, appropriate to his belief that the family embodies his ideals, a fact obvious in their family home. He begins, "Thou art not, Penshurst, built to envious show," as he personifies the estate, adding that this home does not boast touchstone or marble, "polished pillars, or a roof of gold." Rather

> Thou joy'st in better marks, of soil, of air,
> Of wood, of water; therein thou art fair.
> Thou hast thy walks for health, as well as sport;
> Thy mount, to which the dryads do resort.
>   (7–10)

Jonson celebrates the sylvan, or country life, referring to the dryads, or wood nymphs, then to Pan, Bacchus, and the Muses, to represent the fact that Penshurst fits naturally into its surroundings, unlike estates built simply for the sake of pomp. The speaker notes for the readers, as if taking them on a tour of the grounds, important historic events, allowing Jonson to emphasize Penshurst's connection to the past. One oak tree was planted to celebrate the birth of Sir Philip Sidney, later a Protestant martyr for Queen Elizabeth; in various poems of Jonson's era Sidney symbolized civilization. Under another tree the onetime lady of the house, Lady Leicester, went into labor, this fact allowing Jonson to suggest the importance of Penshurst to the future. Another group of trees bears the name *Gamage,* after Lady Barbara Gamage. All areas remain well populated by animals, some of which are domesticated: "Thy sheep, thy bullocks, kine, and calves do feed; / The middle grounds thy mares and horses breed" (23–24). The estate also provides abundant wild game for its owners' table:

The purpled pheasant with the speckled side;
The painted partridge lies in every field,
And for thy mess is willing to be killed.
And if the high-swollen Medway fail thy dish,
Thou hast thy ponds, that pay thee tribute fish.
    (29–32)

Jonson personifies nature and characterizes her as willingly engaging in service to the Sidney family, as if they represent the natural order as aristocrats sharing their abundance. By writing that if the Medway, a nearby river, does not yield fish, their own ponds will, Jonson salutes their husbandry and wise care of the land that has become their responsibility. He looks back to previous inhabitants of Penshurst, suggesting that they also acted in a responsible way to preserve the grounds. By referencing the past and the present, Jonson alludes to a future generation to whom Penshurst will pass in good form due entirely to the Sidneys and their far-sighted attitudes.

Jonson spends many lines detailing the natural bounty of Penshurst, noting the types of wildlife in the pond, orchards, and fruits on vines that "Hang on thy walls, that every child may reach" (44). He alludes to the contrast between the Sidneys and other members of the wealthy landed class, who enjoy the land's benefit only through the sacrifice of those not so fortunate, adding, "And though thy walls be of the country stone / They're reared with no man's ruin, no man's groan" (45–46). Everyone is welcome at Penshurst, regardless of rank, and invited to share in the estate's prosperity. That kindness inspires the visitors to reciprocate. They visit the estate even though they have no special requests to make of the wealthy family:

But all come in, the farmer and the clown,
And no one empty-handed, to salute
Thy lord and lady, although they have no suit.
Some bring a capon, some a rural cake,
Some nuts, some apples; some that think they
    make
The better cheeses bring them. (47–53)

He makes the point that the Sidneys do not need such tribute from neighbors, where the term *clown* means "yokel," but their enlightened natures cause them to accept all such gifts and to invite the visitors to share their "liberal board" in generous hospitality. Jonson counted himself among those fortunate visitors. As he details, Penshurst is a place "Where the same beer and bread, and selfsame wine, / That is his lordship's shall be also mine" (63–64). He again contrasts the Sidneys' hospitality with the forced hospitality at other "great men's tables" (66), where he is directed where to sit and what he can and cannot eat. By contrast, at Penshurst,

Here no man tells my cups; not, standing by,
A waiter doth my gluttony envy,
But gives me what I call, and lets me eat;
He knows below he shall find plenty of meat.
    (68–70)

Even the servant, here referred to as a *waiter,* is not anxious about food, as he will also enjoy the bounty.

Jonson makes clear his belief that the Sidneys have been rewarded precisely because of their generous attitude. He includes the family as part of Penshurst's pride, led by a "noble, fruitful, chaste" (90) lady. Her children, who learn religion and mature each day into gentle spirits,· learn even more from their parents' examples than the books they study, as they "Read in their virtuous parents' noble parts" (97). He concludes with four lines that again contrast Penshurst with the other aristocratic estates. While other noblemen may have built monuments to themselves, the master of Penshurst has constructed a true home to occupy:

Now, Penshurst, they that will proportion thee
With other edifices, when they see
Those proud, ambitious heaps, and nothing else,
May say, their lords have built, but thy lord
    dwells.

BIBLIOGRAPHY

Peterson, Richard S. *Imitation and Praise in the Poems of Ben Jonson.* New Haven, Conn.: Yale University Press, 1981.

Walton, Geoffrey. "The Tone of Ben Jonson's Poetry." In *Ben Jonson and the Cavalier Poets: Authoritative Texts, Criticism,* edited by Hugh McLean, 479–96. New York: W. W. Norton, 1974.

Woods, Susanne. "Aemilia Lanyer and Ben Jonson: Patronage, Authority, and Gender." *Ben Jonson Journal* 1 (1994): 15–30.

"TO THE FAIR CLARINDA, WHO MADE LOVE TO ME, IMAGINED MORE THAN WOMAN" APHRA BEHN (1688)

APHRA BEHN pursues the theme of forbidden love that gained her a reputation as a scandalous woman who wrote poetry, drama, and prose more appropriate for a man. Behn's focus on passion and sex, deemed improper for female RESTORATION writers, but completely appropriate for their male counterparts, elicited the ire of many of her contemporaries. Her work sold well, however, for a time, then remained uncelebrated until almost three centuries later, when feminist critics gave her the credit due her remarkable achievements. In "To the Fair Clarinda" Behn writes of the joys of making love to a hermaphrodite, an individual equally male and female. She formats her first 17 lines as couplets with exact rhymes with the exception of lines 9, 10, and 11, all three of which RHYME. She then indicates a break in flow and manner of address by inserting white space and closing with six lines of couplets featuring eye rhymes.

Behn's speaker begins by addressing her love interest as "Fair lovely maid," then agrees to address her as "lovely charming youth," if that name "more approaches truth." She continues to play with the idea of balance inherent to the presence of masculinity and femininity in one body by using the term *This* to refer to the youth and *that* to refer to the maid. The speaker declares she may "pursue" the youth "without blushes," as long as "so much beauteous woman" remains "in view," a prelude to her claim that "for sure no crime with thee we can commit; / Or if we should—thy form excuses it." In the three rhyming line, Behn continues to emphasize balance as she claims she struggles against Clarinda's "charms . . . in vain," even though her "deluding form" gives "us pain," and "the bright nymph betrays us to the swain." *Swain* was a common label for a shepherd, while a *nymph* was a mythological female being. Behn basically writes that the beauty characteristic of the female induces the speaker to submit to the aggression of the male. She adopts the serpent as a traditional phallic symbol as she concludes the first portion of the poem with the couplet "For who that gathers fairest flowers believes / A snake lies hid beneath the fragrant leaves." She also enjoys wordplay with the imagery of the flowers, as maids gather flowers, but those maids are also often considered flowers to be gathered, or deflowered, by males.

In the final six lines Behn drops the exact rhyme, perhaps departing from the idea of perfect balance. She addresses Clarinda now as neither maid nor youth, but instead as "Thou beauteous wonder of a different kind" and uses a male and female name in the second line, "Soft Cloris with the dear Alexis joined." Here Behn may suggest the joining caused by the act of physical sex. She continues, "Whene'er the manly part of thee would plead," indicating the making of a sexual proposition, "Thou tempts us with the image of the maid." She concludes by referencing mythological figures to comment on, or perhaps criticize, the 18th-century's sharp distinction between love and friendship: "While we the noblest passions do extend / The love to Hermes, Aphrodite the friend." In Greek mythology Hermaphroditus, offspring of the messenger god Hermes and the goddess of love Aphrodite, matured androgynous. Behn's use of the term *noblest* implies that not only is the speaker's love of both man and woman innocent but that those passions are elevated ones, superior to the passions inherent in strictly heterosexual relationships.

"TO THE IMMORTAL MEMORY AND FRIENDSHIP OF THAT NOBLE PAIR, SIR LUCIUS CARY AND SIR H. MORISON" BEN JONSON (1629)

BEN JONSON celebrated two friends, also members of the SONS OF BEN, in the classical ode form. A formal approach, the ode was used only for celebrating serious topics, most notably distinguished events or persons. In this case Jonson salutes an admirable friendship. Henry Morison died, probably of smallpox, at the young age of 20, leaving his younger friend, Lucius Cary, second viscount Falkland, to mourn his passing. Cary, also a poet, became a war hero, and he would die at the Battle of Newbury in 1643 after serving Charles I at court and in Parliament. Of a sensitive nature, and having recently become disillusioned with the political climate, he may have intentionally made himself a target. No doubt his passion attracted Jonson, who was one of several well-known writers to celebrate Cary.

While many poets imitated the ode form, its transformation into English proved a challenge; many English odes had stilted presentation. Petrarch provided a model in Italian and Ronsard in French some decades before any English poets used the form. Although MICHAEL DRAYTON labeled some of his poems odes, they more closely resembled BALLADS. Jonson was the first to naturalize the Pindaric ode in English in the late Renaissance; his poem has long been labeled the first "great" ode in English. Jonson adopts the classic Greek presentation of the ode by a chorus, which moved about the stage, dividing the poem into three portions. The chorus first chanted the *strophe,* then turned to cross the stage in the opposite direction during the *antistrophe,* then stood still to chant the *epode.* Jonson labels the three divisions the *Turn,* the *Counter-Turn,* and the *Stand.* Conforming to a fixed pattern, the four 10-line turns and counterturns incorporate rhyming couplets with varying line lengths, while the 12-line stands are even more complex.

Jonson adopts as his theme the classical concept of friendship, the poem incorporating thought from Plato, Aristotle, and the Stoic philosophers. Friendship is viewed as, according to the critic R. V. Young, "the fruit of shared virtue, as a spiritual reality transcending material circumstances and mortality." Jonson celebrates Morison's life as one of integrity, rather than touting any physical or material accomplishments. This may be clearly seen in the third stanza, or first stand, when the speaker asks,

> For what is life if measured by the space,
> Not by the act?
> Or masked man, if valued by his face,
> Above his fact? (21–24)

Because Jonson's era viewed the Pindaric ode as an impassioned form, his poem contains various startling figures of speech and ideas to emphasize a classic form through original patterns and references. For instance in the first stanza, or turn, an infant of Saguntum,

whose birth occurs as the great warrior Hannibal sacks his town, "looking then about" as he leaves the womb, "Ere thou wert half got out, / Wise child, didst hastily return," at which point his mother's womb is compared to an urn. In stanza 4, or the second turn, Jonson adopts water as an extended CONCEIT for death, rather than using it as the traditional symbol of new life:

> And sunk in that dead sea of life
> So deep, as he did then death's waters sup;
> But that the cork of title buoyed him up.

In the second counterturn, stanza 5, the speaker says, "Alas, but Morison fell young:—/ He never fell, thou fall'st, my tongue," allowing Jonson to pun on the word *fall,* by referencing the Latin *fallo,* which means "to make a mistake." In another rhetorical oddity Jonson concludes stanza 8, the third counterturn, with the word *Ben,* then begins the following stanza, the third stand, with the word *Jonson.* In the next stanza, the final turn, Jonson inserts what George Parfitt has labeled his often used language of morality, the terms *great* and *good.* While those words are abstract, Jonson habitually surrounded them with concrete terms to emphasize the morality of his subject. In this case he describes the two friends as united not by feasts or orgies, "But simple love of greatness and of good / That knits brave minds and manners, more than blood." Ultimately their friendship offered them more in common than had they been related by birth.

Jonson successfully adopts the Pindaric ode to make clear his message regarding the true value of friendship. He concludes with the metaphor of harvest as death, allowing emphasis on the positive effects of a moral life, as he writes of the youthful pair, "Who, ere the first down bloomèd on the chin / Had sowed these fruits, and got the harvest in."

BIBLIOGRAPHY
Parfitt, George. *Ben Jonson: Public Poet and Private Man.* New York: Harper & Row, 1977.

Peterson, Richard S. *Imitation and Praise in the Poems of Ben Jonson.* New Haven, Conn.: Yale University Press, 1981.

Young, R. V. "Ben Jonson and Learning." In *The Cambridge Companion to Ben Jonson,* edited by Richard Harp, and

Stanley Stewart, 43–57. New York: Cambridge University Press, 2000.

"TO THE LADIES" LADY MARY CHUDLEIGH (1703)

Critics judge that LADY MARY CHUDLEIGH endured an unhappy marriage from the evidence in her well-anthologized poem "To the Ladies." Because she begins in her first line comparing wives to servants, noting they differ only "in the name," her attitude toward the woman's place in the domestic sphere becomes clear. Chudleigh's attitude reflects the constraints that remained upon women who had gained little to no legal rights during the 17th century. *The Laws' Resolution of Women's Rights* (1632) explained that females "have nothing to do in constituting laws, of consenting to them, in interpreting of laws, or in hearing them interpreted . . . and yet they stand strictly tied to men's establishments, little or nothing excused by ignorance."

Chudleigh adopts FIGURATIVE LANGUAGE (FIGURE OF SPEECH) to describe marriage as "that fatal knot" that, once tied, "nothing, nothing can divide." Her statement proved true to her times, when men could procure divorces, but women could not. She focuses on a topic that always aroused her ire, the patriarchal ideology that women should be obedient to their husbands. Alluding to the "love, honor, and obey" line so familiar to readers from the traditional religious wedding ceremony, she use italics to emphasize woman's subservience in the line "When she the word *obey* has said." Not only does religion support man's dominance, civil law also protects the male, a point she makes when she adds, "And man by law supreme has made." Once the woman agrees to obey under the laws of the church and of man, "all that's kind is laid aside, / And nothing left but state and pride," where the term *state* means pomp or ceremony. As a subtext Chudleigh seems to suggest that both men and women prove little more than actors in the ritual, assuming roles to which only the wife is later held. Her husband grows "Fierce as an Eastern prince," is overcome by an innate "rigor," and can break his marriage vow with a mere look. But the woman remains "mute," supporting the traditional view of women as most desirable when silent. She has no freedom, may "be governed by a nod," and must remain as fearful of her husband as of God, a statement that supports man's position as a deity. Not only must she "serve" and "obey," she may only speak and behave in a manner that he approves. The speaker of the poem obviously chafes under all these restrictions, warning other women to beware. Chudleigh clearly suggests that to remain single would be more desirable than to marry. She emphatically tells her readers, "Then shun, oh! Shun that wretched state," thereby avoiding the hate of "fawning flatt'rers." Her final command reveals a progressive attitude, as she tells women, "Value your selves, and men despise / You must be proud, if you'll be wise." Women should not feel that pride is sinful, as it will afford them some spiritual independence.

Chudleigh often wrote to friends regarding her disgust for a society that, by design, suppresses its women with ignorance, not allowing them to attend school. All of the aspects of females that exasperate males are specifically bred into the women by those very men. That state of affairs suggests the men are the ones with self-loathing, rather than the women. They design and execute what they later label a disaster, without assuming any responsibility. Unfortunately Chudleigh's poem did not forecast any change, and little would alter over the next 100 years. Women continued to face different standards from those men had to meet, made clear by a parliamentary resolution enacted almost 70 years after the publishing of Chudleigh's poem. The 1770 resolution proclaimed that "all women of whatever age, rank, professions, or degree, whether virgin maid or widow" who attempted any seduction into matrimony of men "by means of scent, paints, cosmetics, washes, artificial teeth, false hair, Spanish wool, iron stays, hoops, high-heeled shoes, or bolstered hips" would face the same penalty faced by those accused of witchcraft. Such misogynistic attitudes would reach far into the 19th and even 20th centuries.

BIBLIOGRAPHY
Ezell, Margaret J. M., ed. *The Poems and Prose of Mary, Lady Chudleigh.* New York: Oxford University Press, 1993.
Ferguson, Moira. *First Feminists: British Women Writers 1578–1799.* Bloomington: University of Indiana Press, 1985.

"TO THE MEMORY OF MR. OLDHAM" JOHN DRYDEN (1684)

Exactly why JOHN DRYDEN

wrote the ode "To the Memory of Mr. Oldham" is not known; no evidence exists of a friendship or professional collaboration between the two. JOHN OLDHAM died of smallpox at age 30 in 1683 after producing a small, but well-received body of poetry in satire as well as some translations. The two poets' shared interest in satire, as well as Dryden's sympathy for the loss of a promising young writer, may have prompted his response to Oldham's death.

Dryden's poem appeared first in *Remains of Mr. John Oldham* (1684), as did Oldham's poem "To the Memory of Mr. Charles Morwent," ironically also focusing on death. However, Oldham's poem rationalized an early death, while Dryden's did not. The poem attempts to clarify their relationship, adopting a classical approach recognizable to informed readers. Dryden co-opts a memory related by VIRGIL about two friends, Nisus and Euryalus, Nisus the older man, a passage Dryden would translate later in that year. The two men competed in a footrace staged by Aeneas in honor of his dead father. While leading the race, Nisus fell, tripped the next fastest runner, allowing Aeneas to win. Critics have noted that Dryden uses the race as an extended CONCEIT representing life.

Oldham had used the political and religious unrest in England as satirical subject matter, as had Dryden. While national instability provided focus for Dryden in *ABSALOM AND ACHITOPHEL, The HIND AND THE PANTHER,* and "The Medal," his approach differed from that of Oldham. Where Dryden's tone may have proved flippant at times, it remained informed, in contrast to Oldham's lighter approach, as seen in a stanza from his "The Careless Good Fellow," couched as a drinking song:

I mind not grave asses who idly debate
About right and succession, the trifles of state;
We've a good king already: and he deserves
   laughter
That will trouble his head with who should
   come after:
Come, here's to his health, and I wish he may be
As free from all care, and all trouble, as we.

Still the fact that both employed satire, not yet a common technique, offered a shared experience for two quite different personalities. Critics point to another of Dryden's odes, "TO THE PIOUS MEMORY OF . . . MRS. ANNE KILLEGREW" in comparison to this ode. In both he expresses frank concerns regarding their talents, yet immediately qualifies those concerns. Of Killegrew he wrote, "Art she had none," but immediately eased the criticism by adding, "yet wanted none; / For nature did that want supply." Of Oldham he wrote that age and maturity, which Oldham lacked, "might (what nature never gives the young) / Have taught the numbers of thy native tongue." Once again Dryden expresses frank judgment of his subject; Oldham's skill in METER was poor. However, he follows with "But satire needs not those, and with will shine / Through the harsh cadence of a rugged line." Some critics, including Ann Messenger, posit Dryden's turns in regard to both of these young poets may indicate that he wanted to recognize the quality of their verse while making clear those same verses lacked his idea of "art." He also seems to suggest that with more maturity that art might have surfaced in both young artists.

In his tribute to Oldham Dryden's first line expresses his regret over the loss, while his second through fourth lines make clear the kinship he felt with the younger man:

Farewell, too little, and too lately known,
Whom I began to think, and call my own:
For sure our souls were near allied, and thine
Cast in the same poetic mould with mine.

Dryden helps clarify his relationship with Oldham at various points by employing allusions to the race celebrated by Virgil. The speaker prepares readers for the first allusion by stating that "our studies" shared a like goal and explains, "The last set out, the soonest did arrive" (7–8). The goal must be death, as Oldham "set out," or was born, "the last," but arrived at death sooner than Dryden. The classical reference then appears in lines 9–10: "Thus Nisus fell upon the slippery place, / Whilst his young friend performed and won the race." Next readers learn that he, "too little" known, need not have grown older: "O early ripe! to thy abundant store / What could advancing age have added more?" (11–12). Dryden may have been thinking of the fact that his own writing career did not even begin in earnest until he was well into his thirties, while Oldham's began and ended at a much younger age.

Dryden does not shy from noting differences in the two poets' stylistic approaches, skillfully inserting a demonstration into his lines. When he writes that Oldham's "generous fruits," or talents, were "gathered ere their prime" (21), he adds they "Still showed a quickness; and maturing time / But mellows what we write to the dull sweets of RHYME" (22–23). He alludes to Oldham's often imperfect and uneven rhyme and uses his famous alexandrine, a line with a METER of six feet, to delay his own rhyme of the specific term *rhyme* with *time*. Such a conscious display of Dryden's own skill allows him to demonstrate his respect for poetry as art. It also allows a contrast between his own approach and that of Oldham, as well as of the classic writers. As SAMUEL JOHNSON would later write of the time before Dryden, "Those happy combinations of words which distinguish poetry from prose had been rarely attempted: we had few elegances or flowers of speech; the roses had not yet been plucked from the bramble, or different colours had not been joined to enliven one another."

Dryden concludes with another classical allusion, to the Roman emperor Augustus mourning the premature death of Marcellus, who should have been his successor. He again echoes Virgil in his closing lines, whose age had hoped to see Marcellus on the throne:

Once more, hail, and farewell! Farewell, thou
  young
But ah! Too short, Marcellus of our tongue!
Thy brows with ivy and with laurels bound;
But fate and gloomy night encompass thee
  around. (22–25).

Dryden found no consolation in the early death; therefore he offered his reader none.

BIBLIOGRAPHY

Johnson, Samuel. *Lives of the English Poets.* Vol. 1. New York: E. P. Dutton, 1958.
Messenger, Ann. "A Problem of Praise: John Dryden and Anne Killegrew." In *His and Hers: Essays in Restoration and Eighteenth-Century Literature,* 14–40. Lexington: The University Press of Kentucky, 1986.
Miner, Earl, ed. *Selected Poetry and Prose of John Dryden.* New York: The Modern Library, 1985.

"TO THE MEMORY OF MY BELOVED, THE AUTHOR, MR. WILLIAM SHAKESPEARE, AND WHAT HE HATH LEFT US" BEN JONSON (1623)

BEN JONSON wrote his famous poem celebrating William Shakespeare to be prefaced to the first folio of Shakespeare's plays. Although many readers may recall Jonson's well-publicized remark that "Shakespeare wanted art," his ELEGY puts to rest any suspicion that he did not admire William Shakespeare. As George Parfitt notes, that particular remark has been incorrectly assumed to represent Jonson's definitive opinion. However, because of Jonson's penchant for epigrams and sometimes terse remarks, as well as the fact that this quotation was recorded by WILLIAM DRUMMOND OF HAWTHORNDEN after a conversation he had with the poet, too much has been made of the statement. While Jonson never pretended complete agreement with Shakespeare's "literary views," he did not believe that Shakespeare did not produce art. He more likely felt that Shakespeare was not artistic enough in terms of Jonson's ideals. Although it may be too reductive an evaluation, for the purposes of discussion it is reasonable to consider that Jonson was considered a writer in the classical vein with an intellectual bent to arouse thought, while Shakespeare wrote to entertain the public and arouse emotion. Parfitt asserts that giving Jonson's offhand three-word comment more weight than his brilliant elegy is unwarranted.

Jonson spends the first 15 lines of the elegy reviewing all the possible ways he might praise a writer who "neither man nor Muse can praise too much" (5). Only in line 17 does he at last begin an attempt to do so with the resounding "Soul of the age! / The applause! Delight! The wonder of our stage!" making clear his honest feelings of admiration. While writers such as Francis Beaumont had alluded to Shakespeare as one who achieved "by the dim light of nature alone," noting by contrast that Jonson was guided by art, Jonson clearly does not agree. He bids "My Shakespeare, rise," writing, "I will not lodge thee by / Chaucer or Spenser" nor "bid Beaumont lie / A little further to make thee a room." Those three poets had been buried in Westminster Abbey, while Shakespeare lay in Stratford. Jonson makes the point that Shakespeare should be apart from that crowded group, adding, "Thou art a monument without a tomb."

Jonson feels strongly positive toward his subject, even if he does allude a few lines later to the fact that his own training in Latin is superior to that of Shakespeare. In typical fashion he elects to overlook Shakespeare's grasp of French and Italian, privileging the classical languages. But he clearly notes that Shakespeare does not remain time-bound, as do certain Greek and Roman poets, and that Britain triumphs in producing a poet "To whom all scenes of Europe homage owe. / He was not of an age, but for all time!" In lines 55–58 Jonson even counters his famous quotation, writing,

Yet must I not give Nature all; the Art,
My gentle Shakespeare, must enjoy a part.
For though the poet's matter Nature be,
His Art doth give the fashion.

Jonson concludes his remarkable elegy by literally lifting Shakespeare to the heights:

But stay; I see thee in the hemisphere
Advanced and made a constellation there!
Shine forth, thou star of poets, and with rage
Or influence chide or cheer the drooping stage,
Which, since thy flight from hence, hath
    mourned like night,
And despairs day, but for thy volume's light.
    (75–80)

Jonson adds to the final line a reference to the volume that was the first collection of Shakespeare's plays. He must be counted among those who performed an invaluable service to later generations by realizing the importance of committing Shakespeare's words to the page for the sake of preservation.

BIBLIOGRAPHY

Parfitt, George. *Ben Jonson: Public Poet and Private Man.* New York: Harper & Row, 1977.
Peterson, Richard S. *Imitation and Praise in the Poems of Ben Jonson.* New Haven, Conn.: Yale University Press, 1981.

"TO THE NIGHTINGALE" ANNE FINCH (COUNTESS OF WINCHILSEA) (1713) ANNE FINCH may have written "To the Nightingale" as early as 1702. It adopts the form of the ode in praise of what Finch terms the "sweet harbinger of spring!" in her first line, meaning one who predicts or acts as a forerunner. Her love of nature and country living was well known, and she portrays that affection in this 35-line poem through her selection of a songbird to make her point regarding the competitive world of poetry and the pressures under which artists work.

Finch stresses in the second line the importance of timing to self-expression as she writes of the bird, "This moment is thy time to sing, / This moment I attend to praise." The speaker explains by noting that she will "set my numbers," where *numbers* are poetic verses, according to the "lays," or songs, of the nightingale. Not only does the poet speaker imply that she finds the bird's music inspiring, she continues explaining that her own song will be as free as that of the nightingale. What Finch expresses is an ideal rather than reality, that each poet should remain completely free of outside influences in her writing:

Poets, wild as thee, were born,
Pleasing best when unconfined,
When to please is least designed. (7–9)

Known to write with an autobiographical intent, Finch is probably reflecting on her feelings of self-consciousness, often expressed in her poetry. She felt unworthy to write, ever mindful of the abundant criticism of females who dared to publish creative work. Although she proclaimed that she wrote only for herself and did not desire praise or notice, as in her "The CIRCUIT OF APOLLO," she likely made such claims in order to conform with Augustan rhetorical tradition.

The speaker continues by explaining that poets write in order to soothe their own troubled minds, not for the pleasure of readers. Unfortunately "Cares do still their thoughts molest / And still th' unhappy poet's breast" (11–12). Finch uses wordplay in employing the term *still* initially to mean "yet again," and in the second line to mean "bring to a stop" or "silence." The reference to the breast reflects on the nightingale's breast, famously pressed against a thorn in mythology. Only while suffering the pain caused by the thorn, which leads to death for the bird, can it produce its best song. The speaker notes the same is true for the poet and then calls for a quiet reverence as the bird performs: "She begins. Let all be still!" (14). Finch could find the stillness she valued in nature, where at times all seemed to stop in order to honor the song of the lowly bird.

The poem shifts tone from one of reverence to one of command, although the voice remains respectful as the speaker calls to her inspiration, "Muse, thy promise now fulfill!" Finch employs ALLITERATION and repetition, her form mimicking the bird's song, as she requests that her poetry might have the same effect on listeners as does the song:

> Sweet, oh! Sweet, still sweeter yet
> Can thy words such accents fit,
> Canst thou syllables refine,
> Melt a sense that shall retain
> Still some spirit of the brain,
> Till with sounds like these it join. (16–21)

As she requests of her muse the gift of musical quality, she adopts the FIGURATIVE LANGUAGE (FIGURE OF SPEECH) of metaphor in suggesting that her syllables can be refined and melted as ore is processed to remove impurities.

However, the speaker immediately admits the impossibility of such an effect in her poetry. She pleads with the nightingale to vary its music to match her own. When that does not happen, the speaker's tone alters, and she tells the nightingale, "Cease, then, prithee, cease thy tune: / Trifler wilt thou sing till June?" where *trifler* suggests someone engaged in frivolity, or action without value. She scolds the bird for doing nothing other than singing while its "business all lies waste, / And the time of building's past!" (29–30). Employing IRONY, Finch pretends to suggest that art deserves only one's limited attention; business or practical matters are more important. She assumes that pretense in order to make a point about poets who feel in competition with one another. The jealous poet who feels outdone may proclaim the more celebrated poetry

as not perfectly in line with societal expectations, simply to have a manner by which to criticize it. As Finch expresses it, poets who covet the gift of others may "Criticize, reform, or preach, / Or censure what we cannot reach" (34–35).

Finch employs the extended CONCEIT of the nightingale's song in order to reflect on what at times could be the painful pursuit of the perfect poem. The poet who would share her work with the public had to prepare herself for attacks, regardless of the poem's quality. Some of the most severe criticism could be expected from fellow poets. Rather than praising work superior to their own, they would attempt to diminish it out of artistic jealousy.

"TO THE PIOUS MEMORY OF THE ACCOMPLISH'D YOUNG LADY MRS. ANNE KILLIGREW" JOHN DRYDEN (1685)

Despite JOHN DRYDEN's subtitle to his ode "To the Pious Memory of the Accomplish'd Young Lady Mrs. Anne Killigrew," describing ANNE KILLIGREW as "Excellent in the Two Sister-Arts of Poesy and Painting," scholars have categorized her art as marginal and forgettable. Feminist critics disagree with those adjectives, claiming that Killigrew's work has never been properly assessed on its own merits. Those who devalue Killigrew's painting and poetry justify Dryden's high praise of her by attributing it to his choice of form. By selecting the elevated Pindaric ode in which to couch his praise, he automatically elevates his subject.

Indisputably beautiful, Killigrew died young and thus provided an immediately sympathetic subject that allowed Dryden to move from ELEGY to panegyric. In addition the suffering of her father, the Reverend Henry Killigrew, an acquaintance of Dryden's, over her loss likely motivated Dryden to the supreme effort that SAMUEL JOHNSON deemed "undoubtedly the noblest ode that our language ever has produced," particularly its opening stanza. That stanza reads, in part:

> Thou youngest virgin-daughter of the skies,
>   Made in the last promotion of the blessed;
>   Whose palms, new plucked from
>   Paradise,
> In spreading branches more sublimely rise,

Rich with immortal green above the rest:
Whether, adopted to some neighbouring star,
Thou roll'st above us, in they wandering race,
    Or, in procession fixed and regular,
    Moved with the heaven's majestic pace.
      (1–9)

The phrase *virgin-daughter* suggests the innocence that Dryden will adopt as a theme. It was a theme Killigrew herself used, and Dryden cleverly co-opts a line from her poem "To My Lady Berkeley," which reads "Though more than man, obedient as a child," converting it to "Her wit was more than man, her innocence a child!" His abundant use of ALLITERATION supports the regal movement of the poem, which is not meant to flow quickly. Rather it suggests the slow and moving style of a pageant or stage presentation, as Dryden had extensive experience in writing dramatic dialogue.

Throughout the ode Dryden uses traditional classic references, such as the "music of the spheres," referencing the supposed emission of musical notes by the planets, in this instance, to welcome Killigrew's birth, and the bees that supposedly clustered on Pindar as an infant to sweeten his lips with their honey. If the bees did not grace Killigrew, the speaker explains, it was only because heaven wanted to welcome her in a more solemn, less vulgar fashion. His speaker also labels Killigrew a *Vestal* in reference to the vestal virgins.

Dryden praises Killigrew's ability as a poet when his speaker tells God that other poets have "Profaned thy heavenly gift of poesy! / Made prostitute and profligate the muse," declaring that she will "atone for all!" However, his speaker begins the next (fifth) stanza by stating, "Art she had none," as if declaring her to be without talent. Feminists might argue that by *art* Dryden means "artifice," which would then make his judgment a positive one; Killigrew worked honestly at her craft, independent of false trappings. That interpretation could be justified by Dryden's constant emphasis of her innocence, her virginity, unassailed by worldly arts. To extend the dispute, those critics who believe that Dryden clearly indicated that Killigrew lacked talent feel his next phrase tempers his criticism. He quickly adds about her lack of art, "yet wanted none: / For Nature did that want supply." As a kindness he claims that Nature supplied Killigrew with charm and beauty to balance her lack of talent. The opposing critical camp can legitimately claim that Nature could represent natural talent, rather than artifice, indicating that Killigrew did not have to depend on tricks of the pen.

The speaker again praises Killigrew's talents when he says she was "Born to the spacious empire of the Nine," referring to the nine muses who inspire art. He continues to emphasize her innocence when referencing her painting by associating her with the pastoral tradition. He states that her pictures often proved superior to her mind's concept, describing them as

The sylvan scenes of herds and flocks,
And fruitful plains and barren rocks,
Of shallow brooks that flowed so clear,
The bottom did the top appear. (108–111)

He later compares her to another bluestocking Restoration poet, KATHERINE PHILIPS, known as "the Matchless Orinda," when he mourns the loss of two talented poets to smallpox. Not only do the two women share early deaths to the same disease and the physical effects of the pox, but because Philips gave to herself and her friends classical nicknames, her reference works stylistically in Dryden's piece. In lines 160–164 he writes,

O double sacrilege on things divine,
To rob the relic and deface the shrine!
But thus Orinda di'd:
Heav'n by the same disease did both translate;
As equal were their souls, so equal was their fate.

Dryden's elevated style creates elegant images such as the "rattling bones together fly," describing the day when dead souls shall rise together toward heaven:

From the four corners of the sky;
When sinews o'er the skeletons are spread,
Those clothed with flesh, and life inspires the
    dead;
The sacred poets first shall hear the sound,
And foremost from the tomb shall bound.
    (185–189)

On that day Killigrew will be among the group "Like mounting larks" that sing of heaven. She especially will help to show others "The way which thou so well hast learned below."

As critics claim, Dryden's images prove classic enough to allow a disjunction between them and Killigrew herself, as they involve so much hyperbole as not to be taken literally. He succeeds in shaping Killigrew as a metaphor for all that is accomplished, cherished, respected, and revered on earth as the arts. In doing so, he makes clear his faith in his own art to lift a topic so mundane as the death of a human above its quotidian station. If some verses appear superior to others, this should not surprise, according to Johnson. After declaring, "All the stanzas are not equal," Johnson explains, "An imperial crown cannot be one continued diamond; the gems must be held together by some less valuable matter."

BIBLIOGRAPHY

Johnson, Samuel. *Lives of the English Poets.* Vol. 1. New York: E. P. Dutton, 1958.
Messenger, Ann. "A Problem of Praise: John Dryden and Anne Killegrew." In *His and Hers: Essays in Restoration and Eighteenth-Century Literature,* 14–40. Lexington: University Press of Kentucky, 1986.
Miner, Earl, ed. *Selected Poetry and Prose of John Dryden.* New York: The Modern Library, 1958.

"TO THE POET COLERIDGE" MARY ROBINSON (1800)

MARY ROBINSON wrote two poems with a focus on Samuel Taylor Coleridge, with whom she frequently corresponded. One focused on the birth of his third son, which she titled "Ode, Inscribed to the Infant Son of S. T. Coleridge." In the second poem, "To the Poet Coleridge," she referenced Coleridge's own work, "Kubla Khan." "To the Poet Coleridge" appeared in her posthumous *Memoirs,* signed *Sappho,* and again in her *Poetical Works.* Coleridge responded to her poem with his "A Stranger Minstrel." That poem by Coleridge appeared with the subtitle "To Mrs. Robinson, a few weeks before her death" in Robinson's *Memoirs.* As the biographer Paula Byrne points out, Coleridge's title responds to a phrase in Robinson's ode inscribed to his son Derwent that read, "accept a Stranger's Song." Robinson divided the 72 lines of "To the Poet Coleridge" into six stanzas with every other line rhyming.

The speaker begins with a tribute to Coleridge's romantic vision: "Rapt in the visionary theme! / Spirit Divine! with thee I'll wander." The wandering will take place "'Mid forest glooms," tracing "the circling bounds / Of thy New Paradise extended," a reference to Coleridge's "Kubla Khan." Robinson employs sensory imagery to make clear that the speaker not only enjoys the vision, but also the abundant sounds encountered while wandering, such as those "Of winds, and foamy torrents blended." In the second stanza Robinson includes specific imagery in describing the source of Coleridge's inspiration as "The mystic fountain, bubbling, panting, / While gossamer its network weaves," again quoting "Kubla Khan" with the phrase "I'll mark thy *sunny* dome." Contrasting with the sunny dome is "Thy Caves of Ice," another allusion to "Kubla Khan." Also presented as a contrast is an "ever-blooming mead, whose flower / Waves to the cold breath of the moonlight hour," those lines referencing Coleridge's "Frost at Midnight" and "Dejection: A Ode," both describing a moonlit meadow. Further imagery includes "the day-star, peering bright / On the gray wing of parting night," and "As summer's whispered sighs unfold / Her million, million buds of gold." Those lines testify to Robinson's sharp sense of sound and rhythm through the use of ALLITERATION, assonance, and word repetition.

Robinson emphasizes again Coleridge's romantic dedication to the spiritual in lines 27–28 as she writes, "Spirit Divine! With Thee I'll trace / Imagination's boundless space!" Her celebration of the release allowed by the imagination through her own art probably related to her long-term ill health, as poetry allowed a freedom her body could not. She repeats references to the "Caves of Ice" and the imaginary state as "thy New Paradise," further emphasizing her alignment of sentiment with that of Coleridge.

Robinson's presentation also makes clear the pain sometimes caused by the blessing of imagination, as its expression originates from visceral effort. She writes in lines 45–46, "And now I'll pause to catch the moan / Of distant breezes, cavern-pent," lines that work on multiple levels. She again reflects on Coleridge's own lines regarding the cave with her use of *cavern* and probably alludes to the idea of inspiration as a literally breathing in with the reference to the breeze. Some dark imagery colors her lines as she mentions the "twilight tints" that are "Purpling the landscape / . . . on the dark promontory's side." The speaker will weave a crown of flowers to represent Coleridge's genius, the flowers decorated with dew, imagery that suggests new life. She follows this allusion by stating that Coleridge opens "to my wondering eyes" the "new creation" that he bids rise; she uses FIGURATIVE LANGUAGE (FIGURE OF SPEECH) to compare the poet's powers of creation to those of God.

In the final stanza Robinson alludes again to "Kubla Kahn" when she writes, "And now, with lofty tones inviting, / Thy nymph, her dulcimer swift smiting," a reference to a "damsel with a dulcimer" in the final stanza of Coleridge's poem. Again Robinson suggests that the life of a poet may not be easy, through her choice of the term *smiting,* a verb that may connote violence. The "ecstatic pleasures" the nymph awakens in the speaker act as an erotic suggestion, particularly as those pleasures are "Far, far removed" from those of mere mortals. The lines "In cadence rich, in cadence strong, / Proving the wondrous witcheries of song!" imitate what they describe, through their own stirring rhythms and use of alliteration. Robinson concludes by repeating again the references to the "sunny dome" and the "caves of ice," ending her poem with the laudatory lines

> She sings of Thee, O favored child
> Of Minstrelsy, Sublimely wild!
> Of thee, whose soul can feel the tone
> Which gives to any dreams a magic all thy own!

Robinson exemplifies the romantic ideal of the sublime through her suggestions of violence and indulgence couched in "lofty tones" and pure sensory experience. Not only does she clarify her admiration of Coleridge and the notions of the Romantics, she also demonstrates her ability to adopt their style.

BIBLIOGRAPHY
Byrne, Paula. *Perdita: The Literary, Theatrical, Scandalous Life of Mary Robinson.* New York: Random House, 2004.

"TO THE POOR" ANNA LAETITIA BARBAULD (1825)
ANNA LAETITIA BARBAULD wrote "To the Poor" in 1795, but it would not be published until 1825. It remains of interest in its strong projection of themes common in Barbauld's work of the mistreatment of marginalized members of society and the responsibility of the church to supply the support that the government often did not. As wife of a minister Barbauld often worked among church members, and she also taught young children, activities that relate to her attack in "To the Poor" on the lack of concern by the wealthy for those living in poverty, especially children.

Barbauld creates a sympathetic but strong persona who uses forceful language to make her point. The poem opens, "Child of distress, who meet'st the bitter scorn / Of fellow-men to happier prospects born," making clear that the distress suffered by the child is a direct result of lack of concern of those born to wealth. The child's distress is heightened because she is "doomed" to observe "Art and Nature's various stores" that "flow in full cups of joy" but she is not privileged to sample. Barbauld attacks those who use the name of religion to excuse their disregard as she continues explaining that the child also observes the wealthy resign to "heaven and fate" the "affliction" of the poor, their excuses allowing them to bear those afflictions "with a patient mind."

The next lines express the pitiable condition of the child:

> Whose bursting heart disdains unjust control,
> Who feel'st oppression's iron in thy soul,
> Who dragg'st the load of faint and feeble years,
> Whose bread is anguish, and whose water tears.

Barbauld adopts a comparison of the child's plight to that of prisoners whose sustenance is bread and water to make clear the child's oppression. With little hope for any improvement in the child's condition the speaker admonishes her, "Bear, bear thy wrongs—fulfil thy destined hour, / Bend thy meek neck beneath the foot of Power;" because the Child can do nothing else. She must commit herself to the mercy of those in power, who apparently have no mercy to spare.

Although the 22 lines of rhyming couplets are not organized into verses, line 13 moves into a second stage in which the speaker focuses on the child's early death as a release from the terror and control inflicted upon her during her brief life:

But when thou feel'st the great deliverer nigh,
And thy freed spirit mounting seeks the sky,
Let no vain fears thy parting hour molest,
No whispered terrors shake thy quiet breast.

Barbauld adopts the traditional approach to death as deliverance from suffering and calls upon religious imagery of the assent of the spirit into the sky to heaven. The poem's persona bids the child not to worry when death arrives, explaining that no earthly force can keep her spirit on earth. Barbauld then blasts members of the aristocracy, writing, "Think not their threats can work thy future woe, / Nor deem the Lord above like lords below." She makes clear that God, as a heavenly Lord, exercises the care over heaven's tenants that earthly lords reject, finding it too burdensome.

In her final four lines the speaker gently urges the child to prepare to meet her maker and then turns her ire upon the church for allowing government control to influence its attitude toward the poor:

Safe in the bosom of that love repose
By whom the sun gives light, the ocean flows;
Prepare to meet a Father undismayed,
Nor fear the God whom priests and kings have
    made.

Barbauld suggests that religion and monarchy have conjured a God in order to use it as an excuse to satisfy their own agendas; this is not the Father who awaits the child. That Father remains "undismayed," untouched by the influence of earthly powers.

According to the scholar Roger Lonsdale, Barbauld showed her poem to a friend soon after writing it, describing it as "inspired by indignation on hearing sermons in which the poor are addressed in a manner which evidently shows the design of making religion an engine of government." Never one to mince words or soften her message, Barbauld expresses dismay over the dangers inherent in the church's sharing with the government a shameful attitude toward the poor. Even worse would be the church's becoming an instrument of the monarchy, pursuing a material agenda rather than a spiritual one. England's treatment of its working class became more and more abusive after the Indus-trial Revolution, which began about 1760. Decreased economic support for workers was exacerbated by the depression sparked by the Napoleonic Wars, which at last ended in 1815. Barbauld's timely poem appeared just prior to the development of forces such as Chartism, a political movement that formed in reaction to working-class discontent with the Reform Bill of 1832 and the Poor Law of 1834. Many saw the bills as discriminatory against workers who faced multiple abuses in the new industrialized society.

BIBLIOGRAPHY

Lonsdale, Roger, ed. "Anna Laetitia Barbauld." In *Eighteenth Century Women Poets,* 299–311. New York: Oxford University Press, 1989.

"TO THE THRICE-SACRED QUEEN ELIZABETH" MARY SIDNEY HERBERT (COUNTESS OF PEMBROKE) (1599)

MARY SIDNEY HERBERT (COUNTESS OF PEMBROKE) dedicated her translation of the Psalms, a project begun by her poet brother Sir Philip Sidney, to Queen Elizabeth. Scholars describe the dedication as complex and brilliantly executed. Many dedications appended to works were responses to patronage, but Herbert needed no financial support for her project. Her dedication instead sought to celebrate a monarch Herbert honestly admired, despite the cool relationship the queen had with Herbert's brother for a time. A staunch Protestant as her brother was, Herbert desired to pay homage to the Protestant queen who had at one time been in peril because of her faith. As the head of the Church of England founded by her father, Henry VIII, to whom Herbert's own father was godson, Elizabeth proved the obvious choice as a figure to celebrate in the context of a religious translation. Herbert could also feel a kinship with the monarch through her gender.

Herbert selected the traditional METER of iambic pentameter for her 12 eight-line stanzas, each with a RHYME scheme of *ababcdcd,* the fixed form appropriate for the solemn occasion. The opening stanza identifies its subject, the queen, in a traditional manner as the poet's inspiration, an inspiration proving much stronger than her own muse. The poet does not take this source of inspiration lightly, as the speaker explains that her muse breaks rhythm in recognizing the queen's control: "And of respect to thee the line out goes. / One instant will of willing can she lose," Herbert adopts the metaphor of rhyming to comment on the Queen's adept dealings, as she notes in a sophisticated use of FIGURATIVE LANGUAGE (FIGURE OF SPEECH) that Elizabeth does not read, but instead receives, rhymes. That thought serves to answer the question as to who may be the one "On whom in chief dependeth to dispose / What Europe acts in these most active times?"

The second stanza expresses Herbert's humility in hoping the queen will accept her verse, acknowledging the royal state and Elizabeth's many preoccupations, but also understanding her power is derived from heavenly decree. In addition the monarch's burden, which she so skillfully accommodates, would be too much for the common person:

> But knowing more thy grace, abler thy mind,
> What heavenly powers thee highest throne
>   assigned,
> Assigned thee goodness suiting that degree,
> And by they strength thy burthen so designed,
> To others toil is exercise to thee. (12–16)

The third stanza remains remarkable in Herbert's comparison of herself to the queen, for just as Elizabeth does a man's job, so does the poet, in completing the work of her brother, although she judges herself less able than Philip:

> The poorer left, the richer rest away,
> Who better might (O might, ah word of woe)
> Have given for me what I for him defray. (22–24)

This allows the transition into the fourth stanza, which further praises her brother, who died a martyr to the Protestant cause. She describes her own grief, unable to stop the tears and sighs his name elicits. She adopts another metaphor in the traditional comparison of writing to weaving, the latter a creative activity deemed acceptable for women. She notes that her brother began the project—"he did warp"—while she completes it—"I weaved this web to end"—even though they used an unoriginal source, "The stuff not ours, our work no curious thing." She comments on "the Psalmist King"

and his roots as a Hebrew, adding that King David has been made an English citizen through their actions. Stanza 5 notes, "And I the cloth in both our names present, / A livery robe to be bestowed by thee." The robe metaphor again aligns Herbert with the queen, as both women assume grave responsibilities. Together with her brother the poet will till the fields, where the fields represent the queen's favor, without any show of ostentation: "And those night fields where sown they favors be / Unwealthy do, not else unworthy till."

Herbert shifts her tone in stanza 6 to admit that Philip's and her work is actually that of Elizabeth, the source of all art, made clear in her allusion to the laurels, which are plants associated with poets. The very leaves complain if forced to drape against anyone other than the queen: "There humble laurels in thy shadows grown / To garland others would themselves repine." The stanza concludes with the thought that Elizabeth not only acts as England's defender, but also as a defender of art, a warrior monarch.

The speaker continues her praise into the seventh stanza, noting that only a king such as King David remains worthy to enter the presence of a queen, thus legitimizing her dedication of the Psalms to the queen. The eighth stanza opens by asking who would not recognize how fitting the match would be:

> And who sees ought, but sees how justly square
> His haughty ditties to thy glorious days?
> How well beseeming thee his triumphs are?
>   (57–59)

The glorious sentiments of the Psalms raise Elizabeth to their height, and as if to exhibit the clever range of the poet, Herbert executes a play on words as she terms the Psalms *holy garments,* adding, "These holy garments each good soul assays / Some sorting all, all sort to none but thee." The first use of the term *sorting* indicates the act of searching through, while the second use *sort* indicates an appropriate type.

Stanza 9 compares Elizabeth to David as a great warrior, while the 10th stanza notes she is his equal. Stanza 10 even suggests that she might be his better as Herbert recalls the slaying of Goliath, for Elizabeth remains a woman, not the traditional warrior. Then she stops herself, noting war is not a proper topic in that circumstance, stating, "But soft, my muse, thy pitch is earthly love; / Forbear this heaven where only eagles fly." Some critics suggest that Herbert indicates war remains an appropriate topic for discussion by men, not for her to mention to the queen. An alternate interpretation is that Herbert expresses her own lack of qualification to join David and Elizabeth in their lofty positions as rulers. This would counteract any claims of presumption that might arise in reaction to her earlier comparison of herself with the queen, emphasizing her humility and comprehension that she is in no way equal to Elizabeth.

In the penultimate stanza Herbert unleashes a volley of hyperbole, heaping obviously exaggerated sentiments upon Elizabeth, where the isle mentioned is England:

Kings on a Queen enforced their states to lay,
Mainlands for empire waiting on an isle,
Men drawn by worth a woman to obey;
One moving all, herself unmoved the while.
(81–84)

She notes that although Elizabeth affects others, they do not affect her, with the assumption that they lack the strength to do so. The queen restores truth, exiles vanity, produces wealth for those who have little, and holds war without vexing others, all of which supplies the poet with excellent subject matter while giving joy to the monarch's subjects:

Truth's restitution, vanity exile,
Wealth sprung of want, war held without annoy,
Let subject be of some inspired style,
Till then the object of her subjects' joy. (85–88)

As Herbert nears the end of her dedication, she returns to addressing her private muse as a mere *handmaid* when compared to the inspiration Elizabeth offers. The stanza concludes with a wish that Elizabeth may enjoy more years and more triumphs than did David, king of Israel and author of the original Psalms.

"TO THE VIRGINS, TO MAKE MUCH OF TIME" ROBERT HERRICK (1648) One of the most famous of the CARPE DIEM poems, ROBERT HER-

RICK's "To the Virgins, to Make Much of Time," remains a popular and widely anthologized work. Herrick considers the transient nature of life, as had many poets before him, echoing Horatian sentiment. In addition to carpe diem Horace's *Odes* contained the theme of the *Eheu fugaces,* the "decay suffered by all living things." Herrick showed high emotion in considering these themes, particularly as applied to the inevitable fading of a woman's beauty. Thus his speaker famously admonishes his audience in his first stanza,

Gather ye Rose-buds while ye may,
Old Time is still a flying:
And this same flower that smiles today,
To morrow will be dying.

As used by the CAVALIER POETS, carpe diem became a tool to convince virginal women to give up their virginity while they remained at their most "ripe," in sexual terms, and the rosebud always symbolized that time of life. While Herrick nods to that tradition in specifically noting his audience as virgins and through his use of the rosebud, his urgency relates to everyone.

The second stanza reminds readers, "The glorious Lamp of Heaven, the Sun," continues to rise, as Herrick adopts a mythological reference to Apollo, the god who pulled the sun across the sky behind his chariot of horses, to add "The sooner will his Race be run, / And nearer he's to Setting." His adopts the FIGURATIVE LANGUAGE (FIGURE OF SPEECH) of metaphor, as the setting sun, signaling the end of day, alludes to the exhaustion of time. The speaker praises youth in the third stanza, noting, "That Age is best, which is the first, / When Youth and blood are warmer." He follows with an admonition that even if one spends those first days in desirable pursuits, those that follow will be "the worse, and worst." In other words young people should exercise their sexual energies and appetites when they can gain the most from them. Time will pass in any event, so they should enjoy all possibilities today.

By the concluding stanza the reader understands that the speaker does not encourage wanton sex. Rather he urges the young to marry so they can enjoy their time and bodies in that legal state. He warns them against being "coy," or falsely resistant to the attention of lovers, advising, "while ye may, go marry." A couple could marry late in life; however, according to this speaker if one loses "but once" her or his "prime, / You may for ever tarry." Unlike in Herrick's "CORINNA'S GOING A MAYING," no specific allusion to death is offered in "To the Virgins." However, the speaker insinuates the flesh may experience a death of will, if it does not respect time and the changes time may inflict.

The theme of the importance of living for the present had appeared prior to works by Horace and other Roman and Greek writers in ancient Hebrew literature, which bore a religious intent. The Hebrew approach remained noncelebratory, contrasting with later "pagan" approaches. The Greek philosopher Epicurus and the Roman Lucretius both stressed the inevitability of death and the foolishness in fearing the end to life. Rather humans should indulge in life's pleasures after admitting that death remains universal and natural, embracing their fate. By the time Edmund Spenser wrote *The Fairie Queene* during the English Renaissance, influenced probably by Tasso, who in turn wrote under the influence of Ausonius, carpe diem had become entrenched in English thought. Spenser wrote of the "passing of a Day," comparing "mortal Life" to "the Leaf, the Bud, the Flower," which "Ne more doth flourish after first Decay." He urged, "Gather therefore the rose of Love, whilst yet is time," as Shakespeare would later.

"TO WILLIAM CAMDEN" BEN JONSON (1616)

William Camden, a famous antiquarian scholar, had served as headmaster of the Westminster School, which BEN JONSON attended, and remained one of the poet's dearest friends. He is thought to be the subject of Jonson's poem "INVITING A FRIEND TO SUPPER" and was responsible for Jonson's humanist values. According to scholars Jonson skillfully imitates Camden's own teaching in the poem "To William Camden" by moving from the topic of pride to piety. He wrote the epigram, a form Camden discussed in his own writings as one in which "our country men now surpass other nations," in order to express his gratitude for Camden's crucial contribution to his life and art. He depicted Camden as a perfect teacher as well as an important writer about the Roman occupation of Brit-

ain; Camden had popularized the shortened form of Britannia, Britain, in his *Remains of a Greater Work Concerning Britain*. As Camden desired to relate modern Britain to the land of the ancients, Jonson would incorporate into his poetry classical ideas and format to relate his writing to that of the ancients. He adopts praise by Pliny of Corellius, a learned adviser, as a model by which to praise Camden. Jonson also models his poem on Pliny's praise of a friend named Titius Aristo and thus emphasizes both Camden's and his own link to ancient Rome.

Jonson begins,

> Camden, most reverend head, to whom I owe
> All that I am in arts, all that I know
> (How nothing's that!), to whom my country owes
> The great renown and name wherewith she goes.

After his self-deprecating commentary on his own lack of knowledge by comparison to Camden's, he references Camden's naming the country *Britain*. The speaker then notes that Britain will never see anyone "more grave, / More high, more holy, that she more would crave." Jonson praises Camden's investigation of "the most antique springs!" and notes that Camden's voice carries great "weight and . . . authority." Jonson is probably recalling his own school experience when he adds that man can hardly ask a question that Camden cannot answer. The final four lines of the poem emphasize the piety Jonson so valued in his teacher:

> Pardon free truth and let thy modesty,
> Which conquers all, be once o'ercome by thee.
> Many of thine this better could than I;
> But for their powers, accept my piety.

Thine in the penultimate line refers to Jonson's fellow students taught by Camden.

Jonson had been fortunate in that someone had sponsored his attendance at Westminster School, which his bricklayer stepfather could not have afforded. Even more fortunate was Camden's recognition of the boy's talent. Critics agree that his dedication and skill helped compensate for Jonson's later inability to attend university. Despite his lack of a complete education,

Jonson maintained a rigorous personal program of study and research throughout his life, modeled after the intellectual pursuits of William Camden.

BIBLIOGRAPHY

Mulryan, John. "Jonson's Classicism." In *The Cambridge Companion to Ben Jonson,* edited by Richard Harp and Stanley Stewart, 163–174. New York: Cambridge University Press, 2000.

TRAGEDY OF DARIUS, THE WILLIAM ALEXANDER (1603)

WILLIAM ALEXANDER's *The Tragedy of Darius* is written in the serious lyrical form known as an ode. A classical form, the ode was always composed in a slightly artificial but learned style and had a dignified tone due to its lofty subject matter. Odes associated with the Greek poet Pindar followed a particular format that varied in scheme and always evinced an elevated style, gaining the label *Great Odes.* Alexander adopts the approach made famous by the poet Horace, whose efforts were titled *Lesser Odes,* because of their more modest aims.

The Horatian ode is characterized by a single stanza type in any consistent form. For *Darius* Alexander designs his stanzas in groups of 20 lines, many with three feet, but others of varying numbers of syllables. Their rhyming pattern is *ababbcddceeecffggfhh,* the final two lines a rhyming couplet. Alexander practices traditional ALLITERATION, as in "Jove's judgment just," and includes classical references appropriate to the ode. He refers to the Far Eastern region labeled *Hydaspes,* the scene a century after the death of Darius I of one of Alexander the Great's most fearsome battles. He also refers to the Tagus River, symbolic of material wealth in the form of gold and jewels. Adopting a traditional approach in featuring the tragic missteps of an exalted individual, in this case Darius I, Alexander reveals a certain moral to his reader.

Information regarding Darius is helpful to understanding the poem. Darius I, known as Darius the Great, was a leading figure in 499 B.C. in the Persian Wars. King of Persia, Darius had conquered broad lands, including Greece. His reign was not peaceful, however, and residents of Athens later helped the Ionians revolt against Persian domination. While the Persian army crushed the revolt, the Athenians burned

Sardis, capital of Lydia. Darius swore revenge and sent a huge fleet of ships to the Hellespont in 492 B.C. His attempt was destined to fail, as a storm wrecked half of the fleet on the Macedonian coast, destroying the Persians' chance for victory. Darius continued to nurse his desire for revenge and increased power to launch a group of 600 ships two years later in a repeat attempt to discipline Greece. The ships with their full cargoes of fierce soldiers arrived at Attica, their generals determined to attack Athens. The Athenians dispatched a runner to seek aid from Sparta, but Spartan forces could not march until the end of a religious festival.

Grossly outnumbered, the Athenian general Miltiades organized his small number of troops to position his greatest strength in its flanks. When the mighty Persian army pushed back its center, the wings enclosed them, rendering the Persian bows and arrows useless against the Greek flanks. The Greek historian Herodotus reported the deaths of more than 6,000 Persians with fewer than 200 Greeks lost. That battle of Marathon became one of the most famous and decisive in the history of war. Darius died before he could launch another attack. His son, Xerxes, would battle Greece, but in the intervening 10 years, the Athenians under Themistocles built a naval force that would prove impossible to defeat.

In adapting Darius's tale and asking readers to apply its moral to their own lives, Alexander participated in a rich dramatic tradition from the ancient Greeks, who associated drama with religious and community values. Because the spoken part of the chorus from Greek drama represented commentary on the action that the audience observed on stage, it offered a logical basis on which to develop poetic forms such as the ode. In offering the audience a chance to observe exalted humans and their foibles in action, the dramatist/poet allows that audience to experience a type of catharsis, or relief from their own burdens. Whereas members of early audiences were not encouraged actually to identify with characters who represented humans of a social rank far above that of the audience members, later focus in drama on the common man did permit such identity.

Poets such as Alexander adopted the ode as a manner of addressing a common reading audience on topics no longer confined to discussion by the aristocracy. This allowed the poet an exercise in execution of form, as well as an opportunity for public address. In part, Alexander warns readers that

Time, through Jove's judgment just,
Huge alteration brings;
Those are but fools who trust
In transitory things,
Whose tails bear mortal stings,
Which in the end will wound.

Because Darius could not accept a small defeat, he later would fall to a far more devastating failure. He desired a "transitory thing," the power that domination of another gives. That desire overcame reason, rendering a once-great monarch a "fool." By suggesting a scorpion or mythological creature capable of delivering grave injury, "mortal stings," with its tail, Alexander warns readers that the false order contrived by humans and in which they place their faith often crumbles before a natural order that directs the universe.

Alexander continues his warning by writing,

How dare vain worldlings vaunt
Of Fortune's goods not lasting,
Evils which our wits enchant?
Expos'd to loss and wasting!
Lo, we to death are hasting.

In those lines the poet makes clear that man bears responsibility for his own downfall. Humans invite the evils that overcome their reason, such as the charged emotion that accompanies power, evils that hasten the death most humans foolishly attempt to avoid. He looks to world history to teach more than mere facts, writing in one couplet, "World's glory is but like a flower, / Which both is bloom'd and blasted in an hour." He exhibits an advantage of the couplet, which can double as an epigram to deliver a strong argumentative flourish, reminding the audience that mortality awaits even the most beautiful. All is transitory, eventually destroyed by the natural effects of time or moved more quickly toward its end by its own actions.

In his final verse, the speaker notes

Long time we toil to find
These idols of the mind,
Which had, we cannot bind
To bide with us one day.

He echoes his concern with human fixation on things transitory, which cannot be bound; by nature's plan they must pass away. By terming human desires "idols of the mind," Alexander emphasizes the false nature of vanity and power, suggesting they are mere abstracts, imagined and without substance. That such imaginary idols should be the only result of long-term toil he finds pitiable. He continues to emphasize the presumption that supports human infatuation with material treasures, which are almost impossible to keep once gained. By adopting an ANTITHESIS for his concluding lines, the poet calls attention to nature's enduring desire for balance, a balance that means all gains must eventually be lost: "Which vex them most that them possess, / Who starve with store and famish with excess."

BIBLIOGRAPHY
Survey of British Poetry: Cavalier to Restoration. Vol. 2. Edited by Editorial Board, Roth Publishing. Great Neck, N.Y.: Poetry Anthology Press, 1989.
Ward, Thomas Humphry. The English Poets: Selections with Critical Introductions by Various Writers and a General Introduction by Matthew Arnold. Vol. 2. New York: Macmillan, 1912.

TRAHERNE, THOMAS (1637–1674)

Any biography of Thomas Traherne must contain terms such as *likely* and *may have,* as little factual information is known of his brief life. Born in Hereford, Traherne's father was a shoemaker, probably related to Philip Traherne, twice elected mayor of Hereford. The relationship seems probable because Philip Traherne probably paid for the education of Thomas and his brother, Philip. Traherne studied as a commoner at Brasenose College, where he received his bachelor of arts degree in 1656. He had received a master of arts by decree in 1661.

In 1656 Traherne began writing his "Early Notebook," to which he added entries for four years. After ordination in 1660 as deacon and priest under the restored Church of England, he received a lifetime living in an appointment to serve Credenhill. That living was augmented by patronage from the countess dowager of Kent, along with the Commission for Approbation of Public Preachers under the Commonwealth, a Parliamentary commission. While at Credenhill Traherne probably participated in a devotional group that included a Mrs. Susanna Hopton, a woman who would prove crucial to the future publication of his meditative poetry. He probably wrote his *Centuries of Meditations* in her honor.

Traherne's religious sensibilities and celebration of a childlike wonder of nature, both common in his poetry, would not be appreciated until the 20th century. As did HENRY VAUGHAN, he took hope in the idea of regeneration, believing that nature existed for his pleasure and that death and decay were crucial to an abundance of new life. Unlike Vaughan, however, Traherne had little use for alchemy or hermetic Christianity and focused instead on the rational approach of emerging science. He also did not incorporate the traditional Renaissance attitude of man as a microcosm modeled on the macrocosm of the universe. Man did not mirror any other world but rather existed as a reflection of God's power seen in the beauty of his creation. Traherne's attitude of praise and thanksgiving inhabits all of his poetry, culminating in a joyous tone that early critics dismissed as unsophisticated and reductive. His work projects belief in both natural and supernatural, or mystic, reasoning. While intellectual, Traherne also trusted intuition as a way of knowing. That trust and its evidence in his poetry would catch the attention of 20th-century postmodern critics.

In 1661 Traherne may have studied religion at Oxford and probably wrote "Select Meditations" during 1662 and 1663. The following year he apparently left university to return to his living at Credenhill, where he spent several years studying Plato. From 1666 to 1668 he may have composed most of the poems in *Centuries of Meditations.* Taking a bachelor of divinity from Brasenose in 1669, he moved to London to serve Sir Orlando Bridgeman, lord keeper of the Great Seal, as domestic chaplain, a position he would retain until his death. During his first year of service

Traherne wrote prolifically, producing probably "Church's Year-Book," *Meditations on the Six Days of the Creation,* and much of *Thanksgivings.* He also probably completed *Centuries of Meditations* and worked on the collection later labeled the *Dobell manuscript.* He also began a "Commonplace Book," which would form the basis for much of *Christian Ethicks* (1675). Traherne's poetry remains deceptively naive, as he closely considered nature and its importance to the mind of God. His meditative approach resembles in form that of biblical poetry, with varying METER and RHYME. Traherne viewed the soul's ultimate union with the deity as a transformation through absorption of God's wisdom.

In 1672 Traherne moved to Teddington, where he continued service to Bridgeman and acted as minister of the local church, as Teddington was Bridgeman's family seat. He researched at Oxford for his publication *Roman Forgeries,* which contained his account of probably forged documents, and probably wrote the final *Thanksgiving. Roman Forgeries* was published anonymously in 1673, and Traherne died the next year. He was buried with honor under a reading desk at Teddington Church. In 1677 the mayor and parish of All Saints, Hereford, received through Philip Traherne Thomas's bequest of five small houses. The Reverend George Hickes published *Thanksgivings* in 1699 anonymously under the title *A Serious and Pathetical Contemplation of the Mercies of God, in Several most Devout and Sublime Thanksgivings for the same.*

Traherne's work had more life in the centuries that followed his death than they had in his own time. In 1717 his *Meditations of the Six Days of the Creation* appeared in the first part of *A Collection of Meditations and Devotions,* authored by Susanna Hopton, the woman with whom he probably engaged in his literary discussions at Credenhill. In 1895 a major breakthrough for later Traherne scholars occurred when W. T. Brooke found *Centuries of Meditations* and the Dobell folio of poems while perusing a London bookseller's stall; the Dobell sequence would be published in 1903 by Bertram Dobell, including the anthologized poem "WONDER." The first published version of the *Centuries* was issued by Dobell in 1908, and the Burney sequence was published as *Poems of Felicity* in 1910, including the popular poem "ON LEAPING OVER THE MOON."

Critics have expended much energy in discussing the arrangement of the entries in *Centuries of Meditations,* and the biographer Malcolm Day focuses an entire chapter on that collection and its analysis. Some see an organization based on Platonic theory, while others think Traherne used his four estates of man, Innocence, Misery, Grace, and Glory, to determine the pattern. Still others see the contents divided into three stages of man's search for God in first, the external world; second, the self; and finally, God's attributes. Day supplies an outline of five sections, all based on the act of "enjoyment": "Century One: Introduction to enjoyment and description of its nature"; "Century Two: The process of enjoyment and its consequences of the soul"; "Century Three: An illustration of the soul's movement toward the attainment of enjoyment"; "Century Four: "The principles of enjoyment and their practice"; and "Century Five: The sources of enjoyment grounded in God." All meditations are unified by an emphasis on the joy derived from knowledge of God, which translates into a relationship with every aspect of the universe.

A definitive work on Traherne finally was published by H. M Margoliouth as *Centuries, Poems and Thanksgivings* (1958), with only a few additional facts discovered over the following decades. However, another manuscript discovery took place in 1964 when James Osborn found Traherne's "Select Meditations." As Day writes, Traherne believed "that ultimate reality consists of the eternal ideas of all things existing infinitely and simultaneously in the Mind of God." God's grace will be gained not through any difficult moral test, but rather through the opening of one's mind to certain mysteries of nature. Traherne's work is imbued with the theme that man must make himself aware of the glories that surround him. That spiritual awakening will result in the achievement of God's grace and eternal renewal.

BIBLIOGRAPHY

Clements, A. L. *The Mystical Poetry of Thomas Traherne.* Cambridge, Mass.: Harvard University Press, 1969.

Colie, Rosalie L. "Thomas Traherne and the Infinite: The Ethical Compromise." *Huntington Library Quarterly* 21 (November 1957): 69–82.

Day, Malcolm M. *Thomas Traherne.* Boston: Twayne, 1982.

Dees, Jerome S. "Recent Studies in Traherne." *English Literary Renaissance* 4 (1974): 189–196.

Grant, Patrick. *The Transformation of Sin: Studies in Donne, Herbert, Vaughan, and Traherne.* Montreal: McGill-Queens University Press, 1974.

Guffrey, George Robert, ed. *A Concordance to the Poetry of Thomas Traherne.* Berkeley: University of California Press, 1974.

Leishman, J. B. *The Metaphysical Poets: Donne, Herbert, Vaughan, Traherne.* Oxford: Clarendon Press, 1934.

Marks, Carol L. "Thomas Traherne and Cambridge Platonism." *Publications of The Modern Language Association* 81 (December 1966): 521–534.

Martz, Louis L. *The Paradise Within: Studies in Vaughan, Traherne, and Milton.* New Haven, Conn.: Yale University Press, 1964.

Uphaus, Robert. "Thomas Traherne: Perception as Process." *University of Windsor Review* 3 (spring 1968): 19–27.

Wallace, John Malcolm. "Thomas Traherne and the Structure of Meditation." *English Literary History* 25 (June 1958): 78–89.

TRIBE OF BEN   Many followers of BEN JONSON gathered to exchange philosophy and poetry in pubs and in literary gatherings with Jonson. They included minor and major poets, such as WILLIAM BROWNE and WILLIAM CARTWRIGHT; the CAVALIER POETS, THOMAS CAREW, ROBERT HERRICK, RICHARD LOVELACE, and SIR JOHN SUCKLING, and Sir Lucius Cary and Cary's best friend, Henry Morison. Jonson celebrated the latter pair in his "TO THE IMMORTAL MEMORY AND FRIENDSHIP OF THAT NOBLE PAIR, SIR LUCIUS CARY AND SIR H. MORISON" (1629). The group labeled SONS OF BEN includes dramatists, such as Beaumont and Fletcher, Richard Brome, Philip Massinger, and James Shirley, among others.

TROCHAIC   See METER.

"TRUE MAID, A" MATTHEW PRIOR (1718)   The four-line ditty "A True Maid" well exemplifies the light approach to verse for which MATTHEW PRIOR was known. Sassy and naughty, the lines contain dialogue and portray in the briefest of scenes the interaction of Rose, the maid of the title, and Dick. The rose had long symbolized romance and a mature woman, ready for the "plucking," in a sexual sense. When Rose speaks of her virginity, readers understand it is in danger because of her mature nature as both a metaphorical and a literal Rose. She begins, "No, no; for my virginity, / When I lose that," says Rose, "I'll die." She seems to be answering a question, as she repeats, "No," and readers assume someone has propositioned her or has asked whether she remains a virgin. Prior adopts a pun with the term *die,* also used traditionally in reference to sexual climax.

Readers meet the other speaker in this microdrama in the third line, when Dick cries, "Behind the elms, last night . . . / Rose, were you not extremely sick?" Dick reveals an intimate knowledge of Rose and her activities, suggesting she may have in Dick's company tempted death the night before. Prior smartly has his characters discuss sex through suggestion and innuendo, with an entertaining result. He also suggests a possible double meaning for the term *True* used to describe the maid in the title, who, we assume, is Rose. Did Rose remain true in the sense that she is sincere and faithful to cultural demands, retaining her virginity, or is she instead true to her desires, yielding to her passions? Dick's assertion of her supposed illness suggests that if Rose has not already lost her virginity, she may be on the way to doing so.

U

"UNDERTAKING, THE" JOHN DONNE (1633)

In "The Undertaking" JOHN DONNE, a poet who exulted in challenging traditional ideas regarding love and gender, counters his era's belief in the false nature of women. He engages in what the scholar Susannah B. Mintz terms "a playful transgressivenes." His speaker admits to knowing a constant woman but holds that he, and other males who had enjoyed the same exposure, keep their discovery quiet. That need for quiet Mintz calls "a space of anxiety in Donne's love poetry." While she views Donne's approach as somewhat enlightened, other critics hold that Donne simply "reentrenche[es] conventional gender roles" despite his seeming attempts in his poetry to blur boundaries between those custom-dictated roles.

Donne establishes a metaphor in the first verse, which he will extend throughout his seven four-line stanzas, that of silence as equivalent to heroism. His speaker begins,

> I have done one braver thing
> Than all the Worthies did
> An yet a braver thence doth spring,
> Which is, to keep that hid.

The term *Worthies* refers to a medieval legend about the individuals who represent the epitome of courage. They included three Jews, identified as Joshua, David, and Judas Maccabeus; three pagans, identified as Hector, Alexander, and Julius Caesar; and three Christians,

identified as Arthur, Charlemagne, and Godfrey of Bouillon. Donne engages in his traditional blending of the sacred and the nonsacred in his allusions to champions of two religions and of English history, suggesting the necessity of spiritual heroism as a basis for physical heroism. This expands the definition of bravery into a spiritual and an intellectual context. That expansion proves necessary to his entire claim. His first stanza makes his entire argument, upon which he will simply elaborate in those to follow.

The second stanza utilizes a comparison to "specular stone," a material supposedly used in classical times to cover windows. It allowed some vision into a structure, but the material no longer existed. The speaker adopts that image to let readers know that he understands that his audience may consider him mad, as he discusses an "art," that of revealing the constant woman, when his listeners believe one does not exist.

By the third stanza he excuses listeners who have never identified constancy and bids them to "love but as before." However, in the fourth stanza he draws in those who, as he has, have made a discovery. He tells them,

> But he who loveliness within
> Hath found, all outward loathes,
> For he who color loves, and skin,
> Loves but their oldest clothes.

Donne adopts outward appearance, enhanced by the false reflection of color and style in a woman's dress, as a metaphor for deception. Others like the speaker have discovered true value, that of internal beauty. He names the valuable internal commodity in the fifth stanza as *virtue*. Then he introduces the aspect of danger imminent in any contradiction of societal expectations. His culture assumed women inconstant, and for a man to proclaim otherwise publicly could put him at risk of disapproval. The speaker wonders whether any man could take such a step, disputing the gender roles assigned by custom:

> If, as I have, you also do
> Virtue attired in woman see,
> And dare love that, and say so too,
> And forget the He and She;

He concludes that stanza with a semicolon, indicating that the discovery and the revelation are not all that is involved.

The speaker continues his conspiratorial whisper in stanza 6, suggesting that his audience not proclaim his accomplishment. To do so would be to challenge

> . . . profane men
> Which will no faith on this bestow,
> Or if they do, deride.

Donne suggests that women will be exposed to even greater humiliation if the men who appreciate them open them up to ridicule by challenging the era's beliefs. He concludes his poem by returning to the topic of courage, as the speaker assures his audience,

> Then you have done a braver thing
> Than all the Worthies did;
> And a braver thence will spring,
> Which is, to keep that hid.

Feminist critics view this final stanza with interest, as Renaissance women found slander one of their greatest dangers. That tradition informed Edmund Spenser's 1590 ALLEGORY the epic poem *The Fairie Queene,* in which slander appeared in the form of the blatant beast that stalked innocent women. It also translated into everyday life, as evidenced by the gift of a ring from Elizabeth Tanfield Cary, the Renaissance playwright and mother to the poet PATRICK CARY, to her eldest daughter. The ring bore an engraving that read, "Be and Seem": A woman should not only be without internal fault, she must also appear so to any who might observe her external actions. In urging men who knew of women's virtues to silence, Donne engages in gender role reversal.

According to popular belief a virtuous Renaissance woman at all times should remain silent and obedient in respect to men. Of course women did not always adhere to public precept, and many enjoyed great freedom within the domestic scene. Donne appears to have been one who encouraged such limited freedom, an idea with which Mintz agrees. She writes that Donne speaks "of gender as a fluid realm of experience" and seems to have been able to consider relationships "outside of a patriarchal ideology" that idealized women and then objectified them as a dangerous and "threatening Other."

BIBLIOGRAPHY

Baumlin, James S. *John Donne and the Rhetorics of Renaissance Discourse.* Columbia: University of Missouri Press, 1991.

Mintz, Susannah B. "'Forget the Hee and Shee': Gender and Play in John Donne." *Modern Philology* 98, no. 4 (May 2001): 577.

Zunder, William. *The Poetry of John Donne: Literature and Culture in the Elizabethan and Jacobean Period.* Brighton, England: Harvester, 1982.

"UPON APPLETON HOUSE, TO MY LORD FAIRFAX" ANDREW MARVELL (1681)

ANDREW MARVELL wrote "Upon Appleton House, To My Lord Fairfax" in the country house poem tradition, probably influenced by BEN JONSON's "TO PENSHURST." Marvell departed from Jonson's approach, however. Whereas Jonson emphasized the lush and productive nature of the estate grounds, Marvell emphasizes the contemplative effect of nature on man. Marvell also does not focus on the entire family occupying the house, as did Jonson. The tradition of praise of retreats was taken from the classics, including work by Horace and Martial, but Marvell does not closely follow the classic pattern as did Jonson; nor does he reproduce the solemn tone of those models. Marvell also departs from tradition in the length of the poem, which totals 776 lines; in the lack of detailed description of the structure, with more attention given to its history, a description of the grounds, and praise of one family member; and in his inclusion of the distinct presence of a speaker. In addition Nigel Smith adds, Marvell participated in a fairly new genre, that of the "prospective" poem, seen also in *Cooper's Hill* by Sir John Denham, a style influenced by the increased popularity of landscape painting. Denham and Marvell "exploited the illusions presented to the viewer by landscapes, and derived social and political commentary from views."

Marvell composed the lengthy poem as a patronage poem for the father of his pupil Mary (Maria) Fairfax. Thomas Fairfax gained fame in the military and then retired to Nun Appleton, one of his several country estates. The original house is believed to have been built from ruins of a Cistercian nunnery, which had been in the Fairfax family since 1542. When Marvell arrived to tutor Mary in 1650 or 1651, a new house may have been constructed. The date of the Fairfax reconstruction remains under debate.

Composed of 97 eight-line stanzas, the poem reflects one of Marvell's favored formats with octosyllabic couplets throughout. Scholars have divided it into six distinctive sections, each with a different focus and emphasis.

The first 10 stanzas describe the structure of Appleton House. They emphasize its humble proportions, reflecting the humility of Fairfax himself, as the first line employs the adjective *sober* to describe its frame, fashioned, the second line indicates, by "no foreign architect." The speaker emphasizes the importance of man's copying nature in building houses that fit his needs, rather than designing grand abodes. He uses as examples in the second stanza the "dens" of beasts and bird's nests, explaining,

> The low-roofed tortoises do dwell
> In cases fit of tortoise-shell:
> No creature loves an empty space;
> Their bodies measure out their place.

The fourth stanza makes clear that "all things are composed here / Like Nature, orderly and near,"

reflecting in their dimensions "that more sober age and mind" in which men had to "stoop / To enter at a narrow loop," an action allowing practice for the day when they would have "To strain themselves through heaven's gate." Marvell associates Fairfax's selection of design for his house with his spiritual nature. The fact that he had to stoop to enter reflects his lack of egotism. When he enters, the speaker notes in stanza 7, the cramped house must endure "the Master great," although the master delights in the small nature of the home. Marvell concludes this section with a comparison to other area estates, noting that at Appleton House "Nature here hath been so free /As if she said, 'Leave this to me.'"

Stanzas 11–35 relate the history of the house, originally a nunnery, and include its relationship to the ancestral family union of the Fairfaxes and the Thwaites. Marvell begins the 11th stanza with the line "While with slow eyes we these survey," using the *w* sounds to slow the reader, imitating the motion he describes. The speaker notes that near the "gloomy cloister's gates" the virgin Isabella Thwaite bloomed, adopting the FIGURATIVE LANGUAGE (FIGURE OF SPEECH) of metaphor to associate Isabella with the preferable natural state. The stanzas relate the family mythology, as the narrator tells readers that Isabella had loved Fairfax's ancestor, William Fairfax, but she was locked in the nunnery to prevent the marriage. Fairfax pursued legal means for her release, in essence performing a heroic rescue that allowed the two to marry, and bears her away from the nuns, "Who guiltily their prize bemonan." Their sons would take possession of the priory, which would pass into the hands of the Fairfax Marvell admired in his poem. Scholars point to the seductive nature of the nuns, who woo Isabella with words loaded with sexual meaning, as demonstrated in the 14th and 24th stanzas:

XIV

> "Here we, in shining armour white,
> Like virgin Amazons do fight.
> And our chaste lamps we hourly trim,
> Lest the great Bridegoom find them dim
> Our orient breaths perfumed are
> With incense of incessant prayer."

XXIV

"Each night among us to your side
Appoint a fresh and virgin bride;
Whom if Our Lord at midnight find,
Yet neither should be left behind.
Where you may lie as chaste in bed,
As pearls together billeted."

Marvell remains critical of the Catholic faith and rituals, characterizing the nuns as opportunists who take advantage of young virgins. He writes in stanza 32 of "the disjointed abbess" who "threads / The jingling chain-shot of her beads," adding of the nuns that "their loud'st cannon were their lungs; / And sharpest weapons were their tongues." Marvell employs the extended metaphor of battle throughout the poem, alluding to Fairfax's military career.

Stanzas 36 through 46 focus on the estate flowers with the use of personification: "Then flowers their drowsy eyelids raise, / Their silken ensigns each displays." They salute "their Governor" with "fragrant volleys" and resemble soldiers on parade presenting their colors. Military references continue, as in stanza 33 the speaker compares the gardener to a soldier who cares for his "gentle forts." Marvell writes of the estate meadows in stanzas 47 through 60, noting the tall "unfathomable grass" provides a home to grasshoppers, which he also personifies. The grass he describes as "green spires," suggesting a spiritual connotation. He features the mowers, as he does in his series The MOWER POEMS, comparing them to "Israelites," "Walking on foot through a green sea," continuing his biblical allusions. He also honors the estate woods in stanzas 61 through 81, with three verses focusing on the river. The speaker emphasizes the human connection with nature, sharing with his listeners in stanza 71:

Thus I, easy philosopher,
Among the birds and trees confer:
And little now to make me, wants
Or of the fowls, or of the plants.
Give me but wings as they, and I
Straight floating on the air shall fly:
Or turn me but, and you shall see
I was but an inverted tree.

In his final stanzas Marvell turns to his young pupil, Mary, whom he greatly compliments by noting the importance of her presence to the natural beauties of the estate. She tends the gardens, and he characterizes her as a nymph, a classical nature creature, who gives order to her surroundings. She represents the entire Fairfax line, whose efforts have imbued new life on the estate. The speaker closes by inviting his listeners to go inside the house as the evening approaches.

This poem remains important for its country house connections but is not read as much as are Marvell's LYRICS. While critics have occasionally attempted to see the poem as a political statement, the results have not proved convincing.

BIBLIOGRAPHY
Chambers, Douglas D. C. "'To the Abyss': Gothic as a Metaphor for the Argument about Art and Nature in 'Upon Appleton House.'" In On the Celebrated and Neglected Poems of Andrew Marvell, edited by Claude J. Summers and Ted-Larry Pebworth, 139–153. Columbia: University of Missouri Press, 1992.
Cousins, A. D. "Marvell's 'Upon Appleton House, to My Lord Fairfax' and the Regaining of Paradise." In The Political Identity of Andrew Marvell, edited by Conal Condren and A. D. Cousins, 53–84. Aldershot, England: Scolar Press, Gower, 1990.
Grossman, Marshall. "Authoring the Boundary: Allegory, Irony, and the Rebus in 'Upon Appleton House.'" In "The Muses Common-Weale": Poetry and Politics in the Seventeenth Century, edited by Claude J. Summers and Ted-Larry Pebworth, 191–206. Columbia: University of Missouri Press, 1988.
Healy, Thomas. "'Dark All without It Knits': Vision and Authority in Marvell's Upon Appleton House." In Literature and the English Civil War, edited by Thomas Healy and Jonathan Sawday, 170–188. Cambridge: Cambridge University Press, 1990.
McClung, William A. The Country House in English Renaissance Poetry. Berkeley: University of California Press, 1977.
Patton, Brian. "Preserving Property: History, Genealogy, and Inheritance in 'Upon Appleton House.'" Renaissance Quarterly 49 (winter 1996): 824–839.
Smith, Nigel, ed. The Poems of Andrew Marvell. New York: Pearson/Longman, 2003.
Thomason, T. Katharine Sheldahl. "Marvell, His Bee-Like Cell: The Pastoral Hexagon of Upon Appleton House." Genre 16 (1983): 39–56.

"UPON COMBING HER HAIR" EDWARD HERBERT, LORD OF CHERBURY (1665)

"Upon Combing Her Hair" by EDWARD HERBERT, LORD HERBERT OF CHERBURY, presents a simple picture of a woman at her toilette, but the speaker's tone is one of praise and exaltation, befitting an elevated subject. Not published until 18 years after Herbert's death, his poems might have provided a bridge from Renaissance poetry, with its innocently romantic themes, to RESTORATION poetry, in which readers expected to find the more salacious themes common in Continental literature. Those readers learned to become appreciative audiences again after the dearth of creative literature that existed during the Interregnum. Along with attending performances in reopened theaters, readers imitated the court's fashionable tastes, and those tastes ran to salacious themes. However, Herbert's work remained strictly of the Renaissance school, as he examined rather innocent ideas of love. He may have objectified women, as had his predecessors the CAVALIER POETS, but his tone remained respectful. No one could accuse Herbert of the rhetorical leer.

Herbert structures five four-line stanzas, adopting the RHYME scheme *abba*. He begins his poem with praise accentuated by repetition of terms and ALLITERATION, appealing to the woman who is the poem's subject to share the wonder of her beautiful hair:

> Breaking from under that thy cloudy veil,
> Open and shine yet more, shine out more clear,
> Thou glorious, golden beam of darling hair,
> Even till my wonder-stricken senses fail.

He engages in hyperbole to make clear the wonder that something as simple as a woman's hair can inspire. His use of the phrase *golden beam* causes the reader to think of the beams of the sun, and his use of the adjective *darling* is meant in its diminutive sense as a term of endearment.

The CONCEIT extends into the second stanza, as the speaker bids the glorious head of hair, "Shine out in light, and shine those rays on far," then references by comparison "the Queen of Love," meaning the Roman goddess Venus, "When she doth comb her on her sphere above, / And from a planet turns a blazing star."

As the celestial references continue, readers learn the hair shines like a star. That type of beauty had such power in Venus's world that it converted a planet into a star. Little wonder then that it could move a mere mortal to a stricken state. Feminist critics would find of interest the fact that the woman remains without face or voice during most of the poem, her hair combed forward to cover her face. Although the comparison to Venus suggests a degree of power, it arises from no facet of the woman's character or intelligence, but exclusively from her physical beauty.

The third stanza suggests that the woman the speaker observes might serve a greater purpose than she even knows: "thou art greater too, more destiny / Depends on thee, than on her influence." That is high praise indeed, as the speaker suggests that the woman's hair "to some one a thread of life must be." The fourth stanza notes her graciousness to the speaker and declares that should her beautiful hair combine with that of Venus, it would be too much to absorb: "those glories which, if they united were, / Might have amazed sense." However, he suggests in the final stanza that "new beauties do arise / While she withdraws these glories which were spread." At that point he focuses on what has been revealed when the hair, or "these glories which were spread," is tossed back away from the face: "thy yet fairer eyes." True to the Cavalier tradition, he turns his gaze on multiple body parts.

Herbert engages his reader by sketching a vivid image of a common daily occurrence. He seems to tell his audience that wonders may be discovered even in their own domiciles. As many poets do, he places a heavy burden on women to remain self-conscious even in private moments, as they cannot escape the male gaze. Critics with a different point of view, however, might argue that the woman demands that men gaze upon the spectacle she creates in the simple task of combing her hair.

"UPON HIS VERSES" ROBERT HERRICK (1648)

"Upon His Verses" by ROBERT HERRICK represents one of dozens of brief poems included in Herrick's more than 1,000-entry collection *Hesperides,* among its secular works. Herrick's upbeat tone framed everyday considerations, including a musing regarding his own pastime of writing. He adopts a traditional metaphor of his poems as his children, used also by MARGARET CAVENDISH, DUCHESS OF NEWCASTLE, among other 17th-century poets. Herrick had no legitimate children, adopting the attitude that his own poetic offspring were just as appropriate for him as were flesh and blood children for more traditional parents. His lines suggest that readers have questioned whether his verses actually belong to him; perhaps he had been accused of lifting his ideas from others. However, he makes clear that is not the case, and he pointedly notes in the poem's opening lines that he does not presume to probe other parents regarding the origin of their children, a gentle rebuke of those who question the legitimacy of his poetry. He notes that he has adopted some of his offspring but that all remain legitimate, hinting that not all parents can make that claim. The six lines of iambic tetrameter go so far as to suggest his offspring might be superior to the children

> What off-spring other men have got,
> The how, where, when, I question not.
> These are the Children I have left;
> Adopted some; none got by theft.
> But all are toucht (like lawfull plate)
> And no Verse illegitimate.

The phrase *toucht (like lawfull plate)* refers to the testing of fine silver and gold by rubbing against a touchstone. That reference allows Herrick to suggest the high value of his work. Ironically in light of the judgmental tone of his poem he probably fathered an illegitimate daughter with a lover named Tomasin.

"UPON JACK AND JILL. EPIGRAM" ROBERT HERRICK (1648)

ROBERT HERRICK placed "Upon Jack and Jill. Epigram" in the secular section of his poetry collection *Hesperides*. Its vulgarity mirrored that in works such as those by Shakespeare, but its utilization of nursery RHYME characters indicates it is not meant to be taken seriously. Its purpose is a light self-deprecation, as it reflects upon the foolishly romantic nature of poets. Herrick subverts the idea that poets are desirable to all women simply because of the tradition of romance attached to their occupation. In the

eight-line verse Jill expresses in certain terms her attitude regarding the poet's life. While Jack, the poet, argues for the aesthetic value of verse, Jill prefers a stomach filled with solid food. A practical woman, she rejects the ethereal kiss that her poet lover feels should satisfy her material cravings:

> When Jill complains to Jack for want of meat;
> Jack kisses Jill, and bids her freely eat:
> Jill says, of what? Says Jack, on that sweet kiss,
> Which full of Nectar and Ambrosia is,
> The food of Poets.

Jack tries without success to convince Jill that poetry offers sustenance suitable for the gods, its "Nectar and Ambrosia" far more spiritually beneficial than meat is beneficial to the flesh. With no wish to live as a starving, near-death poet, Jill desires something other than a poet's food, which is no food at all. Her voice completes the fifth line and continues until the poem's indelicate conclusion:

> . . . so I thought says Jill,
> That makes them look so lank, so Ghost-like still.
> Let Poets feed on air, or what they will;
> Let me feed full, till that I fart, says Jill.

Herrick may suggest that a poet's ingestion of inspiration often results in mere hot air, a product as common and unpleasant as that produced by Jill's gut full of meat.

"UPON JULIA'S CLOTHES" ROBERT HERRICK (1648)

A brief but popular poem, ROBERT HERRICK's "Upon Julia's Clothes" often appears in anthologies. Its six lines offer a masterful imagery with a unity of purpose, rhythm, and RHYME that combine to elevate its common subject matter above its proper station. The speaker begins, "When as in silks my Julia goes," and Herrick adds repetition in the next line, "Then, then (me thinks) how sweetly flows." The parenthetical remark gives a touch of realism to the sentiment, while the flow of Herrick's words imitates that of the silk he describes. The noun in the third line represents the height of sensuality, as the speaker describes what flows so sweetly, "That liquefaction of her clothes." Herrick's introduction of the scientific term *liquefaction* into his obviously artistic creation evokes a hardy contrast and emphasizes the grace within the silks required to reduce them to a liquid, organic skin that flows about Julia's body. The final triplet is the expression of a man exulting in woman's beauty, as Herrick writes,

Next, when I cast mine eyes and see
That brave Vibration each way free;
O how that glittering take me.

The speaker notes the liberated movement of Julia's body with a gaze that is deliberately "cast" in Julia's direction. The speaker remains consumed by Julia's "brave Vibration," seeing her body as a glittering mass that threatens to consume him, as does his passion.

"UPON THE DEATH OF MR. KING" JOHN CLEVELAND (1638)

JOHN CLEVELAND celebrated the life and mourned the death of Mr. Edward King along with others in *Obsequies to the Memory of Mr. Edward King* (1638), which would be reprinted in 1651. JOHN MILTON also saluted the memory of his classmate from Christ's College in his more lastingly famous LYCIDAS (1638). The various elegies inform readers that King had been a fine scholar, a fair poet, and a future clergyman. He died in a mysterious foundering of his ship on a calm day in 1637 between the mouth of the river Dee and the Isle of Angelsea. Cleveland's effort remains notable for one "Clevelandism," as JOHN DRYDEN later termed the poet's "wrestling" words or phrases into contortions of their original meanings and/or order.

Cleveland begins his 54 lines of rhyming couplets by referencing the ELEGY form, often present as music, and he employs the verb *scan*, which traditionally refers to an analysis or measuring of poetry (SCANSION). He writes, "I like not tears in tune, nor will I prize / His artificial grief, that scans his eyes." The use of *artificial* does not apply to the dead Mr. King, but rather to the collection of verses in the volume, as that term sometimes applied to collected poetry. He blends a religious and classical reference as he continues, "Mine weep down pious beads: but why should I / Confine them to

the Muses' rosary?" His pleasurable suggestion of the sacred nature of inspiration is somewhat tempered by the awkward imagery of tears as heavy beads connected to one another and used in what can become a mindless chant.

What follows is the extended metaphor described in Cleveland's time as a "masculine" type. It results in awkward and unfortunate imagery projected through FIGURATIVE LANGUAGE (FIGURE OF SPEECH), as well as RHYME, as the speaker says, "I am no poet here; my pen's the spout / Where the rain water of my eyes runs out." Spouts generally ejected water from gargoyles, introducing a monstrous element into the image. While such figures often decorated churches, no connection to King's intention to become a clergyman is suggested. What follows extends the jarring water metaphor: "In pity of that name, whose fate we see / Thus copied out his grief's hydrography." While *hydrography* means literally "a description of water" and is meant as a reference to King's ocean grave, its juxtaposition to the water reference of tears reduces its effectiveness. Both are salt water, but the figurative expansion of the tears to beads and then to the ocean is neither smoothly nor skillfully accomplished.

Cleveland continues with many classical references incorporated into the next lines, most connected to the ocean. The "Muses are not mermaids" is a line comparing two mythological figures, one that inspires poets, the other often connected to the death of fishermen. A reference to Helicon, rightly a mountain, is meant by Cleveland to refer to Aganippe or Hippocrene, two fountains known to inspire. Declaring, "The sea's too rough for verse," Cleveland reminds readers that Xerxes tried to "fetter th' Hellespont," referencing the tale in which King Xerxes became so frustrated by the interference of the sea with his nautical attempts that he ordered the Hellespont whipped and shackled.

The speaker again mentions his tears, noting they "will keep no channel" and follow "no laws / To guide the streams." Instead, as do waves, they will "run with disturbance," swallowing the poet. In an extension by Cleveland of the wave metaphor, the speaker wonders whether the deceased's expansive virtue can "find a grave / Within the impostumed bubble of a wave?" *Impostumed* suggests a swelling wave, and the speaker wonders whether the winds could not "countermand thy death," and "With their whole card of lungs redeem thy breath?" Cleveland employs the contemporary thought that winds were born at and blew from each compass point, a reference that William Shakespeare employed in his drama *Macbeth*. He asks whether "some new island" might not offer rescue, alluding to the image employed by Milton in PARADISE LOST of whales at sea resembling islands.

Cleveland also references Aristotle, labeling him "The famous Stagirite," as the philosopher was born at Stagira, and refers to Nature as the widow of Aristotle. By noting the widow is "Queen Dowager of all Philosophy," Cleveland alludes to Aristotle as the *King*, with a play on the deceased's name. The poet next states that legend holds that everything present on earth can also be found under sea, probably alluding to the Pliny's declaration in his *Natural History* "Whatsoever is engendered and bred in any part of the world beside is found in the sea." However, "Books, arts, and tongues were wanting," but in King, "Neptune hath got an university," allowing Cleveland to praise King's immense learning and creativity.

In the line "We'll dive no more for pearls," the speaker compares poets and readers to treasure seekers, expanding on the previous metaphor of the sea as a composite of wealth, which King would increase. Using hyperbole to effect, the speaker declares that the hope to meet King and "see / Thy sacred relics of mortality" would "make the seamen prize / His shipwreck now more than his merchandise." King's tomb is compared to the Royal Exchange, the center of English commerce, and Cleveland references destruction by both fire and water and introduces PARADOX by writing, "that dissolves us which doth us compound." He notes that

> We of the gown our libraries must toss
> To understand the greatness of our loss,
> By pupils to our grief, and so much grow
> In learning as our sorrows overflow.

He suggests a role change between teachers, those of the gown, who must become pupils again to learn, and thus gain, from their sorrow. Cleveland concludes with four lines that return to his early reference to

conduits and tears, noting that when those who grieve for King fill

> . . . the roundlets of our eyes,
> We'll issue it forth, and vent such elegies,
> As that our tears shall seem the Irish Seas,
> We floating islands, living Hebrides.

BIBLIOGRAPHY
Morris, Brian, and Eleanor Withington, eds. *The Poems of John Cleveland*. Oxford: Clarendon Press, 1967.

"UPON THE LOSSE OF HIS MISTRESSES"

ROBERT HERRICK (1648)   As did most of his other best recognized poems, the SONNET titled "Upon the Losse of His Mistresses" appeared in ROBERT HERRICK's large collection *Hesperides*. Herrick framed this verse in the same playful tone common in his secular poetry. While the mistresses proved pure fantasy, Herrick seems to enjoy listing "these / Many dainty Mistresses" by name. Those names include "Stately Julia," labeled "prime of all," and Sapho, termed "a principall," or a more important lover. He admires in lines 5–11 "Smooth Anthea, for a skin / White," while "Sweet Electra" is compared to "Heaven-like Chrystalline." With an admirable voice resembling the Lute, Myrha is praised, and "Next, Corinna," not only "for her wit," but for "the graceful use of it." Finally he mentions Perilla, and with her "All are gone; / Only Herrick's left alone." In his loneliness he will "number sorrow by / Their departures hence, and die." Typical of the sonnet format, the final two lines comment on the situation stated in the first 12, although Herrick broke from the serious consideration that underlies the light tone of many sonnets. Herrick wrote many highly erotic poems, such as "The VINE," and the final allusion here to death may be used as it often appeared in Renaissance writing, as a reference to a loss of ability of the male to engage in sexual intercourse due to erection failure.

"UPON THE NIPPLES OF JULIA'S BREAST" ROBERT HERRICK (1648)   ROBERT HERRICK generally framed his erotica with playful intent, and his "Upon the Nipples of Julia's Breast" proves no

exception. Julia was the ideal of woman, considered in a number of Herrick's works, including "The Night-Piece, to Julia" and the well-known "Upon Julia's Clothes." As he focuses on Julia's nipples, the speaker offers three comparisons to dramatic images contrasting red, the color of the nipple, with white, the color of the breast skin. He begins the 10-line poem with a question, "Have ye beheld (with much delight) / A red-Rose peeping through the white?" the first of four comparisons. While the rose traditionally represented women and sexuality, white symbolized innocence or naiveté. Herrick extends the framing of each red image with that of white, suggesting an innocent voyeurism. Later lines describe "a Cherrie (double grac't) / Within a Lily," a strawberry "half drown'd in Creame," and "rich Rubies blushing through / A pure smooth Pearle, and Orient to?" Those comparisons establish through the use of nature metaphors that Julia's breast bears a natural beauty devoid of artificial ornamentation. They also offer images that tantalize and tease, with corresponding terms to describe them, such as *peeping* and *blushing*. Each item in the series seems reluctant to reveal itself, and none burst into the line of sight. Rather each appears only partially visible, the tease representing much of their attraction.

Sexual inferences abound, with the cherry representing a woman's hymen, and the lily symbolizing death, a term used in the Renaissance to mean sexual pleasure or climax. The berry in cream has specific sexual connotation relating to a woman's sex organ and the male production of semen, while the jewels suggest an exotic quality, elevating Julia's breast above that of the common woman. Herrick concludes with a final couplet, "So like to this, nay all the rest, / Is each neat Niplet of her breast." The alliteration in *neat Niplet* creates an auditory pleasure that supports the pleasure produced by the visual imagery. The suffix *-let* on the term *Niplet* acts as a reductive, creating an almost childish term, again equating the speaker's effort to catch sight of the nipple with innocent play. The speaker invites the audience to enjoy a simple, natural phenomenon from their observers' stance. While Herrick writes of other women, none appears in as vivid focus as Julia, who remains the most erotic object of the reader's gaze.

"UPON THE SAYING THAT MY VERSES WERE MADE BY ANOTHER" Anne Killigrew (1686)

In her poem "Upon the Saying That My Verses Were Made by Another" Anne Killigrew uses a technique that became traditional for early women writers, that of defending themselves against charges of what would later be termed plagiarism. Poets including Margaret Cavendish, duchess of Newcastle, had found the need to defend the legitimacy of their writing publicly, but charges that women's poetry was not original seemed to occur more frequently later in the century. The denial by Killigrew remained necessary into the early 18th century, when a doubtful reading public, and many male poets, believed women lacked the intellect and creativity to write poetry. In five stanzas and 62 lines composed of rhyming couplets, Killgrew made her case, adopting classical allusions and a direct reference to a famous predecessor to add support.

The speaker begins with a traditional call to her muse, "O queen of verse," for inspiration. She makes clear in the opening stanza that "The Muse's laurel" proves far more valuable to her than "a crown of gold," referencing the leaves historically identified with poets. She concludes by using the term *holocaust,* meaning a burnt offering, vowing to her muse, "Thou shalt my pleasure, my employment be, / My all I'll make a holocaust to thee." The second stanza describes the joy the speaker feels when writing and the praise her work garnered. However, the promise of fame becomes an empty one, as Killigrew employs Alliteration to call attention to the series *fame, false, flattered,* all related terms with negative connotations here:

> What pleasing raptures filled my ravaged sense,
> How strong, how sweet, fame, was thy influence!
> And thine, false hope, that to my flattered sight
> Did'st glories represent so near and bright!
>   (15–18)

The speaker accepts the blame for her "false hope," a result of her naive acceptance of flattery. Killigrew next refers to the myth of Apollo, Greek god of the sun and of poetry, and the nymph Daphne, adopting that tale as an extended conceit to emphasize the betrayal she felt. Daphne was forced to transform herself into a laurel tree in order to avoid Apollo's lecherous intentions, after she was lured into "rapture and delight" by the duplicitous god. Killigrew's feelings of betrayal are clear.

The speaker admits in the third stanza that her taste of fame "emboldened" her to "commit" her work into a few hands, perhaps those of friends who passed her manuscripts around. Then she adds, "But, ah, the sad effects that from it came! / What ought t' have brought me honor, brought me shame!" She then explains that to others she seemed like "Aesop's painted jay," alluding to a story in which a common jay bird donned the plumage of the beautiful peacock, inciting attack by other birds for his presumption. As the jay assuming a disguise, Killigrew was accused by some readers of falsely representing another's work as her own. They admired her poetry but "scorned" her, thinking she took the laurel wreath from "Another's brow, that had so rich a store / Of sacred wreaths that circled it before." These serious charges quite offended the innocent speaker.

In the fourth stanza the speaker references the poet and playwright KATHERINE PHILIPS, known as "The Matchless Orinda," and a model for Killigrew. She makes clear that Philips had gained glory through her writing, not through any physical beauty. Her "radiant soul" caused her skin, lips, and cheeks to glow like roses and even "Advanced her height, and sparkled in her eye." Killigrew uses *height* metaphorically, meaning that Philips stood high in public opinion. At that time "every laurel to her laurel bowed!" and the speaker wonders why the public questions the authenticity of her work, when Philips's work did not suffer such attack.

The concluding stanza laments that the speaker must endure an "envious age," unwilling to "allow what I do write, my own," where *allow* means to "acknowledge." However, the speaker refuses to be silenced by false charges, as Killigrew again cites classical figures, including Phoebus, another name for Apollo. She also references Cassandra, a princess of Troy to whom Apollo granted the gift of prophecy. However, angered by her rejection of his physical advances, Apollo made all who heard Cassandra disbelieve her, although her prophecies always later proved

true. Thus Killigrew skillfully returns to her previous conceit with Apollo, using it against her detractors. In line 59 she creates a caesura through insertion of a semicolon to make readers hesitate. This allows her to complete her thought regarding her *numbers,* or verses. Then she proceeds to dress down Phoebus in a line that runs into the next, completing her thought through the use of ENJAMBMENT. She emphasizes the importance of remaining true to her art, regardless of criticism:

> But let them rage, and 'gainst a maid conspire,
> So deathless numbers from my tuneful lyre
> Do ever flow; so, Phoebus, I by thee
> Divinely inspired and possessed may be,
> I willingly accept Cassandra's fate,
> To speak the truth, although believed too late.
>   (57–62)

Killigrew's defense represents one of the best of its type. She maintains a strong presence throughout, and her purpose remains to let others have little doubt regarding her firm resolve. The poem stands as a counterpoint to JOHN DRYDEN's famous lines in his ode to Killigrew, "Art she had none, yet wanted none; / For nature did that want supply." Killigrew's studied metaphors, careful use of format, classical allusions, and well-crafted unity of purpose could hardly have originated in "nature." They had to be, rather, the products of a learning and practice necessary to any intellectual or artistic pursuit.

"UPON THE WEAKNESS AND MISERY OF MAN" SAMUEL BUTLER (n.d.)

Published as part of SAMUEL BUTLER's miscellany "Upon the Weakness and Misery of Man" is in the SONNET form of 14 lines and formatted in straight rhyming couplets. While not Butler's strongest effort, which may be found in his landmark *HUDIBRAS* (1662, 1663, 1678), the sonnet clearly expresses his attitudes toward man's self-destructive nature and tendency toward self-delusion. A staunch Royalist forced for a time to work for an officer in Cromwell's army, Butler had ample opportunity to observe the character defects of men supposedly devoted to religious causes, which turned those causes into a means to war and ultimately to control over others. However, in

"Upon the Weakness and Misery of Man" Butler aims at a universal audience, united by their shared human tendency toward ultimately worthless self-aggrandizement, regardless of political leanings.

The first line begins with the simple declaration "Our pains are real things," which contrast with man's pursuit of pleasure: "and all / Our pleasures but fantastical." The speaker indicates that humans simply imagine the pleasure that their private pursuits afford. He goes so far in the third line as to indicate that pleasures actually cause self-inflicted harm to humans, comparing them to "Diseases of their own accord," not easily cured: "But cures come difficult and hard." While earthly delights are easily obtainable, their ethereal, transient nature makes them undesirable, particularly when they often result in long-term consequences that ultimately prove ill to others. Butler selects harshly realistic imagery in his next comparison through the FIGURATIVE LANGUAGE (FIGURE OF SPEECH) of metaphor: "Our noblest piles and stateliest rooms / Are but outhouses to our tombs." By comparing structures of great state and status to outhouses designed to collect human waste, Butler emphasizes the great leveling effect of death and man's ultimate condition as mere detritus.

The poet broadens his consideration to entire civilizations as the speaker continues, "Cities though ne'er so great and brave / But mere warehouses to the grave," with the image of a warehouse indicating that the most glorious of cities act only as holding grounds for foolishly busy humans prior to their deaths. According to Butler, men project a false bravado that fools many onlookers, who can easily be convinced of the value of even a worthless person: "Our bravery's but a vain disguise / to hide us from the world's dull eyes." The *dull eyes* of society may result from constant exposure to deception, which causes its eventual simple-minded acceptance. He may even hint that he and his fellow writers aid in duplicity by immortalizing for profit certain individuals, particularly war heroes. The *bravery* the speaker references may serve as an adequate disguise to fellow mortals or even to one's self but yields no protection against death, which embraces all equally and stripped of any costume. Bravado is "The remedy of a defect / With which our nakedness is decked."

The final couplet acts as it should in a sonnet, to supply a summary of, or response to, the problem presented in the preceding 12 lines. It makes clear that humans will continue pursuit of pleasure, denying its false nature: "Yet makes us smile with pride and boast / As if we had gained by being lost." In this case the final comment expresses IRONY, supporting through PARADOX the clearly expressed condition of man that precedes it. The speaker states sadly that man is so consumed by pride that he cannot even recognize how much he loses by engaging in idle boasting.

V

"VALEDICTION FORBIDDING MOURNING, A" JOHN DONNE (1633)

Literary critics place the writing of JOHN DONNE's "A Valediction Forbidding Mourning" in the year 1611, when he traveled to Europe. He left behind his pregnant wife, and their separation probably inspired his poem. The title term *mourning* suggests the sorrow accompanying death, but Donne writes a love poem, not an ELEGY, and not a *valediction* in the religious sense of a farewell that might be expressed at the end of a religious service. Rather he writes of a farewell in which the partners should resist sorrow, with the knowledge that their love will successfully endure the challenge of separation.

Donne begins a skillful use of FIGURATIVE LANGUAGE (FIGURE OF SPEECH) by comparing the separation of one lover from another to the separation between individuals caused by death. He could draw on a biblical tradition that associated love and sex with death from the Old Testament book Song of Solomon, which describes the marriage of Solomon and a country maiden, referred to as "the Sulammite," with one section describing a temporary separation. The Sulammite tells Solomon in 8:6: "Put me like a seal over your heart, Like a seal on your arm. For love is as strong as death." Donne grounded much of his writing in religious tenets and the Bible's ideas, but he also drew on its abundant poetry as inspiration. The Bible offers much language that could be considered comparable to that of METAPHYSICAL POETS AND POETRY, such as Solomon's lover's comparison of herself to a seal. In the first instance the *seal* reference may have suggested a "signet," but it may also be interpreted in its second usage as "a vehement flame," according to the *Master Study Bible: New American Standard.* Donne's format remains simple, as does his language, the poem consisting of nine four-line verses with the RHYME scheme *ababcdcdefef,* et cetera.

The speaker refers to death in the first stanza but adopts a gentle tone, telling his love,

> As virtuous men pass mildly away,
> And whisper to their souls, to go,
> Whilst some of their sad friends do say,
> The breath goes now, and some say, no;

and concludes with a semicolon, signaling the reader that the initial thought remains incomplete. He selects men of virtue as his focus because their virtue assures them of everlasting life. Their souls may part with their bodies in complete confidence, even if those left behind do not want them to go. He tells his love in the next stanza that they should "melt, and make no noise" as they plan their separation, meaning they should not attract attention to themselves, not crying or making "sigh-tempests." Creating an emotional scene would be treating their love in a profane manner, as then even "the laity" would learn of it. The use of the term *laity,* which refers to those who form a church congregation, allows Donne to suggest the two lovers are not on the same level as common people.

By the third stanza Donne expands his consideration beyond the lovers' bed or room to focus on the entire universe. The speaker notes that when the Earth moves, it may cause fear or harm, prompting those who observe it to wonder about its meaning. Then he adds, "But trepidation of the spheres, / Though greater far, is innocent." *Trepidation of the spheres* references Earth's movement in relation to the other planets and constellations. In Donne's time the Ptolemaic theory described the universe as a series of concentric spheres, with Earth at its center. Donne will extend this metaphysical CONCEIT, later comparing the two lovers to the compass, a drafting instrument with two metal feet, one of which may be fixed at a predetermined spot, while the other moves around it in a perfect circle.

Another metaphor appears in the fourth stanza, as the speaker ranks some "Dull" lovers as "sublunary," meaning those who have fallen below the level of the Moon, with the term *fallen* suggesting angels who fell from heaven because they could not meet its requirements. The dull lovers fell because they share a love "(Whose soul is sense)." Donne uses parenthesis to emphasize how simple the explanation is of these other lovers who do not share what his speaker and partner do. He also makes use of the theory that described the soul as existing in three levels: vegetable, sensible, and rational. While the sensible level would encompass the emotions two lovers experienced, it would remain only a partial knowledge of things spiritual. The rational is also required for complete understanding. The speaker asks that his love move beyond the emotional, including wordplay in the next line, "Absence, because it doth remove / Those things which elemented it," by suggesting *sense* as the root of the term *Absence*. The lovers share a strong relationship, not based only on emotion, but also on logic. Therefore they can accept separation, as emphasized in the fifth stanza, which opens,

But we by a love, so much refin'd
That ourselves know not what it is,
Inter-assured of the mind,
Care less eyes, lips, and hands to miss.

Donne adopts the metaphor of refinement, as he does in other poems, including "BATTER MY HEART," to stress that raw substances, such as ore, must experience stress to achieve their refined end state as valuable metals. The love the couple in this poem share is so valuable they cannot even name it. Because they have realized the rational level of the soul, they can apply logic to help them accept their physical separation.

Donne then draws on the Platonic idea of two souls' joining to form a complete whole as he begins the next stanza,

Our two souls therefore, which are one,
Though I must go, endure not yet
A breach.

He extends the former allusion to the refinement of ore in the next line to another metaphysical conceit. The speaker completes the stanza by explaining their separation constitutes an expansion of their love, "Like gold to airy thinness beat."

Donne introduces the famous compass conceit mentioned in the seventh stanza. The speaker concedes that their souls may be two, but

If they be two, they are two so
As stiff twin compasses are two,
Thy soul the fixed foot, makes no show
To move, but doth, if th' other do.

It offers a perfect image of two parts of a whole in which every movement of one directly affects the other. Having established the metaphor, he extends it into the penultimate stanza, noting that the lovers' relationship not only can withstand the separation but will survive it without ill effect:

And though it in the centre sit,
Yet when the other far doth roam,
It leans, and hearkens after it,
And grows erect, as that comes home.

Psychoanalytic critics would find the implication of a sexual erection, suggested by the terms *stiff* and *erect*, of interest and not out of character for Donne, whose love poetry often contained erotic imagery. They might comment on the extension of the erotic suggestion into the concluding stanza in which the speaker makes clear "Such wilt thou be to me, who must / Like th' other foot, obliquely run;" then mentions "Thy firmness makes my circle just," concluding with the line "And makes me end, where I begun." However, more traditional close readers emphasize the term *erect* as alluding to a straight-backed devotion and a willingness of the lover left behind to stand firm in orienting their love. Thus when the term *firmness* occurs in the next stanza, it reflects on the previous suggestion of strength. The lover who remains is strong enough to guide home again the one who must temporarily leave.

The popular Renaissance idea of the circle and sphere as representing perfection informs the entire poem, offering an image the reader may use to visualize Donne's suggestion of the perfect love. It substantiates the wedding ring as symbolizing a perfect union, an emotion-based idea, but his introduction of the compass, used in logical mathematical pursuits, allows his suggestion that love is more than mere emotion.

BIBLIOGRAPHY

Gardner, Helen, ed. *John Donne: A Collection of Critical Essays.* New York: Prentice-Hall, 1962.

Master Study Bible: New American Standard. Nashville: Holman Bible, 1981.

"VALEDICTION: OF WEEPING, A" JOHN DONNE (1633)

One of JOHN DONNE's more famous poems, "A Valediction: Of Weeping," resembles other of his works in its use of the style of METAPHYSICAL POETS AND POETRY, FIGURATIVE LANGUAGE (FIGURE OF SPEECH), clear logic, and focus on balance. It also suggests a blend of the sacred and the profane with the inclusion in its title of the term *Valediction,* normally associated with the conclusion of a religious service. Donne draws on his naturally skeptical nature and inflated ego to address the act of weeping, common to parting lovers. He also adopts the traditional association of love with death, inherited from the biblical book Song of Solomon. His speaker basically explains to his beloved that tears afford danger, in that one of the lovers might drown.

While such a simplistic explanation of his message reduces it to a humorous exaggeration, Donne refines the theme through his application of poetic format that reflects his passion. That form includes three stanzas, each composed of nine lines. The first, fifth, and sixth lines in each stanza align with the center of the page, calling special attention to their message and their rhymes, with their METER iambic dimeter. All other lines are in iambic pentameter except the final line, which adds one beat in iambic hexameter. The RHYME scheme is *abbaccddd,* momentum interrupted by each midstanza centered couplet. Donne did not often call such attention to his poems' position on the page. It results in a formal effect that seems at first glance inappropriate to its subject.

The speaker begins in a short, centered line, "Let me pour forth," adopting language reminiscent of biblical terminology. Donne might have written simply "let me cry," but the effect would have been greatly reduced. In simple one-syllable words Donne signals his reader that his idea of grief at parting is greater than that represented by a few tears. ENJAMBMENT carries the reader into line 2 with no hesitation on the term *forth,* moving directly into "My tears before thy face whilst I stay here." Donne chooses not to have the speaker refer to his own face first, but instead that of his lover as they stand face to face. This prepares readers for the later Platonic suggestion that the two lovers constitute parts of one continuous whole and perfect union.

The established close position of the speaker and his love allows the reader an image supportive of the next lines. The speaker notes that his own tears reflect his lover's face, "thy face coins them," and that affords the tears value, "And by this mintage they are something worth." Their worth is that they are "Pregnant of thee." Donne shifts to a new metaphor by referring to the tears as "Fruits of much grief," suggesting their careful cultivation. He also reflects on the pregnancy metaphor, as *fruit of the loins* referred to a man's child. He concludes by noting that when his tears fall, containing his love within them, "Thou falls which it bore," further extending the idea of birth through the verb *bore.* Donne offers a strong metaphysical CONCEIT, verging on the absurd, in suggesting that the woman he loves exists in a tear and, moreover, that he, the male, might carry her in pregnancy. However, his extension of that conceit through the following stanzas leads the reader to accept it. He concludes the first stanza with the speaker's noting that when separated "on a diverse shore," "thou and I are nothing then."

The second stanza begins with an image of a grand effect that arises from what at first glance appears to be nothing important:

> . . . On a round ball
> A workman that hath copies by can lay
> An Europe, Afric, and an Asia,
> And quickly make that, which was nothing, all.

Donne adopts the traditional "man as microcosm" view present since classic times and discussed in Sir Walter Raleigh's "That Man Is as it Were, a Little World." His speaker envisions even a smaller microcosm, a whole world in the tiny expanse of a teardrop. He makes that suggestion concrete by asking the reader to envision the construction of a globe. Although only a representation of a world, the globe helps prove Donne's logic. In addition he reflects back on the pregnancy metaphor, as a human being, God's greatest creation, seems to assemble from nothing. His speaker then can compare that assembling of the globe to "each tear / Which thee doth wear, / A globe, yea world, by that impression grow."

The speaker expands his argument by concluding that when the lovers' tears mix, so great is their volume that they "do overflow / This world; by waters sent from thee, my heaven dissolved so." Donne adopts the Ptolemaic view of the universe as overlapping concentric circles, the circle of heaven crossing that of Earth and its waters. He also recalls the creation story from the biblical book of Genesis, in which God first covers the earth with waters, which eventually withdraw to reveal the land. Donne's imagery works in reverse. The lover's immense passion allows her to cover the earth with water that will reach even up to heaven.

By the final verse the speaker has reached the climax of his plea. He begins with the call to his lover, "O more than moon," employing the moon as a traditional symbol of woman. He frames his plea as a matter of life and death, asking her,

> Draw not up seas to drown me in thy sphere;
> Weep me not dead in thine arms, but forbear
> To teach the sea what it may do too soon.

Donne employs the imagery of the male sphere within that of the female, an approach he also takes in "AIR AND ANGELS." The personified ocean can learn from the lovers, in the view of the confident speaker, to resist destructive behavior. The final two short centered lines read, "Let not the wind / Example find," including now in earth, water, and wind all of the natural elements needed for creation except fire, which is suggested by the lovers' passion. The two enjambed lines continue without break into those that follow, so that if read as intended, the passage runs, "Let not the wind example find / To do me more harm than it purposeth." Again the speaker equates his lover's weeping with the most destructive forces on earth, deadly in their effects. He concludes with the Platonic idea that two true hearts may exist as one: "Since thou and I sigh one another's breath, / Whoe'er sighs most is cruelest, and hastes the other's death." He has offered an image of balance through allusions to creation and destruction, life and death.

The scholar Susannah Mintz interprets Donne's focus on tears as his production of a space in which gender differences may disappear. She sees the teardrop's fragile membrane as imitating "the edges between people that Donne is always testing." Its close connection with emotion and the fact that it flows from the inside out symbolize its ability to shatter boundaries. He suggests the dissolution of one boundary in the pregnancy metaphor, as in this case the pregnant male offers a gender role reversal of interest to both feminist and psychoanalytic critics. The tears physically intermingle, his becoming hers and vice versa, supporting concretely the abstract Platonic suggestion that the two lovers achieve perfection in becoming one being.

BIBLIOGRAPHY
Mintz, Susannah B. "'Forget the Hee and Shee': Gender and Play in John Donne." *Modern Philology* 98, no. 4 (May 2001): 577.

"VANITY OF HUMAN WISHES, THE" SAMUEL JOHNSON (1749)

When SAMUEL JOHNSON wrote his poem "The Vanity of Human Wishes," he considered an idea informing all of his writing, whether poetry, fiction, or prose, that false hope produced fantasies rendering man incapable of dealing with the reality of everyday life. At 368 lines in rhyming couplets, this imitation of Juvenal's Tenth Satire proved Johnson's longest poem. His attention to the Latin form and expression is visible in each line, which he attempted to shape in such a way that they would reflect the meaning closest to that of the original. Dense and challenging, the poem dealt, as Johnson often wrote that poetry should, with generalities enabling any reader to apply points to his or her own life. Not to be confused with abstract ideas, the generalities appear in the form of poetic parables about particular famous individuals in history applied to the common man's existence, as well as through personification of emotions, as did medieval morality plays. He achieved this effect by expressing thoughts about abstract values with concrete verbs and strong, clear metaphors. For example, he opens commenting on the necessity of acute observation to man's understanding of his lot, at the same time commenting on what must stand as the exceptional poet's approach to writing:

> Let Observation, with extensive view,
> Survey mankind, from China to Peru;
> Remark each anxious toil, each eager strife,
> And watch the busy scenes of crowded life;
> Then say how hope and fear, desire and hate
> O'erspread with snares the clouded maze of
>   fate.

In these lines Johnson writes of everyday scenes, allowing any reader to form an immediate mental image of his or her own daily activities. He personifies hope, fear, desire, and hate as shadowy figures that stalk man, hoping to trap him in his own destiny. Fate becomes not only a maze through which man must wander, seeking his way out with few clues as to proper direction, but also "clouded," seen as if through a veil that distorts reality. That image allows him to suggest a dreamlike state in which man indulges in fantasies that cripple his ability to cope with the many cruel challenges of life.

The greatest pitfall for humans, the speaker explains in lines 24–27, is the desire for wealth. He labels it "Wide-wasting pest!" in line 23, then elaborates that it promotes crime among humans:

> For gold his sword the hireling ruffian draws,
> For gold the hireling judge distorts the laws;
> Wealth heaped on wealth, nor truth nor safety
>   buys,
> The dangers gather as the treasures rise.

After this caution Johnson launches into lengthy historical descriptions of various once-powerful individuals, noting "How much more safe the vassal than the lord." The speaker explains that the "needy traveler" who moves singing through "the wild heath" enjoys more fortune than a ruler, as "Few know the toiling statesman's fear or care, / The insidious rival and the gaping heir." As did Juvenal, Johnson includes as an example Democritus, representative of a statesman who possesses the power to hear the petitions of others, a power that ultimately breeds his scorn for those who were once friends. And the suppliants who burn "to be great," hoping for Fortune, "mount, they shine, evaporate, and fall" as "Hate dogs their flight, and Insult mocks their end."

The speaker does not remain a mere detached voice but engenders a feeling of brotherhood with readers. As the scholar Howard Weinbrot explains, one way that Johnson involves his reader is through abundant rhetorical questions. He also uses the personal pronoun *we* at several points to be part of his audience and make clear he includes himself in the group that may suffer from faulty perceptions.

Consideration moves on to Thomas Cardinal Wolsey, a onetime favorite of King Henry VIII who falls from grace, mainly because the king feared his power and desired his wealth, and then to George Villiers, duke of Buckingham and onetime favorite of Kings James I and Charles I, eventually assassinated. Also described with details regarding their harsh ends are Robert Harley, earl of Oxford, treasurer for Queen Anne, later impeached and sent to the Tower by the Whigs; Thomas Wentworth, earl of Strafford, once a favorite of Charles I but later impeached and executed; and Edward Hyde, earl of Clarendon, once in favor with Charles II, eventually exiled to Europe. Each finds himself caught up in flattering dreams, which eventually undo him, as they are all ultimately deserted by their fantasies of unending power, through either their own acts or those of others, acts beyond their control.

Johnson personifies Virtue, Truth, Science, Reason, Doubt, Sloth, and Melancholy to address the young man who desires to become a part of the college of Learning, so much so that "The young enthusiast quits his ease for fame," lured into an eventual trap, ironically of his own design. However, the speaker is not without sympathy for those foolish enough to allow fate to do them in:

> The festal blazes, the triumphal show,
> The ravished standard, and the captive foe,
> The senate's thanks, the gazette's pompous tale,
> With force resistless o'er the brave prevail.
> (174–177)

Even courage is not enough to resist the ravages of false pride, suffered by the greatest of men, including Greek and Roman leaders. The speaker includes points from around the world in his cautionary tale, such as Sweden, Moscow, Persia, and Bavaria, where individuals of all backgrounds fall prey to time, which "hovers o'er impatient to destroy, / And shuts up all the passages of joy." Fate is an equal opportunity force, exacting a high price from any who ignore its power. Luxury enslaves, and even favor such as felt by high kings' mistresses dissolves with aging and the loss of beauty. Johnson references Catherine Sedley, mistress of James II, when he writes that "Sedley cursed the form that pleased a king."

A strong example of the use of rhetorical questions occurs in lines 343–348 as the speaker asks,

> Where then shall Hope and Fear their objects
>   find?
> Must dull Suspense corrupt the stagnant mind?
> Must helpless man, in ignorance sedate,
> Roll darkling down the torrent of his fate?
> Must no dislike alarm, no wishes rise,
> No cries invoke the mercies of the skies?

The speaker answers his own questions with reference to God, bidding man to make his petitions to Heaven, which may hear and "raise for good"; however, mankind must "leave to Heaven the measure and the choice." God may actually be kinder than fate, the speaker suggests, but he also makes clear that simply the stirring of a sense of the sacred and the aspiration of "strong devotion" encourages a healthful mind, suggesting that with faith, man can better accept whatever comes his way. Johnson does emphasize love as part of the answer to man's problem, a common approach for him. As Weinbrot writes, "For Johnson, the source of love far transcends human affection. To love one's neighbour is to love God; to use and not bury one's talent is to use God's gift." Johnson stressed in his essays that pleasures remain imperfect "when they are enjoyed without participation." Thus man "applies to others for assistance." He insisted that "No man is born merely for his own sake." "The Vanity of Human Wishes" strongly supports this conclusion.

BIBLIOGRAPHY
Weinbrot, Howard. "Johnson and the Arts of Narration: *The Life of the Savage, The Vanity of Human Wishes* and *Rasselas*." In *Samuel Johnson: Commemorative Lectures,* collected by Magdi Wahba. Beirut: Librairie du Liban, 1986.

VAUGHAN, HENRY (1621 or 1622–1695)

Henry Vaughan was born at Newton-upon-Usk, Breconshire, one of twin boys. He remained extremely close to his twin brother, Thomas. His father, Thomas Vaughan, and mother, Denise Morgan, had one other child who survived, a son named William probably born in 1628. The twins probably studied with Matthew Herbert, as evidenced in Henry's preface to his Latin poem "Ad Posteros." That poem was a part of a collection titled *Poems, with the Tenth Satire of Juvenal Englished* (1646) that Vaughan admitted employed an outdated approach. In this slender edition of the work of one of the CAVALIER POETS, as discussed by Alan Rudrum, Vaughan salutes Herbert as "a man most expert in learning" who "took me under his serene protection, and under his guidance I progressed for six years." He also later described Herbert as his "tutor and always his most cherished friend."

By 1646 Vaughan was married to Catherine Wise, with whom he had a son, Thomas, and three daughters, Lucy, Frances, and Catherine. By 1655 he would marry again, indicating Catherine's death. He took as his second wife Catherine's younger sister, Elizabeth, and they had a son, Henry, and three daughters, Grisell, Lucy, and Rachel.

Both Henry and Thomas Vaughan attended Jesus College at Oxford, the college traditionally attended by residents of Wales, but Henry probably intentionally did not enroll in a degree program in order to save money. Evidence of this fact exists in a 1673 letter to John Aubrey in which Vaughan explains that he did not stay at Oxford, where his father wanted him to study law, "which the sudden eruption of our late civil wars wholly frustrated." Although he later published mainly in English, Vaughan studied the Greek language and Latin classics, as well as Welsh mythology and poetry. He expressed an early interest in "hermetic (mystical) philosophy," studying alchemical and occult literature. As Rudrum explains, an interest in hermeticism led to "heresies" practiced by many as a result of "religious ferment associated with the Civil War." Vaughan later practiced as a physician, and his interest in alchemy related to his interest in medicine and healing.

Probably a resident of London in the early 1640s, Vaughan is likely to have witnessed much of the civil revolt, evidenced by his tone of discomfort in the religious poems of his *Silex Scintillans* (1650). That collection was later celebrated as one of the best examples of 17th-century meditative poetry, and it was reissued with additional poets in 1655. It is noted for lacking direct references to civil unrest but alludes strongly to Vaughan's Royalist sympathies and makes clear his disgust with writers he had previously admired. In the preface he writes of "those ingenious persons. . . . termed *Wits,*" then takes them to task for wasting their time in "a deliberate search, or excogitation of *idle words,* and a most vain, insatiable desire to be reputed *Poets.*" Vaughan's rebirth as a hermetic Christian paralleled his new approach to writing.

Vaughan had prepared the secular verse *Olor Iscanus* ("The Swan of Usk") for publication in 1647, evidenced by the dating of the preface, but it would not appear until 1651. Its tone strongly contrasted with that of the sober and reflective *Silex Scintillans,* as Vaughan attempted to construct traditional Welsh pastoral verse. Critics have noted that *Olor Iscanus* reveals Vaughan's great concern with the political unrest of the 1640s, a fact that may have prevented a cautious publisher from releasing it until it had been edited. For instance, in "A Rhapsody," the speaker proposes a toast "to him / That made his

horse a Senator," a slur against certain individuals in Parliament. Vaughan probably had experienced military service at the time of its writing. A staunch Royalist, he at first criticized Charles I for his part in the execution of the earl of Strafford but later reflected his horror at the king's 1649 execution.

Later anthologized selections from Vaughan's secular poetry include "To Amoret Weeping," which reflects Vaughan's metaphysical bent through the use of outrageous hyperbole, as in the lines "I should perhaps eat orphans, and suck up / A dozen distressed widows in one cup." Rudrum speculates on influence by the Jacobean dramatists in the poetry's "concreteness of moral perception." *Olor Iscanus* also included tributes to the literary greats of Vaughan's age, such as the poet and playwright WILLIAM CARTWRIGHT, the playwright John Fletcher, and the poet SIR WILLIAM DAVENANT among others.

Henry Vaughan would have fought on the side of the throne in the war in which William Vaughan was apparently killed, according to evidence in Vaughan's preface to his "The Man-Mouse." His *Silex Scintillans* reflects great influence by the religious poems of GEORGE HERBERT, as well as immersion in biblical study and the effects on Vaughan of the natural scenes abundant in the Usk Valley. The collection also reflects a theme of trial by God that leads to spiritual epiphany, as Vaughan anticipates God's judgment at the end of time. It produced Vaughan's later most-anthologized poems, including "Beyond the Veil," "The BURIAL OF AN INFANT," "THE LAMPE," "To His Books," "The RETREAT," "The World," "REGENERATION," "SILENCE, AND STEALTH OF DAYS!," "CORRUPTION," "Unprofitableness," "THEY ARE ALL GONE INTO THE WORLD OF LIGHT!," "The NIGHT," and "The WATERFALL."

Little information remains available about Vaughan's life after a return to Newton-upon-Usk in the mid-1640s. He may have served as a judge's clerk but later practiced medicine. In 1652 he published *The Mount of Olives, or Solitary Devotions,* followed in 1654 by *Flores Solitudinis.* Evidence of his medical practice is supplied in his later writings, such as the prose *Hermetical Physic* (1655) and *The Chemist's Key* (1657); he had also included medical allusions in *Silex Scintillans.* In 1689 he turned over ownership of his Newton house to his son by his first marriage, Thomas. He and Elizabeth then moved into a Scethrog cottage. Vaughan apparently requested burial in a churchyard, rather than the more traditional interment within the church. Most critics believe his choice symbolized humility, although some think it indicates that he may have been acting on his belief in nature as a reflection of God. Supporting the former theory, the gravestone inscription reads, "Servus Inutilis: Peccator Maximus," or "Unprofitable servant: greatest of sinners."

BIBLIOGRAPHY

Allen, Don Cameron, ed. "Henry Vaughan: 'Cock Crowing.'" In *Image and Meaning: Metaphoric Traditions in Renaissance Poetry*, 154–169. Baltimore: Johns Hopkins University Press, 1960.

Durr, Robert Allen. *On the Mystical Poetry of Henry Vaughan*. Cambridge, Mass.: Harvard University Press, 1962.

Fitter, Chris. "Henry Vaughan's Landscapes of Military Occupation." *Essays in Criticism* 42, no. 2 (April 1992): 123–147.

Fogel, French. *The Complete Poetry of Henry Vaughan*. New York: W. W. Norton, 1969.

Grant, Patrick. *The Transformation of Sin: Studies in Donne, Herbert, Vaughan, and Traherne*. Montreal: McGill-Queens University Press, 1974.

Hughes, Merritt Y. "The Theme of Pre-Existence and Infancy in 'The Retreat.'" *Philological Quarterly* 10 (1941): 484–500.

Hutchinson, F. E. *Henry Vaughan: A Life and Interpretation*. Oxford: Clarendon Press, 1971.

Leishman, J. B. *The Metaphysical Poets: Donne, Herbert, Vaughan, Traherne*. Oxford: Clarendon Press, 1934.

Linden, Stanton J. "Henry Vaughan: Poet and Doctor of Physic." *Notes and Queries* 45, no. 4 (December 1998): 453–455.

Marilla, E. L. *The Secular Poems of Henry Vaughan*. Cambridge, Mass.: Harvard University Press, 1958.

Matar, Nabil I. "George Herbert, Henry Vaughan, and the Conversion of the Jews." *Studies in English Literature, 1500–1900* 30, no. 1 (winter 1990): 79–92.

Post, Jonathan F. S. "Vaughan's 'The Night' and His 'Late and Dusky' Age." *Studies in English Literature* 19 (1979): 127–141.

Rudrum, Alan. *Henry Vaughan*. Cardiff: University of Wales Press, 1981.

———. "Vaughan's 'Each.'" *Essays in Criticism* 21, no. 1 (1971): 86–91.

Skulsky, Harold. "The Fellowship of the Mystery: Emergent and Exploratory Metaphor in Vaughan." *Studies in English Literature, 1500–1900* 27, no. 1 (winter 1987): 89–107.

Tuttle, Imelda. *Concordance to Vaughan's Silex Scintillans*. University Park: Pennsylvania State University Press, 1969.

West, Philip. *Henry Vaughan's Silex Scintillans: Scripture Uses*. New York: Oxford University Press, 2001.

"VERSES ON THE DEATH OF DR. SWIFT" JONATHAN SWIFT (1739) A satirical poem with a serious purpose, "Verses on the Death of Dr. Swift" was written by JONATHAN SWIFT. In a letter to his friend JOHN GAY, he explained that he had spent months writing a 550-line poem on a "pleasant subject," what might be said about him after his death. The idea for the theme occurred after Swift read a maxim by the French writer François de la Rochefoucauld, which he printed with his poem: *Dans l'adversité de nos meilleurs amis nous trouvons quelque chose, qui ne nous deplaist pas.* That statement translates to "In the misfortune of our best friends we always find something that does not displease us." Known for his witticisms, Rochefoucauld offered a rational approach complementary to that of 18th-century English thought.

As did other of his era's satirists, Swift adopted an edgy humor to examine human nature closely. While general readers might smile at the words, they also often cringed to recognize themselves in the uncomplimentary sentiments. In addition Swift uses his musing to indulge in revenge on many specific individuals who he felt had cheated him out of political appointment. He skillfully leads up to that attack and then applies the verbal "lash" satire inflicted.

Swift acknowledges himself as the poem's autobiographical voice. He mentions his inspiration in the opening of his poem, stating that because Rochefoucauld draws his maxims from nature, he believes them true. Swift shares the ideas expressed in the maxims because, as he states in the third and fourth lines, "They argue no corrupted mind / In him, the fault is in mankind." Again human nature causes one to feel relief when observing suffering of others, simply because the observer has escaped that particular suffering. Swift spends 69 lines considering examples that prove the maxim true and discussing human nature, before he begins the subject of what people will say when he has died. He notes, "We all behold with envious eyes / Our equal raised above our size" (13–14), desiring to be only "an inch" above others to be satisfied. And if

> Dear honest Ned is in the gout,
> Lies racked with pain, and you without:
> How patiently you hear him groan!
> How glad the case is not your own! (27–30)

Because of human nature "The strongest friendship yields to pride, / Unless the odds be on our side:" "Vain humankind! Fantastic race!" (38–39). Swift points out various "follies," such as "Self-love, ambition, envy, pride," that cause us to be jealous of others (40–41). He uses his good friend ALEXANDER POPE in a self-deprecating statement, "In Pope I cannot read a line, / But with a sigh I wish it mine" (47–48). While he pays Pope, and later Gay and the physician and wit John Arbuthnot, great compliment by noting their writing and sense of IRONY as superior to his own, the voice he adopts yearns for superiority. He concludes the prelude to his real topic with the request "To all my foes, dear Fortune, send / Thy gifts, but never to my friend" (67–68). By the time Swift reaches his true topic, he has convinced readers that his attitude is shared by all humans, thus preparing them for the humorous look at the way he envisions his friends' reaction to the news that he has died. In addition readers should share his rhetorical outrage at his enemies, to whom Swift will yield no quarter.

The speaker begins by suggesting the gossip that occurs about him at his advanced stage of life. He feels his friends may speak to one another about his dissipation, including a decaying memory that causes him to tell the same stories 50 times. According to them, "he takes up with younger folks, / Who for his wine will bear his jokes" (93–94). Such description readers can identify with, as the aging Swift's habits are common to the elderly. In addition according to the speaker his poetry suffers, as he requires a full hour to conjure a single RHYME, and "His fire is out, his wit decayed, / His fancy sunk, his Muse a jade" (101–102), where *jade* refers to a worn-out horse. Swift intends a contrast through imagery with Pegasus, the winged horse of

Greek mythology that symbolized inspiration. His friends add with some tenderness of Swift's age that he can even remember Charles II, as proves true; Swift was 18 when Charles died. In a jibe at his own preoccupation with poetry, Swift adopts in line 117 poetic terminology, noting, "In such case they talk in tropes," meaning FIGURATIVE LANGUAGE (FIGURE OF SPEECH) in which one applies a comparison, rather than supply a specific description. As long as they do not share his ailments, they have little sympathy. However, "should some neighbor feel a pain" (135) similar to Swift's, it becomes the main topic of conversation. Swift suggests that people ask after his well-being only in order to be able to speak of their own condition, again a common occurrence that readers will recognize.

At line 147 "Behold the fatal day arrive!" As people ask about Swift they learn he is barely alive, and all decide they must prepare for his death. The first questions are "What has he left? And who's his heir?" (154), as they wonder who might benefit materially from his absence. Swift continually makes certain that readers will recognize the various common reactions as ones they have shared with others. Swift next includes additional references a reader would find familiar. In line 168 he refers to himself as "the Dean," indicating his position at St. Paul's Cathedral, as well as "the Drapier." The latter label recalls his writing letters successfully urging the Irish people to resist the importation of the English halfpence and using the pseudonym "M.B., a Dublin drapier." This heroic action will be referenced again later in the poem, when the tone turns decidedly more cynical.

Swift notes that the news of his death spreads from Dublin to England, as he assumes he would die in Ireland, as in fact he later did. He describes the gleeful reaction of Lady Suffolk, who served George II as mistress and whom Swift knew; of Queen Caroline, who had promised Swift medals when princess of Wales, a promise on which she never delivered; and Sir Robert Walpole, one of Swift's numerous political enemies. He also includes those with whom he interacted through his writing, such as Edmund Curll, a bookseller who published pirated material; Tibbald, meaning Lewis Theobald, a Shakespeare scholar; Moore, or James Moore-Smyth, a self-fancied poet who criticized

Swift; and Colley Cibber, an actor and playwright, completely unqualified to hold the office of poet laureate. An important aspect of satire, the blasting of real people always appeared in Swift's writing. He never missed an opportunity to include criticism for enemies, as well as praise for friends, in his works.

Swift also reflects on those who dismiss the trials of others as God's will, although they might not see their own trials in the same way:

Indifference clad in wisdom's guise
All fortitude of mind supplies:
For how can stony bowels melt
In those who never pity felt?
When *we* are lashed, they kiss the rod,
Resigning to the will of God. (213–218)

Swift does not spare the ladies, writing that his female friends are so tender of heart that they will appear in "doleful dumps." However, their sadness will not interrupt their card playing, as he imagines them saying, "The Dean is dead (and what is trumps?)" (225–28). They discuss attending Swift's funeral, but all manner of excuses arise, each perfectly socially acceptable.

Swift next reflects on the effect his absence will have on the heritage provided by his writing, judging that after a year most will have forgotten his work and will give away his books. They substitute the fashionable pap written by Colley Cibber, with no appreciation for the vast difference in quality between his hack work and Swift's accomplished poetry. Swift's many personal references may be placed in the context of his age, one in which he believed many behaved in hypocritical fashion. While they pretended to seek enlightenment, much of their small effort was simply for show.

However, all is not negative, as Swift imagines a group gathered at a Covent Garden tavern to engage in an informed exchange of ideas. Swift adopts the voice of one of those individuals to say all the things about him, his contributions, and those who had wronged him that he felt the public should consider. The man claims to evaluate him impartially, noting he did not know Swift well. He did know that he "Was never ill received at court" (308) and that Swift had hoped "To

cure the vices of mankind" (314) with his ironic voice, which "Exposed the fool and lashed the knave" (316). Most importantly, "what he writ was all his own" (318), a statement that proved crucial for Swift during an age when disreputable publishers would print plagiarized material, and dishonorable writers would claim others' work as their own. The list of positive attributes continues, including that Swift never borrowed on credit from others, that he proved himself trustworthy, did not put on airs, had no flatterers as allies, and "succored virtue in distress, / And seldom failed of good success" (335–337).

Swift continues with his description of his many positive habits, eventually making the point that had he not so often and so vigorously expressed his honest opinion, he might have been rewarded politically: "Had he but spared his tongue and pen, / He might have rose like other men" (355–356). Again Swift emphasizes the theme of truth in his poetry. The fact that others who had offered much less service to the good of the community than he had been promoted while he was overlooked caused him the bitterness it would cause any deserving person. However, Swift at this point in his life can write, whether sincerely or not, that he preferred that he had remained a virtuous and dependable person to one who gained reward at the expense of others. He mentions specifically, among others, Robert Harley, earl of Oxford, and James Butler, duke of Ormonde. Through the efforts of such men, the speaker avows of Swift,

By innocence and resolution,
He bore continual persecution;
While numbers to preferment rose,
Whose merits were to be his foes;
When even his own familiar friends,
Intent upon their private ends,
Like renegadoes now he feels,
Against him lifting up their heels. (399–406)

Swift deals with several specific instances of real and dangerous personal attacks. Lines 415–420 present an abbreviated account of William Whitshed, the lord chief justice of the King's Bench of Ireland, and his attempts in 1720 to force a jury to find Swift guilty of sedition for publishing an anonymous pamphlet titled *Proposal for the Universal Use of Irish Manufacture.* Although Whitshed commanded the jury to reconsider their innocent verdict nine different times, they refused to convict Swift. Similarly Whitshed presided over the 1724 trial of the printer of Swift's drapier letters, again failing to gain a guilty verdict. A bully dressed in the gown of state, Whitshed was anathema to Swift:

> To save them from their evil fate,
> In him was held a crime of state.
> A wicked monster on the bench,
> Whose fury blood could never quench;
> As vile and profligate a villain,
> As modern Scroggs, or old Tresilian. (415–420)

Swift not only considered Whitshed and others who conspired against him were inadequate public servants, he believed them more villainous and threatening to the public than true criminals. Both Sir William Scroggs and Sir Robert Tresilian whom he references had once held public posts but were involved in plots against the Crown and eventually impeached, and Tresilian was hanged. In Swift's opinion Whitshed deserved the same punishment.

The speaker concludes that he, "the Dean," may have "Had too much satire in his vein," although "no age could more deserve it" (456–458). The voice makes clear that Swift never attacked those who were genuinely dull, not claiming to be otherwise, or those misshapen or unattractive, not pretending to be beautiful. Only hypocrisy in others raised his ire and his pen. The closing lines include the fact that Swift left money to finance a hospital for the insane and that society owed him a debt too late to repay, after his death. The country proved his "satiric touch" (481) necessary, with its indisputable corruption and what Swift saw as a decaying of civic and cultural values.

BIBLIOGRAPHY
Clegg, Jeanne. "Swift on False Witness." *Studies in English Literature, 1500–1900* 44, no. 3 (summer 2004): 461–485.
Downie, James Allan. *Jonathan Swift, Political Writer.* Boston: Routledge & Kegan Paul, 1984.
Fabricant, Carole. "Speaking for the Irish Nation: The Drapier, the Bishop, and the Problems of Colonial Representation." *English Literary History* 66, no. 2 (summer 1999): 337–339.
Rowse, A. L. *Jonathan Swift.* New York: Scribner, 1975.

"VILLAGE, THE" GEORGE CRABBE (1783)

GEORGE CRABBE broke from the tradition that upheld the vision of country life as desirable, idyllic, and free of care, simultaneously upholding the Augustan tradition of logic and rationality in his views. He wanted readers to understand that while rural life offered the beauties of nature and lacked the exposure to physical crime present in cities, it held a great deal of danger. Those perfect spring and summer days celebrated by poets and artists disappeared in reality, replaced by blistering heat that withered crops and grazing lands, destroying farmers' income, and grueling winters that killed their herds and often left the country folk shivering in shelters constructed with too limited resources to make them efficient against the elements. In many instances underfed and lacking good medical care, rural inhabitants suffered illness and early death. Crime also existed, especially along the shores on which writers and musicians often rhapsodized, where a bustling smuggling trade lined the pockets of a few sly masterminds who knew how to take advantage of the rural working class, turning desperate men with families to support into ill-paid criminals. In addition sturdy young farmboys, sorely needed to work the land, were kidnapped, "shanghaied," stolen from their families and forced to serve as sailors, many dying at sea or not returning to their homes for months or years.

Book 1, 332 lines of the lengthy poem written in HEROIC COUPLETS, begins by recalling the pastoral poetry tradition, allowing Crabbe then to move smoothly into reality for an often rude comparison/contrast approach. He begins by referencing "The village life," "youthful peasants and declining swains," who must cease labor, facing old age and deprivation. Then one may observe "the real picture of the poor," images that "Demand a song." He adds, "the Muse can give no more," possibly suggesting a double meaning. Crabbe may use the phrase to suggest that a song of reality is the least a Muse can give those peasants and swains too long idealized by that same Muse. Additionally he may suggest the inability of the Muse to support those who have reached the end of their lives and crave material, not artistic, support. The speaker makes clear that "Fled are those times when, in harmonious strains, / The rustic poet praised his native plains. / No shepherds now, in smooth alternate verse, / Their country's beauty of their nymphs rehearse," allowing Crabbe to include terminology familiar to readers of traditional pastoral verse. By employing the verb *Fled,* he also suggests that those comfortable traditions were chased away, pursued by modern developments. He adds that the only pains felt by shepherds in unrealistic pastoral poetry are "amorous pains." The speaker then asks of all poets, "From Truth and Nature shall we widely stray, / Where Virgil, not where Fancy, leads the way?" The reference to VIRGIL calls to mind the classic pastoral, the veracity of which, Crabbe alludes, modern imagination may challenge.

Crabbe begins his transition with the lines,

Yes, thus the Muses sing of happy swains,
Because the Muses never knew their pains.
They boast their peasants' pipes; but peasants
   now
Resign their pipes and plod behind the plow.

Crabbe's abundant use of ALLITERATION makes uncomfortable thoughts at least sound pleasant. With the repetition of the beginning *p* sound in *pains, peasants', pipes, peasants, pipes, plods,* and *plow,* he creates an echo effect, suggesting a faraway sound of those once ubiquitous pipes. He also draws attention to rhythm and RHYME, which he then mentions in the next two lines: "And few, amide the rural tribe, have time / To number syllables, and play with rhyme." He contrasts his own pursuits, as a poet, with those of people who must perform physical work for a living.

Crabbe later offers abundant evidence to support his idea. He points out that while poets trace the charms of "Fields and flocks" in poetic imagery, "The poor laborious natives" see something quite different. The hot sun at noon plays "On their bare heads and dewy temples," where *dewy* means damp with sweat. That line may take aim at the pastoral ideal of dew freshening the morning and evening flowers, a much more pleasant vision than that of sweating laborers. He wonders,

While some, with feebler heads and fainter
   hearts,
Deplore their fortune, yet sustain their parts:
Then shall I dare these real ills to hide
In tinsel trappings of poetic pride?

Crabbe's accusations against an uncaring audience prove effective mainly because he indicts himself before all others. The use of the descriptor *tinsel* makes clear that much poetry lacks true value, as poets focus more on the form and function of their art than on accuracy in their depictions.

Now having made a full transition from the imagined to the real, Crabbe makes clear his method, explaining through his speaker, "By such examples taught, I paint the cot, / As Truth will paint it, and as bards will not." That truth is not poetically pretty, and the speaker shames other poets who participate in the fabrication. He then speaks to those of that "rural tribe," understanding that

to you the smoothest song is smooth in vain;
O'ercome by labor, and bowed down by time,
Feel you the barren flattery of a rhyme?
Can poets soothe you, when you pine for bread,
By winding myrtles round your ruined shed?
Can their light tales your weighty griefs o'er
   power,
Or glad with airy mirth the toilsome hour?

Crabbe emphasizes art's lack of value to those who often go to bed hungry, and then he illustrates some of those "weighty griefs." They include a merciless nature that transforms heath to "a length of burning sand . . .

Where the thin harvest waves its withered ears;
Rank weeds, that every art and care defy, Reign
o'er the land, and rob the blighted rye.

A scourge of thistles, "sterile soil," and "sickly" blades of grass culminate in "a sad splendor" that "vainly shines around." He alters the landscape so familiar to readers of pastoral in a jarring manner.

After revealing the problems caused by nature, Crabbe begins to describe the ways in which man torments man, referencing first unscrupulous smuggler profiteers:

Here too the lawless merchant of the main
Draws from his plow the intoxicated swain;
Want only claimed the labor of the day,
But vice now steals his nightly rest away.

Not only must the farmer suffer during the light hours, but now in the dark he commits crimes in order to support himself. The speaker recounts his personal experience when seeking peace in the country, noting,

Here, wandering long amid these frowning
    fields,
I sought the simple life that Nature yields;
Rapine and Wrong and Fear usurped her place,
And a bold, artful, surly, savage race.

Crabbe's use of the series proves skillful, as he first uses the repeated conjunction *and* to join *Rapine, Wrong,* and *Fear,* rather than simple commas. This has the effect of drawing out the series and giving all the nouns, each beginning with an uppercase letter, equal and terrible weight. His second series of adjectives provides an interesting mix of two descriptors that could have positive connotations, *bold* and *artful,* followed by two that are without doubt negative, *surly* and *savage.* And it is not only a few who have turned so wicked, but an entire "race." Not all suffer, it is true, but "Where Plenty smiles—alas! She smiles for few— / And those who taste not, yet behold her store, / Are as the slaves that dig the golden ore, / The wealth around them makes them doubly poor." Never is a man so miserable as when he compares himself to those who are wealthy and content.

Crabbe also emphasizes the slow torturous nature of the rural life. In dramatic dialogue a suffering shepherd laments, "'Why do I live, when I desire to be / At once from life and life's long labor free?'" Crabbe's skillful use of alliteration in *life's long labor* stretches the phrase, slowing its reading to imitate the lengthy labor he describes. The voice continues, comparing himself to those who die young, saying, in part,

Like leaves in spring, the young are blown away,
Without the sorrows of a slow decay;
I, like yon withered leaf, remain behind,
Nipped by the frost, and shivering in the wind.

Additional topics for Crabbe's consideration include the second-rate medical care offered to the country poor by "A potent quack, long versed in human ills, / Who first insults the victim whom he kills." These so-called physicians are paid by the parish and reflect an indifference that Crabbe had observed during his brief stint in medical practice. In a powerfully sad description he adds of the "quack," "he wears contempt upon his sapient sneer;" and

In haste he seeks the bed where Misery lies,
Impatience marked in his averted eyes;
And, some habitual queries hurried o'er,
Without reply, he rushes on the door.

Even an individual who has taken an oath to relieve suffering feels no compassion for those who cannot pay his bill.

The only refuge left to the suffering country people is that of their faith, and it offers little more than ritual for comfort. Book 1 closes with a funeral scene of a member of the village who once enthusiastically engaged in sport and labor. Now they follow his body to the grave "and stand / Silent and sad, and gazing, hand in hand." As a final insult "The busy priest, detained by weightier care, / Defers his duty till the day of prayer." When the priest does not appear, the crowd takes little comfort in the knowledge that on church day, he will include the blessing of the dead in his duties: "And waiting long, the crowd retire distressed, / To think a poor man's bones should lie unblessed."

Although later readers may not appreciate the stark contrast between Crabbe's rendition of country life and the traditional pastoral, because of lack of exposure to such classic approaches, they cannot help but admire Crabbe's skillful style and sustained bitter tone. His honesty grates on one's conscience, but his words offer a satisfying read.

BIBLIOGRAPHY
New, Peter. *George Crabbe's Poetry.* New York: St. Martin's Press, 1976.

"VINE, THE" ROBERT HERRICK (1648) Blatantly erotic, ROBERT HERRICK's poem "The Vine" has been labeled by psychoanalytic critics a lyric wet dream, its opening lines reading,

> I Dream'd this mortal part of mine
> Was Metamorphoz'd to a Vine;
> Which crawling one and every way,
> Enthrall'd my dainty Lucia,

where the term *enthrall'd* means "fettered" or "bound." Replete with the FIGURATIVE LANGUAGE (FIGURE OF SPEECH) of hyperbole, the poem offers skillfully developed metaphors, which incorporate imagery from nature while representing in actuality body parts, framed by a playful tone of carnality. Those critical of Herrick's work in his day as sinful and a disgrace to his station based their opinions on works such as "The Vine." Later scholars view the poems as simply celebratory of human nature and physical nature, which Herrick greatly enjoyed.

The speaker's "Tendrils" take by "surprise" Lucia's "small legs and thighs," while his "Nerv'lits" embrace her "Belly, Buttocks and her Waste [Waist]." Herrick sounds much like a schoolboy, exploring his sexual fantasies through the excuse of a dream. The vine "writhing hung" about Lucia's head and "behung" her temples, after which Herrick references the mythical Bacchus, who also found himself "ravisht by his tree." Verbs such as *writhe* and *crawl* suggest actions of a serpent, a traditional phallic symbol and a symbol of temptation and seduction. Eventually the vine makes "All parts" of Lucia "one prisoner," then creeps "with leaves to hide / Those parts, which maids keep unesy'd." Unfortunately for the dreamer, the "fancie" grows so strong it awakens him, after which he experiences an erect penis. Herrick's final two lines describe that experience, as the speaker notes that after his dream he "found (Ah me!) this flesh of mine / More like a Stock [stalk] then like a Vine."

VIRGIL (70 B.C.–19 B.C.)

Born Publius Vergilius Maro near Mantua in Cisalpine Gaul, in the northern region of present-day Italy, the poet whom modern readers would know as Virgil enjoyed an excellent education as he matured on a farm. He traveled to Rome and became a follower of Epicureanism and part of the colony led by Siro the Epicurean on the Gulf of Naples. He began writing poetry as part of that group, starting in 42 B.C., the *Eclogues,* a work that would greatly influence poets of the English Renaissance and beyond. In *Eclogues* Virgil depicts the pastoral Greek life as idyllic, populating his verse with shepherds, shepherdesses, and other figures and allusions that would become conventions during Renaissance times. Virgil's own model was Theocritus, whose pastorals Virgil made more applicable to the common reader by adding humor to ideology. He introduced Greek "Arcadia" to English poets, transforming the rugged landscape of Greece into a landscape of the ideal. He remained interested in revealing truths about human nature through the use of the pastoral trope. Later poets could apply to their own cultures and times Virgil's focus on human passion and ideals, as well as his thoughts on Roman politics and on the power of art, specifically poetry, to transcend human suffering. Because Roman civilization represented the roots of European politics and culture, Virgil became the undisputed patron to whom European poets later turned for inspiration and a model.

Eclogues would be translated many times from Latin into English, with the proper versification remaining in dispute by critics. Virgil employed the METER of dactylic hexameter, with exactly six metrical stresses per line in a strict pattern. For writers in English both capturing the sense of his Latin words and perfectly imitating his style proved challenging. Many employed the alexandrine, a 12-syllable iambic line, to meet that challenge. They also occasionally used a feminine ending, rather than the masculine specific to Virgil, and altered the number of feet and stresses. *Eclogues* also offered a strong example of IRONY, what the poet Horace termed *molle atque facetum,* translated by Guy Lee as "sensitive and witty" or "sensitive and ironic." Lee writes that the power of the *Eclogues* rests in its quality of incantation, or chant and songlike properties, the repetition for emphasis of words and phrases, and its use of ANTITHESIS. Poets of the 17th and 18th centuries would adopt all three artistic techniques.

Virgil also wrote the epic poem titled *Aeneid,* the first six books of which he fashioned after Homer's epic the *Odyssey,* purportedly written during the dark ages of Greece. The last six books he wrote in response to Homer's *Iliad*. He spent his final 10 years at work on the distinctively political poem at the request of Octavius, or Augustus, Caesar, who requested a poem celebrating his feats in strengthening the Roman Empire. Virgil converted the hero's story from one of fearless courage in devotion to political and private ideals to one of a heroism imbued with a sense of justice and an awareness of the humanity in each of the opposing forces.

Although Virgil died before its completion, the *Aeneid* became one of the most important writings in literature. It contemplates and celebrates the establishment of an entire culture, tracing the development of its laws and moral credos. This emphasis makes the work didactic, but also perfect for adaptation as a model by any poet who wanted to engage in verse his era's struggle with political and social order. Thus Virgil's hero became a moral paragon, establishing a new reflection on heroism. The poem celebrates two virtues. *Humanitas,* an empathy we feel for others due to the shared human condition, and *pietas,* loyalty to one's family, culture, and religions, offered excellent themes for adoption. They easily found emphasis in English Renaissance and Reformation poetry, as poets struggled with religious dispute, the king's position as church leader, regicide, plots against the government, the struggle for identity by Parliament, and the right of men to rule. England's 18th century added to that mix of social conflict the rising powers of what would later be termed the middle class and the rumblings of the Industrial Revolution and its redistribution of wealth and power from the country to the city. Virgil's work also gave voice to 18th-century tension resulting from what many viewed as an "occupation" of the English throne by a "foreign" power, the Hanoverians.

Virgil's third influential work, the *Georgics,* celebrates the life of the farm during an era when Italy was torn by civil war. Its four books required eight years for the writing and were influenced by Hesiod, who had produced the first didactic poetry, *Works and Days.* The 2,188 hexametric verses of the *Georgics* contain the famous emphasis on the life of the beehive as metaphor for human society. Virgil depicts the helplessness of humans before the majesty of nature, the hardships

they had to endure in order to produce simple food, the reverence due to deities who controlled various aspects of nature, and an awareness of the seasonal cycles that represent life and death. His combined work so influenced Dante Alighieri's writing of the *Divine Comedy* that the ancient poet appears as a crucial character who acts as the narrator's guide through Purgatory and Hell.

In addition to Dante only a few of the poets influenced by Virgil were MARY ASTELL, WILLIAM BROWNE, GEORGE CRABBE, JOHN DRYDEN, BEN JONSON, ANNE KILLIGREW, CHRISTOPHER MARLOWE, JOHN MILTON, ALEXANDER POPE, and JAMES THOMSON. Virgil's work and influence continue to inspire scholarship as well as artistic production. His poetry remains readily accessible in both print and electronic forms.

BIBLIOGRAPHY

Armstrong, David, ed. *Vergil, Philodemus, and the Augustans.* Austin: University of Texas Press, 2004.

Bowra, C. M. *From Virgil to Milton.* New York: St. Martin's Press, 1967.

Brown, Eric C. "Underworld Sailors in Milton's *Lycidas* and Virgil's *Aeneid.*" *Milton Quarterly* 36, no. 1 (March 2002): 34–45.

Cardinale, Philipp. "Satan as Aeneas: An Allusion to Virgil in 'Paradise Lost.'" *Notes and Queries* 50, no. 2 (June 2003): 183.

D'Addario, Christopher. "Dryden and the Historiography of Exile: Milton and Virgil in Dryden's Late Period." *The Huntington Library Quarterly* 67, no. 4 (fall 2004): 553–576.

Gordon, George. *Virgil in English Poetry.* Folcroft, Pa.: Folcroft Press, 1970.

Guy-Bray, Stephen. "Virgil at Appleton House." *English Language Notes* 42, no. 1 (September 2004): 26–39.

Hale, John K. "Milton's Reading of Virgil's *Aeneid* VI.680 in His Letter to the Vatican Librarian." *Notes and Queries* 49, no. 3 (September 2002): 336.

Lee, Guy. "Introduction." In *Virgil: The Eclogues,* translated by Guy Lee, 11–26. New York: Viking Penguin, 1984.

Levi, Peter. *Virgil: His Life and Times.* New York: St. Martin's Press, 1999.

Spence, Sarah, ed. *Poets and Critics Read Virgil.* New Haven, Conn.: Yale University Press, 2001.

"VIRTUE" GEORGE HERBERT (1633) GEORGE HERBERT stated early in his career that he intended to write lyrics based on spiritual love, rather than tradi-

tional erotic love, and he often used the SONNET form to do so. While "Virtue," a lyric included in his posthumous collection *The Temple,* is not a sonnet, its four four-line stanzas employ various symbols traditionally found in the works of the CAVALIER POETS for a purpose quite different from that of the celebration of earthly love. Herbert's theme that death shall come to all things except a virtuous soul is given emphasis through the use of the symbols common to love LYRICS.

The first STANZA notes that the "Sweet day, so cool, so calm, so bright," which serves as "The bridal of the earth and sky," that is, it weds the earth to the sky, shall die, to be wept over by "The dew." Herbert establishes a pastoral scene, which he then ruptures with the appearance of death, undercutting the calm setting for romance for which readers of his era would be prepared. In addition the death is mourned by the dew, commonly a symbol of cleansing and new life, but here used to signal death.

In the second stanza Herbert introduces a favorite representation of romance and a traditional symbol of the sexually active woman, with the "Sweet rose." However, in Herbert's vision, the rose possesses a "hue angry and brave," its color so intense that it causes "the rash gazer to wipe his eye." Not only does the rose die, before doing so, it spoils expectations of an attractive, alluring blossom, instead offending all who rashly gaze.

In the third stanza it is "Sweet spring," filled with both the beautiful days and the roses Herbert has already described, that meets death. He compares the season of birth and renewal to "A box where sweets compacted lie," but once again, "all must die." Herbert completes his poem by making clear the only survivor will be "a sweet and virtuous soul." He selects a nontraditional symbol for comparison to such a soul, that of "seasoned timber," which, "though the whole world turn to coal / Then chiefly lives." Images of timber and coal hold little romance, yet these are the symbols of life in Herbert's rendition. He successfully turns tradition against itself in a display of stylistic skill.

W

WALLER, EDMUND (1606–1687) Born in Buckinghamshire, Edmund Waller was the eldest child in a wealthy family. His father died when Waller was still an infant, settling an annual income in excess of £3,000 on his son for life. Waller attended Eton and King's College, Cambridge, and was elected to Parliament in his teens. His oratory skills became legendary, as the record of an early visit to King James I established his reputation. Waller enjoyed membership in the circle of Sir Lucius Falkland, a member of the TRIBE OF BEN. The circle, which included BEN JONSON and THOMAS CAREW, gathered at Falkland's home, Great Tew, for philosophical discussions.

Waller wrote his first formal poem, "The Prince's Escape at St. Andero," at age 18; it later appeared in a collection of his works. He married an heiress, and the couple had a son who died and a daughter who survived; his wife died in childbirth when Waller was 25. He then fell in love with Lady Dorothy Sidney, daughter of the earl of Leicester, who became the celebrated Sacharissa of his love poetry. Rumored to have several additional romantic involvements, Waller eventually remarried in his thirties. Not much is written of his wife; the couple may have had 13 children. Although he would lose his seat in the Civil Wars after plotting for the Royalists in 1643, living out most of a near-10-year exile in Paris, he eventually returned home at the invitation of Cromwell, a distant relative. A short time later Waller also regained his seat in Parliament and remained a member for life.

As a poet Waller was noted for his elegiac and panegyric verse, which proved quite popular in his lifetime. Praised by JOHN DRYDEN and ALEXANDER POPE, Waller remained in high esteem through most of the 18th century. However, SAMUEL JOHNSON became the first of many critics to find Waller's verse highly artificial and lacking ingenuity and sincerity. Of a panegyric written to Cromwell, Johnson noted in his *Lives of the Poets* that Waller considered "Cromwell in his exaltation, without inquiring how he attained it; there is consequently no mention of the rebel or the regicide. . . . The act of violence by which he obtained the supreme power is lightly treated." When writing about Waller's praise of Charles II, Johnson remains clearly disgusted with Waller's change of allegiance: "It is not possible to read, without some contempt and indignation, poems of the same author, ascribing the highest degree of *power and piety* to Charles the First, then transferring the same *power and piety* to Oliver Cromwell, now inviting Oliver to take the Crown, and then congratulating Charles the Second on his recovered right." He added that none of Waller's subjects could have considered his work any more than "the tribute of dependence," accusing Waller of possessing a "prostituted mind, that may retain the glitter of wit, but has lost the dignity of virtue."

Later critics found Waller's poetry interesting for its formality and purity of expression in use of the HEROIC COUPLET and "point counterpoint" format. His most widely anthologized works include "The Story of Phoebus and Daphne Applied," "On a Girdle," and the celebrated song "Go, Lovely Rose!"

BIBLIOGRAPHY

Allison, Alexander W. *Toward an Augustan Poetic: Edmund Waller's "Reform" of English Poetry.* Lexington: University of Kentucky Press, 1962.

Chernaik, Warren L. *The Poetry of Limitation: A Study of Edmund Waller.* New Haven, Conn.: Yale University Press, 1968.

Gilbert, Jack G. *Edmund Waller.* Boston: G. K. Hall, 1979.

Hammond, Paul. "Echoes of Waller in Marvell's 'Horatian Ode.'" *Notes and Queries* 38, no. 2 (June 1991): 172–173.

Hillyer, Richard. "Edmund Waller's Sacred Poems." *Studies in English Literature, 1500–1900* 39, no. 1 (winter 1999): 155.

Johnson, Samuel. *Lives of the English Poets.* Vol. 1. New York: E. P. Dutton, 1958.

Kaminski, Thomas. "Edmund Waller, English Precieux." *Philological Quarterly* 79, no. 1 (winter 2000): 19.

"WASHING-DAY" Anna Laetitia Barbauld (1797)

Anna Laetitia Barbauld spent her writing career expressing her opinion that women possess rights to education and economic opportunities equal to those of men. However, she never adopted a militant approach, instead urging women to work within the patriarchal structure of their culture to achieve personal freedom. Acutely aware and accepting of woman's place of subservience to man in the traditional order, she yet bridged the tension between that subservience and personal independence by illustrating ways in which women could assume power. Her focus remained the world of women and nowhere does that world become so clear as in the powerful and moving poem "Washing-Day." Barbauld adopts free verse, abandoning set rhythm and RHYME in order to emphasize the deviation from the order that marked days of the week other than washing day. Simultaneously she illustrates that only to the excluded individual, in this case a male observing the business of washing day, does the wash day procedure appear chaotic. It achieves its own inherent order, specific to the activity, affording the participating women the power of control over a sphere in which men have no part. As the 86-line poem progresses, the community of women featured includes children, servants, washing women, a grandmother, and even the mistress of the house, forming an all-female party, Barbauld does not divide her lines into verses, again avoiding the neat order that any variance from daily routine represents, but, more importantly, promoting a driving momentum that emphasizes the incredible activity of the day.

The poem's first line offers a remarkable comparison of the mundane task of washing to artistic activity; washing requires a lesser Muse than art:

> The Muses are turned gossips; they have lost
> The buskined step, and clear high-sounding
>   phrase,
> Language of gods. Come then, domestic Muse.

She clearly aligns the cleaning of fabric with a creative activity, the term *buskined* referring to high boots worn in Greek tragedies. Barbauld may also have intended to emphasize the wash ritual as akin to a drama, with each individual engaged in a specific role on the domestic stage. The drama, while difficult and demanding, even unpleasant, need not be seen as tragic. In this instance she playfully orders the tragic Muses to become more common, engaging in the gossip that unites a community in work. That interpretation of the opening lines equates to a subversive reading that might be practiced by feminist critics. However, those same lines may be contrarily perceived by Marxist critics as expressing IRONY, making clear that working women have no time for creativity and that the idea of a domestic Muse is ludicrous. Depending upon one's critical view, the poem may be seen as a protest of the burdens of the working class against the power structure or a celebration of women's work as a creative act remaining open only to females. The closing lines' engagement of fantasy elements and emphasis upon literature and the imagination for escape seems to support the latter view.

The poem's speaker next catalogs various topics that workers might include in gossip as the women are "loosely prattling on," including "farm or orchard, pleasant curds and cream," the line's ALLITERATION producing reading pleasure. In addition they might mention such quotidian topics as "drowning flies, or shoe lost in the mire / By little whimpering boy, with rueful face," the reference to the male interesting in its focus on his weakness. The persona then imitates classical poets by calling, "Come, Muse, and sing the dreaded Washing-Day." Muses were traditionally called upon to sing of topics that evoked celebration and joy. Barbauld introduces one of several PARADOXes by suggesting that goddesses might use a light tone to sing of something they dread.

Barbauld's next several lines make clear that in spite of the poem's pleasant tone, the work is unpleasant and remains specifically the task of women. She compares them to oxen or horses, the yoke of marriage pressing heavy on their necks, forcing them to bow beneath the load:

Ye who beneath the yoke of wedlock bend,
With bowed soul, full well ye ken the day
Which week, smooth sliding after week brings on
Too soon;—for to that day nor peace belongs
Nor comfort.

Barbauld uses the term *ken* as "to know or recognize" and emphasizes the flow of that "smooth sliding" with the use of ENJAMBMENT as one line flows into the next.

Any romantic vision of this difficult task of washing disappears, and the speaker emphasizes during that dreaded day "The red-armed washers" have no "repose" or rest; they do not smile or exercise any "quaint device of mirth." The cats scramble to get out of the way, any guests in the home enjoy only a "silent breakfast-meal," the preparation for the task interrupted only "by anxious looks / Cast at the lowering sky." If rain falls to interrupt the work and prevent the washing from being hung to dry

. . . adieu to all
Remains of quiet; then expect to hear
Of sad disasters—dirt and gravel stains
Hard to efface, and loaded lines at once
Snapped short—and linen-horse by dog thrown
    down,
And all the petty miseries of life,

as the linen horse refers to a wooden frame on which linens could be hung to dry. Barbauld next employs an allusion to "Guatimozin," the last Aztec emperor, who died in the 16th century, tortured by Spanish captors. Not only does the idea of torture resonate with the washing chore, Barbauld's readers would have known of the Aztec's stoicism and silence, which became legendary.

The 33rd line shifts out of the dark tone to resume a description of what happens when the washing day remains fair. Through line 57 the focus turns to the hapless master who happens to wander into the middle of the work in progress. The poem seems to divide naturally into a second section as Barbauld emphasizes the power that the work affords the women; it gives them an excuse to ignore, if only for that one day, the male who ultimately benefits from their work. As the master appears, he may foolishly request his usual "'tendance," or service, including his "study swept, or nicely dusted coat," or "stockings mended," but he will receive no assistance even "though the yawning rents / Gape wide as Erebus." The classical allusion to Erebus, noted in Greek mythology as a place of darkness separating the earth from the underworld, to describe the hole in the master's stockings supports a sly joke made at his expense. As he wanders about his estate, he may find his "tender shrubs, / Myrtle or rose, all crushed beneath the weight / Of coarse—checked apron," an "impatient hand" having snapped off branches here and there as decorum gives way to necessity. As if being ignored and having his possessions suffer were not enough, he is told that he may receive a literal slap in the face. The damaged landscaping may "mar thy musings, as the wet cold sheet / Flaps in thy face abrupt." Next the speaker turns her edgy humor against any male guest who may arrive hoping to receive "hospitable rites." He will be met instead with "Looks, blank at best, and stinted courtesy." Barbauld performs a neat play on words using the term *feeds,* as she continues, "Vainly he feeds his hopes / With dinner of roast chicken, savory pie, / Or tart or pudding," none of which he will receive on that day. Instead "the unlucky guest / In silence dines, and early slinks away."

Line 58 begins the final third of the poem. Barbauld has moved from an even tone into a negative one, then a mocking/humorous tone, and finally concludes her poem in a nostalgic tone by employing imagery from childhood. The speaker recalls wash days from her youth. Barbauld encourages reader admiration of all women involved in the task, as the speaker continues, "I well remember, when a child, the awe / This day struck into me." That awe is based on her reaction to the maids who normally treated her with consideration and generosity but became different people on wash day. The speaker recalls that they "looked cross, and drove me from them." She did not receive the "soft caress" and "usual indulgences," which included petting and treats of "jelly or cream" or "buttered toast, / When butter was forbid: or thrilling tale / Of ghost, or witch, or murder." Barbauld makes the important point that the servants generally nurtured the speaker's imagination, meeting spiritual needs, as well as physical.

The speaker joins her grandmother, who watched the small children while other women completed the physical task. The children enjoyed hiding her "spectacles," playing tricks on the "indulgent" older woman, who would have been involved in the vigorous wash work when younger. Barbauld thus emphasizes the wash day as a rite, passed by one generation to another. Feminist critics continually look for such rituals that helped strengthen a materially weak female community. The speaker feels secure, especially as "At intervals my mother's voice was heard, / Urging dispatch." The reader understands that the speaker belonged to at least a middle-class household, as servants were present, but her mother took charge of the domestic duties. The next few lines offer a plethora of images, allowing readers easily to picture the scene through Barbauld's rhythmic series of acts: "All hands employed to wash, to rinse, to wring, / To fold, and starch, and clap, and iron, and plait."

As she launches into her final lines, Barbauld's speaker turns dreamy, creating a fantasy world through the continuing childhood remembrances:

Then would I sit me down, and ponder much
Why washings were. Sometimes through
    hollow bowl
Of pipe amused we blew, and sent aloft
The floating bubbles; little dreaming then
To see, Montgolfier.

The name refers to Joseph Michel Montgolfier, who with his brother invented the first practical hot-air balloons. She terms the balloon a "silken ball" that may "Ride buoyant through the clouds—so near approach / The sports of children and the toils of men." The sudden insertion of the balloon imagery suggests one of Barbauld's favorite themes, the value of human imagination. In this case only imagination allows temporary escape from daily drudgery.

All four of the traditional physical elements are then mentioned in the closing two lines: "Earth, air, and sky, and ocean, hath its bubbles, / And verse is one of them—this most of all." Barbauld admirably emphasizes her message that poetry and literature, products of the imagination, represent the most significant manner of escape from physical concerns. As do the balloons that float above human trials, the imagination carries the mind beyond its quotidian concerns.

"WATERFALL, THE" HENRY VAUGHAN (1650)

As other poetry by HENRY VAUGHAN does, "The Waterfall" focuses on the process that represents the regeneration of man's soul through spiritual action. Vaughn's poetry makes clear his attraction to the idea of an almost daily rebirth, made available through God's grace and evident in signs present in nature. The waterfall offers such a sign, as Vaughan incorporates into his poem the symbolism of water as a means of cleansing and rebirth. The poem opens in an address to the waterfall: "With what deep murmurs through time's silent stealth / Doth thy transparent, cool and watery wealth / Here flowing fall." A master at the use of ALLITERATION, Vaughan often incorporated it, as he does here, for purposes of emphasis as well as rhythm and the building of momentum. The verbal momentum imitates that of the waterfall, which Vaughan uses FIGURATIVE LANGUAGE (FIGURE OF SPEECH) to personify as he comments on the water's fall from high to low: "As if his liquid, loose retinue stayed / Ling'ring and were of this steep place afraid." Critics agree that the water here represents the human soul, which leaps to death out of fear of its present circumstance, falling as "All must descend, / Not to an end," but instead "quickened by this steep and rocky grave." Here Vaughan uses a play on words with the biblical meaning of *quick*, "life," or "those alive." They fall, as if toward the grave, but will "Rise to a longer course more bright and brave." The fall may seem to promise certain death but instead leads to transformation from a state of sin to one of grace, as the soul dies to sin, only to be reborn. It may then rise, either to spend a more fulfilling life on earth or to ascend to heaven for eternity.

Vaughan and his brother Thomas remained keenly interested in acts of transformation, of both physical and spiritual types. The process of transformation remained clear in alchemy, a "science" that fascinated Vaughan. His interest helped lead to his practice of hermetic Christianity, in which the idea of process proved crucial. Hermeticism philosophically held that the created world is unendingly rejuvenated through infinite cycles, with its constant return to its source of cosmic energy. As related by Alan Rudrum, Thomas Vaughan had translated a passage from Cornelius Agrippa that affords a clearer understanding of the Vaughans's hermetic approach to Christianity. The passage makes plain that after "the spirit has failed," it will be "purged from all impurity," at which time it

> changes into innumerable [sic] forms, here into herb and there into stone, or perchance into some extraordinary animal; but now and then into a cloud, a pearl, some gem or metal; and sweetly glittering with blushing flames, it passes continually through a myriad changes of colours, and lives always an operator and magus of prodigies, never wearying with the toil thereof but ever young in strength and energy.

Vaughan adopted some of the imagery of Agrippa, particularly that of the pearl, for use in several of his works.

In the second portion of "The Waterfall," which follows its first 12 lines and the insertion of white space, Vaughan focuses on the cyclical nature of life and death and its promise to humans of improvement. The speaker notes in an address to the waterfall that he has observed the stream and bank where "each drop of thy quick store / Runs thither whence it did before." He uses this observation to comfort humans, "poor souls" who might "fear a shade or night." He reasons,

> . . . since those drops are all sent back
> So sure to thee that none doth lack,
> Why should frail flesh doubt any more
> That what God takes he'll not restore?

Humans may use the lesson of the waterfall, in which the water fragments in order to reunite its many parts after it falls to a new pool, to understand better the idea of regeneration through faith in God in their own lives. The water acts for the speaker as "My sacred wash and cleanser," as well as a "first consigner unto those / Fountain of life where the Lamb goes!" But it only serves to teach a lesson, its importance lying in its symbolism.

Vaughan completes the poem with praise of God and his revelation of grace and the promise of redemption through nature. His use of detail to capture his natural surroundings rivals that of ANDREW MARVELL. However, whereas Marvell focused on his immediate domestic environment, Vaughan embraces all of nature, the wilder the better. He also clarifies nature's service as a conduit to better understanding of God, a means to an end. In this poem, he concludes:

> Oh my invisible estate,
> My glorious liberty, still late!
> Thou art the channel my soul seeks,
> Not this with cataracts and creeks.

Vaughan's practice of hermetic Christianity focuses in his attitude toward nature. While traditionally Christianity emphasized the separation of man from the rest of God's creation, hermetic Christianity emphasized man's intimate relationship with nature. For this reason the later Romantic poets with their emphasis on transcendentalism would embrace Vaughan's work. The alchemy that fascinated Vaughan held strongly to the idea of transfiguration, and hermetic mysticism applied the theory of transfiguration to those who followed Christ's teachings. While one attitude in the 17th century held that a study of nature must be critical and scientific, the hermetic view saw nature and the universe not as the product of an uninvolved clock maker who simply wound it and set it running, but instead as a divine process. The world itself existed as an organism, all energy and all thought finding a home in God's mind.

BIBLIOGRAPHY

Judson, A. C. "The Source of Henry Vaughan's Ideas Concerning God in Nature." *Studies in Philology* 24 (1927): 592–606.

Leishman, J. B. *The Metaphysical Poets: Donne, Herbert, Vaughan, Traherne.* Oxford: Clarendon Press, 1934.

Rudrum, Alan. *Henry Vaughan.* Cardiff: University of Wales Press, 1981.

"WHEN I CONSIDER HOW MY LIGHT IS SPENT (SONNET XIX)" JOHN MILTON

(1652?) Probably the most well-known of JOHN MILTON'S SONNETS, "When I consider how my light is spent (Sonnet XIX)" focuses on the poet's loss of sight and his resultant fear that he may no longer be able to serve God in a blind state. The date 1652 remains its common dating, as that was the year in which Milton became totally blind. The first line adopted as its title, the Elizabethan sonnet employs the extended metaphor of light to represent sight.

The speaker begins by musing on the contrast between the way he spent the days when he could see with his present days, "in this dark world and wide." He notes there exists one "Talent which is death to hide," alluding to the parable in Matthew 25 of the talents a master entrusted to three servants before leaving on a trip. A talent was worth approximately $1,000 in silver content, but more in buying power. When the master returned, he rewarded the first two servants, who invested their talents and returned a profit to their master. However, one servant had hidden the talents away for safekeeping because of fear. According to the King James Version of the Bible, the master called that servant "wicked and slothful" for not assuring that his talents multiplied in his absence. He then not only removed the talents from the errant servant to present them to the obedient servants, he ordered, "Cast ye the unprofitable servant into outer darkness: there shall be weeping and gnashing of teeth." The parable offers an analogy to Christ's leaving behind the faithful to use their talents to convince additional humans to follow the Christian faith. Those who do not do so risk "outer darkness" or spiritual death.

As Milton continues, he describes his talent as "Lodg'd with me useless, though my Soul more bent / To serve therewith my Maker." Critics interpret the poet's talent as his writing. While Milton had continued to write with help, his concerns are real because of his now-total loss of sight. The speaker notes that although he has used up his light, his Soul still desires service. He wants to "present" his "true account," lest his Maker return to "chide" him. He confesses that he would like to ask, "Doth God exact day-labor, light denied," expressing, if not anger, at least frustration that he has been left to labor in the dark. However, patience guides his thoughts to present an answer to the unasked question, "God doth not need / Either man's work or his own gifts." In contrast to the speaker's desperation, patience adopts a gentle tone, explaining that God does not need man's talents, originally his gift to man, handed back to him. Rather, "who best / Bear his mild yoke, they serve him best.'" Now service is cast in the guise of suffering through FIGURATIVE LANGUAGE (FIGURE OF SPEECH) comparing the suffering speaker to a beast of burden. In describing the burden caused by his blindness as "mild," Milton stresses the need for humility in the face of trials and makes clear that suffering in Christ's name and thus in some small way sharing his condition is a positive action, because God's "'. . . State / is Kingly.'"

Finally, Milton shows that he may draw sustenance from the fact that a man can serve, regardless of his condition. Patience's gentle murmur into the poet's ear continues, as his 12th and 13th lines note that hosts of angels are available to carry out holy orders; they at God's "'bidding speed / And post o'er Land and Ocean without rest.'" However, the last line confirms, humans need not compete with such powers that remain beyond their abilities when the voice states, "They also serve who only stand and wait.'"

"WHEN LOVELY WOMAN STOOPS TO FOLLY" OLIVER GOLDSMITH (1766) OLIVER GOLDSMITH's two-stanza poem "When Lovely Woman Stoops to Folly" offers few surprises. In its eight lines with RHYME scheme *abab* Goldsmith eschews suggestion to state that if a woman loses her good reputation, she might as well die. The poem appeared in Goldsmith's

sole, and quite famous, novel, *The Vicar of Wakefield* (1766), in which the title character believes for a time that his daughter had been lured into a false wedding ceremony, was deserted, and ultimately died of grief. While this sentiment represents Goldsmith's typical hyperbole, it also acts as an example of the mid-18th-century fascination of poets with death and suicide, as well as the results of nonconformity with society's unwritten laws, including those demanding purity of women.

The first stanza asks what may be done to rescue the woman who "stoops to folly," that is, engages in sexual dalliance, only to be rejected by her lover:

> When lovely woman stoops to folly,
> And finds too late that men betray,
> What charm can soothe her melancholy,
> What art can wash her guilt away?

The speaker does not deny the duplicity of men, but neither do men suffer the melancholy and guilt foisted onto the lovely woman, at least not while she lives. When Goldsmith uses the term *art,* he means "creative idea" and asks what might be strong enough to cleanse her guilt. The second stanza answers his question. A manner by which she may cover her guilt and hide her shame, as well as invoke regret and remorse in her lover, is to take her own life:

> The only art her guilt to cover
> To hide her shame from every eye,
> To give repentance to her lover,
> And wring his bosom—is to die.

Feminist critics would note the structure of male power over female. The only manner by which the woman can subvert that power is by taking her life. Only then will her lover feel the remorse, regret, and sense of loss that she felt from her lover's rejection. Goldsmith suggests that she suffers an emotional death, and the physical form will follow. The poet Phoebe Cary wrote a parody of Goldsmith's poem titled "When Lovely Woman," which preserved its original form and theme. Additional parodies continue to appear and may consider completely unrelated topics. As an exam-

ple a Norman, Oklahoma, newspaper, *The Norman Transcript,* ran an article titled "When Column-Writer Stoops to Folly" in an August 2005 edition.

"WHEN NIGHT'S BLACK MANTLE"
LADY MARY WROTH (1621)

LADY MARY WROTH began her SONNET sequence "Pamphilia to Amphilanthus," which she included in her prose romance *The Countess of Montgomery's Urania,* with Sonnet 1, referred to by its first line, "When night's black mantle could most darkness prove." The speaker is Pamphilia, a young woman of virtue who attempts to convince her lover, Amphilanthus, of the value of responsible and pure living. Wroth extends the metaphor of night and darkness to suggest danger and the inability to see the future of her speaker. The imagery of the mantle in the first line emphasizes the totality of the darkness. The speaker describes sleep as "death's Image," a common reference that suggests the light of life remains in danger during that time. While she sleeps her "thoughts did move" from a conscious awareness of herself quickly, "Swifter than those most swiftness need require." Wroth emphasizes the trepidation that seizes her speaker in repetition of the term *swift* to indicate how quickly she lost control. Her imagery reflects mythological figures and ideas, as the speaker describes riding in "a chariot drawn by winged desire" and seeing Venus, the goddess of love, with her son, Cupid, god of love. Cupid sits at the feet of Venus "adding fire / To burning hearts," a reference to the belief that Cupid could cause the passion of love by piercing an unsuspecting human's heart. After being shot, the human would fall in love with the next person she saw, losing complete control over who became the object of her affection. The speaker sees Venus hold higher than all of the hearts "one heart flaming more than all the rest," after which she placed it into Pamphilia's breast. Wroth introduces dialogue to dramatize further the scene as Venus instructs Cupid, "Dear, son, now shut . . . thus must we win." The flaming heart is enclosed in Pamphilia, who says that Cupid "martyred my poor heart." When she wakes, she "hoped as dreams it would depart, / Yet since, O me, a lover I have been."

Wroth achieves several purposes with this opening sonnet. She establishes Pamphilia as an innocent young woman, caught up in events beyond her control. She also clarifies Pamphilia's position as a lover, in that she had hoped in vain not to experience the emotions that left her feeling used. The term *martyr* proves especially effective as a description of the speaker, one who dies for a cause greater than she. Wroth allows readers to identify as humans trapped in the same condition, that is, as victims of our passions.

"WHY SO PALE AND WAN, FOND LOVER?" SIR JOHN SUCKLING (1638)

A few songs, such as "Why So Pale and Wan, Fond Lover?" a BALLAD, along with a few LYRIC poems remain from the work of SIR JOHN SUCKLING. "Why So Pale and Wan" was sung by the character Orsames in Suckling's first stage production, a tragedy titled *Aglaura*. Its form is simple, composed of three five-line stanzas with several repeated lines in varying meters. Stanzas 1 and 2 each begin with a question. The first opens with the title question, and readers learn that the "Lover" remains pale and wan as a result of the lack of attention from the one he loves. The adviser reminds him that "when looking well can't move her," why would "Looking ill prevail?" The second stanza opens with "Why so dull and mute, young sinner? / Prithee why so mute?" Following the pattern established in the first stanza, the adviser asks whether "when speaking well can't move her" there is any point to remaining mute. The final stanza breaks pattern to begin with a statement that urges the Lover, "Quit, quit, for shame, this will not move: / This cannot take her." The closing advice is simply to abandon the attempt to win the object of affection, and the speaker adds for effect, "The devil take her!" A strong example of the lighter-weight writing by a member of the CAVALIER POETS, the song nevertheless projects a unity and humor readers may still find attractive. It proved quite popular in its day, perhaps in its contrast to much Cavalier verse in which the lover speaker spends multiple lines exalting his lover's chin or other body part, only to close in despondency.

"WILLING MISTRESS, THE" APHRA BEHN (1673)

APHRA BEHN's "The Willing Mistress" was a song performed in her drama *The Dutch Lover*, staged in 1673. It is sung by a maidservant, who tells her mistress of a sexual experience with a man named Amyntas. *Amyntas* was a favorite name adopted by Behn for the sexual predators in her poetry. Some critics believe it was a nickname for the man with whom Behn became obsessed, John Hoyle. Because Hoyle apparently did not reciprocate her attentions, he could assume the persona in her works of the man rejecting a woman desperate for love. Known for her erotic drama and poetry, Behn scandalized a society that easily accepted themes of sexual excess from RESTORATION period male writers. She seemed to encourage her audience to identify her with the female subjects of her writings, until the private person became indistinguishable from the public character. No doubt this helped sales of her works, all-important to this widow who had to support herself just as any man did. A former spy for Charles II who had experienced firsthand the conflation of power and sex, Behn understandably wrote as her male contemporaries did. In this play the fact that Behn's husband, who probably died in London's plague of 1665, had been of Dutch ancestry encouraged the audience to identify its heroine with Behn herself.

In the brief song, composed of three eight-line stanzas with an *ababcdcd* RHYME scheme, a maid sings to her mistress of her sexual encounter. The title reflects negatively on the mistress, rather than the maidservant, suggesting her guilt by association. Because of her higher social status, the mistress should have silenced her maid, rather than providing an attentive audience. Behn enjoyed a jibe at the upper classes, which enjoyed portraying themselves as positive role models for those of lesser worth.

Behn suggests mythology by developing a secluded "grove" with shade trees as setting, where various classical rapes took place. The trees act as a screen even from the sun, which could not penetrate the darkness to betray the lovers. The dark forest traditionally symbolizes danger, as light symbolizes wisdom; thus the female speaker willingly courts danger although she knows better. She makes clear that she lacks fear as she sits with her lover on "the moss," where they begin "to play / A thousand amorous tricks," or games, "to pass / The heat of all the day." However, their games generate their own heat, as he gives her "many kisses," which she returns, the exchange making her "willing to receive / That which I dare not name." The speaker switches to third person to express her own desire, as she continues,

> His charming eyes no aid required
> To tell their softening tale;
> On her that was already fired,
> 'Twas easy to prevail.

In the second line the term *softening* refers to Amyntas's effect on the maidservant in reducing any protest she might make. The exchange is completely silent, for Amyntas continues his kisses as he "clasp[s]" the maid, "Whilst those his thoughts expressed." Behn may suggest that the female could misinterpret male intentions, believing his kisses to express an intellectual process, when they probably result from simple animal instinct. He is a tender lover, however, from whom the maid fears no danger as she clearly describes him as "gently" laying her on the ground. Behn coyly concludes her song, "Ah who can guess the rest?" well knowing that not only the maid's mistress, but also by extension her audience can easily imagine the direction the action takes.

BIBLIOGRAPHY

Gosse, Edmund. "Mrs. Behn." In *The English Poets: Selections with Critical Introductions by Various Writers and a General Introduction by Matthew Arnold,* edited by Thomas Humphry Ward. Vol. 2, 419–421. New York: Macmillan, 1912.

"WINDOWS, THE" GEORGE HERBERT (1633)

In "The Windows" GEORGE HERBERT uses an extended metaphor to comment autobiographically on the existence of one who acts as the Lord's representative, sharing the sacred message with mankind. Because windows traditionally allow vision from the outside into a building, and vice versa, Herbert sees one who preached, such as he, as serving a similar purpose. God's light, or word, should shine through a religious leader who subtracts nothing from the strength of that word. The simplicity of the sentiment is echoed in the poem's simplicity of form. In three five-line stanzas Herbert's LYRIC easily makes its point.

The poem begins with a direct address to God: "Lord, how can man preach thy eternal word?" The speaker wonders, as in his opinion, man "is a brittle crazy glass." However, in God's temple, a "glorious and transcendent place," man is allowed "To be a window, through thy grace." Because the temple remains transcendent, even a brittle human may gain the strength to serve the Lord's purpose. In the second stanza Herbert expands on the idea of man's brittle nature, writing that the Lord "dost anneal in glass" his story, where *anneal* means to subject glass to a slow process of heating and cooling in order to strengthen it against brittleness. By referencing that process, Herbert makes clear that man must undergo purification in order to serve as a window does. The speaker says to his Lord that after that process, which makes "thy life to shine within / The holy Preacher's," the light changes. Along with the glory it "More rev'rend grows, and more doth win," as Herbert produces multiple meanings in the term *rev'rend*. It means "revered" but suggests an additional adjective with emphasis through the missing *e* on the second syllable, *rend*. *Rend* also indicates a process of reduction for the purpose of purification, while the term in its more familiar form of *reverend* may serve as the noun denoting one who preaches. Without the annealing process, man as window would cause the Lord's light and glory to be "wat'rish, bleak, and thin." As Herbert completes his poem, he further emphasizes the melding process necessary in order for man to become useful to God:

> Doctrine and life, colours and light, in one
> When they combine and mingle, bring
> A strong regard and awe.

However, the next line makes clear that "speech alone," meaning man's words without God's light and glory, "Doth vanish like a flaring thing," like a flame that flares up momentarily, but then dies away, "And in the ear, not conscience ring." Uninspired words will ring only in the ear and immediately die away, as does the flare. But those that are directly from God through the preacher as a conduit will ring loudly in the conscience. The latter ring may be a ring of alarm, one that will lead a man to contemplation and change.

WINDSOR FOREST Alexander Pope (1713)

For decades critics dismissed *Windsor Forest* by Alexander Pope as simple imitative juvenilia. Inspired most obviously by Virgil, it resembled a decorative occasional poem, written to celebrate the signing of the Treaty of Utrecht on April 11, 1713. However, interest was renewed in the poem in the 20th century, particularly after Earl Wasserman demonstrated Pope's use of the description of nature as metaphor for political language. Pope's design proved significant as he adopted his favored theme of *concordia discors,* or harmony through divisiveness, as he would later apply it in *An Essay on Man.* He demonstrated that political harmony related to cosmic harmony, with both dependent upon the order produced by constant tension in forces that sustained them. Wasserman acknowledged Pope's debt to Virgil's *Georgics* but recognized that Pope went beyond his model in actually manipulating the doctrine of *concordia discors* to achieve his desired effect.

Exceeding 400 lines and structured in rhyming couplets, *Windsor Forest* adopts geography, or place, as a trope for man's historic struggle toward peace. He populates the poem with recognizable figures, both historic and mythic, as well as recognizable topography, including rivers. The tension present in nature, and between man and nature, represents the tension that leads to war. He dedicated the poem to George Granville, Lord Lansdowne, who served Queen Anne as secretary of war, crediting him in large part for the peace that the poem's conclusion celebrates. Pope had written the first 290 lines focusing on the countryside prior to 1710. He added the remaining lines later and published the poem in anticipation of the treaty signing, after great victories on land and sea by Great Britain.

As Virgil does, Pope emphasizes man's imperfect nature as he describes the conflict that enveloped civilization from the time of Nimrod, considered the first hunter. He begins by describing the present powerful and wealthy state of Great Britain. He emphasizes its superiority to others by contrasting it to India, which boasts special plants, such as "The weeping Amber or the balmy Tree," which are nothing compared to the English oaks from which "the precious Loads are born," meaning the oaken ships that bear goods around the world. Great Britain remains a place that Pan, the god of flocks and pastures; Pomona, goddess of fruit trees; Flora, goddess of flowers; and Ceres, goddess of grains and vegetation might happily inhabit. He credits Queen Anne with that accomplishment, writing, "Rich Industry sits smiling on the Plains, / And Peace and Plenty tell, a Stuart reigns" (41–42).

Pope next contrasts the bountiful present era with times past. He describes rulers and despots who terrorized man and beast, "Both doom'd alike for sportive Tyrants bled." Instead of reflecting the peace and harmony of natural surroundings,

> Round broken Columns clasping Ivy twin'd;
> O'er Heaps of Ruin stalk'd the stately Hind;
> The Fox obscene to gaping Tombs retires,
> And savage Howlings fill the sacred Quires.
>   (70–73)

Virgil and Pope both associated harmony with an enlightened government, and chaos with the absence of a just ruler or governing body. He mentions specifically the Saxons and Danes and their violent invasions of England, as well as William and Richard, his second son, who was killed by a stag and lay bleeding "in the Forest, like a wounded Hart." Pope employs wordplay with the word *hart,* referring to the stag as well as to Richard's heart. He suggests the violent reap what they sow.

When Pope later describes the victory of Britannia, whose "Standard flies" over those defeated, he makes clear the victory is short-lived. He adopts animals as metaphors, writing of the exultant pheasant that falls prey to a hunter,

> Short is his Joy! He feels the fiery Wound,
> Flutters in Blood, and panting beats the Ground
> Ah! What avail his glossie, varying Dyes,
> His Purple Crest, and Scarlet-circled Eyes.
>   (113–117)

Pope's description makes vivid the loss and waste in the killing of this lovely beast. Other creatures learn from man "each other to undo" (124), as man continues to hunt and destroy. Pope inserts details such as "slaught'ring Guns," "Frosts," "naked Groves," "leafless

Trees," "lonely," "haunt," and "frozen sky" to emphasize the grim reality of man's destructive nature. The later reign of "Th' immortal Huntress, and her Virgin Train" offered some solace, as only in the time of Windsor would England's inhabitants see "As bright a Goddess, and as chaste a Queen; / Whose Care, like hers, protects the Sylvan Reign" (160–163). Pope is probably referring to Queen Elizabeth I, who ruled during a golden age, using the reference also to emphasize the greatness of Queen Anne. Critics have noted that when female references appear in the poem, creating a balance between male and female, peace reigns. However, when only male references are used, discord rules.

Pope also focuses on the creative forces that bring history to life for readers. In the classical vein he calls upon the muses, "Ye sacred Nine! That all my Soul possess, / Whose Raptures fire me, and whose Visions bless," to inspire him. He requests that they "Bear me, oh bear me to sequester'd Scenes" (261). He then mentions *Cooper's Hill,* a mountain celebrated in a famous poem of place by SIR JOHN DENHAM, whom Pope praises as parenthetically as a poet's poet: "(On *Cooper's* Hill eternal Wreaths shall grow / While lasts the Mountain, or while *Thames* shall flow)." The wreaths refer to those placed on a poet's head as a sign of achievement. He also references the poet ABRAHAM COWLEY, who died at the border of Windsor Forest in 1667, his body then conveyed by way of the Thames River to London for burial in Westminster Abbey. He next must pay homage to Granville, addressing him in order to assign glory of the revived woods: "'Tis yours, my Lord, to bless our soft Retreats, / And call the Muses to their ancient Seats." Granville was also a minor poet, explaining why Pope added, "To paint anew the flow'ry Sylvan Scenes," a double reference to Granville's art as well as to the source of the woods' rebirth. He does not neglect the warrior imagery necessary to honor Granville, writing, "Still in thy Song shoul'd vanquish'd France appear, / And bleed for ever under *Britain's* Spear." The song mentioned is that sung by bards to celebrate heroic feats, in this case the defeat of France.

Pope adds more references to the violence that at times engulfed England, including the execution by beheading of Charles I and the destruction by natural causes, including the "purple Deaths" of the Great Plague of 1665 and the "rolling Fire" that destroyed much of London in 1666. In addition "A dreadful Series of Intestine Wars, / Inglorious Triumphs, and dishonest Scars" (325–326), referring to the civil wars, destroyed the peace. Those discordant images contrast well with the harmonious preceding images and those that follow, in which Pope adopts the FIGURATIVE LANGUAGE (FIGURE OF SPEECH) of personification to describe "Old Father Thames" and the many rivers he recalls. This prefaces the praise language of lines such as "Hail Sacred *Peace*! Hail long-expected Days, / That *Thames's* Glory to the Stars shall raise!" (355–356). Thames, representative of Great Britain, shall replace the Tyber of Rome and the Hermes, rumored to have sands of gold, in glory. Eventually the Thames "shall flow for all Mankind, / Whole Nations enter with each swelling Tyde," as Great Britain's glory will stretch to the corners of the globe.

The concluding images echo those of Virgil, in which harmony remains possible only after Discord is conquered, cast into exile along with "Gigantick *Pride,* pale *Terror,* gloomy *Care,* / And mad *Ambition*" as her attendants. They will be joined by "purple *Vengeance* bath'd in Gore," along with Envy, who will feel the bite of her own snakes. In addition Persecution will "mourn her broken Wheel," and Faction will "roar, *Rebellion* bite her Chain, / And gasping Furies thirst for Blood in vain" (415–422). Pope's overblown description remains appropriate to support Virgil's image of Fury chained to the Temple of Janus in the *Aeneid.* Fury as discord must be controlled in order for harmony to reign. That the harmony remains a product of war is the very IRONY that *concordia discors* supports.

Pope follows that crescendo with a call for the golden age to return, another classical reference, as Granville continues to recite through verse "The Thoughts of Gods." The speaker's "humble Muse" will instead focus on the plains and the woods as he passes his "careless Days / Pleas'd in the silent Shade with empty Praise." His song finished, he may celebrate the fact that for "the listning Swains / First in these Fields I sung the Sylvan Strains." While such humility was not characteristic of Pope, it remained the proper tone in which to close his poem, based on his classical models.

BIBLIOGRAPHY

Cummings, Robert. "Windsor-Forest as a Sylvan Poem." *English Literary History* 54, no. 1 (spring 1987): 63–79.

Richardson, John. "Alexander Pope's 'Windsor Forest': Its Context and Attitudes toward Slavery." *Eighteenth-Century Studies* 35, no. 1 (fall 2001): 1–16.

———. Pope's "Windsor-Forest." *The Explicator* 59, no. 3 (spring 2001): 118.

Rogers, Anne. *Pope and the Destiny of the Stuarts: History, Politics, and Mythology in the Age of Queen Anne.* New York: Oxford University Press, 2005.

Rogers, Pat. *The Symbolic Design of Windsor-Forest: Iconography, Pageant, and Prophecy in Pope's Early Work.* Newark: University of Delaware Press, 2004.

Wasserman, Earl. *The Subtler Language: Critical Readings of Neoclassic and Romantic Poems.* Baltimore: Johns Hopkins University Press, 1968.

Williams, Caroline. "Pope and Granville: Fictions of Friendship." *Notes and Queries* 38, no. 2 (June 1991): 184–186.

WINSCOM, JANE CAVE (ca. 1754–1813)

Not much is known of Jane Cave Winscom, other than the biographical information that may be gleaned from her poetry. This makes hers an interesting but frustrating case for feminist critics. Probably born in Wales, she wrote of both her parents, hinting that her beginnings were humble; her father may have practiced Methodism, either personally or also as a clergyman. She probably served private houses or supported herself through teaching. Her poem "Written by Desire of a Lady, on an Angry, Petulant Kitchen-Maid" displays knowledge of servants and the scullery atmosphere, not gained through any privileged position, as her speaker advises a fellow servant:

> Good Mistress Dishclout, condescend
> To hear the counsel of a friend:
> When next you are disposed to brawl,
> Pray let the scullery hear it all,
> And learn to know your fittest place
> Is with the dishes and the grease.

Another poem indicates Winscom's relocation to Bath and future move to Winchester by November 1779. When she published *Poems on Various Subjects, Entertaining, Elegiac, and Religious* (1783), she garnered about 2,000 subscribers, an admirable response. The list included some notables, such as Dr. Joseph Warton, who served as headmaster at Winchester College. Critics believe that Warton's subscription indicates Cave may have had some relationship with the school. By the time of the second edition of her collected poems in 1786, she had apparently married an excise officer in Winchester named Winscom. Her collection would be released in a somewhat expanded third edition (1789), and again in a fourth edition (1794). She developed debilitating headaches later in life, described in "Written the First Morning of the Author's Bathing at Teignmouth, for the Head-Ache," when she sought a cure in waters. She published an ode, "The Head-Ache, or an Ode to Health," in a Bristol newspaper in May 1793 as a plea for advice as to how to handle her affliction. Her description indicates the headaches may have been related to menstruation, as migraines before, during, and after menses were later associated with the menstrual cycle. She writes in part:

> Not one short month for ten revolving years,
> But pain within my frame its scepter rears!
> In each successive month full twelve long days
> And tedious night my sun withdraws his rays!
> Leaves me in silent anguish on my bed,
> Afflicting all the members in the head.

Other poems suggest that she had at least two children, both boys. An obituary after her 1813 death mentions, according to Roger Lonsdale, her having experienced a "miraculous escape from a watery grave, about two years since," labeling her "an authoress of no mean talents; and her domestic character, both as wife and mother, was exemplary."

BIBLIOGRAPHY

Lonsdale, Roger, ed. *Eighteenth-Century Women Poets.* New York: Oxford University Press, 1990.

McKim, A. Elizabeth. "The Headache Poems of Jane Cave Winscom." *Literature and Medicine* 24, no. 1 (2005): 93–108.

"WONDER" THOMAS TRAHERNE (ca. 1660)

Many poems by the 17th-century religious poet THOMAS TRAHERNE were not published until long after his death.

One example is the poem "Wonder," published in 1903 in a collection known as the Dobell sequence, named for its publisher, Bertram Dobell. The poems had remained undiscovered until 1895, when W. T. Brooke found them in a bookstall in London. Influences on Traherne's work included JOHN DONNE, JOHN DENHAM, EDMUND WALLER, and GEORGE HERBERT. As the poetry of Herbert, "Wonder" does not rely on simple form, as Traherne varies his stanza patterns in the eight eight-line verses. He uses the poem to praise nature and its relationship with God, noting that everything from "The skies in their magnificence" and "The lively, lovely air" to "The stars" helped his spirit feel at home on earth, when he descended "like an angel" to discover "How bright are all things here!"

Because the speaker describes all things as "bright," he must include many examples in addition to those from nature. Thus, "The streets were paved with golden stones, / The boys and girls were mine." All people seemed to shine, as the speaker sees the world as if he had the eyes of an angel. He describes all of the rich gems he encounters, including "diamond and pearl and gold," having admitted earlier in the fourth stanza that "Harsh ragged objects were concealed." Also hidden from his sight were "Sins, griefs, complaints, dissensions, weeping eyes," as God revealed only things "Which heavenly spirits and the angels prize," and "The state of innocence" informed all of his senses. He enters that state after a rebirth, prompted by his acceptance of God's grace.

Traherne returns in stanza 7 to the negative conditions that prevent human happiness and often blind men to the positive aspects of their world. Reproduction of the complete stanza aids in the understanding of critical reaction to the poem:

> Cursed and devised proprieties,
> With envy, avarice,
> And fraud, those fiends that spoil even paradise,
> Fled from the splendor of mine eyes.
> And so did hedges, ditches, limits, bounds:
> I dreamed not aught of those,
> But wandered over all men's grounds,
> And found repose. (49–56)

Critics have noted the forced characteristic of the poem's RHYME and METER in order to accommodate the repetition Traherne incorporates in imitation of biblical poetry. His biographer Malcolm Day writes that Traherne's thought or idea drives the poem's construction, noting, "The choice of phrase and word arises primarily out of the force of the idea as it is felt," rather than from any rhetorical convention. In order to capture a feeling of spontaneity, Traherne depends on a "loose relationship" between the rhythm and sound patterns that he incorporates. Day sees this as a positive characteristic. Because Traherne feels little pressure to conform to traditional requirements, his lines project a "supple" quality, enhanced through the simple tools of repetition, including ALLITERATION, assonance, and beat. He did not use FIGURATIVE LANGUAGE (FIGURE OF SPEECH) as often as others of his era, perhaps because metaphor suggests the necessity to use an indirect reference.

In this poem of meditation Traherne's message is that man must simply find his place in the universe, which will lead to a direct relationship with God. Biblical allusions prove a stronger tool than figures of speech. Even his cataloging suggests no hierarchy; all is one in God.

BIBLIOGRAPHY

Bottrall, Margaret. "Traherne's Praise of Creation." *Critical Quarterly* 1 (summer 1959): 126–133.
Day, Malcolm M. "'Naked Truth' and the Language of Thomas Traherne." *Studies in Philology* 68 (July 1971): 305–325.
Ridlon, Harold G. "The Function of the 'Infant-Ey' in Traherne's Poetry." *Studies in Philology* 61 (1964): 627–639.

"WRITTEN FOR MY SON, AND SPOKEN BY HIM AT HIS FIRST PUTTING ON BREECHES" MARY BARBER (1731)

MARY BARBER ranked high in the opinion of the master essayist and poet JONATHAN SWIFT, although later generations did not judge her poetry to be particularly skillful. A woman whose plans never quite reached fruition, Barber yet made a name for herself in Irish literary circles, with Swift supporting the publication of a collection of her poems. In "Written for My Son," Barber places words in the mouth of her child, who supposedly complained about the restraints caused by various articles of clothing. While a feminist critical reading might interpret the poem as containing a message in subtext regarding the oppression of powerless individuals by custom, no indication exists that Barber intended the poem as any type of protest. Rather she frames her child's complaint as a humorous presentation, light in subject and substance.

The poem is formatted in five uneven verses with a total of 56 lines. In straightforward couplets Barber adopts simple RHYMES that satisfyingly imitate a child's voice. She begins with two lines that mimic the limerick form, a clever suggestion of a child's riddle: "What is it our mamas bewitches, / To plague us little boys with breeches?" What follows is a rendition of the effect of binding clothing on the child's body. Examples of lines include

> . . . and then our feet, though young and tender,
> We to the shoemaker surrender,
> Who often makes our shoes so strait
> Our growing feet they cramp and fret.

In the second verse the speaker discusses clothes that are only considered "neat" when "they're so tight we cannot eat," and a hat band that "helps to cramp our brains." By the third verse the persona deviates to consider the IRONY in humans, who are "Fair privilege of nobler natures, / To be more plagued than other creatures!" Those creatures include "The wild inhabitants of air," which "Are clothed by heaven with wondrous care: The beauteous, well-compacted feathers / Are coats of mail against all weathers." The speaker laments, "Man only seems to sorrow born, / Naked, defenceless and forlorn."

The poem concludes with a traditional complaint against Custom, which has "usurped" the throne of Reason. Custom defies Reason's "rules" and

> Delights to make us act like fools.
> O'er human race the tyrant reigns,
> And binds them in eternal chains.
> We yield to his despotic sway,
> The only monarch all obey.

The final two lines are the best of the poem, with the phrase *despotic sway* a strong example of hidden ALLITERATION and the personification of Custom as a monarch effective. Although hardly sophisticated, both the sound and sense of the poem remain pleasing and appropriate to a verse about being a child.

WROTH, LADY MARY (1587?–1651–1653)

Born into a privileged and literary family, Mary Wroth was the eldest of six children. Her father, Sir Robert Sidney, later earl of Leicester, was a poet and a patron of the arts, while her wealthy mother, Barbara Gamage, was cousin to Sir Walter Raleigh. Her uncle and aunt, Sir Philip Sidney and LADY MARY SIDNEY HERBERT (COUNTESS OF PEMBROKE), were widely known for their poetry as well as for the literary circles Lady Herbert held at her home. Mary Wroth's parents instilled in her the family's artistic values as well as the values of community and hospitality. When her father received an appointment in 1588 as governor of Flushing in the Netherlands, she moved in with her aunt. She enjoyed a happy childhood raised at Lady Herbert's estate, which was celebrated by BEN JONSON in "TO PENSHURST." The court became another home for Mary, after the appointment of her father by James I as an earl. She was pledged in an arranged marriage to Sir Robert Wroth, a wealthy landowner and favorite of the king, a union fated to fail.

Contemporaries noted Robert Wroth's jealous tendencies as his wife's popularity at court grew. He gained a reputation as a womanizer and a spendthrift, while Mary's reputation remained pristine, garnering her sympathy of those at court. She began writing poetry and prose and performed in a masque written by Jonson for Queen Anne, *Masque of Beauty*. The Wroths made a handsome couple despite their differences, and Jonson dedicated poetry to them both. He also dedicated his drama *The Alchemist* to Mary. The marriage soon ended with Robert's untimely death in 1614, leaving Mary alone with a son to raise and large debts to manage. Legal matters took away her share of her husband's estate, and within two years of Robert's death Wroth also lost her son. A short time later she began an affair with her cousin, who was also a poet, William Herbert, earl of Pembroke; they had a son and a daughter. Although the arrangement caused her to lose her preferred standing at court, the poet EDWARD HERBERT, LORD OF CHERBURY, dedicated a poem to their daughter.

Wroth continued to write, producing the astonishing uncompleted romance titled *The Countess of Montgomery's Urania* (1621) that contained the first SONNET sequence published by an English woman, "PAMPHILIA TO AMPHILANTHUS." She modeled her ambitious work, the first of prose fiction by an English woman, on her uncle Philip's famous *Arcadia*. The males in Wroth's romance proved unfaithful and irresponsible, as she examines the ideal of fidelity and the double standard in its application mainly to women of her era. Twentieth-century feminist critics found it of great interest, as the female characters have a clear sense of identity separate from their lovers and husbands. Not a roman à clef, the sequence nevertheless suggested real-life courtiers in its characterizations, drawing the ire of several well-placed public figures. Those criticizing her work included the royalist poet MARGARET CAVENDISH, DUCHESS OF NEWCASTLE, who attacked its supposedly lascivious and unsuitably amorous nature in her *Sociable Letters*. The charge proved successful, if untrue; Pamphilia is clearly distinguished by her virtue. She will not yield to Amphilanthus until he demonstrates maturity and fidelity. Wroth based her heroine on a shepherdess in *Arcadia,* a characterization she much admired. After trying in vain to defend *Urania* publicly, Wroth had to recall it, dashing her hopes for the income it should have produced. Little to nothing is known of her life after that scandal.

While Wroth could not publish the completed version of her masterpiece, it was discovered in the 20th century. In addition to the prose romance and the sonnet sequence, the original book contained some 74 additional poems, one written by William Herbert, and others of that group remaining in manuscript form. It included a "crown" of sonnets, poems in a challenging fixed form, such as the often anthologized "IN THIS STRANGE LABYRINTH HOW SHALL I TURN?" Additional commonly published sonnets from "Pamphilia and Amphilanthus" include "MY MUSE NOW HAPPY, LAY THYSELF TO REST," "WHEN NIGHT'S BLACK MANTLE," "MY PAIN STILL SMOTHERED IN MY GRIEVÈD BREAST," and the song, "LOVE A CHILD IS EVER CRYING" and "SWEETEST LOVE,

RETURN AGAIN." This extraordinary output made Wroth the most published woman of her day. Although she had spent a good deal of time at the Jacobean court and her writing occasionally reflected some influence by JOHN DONNE, most of Wroth's work remains remarkable for its freedom from conventions of her day. Rather it echoed the times of the Elizabethan writers, including her uncle. Josephine A. Roberts published much of Wroth's work in a modern edition, and other feminist critics have assured this amazing woman's place in the history of English poetry.

BIBLIOGRAPHY

Beilin, Elaine. *Redeeming Eve: Women Writers of the English Renaissance*. Princeton, N.J.: Princeton University Press, 1987.

Bennett, Lyn. *Women Writing of Divinest Things: Rhetoric and the Poetry of Pembroke, Wroth, and Lanyer*. Pittsburgh: Duquesne University Press, 2004.

Catty, Jocelyn. *Writing Rape, Writing Women in Early Modern England*. Basingstoke, England: Macmillan, 1999.

Elsky, Martin. "Microhistory and Cultural Geography: Ben Jonson's *To Sir Robert Wroth* and the Absorption of Local Community in the Commonwealth." *Renaissance Quarterly* 53, no. 2 (2000): 500–528.

Fienberg, Nona. "Mary Wroth and the Invention of Female Poetic Subjectivity." In *Reading Mary Wroth,* edited by Miller and Waller, 175–190.

Hannay, Margaret P. "'Your Vertuous and Learned Aunt': The Countess of Pembroke as a Mentor to Mary Wroth." In *Reading Mary Wroth,* edited by Naomi J. Miller and Gary Waller, 15–34. Knoxville: University of Tennessee Press, 1991.

Miller, Naomi J. *Changing the Subject: Mary Wroth and Figurations of Gender in Early Modern England*. Lexington: University Press of Kentucky, 1996.

Miller, Naomi J., and Gary Waller, eds. *Reading Mary Wroth: Representing Alternatives in Early Modern England*. Knoxville: University of Tennessee Press, 1991.

Roberts, Josephine A., ed. *The First Part of the Countess of Montgomery's Urania*. Binghamton, N.Y.: Medieval and Renaissance Texts and Studies, 1995.

———. *The Second Part of The Countess of Montgomery's Urania*. Tempe: Renaissance English Text Society in conjunction with Arizona Center for Medieval and Renaissance Studies, 1999.

———. *The Poems of Lady Mary Wroth*. 2nd ed. Baton Rouge: Louisiana State University Press, 1992.

Wall, Wendy. *The Imprint of Gender: Authorship and Publication in the English Renaissance.* Ithaca, N.Y.: Cornell University Press, 1993.

Waller, Gary F. "Mother/Son, Father/Daughter, Brother/Sister, Cousins: The Sidney Family Romance." *Modern Philology* 88 (1990–1991): 401–414.

———. *The Sidney Family Romance: Mary Wroth, William Herbert, and the Early Modern Construction of Gender.* Detroit: Wayne State University Press, 1993.

Weidemann, Heather L. "Theatricality and Female Identity in Mary Wroth's *Urania.*" In *Reading Mary Wroth,* edited by Naomi J. Miller and Gary Waller, 191–209. Knoxville: University of Tennessee Press, 1991.

Wynne-Davies, Marion. "The Queen's Masque: Renaissance Women and the Seventeenth-Century Court Masque." In *Gloriana's Face: Women, Public and Private, in the English Renaissance,* edited by S. P. Cerasano and Marion Wynne-Davies, 79–104. New York: Harvester Wheatsheaf, 1992.

APPENDIX I

GLOSSARY

accent   The STRESS on one or another syllable, especially when poetry is read aloud.

accentual verse   A system of VERSE throughout at least a portion of a poem that depends on a certain fixed number of stresses in a line of poetry; this system, however, allows for any number of unstressed syllables.

allegory   Extended metaphor or symbol with at least two levels of meaning, a literal level and an implied, figurative level; an allegorical narrative tells a story and at the same time suggests another level of meaning.

alliteration   Repeating consonant sounds at the beginnings of words.

allusion   Making reference to something or someone, usually in an indirect manner.

anapest   A metrical foot consisting of two soft stresses followed by a hard stress. See METER.

anaphora   A word or phrase that is repeated at the start of successive lines of poetry.

apostrophe   A turn away from the reader to address another listener.

assonance   Repetition of like vowel sounds, often in stressed syllables in close proximity to each other.

ballad   A narrative in VERSE; the form derives from a narrative that was sung.

blank verse   Unrhymed IAMBIC PENTAMETER.

cadence   The rhythm in language, a pattern that can lend a musical order to a statement.

caesura   A pause within a VERSE line, usually at approximately mid point.

canon   A term originally derived from the Roman Catholic Church having to do with church law, this term also refers to a body of literature that is generally accepted as exhibiting what is best or important in terms of literary art.

collagist poetry   Poetry that employs the organizing element of collage or the bringing together of disparate material to create a new statement or vision.

conceit   Not unrelated to the term *concept,* an unusual supposition, analogy, metaphor, or image, often clever.

connotation   Meaning that is implied rather than stated directly as in DENOTATION.

consonance   Repetition of identical consonant sounds, within the context of varying vowel sounds.

couplet   Two VERSE lines in succession that have the same END RHYME. When the two lines contain a complete statement in themselves, they are called a closed couplet. See also HEROIC COUPLET.

dactyl   A metrical foot consisting of a hard stress followed by two soft stresses.

denotation   The literal meaning of a word or statement, the opposite of CONNOTATION.

diction   Word choice, the actual language that a writer employs.

468

dimeter   A VERSE line consisting of two metrical FEET.

dramatic monologue   An address to an interlocutor (another potential speaker) who is not present; a dramatic monologue has only one actual speaker.

elegy   A poem mourning someone's death.

ellipsis   Part of a statement left out, unspoken.

end rhyme   A rhyme at the end of a VERSE line.

end-stopped   A VERSE line that pauses at its end, when no ENJAMBMENT is possible.

enjambment   A VERSE line whose momentum forbids a pause at its end, thus avoiding being END-STOPPED.

epic   A long poem that, typically, recounts the adventures of someone in a high style and diction; classically, the adventures include a hero who is at least partially superhuman in makeup or deed, and the events have special importance in terms of the fate of a people.

epigram   A brief, witty statement, often satiric or aphoristic.

epithet   A word or phrase that characterizes something or someone.

eye rhyme   Agreement of words according to their spelling but not their sound.

feet   See FOOT.

feminine ending   A VERSE line that ends with an extra soft stress.

feminine rhyme   The rhyming of two words in more than a single syllable.

figurative language   Language that employs figures of speech such as IRONY, HYPERBOLE, METAPHOR, SIMILE, SYMBOL, METONYMY, etc., in which the language connotes meaning.

foot   A configuration of syllables to form a METER, such as an IAMB, TROCHEE, ANAPEST, DACTYL, or SPONDEE. A line of one foot is called a MONOMETER line, of two feet a DIAMETER line, of three feet TRIMETER, of four TETRAMETER, of five PENTAMETER, of six HEXAMETER, etc.

free verse   Poetry lacking a metrical pattern or patterns; poetic lines without any discernible meter.

haiku   A Japanese lyric form consisting of a certain number of syllables overall and in each line, most often in a five-seven-five syllabic line pattern.

half rhyme   A form of CONSONANCE in which final consonant sounds in neighboring stressed syllables agree.

heroic couplet   Two successive lines of END-RHYMING IAMBIC PENTAMETER.

hexameters   A VERSE line consisting of six metrical FEET.

hyperbole   An exaggeration meant to emphasize something.

iamb   A metrical FOOT consisting of a soft stress followed by a hard stress.

iambic pentameter   A five-FOOT line with a preponderance of IAMBIC FEET.

image   Language meant to represent objects, actions, feelings, or thoughts in vivid terms.

internal rhyme   A RHYME within a poetic line.

masculine rhyme   A RHYME depending on one hard-stressed syllable only.

metaphor   An implicit comparison, best when between unlike things, made without using the words *like* or *as.*

meter   An arrangement of syllables in units called FEET, such as IAMB or TROCHEE, and in numbers of feet to make a pattern, such as IAMBIC PENTAMETER; the syllables can be hard- or soft-stressed according to the type of FOOT or pattern to be employed.

metonymy   The substitution of a word that represents an association with, proximity to, or attribute of a thing for the thing itself; this figure of speech is not unlike SYNECHDOCHE.

monometer   A VERSE line consisting of a single metrical foot.

occasional verse   VERSE written to celebrate or to commemorate a particular event.

octave   An eight-line stanza of poetry, also the first and larger portion of a SONNET. See OCTET.

octet   An eight-line stanza of poetry. See OCTAVE.

ode   A lyric poem usually in a dignified style and addressing a serious subject.

onomatopoeia   A word or phrase whose sound resembles something the word or phrase is signifying.

oxymoron   A phrase or statement containing a self-contradiction.

paradox   A statement that seems to be self-contradictory but contains a truth that reconciles the contradiction.

pastoral   A poem that evokes a rural setting or rural values; the word itself derives from the Latin *pastor,* or "shepherd."

pentameter   A VERSE line consisting of five metrical FEET.

persona   The speaker in a poem, most often the narrator; the term is derived from the Latin word for "mask."

personification   Attributing human qualities to an inanimate entity.

prosody   The study of versification; the term is at times used as a synonym for METER.

quatrain   A four-line stanza of a poem, also a portion of a SONNET.

rhetorical figure   An arrangement of words for one or another emphasis or effect.

rhyme   Fundamentally, "agreement," the term specifically indicates the sameness or similarity of vowel sounds in an arrangement of words; there can be END RHYME, INTERNAL RHYME, EYE RHYME, HALF RHYME, FEMININE RHYME, etc.

rhyme scheme   The arrangement of END RHYMES in a poem, indicated when analyzing a poem with the letters of the alphabet, such as, for a poem in successive COUPLETS, AA, BB, CC, etc.

rhythm   A sense of movement created by arrangement of syllables in terms of stress and time.

sestet   A six-line stanza of poetry, also the final large portion of a SONNET.

sestina   A 36-line poem broken up into six SESTETS as well as a final stanza of three lines, the six words ending the first sestet's lines appearing at the conclusions of the remaining five sestets, in one or another order, and appearing in the final three lines; these repeated words usually convey key motifs of the poem.

simile   A comparison using the word *like* or *as.*

slant rhyme   A partial, incomplete RHYME, sometimes called a *half, imperfect, near* or *off rhyme.*

sonnet   A poem of 14 lines, traditionally in IAMBIC PENTAMETER, the RHYME SCHEME and structure of which can vary. There are two predominant types

of sonnets: the English or Shakespearean, which consists of three QUATRAINS and a final COUPLET, usually with a rhyme scheme of ABAB CDCD EFEF GG; and the Italian or Petrarchan sonnet, often with an initial OCTAVE rhyming ABBA ABBA and a concluding SESTET rhyming CDECDE. However, it is important to keep in mind that sonnet rhyme schemes can be very different from the above.

spondee   A metrical FOOT comprised of two hard stresses.

sprung rhythm   Lines or STANZAS made up of a preset number of hard syllabic stresses but any number of soft stresses; the effect is a rhythmic irregularity.

stanza   A group of lines of poetry.

stress   The emphasis when reading a poem accorded to a syllable.

strophe   A STANZA, or VERSE paragraph in a prose poem, derived from classical Greek drama.

syllabic verse   Poetry that employs a set number of syllables in a line, regardless of STRESS.

symbol   A figure of speech that means what it says literally but also connotes a secondary meaning or meanings, and which usually conveys a concept, motif, or idea.

synecdoche   A figure of speech in which a part of something is meant to signify the entirety of the thing, such as a hand that is meant to suggest a sailor whose hands are used in sailing a ship (as in "all hands on deck"). See METONYMY.

synesthesia   The mingling or substitution of the senses, such as when talking about a sound by mentioning a color.

tanka   A Japanese VERSE form consisting of five lines, with the first and third line each containing five syllables and the rest of the lines each containing seven.

tercet   A three-line STANZA grouping.

terza rima   Poetry comprised of TERCETS and an interlocking RHYME SCHEME: ABA, BCB, CDC, etc.

tetrameter   A VERSE line of four metrical FEET.

tone   A poet's manifest attitude toward the subject expressed in the poem.

trimeter   A VERSE line of three metrical FEET.

trochee   A metrical FOOT consisting of a hard STRESS followed by a soft stress.

trope   A figurative or rhetorical mechanism, and at times a motif.

verse   A line of poetry or at times a synonym for *poetry* or *poem*.

vers libre   FREE VERSE.

villanelle   A 19-line poem made up of six STAN-ZAS—five TERCETS and a final QUATRAIN—with the first tercet employing an ABA RHYME SCHEME that is then replicated in the following tercets as well as in the final two lines of the quatrain. In addi-tion, the first and third lines are repeated in lines 6, 12, and 18, and 9, 15, and 19, respectively. The poem's first and third lines, and their subsequent iterations, carry a special thematic weight, and the poem's motifs are brought together in the conclud-ing quatrain.

voice   Not unlike the poem's PERSONA, a sense of a personality or speaker's diction, point of view or attitude in a poem; voice can also simply refer to a poem's speaker.

APPENDIX II

SELECTED BIBLIOGRAPHY

Arp, Thomas R., and Greg Johnson. *Perrine's Sound and Sense: An Introduction to Poetry.* 10th ed. New York: Harcourt College, 2001.

Ashfield, Andrew, ed. *Romantic Women Poets, 1770–1838.* New York: St. Martin's Press, 1997.

Baines, Paul. *The Complete Critical Guide to Alexander Pope.* New York: Routledge, 2000.

Beilin, Elaine. *Redeeming Eve: Women Writers of the English Renaissance.* Princeton, N.J.: Princeton University Press, 1987.

Bermingham, Ann, and John Brewer, eds. *The Consumption of Culture 1600–1800.* London: Routledge, 1997.

A Biographical Dictionary of English Women Writers 1580–1720. Edited by Maureen Bell, George Parfitt, and Simon Shepherd. New York: Harvester Wheatsheaf, 1990.

The Bloomsbury Guide to English Literature. 2nd ed. Edited by Marion Wynne-Davies. London: Bloomsbury, 1995.

Brooks, Cleanth. *Historical Evidence and the Reading of Seventeenth-Century Poetry.* Columbia: University of Missouri Press, 1991.

Bush, Douglas. *The Renaissance and English Humanism.* Toronto: University of Toronto Press, 1972.

The Cambridge Companion to John Dryden. Edited by Steven Zwicker. New York: Cambridge University Press, 2004.

The Cambridge Companion to Virgil. Edited by Charles Martindale. New York: Cambridge University Press, 1997.

The Cambridge Guide to English Literature. Compiled by Michael Stapleton. New York: Cambridge University Press, 1983.

The Cambridge Guide to Women's Writing in English. Edited by Lorna Sage, with Germaine Greer and Elaine Showalter. Cambridge: Cambridge University Press, 1999.

A Companion to Early Modern Women's Writing. Edited by Anita Pacheco. Oxford: Blackwell, 2002.

Christmas, William, ed. *Eighteenth-Century English Labouring-Class Poets.* London: Pickering & Chatto, 2003.

Cook, Elizabeth. *Seeing through Words: The Scope of Late Renaissance Poetry.* New Haven, Conn.: Yale University Press, 1986.

Corns, Thomas N., ed. *The Cambridge Companion to English Poetry: Donne to Marvell.* Cambridge: Cambridge University Press, 1993.

Daughton, M. J. *Progress and Poverty: An Economic and Social History of Britain 1700–1850.* New York: Oxford University Press, 1995.

Dubrow, Heather. *Echoes of Desire: English Petrarchism and Its Counterdiscourses.* Ithaca, N.Y.: Cornell University Press, 1995.

Eger, Elizabeth et al., eds. *Bluestocking Feminism: Writings of the Bluestocking Circle, 1738–1785.* London: Pickering & Chatto, 1999.

Ezell, Margaret J. M. *Writing Women's Literary History.* Baltimore: Johns Hopkins University Press, 1993.

Faderman, Lillian. *Surpassing the Love of Men: Romantic Friendship and Love between Women from the*

Renaissance to the Present. New York: William Morrow, 1981.

Ferguson, Moira. *First Feminists: British Women Writers: 1578–1799.* Bloomington: University of Indiana Press, 1985.

Ferry, Anne. *All in War with Time: Love Poetry of Shakespeare, Donne, Jonson, Marvell.* Cambridge, Mass.: Harvard University Press, 1975.

Firth, Charles H. *The Last Years of the Protectorate, 1656–1658.* 2 vols. New York: Russell & Russell, 1964.

Fox, Christopher. *Locke and the Scriblerians: Identity and Consciousness in Early Eighteenth-Century Britain.* Berkeley: University of California Press, 1988.

Fowler, David. *A Literary History of the Popular Ballad.* Durham, N.C.: Duke University Press, 1968.

Fraistart, Neil, Steven E. Jones, and Carl Stahmer, eds. *Romantic Circles.* Available online. URL: http://www.rc.umd.edu/. Downloaded on May 17, 2006.

Frye, Roland Mushat. *Perspective on Man: Literature and the Christian Tradition.* Philadelphia: Westminster Press, 1961.

George, M. Dorothy. *English Political Caricature: A Study of Opinion and Propaganda.* New York: Oxford University Press, 1959.

Gilbert, Sandra M., and Susan Gubar, eds. *The Norton Anthology of Literature by Women: The Traditions in English.* 2nd ed. New York: W. W. Norton, 1996.

Guibbory, Aschah. *Ceremony and Community from Herbert to Milton: Literature, Religion and Cultural Conflict in Seventeenth-Century England.* Cambridge: Cambridge University Press, 1998.

Harp, Richard, and Stanley Stewart, eds. *The Cambridge Companion to Ben Jonson.* New York: Cambridge University Press, 2000.

Haslett, Moyra. *Pope to Burney, 1714–1779: Scriblerians to Bluestockings.* New York: Palgrave Macmillan, 2003.

Healy, Thomas, and Jonathan Sawday, eds. *Literature and the English Civil War.* Cambridge: Cambridge University Press, 1990.

Herford, C. H., and Simpson, Percy and Evelyn. *Ben Jonson.* 11 vols. Oxford: Clarendon Press, 1954–1970.

Hill, Christopher. *God's Englishman; Oliver Cromwell and the English Revolution.* New York: Harper & Row, 1972.

———. *Intellectual Origins of the English Revolution.* New York: Oxford University Press, 1980.

Holmes, Geoffrey S. *Augustan England: Professions, State and Society, 1680–1730.* Boston: G. Allen & Unwin, 1982.

———. *The Professions and Social Change in England, 1680–1730.* London: British Academy, 1979.

Holmes, Geoffrey S., and Daniel Azechi. *The Age of Oligarchy: Pre-Industrial Britain, 1772–1783.* New York: Longman, 1993.

Hudson, Nicholas. "From 'Nation' to 'Race': The Origin of Racial Classification in Eighteenth-Century Thought." *Eighteenth Century Studies* 29 (1996): 247–264.

Index of Dedications and Commendatory Verses in English Books Before 1641. Edited by Franklin B. Williams. London: Bibliographical Society, 1962.

Knoppers, Laura Lunger. *Constructing Cromwell: Ceremony, Portrait, and Print 1645–1661.* Cambridge: Cambridge University Press, 2000.

Krontiris, Tina. *Oppositional Voices: Women as Writers and Translators of Literature in the English Renaissance.* London: Routledge, 1992.

Landry, Donna. *The Muses of Resistance: Laboring-Class Women's Poetry in Britain: 1739–1796.* Cambridge: Cambridge University Press, 1990.

Lewalski, Barbara K. "Primary Texts and Manuscripts." In *The Life of John Milton: A Critical Biography,* 711–735. Oxford: Blackwell, 2000.

———. *Writing Women in Jacobean England.* Cambridge, Mass.: Harvard University Press, 1993.

Lewis, Peter, and Nigel Wood, eds. *John Gay and the Scriblerians.* New York: Palgrave Macmillan, 1988.

Literature and the English Civil War. Edited by Thomas Healy and Jonathan Sawday. Cambridge: Cambridge University Press, 1990.

Lonsdale, Roger, ed. *Eighteenth Century Women Poets.* New York: Oxford University Press, 1989.

Maclean, Gerald, ed. *Culture and Society in the Stuart Restoration.* Cambridge: Cambridge University Press, 1995.

Maclean, Gerald M. *Time's Witness: Historical Representation in English Poetry, 1603–1660.* Madison: University of Wisconsin Press, 1990.

Manley, Lawrence. *Literature and Culture in Early Modern London.* Cambridge: Cambridge University Press, 1995.

Marcus, Leah S. *The Politics of Mirth: Jonson, Herrick, Milton, Marvell, and the Defense of Old Holiday Pastimes.* Chicago: University of Chicago Press, 1986.

Martz, Louis L. *The Paradise Within.* New Haven, Conn.: Yale University Press, 1964.

———. *The Poetry of Meditation.* New Haven, Conn.: Yale University Press, 1954.

Mellor, Anne K. *Mothers of the Nation: Women's Political Writing in England, 1780–1830.* Bloomington: Indiana University Press, 2000.

Miner, Earl. *The Metaphysical Mode from Donne to Cowley.* Princeton, N.J.: Princeton University Press, 1969.

Nevo, Ruth. *The Dial of Virtue: A Study of Poems on Affairs of State in the Seventeenth Century.* Princeton, N.J.: Princeton University Press, 1963.

Pascoe, Judith. *Romantic Theatricality: Gender, Poetry, and Spectatorship.* Ithaca, N.Y.: 1997.

Peterson, Richard S. *Imitation and Praise in the Poems of Ben Jonson.* New Haven, Conn., and London: Yale University Press, 1981.

Pigman, G. W. *Grief and English Renaissance Elegy.* Cambridge: Cambridge University Press, 1985.

Quintano, Ricardo, and Alvin Whitley, eds. *English Poetry of the Mid and Late Eighteenth Century: An Historical Anthology.* Westport, Conn.: Greenwood Press, 1979.

Rawson, J. *Order from Confusion Sprung: Studies in Eighteenth-Century Literature from Swift to Cowper.* Boston: Allen & Unwin, 1985.

Rogers, Pat. *Literature and Popular Culture in Eighteenth Century England.* Totowa, N.J.: Barnes & Noble, 1985.

Saintsbury, George, ed. *Minor Poets of the Caroline Period.* Oxford: Clarendon Press, 1905.

Schofield, Mary Anne. *Masking and Unmasking the Female Mind: Disguising Romances in Feminine Fiction, 1713–1799.* Newark: University of Delaware Press, 1990.

Scodel, Joshua. *The English Poetic Epitaph: Commemoration and Conflict from Jonson to Wordsworth.* Ithaca, N.Y.: Cornell University Press, 1991.

Shafer, Robert. *The English Ode to 1660.* Princeton, N.J.: Princeton University Press, 1918.

Sharpe, Kevin, and Peter Lake, eds. *Culture and Politics in Early Stuart England.* Stanford, Calif.: Stanford University Press, 1993.

Sharpe, Kevin, and Steven N. Zwicker, eds. *Politics of Discourse: The Literature and History of Seventeenth-Century England.* Berkeley: University of California Press, 1987.

Shattock, Joanne. *The Oxford Guide to British Women Writers.* New York: Oxford University Press, 1993.

Smith, Hilda L. *Reason's Disciples: Seventeenth-Century English Feminists.* Urbana: University of Illinois Press, 1982.

Smith, Nigel. *Literature and Revolution in England, 1640–1660.* New Haven, Conn.: Yale University Press, 1994.

———. *Perfection Proclaimed: Language and Literature in English Radical Religion, 1640–1660.* Oxford: Clarendon Press, 1989.

Snider, Alvin. *Origin and Authority in Seventeenth-Century England: Bacon, Milton, Butler.* Toronto: University of Toronto Press, 1994.

Staves, Susan. *Married Women's Separate Property, 1660–1832.* Cambridge, Mass.: Harvard University Press, 1990.

Strachan, John, ed. *British Satire, 1785–1840.* London: Pickering & Chatto, 2003.

Stevenson, Kay Gilliland. *Milton to Pope, 1650–1720.* Hampshire, N.Y.: Palgrave, 2001.

Survey of British Poetry: Cavalier to Restoration. Vol. 2. Edited by Editorial Board, Roth Publishing. Great Neck, N.Y.: Poetry Anthology Press, 1989.

Swinburne, Algernon Charles. *A Study of Ben Jonson.* Edited by Howard B. Norland. Lincoln: University of Nebraska Press, 1969.

Tillyard, E. M. W. *The Elizabethan World Picture.* London: Chatto & Windus, 1943.

Turner, James. *The Politics of Landscape: Rural Scenery and Society in English Poetry, 1630–1660.* Cambridge, Mass.: Harvard University Press, 1979.

Uphaus, Robert W., and Gretchen M. Foster, eds. *The "Other" Eighteenth Century: English Women of Letters 1660–1800.* East Lansing, Mich.: Colleagues Press, 1991.

Varney, Andrew. *Eighteenth-Century Writers in Their World: A Mighty Maze.* New York: St. Martin's Press, 1999.

Webber, Joan. *The Eloquent "I": Style and Self in Seventeenth Century Prose.* Madison: University of Wisconsin Press, 1968.

Ward, Thomas Humphry. *The English Poets: Selections with Critical Introductions by Various Writers and a General Introduction by Matthew Arnold.* Vol. 2. New York: Macmillan, 1912.

Women, Writing, and the Public Sphere: 1700–1830. Edited by Elizabeth Eger et al. New York: Cambridge University Press, 2001.

Zwicker, Steven N. *Lines of Authority: Politics and English Literary Culture, 1649–1689.* Ithaca, N.Y.: Cornell University Press, 1993.

INDEX

Note: **Boldface** page numbers indicate major treatment of a topic.

A

Abercrombie, Charles 173
Absalom and Achitophel (Dryden) vii, **1–4**, 129, 261, 318, 409
acatalectic line 60
Ackroyd, Peter 67
"Adam Posed" (Finch) **4–5**, 176
Addison, Joseph 79, 157, 273, 325, 326, 388
Address to the Opposers of the Repeal of the Corporation and Test Acts, An (Barbauld) 31
"Aella" (Chatterton) **5–6**, 67
Aeneid (Virgil) 103, 335, 449–450, 462
"Affliction (1)" (Herbert) **6–7**, 20, 206
"Against Them Who Lay Unchastity to the Sex of Women" (Habington) **7–8**, 202
Aglaura, An Account of Religion by Reason (Suckling) 385, 459
Aikin, Anna Laetitia. *See* Barbauld, Anna Laetitia Aikin
"Air and Angels" (Donne) **8–9**, 118, 154, 439
Alabaster, William **9–11**
   The Divine Meditations 10, 11, **115–116**, 375, 376, 377
   and Donne (John) 214
   Sonnet 10 10, 115, **375–376**
   Sonnet 15 10, 116, **376–377**
   Sonnet 46 10, 116, **377–378**
   Sonnet 54 116, 318
Albina (Cowley) 88
Alchemist, The (Jonson) 241, 378, 465

Alexander, Sir William **11**
   Aurora 11, **25–27**, 127
   The Tragedy of Darius 11, 14, **420–421**
"Alexander's Feast; Or the Power of Music" (Dryden) **11–13**, 131, 232, 369
alexandrine 105–106, 125, 410, 449
Algarotti, Francesco 274
allegory 13. *See also* figurative language
All for Love (Dryden) 121, 129
alliteration **13–14**
All the Works of Epictetus (Carter) 56
"Altar, The" (Herbert) vii, **14–15**, 78, 206, 213, 255, 268, 359
"Ambition" (Astell) vii, **15–16**, 23
Anacreon 235
anapestic foot 268, 269
Anatomy of Melancholy, The (Burton) 229, 248, 339, 340
"Anatomy of the World, An" (Donne) **16–17**, 118
Anne (queen of Great Britain)
   Boyd (Elizabeth) on 40
   and Finch (Anne) 176
   and Gay (John) 188, 189
   Pope (Alexander) on 325, 461, 462
   and Prior (Matthew) 329
   Swift (Jonathan) on 105, 388–389
Annus Mirabilis: The Year of Wonders, 1666 (Dryden) vii, **17–19**, 129, 154, 194, 318
"Answer, The" (Finch) **19–20**, 176
answer poems 242
anthimeria 260

antistrophe 323–324, 407
antithesis **20–21**
"Apollo Outwitted" (Swift) 176
"Apology, The" (Finch) **21**, 176
Apology for Poetry (Sidney) 78, 119, 207, 240, 242–243
apostrophe 33, 100, 174, 289, 386, 387, 391, 396
apothegm 57
Apparatus in Revelationeum Iesu Christi (Alabaster) 10
"Apparition, The" (Donne) **21–22**, 118
"Araminata" (Gay) 189, 274
Arbuthnot, John 132, 156–158, 176, 189, 325, 326, 329, 389, 395, 444
Arcadia (Sidney) 154, 207, 466
Areopagitica (Milton) 270, 308
"Argument of His Book, The" (Herrick) 208
Aristotle 22, 74, 119, 316, 407, 432
Arminianism 14, 182, 213, 255
Arnall, William 133
Arne, Thomas 353
Arnold, W. T. 45
Art of Poetry (Horace) 162, 241
Ashton, Thomas 198
Askewe, Anne 28
"Ask Me No More Where Jove Bestows" (Carew) **22–23**, 55
assonance 14, 200, 260, 290, 292, 305, 319, 379, 399, 414, 464
Astell, Mary **23–24**
   "Ambition" vii, **15–16**, 23
   and Chudleigh (Lady Mary) 68, 69
   and Montagu (Lady Mary Wortley) 23, 273, 274
   and Philips (Katherine) 23, 320

Astraea Redux (Dryden) 128
Astrophil and Stella (Sidney) 127, 154, 242
"At the round earth's imagin'd corners blow" (Donne) **24–25**
aubade **25**, 40, 99, 289, 321–322
Aubrey, John 57, 385, 442
Aurora (Alexander) 11, **25–27**, 127
Austen, Jane 91
"Autumn" (Thomson) 220, 223, 395

B

Bacon, Sir Francis 205, 315
Baillie, Joanna 31, 56
Baillie, Lady Grisell 29
ballad **28–29**, 122, 260
   by Burns (Robert) 48, 238, 367
   by Chatterton (Thomas) 5–6
   by Collins (William) 369
   complaint in 75
   by Cowper (William) 282
   by Gay (John) 370, 371
   by Lovelace (Richard) 29
   by Suckling (Sir John) 28–30, 459
"Ballad from Newgate" (Askewe) 28
"Ballad upon a Wedding, A" (Suckling) 28–29, **29–30**, 385
Barash, Carol 184
Barbauld, Anna Laetitia Aikin **30–31**
   "The Rights of Women" 31, **347–349**
   "To the Poor" **415–416**
   "Washing-Day" 31, **453–455**
Barber, Jonathan 32

Barber, Mary **32**
   "Written for My Son" vii, 32,
      464–465
Barish, J. A. 292
Barons' Wars, The (Drayton) 124
Barry, Elizabeth 310, 352
Bassano, Baptista 250
"Batter My Heart" (Donne)
   32–34, 60, 78, 118, 144, 175,
   197, 269, 437
Battle of Agincourt, The (Drayton)
   125
"Battle of Blenheim, The"
   (Southey) 29
"Battle of the Summer Islands,
   The" (Waller) 36
Beachy Head; With Other Poems
   (Smith) 366
Beaumont, Francis 242, 357,
   378, 410–411, 423
Beggar's Opera, The (Gay) vii,
   122, 188, 189–190, **370–371**
Behn, Aphra vii, **34–35**
   "The Disappointment" 35,
      112–113
   "The Dream" 35, 112,
      126–127
   Finch (Anne) on 70, 71
   "Love Armed" 35, **256–257**
   "On Her Loving Two Equally"
      35, **296–297**
   "On the Death of Waller" 35,
      306–307
   and Otway (Thomas) 310
   and Philips (Katherine) 320
   "To the Fair Clarinda" 35,
      406
   "The Willing Mistress" 35,
      459–460
Belle's Strategem, The (Cowley) 88
Bennett, Sir William 394, 395
Bentley, Richard 199
Bergman, David 310
"Bermudas" (Marvell) **36–37**,
   267
Bernini, Gian Lorenzo 177
"Better Answer, A" (Prior)
   37–38, 329
Biathanatos (Donne) 117
Bickley, Francis 329
Blake, William 229
blank verse **38**
   by Collins (William) 74
   by Cowper (William) 89–90,
      92, 384
   by Denham (Sir John) 102
   by Dryden (John) 120,
      121, 129
   by Gay (John) 188
   by Jonson (Ben) 38
   by Marvell (Andrew) 300
   by Milton (John) 38
   by Otway (Thomas) 310
   by Smart (Christopher) 38
   by Smith (Charlotte) 366
   by Thomson (James) 38
Blount, Martha 158, 159

Bodenham, John 154
Boeckel, Bruce 79, 80, 82, 83
Bolingbroke, Henry St. John,
   viscount of 164, 165
Bonny Barbara Allan (ballad) 29,
   38–39
Borough, The (Crabbe) 90
Boswell, James 239, 358, 359
Boulter, Hugh 157
Boyd, Elizabeth **39–40**
   "On the Death of an Infant
      of Five Days Old" vii, 40,
      304–305
brachycatalectic line 60
Bradstreet, Anne 169
"Break of Day" (Donne) 25,
   40–41, 118
Brecht, Bertolt viii, 190, 371
Breton, Nicholas **41–42**
   "Come Little Babe" 41,
      74–75, 349
breve 269
"Bride-Woman's Counselor, The"
   (Sprint) 246
Britannia's Pastoral (Browne)
   42–45, 45, 46, 172
Britten, Benjamin viii, 279, 364
broadside 28, 29, **45**, 282, 355
Broken Heart, The (Ford) 51, 318
Brome, Richard 291, 378, 423
Brooks, Cleanth 53
Broome, William 326
Brown, Eric C. 259
Browne, William **45–46**
   Britannia's Pastoral **42–45**,
      45, 46
   "Fairest, When by the Rules"
      45, **172**
   in Tribe of Ben 46, 242, 423
Browning, Elizabeth 366
Browning, Robert 364, 372
Bruce, Donald 57, 72, 103
Buckingham, George Villiers,
   duke of 1, 49, 129, 352, 440
Bullen, A. H. 41, 74
"Bunch of Grapes, The" (Herbert)
   46–47, 206
Bunyan, John 13, 356
"Burial of an Infant, The"
   (Vaughan) **47–48**, 442
Burke, Edmund 90, 239
"Burney sequence, The"
   (Traherne) 298
Burns, Robert vii, **48–49**
   and Fergusson (Robert) 95,
      97, 174
   "John Anderson, My Jo" 48,
      238
   and Smith (Charlotte) 365
   "Song—For A' That and A'
      That" 48, **367–368**
   "To a Mouse" 48, **397–398**
Burton, Robert 229, 248, 339,
   340
Busby, Richard 128
Busnello, Giovanni Francesco
   266

Butler, Samuel **49–50**
   on Davenant (Sir William)
      97–98
   Hudibras 49–50, **217–219**,
      434
   "Upon the Weakness and
      Misery of Man" **434–435**
Byrne, Paula 351, 414
Byron, George Gordon Byron 54,
   90, 145, 310

C

Cadenus and Vanessa (Swift) 389
Caesar, Sir Julius 223
"Calantha's Dirge" (Ford) **51–52**,
   120, 182, 319
Caldwell, Tanya 103
Camden, William 235, 240, 302,
   419–420
Campion, Thomas, *Observations
   in the Art of English Poesie* 288
"Candlemas Eve" (Herrick) 14
"Canonization, The" (Donne)
   52–54, 118, 268
Cantenac, Jean Benech de 112
canto **54**
"Careless Good Fellow, The"
   (Oldham) 409
Carew, Thomas **54–55**, 60
   "Ask Me No More Where
      Jove Bestows" **22–23**, 55
   "Celia Singing" 55, **63–64**
   "A Cruel Mistress" 55, **93–94**
   "Disdaine Returned" 55,
      114–115
   "An Elegy upon the Death of
      the Dean of Paul's" 55, 60,
      141, **143–144**
   "Epitaph on the Lady Mary
      Villers" 55, **161–162**
   and Lovelace (Richard) 373
   "A Rapture" 55, **338–339**
   in Tribe of Ben 54, 242, 258,
      378, 423, 452
Carmina (Horace) 101
carpe diem poetry **55**, 60
   by Carew (Thomas) 93, 114,
      338, 339
   in *Comus* (Milton) 77
   by Drummond (William) 392
   by Herrick (Robert) 55,
      83–85, 399, 418
   by Horace 55, 84, 418, 419
   by Marvell (Andrew) 55,
      399
   by Pope (Alexander) 337
   by Suckling (Sir John) 311
   by Waller (Edmund) 55, 191
Carter, Elizabeth **55–56**
Cartwright, William **56–57**
   "On a Virtuous Young
      Gentlewoman That Died
      Suddenly" 57, 141, **295**
   "On His Majesty's Recovery
      from the Small-Pox" 57,
      297–298

   in Tribe of Ben 56, 242, 423
   Vaughan (Henry) on 442
Cary, Elizabeth 57, 123, 426
Cary, Patrick **57–58**
Cary, Phoebe 458
Cary, Sir Lucius 58, 242, 406–
   407, 423
Caryll, John 335, 336
*Case of King Charles I Truly Stated,
   The* (Butler) 49
Castara (Habington) 7, 202
"Castaway, The" (Cowper)
   58–60, 89
"Castle, The" (Thomson) 395
catachresis **60**, 67–68, 72, 138,
   159, 260, 268
catalexis **60**
Catherine Henrietta of Braganza
   (queen of England) 1
Catullus 399
Cavalier poets vi, **60–61**. *See also*
   carpe diem poetry
   Alexander (Sir William) as
      11, 26
   Carew (Thomas) as 22, 23,
      54, 60, 63, 93, 114, 143
   complaints by 75
   conceit used by 78
   Donne (John) on 179
   Herbert (George) on 243,
      451
   Lovelace (Richard) as 60, 75,
      258, 396
   Marvell (Andrew) as 25
   Suckling (Sir John) as 60,
      75, 235, 258, 311, 385,
      386, 459
   synechdoche used by 175
   Waller (Edmund) as 60,
      75, 191
Cave, Edward 55, 239
Cavendish, Margaret viii, **61–63**
   and Astell (Mary) 23
   and Cowley (Abraham) 87
   "An Excuse for So Much
      Writ upon My Verses" 62,
      169–170
   "The Hunting of the Hare"
      62, **219–220**
   and Killigrew (Anne) 433
   and Philips (Katherine) 320
   "The Reason Why the
      Thoughts Are Only in the
      Head" **339–340**
   on Wroth (Lady Mary) 466
Cavendish, William 61, 62, 63
Cefalu, Paul 214–215
"Celia Singing: Harke How My
   Celia" (Carew) 55, **63–64**
Centuries of Meditations (Traherne)
   422, 423
Chamberlain, John 10
Chamberlayne, William **64**
Chapman, George 43, **64–65**,
   124, 151, 378
Charles, Amy 206

Charles I (king of England). *See also* Cavalier poets
and Alexander (Sir William) 11
Butler (Samuel) on 49
and Carew (Thomas) 54, 114
Cartwright (William) on 57, 297–298
and Cleveland (John) 72, 87, 102
and Cowley (Abraham) 72, 87, 102
and Crashaw (Richard) 72, 87, 102
and Denham (Sir John) 72, 78–83, 102–104
and Donne (John) 118
drama and poetry under 119, 346
and Hall (John) 203
and Herbert (Edward) 203
Jonson (Ben) on 291
and Lovelace (Richard) 257
Marvell (Andrew) on 215, 216, 265, 287
Milton (John) on 270
Pope (Alexander) on 462
taxation by 80, 82, 128
Vaughan (Henry) on 442
Charles II (king of England) 346. *See also* Restoration
and Behn (Aphra) 34, 35, 459
and Butler (Samuel) 49
and Davenant (Sir William) 98
and Denham (Sir John) 103
Dryden (John) on 1–2, 18–19, 128, 129, 130, 209, 261
and Herrick (Robert) 208
and Killigrew (Anne) 244
and Marvell (Andrew) 266
and Milton (John) 271
poetry and drama under 120, 346
and Rochester (John Wilmot) 351, 352
Royal Society formed by 18
and Sedley (Sir Charles) 321, 357
Waller (Edmund) on 306, 452
Chartism 416
Chaste Maid in Cheapside, A (Middleton) 120
Chatterton, Thomas **65–67**
"Aella" **5–6**, 67
Chaucer, Geoffrey 163, 180, 207, 324, 369
Cherbury, Lord Herbert of. *See* Herbert, Edward
"Christ's Triumph after Death" (Fletcher) 67, 180
"Christ's Triumph over Death" (Fletcher) 67, 180

"Christ's Victory in Heaven" (Fletcher) **67–68**, 180
"Christ's Victory on Earth" (Fletcher) 67, 180
Chudleigh, Lady Mary **68–69**
The Ladies Defence 69, **246–248**, 269
and Philips (Katherine) 68–69, 320
"To the Ladies" 69, 75, **408**
"Church, The" (Herbert) 99, 206, 255
"Church-militant, The" (Herbert) 206
"Church Monuments" (Herbert) **69–70**, 206
"Church-porch, The" (Herbert) 205–206
Cibber, Colley 132, 133, 134, 157, 189, 253, 326, 445
"Circuit of Apollo, The" (Finch) 34, **70–71**, 176, 411
Civic Sermons to the People (Barbauld) 31
Civil War (1642–1651) 79, 85, 87, 103, 208, 346
Clarissa (Richardson) 56
Clarke, Jeremiah 11
Claudian 300
Cleland, John 274
Cleland, William 132
Cleveland, John **71–72**
and Cowley (Abraham) 87
and Denham (Sir John) 102
"Upon the Death of Mr. King" 72, 174, **431–432**
Clifford, Anne 250, 251
Clifford, Sir Thomas 266
Coelum Britannicum (Carew) 54–55
Coffin, C. M. 227
Coleridge, Samuel Taylor 29, 66–67, 350, 351, 359, 365, 414–415
"Collar, The" (Herbert) **72–73**, 175, 206
Collins, William **73–74**
"How Sleep the Brave" 74, **216–217**
"Ode to Evening" 74, **289–290**
"A Song from Shakespeare's *Cymbeline*" 74, **369–370**
on Thomson (James) 396
Colrane, John Hare, baron of 403, 404
"Come Little Babe" (Breton) 41, **74–75**, 349
complaint 75, 111, 283
Comus (Milton) **76–78**, 270, 305
conceit 78
Congreve, William 121, 130, 131, 155, 325, 385, 389
consonance 14, 200, 260, 290, 305, 319, 379
"Constancy" (Suckling). *See* "Out upon It!" (Suckling)

continuous form 183
Convent of Pleasure, The (Cavendish) 62
Cooper's Hill (Denham) 44, **78–83**, 102–104, 136, 147, 310, 427, 462
Copernican theory of universe 228
"Corinna's Going a Maying" (Herrick) **83–85**, 208, 419
Corneille, Pierre 320
"Corruption" (Vaughan) **85–86**, 442
"Cotswold Eclogue" (Randolph) **86–87**, 334
Cotterell, Sir Charles 320
Countess of Montgomery's Urania, The (Wroth) 234, 256, 279, 280, 312, 387, 458, 466
country house poem 107–108, 186, 250, 426–427
Country Wife, The (Wycherley) 121
couplet 183
Cowley, Abraham 72, **87–88**
and Crashaw (Richard) 87, 91
and Davenant (Sir William) 98
and Denham (Sir John) 102
"Hymn to Light" 25, 88
and Marvell (Andrew) 101, 111, 186
"The Muse" 60
on Philips (Katherine) 320
and Pope (Alexander) 87, 325, 462
"The Spring" 88, **381–382**
Cowley, Hannah Parkhouse **88–89**
"Departed Youth" 88–89, **104–105**
Cowper, William **89–90**
"The Castaway" **58–60**, 89
and Crabbe (George) 91
"Crazy Kate" 89, **92–93**
"A Landscape Described. Rural Sounds" 89, **249–250**
on Leapor (Mary) 253
"Light Shining out of Darkness" 89, **254–255**
"The Negro's Complaint" 75, 89, **282–283**
and Smith (Charlotte) 366
"The Stricken Deer" 89, **384**
and Thomson (James) 220
Crabbe, George **90–91**
"The Village" 90, 91, **446–448**
"Cradle Song, A" (Breton). *See* "Come Little Babe" (Breton)
Crashaw, Richard 72, **91–92**
and Cary (Patrick) 58
and Cowley (Abraham) 87, 91
and Denham (Sir John) 102

"Description of a Religious House" 91, **106–107**, 229
"The Flaming Heart upon the Book and Pictures of the Seraphical Saint Teresa" 92, **177–179**
on Herbert (George) 78
"I Am the Door" 92, **228–229**
"In the Holy Nativity of our Lord God" 20, 92, **232–234**
"On the Wounds of Our Crucified Lord" 92, **308–310**
Crawford, Charles 42
"Crazy Kate" (Cowper) 89, **92–93**
Cromwell, Oliver 346
and Cleveland (John) 71, 72
and Davenant (Sir William) 98
Dryden (John) on 128
Marvell (Andrew) on 215–216, 266, 267, 287
Milton (John) on 271, 307
and poetry and drama 120, 194, 346
Waller (Edmund) on 306, 452
Cromwell, Richard 346
Cromwell, Thomas 125
"Crown of Sonnets Dedicated to Love, A" (Wroth) 234
"Cruel Mistress, A" (Carew) 55, **93–94**
"Crumble Hall" (Leapor) 253
Curll, Edmund 157, 444
Curry, Neil 364, 372, 373
Cymbeline (Shakespeare) 369, 370
Cynthia's Revels (Jonson) 240, 299, 333, 362, 363
Cypresse Grove, The (Drummond) 127

D

dactylic foot 268, 269
dactylic rhyme 347
"Daft Days, The" (Fergusson) **95–97**, 173, 175, 397
"Damon the Mower" (Marvell) 267, 275, 276
"Dampe, The" (Donne) 143
"Dance, The" (Suckling) **97**, 385
Daniel, Samuel 124, 207, 288
Dante Alighieri 145, 269, 450
Danvers, Sir John 204–205
Darby, Mary. *See* Robinson, Mary
Darwin, Erasmus 358
Davenant, Sir William **97–99**
and Carew (Thomas) 54
Gondibert 98, 99, **194–195**
and Milton (John) 98, 271
Vaughan (Henry) on 442
Davideis (Cowley) 87

Davies, Sir John 194
Day, Malcolm 423, 464
"Death" (Herbert) 70, **99**, 206, 255, 396
"Death Be Not Proud" (Donne) **99–101**, 118
Defence of Rhyme, A (Daniel) 288
Defense of Poesy (Sidney). See *Apology for Poetry* (Sidney)
"Definition of Love, The" (Marvell) **101–102**, 186, 267, 311
"Dejection: An Ode" (Coleridge) 414
Dekker, Thomas 182, 241, 362
"Delight in Disorder" (Herrick) **102**, 208, 311, 375
Democritus 440
Denham, Sir John 72, **102–104**
  Cooper's Hill 44, **78–83**, 102–104, 136, 147, 310, 427, 462
  and Davenant (Sir William) 98
  and Marvell (Andrew) 266, 427
  Pope (Alexander) on 103, 462
  and Traherne (Thomas) 464
Dennis, John 157, 158
"Departed Youth" (Cowley) 88–89, **104–105**
"Description of a City Shower, A" (Swift) **105–106**, 390
"Description of a Religious House" (Crashaw) 91, **106–107**, 229
"Description of Cooke-Ham, The" (Lanyer) **107–109**, 250, 251
"Description of Walla, The" (Browne) 43–44
Deserted Village, The (Goldsmith) **109–111**, 193
"Design, The" (Pope) 164–165
"Despair, The" (Cowley) 111
Devereux, Robert. See Essex, Robert Devereux, earl of
Devotions Upon Emergent Occasions (Donne) 118
"Dialogue Between the Soul and the Body, A" (Marvell) **111–112**, 267
Dialogues of the Dead (Prior) 329
Dictionary of the English Language, A (Johnson) 239
dimeter 268
Diodati, Charles 270
"Dirge, A" (Shirley) 14
"Disappointment, The" (Behn) 35, **112–113**
"Discipline" (Herbert) **113–114**, 206
"Disdaine Returned" (Carew) 55, **114–115**
Divine Meditations, The (Alabaster) 10, 11, **115–116**, 375, 376, 377

"Divine Poems" (Donne) 213, 214
Dobell sequence 422, 464
Dodsley, Robert 239
Donne, John vi, **116–119**
  "Air and Angels" **8–9**, 118, 154, 439
  "An Anatomy of the World" **16–17**, 118
  "The Apparition" **21–22**, 118
  "At the round earth's imagin'd corners blow" **24–25**
  "Batter My Heart" **32–34**, 60, 78, 118, 144, 175, 197, 269, 437
  "Break of Day" 25, **40–41**, 118
  "The Canonization" **52–54**, 118, 268
  and Carew (Thomas) 54, 143–144
  and Cary (Patrick) 58
  and Cavalier poetry 60
  and Cavendish (Margaret) 340
  and Crashaw (Richard) 309
  "Death Be Not Proud" **99–101**, 118
  "The Flea" 118, **179–180**, 198, 386
  and form 183
  "Go and Catch a Falling Star" 118, **191–193**
  "Good Friday" 118, **195–197**, 236
  "The Good-Morrow" 118, **197–198**
  and Herbert (Edward) 293
  and Herbert (George) 99, 204, 205, 264
  and Herbert (Mary Sidney) 207
  Holy Sonnets 8, 24, 32, 117, **213–215**, 227, 360
  "Hymn to God My God" **223–225**
  "A Hymn to God the Father" 118, **225–226**, 318
  "I Am a Little World Made Cunningly" 118, 175, 198, **227–228**
  "The Indifferent" 118, **231–232**
  and Jonson (Ben) 16, 117, 299, 398, 402
  and Marvell (Andrew) 101, 294
  "Since she whome I loved" **360–361**
  and Suckling (Sir John) 236
  "The Sun Rising" 25, 41, 118, 174, **386–387**
  "To His Mistress Going to Bed" 118, **400–402**
  and Traherne (Thomas) 464
  "The Undertaking" 118, **425–426**

"A Valediction Forbidding Mourning" 14, 52, 60, 78, 101, 118, **436–438**
"A Valediction: Of Weeping" 101, 118, **438–439**
  and Wroth (Lady Mary) 387, 466
"Do Not Go Gentle" (Thomas) 183
"Dooms-day" (Herbert) 99, 255
Draghi, Giovanni Baptista 368
drama and poetry **119–123**
dramatic irony 236
Drayton, Michael **123–126**
  on Alexander (Sir William) 25
  and Browne (William) 43, 45
  and Donne (John) 117
  and Drummond (William) 127
  Endimion and Phoebe 124, **151–153**
  in *England's Helicon* 154
  and Herbert (Mary Sidney) 207
  and Herrick (Robert) 208
  rime royal used by 349
  "Since there's no help" 124, **361–362**
"Dream, The" (Behn) 35, 112, **126–127**
"Dreams" (Herrick) 208
Drummond of Hawthornden, William **127–128**
  and Alexander (Sir William) 11
  and Fergusson (Robert) 173
  "For the Baptist" **182–183**
  and Jonson (Ben) 127, 240, 281, 378, 410
  "Phoebus Arise" 25, **321–322**
  "Then is she gone?" **391–392**
Drury, Sir Robert 16, 117
Dryden, John **128–131**
  Absalom and Achitophel vii, **1–4**, 129, 261, 318, 409
  "Alexander's Feast" **11–13**, 131, 232, 369
  Annus Mirabilis vii, **17–19**, 129, 154, 194, 318
  and Cartwright (William) 57
  Cavendish (Margaret) on 62–63
  and Chamberlayne (William) 64
  on Chudleigh (Lady Mary) 68
  on Cleveland (John) 72, 431
  on Cowley (Abraham) 87
  and Davenant (Sir William) 98, 194
  and Denham (Sir John) 78, 103
  Egerton (Sarah) on 140

"Epigram on Milton" 130, **154–155**
  heroic couplet used by 207
  The Hind and the Panther 13, 130, **209–211**, 328, 409
  and Killigrew (Anne) 130, 244–245, 403, 412–414, 434
  "MacFlecknoe" 130, 133, 236, **261–263**, 265, 273
  and Marvell (Andrew) 267, 301
  and Milton (John) 120, 129, 154–155
  on Otway (Thomas) 310
  on poetry 72, 121, 129
  and Pope (Alexander) 131, 163, 326
  and Prior (Matthew) 328
  and Randolph (Thomas) 334
  Religio Laici 130, 209, **343–344**
  and Rochester (John Wilmot) 129, 352
  "A Song for St. Cecilia's Day" 11, 130, **368–369**
  and Swift (Jonathan) 106
  "To the Memory of Mr. Oldham" 130, 294, **408–410**
  "To the Pious Memory of the Accomplish'd Young Lady Mrs. Anne Killigrew" 130, 141, 244–245, 409, **412–414**
  on Waller (Edmund) 306, 452
Duchess of Malfi, The (Webster) 38, 119
Dudley, Robert 123
Dunciad, The (Pope) **131–136**, 156, 157, 164, 326
Dunlap, Rhodes 143
Dutton, William 36, 266
Dyer, Hugh 136
Dyer, John **136–137**
  and Drayton (Michael) 125
  "Grongar Hill" 136, **199–201**

E

"Easter" (Herbert) **138**, 206
"Easter Wings" (Herbert) vii, **139–140**, 206, 359
Eastward Ho (Jonson, Marston and Chapman) 65, 241
eclogue. See pastoral poetry
Eclogues (Virgil) 42, 260, 449
"Eclogue to Master Jonson, An" (Randolph) 276
Edgeworth, Maria 31, 358
Edwards, Thomas 253
Egerton, Sarah Fyge **140–141**
  "The Emulation" **149–151**
  and Philips (Katherine) 320
  "The Repulse to Alcander" vii, **344–345**

Elegiac Sonnets, and Other Essays (Smith) 365, 366
elegy **141,** 260
"Elegy 19" (Donne). *See* "To His Mistress Going to Bed" (Donne)
"Elegy on Captain Cook" (Seward) 358
"Elegy on the Death of Mr. David Gregory" (Fergusson) 173
"Elegy on the Death of Scots Music" (Fergusson) 96
"Elegy over a Tomb" (Herbert) **141–142,** 204
"Elegy to the Memory of an Unfortunate Lady" (Pope) **142–143,** 325
"Elegy upon the Death of the Dean of Paul's, Dr. John Donne, An" (Carew) 55, 60, 141, **143–144**
"Elegy Written in a Country Churchyard" (Gray) 141, **144–147,** 199
"Elinoure and Juga" (Chatterton) 66
Eliot, T. S. 33, 118, 267, 268, 310, 324
Elisaeis (Alabaster) 9
elision **147**
Elizabethan sonnets 260, 375
    by Alabaster (William) 115
    by Browne (William) 172
    by Drayton (Michael) 361
    by Herrick (Robert) 375
    by Jonson (Ben) 378
    meter used by 268
    by Milton (John) 217, 375, 457
    by Smith (Charlotte) 328
Elizabeth I (queen of England)
    Alabaster (William) on 9
    and Drayton (Michael) 125
    Ford (John) on 51
    and Herbert (Mary Sidney) 206, 207, 330, 416–418
    Jonson (Ben) on 333, 362
    Pope (Alexander) on 462
"Eloisa to Aberlard" (Pope) 142, **147–149,** 325
"Emulation, The" (Egerton) **149–151**
Enclosure Acts 109
Endimion and Phoebe (Drayton) 124, **151–153**
end-stopped line **153,** 154, 196, 319, 362
England's Helicon 41, 125, **154**
enjambment 153, **154**
epic 260
Epicoene (Jonson) 102, 241, 383
Epicurus 351–352, 419
"Epigram on Milton" (Dryden) 130, **154–155**
"Epistle from Mrs. Yonge to Her Husband" (Montagu) 147, **155–156,** 274
Epistles (Ovid) 103

Epistle to a Doctor of Divinity from a Nobleman at Hampton Court (Hervey) 156
"Epistle to Artemisia. On Fame" (Leapor) 253
"Epistle to a Young Lady" (Pope). *See* "Epistle to Miss Blount" (Pope)
Epistle to Burlington (Pope) 164
"Epistle to Dr. Arbuthnot" (Pope) **156–158,** 325, 326
"Epistle to Miss Blount" (Pope) **158–160,** 325
"Epitaph, An" (Prior) 160, 329
"Epitaph on S.P., a Child of Queen Elizabeth's Chapel" (Jonson) **160–161,** 241
"Epitaph on the Lady Mary Villers" (Carew) 55, **161–162**
epode 324, 407
Essay of Dramatic Poesy (Dryden) 72, 121, 129
Essay on Criticism, An (Pope) 135, 157, **162–164,** 325, 347
Essay on Man, An (Pope) 20, 135, **164–167,** 207, 326, 347, 356, 461
Essays upon Several Subjects in Verse and Prose (Chudleigh) 69
Essex, Robert Devereux, earl of 9, 117
Etheredge, Sir George 357
Euripides 269
Eusden, Laurence 156
Euthymiae Raptus (Chapman) 64–65
"Eve's Apology in Defense of Women" (Lanyer) **167–169,** 251
Exclusion Crisis (1678–1681) 1
"Excuse for So Much Writ upon My Verses, An" (Cavendish) 62, **169–170**
"Eyam" (Seward) **170–171,** 358
eye rhyme 106, 115, 249, 347, 376, 399

F

Faerie Queene, The (Spenser) 13, 38, 42, 54, 67, 180, 286, 419, 426
"Fairest, When by the Rules" (Browne) 45, **172**
Fairfax, Thomas 427, 428
Fairfax, William 427
"Fan, The" (Gay) 188
Female Advocate, The (Egerton) 140, 141, 150
Female Page, The (Boyd) 39
"Female right to Literature, The" (Seward) 357
feminine rhyme 347
feminist critics
    on Barbauld (Anna Laetitia) 453, 455
    on Barber (Mary) 465

on Behn (Aphra) 35, 112, 113, 296, 406
    on Browne (William) 44
    on Cavendish (Margaret) 62, 169
    on Chudleigh (Lady Mary) 69, 75, 247
    on Donne (John) 22, 33, 179, 192, 226, 426, 439
    on Dryden (John) 413
    on Egerton (Sarah) 149–150
    on Finch (Anne) 21, 176, 183
    on Gay (John) 189
    on Goldsmith (Oliver) 458
    on Habington (William) 7
    on Herbert (Edward) 429
    on Herbert (Mary Sidney) 207
    on Killigrew (Anne) 75, 130, 412
    on Lanyer (Aemilia) 107–108, 168, 251
    on Leapor (Mary) 253
    on Marvell (Andrew) 187, 287
    on Milton (John) 314, 317
    on Montagu (Lady Mary Wortley) 155
    on Philips (Katherine) 306, 321
    on Pope (Alexander) 148, 325, 337
    on Robinson (Mary) 351
    on Rochester (John Wilmot) 352
    on Seward (Anna Hunter) 359
    on Winscom (Jane Cave) 463
    on Wroth (Lady Mary) 466
Fergusson, Robert vii, **173–174**
    "The Daft Days" **95–97,** 173, 175, 397
Fermor, Arabella 335–336
Ferrar, Nicholas 205, 206
Field, Edward 140
Field, Sarah. *See* Egerton, Sarah Fyge
Fielding, Henry 50
figurative language **174–175,** 236, 268
Finch, Anne **175–177**
    "Adam Posed" **4–5,** 176
    "The Answer" **19–20,** 176
    "The Apology" **21,** 176
    "The Circuit of Apollo" (Finch) 34, **70–71,** 176, 411
    enjambment by 154
    "Friendship between Ephelia and Ardelia" 176, **183–184**
    and Philips (Katherine) 183, 320
    and Pope (Alexander) 4, 19, 176

"The Spleen" 176, **379–381**
    "To the Nightingale" 176, 379, **411–412**
Finch, Heneage 175–176
First Anniversary, The (Donne) 16, 17
First Satire of the Second Book of Horace, The (Pope) 156, 164
Fish, Stanley 77, 313, 318
fixed form 183
"Flaming Heart upon the Book and Pictures of the Seraphical Saint Teresa, The" (Crashaw) 92, **177–179**
Flaxman, John 67
"Flea, The" (Donne) 118, **179–180,** 198, 386
Fleck, Andrew 17
Flecknoe, Richard 236, 261–262, 265
"Fleece, The" (Dyer) 136, 137
Fletcher, Giles **180–181**
    "Christ's Victory in Heaven" **67–68,** 180
Fletcher, John 180, 378, 442
Fletcher, Loraine 365, 366, 394
Fletcher, Phineas 180
"Flower, The" (Herbert) **181–182,** 206
folk ballad 28, 29
Forbes, John 173
Ford, John **182**
    "Calantha's Dirge" **51–52,** 120, 182, 319
    "Penthea's Dying Song" 120, 182, **318–319**
Forest, The (Jonson) 241, 398–399
formalist critics 14, 53
Forman, Simon 251
form and format **183**
"For the Baptist" (Drummond) **182–183**
Fowler, Katherine. *See* Philips, Katherine Fowler
Fragmenta Aurea (Suckling) 235, 385
Fraser, Russell 260
Freeman, F. W. 174
Freemantle, Bridget 252, 253
free verse 183
"Friendship between Ephelia and Ardelia" (Finch) 176, **183–184**
"Friendship's Mysteries, to My Dearest Lucasia" (Philips) vii, **184–185,** 321
"Frost at Midnight" (Coleridge) 414
Fyge, Sarah. *See* Egerton, Sarah Fyge

G

Galen 15, 198
Galileo Galilei 227, 270, 340
"Garden, The" (Marvell) **186–187,** 267, 286

Gardner, Helen 9, 24, 33, 99, 115, 116, 117, 196, 213, 214, 215, 223, 227, 228, 360, 402
Garrick, David 88, 239, 349, 350
Gascoigne, George 41
"Gather Ye Rosebuds While Ye May" (Herrick) 55
Gay, John **188–191**
   and Barber (Mary) 32
   and Montagu (Lady Mary Wortley) 189, 273–274, 354
   and Pope (Alexander) 132, 134, 176, 188, 189
   and Prior (Matthew) 329
   on Robinson (Mary) 349
   songs from *The Beggar's Opera* vii, 122, 188, 189–190, **370–371**
   and Swift (Jonathan) 188, 189–190, 370, 389, 443
   and Thomson (James) 395
Gay, Thomas 188
Gaye, Phoebe Fenwick 188
Gentleman's Magazine 55, 56, 73, 239, 358
George, Lord Anson 58
George I (king of Great Britain) 189, 329
George II (king of Great Britain) 353, 444
George IV (king of Great Britain) 350, 351
Georgics (Virgil) 450, 461
Gifford, William 88
Glorious Revolution (1688) 120, 130, 188, 388
"Go, Lovely Rose!" (Waller) 55, 78, **191**, 453
"Go and Catch a Falling Star" (Donne) 118, **191–193**
"God Moves in a Mysterious Way" (Cowper) 89
Godwin, William 350, 366
Goldsmith, Oliver **193–194**
   The Deserted Village **109–111**, 193
   and Johnson (Samuel) 239
   She Stoops to Conquer 122–123, 194
   "When Lovely Woman Stoops to Folly" 193, **457–458**
Gondibert (Davenant) 98, 99, **194–195**
Gondry, Michel 149
Goodeere, Sir Henry 123
"Good Friday, 1613. Riding Westward" (Donne) 118, **195–197**, 236
"Good-Morrow, The" (Donne) 118, **197–198**
Gosse, Edmund 97, 126
Gould, Robert 140, 150
Gray, Thomas **198–199**, 220
   "Elegy Written in a Country Churchyard" 141, **144–147**, 199

Great Fire of London (1666) vii, 18–19, 118, 129, 313, 346, 462
Greene, Graham 352
Greene, Richard 252, 253, 254, 272
Grierson, H. J. C. 196
"Groans of the Tankard, The" (Barbauld) 30
"Grongar Hill" (Dyer) 136, **199–201**
Grossman, Marshall 108
Grundy, Isobel 273, 274
Gulliver's Travels (Swift) 326, 390
Gunpowder Plot (1605) 10, 202
Gunther, John 100

H

"Habbie" rhyme 95, 397
Habington, William 14, **202**
   "Against Them Who Lay Unchastity to the Sex of Women" **7–8**, 202
Hall, John **202–203**
Hamlet (Shakespeare) 100, 119
Hammond, Brean S. 132
Handel, G. F. 13, 368, 369, 371, 373
Hanmer, Jonathan 188
Hannaford, Renée 338
Happy-Unfortunate; Or, the Female Page (Boyd) 39
Hardin, Richard 124, 125, 151, 314, 315
Hardy, Thomas 146
Harmony of the Church, The (Drayton) 123
Hartmann, C. H. 374
Hawes, Clement 364
Hayley, William 358, 366
"Head-Ache, or an Ode to Health, The" (Winscom) 463
"Heaven" (Herbert) 99, 255
Henley, John 157
Henrietta Maria (queen of England) 57, 61, 87, 98, 102–103, 265
Henry IV (Shakespeare) 37, 124
Henry VIII (king of England) 28, 81, 233, 416, 440
Herbert, Edward **203–204**
   and Carew (Thomas) 54
   "Elegy over a Tomb" **141–142**, 204
   "An Ode Upon a Question Moved Whether Love Should Continue Forever" 204, **292–293**
   "Upon Combing Her Hair" **429**
   and Wroth (Lady Mary) 466
Herbert, George vi–vii, **204–206**
   "Affliction (1)" **6–7**, 20, 206
   "The Altar" vii, **14–15**, 78, 206, 213, 255, 268, 359

"The Bunch of Grapes" **46–47**, 206
and Cartwright (William) 57
"Church Monuments" **69–70**, 206
"The Collar" **72–73**, 175, 206
Crashaw (Richard) on 78, 91
"Death" 70, **99**, 206, 255, 396
"Discipline" **113–114**, 206
"Easter" **138**, 206
"Easter Wings" vii, **139–140**, 206, 359
"The Flower" **181–182**, 206
and Herbert (Mary Sidney) 181, 207, 242
"The Holdfast" 139, 206, **213**, 340
and Johnson (Samuel) 239
"Jordan" (1) 181, 206, **242–243**
"Love (3)" 206, **255**
"Man" 206, **263–264**
and Marvell (Andrew) 101
"The Pilgrimage" 206, **322–323**, 341
"Prayer (1)" 206, 284, **327**
"The Pulley" 206, **331–332**
"The Redemption" 206, **340–341**
"Time" 70, 206, **396**
and Traherne (Thomas) 464
and Vaughan (Henry) 442
"Virtue" 206, **450–451**
"The Windows" 206, **460**
Herbert, Henry **203–204**
Herbert, Magdalene 204, 205
Herbert, Mary Sidney vii, 204, **206–207**
   and Breton (Nicholas) 41
   and Browne (William) 46
   and Herbert (George) 181, 207, 242
   and Jonson (Ben) 207, 378, 404
   "Psalm 58 *Se Vere Utique*" **330–331**
   "To the Thrice-Sacred Queen Elizabeth" 207, **416–418**
   and Wroth (Lady Mary) 404
hermeticism 346, 422, 442, 456
Herodotus 420
heroic couplet **207**
Heroic Stanzas (Dryden) 128
Heroides (Ovid) 124
Herrick, Robert **207–209**
   and Alabaster (William) 10
   "Candlemas Eve" 14
   and Carew (Thomas) 54
   "Corinna's Going a Maying" **83–85**, 208, 419
   "Delight in Disorder" **102**, 208, 311, 375
   on Hall (John) 203
   "His Farewell to Sack" 208, **211–212**

"His Prayer to Ben Jonson" 208, **212**
and Jonson (Ben) 102, 208, 211, 212, 235, 285, 288–289
and Lovelace (Richard) 373
"The Mad Maid's Song" 208, **263**
"The Night-piece" 208, **285–286**, 433
"An Ode for Him" 208, 212, **288–289**
"A Thanksgiving to God" 208, **391**
"To the Virgins" 208, **418–419**
in Tribe of Ben 212, 242, 258, 378, 423
"Upon His Verses" 208, **429–430**
"Upon Jack and Jill. Epigram" 208, **430**
"Upon Julia's Clothes" 208, **430–431**, 433
"Upon the Losse of His Mistresses" 208, **432**
"Upon the Nipples of Julia's Breast" 208, **432–433**
"The Vine" 208, **448–449**
Hervey, Lord John 156, 157–158
Hesiod 450
Hesperides (Herrick) 208, 391, 429, 430, 432
Heywood, Thomas 262
Hilliad, The (Smart) 363
Hind and the Panther, The (Dryden) 13, 130, **209–211**, 328, 409
Hind and the Panther Transvers'd to the Story of the Country Mouse and the City Mouse, The (Montagu and Prior) 328
"His Farewell to Sack" (Herrick) 208, **211–212**
"His Prayer to Ben Jonson" (Herrick) 208, **212**
History of England (Goldsmith) 194
History of the Nun, The (Behn) 35
Hobbes, Thomas 98, 203, 304, 340, 351, 355
"Holdfast, The" (Herbert) 139, 206, **213**, 340
Holinshed, Ralph 124, 125
Holy Sonnets (Donne) 8, 24, 32, 99, 117, **213–215**, 227, 360
"Holy Willie's Prayer" (Burns) 48
Homer
   and Behn (Aphra) 126
   and Chapman (George) 65
   Dryden (John) on 154, 155
   meter used by 269
   and Milton (John) 314
   mock-heroic used by 272
   and Pope (Alexander) 132, 134, 157, 207, 325, 335, 337
   and Virgil 449–450

Hopton, Susanne 422
Horace
    carpe diem poetry of 55, 84,
        418, 419
    and Drayton (Michael) 125
    and Jonson (Ben) 234, 235,
        241
    and Marvell (Andrew) 101,
        186, 215–216, 426
    and Pope (Alexander) 162,
        326
    and Prior (Matthew) 37
    and Smart (Christopher)
        363
    on Virgil 449
Horatian ode 216, 420
Horatian Ode upon Cromwell's
    Return from Ireland, An
    (Marvell) 215–216, 266, 287
Horatio 103
How Milton Works (Fish) 313,
    316
"How Sleep the Brave" (Collins)
    74, 216–217
"How Soon Hath Time" (Sonnet
    VII) (Milton) 217, 271, 375
Hoyle, John 34–35, 459
Hudibras (Butler) 49–50, 217–
    219, 434
Hughes, John 147
Hughes, Merritt Y. 229, 308
Humorous Lovers, The (Cavendish)
    62
Humphrey, Belinda 136, 137
"Hunting of the Hare, The"
    (Cavendish) 62, 219–220
"Hymeneal" (Gray) 198
"Hymn for Christmas Day, A"
    (Chatterton) 65
Hymn on the Seasons, A
    (Thomson) 38, 136, 220–223,
    395
"Hymn to Christ" (Donne) 225,
    360
"Hymn to God My God, in My
    Sickness" (Donne) 223–225
"Hymn to God the Father, A"
    (Donne) 118, 225–226, 318
"Hymn to Light" (Cowley) 25,
    88
"Hymn to the Sun" (Thomson)
    221, 222
"Hymn to the Supreme Being"
    (Smart) 363
hyperbole 175
hypercatalectic line 60

I

"I Am a Little World Made
    Cunningly" (Donne) 118, 175,
    198, 227–228
iambic foot 268
iambic hexameter 125
iambic pentameter 119, 207,
    268–269, 374, 375

"I Am the Door" (Crashaw) 92,
    228–229
ictus 269
Idea, The Shepherds' Garland
    (Drayton) 123–124
identity rhyme 258, 347
Idylls (Theocritus) 42
"I Envy Not Endymion"
    (Alexander) 25–26
"If the Heart of a Man is
    Depressed with Cares" (Gay)
    371
Ignatius His Conclave (Donne)
    117, 227
Iliad (Homer) 65, 207, 325, 335,
    337, 450
"Il Penseroso" (Milton) 61, 200,
    229–230, 248, 270
Imitations of Horace (Pope) 20
"Imperfect Enjoyment, The"
    (Wilmot) 230–231, 352
imperfect rhyme 147, 347
"Impromptu" (Pope) 19
"Indifferent, The" (Donne) 118,
    231–232
Inebriety (Crabbe) 90
Ingelo, Nathaniel 356
instructive poem 266
internal rhyme 93, 198, 280,
    347, 399
"In the Holy Nativity of our Lord
    God: A Hymn Sung as by the
    Shepherds" (Crashaw) 20, 92,
    232–234
"In this strange labyrinth how
    shall I turn?" (Wroth) 234,
    312, 466
"Introduction, The" (Finch) 154,
    176
"Inviting a Friend to Supper"
    (Jonson) 234–235, 240, 419
"Invocation of the Comic Muse"
    (Seward) 358
"I Prithee Send Me Back My
    Heart" (Suckling) 235–236,
    385
irony 174, 236

J

James (duke of Monmouth). See
    Monmouth, James, duke of
James, Richard 208
James I (king of England)
    and Alabaster (William) 10
    and Alexander (Sir William)
        11
    and Chapman (George) 65
    and Donne (John) 117
    drama and poetry under
        119, 127
    Drayton (Michael) on 124,
        125
    and Herbert (Edward) 203
    and Herbert (George) 205
    and Waller (Edmund) 452

James II (king of England)
    and Denham (Sir John) 103
    Dryden (John) on 1, 2,
        18–19, 129, 130, 209,
        210, 261, 343
    mistress of 441
    poetry and drama under 120
James V (king of Scotland) 51
James VI (king of Scotland). See
    James I (king of England)
"January, 1795" (Robinson)
    237–238, 351
"John Anderson, My Jo" (Burns)
    48, 238
Johnson, Esther 382, 388, 389,
    390
Johnson, Samuel 238–240
    on Alabaster (William) 9
    biography of 358, 359
    on Butler (Samuel) 50
    and Carter (Elizabeth) 56
    on Collins (William) 74,
        289–290
    on Cowley (Abraham) 87,
        381
    on Crabbe, George 90
    on Denham (Sir John) 79,
        103, 136
    on Dryden (John) 4, 128,
        129, 130, 131, 209, 328,
        412, 414
    on Gay (John) 188–189,
        190, 370
    and Goldsmith (Oliver) 111,
        193, 194
    on Milton (John) 76, 259
    on poetry viii, 268, 410
    on Pope (Alexander) viii,
        158, 162, 325, 326
    on Prior (Matthew) 38, 160,
        328, 329
    on Seward (Anna Hunter)
        viii, 358
    on Smart (Christopher) 363
    "The Vanity of Human
        Wishes" 239, 439–441
    on Waller (Edmund) 452
Johnston, Arthur 74
Jonathan Wild (Fielding) 50
Jonson, Ben 240–242. See also
    Sons of Ben; Tribe of Ben
    and Alabaster (William) 10
    blank verse by 38
    and Carew (Thomas) 54
    and Cary (Patrick) 58
    and Cary (Sir Lucius) 58
    and Cavalier poetry 60
    and Chapman (George) 65,
        378
    country house poem by 107,
        108, 186, 250
    and Donne (John) 16, 117,
        299, 398, 402
    and Drayton (Michael) 125
    and Drummond (William)
        127, 240, 281, 378, 410
    "Epitaph on S.P." 160–161,
        241

and form 183
and Herbert (Mary Sidney)
    207, 378, 404
and Herrick (Robert) 102,
    208, 211, 212, 235, 285,
    288–289
"Inviting a Friend to Supper"
    234–235, 240, 419
and Marvell (Andrew) 186,
    426–427
"My Picture Left in Scotland"
    240, 281
"Ode to Himself" 241,
    290–292
"On Giles and Joan"
    295–296
"On Lucy" 299–300
"On My First Daughter" vii,
    141, 161, 240, 301–302
"On My First Son" vii, 141,
    161, 236, 240, 268–269,
    302–303, 318
"On Something, That Walks
    Somewhere" 241, 303–304
"Queen and Huntress" 333,
    362
and Randolph (Thomas) 334
"Slow, Slow, Fresh Fount"
    241, 362–363
"Song: To Celia" 241,
    371–372
"A Sonnet to the Noble Lady"
    241, 378
"Still to Be Neat" 241,
    383–384
"To Heaven" 241, 398–399
"To John Donne" 242, 402
"To Penshurst" 107, 206,
    240, 241, 250, 398, 404–
    406, 426, 465
"To the Immortal Memory
    and Friendship of that
    noble pair" 58, 242,
    406–408, 423
"To the Memory of My
    Beloved" 175, 241, 292,
    410–411
"To William Camden" 240,
    419–420
Volpone 119–120, 241
and Wroth (Lady Mary)
    378, 465
"Jordan" (1) (Herbert) 181, 206,
    242–243
Journal to Stella, The (Swift) 382,
    389
Jubilate Agno (Smart) 277, 363,
    364, 372
"Judgement" (Herbert) 99, 255
Julius Caesar (Shakespeare) 379
Juvenal 131, 154, 239, 294, 440

K

Kaufman, Charlie 149
Keats, John 45, 54, 64, 65, 66,
    321

Killigrew, Anne viii, **244–245**
  Dryden (John) on 130,
    244–245, 403, 409, 412–
    414, 434
  and Finch (Anne) 175
  and Philips (Katherine) 244,
    245, 320, 413, 434
  "To My Lord Colrane" 244,
    403–404
  "Upon the Saying That My
    Verses Were Made by
    Another" 75, 153, 244,
    433–434
Killigrew, Thomas 55
King, Edward 258–259, 270,
  431–432
Kingsmill, Anne. *See* Finch, Anne,
  countess of Winchilsea
Kingsmill, Sir William 175
Knox, John 173
"Kubla Khan" (Coleridge) 414,
  415

L

Ladies Defence, The (Chudleigh)
  69, **246–248**, 269
"L'Allegro" (Milton) 61, 74, 200,
  229, **248–249**, 270, 358
Lambert, John 65, 66
Landa, Louis 390
"Landscape Described. Rural
  Sounds, A" (Cowper) 89,
  249–250
landscape poetry 136, 137,
  199–201
Lanyer, Aemilia **250–252**
  "The Description of Cooke-
    Ham" **107–109**, 250, 251
  "Eve's Apology in Defense of
    Women" **167–169**, 251
  and Herbert (Mary Sidney)
    207
Lanyer, Alphonso 250
"Last Instructions to a Painter,
  The" (Marvell) 266
Laud, William 36, 79, 80
Lawes, Henry 57, 76, 184, 270,
  305
Leapor, Mary vii, **252–254**
  "Mira's Will" 253, **272**
Lee, Guy 449
Lee, Mary. *See* Chudleigh, Lady
  Mary
Lee, Nathaniel 121
Leishman, J. B. 283
Leviathan (Hobbes) 304, 340
Lewalski, Barbara K. 168, 251,
  308, 331
Lewis, Anne 240
Lewis, C. S. 313
Lewis, Erasmus 329
libertine poetry 346, 351–352,
  355–356
Liberty (Thomson) 395
Library, The (Crabbe) 90
"Life and Death of Habbie
  Simson" (Sempill) 95, 397

Life of Dr. Darwin (Seward) 358
"Light Shining out of Darkness"
  (Cowper) 89, **254–255**
Lintot, Bernard 157
"Litanie, A" (Donne) 117
literary ballad 28
Lives of the Poets, The (Johnson)
  viii, 87, 160, 189, 209, 239,
  329, 452
local landscape poetry 136, 137
Lodge, Thomas 124
"London" (Johnson) 239
Long, Ada 338
Lonsdale, Roger 416, 463
Lorrington, Meribah 349
Louisa (Seward) 358
"Love (3)" (Herbert) 99, 206, **255**
"Love a child is ever crying"
  (Wroth) **255–256**, 312, 466
"Love Armed" (Behn) 35,
  256–257
*Love Given O're: Or, A Satyr
  Against the Pride, Lust and
  Inconstancy, etc. of Woman*
  (Gould) 140, 150
Lovelace, Richard 60, **257–258**
  and Marvell (Andrew) 101
  "Song: To Lucasta" 175, 257,
    373–374
  Suckling (Sir John) on 29
  "To Althea" 215, **396–397**,
  in Tribe of Ben 242, 258,
    423
*Love Letters Between a Nobleman
  and His Sister* (Behn) 35
Lover's Melancholy, The (Ford)
  182
"Love Swore by Styx" (Alexander)
  25, 26
"Loving and Beloved" (Suckling)
  258, 385
Lucan 17, 216
Lucretius 419
Luke, Sir Samuel 49, 217, 218
lullaby 74–75
Lycidas (Milton) 72, 136, 141,
  258–260, 270, 431
lyric **260**

M

Macbeth (Shakespeare) 432
"MacFlecknoe: A Satire upon
  the True-Blue Protestant Poet
  T.S." (Dryden) 130, 133, 236,
  261–263, 265, 273
MacLaine, Allan H. 173
Maclean, Hugh 338
"Mad Maid's Song, The" (Herrick)
  208, **263**
Magna Carta 82, 83
Maguire, Hugh 28
Malcolmson, Cristina 14, 140,
  205, 243, 255
Malet, Elizabeth 351, 352
Mallet, David 353
"Man" (Herbert) 206, **263–264**

Mangan, James Clarence 28
Manley, Mary Delarivière 40,
  140, 176
Manners, John 49
Manners, Lord Robert 90
Mariam, Fair Queene of Jewry
  (Cary) 57, 123
Marino, Giambattista 54, 63,
  92, 127
Marlowe, Christopher 124,
  151, 339
"Married State, A" (Philips)
  264–265, 321
Marston, John 65, 241, 362
Martial 292, 302, 426
Martinus Scriblerus Club 132,
  135, 156, 189, 325
Marvell, Andrew **265–267**
  "Bermudas" **36–37**, 267
  and Cowley (Abraham) 101,
    111, 186
  "The Definition of Love"
    101–102, 186, 267, 311
  "A Dialogue Between the Soul
    and the Body" **111–112**,
    267
  "The Garden" **186–187**,
    267, 286
  *An Horatian Ode upon
    Cromwell's Return from
    Ireland* 215–216, 266, 287
  and Milton (John) 267, 270,
    271, 300–301
  The Mower Poems 267,
    275–277, 347, 428
  "The Nymph Complaining
    for the Death of Her Fawn"
    267, **286–287**, 347
  "On a Drop of Dew" 25,
    294–295
  "On Mr. Milton's *Paradise
    Lost*" 267, 271, **300–301**
  on Rochester (John Wilmot)
    352
  "To His Coy Mistress" 55,
    101, 267, **399–400**
  "Upon Appleton House"
    174, 275, **426–428**
  and Vaughan (Henry) 456
Marxist critics 44, 453
Mary II (queen of England) 120,
  130, 211, 343
masculine rhyme 347
Mason, William 145
masque 76, 241
Masque of Blackness, The (Jonson)
  241
Massacre of the Innocents, The
  (Marino) 92
Matilda (Drayton) 124
May, Thomas 54
Medal, The (Dryden) 129, 261
Medal of John Bayes, The
  (Shadwell) 130, 133, 261
"Melancholy and Mirth"
  (Cavendish) 61
Meres, Francis 41, 65

Meres, Sir Thomas 356
Messenger, Ann 245, 354, 355,
  409
Metamorphosis (Ovid) 44, 259,
  286
metaphors 174, 268. *See also*
  conceit
metaphysical poets and poetry
  267–268
  by Alabaster (William) 10,
    116, 375, 376
  by Carew (Thomas) 144
  conceit in 78
  by Cowley (Abraham) 267
  by Crashaw (Richard) 309
  by Donne (John) 32, 33, 40,
    52, 120, 143–144, 192,
    195, 197, 224, 227, 236,
    264, 267, 268, 318, 361,
    386, 401, 436, 437, 438
  and form 183
  by Herbert (Edward) 204,
    292–293
  by Herbert (George) 7, 139,
    213, 264, 267, 268
  by Marvell (Andrew) 267,
    399
  paradox in 318
  by Philips (Katherine) 185,
    403
  by Suckling (Sir John) 236
  by Traherne (Thomas) 267
  by Vaughan (Henry) 267,
    268, 283, 342, 442
meter **268–269**, 357
"Methought I Saw My Late
  Espousèd Saint" (Sonnet XXII)
  (Milton) **269**, 271
metonymy 73, 175
Middleton, Thomas 120
Mid-summer Night's Dream, A
  (Shakespeare) 125
Miles, Rosalind 398
Milton, John **269–272**
  and Barbauld (Anna Laetitia)
    30
  and Browne (William) 45
  and Cary (Patrick) 58
  Cavendish (Margaret) on 61
  and Chatterton (Thomas) 65
  and Cleveland (John) 72
  and Collins (William) 74
  Comus **76–78**, 270, 305
  and Crashaw (Richard) 232
  and Davenant (Sir William)
    98, 271
  and Dryden (John) 120,
    129, 154–155
  and Dyer (John) 136, 137,
    200
  and Egerton (Sarah) 149
  and Finch (Anne) 176
  and Fletcher (Giles) 180
  and form 183
  and Gay (John) 188
  "How Soon Hath Time" **217**,
    271, 375

"Il Penseroso" 61, 200, **229–230**, 248, 270

"L'Allegro" 61, 74, 200, 229, **248–249**, 270, 358

Lycidas 72, 136, 141, **258–260**, 270, 431
and Marvell (Andrew) 267, 270, 271, 300–301

"Methought I Saw My Late Espousèd Saint" **269**, 271

"On Shakespeare, 1630" 270, **303**

"On the Late Massacre in Piedmont" **307**

"On the New Forcers of Conscience under the Long Parliament" 270, **308**

Paradise Lost 13, 20–21, 38, 129, 135, 154, 176, 180, 271, 300–301, **313–316**, 335, 432

Paradise Regained 271, 306, **316–318**
Pope (Alexander) on 135, 157, 164

"The Psalm Poems" 271, **331**

"When I consider how my light is spent (Sonnet XIX)" 271, 301, 375, **457**

Miner, Earl 2, 17, 121, 129, 209, 210, 261, 338

Minshull, Elizabeth 271

Mintz, Susannah B. 425, 426, 439

"Mira's Will" (Leapor) 253, **272**

Mirror for Magistrates, The (Drayton) 125

Miscellaneous Poems (Marvell) 101, 186, 216, 267, 275, 286, 294, 300, 399

Miscellany Poems (Dryden) 261

Miscellanies (Pope) 335

Miscellanies (Prior) 328

Miscellanies (Swift and Pope) 132

Miscellanies, Pindaric Odes (Cowley) 87

Miscellany (Dyer) 200

Miscellany (Pope) 326

Miscellany Poems on Several Occasions (Finch) 176, 184

Mistress, The (Cowley) 87, 381

mock-heroic **272–273**

Modest Proposal, A (Swift) vii, 389–390

Mohocks, The (Gay) 188

Monmouth, James, duke of 1, 4, 35, 129, 261

Montagu, Charles 328

Montagu, Lady Mary Wortley viii, **273–275**
and Astell (Mary) 23, 273, 274
and Barbauld (Anna Laetitia) 30, 31
and Carter (Elizabeth) 56

"Epistle from Mrs. Yonge to Her Husband" 147, **155–156**, 274
and Gay (John) 189, 273–274, 354
and Pope (Alexander) 156, 157, 273, 274, 325, 326, 354

"Satturday: The Small Pox" 274, **354–355**

Montaigne, Michele 120, 329, 355

Montgolfier, Joseph Michel 455

Moon-Calf, The (Drayton) 125

Moore, Clement 269

Moore, Thomas 90

Moral Essays (Pope) 165, 326

More, Ann 117–118

More, Hannah 31, 56, 88

Morison, Henry 242, 406–407, 423

Morris, David 133

"Mortification" (Herbert) 323

Mortimeriados (Drayton) 124

"Most Angel Spirit of the Most Excellent Sir Philip Sidney, The" (Herbert) 207

"Mower against Gardens, The" (Marvell) 111, 267, 275–276

Mower Poems, The (Marvell) 267, **275–277**, 347, 428

"Mower's Song, The" (Marvell) 267, 275, 277, 347

"Mower to the Glowworms, The" (Marvell) 267, 275, 276–277

Mozart, Amadeus 13

"Muse, The" (Cowley) 60

"My Cat Jeoffry" (Smart) viii, 38, 60, 174, **277–279**, 363

"My Muse, now happy, lay thyself to rest" (Wroth) **279–280**, 312, 466

"My pain, still smothered in my grievèd breast" (Wroth) **280–281**, 312, 466

"My Picture Left in Scotland" (Jonson) 240, **281**

"My soul a world is by contraction" (Alabaster). *See* Sonnet 15 ("My soul a world is by contraction") (Alabaster)

N

narrative allegory 13

narrative ballad 28, 38

narrative poem 260

Nassaar, Christopher S. 197

Nature's Pictures (Cavendish) 61

"Negro's Complaint, The" (Cowper) 75, 89, **282–283**

Newbery, John 363

Newcastle, duchess of. *See* Cavendish, Margaret

New Historicist critics 14, 79, 149–150, 183, 334

New Inn, The (Jonson) 241, 290

Newton, Sir Isaac 222, 395

"Night, The" (Vaughan) **283–285**, 442

"Night-piece, to Julia, The" (Herrick) 208, **285–286**, 433

Nimphidia (Drayton) 125

Nine Muses, The (Manley) 140

"No blooming youth shall ever make me erre" (Philips) 320

"Nocturnal Reverie, A" (Finch) 176

"Nocturnal upon St. Lucy's Day, A" (Donne) 60

Nokes, David 188, 189, 190, 371

"Noonday" (Thomson) 221, 222

Nosce Teipsum (Davies) 194

"Nox Nocti Indicat Scientiam" (Habington) 14

"Nymph Complaining for the Death of Her Fawn, The" (Marvell) 267, **286–287**, 347

O

Oates, Titus 1, 294

oblique rhyme 347

Observations in the Art of English Poesie (Campion) **288**

Ockerbloom, Mary Mark 176

ode 260

Ode (Gray) 199

"Ode for Him, An" (Herrick) 208, 212, **288–289**

Odes (Horace) 37, 125, 418

Odes on Several Descriptive and Allegoric Subjects (Collins) 74, 289

"Ode on Popular Superstitions" (Collins) 74

"Ode to Evening" (Collins) 74, **289–290**

"Ode to Himself" (Jonson) 241, **290–292**

"Ode to Master Anthony Stafford" (Randolph) 86, **292**, 334

"Ode to the Royal Society" (Cowley) 88

"Ode to Wisdom" (Carter) 56

"Ode Upon a Question Moved Whether Love Should Continue Forever, An" (Herbert) 204, **292–293**

Odyssey (Homer) 65, 126, 134, 325, 326, 335, 449

Of Education (Milton) 270

"Of English Verse" (Waller) 75

"Of His Conversion" (Alabaster). *See* Sonnet 46 ("Of His Conversion") (Alabaster)

Of Mice and Men (Steinbeck) 397

Old Bachelor, The (Congreve) 130

Oldham, John **293–294**, 409–410

Olor Iscanus (Vaughan) 442

"On a Drop of Dew" (Marvell) 25, **294–295**

"On a Girdle" (Waller) 175

"On a Virtuous Young Gentlewoman That Died Suddenly" (Cartwright) 57, 141, **295**

"On Giles and Joan" (Jonson) **295–296**

"On Her Loving Two Equally" (Behn) 35, **296–297**

"On His Majesty's Recovery from the Small-Pox" (Cartwright) 57, **297–298**

"On Leaping over the Moon" (Traherne) vii, **298–299**, 422

"On Lucy, Countess of Bedford" (Jonson) **299–300**

"On Mr. George Herbert's Book, *The Temple*" (Crashaw) 78

"On Mr. Milton's *Paradise Lost*" (Marvell) 267, 271, **300–301**

"On My First Daughter" (Jonson) vii, 141, 161, 240, **301–302**

"On My First Son" (Jonson) vii, 141, 161, 236, 240, 268–269, **302–303**, 318

onomatopoeia 330, 379

"On Shakespeare, 1630" (Milton) 270, **303**

"On Solitude" (Cowley) 88

"On Something, That Walks Somewhere" (Jonson) 241, **303–304**

"On the Death of an Infant of Five Days Old, Being a Beautiful but Abortive Birth" (Boyd) vii, 40, **304–305**

"On the Death of My First and Dearest Child, Hector Philips, Borne the 23d of April, and Died the 2d of May 1665" (Philips) 141, **305–306**, 321

"On the Death of Waller" (Behn) 35, **306–307**

"On the Late Massacre in Piedmont" (Milton) **307**

"On the New Forcers of Conscience under the Long Parliament" (Milton) 270, **308**

"On the Wounds of Our Crucified Lord" (Crashaw) 92, **308–310**

oratorio 232

Oroonoko, The History of the Royal Slave (Behn) 34, 35, 256

Osborn, James 423

ottava rima 123, 124, **310**

Otway, Thomas 121, **310–311**
"The Poet's Complaint of His Muse" 310, **323–324**

"Out upon It!" (Suckling) **311**, 385

Ovid
and Browne (William) 43, 44
and Denham (Sir John) 103
and Drayton (Michael) 124
Dryden (John) on 17
and Marvell (Andrew) 286

Ovid (continued)
  and Milton (John) 259
  and Pope (Alexander) 148
  and Randolph (Thomas) 292
Ovids Banquet of Sence (Chapman)
  64
Owen, Anne 184
Owl, The (Drayton) 125
Oxenbridge, John 36, 266
oxymoron 101, 102, 311. See
  also paradox

P
Pamela (Richardson) 32, 35,
  62, 304
"Pamphilia to Amphilanthus"
  (Wroth) 234, 255–256,
  279–280, 312–313, 375, 387,
  458, 466
panegyric 18, 57, 295, 306,
  412, 452
Paradise Lost (Milton) 13, 20–21,
  38, 129, 135, 154, 176, 180,
  271, 300–301, 313–316, 335,
  432
Paradise Regained (Milton) 271,
  306, 316–318
paradox 268, 318
Parfitt, George 290, 291, 302,
  303, 407, 410
Parker, Samuel 267
Partridge, John 337
pastoral poetry
  by Behn (Aphra) 112–113
  by Browne (William) 42–45,
    172
  by Carew (Thomas) 338–339
  by Crabbe (George) 446,
    447
  by Crashaw (Richard)
    232–234
  by Drayton (Michael) 123–
    124, 125, 151–153
  by Gay (John) 189, 274, 354
  by Herbert (George) 451
  by Marvell (Andrew) 286
  by Milton (John) 76–77, 141
  by Montagu (Lady Mary
    Wortley) 274, 354
  by Pope (Alexander) 325
  by Randolph (Thomas)
    86–87
  by Virgil 42, 260, 449
Patrick, J. Max 211
pattern poem. See shape poem
Pavy, Salomon 160–161
Pembroke, countess of. See
  Herbert, Mary Sidney
Pembroke, William Herbert, earl
  of 256, 378, 404, 465
Penitential Sonnets (Alabaster)
  376
pentameter 268
"Penthea's Dying Song" (Ford)
  120, 182, 318–319
Pepusch, John Christopher 370

Pepys, Samuel 62, 351, 357
perfect rhyme 347
Perry, Ruth 15, 23
Persius 131, 154
personification 174–175
Petrarchan ideal
  Donne (John) on 8, 231,
    400–401
  Herbert (George) on 204,
    243
  Marvell (Andrew) on 400
  Milton (John) on 269, 307
  Pope (Alexander) on 148
Petrarchan sonnets 260,
  374–375
  by Alabaster (William) 115,
    377
  by Alexander (Sir William)
    25
  conceit in 78
  by Donne (John) 17, 25,
    99–100, 361
  by Drummond (William)
    182, 391–392
  by Lovelace (Richard) 374
  by Sidney (Sir Philip) 242
Pharonnida (Chamberlayne) 64
Philips, Ambrose 157, 189
Philips, James 319–320
Philips, Katherine Fowler viii,
  319–321
  and Astell (Mary) 23, 320
  and Chudleigh (Lady Mary)
    68–69, 320
  and Finch (Anne) 70, 71,
    183, 320
  "Friendship's Mysteries" vii,
    184–185, 321
  and Killigrew (Anne) 244,
    245, 320, 413, 434
  "A Married State" 264–265,
    321
  "On the Death of My First
    and Dearest Child" 141,
    305–306, 321
  "To My Excellent Lucasia"
    175, 321, 403
Philips, Sir Richard 351
Phillips, Edward 313, 385
"Phillis Is My Only Joy" (Sedley)
  321, 357
Philosophical Fancies (Cavendish)
  61
Philostratus 371
"Phoebus Arise" (Drummond)
  25, 321–322
phonetic intensives 379
Pierce, Henry 140
Pierrepoint, Lady Mary. See
  Montagu, Lady Mary Wortley
Piers Gaveston (Drayton) 124
"Pilgrimage, The" (Herbert) 206,
  322–323, 341
Pilgrim's Progress (Bunyan) 13,
  356
Pindaric ode 199, 323–324, 379,
  388, 407, 412, 413, 420

Plan (Johnson) 239
Platonic idea
  Cartwright (William) on 295
  Donne (John) on 53, 196,
    197, 437, 439
  Drayton (Michael) on 151
  Habington (William) on 202
  Herbert (George) on 323
  Jonson (Ben) on 407
  Marvell (Andrew) on 101
  Milton (John) on 76, 313
  Traherne (Thomas) on 423
Poems (Barbauld) 30
Poems (Barber) 32
Poems (Cowper) 89
Poems (Drummond) 127, 392
Poems (Gray) 199
Poems (Reynolds) 176
Poems, Chiefly in the Scottish
  Dialect (Burns) 48
Poems and Fancies (Cavendish)
  61
Poems by Mrs. Anne Killigrew
  (Killigrew) 244
Poems Lyric and Pastoral
  (Drayton) 125
Poems of Felicity (Traherne) 298,
  422
Poems on Several Occasions
  (Barber) 32
Poems on Several Occasions
  (Chudleigh) 69
Poems on Several Occasions (Gay)
  189
Poems on Several Occasions (Pope)
  176
Poems on Several Occasions
  (Rochester) 355
Poems on Several Occasions
  (Smart) 363
Poems upon Particular Occasions
  (Carter) 55–56
Poems upon Several Occasions
  (Carter) 56
Poetical Blossoms (Cowley) 87
Poetical Works (Cartwright) 57
Poetical Works (Seward) 359
Poetical Works, The (Crabbe) 91
Poetics (Aristotle) 74
"Poet's Complaint of His Muse,
  The" (Otway) 310, 323–324
Polly (Gay) 190
Poly-Olbion (Drayton) 125
Pond, Arthur 136
Poor Law (1834) 416
Pope, Alexander vii, viii,
  324–327
  and Barber (Mary) 32
  on Carew (Thomas) 55
  on Chudleigh (Lady Mary)
    247
  and Cowley (Abraham) 87,
    325, 462
  and Crabbe (George) 90
  and Crashaw (Richard) 106
  on Denham (Sir John) 103,
    462

  and Dryden (John) 131,
    163, 326
  The Dunciad 131–136, 156,
    157, 164, 326
  "Elegy to the Memory of an
    Unfortunate Lady" 142–
    143, 325
  "Eloisa to Aberlard" 142,
    147–149, 325
  "Epistle to Dr. Arbuthnot"
    156–158, 325, 326
  "Epistle to Miss Blount"
    158–160, 325
  An Essay on Criticism 135,
    157, 162–164, 325, 347
  An Essay on Man 20, 135,
    164–167, 207, 326, 347,
    356, 461
  and Finch (Anne) 4, 19, 176
  and form 183
  and Gay (John) 132, 134,
    176, 188, 189
  and Leapor (Mary) 272
  on literary criticism 162–164
  and Montagu (Lady Mary
    Wortley) 156, 157, 273,
    274, 325, 326, 354
  on poetry 157, 162–163
  and Prior (Matthew) 329
  "The Rape of the Lock" 14,
    19, 20, 30, 54, 176, 188,
    273, 325, 334–338, 354
  on Robinson (Mary) 349
  and Rochester (John Wilmot)
    352, 356
  on Sedley (Sir Charles) 357
  and Swift (Jonathan) 132,
    134, 157, 325, 326, 389,
    444
  and Thomson (James) 220,
    395
  on Waller (Edmund) 452
  Windsor Forest 44, 79, 136,
    157, 325, 461–463
  on writing 158–159,
    162–163
Popish Plot (1678–1681) 1, 261
Pound, Ezra 54
Powell, Mary 269, 270
"Prayer (1)" (Herbert) 206, 284,
  327
"Pressed by the Moon" (Smith)
  327–328, 366
Prior, Matthew 328–330
  "A Better Answer" 37–38,
    329
  and Carew (Thomas) 55
  "An Epitaph" 160, 329
  "A True Maid" 329,
    423–424
Proposal for the Universal Use of
  Irish Manufacture (Swift) 389,
  446
protest poem 72
Prynne, William 49, 50
"Psalm Poems, The" (Milton)
  271, 331

"Psalm 58 *Se Vere Utique*"
(Herbert) **330–331**
Pseudo-Martyr (Donne) 117
psychoanalytic critics 22, 26, 33,
44, 126, 187, 285, 286, 328,
437, 439, 449
Ptolemaic theory of universe 9,
53, 196, 227, 228, 437, 439
"Pulley, The" (Herbert) 206,
331–332
pyrrhic foot 268, 269

Q

Quadruple Alliance 198
quatrain 183
"Queen and Huntress" (Jonson)
333, 362
Questionable Sonnets (Alabaster)
115

R

Raleigh, Sir Walter 117, 230,
289, 439
Ramsay, Allan 173
Randolph, Thomas 276, **334**
"Cotswold Eclogue" **86–87**,
334
"Ode to Master Anthony
Stafford" 86, **292**, 334
"Rape of Lucrece" (Shakespeare)
349
"Rape of the Lock, The" (Pope)
14, 19, 20, 30, 54, 176, 188,
273, 325, **334–338**, 354
"Rapture, A" (Carew) 55,
338–339
reader response criticism 313
"Reason Why the Thoughts
Are Only in the Head, The"
(Cavendish) **339–340**
"Redemption, The" (Herbert)
206, **340–341**
Redpath, Theodore 231
Reform Bill (1832) 416
"Regeneration" (Vaughan) **341–
343**, 442
Rehearsal, The (Buckingham)
49, 129
Religio Laici; Or a Layman's Faith
(Dryden) 130, 209, **343–344**
"Repulse to Alcander, The"
(Egerton) vii, **344–345**
Restoration vii, 3, 120, 121,
128–129, **345–346**
"Retreat, The" (Vaughan) **346–
347**, 442
Reynolds, Myra 176
Reynolds, Sir Joshua 90, 239,
350
"Rhapsody, A" (Vaughan) 442
rhyme 28, 38, 183, 310, **347**,
375
Rich, John 190, 370
Richards, Edward Ames 218
Richardson, Jonathan 136

Richardson, Samuel 32, 35, 56,
62, 253, 304
"Rights of Women, The"
(Barbauld) 31, **347–349**
Rime of the Ancient Mariner, The
(Coleridge) 29
rime royal 41, 74, 75, 123, 124,
347, **349**
Rival Ladies, The (Dryden) 129
Robert Duke of Normandy
(Drayton) 124
Roberts, Josephine A. 466
Robinson, Mary vii, **349–351**
"January, 1795" **237–238**,
351
"To the Poet Coleridge" 351,
414–415
Robinson, Thomas 349, 350
Rochefoucauld, François de
la 443
Rochester, John Wilmot, second
earl of viii, **351–353**
and Dryden (John) 129, 352
"The Imperfect Enjoyment"
230–231, 352
mistress of 310, 352
"A Satyre against Mankind"
60, 352, **355–357**
and Sedley (Sir Charles) 357
Roman Forgeries (Traherne) 422
Romeo and Juliet (Shakespeare)
310
"Ros" (Marvell) 294
roundelay 5
Rowe, Nicholas 176
Rowley, Thomas. *See* Chatterton,
Thomas
Rowse, A. J. 250
Rowton, Frederic 34, 62
Roxana (Alabaster) 9, 11
Royal Slave, The (Cartwright) 57
Royal Society of London 18, 62,
120, 129, 339
Rudrum, Alan 284, 341, 342,
441, 442, 456
"Ruins of Rome, The" (Dyer)
136–137
"Rule Britannia" (Thomson)
353, 395
Runaway, The (Cowley) 88
Ruskin, John 259

S

Sacred Epigrams (Crashaw) 91
Salve Deus Rex Judaeorum
(Lanyer) 167, 251
Samson Agonistes (Milton) 38,
271, 301
Sands, Goodwin 280
satire 122
by Butler (Samuel) 217–219
by Chatterton (Thomas) 65
by Cleveland (John) 72
by Cowley (Abraham) 87
by Cowper (William) 89
by Crabbe (George) 90

by Denham (Sir John) 98
by Donne (John) 116, 117,
118
by Drayton (Michael) 125
by Dryden (John) 129, 133,
236, 261–263, 409
by Egerton (Sarah) 344
by Fergusson (Robert) 173
by Finch (Anne) 176
by Gay (John) 189, 190, 370
by Jonson (Ben) 240, 296,
362
by Leapor (Mary) 272
by Milton (John) 301
in mock-heroic 272–273
by Montagu (Lady Mary
Wortley) 354
by Oldham (John) 293–294,
409
by Otway (Thomas) 310
by Pope (Alexander) 131–
135, 156, 162, 164, 326
by Prior (Matthew) 160
by Rochester (John Wilmot)
352, 355
by Smart (Christopher) 363
by Smith (Charlotte) 366
by Suckling (Sir John) 385
by Swift (Jonathan) vii, 24,
105, 132, 141, 443, 445,
446
Satires (Donne) 116
"Satturday: The Small Pox"
(Montagu) 274, **354–355**
"Satyre against Mankind, A"
(Rochester) 60, 352, **355–357**
Savage, Richard 239
scansion **357**, 431
School for Scandal, A (Sheridan)
122
Scots Vernacular Revival 174
Scott, George Walton 84, 85,
289
Scott, Mary Jane W. 220, 223,
395
Scott, Sir Walter 35, 54, 91, 357,
358, 359
Scriblerus Club 132, 135, 156,
189, 325, 326
Seasons (Thomson). *See Hymn on
the Seasons, A* (Thomson)
"Second Anniversary, The"
(Donne) 16
"Secresie Protested" (Carew) 143
*Secret Memoirs . . . from the New
Atalantis* (Egerton) 140, 176
Secular Masque, The (Dryden)
121
Sedley, Catherine 441
Sedley, Sir Charles 54, **357**
"Phillis Is My Only Joy"
321, 357
"Select Meditations" (Traherne)
422, 423
Sells, A. L. Lytton 145
Sempill, Robert 95, 397
Seneca 160, 303

sententia 262
Serious Proposal to the Ladies, A
(Astell) 23–24
"Sessions of the Poets, A"
(Suckling) 75
Seven Motives (Alabaster) 10
Seward, Anna Hunter viii,
357–359, 365
"Eyam" **170–171**, 358
Seward, Thomas 357, 358
Shadow of Night, The (Chapman)
64
Shadwell, Thomas 130, 133,
236, 261–263
Shaftesbury, Anthony Ashley
Cooper, earl of 1, 129, 209,
261
Shakespeare, William 119
and Cleveland (John) 432
and Collins (William)
369–370
conceit by 78
and Davenant (Sir William)
195
and Donne (John) 100, 231
and Drayton (Michael) 124,
125, 151
and Finch (Anne) 379
godson of 97–98
and Herbert (Mary Sidney)
207
and Herrick (Robert) 430
and Jonson (Ben) 241,
410–411
Milton (John) on 303
mistress of 250
and Otway (Thomas) 310
and Philips (Katherine) 265
and Pope (Alexander) 148,
157, 326
and Prior (Matthew) 37
rime royal used by 349
and Robinson (Mary) 350
son-in-law of 202–203
Shakespearean sonnets. *See*
Elizabethan sonnets
shape poem vii, 14–15, 139–
140, 268, **359**
Shelley, Percy Bysshe 54, 64, 66
Shenstone, William 173
Shepheardes Calender, The
(Spenser) 123, 154
"Shepherd's Week, The" (Gay)
189
Sheridan, Richard 122, 350, 382
She Stoops to Conquer (Goldsmith)
122–123, 194
Shirley, James 14, 262, 378, 423
Sibbald, James 174
Sidney, Lady Dorothy 307, 452
Sidney, Mary. *See* Herbert, Mary
Sidney
Sidney, Sir Philip 206–207
and Breton (Nicholas) 41
and Browne (William) 42,
43, 45
on conceit 78

Sidney, Sir Philip (*continued*)
    and Donne (John) 117
    and Drummond (William)
        127
    in *England's Helicon* 154
    and Herbert (George) 181,
        204, 242–243
    and Jonson (Ben) 240, 378,
        404
    and Milton (John) 217
    on poetry 78, 119
    and Pope (Alexander) 159
    psalm translations by 330,
        416, 417
Sidney, Sir Robert 206, 404, 465
Siege of Rhodes, The (Davenant)
    98
"Silence, and Stealth of Days!"
    (Vaughan) **359–360**, 442
Silex Scintillans (Vaughan) 283,
    341, 342, 346, 359, 392, 442
Simcox, George 91, 106
simile 174
"Since Laws Were Made for Every
    Degree" (Gay) 371
"Since she whome I loved, hath
    paid her last debt" (Donne)
    360–361
"Since there's no help, come let us
    kiss and part" (Drayton) 124,
    361–362
*Sins of the Government, Sins of the
    Nation* (Barbauld) 31
"Sir Eustace Grey" (Crabbe) 90
situational irony 236
slant rhyme 347
"Slow, Slow, Fresh Fount"
    (Jonson) 241, **362–363**
smallpox vaccine viii, 273
Smart, Christopher **363–364**
    "My Cat Jeoffry" viii, 38, 60,
        174, **277–279**, 363
    A Song to David **372–373**
Smith, Benjamin 365
Smith, Charlotte Turner viii,
    364–366
    "Pressed by the Moon"
        327–328, 366
    "Thirty-Eight" 366, **393–
        394**
Smith, Edward 251
Smith, Nigel 36, 216, 267, 275,
    301, 427
Smollett, Tobias 239
Smythe, James Moore 156–157,
    444–445
*Snail: Or The Lady's Lucubrations...
    by Eloisa, The* (Boyd) 40
Sneyd, Honora 358
Sociable Letters (Cavendish)
    62–63, 466
Solomon on the Vanity of the World
    (Prior) 329
Some Reflections on Marriage
    (Astell) 69
"Song—For A' That and A' That"
    (Burns) 48, **367–368**

"Song for St. Cecilia's Day, A"
    (Dryden) 11, 130, **368–369**
"Song from Shakespeare's
    Cymbeline, A" (Collins) 74,
    369–370
"Song of Tavy, The" (Browne) 44
Songs and Sonnets (Donne) 179,
    197
songs from *The Beggar's Opera*
    (Gay) vii, 122, 188, 189–190,
    370–371
"Song: To Amarantha, That She
    would Dishevel Her Hair"
    (Lovelace) 75
"Song: To Celia" (Jonson) 241,
    371–372
Song to David, A (Smart) **372–
373**
"Song: To Lucasta, Going to
    Wars" (Lovelace) 175, 257,
    373–374
sonnet 260, **374–375**. *See also*
    Elizabethan sonnets; Petrarchan
    sonnets
    by Alabaster (William) 10,
        11, 115–116, 375, 376,
        377
    by Alexander (Sir William)
        11, 25, 26, 127
    by Browne (William) 45,
        172
    by Butler (Samuel) 434
    by Donne (John) 32–33, 99–
        100, 117, 183, 213–215,
        360–361
    by Drayton (Michael) 124,
        361
    by Drummond (William)
        127, 391–392
    form of 183
    by Herbert (George) 204,
        242, 243, 327, 340–341,
        451
    by Herrick (Robert) 375
    by Jonson (Ben) 378
    by Lovelace (Richard) 374
    by Milton (John) 183, 217,
        269, 271, 303, 307, 375,
        457
    by Robinson (Mary) 350
    by Seward (Anna Hunter)
        359
    by Shakespeare (William) 78
    by Sidney (Sir Philip) 242
    by Smith (Charlotte) 327,
        365
    synechdoche in 175
    by Wroth (Lady Mary) 234,
        255–256, 279–280, 312,
        375, 387, 458, 466
Sonnet 9 (Alabaster) 115
Sonnet 10 ("Though all forsake
    thee, lord, yet I will die")
    (Alabaster) 10, 115, **375–376**
Sonnet 15 ("My soul a world is
    by contraction") (Alabaster)
    10, 116, **376–377**

Sonnet XIX (Milton). *See* "When I
    consider how my light is spent
    (Sonnet XIX)" (Milton)
Sonnet 42 (Alabaster) 116
Sonnet 43 (Alabaster) 116
Sonnet 46 ("Of His Conversion")
    (Alabaster) 10, 116, **377–378**
Sonnet 48 (Alabaster) 116
Sonnet 54 (Alabaster) 116, 318
Sonnet 61 (Alabaster) 115
Sonnet 64 (Alabaster) 115
Sonnet 116 (Shakespeare) 195
Sonnet 130 (Shakespeare) 78,
    231
Sonnet 135 (Shakespeare) 78
"Sonnet 338" (Petrarch) 17
"Sonnet to Sir W. Alexander"
    (Drummond) 11
"Sonnet to the Noble Lady, the
    Lady Mary Wroth, A" (Jonson)
    241, 378
Sons of Ben 58, 242, **378**, 423.
    See also Tribe of Ben
Sophonisba (Thomson) 395
soul-body dialogue 111
sound **378–379**. *See also*
    alliteration; rhyme
Southey, Robert 29, 67, 90, 253,
    359, 366
Spence, Joseph 274
Spenser, Edmund
    and Alabaster (William) 9
    and Browne (William) 42,
        45
    and Drayton (Michael) 123
    in *England's Helicon* 154
    The Faerie Queene 13, 38,
        42, 54, 67, 180, 286,
        419, 426
    and Fletcher (Giles) 67, 180
    and Marvell (Andrew) 277,
        286
    and Milton (John) 217, 315
    and Pope (Alexander) 325
    and Thomson (James) 395
"Spleen, The" (Finch) 176,
    379–381
spondee 268, 269
"Spring" (Thomson) 220–221,
    222, 395
"Spring, The" (Cowley) 88,
    381–382
Sprint, John 246
Squier, Charles 385
stanzaic form 183
"Stanzas" (Gray). *See* "Elegy
    Written in a Country
    Churchyard" (Gray)
State of Innocence, The (Dryden)
    129
Steele, Richard 24, 388
Steinbeck, John 397
"Stella's Birthday, 1721" (Swift)
    382–383, 388
Steps to the Temple (Crashaw)
    91–92
Still, John 9, 10

"Still to Be Neat" (Jonson) 241,
    383–384
Stirling, earl of. *See* Alexander,
    Sir William
Story, G. M. 9, 115
"Strange News Out of Diverse
    Countries" (Breton) 41
"Stranger Minstrel, A" (Coleridge)
    414
"Stricken Deer, The" (Cowper)
    89, **384**
strophe 323–324, 407
structure. *See* form and format
Suckling, Sir John 60, **385–386**
    "A Ballad upon a Wedding"
        28–29, **29–30**, 385
    "The Dance" **97**, 385
    "I Prithee Send Me Back My
        Heart" **235–236**, 385
    "Loving and Beloved" **258**,
        385
    "Out upon It!" **311**, 385
    in Tribe of Ben 242, 258,
        378, 385, 423
    "Why So Pale and Wan"
        385, **459**
"Summer" (Thomson) 220,
    221–222, 223, 395
"Sun-rising" (Thomson) 221–222
"Sun Rising, The" (Donne) 25,
    41, 118, 174, **386–387**
"Sunset" (Thomson) 221, 222
Surprised by Sin (Fish) 313
"Sweetest love, return again"
    (Wroth) 312, **387**, 466
Swift, Jonathan vii, **387–390**
    on Astell (Mary) 24
    and Barber (Mary) 32, 464
    "A Description of a City
        Shower" **105–106**, 390
    and Finch (Anne) 176
    and form 183
    and Gay (John) 188, 189–
        190, 370, 389, 443
    and Pope (Alexander) 132,
        134, 325, 326, 389, 444
    and Prior (Matthew) 329
    "Stella's Birthday" **382–383**,
        388
    "Verses on the Death of Dr.
        Swift" vii, 141, 253, 272,
        390, **443–446**
syncope 259
synechdoche 175, 184, 216
synesthesia 249, 259

T

tail rhyme 95, 96, 347, 397
Talbot, Charles 395
"Tale Being an Addition to Mr.
    Gay's Fables, A" (Barber) 32
Taming of the Shrew, The
    (Shakespeare) 265
Task, The (Cowper) 89–90, 92,
    249, 384
Taylor, Jeremy 184, 320

Tempest, The (Shakespeare) 98
Temple, Sir William 382, 388
Temple, The (Herbert) 6, 14, 46, 69, 78, 99, 139, 181, 205–206, 242, 255, 322, 451
Temple of Love, The (Davenant) 98
Tennyson, Alfred Lord 145
tercet 183
tetrameter 268
Thackeray, William Makepeace 390
"Thanksgiving to God, for his House, A" (Herrick) 208, **391**
"Then is she gone?" (Drummond) **391–392**
Theobald, Lewis 326, 444
Theocritus 42, 276, 449
"They Are All Gone into the World of Light!" (Vaughan) 268, **392–393**, 442
"Thirty-Eight" (Smith) 366, **393–394**
Thomas, Dylan 183, 359
Thomas, Elizabeth 68, 69
Thomson, James **394–396**
    and Dyer (John) 136
    A Hymn on the Seasons 38, 136, **220–223**, 395
    "Rule Britannia" **353**, 395
"Though all forsake thee, lord, yet I will die" (Alabaster). *See* Sonnet 10 ("Though all forsake thee, lord, yet I will die") (Alabaster)
Three Hours after Marriage (Pope, Gay, and Arbuthnot) 176, 189
Threepenny Opera, The (Brecht) viii, 190, 371
Threnodia Augustalis (Dryden) 130
Thyestes (Seneca) 160
"Time" (Herbert) 70, 206, **396**
"To Althea, from Prison" (Lovelace) 257, **396–397**
"To a Mouse" (Burns) 48, **397–398**
"To Heaven" (Jonson) 241, **398–399**
"To His Conscience" (Herrick) 208
"To His Coy Mistress" (Marvell) 55, 101, 267, **399–400**
"To His Mistress Going to Bed" (Donne) 118, **400–402**
"Toilette, The" (Gay) 189, 274
"Toilette, The" (Montagu) 189, 274
"To John Donne" (Jonson) 242, **402**
"To Lucinda" (Leapor) 253
"To Mr. Addison" (Pope) 325
"To My Excellent Lucasia, On Our Friendship" (Philips) 175, 321, **403**
"To My Lord Colrane, In Answer to his Complemental Verses

sent me under the Name of Cleanor" (Killigrew) 244, **403–404**
"To One Who Said I Must Not Love" (Egerton) **140–141**
"To Penshurst" (Jonson) 107, 186, 206, 240, 241, 250, 398, **404–406**, 426, 465
"To the Fair Clarinda, Who made love to me, Imagined more than woman" (Behn) 35, **406**
"To the Immortal Memory and Friendship of that noble pair, Sir Lucius Cary and Sir H. Morison" (Jonson) 58, 242, **406–408**, 423
"To the Infant Martyrs" (Crashaw) 91
"To the Ladies" (Chudleigh) 69, 75, **408**
"To the Memory of Mr. Oldham" (Dryden) 130, 294, **408–410**
"To the Memory of My Beloved, the Author, Mr. William Shakespeare, and What He Hath Left Us" (Jonson) 175, 241, 292, **410–411**
To the Memory of the Most Renowned Du-Vall (Butler) 50
"To the Nightingale" (Finch) 176, 379, **411–412**
"To the Pious Memory of the Accomplish'd Young Lady Mrs. Anne Killigrew" (Dryden) 130, 141, 244–245, 409, **412–414**
"To the Poet Coleridge" (Robinson) 351, **414–415**
"To the Poor" (Barbauld) **415–416**
"To the Thrice-Sacred Queen Elizabeth" (Herbert) 207, **416–418**
"To the Virgins, to Make Much of Time" (Herrick) 208, **418–419**
"To William Camden" (Jonson) 240, **419–420**
Town Before You, The (Cowley) 88
Tragedy of Darius, The (Alexander) 11, 14, **420–421**
Traherne, Thomas 47, **421–423**
    "On Leaping over the Moon" vii, **298–299**, 422
    and Vaughan (Henry) 346
    "Wonder" 422, **463–464**
"Traveller, The" (Goldsmith) 193
Tribe of Ben 235, 242, **423**. *See also* Sons of Ben
    Browne (William) in 46, 242, 423
    Carew (Thomas) in 54, 242, 258, 378, 423, 452
    Cartwright (William) in 56, 242, 423
    Dryden (John) on 262
    Herrick (Robert) in 212, 242, 258, 378, 423

Lovelace (Richard) in 242, 258, 423
Randolph (Thomas) in 334
Suckling (Sir John) in 242, 258, 378, 385, 423
trimeter 268
trochaic foot 268, 269
"True Maid, A" (Prior) 329, **423–424**
truncation. *See* catalexis
Turner, Charlotte. *See* Smith, Charlotte Turner
"'Twas the Night Before Christmas" (Moore) 269

U

"Undertaking, The" (Donne) 118, **425–426**
Underwood, The (Jonson) 242, 281, 378
"Universal Prayer" (Pope) 164
Untermeyer, Louis 208
Unwin, Mary 58, 89, 249
"Upon Appleton House, To My Lord Fairfax" (Marvell) 174, 275, **426–428**
"Upon Combing Her Hair" (Herbert) **429**
"Upon His Verses" (Herrick) 208, **429–430**
"Upon Jack and Jill. Epigram" (Herrick) 208, **430**
"Upon Julia's Clothes" (Herrick) 208, **430–431**, 433
"Upon the Death of Lord Hastings" (Dryden) 128
"Upon the Death of Mr. King" (Cleveland) 72, 174, **431–432**
"Upon the Losse of His Mistresses" (Herrick) 208, **432**
"Upon the Nipples of Julia's Breast" (Herrick) 208, **432–433**
"Upon the Saying That My Verses Were Made by Another" (Killigrew) 75, 153, 244, **433–434**
"Upon the Weakness and Misery of Man" (Butler) **434–435**

V

"Valediction Forbidding Mourning, A" (Donne) 14, 52, 60, 78, 101, 118, **436–438**
"Valediction: Of Weeping, A" (Donne) 101, 118, **438–439**
"Vanity of Human Wishes, The" (Johnson) 239, **439–441**
Vaughan, Henry **441–443**
    "The Burial of an Infant" **47–48**, 442
    "Corruption" **85–86**, 442
    and Drummond (William) 127
    "The Night" **283–285**, 442

"Regeneration" **341–343**, 442
"The Retreat" **346–347**, 442
"Silence, and Stealth of Days!" **359–360**, 442
"They Are All Gone into the World of Light!" 268, **392–393**, 442
and Traherne (Thomas) 422
"The Waterfall" 342, 442, **455–457**
Vaughan, Thomas 441, 442, 456
verbal irony 236
Verses (Boyd) 40
Verses Addressed to the Imitator of Horace (Hervey and Montagu) 156
"Verses on the Death of Dr. Swift" (Swift) vii, 141, 253, 272, 390, **443–446**
Vicar of Wakefield, The (Goldsmith) 193, 458
Vieth, David 245
"Village, The" (Crabbe) 90, 91, **446–448**
villanelle 183
Villers, Lady Mary 161–162
"Vine, The" (Herrick) 208, 391, **448–449**
Virgil **449–450**
    Astell (Mary) on 16, 450
    and Browne (William) 42, 450
    and Carew (Thomas) 339
    Crabbe (George) on 447, 450
    and Denham (Sir John) 103
    and Dryden (John) 17, 68, 131, 154, 155, 207, 409, 410, 450
    Killigrew (Anne) on 403, 404, 450
    and Marvell (Andrew) 186, 276
    and Milton (John) 260, 313, 450
    Pope (Alexander) on 133, 157, 325, 335, 450, 461, 462
    and Thomson (James) 220, 223, 450
"Virtue" (Herbert) 206, **450–451**
Voiture, Vincent de 158–159
Volpone; or, The Fox (Jonson) 119–120, 241
Voyage (George) 58

W

Waldensians 307
Wall, Cynthia 335
Waller, Edmund 60, **452–453**
    Behn (Aphra) on 306–307
    and Davenant (Sir William) 98
    and form 183
    "Go, Lovely Rose!" 55, 78, **191**, 453

Waller, Edmund (*continued*)
   instructive poem by 266
   and Lovelace (Richard) 373,
      374
   and Marvell (Andrew) 36
   synechdoche by 175
   and Traherne (Thomas) 464
Walpole, Horace 31, 66, 145,
   198, 199, 203
Walpole, Sir Robert 122, 155,
   190, 274, 329, 370–371, 444
Walsh, William 157
Walton, Izaak 206
Ward, Thomas Humphry 11, 87,
   127–128
Warton, Joseph 463
"Washing-Day" (Barbauld) 31,
   453–455
Wasserman, Earl 79, 461
"Waterfall, The" (Vaughan) 342,
   442, **455–457**
Watkins, Rowland 286
Watson, James 173
Way of the World, The (Congreve)
   121, 385
Webster, John 38, 119
Weidhorn, Manfred 258
Weinbrot, Howard 440, 441
"Welcome to Sack, The" (Herrick)
   212
"Were I Laid on Greenland's
   Coast" (Gay) 371
"Were na My Heart Licht I Wad
   Die" (Baillie) 29
West, Richard 145, 198

"What d'ye Call It, The" (Gay)
   189
"When I consider how my light
   is spent (Sonnet XIX)" (Milton)
   271, 301, 375, **457**
"When Lovely Woman" (Cary)
   458
"When Lovely Woman Stoops
   to Folly" (Goldsmith) 193,
   457–458
"When night's black mantle"
   (Wroth) 312, **458–459**, 466
Whipple, Edwin 357
Whitshed, William 445–446
"Why So Pale and Wan, Fond
   Lover?" (Suckling) 385, **459**
Wild, Jonathan 122, 370
Wilkie, William 173
William III (king of England)
   120, 130, 188, 211, 328–329,
   343, 388
Williams, Aubrey 135
Williamson, Marilyn L. 244
"Willing Mistress, The" (Behn)
   35, **459–460**
Wilmot, John. *See* Rochester,
   John Wilmot, second earl of
Winchilsea, countess of. *See*
   Finch, Anne
"Windows, The" (Herbert) 206,
   460
"Windsor Castle" (Otway) 310
Windsor Forest (Pope) 44, 79,
   136, 157, 325, **461–463**
"Wine" (Gay) 188

Winscom, Jane Cave **463**
"Winter" (Thomson) 220, 221,
   222, 223, 395
"Winter Evening: A Brown Study,
   The" (Cowper) 89–90, 249
Winter's Tale, The (Shakespeare)
   350
Wits, The (Suckling) 385
Wollstonecraft, Mary 56, 350,
   366
"Wonder" (Traherne) 422,
   463–464
Wood, Anthony 49, 50, 244,
   266
Woodcock, Katherine 269, 271
Woolf, Virginia 35, 112, 126
Wordsworth, William 66, 90,
   137, 176, 183, 200, 350, 365
Works (Cowley) 88, 104
Works (Crabbe) 91
Works (Jonson) 241, 301–302,
   304, 398
Works (Pope) 147, 176
Works of English Poets, The
   (Johnson) 50
Worlds Olio, The (Cavendish) 61
"Written by Desire of a Lady, on
   an Angry, Petulant Kitchen-
   Maid" (Winscom) 463
"Written for My Son, and Spoken
   by Him at His First Putting
   on Breeches" (Barber) vii, 32,
   464–465
"Written in Juice of Lemon"
   (Cowley) 87

Wroth, Lady Mary vii, 206,
   465–467
   and Herbert (George) 181
   and Herbert (Mary Sidney)
      404
   "In this strange labyrinth
      how shall I turn?" **234,**
      312, 466
   Jonson (Ben) on 378, 465
   "Love a child is ever crying"
      255–256, 312, 466
   "My Muse, now happy, lay
      thyself to rest" **279–280,**
      312, 466
   "My pain, still smothered in
      my grievèd breast" **280–
      281,** 312, 466
   "Pamphilia to Amphilanthus"
      234, 255–256, 279–280,
      312–313, 375, 387, 458,
      466
   "Sweetest love, return again"
      312, **387,** 466
   "When night's black mantle"
      312, **458–459,** 466
Wroth, Sir Robert 312, 378, 465
Wycherley, William 34, 68,
   121, 325

Y
Yeats, William Butler 118
Yonge, Mary 155–156
Yonge, William 155, 156
Young, R. V. 407